A History of Latin America

Robert Jones Shafer

SYRACUSE UNIVERSITY

A HISTORY OF Latin America

D.C. HEATH AND COMPANY
Lexington, Massachusetts   Toronto

For
Stella

Preface

This survey is prepared with a view to being more explicit than is usual about the sources of Latin America's problems with modernization. To this end, for the colonial era (from 1492 to about 1810), the emphasis is on the social factors that still influence Latin America. For the years following Independence, the book seeks a better explanation of the area's development through intense discussion of a few major countries—Argentina, Brazil, Mexico, and Chile—while providing for the other nations sketchier accounts that are expanded whenever major change occurs or disruption of old patterns is threatened. The material for the post-Independence years is organized into three carefully defined chronological divisions, within which the emphasis is on factors critical to the process of modernization: the focus of events since the 1820s.

For the colonial era, heavy stress is put on the class structure and its linkages with the great estate complex; on the prevalent servile and dependent labor systems, largely made up of American Indians, black Africans, and persons of mixed racial heritage; and on the alienation and apathy of the lower classes. Much attention is devoted also to Roman Catholic institutions, to the economic dependence of the Hispanic world on the more developed parts of the North Atlantic world, to the weakness of food production methods (partly caused by lack of incentive for workers), and to the feeble state of manufacturing, which resulted more from the status-ridden social customs insisted on by the upper class in America than from the mercantilistic regulations of Spain and Portugal.

The text stresses, further, that the Spanish and Portuguese colonial systems were strong enough to preserve huge territories against frequent attacks by foes, in large measure because the systems retained the loyalty of the upper classes in America. Also examined is the process of regional differentiation, which later helped shape the independent states. Such factors as great distances and isolation, as well as varied natural resources, racial situations, and historical experience, created regional attitudes that became bases for nationalistic sentiment.

With political freedom, the opportunity for connections with the North Atlantic world increased, and so did economic colonialism, or dependence. A major reason was that the Latin American ruling classes accepted the obvious opportunity for maximum linkage with more developed nations—trading their specialized exports for imports of capital and technical expertise. This decision was well implemented by the institutions and attitudes inherited from the colonial era, which were generally designed to preserve the social status quo—including the great estate and the subservient labor force.

It was otherwise with the initial efforts to modernize through manufacturing or liberalization of the political and social systems. They required changes incompatible with the colonial heritage, changes that were threatening to the immediate interests of the conservative great landowners. In addition, since the lower classes had little incentive for hard work, thrift, or involvement in community affairs, they emerged only slowly from alienation, apathy, and patterns of low productivity. Thus for a long time the culture lacked the flexibility required for superior competition in the industrial age.

Latin American history since Independence, therefore, is viewed as modernization growing slowly against the resistance of old institutions and attitudes—so that both continuity and change are parts of the story. *Modernization* has been defined variously: simply as a transition from "traditional" societies; or largely in material terms, like production, physicians per capita, and transportation capacities; or chiefly in terms of justice for the individual. Liberals are often reluctant to accept the idea that one aspect of modernization is efficiency—of political mobilization, government action, or economic output. They want an ideal of modernization that includes individual freedoms and social well-being. Many regimes in recent times, however, have operated on the premise that at the heart of modernization is economic development, especially industrialization, and "developmentalism" has tended to become a frenzy that drives out concern for other goals.

The following elements have been especially important to modernization in Latin America: class divisions, complicated by race and miscegenation; the relationship between education, communications, and the developing spirit of nationalism as a promoter of integration; regionalism; and, in recent times, the increase of government revenues and functions. Other factors include the growth of political participation, which sometimes seems to promote communications and integration; the perennial problems of monoculture and specialization of exports; the effort to reduce economic colonialism and to diversify production; the slow growth of achievement motivation, with its links to class divisions, education, and communications; the critical role of internal transportation systems; and the pervading influence of violence in public life, most traumatically manifested as the military conspiracy and coup d'etat.

Latin American history, including efforts to modernize, has not followed the same course as that of Europe or the Orient. How could it have? The time schedules of its successes and failures need not be measured against those of France or Arabia. The chronological periods adopted here, therefore, correspond to Latin America's own history, especially to obvious change and the promise of change. Modernization is a differentiating factor even when only modest success has been achieved, because more is almost sure to follow and because even rather unsuccessful attempts have conditioned the actions and emotions of both innovative and resisting groups.

The rate of change certainly increased in Latin America from the 1820s to the 1880s; it accelerated between the 1880s and 1930s, bolstered by the shocks of World War I and the Great Depression; and change moved faster, as in most of the world, after the 1930s. In the dividing or transitional decades of the 1880s and 1930s, the critical changes are identified as economic developments, with their attendant social alterations and transforming attitudes (responsive to both achievement and the hope thereof). Some of the attitudinal changes, however, were due as much to political as to economic ideas, such as the criticism of caudillismo, which was accumulating during the 1880s but was much stronger by the 1930s. Similarly, various early crusades against political instability as a barrier to economic and social development had by the 1930s occasionally been transformed into a rightist or leftist dictatorial government—an authoritarianism with much more technical content than the old caudillismo. In the past forty years, it has become increasingly apparent that authoritarian government in Latin America is compatible with economic modernization and some social progress. Many political leaders nonetheless continue to put individual liberty somewhat lower in priority than national prosperity, security, and independence. This ordering of objectives has been shared by both radical socialism and rightist corporatism.

Latin American leaders at Independence represented small constituencies and had modest dreams. Many leaders today represent greatly broadened, even national, constituencies, and there is no limit to their hopes for the future. If they cannot fulfill their dreams by one set of ideas and methods, they will drive themselves, or be driven by their constituents, to try to fulfill them by others. The enormous area of Latin America is one of the world's battlegrounds between conflicting concepts of how to manage innovation, with the advocates of evolutionary and revolutionary change competing for control of the future.

Three of the nations emphasized in this book —Argentina, Brazil, and Mexico—contain more than half the territory and population of Latin America. Their historical experience and that of Chile does not perfectly reflect that of the other sixteen nations, but the choice permits ample illustration of all the important trends. In any event, the author, after thirty years of giving advice on Latin America to university students and to personnel in government and private enterprise, knows the futility of trying to convey general understanding together with a multitude of exceptions.

R. J. S.
Syracuse, November 1977

Contents

PART TWO / Government and Defense in Spanish America   75

6   The Government of Colonial Spanish America   77

7   International Relations and Defense   98

PART THREE / Social and Economic Conditions in Spanish America   119

8   Population, Class and Caste, and Labor Systems   123

9   The Black Lower Class and Racial Mixture   140

10   Economic Life in Spanish America   156

11   Other Economic Problems   176

12   Some Social Conditions and Institutions   197

PART EIGHT / The Struggle for National Development Since the 1930s   597

MAPS

A History of Latin America

The Mountains of Latin America

ATLANTIC

OCEAN

GULF OF MEXICO

CARIBBEAN SEA

Rio Grande

PACIFIC

OCEAN

Cauca R.

Magdalena R.

LLANOS

Orinoco R.

Amazon R.

AMAZON   LOWLANDS

A N D E S

BRAZILIAN HIGHLAND

M T S.

Pilcomayo R.

Paraguay R.

Paraná R.

Uruguay R.

PAMPAS

Rio de la Plata

Much of the mountain area shown for Mexico and western South America is over
5,000 feet; some of it is much higher, with many ranges over 10,000 feet and peaks
much higher than that. The Brazilian Highland is mostly 1,500–3,000 feet, with relatively
small areas as high as 6,000 feet.

PART ONE

Discovery and Conquest

The speed of the Iberian—and especially the Spanish—penetration of America was astounding, hurried by exciting discoveries of gold and silver and hordes of Amerindians suitable for labor.[1] The hurricane of conquest was essentially complete within a half century of Columbus' discovery; by then lesser but persistent winds of radical reconstruction were blowing.

Five revolutionary processes were swiftly completed or had at least begun. First was the destruction of the great Amerindian cultures, their capacity for growth forever gone. The Spanish tried and abandoned slavery for Amerindians and finally accepted the indigenes theoretically as rational (though wards of the crown), capable of Christianization, even worthy of marriage with Europeans. Those decisions were only partially enforceable, however, since Europeans were determined to exploit Amerindians in mine, field, kitchen, and bed. At the same time began the pandemics of Old World disease, which evolved into a demographic holocaust that consumed 90 percent of the indigenes. Second was the decision to send black Africans as slaves to the New World, and the first hellships began the long mutual agony of blacks and whites in America. Third, a huge and often promiscuous miscegenation began between Europeans and Amerindians, and, with the addition of Africans, created an unprecedented racial melting pot. Fourth, a new society began to emerge, directed by European masters, but molded more than they realized by a vast process of acculturation. For, although the Christian fathers toppled idols and raised crosses, the Amerindians still secretly laid flowers before old images, and black slaves remembered the faiths of their fathers. Europeans transplanted their technology overseas: all the artifacts of the iron age with wheeled vehicles and draft animals where none had

---

[1] Amerindian, increasingly used for American Indians by archeologists and historians, is used only in Chapter 1.

1

been known, together with a marine science undreamed of among Amerindians. But the indigenes clung to many old tools and patterns of work, while contributing to the new American mixed culture, and to the wider world, such delights as the tomato, pineapple, potato, chocolate, and maize. One problem of the new society that received much attention in Spain was construction of a sociogovernmental order for the conquerors that would ensure the control of the crown.

Finally, early Hispanic entrenchment in America actually and prospectively much affected European affairs, as the Spanish sat astride the silver lodes, the tropical agricultural zones, and the best supplies of Amerindian labor. The Iberians built towns and forts, created ports and pioneered the best oceanic routes, and developed paths for inland transport. By the mid-sixteenth century they had such advantages of distance, terrain, climate, and knowledge that foreign intrusion was difficult. Meanwhile, in any case, their foes were busy elsewhere, so even more decades later in the sixteenth century were available for consolidation. The rivals of Spain and Portugal never could eject them. These revolutions developed earlier and more fully in Spanish than Portuguese America, which for a long time was weakly held. Brazil commanded less attention than Portuguese enterprises in the Orient. The conquest of the sparse and primitive Amerindians was a slow process for the few Portuguese who went to America. They and the mother country, nevertheless, did meet the challenges raised by their European foes in the Western Hemisphere. No one in Europe in the 1550s realized how much that was permanently decisive for the Old and New Worlds had been accomplished or set in motion in a few tumultuous decades in America.

1 The Amerindians

From raw grubs to cooked corn cakes comprised a journey of 30,000 years for the Asians who went to America. There, far across the mysterious seas from Europe and the Orient, a great part of the human adventure was played out, unknown to what we call the Old World. The Indians of America over the millennia slowly made their way from a condition little above that of beasts to the cultivation of grain and the making of textiles, the building of temples, and the search for God and the meaning of life. Who was to tell their sages as they recorded the passage of time—for they became notable astronomers—how nearly their great achievements were coming to the day of extinction? They were as unaware of that fate as the Europeans who were to inflict it upon them. So in their separate places white and red people all unknowingly prepared the instruments and attitudes that would decide the outcome of their meeting.

a. Origins, Migrations, Numbers

Migrants from northeastern Asia peopled North America, crossing by land bridge, ice, or boat. That Amerindians are of Mongoloid stock, long living in isolation from Asia, is certain. Even their blood types indicate that. The notion of settlement from the legendary sunken lands of Atlantis and Mu is fantasy. Suggestions of voyages from Africa, Polynesia, China, and Europe (except for a few Norsemen) before 1492 are mere speculation. In any case, small groups of such migrants or lost voyagers could not have accounted for much of the genetic stock of the Amerindians or have had much cultural influence.

The date of arrival is more doubtful. Most likely they came in a series of migrations that began at least 30,000—possibly as much as 70,000 —years ago. Probably the migrants used fire and had some primitive tools. There is evidence of extensive wandering over many centuries. Amerindians were at the southern tip of South America by at least 9000 B.C. The evidence clearly shows a slow development of culture in the Western Hemisphere rather than a sudden intrusion from overseas. Some of the primitive hunters and gatherers of food began to supplement their diet by cultivating plants in the Middle (Meso) American area at least by 3400 B.C. By selection, they improved the strains. With a larger and more certain food supply, habitations became settled, and farmer-village life evolved in a number of centers at least as early as 1500 B.C., which was a few thousand years later than the same development in the Old World. About a thousand years later, true civilizations developed in America, so that when the Europeans arrived, some two thousand years of civilized history lay behind the highest cultures in America. We do not know why farmer-village life and civilization arose a few thousand years earlier in Asia, the Middle East, and the Mediterranean basin. We only know that the different chronologies of development were not grounded in differences of talent among racial groups.

In 1492 there may have been between 30 and 50 million Amerindians in the Western Hemisphere. The number is disputed, especially for Mesoamerica, and it is impossible to feel comfortable with any of the alternatives.[1] The number is important because higher figures support elevated estimates of the quality of Amerindian technology and social achievement generally. That, in turn, bears on the question of the innate abilities of Amerindians, long after the European conquest relegated to subordinate roles in society and denigrated by Europeans as being of inferior talent. The question of numbers at the conquest relates also to the extent of the demographic catastrophe thereafter.

The heaviest concentrations of Amerindians were in Mesoamerica from central Mexico to Yucatán and Guatemala and the Inca realms of present-day Ecuador, Peru, and Bolivia. The disagreement on total population therefore focuses on those areas, not more than 15 percent of the Western Hemisphere. Most of the rest was thinly inhabited. North America north of central Mexico may have had 1 or 2 million; the Antilles less than half a million; South America outside the Inca realms 2 to 4 million, with the densest concentration in the Chibcha areas of present-day Colombia. What is now the enormous republic of Brazil, with more than 3 million square miles, had a sprinkling of Amerindians totaling between 1 and 3 million. Most of these Amerindians outside the higher culture areas were widely scattered in small groups, and some of them were nomadic or seminomadic. Much of America, then, was nearly empty of people.

---

[1] See Chapter 8, Section a, on Indian population.

b.   "Higher" and "Lower" Cultures

This distinction—whatever the terms used—is important in understanding relations between Europeans and Amerindians.[2] Europeans found effective labor in large numbers only where cultures created political systems and productive technologies that permitted concentrations of sedentary population. Labor supply was a matter of consuming interest to the conquerors, although they thought of it in simpler terms. The wonders of the responses of the so-called American Indians to the challenges and mysteries of life were of little interest to European conquerors. They did observe great cultural differences among Indian groups, but the European interest focused on variation in customs of warfare and habits of work. Labor remained a key factor in European actions. Where Indian labor was absent, sparse, or invincibly reluctant or underproductive, other solutions of the labor problem often were expensive or impossible.[3] Hence the location, numbers, and cultural condition of the Amerindians were important determinants of the development of Hispanic settlements and institutions. Although some of the more primitive Indians were induced by the Spaniards to change from intermittent to regular labor, such transformation was difficult and exceptional.

The higher cultures offered concentrated numbers, people accustomed to working regularly under direction, agricultural techniques capable of providing considerable food for both Europeans and Amerindians, and artisan techniques and traditions that could be turned to the construction of European artifacts. The higher cultures also interested the conquerors for other reasons.

---

[2] While the Indian cultures are commonly described in terms of these two categories, all the pairings are subject to some objection. Higher and lower should not be regarded in terms of moral or ethical excellence; similar problems occur with the use of such terms as "civilized" and "primitive," or "complex" and "simple."

[3] See Chapter 8, Section d, and Chapter 9, Section a, on labor systems. Much comment on Amerindian culture occurs in other chapters in connection with its destruction or accommodation with Hispanic culture.

The Amerindian political and social systems that provided the discipline for regular and often state-directed work were autocratic. They had inculcated in the folk a general acceptance of authority that was useful to the Spaniards who replaced the Amerindian rulers. Finally, the greater numbers of people in the higher cultures were important because, as it turned out, prolonged contact between the races resulted in fearful Amerindian mortality.

The lower cultures were different in critical ways. Even when—as was not always the case—they had effective agriculture, the surpluses were not used to develop institutions that permitted the creation of large states. Thus, the Amerindians of the lower cultures seldom had political systems extending over much territory or population, so that the Iberians could not defeat one military force or capture one leader and take over a generally large and subservient population.

c. Relations Among Amerindian Groups

Relations among Amerindian political or cultural groups were weaker than those in Europe, the result of the huge size of the area and the relative simplicity of transport technology. The Indians lacked draft animals, wheeled vehicles, or true ocean-going vessels. They also lacked a monetary system. There was trade between some groups, even some light trade over long distances, but the volume was less and trade was less influential than in Europe. Interchange also resulted from warfare, but, compared with Europe, the effects were attenuated by other factors, including little development of written records and communication. However, that such factors were important in the Amerindian failure to unite against the European invader is difficult to believe. The differences are a matter of degree, not of absolutes, nor are they measurable. Unifying Christian Europe on any question, even opposition to the invading Muslims, was also very difficult.

d. The Natural Environment in America

The distance between the Americas and other continents, together with the state of geographic knowledge and marine technology, meant that cultural developments proceeded in America with no—or little—influence from the rest of the world. Conceivably, such isolation retarded Amerindian cultural development; conceivably, also, it prevented—until 1492—the destruction or absorption of Amerindian culture by others. A certainly fateful result was that the Amerindians had no knowledge of other races, and no inkling of the profound diversity of human culture, for all the great differences between Amerindian culture groups. This lack of knowledge played some role in the European conquest, shocking and confusing the Amerindians as they suddenly beheld white-skinned creatures, sheathed in unknown metal, coming mysteriously from the unknown sea in floating "houses," riding ashore mounted on large "deer," and hurling lightning and thunder from wondrous rods. This surprise factor is, of course, immeasurable, and in any event the Europeans had other great advantages over the Amerindians. Possibly the most fateful result of isolation was the lack of Amerindian immunity or resistance to Old World diseases.

What was the environment in which the Amerindians had developed their varied cultures? The diversity of climate and terrain in America encouraged a variety of human responses to the natural environment. The higher cultures grew in tropical latitudes, but at different altitudes and average temperatures. Generally, they did not have to expend excessive energy on defense against cold, and they enjoyed enough warmth and sunlight for a long growing season—sometimes more than one crop a year. Advantages and disadvantages of climate and terrain were of local importance, but scarcely account for Amerindian development—biologically or culturally—as compared with that in other areas. Healthfulness, fertility, comfort, traversibility were diverse and as favorable as in much of the rest of the world.

The flora was rich and the Amerindians im-

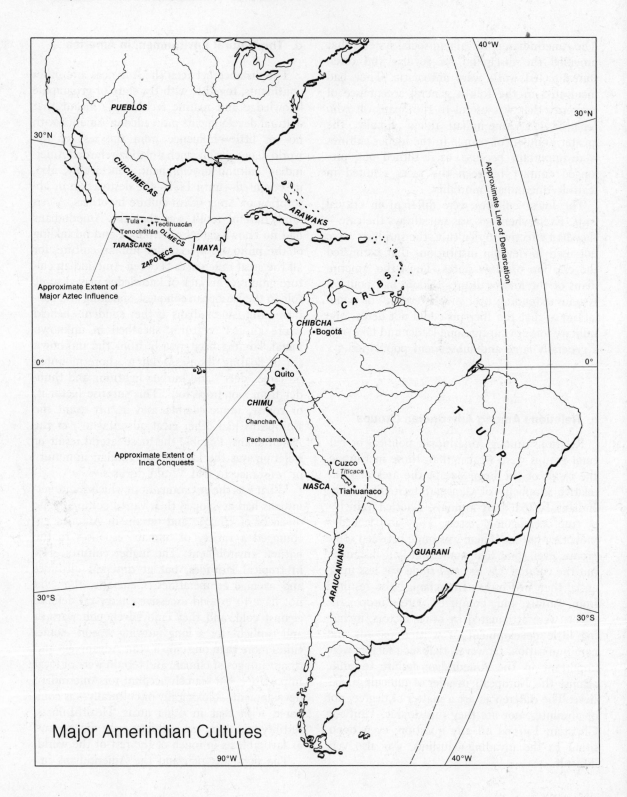

Major Amerindian Cultures

PUEBLOS

CHICHIMECAS

TARASCANS

Tula · Teotihuacán
Tenochtitlán
ZAPOTECS
OLMECS

MAYA

Approximate Extent of
Major Aztec Influence

ARAWAKS

C A R I B S

CHIBCHA
·Bogotá

Approximate Line of Demarcation

Quito

CHIMU

Chanchan

Pachacamac

Approximate Extent of
Inca Conquests

· Cuzco
L. Titicaca

NASCA
Tiahuanaco

T U P I

GUARANÍ

ARAUCANIANS

30°N

0°

30°S

30°N

0°

30°S

40°W

90°W

40°W

proved it by selective cultivation. The development of maize from a wild plant into a widely distributed crop was one of the great victories in the human effort to control the environment. Specialization in food crops often followed lines of climatic variation, but sometimes confinement of crops to parts of America was a cultural decision. In extensive areas the root crop cassava was the staple. The potato, developed in the highlands of the South American Andes, was unknown or little grown in some areas. The hot chiles of Mesoamerica were a localized crop. All in all, the vegetable resources of the continent were ample for the development of the surpluses necessary for growth of economic, intellectual, political, military, and spiritual specialization in human society. Some of the indigenous fruits and vegetables (for example, maize, tomato, potato, pineapple, cacao) would make splendid additions to the nutrition and cuisine of the rest of the world.

The fauna did not equal in variety that of other continents. The Amerindians had nothing comparable to the food resources of cattle, goats, sheep, and swine, or the animal power of horses, asses, oxen, water buffalo; but they still developed adequate diets for large populations. They ate birds, snakes, insects, deer and other mammals, and marine creatures. The important thing was that large populations were as well nourished as they were in much of the Old World, where many people also ate a largely vegetable diet. Deficiencies of animal food were less important than the lack of beasts of burden, a handicap in transportation, communications, and war. The absence of draft animals helps explain why the wheel was not used (it existed in toys). The absence of pack animals (except for the feeble llama) and carts was clearly not, however, a fatal hindrance to cultural development. The Indians of the higher cultures were formidable porters and runners. Conceivably, the lack of attention to the wheel interfered with intellectual development, but this theory is not provable. The lack of draft animals also probably explains the failure to invent the plow. But the digging stick or foot plow served quite well for the production of highly nutritious cassava and maize and other crops and was even superior to the European plow for some intensive agriculture.

Other American resources were adequate. Stone for public buildings and monuments, fortifications, weapons, grinding, and cutting surfaces. Lime for plaster and mortar. Salt for taste and health. Timber for fuel, shelter, implements, and weapons. Clay for pottery and bricks. Fibers and thatch and reeds for many uses. Copper, silver, tin, and gold were used to some extent, but iron was not worked; and metallurgy generally was less influential in cultural development than it was in the Old World. All in all, the natural environment of America was not decisively better or worse than that of the rest of the world.

e. Higher Cultures of Middle America

Mesoamerica was one of the great cradles of civilization. There are more pyramids there than in Egypt, left in the towns and ceremonial centers of various peoples from Honduras to central Mexico, bearing witness to vanished states. Within that area, however, there were enough exchanges of goods, culture, blows, and bloodstocks so that we can speak of a general Mesoamerican civilization. Among its characteristic features was efficient cultivation of improved strains of such crops as maize, beans, squash, and chiles. There developed systems of political and social control over considerable sedentary populations. Mesoamericans had complex cosmological and religious beliefs, including private confession and penance and extensive human sacrifice. They built large structures of stone, typically including pyramids, elaborate residences for the elite, and ball courts. They had an arithmetic and astronomic-calendrical system, much more developed in some groups than others, and always mixed with astrologic lore. Present in many groups were systems of writing, again varying in sophistication. All had markets for local trade and some included commodities from distant—even "international"—suppliers. Into this civilized core were

absorbed over the centuries the "Chichimecs"—
wild tribes—who came from the north, weary of
eating raw grubs and chasing rabbits.

Olmecs

The Olmecs of the hot Gulf Coast may have
devised the writing and calendric system of the
Mesoamerican higher cultures. The Olmec center at La Venta flourished about 800–400 B.C.
and has provided us with one of the oldest dates
in Amerindian glyphs, thought to correspond to
31 B.C. La Venta, as was most usual in Amerindian cultures, was not a city of heavily concentrated population but a ceremonial site with
elaborate structures. There lived a small elite
group, especially priests and governors, with families and servitors, and some craftsmen; and there
repaired on great occasions the surrounding population of farmers.

Olmec influences have been found widely in
Mesoamerica. The history of the Olmecs lay so
far in the past that Amerindians at the time of
the European conquest were unaware that they
ever had existed. A few of them, of course, had
seen, as we can, the huge stone heads the Olmecs
left—helmeted and pouting, the unmistakable
survivors of a long-dead civilization.

Maya

The intellectual achievement of the Maya was
the greatest of ancient America. Politically, however, they remained divided into small city-states,
with related but sometimes mutually unintelligi-
ble tongues, living at various times from Honduras to northern Yucatán and the Gulf Coast
of Mexico. The first and greatest flowering came
in the southern lowlands of present-day northern
Guatemala and southeastern Mexico. A long period of village farming life had preceded, from
about 1500 B.C. until early in the Christian Era.
Toward the end of this village period the Maya
began building pyramids and inscribing monuments. Apparently Olmec traditions, carried on

by other peoples, brought these ideas to the
Maya, up to the second century A.D. Thereafter
the Maya refined and improved what they had
received, though they always retained trade and
other relations with central Mexico.

Their slash-and-burn (swidden) agriculture required much changing of fields as fertility declined. With a complicated pattern of fallow
lands, much territory was always not in use. The
resulting limits on crop production probably inhibited urbanization and the rise of the larger
political units such as developed in the highlands. But the swidden systems of the Maya were
sometimes highly productive, providing a surplus
of the characteristic Mesoamerican crops to support nonfarming ecclesiastics, secular nobles, and
specialist craftsmen. A Maya farmer working under good conditions could supply the food requirements of a dozen persons.

The Maya culture reached its zenith in what
we call the Classic Period, about A.D. 300–900.
Their states were small but firmly organized,
with hereditary elites and rigid social distinctions. Commoners were free workers, probably
having the use of some land from their lineage
groups. There were lesser numbers of serfs, working the lands of the elite, and some slaves. The
system of control, ecclesiastical and secular, was
strong enough to persuade or force the commoners to invest huge amounts of effort in public
labor, either directly on great building projects
or indirectly by supplying food and clothing to
specialists. Maya states also derived income from
exports of edibles and crafted wares.

The most obvious fruits of surplus and control were great elite and ceremonial centers, and
intellectual, religious, and artistic achievement.
The centers were clusters of often magnificent
stone pyramids, columns, plazas, esplanades,
stelae, palaces, ball courts, and causeways.
Around them lived the farming population dispersed in tiny pole, mud, and thatch huts. More
than one hundred centers (some of them post-
Classic) are known in the Maya area. At Tikal,
the largest site, in about six square miles there

were some 3,000 structures, including huts, with a permanent population of possibly 2,000–3,000 political, religious, and economic specialists, and perhaps more part-time inhabitants who were farmers and craftsmen. An even larger population, possibly 40,000, may be described as having had intense interaction with the ceremonial and administrative center. Whether or not this represented "urban" life in historical European terms, it offered some of the cultural advantages of urbanism, as the accomplishments of these city-states indicate.

Their stepped pyramids are spectacular monuments. The one at Tikal rises 229 feet from the ground. Impressive today, stripped by time, weather, vegetation, and purveyors to museums around the world, how much more impressive must they have been when in use with their plaster surfacing intact and painted vivid colors. On ceremonial days the pyramids were surrounded with celebrants bright with mantles, jewels, and colored feathers. Crowds also went to the ball courts, where "games" with ceremonial functions were performed, using rubber balls and special girdles and arm guards.[4] Most Maya sites contain stone stelae, or pillars, carved with figures of men, gods, animals, monsters, and hieroglyphics. The buildings of these centers often were grouped into complexes around plazas and connected by masonry causeways.

The Maya plaster was a durable mixture of burnt limestone and was used not only to face public structures but also to cover interior chambers. In places, plaster surfaces were decorated with magnificently formed and colored wall paintings that deserve to be as well known as those of ancient Egypt.

---

[4] Ball courts have been found from what is now the southwest United States to northern South America. The courts were of various sizes and shapes, and the rules probably varied with time and place, since the ceremony has a known history of at least 2,500 years before the European conquest. Ancient stone monuments depict men apparently clad in the belts and gauntlets of the ceremony. Variations of the game exist today in Mexico.

The Maya positional numeration, including the equivalent of zero, was much better than the Roman. Some of the Maya calendrical and astronomic knowledge was superior to that of classical Mediterranean civilization, and even in a few respects to that of Europe in the time of Columbus. The arithmetic and calendric systems were intimately linked to religion. The Maya had a year of 365 days, but in counting between dates they used the *tun* of 360 days because the other five days were so unspeakably unlucky as to be literally nameless. The Maya, and many other Mesoamerican peoples, used a "calendar-round," which repeated itself each fifty-two years. The Maya also used a "long-count" that indicated time elapsed since a date in their system that now is thought to correspond to about 3000 B.C., presumably based on some mythological event. Calculations that reached a hundred million years into the past probably were, too. Specialists today can read the Maya calendric symbols and relate one Maya date to another; the problem is to relate the Maya system to Christian Era dates, so that developments of the European past can be related in time with developments in Maya history.

Civil and religious institutions were intertwined as they were among the Spanish conquerors. The Maya centers had elaborate religious functions, which also supported civil rule. There was a complex conception of the supernatural and its relation to human beings. It once was thought that Maya pyramids, unlike Egyptian, were not used as tombs, but such a use in America is now well established. A funerary crypt discovered in the 1950s beneath a pyramid at Palenque contained the remains of a great civil leader.

Even more revealing of Maya life are the murals found at Bonampak, dating to the ninth century A.D. and showing a battle and subsequent victory celebrations, with magnificent warriors being saluted with trumpets and prisoners being tortured and slain. Animated and finely colored, a great lord in a jaguar skin is surrounded by his court in gorgeous costumes, including a lady in a white robe who holds a folding-screen fan in one hand. Mummers are disguised as water spirits, gyrating to the rattles, drums, and trumpets of a band. Lords in towering plumed headdresses have blood drawn from their tongues by white-robed Maya ladies, and then perform a dance. The long-dead city almost whispers again with life.[5]

Their writing, combining ideographic and phonetic elements, was the most advanced in ancient America. It included literary, historical, and theological elements. It still is only partially decipherable, partly because Christian zealots burned nearly all the Maya books. We do know that Maya literature, mostly oral, had a heavy spiritual content, including some ominous notes of prophecy. The Maya prophet Chilam Balam cried: "The raised wooden standard shall come! . . . Our elder brother comes. . . . Receive . . . the bearded men, the men of the east, the bearers of the sign of God, lord!" And his prediction seemed to come true in 1517 and thereafter when Spaniards penetrated the area. The actions of the Spaniards seemed to bear out another part of the books of Chilam Balam: "On that day, dust possessed the earth. . . . On that day, a strongman seizes the land. On that day, things fall to ruin. . . . And they are scattered afar in the forests."

The great Maya culture decayed somewhat in the later ninth century A.D. The reasons are uncertain, prominent suggestions being declining fertility of the land, possibly due to the slash-and-burn technique; rebellion against the exactions of the elite; and warfare with external foes. There is evidence for militarism, which may have disrupted the old culture, in the Late Classic Period in the southern lowlands; possibly it was prompted by the need for defense against intruders from central Mexico. In any case, with decay, the older sites in the south were abandoned. Some of the southerners may have moved farther north in Yucatán, where other Maya cen-

ters already flourished. The northern centers continued to the time of the Spanish conquest, sometimes disturbed by warriors from central Mexico, who established dynasties at some of the city-states. In the northern Maya area the Spaniards found a culture still using impressive ceremonial centers, with a social organization and community spirit that permitted fierce opposition to the conquerors. The culture had long ago lost, however, its innovative drive.

Teotihuacán

In the highlands of Mexico many great cultures flourished and died. One had its center at Teotihuacán in the Valley of Mexico, near the present-day Mexico City. Founded about the time of Christ, it died violently, presumably in war or rebellion, about A.D. 700. Teotihuacán was one of the greatest of the few true cities—as opposed to towns at ceremonial centers—in Indian America, and in terms of area (seven square miles) one of the largest preindustrial cities in human history. The population may have been on the order of 100,000. Probably high agricultural yields in the Valley of Mexico, an intermont basin with internal drainage and a large system of lakes, permitted this concentration. Some rich bottomlands in river valleys could be cultivated continually, receiving rich flood silt. Some fields were given fertilizer of excreta and garbage. Mountain terraces were used. Around the lakes, *chinampa* agriculture (sometimes on what originally were artificial islands or peninsulas) was highly productive, using irrigation, rotted vegetation, and rich mud, plus seed beds to aid the planting of a succession of crops during the year. The remains of the city and the still-standing gigantic pyramids awed the Aztecs nearly a thousand years after the fall of Teotihuacán, as they excite the wonder of visitors today. The Teotihuacanos had Mesoamerican writing. Their military and economic reach was long, possibly as extensive as that of the later Aztecs, spreading into what is now Guatemala, where the

---

[5] After a description in Michael D. Coe, *The Maya* (New York, 1966).

highland Maya fell under Teotihuacano domination.

Some Other Civilized Peoples

Higher cultures arose in Oaxaca, south of the Valley of Mexico. Those associated with the vast archaeological sites at Monte Albán and Mitla were developed by people who spoke Zapotec. Some still live there. In the great days of Monte Albán (about A.D. 300–900), the characteristic cultural elements were present in the calendar and writing. Mitla developed later, but we have some of its folding deerskin books (with "writing" much simpler than that of the Maya) that carry its history back to A.D. 692.

Cholula, in a valley a hundred miles southeast of Teotihuacán, was a major center before the destruction of the latter and continued an important place until the time of the Spanish conquest. Over many centuries the local inhabitants, absorbing many conquerors, built a huge pyramid that was the largest structure in ancient America and was sacred to Quetzalcóatl. Begun in the time of Teotihuacán's greatness, it consisted of four pyramids superimposed upon one another; the final structure was 180 feet high and covered 25 acres. Long before the Spaniards came, it was left untended, taking on the appearance of a brush-covered hill. But the local people remembered that it had been sacred to the Feathered Serpent in the days of the giants.

Far from the highland sites of Monte Albán, Mitla, Teotihuacán, and Cholula, in the lowlands of Veracruz what we call El Tajín was at the peak of its civilization from A.D. 600 to 900. The center lay in a fertile valley that produced maize, cacao, and vanilla. The nucleus of the center covered some 150 acres, but much of it and surrounding subsidiary ruins remain unexcavated. Some of the uncovered buildings are marvelously symmetrical pyramids. There are palace-like buildings with colonnaded doorways, roofed with concrete slabs poured over wooden scaffolds. The drums of some columns are carved in reliefs showing winged dancers, eagle knights, and

numerals testifying to the literacy of the builders. El Tajín has seven ball courts! Some have stone bas-reliefs showing the games and the sacrifice of the losing captain. Fire apparently destroyed El Tajín, probably started by wild Chichimecs from the north at about the beginning of the thirteenth century.

Those barbarian tribes of the north always had pressed against the civilized peoples of central Mexico. Among the Chichimecs were the Toltecs, an assortment of tribes who spoke Náhuatl (the language of the Aztecs), who entered the area of sedentary peoples in the tenth century A.D. The Toltecs acquired the local culture and built a center at Tula, not far north of the Valley of Mexico. They quickly established wide influence and hegemony in much of the central highlands. Their King Topíltzin, identified with the long-venerated (even in Teotihuacán) Feathered Serpent god (Quetzalcóatl in Náhuatl), was ejected in a civil war toward the end of the tenth century. He and his followers apparently fled to Yucatán, where they established a dynasty at the Maya center of Chichén Itzá. Maya legend tells us that the Feathered Serpent (Kukulcán in Yucatec) did indeed arrive then. Tula of the Toltecs some time thereafter fell on hard times, and finally in the twelfth century the Toltecs moved their capital to the Valley of Mexico. Thereafter they dispersed in all directions, some even to Guatemala. But they remained a great legend, the men of a golden age, to those who came later. The ruins of their temples, palaces, and ball courts are still visible in the fields near the village of Tula today.

Aztecs

Chichimec tribes continued to press into central Mexico. Most of them were Náhuatl speakers. Some, like the Acolhuas and Tepanecas, preceded the Aztecs into the Valley of Mexico in the thirteenth century. The little band of Aztecs (better called the Colhua Mexica) found itself shunted to the least desirable parts of a long-populated valley. By the middle of the fourteenth century they lived on some marshy islets at the western rim of the great lake that filled much of the Valley of Anahuac, or Mexico. The Aztecs slowly increased. Then later in the century they began to serve as mercenary soldiers, winning loot and a bigger place for themselves in the valley. Thereafter they rather quickly made themselves the predominant power of Middle America, skillfully employing the usual methods of conquest. They increasingly refined their political and religious institutions for the conduct of war. A great bureaucracy administered the state and kept records on deerskin and *agave* paper. Their script, a pictograph system, was adequate for such purposes, though inferior to Maya writing. The gods cried out, according to Aztec belief, for prisoners, whose hearts held up to the sky would ensure the progress of the sun and stave off the end of the world. Thus did religion, requiring a daily task of supreme importance, reinforce the political and economic ambitions of the state.

The polity and economy provided larger battalions and firmer direction of all elements of the society. The wise men burned the books of other peoples and proclaimed the Aztecs the descendants and heirs of the Toltecs of fabled Tula, the type of political lie many societies develop. Through alliances, treachery, and war, by 1500 the Aztecs had made conquests as far as the Gulf of Mexico and south to Guatemala. Not all of that area was held by the Aztecs, and some powerful groups remained unconquered. But the "empire" included possibly five million people (some estimates put it higher), in various types of relationships. Tribute flowed into the capital at Tenochtitlán, by then a veritable metropolis built into the lake, possibly with a population of well over 100,000. Food came from an area of some 125 miles in all directions from the city, but tribute in such luxuries as cacao, feathers, honey, skins, jade, and metals came from much farther.

Both military and religious institutions were important, and reinforced each other, under con-

trol of the elite. The monarch was a priest as well as a noble and by the time of the arrival of the Spaniards was regarded as a demigod. The elite were educated in part in priestly schools, but those who became great military captains surely were much like their counterparts in other cultures. War was a very important occupation among the Aztecs. Religious beliefs certainly influenced many of the actions of government, including the continual warfare, staged in part to obtain the incredible numbers of human sacrifices required by their beliefs. The god Huitzilopochtli demanded human hearts atop his pyramids. There is reason to suppose, however, that the sacrifice system was created as an instrument of statecraft, and the religious justification of it developed later. Some of the wars were fought with fellow Náhuatl speakers in neighboring states, sometimes on a basis of agreements among the elite and unknown to the common folk, so as to ensure a flow of prisoners to go under the knife at the top of the great blood-blackened pyramid in Tenochtitlán.

Much Aztec art reflects the brutality of the religion, featuring skulls and the wearing of skins flayed from human bodies. But there were other motives for warmaking. Estimates are that possibly half the inhabitants of Tenochtitlán subsisted on tributes from defeated or frightened peoples.

The society was rigidly hierarchical. Commoners, the majority of whom were farmers, were required to work and to pay tribute in kind and in labor to the state. There were also serfs on the estates of nobles, and some slaves. There were specialized groups of distinguished military leaders, administrators, long-distance merchants (who also acted as spies for the state), artisans, and porters—important in a society without draft animals. Tenochtitlán also was supplied by fleets of canoes on the great lake and the canals of the city. Some of the muckland of the lake margins was marvelously fertile and supported a large population in the Basin of Mexico. This region was divided into sixty units, each with a town as its center, administered by a local elite, and paying tribute to Tenochtitlán, Texcoco, or Tlacopán.

The great markets at the twin cities of Tenochtitlán-Tlatelolco were described as enormous by the Spanish conquerors. Used as media of exchange were cacao beans (sometimes counterfeited), cotton cloaks, and quills full of gold dust. Even the smaller towns in densely populated central Mexico had better-developed market systems than the Maya areas.

The Aztecs were the sophisticated heirs of many centuries of civilization in Mesoamerica. Although the Aztec culture, like the Roman, had repellant features, the ideal upper-class Aztec was, like the ideal Roman, austere and responsible. There were, of course, great differences—fundamental and superficial—between European and Aztec culture. Unfortunately for the Aztecs, most Europeans saw only the differences, and found them hateful. The results of that European attitude fully justified the strain of melancholy in Aztec poetry:

Even jade is shattered.
Even gold is crushed.
One does not live forever on this earth.
Perhaps we will live a second time?
Thy heart knows: Just one time do we live!

f. Higher Cultures of South America

The other important cradle of civilization in America comprised the central Andes and river valleys of the adjacent desert coast of Peru. An intensive agriculture developed, using hoes, clod breakers, and the foot plow, a pole with a sharp wooden or bronze tip, with a crosspiece near the tip for foot pressure, like a spade. Maize grew at elevations up to about 12,000 feet, and above that a specialized high-altitude grain, *quinoa*. This area was the original home of what some people much later called the "Irish" potato. Along the coast fertilizer consisted of fish heads and *guano* made from bird droppings which accumulated on arid coastal islands. Llama dung fertilized highland fields. Guinea pigs provided

the only meat that many commoners had. The little creatures scavenged scraps in lowly homes and were further fattened on greenery. Highlanders kept great herds of camel-like llamas and alpacas, the latter for fine wool, the former for meat and as beasts of burden (although limited to about one hundred pounds).

Pottery making existed by 1000 B.C. Quite early, especially in the coastal valleys, some of the finest wool and cotton textiles of Indian America developed. The most advanced metallurgy in the hemisphere included riveting objects of sheet metal and final soldering of the edges. But Spanish iron tools quickly replaced Amerindian copper and bronze ones following the conquest. In fact, native metal-working techniques disappeared so fast that even early Spanish chroniclers did not find out about them.

Some coastal peoples had wooden rafts with centerboards and steering sweeps, which they used for coastal traffic and in gathering the products of the sea. Before A.D. 600 the Mochica culture built an irrigation canal seventy-five miles long. Before the ninth century A.D. the coastal cultures were building elaborate religious edifices. Later, some of them controlled more than one river valley and built roads between them. Chan-Chan, the Chimu capital, covered some six square miles and had at least ten large walled rectangular enclosures, built of mud bricks, and a population of possibly 50,000. Art became elaborate and institutions and beliefs increasingly sophisticated.

Cultural development also proceeded in the highlands. The great classical site was Tihuanaco, a religious ceremonial center built of monolithic stones on the shores of Lake Titicaca. Among the groups of those high mountains the little tribe of Incas slowly rose to prominence. They were stabilized at Cuzco about A.D. 1200, but did not become a conquering and imperial power for more than two centuries. Then, from 1438 until the time of the European intrusion almost exactly a century later, they speedily conquered most of present-day coastal and highland Peru, Ecuador, and Bolivia, and parts of northern Argentina and Chile. This territory extended from north to south more than 2,000 miles. The east-west extent was much less, from the Pacific, where the coastal plain often was narrow and inhospitable, through those restricted basins of the Andes where cultivation was possible, to die on the slopes down to the Amazon basin and vast wet forest lands beyond. The eastern boundary was an impenetrable barrier of vegetation, tangled water courses, humidity and heat, and warlike primitive tribes.

How did the Incas hold such a vast and varied area together in an empire? They were superior to all Mesoamerican peoples in the effectiveness of their military and political institutions. Like the Aztecs, they came late to power, and much of their culture was learned from the peoples they conquered. The imperial talent, however, was uniquely Incan: the Incas produced three great rulers from 1438 to 1527. Inca expansion was conducted with a rapidity and skill seldom matched in human history, especially in a culture without horses. The military accomplishment did not depend on technological superiority, but on will, superior organization and supply, leadership, and a persistence quite different from the more usual intermittent military activity of Amerindian states.

In addition to military talent, which many other peoples also have had, the Inca had something rarer, the sort of imperial skill displayed by Rome. For administration the Inca used an effective method of damping or isolating dissidence by integrating conquered populations into the Inca system. They encouraged use of their own Quechua language and required conquered peoples to accept the Inca state religion, although they could also keep their own gods. Conquered nobles were permitted privileges; some even retained their own lands. Some doubtful groups were moved among faithful populations where they could do a minimum of harm and be indoctrinated by example.

A great system of roads, some taken over from earlier peoples, some built by the Incas, assisted in maintaining the empire. Suspension bridges of

fiber cables spanned immense gorges. At one place the Incas built a pontoon bridge, and at several places used what we would call a breeches buoy, with a basket that slid along a cable. In areas that were marshy or subject to flooding, the roads ran on earth causeways, pierced with culverts roofed with stone slabs. Sometimes the road surface was paved with flat stones. The roads ran the length of the empire, both in the mountains and on the coast. At intervals were rest houses for official travelers; no others were permitted in the rigidly regulated Inca society. Also at intervals were relay posts for state runners, who moved messages 150 miles a day and could carry fish from the Pacific to the Inca, deep in the mountains at Cuzco, before the stench became unacceptable.

Like most advanced cultures, the Incan was hierarchical, with a small elite ruling the masses. The Sapa Inca ruled the empire, and was so absolute a monarch that he often sat behind a screen, too holy for the common gaze. A subject had to approach him barefoot with a token burden on his back. The Sapa Inca operated through a large bureaucracy made up of two types of nobles: those of the Inca line, who filled the higher posts; and nobles of merit and service (*curacas*) who were named to complete the staff, a dual system similar to some developed in the Old World. Both types of nobles in Inca America were hereditary and exempt from the ever-present required labor. Included in the upper class were the persons in and attached to the ecclesiastical apparatus, which was also headed by the Inca. The Inca had no writing. The administrative burden of so large an empire was eased by the *quipu*, a system of colored and knotted strings that served as a record and as a mnemonic device and was the responsibility of a special class of accountants.

The masses were kept in order by rigid organization; heavy required work and tribute; provision for the sick, the aged, the orphan, and the widow; harsh penalties for unauthorized behavior, including moving about; and the awesome sanction of divine will, unambiguously interpreted by the bureaucracy. These regimented commoners were grouped into kinship groups as *ayllus*. Among pre-Inca highland peoples each ayllu acted as an economically self-sufficient unit. Under the Inca, the ayllu lands theoretically were divided into three parts, with the produce to go to the emperor (Sapa Inca), the Sun (church), and to the ayllu. There were, however, many variations. The Incas grouped ayllus into provinces, which in turn were grouped into the four quarters of the empire. At least in theory close regulation also governed crop tending, animal herding, artisanship, construction of public works, tax collection, labor rules, food storage for bad years, religious observance, marriage, and many other facets of life. So comprehensive a system of regimentation could not work perfectly, but probably the incidence of compliance increased with time as the empire was consolidated.

Much of the luxury of the upper class was concentrated in Cuzco, with its large stone or stone and adobe brick buildings. Some commoners lived in the town, but many more lived in surrounding clumps of adobe and thatch huts. The narrow streets of Cuzco had a stone drainage gutter in the center. The buildings for the elite were designed by professional architects who used clay models to plan for the capital as well as the empire's palaces, temples, roads, storehouses, agricultural terraces, irrigation systems, canalization of streams with stone banks, forts, baths, and tombs. Inca building was technically the best in Indian America, though not as spectacular in appearance as many Mesoamerican structures. Much Inca building was lost when Cuzco was torn apart and rebuilt according to Spanish tastes and needs. But the surviving stone work of the Incas remains beautiful and distinctive today. It consists of polished stones, either cut to uniform size and laid in regular courses or put together with irregular shapes. In either style, the stones fit marvelously without mortar. The outer surfaces are finely polished, and the stones are beveled inwards at the outer face edges, producing a pleasing shadow effect.

The roofs were of thick thatch arranged in a decorative pattern.

Life for the elite of Cuzco was luxurious. Servants were plentiful. Only the nobility was permitted to chew coca leaves, which released a small amount of cocaine. Vanity and the esthetic sense were gratified. There were gardens of artificial flowers made of precious metals and jewels. The great temple of the sun cult was lined with slabs of gold. Clothing, diet, amusements, and all other aspects of daily life were immensely more pleasant than in the huts of the lower order.

Much Inca literature was in poetic form, suitable to public recitation and to memorization among a people without writing. Most of it was lost, partly because it had so high a religious content that Spanish missionaries did what they could to suppress it. Versions that we have in Spanish include: "Oh ... ever-present Viracocha ... Thou who art from the beginnings of the world until its end! Thou gavest life and valor to men, saying, 'Let this be a man,' and to the woman, saying, 'Let this be a woman'.... Grant them long life and accept this our sacrifice, Oh Creator!" Clearly, that sounded too much like ancient Hebrew prayer to make Christian priests comfortable. Another recorded bit of Inca literature sang, "I was born like a lily in the garden, and so also was I brought up. As my age came, I grew up. And, as I had to die, so I dried up and I died."

These fragments, like Mesoamerican literature that has come down to us, showed the Amerindians similar in many sentiments to Europeans. But the conquerors did not want to see that. In any event, few Spaniards knew of that literature, partly because of lack of interest, partly because of heavy mortality and changed circumstances among the cultivated Inca upper class. The higher culture was not a part of the equipment of Inca shepherds and potato diggers, any more than peasants in Europe quoted the songs of the troubadours.

There has been much dispute among scholars about the quality of Inca life. At one extreme is the view that it was an admirable "communistic" society, in which all men were protected and cared for from cradle to grave. Adherents to this position cite Garcilaso de la Vega, "The Inca," son of a Spanish conqueror and an Inca princess. He wrote in praise of his mother's people—long after his father had set her aside for a Spanish woman, "No thoughtful man can fail to admire so noble and provident a government." A modern judgment is that the Incas erected what we would call a police state and that their society seems to have made little provision for a sense of joy or even minimal liberty to give spaciousness to people's lives. Possibly theirs was no more dispiriting in this regard than other hierarchical societies in ancient America or many that existed then and later in the Old World. At the least, the Incas' economic, political, and military achievements marked them as a people of impressive talent and will.[6]

g. Other Amerindians

Some other Amerindians were essentially sedentary. Among these other settled groups were the Arawak-speaking people of the widespread Taino culture in the Caribbean islands of Española and Cuba, the first centers of Spanish activity in America. Also sedentary were the Pueblos of what is now New Mexico, who lived in adobe apartments and supported themselves largely by tending crops. The Chibchas of modern Colombia were farmers with good agricultural skills and well-developed crafts, including impressive gold work. Many other culture groups, however, were nomadic or seminomadic and most of them few in numbers. Some of the relatively primitive groups were pacific or were ineffective warriors; others were formidable in battle, like many of the Amerindians encountered by Spaniards on the northern shores of South America or the Araucanians of Chile and many

Indians of northern Mexico. Few of these peoples were accustomed to rigidly scheduled work, and they reacted poorly—by death, flight, or inefficient performance—to European systems of forced labor. On the other hand, they had knowledge of the environment, skills, and at least a marginal usefulness as labor, so that their largely negative role in the conquest, from the Spanish point of view, was supplemented by a few positive factors.[7]

h. The "Lost Future" of the American Indians

Some writers have maintained that the Amerindians were decadent when the Spaniards arrived. Part of the argument is political: for example, that the Aztec system was at the limits of its capacity for control and that the enemies it had created were certain to tear the system apart, as indicated by aid the Spaniards got from Amerindian groups during the conquest. We cannot know, however, that there might not have been sufficient change in the Aztec system to increase its effectiveness. Recent research suggests, in fact, that the Aztecs at the time of the conquest were reducing the power of the independent enclaves in central Mexico. We know that the Aztecs had successfully overlaid the old clan organizations with a class and hierarchical system more suited to the needs of the empire. Possibly their social organization would have continued to evolve usefully. Finally, we cannot know that the historic eclecticism of central Mexico would not have thrown up a new people capable of greater achievement.

What was there about the culture history of the Andean region to suggest the probable appearance of a people of such political talent as the Incas? Nothing. Commentators have claimed that the Inca system was breaking up when the

---

[6] Such achievements lead many scholars to describe the Inca as a true civilization; a few maintain that the term must be denied cultures without writing.

[7] See Chapter 15 on the Tupí of Brazil. Others of the more primitive Indian culture groups are commented on in other sections dealing with their effect on the history of the colonial era.

Spaniards arrived, and indeed there had been recent civil war. But civil wars were common in the Roman and other long-enduring systems. The claim that the civil war in Peru was indicative of the fact that the Inca system had outrun its cultural and technological resources cannot be proven, because we do not know whether instability would have been permanent or crippling. Inca achievement was sufficiently remarkable to permit us to suppose that it might have endured longer and been extended.

Some historians have believed that Amerindian cultural achievement peaked among the Classic Maya, that it decayed among them thereafter, and that it never was matched in other culture groups. But labeling the Maya at the conquest as culturally decadent requires overlooking conditions not associated with decadence: It was a healthy population, with a satisfactory agriculture and commerce and an impressive determina-

tion to defend itself against invaders. The Maya clearly had declined intellectually from their great days, but who can tell what revivals might have occurred, since there is no reason to believe that the human stock had deteriorated? Our understanding of the rise and fall of human cultures is not so perfect that dicta on such matters can be taken seriously. Furthermore, we cannot know that there were no stimuli that would have set off intellectual growth among the triumphant Incas, whose energies had been poured largely into war and administration. We must point out again that our understanding of human intellectual history is too feeble to permit confidence in sweeping judgments on the Amerindians.

In any event, the destiny—or history—of the Amerindians was conquest by Europeans and the processes of somatic and cultural amalgamation that played so large a part in the history of the other continents.

The Amerindian Civilizations

The Amerindian civilizations produced agricultural surpluses that supported artisans, priests, administrators, and warriors. Their stone monuments testify to social organization and a long development of building skills. Artistic products were often charming and impressive.

This basalt figure of a bearded man, possibly a portrait, is from the Olmec culture that existed in the lowlands along the Gulf of Mexico centuries before the Aztecs. It may have been carved some two thousand years before the Spaniards arrived in Mexico. *Carlos Lazo de la Vega*

A Maya mural at Bonampak, in southeastern Mexico, shows musicians in an elaborate, colorful ceremonial procession. *Courtesy of United Fruit Company*

The Great Pyramid at the Maya ceremonial center of Chichén Itzá in Yucatán, Mexico, with the columns of another structure in the foreground. *Hamilton Wright*

Fragment of a tapestry from a coastal desert culture of Peru. Woven in a design of animal and human figures, using vivid colors, this bit of cloth is from 700 to 1,000 years old. *Courtesy of the Museum of the American Indian, Heye Foundation*

Ancient Inca walls at Sacsahuamán, Peru, closely fitted without mortar. Notice, on the far right, a white-shirted climber resting. *Peter Menzel*

2 Europe and Iberia

Why is not Mexico's culture heavily Chinese rather than Spanish? Or Brazil's French rather than Portuguese? Or Peru ruled by an Inca and the documents of state printed in the Quechua tongue? Because Europeans were ready sooner than Asians for expansion overseas—they forged and dominated the Oceanic Age. Because Spaniards and Portuguese were ready before other Europeans to exploit new opportunities overseas. Because the American Indian civilization did not match the European in some critical ways. Thus, Europe in general, and Spain and Portugal in particular, enjoyed advantages. In other times we said they were "superior." Today, however, superiority seems a murkier concept than it once did. We now know that the local, temporary, and partial advantages that subdued Indians and enslaved black Africans were merely technological rather than moral or intellectual. Africans, American Indians, and Asians contested European pretensions during the Oceanic Age; other Europeans contested those of Spain and Portugal. Neither Europe in the larger contest, nor Iberia in the smaller, established permanent hegemony, but they tried.

a. The Expansion of Europe

The great expansion of Europe went on for five centuries, from the fifteenth, when the Portu-guese traveled to Africa and Asia, to the early twentieth, when resistance to European domination plainly was the wave of the future. The expansion was grounded in European desire to inquire, to build, to acquire, and to rule. It was a movement of bodies and genes, of economic aims and systems and ties, of technology, of language, and other aspects of culture. A major flow was from Iberia to the Western Hemisphere, where in a few decades after 1492 Spain and Portugal took over a large part of the earth.

In that huge region from Florida and Texas and California, through Mexico and the isles of the Caribbean and the great continent to the south, to the edges of the polar sea, the Hispanic pioneers set up the first large-scale modern European colonies overseas. European expansion into Asia and Africa in the sixteenth to eighteenth centuries was smaller and more superficial. In the Hispanic American colonies occurred the largest mingling of European with other bloodstocks—Indian and African Negro—and a series of catastrophic clashes between European and other cultures, in which gods died or were transformed, languages perished or were twisted, technologies mingled, and systems of power and control were modified. After the revolt of Britain's thirteen colonies in North America, new outlooks were created in the Hispanic colonies in the early nineteenth century that were part of the first great wave of modern anticolonialism.

The Hispanic expansion to America involved two of the larger "accidents" of modern history: the fact that the peoples of Europe rather than those of Asia, Africa, or America were ready to expand; and the chance that Spain and Portugal were able at that precise time to concentrate on overseas expansion in a way not open to, for example, Frenchmen, Germans, Russians, or Englishmen. These things were not, of course, really accidents, but merely history—the way human developments worked out in fact as against the way they might be expected to work according to social theory or the relative merits of culture groups. The technology and cultural drives necessary to effective exploration and to attempted domination of the world that Europeans developed gave them large advantages over Oriental peoples, who were their equals in ability and total achievement, and even larger advantages over the talented but less developed peoples of Africa, Oceania, and the Western Hemisphere.

The new colonial processes, molded by then current conditions, later were sanctified by their beneficiaries as being the result of superior talent, virtue, and energy. Rivals of Spain and Portugal, however, condemned their American conquests as the result of chance. Elizabeth of England in the sixteenth century took that view; newly unified Germany of the late nineteenth century viewed the far-flung colonial outposts of British, French, Spanish, and Portuguese culture, people, power, and wealth as the unfair result of historical accident.

The total list of influences behind the expansion of Europe is not seriously argued; their relative importance is. Some scholars emphasize changes in motivation, such as restlessness, individualism, curiosity, the questing spirit of the Renaissance, or the desire to find a new route to the spices of the East. Others stress cultural or technological changes that made expansion more attractive or feasible: better ships and sail patterns, navigational aids, or the relatively centralized and effective governments of Portugal

and Spain. Accepting those influences, we may also be sure that much of the drive for expansion was economic, political, and religious—factors old in European culture. Only the proper stimulus was necessary to attach those motives effectively to overseas exploration and conquest. Such factors pushed Portugal and Spain in the fifteenth century into occupation of the Atlantic isles of Madeira, the Canaries, and the Azores, and led Portugal slowly south along the coast of Africa on the way to the distant Orient. Those enterprises involved not only oceanic voyages, but the conquest of natives (in the Canaries and Africa), the development of tropical plantations, and the use of forced and slave labor—all of which were to be important in America.

b. The Portuguese Voyages

Portugal led the way to America psychologically and technically in the fifteenth century, using late medieval ideas and marine technology to move into unknown seas. The Portuguese knew of the Atlantic islands in the mid-fourteenth century, and in the fifteenth century Portugal fastened its hold on Madeira and the Azores, while Castile took the Canaries. Portuguese accomplishments in African waters by the 1470s made certain the eventual rounding of the Cape of Good Hope and passage by the eastern sea route to Asia. That bold venture ensured the discovery of America even if Columbus had never lived, for frequent voyages from Europe around Africa made it certain that weather, navigational errors, or marine accidents would push vessels to South America. Thus, whether the Portuguese Cabral, arriving on the coast of Brazil in 1500 with an Asia-bound fleet, had sailed deliberately to America or arrived accidentally is not important.

How did tiny Portugal come to lead Europe along the sea route to the Orient? Portugal had fewer than a million inhabitants in the fifteenth century. It had the advantage, however, of a "modern" government—a centralized national dynastic state, without those strong regional or political divisions that reduced the capacities of most European peoples. The meager resources of Portugal could thus be concentrated in a manner often difficult to match in richer but divided or strife-torn France, England, the Germanies, or Italy. It had the advantage, also, of an oceanic —as opposed to an inland sea—position, and the nautical skills and vessels that could withstand the battering waves of the Atlantic. Its ports were conveniently located with regard to the African enterprise. Its location and poverty insulated it from the attentions of Europe's warring states, and it lacked the resources to develop martial ambitions of its own, generally being content to fend off Castile. The sparseness of Portugal's internal resources tended to encourage fishing and other maritime enterprise. Its nobility often participated in commercial ventures. But none of those factors would have enabled it to compete successfully with the English, Dutch, French, Germans, and Italians had those peoples fought for the African enterprise in the fifteenth century.[1] When some of them did compete in Africa and the Orient, in the sixteenth and especially the seventeenth centuries, they dispossessed Portugal of much of its holdings. The fact that they did not compete in the fifteenth and much of the sixteenth centuries was the greatest advantage of the Portuguese: "accident," or history, or the conditions of the time, distracted potential rivals with other tasks—dynastic, civil, and international wars; religious turmoil; regional rivalries.

In 1415–1460 much of the Portuguese activity was inspired by Prince Henry, the "Navigator." He built on a Portuguese tradition of voyaging between the Iberian Peninsula, the Canary Isles, and the coast of Morocco to trade and to fish. Portuguese traders dealt largely in wine, fish, and salt, finding that to break into the more profitable but monopoly-ridden Mediterranean trades, protected as they were by powerful fleets, was

impossible. Henry combined interest in the trade and gold of Africa with crusading aims—to smite the Muslim, turn pagans into Christians, and ally with Christian rulers in Africa, including the legendary Prester John. For decades he encouraged and subsidized mariners and mapmakers. His activity was the result of an accumulation of European advances in the marine art, and of his own—and some traders'—interests in Africa. It owed little to the upsurge of the spirit of quest associated with the Renaissance or to revolutionary ideas about the shape and size of the globe. In later years, however, after Henry's time, Portugal's maritime enterprise was heavily influenced by belief in the sphericity of the earth and by the specific desire to find a sea route to the spices and other goods of the Orient.

The Portuguese benefited in the later years of the fifteenth century, as did other Europeans, from technical improvements in navigation and in ship construction and rigging and from the growth in Europe of interest in the study of geography and cosmography. Much of the last concentrated on classical—often Ptolemaic—ideas, which contradicted the religiously oriented views of medieval Europe and encouraged speculation about the earth. Printing with movable type (developed in the middle years of the fifteenth century) spread interest in such activities, through production of academic treatises, charts and maps, and the popular travel accounts of such medieval European explorers of the outer world as the Polos and John of Plano Carpini. There was also increased circulation of manuscripts containing sailing directions and of navigational manuals.

Although the exploring ships were standard or modified merchantmen of the later Middle Ages, many improved types were being developed during the fifteenth century. Hulls were strengthened, keels and rudders were improved, rigging was altered. The simple square sail, known in the Mediterranean since ancient times, was divided into units for easier handling, and combined with the Arabic lateen sail to give added maneuverability. With these and other changes came ships that could better meet the conditions

---

[1] Those qualities of Portuguese culture that were important to the settlement and development of Brazil are discussed in the appropriate chapters in connection with that colony.

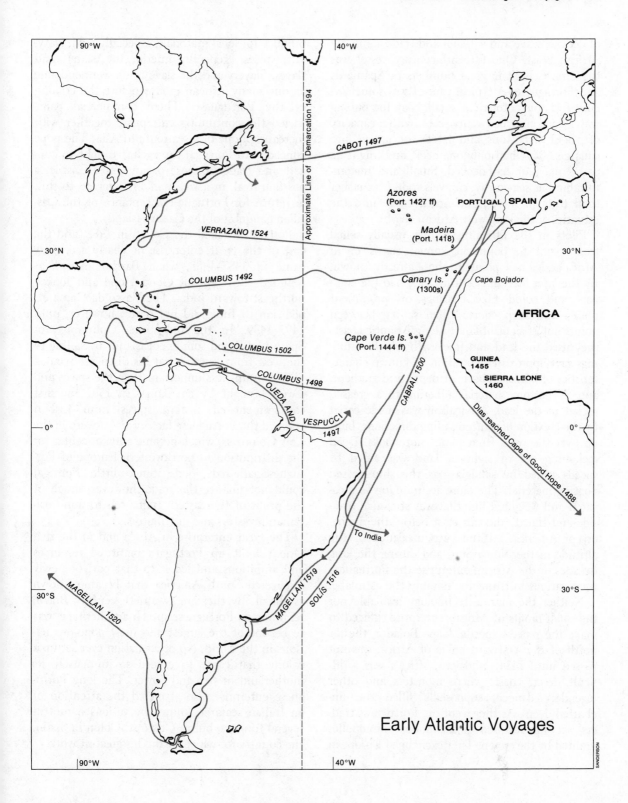

CABOT 1497

VERRAZANO 1524

COLUMBUS 1492

COLUMBUS 1502

COLUMBUS 1498

OJEDA AND

VESPUCCI 1497

CABRAL 1500

Dias reached Cape of Good Hope 1488

To India

MAGELLAN 1519

SOLÍS 1516

MAGELLAN 1520

Approximate Line of Demarcation 1494

Azores
(Port. 1427 ff)

PORTUGAL SPAIN

Madeira
(Port. 1418)

Canary Is.
(1300s)

Cape Bojador

AFRICA

Cape Verde Is.
(Port. 1444 ff)

**GUINEA
1455**

**SIERRA LEONE
1460**

90°W   40°W

30°N   30°N

0°   0°

30°S

90°W   40°W

Early Atlantic Voyages

SANDERSON

of oceanic wave and weather and trade along the African coast. One fifteenth-century vessel was the caravel, built in great numbers by Spaniards and Portuguese. A typical caravel was some seventy feet long (today, a small boat for pulling water-skiers may be twenty feet), with a capacity of about sixty tons and lateen or lateen and square sails. It had only one deck, and might be partly open or half-decked. Small and uncomfortable but seaworthy, caravels rode over rather than through waves, and nosed easily into the estuaries of the long west African coast.

Pilots in the fifteenth century usually sailed from point to point on known coasts or in Africa added new points to those already known. By the later fifteenth century they had the compass and could take bearings on prominent points and keep course when sailing between points out of sight of land. Along Atlantic coasts they used the lead and line, with which soundings gave approximate position by known characteristics of bottoms, both by depth and gradient, and by bottom material adhering to a greased socket in the lead. Navigation was made easier by the creation of written sailing directions, built up over the years from pilots' notebooks. Dead reckoning out of sight of land was aided by speeds timed by sandglass as the ship passed floating material. The more accurate *log* (a measured and weighted line that was streamed overside and timed) did not exist before the discovery of America. Latitude was measured by the altitude of the North Star, and during the long decades of the African enterprise the Portuguese used various instruments, notably the astrolabe.

Neither the marine technology available nor the small profits of African enterprise sufficed to make the process speedy. Cape Bojador, the far north of the westward bulge of Africa, was not passed until 1434. Northern Africa's was a difficult desert coast, where monsters and other legendary dangers supposedly filled the uncharted deeps. As they went on, Portuguese traders set up fortified posts under monopolies granted by the crown. They exchanged European produce for local materials, especially gold, ivory, salt, spices (generally inferior to Asian), and slaves. Slavery and the slave trade were endemic among many African groups before the coming of the Portuguese. These commercial gains fueled the continuing enterprise, together with increasing hope of a sea route to Asia. The pope conceded to Portugal the exclusive right to convert and trade in those pagan lands. Castile, a possible rival, in a treaty in 1479 agreed to this, in return for Portuguese acceptance of the Castilian conquest of the Canary Islands.

Portugal reached the Congo in 1482, and the end of the great enterprise of nearly a century came in 1487–1488, when Bartholomeu Dias rounded the Cape of Good Hope and looked northeast toward India. The Vasco da Gama expedition to India did not occur, however, until 1497–1499. In the meantime, Columbus for Spain had found some poor islands by sailing to the west from Europe, but his discovery seemed to Europeans less important than the spices and jewels brought by da Gama. In 1501 the first consignment of eastern spices from Lisbon reached the Portuguese factory at Antwerp in the Low Countries, which became a major center for the distribution to northwestern Europe of Portuguese-gathered goods. Since little Portugal could not finance the trade, however, much of the profit of the eastern traffic fell to non-Lusitanian investors and distributors.

The great enterprise in Africa and in the rich Orient built up Portugal's maritime resources and ambitions and led it to that part of newly discovered South America that became known as Brazil. By the late twentieth century Brazil, retaining its Portuguese speech and heritage, was to be one of the largest and most populous nations in the world. No other nation ever set up a colony that came to exceed so immensely its motherland in size and power. The long Portuguese enterprise also attracted the attention of an Italian seafarer, known by various names in several tongues, but as Cristóbal Colón in Spain, the country for which he did his greatest work.

c. Spaniards and Other Europeans

The Spain of Columbus was well suited to the overseas exploration, conquest, and colonization to which he led it. It had effective government; national pride and ambition; missionary zeal; resources of men, money, ships, and the other requirements for conquest overseas.

Spain, like Portugal, was a leader in the creation of a unified national dynastic state, with the reduction of regional rivalries, the control of the great nobility, the relative ensurance of the succession to the throne, and the damping of the pretensions of parliamentary institutions, which in western Europe in the later Middle Ages had begun to contest the powers of monarchs. The Spain of many kingdoms, exacerbating regional rivalries and frittering away "national" resources in internecine strife, was potentially united by the marriage in 1469 of Isabella of Castile and Ferdinand of Aragon. They soon succeeded to their thrones and, though separate rulers, cooperated closely. Spain was fortunate that both had ability and determination. Among their achievements were reduction of the powers of the nobility, improvement of the administrative and fiscal agencies of government, and (in 1492) the conquest of Muslim Granada. Furthermore, they left to their heirs a united national dynastic state. It became full reality in 1516, when their grandson Charles inherited all their realms, although for most of the years from Isabella's death in 1504 to his own in 1516 Ferdinand was in effect ruler of a united Spain.

The monarchy in Spain still had to fight off the last important efforts to make the parliaments (*Cortes*) effective; in addition, regional customs and traditions, even distinct dialects and languages, somewhat reduced the effectiveness of national unity. So Spain was fortunate that no great rivalry for America arose during the half century after its discovery while the crown continued with consolidation of the new nation and its institutions of government. Nevertheless, even by 1492 the consolidation of Spanish power was

impressive; and thereafter its expressions in policy—especially the mounting of military operations in Europe and America—were critical to the success of the conquest and colonization of Spanish America. During the first decades of the American conquest Spain was recognized as the greatest power in Europe, with renowned soldiers and fleets and a consolidated position in the Peninsula. Charles I of Spain represented the union of the realms of his grandparents Isabella and Ferdinand and the position of his father (Philip of Burgundy, a Hapsburg) in the rich Low Countries, on the borders of France, and in the Germanies.

The importance of national pride and ambition and of missionary zeal is more difficult to measure than effective government. The Europeans of the day certainly considered the pride of the Spaniard legendary. It was a pride founded in military victory, triumph over the Muslim, and in a profound xenophobia that owed something to the peculiar institutions of Spain developed during long centuries of rule by Roman, Visigoth, Muslim, and regional Spanish princes. The zeal of the Spanish Catholic in conversion of the infidel is, if anything, even clearer. Monarch in Spain and conquistador in America were driven in part by a passion for the Christian faith. The religious zealotry, no less than the national pride, of Spain was a legend in Europe in the years of the conquest of America.

The physical resources of Spain were sizable but not lavish. It had ships and seamen, and an oceanic as well as a Mediterranean maritime tradition and technology. Its fiscal resources, public and private, were at least equal, as the event proved, to the conquest and more adequate than they would have been before the consolidation of the realms. There was no doubt that Spain had men suited to the enterprise and eager to go. Some of these were minor nobles—*hidalgos, caballeros*—whose status entitled them to little more than some legal exemptions, respect of a sort from inferiors, and a keen desire to follow the traditional upper-class path to war and fame and fortune. Others were of the proletariat or lower middle class of a poorly developed country with what we would call much un- and underemployment and little expectation of improvement. Some of these, like Francisco Pizarro, proved as adept conquerors as any *hidalgos*. Spain had an unusually large aristocratic group with a traditional attachment to military activity, but such groups and attitudes were found in many countries. By no means did all the Spanish nobility go to America, and many commoners did.

All these conditions and qualities made the Spaniards at least as well prepared for the American enterprise as any other European national culture group and better prepared than most. We cannot be sure, however, how others would have performed had theirs been the chance. The matter is of some importance because of the long-continued "black legend" of excessive Spanish cruelty, avarice, and mismanagement in America as well as the notion of superior Spanish military ardor and ability. Some of this legend grew from events in America or from misinformation or deliberate misinterpretation or exaggeration, some from foreign estimates of Spanish character and institutions, amply influenced by national rivalries and jealousy. The question therefore arises: Just how different was Spanish culture from that of Europe generally? One answer is that although there was variation within the European culture area, the varieties formed a describable whole, just as did such cultures as the Chinese or Maya. Spanish culture certainly had unique elements and, within the limits of the western European "norm," gave to Spanish America its special institutional and traditional aspects within the general Occidental culture.

Englishmen or Frenchmen, however, under different historical circumstances, could have conquered the Aztecs and Incas much as did Spaniards, and some of their "solutions" to problems of the colonial era might have been similar. The differences between Spanish and French and English culture were not so profound that they were not similarly interested in silver and gold, profits from tropical produce, forced labor

of Indians and enslavement of black Africans, and the triumph of Christianity over other faiths.[2] Lists of medieval holdovers in Spanish culture or of Muslim influences or other peninsular peculiarities help in a minor way to explain specific Spanish acts in America, but scarcely at all to establish Spanish superiority over other Europeans for the tasks of conquest and colonization. Especially, we cannot compare Spanish *caballeros* of 1520 with English religious radicals of 1620 or suppose that the kind of Englishmen who would have engaged in the conquests of Mexico and Peru in either the sixteenth or seventeenth centuries would have been much different from Spaniards in their conception or execution of conquest.

The Spaniards did have some institutions to transfer to America that seemed especially well suited to local conditions. But they always were modified—by deliberate decision or by circumstances—in the American environment; we cannot know how the English or French might have modified their institutions in Mexico or Peru. The fact is that judgments of the suitability of Spanish ideas and institutions to America largely depend on their use in the specific cultural environment, which in critical areas meant large numbers of Indians of sedentary habit available for labor, not only in agriculture but in silver mines—two conditions not encountered in English or French America. The Spaniards could not claim to be unusually fruitful in arts or sciences or in commerce, industry, or banking. They did things in the European way and often less well than the best practitioners in other lands. That Spaniards emphasized their "differentness" is a fact, and insofar as that self-image affected their actions and the reactions of their foes, it had some importance. Naturally Englishmen and English Americans would exaggerate those differ-

2 Discussions of Spanish and Portuguese institutions and habits of thought, together with comparisons with other European national groups, occur in many appropriate places in the following chapters: for example, 6, Section a, on institutions of government in Europe; 8, Section b, class and caste in Spain and America.

ences in order to condemn Spanish "depravity," and Spaniards and Spanish Americans would reject Anglo-American propaganda and celebrate their own superior institutions and virtues.

Finally, there is no question that the Spaniards were aided in the American enterprise by the relative weakness of competition. The extra-European world was neither interested nor politically or technologically prepared to compete. In Europe, Russia was weak and not a maritime power; Italy was divided and its effective and rich merchant states were involved in a profitable economic system of their own; the Germanies were fragmented and much distracted with continental warfare; the rich Low Countries were under Spanish rule or French attack; England was relatively underdeveloped and spent much of its energy in the sixteenth century on dynastic rivalries; France, the richest land in Europe, wasted its substance on foreign wars and on a series of ruinous internal religious and dynastic conflicts. "History" for nearly a century after the discovery of America seemed to conspire in favor of the overseas enterprises of Spain and Portugal.

3 Early Discoveries in America

Treasure hunters are a restless lot. There is always a new place to search. So for twenty-seven years the first generation of Europeans in America, especially in the Spanish area, were always on the move. The *entrada*—exploratory penetration—was the characteristic institution of those years. The men of the first generation were transients to they knew not where. They would not rest until they found it—whatever "it" was. The first enthusiasm about Columbus' landfall to the west was soon dissipated as rich India and Cathay were not encountered. A few searched on for a strait to the wealth Portugal had found by sailing east. A few found gold or pearls. But the Indies—as the Iberians called the new lands —seemed poor. Intellectual curiosity certainly did not sustain many of the conquerors. They cared little for the strange flora and fauna of the Indies; even the Indians engaged only the attention given beasts of burden, and they dwindled toward extinction in a few years without much notice from the marauders. So, few Spaniards or Portuguese in 1492–1519 went to those lands of little promise, and few of them found fame or fortune. But they looked for it. Brazil was little settled, but Spaniards unceasingly put out from their little hut clusters in the Caribbean to probe the unknown land and seas. They were not sure what they were looking for, but they knew

it when they found it in 1519 and thereafter. When they found it, they took it, and their restlessness ended. They ceased to be transients. As solid citizens they settled down to build a system that lasted three hundred years.

a. Columbus and the Discovery

Columbus, far from alone in proclaiming the sphericity of the earth, was more notable for his determination in the face of indifference to reach the Orient by sailing west. The Portuguese government, to which Columbus applied in the 1480s, declined to support him, because its experts thought he underestimated the length of the voyage—as he did—and because it was satisfied with the progress of its movement along the coast of Africa. Isabella of Castile finally agreed to help finance the enterprise, because it was a peaceful and cheap way of competing with the Portuguese. The crown provided some funds for the expedition and extracted some from the little town of Palos in the form of fines. Private investors also supplied capital, rather less than usually was the case with later American exploration, generally licensed by the crown but paid for by the venturers.

Isabella's counselors had only faint and generalized hopes for success. The contracts between the crown and Columbus spoke not of Asia, but of "certain Islands and Mainland in the Ocean Sea"; and they conferred great powers and possessions upon an obscure mariner now named admiral, viceroy, and governor. With these glorious sanctions—on which he had insisted—Columbus skillfully made his way to the Spanish Canary Islands—destined to be an important way station on the route he pioneered—and on west for nearly five weeks into unknown seas. He made the most famous landfall of maritime history in the Bahamas, and moved on to the coasts of Cuba and Española, leaving in the latter some men in a tiny settlement named Navidad. During the voyage, Columbus found numerous opportunities to convince himself, and to declare, that he was in the Orient of his dreams—an opinion he maintained for years in the face of the evidence and the skepticism of other observers. Poor Columbus! He found neither Cathay nor the great power he desired and not a tithe of the wealth he expected, nor was his name attached to the wondrous continent he found for Spain and the Occident.[1]

Isabella and Ferdinand honored Columbus as he deserved for his astonishing—if somewhat ambiguous—voyage. There was considerable excitement in Europe at the news—and dismay in Portugal. Columbus received large powers for

new activity, and in 1493 sailed with 1,500 men in seventeen vessels. On an expedition that lasted until 1496, he discovered Jamaica and Puerto Rico and some of the Lesser Antilles, further explored the coasts of Cuba, and continued with the work of colonization. He made a third voyage in 1498–1499, discovering the coast of South America in the area of Trinidad and the mouth of the Orinoco; and a fourth in 1502–1504 in which he explored some of the shores of Central America. The great mariner died in 1506, disappointed in his hopes of the East (which he always claimed to have reached), unaware of most of the marvels of the enormous continent that came curiously to be called by the name of a more obscure seaman, Amerigo Vespucci.

On Columbus' return from his first voyage, Isabella and Ferdinand petitioned the pope, who was a Spaniard, for such exclusive rights over pagan areas as the papacy had conceded Portugal in Africa and had earlier given to other Christian sovereigns. The resulting series of papal bulls in 1493 granted Castile those pagan lands west of a line one hundred leagues beyond the Azores and Cape Verde Islands and running grandly from pole to pole. In return for this colossal—as it proved—grant, Castile was to Christianize unbelievers. Although no one then knew what the grant embraced, King João II of Portugal bitterly protested. What threatened to be an ugly dispute was smoothed over for a time by the Treaty of Tordesillas (1494) between Spain and Portugal, moving the line of demarcation to 370 leagues west of the Cape Verdes. Portugal's enterprise in Africa received not only more protection, but, as it turned out, an area (Brazil) on the American continent.

The lines of demarcation were important—but not entirely conclusive—in dividing the American and Asian activities of Spain and Portugal,[2] but had no effect on their potential rivals. Although Catholic princes sometimes accepted

---

[1] There is today little scholarly interest in other "discoveries" of America, because they can have had small effect upon Amerindian development and certainly meant little to Europe. That is, such as may have occurred played a small role in history. It is agreed that Norsemen visited North America but that this had no important influence on European geographic thought, or on Columbus' ideas. There is rather persuasive evidence that Bristol seamen fished off the Grand Banks long before Columbus' voyage. For one thing, their descriptions of the banks indicate it; for another, where else in that direction would they have caught such large quantities of fish? They took the fish back dried, presumably on the North American continent. The evidence is less satisfying for the claims for voyages to America by early modern Welsh or French or Portuguese mariners or fishermen, and even less so for earlier medieval and ancient Greek mariners. There also are theories of African, Chinese, and Polynesian voyages to America, supported with a variety of unconvincing arguments, documents, and suppositions.

[2] Later treaty adjustments of Spanish and Portuguese claims were made, for Asia in the sixteenth century, for South America in the eighteenth.

papal pronouncements on nonspiritual matters, they often did not; and, of course, after the beginning of the Protestant Reformation in a few years, some monarchs would accept none of the views of Rome. Both public and private interests outside Iberia soon greeted Columbus' discovery as an invitation to action. Among others, Henry VII of England sent the Italian John Cabot in 1497–1498 on voyages that reached Newfoundland and probably the northern part of the present-day United States. News of this English activity caused some alarm in Spain and the Spanish Caribbean. In 1500–1502 Gaspar and Michael de Corte Real explored for Portugal to the north of Newfoundland.

b. Early Spanish Explorations

For nearly three decades, exploration was confined chiefly to the Caribbean isles and the shores of Central and northern South America. There were, however, some other penetrations. The coast of Florida was sighted in 1513, but Spanish exploration of North America did not begin until later. The Portuguese began settlement of Brazil. The Spaniard Juan Díaz de Solís in 1515–1516 reached the Plata estuary in southern South America. The expedition of Magellan in 1519–1521 sailed from Spain around South America, across the Pacific, and around Africa back to Europe. This first circumnavigation of the earth confirmed its sphericity (of which the informed had had no doubt for years), the fact that the lands discovered by Columbus were in the midst of vast seas and remote from Asia (hence that the westward route to the riches of the East was difficult), and established some Spanish rights in what became the Philippine Islands.

The chronological divide of 1519 is important because in that year the Spaniards first clearly opened relations with Indian cultures that promised large rewards in labor, precious metals, and missionary effort. Before the invasion of Mexico in that year, what was found, together with the hope of locating a strait leading to Asia, was

sufficient to stimulate a small-scale continuing effort, but not to draw the men, enthusiasm, and investment that followed thereafter.

Problems and Methods

Until 1519, the explorers faced serious problems. Funds often were lacking for the purchase, hire, or proper repair of vessels. Ships built or reconstructed during expeditions were badly made of driftwood or green timber hacked from the forest. Tropical ship borers were a serious pest. Winds and currents were unpredictable, even when they were well known; hurricanes could be deadly. Explorers suffered terribly from starvation. The climate of the islands was benign, but in places in South and Central America the Spaniards found arid wastes, tropical foliage and heat and humidity, clouds of insects, areas of nearly impenetrable marsh, river, and tangled vegetation. Heavy European clothing or the metal armor or cotton quilting sometimes worn for protection caused great discomfort. Armor was necessary because expeditions encountered many warlike Indians, especially on the mainland. Some were cannibals. Some used poisoned darts, which the Spaniards viewed with much the panic that Indians showed before the jaws of the huge European war dogs. At least one Spaniard clapped red-hot armor plate over an arrow wound in the hope of drawing the poison.

A few Spaniards in a huge area of sea and shore were probing the unknown. The same uncertainty slowed them that had made the Portuguese venture along the African coast a series of tentative thrusts that sometimes stopped just short of what later proved a valuable find. Balboa took three years crossing the narrow neck of America—less than a hundred miles—partly because he did not know that the "South Sea" was so near. Even when territories had been discovered, they usually remained vacant of Spaniards for years, and were seldom visited. Columbus, returning from Central America on his last voyage, had a terrible time beating east against the wind, abandoned two ships riddled with worms, and then spent more than a year marooned on isolated Jamaica.

Palaver with Indians both aided and misdirected the explorers. Even with interpreters such communication could be misleading; without them it depended on sign language and sketches. Geographic data obtained from Indians sometimes proved accurate; at other times, insistent questioning of Indians about gold, often punctuated with torture, simply produced lies. Sometimes the misdirected effort arose from European eagerness—shared by Columbus—to hear Indian words that could be interpreted as gold.

Despite difficulties and small returns, there were always Spaniards ready for voyages in leaky vessels, and for *entradas* (penetrations) by land into new territories. An *entrada* consisted of a small group of Spaniards, possibly with a few horses; often with war dogs; swords, lances, crossbows, a few clumsy firearms; and ideally, swarms of Indians. If an *entrada* did not start with Indians, it hoped soon to acquire them. They were important as porters, carrying the body armor of the European warriors (unless attack seemed imminent), chests of trade trinkets and other impedimenta, cooking pots, and food. They also made fires, hauled water, pulled off boots, gathered horse fodder, and served as sex partners. Above all, the porters died—of overwork, disease, and starvation and malnutrition. The Indians of an *entrada* usually far outnumbered the Spaniards, but in many cases (both in the early Caribbean and in the later decades of the great conquests) the records do not even mention their existence and do not number them even though there may be a figure for swine.

The Spaniards employed various methods in dealing with Indians met by *entradas*, depending partly on the temperament and intelligence of the Spanish commander. They sometimes gave trinkets to the Indians or traded them for gold. The amount of gold thus obtained did not often satisfy, and more drastic measures followed. Sometimes peaceful arrangements could be made with the *cacique* (an Arawak word for chief that the Spaniards carried from Española to all the language areas of America). Sometimes, on one pretext or another, the *cacique* was made prisoner and held hostage for his people to force an agreement. Columbus used this tactic as did two generations of Spanish conquerors in America after him—and as had unnumbered warriors of the Old World for thousands of years. In Española a deliberate policy of eliminating the *caciques* finally was adopted.

The explorers often inflicted terrible punishments on Indian individuals or groups. Ojeda in Española in 1494 lopped the ears of an Indian in public on a charge of stealing. Such punishment was, of course, no more than occurred in Europe, but in America such "justice" often fell with little or no investigation, sometimes chiefly to overawe the populace, without regard for the guilt of the individual. Soldiers in all ages had done the same. There was also some casual cruelty to Indians. Occasionally fierce Spanish war dogs were set on friendly Indians as a sport. If this kind of "sport" says something about the callousness of rude, lower-class, irregular warriors, one can also easily understand that almost any activity was a relief from boredom in the encampments of the conquest.

Along with such aggressive methods, the Spaniards protected themselves with little forts. Isabela in Española was built in 1494 with a moat and parapets. Columbus built forts to protect the gold fields in the interior of Española. As with many built later in the islands and on the mainland, they sometimes were of parallel timber courses between which earth was tamped. Even such simple protective works posed virtually unsolvable military problems to the weapons and the military habits and resolution of the Indians.

The Islands

The most important early center of exploration was the large island sometimes known by the Indian name of Haiti, but more often by the name Columbus gave it, Española, corrupted by the English to Hispaniola. Columbus returned to

Española on his second voyage to find that the settlers he left at Navidad had been killed by Indians. Thus, very early, the usually peaceable Arawaks of the isles showed there were limits to their tolerance of the habits of Europeans. Other settlements soon appeared in Española, the most important being Santo Domingo on the south coast, established by Bartholomew Columbus in 1496, and now the oldest European town in the Western Hemisphere. Spanish expansion through a good part of Española proceeded rapidly against feeble Indian opposition, accompanied by enforced labor by the aborigines in gold working, agriculture, grazing, construction, and other endeavors. The island became a center of supply, of administration and justice, of recruitment for expeditions, of financing for enterprises, of haven and repair for ships, and of knowledge and experience about the strange and often dangerous New World.

The basic exploration of the shores of the other islands required about a decade and a half, culminating with the circling of Cuba in 1508, but most of the island coasts were well known before then. Columbus discovered Puerto Rico and Jamaica early, but their conquest and settlement began only in 1508–1509. Cuba's conquest began in 1511, and it became thereafter an important center for exploration to the west. The smaller islands received scant attention. The Spaniards carried the peaceable Indians of the Bahamas into slavery, some in the deadly pearl fisheries of Tierra Firme. Of the great chain of the Lesser Antilles, stretching from Puerto Rico to the mouth of the Orinoco River, some were uninhabited, others held formidable Carib Indians. The Spaniards did not settle these islands, both because they had better land on the larger islands and because they were subject to Carib raids. Even in the early seventeenth century, when the English, Dutch, and French began to occupy the smaller Antilles, they met some Carib resistance.

Tierra Firme and the South Sea

The northern coasts of South America, which the Spaniards called Tierra Firme—the main-

land [3]—were first touched by Columbus. In 1499 the crown issued licenses to private investors for voyages to Tierra Firme, interpreting it as being outside the authority of Columbus. The result was four voyages in 1499–1500, by which Juan de la Cosa, Alonso de Ojeda, and the Italian Amerigo Vespucci surveyed the coast from the northern part of present-day Brazil to beyond what we know as Lake Maracaibo. Pearls gave their name to part of the coast of Venezuela. In 1500–1502 Juan de la Cosa and Rodrigo de Bastidas sailed even farther west, beyond the Gulf of Urabá, at the edge of what later was known to be the narrow Isthmus of America. They returned to Spain via Española, where the gold ornaments they had collected excited interest. In 1502–1503, as has been noted, Columbus in Central America explored a long reach of shore from the Bay Islands of Honduras south and east well into the present Panama. His and the Cosa and Bastidas exploration had, in fact, shown that the coast was continuous from present-day Brazil nearly to Mexico.

Other expeditions went to western Tierra Firme, looking for gold, for a water passage to Asia via the Gulf of Urabá, and for Indians to enslave. But in 1508 there still were no permanent European settlements anywhere in America but in Española. In that year, in Spain, western Tierra Firme was divided at the Gulf of Urabá between Diego de Nicuesa, well-to-do resident of Española, and a partnership made up of the experienced pilot Juan de la Cosa, that prototype of the reckless conquistador Alonso de Ojeda, and Martín Fernández de Enciso, a lawyer of Española. Both groups made preparations at Santo Domingo, largely at their own expense, since the crown depended on private enterprise to finance the conquests. The expeditions sailed at the end of 1509 with about a thousand men.

While Enciso stayed in Santo Domingo, Ojeda took their expedition to South America east of the Gulf of Urabá, where they suffered shipwreck, starvation, and poison arrows. Ojeda returned to Santo Domingo to nurse his wounds, and the survivors, including Vasco Núñez de Bal-

---

[3] The English translated this name as the Spanish Main.

boa and Francisco Pizarro, moved west of the gulf into the Isthmus of Panama, where they lived precariously in a hut-cluster on the Caribbean shore. As the conquerors often did, they organized a municipality, grandly calling it Santa María de la Antigua del Darién. They could now claim ancient Spanish rights of self-government (with undefined limits and subject to crown approval). To this outpost came the lawyer Enciso, claiming his right to rule under the royal grant. The men would have none of him, preferring Balboa, a man suited to leadership of a semimilitary camp on the edge of the unknown, menaced by starvation and Indians. So lawyer Enciso went to Spain to complain. Then Nicuesa arrived from the north half-dead, with the remnants of his disastrous expedition, and claimed power. He and a few partisans were pushed into the sea in a bad vessel and never heard of again.

Balboa sent the king a store of gold ornaments and news of Indian accounts of a sea to the south, and asked powers for further exploration. The king in 1511 recognized Balboa as governor at Darién, but in 1513 sent a fleet under an old courtier and soldier, Pedrarias Dávila, as captain-general and governor of Golden Castile—not the last public-relations name bestowed on poor parts of Spanish America. Meanwhile, Balboa had reached the Pacific and sent word to Spain, with pearls and gold. In response, Ferdinand in August 1514 named Balboa Adelantado of the Shores of the South Sea and governor of the provinces of Panama and Coiba but left him subordinate to Pedrarias. The crown, as was its common practice, thus simultaneously encouraged initiative by new men and curbed their authority.

The Pedrarias fleet found Balboa's little group barely subsisting on food grown by Indians. The sudden increase in demand for food could not be met. Soon Spaniards in silks died of hunger and disease in the dust between the huts within the log palisade, begging aid of their fellows, who stared at them with the indifference born of fear and their own need and suffering. Many of the surviving Spaniards fled to the islands, while Pedrarias governed as a tyrant, disdaining the

experience of Balboa, who had obtained Indian collaboration by controlling Spanish exactions. Finally, Pedrarias had Balboa executed in 1519 after a dubious trial. The experience of the Spaniards at Darién from 1509 to 1519 illustrated many of the features of confusion, violence, conflicting authority, and small profit that marked the early days in the Caribbean.

Approaches to Mexico

In the meantime, other disappointing expeditions were sailing north and west of Darién. In 1515 Governor Velázquez of Cuba sent ships westward, having heard from Cuban Indians that men came from there in canoes. His men sailed from Santiago de Cuba to the isles of the Bay of Honduras discovered by Columbus, took slaves and gold, and pioneered the best return, with wind and the Gulf Stream via the Yucatán Channel to the uninhabited harbor that later became Havana. In 1517 an expedition, largely financed by a Cuban resident, Hernández de Córdoba, went west from the harbor of the future Havana to the coast of Yucatán. It found Maya settlements with fine stone buildings and other signs of wealth. The inhabitants were unfriendly and belligerent, no doubt because of recently gained knowledge of European ways. In any event, the looting of temples of golden objects by the men under Hernández de Córdoba soon provided sufficient reason for warfare. All along the coast the Spaniards found the Indians ready to fight. The expedition made its way back to Cuba, with heavy losses but intriguing information. The news impelled Velázquez in 1518 to send an expedition under Juan de Grijalva, which surveyed the coast of present-day Mexico from Yucatán to the north. The further evidence it found of wealthy peoples increased the excitement in Cuba, which had few attractions for Spaniards in any case.

By 1519 it was the turn of Cortés, and the conquest of fabulous Mexico began. In the meantime, in the decades between 1492 and 1519, the Spaniards were trying to adjust to the strange new lands and peoples of the Indies.

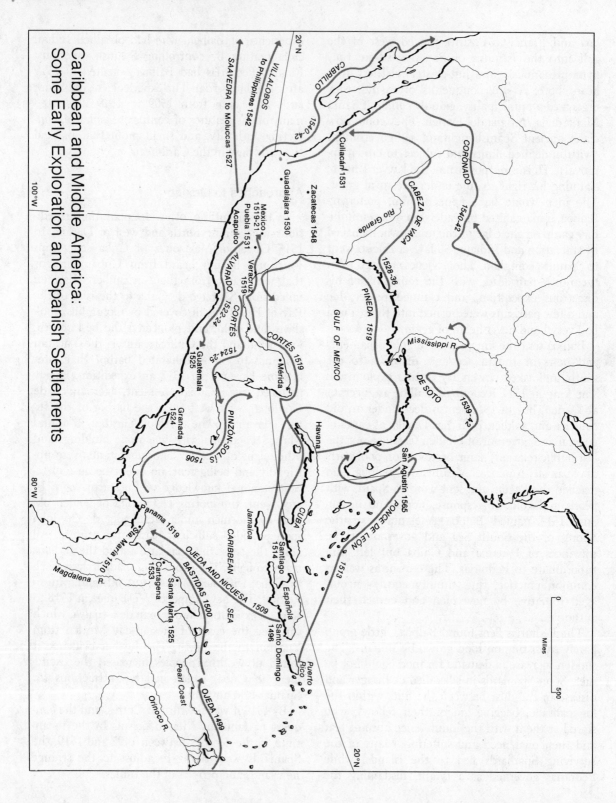

Caribbean and Middle America:
Some Early Exploration and Spanish Settlements

c. Life in Early Spanish America

Government

Columbus tried to use his wide powers of government in 1492–1498, chiefly in Española, but had trouble compelling obedience. The Spaniards were violent and intractable adventurers, frustrated by small profits and boredom. Communications with distant Spain were slow, and contradictions in testimony made punishment of misdeeds even slower. No leader could have prevented idleness, factionalism, disobedience, abuse of Indians, and feverish search for gold. Columbus had additional problems. He was handicapped by his arbitrary manner, by the fact he was a foreigner as were the brothers to whom he gave substantial power, and by his lack of prestige, social rank, public service, and the military experience that was needed to lead adventurers effectively. Furthermore, the initial system was a monopoly, owned by Columbus and the crown. He had the right, which the settlers resented, to decide many priorities of effort. The crown soon joined the settlers' opposition. There was resentment when Columbus made brother Bartholomew an *adelantado*—a Spanish military office for frontier areas menaced by Muslims, and a position much used in America. Bartholomew had energy and some ability, but neither adequate authority (since it came but indirectly from the crown) nor respect to control the settlers. Complaints, mostly justified, about Christopher's lack of ability as a governor accumulated in Spain. By 1496 the crown was aware of his unsuitability in that role.

In 1497 Francisco de Roldán led a revolt against the Columbus regime. The Roldán band went far into the interior, to live among the Indians. Other Spaniards also were living in Indian communities, which they often tyrannized, a problem that would exist for centuries in America. The situation in Española became so nearly anarchic that both Columbus and his enemies requested royal intervention. The crown grants of discovery and government in Tierra Firme, beginning in 1499, initiated reduction of the ex-

cessive powers granted Columbus. In 1500 it sent Francisco de Bobadilla to Española as an inspector empowered to take over the government. Impressed by the complaints against the Columbus brothers, he sent them to Spain in chains. Ferdinand and Isabella repudiated the arrest but did not restore Columbus' governing powers. He thereafter received a percentage of royal revenues from the Indies and retained his title of Admiral of the Ocean Sea and rights of discovery, but his governing career was over.

Bobadilla could not control the settlers and was replaced in 1502 by Nicolás de Ovando, who came with a fleet and 2,500 men, a large investment by Isabella to try to establish the colony firmly and Christianize the Indians. During his seven-year tenure the Spanish population grew, and food and gold production rose. He scarcely tried to protect or Europeanize the Indians. He was succeeded in 1509 by Governor Diego Columbus, son of the discoverer, who lacked the powers in all the "isles and main" of the original Columbus contract.[4] He also was restricted by increased supervision from Spain; by a royal treasurer; and in 1511 by the creation of a high court (*audiencia*) in Santo Domingo.

The crown continued to experiment with administration for America in 1516 by appointing to succeed Diego Columbus a committee of three friars of the Order of St. Jerome (Hieronymites). The friars, following orders, tried to improve the lot of the Indians, with little success. Their rule ended in 1520; by then the focus of interest had shifted to Mexico.

In the meantime, the colonial administration in Spain during the first three decades also was experimental. From 1493 to 1516 Bishop Juan Rodríguez de Fonseca had chief authority over America. He was competent, unscrupulous, and mostly interested in revenues for the crown. Possibly no administrator could have done much

---

[4] Diego was suing the crown for his rights under the contract. A settlement in 1536 left the family rich and titled but with no governing rights in America. A final settlement occurred in 1564.

better, given the information available, the attitudes of the monarchs, and conditions in America. Fonseca did see to formation of the Casa de Contratación (House of Trade) in 1503, which for more than two centuries was an important center for trade policy and administration and other American activities. In 1516–1518 colonial affairs were under Cardinal Francisco Ximénez de Cisneros, regent for the mad Queen Juana and her minor son Charles. Thus, for nearly three decades the Spanish government was feeling its way with no sense of great urgency. The amazing discoveries in Mexico, beginning in 1519, would change that situation.

Relations with Indians

The conquerors considered the Indians inferior beings and had little interest in their souls, although they occasionally ignored safety and gain to smash idols or help friars with baptisms. What they wanted to know of Indians was: (*a*) Had they gold or knowledge of its location? (*b*) Were they pacific or formidable warriors when aroused? What would it cost to control or exterminate them? (*c*) What geographic data could they supply? (*d*) Could they help with problems of food, shelter, and general supply? The Indians did provide information and instruction in the use of indigenous crops, including the bitter yucca from which cassava bread was made, and many artifacts—hammocks, pottery, baskets, light cotton fabrics. Indian women were objects of some interest for rape, concubinage, and even marriage.

Especially, Spaniards wanted to know (*e*) How useful were Indians as labor? Thus, for most Spaniards, the only distinctions of importance were between friendly and unfriendly Indians, and between those that had or had not a well-defined class system and despotic government, conditions that aided conquest and control of labor. Lacking interest in social analysis, the conquerors distinguished between Indians primarily in terms of military or police problems. They quickly reduced Indians, where possible, to

forced labor or slavery. The death of Indian porters on *entradas* was but a fraction of the loss, especially in the settled agricultural communities of the peaceful Indians of the Taino culture in Española and Cuba. Their military capabilities were small. Flight was difficult with the sea at their backs. Their class system made subordination habitual, so conquest could be accepted more readily than by the more democratic and warlike Caribs.

The island of Española held more Indians than the other Antilles combined. Between 1492 and 1519 its population fell from possibly 150,000 to a few thousand, from a combination of warfare, forced labor, slavery, disruptions of food supply and the demands thereupon by the Spaniards, and a failure to reproduce that resulted from a number of causes. Many died of disease, complicated by weakness from malnutrition and abusive labor, and to some extent by a despair that led to mass suicides, but probably more importantly to a loss of desire to live. Similar declines occurred in the smaller populations of Jamaica, Cuba, and Puerto Rico. The warlike Caribs of the Lesser Antilles resisted much longer.[5] The typical Spaniard in the islands found the Indian population decline inconvenient; a few clerics found it horrifying and began to protest.

Spaniards enslaved Indians almost at once. Columbus on his second voyage sent several hundred to Spain to be sold as slaves. Isabella angrily freed them and returned them to the Indies. New slaves in the meantime were being created in Española as retaliation for the first Indian rebellion in 1494. Armed resistance to Spanish rule and apostasy by "Christianized" (usually merely baptized) Indians for years were considered adequate grounds for enslavement, as were sodomy and other "pernicious" practices. Columbus, recovering from his rebuke by the queen, sent more Indians to Spain to be sold into slavery. His pursuit of wealth and lack of interest in Indians as human beings mirrored the view of most of the invaders of America—

---

[5] See Chapter 8, Section a.

including the English a century later. Church and state in Spain acted but feebly to control Indian slavery for some years, although Isabella and the church always proclaimed the principle that Indians were subjects to be Christianized as soon as possible. But when enslavement for "proper" cause occurred, Isabella demanded her share of the profits. Isabella permitted slaving in western Tierra Firme in 1503. Ferdinand, regent for Castile for some years after Isabella's death in 1504, legitimized the enslavement of the Caribs in the Lesser Antilles and was generally less interested than his wife in Indian welfare.

The biggest impact on the numerous tractable Indians in Española and Cuba came not from slavery but from labor services granted to Spaniards. From the beginning, Indian leaders made gifts to Spaniards of goods and labor, and Spanish demands and seizures enlarged this tribute. Before long, Columbus made allotments (*repartimientos*) of Indians to Spaniards in response to irresistible demand. Soon such allotments were confusingly connected at times with the Spanish institution of *encomienda*, whereby lands and peoples taken from the Muslims during the long Reconquest of Iberia had been assigned to Christians.[6] In the earliest days in America, the allotment of Indians owing labor service was unregulated and scarcely distinguishable from slavery. In addition to labor, tribute in gold was instituted in 1495, and other types of payment (for example, cotton cloth and foodstuffs) soon were included. Indian labor was used in Española by the Spaniards without regard for its preservation.

Most of the conquerors were men of crude and violent habits and largely sincere in their decision that Indians were inferior creatures, "dogs" as they called them from the beginning. Spaniards considered that their actions were justified by the fact that they were building a civilized Christian society that must be made secure and profitable for the new and legitimate ruler. Spanish treatment was so disruptive of Indian production and life generally that the population decline in Española already was well advanced by 1496.

Although Isabella had doubts about allotment of Indians, she permitted Governor Ovando to assign to individuals or to the crown almost all the male Indians of working age. The crown could not be certain of the extent that the allotment system damaged the Indians, or its potential dangers to the crown, or what other labor system might be effective at bearable cost. So brutality, confusion, and waste were enormous. The language barrier meant that much instruction in new tasks (working gold, tending pigs, growing radishes) had to be by example. The Spaniards did not spare beatings to enforce learning or demands for labor or tribute or even acquiescence in conversion to Christianity. The clergy often agreed that such methods were necessary, given the needs of civilization, the faith, and Spanish rule.

The few early Franciscans in Española did little to mitigate the practices that were flaying the Indians unmercifully. When the Dominicans arrived in Española in 1510, however, they began their condemnation of abuses, which never was stilled thereafter. Friar Antonio de Montesinos in 1511, preaching to the Spaniards of the island, thundered

> I who am a voice of Christ crying in the wilderness of this island [say] that you are in mortal sin ... for the cruelty and tyranny you use in dealing with these innocent ... Indians. ... Are these not men? ... Are you not bound to love them as you love yourselves?

Yes, if they were men. But most Spaniards skirted that Christian difficulty by denying that the Indians were fully men. Those who heard Montesinos in 1511 certainly did so and continued their charges that Indians were lazy, idolatrous, superstitious, childlike, prodigal, dishonest, sexually depraved, improvident, drunken, and gluttonous—a people who could never learn to live in freedom after the Spanish manner.

Such charges piled on the desks of officials in Spain while other piles contained denunciations of abuse of the Indians. King Ferdinand was sufficiently impressed by the latter to issue in 1512–1513 the "Laws of Burgos" to regulate

---

[6] See Chapter 5 for discussion of *encomienda*.

forced labor. The laws permitted the *encomienda*, adopting the view that the Indians required the discipline and guidance of commendation to Christian care. In return they were to provide their masters with labor. The laws also allowed local judges to free Indians when they became good Christians and capable of self-government. The Laws of Burgos were quite ineffective. The Spanish colonists were uninterested in the regulation of abuses or preparing Indians for self-government.

Economic and Social Conditions

Both Spaniards and the Indians of Española and Cuba had class systems with hereditary rulers, nobles, and lower classes. The Spaniards used the Indian system to establish control, by ruling through Indian leaders, the *caciques*. At the same time, the Spaniards made clear that all Indians were an inferior breed. The complexities and rigidities of the class situation increased with the birth of half-breeds (*mestizos*) and with the import of African slaves. A few of the latter were taken to Española early in the sixteenth century as miners and endured the labor better than Indians. King Ferdinand supported this policy. An increase in the supply occurred about a decade later, when in 1517 the Hieronymite fathers asked that Negro slaves be brought from Africa. So a license was granted in Spain to some Genoese to supply 4,000 blacks to America, and they began to do so in 1518.

The Spanish population of the Caribbean in 1492–1519 was small, and mortality was higher for Spaniards than in Europe. Española held the largest portion—only 10,000 at the peak of prosperity in 1509. Most Spaniards were from the Peninsular lower or lower middle class or of the very minor nobility (*hidalgos*). The towns of America before 1519 were tiny. Some of the early settlements did not organize municipal government. Santo Domingo, although a city (*ciudad*), was in size a small town. Santa María in Darién was merely a camp, with a wooden chapel and a gibbet in the dusty plaza. Santiago de

Cuba was but a poor hamlet when Cortés sailed for Mexico in 1519. In that year the town of Panama was founded on the Pacific, a few huts just above the stinking mud flats that appeared at low tide.

Pearls, and especially gold, were the most valuable products of the region, and received special legislative treatment by the crown to protect its revenues. The first voyage to the Pearl Coast in 1499 brought back fifty pounds of pearls, and soon after came efforts to keep most Spaniards out of the pearl area. The efforts were fruitless, but the pearl areas were easier to control than the gold fields in Española and Cuba. When Ovando's fleet arrived at the former in 1502, many newcomers took off at once for the mines.

Much of the washing of the gold was badly done by inexpert Indians and ignorant Spanish supervisors. Considerable ancillary business grew up around mining: selling supplies, transporting, policing, smelting, government assaying and stamping and collecting revenues, and smuggling. But gold mining had about petered out in Española and Cuba by 1519.

Only small land grants were made. There was no motive for building large estates. A few Spaniards made money by selling foodstuffs to towns, mines, and *entradas*. The island Indians allotted to Spaniards retained their old agriculture, using a digging stick to plant highly nutritious root crops. They also were put to work cultivating European plants. European animals multiplied rapidly. Before long, the islands could export modest amounts of hides, tallow, lard, and dried, smoked, or salted meat. Agricultural exports were, however, little developed. A small effort to raise oriental pepper failed. Sugar cane was carried to the islands from the Canaries, but for years was consumed locally in the Indies as crude syrup. Not until the end of the period, possibly in 1515, were the first mill and reduction works of the complicated sugar-processing industry erected by experts from the Canaries.

European crafts were practiced, some reluctantly by Spanish amateurs, some by Indians or mestizos more or less trained for the work. A few carpenters and masons came from Spain. Diego Columbus had a small stone palace put up in Santo Domingo, but most structures in 1519 were wooden. The production of Indian artifacts began dying out with the Indians. The islands and the shores of the mainland were in 1519 little populated or developed, and their few European inhabitants soon showed a decided preference for life in Mexico.

d. Early Brazil

Brazil as a European colony developed even more slowly than Spanish America. In 1500 the fleet of Pedro Alvarez Cabral, en route to India, landed in what he named the Land of the True Cross, soon called Brazil. Probably the "discovery" was due to weather problems or navigational error.[7] The king of Portugal at once claimed the territory as being on his side of the line of Tordesillas. The next year a Portuguese fleet found the brazilwood that gave its permanent name to the Portuguese territory and explored the coast far into present-day Argentina. In 1502 license to trade in Brazil was granted, and thereafter a modest traffic developed. The few hundred Portuguese who intermittently frequented the coast lived in huts. No towns existed. Relations with the primitive Indians were sometimes friendly, sometimes not. As did the Spaniards in the Caribbean, the Portuguese sired large numbers of children by Indian mothers. For thirty years the Lisbon government was reasonably content with this situation. It made small profits from licenses to export dyewood and such tropical curiosities as nuts, monkeys, and parrots. Sugar was carried to Brazil from Portuguese Madeira and the Cape Verde Islands in the 1520s, but the industry was unimportant for several decades thereafter. The bulk of Portuguese attention and resources were being devoted to the great enterprise in India.

During most of these years French woodcutters and traders, encouraged by their government, were active on the coasts of Brazil. They built tiny settlements. Occasionally, French vessels preyed on Portuguese ships. The Portuguese rooted out the French when they could, and even set up a few armed posts on the coast. By 1530 there also was some fear of Spanish intrusion into Portuguese territory. In that year the Portuguese government decided to protect the Brazilian flank of the route to India. A small fleet was sent, carrying some four hundred men, commanded by Martin Afonso de Sousa. They were to expel any French they encountered and to plan a stronger Portuguese position in the Indies. They founded São Vicente, on the coast some two hundred miles south of present-day Rio de Janeiro.

Sousa, on his return to Portugal, helped plan further strengthening of the colony. The heart of the plan was division of the coast of Brazil into fifteen captaincies, of different sizes, with territory extending into the unknown interior. These lands were granted to wealthy Portuguese willing to invest in the development of Brazil. But by 1548 the Portuguese population of Brazil was only some 2,500, and the French still were active there. In the meantime, the Spaniards had conquered rich Mexico and Peru and made prodigious explorations into central North America, all through Central America, and along the coasts and into the interior of South America from its Caribbean shores south to Chile, the Plata estuary, and Paraguay. In the mid-sixteenth century little Portugal seemed in a doubtful position to hold Brazil against its European competitors.[8]

---

[7] Spaniards had touched what is now northern Brazil before 1500, as has been noted. A few scholars maintain that Cabral was ordered to sail west in 1500 in the hope of finding new territories.

---

[8] See Chapter 14 for extended discussion of early Brazil.

4 The Great Conquests

After three decades of disappointment in the Caribbean, the Spaniards suddenly came upon the rich cultures of Mesoamerica. The conquests that followed were as ugly as most in history, including many in pre-Columbian America. They involved a frenzy of looting, murder, rape, and branding of Indian slaves. The disruption of social structures and habits of work, together with the huge appetites of Europeans (often complained of by Indians) and the introduction of European diseases, caused hunger, malnutrition, and death at an accelerating rate.

The attitudes of historians toward the brutalities of the conquest have varied widely. Some still speak of the conquerors in terms of valor, and certainly the men were brave; but there is a growing stress on the valor of the Indians, an insistence that they did all they could to repel the invaders. We are now reluctant without clear evidence to say or imply that large groups of men are "inherently" cowards or "naturally" slaves. Occasionally historians gloss over the brutalities of Spaniards on the grounds that they were little different from other Europeans, or Asians, or American Indians, in dealing with weaker peoples. In any event, the Spanish victory over the higher Indian cultures was rapid and thorough. The Indian cultural systems were so shattered that they were incapable of further in-dependent growth, although many elements remained to be combined with European culture. The rapidity and violence of the conquest of the higher cultures reflected the fragility of the Indian politicosocial order in the face of a crisis of warfare with an overwhelmingly superior foe bent on absolute subjugation.

The conquests of Aztec and Inca occurred during two decades beginning in 1519. There were other, smaller conquests then and later. Immense areas were explored and found to be of little interest, lacking Indians or other attractions. The conquest of populous sedentary cultures focused new attention on America—by the crown, Spanish adventurers and investors, the church, and by hopeful foreign capitalists and intruders. It also created new centers from which further exploration could be mounted. Some of the new areas proved rich in silver, and in, mid-century this wealth stimulated yet more movement of Spaniards and capital and fathered a new need for Indians and blacks as labor. Much of the Western Hemisphere thus was quickly surveyed in a few decades after 1519. While exploration, conquest, and expansion of towns were occurring, all sorts of economic, political, and social institutions were being destroyed, created, or modified. The process continued throughout the colonial centuries.

a. North America

The Road to Tenochtitlán

In Cuba in 1518 there was excitement at the gold and tales of wealth brought from the coasts of Mexico by Grijalva. Governor Velázquez prepared another expedition. He got authorization from the Hieronymites ruling in Santo Domingo but also sought independent authority directly from Spain. Such efforts to break off new jurisdictions by negotiation with Spain were common during the conquest years. They not only were a normal consequence of ambition but also made sense because of the inadequate and long-delayed information available in Europe and because no one could be sure what methods, jurisdictions, or persons could best serve the crown in new situations. New jurisdictions gave talented new leaders a chance to perform.

Velázquez chose for the Mexican venture Hernando Cortés, a prominent *hidalgo* in his thirties, better educated than most, and restless because of the lack of opportunity in Cuba, a bucolic outpost of empire that offered little outlet for ambitious adventurers. Cortés' unrest had in the past led him to plot against Velázquez. He now put such enthusiasm and energy into his new command as to inspire suspicion in the governor, who prepared to replace him. Cortés, forewarned, sailed with his unfinished fleet from Santiago de Cuba. His legal position was ambiguous, if not worse, but most of the men supported or acquiesced in his action, awaiting events.

The little fleet carried some six hundred men, sixteen horses, dogs, two dozen cranky firearms (tiny field guns and clumsy handarms), crossbows, lances, swords, and armor. The first landfall, early in 1519, was on the island of Cozumel, off the coast of Yucatán. Immediately, relations with the Indians repeated experience in the Antilles and prefigured a multitude of actions in the following decades. Pedro de Alvarado stormed ashore with some men, plundering and taking Indians captive. Cortés returned the loot and smoothed things over with the Indians. To the invaders came Aguilar, a Spaniard long castaway among the Maya, who became an interpreter for Cortés, a great stroke of luck.

The expedition sailed west in the Gulf of Mexico along the shores of Yucatán and landed in what is now the state of Tabasco in Mexico. It found the Indians hostile, and read them the *Requerimiento*. This remarkable document had been prepared in Spain a few years before for the instruction of newly discovered heathen in the Indies. It was first read to Indians in South America by the Pedrarias expedition before it arrived in Darién in 1514. The *Requerimiento* was an elaborate exposition—in Spanish—of the Christian faith (not omitting the Roman view of the trinity) and the church-given rights of the potent Spanish monarch (with a list of his dignities) over unbelievers. The folk of the Indies were to understand, accept, and embrace this, on pain of sanctified castigation. In 1519 in Tabasco the *Requerimiento* was read three times, Aguilar attempted a translation, and the Indians attacked. Although one of the participants, Bernal Díaz, later wrote that the Indians came at them like "mad dogs," the Spaniards prevailed.

Cortés, a clever man, at once dealt amicably with the Indians, who let him set up an altar with a cross and images of the Virgin and Child. The Indians also provided such gifts as the always acceptable gold and women. One of the latter was Doña Marina (as the Spaniards called her), an Aztec who had been sold into slavery with the Mayas and who served Cortés as another interpreter. Marina was a woman of ability who gave her loyalty to the Spaniards, as many Indian men and women did, joining the obvious wave of the future. Marina was Cortés' mistress and was passed on to the beds of other prominent Spaniards.

Continuing along the coast, Cortés bolstered his legal position by having his partisans urge him to name members of a municipal government for the Rich Town of the True Cross (Veracruz), a hut-cluster on a hot and pestilential coast. These officials, named by Cortés, then declared the "authority" of the town over the new and unknown territories and named Cortés captain-general. The town wrote the king a justification of its actions, together with the supposed misdeeds of Velázquez. It sent along for crown and officials in Spain the loot so far gathered, which Cortés induced the men to relinquish, no mean leadership feat in itself. Some justification existed in Spanish tradition for such municipal action, as in the case of Balboa. In any case, the crown was known sometimes to tailor its policy to deeds, especially when the deeds were wrapped in treasure. The first reactions of government in Spain in this case were ambivalent; it awaited events in this new and apparently promising land. In 1519 Mexico was not a matter of importance, just another small foray into the distant wilderness. The statesmen of Spain were busy with great armies and plans for war in Europe, with the *comunero* rebellion in Spain, with the new position of young Charles I of Spain, now also Charles V of the Holy Roman Empire, and the problem of joining the disparate interests of the many domains of the monarch.

At Veracruz, Cortés set up a fortified encampment, where his most important activities were collecting information and bringing more Indian groups to Spanish allegiance, which he generally accomplished peaceably. Nearly all physical labor was performed by Indians. There usually was little difficulty in securing them. Indian leaders who had been defeated or prudently succumbed without resistance hastened to provide laborers. When these offers were insufficient, the Spaniards usually could easily seize Indians of the sedentary cultures and require them to work. After all, these were class societies, and Indian leaders nearly always eagerly volunteered the labor of others to guarantee their own position under the new lords of the land.

Cortés received from the distant Aztec ruler, Moctezuma, both gifts, including gold and silver ornaments, and requests that the intruders depart. The latter seemed like pleading and a confession of weakness. Also encouraging to Cortés was his knowledge of the legend of the return of the white god Quetzalcóatl. Their victories over

Indians also reassured the Spaniards as well as the fact that many Indians submitted without fighting. Clearly the Europeans sometimes could overawe Indians with horses and firearms and insistent arrogance. Finally, these were intrepid adventurers, to be discouraged by almost nothing.

Nevertheless, and although the gifts from Moctezuma were tempting, there still was dissension in the Spanish camp, especially among partisans of Velázquez; so Cortés disabled the ships to prevent defection by sea. After several months at Veracruz, the Spaniards set off by land to the north and west. Thus began the march to Tenochtitlán that has been celebrated variously as a glorious epic of Spanish arms, a victory for Christ, banditry on a heroic scale, a crime against humanity, just one more case of might making right in international affairs, and one of the chief episodes in a clash between incompatible cultures.

Cortés set off with some four hundred Spaniards, having left more than one hundred men at Veracruz. They had the usual Indian bearers. As they marched, they saw rearing out of the first range of mountains the lofty snowcapped cone of Citlaltepetl (Pico de Orizaba), which at times seemed to float in the sky over lower cloud layers. At the Totonac town of Cempoala on the coast the Spaniards heard, not for the first time, of bitter enmity for the Aztecs—another reason for Spanish optimism. More Indian help was provided, with Cortés astutely committing the Cempoalans against the Aztecs. At the same time, Cortés made sure that news went to Moctezuma assuring him of Spanish friendship. The expedition turned inland. Two hundred Indians dragged and pushed the guns. They went out of the humid coastal plain into the cooler, rich upland slopes and valleys, a land of benign climate, bright with flowers and birds. At Cocotlán, as always, Cortés told the Indians that he came from a distant king "to warn the great Moctezuma to desist from human sacrifices . . . and to require from him submission to our monarch." Cortés also told the local Indians "to renounce your human sacrifices, cannibal feasts, and other abominable practices, for such is the command of our Lord God." He then prepared to erect a cross, but Father Olmedo dissuaded him, saying that there would be better occasions, when ignorant people would be less likely to commit indignities against the cross. This was not the last occasion during the Spanish conquest on which the friars were more prudent than the soldiers.

They went farther into the mountains, into the typical high, drier, upland country of central Mexico, with its arable plateaus and valleys and cultivated fields of maize, squash, maguey, and other crops. There the way was blocked by the Tlaxcalans, only some eighty miles from Tenochtitlán. The Tlaxcalans were formidable warriors, unsubdued by the Aztecs. Although they thought that the Spaniards might be supernatural beings, they attacked them repeatedly for several days with their inferior weapons—slings, darts hurled from throwing sticks, spears, and obsidian-bladed club-swords that could fell a horse. Bernal Díaz, who was there, claimed there were 40,000 warriors against 400 Spaniards (plus Indian allies). But he also wrote that the Indians did not know how to attack all at once without confusion. Díaz said the Spaniards at times were so hemmed in they could scarcely move. But he made clear that they moved enough to inflict much heavier casualties on the Indians than they received. He noted that the bunching of the Indian horde made it vulnerable to the guns. The Tlaxcalans finally responded to Cortés' repeated threats to destroy them if they continued to resist. Apparently they ceased because they were wearied of their disproportionate losses and because they had been disabused of their supposition that Cortés was an ally of the hated Aztecs. The Tlaxcalans allied themselves with the Spaniards.

The little band of Europeans and more numerous Indian bearers and warrior allies went on over usually easy terrain in the high mountain valleys some twenty miles to Cholula. This important town, long a religious center, was near the site of present-day Puebla and was domi-nated by the Aztecs. The Spaniards were received at Cholula with a show of cordiality, but in fact an ambush was planned with the aid of a nearby Aztec army. Doña Marina discovered it, and Cortés put some thousands of Cholulans to the sword. Such terroristic methods were, of course, used by Indians in their own warfare. Cortés turned the Cholulans into allies, though not without difficulty in persuading the Tlaxcalans to cooperate with old enemies. The Aztecs made no further move to stop the Spaniards, and they marched in a few days over a mountain pass and into the Valley of Mexico.

The "topless towers of Ilium" can have been no more wondrous a sight to Greeks than the great basin of Anahuac, or Mexico, to the men of Cortés. They came down from the mountains in November 1519 and were met by important men from various towns in the high valley. The sun shone on the great lake; in the western waters seemed to float the twin cities of Tenochtitlán-Tlaltelolco, interlaced with canals, dominated by the great pyramid, swarming with more than 100,000—and possibly as many as 300,000—inhabitants, one of the great cities of the world. Bernal Díaz later wrote that it had seemed a scene of enchantment from a romance. They crossed a causeway leading through the water to the city, escorted by an emissary of Moctezuma, borne in a jeweled litter.

The bewilderment and indecision of Moctezuma was pitiful. For several years there had been portents of disaster, darkly interpreted by priest-astrologers. Then came news from the coast of the intruders, and Moctezuma sent spies among them. They sent messages and excellent colored paintings of the invaders. Clearly the whites were hearty feeders, and they coupled energetically with Indian women. Still, Moctezuma worried that they were the gods of the Quetzalcóatl legend or at least their emissaries. A messenger from the coast reported of a cannon:[1]

---

[1] Recorded from the recollections of Indians after the conquest.

A thing like a ball of stone comes out of its entrails; it comes out shooting sparks and raining fire. The smoke that comes out with it has a pestilent odor, like that of rotten mud. This odor penetrates even to the brain and causes the greatest discomfort. If the cannon is aimed against a mountain, the mountain splits and cracks open.

So from a distance Moctezuma had tried gifts and veiled menaces and then the trap at Cholula. Its frustration merely convinced the Aztec ruler that the newcomers were omniscient. Probably few of the prominent men of Tenochtitlán shared the views of the weak, pacific, imaginative Moctezuma, but he was the absolute and almost godlike ruler of his people.

Moctezuma was borne out to meet the Spaniards and apparently greeted them as the fulfillment of the Quetzalcóatl legend. Whether Cortés at this time represented himself as the subject of a great ruler overseas or as a god is not clear. In any event, he and his followers went to live in the city in quarters next to Moctezuma's, in the heart of Aztec power. Fortunately for them, Moctezuma continued to be paralyzed by indecision. Some of his advisers urged him to oppose the intruders. They were sure that the whites were men who bled, ate, copulated, and squabbled over loot. But for the moment such advisers were restrained by the traditional civil and religious prestige of Moctezuma. Such a crisis of indecision was not novel in the history of human affairs.

Defeat of the Aztecs

The prospect was not alluring to the Spaniards, and they were nervous. They were trapped in an island city. Cortés saw their position being endangered daily by his men, who roamed the countryside, looting; and by interference with the Indian religion, which the Spaniards found horrifying, both for its elaborate paganism and for its human sacrifices. The Indians later testified that when the Spaniards entered Moctezuma's treasure room, they "grinned like little beasts and patted each other with delight." The greed

and lust of the Spaniards convinced many Aztec leaders that the invaders were all too human. Faced with rising Indian resentment, Cortés used the ancient tactic of seizing the enemy chief. Plenty of plausible pretexts were available; he used the one that the Aztecs had seized some of Cortés' men on the coast. Moctezuma was escorted by Cortés and a handful of men to the Spanish quarters without difficulty, then had his guilty coastal officials brought to Cortés, who burned them at the stake. Cortés also imprisoned the rulers of some other city-states in the valley and made Moctezuma order the collection of treasure.

In May 1520, after some six months of this nerve-racking situation in Tenochtitlán, Cortés had to hurry to the coast to meet an expedition sent against him by Velázquez, led by Pánfilo de Narváez. Defeating this threat, and enrolling most of Narváez' men in his own forces, Cortés returned to Tenochtitlán, hurried by the news that the Spaniards were hemmed in by threatening Aztecs in retaliation for having massacred Indians at a religious ceremony.

Cortés tried to conciliate the Aztecs, releasing Moctezuma's brother Cuitlahuac, who promptly assembled the Aztec council, which deposed Moctezuma, installed Cuitlahuac, and decided on war. Moctezuma, true to his gentle nature, and with promptings from Cortés, tried to reason in public with his people and was fatally stoned for his pains. On the Sorrowful Night (Noche Triste) of June 20, 1520, Cortés began to retreat from the island city. The Aztecs had cut the western causeway, and bloody skirmishes occurred at the breaches, with Aztecs attacking from the rear and from canoes in the lake. The Spaniards lost most of their treasure and more than a third of their European army of 1,300, as they retreated out of the valley and over the mountains to Tlaxcala.

There Cortés rebuilt with the aid of Spanish recruits coming from the Caribbean at news of the wonders of Mexico. The Spaniards and their Tlaxcalan allies descended upon neighboring cities, reading the *Requerimiento* to the Indians, and branding recalcitrants on the face as slaves. In the meantime, smallpox in central Mexico began the decimation of the Indians by European disease that played such a prominent role in the depression of their spirits and the disorganization of their societies.

In the spring of 1521 Cortés returned to the Valley of Mexico, with about six hundred Spaniards, including forty cavalry, a few guns, and many Indian allies and porters. It required thousands (reports said 15,000!) of porters to carry thirteen dismantled ships built at Tlaxcala. The invading force made a column six miles long. Cortés set up his base at Texcoco, a town of some 30,000 on the lakeshore. It had a long history of rule in its own area and a grudge at having recently fallen under the domination of Tenochtitlán. From Texcoco, Cortés sent expeditions against many towns. The ships swept the lake of Indian canoes. Assaults along the causeways to Tenochtitlán began late in April and failed. More Spanish prisoners were taken to have their hearts torn out on the altar of Huitzilopochtli.

So with the aid of the ships, Cortés tore down the city, filled the canals with rubble, opened up space for cavalry to maneuver. The Aztec resistance was fanatical, under the dead (of smallpox) Cuitlahuac's successor Cuauhtémoc, and lasted three and a half months, until most of the city was leveled and the surviving Aztecs were starving. Few people in history have shown such desperate courage. Recent historical research suggests that 240,000 Aztecs died during the siege and that 60,000 survived. With the surrender in August 1521 died much of the Aztec culture and all of its potential for growth. The following Aztec lament was recorded after the conquest:

> Broken spears lie in the roads. We have torn our hair in our grief. Worms are swarming in the streets and plazas and the walls are splattered with gore. Our city is lost and dead. . . . Nothing but flowers and songs of sorrow are left in Mexico and Tlatelolco, where once we saw warriors and wise men. You, the Giver of Life, you have ordained it.

With the extinction of Tenochtitlán, the other towns in the valley offered allegiance to Cortés. He sent expeditions in all directions, distributed lands to Spaniards and Indian *caciques*, and tried to decide how to regulate Indian labor. In the meantime, Spaniards simply used Indians as laborers, either under the undefined grants of *encomienda*, by gift (free or forced) from Indian leaders, or by direct compulsion. Spanish towns were set up. A great treasure was sent to Spain to help persuade the crown of the value of the Cortés leadership. A French corsair captured the treasure ship in the eastern Atlantic. The European warfare over America had begun. It was to last three centuries.

By the time Tenochtitlán fell, the next stage of relations between Europeans and Indians had been going on for two years in some areas of Mexico. The other peoples of central Mexico would succumb, many of them without fighting. Indian society was devastated by Spanish levies on its supplies and manpower, lines of authority were fractured, women violated and transported, habits disrupted. While the waves of the conquest moved on to distant shores, they left behind wreckage and new demands, Spanish posts, personnel, and lines of communication. All was part of the basis for a new social synthesis.

The North and the Pacific

Much of the area within a few hundred miles of the Valley of Mexico was quickly penetrated and brought under Spanish control in the 1520s and 1530s. Nuño de Guzmán in the 1530s completed the conquest to the north and west into what became Nueva Galicia (including the present-day Mexican states of Michoacán and Jalisco), which later ruled much of northern Mexico, or New Spain. Guzmán was one of the most brutal of the conquerors. Complaints multiplied, but officials in Spain could not easily be certain of conditions in America. Every governor was denounced by letter-writing rivals with so little regard for the truth that officials knew the necessity of checking and double-checking accusations.

Finally, the odor of Guzmán's crimes became unmistakable.[2]

Interest in northern exploration was stimulated in 1537 by news of the experiences of Cabeza de Vaca. He had been shipwrecked in 1529 with the Pánfilo de Narváez expedition to Florida and the Gulf Coast. He walked and lived among the Indians for eight years of suffering and endurance before arriving at the Spanish settlements in Mexico. He had heard tales from the Indians, he said, of rich cities to the north. A series of expeditions soon carried Friar Marcos de Niza, Francisco de Coronado, and others north to what became Arizona, New Mexico, Texas, Oklahoma, and Kansas. They found little of interest.

The absence from New Galicia of so many Spaniards on the Coronado expedition encouraged the Indians there to revolt, and the Mixton War of 1541–1542 caused the viceroy to send 450 Spanish reinforcements and some 30,000 Tlaxcalans and Aztecs. Pedro de Alvarado, now preparing an oceanic adventure to the East Indies, was pulled into the Mixton War and killed as he charged his horse at an Indian position in his familiar reckless fashion.

In the 1540s and thereafter much Spanish movement in New Spain was channeled by the discovery of silver deposits: in Michoacán in 1542 and more distant Zacatecas in 1546. Warlike Indians in Zacatecas and other northern areas made the connections with Mexico City unsafe for half a century. The northern mining camps drew not only miners but commercial farmers and stock raisers and merchants, and Guadalajara became a supply center for the mines. Mining rushes stimulated slave raiding, which in the mid-sixteenth century carried into distant Texas. Exploration and slave raiding did not always result in subjugation of the Indians of the areas traversed. The Durango region was not won until the conquest by Francisco de Ibarra in the 1560s. Far northeastern Nuevo León was created in 1579, and it stretched into what is now Texas. But few Spaniards lived in those vast reaches of the periphery of New Spain. The little town of Monterrey was not founded until 1590, and did not become a great city until the twentieth century. Farther west and north, slave raids were made, the Pueblo Indians were found, some gold was located in what is now Arizona, and the far outpost of Santa Fe was set up in 1609, isolated and barely able to survive.

Spaniards explored the eastern shores of North America in the 1520s, but they found little of value. A colony founded in Carolina quickly failed. Hernando de Soto in 1539–1542 explored much of what became the southern United States. That territory also was a disappointment. Florida also was found worthless by Ponce de León in 1513 and 1521, by Narváez later, and by other Spanish expeditions in the 1540s and 1550s. Then in 1562–1564 a French settlement was set up on the north Florida coast, on the flank of Spanish shipping routes from America to Spain via the Florida Channel. So Spain sent Pedro Menéndez de Avilés, who killed the French, explored the coast as far as Chesapeake Bay, founded some small and short-lived missions, and in 1565 created the fortified post of St. Augustine, which endured more than two centuries as an important bastion of empire.

Exploration by sea in the Pacific began early. Ships sent by Cortés in the 1520s explored the coast to the Gulf of California and crossed the Pacific to the East Indies. Later expeditions went west across the Pacific or north along the coast of North America, searching for a strait and coming near the northern limits of the present-day United States by the 1540s. In 1562–1564 a round trip by Miguel López de Legazpi and Andrés de Urdaneta between Mexico and the Philippine Islands found that the best eastward passage was in the north Pacific. The California coast thus became an important part of the route between Mexico and the Orient, and expeditions set out to find harbors there. Meanwhile, Manila had been founded in the Philippines in 1571, and before the end of the sixteenth century the

---

[2] See Chapter 5, Section c, for more on Nuño de Guzmán.

galleons had begun regular trade between the Orient and Acapulco.

Yucatán and Central America

Central America fell quickly to conquest. The Yucatecans were more stubborn, and there the process took about twenty years. Late in 1523 Cortés sent Pedro de Alvarado south toward Guatemala, and Cristóbal de Olid to Honduras. Olid threw off his allegiance to Cortés, whereupon the latter made the unfortunate decision to lead an expedition of chastisement by land. This expedition turned out to be an epic example of Spanish methods of movement during the conquest, of their imposition of impossible burdens on Indians, the luxury of camp life where possible, ruthlessness toward supposed Indian opposition, and the enormous Spanish capacity for enduring hardship when necessary. They started with battalions of Indian bearers, concubines, grooms, acrobats and musicians, other attendants, the prisoner Cuauhtémoc, needed supplies, and such fancy baggage as dinner plate. The difficulties of the terrain, together with supply problems, led to the usual frightful mortality among the Indians. Cortés had Cuauhtémoc hanged on a charge of conspiracy to revolt, which even the later chronicler Bernal Díaz, a member of the expedition, thought unproven. To crown the disasters of the expedition, they found in Honduras that Olid was dead. Cortés returned to Mexico City after an absence of twenty months to find the Spaniards there wallowing in a morass of brutality, greed, and factionalism. The temptations of the new environment and the weakness of controls surely made such degeneration almost inevitable.

Alvarado went through southern Mexico to Guatemala, a distance of some seven hundred miles, subduing many Indian groups with his usual brutal efficiency, disappointed that their wealth was not equal to that of central Mexico. He founded the city of Guatemala in 1524 in the midst of a large sedentary Indian population. Pedrarias had remained in Panama since the ex-

ecution of Balboa in 1519 and sent forces northward, which met and clashed with those of Alvarado. Costa Rica (Rich Coast) proved anything but, as did Nicaragua and Honduras, and El Salvador and Guatemala were little better. Old Pedrarias moved to Nicaragua as governor in 1527, dying there for his sins, as an old man, in 1531. Alvarado went by sea in 1534 intending to join in the conquest of Peru, but was bought off by the Spanish leaders already there. The stubborn resistance of the Maya of northern Yucatán was broken by the Montejo family in 1527–1546; the lowland Maya of remote Petén were not fully conquered until 1697, but they were isolated and of no consequence.

b. South America

Conquest of the Incas

The approach to Peru was as prolonged as that to Mexico. The explorers in both cases were delayed and misled by distance, winds and currents, problems of finance and supply and leadership, and difficulty in interpreting apparently ambiguous information. As it turned out, the penetration of Peru might have come by land from the Río de la Plata and Paraguay to the east or by ships sailing from Spain to the Pacific, but that did not happen. Spaniards entering South America from the south Atlantic coast penetrated some distance into the interior and had news of the rich and advanced Indian culture of the Incas, but they did not reach that domain. A Spanish ship sailed around Cape Horn and north in the Pacific to Mexico before Pizarro's contact with the Incas but without learning of those rich lands. Thus, Peru was reached and conquered by Spaniards from Panama.

After Pedrarias had contrived the execution of Balboa in 1519, he moved to Panama on the Pacific. While he turned his attention north and west to Central America, which seemed more promising in Indians and gold, the inhospitable tropical coast to the south discouraged explorers. It finally was penetrated by a partnership of

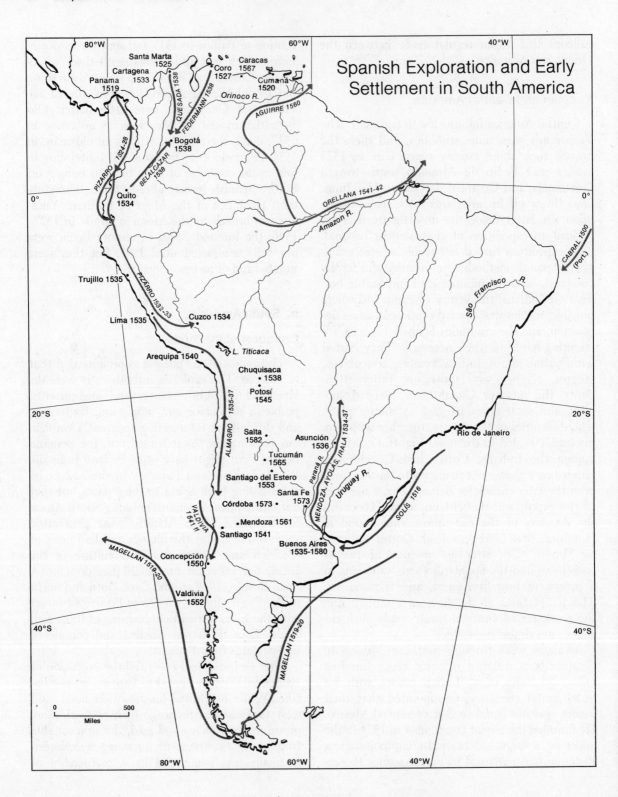

Spanish Exploration and Early
Settlement in South America

three men of Panama: Francisco Pizarro—an illiterate Spanish peasant turned soldier with Ojeda
and Balboa—who had acquired some property
in this little tropical outpost; Diego de Almagro, another illiterate peasant turned conqueror; and Hernando de Luque, a priest. They
had a contract providing equal shares in all their
discoveries.

After terrible sufferings during voyages in
1524–1528, they finally came to unmistakable
evidences of a wealthy culture at Túmbez in
what is now northern Peru. Pizarro went to
Spain and secured a royal grant with his news
and presents of gold and silver ornaments. He
received for himself the titles of Governor, Captain-General, Adelantado, and Alguacil Mayor
of Peru, with salary to be drawn from the conquered territories. He collected lesser titles for
his partners, which they naturally resented.

Pizarro was back in Panama in 1530, with four
brothers and a cousin. Assembling a small expedition took nearly two years, but they finally
set out in 1532 with fewer than two hundred
men and a couple dozen horses. They came again
to Túmbez, subdued the Indians, and learned
that since Pizarro's departure four years before,
the Incas had fought a civil war, a contest for
power between Huascar and Atahualpa, sons by
different mothers of the deceased Inca Huayna
Capac. Atahualpa's forces were winning, and he
held Huascar captive. Also at Túmbez, Pizarro
was happy to receive reinforcements, led by Hernando de Soto, by sea from Nicaragua.

Pizarro founded a town, San Miguel, as a base
and appointed officials before the conquest had
more than begun. Then in November 1532 Pizarro moved into the mountains toward Cajamarca, where Atahualpa and one of his armies
were located. Pizarro had fewer than two hundred
men, a sizable number of horses, but almost no
firearms. In these ranges, where the passes were
higher than those in Mexico, men and horses suffered from cold and altitude sickness. The Spaniards nervously noted that the narrow defiles
were perfect for ambush. Apparently Atahualpa
could not take this little band seriously, although

why he did not try to prevent the penetration is
uncertain. Assorted theories claim that he was too
preoccupied with the civil war with partisans of
Huascar, reluctant to divide his forces, waiting
for reinforcements, drawing the Spaniards into a
military trap in the interior, and/or confused
with regard to Spanish intentions because Pizarro was sending cordial messages while at the
same time deposing Indian rulers of the Atahualpa faction. These explanations are plausible
but all is speculation, even on the part of contemporary Spanish chroniclers.

At Cajamarca the staggering size of the Inca
army appalled but did not discourage the Spaniards. Pizarro had talked to Cortés in Spain and
knew about Indian military weaknesses. He invited Atahualpa to dine, and that poor innocent,
having no conception of the audacity and fighting capabilities of this tiny band, accepted, and
was seized as a hostage. His escort and part of
the surrounding host were slaughtered almost at
will by the Spaniards. After this fearful demonstration, the Inca army disintegrated, some going
home, some taking service with individual Spaniards. Atahualpa offered a roomful of treasure as
ransom, and Pizarro agreed. A few Spaniards
went to the Inca capital at Cuzco and were impressed with the great public buildings and dwellings of nobles, of beautifully fashioned and fitted
stone; gardens of artificial flowers of gold and
silver and precious stones; colored and figured
fabrics of vicuña thread that made the finest
sheep's wool cloth seem harsh. They especially
were impressed with the seven hundred two-foot
slabs of gold that lined the Temple of the Sun.
A chronicler soon noted that the slabs averaged
four to four and one-half pounds when melted
down—nearly two tons of gold! These slabs, plus
other treasure, were heaped up for Atahualpa's
release. But Pizarro had him executed on
trumped-up charges. The last of the effective
Inca rulers accepted Christian baptism to earn a
less terrible death than burning at the stake.

Pizarro and some five hundred men—more
reinforcements had arrived—pushed on through
the mountains to Cuzco in November 1533. The

usual events occurred: plunder, torture of Indians to reveal more treasure, impressment of labor, division of buildings, appropriation of women, establishment of Spanish municipal government. The conquest was really over, although one large rebellion occurred thereafter. In 1536–1537 Manco Capac, whom Pizarro had set up as a puppet Inca, became outraged at his treatment by the Spaniards, and besieged Cuzco with an Indian horde. His forces have been estimated as high as 180,000, a figure that seems unlikely for reasons of supply. Even 80,000 would have been far more than necessary to defeat the few Spaniards in Cuzco if Indian weapons had been equal to the Spanish; even 40,000, or 10,000, would have been a huge superiority in numbers. It was a forlorn hope. Manco could not subdue the two hundred Spaniards (plus Indian servitors and allies) in Cuzco, nor could he indefinitely prevent Spanish reinforcement of the town. Although the conquest of Peru was over, consolidation of the Spanish position came only after a period of factionalism, assassination, treason, and civil war.

Further Penetration of South America

Almagro went to Chile in 1535–1537 with a big expedition. During a staggering march of nearly 3,000 miles, over high passes and through desert wastes, many times more Indian bearers died than Spanish conquerors, as usual. The pleasant lands of central Chile held little treasure, and the redoubtable Araucanian Indians were difficult to turn to labor, so Almagro returned disgruntled to Peru. The Spanish occupation of Chile was carried out by Pedro de Valdivia, beginning in 1540, under a commission from Pizarro. The settlements for some years barely survived. The Araucanians were not only intractable and valorous but adaptable enough to use firearms and horses. In Lautaro, one of their early leaders, they produced an impressive guerrilla chief.

Quito was conquered in 1533–1534 by Sebastián de Belalcázar, a subordinate of Pizarro. He had the help of local Indians who detested the rule of the Inca Ruminahui, who had tried to set up a government there after the death of Atahualpa. Belalcázar continued north from Quito into what is now Colombia, founding Popayán in 1536 and Cali in 1537. He went on with the usual swarms of Indians and the herds of swine that accompanied some *entradas*, reaching the land of the Chibchas in 1539, where he met two other bands of Europeans.

Gonzalo Jiménez de Quesada had come south from the Caribbean through the morasses of the Magdalena River country and found gold among the Chibchas on the high plateau of Cundinamarca. He collected considerable treasure, applying torture to Indians to extract more, and founded the town Santa Fe de Bogotá. The third band was led by Nikolaus Federmann and came from Venezuela to the east. It was the result of a grant by Charles of Spain to the Augsburg merchant-bankers, the house of Welser, making them proprietary lords of Venezuela in compensation for loans to Charles. Despite this convergence of three bands at Bogotá, northern South America scarcely had been touched by Europeans, since few areas offered precious metals, many of the Indians were intractable, and the terrain was difficult.

In Quito, Gonzalo Pizarro became governor in 1539, and went east in the Land of Cinnamon to search for El Dorado—the Golden King—with an *entrada* of 210 Spaniards, 4,000 Indians (the usual round numbers), and 5,000 swine, dogs, and llamas. They quickly learned that the Amazon lowlands were a death trap. None of the Indians returned to Quito though some of the Spaniards did. Francisco de Orellana broke off from the Pizarro party and descended the river to the Atlantic, seeing nothing of value in all its vast length, only lush vegetation and a sparse and primitive Indian population.

In 1516 Juan de Solís had sailed from Spain to the South Atlantic and discovered the great estuary he called the River of Silver. While he was probing the river system that drained into the estuary of Río de la Plata, Indians captured him and devoured him in sight of his companions. Sebastian Cabot went out from Spain in 1526 and further explored the area. In 1535 a large fleet left Spain for the Río de la Plata under Pedro de Mendoza. This group founded a mud-hut town called Buenos Aires (Good Airs), but it soon failed because of the hostility of the primitive Indians and the lack of other attractions. Mendoza returned to Spain. His lieutenant-governor, Juan de Ayolas, went far up the great river system and founded Asunción on the banks of the Paraguay River among friendly Guaraní Indians. Paraguay, in the heart of the continent, became the center of Spanish activity in the area. Buenos Aires, at the mouth of the estuary, one day to be a position of great strategic and economic importance, was not refounded until 1580. The Indians of what is now Argentina were intractable throughout the colonial period.

c. The Why of Spanish Victory

The astonishing victory of the "hundreds over the millions" was not due to Indian cowardice. The fact that the Spaniards prevailed militarily whenever they considered victory worth the investment simply showed an invincible superiority. They often did have an early advantage in that the higher Indian cultures doubted the propriety of resisting possibly supernatural beings. That attitude soon was replaced, however, by conviction of the all-too-human qualities of the invaders. Furthermore, the easy surrender and eager collaboration of some Indian leaders was induced less by religious awe than by a simple desire to join the winning side.

The fact that the Spanish was the winning side rested first of all on technological superiority. The Spanish crossbow was more lethal than Indian bows; Spanish iron-tipped lances were better than stone and bone; steel swords outperformed wooden bludgeons set with obsidian flakes. Bernal Díaz rhapsodized on the saving qualities of Spanish blades. Spanish armor turned off or minimized Indian blows. Firearms usually were few but unmatched in range, and did some killing, especially because the Indian hordes were so crowded together. That some of the effect was psychological does not detract from their value; the object of war is not killing but breaking the enemy's will to resist.

Horses were important in breaking that will, as the conquerors said themselves. The lances and swords of Spaniards were much more terrible from the height of a horse's back or with the weight of its charge behind them. The horse's body contributed battering power, which not only damaged Indians but disorganized them and gave them a sense of being outmatched. And the mobility of the cavalry was a great advantage. Used as a reserve, the little cavalry forces were immensely effective, again not only for the death they dealt but for the disorder and sense of inferiority they induced. Even ten horses bearing armored lancers at a gallop, offering skewers driven by a half ton of thundering animal power, might make the bravest warrior cringe. The Indians had no experience with the methods required to defeat cavalry with infantry. The obvious little devices that occurred to them were not enough. Asiatic and European tactics for the solution of this problem have involved intricate combinations of unit organization, training, armament, armor, communications, and position and movement on the battlefield.

Some commentators have said that the Indians did not understand "human sea" tactics, did not press their attacks, regardless of losses, until their numbers overwhelmed the Spaniards. Such tactics are easy to understand; what is difficult is arranging the necessary motivation and training. Military history suggests that soldiers become discouraged when chopped up by a technically superior enemy. Seas of Indians tried in vain to destroy small bands of Spaniards in Tabasco, Tlaxcala, Tenochtitlán, Yucatán, Cuzco, the Mixton War, and other places. They showed great valor, but usually failed; they were only human. Military history is full of small forces beating much larger armies that suffered inferiorities of leadership, organization, training, or weapons.

The extreme rigidity of the Indian social organization was a weakness. Lacking the European spirit of individualism, Indians were more prone to panic on the battlefield when a leader was killed or when they were stunned by the slaughter wreaked by Spanish weapons. There were many cases of sudden flight or supine surrender. Furthermore, when the armies of the higher cultures were defeated and most upper-class leaders killed, captured, or in flight, the common folk tended to accept the defeat as decisive, and they offered no further resistance.

Therefore, the higher cultures could not adopt their potentially best strategy for prolonging resistance. The folk were sedentary farmers, with no tradition of guerrilla warfare as practiced by their socially less developed Indian cousins. There were no plans to withdraw into remote redoubts. The leaders had insufficient information and opportunity to make such a decision before the military crisis was upon them. The decision would have required much emotional and logistical preparation. Not many complex societies have been able to make such plans in the face of sudden and overwhelming invasion.

Indian "disunity" was a fortunate thing for the Spaniards, but there could have been nothing else. Different cultures with different languages were often unaware of each other and in other cases were bitter enemies. Some animosities between Indian groups were so intense that they fought enthusiastically for the Spaniards against traditional foes. Indian allies also fought against distant and previously unknown Indians. Partly, these alliances were just collaboration with the winner, not unknown in Europe, and were no more remarkable than European division in the face of Muslim invasions in medieval and early modern times.

This Spanish mastery over the higher Indian cultures was not entirely transferable to warfare with more primitive Indians. In those cases, effectiveness was sufficiently reduced so that often trying for victory in the sense of permanent control was not worth the effort. The more primitive Indians often fought in small bands, avoided

pitched battles with strong Spanish forces, kept refuges at their backs for retreat, and used guerrilla methods—ambush, sniping, raid, and withdrawal. Most of them were organized into relatively small groups, and could travel fast because their possessions were easily transportable or replaceable. To kill many of them at a time was difficult, and no victory gave much territory or conquered labor to the victor. Araucanians, Caribs, Apaches, and many other Indian groups did not surrender, but dispersed and fought another day. Endless skirmishes were wearing on Spanish nerves, property, and life itself. In some places, where the Spaniards were too little interested to make the investment required to stop them, these skirmishes went on for centuries. So frontier communities were left largely to their own defense. Even so, more primitive Indians could have been controlled by the Spaniards, if only military considerations had been involved. As usual, the important consideration was balancing cost against profit. The difference was apparent when private persons and government poured resources into protecting a new silver discovery.

Probably even the most miraculous of Indian decisions on cooperation or strategy could not have done more than delay the conquest and make it more costly. Individual Spaniards and crown and church would have been willing to pay a higher price than the quite modest one that conquest in fact required. The lure of gold and silver alone would have continued to draw individuals to the effort, bringing more numerous firearms and cavalry. Even assuming an unlikely Spanish abandonment of the effort or a military stalemate, also difficult to imagine, either surely would have meant that eventually Spain's European rivals would have interfered in their own interest. They would have either ousted the Spaniards and completed the conquest or stimulated the Spaniards to increase their own efforts.

The Indians were truly doomed. The European culture was technologically superior, and that technology had been applied with some care to military affairs. To ascribe the Indian defeat to disunity, religious fear, or strategic or tactical errors is misleading. Those factors were important in the historical conquest, but a greatly improved Indian performance would have made no difference. The longer the fighting continued, the more the European superiority would have been decisive.

Today we feel the special sadness for the extinction of the Indian civilizations that we feel when a biological species disappears. We feel somehow lessened, made poorer.

d. The Black Legend of Spanish Cruelty

Undeniably the Spaniards of the conquest were cruel to the Indians. Cruelty had been common in international and domestic affairs in the Old World for several thousand years, and American Indians had been cruel to each other. Many atrocities of the conquest were committed by Indian allies of the Spaniards. There is no reason to suppose that if Englishmen, Frenchmen, or Dutchmen had conquered Mexico and Peru, they would have been kinder than Spaniards. Visions of English Pilgrims charming Aztecs and Incas with book and bell scarcely reflect what we know of English society in the sixteenth and seventeenth centuries. The lure of loot and Indian labor would have drawn from England to Mexico and Peru such adventurers and flint-souled businessmen as went to Virginia and India to find profits and not to plow; and English peasants and scaff and raff from the towns would have shown precisely the energy, greed, and unthinking ruthlessness of Pizarro, who according to legend prepared for the great adventure in Peru by tending swine in Spain.

Misunderstandings, prejudice, and exaggeration have muddied this essential truth in literature and legend. Some have supposed that the atrocities committed by Spaniards against Indians comprised their whole relationship, which was far from the case. Spaniards mingled their blood with Indians on a large scale, sometimes recognizing their offspring as legitimate. They wished to Christianize the Indians, and they certainly wanted to preserve them as laborers. Critics who emphasize three hundred years of forced Indian labor do not always mention the cruelty of Russian or Chinese elites to their peasants; the way of Englishmen and Frenchmen with black slaves; or that the Anglo-American failure to force much labor from Indians in North America was not for lack of trying, but because the cultural groups there were unsuited to such use, precisely as was true of Indians in Argentina, northern Mexico, and southern Chile.

Condemnation of Spanish abuse of Indians sometimes has been coupled with celebration of Indian innocence and virtue. In the sixteenth century, Bartolomé de las Casas, the great defender of the Indians, although he deplored many Indian customs, slighted those defects in order to concentrate on the misdeeds of his fellow Spaniards. In the eighteenth century there was a European .fad for rhapsodizing about Indians as "noble savages." Intellectuals thus found in the Indian theme a way of expressing their views of their own society. Since they were interested only in their own place and time, these writers naturally did not allow fear of speaking from an almost total lack of knowledge of Indian culture to impede their eloquence.

The Spanish conquerors, as has been noted, did not celebrate Indian virtue. The Spaniards' usually sincere statements of disdain and loathing formed an important body of self-justification for violent acts of "reform." Twentieth-century scholars tend to shrug off such biased testimony. On the other hand, there has been much recent study of such unsavory preconquest Indian practices as human sacrifice, slavery, serfdom, drunkenness, infanticide, torture, and the lack of freedom and choice for the individual. While there are few to assert that these defects justified conquest, their presence at least suggests that the Spaniards did not destroy the Garden of Eden.

The reason for much of the legend of unusual Spanish cruelty stems from elaboration by Spain's enemies in Europe, especially by Englishmen.

Colonial Spanish America

The Conquest. The episodes of the conquest in New Spain (Mexico) are shown in the Lienzo de Tlaxcala, a painted account set down by Indians about thirty years after the event. It emphasizes the role of the Tlaxcalans as allies of the Spaniards in conquering other Indians.

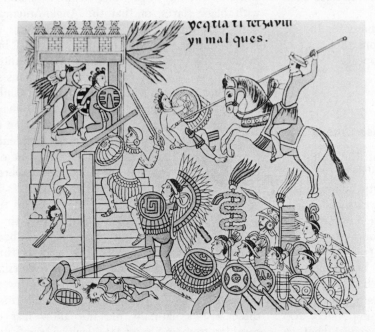

Spaniards and their Indian allies attack the Aztec defenders of the great temple at Tenochtitlán, the large and powerful center of the Aztec Empire that later became Mexico City. *Lienzo de Tlaxcala*

In the center panel the last Aztec ruler, Cuauhtémoc, surrenders to Cortés (seated). Behind Cortés stands Dona Marina, an Indian woman who greatly aided the Spaniards; she is accompanied by one of the new wonders of America—a turkey. In the top right corner, Cortés receives Cuauhtémoc's wife and family. Below, a Spanish soldier guards Indian notables. *Lienzo de Tlaxcala*

Details of the fighting in Tenochtitlán, with the Spaniards and Tlaxcalans using horses, cannon, and handguns, sometimes from within portable wooden shelters. *Lienzo de Tlaxcala*

Spanish Officials. After the conquest, the great task for Spain was to set up a government that could control the often turbulent conquistadors and could Christianize, organize, and exploit the great Indian populations.

Luís de Velasco, viceroy in New Spain and later in Peru during the sixteenth century, capably used the great powers of the highest office in the Indies for the glory and profit of the crown and the advancement of the faith.

Poma de Ayala, a seventeenth-century descendant of the Incas, drew this scene of a *corregidor* and a priest gambling in Peru. The wealth they squandered in pleasure was, of course, derived from those they were supposed to govern and cherish. A *corregidor* was a provincial official, notorious for mistreating Indians. The church itself played a big role in pacifying and controlling the Indians, especially by persuading them to pay taxes in labor or goods. Poma made many similar sketches protesting the exploitation of the Indians.

Upper-Class Life. The creoles and peninsular Spaniards of the small upper class enjoyed privileges that set them far apart from the huge lower class.

Sor Juana Inés de la Cruz, a member of the upper class in seventeenth-century Mexico, entered a convent as did many girls of colonial Spanish America, not from a sense of vocation but for the convenient and socially acceptable lifestyle. Discipline for such residents was sometimes lax, and living conditions were pleasant. Sor Juana, who had been a child prodigy, became a woman of great learning and a notable poet who celebrated both sacred and romantic love. Miguel Cabrera painted this in 1750 from a simpler self-portrait and gave her the background of a scholar's library. The painting hangs in the National Museum of Mexico. *Courtesy of the Latin American Collection, University of Texas*

Torre Tagle Palace, in Lima, was an upper-class residence of the eighteenth century. A prototype of the neo-Hispanic architectural style, it reflects the luxury and charm of colonial life for the fortunate minority. *Peter Menzel*

Interior of an old, opulent home in Antigua. Once the capital of Guatemala, Antigua contains some of the finest Spanish colonial buildings. *Jane Latta*

Aristocratic lady of Peru in the eighteenth century.

As the great power of the sixteenth century, Spain was a target for envy. Finding ammunition in Spanish history and habits was easy. The pride of Spaniards was notorious and resented. Envy of the riches of its American possessions led to charges of unusual avarice, a comic suggestion in view of the history of the profit motive in England and France. Useful data on atrocities could be mined from the writings of Spaniards, especially Bartolomé de las Casas, damning the Spaniards from their own mouths.

Spain's resistance to Protestantism made it a special object of loathing by the enemies of Rome. The profundity of the Spanish faith and the zeal to preserve its purity, as seen in the Inquisition, seemed to Protestants a different proposition from the bigotry of Calvin in Switzerland. The cruelty of Spaniards to Jews and Muslims naturally was regarded by Englishmen as being of a different order from their own conquest and rapine in Ireland, to say nothing of their own medieval expulsion of Jews. The English were also afraid, with good reason, of Spanish schemes both to restore Catholicism in England and to restrict its political independence and overseas activities. With all this motivation for fear and envy of the Spaniards, no wonder English writers exploited such themes, and Englishmen believed in their validity.

This exaggerated notion of Spanish cruelty and avarice became imbedded in English popular and formal history. It was carried to English America and there reinforced by continued rivalry and warfare between the "dons" and Englishmen in Europe and America. Various accretions to the mother lode fattened the legend in English America and the United States. One of the most ludicrous was the view that English stock represented family affection, social stability, and civilization generally, whereas Spaniards stood for none of these. This view rested on a picture of Englishmen coming to America with wives and children clinging to their hands, whereas Spaniards came as unattached males, lusty and untrammeled, interested only in dusky loins and gold. The picture was absurd as history, merely propaganda and ego-bolstering prejudice. The barest acquaintance with the facts makes clear that Spaniards in America were strongly attached to family ties and a stable social order.

Hispanic resentment of such distortions resulted in a countermovement of historical argument. The notion of unusual Spanish brutality and avarice and inferior contributions to civilization was labeled early in the twentieth century a "black legend" of lies and misinterpretation. The corrective was needed, for the Spaniards were much like other Europeans in their cruelty, avarice, love of family, and interest in social order and civilization.

5 Consolidation of the Conquests

The genius of Spain in America appeared less in the conquests than in their consolidation. Fortunately, Spanish institutions and will were equal to bringing order out of an appalling mess. From the 1520s to the 1540s crown control of the new lands was in doubt. The colonists' determination to possess the Indians threatened Spain's hold on the European element of the new society as well as its ability to perform its Christian duty for the conquered peoples. A humane and prudent Indian policy had to be hammered out and a civil society created for the European community in America that would be securely under crown control. Those efforts aroused bitter conflicts of interest and belief in Spain and America, but out of them came institutions that endured for more than 250 years.

a. The Conquest as a "Period"

The conquest as a military process ended early in the larger Caribbean isles. It was virtually finished in the mainland areas of the great cultures by the 1540s. In some areas there was no military conquest, because there were few Indians or because they were pacific or withdrew. On the other hand, military operations against Indians in some areas continued to the end of the colonial era. Although this continued warfare was of local concern, it did not greatly affect Spanish decisions on the consolidation of the conquest or the development of institutions in the major centers of the empire. The conquest as a period also must be considered to include those years during which physical coercion was accompanied by the first important efforts to erect administrative, spiritual, and other methods of control. Those efforts to consolidate began early in the conquest period, but the need became acute with the great conquests from 1519 to the mid-1530s. Most of the essential Spanish decisions on conquest and consolidation were made before the end of the 1550s.

The dramatic events in Mexico and Peru captured the European imagination. An enormous literature has appeared on those events, much of it celebrating the physical valor and military deeds of the Spaniards. Other popular themes have been treasure, the splendor of Indian culture, Spanish cruelty, and the winning of new souls for Christ. In our own time there has been a reappraisal, with more attention to what the Indians lost and less to the doughty sword arms of the European marauders, with emphasis upon the conquest as preparation for the processes of cultural fusion that came thereafter. Seen in that way, the conquest had special importance for the entire colonial period because of the erection then of institutions that endured. Partly because of emphasis on this question of institutional foundations, the conquest sometimes is made— explicitly or implicitly—nearly coterminous with the sixteenth century,[1] a misleading simplification. The early foundations were important, but no more so than the evolution and operation of those institutions throughout the colonial era. Two important subjects do require discussion in terms of precisely the period of the conquest: the great decisions on the status and treatment of the Indians, and the problem of crown control of the conquerors.

b. The Evolution of Indian Policy

The disastrous results of European-Indian relations before 1519 multiplied during the great conquests. The crown was far from the scene, flooded with vague and contradictory information, and badgered by the spokesmen of various interests. Colonists in America and their supporters in government called for "practical" measures for development and defense of the new territories and erection of institutions that would Christianize and cherish the Indians. Some churchmen supported this plan, either convinced by the practical arguments or believing the Indians a corrupt and inferior breed. Other churchmen supported an opposing policy of radical measures to protect the Indians, regardless of damage to the material interests of the colonists.

Early Experiments

The crown tried to reconcile the somewhat ambiguous voice of conscience with the wishes of the colonists. Isabella and Ferdinand attempted to limit Indian slavery while they permitted some to continue, issued the Laws of

Burgos of 1512–1513, and suggested Indian self-government in Española. The governor at Santo Domingo in 1508–1514 did give a few Indians land on which to develop a European-style life, but his experiment was a failure. Soon thereafter, the Hieronymite fathers in Española canceled the allotment of Indians to absentees, put miners on wages, and tried to stop voyages to the Pearl Coast, which frequently involved slaving.

The Hieronymites looked for evidence that the Indians might become civilized and live in freedom, but the Spanish colonists told them that the idea was mad, that Indians were subhuman. Convinced, the friars instead in 1518 collected the miserable remnants of the Indian folk into villages of four to five hundred. Just at that time a plague of smallpox carried off a third of what remained of the once great Indian population. These failures did not quite kill the theory that Indians could absorb sufficient European culture to govern themselves, liberated from the forced-labor system. In 1519 a judge, Rodrigo de Figueroa, arrived in Española from Spain with authority to probe the capacity of Indians to live in such a manner. Figueroa tried some villages of free Indians, with little success. In 1520 he received from Spain an order to free Indians from subordination and forced labor "with all convenient speed." So far as the colonists were concerned, no speed toward such an objective was convenient. In any event, there were few Indians left on the island. Yet another effort at self-government was tried, in Cuba in 1526–1535, and failed.

Some of these early efforts were suggested or supported by Bartolomé de las Casas, a well-educated priest who arrived in Española in 1502. For some years, there and in Cuba, he functioned as a chaplain and received allotments of Indians, which he used for profitable enterprise. In 1514, at the age of forty, Las Casas became convinced that Indian policy was horribly wrong. He renounced his *repartimiento* of Indians and went to Spain in 1515. Thus began a remarkable career of Christian love, political agitation, travel and administration, and doctrinal polemics that

---

[1] See Chapter 11, Section f, for discussion of the seventeenth "century of depression" and the eighteenth as a time of limited "prosperity"; and Chapter 14, Section b, for the eighteenth as a century of very limited "reform." The duration and, even more, the importance of such trends are doubtful, and should be viewed with caution.

ended only with his death, at more than ninety years of age, in 1566.

Beginning in 1516, after Cardinal Cisneros became regent in Spain, Las Casas helped plan new legislation for the protection of Indians. When Cisneros sent the Hieronymite friars to govern in Española in 1516, with orders to aid the Indians, he sent with them Las Casas as defender of the natives. Las Casas soon protested Hieronymite willingness to accept the advice of the colonists regarding Indians. The settlers then became so hostile to Las Casas that he took refuge in the Dominican monastery of Santo Domingo, not the last time that he was threatened with physical violence by angry Spanish colonists.

Returning to Spain in 1517, he spent three years trying to get concessions for the Indians. He advocated creation of European communities organized to cherish rather than exploit the natives. They were to include friars for peaceful conversion, and Spanish farmers, with other Spaniards forbidden entrance. In 1520 the government declared that Indians were free men and were to be Christianized with that in mind, and Las Casas got a grant for his experiment on the Pearl Coast of northern South America. It proved a disaster. Most of the friars assigned to the project failed to reach the Indies because of storms. Two existing Dominican missions that were to be used were destroyed by Indian attacks in 1520. Support in Spain for the venture was cut by the great *comunero* rebellion, which drew most of the crown's attention. Instead of the fifty farmers Las Casas expected to receive, he was assigned seventy proscribed political agitators. Financial support for the venture was too small. When Las Casas arrived at Puerto Rico in 1521 his little group of malcontents destined for farming promptly deserted and joined the Ponce de León expedition for the conquest of Florida. Of course. A Spanish peasant who landed in America at once thought of himself (unless he were exceptionally stupid) as a celestial creature, far above the alien Indians. He would not farm where earth-grubbing was associated with a lower

caste. He could declare himself a *caballero*, without old neighbors to point out his peasant forebears. America was a great opportunity for a poor boy from Spain.

Las Casas clashed with the governor in Española, who was bent on attacking the Indians who had killed the Dominican friars on the Pearl Coast. The governor rejected the prohibition on movement to Las Casas' "insulated" area, a typical case of decision in Spain being outrun by events in the Indies. So Las Casas compromised, getting local aid for his venture but permitting Spanish intrusion in his assigned area. He went to the Pearl Coast, but the venture collapsed before the end of 1521. Spaniards continued slave raiding in the area, as did the few soldiers Las Casas had assigned to him. Nearby Spanish officials would not aid Las Casas. Indians attacked the mission area.

Las Casas met hostility and ridicule when he arrived again at Española in January 1522. He reproached himself for the deaths on the Pearl Coast, and for agreeing to slave raiding. He became a Dominican and spent more than a decade in Española, mostly in his monastery, studying, writing on the history of relations between Indians and Spaniards, and carrying on a voluminous correspondence. He was developing two reputations, depending on the point of view, from Mexico to Spain: a model religious or a dangerous agitator. In the early 1530s he was part of an official visitation to the Dominican province in Mexico, where he helped reestablish discipline, over fierce opposition from some Dominicans and from the municipal government of Mexico City. Back in Española, in 1533 Las Casas was confined to his monastery by local government order (later confirmed in Spain) for persuading a dying Spaniard to free his encomienda Indians and to leave his goods as reparation to Indians for his extortions. He was let out in January 1534 to risk his life in the remote mountains persuading the rebel Indian Enriquillo to give up his armed resistance.

Las Casas was in Panama in 1535, deploring slavery and the corruption of officials. He went on to Nicaragua, writing king and council for permission to try peaceful penetration of unconquered Indian areas. The civil officials of Nicaragua forced him to leave the province. In Guatemala he received support from some churchmen for his efforts to protect the Indians, but some joined the civil society in opposition. He did get local agreement to a trial of peaceful conquest in what was called the Land of War because of the intransigence of the Indians. The friars entered the territory in 1537 and had enough success to feel justified in renaming it the Land of True Peace. But much local Spanish opposition remained, and the method required more support, so Las Casas went to Spain, arriving in 1540.

He secured further authority for peaceful conversion in Chiapas (now the southernmost state in Mexico), with Spaniards other than friars barred from the project area. At this time Las Casas became busy with the important New Laws (which will be treated later), but he did not forget the Chiapas venture. In 1543 he accepted the bishopric of Chiapas, recruited forty-five Dominicans, and sailed in July 1544. Three of his friars deserted in Puerto Rico. He was in Chiapas in March 1545 and issued a pastoral letter barring absolution in cases of extortionate abuse of Indians unless the guilty set the Indians free or restored their property. This order ensured his repudiation by the Spanish community. He could not even get treasury officials to pay out funds due him and his favorite venture. Before long Las Casas was ordered to a bishops' conference in Mexico (1546), where he again raised a storm by advocating his doctrine of restitution to Indians. Although a majority of the bishops supported the idea, civil officials would not implement it, the fate of much of Las Casas' activity. He was back in Spain in 1547, never again to visit the Indies.

Spaniards in Chiapas and Guatemala continued to complain that Las Casas was a danger to the Spanish hold on America. Las Casas resigned his bishopric in 1550; he was then seventy-six. The experiment in the Land of True Peace

was abandoned later in the 1550s. We have, thus, surveyed three experiments for preservation of the Indians that failed: settling them in villages to develop European habits as free subjects of the crown; combining Spanish farmers with friars in a benign arrangement with Indians; and peaceful preaching to achieve conversion and pacification.

Encomienda and Slavery

Abolition of encomienda and of Indian slavery were also important aims of Las Casas. Law and practice on those matters long were confusing and contradictory.[2] Little impeded the allotment of Indians in Española and Cuba except their rapid extermination. Early allotments were called just that, *repartimientos*, and the term remained in use even after the concept of encomienda was asserted. Spaniards wanted the simple allotment, not commendation to their care (encomienda), of the Indians, since the latter involved reciprocal obligation. The Laws of Burgos of 1512–1513 permitted encomienda but accepted the doctrine that Indians by nature required Christian supervision. The provisions for protection of Indians in those laws were ineffective. A few years later, in New Spain, Cortés and other commanders granted Indians in encomienda. At the same time other Indians were being enslaved on a variety of pretexts, or none. In fact, *encomenderos* in New Spain sometimes branded their encomienda Indians as slaves. By that time the crown's doubts about encomienda pertained not only to the abuse of Indians, but to the desirability of controlling the Spanish *encomenderos*.

Few Spaniards in the Indies received encomiendas. A few encomiendas were granted to upper-class Indians, reflecting a fitful interest in Indian rights but even more the Spanish policy of using the Indian elite to help control the Indian masses. Spaniards in America constantly com-

---

[2] See Chapter 3, Section c, for the early history of Indian allotments in the islands; and Chapter 8 for comments on the later history of encomienda and slavery.

plained that there were not enough allotments for the men who had spilled their blood in the conquests. The 714 Spanish holders in Española in 1514 had an average of 26 Indians each, and the Indian population was declining rapidly. In the populous Valley of Mexico only 30 encomiendas were granted, with an estimated 180,000 tributary Indians (heads of households), so a few men were greatly favored. The holdings of Cortés within and without the valley were unique: officially, 23,000 tributary Indians, but actually many more. In Chile there were few suitable Indians, so that in 1546 the 60 *vecinos* (full Spanish citizens) of Santiago complained that some *encomenderos* had fewer than 100 Indians. In Peru and Mexico some had more than 2,000 Indians, although such large numbers were unusual. In Peru in the 1550s *encomenderos* totaled 480 of a Spanish population of some 8,000. Lima at the beginning of the seventeenth century had about 2,000 *vecinos,* but only 30 were *encomenderos.* In all Spanish America in the late sixteenth century there were some 160,000 Spaniards (creole and peninsular), of whom only about 4,000 were *encomenderos.* Even with all their Spanish employees and relatives, that was probably less than a quarter of the Spanish population.

Encomienda was a delegation of the royal power over the king's Indian vassals in the collection of tribute. Tribute, the holders always assumed, meant tribute in labor and in commodities, although only labor was mentioned in many of the early grants. The grants either named an Indian ruler or official and his dependent population or named towns and their inhabitants. The reciprocal duties of caring for the Indians that were theoretically a part of encomienda have been noted, as well as the fact that the *encomenderos* often ignored them. In fact, often the allotment of Indians was simply that, the way it had begun in Columbus' time, with no discussion of reciprocal duties. Columbus did not establish the allotment of Indians in imitation of encomienda in Spain, but as an obvious response to an immediate need.

Then the connection with the old Spanish encomienda of the *Reconquista* against the Muslims was established in the following years. But unlike the practice in Spain, an American encomienda grant did not give title or other rights to land or general jurisdiction over the conquered population. In the Indies it was a system of private and unpaid labor and of control over tribute in commodities. *Encomenderos* were men of some consequence in the conquest society, busy with affairs, often holding public office especially in town councils. They were interested in extracting what they could from their Indians, without reference to Indian welfare. *Encomenderos* did not live among the Indians but rather in the Spanish towns. Majordomos or overseers and business managers handled their affairs, depending in turn on collaboration with the local Indian leaders—often called *caciques* or *curacas* by the Spaniards. Those Indians in their turn had lesser Indian assistants. The majordomos and their assistants, and the Indian ruling class at the local level, collected the tribute and arranged the labor drafts.

Several features of the system may be emphasized. (*a*) The colonial elite thought of it as providing nearly "costless" labor. (*b*) It was a system of almost unrelieved exploitation for more than half a century. For years encomienda rights were not defined. When definition began, the *encomenderos* and their agents continued to act as they pleased. Although we do not have much record of the operation of encomiendas, we have plenty regarding overwork, physical abuse, seizure of Indian buildings and commodities, even the selling of tribute back to the Indians giving it. Civil and ecclesiastical authorities, lacking strong coercive instruments, could do little to control abuses in the huge areas and among the many Indians involved. The economic, physical, and psychological weight of *encomendero* greed and tyranny was heavy. (*c*) The holders insisted on their right to bequeath encomienda grants. The crown feared such rights would create a hereditary nobility that would be difficult to control. (*d*) Through encomienda vast construction work was done, helping build the Spanish town in America, as well as enterprise in the countryside. (*e*) Through encomienda much crude acculturation was accomplished. It provided interchange between Spaniards and Indians, assisting creation of a new society. An aspect of this was the sensible Spanish decision to use Indian governmental and labor customs and personnel. In fact, probably no other type of arrangement would have worked nearly so well. Both the mass of the Indian workers and their traditional supervisory personnel accepted with relatively little protest a continuation of their labor habits. Many of their tasks remained the same as before the conquest, especially in the production of such Indian crops as maize, beans, potatoes, and squash; wood gathering; water hauling; pottery production; and the like. They had, of course, also to learn how to grow European crops, tend European animals, and make European structures and artifacts.

The *encomendero's* agents decided how best to use labor, within the limits of Indian capacity to resist. They often followed preconquest Indian labor practices, but were under little compulsion to do so. They dragged encomienda Indians off on new expeditions of conquest in distant regions, and few of them returned. They took encomienda Indians to the new Spanish towns to build their houses and act as servants. Sometimes the overseers did not use the rotation system to which the Indians were accustomed in giving labor services to the state in preconquest times. Indians in the countryside built for their *encomenderos* mills, storage sheds, stables, residences for majordomos, corrals, and other structures. Usually, the Indians were afraid to complain or found complaint ineffective. No wonder, since *encomenderos* and their agents in fact exercised governmental rights over the Indians granted to them for limited purposes. The near invulnerability of the *encomendero* position made possible such extreme measures as branding encomienda Indians as slaves without a shadow of justification. They stole lavishly from the Indians land and other property over which encomienda grants gave them no rights whatever.

Some early crown assertions against encomienda and slavery, and in favor of freedom for Indians, have been noted. The crown objected to encomienda because personal service not only interfered with Indian freedom but made the Indians servants in perpetuity. Also, experience showed that encomienda led to maltreatment that had something to do with depopulation. Finally, *encomenderos* clearly thought of themselves as lords of the land, an unnerving thought to a government that had had too much recent experience with unruly nobles in Spain.

In 1523 Cortés was ordered not to grant encomiendas. Such orders were virtually ignored, and in 1526 the institution of encomienda was legalized for New Spain, although an encomienda was supposed to consist thereafter of a maximum of three hundred tributary Indians (many were, in fact, much smaller). In 1528 the crown again confirmed encomienda and apparently was inclined to make it permanent and hereditary, something the conquerors passionately desired.

In 1530, however, the crown decided to restrict encomienda by appointing *corregidores*. The *corregidor* was a royal official who had been important in Spain in enforcing crown authority in independent-minded towns. He was now appointed to local jurisdictions in America, partly to administer Indians under the crown.[3] Then in 1536 the Law of Inheritance for Two Generations allowed *encomenderos* to leave their Indian allotments to the first generation of their heirs (a widow or first descendents). The crown obviously was having difficulty coming to a final decision. By now Spaniards had been in New Spain for seventeen years, and towns, farms, churches, workshops, and government structures had been erected. The existence of many highly vocal interests made a touchy business of any tampering with the labor system on which the ruling class depended.

Thus by the later 1530s the questions of Indian slavery and forced labor by commendation or allotment had agitated the Spanish world for

---

[3] See Chapter 6 for more on the *corregidor*.

nearly forty years. All sorts of opinions still were being offered to the crown. In 1537 a papal bull (*Sublimus Deus*), in part inspired by Las Casas, declared that Indians were "truly men," capable and desirous of understanding Christianity, free, not to be enslaved, and entitled to their property. When in 1540 Las Casas arrived in Spain from his initial success in the Land of True Peace in Central America, he entered the controversy. His writings included what became the famous "Very Brief Account of the Destruction of the Indies," later (1552) printed in Spain and reprinted in other languages as propaganda against the Spaniards. It sacrificed accuracy to the higher goal of illuminating a moral point and showed the Spaniards slaughtering without compunction impossibly large numbers of Indians.

King Charles in 1542 was persuaded to issue the New Laws, remarkable not only for their bold exposition of the reform view but for the commotion they provoked in America. Probably the king was influenced by considerations both of religious duty and of sound government. The New Laws outlawed enslavement of Indians (presumably ending the practice of justifying it for cannibalism, apostasy, viciousness, warfare, and so on) and freed those who previously had been enslaved improperly. Prohibitions were laid on dangerous types of labor for Indians. Encomienda was declared virtually at an end: those improperly held were voided; *encomenderos* who mistreated Indians were to lose them, including the chief figures in the brawls of the conquerors in Peru; those named persons with unreasonable numbers of Indians in Mexico were to lose some; Indians held in encomienda by royal officials and prelates were forfeit, nor were such personages ever again to receive them; and all encomiendas were ended with the lives of the current holders, the Indians then reverting to the crown.

Fierce opposition arose in America to this grand design. *Encomenderos* were supported by many friars for selfish, practical, and moral reasons. The fact that Indians, on learning of the New Laws, abandoned both their *encomenderos* and their priests reinforced the conservative view among the religious. *Encomendero* representatives were sent to Spain to protest the New Laws. Although the *encomenderos* were a minority in America, they were community leaders. Furthermore, the majority of Spaniards who lacked encomiendas was not organized. The immediate problem for the crown was the resistance movement.

Almost as striking as the opposition was the quick retreat by prudent officials. The viceroy in Mexico did not enforce the New Laws. A more rigid attitude in Peru caused rebellion. The crown itself retreated in 1545–1546 by repealing or suspending many of the New Laws. In spite of this retreat, however, subsequent legislation chipped away at encomienda, since the crown could not accept an institution that threatened creation of an uncontrollable upper class.

The more gradual crown effort to reduce encomienda met less resistance because of the failure of revolt in Peru; improved imperial machinery in America; and the growth of an elite population with no stake in encomienda. In Peru in the mid-sixteenth century the crown effort to reduce encomienda while providing aid for the increased Spanish population took the form of new towns which granted small haciendas, a process that the *encomenderos* resented.[4] The lack of interest in New Spain was evident in the 1560s when a few *encomenderos* talked wildly against an apparent crown decision to destroy encomienda definitively. The so-called Avila-Cortés (son of the conqueror) conspiracy involved at least reports of a plan for an independent kingdom. It also involved the improper business interests of *audiencia* judges who sympathized at least with the economic complaints of *encomenderos*. It came to involve friction between *audiencia* and viceroy, investigative judges sent from Spain, and a spate of jailings, executions, exile, even torture of young Cortés, the second Marqués del Valle. Everyone was relieved when the mess was resolved. Most of the slight resistance to the later reductions of encomienda occurred because of the demographic catastrophe among the Indians,

---

[4] See Chapter 10, Section d.

which reduced many encomiendas to valueless shells—communities without people. Furthermore, other Indian labor systems were developed, and Spaniards used them successfully.

The repeal of the New Laws was not of prime importance in determining the condition of the Indians. If all Indians had come under the crown in the 1540s, probably their lot would not have been happier. The decline in the population would have occurred anyway from the effects of European disease and the abuse of Indian labor. Transferring Indians to the crown probably would have done little to protect them from demands for forced labor by church, state, and private individuals. The fact that after encomienda had lost its importance, other systems of forced labor were used indicates how little the effect would have been. The colonists always demanded a secure and low-cost supply of labor; the government could tinker with the method but could not oppose the demand.

Decline in the value of encomienda had several aspects. One was that fixed expenses—such as supervisors, the church, taxes—outran income in the middle and late sixteenth century. *Encomenderos* could not reverse the process. Another source of change was that when an encomienda holder lacked heirs, the Indians reverted to crown control. Encomiendas disappeared not only with the death, but also with the movement (authorized or unauthorized) of Indians. Various rules regarding the number of generations that encomiendas could last chipped away at them. As important as the decline and movement of the Indians was the crown's campaign to strip encomienda of its labor function, leaving only the commodity or money tribute to the holder. A serious effort to do this began in 1549. Crown Indians no longer owed service (at least under this system), merely commodities or money. Enforcing the rule on the private *encomenderos* took somewhat longer, but the reform obviously was a success long before the end of the sixteenth century;[5] by then, in any event, the Indian population was much reduced. With population change encomienda became an inefficient way of allocating labor.

Little remained of encomienda in most places in the seventeenth and eighteenth centuries. In Paraguay and the Plata area encomienda Indians still were giving labor and tribute in the later colonial era. But among the great Indian populations of Middle America and the Andes the institution long since had ceased to be of consequence.

The Doctrine of "Just War"

Throughout all these years, there was discussion of the right of conquest, of the doctrine of "just war." The issue came to a head in the late 1540s and involved debate among learned churchmen. If the pious doctors could not agree, who can wonder at the doubts of the crown? One contestant, the jurist Juan Ginés de Sepúlveda, had years before composed a treatise arguing that war against Indians was just. Las Casas, who had several times requested a ban on licenses for expeditions of conquest, entered the contest. The anticonquest view seemed to be predominant, as seen in orders of 1549 for stringent restrictions on the licensing and conduct of expeditions of conquest. Then in April 1550 the king ordered suspension of all conquests until the moral issue was resolved, a remarkable demonstration of the importance to the greatest monarch in Christendom of religious faith and ideas of justice.

Judges were named and arguments presented to them in Spain in 1550–1551. Spain could not claim to be recovering Christian lands in America, as it said of military actions in North Africa. Sepúlveda declared that war against Indians was justified by their sins and barbarity, the necessity to protect Indians from each other, and by the imperious demands of Christianization. He relied on Aristotle's assertion that some beings are by nature inferior and subject to the rule of superiors, and on his own judgment of the quality of Indian culture. Las Casas, who knew more about Indian culture than Sepúlveda, declared that it

---

[5] See Chapter 6, Section b, on the history and strength of the *tributo*.

was of sufficient quality to negate Sepúlveda's claims. This question had been argued in one form or another for decades. The judges were confused by the charges and countercharges and came to no clear-cut decision.

Although various actions by the crown indicated its sympathy for the views of Las Casas, the view that the security of the empire and the needs of religion required a compromise overrode that sympathy. For some years after the great debate of 1550–1551, the king permitted viceroys in the Indies to license expeditions. Las Casas continued to battle against conquest until his death in 1566. In 1573 Philip II issued an order requiring that unsubdued Indians receive extensive explanation of the good intentions of the crown and the necessity of submission and that Indian vices be reformed only gradually. In any event, only the minimum of force was allowed, and no Indians were to be enslaved. The order was vague and never fully enforceable in the vast reaches of America. The crown itself in the later sixteenth and early seventeenth centuries occasionally permitted strong measures, even enslavement, against obstreperous Indians.

While these events were occurring, the regular clergy were preaching, converting, and teaching. They sometimes slightly mitigated the severity of civil demands upon the Indians. Bishop Zumárraga in the early days in New Spain created an Indian court, and tried to make the charges brought there to bear upon the conquerors, with small success. Other early efforts of the friars in Mexico included Peter of Ghent's school for Aztec boys and Vasco de Quiroga's small communalistic Indian communities based on the *Utopia* of Sir Thomas More. Neither had much effect. Even less was accomplished in Peru in early decades to protect and instruct the Indians. In Mexico, at least, large numbers of Indians quickly developed strong attachment to the friars, in contrast to their reactions to *encomenderos* and civil officials. They made voluntary contributions of labor and materials to church building and to the sense of identification with new parishes or individual clerics. The attachment declined severely within a few years, but it already

had made a contribution to the establishment of the new society.

Indian suffering did not come about primarily as a result of a decision by the Spanish crown, which wished to act justly but not at the expense of prudent government. The nature of European culture made the cruelties of the conquest inevitable, especially under the difficult conditions of communication and control between Spain and America. European culture was no more cruel than that of the Indians, among whom pity for the weak was little evident. Christian conscience among the Spaniards produced at least a considerable effort to deal decently with the Indians. Certainly there was virtue in the final decision that the Indians were people to be brought somehow to Christ and civilization. That conclusion was better than slavery, as the history of the black African in Hispanic and Anglo-America testified.

In summary, the crown: (*a*) was consistent in its position that the Indians were free; (*b*) permitted slavery when the Indians "deserved" it and insisted on a share of the profits; and (*c*) early permitted collection of tribute from the Indians in the form of labor and commodities while vacillating as to the conditions necessary for regulation of these processes. If the legality of conquest itself is accepted—and human history is full of acceptance in many forms—the crown must be conceded a considerable measure of responsibility and conscience in pursuit of its functions in the realms of high state policy, religious obligation, and practical governance. Hispanic treatment of Indians, in the colonial period and thereafter, was at least as decent and responsible as that of the British and their successors in the United States.

c. Controlling the Conquerors

There was abundant reason for the crown's desire to limit encomienda as a means of controlling the conquerors. The latter viewed their actions as having the sanction of cross and crown, and of the moral, cultural, and military superiority of Europeans. They asserted that their valor and sufferings, together with their great gifts of new subjects and resources to Spain and Rome, entitled them to honor, place, and riches. Some of them did, in fact, receive considerable rewards; others remained poor and unsung, perpetually pestering the crown for aid. In addition, the crown's desire for greater control of the men of the Indies was stimulated by the conquerors' habit of bickering about orders from Spain or simply disregarding them.

The evidence surely required that prudent monarchs act on the supposition that a threat to royal rule existed. They did not have available our hindsight, which suggests that they could count on the fundamental allegiance of most of the men of the Indies. Only a few of the conquerors were obstreperous to the point of rebellion. There always would be Spaniards willing to support the crown's cause, either out of loyalty and conviction or desire to be on the winning side. The union of the church with the state in opposing dissidence made schism all the more unattractive. The resources of the crown made it safe against open rebellion so long as the bulk of the Spaniards in America did not unite at one time against the mother country. Such unity did not come about in the conquest period.

The desire of the crown to diminish the importance of the conquerors did not denote "ingratitude." The conquerors had been given or had taken too much in the beginning for a sound system of control from Spain. Grants made when conditions were unknown had to be adjusted in the light of reality. The crown understandably feared the growth of a group capable of contesting its power. In addition, the conquerors often were ignorant, shortsighted, and parochial, and they appeared to despise calm discussion and compromise. In the government and bureaucracy in Spain, on the other hand, were many polished, learned, and sophisticated men, with a habit of decision making that was patient and cautious. To the personnel of this apparatus, the conquerors were tolerable as the rough tools of conquest but not as instruments of permanent governance.

The crown preferred to send from Spain offi-

cials who, it was confident, thought first of its needs and only secondarily of their own interest. This attitude has been noted in the cases of Columbus and Balboa, and will be remarked later in those of Cortés and Pizarro. Also noted was the early institutionalization of authority in Spain by creation of the *Casa de Contratación* at Sevilla (1503) and in America by erection of an *audiencia* (high court) in Santo Domingo in 1511.

The conquest of Mexico magnified the stakes and the responsibilities and the crown's perception of the desirability of tightening its hold on the Indies. In Spain, the Council of the Indies was created in 1524. An *audiencia* was created for Mexico in 1528, although the first viceroy did not arrive there until 1535. In addition, an increasing number of ecclesiastical personnel and institutions tied Spaniards to their God-given king.

Important as were these decisions, even more critical was the fact that most Spaniards in America were inclined to accept the general rule of state and church, however they caviled at details. This loyalty and perception of community and of parallel interest, more than anything, guaranteed the system throughout the colonial centuries. Important also in retaining allegiance and in bolstering loyalty was the fact that officials early decided to use discretion in accommodating European fiat to Spanish opinion in America, as has been noted in connection with Indian policy.

New Spain

Hernan Cortés ruled Mexico for only a few years. King Charles bolstered (1522) the shaky legal foundations of his early actions when he recognized Cortés as governor and captain-general. At the same time the king began to circumscribe Cortés' sphere of activity by sending justices and treasury officials. Cortés, immensely active, sent expeditions to conquer Indians, founded towns, manufactured gunpowder and guns, built ships on the Pacific, promoted European crops and animal husbandry. He had to accept the demands of his men for encomiendas although he tried by ordinance (1524) to put the institution on a reasonable basis. He directed bachelors to wed and told married men to bring their wives from Spain. He supported the work of the friars. When a group of twelve arrived in 1524, walking barefoot the two hundred miles from the coast to Mexico City, Cortés met them with public veneration, kissing their grimy robes.

Cortés was in his thirties when he began this complex work of construction—an intelligent, energetic, and attractive man. Although he showed considerable aptitude for government, scholars argue about both this ability and the value of his activity as a builder. In any event, his opportunities were somewhat restricted. Not only was this the most turbulent part of the postconquest period, but Cortés' authority was by no means accepted automatically. It was compromised by his personal business activities, which made it difficult for him to pose as a disinterested public servant. The great disparity between his holdings and those of the other conquerors was a source of dispute and complaint. Furthermore, his former lowly estate was remembered; some Spaniards did not think of him in terms of a person deserving the greatest respect and obedience. Then his disastrous expedition against Olid in Honduras (1524–1526) left central Mexico without a firm executive authority. While Cortés pursued remote and partly personal interests, conditions in the heart of New Spain deteriorated, as officials quarreled among themselves, scrabbled for advantage, and persecuted Cortés' partisans.

The friars, so firmly presented to the Indians by the renowned Malinche (as they called Cortés) as beings to be loved and obeyed, forwarded consolidation. Few in number in the early years, the friars labored valiantly with the multitude of disorganized and bewildered Indians. Their preaching increasingly included a smattering of Indian tongues, and they fleshed this out with sign language and pantomimes. However little the Indians understood Christian

doctrine, they could identify some Christian ideas or practices with their own, which had included incense, baptismal rites, confession, emphasis on chastity for girls, monogamy, genuflection before holy objects, and punishment for adultery. The friars found it useful to organize Indians into brotherhoods (*cofradías*) to attend to the Christian celebrations, which proved popular with the Indians for both religious and social reasons. The friars persuaded Indians that some Europeans were interested in their welfare, thus performing a role in pacification and adjustment.

News of the sorry state of New Spain poured across the sea, much of it ascribing evils to Cortés. The king ordered a probe of Cortés' use of his powers, and the investigator arrived in Mexico soon after Cortés' return from Honduras. The subsequent tangle of charges and countercharges made Cortés glad to leave Mexico for Spain in 1529, hopeful of a solution to his problems by the crown. He arrived at court with a retinue of Indians, exotic flora and fauna and handicrafts, and some of the always pleasing treasure of America. The king received him cordially; named him Marqués del Valle de Oaxaca, with many Indians in encomienda; and confirmed him as captain-general (but not as governor), empowered to explore further in America.

In the meantime, just before Cortés left for Spain, the crown had established the *audiencia* for Mexico. As long as this court lasted (1528–1529), its judges, headed by Nuño de Guzmán, were a disgrace. They committed arbitrary and brutal acts out of avarice and malice. Nuño de Guzmán was an educated man of good family, who in America became a barbarian when faced with freedom from restrictions and with great opportunities for theft, murder, slaving, and arbitrary command. Guzmán had been governor of Pánuco in eastern Mexico, whence he shipped Indian slaves to the Caribbean. The many complaints against the judges led to their being replaced in 1530. For the next five years the new judges were fairly successful in exercising control over the central part of New Spain. They punished some of the crimes of the first magistrates. Their reach was restricted, however. Many areas remained turbulent and in violation of the letter and spirit of the law. Nuño de Guzmán and his followers had marched far to the northwest, where they spent the next seven years ravaging the area, selling Indians into slavery, granting encomiendas of Indians, and founding Spanish towns. Guzmán was a typical conquistador in his interests, being remarkable only for his position and opportunities.

Cortés returned to New Spain in 1530. He found that he had little authority. The new *audiencia* judges would not allow him to enter Mexico City, lest his presence create disturbances. They feared not only the friction between supporters of Cortés and other groups of Spaniards, but also the respect Cortés received from the Indians. Cortés continued his interest in Pacific exploration, built a palace at Cuernavaca in his marquesado, and developed his holdings. But he still was plagued with complaints against his property and rights, teased by the litigation that was to be so prominent a phenomenon of the colonial centuries in America.

The arrival of the first viceroy in 1535 further indicated that the crown would not give Cortés a high post in the Indies. In 1540 he returned to Spain, this time to be received coldly at court. He was eager to play an important role in Europe, but was not used. Cortés never returned to America, dying in Spain in 1547. The greatest repudiation of his career still lay far in the future. In recent times he has been rejected by the European-Indian culture of Mexico that was conceived in the blood and social disorientation of his years in the Indies. Not a statue of Cortés exists today in Mexico, but Cuauhtémoc, whom he defeated and executed, is lauded as a great representative of the Mexican nation.

Antonio de Mendoza served as viceroy in New Spain from 1535 to 1550. He quickly demonstrated the soundness of the decision that consolidation of rule in America could be powerfully promoted by this immensely prestigious office. Mendoza was a man accustomed to command, a member of a great Spanish family, much experienced in the service of the crown. He came as the direct voice of the king. In addition to his great executive powers, he was president of the *audiencia*, vice-patron of the church, and commander of the armed forces. Generous pay and perquisites, a style of life that signified the lesser positions of others, and ceremonies, honors, and precedence that constantly reinforced the impression of his power—all emphasized his authority and prestige.

Mendoza was a man of energy and ability. He helped in many ways to build the new society and consolidate the Spanish hold on Mexico. He promoted the economic and intellectual life of the land and fostered the church, but his greatest achievement was precisely in ensuring an adequate acceptance of Spanish rule. He was the authority who declined to implement the New Laws in New Spain, specifically because disturbances, even rebellions, might damage the fundamental goal of control and consolidation. In his time, also, the great silver strikes began. The problems of their exploitation, defense, and control created additional reasons both for governmental firmness, which Mendoza was well able to supply, and for colonial perception of the value of effective government.

Peru

The conquerors proved more difficult to bring to order in Peru than in Mexico because of a number of unfortunate local circumstances. Almagro the Elder returned from the arduous and unprofitable expedition (1535–1537) to his Chilean grant, burning with resentment that his partner Pizarro had received richer territories from the crown. He therefore seized Cuzco, claiming that it was on his side of the boundary between their grants. His men followed him, not only because he was a popular leader, but in the hope of profit. In Peru, as in New Spain and everywhere in the Indies, there was not enough Indian labor to supply Spanish demand. Almagro's men saw a simple answer in violent redistribution. There followed a civil war between Almagrists and Pizarrists. The former lost the final battle (1538), deep in the sierra of Peru, watched by Indians on the surrounding heights, who doubtless hoped that all the invaders would die in agony. The victors executed Almagro, scarcely salve for the wounds of the vanquished. Even more a guarantee of continued factionalism was Pizarro's decision to confiscate the holdings of the "Men of Chile," including those of the slain leader's mestizo son Diego.

The king, weary of the disorder in Peru, sent a lawyer, Vaca de Castro, to investigate affairs. While the lawyer was slowly proceeding toward Peru, the "Men of Chile" were stewing in poverty. Old Pizarro had little talent as a conciliator, nor was he much alarmed at the signs of dissidence among the followers of Diego Almagro the Younger. Pizarro paid for these errors when in June 1541 he was assassinated in his home in Lima by the Almagrists. Another civil war ensued in 1541–1542.

Vaca de Castro sailed from Panama south along the coast, then went inland to Popayán, where Belalcázar greeted him as the successor of the murdered Pizarro. The king's envoy then made his way through the Andes, while many groups in Peru declared their loyalty to the crown. The little armies met in September 1542 and the loyalists won a bloody victory. Almagro the Younger and some others were executed. Immediately, the possibility of further trouble appeared in the claim of Gonzalo Pizarro to succeed his dead brother as governor. Vaca de Castro managed to persuade him to retire to his holdings in Chuquisaca but accomplished little else because word soon arrived that a viceroy was coming to Peru.

Blasco Núñez Vela, the first viceroy of Peru, quickly and disastrously demonstrated the danger of confiding the great power of that office to a man of limited vision. Núñez was the archetype of the professional soldier out of his element, dictatorial where at least temporary compromise was needed. He could not understand that his chief goal must be consolidation of Spanish rule; instead, he obstinately tried to carry out the letter of the New Laws he had been sent to enforce. Nor was he inclined to listen to the prudent counsel of the judges sent with him to form an *audiencia* at Lima. He moved through Panama early in 1544 declaring Indian slaves freed and went on to Peru where he did the same. The *encomenderos* protested, and the Indians began to act as though they were in fact liberated.

Núñez' habit of precipitate action and his lack of skill at compromise soon led to a conspiracy somewhat reluctantly led by Gonzalo Pizarro. It also led the *audiencia* to have Blasco Núñez Vela deposed, arrested, and sent to Spain. He was released, however, on shipboard en route to Panama, on the grounds that the *audiencia* had exceeded its authority. Such conflicts over jurisdiction were to be common in the colonial era, as were the dilemmas and opportunities they presented to Spaniards in general on this far rim of the crown's domain.

All was now in motion for yet another civil war in Peru. Blasco Núñez Vela gathered forces in the interior of Peru until forced north by Gonzalo Pizarro. The latter came the long way from high Charcas to coastal Lima, where in October 1544 he intimidated the *audiencia* by hanging some "deserters" from his cause. The judges accepted him as governor until the king would determine what further notice to take of unhappy Peru. Núñez and Pizarro were, naturally, looting the Indian countryside during their movements and proceeding with the aid of swarms of native bearers.

Gonzalo Pizarro sent a fleet to Panama, captured the ships there, hanged some of the officers, and took control of the isthmus. He also drove Blasco Núñez far north through the mountain chain, through Quito to Popayán, where Governor Belalcázar loyally supported the king's man. In June 1546 Núñez was killed in a battle with the Pizarro forces near Quito. Gonzalo Pizarro pulled back from this victory nearly a thousand miles to Lima. From there he sent a lieutenant to quell dissent in Charcas, hundreds of miles into some of the most formidable mountain terrain in the world. From Charcas soon came news of the discovery in 1545 of silver at Potosí. A fevered rush began to what was to prove one of the most fabulous lodes ever discovered. It might have financed the independent kingdom that some of Gonzalo's men said was now his only recourse. Poor Gonzalo Pizarro, however, dreamed of reconciliation with the crown, while the king considered his treason unforgivable.

King Charles now retrieved the blunder of Blasco Núñez Vela by sending to Peru the priest Pedro de la Gasca, a splendid example of the talented and loyal personnel the monarchs of Spain had available (when they were wise enough to use them). Gasca was made president of the *audiencia*, with great authority to appoint or remove officials, to cancel many of the New Laws, and to redistribute Indians. Much of his power was deliberately kept secret (on his advice) and he carried blank orders from the king that he could fill in as he wished.

In Panama Gasca won over Pizarro's men with amnesties, even the men of the fleet that apparently blocked his way to Peru. In 1547 he was in Peru, still reminding Spaniards of the penalties for treason, but offering amnesty and spreading the word of King Charles's retreat from the New Laws. The captains and their men began declaring for Gasca and the king. By early 1549 Gasca had an army of nearly two thousand, by far the largest yet seen in Peru. When it finally faced Gonzalo Pizarro near Cuzco, the latter's men simply walked over to the representative of the crown, and the rebellion was over. Gonzalo and some others were promptly executed.

Gasca's performance was masterly, but it clearly was made possible by the reluctance of Spaniards to be branded as downright rebels. Gasca spent a few months distributing the encomiendas that were confiscated from rebels, a task that could not possibly please all Spaniards in Peru. At the end of 1549 Gasca handed his authority over to the *audiencia* and departed for Spain. Soon thereafter (1551) Antonio Mendoza came from Mexico to be viceroy of Peru. The conquest could now be said to have been consolidated in the sense of general acceptance of peninsular authority. Mendoza soon died, and the *audiencia* was the supreme authority in Peru in 1552–1556. Although it faced the Girón Rebellion (1553–1554) over the perennial encomienda problem, by conciliation it isolated Girón, then had him executed.

The civil wars of the conquerors in Peru delayed regularization of the new Indian society. For all the horrors of the process in central Mexico, it was achieved more rapidly and with less suffering than in Peru. The movements of armed bands of Spaniards in Peru brought with them seizure of supplies, wanton robbery, rape, and large-scale drafting of porters. The latter, in at least some notorious cases, were chained together by the neck. When a man fell, he was beheaded as the most convenient method of removing him from the line. No wonder that under the conditions of turmoil in Peru the early clergy did much less than in Mexico to Christianize and pacify the Indians.

The divisions of the Spaniards in Peru affected their relations with the Indian resistance group. Manco Capac's siege of Cuzco had largely spent itself when Almagro arrived there in 1537. Almagro then drove Manco into a mountain fastness, from which the movement could make only nuisance raids against Spanish positions. Almagro conferred the scarlet fringe of supreme Inca authority on a young noble, Paulu. This collaborator and some Indian fellows aided Almagro during the civil war. Manco lived on in his refuge until his death in 1545. He sent captured Spanish arms and armor to Vaca de Castro, preferring him to the hated conquerors. Manco's successor soon succumbed to Spanish blandishments, went to Cuzco, and in 1559 abdicated in favor of the king of Spain. Life in a wilderness redoubt might appeal to honor, but it was uncomfortable. The Spaniards preferred this outcome, if the Indians accepted it. But claimants to the scarlet fringe remained in the remote refuge until the Spaniards in 1571 captured and executed the last Inca, Tupac Amaru. The end to a nagging claim was gratifying, but it was not a major factor in compelling Indian obedience to the new order.

Indians in vast peripheral areas bore arms against the Spaniards throughout the colonial centuries, but in the heart of the system, among the concentrated populations of Middle America and the Inca lands, a certain minimum of obedi-ence came with the conquest, and its regularization only awaited the consolidation of crown control over the conquerors. By the middle years of the sixteenth century, that had been achieved. A clearer road now apparently lay ahead for the great tasks of Christianization and exploitation. No one could then guess how complex, how puzzling, how almost infinitely aggravating and almost unmanageable, would be the process of trying to understand and impose some control upon the emerging new society.

PART TWO

Government and Defense in Spanish America

In both government and international relations the Spaniards displayed much persistence and endurance, qualities often more useful than intermittent brilliance. Such qualities were needed, because Spanish dominions and interests were under nearly constant attack during most of the colonial era by the British, French, and Dutch. Spain was successful in preserving most of the territory it strongly wished to keep but did less well in protecting communications, trade, or populated places on the coast, especially in the Caribbean. Spain's army and navy provided much of the defense, either directly in America or indirectly by tying down enemy forces in Europe. The entrenched position of the colonial society, which posed a formidable barrier to penetration of the interior, also provided defense. That barrier was founded on strengths built into the colonial society, aided by distance and terrain. The government and social system were hierarchical and well suited to the aims and traditions of the predominantly Spanish ruling minority and to the cultural history of most of the lower class, largely of Indian and black African heritage. Class and caste provided a privileged minority devoted to defense of territory—but not of Spanish monopoly trade—against foreign foes and lower-class rebellion. These powerful motivations preserved upper-class unity even when the creoles (roughly, whites born in America) greatly outnumbered the European-born and resented the pretensions of the latter. Status set a man's place in (or absence from) government, and it helped shape government forms and actions, including those relating to the lower class. Although the masses often were turbulent, they could not successfully rebel against the armed solidarity of the elite. In addition, more often than not the lower class was apathetic, alienated, and subdued by lack of opportunity and by the violence, actual and threatened, that sustained the class system. The huge lower-class labor force produced the Mexican and Peruvian silver that built warships and forts. It produced the logistic support for the upper class that would have made the interior of Hispanic America nearly unconquerable at bearable cost if the French and British ever had reached the interior.[1] Much fuss was made then, and has been made since, about the contradictions and inefficiencies of the governing system. They existed but were compensated for by accepted detours around the rigidities of the formal structure. The system directed and defended a large and complicated social and economic order with considerable success for three hundred years.

---

[1] See Chapters 14 and 15 on similar strengths in Portuguese America.

6 The Government of Colonial Spanish America

Damning the government comes naturally to citizens enraged by its inanities and to armchair critics—including historians—who judge that they could do better. Colonial Spanish Americans certainly complained wrathfully about government. But that government was effective by several measures. It aided the generally successful defense of the realms for three centuries. It guided and guarded a large system of economic production and distribution and collected sizable revenues. It was strong enough to function in years of weak kings and poor wartime communications. It kept the loyalty of its active citizens, for all their grousing. It was not a fragile system.[1]

It endured, furthermore, in the face of great problems. First, few governments have had to grapple with so heterogeneous a society: minorities of Europeans and of black slaves, an initially huge majority of Indians, and an ever increasing population of mixed blood. Second, Spain insisted on many measures to aid the Indians, which added cost and complexity to the system of government. Third, problems of information for decision making were formidable. Distances made communications slow. Variations in interest and points of view created conflicts or am-

biguities in reports, petitions, and complaints. The fact that much that happened in America was alien to European experience distorted the reactions of officials. Fourth, there was slippage between the general wishes of a busy monarch in Spain and the interests and beliefs of the bureaucracy in the Indies. Finally, Spaniards had the usual human desire to believe what was convenient.

The bases of the system were laid in a few decades of trial and decision, so that by the later 1520s a panoply of civil institutions provided for centralized authority, although it was not yet secured. The church organization paralleled and supplemented, and to some extent interpenetrated, the civil government. In addition, there was the de facto power of *encomenderos* over Indians. Although the encomienda was nearly eradicated after a few decades, its de facto governing power in the countryside was replaced by another form of private government on haciendas. There also was de facto governing power over black slaves. Finally, Spain provided self-government of a sort for the Indian village. This experiment evolved from an ideal of insulation from the Spanish society, a noble conception, even though it could not be strictly enforced. Complex relationships, then, were characteristic of government for Spanish America.

---

[1] See Chapter 3, Section a, Chapter 5, Section b, and Chapter 7, Section a, on Spanish justification of the conquest and subsequent rule in America.

a. Institutions of Government in Spain

Royal Power

Loyalty to the crown, however, was becoming less complex. The ancient belief that sound criticism of the king was not disloyal had been diluted, and group (noble, bourgeois) interpretations of loyalty were less offered or tolerated. The increased importance of royal authority thus was supported by a more unthinking loyalty to the crown. Other agencies of government—parliamentary, municipal, corporative—had become relatively unimportant. In view of this concentration of authority and respect, it was unfortunate that in 40 percent of the years 1492–1815 the kings of Spain were low-grade mediocre or quite incompetent. On the one hand, a good king did not guarantee a golden age; but on the other, a bad one was a guarantee of misery. Fortunately for Spain's international relations, monarchies of other nations also turned up some feeble-minded, vicious, or reckless princes.

Charles I (1516–1556), grandson of Ferdinand and Isabella, inherited the realms of Castile and Aragon, including Castile's American lands. Charles and his son Philip II (1556–1598) carried on the policies of Ferdinand and Isabella in consolidating royal authority against the greater nobility and the bourgeoisie. The powers of the parliaments (*cortes*) of the Iberian kingdoms were further curtailed, almost to extinction. The great *comunero* revolt of 1520–1521, originally both bourgeois and aristocratic, brought reduction of the power of both elements. New or strengthened institutions, such as the royal council and the crown's *corregidores* in towns, consolidated central authority.

Ferdinand and Isabella and their successors fostered centralization and uniformity in administration by favoring for many offices university-trained lawyers (*letrados*), often from families of the lesser nobility or the bourgeoisie. They owed their position and allegiance to the crown, and their legal training in Roman law made them partisans of centralized monarchic authority. Members of the higher nobility were, however, continuously used for many important civilian and military posts.[2] The church accepted the domination of the throne, the more easily in that Charles and Philip were the chief pillars of Roman Catholic resistance to the Protestant Reformation that began in 1517.

The centralizing process was impeded in Spain by regional institutions and culture: Catalan, Basque, and others. Centralization was hindered also by the privileged corporations inherited from the Middle Ages, as in all Europe—nobility, church, craft guilds, and others. Both regionalism and medieval institutions also hampered standardization of culture and outlook on domestic and international policy, and more effective arrangement of social and economic institutions and habits. Those things proceeded more rapidly in the sixteenth to eighteenth centuries among the rivals of Spain—the British, French, and Dutch. The Spanish governing system was not very responsive to changing conditions in the western world, because of the lack of bourgeois access to decision making in an effective legisla-

---

[2] See Chapter 8, Section b, for more comments on the complex role of the class system in Spanish and Spanish American society, especially in formal and informal modes of governance.

The map shows the approximate allocation of territory during most of the colonial era. Bear in mind that (1) most of the boundaries between Portuguese and Spanish territory in South America not only were indefinite but also ran through land that was lightly populated and not much valued. Consequently there was little interest in the exact location of boundaries. The same was true of North American land west of the Mississippi River. (2) Although for nearly two centuries Spanish America was divided between the viceroyalties of New Spain and Peru, areas distant from the viceregal capitals had considerable administrative independence—even, at times, explicit freedom of action.

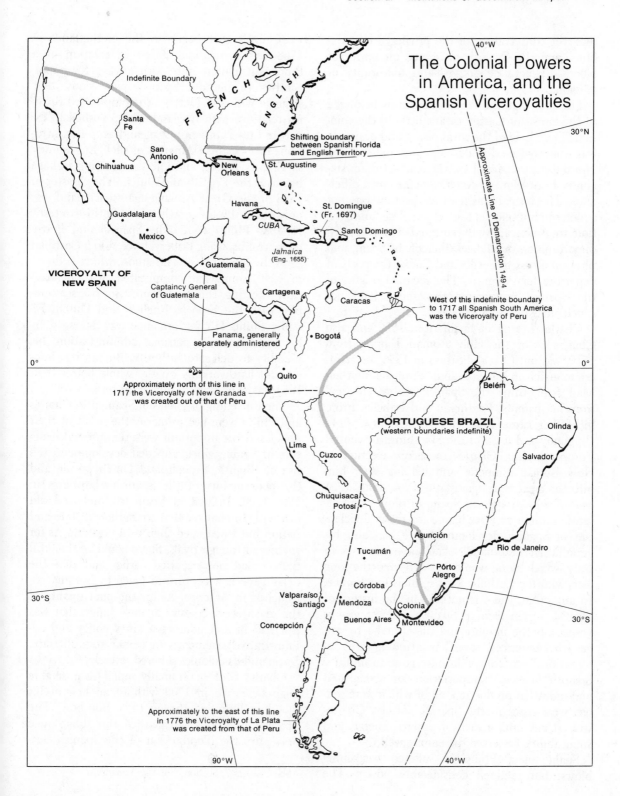

The Colonial Powers in America, and the Spanish Viceroyalties

Indefinite Boundary

FRENCH

ENGLISH

40°W

30°N

Approximate Line of Demarcation 1494

Santa Fe

San Antonio

Chihuahua

New Orleans

St. Augustine

Shifting boundary between Spanish Florida and English Territory

Havana

St. Domingue (Fr. 1697)

CUBA

Santo Domingo

Guadalajara

Mexico

Jamaica (Eng. 1655)

VICEROYALTY OF NEW SPAIN

Guatemala

Captaincy General of Guatemala

Cartagena

Caracas

Panama, generally separately administered

Bogotá

West of this indefinite boundary to 1717 all Spanish South America was the Viceroyalty of Peru

Quito

Belém

0°   0°

Approximately north of this line in 1717 the Viceroyalty of New Granada was created out of that of Peru

PORTUGUESE BRAZIL (western boundaries indefinite)

Olinda

Lima

Cuzco

Salvador

Chuquisaca

Potosí

Asunción

Rio de Janeiro

Tucumán

Pôrto Alegre

Córdoba

Valparaíso

Santiago

Mendoza

Colonia

30°S

Concepción

Buenos Aires

Montevideo

30°S

Approximately to the east of this line in 1776 the Viceroyalty of La Plata was created from that of Peru

90°W   40°W

ture, the conservatism of the privileged corporations, and the Spanish insistence on purity of blood—*limpieza de sangre*—and uniformity of religion.

The fact that the American realms belonged to the crown of Castile meant little to the colonies. The whole of the royal power and resources was what mattered in development and defense. Nor did the transfer of Castilian rather than Aragonese institutions to America make much difference. The formal Castilian connection was not a determining element in channeling immigration to America; what mattered was perceived opportunities, or the lack thereof, in Spain, and physical access to Sevilla and Cádiz, the ports of departure for America. The regional origins of the Spanish immigrants to America did not much affect developments.

Charles I, king of Spain from 1516 and also Charles V of the Holy Roman Empire from 1519, was until his abdication in 1556 the greatest monarch in Christendom. From his mother, Mad Joan, came the Spanish realms she had from her parents, Ferdinand and Isabella. From his father came the rich Low Countries and Burgundy and a tie to the Hapsburgs of central Europe, leading Charles to secure election as Holy Roman Emperor and helping steer him into the great wars against the Protestants. The cost of that struggle to Spain, in money and attention, often receives blame for many deficiencies of Spanish development. He had also his grandfather Ferdinand's Aragonese interests in Italy, which alone would have ensured the long wars with the Catholic King Francis I of France. In any event, there is nothing in the history of Spanish regionalism or Spanish interest groups (especially the nobility and the church) to suggest that resources "saved" by avoiding some international warfare would have gone to improve Spanish finance, transportation, or agricultural and industrial production, all of which were serious weaknesses in the Spanish society. Charles was, at any rate, a man of probity, energy, and some ability; he served the empire well.

Spain under Philip II suffered weakening blows, but retained considerable power. The great revolt that began in the Netherlands in 1568 was costly, and it led to creation of a Protestant Dutch state with an eye for opportunities to plunder Spanish possessions. The struggle with the Dutch also complicated Spanish relations with England. Philip wished to extirpate Protestantism in England, stop the intrusions into Spanish America of such Englishmen as Francis Drake, and cut the growing linkage between the English and Dutch. The disaster in 1588 of the Great Armada against England was only one of Philip's costly efforts in this contest.[3] In 1580 Philip united the Spanish and Portuguese realms, using bribery, force, and a Castilian claim by inheritance. The union, which endured to 1640, somewhat complicated, without basically affecting, the great contest for overseas empire with the French, English, and Dutch. Finally, Philip II's performance was damaged by his obsession with personal administration, his inability to delegate authority. But he was honest and hardworking, on the whole better than the average of kings in human history.

The worsening problems of Spain after Charles and Philip were not primarily the result of their policies. More important were the internal structure of Spain, which impeded development; the rise of English, French, and Dutch power; and the poor quality of the Spanish Hapsburgs in 1598–1700. Influential Spaniards preferred old privileges to changes that strengthened state and nation but threatened their own position. As for the rise of foreign rivals, Spain could be thankful that it had not occurred earlier and that the delay gave it a century of grace to become entrenched in America. As for the poor quality of the seventeenth-century Spanish kings, that was just bad luck. Under such kings policy and administrative weaknesses are certain to proliferate. Spain and its colonies suffered severely.

Charles II of Spain finally ended his miserable reign by death in 1700 without an heir of his blood, willing his throne to a Bourbon. The Spanish Bourbons safeguarded this inheritance only after the bloody War of the Spanish Suc-

---

[3] See Chapter 7, Section c, on the Armada.

cession (1701–1714), fought by England, Holland, and Austria to try to prevent such a concentration of dynastic power in Bourbon Spain and France. The three Spanish Bourbons of 1700–1788 were more talented than the seventeenth-century Hapsburgs, and they imported to the peninsula French institutions and ideas that somewhat improved Spanish performance. Charles III (1759–1788) made an especially great effort to modernize Spain and the imperial administration.[4] The last Bourbons before Spain lost America were Charles IV (1788–1808) and Ferdinand VII (1814–1833). Their reigns were divided by a regime imposed by Napoleon Bonaparte. Even the horrors of that French invasion and rule were hardly more damaging than the passive ineptitude of Charles IV and the active incompetence and malignancy of his son Ferdinand.

Casa and Council: Great Agencies of the Crown

The crown's ideals of monopoly, privilege, and bureaucratic regulation were illustrated by creation in 1503 of the *Casa de Contratación* (House of Trade). Its purpose was to foster and police commerce and navigation. For about two centuries it was at Sevilla, the commercial and financial center of Castile. Its merchants and moneylenders had great influence with the crown. Its economic and political influence compensated for the fact that although it was an Atlantic port, it was well up the Guadalquivir River in southwestern Spain. The *Casa* was charged with the impossible task of establishing a Spanish monopoly of trade with the America realms. In pursuit of that aim, it agreed to creation of the Sevilla *consulado* (merchants' guild), whose members received the exclusive privilege of trading with the Indies. The *consulado* had extensive economic and judicial duties in connection with the overseas traffic. The merchant houses thus

were allied with the government in policing the system in the only way that proved possible—by an agreed-upon method of at once abandoning the closed trading ideal and letting in foreigners, while retaining the monopoly of Sevilla. Monopoly operated in other aspects of the economic life in Spain, but the American monopoly, supervised—even in evasion, by letting in foreigners —by the *Casa*, was the greatest.

The *Casa*'s duties grew with the American colonies. It licensed and regulated shipping and emigration. It provided research, records, and training in geography, navigation, and pilotage. It collected some taxes and trade duties, handling royal revenues shipped from America, which gave it an important treasury function. It assisted with overseas communications, serving some of the functions of a postal service. The *Casa* also had judicial authority over problems arising from trade and navigation. It supervised the convoy (*flota*) system for commerce with America that was important from the mid-sixteenth to the mid-eighteenth centuries. Early in the eighteenth century the *Casa* lost some of its powers to a new Ministry of Marine and the Indies, and the *Casa* was moved (1717) to the coastal city of Cádiz, partly because navigation on the Guadalquivir was dangerous and costly. It gradually lost power thereafter, especially as the restricted port system was abandoned in stages after 1763. The *Casa* was abolished in 1790.

The Council of the Indies (*Real y Supremo Consejo de las Indias*) was created in 1524. It did for American affairs what the Council of Castile did for that kingdom: governed in the king's name, subject to royal orders and confirmation. The crown dictated some appointments and made other decisions as the result of a multitude of pressures and petitions. But the king could not be privy to more than a small fraction of the activities of the Council of the Indies. The council therefore made most decisions itself in light of its understanding of royal policy, national needs, and pressures brought upon the councilors and their staff.

The council developed and dispatched masses of legislation for America. Reading it today, one

---

[4] For eighteenth-century changes see Section c of this chapter; also Chapter 11, Section d, and Chapter 17, Section b.

is impressed by the quantity and by the knowledge shown of conditions in America; alas, one also is impressed with the efforts to legislate into existence conditions that previous legislation had failed to secure. The council also had great powers in the appointment of civil and ecclesiastical officials, and in confirming appointments of minor officials made by the upper levels of bureaucracy in America. The council was the final appeal court for civil cases from America. It controlled the process of review (*residencia*) of the administrations of retiring officials in America. It had a hand in policy and administration of defense and in economic affairs, including commerce and mining. It corresponded not only with officials but with private individuals and was at the heart of the investigative net so typical of the system.

The council sent inspectors (*visitadores*) to probe difficulties and make recommendations. The *visita* might have a mandate to investigate a small area or even a single official, but great general *visitas* had wide-ranging jurisdiction. The principle of the *visita* was first applied in 1499 when a *juez pesquisidor* (judge inspector) was named in Spain to investigate the Roldán rebellion in Santo Domingo and the alleged maladministration of Columbus. The first *visitador-general*, a member of the Council of the Indies, was sent to New Spain in the 1540s to enforce the New Laws. The visitors-general clashed with the viceroys, who were not in all respects responsible to the visitors-general. Possibly the institution did something to make administrators cautious about dishonesty and indolence, but much contemporary comment suggests that they often were only moderately effective. The system was too big to yield easily to such a method.

The Council of the Indies over the years became a considerable bureaucracy. Many men of capacity, training, and experience of Spanish and American affairs either sat on the council or served it in subordinate capacities. It frequently bogged down in its own procedures and in the paperwork that was characteristic of the Spanish bureaucratic system. The council progressively

lost power after 1714 with the development of the ministry system of the Bourbons, which began to replace the conciliar Hapsburg institutions. By the 1760s the Minister of the Indies had taken over the Council of the Indies' role in policy making, reducing the council to an advisory function. It revived somewhat in 1773 with a decision to make it equal to the Council of Castile and to give the Council of the Indies more men with American experience. When in 1790 the Ministry of the Indies was abolished and American affairs divided among five ministers with functional areas of administration for the empire, the Council of the Indies was the only governmental body dealing exclusively with America.

Spanish Policy for America

Spanish royal policy, based on Castilian crown ownership of America and a supposition of European superiority, assumed that the colonies existed for the benefit of Spain. It was one reason for concentrating appointive and other authority in Spain and for encouraging direct communication by residents and officials in the Indies with the crown, sometimes coming close to spying. Spanish officials in America were restricted in business and property holding and in marrying into creole families. All these measures were meant to ensure an administration with European orientation and loyalty to the crown.

That aim, together with a desire to reward deserving or importunate Spaniards, also underlay the policy of giving most high offices—civil and ecclesiastical—in the Indies to peninsular Spaniards. But that practice was not law. By law, Spaniards (meaning people thought to be sufficiently white and Europeanized) were not divided into those born in Spain (those of the Iberian Peninsula, hence *peninsulares*) and *criollos* (creoles, born in America), but the terms and their equivalents were used in a number of contexts. Whether the division between the two groups that often were lumped as *españoles* was serious enough to make useful a discussion of two classes depends on the point of view.[5] Both groups considered themselves elevated above the non-Spanish, meaning colored, population, on racial and cultural bases. Both deprecated the encroaching ways of partly Europeanized mestizos and mulattoes. Peninsulars and creoles of equal economic resources had similar life-styles. They did mingle socially, and they intermarried. From lower in the social system, they were indistinguishable. But until 1813 there were only 4 creole viceroys; 14 creoles among the 602 captains-general, governors, and presidents; and 105 among the 706 bishops and archbishops. Nearly all the intendants of the late colonial era were peninsulars. The figures on the overall exclusion of creoles from high office are so stark as to admit of little argument, even though creole appointments to some offices (for example, *audiencias*) increased with time.[6]

Creole animosity against peninsulars also had other bases. Peninsulars controlled the most lucrative commercial activity. Poor Spaniards emigrated to the Indies, worked hard, often aided by other peninsulars, became well-off, and married creole women. Both these types of peninsular success rankled with creole men. Peninsulars sometimes claimed superiority on the basis of their pure Caucasian (they said Spanish) heritage. It was known that some creole families had Indian or Negro ancestry.[7] Peninsulars sometimes said that creoles were indolent, and exclusion from office certainly closed them off from one form of activity that they would have been happy to undertake. Peninsular Spaniards—and other Europeans—came (especially in the eighteenth century) to impute a general spiritual, physical, and intellectual degeneracy to American stock and residence. This attitude naturally embittered the creoles. They expressed their bitterness in terms of contempt for peninsulars: *gachupines* (spurred ones) or *chapetones* (tenderfeet, who did not understand or adapt well to America). It took the form of nasty disputes and brawls.

Although this tension was of some consequence, it did not seriously disrupt society. Creoles often aped and courted peninsular officials and their families. Bitterness did grow with time, as a matter of accumulation and as the creole group more and more outnumbered the peninsular. It played a role in late colonial dissatisfaction that merged into the wars for Independence. Even at that late date, however, creoles and peninsulars were united against the lower orders. For most of the colonial period, that sense of common cause was more important than the divisions between peninsulars and creoles.

The metropolitan bias in government also took the form of "mercantilism," a set of policies designed to keep the colonies economically tied to and profitable for the metropolis. That policy was expected to bolster both the economy and the military power of Spain. In its simplest form, it meant a closed trading system, with colonials forbidden any commerce except with Spain and Spanish merchants; and colonial concentration on raw-material production, which in turn meant that manufactures would be bought from the metropolis. In practice, economic policy for the colonies was complicated by many factors: (*a*) a narrow concern for crown revenues; (*b*) the policy of trying to channel traffic through the single port of Sevilla; (*c*) a failure to provide the Spanish manufactures to service the raw material–producing colonies; (*d*) the impossibility of preventing all competing manufacture in the Indies and willingness at times even to encourage it. There never was a completely closed Spanish economic system; it became more porous with time, and efforts to enforce the theory and law were expensive and ineffective.

A part of the general goal of monopolizing American resources was the extensive emphasis on America as a source of royal revenues. The crown was forever in need of more. That need made support and regulation of silver mining and of silver shipment matters of much concern, a

---

[5] See Chapter 8, Section b, for more comment on creoles and peninsulars in the class system.
[6] See Chapter 17, Section c, for comment on the issue in the late colonial era.
[7] "Negro" is Spanish for "black."

concern grounded in the prevailing belief that wealth consisted of hard money or bullion (rather than the later idea that it consists of production and the raw materials and social institutions that sustain it). Concern for royal revenues underlay the policy of permitting great independence to treasury officials.

Another area of policy can be called the dream of a well-ordered and disciplined society. It involved efforts to control all aspects of life, including bolstering the system of privilege in many ways. Class lines were a prop of the system. The privileges of the corporations were a part, including the juridical systems of ecclesiastics, merchants, and military officers. One aspect of this control was discrimination against creoles. Another part of the ideal was maintaining the elite population—including the creoles—as unassailably of Spanish and Roman Catholic stock. Spain devoted a considerable effort to that ideal, the Inquisition being only one of the agencies charged with the task. Another ideal was control of publication, reading, discussion, even of thought.

The policy was to cherish the Indians, maintain the church in its work with the Spanish population of America, and defend the realms with military force. All those things required heavy expenditure and floods of legislation. The crown never doubted the importance of any of those complex policies. Defense alone included provision for the army and militia, naval forces in Spain and America, fortifications, supply, transportation, and other functions.

There were other notable features of government. (*a*) Officials served limited terms, at the king's pleasure. Rotation and dependence thus were theoretical barriers to accumulation of power. But rotation may have accelerated corruption, an uncertain or short term of office suggesting a need for rapid profit. (*b*) Government institutions had a mixture of judicial, legislative, and executive functions, in the mode of the day. (*c*) There was much overlapping of jurisdiction, as between viceroy or captain-general and *audiencia,* and between church and civil govern-

ment, providing some check on the concentration of authority. The overlap also encouraged litigation and jurisdictional squabbles. The resultant delays in decision making encouraged the use of informal methods of solution—bribery, collusion, and violence. Jurisdictional quarrels, involving administrators or courts, were often acrimonious, sometimes bloody. (*d*) There was no legislative authority with elected representatives, comparable to the English parliament or the provincial assemblies of English America, to check executive or administrative action. (*e*) From the late sixteenth century through the rest of the colonial era there was increasing sale of public offices. (*f*) There was much discussion in Spain of changes in the governmental system and relatively little significant action. (*g*) Finally, the governmental system was notable for insistence upon documentary reporting and detailed accounting. Not for Spain the indifference—or permissiveness—that Britain later showed toward its American colonies. Spain considered that responsibility demanded detailed decisions on social order and continual supervision.

b. Government in America

Church and State

Union of church and state seemed natural to Spaniards. There was no popular interest in freedom of religion. Spaniards were loyal to Catholicism. The crown did not feel threatened by a state within a state, since it controlled the secular church from parish priest to archbishop, except in questions of religious doctrine and discipline. Crown control of the regulars—members of orders, called friars, who lived by rule—was less firm, since they came under the heads of their orders—Augustinian, Franciscan, Dominican, Jesuit, Mercederian. But the crown defined the sphere of action of the orders. The regulars, unlike the secular clergy, were not generally a part of the imperial administration. A shortage of secular clergy during the conquest, however, required the use of regulars for religious functions that in Spain would have been performed by the secular clergy. The early friars were not only missionaries but administered the sacraments. They were soon replaced in this role in the Spanish towns, although they retained monasteries there. Their jurisdiction then was confined to their missionary Indian areas, where they continued to play an important part in conversion and pacification and in the defense of frontier areas. The secular church constantly agitated for reduction of the missionary and other roles of the regulars. Clashes between seculars and regulars were incessant, and sometimes violent.

Royal power in church administration, called the patronage (*patronato real*),[8] included the right to appoint ecclesiastics, set the geographic boundaries of church jurisdictions, collect the tithe, and control dissemination of papal edicts. These formidable powers in effect let the crown mold civil and ecclesiastical government into a royal whole. The church saw not only that the faith stayed pure, but also that the faith was equated with loyalty to the state. The church preached acceptance of government actions. It controlled most schooling, kept vital statistics, provided social assistance (hospitals, orphanages), owned great properties and employed many people, lent money, conducted courts for certain types of cases and persons, decided questions of birth, marriage, and death that were important for many civil purposes, supplied ecclesiastics for civil positions, and served as a vast information network. Many of its functions duplicated or overlapped those of civil administration.

The first bishops in America were dependent on the archbishop of Sevilla, but after 1545 archbishoprics were set up in America. Inquisitorial powers in America were in the early decades in the hands of the bishops; then in the 1570s Tribunals of the Holy Office were created for Lima and Mexico City, and in 1610 a third at Cartagena. On the whole the church must be judged to have been a pacifying rather than a disturbing factor. Even when creoles complained of the distribution of church offices or church wealth or of ecclesiastical contentiousness, there was no desire to do away with the church. The elite never thought of a society without a strong church until a few people fell under the influence of the Enlightenment late in the colonial period.[9]

Viceroys and Captains-General

The most important position in America was that of viceroy, created in 1529 for New Spain (Mexico City), in 1542 for Peru (Lima). Until the eighteenth century, all of Spanish America theoretically was under the jurisdiction of one of them, although many areas were so distant from the viceregal seat that the viceroy's power was nominal. In 1717 a viceroyalty of New Granada was created, its seat at Bogotá, with jurisdiction over what are today Venezuela, Colombia, and Ecuador. It was dissolved in 1723, recreated in 1739, with Panama added to its jurisdiction. In 1776 a fourth viceroyalty, Río de la Plata, was created, with its seat at Buenos Aires, partly to tighten defense of that increasingly important area, threatened by the expansion of Portuguese Brazil. Captains-general functioned much like little viceroys, especially those in areas like Guatemala and Chile, which were remote from the viceregal capital. Although the first captaincy-general as a separate administrative area was not created until 1550, the office itself was granted earlier.

Viceroys and captains-general were appointed in Spain and had great prestige as direct representatives of the king. Nearly all were peninsular

---

[8] Given in papal decrees in 1493, 1501, and 1508, and clarified in later pronouncements. The papal bull of 1493 gave the Spanish crown title to the Indies, the obligation of converting the Indians, and the rights and privileges earlier popes had given Portuguese kings in overseas discoveries, including the right of presentation to ecclesiastical office.

[9] See Chapter 10, Section e, on the church and the economy; Chapters 12, Section c, and 17, Section a, on the church and the Enlightenment at the end of the colonial era.

Spaniards. They headed civil government, secular church, and the military system. The viceroy, with responsibility for all aspects of justice and life, also carried the title of governor, signifying duties in the revenue field; that of president, or head of the *audiencia* or high court; and that of vice-patron, with control of the *patronato*. Fiscal affairs were a prime concern of viceroys and captains-general in line with the crown's constant interest in revenue. They had legislative powers; though subject to approval from Spain, the legislation went into force upon proclamation in America. They had appointive powers to the civil and ecclesiastical administrations. They had to sustain the crown's interest in its Indian wards. In the early days, they made new allotments of vacant encomiendas. Their discretionary powers were so great that sometimes they decided that legislation from Spain was not suitable for America. Then they used the formula "obedezco pero no cumplo"—I obey but I do not carry out—expressive of the view that kings could properly issue only just and reasonable orders and that the duty of vassals was to protect them from error due to bad advice. Since most viceroys served only three to eight years, they had none too much time to become acquainted with their great realms but sufficient to learn the intractability of the problems.[10]

Audiencias

The *audiencia* judges (*oidores*) embodied both the crown's strong concern for the juridical system and its ideal of a prudent fragmentation of royal powers. The *audiencias* were chiefly courts in the early years in America, although legislative and administrative duties quickly grew out of need in the new lands. An *audiencia* was a court of first instance for some cases and the highest appellate court in the Indies. It had supervisory powers over lower courts. Personnel

varied with the importance of the *audiencia* jurisdiction and included a number of staff members in addition to, of course, the judges. The latter were trained in law, appointed from Spain, and mostly peninsulars. They often served rather long terms of office, so that *oidores* might provide more continuity of experience in an area than the viceroy or captain-general. Ten *audiencias* were established in the sixteenth century; twelve existed at the end of the colonial era.[11]

The *audiencias* provided counsel to viceroys and captains-general. This relationship often did not work smoothly. Sometimes the *audiencia* rallied opinion against the other officials. The *audiencia* might assume the powers of the viceroy or captain-general, either because the office fell vacant by death or illness or prolonged absence or because the *audiencia* decided that the official was not performing acceptably. These relationships naturally varied with the leadership talent of the viceroy or captain-general. The powers of *audiencias* also varied with their distance from the seat of a viceroy or captain-general. The *audiencias* at Mexico City and Lima were presided over by viceroys and felt the continual weight of viceregal power. Other *audiencias* were freer to pursue their own views. Occasionally, an *audiencia* president was the chief official of an administrative area for long periods, as in the *presidencia* of Quito. The president of the *audiencia* of Nueva Galicia was also governor during much of the colonial era. *Audiencias* also had influence through their power to appoint, or aid in appointment with the viceroy or captain-general, the investigators (*jueces pesquisidores*). The investigators conducted what amounted to local *visitas*, looking at the records of officials of the level of *corregidor* and lower. After such an in-

---

[10] See Chapter 5, Section c, on the powers and accomplishments of the first viceroy of New Spain.

[11] The earliest were Santo Domingo, 1511; Mexico, 1528; Panama, 1538; Lima, 1542; Nueva Galicia (in west central Mexico), 1548; Bogotá, 1549. At the end of the colonial era they were Nueva Galicia, Mexico, Guatemala, Santo Domingo, Caracas, Bogotá, Quito, Lima, Cuzco, Chuquisaca or Charcas, Santiago de Chile, Buenos Aires.

vestigation, the *audiencia* might suspend an official or take other action.

The crown placed great reliance in the *audiencias*. It encouraged them to act against viceroys and captains-general that they thought were mismanaging their offices. This freedom guarded against that concentration of authority that the crown so much feared. These important judges were subject to regulations designed to reinforce their attachment to royal interests. Efforts were made to isolate them from the community by requiring them to live together in *audiencia* quarters, forbidding them to engage in business, and discouraging social intercourse (including marriage) with the population. Enforcing such rules in a meaningful way, however, was impossible. The opportunities for profit available to *oidores* were irresistible. They did have social relations with creoles and sometimes married into creole families. On the whole, *oidores* were loyal and useful servants of the crown; some were perceptive analysts of the new society they were helping to mold and govern.

Some Other Officials

Audiencia districts were divided into the jurisdictions of *corregidores, alcaldes mayores,* and *gobernadores.* Their functions were identical, so we will refer to all as *corregidores.*[12] They sometimes were appointed by the viceroy, but the tendency was progressively to reserve that power to Spain. *Corregidores* early collected tribute from Indians that were under crown jurisdiction; then their authority quickly extended to encomienda Indians and became general for government in assigned districts. The *corregidor* was in intimate touch with the lower officials who actually executed the law, some of them Spaniards, some of them Indians. At the levels below the viceroys, captains-general, and *audiencias* corruption occurred on a broad basis. The *corregi-*

---

[12] See Chapter 5, Section b, on the introduction of *corregidores* to America.

dores were notoriously greedy. They milked their territories not only as administrators but as magistrates of courts. They also worked closely with town councils, another government organ much used for private profit.

Corregidores became especially malodorous for their use of the *repartimiento de bienes* (allotment of goods), a system of forced sales, chiefly to Indians. *Corregidores* borrowed money to buy their offices, then had to do enough business to pay off the debt, bribe witnesses and investigators, and make a profit. They did so in part by forcing Indians to buy goods (for which much of the officeholder's credit had gone), sometimes useless trinkets, and at inflated prices. In the process of trying to collect payment, *corregidores* often sold or hired out Indians who were delinquent in their payments, found ways to compel Indians to cultivate fields, and used their office to engage in trade in local products. *Corregidores* did this last both on their own account and as middlemen between producers and merchants. We even have evidence of *consulado* (merchant guild) members in such arrangements paying the sales tax obligations of provincial officials.

Special powers of government belonged to the privileged corporations: *consulado, gremio* (craft guild), organized miners, church, medical office (*protomedicato*), the military, universities, and others. There was a constable (*alguacil mayor*) to carry out the orders of *corregidores* and to police the towns. Rural banditry, including cattle rustling, resulted in the importation (1552) to Mexico from Spain of the institution of the *Santa Hermandad* (Holy Brotherhood), which apprehended wrongdoers and turned them over to its own court. The *residencia* was a hearing at the end of an official's term, inviting charges from the public. Officials had an additional motive for graft in the need for funds to purchase immunity or a good result from the *residencia.*

Escribanos were necessary to make the wheels go round. They were permanent staff members with many tasks, from routine record keeping and filing to the typical Spanish notarial function of certifying the authenticity of acts and instruments. *Escribanos* served *audiencias*, *cabildos*, viceroys, treasury agents, *consulados*, and others. *Escribanos* registered deeds or mineral rights, certified freight cargoes, received and recorded obligations at customs houses or looked after the property of deceased persons. *Escribanos* not only prepared the voluminous official documents, on the required stamped paper, and were the custodians of many records, but they prepared the agendas of meetings and inevitably guided the work of officials who were busy, new on the job, or lazy. *Escribanos* were paid fees, as was then the practice in Europe for such services. In addition, their functions gave them chances to profit from deals with private citizens. The position of *escribano* thus was coveted and commonly sold either for life or a term of years. Sometimes the offices were auctioned. There was much variation in practice and much opportunity for abuse, so that the tendency of the crown after the late sixteenth century to make such appointments or sales a royal monopoly was meant to improve the system. Other minor offices in addition to that of *escribano* were sold.

The Revenue System

Taxes were no more popular in Spanish America than elsewhere. Complaint and evasion were inevitable accompaniments of the revenue system. However, to calculate the importance of the revenue system is difficult. Disposable revenues rose gradually in the sixteenth century to peak about 1600, then declined and generally remained at a lower level until after the mid-eighteenth century. The decline was related to the great reduction of Indian population, problems in the production and shipment of silver, and to grievous military weaknesses and consequent losses to enemy action. The late colonial increase reflected population growth, higher silver production, improved transportation, and enlarged markets for agricultural and pastoral products. In the late period, public revenues rose abruptly in New Spain, in totals and on a per capita basis: from some 4 million pesos in 1746 to 20 million in 1800, much of the change coming from new levies on tobacco and *pulque*.[13]

Much of the crown's revenue, throughout the colonial period, was put back into the civil, ecclesiastical, and military administrations in America. At the end of the colonial era expenses probably averaged about 80 percent of American royal revenue. Peru and Mexico had surpluses to subsidize poorer American realms. In the late colonial era, in some years when public revenues in New Spain were about 20 million pesos, possibly 30 percent went to Spain and 17 percent to other parts of Spanish America, leaving about half for New Spain. That realm, though the richest in Spanish America, nearly always had revenue problems, and by one accounting method or another was often in arrears on payments.

The American revenue system did not make the kings of Spain rich beyond the dreams of avarice. There were limits to what could be milked from America, because excessive demands led to increased evasion and bribery. Great reliance was placed on records and audits, but the paperwork often was in arrears. The weight of Spanish revenue demands was not excessive by the standards of the time, especially when it is remembered that exemptions were granted, much evasion occurred, and much of the revenue went for American purposes. The system was "regressive," that is, bore heavily on the poor, but in most of the world all social arrangements bore heavily on the poor. The problem of the poor in Spanish America was not so much taxation as low remuneration. The general rate for public levies in the colonial era was low, no matter what the colonials said. Collections in late colonial New Spain averaged only about three pesos per capita, about the pay of an unskilled worker for a week.

How adequate were public revenues for the

---

[13] *Pulque* was made from the century plant (*maguey* in Mexico) by the pre-conquest Indians and widely consumed in the colonial era. It has an alcoholic content comparable to beer.

needs of society? Spain defined such needs narrowly; therefore, only limited funds were needed. Much public revenue went to collection costs, civil and ecclesiastical salaries and expenses, and to military expenditures. Little went for social development in health, education, or transportation. Nevertheless, during most of the colonial era the revenue system was far from crippling in its extent, its inefficiency, or the amount of complaint it caused. When the creole elite finally came to devote more attention to the matter, the chief change it wanted was lower taxes for itself, higher for the poor, and the ability to draw on the revenues without competition from peninsular Spaniards and imperial policy.[14]

Viceroys and captains-general nominally supervised the system in the early years, but treasury officials often were nearly independent; it is no wonder they conflicted with other officials. They were known as the "royal officials," an indication of crown interest in revenues. Important towns had them as residents, to handle taxes and other revenue matters only nominally under the *corregidor*. As early as 1554 in New Spain there was a Supreme Commission of the Royal Treasury in Mexico City, consisting of the viceroy, the senior *oidor* of the *audiencia*, plus its *fiscal* or state attorney, and the three treasury officials resident in the city. Early in the seventeenth century the crown established Accounting Tribunals (*Tribunales de Cuantas*) in several big American cities.

The senior "royal official" was the treasurer. He was accompanied by a comptroller and sometimes by other specialists. Duties depended on the revenue possibilities of an area. The officials kept a strongbox; supervised tax farmers (private tax collectors), the sale of offices, and the selling of Indian tribute paid in kind; made distributions of state funds upon proper authorization; and shipped revenues to the *Casa de Contratación* in Spain.

Revenue devices were numerous, and none accounted for a large share of the total collected. The *quinto*, royal fifth, went to the crown from the production of precious metals, although it was often lowered or even waived, to stimulate production. The *quinto* also was massively evaded.[15] Ecclesiastical tithes brought in considerable income. The papacy granted those for America to the Spanish crown in 1501, with the proviso that the crown fully support the church. The tithe affected all agricultural and livestock activity, including royal property. It was not generally collected from products that were otherwise taxed, such as silver, or industry and craftsmanship. Indians generally were exempt, although in the early decades there was much argument over the matter; instead, funds were taken from Indian tribute to support the church. The government spent most of the tithe on the church, and even sometimes put in additional funds. Collection was sometimes by the royal treasury, but often turned over to a bishopric, which then farmed it.

The tribute (*tributo*) paid by adult male Indians and by some *castas* (racial mixtures) was a sizable source of revenue, which went at first to the *encomenderos*, but soon to the crown as it took over encomienda Indians. In New Spain the tribute averaged about five pesos a year. It sometimes was the largest single source of public revenue, but that was only 17 percent in New Spain in 1746 and a much lesser percentage in later years. The *avería* was a tax on imports and exports to finance the *flotas* or convoys. The *almojarifazgo* was a duty on goods in trade between Spain and America. Its rates were seldom more than 10 percent and often much less, and some goods were exempt. Customs duties brought little revenue and probably had little effect on trade.

The *alcabala*, a sales tax, was one of the more important imposts. It was first applied in parts of America in 1575 at a rate of 2 percent (as

---

[14] See Chapter 17, Section c, on tobacco monopolies and more efficient tax collection and their influence on creole dissent in the late colonial era.

[15] See Chapter 10, Section g, for more on crown income from precious metals.

compared with 10 percent in Spain). Its application was complex. Some sellers paid the tax daily, some by the week, some less frequently. It was not paid on all sales, either by regulation or by practice. Many items, like bread and grain, were exempt. There was much exemption for Indians, especially for things they produced themselves. It was often paid as a lump sum to cover a class of sales: by a tax farmer; or by types of craftsmen or merchants; or sometimes by the *consulado* of Sevilla for noninspection of goods in *flotas*. The *alcabalas* were not so ruinous as colonials asserted. The "multiplier effect" sometimes cited, with the stated amount collected again and again on the same goods, did not occur in many cases. If the *alcabala* of the moment was 6 percent, much less might be collected if the *consulado* paid a lump sum for its district, to be recovered by itself as tax farmer at a low rate negotiated with the crown. It appears that *alcabalas* were felt most in large towns. In late colonial New Spain the Mexico City district produced half the total receipts of the *alcabalas* for the realm. The provinces in much of Spanish America could not be tightly administered for tax or other purposes; furthermore, in many cases commercial life in the remote and poorer areas was feeble.

Other revenue came from sale of public offices. Royal officials on appointment paid part of their salaries (*mesada, media anata*). There were monopolies on salt, playing cards, stamped paper for legal proceedings, quicksilver, and in the eighteenth century in New Spain one on the storage and sale of snow. The tobacco monopoly was established in different American areas, beginning in the 1750s, and at once became a big revenue producer. In New Spain, following its introduction in 1765, it became the greatest single source of public revenue. There in 1803 it raised about 8 million pesos, compared with 6 million for all mining levies. Much of its apparent usefulness was illusory. The administrative costs of the tobacco monopoly were especially high and took much of the money collected. Most monopolies were leased or farmed to public or private bidders, as were taxes, including the tithes. Late in the colonial period the crown

veered toward more administration by treasury officials, a practice that tended to yield more revenue, with results more pleasing to Spain than to taxpayers in America.

There were other miscellaneous levies. The *bula de cruzada* was an ostensibly voluntary indulgence, but in fact was required to be bought. Originally sold to support medieval crusades, it supports the truism that taxes seldom are temporary. The crown (and sometimes local officials too) taxed the sale of alcoholic beverages, after some early efforts to prohibit the manufacture of intoxicants. In late colonial Mexico nearly a million pesos a year was realized from the tax on *pulque*, almost as much as came from the Indian tribute. Numerous other levies were enforced in Spanish America, and when all else failed to bring in enough and the crown was desperate (rather common), forced loans or gifts were exacted.

Municipal Government

Discrimination against creoles in government stopped short of the town council (*cabildo* or *ayuntamiento*). That concession by the crown was sensible and quite safe. It gave creoles a sphere of public honor and decision making without giving them power that could threaten the empire. For one thing, imperial officials retained actual and potential power in municipal affairs. For another, the *cabildo* was run by the local elite, which generally supported the status quo. As large landowners resident in town, creole magnates used the *cabildo* to help direct the pricing and supply systems in such ways as to favor themselves as suppliers. Sometimes, to be sure, this activity had to give way to their responsibility for the care of the general population. Food riots, especially, were apt to have an effect on the balance of considerations. Generally, however, the *cabildo* served the interest of the creole elite.

Creoles in the *cabildo* thus had little motive to object to the municipal system. When an individual town did have a grievance, it had little leverage to bring to bear on the crown, and effective communication between towns for political purposes was forbidden. There was a small amount of consultation among representatives of different *cabildos* in the sixteenth century, but the crown put a stop to it (it had also curtailed communication among towns in Spain by the virtual suppression of the parliaments of the peninsular realms). Meetings of representatives of different towns in America would have been contrary to the spirit and sense of prudence of the imperial administration. There were only a few creole comments even at the end of the colonial era that the policy of discouraging communication between provinces was damaging. The towns did, however, send representatives (*procuradores*) to Spain as lobbyists with the imperial administration there.

The early *cabildo* in the Indies theoretically had power over huge territories. That power soon was cut down by the multiplication of towns and other agencies of government. Members of the early *cabildos* were either appointed by conquerors or elected. When election occurred, then and later, voters were the *vecinos*, a small elite of property holders. The offices of *regidor* (councilor) and *alcalde* (magistrate) sometimes were sold by the crown by the middle of the sixteenth century. Before long, resale was permitted; also, some purchased posts became hereditary. It sometimes is suggested that a rough-and-ready democracy of the conquest era unfortunately was suppressed by a centralizing and avaricious crown. This theory misleads by slighting the fact that the creole oligarchs were as interested in privilege as the crown. In the early years some *cabildos* were composed solely of *encomenderos*, many of them born in Spain; in later years American-born hacienda owners were predominant.

The *alcaldes* not only held the local court but usually presided over the meetings of the council. There were specialized *cabildo* offices, sometimes filled by *regidores* assigned to carry out a town function. One official who was not himself a *regidor* was the city attorney (*síndico*), who was chosen by the *regidores*.

The *cabildo* built and maintained streets, bridges, drainage systems, and public buildings; supervised weights and measures, meat slaughtering, and markets; tried to ensure adequate supplies for the town; and set and attempted to police prices. It managed the pasture and woodlands owned by the town, sometimes leasing them to private persons. It maintained a jail, a gibbet, a constable, and a night watchman. Its public-order functions extended into rural areas and encompassed action against stock rustlers and illegal animal slaughter and woodcutting. It performed ceremonial functions for such events as the arrival of viceroys or bishops and important dates in the lives of princes. Municipal revenues were insufficient for extensive execution of many of the *cabildo* functions. *Cabildos* received help in some of these duties by such private corporations as the *consulado* and the craft guilds (*gremios*) as well as by other echelons of government.

Although the scale and importance of *cabildo* activities are disputed, they often were highly useful. Not all *cabildos* were pushed aside by other agencies. Those in areas remote from the seats of important officials were the freest, but they also tended to have the least population and revenue and were either dependent or quiescent for that reason. When they were under the eye, and to some extent the hand, of viceroy or captain-general or *audiencia*, they were also in a place with more revenues and larger affairs to consider.

The role of the *cabildos* weakened in the seventeenth and eighteenth centuries. Some towns had difficulty finding men willing to serve. In others, however, *cabildo* office remained a matter of creole competition. The new intendants in the late colonial era, given extensive power over the *cabildos*, found many of them moribund. Some intendants tried to stir the *cabildos* to greater efforts. New spirit in the *cabildos* then sometimes became linked with local complaints about the government and even with the rising creole self-consciousness that came to play a role in independence.[16]

---

[16] See Chapter 17, Section b, on intendants.

The *cabildo abierto* (open *cabildo*) was not a town council meeting but a gathering of the local elite, including higher ecclesiastics, to consider an emergency. It might be called by the *cabildo* or by the governor. It was as oligarchic an institution as the town council. A meeting of a few score—that was the order of magnitude—of the local elite, rather than a dozen in the town council, merely gave the local magnates a better opportunity to agree on policy. In any event, open *cabildos* were not common and not important. A few occurred in the conquest period and a very few thereafter before the late colonial era. The chief historical role of the *cabildo abierto* was in the Independence period, when the institution was suddenly and briefly used in a time of unprecedented crisis.[17]

The Juridical System

The system of civil justice included the *audiencias*, courts held by such provincial officials as *corregidores*, and the *alcalde's* town court. Appeal sometimes could be made from the *audiencia* to the Council of the Indies. In addition, we have seen that *encomenderos* and hacienda owners settled disputes for dependents. Indian villages accepted the decisions either of their own leaders or of *corregidores* in disputes; or they appealed to higher magistrates, who were under orders to give special attention to Indian cases. Courts for Indians—*juzgados de indios*—were created in Mexico and Peru late in the sixteenth century. Indians sometimes were provided free legal counsel.

Spain devoted great attention to the juridical system because of its ancient conviction of the importance of law and the magistracy to maintenance of the power and legitimacy of the monarchy. The government depended heavily on the trained lawyer and magistrate. He was a trusted royal official without the exaggerated special interest and loyalties of the great families. As a class lawyers and magistrates were dedicated to

---

[17] The Indian *cabildos* are discussed later in this Section.

patient unification and orderliness in society. To be sure, private lawyers in America also were dedicated to promoting litigation, as the colonists early complained, begging the crown to prohibit more immigration by lawyers. The dependence of the crown on the ordinary courts was only in a minor way diluted by the grant of some special tribunals to such privileged corporations as the church, military, and merchants.

Much of the special legislation for America was public law. In the private law, the elite in America often simply followed Spanish practice, precedent, and codification. Thus, matters such as the family, testaments, and property and obligations did not require special legislation. On the other hand, there were some legislative changes for America in this large area, and other changes were developed by interpretation and practice in the courts of the colonies. Many differences from Spanish private law concerned problems relatively or entirely unknown in Spain, such as those relating to mixed marriages, Indians, or American labor systems. Private law followed Spain in considerable legal discrimination against women, for example, on questions of adultery or bigamy. On the other hand, the law on the inheritance of property treated women fairly. The Roman legal system lacked the jury and the binding precedent of judicial decision that was a feature of English law. Not being a part of the tradition, they were not missed.

The body of special American law, issued in Spain or the colonies, became so large that consultation was a chore, made worse by poor organization. New legislation seldom entirely canceled out old. Even for *audiencias*, the typical collection of laws was a jumble of papers in a storeroom. Occasionally, someone would prepare a list of titles, called a *cedulario* after the name of a legislative instrument, the *cédula*. No *cedulario* covered much of the documentation. More serious efforts at collection were made in Spain, without major result until publication in 1680 of the *Recopilación de las Leyes de las Indias*. The *Recopilación* included more than 6,000 laws, but only some of the major ones, leaving much to the storage rooms and to the common law of Spain. The profusion of law and its poor organization were among the factors making for long delays and solutions outside legal channels. There was much creole complaint about the courts. They did not serve the creole elite too badly, however: the prevalent bribery favored them; the delays could be an irritant but were sometimes an advantage; and at least the courts were partial to the elite over the masses.

Law and Government for Indians

There were special laws and institutions for handling Indians, often designed to protect them. They proved, however, very difficult to implement because of lack of cooperation from upper-class whites and problems of misunderstanding and diffidence among the Indians. Efforts were made to use Indian institutions and officials in a new system of collaboration and control. The Indians had special church administration, taxation, and labor systems. They were largely exempt from the Inquisition and the *alcabala*. They had some special judicial tribunals, such as the *Juzgado General de Indios*, set up in New Spain in 1573. Where such tribunals did not exist, the *audiencias* had an especial obligation to help Indians. Of course, the Indians suffered insofar as the juridical system in practice discriminated against the poor, and from the general presumption of their lack of capability as compared with Europeans. The weight of several Indians' testimony was required to equal the word of one white.

Population decline among Indians led to formalization of the policy of Indian segregation, whose beginnings we have seen in early Española. This policy led, especially in areas of great Indian population, to the ideal of the *república de indios*, the community in the countryside separated from the Spanish community. The crowding of some Indians in Spanish towns into special wards (*barrios*) had a different purpose. The rural segregation was diminished by intruding residents—white, mestizo, mulatto—who seized property and authority and contributed to *mestizaje*; by

economic conditions and exactions (like the tribute), which led to Indian vagabondage; and by the usurpation and interference of the haciendas.[18] Much of the putative value of segregation was not realized because of the activities of Spanish officials, most notoriously the *corregidor*. He forced Indians to buy goods (the *repartimiento de bienes*), often ones the Indians did not want, at inflated prices, stole their property, abused their labor, and aided other outsiders who oppressed them. Indians were favored, as a child-like race in tutelage, by being seldom fined, imprisoned, or executed. They were prohibited from borrowing large sums to keep them out of activities requiring much capital. These and other regulations marked the Indians as a special group, even if much of the legislation on Indians was not enforced to the letter.

The Indians continued to have a role in local government under the Spaniards, who used members of the preconquest official class. Some Indian offices under the Spaniards long retained hereditary features. Such officials often were called *caciques* in New Spain and *curacas* in Peru, the former name being a Spanish import from the Caribbean to the continent, the latter native to Peru. These Indian collaborators were folded into the upper class by being declared *hidalgos*. They received power, property, titles, and privileges; in return they performed political, economic, and social functions in the interest of the elite of which they were a special part. In the early years of the conquest period the Indian masses were content to deal with accustomed officials, who could explain what was expected of them under the new regime, and, hopefully, would try to protect their interests. The Spaniards needed their orders translated into action, and the *caciques* were able and eager to do so. The upper-class position of the Indian nobility, however, had limitations. Their property was but a fraction of that held by Spaniards, and their

---

[18] See Chapters 8 and 9 on *mestizaje* (race mixture), loss of Indian lands to haciendas, Indian vagabondage, and related subjects.

governmental powers were exercised at the lowest level, only over Indians, and under Spanish supervision.[19] The Indian upper class was of more consequence early in the colonial period than later, quickly losing much of its authority, both because the Indian laborers became disillusioned by their collaboration and rapacity and because the Spaniards gradually gave their authority to other officials.

The Spaniards, before long, began to require election of Indian officers on the Spanish town model. In New Spain it took several decades, until after the mid-sixteenth century, to get the Indian *cabildo* well established. By the end of the sixteenth century, in several places in the Indies, the Indian *cabildo* seemed to be working fairly well. It did not precisely duplicate the Spanish model. Elections were supervised by Spanish officials. Many factors complicated the development of the Indian *cabildo*. It cut into the role of the older Indian governing system at the local level. In Peru the new *alcaldes* of the *cabildo* and the *curacas* deriving from the Inca system divided authority, but the *alcalde* in time came to have more than the *curaca*. Some Indian villages in the Indies used the *cargo*, by which men with property were forced into local office by community pressure and required to expend their substance for public purposes, even *fiestas*. To enforce the rule that all *cabildo* members should be Indians proved impossible, reflecting both *mestizaje* and the presence of predatory intruders in the Indian communities. Sometimes, Indian *cabildos* had authority over the collection of tribute and over the provision of labor drafts under *repartimiento*. They also had many of the functions of the Spanish *cabildo* with reference to town supply, building, and policing. They defended the town lands against usurpation. They held courts and maintained a town jail. Some had *escribanos*; some of them in New Spain for decades kept records in Náhuatl (in

Roman script), and others continued the preconquest picture writing for a time.

The church tended to support close Spanish control of the Indians, especially after the optimism of some of the early idealistic friars had been diminished. In New Spain, church support of strong controls increased as the early Indian enthusiasm for Christianity waned. Church attendance declined as the *caciques* found it difficult to herd their people to Christian services. So Indian alienation from the church was a factor in strengthening church support of Spanish control in general.

Tribute was one of the marks of Indian status, though it also was paid by some of the *castas*. It was similar to head taxes paid by peasants in medieval Europe. We have noted the tribute of services and goods during the heyday of the encomiendas, the early elimination by the crown (in many places) of the service feature, and the widespread conversion of the Indians from a private to a crown relationship. The tribute in kind might be paid (depending on region) in fodder, eggs, fish, fuel, chickens, stone, lumber, maize, or other products.[20] There was much abuse in the amounts set, which at least originally were often founded on preconquest tribute practice among the Indians. Population decline caused additional abuse, because of the tendency of officials to try to offset the fall in the number of tribute payers by raising the assessment, just as they tried the same solution in connection with labor drafts.

In the late sixteenth century the big sedentary Indian populations of Mexico and Peru were largely converted solely to commodity tribute, and labor was being handled in other ways with the decline of encomienda. Commodity tribute was collected several times a year by *corregidores*, working through assistants and local Indian government, and then a factor of the royal treasury sold the tribute at auction. Commodity tribute over the years tended to be commuted to money payments, as Indians gained more coinage by

---

[19] See Chapter 8, Section c, on the social position of the Indian upper class and Section d on *caciques* and the labor system.

[20] See Chapter 3, Section c, for early tribute in Española.

wage labor. Tribute generally ran between five and eight pesos per tributary. In the late colonial era in New Spain the average tribute was about five pesos for each tributary head of a household, which was on the order of 2 percent of what a tributary might earn in a year. For poorer tributaries, however, the weight of tribute was considerably more than 2 percent of earnings.

c. Eighteenth-Century Changes

Some eighteenth-century developments represented important changes in institutions that would be carried over to the independent republics.[21] The eighteenth-century changes in the Spanish administrative system were not, however, so important. It is easy to exaggerate their influence because (a) the government talked as though it expected fundamental improvement from the administrative changes; (b) they occurred about the same time as some changes in the closed port trading ideal, seeming to make a package of "reform" even though neither had much of the effect that Spain wanted; and (c) both changes turned out to have been put into effect near the beginning of the wars for Independence, inviting a presumption that the former must have been radical enough to help bring on the latter.

Important administrative changes were discussed in the first half of the eighteenth century, but little was put into effect until the 1760s. We have noted for the earlier part of the century the reduction of the powers of the Council of the Indies and of the *Casa de Contratación*, which continued after mid-century. The *flota* system was virtually dead by mid-century. Some efforts were made to improve communications with the Indies early in the eighteenth century

by using postal ships. Such efforts continued later, but communications remained a serious administrative problem.

Most of the changes after mid-century were unremarkable. Alterations in taxes and revenue administration had some effect on trade and production but little on the administrative system generally. An economic change with effects on administration was the virtual extinction of the limited port ideal after 1765. This was labeled *comercio libre* (free trade) but was in fact merely free trade within the empire. *Comercio libre* stopped neither contraband nor peninsular and creole evasion of the various trading regulations that remained, and commerce continued to require much government activity.[22] Another change was an effort by Charles III to reduce somewhat the powers of the church. He ousted the Jesuits and tried to restrict the *fuero* that permitted churchmen to be tried in their own courts.[23] At the same time in the late colonial period, the crown recruited more of its officials from the military and fewer from the church. Another change was the decentralizing of territorial administration with creation of two new viceroyalties (New Granada before, and La Plata after, mid-century); new captaincies-general for Cuba (1764), Venezuela (1777), Chile (1778); and *audiencias* at Caracas (1786) and Cuzco (1787). In 1776 was created the vast General Commandancy of the Interior Provinces, stretching from the Pacific across what is now northern Mexico, New Mexico, and Texas. It later was subdivided and otherwise modified.

The creation of the viceroyalty of La Plata was especially significant. It reflected long-standing worry about the contraband activities of the population of the south Atlantic seacoast and Plata River system, especially at Buenos Aires and Montevideo; the difficulties of communication between that area and the viceregal court at Lima; and the escalating fear of foreign encroach-

---

[21] For example, the increase of hacienda and peonage, race mixture, creole-peninsular tension, and the creole desire for high public office; certain economic changes, like the development of Cuban sugar and the Plata area's cattle business; the increasing intellectual sophistication of a part of the creole upper class.

---

[22] On the *flota* see Chapters 7 and 11, Section d; on *comercio libre* see Chapter 11, Section d.
[23] See Chapter 12, Section c.

ment. The Portuguese, who often had British support, persisted in pressures on the Spanish Jesuit Indian missions of the interior and in the Banda Oriental (present-day Uruguay). The British, on their own account, briefly took a harbor in the strategically located Falkland Islands in 1764, were driven out by the Spaniards, were back in 1771–1774, and apparently meant to return. Furthermore, the cattle business of the Plata areas began to increase notably in mid-century. About that time the Spaniards made some strong military efforts to support their claims to what is now southern Brazil.[24] Such considerations led to creation of the viceroyalty of La Plata in 1776 with its seat at Buenos Aires.

Introduction of the intendant system to America was the change that seemed most striking. The new Bourbon monarchs of Spain began establishing intendancies in Spain in 1718 on the model of the institution in France as part of their drive for more uniformity, centralization, and efficiency in the Spanish government. This introduction occurred at the same time that the Bourbons were reducing the power of the old council system with new ministries. Extension of the intendancy system to America was long delayed, being first applied to Cuba in 1764, partly because of the need to improve the strength of that island, which had been captured by the British in 1762. The intendancy system thereafter was extended in stages to various areas of the Spanish Indies until by 1790 nearly all had it.

The intendants replaced governors, *corregidores*, and *alcaldes mayores*, combining their functions with those of the treasury officials in the new office. Thus, most of the American realms were given uniform divisions, the *intendencias*, which were subdivided into *partidos* headed by *subdelegados*. The *audiencias* and viceroys remained. New Spain had the most intendancies (twelve), headed by a superintendent, and they included the territories formerly under some two hundred *corregidores* and *alcaldes mayores*. Intendants were few enough in

number to be given high salaries and thus better men were attracted. Many of the intendants were energetic and honest. Many were military men. All were peninsular Spaniards. The much more numerous *subdelegados* were not well paid and were no improvement over *corregidores*.

The intendancy was supposed to strengthen the administrative system by making it more uniform and by giving the intendants more power than the officials they replaced, with rank equivalent to captain-general. They had great authority over administration, military affairs, finance, and economic development. Increasing revenue was the chief aim of the system, partly to provide the wherewithal to fend off the British. The intendants also were to push such reforms as abolition of forced Indian labor and of the *repartimiento* of goods. In a few places the friction between viceroys and *audiencias* on the one hand, and intendants on the other, interfered seriously with administration. Much adjustment was required, often under difficult wartime conditions. As matters developed there was not much time for trial, because the imperial crisis of 1808 soon was upon the Spanish world. The intendants were not long on the scene in America.

Insofar as the intendants managed, or attempted, a more rigorous administration, they were less acceptable to creoles than the sloppier system that so long had permitted the American elite to escape much of the theoretical rigidity and rigor of the imperial regimen. Another unexpected result came from the authority given intendants to exercise wide powers over *cabildos*. Rather than smothering those creole municipal councils, the intendants often stimulated them to new efforts, sometimes not pleasing to the imperial administration. Finally, the effect of the intendancy system on improving revenues and production was small. The life span of the system coincided with some improvements in trade and production and with large increases in public revenues, but the intendant usually had nothing to do with these developments.[25]

---

[24] On Spanish-Portuguese relations in America see Chapter 7, Section f.

[25] See Chapter 17, Section b, for more discussion of the intendant.

d. The Quality of Government

The government managed society according to the oligarchic aims of its directors. These aims included containment of the discontent of the numerous poor, subject, and dependent peoples within limits of either passive and grumbling complaint or localized disorders against specific ills. It also supervised a nicely balanced relationship of collaboration and antagonism between crown and creole. Although creoles resented exclusion from high office, they remained loyal, because they were collaborators with the state in control and exploitation of the lower class. The creoles did not want popular government but rather more control of the oligarchic system for themselves.

Paperwork was heavy and may have slowed action excessively; but good information, often provided on a regular schedule, was useful. Graft was common, as it was in most governments of the time. Also common at the time, and difficult to judge, were the effects of bureaucratic routine, hierarchical rigidity, tax farming, the sale of public offices, and the mixture of executive, legislative, and judicial functions. The cost of administration certainly was rather high, partly because offices were created merely in order to sell them; on the other hand, offices provided jobs, attracted people to America, and helped in the accumulation of capital, some of which went into productive enterprise. The absence of a jury system did no violence to feelings, because it was not part of the Roman legal system, nor is there evidence that the latter promotes justice less effectively than the Anglo-American. The lack of a broadly based legislature supposedly contributed to a fatal rigidity in the system. However that may be, it did not dilute the loyalty of the upper class.

The often cited "rigidity" of the formal structure did not exist in practice. The system bent to need quite nicely. The variety of institutions and the overlaps of jurisdiction can be as easily praised for providing flexibility as blamed for creating confusion. Flexibility was provided also by cutting old jurisdictions into new *audiencias*, captaincies-general, and viceroyalties. It existed because the operation of a provincial government often depended on its distance from the next higher echelon in the system, and distance from Spain in times of delayed communications. Flexibility and reform and bypassing were promoted through the inspection system of *visitas*. Graft provided flexibility, in that it permitted circumvention of paperwork by means of what in our day has been called external coordination. In addition, flexibility resulted from "goal ambiguity," or conflicting aims within the system, which in effect left to subordinate officials some share in their reconciliation. To be sure, in many cases flexibility was not attained, and action did not occur when it was urgently needed, but the legendary total rigidity did not exist.

The system did, however, fall more and more out of adjustment with reality in a changing world. Spain's misfortune was that as this happened in the eighteenth century, the country also faced expensive and dangerous international wars, and that both those factors coincided with some increase in creole dissatisfaction.

Massive use of coercion and persistent avoidance of some aspects of the legally constituted governmental system are often said to have fastened upon the creole elite an affection for "aggressive individualism" and a lack of respect for law. Such behavior by an elite ruling by discrimination and violence over a large socially submerged population was to be expected. It was not purely Spanish, nor was it an indelible preference, but merely a reaction to cultural conditions. It was, nevertheless, one of the notable parts of the colonial heritage to the independent republics of the nineteenth century.

International Relations and Defense

Military force was the critical element in the contest of the Atlantic powers for overseas hegemony after the discovery of America. The English, French, and Dutch were not fools. They preferred to conquer valuable Spanish territories in America. When they could not, they made do with secondary choices of territory and with illegal methods of capturing trade. They would have chosen Mexico and Peru over Massachusetts and Québec, but they could not get those centers of Indian population and mining. They also would have been glad to acquire such strategic territories as Cuba, the Isthmus of Panama, and the Río de la Plata basin, but for one reason or another did not. What Spain lost was some Caribbean islands that it could not exploit; they became rich slavery-based plantation colonies of the British, French, and Dutch, and centers for contraband and military action against Spanish settlements. Their existence was dangerous but not fatal. Also worrisome rather than critical for Spain was French expansion in the Mississippi Valley and east and west from there. The English settlements on the Atlantic seaboard for some years were not alarming, although ultimately British and United States expansion in North America would roll over Spanish and Mexican claims to lightly held territory from Florida

to the Pacific. The Portuguese in Brazil swept across large areas that Spain claimed but could neither populate nor protect. Spain, however, held firm north of the strategic estuary of the Plata.

For most of the sixteenth century Spanish America suffered only military raids and minor invasions by traders. Spain had time for entrenchment in America. In the seventeenth century the European assault took over eastern North America and important positions in the Caribbean isles; slashed heavily at shipping and coastal points in America, especially in the Caribbean; and captured most of the market for imports. Spain was compelled to agree to provision of capital and manufactured goods by the more developed states, but demanded that America use them only through regulated Spanish commercial channels. Spanish-Americans accepted Spain's surrender without the condition. In the eighteenth century Spain's military position was bolstered somewhat by economic improvement, by a great French-English duel over North America, and by a tendency of Bourbon France to ally itself with Bourbon Spain against the nearly unmanageable strength of expansionist Britain in commercial and financial alliance with the Dutch. The rising scale and complexity of warfare increased the importance to military contest of economic power, and in that competition Spain continued to lose.

Spain long retained one of the most extensive empires in history against determined foes, not only because of advantages of early entrenchment, distance, topography, and squabbling between its rivals, but because of the existence in the Spanish world of notable military resources, skill, and valor. Its economic resources, however, were less formidable, and as time went on, the Spanish world became ever more dependent economically on northern Europe for manufactures, capital, and merchant shipping.

a. Spanish Claims

The will of father Adam not being clear, as a French king noted, rival European monarchs claimed territorial jurisdiction on various grounds. Spanish kings cited papal edicts about their rights as missionary princes who were first on the land. Other monarchs denied papal authority in the matter. Spain also claimed rights of discovery, conquest, and occupation, according to the theory and practice of states, reinforced in the seventeenth century and thereafter by new theorists of "international law." Those claims also were contested. How much territory does a "discovery" cover? Does landfall in the Bahamas confer rights on the shores of lakes Ontario and Titicaca? How much occupation is required to confer jurisdiction? How many Spaniards per square mile for how many years? How far from outposts like Santa Fe (in what later was called New Mexico) or St. Augustine in Florida did the Spanish writ extend because of discovery and use? The answer is that Spain followed the usual modest practice of nations by claiming everything and used whatever arguments were available for its own interpretation. It claimed the Western Hemisphere from pole to pole, except for Portuguese Brazil, and the boundaries of that were long in dispute.

In fact, however, Spain tacitly accepted the French and English settlements in North Amer-

ica in the early seventeenth century, although not until 1670 (in the Treaty of Madrid) did it formally agree to a boundary between Spanish Florida and English America at the Savannah River. Spanish reaction to European encroachment in the Caribbean was more violent and sustained, but there was also tacit acceptance of European settlements before they were recognized by treaty. By the 1670 treaty, Spain accepted England's possessions in the Lesser Antilles and its conquest of Jamaica in 1655. In short, Spain kept what it could hold; theory had little to do with the matter.

The Spanish claim to a trade monopoly with its American colonies followed the norm of many imperial powers in history, as did the refusal of its foes to honor the claim. Spain retreated quite early from its extreme claims of monopoly when it permitted foreign investment in the supposedly closed trading guild of Sevilla and when not all commercial intruders in America were hung as pirates.

b. Factors in Defense

To have geographic and historic circumstances favor your defense is pleasant. The Spaniards enjoyed five such advantages. First, problems of distance, terrain, and climate helped rather than hurt the Spaniards, because they were first on the ground and became well established in America. They knew the best communication and supply routes and often controlled them all or key points on them. Distance and terrain made attempts to invade the mineral-rich mountain interiors of Mexico and Peru especially hazardous, and nobody made a sustained effort at such invasion.

Second, the military technology and doctrine of the day made foreign intrusion chancy. Sailing ships with primitive guns, battered by storms and idled in calms, with tough problems of supply and reinforcement, sometimes could not take prepared Spanish positions. Military timidity or prudence often led to limited or quickly abandoned efforts. That familiar element in military history was promoted by badly designed command structures, especially when both naval and ground forces were involved; by poor staff work; and by the presence of many amateur or incompetent officers, purchasers of their commissions or recipients of their appointments through the blatant favoritism of the day. The Spaniards benefited time and again from British military stupidities. Oliver Cromwell took advice from Thomas Gage, one-time friar in Spanish America, who said the colonies would quickly collapse under determined assault. He could hardly have been more wrong! Cromwell sent an expedition against Española with dual and equal commanders, a silliness of great value to the successful defenders. Cromwell's team of planners could not even judge the true resources of Britain's own island of Barbados as a possible element in the attack on Spanish America.

When Spaniards endured an attack for a time, those factors often worked against the offensive force. Even naval tactics became increasingly conservative, till by the mid-seventeenth century they dictated in-line formations that worked against destruction of fleets. Naval commanders feared to concentrate forces and violate the in-line norm lest a defeat lead to their court-martial. Also favorable to Spain was the lack in Europe of well-developed strategic concepts, including a sophisticated definition of objectives. When large aims were suggested, they were difficult to sell to military and civilian leaders. England had great plans for attacks on Spanish America at various times (Drake in the sixteenth century, Cromwell in the seventeenth, and other leaders in the 1740s–1760s), but they were not sufficiently believed in, worked out, or pursued. Thus, the state of military and strategic thinking helped the defending power.

Third, other methods of intrusion were alluring substitutes for expensive and dangerous assaults on the forts and mountains of Mexico and Peru. Spain's foes could settle unoccupied areas of America more safely and more cheaply. Also, there were profits to be had from small Caribbean sugar-producing islands that were easier to take than the great silver mines of the continental interior. Fourth, there was much profit in investing in Spanish mercantile houses in Sevilla or illegally selling goods (including slaves) directly to America. A last external factor that favored Spain's defense was that its rivals were often distracted by internal difficulties or by warfare or by competition with each other.

Spain supplemented these advantages with defensive efforts that were intelligent, sizable, and often effective. First, the extent of the early settlements made rooting out the Spaniards difficult; and the system of expansion by missionaries, sometimes with the aid of small military garrisons (*presidios*), was part of the military strength of the empire. To small numbers of friars and soldiers must be added the pacified Indians, who were auxiliary military and supply forces and who reduced the defense problem on Spain's frontiers. The missions and *presidios* existed in areas difficult to traverse because of distance, terrain, climate, and hostile Indians. French and British forces brought to bear on them in Texas, Florida, and Georgia often were too weak to resolve the contest.

Second, the Spanish social system in America sustained the empire. The elite was loyal. It traded with the enemy, but despised them because they were not Spaniards, even more when they were Protestants. The lower classes were on the whole quiescent. The *castas* thus provided labor, supplies, and fighting men. They were not an important internal danger that could be useful to Spain's enemies, so long as the latter could not get at them effectively to move them to action. Francis Drake and others could get only the few Indians and runaway blacks with whom they came in contact to act with them against the Spaniards.

Third, Spain's naval force in Europe and America often was sufficient to force rivals to expect that it could take damaging action. Spain, in Europe and America, usually had some money for naval purposes. There were timber, iron, fibers, and artificers. Shortages, high prices, and embezzlement in the Spanish maritime industry had some counterparts in all countries and were in any event not absolute barriers to the creation and maintenance of naval power. Much of this was by private or semiprivate vessels. In the sixteenth century Spanish maritime forces did well in frustrating intruders; in the seventeenth they did much less well, but were not completely helpless. Spanish ships did not disappear from the seas. The "bankruptcies" of the monarchs were not like the liquidations of petty merchants. Funds were scraped together by repudiating debts, including those to bankers, and by seizures of property, forced gifts and loans, and other shifts. Some of the money went to military, and specifically naval, purposes. In the eighteenth century there was a considerable revival of Spanish naval strength. Havana's naval construction and repair yards were unmatched in the Caribbean.

The convoy—*flota*—system, begun in the 1520s, had developed by the 1560s into the practice of sending two fleets a year. This system soon was altered. The deficiencies of the *flota* system were considerable—many years no convoys sailed —but it was not contemptible.[1] The merchant vessels were sufficiently armed to be of use against some attackers. Additionally, the escort vessels sometimes were detached in America to patrol the Caribbean. Although foreigners captured a few treasure shipments from America to Spain, most got through. Insufficient Spanish naval strength had its main effects not on capture of eastbound fleets with their treasure, but on delaying them; seizure of other vessels; interruptions of legal trade and the growth of contraband; seizure, sack, and ransom of coastal towns and inhabitants; and acquisition of territory in America.

Fourth, Spain had enough resources in ground forces in Europe to protect the homeland. Until the late seventeenth century they played an important role in campaigns in France, Italy, and the Germanys, and until the eighteenth held parts of the Netherlands. By the peace of 1659 the France of Louis XIV had usurped the ascendancy of the Spanish military but had not extinguished Spanish force.

Ground forces in America were often of poor quality. The "regulars" were few in number and were found mostly at major ports, at fortifications, in viceregal guards, and in a few frontier situations. Their usefulness varied. Some units were burdened with enlisted men from the lower class, including convicts and vagabonds, who were badly treated, trained, and supplied. The militia was even less reliable. Both regulars and militia were often either badly paid or not paid at all. Units sometimes were disbanded for lack of funds. Presidio garrisons sometimes were absorbed in the business of remaining alive, plagued with cheating pay masters and dishonest provision systems, and encumbered by their families. Civilians given the name of militia, suddenly called upon to repel European invaders—buccaneers or soldiers—were just as effective as the militia of George Washington's despair. Their understandable fears of howling pirates or European troops were not overlaid with disciplinary restraints or considerations of military honor, experience of their own capacity for inspiring fear, or confidence in their preparation. In many cases they had property and families at hand to defend, hostages to fortune. Often they fell into panic.

Most American units certainly were inferior by European standards. Those standards, however, were seldom pertinent in Spanish America, where armed men had little occasion to face European troops for any length of time and then could do so from fortified places. Regular units at fortified ports sometimes gave a good account of themselves. Even civilians sometimes did so. It was especially important that they usually could flee to the interior, returning to fight another day. Their mere existence nearby inhibited further penetration by the invaders. What this meant was that so long as the upper class was loyal to Spain, America's defensive capabilities were greater than the results of individual actions suggested.

Changes in the military system in America were made in the second half of the eighteenth century. They came in response to the general desire of the Spanish Bourbons to improve de-

---

[1] See Chapter 11, Section d, on the *flota*.

fense; to the increased perception of danger as the British won great victories in the Seven Years' War; and to changes that increased the privileges of military personnel in Spain. The reforms increased the number of military in America, both regulars and militia, which the creoles approved because they improved defense against Indians and foreign foes and brought money into the area. Military measures in the northern reaches of New Spain responded to new pressures from Britain and later from the United States. A new Commandancy-General of the Interior Provinces took much of the north of New Spain from the viceroy's control.

The expanded regular units did not come from Spain, because transporting them would have been too costly, but were organized with mostly American personnel. The total number in regular units was much less than in the expanded and presumably improved militia. Adjustments in these reforms were made for years, since obviously the quality of the enlarged force was poor. The militia reform began in Chile in 1759. It extended to New Spain in 1764, and by 1800 the army there had some 30,000 personnel, of which 24,500 were in the militia. The reform provided small gratuities for service, but the men had to pay for their own billeting. Few made money from military service. The reform did not improve discipline, always one of the defects of the militia and of most of the "regulars." The new militia offered the lower-class soldiers a trifle more income and prestige than they enjoyed in civilian society. Some joined because their employers were officers. Certainly the duties were not arduous. There was not enough drill or other instruction to make it a burden—or an effective army. Few of these militia ever were tested in combat. The great effect of the "reform" was not military but political: the creoles were delighted with their new titles.[2]

Fifth, Spanish fortifications and other prepared positions often were decisive. Havana and Cartagena were strongholds by the end of the sixteenth century, and improvements were made until the close of the colonial era. Famous Italian engineers planned some of the works, and Spain spent great sums on them. Cartagena was taken several times but never retained, and after each loss and return the Spaniards made it stronger than ever. San Juan de Puerto Rico in the late colonial period was heavily protected with three fortresses and a number of smaller works. Santo Domingo, Portobelo, Veracruz, and other ports had stone works and guns that repelled many attacks. Isolated Acapulco had a small star-shaped fortification on a hill overlooking the harbor, although it was only a modest tropical village except when the once-a-year Manila galleon arrived.

Lesser works were erected at various places. Even the poor region of Central America ultimately had three major and six minor defensive works. Coastal towns sometimes had stone walls. An earthen pit or a modest log, earth, or stone wall could help protect the guns, which had the advantage of a stable platform as compared with those on invading ships. Furthermore, the guns were laid out so as to cover surveyed target areas.

Finally, invading forces that were held up by fortifications often suffered terrifying losses from tropical disease. Cartagena, Veracruz, and Havana had notorious defenses of that sort. The commanders of the British forces that took Havana after a siege in 1762 reported that their forces had 646 killed and 6,008 dead of sickness! Thus, the flexibility that sea power gave to pirates and invading navies often was reduced by other factors.

c. A Century of Grace After 1492

Spain's Rivals

Spain had four important rivals for American empire. None of them was nearly so dangerous in the sixteenth century as later. England, smaller than Spain, was in the sixteenth century disturbed by its conversion to Protestantism and by

---

[2] See Chapter 17, Section b, for important effects on Independence and on the life of the new republics.

dynastic conflicts. The caution of Elizabeth (who reigned 1558–1603) in foreign affairs reflected the weaknesses of her personal position and that of her country. England's later growth made it increasingly formidable. France was populous and rich in the sixteenth century, but rent by dynastic conflicts, complicated by religious strife, and in the seventeenth and eighteenth centuries often distracted by European warfare and by the great colonial rivalry with England. Portugal's limited resources were committed to India and the East Indies and to only a modest activity in Brazil, where it did little in the sixteenth century. The Dutch were under Spanish rule until 1568, when they began their war for independence. War limited their overseas actions until the next century, when they became serious intruders into the Spanish and Portuguese systems. The German- and Italian-speaking peoples were fragmented into many states and fully occupied with European affairs. Beyond them were Slavs and Muslims who were unconcerned with competition for American empire.

Early Penetration

You can't kill an eagle with a flyswatter. While its foes spent half a century proving that maxim, Spain simply grew stronger in America. The piddling activity of its rivals was little more than coastal exploration, nosing into inlets and rivers in search of precious metals or rich Indian cultures or a passage to the Orient, or making small raids on Spanish positions. The English did almost nothing for long after the Cabot voyages in the late fifteenth century. Although the French did more, the chief result was stimulation of Spanish defense. France sent Verrazano in 1524 to explore parts of the north Atlantic coast. In 1534–1542 Jacques Cartier made voyages to the St. Lawrence area. But the French found little to tempt them. The Spaniards reacted to these and the few other foreign voyages in the north Atlantic area by explorations and patrols of their own. In the Caribbean, French raiders in the 1530s and thereafter sacked some Spanish towns,

took ships, captured treasure. In that area the Spaniards reacted with increased vigilance, armament, small fortifications, and by 1521 a tax (*avería*) on exports and imports to support convoys and other ways of guarding connections with America. After 1526 regulations often forced Spanish merchantmen to sail in fleets and carry armament. After 1537 royal naval vessels often were used to convoy bullion shipments to Spain.

Foreign penetration became somewhat more serious in the second half of the sixteenth century, but by that time the Spaniards were more deeply entrenched in America. Most of the penetration was by Englishmen. In the 1560s merchant John Hawkins attempted to open peaceful trade with Spanish America, with approval by Queen Elizabeth and financial support from Londoners. He found Spanish colonists in the Caribbean eager to trade, although threatened with punishment by Philip II. Spanish officials were ready, for a price, to collaborate with such violations of the closed trading ideal. The last Hawkins expedition (1568–1569) was trapped by a Spanish fleet at Veracruz, and four of his six vessels lost, although he and his cousin Francis Drake escaped. This experience virtually ended English support for efforts at peaceful trade within the Spanish system; henceforth, undeclared war was an accepted necessity.

Drake became the most notable English intruder in the latter part of the sixteenth century. From a base on a deserted Caribbean coast, with fewer than a hundred Englishmen and some Indian and Negro allies, he took Nombre de Dios on the isthmus in 1572, capturing the silver shipments from Peru to Europe. In 1573, from the same base with even fewer Europeans, Drake crossed the isthmus, took the town of Panama and the silver there, and returned to England a national hero. He left England again in 1577, rounded Cape Horn, sacked towns in Chile and Peru, harassed Spanish shipping in the Pacific, and went westward round the world. In later years Drake attacked Santo Domingo, Cartagena, and St. Augustine, capturing considerable booty, but he failed in an effort in the 1590s, with a large force, to establish a permanent base in Panama.

The French, after the abortive efforts of Cartier, did not try settlement until 1562, when the Huguenot Jean Ribaut established short-lived Charlesfort at Port Royal in present South Carolina. This was an unpromising environment, as the Spaniards had found in 1526–1528, when they tried to colonize in the area under Lucas Vásquez de Ayllón. The Charlesfort settlement failed. The French tried again, in 1564, when René Laudonnière founded Ft. Caroline on the St. Johns River, near present-day Jacksonville. Spain in 1565 sent Pedro Menéndez de Avilés as *adelantado* of Florida. In that year he founded the town of St. Augustine, about forty miles south of Ft. Caroline, from which he quickly ousted the French. Although there was skirmishing between French and Spanish forces for a few years thereafter, this incident really ended the French venture on that coast. Menéndez also sent exploring parties inland, tried to found other settlements, and imported Jesuit missionaries. None of his efforts were successful. St. Augustine remained, however, and was fortified, becoming an important bastion of empire, guarding the treasure ships bound for Spain, and a salient against the intruders living farther north along the coast. It was some five hundred miles from Havana, which guarded the Florida Channel between Cuba and the Florida Keys, the route of the galleons to Spain.

The Great Armada

Philip II of Spain had bad luck with England, but the facts are not as bad as the English legend pretends. Philip wed Queen Mary of England in 1554, hoping to promote diplomatic détente and permanent restoration of Catholicism in England. He achieved neither. After Mary's death in 1558, Queen Elizabeth hinted at marriage with Philip but never came to the point. She began aiding the rebellious Dutch provinces against the Spaniards. Her support of

attacks on Spanish America by Drake and others was imperfectly camouflaged. She again demonstrated her unregenerate Protestantism in 1587 by executing the Catholic contestant to the throne, Mary of Scotland. Open war between England and Spain began in 1588.

Philip had determined on invasion and gathered a great fleet. The campaign was badly managed, chiefly because of Philip's poor decisions. His choice of an inexperienced commander-in-chief was foolish; even worse was his failure to insist on a secure naval base in the Netherlands, in spite of advice about its importance. Dutch and English action secured the best harbors against seizure by the Spanish armies in the Low Countries. The result was that the great fleet sailed from Spain into the English Channel in 1588 with no satisfactory haven against weather or English harassment, or for supply and repair. All this was especially necessary for a fleet heavy with ground forces and weapons for the invasion of England, and expecting to take on more in the Low Countries. The fleet was broken up and most of it lost because it had no refuge against bad weather, which was more lethal than losses to English action.

Anglo-American tradition and literature exaggerate the results of the defeat of the Spanish armada. The loss of the fleet was damaging, but it did not cause fundamental decay of Spanish strength. Although the financial loss was considerable, Spain quickly rebuilt her naval force. It soon was more formidable than before. The 1588 campaign did not itself confer any new physical strength on the English, and how much English courage and aggressiveness were inflated by victory is difficult to know. The superior maneuverability of English ships in 1588 often is celebrated, but English naval victories in succeeding centuries ordinarily came not from superior maneuverability but from weight of metal.

Most misleading is the notion that with defeat of the armada the Spanish empire "went into decline." There were many reasons for its decline, and it was that, not a collapse. It did not become instantly incapable of defending its dominions. Some notable fortifications were built in the 1590s in America. Drake's grandest scheme was beaten off in that decade. Spain's later difficulties were due chiefly to the growing strength and changing aims of her rivals. English, French, and Dutch settlement in the Western Hemisphere in the seventeeth century does not demonstrate a drastically reduced Spanish defense capability; Spain could not have prevented such settlement in the sixteenth century either, had it been mounted with vigor on a sustained basis. The defeat of the armada may even be interpreted as useful to Spain, insofar as it ended the dream of bringing England to heel by invasion. It is difficult to imagine such efforts as having any result more important than great expense to Spain and ultimate failure. The European powers have not found conquests, much less control, of each other to be easy.

d. Seventeenth-Century Encroachment

The Spanish system staggered under many blows in the seventeenth century, but it did not collapse. It suffered bad rulers, an overly ambitious European foreign policy, stronger rivals paying more attention to overseas affairs, and a plague of buccaneers. In the first half of the century, Spain reeled under heavy military expenditures for the Thirty Years' War (1618–1648), for a great revolt in Catalonia in 1640–1659, and for the effort to contain foreign encroachment and brigandage in the Caribbean. More and more decisions concerning America became entangled with the strategy and diplomacy of European affairs. Whereas at the beginning of the century Spain's military situation was worrisome, by mid-century it had degenerated to a condition of obvious peril. Assaults on Spanish positions in America—especially in the Caribbean—continued to the end of the century. "No peace beyond the line" was an informal agreement, dating from the mid-sixteenth century, that west of the Azores and south of the Tropic of Cancer the powers could snipe and smash at each other without leading to warfare in Europe.

In the seventeenth century it came to seem in very fact that there never was peace beyond the line.

New Caribbean Colonies and Buccaneers

Finally, the rivals of Spain began settling in America. They took only small parts of the Caribbean area in the seventeenth century but made them profitable as sugar-farming regions, as centers for contraband with Spanish settlements, and as military bases. The British, French, and Dutch eased the Spanish problem by jostling each other for position. Most of the lesser islands they seized had not been occupied by the Spaniards. Spain was uninterested in their economic exploitation because its resources, policy, and interests were concentrated in other areas. Spain had more good sugar lands than it used in the Greater Antilles. Government and colonists were more interested in opportunities offered by the silver mines and large Indian laboring populations of the mainland. The business element in Spain was occupied with aspects of the closed trading system and its monopolistic privileges. In fact, the use of chartered trading companies by the three intruding nations showed the growing influence of the bourgeoisie among Spain's rivals. The tardiness of adoption of the trading company in Spain for overseas ventures was indicative both of other policies and interests and of the lesser vigor and influence of the Spanish bourgeoisie. A strategic rather than an economic occupation of the lesser islands might have been mounted, but it would have required reduction of Spanish strength at other points that were considered more essential, such as Havana, Santo Domingo, Veracruz.

The English took over many of the Lesser Antilles without much opposition from the Spaniards. They seized St. Kitts in 1623–1625 and Nevis in 1628, were ousted from both in 1628 by the Spaniards, but quickly reoccupied them. They settled other small islands, positions in Guiana, and islands on the Mosquito Coast of Central America. In 1655 the English seized the large but almost unpopulated island of Jamaica. Oliver Cromwell had grander plans to dismember the Spanish empire, but they failed. Jamaica itself was a damaging loss because of its ideal position as a military and smuggling base. In the 1670s and thereafter Englishmen, including buccaneers, were living in Belize in Central America, cutting dyewood and other timber. It eventually became the colony of British Honduras.

Dutch settlements were largely made through the efforts of the Dutch West India Company, founded in 1621. This joint-stock company was to maintain warships, conquer, settle, and exploit, all blanketed with a promise of Dutch government aid in wartime. Dutch settlements before mid-century included Tobago, Curaçao, Saba, St. Eustatius, and St. Martin. The Dutch also began settlement in Guiana. About the same time (1624–1661) the Dutch were taking parts of Brazil, but Brazilians finally ousted them. In the second half of the century the Dutch pushed exploitation of their Caribbean position, but did little to add to their territorial holdings, as they were tied down by ventures in the Far East and wars with Britain. A growing Dutch-British economic and military alliance culminated in 1689 with the accession to the British throne of the joint monarchs William of Orange and his English wife Mary, daughter of James II.

The French used several trading companies. They took Martinique, Guadeloupe, and Dominica in 1635 and established a position in Guiana. There were fourteen French isles in the Caribbean in 1664. France's greatest Antillean prize was St. Domingue, settled in the second half of the century, in the western part of Española. French settlers there engaged in piracy, agriculture, and stock raising. In 1665 the West India Company named a governor. After the great War of the League of Augsburg, Spain in 1697 ceded the territory to France. Also, late in the seventeenth century, the French were establishing claims on the Gulf of Mexico.

Privateering, piracy, and undeclared war flourished in the Caribbean in the seventeenth century. It became heavily polluted with thugs and thieves, who were called buccaneers after the grills on which they cooked meat. They were a violent and heedless lot, living mainly by piracy, plunder, and ransom. Terror was a favorite tactic, often effective in producing panic and payment; it also was a pleasure for some of the notably brutal individuals who belonged to the "brotherhood of the coast." Some buccaneers did grow food and make sales to contrabandists. Some went into stock raising and logging. In a few cases they helped found permanent and peaceful settlements.

The main reason for the growth of buccaneering was that the French, Dutch, and British governments, with their new positions in the Caribbean, were not interested in limiting practices that either benefited their citizens or reduced Spanish strength. On some occasions those governments gave sanction to cutthroats to prey on Spanish America. Occasionally, buccaneers fought for pay for the national rivals in the area. In the second half of the seventeenth century buccaneering reached a peak of semiorganized violence. The governors of British Jamaica and the French colonies often provided buccaneers with commissions to raid, clothing their activities with some shred of legitimacy. Governments and individual officials claimed shares in the profits of such ventures. Henry Morgan, from the Spanish point of view one of the most notorious "Lutheran" pirates, crowned his career with the governorship of Jamaica. It is difficult to be more incensed at this than at Francisco Pizarro's being made a marquis.

Spanish American coastal towns lived in fear of plunder, rape, torture, and murder. Some were hit again and again. Santo Domingo, Havana, Cartagena, Panama, Portobelo, and Veracruz were likely places to find treasure and persons worth ransom, but they also were difficult to take. Smaller places sometimes yielded surprising booty. The relatively undefended coast of Venezuela became infested with intruders, especially Dutchmen, who early in the century almost monopolized the trade in salt. In some places intruders could get agreement with Spanish officials

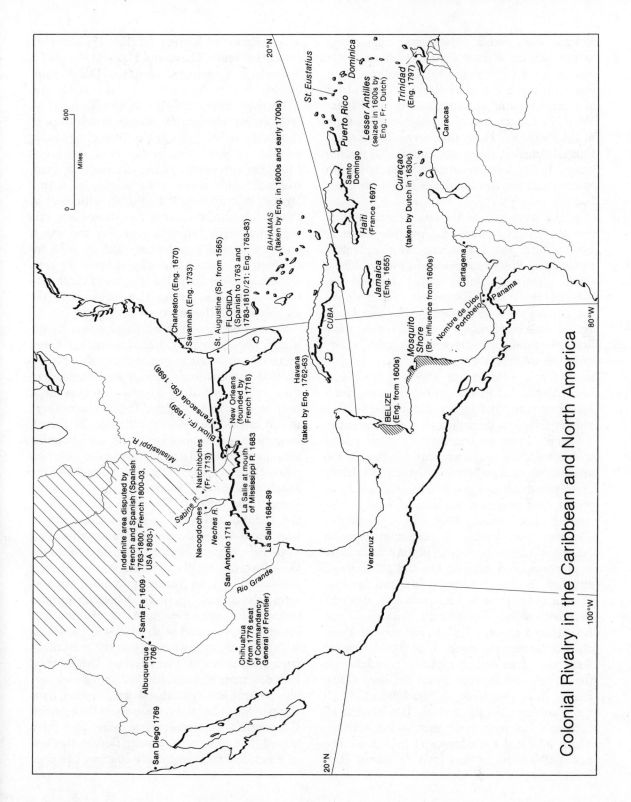

Colonial Rivalry in the Caribbean and North America

St. Eustatius

Dominica

Puerto Rico

Lesser Antilles
(seized in 1600s by
Eng., Fr., Dutch)

Trinidad
(Eng. 1797)

Caracas

Santo
Domingo

Haiti
(France 1697)

Curaçao
(taken by Dutch in 1630s)

BAHAMAS
(taken by Eng. in 1600s and early 1700s)

Charleston (Eng. 1670)

Savannah (Eng. 1733)

St. Augustine (Sp. from 1565)

FLORIDA
(Spanish to 1763 and
1783-1810/21; Eng. 1763-83)

Jamaica
(Eng. 1655)

CUBA

Cartagena

Nombre de Dios

Portobelo

Panama

*Mosquito
Shore*
(Br. influence from 1600s)

Pensacola (Sp. 1698)

Biloxi (Fr. 1699)

New Orleans
(founded by
French 1718)

Havana
(taken by Eng. 1762-63)

BELIZE
(Eng. from 1600s)

Mississippi R.

Natchitoches
(Fr. 1713)

Sabine R.

Nacogdoches

Neches R.

La Salle at mouth
of Mississippi R. 1683

La Salle 1684-89

San Antonio 1718

Indefinite area disputed by
French and Spanish (Spanish
1763-1800, French 1800-03,
USA 1803-)

Santa Fe 1609

Albuquerque
1706

Chihuahua
(from 1776 seat
of Commandancy
General of Frontier)

Rio Grande

San Diego 1769

Veracruz

500

Miles

0

20°N

20°N

80°W

100°W

to trade, using various subterfuges or agreement to pay ransom without fighting. Although the bulk of the activity was in the Caribbean, there was some along the Gulf Coast at such places as Campeche and Veracruz, and in the Pacific. When buccaneers lost or abandoned their ships in the Pacific and made their way on foot across Central America, they sometimes raided interior towns. In the late seventeenth and eighteenth centuries pirates developed ties in British Carolina and New York.

In the latter part of the seventeenth century the new colonial powers in America began to turn against the buccaneers. As the Dutch, French, and British possessions in the Caribbean became more profitable, sound business demanded relief from lawlessness. Furthermore, the powers now had less use for the buccaneers against the Spaniards, because they were more firmly established and because Spanish ability and will to oust them had declined. English naval vessels were used in 1685 to harry buccaneers. Dutch and French action followed over a period of years, and by the end of the century buccaneering was dwindling to a minor menace.

Spanish losses to buccaneers and to raiders with some color of government sanction in the seventeenth century were immense. The booty came from captured towns and ships. Foreign profits from increased contraband soared. The Spanish closed trading ideal was so thoroughly disrupted that possibly 90 percent of Spanish American imports by the end of the century were from contraband sources. On the other hand, although the loss of treasure, life, and freedom of action was great in the Caribbean, it might have been worse. The treasure ships could not be kept to a regular schedule, but most of them did get through to Spain. Only three treasure fleets were destroyed or captured completely in the seventeenth century. Spain did keep Cuba, Puerto Rico, two-thirds of Española, nearly all the Caribbean coasts, and all the hinterland. Spaniards did have some successes in warfare, which inhibited the advance of their foes. The new fortifications at San Juan de Puerto Rico

were helpful in beating off the 1595 English expedition under Drake and Hawkins. In 1605 a Spanish fleet destroyed nineteen Dutch ships loading salt in Venezuela. In the 1620s and 1630s there were a number of Spanish naval attacks on intruders in the islands. Dutch ships in the Pacific in the 1620s found themselves unable to take the port of Callao in Peru, much less Lima, the rich capital of the viceroyalty of Peru, which lay only a few miles inland. In 1641 a Spanish fleet destroyed the British settlement at Providence on the Central American coast, taking some eight hundred prisoners and much booty. Cromwell's ambitious plan of 1655 for conquest in Spanish America suffered an early setback at Santo Domingo. The seventeenth century was a purgatory for the Spaniards in the Caribbean, but they were not destroyed.

Spanish defense included naval action, fortification, raising troops to defend towns, flight, and protective destruction or scorched-earth tactics. In 1605 the Spaniards depopulated the western third of the island of Española to prevent it from supporting smugglers. This heroic measure merely opened the door to settlement by French buccaneers and annexation by France. A similar measure was tried later in Venezuela, when tobacco fields near the coast were burned and the inhabitants moved inland so they could no longer trade with the Dutch. In the same area, the Spanish authorities poisoned salt works to stop forbidden trade in that commodity. Fast dispatch boats improved communications. *Guarda-costas*, small enforcement vessels, were authorized by local Spanish governors. Such efforts helped preserve much of Spanish jurisdiction in the area. Finally, naval attrition and losses of treasure and some islands in the Caribbean had only indirect effects on the great mainland settlements of the interior. These effects included trade dislocations, but sometimes they also brought new contraband opportunities, damaging to Spain but not necessarily to the colonies. Government communications were also interrupted, but those were usually slow in the best of times, and the bureaucracy continued to operate throughout the seventeenth century. Caribbean losses were less costly to Peru and Mexico than to Spain, and America would have benefited more from a reform of Spanish financial and economic policy than from retention of Jamaica or better control of buccaneers and contrabandists.

Early Settlements by Intruders in North America

Boston and Québec caused few chills of fear or fevers of envy in Spain. English North American settlement, which began with Jamestown in 1607, during the next century expanded along the coast from Maine to Carolina, but did not go inland over the mountains. So Spain made but a feeble response to colonies so distant from vital Spanish centers. Britain, furthermore, became involved in a deadly conflict with the French in Canada, which reduced the British threat to the interior of the continent. Thus, Britain's activity in North America seemed less dangerous than its warfare, contraband aggression, and colonization in the Caribbean. French Canada seemed to Spaniards no more a peril than the British North American colonies. After the foundation of Québec in 1608, French expansion west and south was slow and weak. Not until 1683 did La Salle emerge at the mouth of the Mississippi River, arousing serious Spanish alarm about French intentions in North America. By that time Spain had been digging herself into America for two centuries.

Relations Between Spanish and Portuguese America

The world scarcely knows the history of one of the most important contests for territory in modern times: between the Spanish and Portuguese empires in South America from the sixteenth through the eighteenth centuries. Even though much of the territory involved was poorly suited to agriculture, some of it was valuable for grazing. Furthermore, some places had great strategic value, controlling trade routes and leading to possible encroachments on potentially valuable agricultural lands in south central Brazil and in what is now Argentina.

At first, there seemed little reason for conflict. The growth of Brazil in the sixteenth century was too small to cause much alarm in Spain; in the early seventeenth century, however, a larger westward movement by Brazilians across the line of Tordesillas increased Spanish concern,[3] although Spanish reaction still was more limited than it was to be in the eighteenth century. No important effort was made to solve this problem through the union of the Spanish and Portuguese realms that Philip II engineered in 1580 and that endured until 1640. The Spaniards did not use the sixty years of what the Portuguese regarded as a Babylonian Captivity to try to absorb Brazil; they had enough other problems without so presuming on a connection that was in every way distasteful to the Portuguese.[4] The Spaniards did make efforts to try to control Portuguese-Brazilian traders in Spanish America: Some were compelled to register with Spanish authorities, and some were expelled. More important from the point of view of territorial jurisdiction, nothing was done (or probably could have been done at bearable cost) to inhibit the movement of Brazilians in the great wild heart of the continent.

In the 1630s *bandeiras* from the São Paulo region of Brazil, roaming the vast hinterland for Indian slaves, reached the Spanish Jesuit missions in Paraguay. The Spanish Jesuits had arrived at Asunción in 1605 and quickly moved south, converting Guaraní Indians and collecting them into villages (*reducciones*).[5] These were far from the Spanish town of Asunción, whose inhabitants opposed the Jesuit control of so much Indian labor and were uninterested in protecting

---

3 See Chapter 14, Section f, on Portuguese expansion in America.
4 See Chapter 6, Section a, on the 1580–1640 union of Spain and Portugal.
5 See Chapter 13, Section i, on the Jesuit *reducciones* of Paraguay.

the missions. After the Brazilian *bandeirantes* struck at the Paraguay missions, the Jesuits organized the Indians for war. They found, however, that the Paulistas were too tough and persistent, so the Jesuits soon moved many of their Guaraní charges southward. The Brazilian raiders followed. But the Spanish Jesuit mission system in the Paraguay area remained a barrier to Portuguese expansion. After a Paulista attack in 1676, the Jesuit military system was improved, and troops were available on an alert basis for use by Buenos Aires.

Generally, however, the Spanish and Portuguese governments did not for many years make much contribution to this contest. It went on in the interior of the vast and roadless continent, in an area of little apparent value. While the Portuguese colonial pressure against the Spanish Jesuit positions continued, it was paralleled by another expansion, hundreds of miles to the east, where Portuguese Brazilians moved south from São Paulo into Santa Catarina in the mid-seventeenth century. This territory was also unoccupied, save for a few Indians, and disputed between Spain and Portugal. There was, then, at least a potential Portuguese threat by two routes to the Banda Oriental (East Bank) of the Uruguay River, approximately the territory of the present republic of Uruguay, and to the Río de la Plata estuary, its southern boundary, which was the river entrance to the Spanish interior provinces of Paraguay, Tucumán, and far-off Upper Peru.

Portuguese or Brazilian trade into Spanish America by the beginning of the seventeenth century went largely to the Plata estuary, where Buenos Aires was founded by the Spaniards for the second time in 1580. The Plata was the indispensable key to the Spanish defensive position in the southern part of the continent. Heavy trade grew up by way of Rio de Janeiro and Buenos Aires, especially in slaves from Portuguese Africa and manufactured goods of non-Portuguese origin, largely British, French, and Dutch. From the estuary, shipping went up the river system. Some went to Paraguay, but the

largest amount was off-loaded to cross the plains by ox cart and mule back to Córdoba and Tucumán and to silver-rich markets in the mountains of Upper Peru. The trade grew because of high prices and scarcities in Spanish America caused by the Spanish closed trading requirements: European goods were expected to go to Upper Peru via the long and expensive route through Panama and Lima. Peninsular and creole Spaniards in Buenos Aires and many other places in the Indies supported smuggling, while retaining their dislike of foreigners and their loyalty to the political connection with Spain. The entire system was given impetus by the union of Spain and Portugal in 1580–1640, which diluted Spanish enforcement of regulations in the case of the Portuguese. Many Portuguese merchants came to reside in Spanish American towns. For several decades after 1640, however, the Portuguese share in contraband trade with Spanish America was much reduced by Spanish action consequent to the rupture of the union of the monarchies. The Portuguese war for independence from Spain went on intermittently until 1668.

In 1680 the Portuguese crown made a bold move in ordering the foundation of Colônia do Sacramento on the Plata estuary, in the territory of present-day Uruguay, only a few miles and one day's sailing from Spanish Buenos Aires. Portugal hoped to bolster its territorial claims in the strategic estuary region, to recover some of its trade with the Spanish colonies by offering a convenient entrepôt for slaves and merchandise, and to exploit further the cattle roaming the surrounding plains. Colônia realized only a small part of what Portugal hoped for it, partly because it was difficult to support militarily, partly because other routes were available for contraband and for the hide business. It was a challenge, nevertheless, that the Spaniards could not ignore. They destroyed Colônia in 1680, only a few months after its foundation. It was reestablished in 1683, because Spain permitted the Portuguese back in order to secure positions elsewhere; these imperial considerations took precedence over local issues. The same thing would happen several more times, with Britain especially supporting Portugal's territorial and economic pretensions. The rivalry between Spain and Portugal in southern South America would continue in the eighteenth century.

•

e. The Rewards of Endurance, 1701–1800

Changing Conditions: Gain and Loss

Spain's stubborn endurance in the seventeenth century had its reward in the eighteenth. For one thing, the ghastly Spanish Hapsburgs died out, and the new Bourbons improved administration. They strengthened the navy and American fortifications, and to some extent the ground forces. They undertook defensive territorial expansion in America. The defensive strength of the system also benefited from economic and demographic growth, especially after mid-century. A second gain was that France and Britain became somewhat distracted from Spanish America by a duel over North America. A third gain was the continued decline of buccaneering. Yet another Spanish gain was that France tended in the eighteenth century to ally with it against Britain. Of course, the other side of that was the increasing power of Britain that induced such alliance. British strength finally was too much for France, and Britain thrust it entirely out of North America in 1763. That victory left Spain more nakedly and more dangerously exposed to British and British American might, though it still enjoyed either alliance with France or parallel policies for opposing Britain. The British, fortunately for Spain, used their power badly with reference to Spanish America. From the 1740s to the 1760s Britain had schemes for drastic penetration of Spanish America, but they were either poorly executed or not even attempted. After that, Spain had the good fortune that Britain was involved in a quarrel with its North American colonists in 1763–1783. But even that did not end the expansion of British America. Frontiersmen began to move over the mountains before the American Revolution. Then after 1783 the

westward movement in the new United States became a flood.

Some of the advantage gained by the improved Spanish administration, economy, military organization, and diplomatic position was used for defensive expansion. The fact that the French and British positions in North America by the late seventeenth and early eighteenth centuries were coming perilously close to the Spanish outposts further promoted Spain's moves. The resources of the vast region were not needed by Spain; the territory involved merely represented space and military points to fend off movement toward the rich heart of Mexico. The expansion was a gigantic delaying action. The individual actions were much less important than the great objective they helped gain for Spain: yet another century for consolidation in the heart of the empire. The local strength of Spanish positions increased only marginally, being but lightly bolstered with a few colonists and soldiers. Florida, Louisiana, Texas, and California received only the small reinforcement that could be spared from defense and exploitation of what were then much more important territories. The North American positions finally were lost, but they had been buffers, not integral parts of the empire. The loss was inevitable because in the eighteenth century the Spanish world continued to fall behind Britain and France technologically and economically, and thus militarily. Spain's ability to protect the heart of the empire depended mainly on consolidation and growth there rather than on defensive expansion. And in any case, expansion was more important in South than in North America. In terms of actually integrating new or loosely held territory into the empire, the most important arena for Spain and its heirs was the contest with Portugal in southern South America. The Río de la Plata basin and adjacent areas were a rich prize and essential to Spanish communications. There was also a larger local Spanish American population with which to work than in the wastes from California to Florida. No empire can do everything. Spain accomplished a great task in preserving as much as it did.

In the War of the Spanish Succession (1701–1714), Spain had to fight for its new dynasty. Various states, including Britain, wanted to prevent union of French and Spanish strength as a French Bourbon mounted the throne of Spain. There were fleet actions and amphibious operations in the Caribbean. The fortifications at Cartagena made it an important base for allied France and Spain. A British fleet surveyed the complex of fortresses in 1711 and judged it too strong to be taken. Extensive warfare occurred in Europe and some in northeastern North America involving French and British. There was much small-scale action in southern North America involving Spaniards. The treaties at the end of the war transferred French Newfoundland, Nova Scotia (Acadia), and the Hudson Bay settlements and claims to Britain; also to Britain went Spanish Gibraltar and the *asiento* (license) for supplying the Spanish colonies with slaves and some trade goods. The remaining Spanish Netherlands were ceded to Austria. Spanish and French losses certainly justified increased fear of British strength and intentions. The *asiento*, as a legal wedge into the Spanish closed trade ideal, was to prove especially troublesome in America. The treaty provisions as a whole were illustrative of the interconnections of European and American issues. The Spanish government necessarily adopted an imperial point of view, and its decisions—on treaties and many other matters—were bound to irritate colonials who had a more parochial interest.

Spain in North America, 1680s–1740s

Defense expenditures in remote areas were part of the imperial point of view. These outlays increased from the late seventeenth century as Britain and France extended their positions in North America. The Spanish mission system among the Apalachee and Creek Indians, in western Florida and in what became Georgia, met British expansion from Carolina. In 1702 a British force from South Carolina attacked St. Augustine but was driven off. In succeeding years the British destroyed much of the Spanish mission system among the Apalachees. The Spaniards attacked British settlements in Carolina. In 1716, the Carolinians established a fort on the Savannah River. Soon thereafter the buffer colony of Georgia was formed, with Savannah founded in 1733. Other British settlements followed. Spanish resistance had achieved delay, all that could be hoped from a modest defense investment.

Conflict between Spain and France in North America involved territories from West Florida to Texas and far north into the interior of the continent. Spanish fears were aroused in the later seventeenth century by reports that France planned attacks on New Spain; they became greater when La Salle reached the mouth of the Mississippi from Canada in 1683. In 1684 news arrived in Spain that La Salle would found a colony on the Gulf Coast west of the Mississippi. He did so that year on the coast of Texas, and it endured until 1689. That was a long but poorly supported step toward the mines of New Spain, which La Salle hoped to reach.

These and other reports of French activity brought Spanish response. In 1686 a Spanish expedition in southeastern North America explored west by land from Apalachee to Mobile Bay. Far west of there, in 1686–1688 Spaniards in five coastwise expeditions explored the Gulf of Mexico from Veracruz to Texas; one of them discovered the wrecks of La Salle's vessels. Meanwhile, expeditions went in 1686 from Monterrey and Monclova, in the northern interior of New Spain, to the east. They reached the gulf at the mouth of the Rio Grande and moved north of there in 1687–1689, finding the remains of the La Salle settlement at Matagorda Bay, just after it had been destroyed by Indians. In 1690 a Spanish expedition crossed Texas from the south and founded two missions among the Asinai (Tejas) Indians on the Neches River, near the present boundary of Louisiana. But the Asinai Indians were hostile and communications with New Spain poor, so in 1693 the missionaries withdrew. The eastern Texas project was abandoned for a time, and Spain focused attention on West Florida, which was in danger from the British in Carolina and the French from the Mississippi area.

Spain and France made a series of further moves in the 1690s and early eighteenth century. The French in 1699 settled at Biloxi but in 1702 moved from there eastward to Mobile Bay, closer to Pensacola. Then, after their collaboration in the War of the Spanish Succession, France and Spain in 1713 continued their rivalry in North America. The French tried to open trade with the Spanish colonies in New Spain. In 1713 a French expedition went to Natchitoches in what is now western Louisiana. In 1718 French New Orleans was founded. The Spaniards, in the meantime, after the withdrawal from eastern Texas in 1693, had discussed further efforts in Texas but did little until French traders began arriving there in 1714. A council of war in Mexico decided to reoccupy eastern Texas with missions, a garrison, and a small Spanish colony. An expedition in February 1716 left Saltillo with sixty-five persons, including nine friars and twenty-five soldiers. It went through the great vacant spaces some six hundred miles from Saltillo to eastern Texas and established a mission and presidio among the Asinai Indians. To support isolated eastern Texas, an intermediate post was erected at San Antonio, between Monterrey and eastern Texas, with a mission, presidio, and town.

War between France and Spain began in early 1719 because of dynastic rivalries between them in Italy. In America it became a frontier conflict over a vast area. In 1719 the French from Mobile took Pensacola. The French from Natchitoches drove the Spaniards from eastern Texas to San Antonio. In 1720 an expedition under Pedro de Vallazur went from New Spain all the way to the South Platte River, where Indians using French weapons wiped it out. Although peace was concluded in Europe in 1720, maneuvering continued in America. The governor of Coahuila left Monclova in 1720 with an expedition of more than five hundred armed men, and by 1722

he had reestablished the mission and presidios in east Texas. The French objected that he had improved the Spanish position. Texas was made a province separate from Coahuila at this time, with its capital at Los Adaes (now Robeline, Louisiana), not far from the French position at Natchitoches. But in succeeding years Texas remained little populated. By these and other actions Spain secured Texas against France, which had enough other territorial problems to engage it, and in any event had again become allied with Spain. But Spanish efforts in Texas—and in the Floridas, Carolina, and Georgia—only kept a finger in the dike and attempted no radical improvement of the Spanish position there. That policy was certainly sensible.

The Wars of 1739–1783

War occupied more than half the years between 1739 and 1783. In the three big wars, France bore more of the fighting with Britain than did Spain. France also bore most of the territorial losses in America. The Spanish loss of the Floridas in 1763 was offset by the transfer to it of Louisiana by France. The American Revolutionary War cut into British ability or desire to hit Spanish America, and Spain got Florida back. The big dangers for Spain from the American Revolution did not stem, however, from Britain. One was the expansion of the British colonists in North America, which Britain could not even control before their independence and which Spanish frontier actions thereafter could affect but little. The other danger was that possibly Spanish American colonials might be moved to imitate the revolution. The inception of that North American revolt was entirely beyond Spanish control, and its success was due only marginally to Spanish participation in the war against Britain.

The 1714 peace, ending the War of the Spanish Succession, had been merely a truce. Spain and Britain were on a collision course. British merchants had traded heavily and illegally with Spanish America for years. They simply rejected

Spain's claim that it was entitled to keep them out. The fact that they abused the new *asiento* of 1714 by sending more trade goods into Spanish America than the license allowed changed nothing. A change was attempted, however, by Spanish officials after the War of the Spanish Succession. They tried to tighten controls. One way was by commissioning *guarda-costas*, private profit-seeking vessels. The ships' gains were shared by the commissioning officials and even by the magistrates who decided disputes that arose over procedures and values. The natural result was that British rights received little attention from Spanish mariners or judges. British mercantile interests complained to London. One Captain Jenkins, claiming to have lost an ear to brutal Spanish coast guards, helped whip up a "patriotic" war that began in 1739. Although France did not join this War of Jenkins' Ear, it did make public its alliance with Spain and gave notice that it would not let Britain expand in the West Indies. The first Bourbon Family Compact, thus announced, had been concluded secretly between France and Spain in 1733.

Britain decided to try again to dismember the Spanish empire. In 1739 it took Portobelo in the Isthmus of Panama as a first step in an effort to control that strategic area. The plan came to grief in 1740 when a large amphibious assault under Admiral Vernon failed miserably at Cartagena, partly because of incompetent planning in Britain and leadership at Cartagena. Vernon also failed in an attack on Santiago de Cuba. These disasters ruined the plan to seize the isthmus by collaboration between Vernon in the Caribbean and a squadron under Commodore Anson in the Pacific. Anson's unsupported attacks on the Spaniards in the Pacific had little effect except to alarm Spain further and stimulate more defensive preparations. By 1740 the war had merged into the general War of the Austrian Succession (ended in 1748), and again American and European issues became inextricably mixed in policy decisions. Spain lost no territory in the peace settlements; it had shown considerable defensive capability; and it secured termination of

the British *asiento*, a gain of more symbolic than practical significance. Most important, the war had further aggravated British-French rivalry, and it was clear that another war loomed ahead. The fate of the Spanish empire thus depended heavily on what the other powers were determined and able to do, not just to the Spanish world, but to each other.

The next war soon began, with clashes between France and Britain during the expeditions of George Washington and Edward Braddock on the Virginia frontier in the early 1750s. In 1756 that conflict merged into the general European Seven Years' War (ended in 1763). It involved not only the usual campaigns in Europe, but a widening of the British-French colonial duel from Canada and the West Indies to African waters and the Indian Ocean. In 1761 France persuaded Spain to agree to the second family compact, and in 1762 to join the war against Britain. One immediate result was that Britain took Havana, a shattering blow to the Spanish position.

The peace of 1763 had a more drastic effect on colonial matters than anything before it. France had to give up huge possessions in India and North America. Britain solved the Canadian problem by simply insisting on its ownership of the whole of France's claims there and east of the Mississippi River. The French ceded their trans-Mississippi claims ("Louisiana") to their ally Spain, both as compensation for losses and for the defense of the Louisiana country against the rampaging British, which the Spanish were better able to carry out. Spain traded its Floridas to Britain in return for Havana. Spain clearly now faced a great threat from the British.

Soon the American Revolution (1775–1783) presented Spain with the chance to help its ally France against Britain. It had doubts, however, as to the wisdom of aiding a colonial people in America to independence, fearing the effects on Spanish Americans. Spain finally did enter the war, reluctantly, in 1779, reconquered positions in former Spanish Florida, and seized British Honduras and the Bahamas. Spanish Louisiana gave aid to American rebels in the Ohio country. After the peace it seemed that the effort had not been worth the expense. Spain did get its Florida possessions back from Britain. But the latter granted to its victorious colonies the territory from the Appalachian Mountains to the Mississippi, thus giving the new United States a common frontier with Spanish Louisiana and Florida. Another unfortunate result from the Spanish point of view was that France's expenditures in the war helped bring on the French Revolution only a few years later (1789), transforming Spain's ally into a new and uncertain, and soon aggressive, power.

Spain in North America, 1763–1800

Spain in the late colonial era built a huge paper tiger in North America. By the decisions of 1763 it held all the Gulf Coast west of British Florida to Mexico and everything west of the Mississippi to the sea except for some disputed parts of the Pacific coast. But there were almost no Spaniards in that huge area. Expansion from New Spain in the west had by the end of the seventeenth century reached into Lower California and soon thereafter into what is now Arizona. That country was difficult and subject to Indian raids. In the Pacific north of Lower California the Spaniards had often cruised but never settled. They became worried, however, about Russian expansion south from Alaska, where subjects of the Czar were fur trading in mid-century. To counter the Russian movement, Spain in 1769 sent from Lower California a military expedition by land and sea under Gaspar de Portolá, accompanied by the missionary Friar Junípero Serra. A mission and presidio were founded at San Diego, within the borders of the present-day United States, in 1769. A few other towns, presidios, and missions were set up in succeeding years from San Francisco (1776) to Los Angeles (1781).

To counter rumored Russian expansion, in 1774 the viceroy of New Spain sent the Juan Pérez expedition north by sea. It explored Nootka Sound in the vicinity of the present Canada–United States border. There were expeditions by Spaniards to the area in the later 1770s. In 1778 the English explorer Captain James Cook reached Nootka Sound and a diplomatic crisis ensued. By treaty in the 1790s Spain agreed that other nationals could trade and settle north of San Francisco where the Spaniards were not in possession of the territory. Also in the 1790s the new United States began asserting claims to the area by right of exploration.

Spain had acquired Louisiana from France in 1763 for strategic reasons. She did little to develop the vast territory. It proved a drain on Spanish resources. Even getting sullen acquiescence in the new regime from the French inhabitants required a considerable military effort, and they needed coddling thereafter. There were only about 10,000 non-Indian inhabitants in all the poorly defined territory. Most of the non-Indian population was in the far south, near the Gulf of Mexico and New Orleans. Most of the potential immigrants, as the following decades would prove, were in British America. In the Indian lands to the north and west, Spain depended on French traders rather than trying to expand its own missionary system. The Spaniards ultimately supported traders far up the Missouri River, and opened overland trading routes between far-off Santa Fe in New Mexico and St. Louis on the upper Mississippi, Natchitoches in what is now Louisiana, and San Antonio in Texas.

Unfortunately for Spain, its positions were merely flimsy outposts in the wilderness; it was overextended. The thin commercial and communications network of the interior soon was menaced by British-American traders. At the time of the American Revolution, Spain lost the Missouri trade to the British, so the northern part of the Louisiana country was passing out of its control. During and after the American Revolution, Anglo-Americans moved west of the Alleghenies, and by 1800 citizens of the United States both within and outside Louisiana were putting pressure on New Orleans and West Florida.

One result of the Spanish advance into Louisiana was that it led to a decision that eastern Texas could be allowed to decay. Nor did the rest of Texas receive much attention during the half century from the acquisition of Louisiana in 1763 to the independence of Mexico in 1821. Texas lay virtually unpopulated when citizens of the United States under Stephen Austin were allowed to enter in the 1820s. It is open to question whether Spanish ownership of Louisiana in 1763–1800 (when it was retroceded to France) was worth the expenditure. Texas would have been a more feasible defense line. It would have been closer to reinforcement from Mexico and increased the logistic strain on invaders coming by land. Possibly the strongest justification for the delaying action on advanced lines in Louisiana was that building a strong loyal population base in Texas would be difficult. Thus, if Louisiana fell to an aggressive enemy, a defense would have to be improvised for Texas from outside resources in any event.

The wars and frontier action of the years to 1783 posed worry enough, but the big disasters were yet to come: the accession to the Spanish throne in 1788 of the incompetent Charles IV, and the wars of the French Revolution and Napoleon in 1792–1815.

f. Continuation of Spanish-Portuguese Conflict

In the eighteenth century, Spanish-Portuguese rivalry in America continued to be of major consequence in the disputed lands of the south and of minor importance in Amazonia. The disputed southern lands formed a great wedge from the Atlantic to the Uruguay and tributary rivers, some 250 to 325 miles inland, and from the estuary of La Plata some 650 miles north to the eastern borders of Paraguay and almost to the southern boundary of the Brazilian state of São Paulo of today. This great wedge comprised some 250,000 square miles, roughly the present-day republic of Uruguay, the Argentine state of Misiones, and the Brazilian states of Rio Grande do Sul and Santa Catarina—an imperial domain in European terms. It was lightly populated but clearly had economic potential. Strategically, much of the area seemed essential to the protection of other territories: for Spain, the entrance to the continent toward Paraguay and the land route to Tucumán and Upper Peru; for Portugal, the supply and protection of her central position in São Paulo, Minas Gerais, and Rio de Janeiro.

Paulista pressure on the Jesuit missions no longer was much of an issue, because the latter had moved south of easy reach by the *bandeiras*, and more important because imperial interest after the late seventeenth century was concentrated on the Plata estuary and the shores of what is now southern Brazil. Colônia do Sacramento, on the estuary, which was restored to Portugal in 1683, maintained a precarious existence thereafter, an isolated military-commercial outpost far from the rest of Portuguese America. It was an aggressive assertion of the Portuguese claim to a boundary at the Plata. In 1705 Colônia fell for a second time to Spanish troops, only to be restored again by treaty because of European considerations and reoccupied by the Portuguese in 1716. At the same time, expansion south from São Paulo into Santa Catarina was proceeding but slowly. South of Santa Catarina lay Rio Grande do Sul, where the Portuguese began to take possession in 1737, a large stride toward the Plata estuary and toward closing the gap between Colônia and the rest of Portuguese America. In 1735–1737 an undeclared war in the Plata area involved attacks on Spanish Montevideo and Portuguese Colônia before the two powers agreed to try to settle their American problems. Tension continued until a treaty was finally concluded in 1750. The Spaniards were convinced that Colônia drew off much silver from Peru by illicit trade, that Portuguese claims on the estuary retarded Spanish development there, and that the Portuguese position represented a continual threat of British involvement on the side of its ally. Portuguese statesmen had

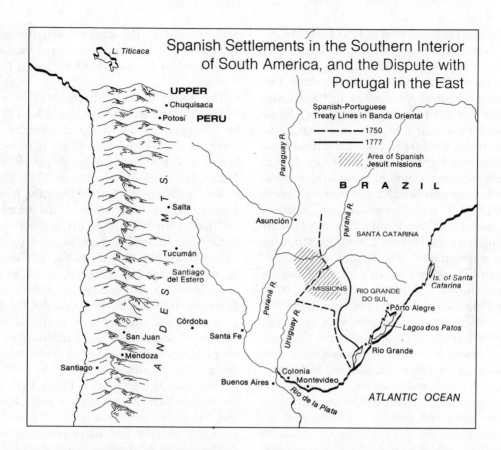

Spanish Settlements in the Southern Interior of South America, and the Dispute with Portugal in the East

become convinced that Colônia was indefensible and that it was better to concentrate on the defense of Rio Grande do Sul, which was held only lightly on or near the coast. Portugal wanted expansion into the interior, including the Spanish Jesuit Seven Missions area, to consolidate its hold on coastal Rio Grande.

The Treaty of Madrid (1750) was a compromise that generally accepted the principle of *uti possidetis*—actual possession—for the determination of territorial jurisdiction, a principle that made much sense for all of Latin America with its huge territories, small and scattered populations, and unsurveyed boundaries. Exceptions to the principle in 1750 were that Portugal gave up its claims to Colônia and the rest of the Plata estuary, and Spain ceded the Jesuit Seven Missions area between the Ibicuí and Uruguay rivers, promising to move the Jesuits and Indians

out of it. Commissioners were to set the boundaries. The line was to run generally through present-day southern Brazil, leaving part of it and the present republic of Uruguay to Spain. There was opposition to the treaty in Spain, Portugal, and the Seven Missions. Combined Spanish-Portuguese armies of some four thousand troops finally were required in 1754–1756 to defeat Indian resistance to movement. So many disputes and suspicions arose that the two countries in 1761 agreed to abrogate the treaty of 1750.

Spain had by that time determined to challenge Portuguese settlement far to the north in Rio Grande do Sul and Santa Catarina. At the same time, Spain's blockade of Colônia was tightened. In 1762 Spain and Portugal were at war, and Colônia in that year was captured for the third time by the Spaniards. Governor Pedro de Cevallos of Buenos Aires took an expedition of about one thousand men in 1763 from Montevideo, through the Banda Oriental to coastal Rio Grande do Sul. There he heard of the end of the Seven Years' War and had to cut short this promising offensive. Ambiguities in the treaties after the war led to more disagreement: Spain claimed for the next fourteen years that it had only to return Colônia to Portugal but retained its rights far to the north in Rio Grande do Sul. Portugal of course disagreed. Spain's claim represented a dangerous Spanish penetration toward the heart of Brazil. Portuguese and Brazilian forces were ineffective in attacking the Spanish position, at times because Lisbon preferred to discuss a compromise. The Spanish offensive resumed in 1773, when Governor Vértiz of Buenos Aires marched an expedition seven hundred miles through the Banda Oriental and into Brazil to a point north of the Spanish position on the coast, about the latitude of Pôrto Alegre, the new Portuguese capital for the Rio Grande area. But Vértiz was beaten and retreated to the Spanish position on the Lagoa dos Patos, the great navigable lagoon on the coast. By the mid-1770s, the area was dotted with Spanish and Portuguese fortified positions. By 1775 Portuguese minister Pombal had decided to give up Colônia in order to protect Santa Catarina and Rio Grande. Although he soon changed his mind, his idea was an indication of his appreciation of the threat to central Brazil.

Victories by Portuguese and Brazilian troops over Spaniards in Rio Grande do Sul in 1776 nearly ruined the Spanish position. The next year, however, a great fleet under Pedro de Cevallos came from Spain, with 116 sail, nearly 10,000 troops, and supplies for six months. Cevallos was named first head of a new Viceroyalty of La Plata. The expedition took the Island of Santa Catarina, well to the north of the Spanish position in Rio Grande on the Lagoa dos Patos. Cevallos then tried to land in the *lagoa* but was prevented by storms, so he sailed south and took Colônia, which thus fell to the Spaniards for the fourth time since its foundation in 1680. Cevallos

had dismantled the military installations and walls of the fortress and had started back to Rio Grande when news came of an armed truce in Europe.

The Treaty of San Ildefonso (1777) was influenced, as was usually the case, at least as much by European as by American issues. For one thing, Spain realized that it might soon be involved in the war for independence of Britain's North American colonies. As in 1750, Portugal ceded Colônia and retreated from the hope of a boundary at the Plata estuary. It did get a boundary line in the north that left it the Lagoa dos Patos, where there had been so much fighting in recent years, but it gave up the interior Seven Missions area it had gained by the 1750 treaty. Spain gave up its conquest of Santa Catarina Island to the north of the Lagoa dos Patos. The 1777 treaty did not end the territorial conflict between Portugal and Spain and their successor states in America. In 1801 Portugal seized the Seven Missions area and added it to Rio Grande do Sul, and in later years it invaded the Banda Oriental, which did not emerge from Argentine and Brazilian contention until 1828 as the permanently independent nation of Uruguay.

This record of warfare in the disputed lands of southern South America was indicative not only of the importance Spain and Portugal attached to the territories, but of the military resources, local and imperial, that Spain and Portugal could call up at need.[6] Those resources were much greater than this sketch has indicated, especially for prolonged defense in the interior. The rivals of Spain and Portugal were aware of those facts. To carve up Spanish or Portuguese America would have been an even more expensive venture than one or two centuries earlier. The Hispanic societies in America in three centuries became too strong for easy conquest.

---

[6] In 1775, just before the large expedition was sent from Spain against Santa Catarina and Rio Grande do Sul, Spain mounted a 400-ship, 40,000-man assault on Algiers in Africa.

PART THREE

Social and Economic Conditions in Spanish America

The white minority thrust into inferior status the lower class, which was nearly all Indian, black African, or racially mixed. Most blacks and some Indians were slaves; many Indians endured forced labor, and most were supervised wards of the crown; the mixed breeds lived amid prejudice and discrimination. It was a system of accepted and codified privilege. Status affected almost every aspect of life: access to government, including the courts; marriage; relations with the church; economic opportunity, and notably anything heavily dependent on government sanction, investment capital, landholding, or the use of large amounts of labor. While the upper class feared pretension in the lower, the latter was marked by poverty, apathy, alienation, and an accustomed use of violence.

The Spanish and Portuguese world increasingly became a subservient element in the North Atlantic economic complex. The ruling class in Spain and Portugal accepted that position because their relatively inflexible politicomilitary and economic situations permitted other powers to impose costly economic terms upon them. Iberia accepted the terms because its elites did not want to adopt the internal reform necessary to the creation of institutions that permitted economic development, lest that disturb the dominance of the upper class. That class thus accepted increased dependence on external industrial, commercial, and financial forces. In Spain the decision resulted in large measure also from an insistence on foreign policies that had important religious and political motives but were only partly connected with economic considerations. Those policies helped determine expenditures in the Spanish world and reduced the possibility of stimulating economic development and improving defense of the Atlantic trading system. Thus, dependence shored up social patterns—social rigidity, including controls on bourgeois authority and innovation, great estates, a subservient peasantry, and intellectual and technical backwardness. Portugal sustained itself largely by agreeing to British domination of much of its commercial-industrial system. The

Spanish world was much stronger and was sustained by its internal resources, including bullion from America and a strong offensive and defensive military position.

The economy of Spanish America was marked by low productivity and purchasing power; scarce and poorly organized capital available only to a small minority; land transportation so costly as to be a major barrier to effective economic activity; massive use of monopolistic practices; rather limited exports, especially when the large silver flow is considered a special case; little exchange between the American realms; a widespread but small-scale manufacturing or handicraft sector that found competition with European-made goods progressively more difficult; and the growth of the great estate system and its accompanying peon labor. These things grew out of social policies in the Spanish world and European advantages in production and distribution, and neither could be easily changed. That was not perceived by those colonials who developed the idea that freer trade and generally lessened economic restriction would work a magic transformation. The later experience of the independent states showed the difficulty of breaking the circle of poverty and dependence, of reducing European sales to America or increasing American sales abroad, of altering property patterns and the productive culture of the region.

All aspects of society, including the economic, were affected by the church. It inculcated some Christianity among the lower class, although belief remained mixed with African and Indian elements, because of both insufficient church services and the church's concentration of interest on the Spanish society. For the upper class, the church helped define political loyalty and regulate reading, education, and public expression. Formal instruction was extended to only a tiny minority. Education for the elite had a humanistic emphasis; this, combined with censorship and fear of intellectual innovation, made the Spanish world a technological backwater as other European peoples pressed on into the scientific and industrial age.

Within these patterns there were considerable variety of detail and mix, continual change, and notably in the eighteenth century, a simultaneous persistence and alteration of institutions: (*a*) Strong class lines and socioracial distinctions amounting to caste continued to the end. (*b*) Class structure was complicated by the accumulating influence of *mestizaje* (race mixture), which made increasingly difficult the application of socioracial distinctions and was a source of fluidity, pressure, and tension in the society. (*c*) Indian slavery virtually ended, but forced and dependent Indian labor continued to the end. Black slavery declined in some areas, notably New Spain and Peru, and increased in others, especially the Plata and the Caribbean. There was a modest increase of free wage labor. (*d*) The haciendas grew to the end and with peonage were to be a continuing influence after Independence. (*e*) The governmental system was relatively unchanging, and creole dissatisfaction with it increased toward the end of the period. (*f*) In the economic realm there was much change in details over time but little in fundamentals, although regional activity often altered substantially. Economic growth in the eighteenth century increased creole impatience with Spanish restrictions, especially where agricultural and pastoral export opportunities increased. For nearly three centuries, however, creoles collaborated with peninsular Spaniards in the government, exploitation, and .defense of the realms.

8 Population, Class and Caste, and Labor Systems

One dominant and two subordinate races, plus exploitation and promiscuity, resulted in race mixture and bastardy—important though unplanned results of Spain's activity in America. The ingredients were a few hundred thousand Spaniards, about a million blacks carried from Africa in chains, and 30 to 50 million conquered Indians. Another unplanned result of the conquest was that millions of Indians died of abuse and Old World diseases. Enough remained, however, to make Indians the largest element in the racial stew. The racial situation complicated the class system carried from Europe, so that a *socio-racial* structure resulted. No aspect of life in the colonial era was more formative of institutions and attitudes, of pride and misery and bitterness, than notions of class and caste. Those divisions by status were especially reflected in colonial labor systems, and the "degradation of the labor forces" was the "predominant social legacy" of colonial Latin America.[1]

a. Population

Race and Numbers

Dense populations of Indians existed in 1492 chiefly in what are now Guatemala, central and southern Mexico, and the mountain and coastal regions of Ecuador, Peru, and Bolivia. In those areas, comprising only some 15 percent of North and South America, lived 80 to 90 percent of the Indians. Most estimates of the Indian population at the conquest range between 30 and 50 million, but many lower and higher figures have been offered.[2] The Indian population dwindled sadly for about a century after the first contact with Europeans and then increased modestly after the low point of the seventeenth century. Indians almost disappeared from the Antilles.[3] The best-regarded studies for central Mexico show a horrendous Indian decline, from possibly 19 million in 1519 to about 1 million in 1605. In the Inca area, Indians declined from some 5 million at the conquest to 1.5 million in 1561 and to 800,000 in 1800. In the central Mexican and Inca areas the dwindling of the Indians was seen in reduced

[1] Stanley and Barbara Stein, *The Colonial Heritage of Latin America* (New York, 1970).

[2] Latter-day specialists have used a variety of concepts and sources, some of them ingeniously contrived, without ending the controversy. See Chapter 1 on the importance of the dispute, and also for the geographical distribution of Indians.

[3] The Caribs in the Lesser Antilles put up a serious resistance to French, British, and Dutch settlement in the seventeenth century, but by 1660 they were practically confined to the islands of Dominica and St. Vincent, where there were as yet no permanent European settlements.

work forces and tribute rolls, abandoned huts, and once productive fields gone to weed.

The white population of Spanish America was small for many decades. There were only some 100,000 whites in the mid-sixteenth century, and 160,000 in 1574. In the sixteenth and seventeenth centuries, only 200,000 to 300,000 Spaniards went to America. When, therefore, the white population of Spanish America toward the end of the colonial era was estimated at 3 million, most of them were creoles, since peninsular Spaniards were still few in number. The creoles often had some Indian or black genetic heritage.

Possibly 1 to 1.5 million black slaves were carried to colonial Spanish America.[4] There were few in the conquest period, and perhaps only 54,000 in 1575. Some 200,000 were taken by 1650, probably more than half of them to New Spain. During much of the colonial era the largest black slave and Afromestizo population was in Mexico and Peru, with the next most important concentration in New Granada. After the mid-seventeenth century, increased imports of slaves built up the black populations of Cuba, Puerto Rico, New Granada, Venezuela, and the Plata area. There were blacks and Afromestizos in the Spanish towns; in all the major mining areas, notably north central New Spain, Upper Peru, and in the gold placers of the western lowlands of New Granada; and in the sugar industry in the Caribbean, the subtropical valleys of Mexico, and the river bottoms of the Peruvian coastal desert. Blacks worked on cattle haciendas, often as supervisors, and in tropical ports, where they endured the work better than Indians. The percentage of black African stock in Spanish America was less than in Portuguese Brazil or in British North America because the Indians of Peru and Mexico provided ample labor. Alexander von Humboldt, who lived in Spanish America at the end of the colonial era, estimated

that in 1810 there were 776,000 Negroes there, about 4 percent of a total population of 17 million. In the United States in 1820 some 18 percent of the 9.63 million was black or mulatto. Brazil at the end of the colonial period (1822) had a population of some 3.61 million, and more (perhaps much more) than half was black and mulatto.

After the total population of Spanish America sank to a low point of possibly 5 million early in the seventeenth century, it began to grow. The rise in numbers was especially marked in the eighteenth century. The total of some 17 million at the end of the colonial era was still heavily (possibly 50 percent) Indian, although some areas had very few Indians. By then on the order of 30 percent of the population was of mixed racial heritage, 12 to 19 percent was white or largely white, and 4 to 6 percent was black or largely black. So the three colonial centuries left Spanish America with a population smaller than at the conquest, with a multiracial character.

Settlement Patterns and Movements

The largest Indian populations remained in the mountains where they were at the conquest, and much of the white population, with its black slaves, also moved there. There were several reasons. Indian laborers who moved out of the highlands did not perform well and died rapidly; so it was most efficient to use Indians in agriculture in areas they were accustomed to. The great mining areas were in the mountains. Higher elevations were more healthful and offered more protection against intruders. Populations were smaller in other areas, especially before the latter part of the eighteenth century.

The European Town in America. The Spaniard in America was essentially a town dweller. In Old and New World, town life was more comfortable and pleasant than rural, and the town was the center of power and preferment. Privileged Spaniards in Europe generally preferred town life, and even Spanish peasants who

---

[4] The data are spotty, but probably that order of magnitude is correct. The fact that slaves often were introduced illegally contributes to the shakiness of the estimates. See Chapter 9, Section a, for more statistics on the slave trade and on black and Afromestizo populations.

went to America lived in town. Towns were established during the conquest to authenticate the actions of captains; to serve as administrative, supply, exploration, and military centers; to handle the allocation of housing lots, facilitating the erection of residences for the conquerors; and to direct the building of churches and such other appurtenances of civilization as gibbets, jails, and cemeteries. The Spanish towns, as time went on, held many Indians, blacks, and people of mixed race, who did most of the work. Sometimes Indians inhabited special districts in the Spanish towns, but often they lived in the houses of their masters. The racial variety of Spanish towns in America made them very different from those of Spain.

There was nothing about the countryside to appeal to Spaniards, except the prestige of estate ownership and the possibility of profits (preferably by absentee ownership). Travel was tedious and perilous. A person on country lands was isolated, forced to associate only with family, a few neighbors, and chance travelers. So upper-class landowners left estate operation to majordomos. Even to sell the produce of the estate or arrange to add to holdings or to improve one's title or borrow money, the city was the place for the landowner to make the arrangements.[5]

There were 225 Spanish towns and cities in Spanish America in 1580, and 331 in 1630. Some were mere hamlets with a handful of Spanish householders. Mexico City, the largest, assertedly had 30,000 people in 1524, most of them Indians (there were only some 12,000 Spaniards in all Mexico as late as 1570). In 1800 the population of the city may have been about 140,000, which was large even for European cities at that time. Lima as late as 1700 had only about 30,000, but it grew to 80,000 in the course of the century, whites always comprising a minority of the inhabitants. Buenos Aires grew slowly from its permanent establishment in 1580, to some 10,000 in 1744, and 40,000 in 1800. Potosí, the silver town

in the mountains of Upper Peru, may have reached 150,000, but it fell off quickly when silver production dwindled. Havana was a small town until the eighteenth century; it had some 48,000 people in 1791, and 80,000 in 1817. Guatemala had possibly 25,000 in 1800. Montevideo, founded in 1726, had about 7,000 in 1820. The towns were the vital points of the empire, residence of the governmental, economic, and spiritual lords of the land, nodal points for the hinterlands.

Indian Villages.   Much of the population of Spanish America lived in Indian villages. Some concentrations continued from preconquest times, and others resulted from Spanish congregation of Indians. Many aspects of village life were relatively unchanged from the days before the conquest, and we have seen that the Spanish administration made some effort to insulate it from change.[6]

Latifundios.   The great estates (*latifundios* or haciendas), depending largely on Indian or mestizo labor, appeared in the seventeenth century and grew throughout the rest of the colonial era. They became an important type of residential pattern. Often the population of the estate was not large, but its continuance depended on controlling many of the Indians living in villages nearby. Population was also clustered on tropical agricultural estates, or plantations, worked by black slave labor.

Mining Camps.   Most mining camps remained just that; only a few turned into sizable towns. The larger camps had considerable elements of Indian forced labor or black slaves, although free wage hands increased over time. The camps usually were in isolated situations, with predominantly male, and often boisterous, populations.

---

[5] See Chapter 10, Section d, on the residence of *hacendados* in town.

[6] See Chapter 6, Section b, on law and government for Indians; and Chapter 8, Section b, for the Indians and class and caste, Section c, the Indian upper class, and Section d, the Indian lower class.

Those factors, together with concern for the royal share of the product, caused the government to give them special legal, administrative, and other attentions.

Ports. These specialized towns were distinguished by occupations connected with seafaring and maritime traffic, with cargo movement and storage, customs houses, and attention to defense. Sometimes, too, they were distinguished by unsalubrious and fatiguing climate and by the attentions of pirates and the more formal foreign enemies of Spain. Some ports were given elaborate fortifications. They were also noted for the temptations of contraband trade with foreigners and for the inability of private and public figures to resist such temptations. Their size and location were determined by economic, military, and administrative factors. The vigor, or even the existence, of some depended almost entirely on public policy rather than on private economic activity.

Missions and Presidios. Not many Europeans resided at most missions, which were in frontier areas afflicted with problems of pacifying and Christianizing Indians and sometimes pressures from foreign powers. There might be only a single friar or at most a handful; sometimes a small military post, often with a dozen or fewer men; possibly a merchant or two, more or less permanently established adjacent to the *presidio*. The number of Indians at a mission varied from a few score to several thousand.[7]

Others. Other places of work and residence held small numbers of people: fishing villages by the sea; the camps of woodcutters, charcoal burners, sawmill operators, and shipwrights; salt works; great conventual structures in the countryside, often with only a few European religious and many Indians who aided them in their religious work, tilled the gardens, ran the kitchens,

and scrubbed the floors. Other small concentrations of population were pearl fisheries, independent settlements of runaway slaves, semipermanent pirate havens, the shifting or permanent shelters of "wild" Indians, the camps of muleteers, and the communities of professional bandits who scourged many parts of Spanish America.

Wherever they lived people generally stayed put. To move meant exchanging family, friends, accustomed methods of earning and borrowing and community aid for hunger, the fatigues and dangers of travel, and fears of unknown perils. A minority of Indian villagers became vagabonds or grasped new enterprise and moved out of their natal valleys to try mule skinning or silver mining. Those who remained behind had little incentive to explore widely. Most residents of Spanish towns were no more mobile. It was, then, a society in which a person tended to stay in a locality, as was true of most of the world. Most people observed little of what went on outside their valley or town nor were their horizons broadened by literacy or by the institutions of the civil and ecclesiastical administrations.

b. Class and Caste in Spain and America

Class divisions and special privilege were the norm in Spain and the rest of Europe when America was discovered. They certainly were as strong an element in Spain as anywhere, having been nurtured by the *Reconquista*, the long military struggle against the Muslims. All the European nobility were set apart, however, by titles, privileges, immunities, and differential courtesy. In Spain, although the upper nobility were town dwellers, they were distinguished as the owners of country estates. That association of upper-class status with land inevitably was transferred to the Indies. The Spanish nobles were also set apart by their life-style, though rich merchants might equal them in ostentation and poor clerics surpass them in learning. The *hidalgos*, a numerous lower nobility, had legal privileges and some social distinction but usually little property. Hug-

---

[7] For the exceptional situation in the Jesuit missions of Paraguay, see Chapter 13, Section i.

ging their status, they despised manual labor as tainted with social inferiority. There was vertical mobility in Spain but not much. Not many poor boys became learned prelates, gained distinction in military forces dominated by the aristocracy, or elevated themselves by accumulating wealth. Although much of the barrier to social mobility was economic, it was also social. Poor boys were taught by the church to accept the place God had given them.

The crown depended on church and nobility for services and support, although it also used the bourgeoisie to control those privileged groups.[8] This helped fragment power to the benefit of the crown. The greater nobility were channeled into a relatively few high positions and roles as courtiers. In Castile and León, not long after the discovery of America, 13 percent of the population was noble (mostly *hidalgos*) and thus paid no taxes. In addition, they seldom worked, and thus were a burden on the rest of the population. Peasants were a large majority and few of them were landowners. Of peasants and the urban proletariat, the crown expected loyalty and uncomplaining labor. The nearly dead Iberian parliaments (*cortes*) were organized by estates—nobility, clergy, and wealthy townsmen; that is, there was no direct representation for the proletariat. In summary, the crown depended on a system of class distinctions and privilege as a method of social and political control. It granted special rights (*fueros*) to such groups as towns, the church, merchant and craft guilds, universities, and the military. Thus it further fragmented the privileged minority in Spain, making portions of it dependent on the crown in different and sometimes conflicting ways.

Division and privilege were fortified by religious and racial distinctions in minor but not insignificant ways. There was some discrimination against the small group of Negro slaves in Spain. More important were discrimination and persecution of Muslims and Jews, even of con-

verts to Christianity from those faiths because of fear that conversion had been insincere, as sometimes was true. Persecution occurred, also, because of sheer bigotry and because of a variety of pressures for it from within Spanish society, including some of an economic nature. Some *conversos* (forced or voluntary Jewish converts to Christianity) contributed to persecution of Jews as a means of solidifying their own position as "New Christians." Some of the latter had married into prominent "Old Christian" families.

Then in America the crown depended on a privileged class,[9] and it, in turn, depended on the imperial system to help maintain its position against revolt and encroachment from below. The church fully supported the class system in Spain and America. Poor Spanish immigrants to America, far from quarreling with the class system, wanted to move into the elite. The Spaniards who went to America did not include groups believing in types of egalitarianism; there were no Pilgrims or Quakers in Mexico and Peru. Although there were great differences of property and status between whites in colonial Spanish America, most of them stood together against all the rest of the inhabitants.

In this critical way the Spanish use of social distinctions as a method of control was reinforced in America by the presence of large conquered or enslaved populations. The fact that the latter were non-European meant that the factors of race and subordination inevitably were intermingled, so that we can speak of *socioracial* distinction and discrimination in America. Class division was made the easier for the Spaniards because many Indians were also accustomed to privilege and subordination in their own hierarchical social systems. Division was provided by the law that made Indians, and often also free mulattoes and blacks, subject to the tribute, a head tax that distinguished them from Spaniards (peninsular and creole). A similar tax distinction existed in Spain between peasants and

---

[8] See Chapter 6, Section a.

[9] See Chapter 10, Section a, for a discussion of privilege and concentrated wealth.

nobles (including *hidalgos*), suggesting that in America all Spaniards were *hidalgos*.

The vanquished Indians and the black African slaves became fixed in the minds of their conquerors and owners as being both subordinate and inferior. This attitude derived not only from the weakness and servility of the Indians and Negroes but from what was thought to be their lower culture, including dress, language, and recent and only partial conversion to Christianity. These notions were intensified by fear, by the felt need of the upper class to build the sense of subordination as a barrier against revolt. The elite felt more menaced by the masses in America than in Spain, partly because of the recency of the conquest and enslavement. The class system could not be thought as securely entrenched as in Europe. Partly, the menace leapt to the eye because the physical differences between white rulers and darker ruled made obvious the numerical disparity between them.

c. The Upper Class in America

The most important aspect of the system of socioracial distinction was the division between whites and others. Thus, for most purposes we can regard creoles and peninsulars as parts of one Spanish upper class.[10] The Indian *caciques* for some purposes were conceded by the Spaniards to be upper class, as they legally were. But their privileges did not affect the inferior status that the bare fact of being an Indian almost always gave, certainly in the minds of most Spaniards. They had some power, especially in the early decades, but it declined in time, partly because with the fall in the numbers of Indians the Spaniards squeezed property out of the *cacique* class. At the end of the colonial era the social status of a *cacique* was far below that of a creole. *Caciques* were never, in fact, automatically accepted by all Spaniards as social equals; acceptance depended on their wealth, manners, and way of

---

[10] See Chapter 6, Section a, for a discussion of creoles and peninsulars.

life. The property of *caciques* did make their female heirs attractive to Spaniards as wives.

Non-Spaniards were tagged as "something else." Although the position of poor Spaniards doing manual labor was ambiguous, many poor Spaniards did hold themselves up as superior beings just because of their race and the cultural eminence that was presumed to be inescapable from that race. Thus, Humboldt at the end of the colonial era observed, "Any white person, although he rides his horse barefoot, imagines himself of the nobility." He also observed that the few poor whites working in agriculture did so away from their villages to avoid display of such disgraceful activity. But the origins of most Spaniards who migrated to America were lower or middle class. There was little to attract the upper class of Spain to the Indies. The ultimate seat of power was in Spain. European diplomacy and war seemed more important than disputes over a distant wilderness. Social and institutional life in Europe were better developed, and they involved the traditional families of distinction. The few great nobles of Spain who went to America did so only briefly as holders of imperial office. A fair number of poor *hidalgos* went to America, hungry for property and flaunting their status. Even more lower-class Spaniards in America claimed *hidalguía*, clawing upward in a society where status was almost everything.

There were legal restrictions on migration to Spanish America by Jews or Muslims and by Spaniards with traces of such heritage. Protestants were also excluded. Foreigners generally were banned. Despite legal and illegal exceptions to these rules, most European residents were Spanish Roman Catholics. Most of the migrants were men, partly because of legal restrictions on the migration of unattached Spanish women.

Although a majority of Spanish migrants went to America from southwest Spain, the contribution from other areas was substantial. The latter, however, did not contribute to the new colonial culture even a proportionate share of "unplanned" (not determined by church or state) traits. In the early years colonists were heavily from southern Spain, and the cultural forms they took with them became well imbedded, so that competing forms—of plows, speech, cooking—were not needed in the simple frontier environment. Why teach an Indian more than one Spanish term for a thing or more than one way of performing an operation? Furthermore, not only was the material culture of southern Spain adequate for use in America, but the costs of transportation in Spain made bringing competing forms of plows, tools, and the like from other parts of the Peninsula irrational.[11]

Since the Spaniards were part of a highly class-conscious tradition, in the Indies they continued to place emphasis on family, heritage, title, precedent, office, and great deeds deserving of distinction. Hernando Pizarro rather despised his illegitimate and illiterate half-brother Francisco, despite the fame, honors, and property achieved by the latter in his old age. But Francisco, and many another Spaniard in the Indies, worked hard and successfully to improve his status. Commonly Spanish immigrants asserted a higher social origin than they had in Spain. With money, the claim was listened to with increased respect, and they bought their way by marriage into the acknowledged upper crust. The originator of the new family might be sneered at for his origins and lack of graces, but his offspring would blend nicely into the creole upper class.

Getting ahead in the Indies, however, was complicated by the fact that many Spaniards would not do manual labor. The most acceptable occupations were landholding, government, and the church. Being a merchant was somewhat less prestigious, although rich ones could hope for acceptance by the upper group of creole landholders and peninsular officials. A few very rich artisan-proprietors, especially in jewelry and gold and silver work, were somewhat lower down the social scale, and small Spanish artisans much below.

---

[11] A similar filter may have operated in favor of the culture of a relatively restricted area of West Africa, which was carried to America by black slaves, tending to override much other African culture.

A man could become rich enough to be part of the economic elite without having been accepted in upper-class society. Such gradations within the Spanish group were clear at the time and made operational by differential courtesy, access to prestigious government and charitable offices, precedence in processions and in seating in church, ease or difficulty of intermarriage with the highest circle of society, and by social intercourse, for of course the select few knew exactly which persons were fit by status to enjoy their personal intimacy. Lacking other opportunity, an immigrant with claims to *hidalguía* (warranted or bogus) might become the client (with or without regular functions) of a wealthy and powerful man who needed messengers, advertisers, witnesses, and informal guards, and appreciated that a sizable retinue added to his consequence. Some of the poor Spaniards who swarmed around the rich and powerful in the Indies were, inevitably, threadbare cousins and nephews from the Peninsula.

There were, therefore, whites who were upper class only insofar as they could claim inclusion in a racially superior group, together with the privileges that all whites enjoyed by reason of legal discrimination against the lower class of color. But to lump such poor Spaniards (creole and peninsular) with other whites as part of a monolithic upper class is misleading. Although they could claim some aspects of status superior to Indians or Negro slaves or mestizos, they were far from the governing, economic, and social elite. Some of these *españoles* or whites worked with their hands for little pay, some even as farmers. There were Spanish servants, peddlers, and men who sank into vagrancy or criminality or moved into Indian villages to prey on the people. Such choices by whites might result from lack of talent or bad luck, but sometimes were a matter of temperament. Invincible laziness or preference for low life could find plenty of outlets in the gentle climate and violent social conditions of the Indies.

Some passage of Indian and Negro blood into the upper class was permitted, but the terms of passage emphasized that an exception was being made. Persons only partially of white ancestry sometimes were accepted into the upper class after purchasing government documents certifying their whiteness. Generally, the less the taint of non-Spanish ancestry, the easier the passage into the elite, although in some cases ancestry was less important than money or marriage ties. If his skin was very dark, a man might have to be satisfied with a more ambiguous documentary "proof" of bleaching. Although there was race in this purchase of status, the individuals could not be accepted socially, as opposed to legally, if they did not live (dress, eat, talk) in the European manner, which was a class matter. Of course, they could not change those habits without money, which also was needed to buy the certificates. So the socioracial system of distinction concentrated property in the hands of the elite, and made difficult the accumulation of wealth required for access to ultimate change in status.

Upper-class families were sensitive about the racial question. Each knew its own ancestry and much of that of its friends. Grandmothers of color could not always be hidden. Unkind remarks about such forebears in other families were bound to occur in a society constantly aware of race and its relation to social subordination.

The white upper class monopolized office in the civil, military, and church administrations. Most of the ranks of secular and regular clergy also were creoles or peninsular Spaniards. The upper class was the beneficiary of the special privileges (*fueros*) given the nobility, clergy, merchants, mine owners, and universities. A few creoles acquired titles of nobility. A considerable number of creoles acquired entails (*mayorazgos*) to protect their great rural properties from fragmentation, one means of trying to assure the continued eminence of the family and to prevent the partition of property. Although they did not always succeed, and although wealthy families became impoverished and new families rose to property and eminence, the group remained small, with an unchanged position of privilege.

The creole upper class was, of course, much larger than the peninsular and conspicuous for the way in which it set itself apart from the lower class by indulging in luxurious display, in mansions, furnishings, ceremonies, chapels, coaches and sedan chairs, and personal adornment. Material wealth put the upper class at an almost unimaginable distance from the rest of society. No wonder Spaniards (creole and peninsular) spoke of themselves as alone being decent people (*gente decente*). For them to discriminate against the other orders in matters of dress, bearing arms, taxation, access to the courts and treatment therein, and many other things came as naturally as breathing. A homely example is that when dishonest weighing of meat was detected at the Mexico City slaughterhouse in the sixteenth century, the punishment for a mulatto, mestizo, Indian, or black was a hundred lashes, and for a Spaniard only a fine of twenty pesos. Even if that punishment was not perfectly carried out, the distinction was invidious.

The oligarchic idea was never seriously threatened, remaining alive even when poverty and lack of material distinctions made its implementation weak. The so-called democracy of life around the campfires of the conquest was, of course, accompanied by a strongly marked distinction between knights (*caballeros*) and foot soldiers (*peones*). It was reflected in the division of loot (including women), the distribution of town lots and encomiendas, and the awarding of office. The class system remained essentially intact in the colonial areas where poverty is said to have reduced class distinctions. Such relative egalitarianism has been attributed to poor areas of what later was Argentina, but class survived to show renewed vigor when conditions permitted: for example, in the town of Córdoba in the seventeenth century and in Buenos Aires in the eighteenth. Finally, the class system not only endured even under adverse economic conditions, but the ranks of the upper class remained small. There was movement within and without it, but its exclusivity and power remained essentially unchanged.

d. The Lower Class in America

There is no one best way to describe the divisions of the lower class. It is useful to start with four categories: Indians, blacks (*negros* in Spanish), mestizos, and all other mixtures. The problem is partly to distinguish between legal condition and social status. As has been noted, all Spaniards were legally equal, but peninsulars claimed a *social* status somewhat above that of creoles. In legal condition, Indians ranked immediately after Spaniards, with many special protections and privileges, but in social status Indians ranked below mestizos, because the latter served the Spaniards more intimately as supervisors and other sorts of employees and were considered the intellectual superiors of Indians. That social ranking of mestizos generally was accepted in colonial society, although they sometimes were officially lumped with the other *castas de mezcla* or racially mixed persons of low estate. The comparative social rankings of Indians and blacks within the lower class varied according to many circumstances—for example, Indian holdings of black slaves, and positions held by free blacks and mulattoes as foremen over Indian and mestizo laborers.

Ambiguities were inevitable in such a society. An Indian moving to town and adopting the Spanish language and some Spanish clothing and habits was apt to be classified as a mestizo because of the way he lived or because he declared that he was mestizo. Spanish officials complained of this type of "passing." Matters of status were an almost obsessive preoccupation of the populace. If persons gave their socioracial rank for legal purposes, their statements usually had to be accepted, for who could prove a lie? Although lying to be whiter was most common, a mestizo might declare himself Indian to escape the Inquisition, or an Indian might claim to be mestizo to escape the tribute or the forced labor drafts.

The many subdivisions of the lower class were chiefly founded on race. People knew they lived in a "society of castes." On the other hand, assignment to such a subdivision was partly a matter of the property of the individual and his manner of life. In the minds of the elite, the lower class was tainted not only by race but (probably more importantly) by subordination, irrationality, poverty, bad habits of all sorts that were thought to be ineradicable, and by a pervading bastardy.

The Indian Lower Class

The reluctance of Spaniards to marry Indians suggested early that the latter would become an inferior caste. By 1501 the crown encouraged such unions, but the response was small and confined largely to Spaniards of the lowest status. A special effort was made to encourage Spaniards to wed the female heirs of *caciques* to Europeanize that group. There were early orders for *encomenderos* either to marry Indians or send for their wives in Spain. None of these efforts had much effect. Spanish resistance to marrying Indians was seen in their abandonment of concubines for European wives during the conquest. Pitiful cases occurred of Indian concubines trying to whiten their skin to compete with Spanish women. Intermarriage of Spaniards and Indians became rarer. By the mid-seventeenth century the jurist Solórzano in Peru could state, "Few honorable Spaniards marry Indians or Negroes."

Being an Indian was a very special thing, subject to burdens imposed by the Europeans. Indian status was marked by the tribute or male head tax; by forced labor; and by exemption from tithes, the sales tax, military service, and some of the attentions of the Inquisition. Sometimes there were restrictions on Indians as participants in Christian sacraments, as witnesses in court, as users of horses or weapons, and as wearers of European-style clothing. Indians, considered "minors" as a class, could not enter into binding contracts without the approval of Spanish authorities. Some of these restrictions were lifted for Indians in trades. Viceroy Toledo in Peru in the later sixteenth century exempted from forced labor in each Indian village a blacksmith, a shoemaker, and a dyer. A royal decree later

(1618) freed all Indian artisans from labor levies. But that affected only a minority of the Indian population.

Efforts were made to segregate and protect Indians in Spanish towns, but a much bigger effort was the Indian villages. A long series of rulings, beginning in the sixteenth century, tried to keep blacks, mixed breeds, and finally Spaniards out of the villages. Many villages were created partly to provide such protection, but they were also meant to aid Christianization; improve the availability of labor, increasingly a problem as the population dwindled; help with training in new productive techniques; and provide better supervision by civil and ecclesiastical authorities. The Spaniards gathered Indians into many new settlements—civil *congregaciones* and ecclesiastical *reducciones*.

Other efforts at protection included Indian courts; the phasing out of encomienda, with many of those Indians becoming wards of the crown; and the *corregimiento*. Other benign aspects of Indian status were that they seldom were fined, sent to prison, or executed; and usually, after the conquest decades, they were not subject to slavery except for rebellion. But Indian opportunities to improve their status declined with time, as economic needs prompted Spaniards to increase the pressure for labor on the declining Indian population. That decline was one cause of the decay of the position of Indian *caciques*, and of reduction of the preconquest distinctions of status that Indians had retained within their own community and which the Spaniards neither understood nor cared about.[12]

None of these measures interrupted the terrible wastage of the Indian population in the sixteenth century, and congregation probably aggravated the effects of disease, the worst cause of mortality. Disease did increase from disruptions of food production due to labor drafts, slavery, resettlement, and warfare; and from weakness produced by overwork and beatings. It may be

that mortality in the sixteenth century was increased by sheer despair and a reduction in the will to live. The decimated Indian population in some places increased in numbers modestly in the seventeenth century and more in the eighteenth.

Labor Systems for Indians

The labor systems of colonial Spanish America were a critical part of the complex of status, discrimination, and coercion imposed by the upper class. That complex had such wide effects that the term "aristocratic dispensation" is useful, indicating elite control and fashioning of critical parts of such institutions as labor, property holding, government, and education. Those were the *operational* effects of class and discrimination. Those effects mostly were imposed from town, where the elite resided, onto the rural areas where most laborers lived. Thus, much of the story of labor is a part of the domination of the countryside by the Spanish town. It also is the story of Spanish heedlessness of the spiritual elements involved in labor. Spaniards did not understand the use of incentives and were negligent of the ceremonial or ritual elements in preconquest labor. Both those errors contributed to poor Indian performance and to the Spanish notion that Indians were invincibly lazy.

Spaniards and preconquest Indians were familiar with more than one type of labor system. Many types were used after the conquest, often mixed together in a community or even in a single enterprise. One sugar hacienda in New Spain in the sixteenth and seventeenth centuries used five different types of Indian labor (plus black slaves). In some times and places one mode or a combination of modes of labor would be dominant, but the situation would be different elsewhere. In the conquest and immediate postconquest decades, slavery and encomienda (both unpaid labor) were dominant. Then came *repartimiento* (forced and paid labor) as a dominant, but not exclusive, mode from the later sixteenth to the mid-seventeenth centuries, especially in

---

[12] See Chapter 5, Section b, on encomienda; Chapter 6 Section b, on Indian villages and on the *corregimiento*.

New Spain and Peru. In the meantime, all sorts of free labor systems were being developed. One was peonage, largely a development of the middle and late seventeenth and the eighteenth centuries. In all those systems, the laborers were supervised by overseers and foremen rather than by the owners of enterprises. Such supervision often was brutal, and Indian, mestizo, black, mulatto, and white foremen were equally demanding.

Most manual labor performed for the upper class was forced or dependent and performed by nonwhite or mixed race persons. All these systems (plus slavery for blacks) involved some coercion or the threat thereof and required extensive support by public authority. The submissiveness required of either forced or dependent labor was supported not only by law, custom, and economic, social, and psychologic need but by the intellectual and moral resources of statesmen in church and civil government. Although church and state also engaged in activities—legal, rhetorical, and physical—to protect laborers, they were only occasionally and mildly successful. Labor had little protection against exploitation.

There was a large element of periodicity in all forced and dependent Indian labor except slavery. That is, laborers left their Indian communities, voluntarily or involuntarily, only for stated periods of time, some of them quite short. This was in accord with ancient Indian tradition and with the Spanish policy of trying to keep the Indian and Spanish communities separate. Such periodicity helped Indians to retain their own social and economic practices. Indians, nevertheless, used many dodges to avoid forced labor. An Indian who became an artisan in a Spanish town and adopted some European habits might claim to be a mestizo and thus avoid labor drafts. Or he might shift residence frequently to avoid that obligation. Some became vagabonds, the subject of much complaint by the whites for several reasons, including the difficulty of inducing them to work. As time went on, more and more of the lower class, including Indians, converted to free labor. The system was made up, however, largely

of unskilled and semiskilled labor, and the forced or dependent labor systems that affected the vast majority were the dominant modes of the colonial era.

Indian Slavery and Encomienda. Indian slavery gradually came under crown control. Although never quite exterminated, in the seventeenth century it dwindled to insignificance. Some modes of apprenticeship, service, and peonage, however, somewhat resembled slavery in practice, since the Indians could not always obtain legal recognition of their rights. An Indian forced by rigged debts to labor in a textile workshop, sometimes chained in place, in effect was enslaved; as was an orphan sold into service, occasionally by ecclesiastics, in payment of fees owed by the orphan's deceased father. The drastic decline of encomienda in the second half of the sixteenth century has been described.[13]

Repartimiento. As the labor aspect of encomienda became less important for most residents of Spanish America in the mid-sixteenth century, it was paralleled by new systems of forced labor, many of them involving wages. Unpaid Indian labor remained, not only where encomienda lingered, but in other systems of obligation. Various Indian cultures had differing types of semislaves and serfs, and some of those forms continued in the Spanish period. Some such obligations complicated the assignment of Indians under the new contract systems, the most prominent of which was *repartimiento*. The allotment (*repartimiento*) of Indians on a permanent basis to individual Spaniards as unpaid labor, associated with encomienda, was supplemented in the mid-sixteenth century by a different sort of *repartimiento*. This later *repartimiento* was forced—but paid—labor, allotted by state officials to applicants for specified short periods of time.[14] Although most frequently ap-

---

[13] See Chapter 5, Section b.
[14] For yet another use of the term *repartimiento*, as a forced sale of goods, see Chapter 6, Section b.

plied to Indians, it was often also applied to persons of mixed race. The system helped meet the problem of drastically declining Indian population by meeting the labor needs of the elite more rationally than did the permanent allotment to the few *encomenderos*. Church, state, and private users of labor all needed the system.

Similar systems of conscripted or forced labor have been common in human history, and *repartimiento* sometimes is described as a *corvée*. It certainly had been used by the higher Amerindian cultures before the European conquest. *Mita* was an equivalent institution in the Inca culture, and in the Peruvian area it bore that preconquest name throughout the Spanish period. In New Spain it sometimes was called by the Indian term *cuatequil* but was usually called *repartimiento* of labor, the commonest term for it.

Indians subject to *repartimiento* were assigned to duty by locality, with specified numbers to serve for a stated period. They were supposed to be able-bodied adult males, and communities were not supposed to be crippled by excessive levies. Spanish officials set the quotas, with some attention to the size of the communities involved. At the head of the system were Spanish officials sometimes called allotment judges (*jueces repartidores*), with staffs to aid them. The local Indian *caciques* helped fix the quotas, collected the laborers, and conducted them to the *juez repartidor*. Then the *juez repartidor* assigned Indians to Spanish employers or their agents. He collected fees from the employers, which went to pay the underlings of the *juez* and the Indian local officials, and to line the pockets of the *juez*. The Indians spent their period working under overseers. The small wages of the laborers were supposed to be paid before they were released from the draft. Some of the work periods were as short as a week, some much longer. Draft quotas were lowered at times because of epidemics or local needs for labor, but the clamor for *repartimiento* often made this impossible, so sometimes the draft imposed a crushing burden on a community.

Massive evasion of the regulations, plus economic need, led to frequent efforts at tighter control. Indian *caciques* were allowed to retain their bound or serflike labor (*mayeques* in Mexico, *yanaconas* in Peru) in the early years of the *repartimiento* system, but later, as the Indian population declined, *caciques* had to allow their serfs to be included in *repartimiento* quotas. The same pressure led local Indian officials to force females and cripples onto the quota rolls and compel them to pay for exemption, and employers to retain Indians by force beyond their terms.

Not only were the quotas both evaded and legally raised, but there were violations of the rules on distances Indians could be transported from home areas or on supervision of such especially arduous and hazardous tasks as mining. There was bribery of officials by employers to wink at abuses. Wages were not only low but sometimes uncollectable. Some *repartimiento* labor was marked by high mortality. It sometimes seriously disturbed Indian family, social, and economic life. The hated draft led Indian women to marry into mestizo status to have sons free of the obligation. It led Indians in Peru to move to *yanacona* (serflike) status to avoid the terrible *mita* of the mines. Indians moved to town and became artisans at wages much higher than those of *repartimiento* labor, so that they could buy exemption or substitutes.

Repartimiento gangs did a great deal of work. They constructed public buildings, aqueducts, granaries, ecclesiastical structures, streets, bridges, and flood control works. They played a large role in mining. There was considerable *repartimiento* labor for a few decades in agriculture, but it tended to be less useful in farming and grazing because too much rotational labor was costly in those enterprises. The government generally channeled *repartimiento* labor to other uses.

In New Spain the *repartimiento* system had its chief effects from the late sixteenth to the midseventeenth centuries. The crown always expected it to be temporary and to be replaced by more humane systems. In the late sixteenth century the crown tried to restrict *repartimiento* and encourage free Indian labor and black slavery. It made a notable effort to prohibit *repartimiento* for occupations that were arduous or dangerous, as in textile factories, sugar mills, and indigo works. Not only was the prohibition difficult to enforce, but the replacement systems sometimes were worse than *repartimiento*. In 1632 the viceroy of New Spain decreed the end of all *repartimiento* except in mining—not the first time that had been tried. The 1632 edict was accepted by the elite without protest, because *repartimiento* no longer was important to it except in mining. In mills, new, ostensibly free systems of labor served acceptably from the employers' point of view. In agriculture, *repartimiento* had been replaced by private contract systems and by peonage. And other exceptions and adjustments made *repartimiento* unnecessary in most places. In Mexico City, for example, the declared abolition of 1632 did not affect the big special *repartimiento* for flood control. The draft for this heavy and dangerous work had been begun during the inundation of 1555–1556. It was considered of critical importance and simply not regarded as part of the prohibition of 1632. In New Spain other remnants of *repartimiento* continued until the end of the colonial era. Reduced *mita* drafts continued in Peru. The institution thus retained some usefulness, although its general unacceptability had long since lessened it. There was too much Indian resistance to be worth attempting to overcome. And the labor often was too costly in terms of administration, travel, and performance.

Peonage. Peonage was a system of free, remunerated, but "dependent" labor on great estates. The dependency was as much economic and psychological as directly legal. It began in the sixteenth century in response to various conditions. One was the decline of the Indian population, which meant that *repartimiento* hands were less abundant, a situation made worse for agricultural estates by the crown policy of turn-

ing *repartimiento* away from them. Also, Spanish estates were increasing in size, so that proprietors had a rising interest in secure sources of labor. At the same time, the Indian society was so depressed economically that it was willing to undertake wage labor that paid more than *repartimiento*. Indians began doing voluntary work for wages, with and without contracts, as *gañanes*, *naboríos*, *tlaquehuales*, and *peones*. Many still lived in their villages. Some accepted the liabilities of peonage to escape tribute and labor service in the villages or to earn the tribute payments. Spanish estate owners invited workers to settle on or near their holdings and often acquired the duty of collecting the tribute. The crown complained of the ways Indians were pulled near or onto private lands but did nothing effective about it.

An element in holding peons to the estate was debt. This simple device occurred as easily to employers in colonial Spanish America as to southern landowners after the United States Civil War. A poor, socially submerged, diffident population was given access to cash or goods, agreeing to work until out of debt. The Indians bought because their needs sometimes were desperate and because they were tempted by tools or luxury goods (a knife, a ribbon, a sweet). Getting out of debt was difficult because their income was low, prices were inflated at the hacienda store, records were doctored, and the society was such that recourse to authority or law seldom was effective and might be dangerous. By the sixteenth century the problem was of such proportions that the crown tried to limit indebtedness, which also was used early to try to control labor in *obrajes* or workshops.

Probably, however, other considerations were more important than debt to the peons, who perceived advantages in the system in addition to escape from village obligations. Although formal wages were low, peons often received daily issues of food and sometimes of strong drink, the use of personal garden plots, some access to hacienda facilities (church, workshops, tools), and some protection against the numerous marauders and speculators—some of them civil or ecclesiastical functionaries—who constantly preyed on Indian villages. Of course, the hacienda connection did not protect peons living in nearby villages from incursions against village lands by their own *hacendado* or *patrón*.[15] As another form of compensation, peons, through their own activity or that of relatives or friends, surely siphoned off supplies from kitchens, storehouses, and fields. Some of this had to be known to the hacienda owner and his overseers. The practice, common among servants and other workers in Latin America today, is an inescapable concomitant of a society with a huge underprivileged labor force. In addition to all these reasons why peons preferred to stay dependent on the hacienda rather than flee, one can plausibly suppose that flight was impeded by the conservatism of peasants who feared to leave their accustomed lives and venture into the unknown reaches of a society where violence in human relations was prevalent.

There were peons who were permanently resident on the estate and others who were seasonal workers. The former were the minority, and they were only a part of the resident population. Others included supervisory personnel of a higher socioeconomic category. Most of the peons commonly lived chiefly in surrounding Indian villages and went to the estate intermittently. Some hacienda owners forced Indians off their own lands, partly to possess the latter, but partly to make the Indians dependent on the hacienda. Other hacienda owners encouraged Indians to settle on the fringes of the hacienda in villages, so that they could be called on when needed. The amount of labor that peons provided varied, depending on local custom and on the character of the supervisory system. Some worked hard for little return. Peruvian peons in the late colonial era were, according to report, especially notable

for hard work, drastic punishments, and perpetual debt. Even there some of the drastic punishment was surely due to the fact that peons were succeeding in evading work, doing it badly, or engaging in the sort of molasses-slow activity that is one of the best refuges of forced or dependent labor groups.

Although peonage had beginnings in the sixteenth century, it grew much larger in the seventeenth and greater yet in the eighteenth with the growth of haciendas. Furthermore, peonage not only became the dominant labor system in many of the agricultural and grazing ventures of the elite during the second half of the colonial era, but it continued as an institution of major importance in independent Latin America in the nineteenth and twentieth centuries. Development in the colonial era was not uniform, however, in time or characteristics. Where encomienda labor lingered longest, as in Chile, or where *repartimiento* persisted, as in Quito, Peru, and Guatemala, there was less need for peonage. Also, not all peons entered that condition from Indian villages. Some had been vagabonds and some were mestizos. Despite variations of time and place, the system did grow progressively more widespread, more and more the dominant labor system for rural areas, a system of practically hereditary rural workers.

Obrajes. Labor in *obrajes* (workshops) showed some features of dependence, some of theoretical freedom, but mostly those of force and fraud. It began quite early in the colonial era as essentially a system of free contract labor, almost at once supplemented with debt as a means of trying to keep workers. *Obraje* employers may have been the first to develop supplementary techniques of labor recruitment distinct from encomienda, slavery, and judicial sentence. *Obrajes* making woolen cloth existed at least by the 1530s in New Spain. Workshop owners early had to find labor outside *repartimiento*, because the crown cut down on that source for *obrajes*. A few *obraje* workers were Indian slaves from frontier areas. A few Oriental slaves were im-

---

15 *Patrón* must be rendered into English as something like "a combination of boss, patron, and uncle." The relationship was—and still is—of importance in towns as well as in the countryside in Latin America.

ported from the Philippine Islands to serve in Mexican *obrajes*. Most *obraje* labor in the early decades, however, consisted of free Indians; with time, other *castas* became increasingly important. Supervisors and guards usually were Spaniards, mestizos, blacks, or mulattoes. The *obrajes* were notorious for the illegal detention of workers and for physically abusing them. The owners' lust for profit was aggravated by a system of remunerating the majordomos in accordance with the work they screwed out of the crews.

There were other abuses. Owners negotiated with Indians who needed money, sometimes sealing the bargain with written contracts before judges. Once in debt, workers found it hard to escape, both because of manipulation of the amounts and because of forceable detention. They ran up bills for food and for the intoxicating drink that was their one escape from misery. Locking workers in was sometimes justified on the grounds that the *obrajes* received convicts from the state as workers, but the method also was used to keep free workers from escaping. The abuses of sentencing Indians to serve in *obrajes* were prohibited by legislation but continued throughout the colonial era. *Obrajes* also took in Indian children as apprentices or were assigned orphans by the courts and then locked them up for life.

Although the scandalous conditions in *obrajes* were recognized early by the government, which issued tough-sounding ordinances and appointed inspectors, little changed. A *cédula* in New Spain in 1601 prohibited the use of Indian labor for textile mills except in *obrajes de comunidad* (owned and operated by Indians) and recommended that black slaves replace Indians. Neither was done. The profits were too great. Further, the argument was that clothing shortages would result from interference with *obraje* production. The brutalities the state permitted in the *obrajes* were the only means of holding the workers under conditions of low wages and inhuman treatment. Debt slavery alone would not have held them. The workers had to be locked in and sometimes chained in place.

Free Labor

Free labor began to develop in the sixteenth century, although a large group of peons in the seventeenth and eighteenth centuries was only nominally free, being heavily dependent on the hacienda or bound by debt. While some Indians were taking the route into peonage, others signed private labor contracts with Spaniards that gave them some freedom of choice and opportunity to bargain. Others just did casual labor and had no room to maneuver. Best-positioned were wage laborers in critical supervisory positions in agriculture, grazing, mining and smelting, sugar, grist and sawmills, and some other enterprises, and those who worked as artisans. Some miners received not only high wages but shares of production. Although Spanish America remained a miserable area for the laboring man, at least his condition improved a trifle from the depths of wide-scale application of slavery, encomienda, and *repartimiento*. Still, in colonial Peru no more than 5 percent of the economically active population ever was fully paid in cash for its labor.

Decay of the Indian Way of Life

Retention of at least a part of the traditional Indian life depended on a number of factors. Forced and dependent labor, appropriation of some community lands, and the great loss of life during epidemics damaged it. Then it suffered shocks as the Spaniards moved the smaller populations into new villages. The church formed villages largely for purposes of Christianization. The civil administration was interested in concentration of a reduced labor supply. In any event, the life of the village depended to some extent on the location of the community with reference to Spanish towns, mining camps, or haciendas, or well-traveled roads or trails, or on the value of Indian lands. Some communities quite near the Valley of Mexico were in such remote mountain locations or had such marginal land that they retained much of the old folk culture to the middle of the twentieth century.

Indian communities in many respects tried to make of their place a closed environment, in well-justified suspicion of the outer world, from which came clouds of tribute gatherers, ecclesiastics with hands out, private commercial plunderers, or wandering adventurers looking for someone to dominate and bilk.

Such isolation, although often encouraged by the crown,[16] many times could not be achieved because both Spaniards and Indians decided against it. Church protection of Indians in communities was sometimes weak. Neither church nor state, in fact, possessed the power to prevent Spaniards—officials and private individuals—from practicing large and petty tyrannies upon the Indians, penetrating the ideal of the *república de Indios*. Spaniards moved some Indians to the new Spanish towns, by a variety of methods. Yet other Indians chose to move to Spanish communities, either in desperation at the deterioration of conditions in their own communities or from a more optimistic belief in the opportunities to be found among the new lords of the land. Some Indians in the Spanish towns took readily to European culture while working at European crafts or as servants in Spanish residences, porters in public buildings, street sweepers, peddlers and street hawkers, and market personnel.[17]

On the other hand, Indians in town and even more those in the old communities retained much of the old daily life: foods and their preparation (though European chickens and swine were accepted readily), housing, clothing, amusements, folk medicine, and superstitions and religious beliefs (though mingled with Christianity). European crops, tools, and animals were adopted or cared for either because Spaniards insisted or because they offered clear advantages to the Indians. There thus was some use of European plows, metallurgy, iron and steel hatchets, saws, other hardware, fishing devices, sheep's wool, and the Spanish flat-bed loom.[18] But often

European looms, hardware, pottery methods, and other aspects of culture existed side by side with Indian methods.

Indian rural society also retained status or distinction systems of the preconquest period, for ordinary individuals or for functionaries, at levels below nobles and principal rulers, which the Spaniards eradicated. In some rural areas postconquest Indians long had less consciousness of the Spanish status system than of their own earlier system. That did not matter to Spaniards. They had small interest in holdovers that did not affect their own system of political and economic management, and often remained unaware that Indians retained some of their own system of status and appointment.

In Peru, Indians had the old distinction between upper-class *curacas* and commoners, which the Spaniards used, and another between all Indians who participated in kin groups (*ayllus*) and those—*yanaconas*—who did not. The *yanaconas* were specialized retainers, sometimes called serfs by European writers, who had lost their kin-group relations. The bulk of the Indians were neither *curacas* nor *yanaconas*. An Indian's kinship group was of prime importance to him because it determined much of his access to land, assignment to work, and place in ceremonies, worship, and diversions. To be sure, some Peruvian Indians did take up positions in the new Spanish system, as headmen cooperating with *encomenderos* or *corregidores* or as members of Indian *cabildos*. Some of them, however, at the same time secretly carried on functions in Indian religious ceremonies, and the land they worked had to come from that belonging to their *ayllus*. Although the kin-group assignments never disappeared in the Inca area, they came under increasing pressure from the Spanish culture, as Spaniards upped their economic demands and more Indians collaborated with the Spanish governing system.

Whether the Indians were worse off physically after the conquest than before—aside from Old

---

[16] See Chapter 6, Section b, on government and law for Indians.

[17] See Chapter 3, Section c, for the earliest adjustments of the Caribbean Indians to European culture.

[18] See Chapter 8, Section c, on the differential origins of Spanish cultural traits and tools in the southern provinces.

World diseases—is difficult to know. In both periods they suffered from war, forced labor and slavery, rigid class systems, taxation, and demands from an ecclesiastic establishment. Probably Indian peasants in colonial Spanish America lived about as well—or badly—as the less fortunate peasants of the time in eastern Europe and Asia. Their lot certainly was not rosy, as pointed out by the secret report of the Spanish naval officers Juan and Ulloa in the middle of the eighteenth century. It stated that two centuries of effort in Peru had failed to improve the condition of the Indians. Juan and Ulloa, however, had no way of measuring the physical condition of the Indians of their day as against that of preconquest times.

As for the spiritual or psychological condition of the Indians of the colonial era, it is difficult not to suppose a deterioration. Some of this, however, may be illusory. We know that most preconquest Indians did not have freedom of opinion, government, movement, or social relationships. Most of them were hemmed into an inferior class that was tightly regulated and heavily regimented. Their horizons were limited; they had the conservatism and parochial prejudices and short vision of peasants everywhere. Possibly things worsened after the conquest in that the accustomed inferiority of the masses became accompanied by consciousness of belonging to an alien and despised group, even more separated from the Spanish lords of the land than they had been from the haughty oligarchs who ruled them before. We do know that the Spaniards generally despised the Indians, often describing them as sulky and spiritless. The fact was, of course, that their natural human joy in laughter was choked off by their need to present an inscrutable face to the alien elite. So low did they sink in the esteem of other groups that Juan and Ulloa reported that Indian nobles were even disdained by mestizos. Indian resentment and hatred simmered, however, beneath their stony facial masks. They were ingenious in ways of subverting Spanish demands by procrastination, partial obedience, misinformation, pretended misunderstanding, and litigation.

Indian tumults were numerous, and the Spanish overlords feared rebellion and race war. Shortages of food and high prices were a common cause of Indian rioting, as were unreasonable exactions in goods, money, and labor. But there were only two large-scale rebellions with more than short-term goals, clear testimony to the effectiveness of the system of control. The rebellion of Tupac Amaru in Peru in the 1780s may have involved a hundred thousand Indians.[19] Even larger-scale and bloodier was the Indian response in Mexico to the call from Father Hidalgo in 1810, when the Indians seemed bent on killing every white person they could find.[20] Despite those two exceptional massive indications of latent hatred, and despite the thousands of smaller incidents of Indian violence in protest against conditions, the Spaniards maintained control with relative ease. Indian outbursts were sporadic, poorly sustained, and usually quickly controlled.

Many unpacified Indians became more dangerous as they acquired horses and guns. They descended from their refuges upon Spanish settlements, to seize women, horses, guns, and other loot, and to kill Spaniards. The latter, in turn, raided Indian country, burned villages, enslaved the inhabitants, and set up forts and missions or settlers in the hope of controlling or pacifying the Indians. Northern Mexico never was pacified, although the menace gradually was pushed northward. Also troublesome to the end of the colonial era were Indians in the extensive forested lowlands of present-day Colombia, Venezuela, Ecuador, and Peru, the forests of Chile, and the southern plains of Argentina. Even the tiny Spanish settlements in Costa Rica had to carry on a long struggle to pacify the Indians of the Talamanca Mountains. Between frontier warfare with some Indians and coercive domination of others, the upper-class managers of the Spanish American colonial system built up a bitter legacy of distrust and hatred in the Indian lower class.

---

[19] See Chapter 17, Section c, on the Tupac rebellion.
[20] See Chapter 19, Section d, on the Hidalgo uprising.

The Black Lower Class and Racial Mixture

a. The Black Lower Class

Blacks in Spanish America comprised a smaller percentage of the population than in Portuguese or British America, and they were unevenly distributed geographically. Most pure-blooded blacks were slaves, though the percentage of freedmen grew with time. Black, Indian, and white interbred frequently, and many of their racially mixed (Afromestizo) offspring were not slaves, but most of them remained in the lower class. The slave status of most blacks contributed to a low Spanish regard for the pure race and its mixtures, and they were subject to extensive discrimination and restriction. Much of the restriction, however, was directed at slaves rather than at blacks, and the latter in many contexts were considered more capable than Indians. Although prejudice against black racial stock was somewhat less than in British America, most obviously in the treatment of the numerous free blacks and Afromestizos, it was very strong.

The Slave Traffic

Many human societies had slavery before the discovery of America, and the lot of such chattels never was enviable. In the fifteenth century Portugal began selling black African slaves in Europe. Sevilla had both black and white Muslim slaves in the time of Columbus. By the seventeenth century the Atlantic slave system at times involved the Dutch, British, French, Danes, Swedes, Germans, Spaniards, and Portuguese. All the colonial powers in America used black slaves. The slave trade was sanctioned by governments and by Catholic and Protestant churches. It was also sanctioned by some black African cultures whose leaders sold blacks to whites. Europeans thought black slavery economically sound. As heavy laborers in fields, ports, and mines, black slaves often were essential where other workers were not available or did not perform well. Black slaves also performed well in many supervisory and skilled positions. Although we know of cases where free labor outperformed slave in the colonial era, large-scale free labor in plantation agriculture in the Caribbean, in coastal Peru, and in some other places could not be had on terms—social, political, and economic —that the elites were interested in paying.

There is some mystery regarding the lack of protest against black slavery in the Spanish world, because its presence contrasted with the restriction of Indian slavery. Some worthy Spaniards, including Las Casas at one time, supported black slavery to relieve Indians of excessive burdens. Did the Spaniards consider blacks natural slaves because they knew some of them in that condition in Spain? It is difficult to place much confidence in that argument, since Europeans knew that there had once been enslavement of Europeans, that there were free blacks in Africa, and that American Indians made slaves of each other. Nor had Indian cultural achievement impressed many Spaniards with Indian superiority over black Africans. There was some early Spanish expectation that black slavery would be temporary. Some ecclesiastics feared that too many Africans in America would interfere with Christianization of the Indians by encouraging pagan ideas, and they advocated importation of only Christianized blacks, but that idea came to nothing. None of this was of much consequence in the "decision" to enslave blacks.

It was convenient for an untroubled sense of Christian justice for Spanish leaders to adopt a protective attitude toward Indians and stop their enslavement. At the same time, it was convenient both for conscience and for a sense of the requirements of statecraft and economic life to permit black slavery without an upsetting debate as to its justice. In sum, the justice of black slavery was scarcely considered by Spaniards or other Europeans. Kings and bishops found the system acceptable. Religious orders in Spanish America owned black slaves. If the dedicated Society of Jesus believed in black slavery, what Spanish layman could think otherwise?

Black slaves were carried from Spain to America in the time of Columbus. For a few years they came from the slave population of Spain but soon were supplied directly from Africa. Charles I granted the first license for such supply in 1517 to a Flemish favorite, who sold it to Genoese merchants. In 1528 the first monopolistic contract (*asiento*) was let. A few black slaves accompanied Cortés in the conquest of Mexico. Pizarro's agreement with the crown on Peru in 1529 included a license to import fifty-two African slaves a year. Other such privileges were granted in the conquest period. For a while, nonmonopolistic contracts for slave supply were made with Spaniards, Portuguese, Italians, and Germans. In the 1560s and 1570s the Portuguese, who had the advantage of good stations in Africa and connections with Brazil and could outperform other suppliers, took over the trade. Late in the sixteenth century Spain returned to monopolistic *asientos*, all with Portugal during the union of the two crowns in 1580–1640. The Portuguese had papal authority to take Africans by force, but they usually bartered with blacks in Africa for their supplies of slaves. Although license was for introduction of a specified number of black slaves into Spanish America, the entrepreneurs also expected to profit from other goods sent in the slave ships.

Spanish merchants naturally protested both the Portuguese monopoly of the slave trade and the introduction of other goods in the slave ships. But Spain used foreign suppliers because it had no territory in Africa where slaving was possible and because Spanish maritime entrepreneurs were busy elsewhere. The most famous *asiento* was that of 1713–1750 (with interruptions), which the British got for their South Sea Company as the result of victory in war.[1] The system of monopoly contracts for slaves ended in 1773. Some Spanish merchantmen entered the trade, partial *asientos* occasionally were signed, and smuggling of slaves continued. Expanded British permission to Spaniards to buy slaves in Jamaica and some other British colonies in the eighteenth century aided smuggling. Thus, over its long and sordid history, much of the profit of the slave trade to Spanish America went to non-Spaniards.

Most contracts counted slaves in *piezas de Indias*, a concept that varied but generally meant a young adult male of a certain size and physical condition. Parts of *piezas* were females, youngsters, the small, puny, ill, and handicapped. Conditions on the slave ships bearing these full and partial "pieces" to America often were unspeakable, and mortality was high. Such conditions resulted from fear of the captives, from greed combined with callousness or inhumanity, and from ignorance of hygiene and preventive medicine, as

---

[1] See Chapter 7, Section e.

seen in the fact that at times a higher proportion of crew than slaves died. Because of their greater value, more men than women were carried. When the slaves arrived at the markets of America, they sometimes died and rotted in bare cells in such tropical ports as Cartagena, dead mouths filling with flies (according to reports) while unheeding traders skirted them to prod and bid for the poor souls who were still alive.

In the larger distribution centers the black slave business made fortunes for some merchants, and attracted others—officials, sailors, artisans—to try to turn a peso in the trade. Slaves were so valuable that they were often put up as collateral for loans. Cartagena became a considerable slave mart in the late sixteenth century and long remained a distribution center for New Granada, Peru, and some other areas. From the late sixteenth century to well into the seventeenth the single best market for slaves at Cartagena was Peru. Merchants went from Lima to Cartagena to buy slaves and combined this traffic with dealings in other commodities. In those years they could control the distribution of slaves not only to the coastal and highland areas of Peru but also to Quito and Chile. Many of these merchants were Portuguese, and some were "convert" Jews. One in the early seventeenth century was among the wealthiest merchants in Lima. His operations at Cartagena showed that a large number of persons was involved in the slave traffic, because he bought slaves in small lots from pharmacists, sailors, and others. Most of his sales in Lima also were in small lots, because few persons owned large gangs of slaves.

The slave trade began slowly. Of the 1 to 1.5 million carried to Spanish America by 1810,[2] possibly fewer than 100,000 arrived before the year 1600. Beginning in the late sixteenth century, however, the annual introduction of black slaves was on the order of 10,000 persons. At the end of the colonial era as many as 75,000 were introduced in some years. Of blacks imported by 1650, New Spain probably received well over one-half. Thereafter its importance as a black slave market declined in relation to other areas of Spanish America, and its proportion of total imports from the beginning to 1773 was probably less than one-third, with most of those being taken to Mexico before the eighteenth century. Mexico's early heavy use of black slaves was the natural result of the area's rapid pacification, large European community, and great economic opportunities. The later decline of its importance as a slave market was due to the development of large numbers of free laborers of mixed blood and the increase of the Indian population. At the same time, the population and economic production of other parts of Spanish America were increasing.

After the 1770s many more Africans were imported to Spanish America, in response to the expansion of export agriculture, notably in Cuba but also in Puerto Rico and Venezuela. New Granada remained an important market for black slaves, especially for the gold fields. Large streams of blacks were sold to Peru and smaller numbers to all the other provinces of Spanish America. Of slaves imported to Spanish America in 1774–1807, Cuba received more than one-half, Venezuela on the order of 12 percent, New Granada (present-day Colombia and Ecuador, with reexports to Peru and Chile) another 12 percent or so, the Plata basin some 8 percent (including those provided to Upper Peru), Puerto Rico 6 percent, Santo Domingo 3 percent, and Mexico and Central America together less than 3 percent.[3]

After 1807 the only significant flows of black slaves to Spanish America were to Cuba and Puerto Rico, the others being cut off by international war, the struggles for Independence, the abolition of the British slave trade, Britain's interest in driving all nations from the traffic, and

---

[2] In 1810–1865 more than 600,000 additional blacks were carried from Africa to Cuba and Puerto Rico, more than 90 percent of them to Cuba.

[3] The statistics are uncertain, but the general picture of distribution is sound.

a lack of demand for additional slaves in much of Spanish America.

The Life of the Black Slave

Occupations. Most black slaves did brute manual labor, although the proportion in other occupations was slightly higher in Spanish than in Portuguese, French, Dutch, or British America because export agriculture was not so well developed in the Spanish realms. The number of field hands increased in Spanish areas, however, late in the colonial era, with the growth of export crops in Cuba, Puerto Rico, Venezuela, and New Granada. All European holders treated unskilled black laborers in the Western Hemisphere inhumanly.

Brutalization of the Africans began on the slave ships. Some of their culture was peeled off, both because they were uprooted from its sources and because different language groups were mingled. That mixing was sometimes deliberate, on the ships and later, so that communication for purposes of rebellion would be minimized. The slaves in America learned some Spanish (or Portuguese, English, Dutch, French) in order to survive and avoid the beatings thought necessary to help them learn their jobs. The skills they brought from Africa were seldom used, and unskilled manual laborers were especially subject to heavy work demands and discipline. Slaves were predominantly males and had relatively little normal sexual or family comfort. Field hands had slim chance of manumission. They were treated with worse than contempt, with the indifferent force employed against animals. They died like flies.

A minority of black slaves in Spanish America, those in skilled or supervisory jobs and servants in wealthy homes, were better treated than field hands, rough miners, or dock wallopers. Black slaves, free blacks, and mulattoes were more numerous in such positions in Spanish than in British America partly because of the scarcity of poor whites in the former. Often slaves were chosen for such positions because of certain qual-

ities: appearance (especially for concubines, but to some extent for ordinary servants, also), intelligence, tractability. Either they had become Europeanized faster than other slaves—an element in their selection—or their new positions hastened the process. Capability in the Spanish language was critical. Slaves in such jobs were cleaner and better clothed. Those qualities and habits, together with their necessarily close contact with the owner class, made them seem to the latter more human than the brutish field hands. Skilled black and Afromestizo artisans (slave and free) were more common in the towns of colonial Spanish America than in British America, and the same apparently was the case with supervisory positions in agriculture, mills, and elsewhere.

Slave nurses, some of whom suckled their white charges, were especially likely to receive decent treatment, even affection. Other types of servants benefited from household relationships. White children who were provided sweets by slave cooks, driven by black coachmen, pushed in their swings by footmen, tended by slaves in illness, who shared treats and tears and laughter to some extent, regarded the slaves with feeling. Slave women favored by whites with their sexual attentions might receive some "compensation." Certain skilled slaves—like blacksmiths or mill specialists—were well treated because of the value of their services. Black slaves performed menial tasks in all sorts of religious and civil government institutions. At times, black slave artisans and vendors worked with the public in order to share their earnings with their masters.

Marriage and the Family. Slave marriage was legal in Catholic areas of Europe and America, in part to avoid the sin of fornication. In Spanish America black slaves had the right, in both civil and canon law, to marry even without their masters' consent. But only a minority of black slaves did marry, and marriage was especially rare among field hands. Possibly in nearly all Spanish areas fewer (often much fewer) than 20 percent of all black slaves were married. This was so well known that the elite assumed that men of color were of illegitimate birth. Much de facto marriage existed, however, as in British America. It may be that the legal right of black slaves to marry had some effect upon general attitudes toward blacks, inclining the elite to regard them somewhat as fellow human beings. Probably this factor should be related not to slavery but to its effects on race prejudice and discrimination.

There was legislation to preserve the integrity of slave families, but the owner of the parents owned the children. In fact holders separated families by sale, and slave family life was unstable. Separation of slave families is difficult to quantify; it happened in spite of law in Spanish America, and it happened less often in English North America than abolitionists claimed. In Spanish America (and all tropical America) the slave population did not reproduce itself, so imports were required just to maintain the size of the slave force. Among the major reasons for the low reproduction rate was that about two-thirds of slave imports were male because men were thought better for heavy labor. Furthermore, Spanish American owners thought that importing slaves was more economical than rearing them. Slave breeding thus was not encouraged in Spanish America, and it differed in this way from North America.[4] In addition, the way many male slaves lived discouraged the production of slave children.[5] In at least a few cases, slaves practiced contraception rather than bring children into a life of misery. The production of Afromestizo children was a different matter. The lack of a legal barrier to black or Afromestizo marriage with other socioracial groups had impor-

tant consequences. It produced slave children only when the mother was a slave. It did not, however, increase the opportunity of the black male slave to elevate himself.

Much of the black condition can be only tentatively described, since neither blacks nor the upper class kept much record of how blacks lived. Sexual exploitation of slave women by whites can scarcely be quantified. Statistics on race mixture are notoriously unreliable. Finally, there was much variation in Spanish America at different times and places.[6]

Slave Religion and Education. Spanish American black slaves gradually became partly Christianized but not because they received much formal instruction in religion. Free blacks and Afromestizos were considerably more Christianized than slaves. Church and crown had a theoretical commitment to Christianization of slaves, but often the execution was little more effective than the baptism of slaves before embarkation in Africa. To be sure, crown and church lacked resources to Christianize slaves deeply, but they also lacked the will in face of their other obligations and the disinterest of slave owners. A few slaveholders were hailed before ecclesiastical courts for working their slaves on Sunday rather than letting them go to Mass, but such abuses were uncontrollable. The evidence is weak for the claim that blacks in Catholic colonies received more religious attention than in Protestant. If Spaniards felt a greater obligation to baptize blacks, they did little more about it, whereas some English North Americans recognized that blacks had redeemable souls and encouraged conversion.

---

[4] It is not clear, however, whether the high reproductive rate of slaves in the United States was due to the celebrated "stud farms" of abolitionist literature or to the existence of stable nuclear black families.

[5] In some urban areas of Spanish America the sex ratio among blacks was about in balance, but not among slave-labor gangs at mills, plantations, and mines. Second-generation blacks ordinarily reproduced better than those born in Africa.

---

[6] The nonwhite population of the United States in 1860 was only 7.7 percent mulatto. There probably were larger percentages of mulattoes in most Spanish American provinces about 1800, but they were much smaller in Peru and Mexico than in Cuba or New Granada. Although there were many *zambos* in Peru and Mexico, they were not often identified in statistics.

Under those conditions slave religion necessarily retained a large component of African belief, sometimes Muslim but usually animistic. A minority of black slaves became more Christianized because their occupations gave access to the faith and encouraged emulation of the elite. The *cofradías*—sodalities—of blacks in towns were regarded with suspicion by the elite, although they were in fact harmless groups for worship, recreation, and burial services. In any event, they enrolled only a minority of the black population. Christian institutions sometimes showed more interest in the economic value than the spiritual needs of black slaves. Branches of the Holy Office claimed immunity from secular criminal prosecution for their black slaves. There were, of course, some saintly ecclesiastics who devoted their lives to black slaves, such as the Jesuits Alonso de Sandoval and Saint Peter Claver at Cartagena. Church institutions in other places cared for old and sick slaves on their estates and operated a few town hospitals for blacks.

Most Spanish American owners had no interest in the slaves' cultural condition except what they could observe of the relationship between African tribal origins and such traits as docility, willingness, and hardihood. Owners thought education for slaves was dangerous, and very few became literate. Slaves often kept a part of their African language, music, and folklore. They came, of course, without artifacts, and duplication of African forms in America was often neither convenient nor permissible.

Slave Mortality. Black slave mortality was high, mostly because of abuse, including overwork; poor diet and housing; and disease, which was the more deadly because of the way the slaves had to live. Gang issues of imported food in some places were inadequate, as were the conditions of slave cultivation of crops. Caribbean plantations led in slave mortality, because of the greater prevalence of "fevers" (which made for high white mortality, too). Even in the more favorable climatic conditions of coastal Peru,

blacks and Afromestizos suffered far higher mortality than Spaniards.[7]

The mortality of slaves should be a key to their conditions of existence. The English North American colonies come off best in this regard, but since being a slave in the English West Indies was much more dangerous, the presumption is that a good climate and freedom from disease were more important benefits than recollection of Christian precepts or the beauties of the common law. Field hands everywhere died after a few years (often less than ten) of animal-like existence; house servants and town artisans and janitors were less abused and lived longer. The last statistical and moral judgments have not been rendered on this horrible competition to establish relative guilt for a wastage of life that was dreadful at best.

Slave Control and Discipline

A good part of Spanish legislation at all levels that touched slaves was repressive. Spaniards were constantly concerned about poor work performance by slaves, criminality, immorality, escape, and possible rebellion. Exaggerated reports and rumors about slave misdeeds and intentions were common, the usual concomitant of fear. The fear was seen in shifting views of different "types" of slaves. Sometimes opinion favored the common rude African imports (*bozales*) on the grounds that they were cowed and ignorant and easy to discipline. In this view, disciplining black slaves who knew Spanish ways was difficult. The partly Hispanicized slaves were known as *ladinos* if born in Africa and *criollos* if born in Spain or Portugal.[8] Some of them were superior slaves, but

---

7 There was Spanish legislation requiring slave owners to feed and clothe slaves decently, but it could no more be enforced than the rules on Christianization. The famous Royal Instruction of 1789 stated some relief for slaves, but those provisions were unenforceable; the main intent and effect was to extend slavery by promoting a free slave trade.

8 *Ladino* also was used in place of *mestizo* in other contexts; *criollo*, of course, was also a Spaniard born in America.

others were thought too knowing of European ways to be easily controllable. Such comfort in contemplation of *bozales* was replaced at other times by fear that recently arrived African slaves had retained too much memory of Africa to be easily disciplined. The upper class was simply fearful of all slaves.

So slaves were subject to severe restrictions and to draconian punishments for misdeeds. There were prohibitions against slaves congregating; there were efforts to regulate their morals and dress and to restrict their diversions. In some places in the late colonial period there was some softening of severity but not in the West Indies, where the proportion of blacks to whites was greatest. Many contradictory actions bore on slave use of weapons. In the first half of the sixteenth century slaves at times were armed to aid Spanish forces; at other times they were forbidden to bear arms unless with their masters; and at others they were prohibited from bearing arms under any circumstances. A slave curfew at Lima in 1535 called for loss of a slave's genitals on a second violation. Enough lashes to cripple or even kill were prescribed for various offenses. Although owners and overseers ordinarily did not cripple valuable workers, there were cases of sadistic treatment of slaves. And Spaniards who killed slaves or free persons of color seldom paid heavily for doing so.

Blacks reacting against slavery used such combative responses as malingering, sabotage, lying, stealing, sullenness; and such collaborative methods as toadying, spying for the masters, and acceptance of supervisory positions with disciplinary functions over their fellows. They also resorted to flight. They could try to claim the status of black freemen in a new Spanish community, settle in an Indian village, or search for a refuge in the wilderness. Slaves escaped from the mines of north central New Spain and took to the mountains, allying themselves with Indians to raid Spanish ranches and travelers. In some places flight was aided not only by mountains but by great spaces, forests, and swamps;

in others, it was more difficult. Slaves in coastal Peru found the open desert terrain unconducive to flight. Much effort was expended by the Spaniards to prevent flight and to find fugitives. Royal decrees in 1571–1574 formed a fugitive slave code and a system of slave control. Brutal punishments were provided for flight. Absence for six months merited death, although the sentence was sometimes reduced to castration. There were rewards for the capture of fugitives and penalties for aiding them. Flight was a chancy proposition. In Peru, at least, most slave runaways were soon captured.

Long-term slave refuges or settlements, *palenques*, existed. Their inhabitants were known as *cimarrones*. There were notable refuges on the Mosquito Coast of Central America, in Panama, Quito, and on the north shore of South America. At the beginning of the seventeenth century, in the mountains and lowlands of eastern Mexico, there were some small settlements of escaped black slaves. Bands of them preyed on mule trains and the plantations and towns of the area. Spanish efforts to control them failed. A considerable military effort attempted to root out the settlement ruled by a talented black, Yanga (or Ñanga). The viceroy accepted a compromise, agreeing to Yanga's demand that his *palenque* be considered a free town, with its own *cabildo* and Yanga as governor, with his descendants to succeed him. In return, Yanga agreed to chase fugitive slaves and aid the crown against external foes if necessary. So the new town of San Lorenzo de los Negros was established in 1612 and lasted many years. But this case was the only one of the sort in New Spain. If the problem had multiplied, the Spaniards would have made the investment necessary to deal with it.

The slave reaction that the Spaniards most feared was rebellion. It haunted them throughout the colonial era, but in three hundred years never proved serious. There was a slave revolt in Española in 1522, another in Mexico in 1523. In 1537 the government in New Spain uncovered what it thought was a plot for a general slave revolt in collaboration with Indians—the ultimate nightmare—including the planned murder of all Spaniards and creation of a Negro kingdom. Some alleged conspirators confessed under torture and were drawn and quartered. Revolts in the 1540s led to a number of restrictions on blacks, including curfew and a prohibition on three or more gathering in public without their masters. Although there were other small black slave uprisings in Spanish America, and many alarums and excursions, the great bulk of the black slaves remained closely restricted, did not riot, and did not escape to the mountains.[9] Such actions required risks that most human beings are not able to accept. Black slaves merely acted as people usually do when faced by unconquerable coercive force.

All European groups in America were preoccupied with slave flight and criminality and were terrified of slave rebellion. Regulations for the punishment of black misdeeds were strict everywhere. They were not always enforceable, and sometimes, when used, they were modified. Whether a white who murdered a black in 1800 was more strictly punished in Spanish America or in the United States is apparently arguable. What is not arguable is that in both areas to murder a black or an Indian was safer than to kill a white. There was a bit more violent rebellion among black slaves in Spanish than in English North America, but that is insignificant compared with the fact that in none of the European slave areas in the Western Hemisphere were serious rebellions common. The reason for the lack of large-scale violent resistance was that the conditions of slavery in plantation agriculture, in mills, mines, and other places requiring heavy manual labor, made slave rebellion difficult and dangerous. Slaves in other occupations in Spanish America seem not to have been much interested. They sought escape into the Spanish society for themselves and their progeny, through miscegenation and progressive integration.

Comparative Slave Systems

As indicated above, slavery was inhuman in all areas of the Western Hemisphere. Rather than degrees of benignity, one must speak of small variations in inhumanity. The decency of Spanish and Portuguese laws mattered little; what did matter was their lack of enforcement. It is no longer possible to accept the dicta of abolitionist polemics in the United States or the ramblings of foreign travelers in Brazil who "learned" that jolly slaves and indulgent owners were the norm there. What is needed are improved statistics on slave mortality, manumission, and occupations and living conditions. On the matter of sexual exploitation of slave women, it is no longer enough to dress up fragile data with rage. Is the immense amount of miscegenation in Spanish America to be considered chiefly an indication of lack of repugnance for the black race or chiefly exploitation? Is the reproductive success of black slaves in English North America and the United States evidence of especially foul exploitation—slave breeding—or was it more abhorrent to follow the Spanish practice of not encouraging reproduction but of continually replacing the slave population with imports from Africa? Can we make much of the fact that slaves, and free blacks and Afromestizos, were armed more often in Spanish than in English North America? Apparently, arming slaves reflected desperation in the great reaches of Spanish America rather than superior trust, since the Spaniards worried about the black militia.

It seems that all European powers in America were about equally guilty of accepting slavery, although there was more protest from white minority groups in English America than in Hispanic. All European powers regarded slaves as chattels who were essentially rightless. They were

[9] It has been suggested that possibly the low level of unrest among Peruvian black slaves was due to the fact that although their lives often were bleak, they were "rarely grindingly harsh." It is easier to believe this of servants and skilled slaves than of rough workers, who more likely merely were too cowed to protest much.

treated as such regardless of some protective legislation. They had almost no civil rights anywhere; the exceptions, while somewhat more prevalent in Hispanic than in English America, meant little in fact. Courts in all the colonies seldom protected slaves and nearly always were severe with their misdeeds. As to slaves, Catholicism and Protestantism were about equally unfeeling, but a difference in favor of Catholic Spanish and Portuguese America was notable in regard to free blacks and Afromestizos. Finally, some conditions seem to have brought especially harsh treatment of slaves in all colonies: a prevalence of blacks, especially slaves, as a large part of the population; and the presence of supervisors in large commercial operations—sugar, mines, and cotton—who were fearful of lax discipline, tied to output goals, and relatively impersonal in attitude toward labor gangs.

The comparative "profitability" of slavery in different European colonies is subject to conflicting interpretation. To many it seems to have been least profitable in Spanish America simply because the sugar colonies of other nations made such large cash gains, but that is only one way of measuring profitability. Significantly, important interests found slavery still profitable in the nineteenth century in the United States, Brazil, and Cuba. In most of Spanish America, however, by the Independence period sizable numbers of leaders considered black slavery economically unnecessary and morally indefensible.

Freemen of Black Heritage

There were fewer black than partially black freemen. Children born of slave mothers, regardless of the race or status of the father, were slaves. Manumission, however, was more common than in English America, though far from widespread. Spanish fathers sometimes freed their mulatto offspring. Black slaves could achieve freedom by gift of the master and had the legal right to buy their freedom. Manumission by purchase was rare, however, because for a slave to accumulate the price was difficult; sometimes,

also, the owner resisted. In any event, gang laborers probably almost never became free by any method in Spanish America. Figures for colonial Peru show not only that manumission was more common in urban than rural areas (which included the commercial farms with black gang labor), but that adult males of thirteen to thirty-five almost never were freed. Of those manumitted 82 percent were women and children. Practice varied in time and place, however. In late colonial Venezuela, for example, some slave owners freed slaves because they could make more money renting them marginal land. Manumission in Spanish America could be by testament of the owner, and might be unconditional, or it might depend on future service or other obligation before taking effect. It even occasionally happened that a slave who lacked written evidence of a dead master's intent to free him could persuade a court of the fact.

Possibly about 90 percent of the black slaves in Spanish America could not expect to buy or be given their freedom. There was some motivation for town slaves in Spanish America to try to accumulate money to buy their freedom, but few managed to do it, so it scarcely was much of an incentive. Hence to consider manumission alone the "great divide" between the legal status of slaves in Hispanic America and in English North America and the United States is misleading. The fact is that, of all slave areas, only in the southern United States did legislation finally try to block all emancipation and right of manumission. What needs to be added as part of the "divide" is that many of the free colored of Spanish America entered that condition because they were born of free mothers. Slaves could breed freemen with free mothers; they could even marry into other sociracial groups. It was the massive miscegenation in Spanish America and the free status of so many people of mixed blood that as much as manumission created a large group of free colored. Finally, it is worth suggesting that although slave owners in Spanish and English colonies were equally unfeeling toward their slaves, the Spanish attitude toward freemen of African blood was somewhat more generous, even though always a riot of prejudice and disdain.

Distribution of Black African Stock in Spanish America

The distribution of blacks and people of partially black ancestry changed greatly with time in Spanish America. We have seen that the early large traffic in slaves to New Spain was superseded in later years by larger flows to other areas, ultimately and most notably to the Caribbean islands and northern South America. Such changes were due to a variety of conditions, including domestic and international markets for commodities and the condition of local labor supplies. One of the largest changes in labor supply occurred with the growth of *castas* of mixed Indian, white, and black heritage. Reproduction involving blacks and other races varied among areas, especially in response to slave occupations (field gangs had limited opportunities), local health conditions, and the size of the local Indian and white groups. By about the year 1800 the population with a black African genetic heritage in Spanish America probably was on the order of two million, a quarter of them slaves.

There were some 550,000 black slaves in what became the eighteen republics of Spanish America;[10] of those, some 400,000 were in Cuba (212,000), Peru (88,000), Venezuela (88,000), Colombia (70,000), and Santo Domingo (30,000). None of the other major provinces had more than about 15,000.

There were some 1,500,000 free Negroids in Spanish America about the year 1800. It is difficult to untangle the figures on the populations and activities of free blacks from those of freemen only partly of black genetic heritage. Even legislation of the Spanish system sometimes simply lumped together all freemen with African blood. Nearly half of the 1,500,000 were in New

Spain (600,000); they were mostly mulattoes and zambos, well on the way to absorption into the generally Indian and mestizo population of the realm. The other largest blocs were Venezuela, 440,000; Colombia (including Panama), 140,000; and Cuba, 114,000.

New Spain in 1650 had 35,000 blacks and more than 100,000 Afromestizos (mixtures of black with white and Indian). Although black stock was widely dispersed, a large concentration was in the Valley of Mexico, with more than 20,000 before the end of the sixteenth century, and 50,000 at a later peak, including slave and free, black and Afromestizo. For many years the blacks and Afromestizos were thought a danger to order. But with time they were increasingly assimilated into the sea of Indians, the more easily in that only some 20,000 black slaves were imported to New Spain in the eighteenth century. In 1800 the black slave population was less than 10,000.

Although blacks were taken to Peru early, they were not numerous. They lived mostly in Peru's coastal area, where the Indian population died off with special rapidity. The larger Indian population of the mountains survived better, but the crown generally resisted transportation of highland Indians to the coast, both because they did not survive well there and because they were needed for the mines of the sierra. Much of the Negroid stock worked in the irrigated agriculture of coastal valleys, but the largest single concentration was in Lima, which in 1586 had an estimated 4,000 blacks, mulattoes, and zambos, of which some 25 percent were free. The percentage of black freemen was much less in rural areas. Lima had some 13,000 Africans in 1619, and in 1650 a colored population of some 30,000, only 10 percent of it free. In later years the free colored group grew in relation to the slave, and in 1792, of the total Afro-Peruvians (less than 8 percent of the Peruvian population of 1.07 million), a bit over half was free.

New Granada received black slaves from the last quarter of the sixteenth century. Most were used in the Pacific gold fields or in commercial

---

[10] The figures often included mulatto slaves.

agriculture and other tasks in the Caribbean low-lands. Cartagena received as many as 1,500 slave imports in some years in 1580–1600, and 2,000 in many years thereafter. Possibly 200,000 were imported in the entire colonial era for use in present-day Colombia, Ecuador, and Panama. There were some 72,000 black slaves in New Granada in 1810, and the Afromestizo population was very large. The relatively small Indian population, and the fact that many Indians were not accustomed to disciplined labor, opened the way to an increase in those with an African genetic heritage, especially in the north and west of New Granada, rather than among the more numerous and sedentary Indians of the center and south.

Cuba, Santo Domingo, and Puerto Rico, during the first two and a half centuries of the colonial period, suffered extinction of their Indians and received modest numbers of whites and blacks. Among the small populations, the black element was well entrenched when the great expansion of the sugar industry in the later eighteenth century increased slave imports. Cuban slave imports may have been only 13,000 up to 1773; they were 119,000 in 1774–1807, and 568,000 in 1817–1865. Before 1789, the sugar *hacendados* and merchants of Cuba complained of an undersupply of slave imports. These were much facilitated in that year by a Spanish decree authorizing free commerce in blacks for two years. It was later extended. By the early nineteenth century, so many slaves had been introduced that even former proponents of mass imports thought the trade had been carried too far. The total population rose from 171,620 in 1774 to 552,033 in 1817, while whites declined from 56 to 43 percent, and the black slave population increased faster than the free black. The free black and mulatto group was, however, notably large in Cuba, rising in 1774–1817 from 18 to 21 percent of the total population.[11] The free col-ored population continued to increase in Cuba in the nineteenth century up to the time slavery ended in 1886, even though manumission of slaves in nineteenth-century Cuba was rare. Slaves in Cuba numbered 44,300 in 1774 and 199,000 in 1817.[12] As always in Hispanic America, newly imported black slaves did not nearly reproduce themselves, and fresh imports were needed constantly. A census of Cuba in 1827 showed a total population of 704,000, made up of 311,000 whites, 286,000 slaves, and 106,000 free blacks and mulattoes, making freemen of African heritage 15 percent of the population, compared with some 8 percent in the South of the United States in 1822.[13]

The slave populations of Spain's other Caribbean colonies grew more slowly. Puerto Rico's went from 5,000 in 1765 to 13,300 in 1802 to 21,700 in 1820. Santo Domingo's slave population in 1790 was an estimated 15,000, some of them mulattoes.[14]

In Venezuela possibly 120,000 black slaves were imported during the colonial era, more than half of them in the eighteenth century. The relatively small and primitive Indian population made for a lesser dilution of the African genetic heritage than in some areas. The importation of some 30,000 blacks in 1774–1807 helped strengthen a slave interest that was stronger at Independence than in many parts of Spanish America. Free blacks, zambos, and mulattoes by

---

[11] A recent study of the subject could not be sure, however, whether the fact that the free black and mulatto population of Cuba kept pace with the rapid growth of slaves in the later eighteenth century was due to manumission or to good living conditions and a high rate of natural increase.

[12] There were at least 12,000 mulatto slaves in Cuba in 1791.

[13] In the United States in 1860 possibly 11 percent of persons of black ancestry were freemen; in the 1870s in Cuba the percentage was 38, and it was much higher than that in Brazil.

[14] The huge increase in the black African population of the Caribbean had been occurring even earlier in the English, French, and Dutch colonies there, and their islands became more black than the Spanish. The most spectacular growth was in Haiti, where blacks were not numerous until the territory became French in 1697; thereafter, Haiti was built into a large-scale sugar producer that was the envy of other powers. French Haiti in 1788 had 520,000 inhabitants, of which about 87 percent were black slaves, 8 percent white, and 5 percent free blacks or mulattoes. English Jamaica at the same time was some 90 percent black, mostly slaves.

that time in Venezuela numbered more than 400,000.

In parts of the Captaincy-General of Guatemala black slaves were of some consequence, but they were far outnumbered by Indians in the more heavily populated sections of the provinces of Guatemala and Salvador. In the Plata area black slaves were for many years chiefly of interest as commodities being forwarded to Peru, although there were small groups at such towns as Buenos Aires, Córdoba, and Tucumán. The importation of blacks through La Plata ports (especially Buenos Aires and Montevideo) greatly increased during the second half of the eighteenth century, when they handled about 50 percent of all those coming through there during the colonial era. In the interior areas the black stock tended to be assimilated with the Indian. Buenos Aires, with almost no Indians, was a different case. Late in the colonial era, as the port's prosperity grew, more black slaves were brought for use there. Some 20,000 blacks and mulattoes lived in and near the city at the end of the colonial era, a sizable proportion of the local population.

b. Race Mixtures in the Lower and "Middle" Classes

Race mixture, and attitudes toward it, were a greater dividing line between Hispanic and English America than manumission. There was little barrier to race mixture in colonial Spanish America, in law, custom, religious belief and admonition, or opportunity. When early conquerors chose to divide up Indian women, who was to stop them? Bernal Díaz complained that Cortés' captains reserved the best-favored women for themselves. Some Indian women were gifts to Spaniards by Indian leaders, a custom in some culture groups. Numerous Indian women gladly allied themselves with Spaniards, choosing to attach themselves to the lords of the land, as many Indian men did also. Partly they desired to endow children with the blood of the conquerors, a common phenomenon among conquered peoples. Indian women held in encomienda often

worked in the town house of the *encomendero* and easily became concubines, as churchmen complained. The crown's attempts to prohibit personal service in houses were unenforceable. Some Indian men did object. Encomienda Indians in Yucatán rose against concubinage in 1546, killing Spaniards and the Indian women who served them.

As time went on, upper-class males became surrounded by a veritable racial bouquet of available women. Some became wives of Europeans; many more served them as casual partners or as mistresses, in any case bearing children of increasingly complicated racial heritage. The willingness of the woman of mixed blood was ensured both by economic need and by hope of advancement for self and offspring. As black and mulatto slaves became available, they were bought at premium prices for their comeliness. The opportunities of the ruling class were irresistible. Boys partook of these delights at an early age and were less likely to assume responsibility for their offspring than their elder brothers and fathers. Even sizable numbers of ecclesiastics had liaisons that produced children. There is no reason to believe that any unusual degree of sexuality was involved in this impressive amount of miscegenation; opportunity was what was unusual.

Race mixture also went on massively between lower-class partners. The unchanging crudity of their material existence promoted it. There could be little prudery in the dark holes back of city kitchens, at night in the camps of labor gangs being served by their women, or in the huts and shacks or scrub of the countryside. Mixture also was promoted by the lack of barriers of cultural or racial repugnance or of religious prohibition or surveillance. The government tried to discourage unions between Indians and blacks, but many occurred. There was effort to protect Indians in their villages, but all sorts of authorized and illicit outsiders came in and had children by Indian women. The latter sometimes agreed because the children would not be liable to the Indian tribute or labor drafts. Blacks married free Indians in the hope that their children would be free. Although the law required that children assume the status of the mother, it sometimes was violated. In the Spanish towns the lower classes mingled and remingled without letup. Sometimes Indians built squatter settlements near Spanish towns to offer themselves as labor; other Indians lived in special sections of Spanish towns or in the houses of their masters. Men of African stock found great opportunity not only with Indian women and with women of mixed blood, but occasionally with married Spanish women. The census estimates of the colonial period probably always put the mixed stocks too low. The process of mixture was much accelerated in the eighteenth century, and the effects were of some consequence in the crises that led to Independence. In New Spain, the largest unit of the empire, by the end of the colonial period at least 40 percent of the population was of mixed racial stock. The offspring of these casual, temporary, or permanent unions often enjoyed little care, so that hordes of racially mixed children were sporadically or permanently waifs who survived by accident, charity, and their wits. The unavoidable illegitimacy and vagrancy of the man of mixed blood made him especially detestable to the elite.

Although *mestizaje* (mixture) of Spaniards and Indians began at once, some decades passed before it became a subject for discrimination. The number of mestizos began to cause alarm, partly out of fear that they might not be loyal during Indian rebellions. The same attitudes developed toward the smaller group of mulattoes. In the middle of the sixteenth century, legislation began to restrict the rights of men of mixed blood. They were not to have Indians in encomienda, not to live among the Indians, not to hold certain offices. The concept of the *casta* was loaded onto mestizos, mulattoes, zambos, and even onto pure blacks. The concept of caste came easily to Spaniards, who believed in "purity of blood," free from Muslim or Jewish mixture.

The terminology for race mixture gradually grew more elaborate, until in the eighteenth century there were some one hundred terms for racial combinations. *Mestizo, mulato,* and *zambo*

(Indian and black) were the primary mixtures. Terminology was not uniform for all Spanish America. In one system, Spaniard plus *Indian* equaled *mestizo*; mestizo plus Spanish woman equaled *castizo*; *castiza* plus Spaniard equaled Spaniard; Spaniard plus *mulata* equaled *morisco*; a *morisco* woman and a Spaniard produced an *albino*; and on and on by steps to a *coyote* woman and an Indian begetting a *chamiso*. Two often cited terms that show the white bias of the system are *tente en aire* (suspended in air), the offspring of a mestizo couple whose children often showed no change of type (that is, movement toward or away from whiteness), and *salta atrás* (throwback), a child of a *mestiza* and an Indian. Only part of the elaborate terminology was much used, but it reflected the interest of the late colonial society in the subject, and it helped reinforce the prejudice on which it was based. As Humboldt remarked early in the nineteenth century in New Spain, everyone was fascinated with "the fractions of European blood which belong to the different castes." The terms for the primary mixtures were in common use and sufficed with a few others added, like *castizo* (light mestizo) and *coyote* and *cholo* (dark mestizos).

Mestizos were the favored mixture in law and practice. They were considered *gente de razón*, capable of reasoning, which put them a notch above Indians, who were thought to be more childlike in that respect. This opened the door to some minor offices, but only a few mestizos attained such posts. They were similar to Spaniards in that they paid the *alcabala*, were liable to military service, and were subject to law in the same ways as Europeans. Some mestizos were freed of the labor draft and the tribute quite early, and later they scarcely could be held to either. In Peru by the eighteenth century the *cholo* (offspring of an Indian and a mestizo) was freed of the *mita*, though not of the tribute. Mestizos were lumped with Indians by various sorts of legislation—often unenforceable: for example, against access to cattle branding irons or to Spanish residential areas in towns. There was, in fact, ambiguity and contradiction regarding the access of mestizos to different institutions, such as the church, craft guilds, and universities.

There was no ambiguity about the need of the upper class for the services of mestizos in many tasks. Some mestizos thus accumulated property and status considerably above that of the bulk of the lower class. Even so, they were but a tiny minority. This minority is sometimes called a "middle class," but it was far from resembling the historical bourgeoisie of the European world in function or in self-image. Its access to power was almost nil, thus making it quite different from the bourgeoisie of Western Europe in the centuries after the discovery of America.

Men of African descent suffered more discrimination than mestizos. The free *mulato, zambo,* and *negro* suffered the restrictions on mestizos and also had to pay tribute like the Indians. This requirement was sometimes difficult to enforce, its legality was argued, and at times it was simply forgotten by all parties. The Spanish attitude toward mixtures of Indian and black stock indicated a low view of both: Such persons were thought to inherit the worst traits of the races of their parentage. The town council of Lima vented an early distaste for free Africans in 1574 by calling free blacks, mulattoes, and Afro-Indians "gente de mal vivir" (people who led bad lives), partly because they caused trouble among slaves and tried to control them. Free blacks and Afromestizos sometimes were subject to requirements that they hire themselves out to and live with Spaniards. Again, although there were campaigns—some by *cabildos*—to enforce such rules, enforcement was difficult. Another problem was that free Africans might be subject to curfew and arms laws, together with black slaves, and at the same time be required to serve in the militia. Sometimes the militia duty could be done in noncombat and service roles, but not always. There were serious prohibitions against black officers in the militia, and these were only slightly moderated by the militia reforms after 1763. In any event, the contradiction between discrimination and military service was palpable.

Free blacks and mulattoes were like Spaniards in being subject to the Inquisition. Men of black heritage might be sent to forced labor in the mines. They suffered other restrictions in law and practice. Peninsulars and creoles generally opposed the marriage of whites to blacks or mulattoes, and little of it occurred. New laws of the late colonial era (1778, 1805) increased the difficulty of *casta* marriage with whites. Free and slave women of black descent were subjected to sumptuary legislation, which was difficult to enforce: against using silk, pearls, or gold; or wearing the mantilla on the head; or even sleeping in canopied beds. The pretense was that such luxury must represent the fruits of prostitution. Men of African heritage found buying even minor public office difficult, and if they did so, they might have the sale canceled because of white protests. Race prejudice is starkly revealed in the fact that a quadroon in office was less objectionable than a mulatto. Blacks were kept from church positions both because of their socioracial status and because of their illegitimacy. Their access to education was restricted by both low income and discrimination. When the Jesuits of Lima tried mixing races in their academy, Spanish protests killed the experiment. In 1763 persons of African blood were excluded from receiving doctorates in Spanish American universities, an indication of continuing discrimination, even though exceptions occurred thereafter. Finally, could anything be more eloquent of prejudice and discrimination than the prohibition in 1614 by the Lima *cabildo* of coffins for those of African descent as an affront to the superior status of Spaniards?

Men of African blood were, however, much needed in society. Even when Spanish artisans tried to restrict blacks, the community might decide otherwise. The Lima *cabildo* sometimes gave a black carpenter a license if he swore he had been a master worker in Spain. The free Afro-Peruvian thus pursued his individual advantage. There was no incentive to develop a sense of racial solidarity. The conditions of existence were so hard, materially and spiritually, that he focused on his individual plight and had no psychic resources or material treasure to spare on projects for improving the lot of his racial fellows. The route upward was through money and bleaching.

Blacks worked mostly at menial tasks. Many were quite evident in the community as vendors, artisans, inn- and storekeepers, bakers, confectioners. Their incomes were low, with few exceptions. A few Afro-Peruvians did own slaves. Using money and bleaching, a few men in the late colonial era appealed to the *audiencias* for judgments that they were white. In the same period mulattoes (sometimes called *pardos*) were given an opportunity to advance by being allowed to buy licenses that made them legally white. They were called *cédulas de gracias al sacar* ("thanks for the exclusion" or "exemption"), certainly a racist term. Apparently, the sales served the crown's need for revenue and were intended also to dilute the growing restiveness of the creoles. What such a purchased change of status meant immediately to an individual is not clear. One report stated that it only meant that the individual's wife could dress differently. In any event, black and Afromestizo labor, slave and free, was important to many areas of Spanish America at various times. In some places the black stock became less important with time and sometimes was assimilated to the point of disappearance from the public eye; in others, its role increased.

Mixture in the eighteenth century proceeded to the point where it led, on the one hand, to hardening of discrimination as a result of upper-class fears and, on the other, to a situation where making sense of the socioracial categories, or what they meant in practice, became baffling. There were Indians who had black slaves, and black farmers using servile Indian labor. The Indian villages became increasingly mestizo in blood and custom, as the result of three centuries of residence there by officials, vagrants, churchmen, and adventurers of all combinations of racial stock. Mixed-blooded children were issuing from concubinage and common law marriages by the hundreds of thousands. Lesser numbers came from legal intermarriage of all sorts, even between Indian *caciques* and Spanish women of good family.

"Passing" to a higher socioracial category than was justified by one's actual heritage (if fully known) was thus the road upward for the lower class. It could be done by marrying whiter and thus improving the social status of the offspring. It could be done by buying from the government a bleaching document. It could be done by lying. Claims could be disputed but doubts could scarcely be verified. Who could naysay a self-proclaimed quadroon? Thus, although the elite openly despised the colored, it did permit slow assimilation. Its racial prejudice took the form of at least slightly softening contempt as the degree of whiteness increased. Why this was the case is unclear. One of the unproven assertions is that the darker skin of Mediterranean whites made it easier for them than for northern Europeans to accept racial mixtures. In any event, the Spanish attitude was different from the English North American prejudice—that a trace of black heritage was the same as 100 percent. English North Americans simply would not accept racial mixtures, although of course they fathered them. The Spanish attitude, together with acceptance of persons of some black and Indian ancestors into upper-class ranks, made the burden of nonwhite blood a trifle easier to bear than in English North America. But that small colonial difference came to be more important in the course of the nineteenth and especially the twentieth centuries.

Discrimination became such a tangle that generalization is difficult, since it varied from place to place and time to time, in guilds, *cofradías*, *consulados*, universities, the church, and other places. The more the mixed population grew, the more the elite tried to discriminate and the less it was able to control the situation. At the end of the colonial period, socioracial conditions were in such confusion that an official in New Spain declared, "Nobody dared to classify the *castas*," because if classification were done rigorously, it would uncover dark stains in families that thought them erased by time.

c. Effects of the Socioracial System

Men of the lower class reacted in various ways: with apathy, sullenness, frustration, alienation, spasmodic rage, "criminality," and efforts to find the best accommodation by work or wit within an unsatisfactory system. It has been remarked that all they had was "survival techniques and the acquisitive instinct." Since they often could not exercise the latter, alienation became "their tent, hut or hovel, anomie their landscape." Indians often seem to have reacted with apathy. They did rage and revolt on many occasions. Furthermore, insofar as they could insulate themselves in their villages, they had an acceptable physical and psychological "answer" to their subordination. It has been said, however, that the destruction of much of their way of life left them with "damaged souls."

Fleeing slaves, if they were fortunate, might found or reach semi-independent settlements of their fellows, or they might become buccaneers or take to the mountains for a career of banditry. The reaction of the mestizo is of especial interest because that was the predominant stock in a number of areas before the formation of independent republics. The mestizo is commonly regarded as one without deep roots in either culture in the colonial period, thus psychologically adrift while economically striving. Many mestizos were quite aggressive in searching for place or security, and this striving, together with their numbers, alarmed the elite and led to emphasis upon what were thought to be the mestizos' less lovely habits. Such efforts at psychoanalysis of the mestizo class are of value insofar as they indicate that miscegenation and socioracial discrimination over a period of three centuries were historical processes of great importance, however little they resemble such spectacular events as battles and sieges, great silver strikes, corn riots, and gorgeous shows to welcome new bishops and viceroys.

There is some reluctance among scholars to stress the racial element in this system. It certainly was not uncomplicated caste—that is, birth was not the sole determinant of member-ship in the socioracial groups, and there was at least some limited vertical social mobility. The last factor is what encourages judgments that the discrimination and prejudice involved in the system were social, not racial. Yet there still was stratification not only by wealth and habits, but by color and physiognomy. It has been well said that for Hispanic America the tragedy was that the inequalities of Europe were reinforced and complicated by race. The emphasis on white purity among the elite cannot be described simply as a matter of class; there were elements of race or caste in it also.

However the system of status, discrimination, and prejudice during the colonial centuries is described, it did help to maintain the grip of the elite, to defend the social order from attack within and without. That was one kind of effectiveness or success. But the system of control and division, and the reluctance to accept spiritually the equality of the lower-class stocks, meant that their abilities had to be denigrated. That habit was reinforced by what the upper class interpreted as evidence in habits of life and work: that is, that the lower classes were dirty, ill-mannered, improvident, and such traits must show lack of ability or will or virtue. The elite had neither the knowledge nor the desire to arrive at any different judgment. Thus the early generations of Latin American republican leaders after Independence thought their proletariats poor material for the construction of modern nations. Both the interests and the inherited convictions of the elite entered into this judgment, and in that sense the socioracial system of the colonial period was a failure. It did not prepare the Spanish Americans for what lay before them. In Spanish America (and in Spain) the class system impeded development in the industrial age. That development demanded ever broader use of the physical and intellectual abilities of the masses. The upper classes hesitated to allow such use.

10 Economic Life in Spanish America

"Early to bed and early to rise" in colonial Spanish America was less likely to make "healthy, wealthy, and wise" than in Benjamin Franklin's homeland. Economic opportunity was quite limited for most people, as it was, of course, in much of the world. A few people, however, did quite well. Some of them were creoles, but many of them finally decided that their profits were being intolerably limited by Spanish regulation.[1] All colonial powers, of course, believed in the mercantilist regulatory system. Regulation, however, depended on policing, and Spain's effort was much too feeble to be a decisive element in American economic life. Spain scarcely tried to control production in America, and its sizable efforts to control international trade were an expensive failure because Spain itself let some foreign goods flow to America, and Americans bought many more illegally. Spain's military and naval power could not prevent it, being unequal to the belligerent economic policies and military force of the British, French, and Dutch.

a. The System

Among major reasons for limitation of opportunity to a few people in Spanish America were strict class lines, property concentration, monopoly, and privilege. The system of privilege forced most work onto men of color for little return. On the other hand, *hidalgos* had exemptions from direct taxation and from imprisonment or attachment of property for debts. Encomienda grants went to a few men and helped them accumulate income and property. Land grants were channeled to the elite, who also squatted on Indian lands and beat off protests. Elite economic activity had support in entail, mortmain, *repartimiento*, in props to the hacienda system and peonage, and in advantages in the courts.[2] The elite dominated the *cabildos* with their powers to distribute land, allocate its use, fix prices, adjudicate disputes, and influence labor systems. Only the elite could make much money from mining, because of their access to capital, official favor, and wholesale commerce. Also a part of the privileged system was Spain's ideal of a limited port system, a Spanish monopoly on commerce and shipping, and other commercial regulations designed to benefit favored groups. Finally, the tight control of the elite was furthered by family ties. The damping effect of all this on

[1] See Chapter 6, Section a, on mercantilism, Chapter 11, Section d, on trade regulation, and Chapter 17 on late colonial economic complaints.

[2] See Chapter 5, Section b, on encomienda, Chapter 6, Section b, on the *repartimiento* of goods and other exactions and business practices that involved official authority or force, and Chapter 8, Section d, on the labor *repartimiento*.

incentive among the masses was a factor in their low productivity and lack of a psychology of thrift. They knew that "early to bed and early to rise"—hard work—brought small reward.

Franklin's fascination with science and technology, no less than his middle-class economic optimism, had but weak counterparts in the Spanish world. The sugar plantations in the Spanish Caribbean, for example, were notoriously inferior to those of French, British, and Dutch areas. Spanish knowledge of that ignorance led reformers in the late eighteenth century to assail it as a barrier to improvement of the economy. The intellectual climate of the Spanish world did not favor the acquisition of new ideas and techniques. Control of publication, study, and expression hurt science. Laymen feared to depart from privilege and monopoly. The church too often thought new ideas dangerous to faith and morality.

Also damaging to economic life in America were heavy freight charges due to great distances and rough terrain. It was hurt also by low popular incomes, which restricted the internal market, nor did popular incomes increase over time as happened in some Western European nations and their colonies. Well-to-do small farmers, merchants, and craftsmen were not numerous in Spanish America.

Yet another factor was the mingling of European and Indian economic systems. Leftist theorists in the late twentieth century overstated the effects of that by claiming that after the conquest Latin America was not feudal.[3] Spaniards introduced money and the capitalist system. The fact was, however, that in most of Spanish America the Indian society felt only limited effects from capitalism. Many Indians scarcely produced for the market. Furthermore, they remained "feudal" in suffering many noneconomic forms of coercion (like the class system) that took their production and labor. The Latin Americans who from Independence to the late twentieth century insisted that "feudalism" was a prominent part of the colonial system were using a term

with useful general connotations, whatever its acceptability among Marxists.

The Spaniards also introduced new transport, better mining methods, new forms of manufacturing and craftsmanship, new food crops and animals—swine, goats, sheep, cattle, fowl, fruits, vegetables, cereals—and demands that they be prepared or used in European style. They also introduced such tools unknown to the Indians as the plow, saw, wheelbarrow, and foot treadle loom. They wanted European meat, wine, olive oil, wheat bread, and pastries to be available from American sources as soon as possible. Francisco Pizarro lived to see the first oranges ripen in Peru. Many another conqueror labored to grow pears and barley and to instruct Indians in the intricacies of baking with wheat flour. Still, the Indians clung to many of their old ways, accepting some European products more readily than others.

Spain and Latin America at the beginning of the nineteenth century still were lands of the aristocratic dispensation, with a feeble middle class and few of the marks of the bourgeois egalitarianism that was to distinguish the coming age in the Occident. They had long faced competition from the more successful economic systems of Britain, France, Holland, and finally the United States. Manufactured goods poured into the Spanish world from other lands. The factors that had kept the Spanish world economically "colonial"—dependent on better-developed areas—increased rather than decreased with time, and the new nations inherited them along with independence from Spain early in the nineteenth century.

b. Finance

The elite controlled investment capital. A worker's income did not permit even an interest in saving, when a field hand worked more than three days to earn the price of a chicken and twenty for his tribute payment. The elite caused capital shortages by heavy expenditures for luxurious living and for land—the latter partly for

---

[3] See Chapter 34, Section d, on dependency theory.

prestige rather than profit. Much of the rest of investment went to mining, commerce, and government. Lesser funds went into industry, transportation, and social services. Furthermore, since America was a debtor area, funds went abroad in payment of charges for imports and taxes. The result was shortages of coins despite the heavy American production of gold and silver pieces, with the first mint having been created at Mexico City in 1536. Another feature of the system was wild price fluctuation due to transportation and communications problems, lack of storage facilities, bad weather, plant and animal diseases, and monopolies. There were 600 percent changes in wheat prices in a few years in New Spain. Great price rises—and short supply—of maize provoked serious riots.

The only banks in the Indies were a few that invested in silver mining. Merchants and the church were the most important sources of loans. Merchants financed not only commerce, but also mining, agriculture, and stock raising. The church was heavily involved in lending, usually on mortgages. Some wealthy craft guilds lent money. Sometimes estate owners could lend money, though they were typically land-poor borrowers. There were specialized lenders who financed the purchase of public offices. Contributions came from foreign sources, which sent capital into Sevilla's merchant houses, into foreign companies that received *asientos* to supply African slaves to Spanish America, and into loans to the Spanish crown. The bulk of the capital, however, was domestic. Much of it went for military expenditures in Europe and America, payment for foreign goods and loans, luxury, and largely unused land. Hence, modern critics condemn misuse of the great capital resources of the Spanish system. That is, however, merely an economic point of view. Could Ferdinand and Isabella of Spain abandon the faith to Protestant attack merely to save money? Could the class system be abandoned in order to ease the way for better investment in land? What else could the elite of the Spanish world do but act according to their own vision of proper social arrangements

and public policy? That their vision coincided with their own class interest was merely human.

c. Transportation and Communications

Water transport usually was cheapest and fastest in that day but was poorly developed in Spanish America. Traffic by sea was sizable but not as well developed as in Britain, Holland, or British America. There was enough traffic, however, so that ships were built at times in most American coastal provinces. Such shipbuilding did not become a major industry because seaborne traffic faced too many problems in Spanish America. The worst was that many regional economies in the area produced the same or similar commodities, making trade between them small and intermittent. That fundamental difficulty remained in Latin America in the nineteenth and twentieth centuries. Another of the colonial difficulties was competition from contrabandists. In addition, piracy and warfare made ocean traffic risky. A sizable problem was government restriction on trade and on ship movements. Finally, there was no big fishing industry to give support to shipbuilding, supply, marketing, and the training of mariners. Thus, although shipping occurred between scores of ports in Spanish America and between there and a smaller number of ports in Europe and Asia, it was on a small scale. Spanish America did not become a shipbuilding or ocean-carriage power.

Few rivers were commercially important. The largest navigable systems had little traffic: the Magdalena-Cauca, the Plata, and the Orinoco. Rivers in the mountain areas of greatest population were not navigable. The terrain required the use of costly land transport. Much of it went by pack mule, because even to provide a modest one-way dirt track for carts in the mountains was too costly.

A long-distance cart road was hacked out of the mountains between Veracruz and central Mexico in the mid-sixteenth century because of the great silver strikes of the 1540s. Carts were useful for heavy or bulky materials like mining and refining machinery and timbers. A heavy two-wheeled *carro* was developed as sort of a moving fortress that provided protection against Indians and bandits. It carried more than two tons, and was drawn by sixteen mules. But the road fell into ruin in the first half of the seventeenth century, because demand from the mines waned, and the new haciendas tended to be self-contained. Given these developments, plus labor shortages, the government decided not to keep up the road. In the seventeenth century and most of the eighteenth the route was a mule track. Then economic revival in the late 1700s led to construction of a new Mexico City–Veracruz road, via Jalapa, a bit longer but less mountainous. Some other long-distance routes were used by carts and wagons of several types, usually pulled by mules or oxen. Cart and wagon routes were gradually extended to cover a huge area, from the Valley of Mexico to the north as far as Chihuahua near the present-day Mexico–United States border. There was cartage in the eighteenth century from Lima in Peru north to Paita, where pack mules took over for further carriage into the mountains of Quito and New Granada. There was heavy cartage, using great two-wheeled vehicles, between the Plata River system and Tucumán, across the rolling plains of what now is northern Argentina. North of Tucumán to Upper Peru traffic was by mule pack. The 550-mile cart route between Tucumán and the river ports existed because of the favorable terrain and because the silver of Peru could almost ignore freight charges.

Colonials complained often about the foul roads of the Indies, but neither government nor private enterprise would spend much on road building or maintenance. Merchant guilds had some responsibility but accomplished little with their limited resources. The poor sometimes were subject to *corvée*—forced or public labor on roads and tracks. Much of the effort on roads went to service the richer mining areas and a few major towns.

Some transport was by human porter, which had been a large-scale Indian activity before the conquest, using efficient pack frames and tumplines. The llama had been the only working animal and existed only in the Inca area. Even there, porters had been used, because llamas would carry only about one hundred pounds each and men moved faster. After the conquest, backpacking was mostly by Indians, though other *castas* participated. Forty porters bearing fifty-pound loads would carry a ton. By the mid-sixteenth century pack animals had so increased that shippers lost much of their interest in porters.

For more than two and a half centuries most land transport was by pack animal, chiefly mules. A muleteer (*arriero*) with a small train (*recua*) of twenty animals could transport about two tons. Some large strings represented considerable capital and were owned by men of standing. Small owner-workers also were common. The mule skinners were lower-class men, Indians or *castas*. Packing, covering, and lashing of loads were matters for experts. There was a severe limit to the size and weight of items of cargo, and loads had to be distributed equally on each side of a mule. Encampments of *recuas* at junction points or prominent supply posts were lively places with much drinking, fighting, trading, whoring, and other entertainment.

Land freightage was so costly that small producers often sold out to larger ones who could afford the charges. In the eighteenth century more than one-third of the indigo production of the Captaincy-General of Guatemala was by small growers in El Salvador, Honduras, and Nicaragua who could not afford to transport their produce to Guatemala City. They sold their crop to peddlers or to *corregidores* or to large planters, or they took their produce to one of several provincial fairs for the same purpose. The large planters owned mule *recuas* that transported the indigo they produced themselves or bought at the indigo fairs. Everywhere, the shipment of even maize over short distances was impossible at times, partly because of travel costs and poor circulation of market information. At times transportation difficulties, often complicated by foreign naval activity, caused diversion of traffic from the Isthmus of Panama to Cape Horn or the Acapulco-Veracruz route across Mexico. The latter could raise the price of goods severely.

Upper-class travelers rode horses and mules. Spanish riding mules had an international reputation: Spanish kings gave them as presents to brother monarchs. Mules were better on mountain trails than horses. Chairs or slings might be hung between mules or carried by porters. Carriages were a late development, often used only in or near town, although a few long-distance routes were developed late in the colonial era. The carriage route from the port of Valparaíso to Santiago, in Chile, about seventy miles, was opened only in 1795. An overland carriage journey anywhere was a tooth-jarring experience. Travelers in the Indies found shelter and food at inns, monasteries, and private residences, or they camped in the open. Travel was slow, uncomfortable, and dangerous, because of health hazards and action by hostile Indians and bandits. For the same reasons the communication of information was also slow and uncertain.

d. Landholding

The great estate or hacienda in colonial Spanish America was the heart of the aristocratic dispensation, desired by private individuals and the church and protected by public authority.[4] Much of colonial life depended on aspects of great estate management. It was a prime element in the access of the creole elite to power, wealth, and prestige. A critical aspect of hacienda history was the acquisition of Indian community lands. The church supported *latifundio* and had vast holdings of its own.[5] In addition to great estates,

───────────

[4] Other terms besides hacienda also were used for great estates—for example, *estancia*, although the latter also sometimes meant a small holding and had other meanings.

[5] *Latifundio* derives from *latifundium*, the great estate of the Roman empire, and is a general term for the great estate system.

Spanish towns and Indian communities owned land. There were also small individual landholders, but they labored under legal and economic difficulties and played only a paltry part in public affairs. The system of landholding was a great difference between Spanish (and Portuguese) America and much of British America.

Types and Functions

During the conquest, interest in land was overshadowed by the lure of gold, pearls, and *entradas*, which made for impermanence of residence and little concern for rural estates. But Spaniards early acquired small land parcels. (Under Spanish law, title to land did not include subsurface resources, the exploitation of which required separate royal license.) On foundation a town had or assumed authority to assign lands for common use: for general and specialized pasture, such as for team oxen or cattle due for slaughter; woodlands; fields for cultivation, to be parceled out and supposedly given for use by drawing lots. The settlers also received, as individuals, residential lots in town and rural lands, from an expedition leader who had license to apportion them or who hoped later to receive approval of his acts. Once such apportionments had been made, to rescind them was legally and politically costly. Foot soldiers of the conquest were granted as rural lands *peonías*, "one-family farms," each typically about twenty acres. Cavalrymen received *caballerías*, about five times as large as *peonías*.

Other types of grants were made from the extensive royal lands (*realengos*) by town councils and royal officials. Some ten thousand land grants were made in New Spain in the century after the conquest. A *merced* was a grant, either of use or ownership, and the former type might slide into the latter over time. Generally, *mercedes* were granted beyond the common pasture lands of the Spanish towns. Some were distributed by conquerors, more by towns. Often the grants did not give boundaries, or they were ambiguous. Very early there were disputes about the nature of municipal rights in distributing such lands. Regulations stated that land was to be actually used, not just accumulated. Sometimes *mercedes* could be passed to heirs, with payment of fees to the town; but difficulties arose from regulations that provided that *mercedes* should pass to heirs as holdings in common (*haciendas comuneras*), which created problems of administration, and made sale of rights almost impossible.

Acquiring land through legal means was often costly and time-consuming, so there was much squatting without title, sometimes on land belonging by tradition and use to Indian communities. There were forced and fraudulent sales of Indian lands by the *caciques* and by Indian *cabildos*. Great confusion reigned because of fraud, force, poor definition of boundaries, Indian community claims, sales and subdivision and combination. In the late sixteenth century the crown's need for funds increased its interest in selling royal lands, which created pressure for better titles. As early as 1571 use was made of *composición*, whereby titles could be cleared or acquired, or boundary disputes settled, by money payment to the crown. This favored the wealthier owners. Requirements for proof of title were tightened in the eighteenth century, leading to a plague of *denuncias* against occupiers as the law provided. Again, this worked in favor of the wealthy. At the end of the colonial period there still were big problems with titles and boundary disputes, but the growth of great estates had overshadowed everything else in connection with land.

The Great Estate—Hacienda

Accumulation of Estates.   Few large landed holdings came from single grants. The *marquesado* of Cortés and his heirs in New Spain was an exception that the crown came to regret. The haciendas were built up by accumulation. Spaniards in America passionately desired large properties, not surprisingly when agriculture and grazing were the chief sources of wealth. In such

societies, large landholdings worked by dependent labor almost inevitably confer social distinction and political power upon the owners. A system of great estates—held by a civil and ecclesiastical elite—was a feature of Iberian society in Europe. The system was the easier to hold together because the Spaniards brought from Europe the system of entail (*mayorazgo* in Spanish), which forbade the sale of the whole or parts of an estate. Not all estates were entailed, but there were enough to make entail a prime target of reformers after Independence. The equivalent institution for church estates was mortmain (dead hand, *mano muerta* in Spanish). Despite such aids to stability in landownership, civil estates and church lands were sold during the colonial era.

Much else in law and practice favored the creation and retention of great estates. The common lands of Spanish towns were available on a privileged basis to estate owners, who dominated the town councils. They arranged, for example, to pasture their cattle on common lands. *Hacendados* had advantages in the labor market, in the system of price controls (some of which they set themselves through town councils), and in access to capital. There was legislation on the size of grazing lands and on requirements for erecting buildings and other improvements on holdings, but it was little enforced. Other advantages for the elite were physical force to dispossess and beat off Indians, superior access to legal talent, preferential treatment by the courts, and political clout with administrative officials in disputes with Indians. Although there were areas where Indian communities protected their lands quite well against *hacendados* and were not driven into peonage, that was not typical.

All this was inevitable, given Spanish tradition, the heavily agricultural base of the colonial economy, and social stratification in America. The small freehold farm was not typical of Spain, and there was nothing about American conditions to make the situation different there. Quite the opposite, for the process of land accumulation by a minority of Spaniards was facilitated in such areas as New Spain and Peru by the decline in the Indian population. The Spanish policy of concentrating the remaining Indians into fewer communities intensified the effects. Spaniards could claim land vacated by the congregated Indians. The decline of Indian labor also upset the food supply to the Spanish towns. Thus, the hacienda grew partly as a more efficient way of production, using peonage to ensure a labor force. It also grew because smaller Spanish holders usually lacked the capital to develop production properly and because in many areas agriculture simply did not appeal to very many Spaniards as a likely way of making profits. The fact was that although demand for agricultural and pastoral produce grew with time in America, the absolute amount was much less than the haciendas could have provided had they increased production only modestly. Some small haciendas did survive to supply Spanish towns.[6]

Another reason for increased land grants was a need for political gifts. With no more Indians to allot in encomienda and a limited number of public offices to parcel, what but land was left to reward men for service or to ensure their loyalty? The viceroys in the 1550s and 1560s increasingly used land grants for such purposes, and the first towns were established whose founders received no encomiendas. Also, the silver discoveries of the 1540s made commercial agriculture, hence landholdings, seem more attractive, to serve the rich mining camps.

Land accumulation, therefore, accelerated in the late sixteenth century, but haciendas did not exist until the seventeenth. By 1700 they were a dominant institution. Although encomiendas were allotments of Indian service and not land grants, some *encomenderos*, as men of influence, money, and property in town, had advantages in the acquisition of land. In Chile *encomenderos* even cited their encomiendas as justification for

asking for land (*mercedes*) within the areas where their encomienda Indians lived. Even when a creole family lost its lands, it merely meant that another elite family took over, or it was parceled to other large owners—that is, the replacement of hacienda families by men rising from below into the creole elite did not disturb the process of agglomeration of land into fewer hands.

The church became a huge landowner. Its institutions received early grants from conquerors and town councils and from newly converted Indians. They accumulated land by pious gift. Both the secular and the regular clergy benefited, but especially the latter. Church institutions owned some land outright; to some they held partial title through mortgage lending. As early as 1535 the crown tried to limit church holdings in America, listening to complaints from colonists and remembering the vast estates of the church in Europe. Discussion and action on the matter continued throughout the colonial era, with little effect. Estimates put church-dominated land (including mortgage interests and rentals) at the end of the colonial era at over one-half of the productive or usable land in Spanish America, which was an exaggeration. The church did have large holdings, however, especially in areas where climate and soil, labor and markets, were favorable to productive use.

***Character and Effects of* Latifundismo.** The most important thing about the hacienda was not the land or its produce, but the social system of which it was the center. Hacienda resembled the medieval European manorial system in concentration of property holding, class divisions, and a synthesis of socioeconomic elements. They were also alike in displaying, beneath apparent uniformity, a considerable variety, growing out of varying geographic and social conditions. No wonder *latifundismo* was not precisely the same in Chile, central Mexico, and Cuba. Some critical elements, however, were found almost everywhere it existed.

First, concentration of landownership bol-

---

[6] They were called by various names—*chacras* in Peru. There is no clear way of differentiating between the huge manorial haciendas and the "small" ones, although 359 acres has been suggested as the dividing line in colonial Peru.

stered the class system by making the rural population almost hereditarily poor, dependent, diffident, undemanding, and unambitious. Subordination was part of the Indian heritage from preconquest society, and under hacienda it was reinforced. Diffidence was the inevitable stance of the peon, standing before the master or majordomo, barefoot or sandaled, in rough cotton shirt and drawers, straw hat in hand, patient, humble, hopeless. In the second place, governmental and social power became concentrated in hacienda owners, often acting through managers and supervisors. They acquired these powers by assuming them when other authority was not present; having them thrust upon them by peons who needed adjudication of disputes and guidance and aid in a weary life; and having them granted, both implicitly and explicitly, by the imperial government. For another thing, ownership of a great estate was part of a mystique of superiority. True, it was a source of income, and it helped signify a person's worthiness for place on the town council. But the latter possibility, more than conferring power, meant social distinction. Largely for that reason, a man who made a fortune in trade or mining used it to buy estates. The glory of being a *hacendado* went beyond economic terms. A fourth element was that poverty and lack of opportunity among peons resulted in sloppy work habits and a lack of incentive to save. Furthermore, although there were differences between ecclesiastical and other rural estates, both contributed to concentration of ownership, low social mobility, and apathy among workers.

Hacienda also contributed to the decline of the Indian village, the *república de indios* of Spanish social theory, by usurpation of Indian lands and by attracting some village Indians to live on the hacienda. The latter was not typical, however; haciendas usually encouraged Indian communities to live outside but near the estate boundaries, as a reserve labor force. Much Indian labor on the haciendas remained periodic, though the permanent labor force gradually increased. The availability of labor was enlarged by

the disruption of the village that, we noted, resulted from the presence of all sorts of drifters and exploiters, and by the great increase in the mestizo population, some of which was sopped up by the haciendas.

Hacienda was a link between the growing Spanish towns and the dwindling Indian villages. The *hacendados* lived in town most of the time, where they were part of the upper-class front (creole and peninsular) against popular turbulence and social pretension.[7] Haciendas helped regulate rural society and economic flows from it to town. Some *hacendados* received periodic personal service by Indians in their town houses, reflecting practice in preconquest times and under encomienda. The manager—*mayordomo*— of a hacienda spent some time in town on financial, marketing, and supply business. Under the majordomo were supervisors or foremen who stayed on the estate and bore such titles as *calpisque* or *capataz*.

Haciendas were largely devoted to agricultural and pastoral pursuits, sometimes specializing to some extent in one or the other. Some grew sugar cane and had elaborate and expensive industrial works. They usually sold their product locally, however, because mainland haciendas generally were inconveniently located for participation in the Atlantic sugar trade.[8]

The overseas export sugar business was associated not with the system of free yet dependent peons, but with tropical plantation agriculture using black slave labor. Whereas haciendas were held as much for their contribution to social status as for profit, plantations were geared to the latter. The plantation, unlike the typical hacienda, was closely linked to international commerce and lacked the feature of supplying local towns that was so prominent with hacienda. The frequent paternalism of the owners of haciendas toward labor did not exist on plantations, where

---

[7] See Chapter 8, Section a, on the preference of Spaniards for town life.

[8] Brazil, however, was conveniently located for that. See Chapter 15, Section b.

slaves were mere cogs in a machine. The subsistence production of the hacienda often was conspicuously absent from plantations, which concentrated on their cash crop and bought much of the food required for the slaves. Plantations did not become prominent in Spanish America until the eighteenth century.

Most haciendas had varied activities, including agriculture, stock raising, milling, and artisan crafts. Largely this variety came from the Spanish interest in profit that we saw in *encomenderos* who put Indians to building mills before haciendas existed. Varied production or hacienda self-sufficiency, in fact, usually was the only reasonable course. Maximum production made little sense to the *hacendado* at that time; nor did rigid specialization. Some measure of specialization, however, was common. The attractive choice, rather than maximum production, was to arrange monopolies, maintain high prices, and exploit a limited market. So the hacienda was largely self-sufficient, but also was market-oriented—with a monopolistic bias.

So why did the *hacendado* thirst for more land when he did not fully exploit what he had? The motive was partially social ambition and pride. But it was also good business, because monopolization of land inhibited the rise of nearby competitors. Furthermore, if haciendas had produced commodities on all their land, they would have flooded the market, which happened frequently in any event. Hacienda production was limited by the size of urban markets, fluctuating demand from the mining areas, and the lack of export markets for most agricultural and pastoral products. The most market-oriented landed enterprises in the Spanish Indies were sugar operations. But they did not typically become rigidly specialized, raising much of their own maize, wheat, and cattle. This situation did change in the late colonial era, but in limited areas such as Cuba and Puerto Rico.

Labor and social conditions under hacienda and peonage were less oppressive than under encomienda and *repartimiento*, and the peon can

be described as "satisfied" in the sense that the hacienda offered a refuge, protection, a certain minimum of more or less guaranteed subsistence. The flow of seasonal workers showed that they perceived advantage (as did the hacienda resident force) in the connection. "Locking in" peons, as was done with workers in *obrajes*, was not necessary. Thus, peons "enslaved themselves" by hoping for beneficence from the *patrón*, even though they knew that owners and managers were far from generous. Many Indians had little choice but peonage, either having lost their land or being unable to sustain themselves and meet tax and other obligations by means of Indian community production.

A large slice of late colonial life can be seen on the rural estate, with its croplands and pastures, corrals, grist mill, blacksmith and carpentry shops, cart and plow oxen, pack mules and burros, riding horses for travel and supervision and cowpunching, walls and gates around the headquarters compound, its chapel and sometimes a resident priest. There were also residences for the majordomo and his assistants and foremen—not elaborate, but better than the huts of the resident or temporarily employed peons. Great hacienda houses for the owners generally were a late development, mostly of the eighteenth century or after Independence in the nineteenth. On and around these baronies the peons shuffled from cradle to the grave in isolation from the world.

e. The Church and the Economy

The church was a big economic factor. We noted its landholdings and income from tithes. It received gifts (labor, goods, property, money), forced labor, and interest on loans. Service fees, as for weddings and funerals, caused complaint, but efforts to fix charges failed to dampen clerical avarice. Gifts took many forms, but real property and money income were most important. Pious persons of low and high estate gave materials to build churches or commodities to sustain clerics. Poor Indians often gave free labor for church activity; sometimes they were persuaded to give it. The church received *repartimiento* labor. Ecclesiastical personnel and institutions were exempt from most taxes (including the sales tax) on goods they produced for themselves or on nonprofit transactions. But definition and enforcement were difficult and caused bickering.

Much money income came from endowments and annuities and from lending operations. To put a girl into a convent, a father usually had to provide a dowry, which could take the form of an annuity. Other similar gifts of income were made for such pious purposes as perpetual prayers for the testator. Money income came from church loans, important in a society with little liquid capital and no banking structure. The church used many devices to circumvent ecclesiastical injunctions against lending for profit.

Church property sometimes was badly managed, although that of the Jesuits seldom was. The numerous monasteries with a handful of residents represented poor use of resources and made finding competent full-time managers in the religious community difficult. Many properties were poorly run simply because those in charge were amateurs. Even though managers often hired majordomos, usually lawyers or notaries, the capacity of the religious to choose or supervise the majordomos often was defective. Some religious houses had financial difficulty both for these reasons and because of their inability to attune their expenditures to their income.

The lay elite and the government often objected to the church's wealth and to some specific economic activities. Efforts were made to stop church accumulation of real property as early as the 1530s and were often repeated thereafter. An especially great effort was made in the eighteenth century. Some complaint came from colonials; some grew out of crown search for income. Decrees in 1717 and 1734 tried to prevent creation of new conventual establishments and restrict the number of novices admitted to the orders in America. A pronouncement of 1754 forbade clerical participation in the drafting of wills. None of this had much effect. Jesuit properties were seized in the 1760s, though not primarily because of the order's wealth. Wartime necessity in the 1790s and early nineteenth century led to more efforts.[9]

To argue that reduction of church ostentation and luxury would have freed funds for productive uses is unrealistic. Probably the crown would have used the savings for administrative and military purposes. Whatever additional land the colonial elite might have acquired from the church probably would have been left unworked or the profits from its exploitation largely eaten up by luxury. That is what happened with much of the Jesuit land acquired in the eighteenth century and some of the larger church lands acquired by estate owners in the nineteenth.

f. Agriculture and Stock Raising

Most people tilled the ground or tended animals, especially the former. Few gained more than a hovel and a spartan diet for their labor. This condition resulted from poor technology; bad organization of transport, communications, and markets; and governmental and social controls in favor of the elite. Government especially molded agriculture and grazing by regulating landholding and labor. It also tried to control prices and production. Although such controls had some important local and temporary effects, they were less telling than other factors.

The total value of agricultural and pastoral production was considerably larger than that of mining, but it was very fragmented and often not translated into money. Farming was marked by the existence (and sometimes the mixture) of Indian and European crops and techniques. Stock raising was almost entirely European as to types of animals and methods. Indians, Negroes, and persons of mixed blood quickly got into live-

---

[9] See Chapter 18, Section b, on the liquidation of church properties in 1805–1809.

stock raising, either as small farmers or as employees.

Specialization in agriculture or stock occurred, being most exaggerated on tropical plantations—notably sugar lands—but also on stock haciendas, or truck gardens serving towns. Mixed production, however, was most common. Individual Indians not only engaged in subsistence farming, but raised a few scrawny chickens and sometimes pigs. Farming and stock raising in different areas were powerfully affected by the local taste in diet and by climatic factors. Commercial activity in agricultural-pastoral commodities was affected by the growth of Spanish towns and mining. Late colonial agriculture benefited from the spread of crops to areas that had not grown much before. This growth resulted largely from European demand during the Bourbon years rather than from agricultural promotion efforts, and from the use of more land and labor rather than from technological improvement.

Agriculture—Regional Variation

Crops, fertility, climate, technology, and market opportunities varied widely. Much of the area inhabited by the higher Indian cultures depended on maize, although in the mountains of Peru potatoes and the high-altitude grain *quinoa* also were important. Parts of the Caribbean lowlands and the Plata basin grew manioc, often along with maize. Efficient wheat production was possible only in a limited number of places near large markets. Wet tropical lowlands were generally not suitable for either wheat or maize. Other crops requiring rather narrow ranges of natural conditions were sugar, cacao, and to a lesser extent tobacco. Some crops were produced in great quantity in certain areas and almost nowhere else, for example, hot chiles in Mexico. Most production was for consumption by the grower or entered into only small-scale local exchange. Distant markets were not easy to develop, because of communications difficulties (affecting demand and prices) and costly transport. Some distant sale was possible for specialized

crops or to specialized markets, particularly sale of grain and truck-garden produce to mines, ports, and towns.

Agriculture—Technology

The mixture of Indian and European crops, techniques, habits, and superstitions was important. There were obvious additions in European grains, fruits, vegetables, and herbs. All of these the Indians proved willing to grow for sale to the elite under certain conditions of compensation or coercion. Only some of them were the Indians willing to grow for their own use. Wheat, for example, was sometimes grown but usually not consumed by Indians. Although there was some irrigation and use of fertilizer, employment of both generally was deficient. Indian farmers were as much at the mercy of disease, worms, insects, birds, and the weather as European and probably did the same amount of praying and cursing.

An important change was introduction of the plow and of the animals (chiefly oxen) to draw it, primarily in the large-scale production of wheat and maize. Most Indian farmers either retained the wooden digging stick or foot plow (*coa*) or new and more efficient variations of it with iron blades. The *coa* has a bad reputation with some twentieth-century writers because some have a short handle that requires stooping and because it is a hand instrument associated with small-scale cultivation. Colonial writers pointed out, however, that it was valuable in close weeding and in soil dibbling to encourage root formation. It certainly was well suited to the traditional agriculture of the Indians. Few farmers could afford to own or share the use of plows and draft animals and associated equipment. Although plow culture usually permitted more rapid work and cultivation of larger plots, the former was not essential and the latter not available. Equally critical was the fact that plots worked with *coa* or hoe often gave greater yields than plowed lands. A small space would give high nutritional value where devoted, under proper conditions of soil and climate, to maize, yams, plantains, or manioc. But Indian cultivators tended to be pushed onto plots undesirable from every point of view: slope, distance from residences and markets, availability of water, and fertility.

A prominent activity was commercial cultivation on haciendas of barley, oats, rye, maize, and wheat. By the 1540s wheat production was large in the Puebla area of central Mexico. Markets included the capital and the fleets at Veracruz. By the late sixteenth century the Antioquia area of present-day Colombia sent wheat to Cartagena, partly for the fleets. In some areas two wheat crops could be grown a year, one using the seasonal rains, the other, irrigation.

How efficient was the hacienda? The owners served wider markets than the *encomenderos*, and greater production on haciendas was one reason for hacienda development under conditions of declining Indian population that made supplying Spanish towns difficult. But much hacienda land was idle. Was idle land an important result of *hacendado* interest in a life-style rather than in profits? Probably not; probably most owners preferred more profits. Various other factors, however, restricted the perception of opportunities for more production on the hacienda. These included labor and distribution problems, and above all limited markets. Hacienda production had to be restricted because gluts made commodities unsalable.

In the sugar industry there were many small operators, but the larger ones had advantages because the cane fields required careful preparation and processing operations were expensive. The cane fields of the Cortés family in New Spain were plowed several times, clods were pulverized, irrigation courses were carefully laid out. Cane cutting was with steel knives much like the machete of today. The sugar industry spread widely in various provinces in the sixteenth century. Its success was fueled by high per capita consumption in America, and it figured in inter- and intracolonial trade. Some sugar was shipped to Spain. But until the late colonial era Spanish American sugar operations were relatively backward, and its sugar entered little into international trade.[10]

Agriculture—Regulation and Distribution

The government had considerable influence on agriculture. It encouraged the introduction of plants from Europe, provided defense for food shipments in America, helped build and maintain roads and ports, supported prices through various agencies, built local market structures and granaries, and helped provide labor. Some efforts were made to prevent animal encroachment on cultivated fields, without notable success. On the other hand, public authority also did some things to restrict agriculture. Pricing policies sometimes had that effect, as did the reallocation of village lands.

Government regulation of the vine and olive tree included early encouragement, later restrictions and prohibitions, much disobedience, and uncertain effects on production. Grape and olive crops were small before the 1550s. Local oil in large quantities was not available in Peru till the end of the sixteenth century. When the local product did become plentiful, Spanish merchants won regulations against it. But grape vines and olive trees continued to exist in many places where nominally prohibited. Cheap varieties of wine and oil inevitably were produced in America because inspection was difficult and because usually shipping the cheaper varieties from Europe did not pay. Another example of government effort at control was in the cultivation and processing of indigo in Guatemala in the second half of the eighteenth century. Many measures were tried but probably had little effect compared with basic problems of local production and the state of the European market, especially in view of competition from producers in other parts of the world.

The most important government operations of this sort dealt with basic foodstuffs, especially

---

[10] See Chapter 11, Section d, for more on sugar exports.

wheat and maize.[11] Shortages of maize in New Spain in 1575–1585 led to a large increase in regulation. The shortages resulted from a combination of labor decline during epidemics and bad weather for crops. With shortage came speculation and high prices, and suffering and complaint among the poor. The situation became so bad in Mexico City that the *cabildo* demanded that forced labor be channeled solely to food production. The viceregal government tried various devices, some of which had been used before: aiding the *cabildo* to buy grain, requiring Indian tribute to be paid in maize and wheat, trying to make the Indians grow more grain, pegging maize prices, and ordering confiscation of maize by officials in the countryside for distribution at set prices. The *cabildo* finally asked for and was given the royal-tribute maize in a large area around the city at moderate prices, and also sequestered some private-tribute maize.

It also established an *alhóndiga* (public market for grain) and a *pósito* (granary). These were Spanish institutions in the Peninsula. To the *alhóndiga* were to come sellers of grain, with provisions against speculation by middlemen. Prices were regulated. It became a large operation, requiring laborers, clerks, and members of the *cabildo* as supervisors. There were special provisions for popular purchases and restrictions put on such commercial buyers as bakers. *Alhóndigas* were set up in other towns in addition to Mexico City.

The *pósito* was to accumulate surpluses for poor crop years and regulate prices downward by sales in those years and upward by purchases in good crop years. In fact, it let its supplies decline in good years, so that in bad years the city had to build stocks at high prices. The *pósito* supervised sales from its granaries.

The Indians were guaranteed 25 percent of all maize distributed by the city. Operation of the *pósito* turned out to be a maize subsidy by the royal government, since it sold royal-tribute

maize to the city at moderate prices in years when it could have received high prices for it. Such efforts did not eliminate speculation in grain or guarantee a sufficient supply at all times, as food riots in later years attested. In 1720–1810 in New Spain there were ten crises in which maize was in very short supply and prices too high for popular income.

Poor functioning of short-distance food distribution was the result not only of manipulation by government but of inaccurate information and costly transport. These factors led to stultifying speculation by private merchants. Maize riots due to shortages and high prices might occur within a hundred miles of areas with a glut. Official shipping restrictions also inhibited long-distance trade in agricultural produce. Possibly more important was the fact that most provinces grew similar crops. Only a few interprovincial exchanges achieved any size. The small trade between the republics in the nineteenth and twentieth centuries strongly suggests that the possibility of much more trade in the colonial era was remote, regardless of official policy.

Exports of agricultural products to Europe were mostly tropical produce, with sugar the most important, although cacao and indigo at times enjoyed considerable demand. Although Spanish American sugar was an item in European and intercolonial trade in the sixteenth century, it was less so than sugar from British, French, Dutch, and Portuguese areas, especially before the late eighteenth century, when Cuban production and exports rose rapidly. In short, distant markets for American agricultural products, in the Western Hemisphere or Europe, were not sufficient to affect the bulk of agricultural activity in the Indies.

Stock Raising—Culture

Animals brought from Europe to America multiplied rapidly: horses, cattle, sheep, goats, asses, swine, chickens. Horses and asses were mated to produce mules. Male cattle were castrated to make oxen. The tiny Chilean settlements in 1545

---

[11] Other foods also were subject to regulation, including eggs, meat, fowl, vegetables, and fruit.

claimed 8,000 swine descended from an original boar and two sows. Although government concessions in Spain favored sheep raising, that pattern was not followed in America, where sheep flocks were sizable but much less important than cattle herds. Wool production enjoyed little encouragement, and America did not produce enough for its own needs. The sheep business involved a good many Indians in America. Depopulation in the sixteenth century promoted use of vacated lands as sheep ranges. Close sheep cropping also increased soil erosion in lands with steep slopes and sparse vegetation. In the sixteenth century there were large sheep flocks in New Spain and Peru. Essentially, however, Spain opposed competition with its own wool.

Spain had a small-scale cattle system in the humid north, producing meat and dairy items as in other parts of Europe. In the south of Spain, especially in Andalucía, there developed large-scale cattle raising that was unique in Europe, with a wild, tough bovine type and the focus on hides (though some meat was used) with no dairy output. This system was based on demand for hides, large and lightly populated pasture lands in Andalucía, and the unique abundance and cheapness of horses there. The feral cattle and large ranges made cowpunching by horseback essential. Contributing factors were the Spanish elite's prejudice against agriculture as involving vile peasants and infidel Muslims and pleasure in use of the aristocratic horse. This activity in southern Spain was the origin of cattle ranching using large ranges and herds, roundups (*rodeos*), horses, a suitable saddlery, lariats or lassos, corrals, brands, and many other items that were carried to Spanish America and from there inherited by the western United States.

Cattle existed on all the larger haciendas in America, partly because there was surplus land for which there was no better use than pasture. In addition, large-scale cattle haciendas gradually developed. Many were in frontier areas and received generous land grants from a government anxious to control nomadic Indians and possible foreign intruders and in some cases to provide meat and work animals to local mines. A cattle hacienda had fewer personnel than one specializing in agriculture, and those cattle personnel tended to be heavily mestizo and mulatto, although there were Indian and black cowboys (*vaqueros, gauchos, llaneros*). They were free wage hands. They bestrode the aristocratic beast, acquiring a psychic and physical mobility that made cowboys more aggressive than peasants.

Cattle ranches might also raise horses and breed mules. The three animals were *ganado mayor* (major stock), and treated in special ways (for example, they had different pasture requirements) as compared with *ganado menor* (minor stock). Stock-raising lands went by several names, including *estancias* and haciendas. Indians also often kept a few chickens, swine, or goats of their own, but less often cattle, mules, or horses.

Stock Raising—Investment and Support

Large-scale stock raising was dominated by the elite. It required capital and government support. A seat or a friend with a seat in a *cabildo* was useful because of its power to grant use of municipal lands, regulate water use, let contracts for meat or hide slaughter, set prices, and supervise butchering and sale. Around some towns the wild cattle belonged to the *cabildo*, and it licensed hunters to bring them in for slaughter. The *cabildo* of Mexico City early (1537) created a *mesta* (stock raisers' guild), on royal order. Unlike the *mesta* in Spain, which was chiefly a sheep raisers' guild, Mexico's was a cattlemen's organization. It helped register brands and control rustling through a special rural police and a court system. But in the great spaces of Mexico law enforcement was difficult. Late in the sixteenth century there was fear of extinction of cattle by overkill. This led to prohibition of slaughter without license, even by owners for their own use. Indian towns were not to build public slaughterhouses. Such measures still existed late in the colonial era, although it was clear that cattle were not being exterminated. In frontier Texas in the eighteenth century settlers objected to paying official fees for licenses to round up wild cattle and horses. They also refused to obey rules on butchering. Troops guarding the herds of military posts insisted on slaughtering cattle illegally for their own use.

Stock Raising—Distribution and Processing

Sales of meat, hides, and tallow to towns and mining settlements were important. Cattle drives to such places sometimes covered long distances. Cattle were driven from what is now northwest Argentina to Potosí in the mountains of present-day Bolivia. Late in the colonial period cattle were driven from Texas north to Louisiana and south into Coahuila. Cattle occasionally were driven two hundred miles from the Bajío to Mexico City. Small cattle raisers in Nicaragua either sold to big producers or drove their herds to the provincial fair. Big Nicaraguan and Honduran cattlemen drove herds of 40,000 to 50,000 in the 1750s to the annual cattle fair at Guatemala City. There they bartered their stock, which usually was pledged beforehand to buyers for credit earlier received in domestic goods and cash. The goods they distributed to local officials (*corregidores*) in their home districts, to small stock raisers, and to other middlemen and consumers.

Animals for transport and labor were much in demand. These included riding horses and mules, cart and plow oxen, pack animals, and beasts to turn mill wheels and windlass hoists, drag ore pulverizers, and do other work. Mules were driven or shipped from Nicaragua to Panama for the isthmian traffic, because breeding mules in that hot climate was not feasible. Venezuela and New Granada sent thousands of mules annually to the Antilles, as did Tucumán to the silver-rich mountains of Peru. In indigo processing animals drove wheels that beat indigo solutions to induce coagulation. Animals were important in mineral processing and supply operations. As mines became deeper and encountered more drainage problems, more animals were needed at

the vertical shafts to operate whims (hoists). One drainage operation in New Spain at the end of the colonial era involved more than a dozen hoists, using 660 mules; another effort in a single shaft used 8 hoists, operated by some 800 horses in shifts.

The traffic in hides was sizable, for American and European markets. Leather went into harness and saddlery, bags and buckets for specialized functions (carrying ore, shipping indigo and mercury), coach springs, ties for packages, furniture, shoes and boots, clothes, and belts for machinery. Spanish leather work was famous, and the skills were carried to America. Exports from some of the smaller producing areas were in the tens of thousands of hides. The fleet of 1587 took some 35,000 hides from Santo Domingo and 75,000 from New Spain.

The hide trade increased with the years. Contrabandists traded in hides from the sixteenth century and in the seventeenth went increasingly to the Plata area. By the latter century, Spanish officials there were enthusiastic about the hide trade. But nearly everywhere the greatest increase in hide traffic came in the eighteenth century because of rising demand from a Europe in which population, industrial production, and wealth were zooming. The most spectacular effects were in the Plata area. The annual export of hides from Buenos Aires rose from some 150,000 in the 1770s to about 1.5 million by the early 1790s. New Spain did not develop large hide exports, despite the great size of its herds.

Other cattle products were less important: bone, tallow, grease, hair, hooves. Tallow had a large market—for cheap candles, soap manufacture, and lubricants. It was made at home as well as commercially from cattle, sheep, and goats. The best tallow came from sheep's kidneys, so that slaughterhouses were not supposed to pare the fat from sheep's kidneys before selling them to consumers. This and other malpractices were important enough to cause big town *cabildos* to appoint tallow inspectors. Meat, especially beef, had a big market in America, but little was exported. Driving cattle on the hoof solved the transport problem and provided fresh supplies in a day without refrigeration. Dried and salted and pickled beef were used only in small quantities until the end of the colonial era. Then demand increased rapidly to feed black slaves in the growing sugar industry in the West Indies of several powers and in Brazil, as well as the sailors in the burgeoning merchant marines and navies of Europe. The area around Buenos Aires, especially, in the late eighteenth and early nineteenth centuries enjoyed new demand for preserved meat.

g. Mining

The size of the torrent of treasure from Spanish America cannot be known exactly, because the official figures are deficient and because much went to contrabandists or escaped registry in America or in the fleets. The assay offices in the Indies were supposed to record the amounts, but many owners preferred not to submit to assay and the accompanying taxation. As early as the late sixteenth century, an observer guessed that between one-third and one-half of American treasure went unrecorded.

During the conquest, pickings were small by later standards and consisted mostly of gold from placer mining in the islands and from seizure of accumulated gold and silver ornaments of the Indians. When the great silver deposits were found in the 1540s and thereafter, large-scale mining began. A great spurt came in the 1550s from Potosí in Peru and Zacatecas in New Spain. A second jump came after 1580, due partly to the introduction to Peru of the mercury amalgamation process developed in New Spain and to exploitation of the mercury mines at Huancavelica, Peru. During the subsequent boom, Peru accounted for some 65 percent of American silver sent to Sevilla. The silver cone of Potosí, in the rarefied air of the Andes, was accounting for 70 percent of Peruvian silver and became a legend of riches.

Then, about 1605–1635, Mexican production steadily expanded, while Potosí's declined, but after 1635 Mexican production fell off more than

Peruvian. Apparently the crown diverted European mercury to Peru (because it made more from taxes on Peruvian silver). Furthermore, a decline in mercury production in Spain created a supply problem. Silver output in Peru went down slowly in the seventeenth century and more rapidly in 1690–1730. Thus, there was a mining depression in Mexico about 1635–1689, whereas the worst phase of the depression in Peru came after 1690. Total production in Spanish America was, nevertheless, large in the seventeenth century of "depression."

In the eighteenth century Mexican silver boomed, with an especially sharp increase in the 1770s. Mintage quadrupled from 6 million pesos in 1706 to 24 million in 1798.[12] By the latter date, Mexico accounted for some 67 percent of the Spanish American total. In 1800 Mexico minted nearly five times as much silver as in 1632, whereas the combined viceroyalties of Peru and La Plata did not regain their 1600 level of 10 million pesos a year until the 1790s. If the Mexican production in 1798 is put at 25 million pesos, and that taken as 65 percent of Spanish American total production, then the latter in that year was some 36 million. Silver production had not quite come back to the peak of the early seventeenth century, but it was large, and the accumulating production huge. Other mining was insignificant in comparison with silver.[13]

The silver of colonial Spanish America, including such coins as the famous "pieces of eight," helped finance Spain's wars, stimulated price inflation there and elsewhere, and played some role in diverting attention from agriculture and indus-

---

[12] Mexican mintage in the colonial era was about 2 billion pesos, probably about half of all produced in Spanish America. That total of something over 4 billion pesos must be judged beside the prevailing good daily wage of one peso or the ability to buy 100 pounds of corn for the same amount. Although it is impossible to state simply how much 4 to 5 billion pesos was "worth" then in comparison with today, a multiplication by 50 would not be extravagant.

[13] There was sizable gold production in New Granada and small operations in many places. There was some copper mining, notably in Chile; and small amounts of lead, zinc, and iron were produced in colonial Spanish America.

try. None of these effects in Spain was inevitable. The crown might have made other decisions on warfare, factors in addition to silver produced inflation, and Spanish neglect of agriculture and industry came from social structures and attitudes that depended little on American treasure. Certainly the *flota* system had as one aim the protection of bullion shipments from America to Spain, but that could have been done without a closed trading and limited port policy.

Mining in the Spanish Indies sopped up large accumulations of capital; moved population to mining areas; stimulated agriculture, grazing, transport, trade, and some industries and crafts; and made the Spanish enterprise in America larger and more complex than it would have been otherwise. The effects were felt far from the major mines. There were thousands of mines and washings in Spanish America, most of them unprofitable or barely of value to a lone prospector. By 1800 New Spain alone had some 5,000 mines. There were uncounted numbers of abandoned holes and hopes in such a poor province as Honduras.

Mine labor powerfully affected Indian life in some places. The *mita* for mining in Peru was some 16,000 men at any one time. Most of these were for Potosí and drawn from surrounding districts within some hundreds of miles. In those regions they constituted possibly 14 percent of the adult males. At least in those areas, such a percentage, with addition of their families, was large enough to have a drastic impact. Miners were, however, a minority of laborers in Peru and other provinces. The total labor force in all Peruvian mines—*mitayos* and free labor—at its peak may have been 50,000; with their families, this was on the order of 10 percent of the Peruvian population.

Abuses of mining labor were horrible during the mining fever in the middle decades of the sixteenth century, when there was confusion regarding controls by government and church. But as the institutions of the colonial period developed and the decrease in Indian population progressed, mine labor systems were regularized. For

some years in New Spain labor came largely from *repartimiento*, but by the mid-seventeenth century free labor was predominant, and before long was almost the only type of mining labor there. Even in the late sixteenth century in some areas of New Spain most mining laborers were free Indian specialists as the Spanish responded to Indian willingness to work for wages when they were high enough.

In Peru, the *mita* was regularized in the 1570s by the capable viceroy Francisco de Toledo (served 1569–1581) and remained until abolished in 1812. Even in Peru, however, considerable free Indian and *casta* labor worked in mining, especially in the eighteenth century. Why forced mining labor remained more important in Peru than in Mexico or why the records indicate more Peruvian Indian fear of the mines is unclear. One reason was that cheap Indian labor concentrated at Potosí, with higher taxation of the metal there than in Mexico, made for high production and income to the crown. Even in the eighteenth century, when both Potosí and Huancavelica depended mainly on free labor, the *mita* was continued, presumably as a way of subsidizing a production afflicted with rising costs due to changes in mining conditions.

Work in the mines was not pleasant. At the 12,000- to 16,000-foot elevations of Potosí it was especially uncomfortable. The Peruvian *mitayos* worked one week in three and often hired themselves out as free workers during the other two weeks, for which they received not only wages but small shares in production. One-third of the *mitayos* were underground; the others mostly worked in the laborious ore-reduction processes. Underground work was heavy, frightening, and dangerous. The digs were narrow, which did not improve ventilation or fear of suffocation. Light came from tallow candles, flickering and dim. Much of the work consisted of pecking at the mine face with picks and iron bars, loading ore into baskets, trudging to ladders, basket on back, to climb to the surface. In most shaft mines movement was by rickety ladders between wooden platforms. The ladders were leather steps tied to poles, sometimes double, so that two files of Indians could use them. The bearers went up these swaying contraptions with one-hundred- to three-hundred-pound loads of ore, and candles on their thumbs to show the way.

Why did many take up mining voluntarily? Surely because the chance of good income in other occupations was not promising. Not only were wages high, but miners got shares of production and stole what they could. Workers sold their shares and pilferage to independent refiners, who operated near the great integrated enterprises that mined and refined. Indians coming off shift were examined with care, their hair and orifices getting special attention. In Mexico the most successful method of smuggling out silver was in clay suppositories up the anus.

How much did mining affect other sectors of the economy? Public authority certainly gave great attention to mining, but less silver would probably not have much improved official attention to other sectors, although some Spanish writers suggested that this would happen if minerals were less stressed. There is nothing about Spanish economic performance in the Peninsula to encourage the notion. Nor was Spanish American sugar production before the late colonial period such as to inspire confidence in readiness to pursue that line of innovation. Mining certainly promoted other lines of output, so that less mineral production in fact would have meant less agricultural and industrial production in America. Less silver would probably not have led to a freer trading system overseas or between American realms.

The government went to great lengths to help with mining problems and secure its own profit. All precious ores were crown property, for which only working rights could be acquired by private parties with the obligation to work the claim or lose it. Government gave help in defense of mining camps and supply routes, provision of labor, and tax reductions. The *quinto* (fifth) was the crown's share of production, but in New Spain in the 1540s it began making reductions to aid mining, and later concessions by the end of the

seventeenth century made the usual tax a tenth. There was some reduction to a tenth in Peru in the seventeenth century, but not for its greatest producer, Potosí, which was kept at the full *quinto* into the eighteenth century, when increased costs brought reduction. Late in the eighteenth century risky and costly mines in New Spain got exemption from the *quinto* until investment was recovered.

Very important was the crown monopoly on mercury, needed in one process of ore reduction. The crown made a profit on its sale and used it to regulate production. Essentially, Peru worked with local mercury from Huancavelica; New Spain used mostly mercury shipped from Almadén in Spain, plus some other European and some Huancavelica mercury. High freight costs were a significant factor in the use of mercury. The cheapest route from Huancavelica to Potosí, both in the mountains of Peru, was west from the former to the sea, then south in the Pacific to Chicha or Arica, then inland again, far to the east into the mountains to Potosí. Typical of Spanish economic policy, generally dominated by the immediate need for public revenues, the crown usually kept the price of mercury high and only slowly yielded to protest and argument. The intelligent policy of the ministers of Charles III in the later eighteenth century in lowering mercury prices had immediate results in higher silver output.

The problem of capital for mining was always worrisome. Investment came from merchants, public officials, and from estate owners who could make or borrow the cash. The many small mine owners at Potosí depended heavily on the large owners, who also had ore-reduction plants. Also lending money there were about a dozen silver merchants, who bought silver to take to the mint, but they were eliminated by a bank after 1751. In New Spain silver merchants and specialized silver banks provided credit. For some of the big projects in eighteenth-century Mexico several men put up shares. Investment in mines often brought terrible loss and not uncommonly bankruptcy.

Technical problems abounded in mining. Different types of ore required different mining and reduction methods. Much of the boom-and-bust history of silver mining was related to changes in ore types and locations. Gunpowder was used for blasting at Huancavelica at least by 1631 but in most places not before the eighteenth century. Drainage could be a terrible problem. It was more common in the eighteenth century than earlier, because the mines generally did not get down to the water table (four hundred to six hundred feet in Mexico) before 1700. Potosí during most of its history was able to work from adits, horizontal penetrations of the peak, from which branched many work shafts. As miners worked down from the top of the fabulous mountain, however, they needed larger adits, which increased costs. Potosí miners finally got down to the water table, and in 1789–1810 a six-foot drainage adit was driven over a mile into the mountain at great cost. A Mexican drainage adit of some 750 feet in 1617 was installed with government aid. Such efforts often received favors from government in the form of tax reductions or even by direct public investment, though such help was not common. In Mexico in the late colonial era, the Count of Regla took thirty years to drive an adit more than one and a half miles long. Zacatecas mines after 1732 were abandoned one by one because they were deep and waterlogged. They revived in the 1760s with new capital, cheaper mercury, and lower taxation.

Vertical shafts of great depth were not common, though in Mexico a number grew deeper than six hundred feet. At more modest depths they could be operated with the platform-and-ladder method. As they went down, hand hoists could be used to depths where the time and technical characteristics involved became marginal; then they used whims (hoists) powered by horses or mules. Some whims could handle loads of more than half a ton. By the late seventeenth century in some places there were shafts with more than one whim. In the late eighteenth century the great Valenciana mine had eight whims in one big octagonal shaft going down more than 1,800 feet. That shaft cost a million pesos.

Once the ore was aboveground, other technical and financial problems arose. Reduction of the ore was by smelting, or by the amalgamation process with mercury after its development in New Spain in the 1560s. Amalgamation was a complicated process calling for skilled personnel.[14] Smelting was still sometimes preferable, because of the type of ore or mercury shortages. The early clay furnaces at Potosí were an Indian model, fueled by dried grass and llama dung. The Indians were grinding the ore by hand, but using the European method of adding lead or litharge to facilitate the separation of silver from the ore. At various places in America women and children pounded ore by hand; at others, ore went through stone grinding mills.

In the 1570s at Potosí, as high-grade ores suitable for smelting petered out, the mercury amalgamation process was introduced. Spaniards built stamp mills, furnaces, and vats. Heavy drags were introduced to help break up ore. The mills were mostly driven by waterpower at Potosí. Ore reduction by amalgamation in Peru was always in containers, whereas in Mexico open patios often were used. The separation of silver in containers in Peru was accomplished in ten to fourteen days, whereas it often took much longer in Mexico by the patio process. The yields of metal from ore are not certain. Possibly losses varied between 10 and 14 percent, some of it due to technical

---

14 After some of the rock was washed from the pulverized ore, the remaining sludge was spread in a yard (*patio*) to form a cake (*torta*), often 100 feet by 2 feet. A specialist then added salts, lime, or copper pyrites, "cooking" the cake several days while he judged its condition by taste, smell, and touch. Then he added mercury cautiously. The cake was tromped by men and beasts, then tasted again and more chemicals added. This might last for one to five months, until the expert sent the mixture to the washing vats, where the heavier premercury amalgam settled. After this, much of the expensive mercury was recovered by heating and pressing. Although the process was a lengthy one and a heavy consumer of labor, a high percentage of silver was obtained.

problems, some possibly to unwillingness of workers to permit assays that might reflect on their performance.

Knowledgeable foreigners tended to be critical of the technical level of silver mining in America. There was also foreign criticism of Mexican mining as being too small-scale. These criticisms were not wholly justified. Deficiencies were being overcome to some extent in the last three decades of the eighteenth century. Greater investment, technical improvement, and larger-scale operations were encouraged by enlightened government policies. Taxes were reduced and gunpowder and mercury prices lowered. It was specifically contemplated that financial aid would lead to improved technology. Costs were in fact reduced for some operations, more money went into mines, and production increased. The scale of activity was escalating. Finally, one mine in Mexico had weekly expenses of about 20,000 pesos (some 1 million a year), with a work force of 2,500. Owners pressed for new advantage by ending all metal shares for workers and by paying wages partly in goods (an illegal practice). Still, many ventures were financial and technical failures, at least in part because some mines simply were marginal operations, given the conditions of the time.

11 Other Economic Problems

a. Manufactures and Crafts

A fundamental weakness of the Spanish American economy was the fact that the Spanish system left large unsatisfied demands that had to be met by foreign suppliers. The problem was not primarily lack of capital but Spain's choice to use its capital for other purposes, including costly wars that sometimes had little economic motivation. In any event, in sixteenth- and seventeenth-century manufacturing there were no huge costs for machinery; equipment cost less than materials and labor. The chief problems were attitudes and the social structures on which they rested. There was little interest in industry and much fear of intellectual and educational innovation. Efforts to promote technical education and better productive processes in Spain were weak. But even the technological advantages of Spain's rivals were far from large barriers in the sixteenth and seventeenth centuries. Textile-making methods, for example, changed little. Those changes made a difference, but more important were two new marketing ideas: to sell cheaply by sacrificing some quality in production; and the decision by the French, English, and Dutch to use aggressive methods to push their expanded production of cheaper wares. Spain was not the only country to suffer from the actions of the North Atlantic manufacturing and commercial aggressors. Venice clung to quality textile production and lost many markets as a result. Technological backwardness did begin to hurt Spain badly in the later eighteenth century, when the new steam-driven machinery of her rivals, especially Britain, ushered in the Industrial Revolution. In 1803 wealth produced in Spain from the "mechanical arts" was less than one-fifth of that produced in either Britain, France, or Germany.

There was much fabrication in Spanish America of articles that cost too much to import. The upper class bought many locally made articles that were serviceable and cheap. The poor could afford only local wares, made by themselves or by simple craftsmen. The Indians had a strong craft tradition, to which they added European elements. Colonial fabrication was carried on largely in the huts of the users, or in small shops, and usually exchanged by barter or for only small sums of money. That fabrication nearly satisfied demand for most cheap products, from chocolate beaters and other household utensils to common footwear and leather buckets. A great range of inexpensive items was readily exchangeable for money or produce. The cost of importing all manufactures would have been astronomical, and no one considered doing so. Nevertheless, the amount that was imported was large enough to be quite costly.

Although many fine goods were supplied by European producers, mostly non-Spanish, some were also made in America. Fine goods, including gold and silver work, were made in shops in the Spanish towns of America, often guild-regulated and involving a small group of workers with advanced techniques, aided by rough laborers. A few of the largest establishments could be called factories. Sugar making and ore reduction involved substantial numbers of workers, many highly skilled; much investment in equipment and raw materials; and some "machinery" with moving parts—belts, ropes, cams—driven by animals or waterpower. The large textile workshops (*obrajes*) were factories in the sense that they brought together some scores of workers and had sizable production and specialization. Also common were gristmills, using gears or belts and animal or waterpower, sawmills, large workshops for making chinaware and glass, and works that processed the indigo plant into dyestuff. Steam power was not used in the eighteenth century; even in Spain it was used then only in relatively progressive Cataluña. Men with money in most parts of the Spanish world were less interested in industrial development than in commerce, mining, grazing, and agriculture.

Spanish regulations banned or limited some colonial fabrication, but other official actions encouraged it. Furthermore, enforcement of restrictive rules was often lax. Restriction, encouragement, and evasion existed in all three colonial centuries. Although restriction killed some fabrication, there was no general industrial paralysis decreed from Spain. Complaining colonials often were ignorant of some of the factors involved or testified as interested parties. Spanish restrictions, though not helpful to colonial fabrication, were of minor importance. They had no influence on rough goods and cheap items and were not intended to. For the other items, market factors usually were the governing element. If American goods could compete, they usually were produced and sold. The problem was that they sometimes could not compete with Spanish goods in quality or in price, and they often could not compete with foreign goods in either respect. The problem of foreign competition worsened with time. There was much late colonial complaint about damage to American output from foreign manufactures. The more advanced European nations were expanding their manufacturing, shipping, and financial strength more than the Spanish world was. This hurt the textile industries of Quito and Puebla. It also hindered the sale of the textiles and wine of the Tucumán area in the markets of Buenos Aires and Montevideo. The Spanish world was not competitive in the new industrial age.

How large was industrial output in colonial Spanish America? We have no very precise idea. Humboldt, at the end of the colonial era, put the value of all manufactures in New Spain at 7 to 8 million pesos a year and minerals at 25 million, with agriculture 30 million. His figure for manufactures is too low if all homemade or rough craft products are included. The question becomes: What purpose is to be served by valuing them? On the one hand, they certainly represented a huge amount of worthwhile production. On the other hand, they did not represent a dynamic element, did not contribute to investment funds or to the taxes that were used for so many necessary purposes. Home industry did produce clay griddles for corn cakes, clay pots for water, rough skirts and trousers, and a host of other items.

The largest industry after food processing was textiles. Most yarns, threads, and fabrics were made in homes or simple shops for family use, for retail sale by the maker, or on a piecework basis for *obraje* owners. One specialized line was silk. Mulberries and silkworms were carried from Spain to Mexico in the 1520s. The industry grew considerably in the sixteenth century. Yarns were sold to the silk-weaving guilds in Mexico City and Puebla. Fabrics were sent to Peru. The quality of workmanship became quite good, with Spanish artisans teaching Indians the craft. The silk industry declined in New Spain from about

1580 and never recovered, because of competition, beginning in 1565, from cheaper and finer Chinese silks brought from the Philippines. Indian population losses also hurt the industry. Oriental raw silk was more and more used in the Mexican industry. Despite these problems, there were some 14,000 silk workers in *obrajes* in Mexico City, Puebla, and Oaxaca in the late sixteenth century.

Commercial production of woolens was carried on under both upper- and lower-class ownership. Early in the sixteenth century Mexico City had about twenty-five *obrajes* manufacturing cloth and ten making hats. Other towns also had *obrajes*. Many *obrajes* had fewer than fifty employees; more than a hundred was rare. Specialized functions included wool washing, carding, spinning, dyeing, weaving. In the first half of the eighteenth century colonial textiles began to decline because of European competition in cheap lines. Still, in 1803 Humboldt found in Querétaro, a small town, not only twenty *obrajes* but three hundred smaller textile workshops. By that time, however, Mexico was far from supplying all its cheap fabrics. Bishop Abad y Queipo claimed in 1805 that the clothing industry there could not dress and shoe a third of the population, so much of the supply came from abroad.

Most notorious were Spanish-owned *obrajes* in Spanish towns. Some were owned by the clergy. There were also *obrajes* run by and in Indian communities. A typical *obraje* was a large hall, into which were crowded workers, equipment, and primitive living arrangements. Locked doors and guards prevented escape. Sometimes families were separated. Much use was made of beating, and some of chains. Food, ventilation, and sanitation were poor. The owners ran the *obrajes* through majordomos, whose compensation depended on output, which they screwed as high as possible.[1]

Of the extensive milling industries, we have mentioned ore reduction and saw- and gristmills. Especially impressive were the larger sugar mills.

The Spaniards brought the industry from Europe and the Canary Islands. Mexican production grew rapidly. Hernán Cortés began a sugar works some sixty miles from Mexico City, where lower elevations made cane culture feasible. By 1600 in that Cuernavaca-Cuáutla area, a dozen mills served the big Valley of Mexico market. Peru had a large sugar industry; and many other provinces produced sugar. Mill owners had to invest in great timbers to sustain cane presses, heavy metal bearings, vats, pottery products, animals (a sugar hacienda might need five hundred oxen alone, for plowing, pulling cane carts, turning presses), firewood, black slaves, wages for free labor, tools, and other items.

There were many other manufactures. (*a*) The metal-working industries, small-scale but important, included locksmiths, gunsmiths, swordsmiths; farriers to make horseshoes (and doctor horses); and jewelry and silver fabricators. The industry turned out a great variety of work in iron, steel, gold, silver, copper, and bronze. Wares included decorations, tools to make millstones, railings, fittings and fasteners for many uses, cannon, bells, nails, and a variety of hardware. The royal mints used elaborate machinery with moving parts made of wood, metal, and leather. (*b*) The food-processing industry—in addition to gristmills—was extensive: fermentation and distillation of alcoholic beverages; baking; the making of lard, olive oil, confections; and butchering and meat preservation. (*c*) There was a huge pottery and ceramic production in Spanish America. Much was by small Indian producers, mostly cheap ware without glaze or extensive firing. Fired and unfired bricks were made. A Spanish brick maker of Lima in the 1550s was selling his product by the tens of thousands. Fine glazed tiles and chinaware were made at such centers as Puebla in Mexico. Glassware also was turned out for the luxury trade. (*d*) The large production of leather objects required a tanning industry. (*e*) The wood-working industry made a multitude of objects: crucifixes, linen chests, great doors for public structures, barrels, heavy framing for mills and other buildings. (*f*) Ship-

---

[1] See Chapter 8, Section d, on labor in *obrajes*.

building went on at many places. (*g*) The tobacco industry grew greatly in the seventeenth and especially eighteenth centuries. Some tobacco factories had the largest employment of any industrial establishments in Spanish America. The Mexico City factory had 9,000 employees long before the end of the eighteenth century; that at Querétaro had about 3,000 turning out cigars and cigarettes. (*h*) Other types of fabrication in America included gunpowder, a royal monopoly but also made illegally; various chemicals; hats; clothes; lace; rushwork (basketry, mats); feather work; soap; fireworks; processed indigo; rope and cordage; and pitch.

Guilds of arts and crafts (*gremios de artes y oficios*) were transplanted from Spain. Mexico came to have more than a hundred, including tanners, rope makers, gilders, makers of harness and saddle trappings, coach makers, wax and candle makers, grocers, gold beaters, tavern keepers, hatters, potters, weavers. They were regulated by the town councils, and usually had ordinances that dealt with labor conditions, the quality and price of goods, and journeymen and apprentices. The statutes of the tavern keepers permitted sale of only one kind of wine at a tavern; the grocers' statutes regulated credit, required the owner to provide an outside light, and said that there could be but one store at an intersection. Guilds restricted movement from the rank of master to journeyman, as they had in the Middle Ages. In America, this practice was complicated by efforts to discriminate against Indians and *castas*. Although much restriction was effective, to keep *castas* and Indians out of the guilds entirely proved impossible. To keep non-Spaniards from making goods outside the guild system was even more difficult. The guilds tried to prevent combinations in restraint of trade. They also took part in public celebrations and promoted brotherhoods for worker assistance.

b. Other Extractive Pursuits

Lumbering was an important activity. Great timbers were needed for ships and for public and private buildings. Even when large structures of stone and adobe were built in cities and on rural estates, timbers were often needed for roof framing and working beams. Mines needed timbers and other lumber. Other uses for wood included furniture, receptacles, yokes, blocks for rope hoists, and the bodies, wheels, and tongues of carts. Much wood was used for fuel, both directly and as charcoal. Many industrial operations required wood for fuel. Huge quantities were needed for cookery, private and commercial. In populated areas the hills were combed for sticks and twigs. Indian wood gatherers tottered into town with towering loads on their backs. Out in the hills, charcoal burners plied their craft.

Fishing was poorly developed. In various places individuals caught fish for their own use. Commercial fishing was limited by problems of storage and transportation. Indians did carry fish from lakes to markets in town, but ocean fishing involved only small individual enterprises and vessels, partly because there were few sizable seaside towns in which to market fish. Little was done to develop the dried and salt fish industry. Salt making by evaporation and mining was widespread to supply needs for cooking, food preservation, and other purposes. Various public authorities tried to foster or control the business. Venezuelan salt long was a matter of international rivalry, especially due to Dutch activity. The *cabildo* of Buenos Aires in the seventeenth century, when it was a mere village, let contracts for wagon trains to get salt at distant mines. In the late eighteenth century this became a more important business because of the growth of the cattle industry and the salt meat trade in the area.

Cochineal was a valuable dye extracted from an insect gathered by Indians. Vanilla was sometimes gathered from wild plants, sometimes cultivated. Pearling was a small industry. Hunting was extensively practiced, sometimes for the market. Rock quarries were exploited. There was gathering of honey, feathers, precious and semiprecious stones, berries, herbs, roots, insects, lizards and snakes, the paddles and fruits of *nopales* (a cactus), and maguey plant spines for needles and punches, and fibers for ties, net bags or carriers, shawls, and other uses. Some of the items gathered were used as food, others supposedly had medicinal or magic properties.

c. Professions and Service Occupations

Lawyers were so numerous that colonials declared them a plague. Some moved on from private practice to public office, in executive positions and as magistrates. European-style medical men were less numerous or well placed in society, a reflection of the feebleness of their grasp of human infirmities. The poor had to make do with the advice of pharmacists, home remedies, or the lore of folk curers, who practiced extensively. Notaries were essential for much public and private business. Spanish tailors and hosiers became numerous. There were teachers at the universities and lower schools. Servants were legion. Few received money wages. Instead, they had room and board, sometimes for their families also; gifts of clothing, medical help, and aid with religious obligations; and chances to pilfer. Also in the service sector were barbers, who not only cut and shaved but bled and did minor surgery; pharmacists; the many members of the civil and ecclesiastical bureaucracies; the few military; guards and night watchmen; cowboys; butchers; mule skinners; the important class of majordomos, managers, foremen; janitors and doormen in public institutions; water sellers; backpacking cargo carriers; and cobblers.

d. Overseas Trade

Overseas trade here means that between Spanish America and Europe, Brazil, the Philippine Islands, and English-speaking North America and the United States.[2] Spain would have preferred that the trade be in Spanish-made goods, but as it could not provide them, it tried to maximize sales of Spanish goods while channeling the sale of foreign wares through a regulated trading system. The aggressive British, French, and Dutch participated in the regulated Spanish system, but also traded illegally with America, both by corruption of the channeled system and by direct voyages across the Atlantic. During three centuries of overseas trade there was much variation in law and practice, but Spain always aspired to a monopoly and close regulation and licensing, common aspirations in trading countries. Although contraband traffic and other violations of the control idea were massive, such evasions were more important to the Spanish government and merchants than to creoles, who appreciated the fact that leaks in the theoretically closed system introduced a flexibility valuable to them. Creoles—and Spanish officials who collaborated with them—were loyal to the Spanish political connection, but insisted on accepting illegal foreign supplies because the alternative called for sacrifice. Spain itself accepted dependency on foreign goods but wanted to impose its own definition of it on America. The Americans were handicapped in that during most of the colonial period many of their goods could not be traded, either because there was no demand for them, or because transport costs priced them out of the market. By the late sixteenth century much Spanish American trade was legally or illegally in foreign goods. In the worst times of the seventeenth century the proportion may have been 90 percent and it was as bad in the worst years at the end of the colonial period. The aggressive foreign penetration of Spanish American markets often was aided by military force, and in wartime especially the Spanish regulatory system foundered.

Regulation in Theory and Practice

Selected Ports, Monopoly, Licensing and Taxation. The theory was to channel traffic between Sevilla or Cadiz in Spain and a few designated ports in America. Many exceptions were al-

---

[2] On long-distance "overseas" trade between Spanish American areas, see Section e of this chapter.

lowed, but it remained a cornerstone of policy. The bulk of the legal traffic from Europe went from Sevilla or Cádiz to Portobelo on the Isthmus of Panama for transshipment to Lima and South America, and to Veracruz for the supply of New Spain. A smaller amount went to Cartagena for the coast and hinterland of New Granada. And under a variety of rules legal cargoes from the two Spanish ports went directly to other American ports, including the West Indies and Buenos Aires. Government thought the limited port theory would keep traffic in Spanish hands and ease tax collection. Merchants in southern Spain, who controlled the trade both there and in America, were happy to have a monopoly. Government usually found that having select groups (merchants, artisans, graziers) organized and responsible for their specialized economic activities was convenient, assisted regulation, and made collection of taxes easy even in advance of the due date for payment.

Trade, even between permissible ports, had to be licensed by public authority. The license often was a tedious requirement. It meant clearances showing payment of taxes and inspection for prohibited articles. Customs duties, usually collected in Spain, were not high, but other taxes and fees sometimes were. Limits were set on the maximum and minimum sizes of ships, and there were regulations on their condition and on supplies and the training of crews. The trade was supposed to go in Spanish bottoms and consist of Spanish goods.[3] But Spain early suffered shortages of ships and seamen for American trade. Even more strikingly, Spain did not produce enough commodities for American demand, so that European goods entered Spain and were carried through the limited port system to America by Spanish merchants, who took a profit on the transactions, but had to pass the bulk of the payment to the foreign suppliers. There thus was a big hole in the monopolistic theory even if the limited port system could be enforced. In addition, foreigners carried goods directly to America in their own ships, outside the legal system.

Flotas, Registros, and Contraband. During much of the colonial era the ideal was for traffic to go periodically in fleets (*flotas*) convoyed by warships. The fleet idea arose in the 1520s, but was not regularized till mid-century. Even before then the concept was to supply New Spain through Veracruz and all South America through the Isthmus of Panama. In the 1560s there were two fleets a year—one to New Spain and one to Tierra Firme, Cartagena, and Panama. The two combined the next year and returned to Spain by way of Havana in Cuba, thence northeast to get the trade winds to Europe. Ships from the fleet were commonly detached to supply Venezuela and the islands and minor ports of Central America. The ships to South America came to be called the Galleons and those to New Spain and the islands the Plate Fleet.

Schedules and the number and tonnage of vessels varied. There were fleets with sixty vessels; most had far fewer. The fleet system was much battered in the seventeenth century and played out in the eighteenth. Freight rates in the fleets often were high, partly because of artificial restriction of the fleets by the monopolistic merchants. The fleets did help prevent capture of treasure on the high seas by foreigners. At the same time, they helped rivet the limited port system upon the Spanish portion of overseas trade.[4]

The size and scheduling of fleets varied because of deficiencies in Spanish shipping and naval strength and even more because of warfare and buccaneering. In some years in the seven-

---

[3] Though not fully developed at once, this policy soon became firm. By 1538 royal order excluded foreigners from trade and navigation in the Spanish Indies.

[4] The slave trade was outside the *flota* system. Other aspects of *flota* history are of interest: for example, inspection of cargo often was cursory, sometimes because of bribery; official assessment of cargo values sometimes was arbitrary; even the warships carried illicit cargo, sometimes with the connivance and in the personal interest of commanders of high repute. This sort of conduct was common in Europe at the time: commanders expected to profit from their official positions.

teenth and early eighteenth centuries, no fleets sailed to the Caribbean; contraband increased as a result. In addition, when Spain was allied with France during the War of the Spanish Succession early in the eighteenth century, it let Frenchmen trade in the Caribbean and around South America to Chile and Peru. After the war, the fleets were revived, but they did not go annually. The system could not be sustained, partly because markets glutted with contraband could not absorb the higher-priced goods of the fleets. The fleets were abolished in 1740, permanently for the Galleons, and the Isthmus lost its role as a transshipment area. Thereafter, all goods to Peru, Chile, and the Plata went directly, either by legal vessels or as contraband. The New Spain fleets were revived in 1754 and sailed intermittently to 1789, then were abandoned.

Many nonfleet vessels (*registros*) were licensed for overseas trade, beginning in the sixteenth century. They were supposed to go only to the ports assigned them. Many situations resulted in permission for *registros*: suspension or inadequacy of the fleets; the peculiar problems of the far-off Plata area; or wartime navigational hazards or local plagues of contraband. In the eighteenth century *registros*, while clearly more effective than the fleets, still had to be licensed by the *consulado* at Cádiz. In 1740 *registros* were allowed to operate around South America into the Pacific. During all those years, of course, many Spanish ships had been going to America without license or disobeying the rules even if licensed. Spain really was trying to *control* shipments of foreign goods, knowing that they could not be excluded entirely.

A number of other breaches of the closed trading ideal resulted from Spanish action. In the mid-sixteenth century the crown permitted carriage of unregistered goods if the fact was declared to the *Casa* and fines paid. Sometimes foreign ships loaded directly into the fleet in Spanish waters, without going through the *Casa's* registration procedures, and received American silver back in the same direct way. The fact that

many foreign merchants were allowed to live in America was admission that the closed trading ideal would not work.

Many Portuguese traders operated in Spanish America, especially in Peru. Some were specialists in the black slave trade via the Isthmus and the Caribbean. More conducted illegal traffic from Peru to the Plata area. That trade started in the 1580s and was fostered by Spanish residents and officials, sometimes by legal but more often by illegal means. The services of the Portuguese merchants were so useful that they generally survived the suspicion of a Jewish taint. The Inquisition at Lima in 1635–1639 swept up about eighty persons and executed twelve, some by burning. One of the arrested Portuguese was Manuel Bautista Pérez, who had been in the African slave trade in America since 1612 and was possibly the richest merchant of Lima. A few years later (1646) the government made another effort to control the Portuguese in Peru by registering some 6,000 of them.

Efforts to control contraband encountered three major difficulties: few creoles would cooperate, officials were easily bribed to overlook violations, and the crown periodically had to relax its ideal because of political or strategic considerations. Even monasteries and convents in America were sometimes used as warehouses and distribution centers for contraband. Landing goods illegally at isolated places in the great spaces of America was easy. Colonial ships could go to foreign isles in the Caribbean and buy contraband, and foreigners poured goods through those islands into Spanish America. The Dutch in 1637 captured Curaçao, off the South American coast, and made it an important contraband center. One of their accomplishments was a monopolistic grip on Venezuela's cacao exports and its imports of European commodities.

The Plata area illustrates the complexities of policy on contraband. In 1573 Paraguayans founded Santa Fe between Asunción and the Atlantic and used it to trade west across the plains with Potosí in sugar, wine, wax, grains, and cattle. They met some competition from Tucumán. They soon ran into a worse problem with Tucumán, when Paraguay in 1580 refounded Buenos Aires for trade with Brazil. The Paraguayans found they could not break into the traffic between Tucumán and Brazil, in which the former supplied cattle, grain, and silver, and received in return sugar products, wine, slaves, and manufactures (mostly Dutch). To make matters worse, royal officials at Buenos Aires protected the contraband element in this traffic. The Paraguayans threatened to abandon the city. Since Spain wished to maintain Buenos Aires for strategic reasons, it made concessions before long. In 1602 the city of Buenos Aires received license to export a limited amount of wheat, jerked beef, and tallow to Brazil in exchange for such things as clothing and household goods. This move turned out not to be helpful to the Paraguayans at Buenos Aires because Portugal had the ships, and the poor Spanish Americans had to sell the Portuguese their new *permiso* rights. Thereupon the Portuguese bought grain and meat from Córdoba, far in the interior in Tucumán province, rather than from Buenos Aires province. With different areas of Spanish America at odds, each supported by some royal officials, effective control of contraband was more difficult than it would have been without that division.

Paraguayans then suggested that they could control shipping with *registros* trading directly with Sevilla and with some rights in Brazil as well as the African province of Angola. So in 1618 Spain authorized two ships a year between Sevilla and eight cities of La Plata, with some rights to trade through Brazil. This route, too, fell into the hands of contrabandists. Then in the 1640s Spain tried to cut off trade between Buenos Aires and Brazil during the war for Portuguese independence from Spain. But excluding the Dutch contrabandists in this traffic was difficult. They had the ships and goods, and creoles and Spanish officials permitted or welcomed their activity. Potosí and Tucumán still provided contraband. Some residents of Buenos Aires needed

foreign ships to take out their increasing hide exports. This left the anticontraband residents of Buenos Aires outmatched.[5]

Smuggling became more difficult to control in the eighteenth century because of eased official restrictions;[6] improved communications; the growth of legal intercolonial trade, increasing the number of vessels and routes; warfare; and more determined action by the intruding powers. It might be supposed that the lowering of Spanish duties late in the century, which reduced the price differential enjoyed by contraband, would make a difference. It did not, because the quality and price of illegal goods still were often sufficient to determine decisions. The flow of foreign goods was increased by creation of the Dutch free port at St. Eustatius in 1737. Then in 1766 Britain designated certain free ports in Jamaica and Dominica, which meant that stated goods could use them on payment of small duties. Finally, the great wars of 1792–1815 punched new or wider holes in the Spanish trading ideal. Spain in the 1790s felt compelled by America's need of supplies to allow officially some neutral trade. From then until 1815, mostly years of war, Spain's ability to channel traffic continued to decrease. The closed trading ideal had been fraying for three centuries. Finally, it was in complete disarray, because Spanish capa-

---

[5] The problem in the area was, in fact, even more complex. Contraband also was promoted by an *asiento* of 1595 to a Portuguese to take six hundred black slaves annually to Buenos Aires to help in its defense; in fact, the slaves were sold to Potosí for silver. Spain suspended the contract but could not stop illegal traffic in slaves to Potosí. Another gap was that unlicensed ships, if they were Spanish or sometimes of allied powers, could enter port on a claim of hazard to ship or crew (for example, from weather, lack of supplies, need for repairs). It was used as a subterfuge for trading, with bribes to avoid the confiscation supposed to follow such chicanery.
[6] For example, joint stock companies for trading with America were given royal licenses in the eighteenth century. They generally were backed by northern Spaniards. These breaches of the old monopoly were protested by the Andalusian merchants. Only the Caracas Company had a measure of success.

bilities were declining and because creoles had had enough of it.

Consulados and Merchants. Overseas trade was handled by merchant houses in Sevilla and Cádiz, with offshoots in America. Sevilla at first had advantages of location, and there was little competition when the American trade was small. Merchants in Sevilla naturally wanted as much monopoly as possible. The Sevilla *consulado* was created in 1543, on the model of other merchant guilds, but even before then a more informal organization had a privileged position. Traders with the Indies were supposed to belong to the *consulado*. Power and profit thus accrued to merchants in Sevilla and Cádiz (which soon shared the monopoly). Since Spanish goods could not fully supply America, however, the Spanish merchant firms early took in foreign partners and capital. Thus, regardless of the fact that Spaniards controlled *consulado* offices and procedures in Spain, the profits had to be divided according to investment, and the *consulado* had to submit to pressure from foreigners. Sevilla and Cádiz did manage—with some small variations in Spanish regulations—to maintain their monopoly position in Spain until the late eighteenth century.

Consulados were created at Mexico City in 1592 and Lima in 1613, but long before then merchants were organized in America, accepted as a privileged special interest group, and supported in their monopolistic practices. Merchant firms in Spain maintained control of or close collaboration with firms in America, either through the use of relatives in both hemispheres or by Spanish advantages in marketing or access to government. The firms in Mexico City and Lima had branches in other American towns, and the latter sometimes were organized as deputations or branches of the two *consulados*. Inevitably, there were differences of viewpoints between the deputations and the *consulados*, notably over the concentration of mercantile justice at the *consulado* seats, an inconvenient and expensive measure for merchants in the provinces, resulting in

a high proportion of decisions unfavorable to the latter. Merchants in provincial towns were supported by other elements of the local elite.

This regional tension increased with the growth of creole participation in commerce, which came only slowly at the wholesale level. There were requests for more *consulados* in America. One was established at Bogotá in 1695–1713, but commerce there was too feeble to sustain it. Before the middle of the seventeenth century merchants in Guatemala asked for a *consulado*. They had a commercial deputation from 1729, and at least by 1772 could convoke assemblies of businessmen (*juntas de comercio*). Such pressures led to actions against American merchants by the Spanish monopoly, as in 1729 when the *consulado* (by then at Cádiz) prohibited American merchant houses from acting as agents of the Cádiz exporting firms. The founding of new American *consulados* was always opposed by the merchants of Lima, Mexico City, and Sevilla and Cádiz, and none were erected there until the 1790s.[7]

The judicial function of *consulados* was not simply a matter of conferring more privilege but of providing for that speedy decision by experts on commercial matters that mercantile law long had recognized as desirable. A rather different result was that sometimes the mercantile courts in America favored merchants over the local producers with whom they traded. That trade arose because wholesale merchants often shipped goods back to Spain, and so were involved in intraprovincial traffic in America. Another problem was that *consulados* ran afoul of *cabildos* and viceroys trying to ensure supplies at bearable prices. In disputes of all types, however, the *consulados* had great strength in capital resources, business connections and expertise, and shipping and land transport facilities.

The crown supported the system because it could easily "request" gifts (*donativos*) from the organized merchants. The *consulados* also were

---

[7] See Chapter 17 for the new *consulados* and creole complaint.

called on to help manage loan operations of the perpetually embarrassed royal treasury. The financial power of merchants was demonstrated by those who paid sales taxes and tribute on behalf of *alcaldes mayores* and *corregidores,* who were middlemen in the domestic trade of America. The *consulados* provided a mechanism for pooling and identifying funds for investment in mercantile and such other forms of activity as mining. The Mexico City *consulado* had the contract for the *alcabala* in and near the city from 1602 until 1753. The crown liked the arrangement because it got the tax in a lump; the *consulado,* because it could be sure its tax liability would not be suddenly changed, and that the tax collection would not fall into unfriendly hands.

This system of large and monopolistic partnerships was no place for small merchants. In addition to the ordinary capital needs of such business, there was much delay in payments. It was difficult to control agents, who were fertile in schemes for personal enrichment. The crown had a nasty habit of sequestering private bullion shipped to Spain. Shipwrecks and buccaneers and foreign navies caused losses. Thus loans for commercial ventures carried high interest, up to 35 percent. The wholesale merchants generally tried to make their profit through control of supplies and prices and by concentration on what we would call a high unit profit, by manipulation of prices through planned shortages. Sometimes things worked that way, and there were many complaints about short supply and price gouging. Unfortunately for the monopolists, foreign and Spanish contrabandists introduced massive supplies of goods. *Consulado* merchants often found either that there was no market for what they had brought from Europe, or that the market was limited and choosy.

Fairs. The major international exchange in the legal traffic occurred at fairs (*ferias*) at Portobelo for Peru, Chile, and Buenos Aires; for New Spain at Veracruz or Jalapa; at Cartagena, which served the hinterland toward Bogotá, the gold mines of the western sierra of New Granada, and

frequently Lima and South America; and at Acapulco for the Oriental trade with the Philippine Islands. There were other fairs that also involved items in international traffic.

Such fairs met only when fleets arrived. At Veracruz, a hot and unhealthful tropical port exposed to attack, goods usually were pushed rapidly to Mexico City for the conclusion of trading. Veracruz lost much of its trading function in the eighteenth century, when the crown made Jalapa, seventy-five miles into the highlands, the site of the fair. It first met there in 1724. For a few weeks it would bulge not only with the men of the fleet but with people who poured in from near and distant New Spain—merchants, mule drivers, priests, officials, petty vendors, whores.

In the isthmus, a fair developed only after 1574, at Nombre de Dios. In 1597 it was moved to Portobelo. In good years it was larger than the fairs at Cartagena and Jalapa. The fleet stopped at Cartagena, unloaded goods for the fair there, and waited till news came that the fleet from Peru was on the Pacific side of the isthmus. The fleet from Cartagena might arrive at Portobelo with 4,000 to 5,000 persons. Panama City was nearly emptied during this season. Food and lodging prices went sky-high at Portobelo. Many had to stay in temporary structures. Officials inspected the ships before they could unload. Meanwhile, representatives of the merchants of Spain and Peru set prices. Tents of ship sails were made ashore for the cargo. Merchants hired shops and houses to display their wares. Seamen had stalls to sell on their own account small articles they had brought. The bullion from Peru lay piled on the ground. Most of the transactions were handled by agents of the merchant houses, and occasionally they did business more on their own account than for their employers. If there was no glut of goods due to contraband, the prices set might allow profits of 100 percent—less than it seems because of the many risks involved. The Portobelo fair ended in the mid-eighteenth century, killed by contraband and by the Spanish commercial reform of 1720, which allowed registered ships to sail from Spain directly to western South American ports via Cape Horn. The last galleons visited Portobelo in 1737; thereafter, the fairs became smaller and finally ended.

The Philippine Trade. Trade with the Philippine Islands had a separate strict and monopolistic structure. Spain could not conduct the Philippine trade around Africa, because those seas were controlled by other nations, so it was developed via Mexico. The first Chinese goods arrived at Acapulco in 1573, and the process began of exchanging the silver of Mexico for the luxury goods of the Orient, especially silks. The Sevilla monopolists objected. The Philippine trade competed with the silk industry of Spain, which was being hurt even before then by a new silk industry in New Spain. Supporters of the closed trading system quickly stopped direct trade between Peru and the Philippine Islands, which began in the 1580s. They also tried to stop the transshipment of Oriental goods from New Spain, especially to Peru, but that proved more difficult.[8]

Acapulco had a good harbor but was an isolated, tiny village. The commercial route between the port and Mexico City was about three hundred miles, mostly a mule track. After 1593 there were supposed to be two ships a year of set tonnage from the Philippines to Acapulco, but the legal limits always were exceeded. At the end of the sixteenth century the legal limit for the two Manila galleons was cargo valued at 250,000 pesos. The trade peaked in the late sixteenth and early seventeenth centuries. In 1597 some 12 million pesos of bullion were sent from Acapulco to Manila, but 3 to 5 million was more usual, and the total sometimes was nearer 2 million. No wonder Mexican coinage finally became common in China!

From the Orient came such things as printed calicoes, raw silk for manufacture in Mexico (until the mid-seventeenth century, some even crossed Mexico to Spain), spices, muslins, coarse cotton shirts, silk stockings, jewelry, porcelains, aromatic oils. To the Orient went silver, cochineal, iron, cacao from Guayaquil, wine, oil, wool (some from Spain). The Spanish government continued to discuss the valuable and difficult-to-control traffic, although the importance of the problem declined after the mid-seventeenth century. In 1784 restrictions on the trade finally were repealed, a part of the general move toward more freedom of commerce in the late eighteenth century. In 1785 the Royal Philippines Company was created as a monopoly.

Commodities and Markets

By the end of the colonial era Spanish American imports, including contraband, probably were something over 60 million pesos, and exports nearer 70 million (and occasionally even more in the early nineteenth century). By that time exports of gold and silver were something over one-half of total exports, whereas earlier the proportion had been much greater. A two-way flow of some 150 million pesos yearly was immensely valuable, worth billions of dollars in terms of our present-day price levels. It was well worth the great attention that Spain and her rivals gave it.

Overseas trade was small for several decades after 1492, then increased with the great mainland conquests, especially with the discovery of silver mines. In the late sixteenth and early seventeenth centuries gold and silver were annually at least 80 percent of the value of recorded cargoes from America to Spain, and 95.6 percent in the peak year 1594. Bullion shipments declined in the first half of the seventeenth century, because of foreign intrusion, production and shipment problems, and retention of silver in America by the growing creole elite; they increased late in the seventeenth century and grew rapidly in the eighteenth. Since bullion was the chief fuel of the overseas trade, that trade followed the ups and downs of bullion production in New Spain and Peru.[9]

---

[8] On transshipment from New Spain to Peru, see Section e of this chapter.

[9] See Chapter 10, Section g, on silver production.

The total overseas trade of Spanish America increased sharply in the late eighteenth century, but the amounts and the significance of the increase are uncertain. In any event, the foreign trade values were not high enough to permit transformation of society, even if those most profiting had been interested. Equally important, the rate of increase could not be sustained. A small element was United States activity, but it was not large enough to affect the totals much. In 1800 United States exports to Spanish America were some $10.5 million, equivalent to the same number of pesos.

Overseas trade, although far from dominating the economy, was a dynamic element. It involved concentrations of capital, decisions on investment in productive enterprise, use of resources for transportation. The activity created ripples of influence as payments were made for goods, labor, and services. It represented achievement motivation, accumulation of capital, risk taking, in an environment where such things were unknown to most of the population. It engaged much government attention, because it was important to public revenues and because it drew to the Spanish world the attentions of foreign capitalists and adventurers.

Imports from Europe in the first half century or so included all sorts of supplies, even a few low-priced bulk goods such as wine, flour, and oil. As American production increased, most imports were high-priced items, generally from non-Spanish Europe or the Orient: such finery as fabrics, stockings, cloth-of-gold ruffs, gloves, hats, laces; fancy ham and wines; black African slaves; hardware, porcelain and glassware, rugs, saddlery, musical instruments, spices, mortars and pestles, bells, candlesticks, folding desks, opium, religious images, glue, and books.

The history of colonial Spanish American exports shows that the values were usually small for items other than bullion. Some growth occurred in a few commodities in the late colonial era, much of it quickly and drastically reduced by other world producers. There is some evidence that better Spanish policy might have improved exports as it did in the case of Cuban sugar. But

Cuba had greater advantages of land, climate, and location for sugar culture than most Spanish American producer areas for that crop, or for cotton, indigo, or wheat. Probably Spanish policy could not have much improved American exports elsewhere than Cuba.

Cattle products, chiefly hides and secondarily tallow, had a modest market almost from the beginning. Some were sold to contrabandists. The poor Caribbean islands were always eager to eke out their slender incomes with hide sales. Few hides were exported from the big realm of New Spain. The great boom in hide export was in the Plata area late in the colonial era. The annual export of hides from Buenos Aires was some 150,000 in the 1770s and by 1790 nearly 1.5 million. Preserved meat exports from La Plata also began to be of some consequence then. Even so, total exports of the Plata area early in the nineteenth century were only some 7 million pesos, and metals accounted for 5 million of that.

Sugar was another of the small, nonbullion exports of Spanish America. Some was sold in the sixteenth century to Spain and to contrabandists. Only toward the end of the eighteenth century did it achieve notable value. New Spain's large sugar output and internal distribution of sugar never led to large exports. The big change came in Cuba, where the industry was puny for two and a half centuries, then flowered in the later eighteenth and nineteenth centuries. The British, during their brief rule in the isle (1762–1763), greatly stimulated commerce, to the joy of the Cuban elite. This reaction alarmed Spain as to Cuba's future, and led to execution of the reforms for America that the Bourbons so long had pondered. Loosened trade restrictions, reduction of duties, and government aid in importing African slaves also aided the industry. The Cuban elite was encouraged to improve sugar technology. Useful also was increased European demand due to population growth, wartime demand, price rises, and enlarged purchasing power in the new industrial age. The Cuban industry benefited also from interruptions in Haitian sugar output after the revolution began there in the 1790s.

Exports of sugar from Cuba were 480,000 *arrobas* (one *arroba* equals about twenty-five pounds) in 1765, more than doubled to 1.1 million in 1790, nearly doubled again by 1800, rose another 66 percent in 1800–1820, and continued upward thereafter. Export-import values in Cuba rose from 2.06 million pesos in 1770 to 16.67 million in 1790. Public revenues rose in Cuba from 163,000 pesos in 1760 to 532,000 in 1770 to 12.2 million in 1790. No wonder Spain was enthusiastic about this development! Still, although methods were somewhat improved, technology did not match the best levels in the sugar industries of other European powers in the Caribbean. Cuba's natural advantages, however, were enough to offset this technological disadvantage.

Cacao was little exported in the sixteenth century, although it was much traded within America. Exports grew thereafter with Venezuela and Guayaquil prominent suppliers as Europeans developed a taste for chocolate, especially in the late eighteenth century.

Indigo exports from the Captaincy-General of Guatemala were of some consequence late in the sixteenth century, and grew in the seventeenth and eighteenth. At its peak, however, indigo exports from the area were worth only 2 million pesos a year and they began to decline at the end of the eighteenth century. At that time Venezuela became an indigo exporter, reaching a peak of some 1.25 million pesos, then declining long before Independence. Not only was this dyestuff limited to a few areas as a modestly valuable export, but by the late 1780s it met serious competition in the European market from cheaper Asiatic producers.

Cochineal, a red dye extracted from an insect, was exported from New Spain. In the late colonial era cochineal exports out of Veracruz were worth only 2.5 million pesos annually, a very distant second after silver. Vanilla also was exported early from New Spain. Its value was modest. Cultivation was abandoned in the eighteenth century, and thereafter it was collected by Indians from wild plants. At that time, the international market for vanilla was being taken over by non-Spanish producers.

Tobacco was not an important export. Little was shipped overseas in the sixteenth century, when it was not popular in Europe. As the international market increased, growers outside the Spanish world produced most of the supply. When tobacco monopolies were established by Spain in the American provinces in the eighteenth century,[10] public revenues benefited, but the system meant restricted production, low harvests, and high prices, and usually left little for export. Tobacco export growth was notable only in Cuba, where by 1820 it was worth some 5 million pesos, a large sum for nonmetallic exports from Spanish America. Even Cuban exports were restricted by pricing policies that drove buyers to the cheaper product of the United States.

Cotton during most of the colonial period was not an export crop. In late colonial times output grew in Venezuela, due to the Industrial Revolution in Europe, but exports only went to 1,100 tons a year. Meanwhile, the United States and other non-Spanish producers supplied most of world demand. Coffee became an American crop and export of any consequence only in the 1770s, especially in Venezuela and Cuba, and chiefly after the Haitian revolution of the 1790s hurt production there. Again, the values were small. Many other items were sent at times to Europe in small quantities, such as pearls, dyewood, quinine, and candied sweet potatoes.

Changes in the Late Colonial Era

Some Spaniards realized in the seventeenth century that America could sustain foreign trade without the Spanish connection.[11] In the eighteenth century officials in the Indies advised that the increasing economic independence there could lead to political freedom. The Spanish Bourbons in the first half of the century did little, however, but discuss changes. Modifications in the fleet system and the *Casa* had little effect.

---

[10] See Chapter 17, Section b, on reaction to the tobacco monopoly.
[11] See Chapter 17 on colonial attitudes during the late colonial era.

France, by the time of its 1761 Family Compact with Spain, wished to promote the economic and military strength of its ally. Its suggestions were less influential, however, than Spain's shocking losses of Manila and Havana to England in the Seven Years' War. A commission in 1765 emphasized to Charles III some of the well-known ills of the old system, assailing the Cádiz monopoly, the fleet system (then moribund), and the trade duties. It hoped that correction of those things would reduce the notorious incidence of smuggling. The same commission, however, deplored damage to Spain from nonenforcement of restrictive legislation on American vineyards and olives, liquor manufacture, and textile making, and even the Philippine trade, as diverting silver that might be spent in Europe. All this scarcely suggested attitudes favorable to innovation. The restrictive ideal was far from dead.

Commercial reforms began with decrees in 1764–1765 opening trade between major ports in Spain and its Antilles, lowering and simplifying duties, and permitting trade between the Philippines and Spain via Cape Horn. During the next quarter century Spain spasmodically loosened its grip on parts of the system. In 1778 a general Free Trade (*Comercio Libre*) Regulation authorized it for all American provinces except New Spain and Venezuela and with most major ports in Spain. Its implementation was in fact stretched out over several years, and it was not extended to New Spain and Venezuela until 1789.

Partially opening ports was only part of the reform effort. Other reform decrees rained upon the system, altering distribution patterns and the direction of mercantile profits, but not much increasing the production—wealth—of the system.[12] Furthermore, the system still did not admit foreigners. An open system was not created,

but what we would call a form of limited "imperial free trade." Even within the empire, newly legalized flows of trade remained subject to much licensing, regulation, and taxation, although these restrictions were somewhat lightened.

The remaining rules, furthermore, perpetuated some inequities and did not destroy the monopolistic system. Cádiz retained the largest part of the legal American trade, and monopolistic merchants in America who were allied with Cádiz suppliers did not lose all their advantages, either in law or in practice. The 1765 decree let natives of Cuba and the West Indies take their own products to Spain on the same conditions as Spaniards, but that privilege was not granted to other American realms until 1796. Then Spanish Americans were authorized to voyage to the privileged ports of Spain in their own ships, laden with American goods, and return with merchandise, provided they conformed to the tariff of 1778. But this 1796 permission was immediately diminished in value by wartime interruptions of trade. Even the wartime concessions to neutral traders retained many rules to try to protect Spanish profits.

The changes in America should not be exaggerated. With the reforms, prices dropped within the system. But reductions were insufficient to diminish contraband, so the advantage to the system was slight. A somewhat larger mercantile community was created, with smaller operators, more small vessels, more flexible sailings, use of more ports. But those things occurred only on a small scale. Fundamentally, the system was little altered. Veracruz retained its privileged position in New Spain, both by law and by the facts of business life. In Spanish America generally, free trade did not destroy the advantages entrenched merchants had in experience, capital, close ties between American and Spanish operations, and control over American producers—for example, loans, and manipulation of markets and prices. In Central America, for instance, where the free trade regulation of 1778 was put into effect in 1781, it was used to try to cut into the monopoly operated by Guatemala City merchants. One method tried was to shift traffic from the monop-

---

[12] For example: decrees of 1772 and following years reduced duties below the 1764–1765 provisions; in 1774 trade was permitted in the Pacific between all parts of the empire, removing old barriers between New Spain and Guatemala and between New Granada and Peru; a 1782 decree freed New Spain's grain and flour exports of many restrictions—but not of registering at Veracruz.

olistic route through the port of Santo Tomás to the ports of Omoa and Trujillo. It failed. The Guatemala City monopolists prevented such a shift largely by means of their established advantages in capital, connections, and expertise. The experience of the late colonial period showed—as would the nineteenth and twentieth centuries—that government-decreed commercial changes often were one thing on paper and another at the places where business was conducted.

The legal trade of the empire increased under the new rules, but so did contraband. Legal traffic possibly doubled between 1778 and 1800, not remarkable in view of general demographic and economic developments in the world. Much of the increased legal trade still was in non-Spanish goods. Improvements in the legal traffic were often obscured by interruptions of warfare, especially in 1792–1815. The total increase in trade, legal and illegal, was more the result of changes in demand in America and Europe than of tinkering with imperial trade rules. The encouragement the changes gave to smaller merchants in America drove some large wholesalers to move funds into mining and land, but their actions had minimum effects on the economy. More important was the effect of the reforms in stimulating creole mercantile ambition. We noted this growth of interest long before the *comercio libre* was enacted. The latter boosted that ambition, as did creation of new American *consulados* in the 1790s.[13] American merchants were also stimulated by the growth of trade, the perception of new opportunities, and a natural human impatience with remaining restrictions, once some had been removed. For example, in Buenos Aires some merchants continued to favor the Spanish monopoly because they were part of it, but most creole traders wanted to expand into still forbidden traffic, and they were supported by most of the creole cattle producers.[14] The Spanish

commercial reforms of the late eighteenth century, therefore, did as much to unsettle as to strengthen the system.

e. Trade Within Spanish America

Trade within Spanish America was greater in volume and value than overseas trade but different in character. First, most people engaged only in petty transactions, some of it barter. Almost none of that activity permitted accumulations of capital. Second, most trade was over short distances. There was little long-distance shipment of grain, garden produce, cheap pottery, clothing, or other common household and work supplies. Finally, wholesale traffic involved some trade in relatively small areas and some that ranged over considerable distances.

A great increase of trade would have been difficult to arrange. Natural obstacles were one problem. More important was the fact that the elite would not permit much change of expenditure or other policy. Spanish restrictions were not what mattered as much as creole-peninsular social aims, which meant few people with money or goods for other than petty transactions. Productive initiative and efficiency and high popular incomes were not encouraged. These deficiencies of production in America affected not only overseas trade, as we have seen, but trade within America. Late colonial exports of flour from Mexico to Havana, for example, ran into competition from lower-priced supplies from the United States.

Some trade within Spanish America was by wholesalers also involved in traffic with Europe and the Philippines. They had great advantages in capital, know-how, ability to influence government and enter into marketing agreements with officials, and in commercial linkages, communications, and transportation. They supplied funds (credit or money) to American producers,

---

[13] See Chapter 17 for more discussion of the new *consulados*.

[14] That the increased trade in a small market like Chile could hurt merchants by saturating the market is true, so

that as late as 1814 there was mercantile interest in restricting trade. Of course, throughout the history of commercial activity in colonial America there were differences between traders on the basis of variant interest.

so the latter could pay off their lesser creditors and dependents, buy goods, get on with their next crop. This activity not only facilitated the distribution of goods imported from overseas by the large merchants, but gave them cargoes for shipment back to Europe, and profits on exchanges of goods that remained in America.

Long-Distance Trade Within America

Although there is no way of distinguishing sharply between long- and short-distance trade, the extremes are clear: a few miles from fields and cottage workshops, or shipment between Mexico and Peru. On the whole the latter was a minor trade, although at times a few routes handled sizable cargo values. In 1802 imports and exports between Veracruz and Spain totaled some 54 million pesos, whereas exchange between Veracruz and American ports was worth only 6.18 million.

Many regulations sought to control long-distance American trade. Some aimed at exchange in commodities that were exported in significant values from Spain, like wine, raisins, olives, almonds, silk. Others tried to control the movements of gold, silver, and Oriental wares. Others discriminated against American in favor of Spanish wholesalers. In 1729 the *consulado* at Cádiz was so afraid of competitors in America that it prohibited American merchant houses from acting as agents of Cádiz firms.

Although there were general Spanish restrictions on traffic between American provinces, they were less important than the fact that much of the limited long-distance trade was in items that were producible in many places in America. Their competition could not be reduced by Spanish decrees. Freedom from Spanish restrictions after Independence had virtually no effect on commercial interchange between the new Spanish American nations; they could not absorb each other's products or satisfy each other's needs. Nor could decrees cancel the limitation of low American purchasing power. What America needed was higher production and better

commercial relations with Europe. Some of the small long-distance trade was hurt by the late colonial reforms. This was the case with Tucumán's sales to the Plata littoral, but even there the main problem was not regulation but European competition allied with the determination of the littoral to sell to Europe and buy from it. Spain did not have the resources to make Tucumán competitive with Britain or to coerce Buenos Aires.

Few American-produced items were of consequence in long-distance traffic in the hemisphere. Animals, for meat or work, could be driven at relatively low cost. A few other foodstuffs besides meat on the hoof occasionally went long distances to mines, ports, and visiting fleets. Silk goods made in New Spain were shipped various places, especially to Peru; and some American-made woollens and cottons were carried considerable distances. Mercury was a valuable commodity, sometimes sent from Peru to New Spain. Its movement from the mines at Huancavelica to Potosí in Upper Peru also involved a long and circuitous route. Coca (source of cocaine) was moved from its hot croplands east of the high Andes to Indian laborers in mine and mountain field. By the end of the sixteenth century, Potosí alone spent some 5 million pesos a year on coca. Even a full list of items would not be impressive, and the values involved were small.

Trade Between North and South America in the Pacific. Traffic between the continents in the Pacific began with the conquest of Peru. For many years it was small, in the 1550s on the order of half a dozen ships a year. In the 1560s and 1570s only some 200,000 pesos' worth of goods left New Spain for Peru annually. Peru needed European-style goods for some decades during the conquest and civil wars. Production long was poorly organized in Peru, and Mexican-made goods were cheaper. So Peru imported Mexican armor, crossbows, sugar, horses, slips of fruit trees, woollen drawers for children, napkins, hats, razors, saddles, and hairnets. Many of these items were in short supply in New Spain, and went to Peru because of Mexican need for silver to supply a medium of exchange and to meet debts to Spain. The result sometimes was an increase in prices in Mexico, which caused complaint there. Mercury in the 1560s joined silver as a Peruvian export to New Spain, and late in the century wine was added. There were also exchanges between New Spain and Central America and between the latter and Peru.[15]

The intercontinental trade in the Pacific was at first unregulated by the crown, though local licensing and control soon were imposed, whereupon the crown decreed that such traffic was free to all its subjects in the Pacific. But a maze of inspection and rules followed: registry of cargo and passengers in order to collect taxes, watch for foreigners, control vagabonds and criminals, and to enforce restrictions on the movement of such items as precious metals and weapons. The large number of licenses needed drew many complaints. On the other hand, Spanish monopolists early argued that the Pacific trade was inimical to the Atlantic trade. The big complaint, however, began with the Manila galleons and transshipment of their Oriental goods from Acapulco to Peru in the later 1570s. By the end of the 1580s reshipment of Chinese goods had greatly increased the Mexico-Peru traffic.

Peruvians bought Oriental goods in preference to European, hurting an Atlantic trade that was at the same time being damaged by interruptions in the fleets and by crown seizure of specie to meet government needs. The expenses of the Atlantic fleets had to be met even when cargoes were low. The Peruvian merchants at Acapulco were buying Chinese textiles because they were both higher quality and cheaper than equivalent European wares. In addition, Peruvians had the

silver to outbid Mexican merchants for European goods, both from legal channels and from contraband. The flow of silver from Peru to Mexico in the early 1590s was 2 to 3 million pesos, most of which went on to the Orient. The flow was bigger in the late 1590s. The Mexico City *cabildo* claimed that in 1597 Peruvian and Mexican specie sent to the Orient from Acapulco totaled 12 million pesos. Possibly 8 to 10 million of that total came from Peru. By then Mexican-made goods going to Peru were only 10 percent of the total taken from the former to the latter, the rest being Oriental wares.

This great expansion brought new control measures in the late 1580s and 1590s, met by the merchants with dodges, including bribery and smuggling. More laws in the seventeenth century tried to control transshipments of Oriental goods to Peru. Exports to Peru of Mexican manufactures still were permitted, but they were minor. The legislation had only a limited effect. In 1631 the crown, under pressure from the Sevilla merchants, forbade all trade between Peru and New Spain, a prohibition that lasted into the eighteenth century. A customs house was set up in 1646 at Acapulco to combat contraband. It nevertheless continued. In 1697, for example, two Peruvian ships took over 2 million pesos to Mexico for the trade. So many Peruvian coins circulated in Mexico that they were called *peruleros* there. The problem eased in the eighteenth century, partly because of lower silver production in Peru and much higher in New Spain. That is, local conditions, not the regulatory system, caused the change.

Other Long Routes in America. We have noted the long routes between Upper Peru and the Atlantic, and between Peru and Panama and Central America. Peru also traded with Chile, largely transshipping European goods, although some American commodities were involved, notably Peruvian sugar and Chilean wheat. There was also long-distance but small-scale intracolonial trade in the Caribbean. A sharp rise in New Spain's wheat-flour market in Cuba in the

---

15 Peru in the sixteenth century traded directly with Central America for cacao and pitch and tar. Sometimes the Central American cacao was worth more than the total of imports from New Spain. Peru had some trade with Panama that was independent of the channeled port and *flota* system, notably in black slaves and some Caribbean items—for example, pearls. Even much later, in the 1790s, indigo went by sea from Central to South America in the Pacific, paid for by silver and some other items.

late colonial era resulted from the growth of Spanish population and income in Cuba as the sugar boom began. But English-speaking North America soon offered the Cuban market prices and delivery schedules that New Spain could not match. Exemptions (1782) from the sales tax for Mexican flour exports to the Caribbean islands could not overcome North American advantages in production and distribution. North Americans even sailed to Veracruz in New Spain, trading flour for cacao, indigo, and other products.

The history of exchange between New Spain and Venezuela shows in the first place the small values involved, and secondarily Spanish restrictive ideals and the influence of contraband. The trade was small for a long time until about 1620, when regular shipments of Venezuelan (Caracas and Maracaibo) cacao began to New Spain, which formerly depended on imports from Central America and Guayaquil. The trade grew modestly until the early eighteenth century, but most cacao still was handled by contrabandists.[16] Spanish goods could not compete with illegal foreign imports in Venezuela, and the cacao went to pay for the latter. In the mid-eighteenth century the cacao traffic to New Spain increased notably, then fell precipitously after 1774. In the 1740s it was claimed that the cacao trade with New Spain was some 600,000 pesos a year and was Venezuela's only source of silver. Venezuela took only small cargoes of such other Mexican items as pottery, flour, and forbidden Chinese wares. Even if this modest flow to New Spain had been expanded to include all the latter's cacao needs, which were not large, it would have been of no value to the system, since it would merely have cut cacao exports from Quito, Guayaquil and Central America.

The redirection of New Spain's cacao imports in the mid-eighteenth century was partly due to the operations of the monopolistic Caracas

Company, formed in Spain in 1728.[17] Its energetic, if often despotic, stimulation of production and distribution in Venezuela was aimed not only at profits but at reduction of contraband and at redirection of trade toward Spain. It had considerable success in both aims. Its operations certainly showed the Spanish goal of favoring trade with the Peninsula. A royal decree of 1741, issued under pressure from the company, ordered the latter to send at least 40,000 *fanegas* of cacao annually to Spain, before any went to Mexico. It also forbade all innovations in trade between Venezuela and New Spain, a rather typical example of the Spanish mercantilist attitude. Small as cacao exports from Venezuela were, they usually accounted for the bulk of its shipments, being 75 percent in 1775, but down to some 60 percent in the later years of the eighteenth century, as Venezuelan indigo enjoyed a brief, small-scale flurry in foreign trade. Venezuela's cacao exports were important to a poor province but much less important to wealthier New Spain and of little consequence to the entire Spanish system.

Shorter-Distance Trade: Wholesale and Retail

The largest trade was in or within a few miles of towns. There also was considerable travel of a hundred or so miles to supply towns and mining camps. Much of the exchange took place in markets in accordance with old Spanish and Indian tradition. Regional, town, and *barrio* (ward or town section) markets were held in streets or plazas. Some retail sales were handled in shops by craft-guild members. There were many peddlers both in town and in the countryside. Yet another retail outlet, largely developed in the eighteenth century, was the hacienda store.

Some *barrios* and villages specialized in certain products. In addition, the medieval tradition of retail specialization remained strong among the

---

[16] Of the 1749 crop of some 120,000 *fanegas* (one *fanega* equals about one and one-half bushels), 25,000 went to New Spain, 3,000 to the Antilles, 6,000 to the Canaries, and much of the large remainder to contrabandists.

[17] See Chapter 13, Section g.

Spaniards, as seen in prohibitions on mixed sale of beef, mutton, and pork. Some markets were daily affairs, partly because purchasing power was low and partly because food storage was difficult. Larger markets offered a great variety of food and handicrafts. Some Indian vendors sat all day on the ground in front of neatly arranged piles of potatoes, beans, squash, or crude cooking casseroles or wearing apparel. The markets also drew hucksters of drinks and food, hawkers of religious amulets, love philters, and other placebos for human need, together with pickpockets, beggars, and prostitutes.

Both wholesalers and retailers were involved in short-distance trade, but some of them had little more in common than the profit motive. There was a great gulf between a big wholesaler who belonged to the *consulado* and a petty hawker of tobacco. Most retailers made too little money to move on to the wholesale level. Furthermore, such a move also required energy, intelligence, and luck. Many hazards, even ruin, lurked just around the corner. Supplies might be interrupted by drought, transport difficulties, or monopolistic price gouging. The retail merchant suffered from arbitrary and greedy demands and seizures by tax gatherers and other public officials.[18] Application to magistrates might be fruitless or too costly even to undertake. Small merchants had little with which to resist such disasters. Their savings were tiny and credit scarce and expensive. The system of favoritism and monopolistic trading made rising from petty retail traffic to the wholesale level difficult. One aspect of this was the influence of local officials on business, as we have seen. *Corregidores* not only did extensive business with Indians, but they bought and sold from local Spanish producers and often had business connections with large regional traders, including those in the provincial capitals.

A small trader found it difficult to work his way into such networks. A part of the control of wholesale operations by small groups of middlemen (operating as buyers, sellers, and financiers) was the tendency for commercial houses with large overseas interests also to get involved in sale of American products. They did so not only to export such items to Europe but also to supply retailers, contractors, or other middlemen in America. The grain and cattle businesses were notable examples. Such commercial houses thus played a role in control of American supplies and monopolistic pricing of them. The clerks or peddlers who moved into the commercial houses often were Spaniards, favored by their countrymen who dominated the firms. Many creoles with connections and capital thought commerce demeaning, but those who went into it—and by the late colonial period they were numerous—had advantages not available to a petty purveyor of the lower class.

This sort of wholesale trade in American products, sometimes combined with operations in exports, contributed to hostility between the merchants of different areas. It even existed between members of the same *consulado* who were resident in different towns. Merchants in Guadalajara, and their allies in other segments of society there, sometimes thought that the Mexico City *consulado*, several hundred miles away, was not interested enough in their problems. The same tension existed between port of Cartagena merchants and those of the mountainous hinterland. Merchants at Córdoba, in the interior of South America, often complained of those at the port of Buenos Aires. Such tensions grew with time, partly because merchants coming out of the constantly growing creole population became more important in relation to the peninsular-born merchant group. The rise of creole merchants was partly a result of intermarriage between creoles and peninsular merchant families. A final type of friction involving commerce should be noted: between *consulados* and *cabildos*, allied on some matters but not on others.

Meat supply in Spanish towns was as much

---

[18] At least in eighteenth-century New Spain, ambulatory vendors were not required to pay the *alcabala de reventa* —sales tax on second and further sales of items until they were "used up." The *consulado*, as *alcabala* farmer, also sometimes did not try to collect from the smallest retailers, whose businesses were too petty to justify the trouble.

regulated as grain. It was under *cabildo* jurisdiction, but other officials often played a role. Regulation involved supply, distribution, price, and sanitation. Essentially, Mexico City's meat was provided ten months of the year by contractors. The other two months any livestock owner could slaughter and sell. The contract price was set by bidding. The winner had to post bond in guarantee of performance. He won a monopoly but had to maintain proper supplies at the set prices. It took close inspection to fight filth, price gouging, short weights, and sale of diseased meat. Mexico City in the sixteenth century came to have four slaughterhouses. A provision that no person could have the contract for more than one of them reflected government fear of some of the effects of monopoly, especially shortages of supplies and exorbitant prices due to cornering. A slaughterhouse inspector, appointed by the *cabildo*, kept records of the sales tax levied on beef and mutton, which supported the city water supply. The official meat cutter, licensed by the *cabildo*, had to be a Spaniard. A continuing short-weight problem was countered with double checks, on two scales. The sanitary problem can be guessed from demands that meat be kept on hooks, not on the floor.

f. Summary of the Economy

The socioeconomic system of Spanish America channeled income to mine owners and *hacendados*, to some Spanish and other European wholesale merchants and manufacturers and shipowners, and to church and state agencies and personnel that tapped those concentrations of wealth. The favored group in America lived well. Observers noted the luxury of the creole elite. Their life-style depended heavily on free or cheap labor, land gifts or grabs, commodity exchanges, and payments in kind. They were land-poor. Their luxury indicated heedless expenditure as much as actual wealth.

The seventeenth was in some respects a century of depression in Spanish America. There was a dramatic decline in silver output and the activities and jobs damaged by that—government revenues and bureaucrats, mining investors and import merchants, and the suppliers of mining camps. The damage as it related to exports and imports was worsened by the coincidental flaying of Spanish shipping and coastal points in America by foreign foes and buccaneers. That and production decline in Spain contributed to a rise in contraband. Coincidental with the mining and export-import depression, there was trouble with production for the American market due to the terrible decline in Indian population. As populations were moved around and new labor and production systems tried, there were problems even with basic food production.

Most creoles were not upset by Spanish export losses. In fact, some creoles benefited from stimulation of local production and trade by dislocations of maritime traffic. In addition, a few areas in the seventeenth century somewhat improved exports of hides, indigo, and other products. Such local improvements often depended on the condition of foreign demand and competition more than on initiative in production and distribution in America and relationships to profits in silver production or to the warfare in the Caribbean. Long-distance trade between Spanish American provinces and exports overseas to Europe were small in commodities other than silver, and those commodity exports did not vary in accordance with investments in productive facilities by silver investors or other capitalists. Finally, the bulk of the population was little affected by any slowdown in mineral output, interruption of imports, or violence at coastal points.[19] The decline of population and the shortage of labor affected more people than did the lower silver production. Depression in the seventeenth century was important, but not as meaningful as *latifundio*, the continuing class and caste systems, servile and dependent labor, and low popular purchasing power.

---

[19] See Chapter 7 for the limited extent of Spanish military losses in the seventeenth century.

The economy improved somewhat in the eighteenth century. The upturn was not as remarkable, however, as creoles at the end of the century claimed. They were then irritated by wartime regulations and claimed that recent glorious prosperity had been brought to penury by Spanish folly. Lucas Alamán, who wrote in early republican Mexico, warned of such exaggeration, noting that the celebrated Humboldt had given creoles an inflated notion of the wealth of their country, building dreams of growth that facts did not support. Just so. It was a limited prosperity in a late eighteenth-century Mexico that enjoyed increased silver output but suffered shortages and high prices for maize, bringing severe hardship. "Prosperity" in colonial Spanish America means little except as applied to the elite or to the condition of the treasury. For the masses, there were degrees of poverty. Economic growth in eighteenth-century Spanish America did not initiate processes that led to continuing improvement in the nineteenth century. Nearly all nineteenth-century growth came from foreign demand.

The defects of the Spanish American economy were the result of many things more important than Spanish policy. Two were critical: the unalterable creole support of the aristocratic dispensation, and the determination of Spain's rivals to do business with the Spanish Indies. Others, some related to creole compulsions or to Spain's policy imperatives, were a fitful and selective interest in productive technology; the insistence on forced and dependent labor systems, which helped keep most workers at low income levels, without much incentive; insufficient capital, much of it used for what we would call nonproductive purposes; deficiencies in the transport and communications systems, some being an unavoidable burden imposed by the physical environment; and the concentration of the best land in a few hands. Add these things to the crown's fixation on bullion, due to the ideas of the day and to the constant crisis of state need in Spain, and it seems unsurprising that the economy of Spanish America did not develop like those of Britain or its colonies in North America.

With all these problems, the opportunity did not exist for a rapid and widescale development. To hint that such development might have occurred if Spain had adopted some magic formula or if the destruction of the wars of 1792–1824 had been averted is misleading. Most people with capital in America saw no reason to put money into agriculture or manufacturing for export. In the sixteenth and seventeenth centuries, especially, agricultural and pastoral exports were small and apparently would have been difficult to develop. Both Spain and Spanish America during the sixteenth to eighteenth centuries became increasingly "colonial" in the modern economic sense—subject to pressure and imposition by other states, especially Britain, France, and Holland. The Independence struggle (1810–1824) in Spanish America scarcely affected underlying socioeconomic structures, and it did not reduce economic dependence or colonialism. Since the rupture of the Spanish empire, both Spain and her former colonies have struggled to break out of their poverty and dependence. The difficulties they have met indicate the profundity of the political, social, and economic chasm into which they fell.

12 Some Social Conditions and Institutions

Drunkenness, illness, crime, and prayer tell as much about life in the colonial era as class and race or property and work. They suggest something of the life of the heart, soul, and mind. Family life, the schoolroom and university hall, the games people played, the books they wrote and read, and even those they banned also have their tales to tell. So do stately town halls fronted with shadowed porticoes, where the colonists walked safe from the tropical sun, and a multitude of great churches, with glazed tile domes of green and blue and yellow; soaring towers; stone angels, saints, and cherubim, sometimes with the features of an Indian stonecutter to proclaim that this was the New World.

a. Family Life and Recreation

The upper class lived in towns because life was more comfortable and interesting there.[1] Not that there were no drawbacks. Residents complained of dust, mud, and dung in the streets; thieves and beggars; epidemic disease; and the snarled traffic of coaches, carts, sedan chairs, mule trains, people on horseback, and even sheep, cattle, and goats. The upper class growled that in town many of the *castas* became

"uppity." Still, such things were a small price to pay for the variety of clothes and food, neighboring friends, news of the world, theaters, musical performances, festivals, illuminations, fireworks, bullfights, gambling, access to government favors, and the charming bustle that gave a sense of participation in the world instead of the dull isolation of the countryside.

The power of the upper-class man over wife and children was legally and customarily heavy. Clerical authorities preached wifely obedience and inferiority. The upper class married in church. Daughters received the close attention of *dueñas* (chaperons), and they were wed with father's consent and often by his arrangement. A notable minority of women, however, elected to enter convents rather than marry. In many cases, they led a pleasant, pampered life in the convent, with servants, music, and social events.

The average upper-class woman was home-centered, but did go out. Visits to church permitted mutual ogling with men and the passing of notes. Women visited shops. There were promenades, afoot or in carriages, in certain selected spots where their class congregated at set times. There were gala occasions at the viceregal courts that included women. Also important was the fact that inheritance laws were fair to women. Primogeniture was uncommon, so it did not bar

---

[1] See Chapter 8, Section a, on towns in Spanish America.

women from owning property. Some women inherited encomiendas and ran considerable establishments. Upper-class women had enough freedom so that charges of adultery were brought against them; not all the charges can have been false.

Upper-class families inherited the Spanish affection for family ties and often lived in large dwellings occupied by several generations and kinds of blood and other relationships. Men who made money in the Indies quickly attracted as aids and pensioners all sorts of relatives and flunkeys. Houses came flush to the street and kept family life hidden from the world. Many had pleasant interior courtyards and gardens. Upper-class families enjoyed many servants. One of their duties was preparation of a rich and nourishing diet, which included many dishes of American origin, or Spanish dishes with American ingredients, spiced to suit the palates and obstinacy of Indian cooks. The elite in Paraguay ate cassava in several forms and drank the invigorating local *yerba mate*. In Mexico they ate *tortillas* (thin corn cakes) and grew accustomed to a liberal use of hot chiles. Pastries, preserved fruits, and other confections were a passion with creoles everywhere, a taste happily served by the widespread sugar production of the Indies. Upper-class dress followed European modes and led to purchase of large quantities of stuffs, lace, ruffs, shoes, boots, buckles, mirrors, and other articles. The luxury of this interest stares out of colonial paintings that have survived.

Among the poor, sexual relations sometimes were promiscuous, but in many cases stable man-woman relationships were maintained. In Indian villages promiscuity was often punished harshly. The dirt of common dwellings had a relationship to disease, and the elite knew that intimacy with the pustules of plague victims was one undesirable feature of popular housing arrangements. The diet of the lower class was as adequate as that of most of the world's poor. It was meager in variety, with reliance on a few staples, depending on region: cassava, maize, potatoes, beans. Meat and fish were as rare as in most of the world. But in such places as the plains of the Orinoco or La Plata or the cattle regions of New Spain, cowboys ate little but beef. Sometimes they would even eat the tender tongue and leave the rest of the carcass to rot.

Lower-class clothing was adequate, especially in the great areas that seldom or never suffered freezing temperatures. In some mountain regions wool textiles were woven at home by poor Indians, or made in commercial workshops (*obrajes*). For the feet, the mode was sandals or nothing. The most important thing about Indian clothing, aside from its simple adequacy, was that it was different from that of the elite. Dress distinctions set the classes well apart. Indians wishing to be considered mestizos adopted some Spanish dress; mestizos wishing to pass as creoles had to amass sufficient wealth to ape them. Or, from the opposite viewpoint, the elite deplored the tendency of the lower orders to forget their place by dressing too fine.

For leisure pursuits, upper-class homes knew European card, dice, and board games, dolls, swings, and blind man's buff. Parties at home were popular, and wine and liquor flowed. There were excursions to the country. Tobacco came into fashion in the seventeenth century. For men there were horse races and bull, cock, and dog fights. In large towns important figures could visit convents to be regaled with conversation, sweetmeats, and musical concerts. Gambling was such a passion that the crown early prohibited cards, but finding the rule impossible to enforce, created a monopoly of playing cards. Elegant commercial eating or drinking places did not exist. Cafes were just coming into being late in the eighteenth century. Lima's first *cafée público* was opened in 1771, and twenty years later some of the elite still feared that it led to promotion of the spirit of faction. The same doubt arose in Mexico, where the first coffee house opened in the capital in 1785. The viceroy in 1790 thought that such places should be prohibited because periodicals were read and discussed there!

There was religious and secular drama. Early

missionaries used religious plays to teach the Indians, sometimes in Indian languages. Before long the church tried to restrict such performances because Indian players and audiences were delighted with the drama and ignored the message. Some performances in the sixteenth century at church altars, in monasteries, and in the streets satirized civil authority. At Santo Domingo in Española in 1588 a church-sponsored farce abused government officials. The *audiencia* deported the author, a churchman, whereupon the archbishop accused the magistrates of exceeding their authority. Church-sponsored farces were, however, increasingly suppressed in the later sixteenth century although never entirely eliminated. The secular theater began late in the sixteenth century in Mexico and Peru. It continued thereafter, often with vice-regal encouragement. Even opera crossed the sea to Spanish America late in the colonial era.

Although some upper-class entertainments were elaborately luxurious and some were licentious, most were neither. Hernán Cortés showed a pretty taste for fancy banquets. Several viceroys were addicted more to pleasure than to business. Some lesser officials led such scandalous lives that they suffered condemnation, dismissal, and fines. In some cases, however, a long time passed before they were brought to book. The lower-class mistresses of upper-class men seldom caused trouble if they did not flaunt themselves luxuriously in public. Some of them, however, insisted on doing so.

Certain public ceremonies and festivities assumed great importance because of the scarcity of commercial and private recreation. All classes watched or played a role in these. Religious celebrations often were grand, with elaborate processions, and much upper-class jostling for place. There was excitement at the arrival of a new viceroy or archbishop. In New Spain such an occasion involved two hundred miles of activity, in Veracruz, along the road to Mexico City, and near and within the capital. In Quito in 1631 news of the birth of a Spanish prince launched nine days of fiestas, after a month's preparation.

There were bullfights daily. The great plaza was decorated. Soldiers paraded and fired artillery. In a great procession through the streets, a religious image was escorted by all manner of civil and ecclesiastical authority. On following days pageants were put on in the streets by various groups, including the guilds and their *cofradías* (brotherhoods). Indians acted out a mock battle of Inca times.

Other opportunities for recreation varied. At one extreme was the city of Potosí, with 100,000 inhabitants and a mountain of silver, which about the year 1700 offered fourteen dance halls, thirty-six gambling houses with professional gamesters, a theater, many grog shops, and unnumbered prostitutes, some with fancy houses and rich ancillary entertainment. On the other hand, most people lived in small towns and villages, where public celebrations were modest and infrequent and commercial wares simple. The Indians and *castas* became fond of fireworks, which the Spaniards brought from Europe. Even small towns in America sometimes had a fireworks maker. Some towns in Mexico and Guatemala had the tradition of the spectacular *voladores* (flyers), Indians who dove off great poles to unwind to the ground on twisted ropes, flying in huge circles as a turntable at the top rotated. There were gossip, gambling, strong drink, and quite a lot of fighting with knives. But for most people in the countryside the day was for work, the night for sleeping, a routine seldom relieved except for Sunday market and church.

b. Intoxication, Health, and Crime

Intoxication

Intoxication was not only recreation but also therapy for the lower class. Many Indian groups, before the conquest and after, used intoxicants: hallucinogenic fungi and other plants and alcoholic drinks. The Spaniards in Peru widened the use of coca leaves (source of cocaine) as a business proposition. The Indians bought coca to deaden the dreary round of labor under the con-

Colonial Spanish America

Life of the Lower Class. In the lower class were Indians, blacks, and people of mixed racial heritage.

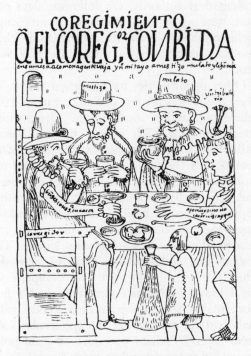

Above—a Spanish *corregidor* (official) in Peru invites to his table "men of the lower class," as the legend at the top of the picture states—a mestizo, a mulatto, and a tributary Indian. This was drawn by Poma de Ayala, who is described on page 56.

Above right—Poma de Ayala in the early seventeenth century shows a Spaniard abusing a heavily laden Indian, a common occurrence in all Spanish America.

Right—a fanciful European version of Indians mining silver at Potosí in Upper Peru (now Bolivia). The miners did use candles and hand tools, and they laboriously carried the ore up unsteady rope-and-stick ladders. The work was heavy and dangerous. *Courtesy Rare Book Division, The New York Public Library, Astor, Lenox and Tilden Foundations*

Cathedral altar, Mexico City. Such lavish decoration was common.

Above—the church of La Compañía, Quito, Ecuador. The amazing number of churches, convents, and monasteries represented a conspicuous part of public expenditures in Spanish America. Secular structures included viceregal palaces, municipal buildings, and mints. *Peter Menzel*

Right—the fortress of El Morro, San Juan de Puerto Rico, was built gradually over the years. Havana, Cartagena, and many other places also had formidable military bastions. *Courtesy of the Commonwealth of Puerto Rico Tourism Development Company*

querors. Many Indians before the conquest drank heavily, at least on occasion. Drink frequently had a socioreligious function, giving relief from the round of monotonous toil and tending to bind the community together. Among the higher cultures, it usually was rather closely controlled by the state. These traditions continued to influence drinking after the conquest, although the hold of the old religion and customs slowly decayed.

Alcoholic drunkenness certainly increased after the conquest. The poor of the colonial era had good reasons for drinking. Like coca, liquor was an escape from physical misery and a society in which they felt alien. Furthermore, it was cheap when the drinks often could be made at home, like *chicha* in Peru and *pulque* in Mexico. Drinking was promoted by commercial makers and sellers of intoxicants, and encouraged by employers to keep the lower orders in debt and subservient. Mexico had large upper-class producers of *pulque*, and some of them also owned retail outlets. The drink was made from the common maguey plant with little expense to the producer. The state approved because it derived tax revenues from intoxicants.

At the end of the seventeenth century Mexico City had thirty-five authorized *pulquerías*, simple bars for the poor, where customers sat together on benches at long tables. If the proprietors did not display the classic sign of later years, they would have subscribed to the sentiment:

> Keep coming in, keep drinking,
> Keep paying up, keep leaving.

Religious and civil government made many efforts to control the sale of alcohol, both to limit drunkenness and to ensure revenues from it (scarcely compatible goals). Measures taken in the late sixteenth century in Peru showed some attitudes toward the problem. The government decided that wine and *chicha* were identified there with pagan rituals, so the clergy was authorized to search out and destroy supplies. The *audiencia* at Lima, however, did allow Indians to buy two pints of *chicha* a day in licensed taverns, but it tried to control home brewing. Thus, the "interests" or crying needs of both elite and proletariat made lower-class temperance a sometime thing. It should be noted, finally, that drunken brawling by men of the upper class was sufficiently common to suggest to the commonalty that alcohol was not repugnant to old Christians.

Health

People in all the world in those days were more inured to suffering from disease and injury than we are. The life span was short but on the average longest among the privileged whites. Infant, child, and maternal mortality were especially high. There were recurrent epidemics. A chronicler of the conquest said that in some areas smallpox left half the Indians dead "in heaps like bedbugs"; and as late as 1779 smallpox devastated Mexico City with a 20 percent mortality. The disease terrified communities. In a few days it could make a vigorous person a pustuled, oozing horror.

The relationship between sanitation and disease was known, but only imperfectly. Gastroenteric disorders were endemic, debilitating, and frequently fatal. Much effort was expended to ensure pure drinking water. Aqueducts carried water to the larger towns, and their great arches still march across the countryside, witness to the Spanish tradition of civic responsibility. Public wells and springs were common. Colonial descriptions of slaughterhouses indicate that they were fragrant. They sometimes contaminated water supplies, but they would have been worse without supervision. Sewage was not well handled because of the expense, engineering problems, and inadequate appreciation of the dangers involved in raw sewage.

Physicians trained in the European style were relatively helpless until the eighteenth century, when in all the European world there developed a new appreciation of anatomy and disease. In Spanish America the new medical education and vaccination were introduced in the middle and late eighteenth century, under both public and private auspices. The institution of the *proto-medicato*, or public health office, had been early brought from Spain. Where there were *protomedicatos*, they licensed medical and pharmaceutical practitioners. Unfortunately, the *protomedicatos* were too few in number and were understaffed. The physicians they dealt with were great believers in purges and bleeding, which often did more harm than good. Considerable surgery was done by barbers. Most people, however, had to use folk doctors or home remedies. For some simple disorders herb mixtures did well enough.

Hospitals were built and supported by government, church, and individuals. Aid for hospitals and foundling homes came from church funds, municipal governments, alms, bequests, and from the *cofradías*, or brotherhoods, which served hospitals without pay. The governor in Santo Domingo on royal orders established in 1503 a hospital for poor Spaniards and Indians. Later, in many provinces special hospitals were established for *castas*, lepers, women, sailors, and poor clerics. Hospitals cared for not only the sick but the old and crippled and abandoned infants, and they gave alms to the poor. The *cofradías* that supported them were organized by all classes. Hernán Cortés was a generous member of the Confraternity of Our Lady, which built and supported a great hospital in Mexico City. In the sixteenth century in Lima the managers (*mayordomos*) of hospitals often were leading merchants, who had the business acumen to run them and their endowments and coveted the public honor involved. *Cofradía* members might give money or free nursing care. Most craft guilds had parallel *cofradías*, which sometimes supported hospitals and helped bury the guild members. Many small Indian towns had simple hospitals, served by Indian *cofradías*, whose members took turns as nurses.

In 1580 Spanish America had twenty-two hospitals in thirteen cities; in 1630 there were ninety-four in sixty-five cities, about 35 percent of the cities in the area. By the end of the eighteenth century, Mexico City had nine government-sup-ported hospitals and several private ones. This total represented a considerable effort. There were complaints, however, that the hospitals were badly managed. During epidemics, people, with reason, feared being sent to isolation hospitals, which were meant to restrict contamination rather than to treat the afflicted. Isolation at home or flight were the best measures during epidemics, but only the upper class could afford either.

Crime and Public Safety

Colonial Spanish America was massively affected by violence. The upper class thought itself privileged to treat the lower as it pleased. The brutalized lower class stole and committed bodily violence, out of need and frustration, and without any sense of identification with upper-class rules and institutions. People who had made enough money to rise out of the proletariat and could not enter the elite for either monetary or social reasons did not have modern bourgeois ideas on "middle-class" virtues; instead, they identified with the upper class. Colonials often attributed crime to vagabondage, and no doubt there were linkages between them; but the attribution really shows the lack of upper-class interest in the social bases of crime and reliance on the punitive philosophy of the law of the time. They were far from unique in these attitudes among governing groups in the world.

Crime was serious in both urban and rural areas. Shippers and travelers went prepared to defend themselves. The streets of cities sometimes were unsafe even in daylight. They were worse after dark, because extensive street lighting was just coming in at the end of the colonial era. Careful citizens went armed in groups and carried lights.

Lower-class crimes against the upper class were less numerous than crimes of violence visited by lower-class people on each other. *Castas* also fomented riots out of ill will or the attraction of profit from looting. To be sure, Spaniards sometimes did the same. The upper class, of course, emphasized the crime and disturbance created by the riotous and "criminal" lower classes. Much of that activity was concentrated in a minority of outcasts. They were called *léperos* in Mexico. The outcast's understandable defiance of a society that rejected him reinforced upper-class disdain for a barbarism it thought natural to people of inferior race and illegitimate origins. Long after Independence, Spanish America would retain a high level of violence, as well as the attitude that nothing better could be expected of the lower orders.

Even some tiny villages founded by Spaniards in the early years in the Indies received at once a gibbet and a town constable (*alguacil mayor*). This constable, with assistants in larger towns, patrolled, pursued, jailed, and carried out the decisions of magistrates (*alcaldes*) of the town and higher officials. Constables had some difficulty with the tradition of church sanctuary and clerical protection of laymen who sought it. Their worst problem, however, was a staff wholly inadequate to the amount of crime. Jail buildings were simple, sometimes private structures. That problem was relieved by renting prisoners out as labor.

The *Santa Hermandad* (Holy Brotherhood), a rural constabulary, was exported to New Spain in the 1550s. Its functions were assigned at that time to the stockmen's association (*Mesta*), transported from Spain to Mexico in 1537. It later was established in other towns in New Spain, but never elsewhere in America. Even before 1537 rural crime, including rustling, had agitated stock owners. The vast and brutal uprooting of the Indian society had driven many men to banditry as a profession. By 1550 brigands waited near likely spots on the main roads of New Spain, especially near towns. Banditry was not to be well controlled in Mexico until near the end of the nineteenth century.

Alcaldes de Mesta were elected annually from among the town councillors of Mexico City; thus their cattle-protection and general police functions both were in the hands of a city oligarchy that more and more developed important hold-

ings in the countryside. The *Alcaldes de Mesta* acted for the *Santa Hermandad* both as a police court and director of constables, in the city and the surrounding areas. In 1710 the functions of the *Santa Hermandad* were taken over by the court of *La Acordada*, whose agents—reputedly to the number of 2,500—served without pay but with privileges and honors. *La Acordada* had jurisdiction over virtually all of New Spain. It became famed for summary and terrible punishment—often hanging or shooting with arrows. It somewhat cut down rustling and rural banditry but could not completely eradicate the problem.

c. Religious Beliefs and Structures

Church organization did not change much during the colonial era, except that bishoprics multiplied, and the secular organization progressively replaced the regular.[2] By 1545 there were three archbishoprics (Santo Domingo, Mexico, Lima); at the end of the colonial era there were ten archbishoprics and thirty-eight bishoprics. A count of monasteries about 1630 showed 334 in 122 towns, about 74 percent of the towns in the Spanish Indies. There were twenty in Mexico City and twelve in Lima. The count also showed seventy-four nunneries. Some of the monasteries and nunneries, however, had very few residents.

Personnel and treasure were dedicated to religion by the elite far out of proportion to the numbers of that group. At times the separation of socioracial classes in towns was emphasized by attendance at different temples by whites, blacks, mulattoes, and others. The church had its least effect upon the black slaves. Free blacks became Christians rather more readily than Indians, presumably because the blacks were more separated from their old cultural roots and lived closer to Europeans. Mulattoes, like mestizos, generally

---

[2] For the church of the conquest, see Chapters 4–5; for church and government, Chapter 6; church and expansion and defense, Chapter 7; church and the economy, Chapter 10.

accepted, if they did not practice, Christianity.[3]

The church seemed to have a tremendous opportunity among the Indians of New Spain in the 1520s; there was little opportunity in Peru until after the civil wars ended in mid-century. By then the Indians were suspicious of all Spaniards. There was great excitement among the friars in early New Spain, some of them driven by an idealism based in part on the church reforms in Spain of Cardinal Ximénez de Cisneros early in the sixteenth century. Indians flocked to be converted, build churches, serve the friars. It must have been an inspiring experience for an idealistic friar of those days to stand in the second-story open altar space set in the facade of a new church and preach to a multitude of Indians standing reverently in the bright sunshine. It brought to mind the apostolate of the early church. But Indian enthusiasm cooled, because of clerical greed and the church's inability to protect the Indians from the conquerors.

Each encomienda was supposed to have a *doctrinero* to convert and serve the Indians and act as the *encomendero's* private chaplain. Each hacienda later had a priest with such dual functions. But encomienda Indians and others felt badly served and, as we have seen, Indians greeted the New Laws of 1542 as an invitation to abandon not only the *encomenderos* but the clergy as well. Priests had great retinues of Indian assistants for some decades, but by the early seventeenth century such service was restricted. The assistants did not relieve the problem of a shortage of clergy for pastoral work. That shortage was aggravated in the countryside by the preference of the clergy for town life. The church would not, however, permit an Indian priesthood or even let many mestizos and mulattoes take holy orders. There were a few Indian clerics and a few more mestizo and mulatto. Peninsular and creole clerics agreed on such restrictions. Sadly, one element in their position was interest in the income and perquisites to be drawn by themselves from Indian parishes.

---

[3] See Chapter 8 on religion and blacks.

The Indians in their suspicion and disillusion adopted ambiguous attitudes toward church and faith. On the one hand, they showed reverence for Christianity, especially for local saints and manifestations of the virgin. The church welcomed belief in the vision of an Indian virgin who appeared in 1532 to a poor Mexican. She quickly became the venerated, dark-skinned Virgin of Guadalupe. But Indians also mingled old religious beliefs with Christian and even carried on parallel preconquest and Christian rites. Spanish priests in the seventeenth and eighteenth centuries sometimes were shocked to stumble upon pagan survivals. One curate found that his rural parishioners had "priests" of the old cults and worshiped an array of thirteen gods. The Indians at times showed great respect for Christian clerics but at others were willing, even eager, to get along without them—indeed, the sacraments usually were a small part of the Indian worship system. Such ambivalence makes any estimate of the hold of Christianity on the Indians difficult. It was enough to keep them somewhat attached to the church; but the attachment was not sufficiently clear to let anyone predict how Indians would react to a given issue involving the church. Indians sometimes were fanatically devout; at others, they cared little for the views of the clergy.

Did the church, then, neglect or throw away a great opportunity among the Indians? The answer must be no. A vastly greater opportunity than it seized did not exist. Spaniards in America would not support the radically better life for Indians that would have been required to make them conventional Christians. Nor were the state or the ecclesiastical hierarchy willing to go far in an effort to coerce Spaniards to be kind to Indians. In this they were no weaker than the clergy who dealt with slaveholding planters in colonial Virginia and slave-ship owners in Massachusetts.

Anyone with pretensions to social standing in a Spanish town in America was an active church member, although piety was more conspicuous among women than men. All the upper classes and pretenders to that status were baptized, wed, and buried in the church. Benefactions to the church were frequent. Influential prelates often received great deference, but if it was perceived that one had abused his authority, deference disappeared. It also disappeared during factional strife. Thus, many an ecclesiastical dignitary suffered verbal abuse and threats, and some went into hiding in fear for their safety.

Local holy men and women, often reputed saints, sensitized people to religion and the problems of life and mortality. All classes could be deeply moved, even to the edge of hysteria, by disasters—floods, earthquakes, volcanic eruptions, droughts, epidemics, attacks by corsairs—especially when they occurred in groups or were accompanied by comets and other portents and when worked over by eloquent preachers. A reputation for miraculous healing powers could excite a population that was unable to alleviate suffering. Mariana de Jesús, a seventeenth-century creole damsel of Quito, was such a reputed saint. She practiced physical mortification, good works, and prayer more rigorously than women in the convents, where many residents entered with dowries and servants and spent their time in embroidery, fancy cookery, musical diversion, and pleasant conversation. The miracles attributed to Mariana included bringing the dead to life. Her death in 1645 brought an outpouring of grief by high and low. The people had "canonized" the "Lily of Quito" long before the Holy See made her sainthood official.

The upper class thought of Spanishness and Catholicism as two sides of one coin. Thus, the Holy Office of the Inquisition in its function of ferreting out heretics may be thought of as a "popular" institution. Most colonials had nothing to fear, and a deep detestation of unbelievers. The Inquisition was founded under the bishop of Santo Domingo in 1517 and remained under control of the bishops in the Indies until 1569, when the king founded tribunals of the Holy Office of the Inquisition at Mexico City and Lima. A third was set up in New Granada in 1610. The Inquisition did much investigating

during the two centuries after 1569, but only a few thousand cases were prosecuted after such probing. About a hundred persons were burned as a result of its action. The Indians did not come under the Holy Office. Indian heresy was investigated under episcopal authority.

Crown and miter hoped that the Inquisition promoted religious solidarity in the Indies and that this promoted civic solidarity. Possibly it did, while also creating some fear. People were cautious about attacking the Holy Office, even late in the eighteenth century when it had lost some of its influence. Reasons for caution were the Inquisition's notorious secrecy, fondness for torture, and abuse of authority by its officers. *Audiencias, visitadores generales,* and the Council of the Indies denounced men who exceeded their authority in the Holy Office. A governor complained to the king in the seventeenth century that the Holy Office in Cartagena de Indias had "terrorized" the province by seeking "to become the master of everything," with one inquisitor using intimidation to gain favors, including special prices in the slave market.

Other problems involving the church have been mentioned: complaints about church wealth; and conflict between seculars and regulars, and ecclesiastical and civil courts, and great prelates and civil officials. Churchmen engaged in a marvelous variety of squabbles, lawsuits, and physical bouts. Friars even buffeted nuns in arguments over jurisdiction. Such matters often involved income. In the seventeenth century in Mexico the Jesuits refused to pay to the bishopric of Puebla tithes on a farm bequeathed to the order. The dispute went to court. It led to vituperative sermons, excommunications, and even that terrible weapon the interdict. Finally the Jesuits were pronounced wrong by the Council of the Indies, the papacy, and the general of the Jesuit order in Rome. In this way a relatively minor matter, but one involving questions of money, principle, and precedent, led to an extraordinary amount of trouble.

Competition between peninsulars and creoles agitated the church. For the secular church it was settled by reserving most of the episcopal seats for peninsulars. In the history of colonial Mexico, only 32 of 171 bishops and archbishops were American-born; in Spanish South America, only 64 of 535. The decision in the case of the orders was no less aggravating to creoles. By the early seventeenth century some houses had a majority of creole friars. The peninsular-born friars said creoles were ineradicably tainted by American birth or by being suckled by Indian wet-nurses. Creoles said peninsulars had been failures in Spain and did not understand American conditions. The fact is that many men entered the orders, in Spain and America, not because of a vocation but because of lack of other opportunity. Discipline was lax, except among Jesuits.

The number of creole friars came to give them an advantage in the election of heads and councils of the administrative provinces of the orders. The outnumbered peninsular friars demanded the *alternativa,* a system of rotating creoles and peninsulars in office. Although there were doubts in church circles in Europe about the wisdom of the *alternativa,* the Spanish government accepted and sometimes insisted on it for the orders. It was applied in America in many cases in the seventeenth century. It was a gross extension to the orders of discrimination against creoles, and irritating to prominent creole families with sons in the orders.

The church's missionary efforts in terms of defense and expansion have been mentioned. Missions also had economic effects, involving hundreds of thousands of Indians, agricultural and pastoral operations, buildings, handicrafts, transport, and trade. The northern missionary effort in New Spain finally reached Texas, New Mexico, Arizona, and northern California. There were missionaries nearly everywhere, at one time or another: Chile, La Plata, Costa Rica, Venezuela.[4] In the province of Mainas, in the lowlands east of the mountains of Quito and Peru, a handful of Jesuits built a mission system in the seventeenth century that covered an area of 1,300

by 700 miles. They congregated some 100,000 intermittently warlike Indians into villages of 2,500 to 5,000. But the Indians often fled, sometimes for fear of epidemics, sometimes in preference for their traditional system of moving about the great rain forest to plant their maize and manioc in virgin soil. The missions of Mainas decayed in the early eighteenth century with Indian revolts and with slave raiding into the area from Portuguese Brazil. By 1762 the Mainas missions held fewer than 20,000 Indians.

Whether the position of the church altered substantially in the Bourbon century is disputed. The fairly numerous Bourbon efforts to curb its wealth were timid failures. There was little change in ecclesiastical discipline. The orders suffered some decline in numbers and prestige, probably in part because of the *alternativa.* Both the regular and secular branches permitted more members of somewhat lower social status, but not a great invasion of *castas.* This slight liberalization did mean that more of the creoles who went into church positions (or their families) had at some time risen to creole status out of the *castas.* Such ultimate lower-class origins became of some moment during the Independence period, when many parish priests sided with that movement, whereas the hierarchy was loyal to Spain.

Much argument that the church changed in the eighteenth century relates to the Bourbon regalists who insisted on the supremacy of the civil over ecclesiastical power. They tightened control over church appointments but without much altering church operations. Some important regalists in Spain who opposed church influence in Hispanic affairs were partisans of the rationalism of the eighteenth-century Enlightenment.[5] That led them to encourage some lightening of the censorship, at least before the frightening French Revolution began in 1789. But the most drastic regalist effort was against the Jesuits. Regalists and rationalists in several European countries in the eighteenth century

---

[4] See Chapters 7, Section b, and 13, Section i, on missions.

[5] See Chapter 17, Section a.

criticized the Society of Jesus. Its discipline, influence, and penchant for intrigue to gain its ends led to claims that it was excessively devoted to the interests of the church, even a state within the state. Portugal took this line, reinforced with the charge that the Jesuits plotted assassination of the king, and expelled them from Portuguese realms in 1759.[6] Charles III of Spain had the general motives of the enlightened despots of the day to justify his expulsion of the Jesuits from the Spanish realms in 1767. He also objected to Jesuit support of resistance by the Guaraní mission Indians to execution of the Portugal-Spain Treaty of 1750 and claimed they were involved in a rebellion in Spain in 1766.

In Spanish America the expulsion was carried out rapidly and secretly. The 2,154 Jesuits went into exile in Europe as submissive subjects. Only a minority was creole, so not many relatives and friends in America were irritated. Some of the creole exiles were bitter, but few protested actively.[7]

Regalism probably affected the faith in America very little. The new rationalists were a small minority. The expulsion of the Jesuits did not affect the Christianity of most Indians. Efforts that have been made to find a vast creole resentment at the expulsion have failed. Removal of the Jesuits hurt upper-class education some by removing teachers, but formal education was not a large part of Spanish American life. The expulsion did not threaten the overall role of the church in society, so conservatives did not consider that their view of that society was under attack. They specifically did not so consider the seizure of Jesuit real estate, being happy to acquire it themselves. The same attitudes toward church property were to be evident in the independent republics of the nineteenth century. In the eighteenth century and later a man could be conservative on political and religious matters

but be willing to relieve the church of some of its land. Upper-class laymen did want the church to have considerable property and income, approving of its sizable expenditures for personnel, ornamentation, oil, incense, and the construction and maintenance of churches and ecclesiastically funded hospitals, schools, and universities.

Churchmen and women in large measure reflected the upper-class civil society. They condoned slavery, played the businessman and woman, sometimes were licentious (more a male failing at the time), often fleeced Indians in collaboration with civil officials, frequently were idle when the population needed more service, sometimes were ignorant and superstitious, supported an educational system for a small minority, and generally were full supporters of the aristocratic dispensation.

The church was important, however, in molding and guarding a Spanish and Christian system, and in transmitting to America many aspects of European culture through education and intellectual life, architecture, painting, sculpture. Beneficent activity also reflected Christian and upper-class Spanish ideas. Although there was a secular as well as a religious role in poverty relief, the tone was set by the church. It preached charity together with the holiness of accepting God's assignments to misery. An end to "indiscriminate" almsgiving was advocated by a small reform group in Spain and America in the eighteenth century. The aim was to concentrate charity on work for the "deserving" poor. Most upper-class Catholic Christians in Spanish America nevertheless retained an unreflective belief in indiscriminate almsgiving and in their other traditional beliefs and habits.

d. Education, Intellectual Activity, Literature, and Art

Education

Education reflected the system of privilege. Schools and universities were provided mainly for the sons of the elite. The church, political

---

[6] The Jesuits also were expelled from France, Austria, and the Kingdom of the Two Sicilies, and abolished by the papacy in 1773.

[7] See Chapter 17, Section b, on the expelled Jesuit Viscardo.

processes, and economic and social conditions discouraged the acquisition of literacy by the popular classes. Elementary education was simple. Sons of the conquerors got a bit of reading, writing, and calculation drummed into them by their fathers, relatives, or clerics. Before the sixteenth century was over there were what amounted to parish schools, run by clerics for fees, where sons of the elite learned by rote a few letters and numbers and the catechism. Memorization was assisted with knotted cords across the palm, on the prevailing theory that "learning enters with blood." A few upper-class girls went to classes for a year or two in convents, learned a bit of religion, and became barely literate. There were provisions for Indian schools, even decrees that each village should have one, but the results were scanty. There came to be a few municipally supported elementary schools, and a few private classes for pay were offered in towns, some by *castas*. But all these methods of imparting a crude knowledge of letters and numbers touched but a small minority, although increased numbers of schools toward the end of the colonial era modestly improved the situation for women and for members of the nonprivileged class.

The Economic Societies of Friends of the Country, active in Spain after 1764, and in America from the 1790s, tried to promote primary instruction because literacy was so rare that they could not get on with their major interest in technical training. The Havana society declared in 1795 that from the deficiency of education, "It resulted that many talents descended to the sepulcher without ever being useful." But that was a late colonial idea and held by only a tiny minority who thought of themselves as being enlightened and who had the novel notion that literacy training ought to be equated with patriotism.

Colegios, run by friars, were what we would term a combination of secondary or preparatory school and seminary. Sixteen cities in Spanish America had *colegios* by 1630, and others received them later. The Jesuit *colegios* became especially renowned. Students were mostly sons of the elite who could afford the fees. The church did provide some free schooling to promising poor boys, not only because they were wanted as clerics, but because making use of obviously talented boys who were fortunate enough to make their potential known was traditional. Few boys of any class would advance much beyond simple literacy if they did not attend a *colegio*, where attention was chiefly directed to theology, Latin, and to philosophy selected for its reinforcement of Roman Catholic positions. Not only was Latin the indispensable tool for higher studies, but it was a major means by which students were inculcated in habits of study and a few captured by the love of learning. With Latin came some ancient history and literature and even some mild brushes with social comment. We may be sure that sturdy descendants of the conquerors often gagged over their Latin texts, but we know that the great teaching and intellectual traditions of the church turned a few into respectable scholars, usually with careers as clerics or civil lawyers.

Some twenty universities were decreed established, but not all of them operated. Some were eighteenth-century creations and had little time to develop before Independence. Those at Mexico City and Lima went into operation in the mid-sixteenth century. Mexico City from 1553 to 1775 conferred some 30,000 bachelor's degrees, about 1,000 doctorates, and some master's degrees, an average of about 140 degrees of all types per year. The universities of Lima, Guatemala, and Córdoba (in present-day Argentina) had long and rather vigorous lives. There was less vigor at most of the others. Possibly 150,000 degrees were granted by all the colonial universities.

Although most university students were from the creole elite, laws at times permitted admission to Indians and *castas*, although they seldom applied or were accepted. An increased eighteenth-century upper-class alarm at the rise of the *castas* was reflected in new edicts requiring proofs of legitimacy and purity of blood to enter the universities.

The universities put a polish of learning on the sons of wealthy creoles. They also provided lawyers for practice and the bench, educated men for the civil bureaucracy generally, and churchmen. Thus the faculties of law and theology were the most important. A few men took degrees in medicine or mathematics (engineering or surveying were the careers involved), but the fields were little esteemed. Some efforts were made to promote the study of Indian languages through the universities, with meager results.

The ideas expressed in the universities naturally reflected those predominant among learned men of the upper class, especially in the church. University study was not meant to be innovative. Reliance was on neither invention nor experiment, but on authority (Christian scriptures and commentaries, St. Thomas Aquinas, Aristotle), and on memory and rhetorical flourish. A typical subject for elucidation was: "If a sacrament administered by a demon or a fallen angel would be a real one." An ability to recite from memory was greatly admired, and sometimes eleven-year-old boys did so for the edification of learned doctors and their guests. Also thought admirable were such feats as arguing four topics alternately, a sentence to each, never faltering, never mingling one argument with the other. Such sterility was evident in most European universities of the time, and much of the intellectual invention of those centuries occurred outside their halls.

University professors were part-time instructors, spending their main energies at other work, chiefly in the ecclesiastical or civil establishments. Men competed for university chairs because of the prestige involved; the income was low. There were important ceremonies at the universities, attended by the great men of the community. When the university of Mexico City was inaugurated, the viceroy and members of the *audiencia* attended classes for a week. The prescribed medieval regalia for a professor made a brave show during many public processions and celebrations.

The acceptance of new ideas in the American universities was retarded for some time by conservatism and the system of controlling reading and speech. Then the disturbing rationalistic ideas of Descartes arrived in the late seventeenth and eighteenth centuries, rather tardily after their announcement in Europe. They often could be introduced only in disguised forms. The ideas of the eighteenth-century Enlightenment, however, came more rapidly to the universities of Spanish America, which were by the second half of the century in closer communication with the rest of the Occidental world. That was important to the generation that led the Independence movement in the early nineteenth century. At least, it may be said of the university system in colonial Spanish America that it was much more impressive than anything done in the field by the French, British, or Portuguese in the Western Hemisphere.

Censorship and Other Controls

Both church and state restricted the publication and dissemination of reading materials and the expression of ideas. Permission was required for legal publication. Lists of authors who were completely banned and of works that were condemned in whole or in part were issued. Materials were proscribed on the grounds of heresy, superstition, immorality or obscenity, or even extravagance in the romances of chivalry that the conquerors liked to hear retold around campfires. The Lutheran revolution that began in the 1520s increased censorship in the Catholic world. By 1559 the Roman Inquisition called its list of prohibited and expurgated books the "Index." Late in the colonial era, censorship turned heavily against the philosophical and political radicalism of the Enlightenment, which was alarming to both state and church. These rules did not much interest the elite, few of whom spent much time reading or were likely to utter proscribed ideas. Still, there was some basis for the saying, "Concerning the King and the Inquisition, Shhh!"

How much was the life of the mind inhibited by rules? Prohibited books certainly circulated, often with the connivance of the authorities.

Although censorship did not stimulate intellectual life, possibly it did not much inhibit it before the eighteenth century. Most people, even learned men, did not want to depart far from the old ideas. Possibly the restrictions did not much dampen good work in theology, law, literature, history, linguistics, descriptive biology; they were more of a barrier in philosophy, physics, and political economy. They did a good deal to restrict the incidence and content of newspaper publication. Both these areas of inhibition—in philosophy, physics, and political economy; and in newspaper publication—were important to the coming of Independence.[8]

Printing, the Book Trade, Libraries

Presses operated in Mexico City in the 1530s, at Lima in 1584, and at other cities later. Printing did not spread rapidly because paper was dear, the book market small, and competition with Spain difficult. As many as 10,000 books annually were shipped legally from Spain to America early in the seventeenth century, and others went that were not declared. There were twenty-five printing presses in Spanish America in 1800, ten of them in New Spain. Most works published in America were on religious subjects.

Libraries were connected with institutions of learning or the church or were in homes. Books were not numerous in creole houses, any more than in those of colonials in English-speaking North America. The institutional libraries consisted, at most, of a few thousand tomes. The first public library in Spanish America was opened by the Havana Economic Society in 1793, and in 1794 it had 1,500 volumes, nearly two-thirds of them on loan from private collections. Spain thus extended to America its own techniques and attitudes toward printing and the sale and acquisition of books. They served the purposes that church, state, and most active citizens thought most important. Restrictions were not of much importance to society, or to the

---

[8] See Chapter 17, Section a.

perspective of history, until the end of the colonial period.

Newspapers and Broadsides

Broadsides—usually a single printed sheet—for distribution and posting were issued in the early seventeenth century. Some announced news, such as ship arrivals, government orders, appointments to office; some were scurrilous attacks on individuals, which also had been done earlier in manuscript form. The first newspaper was the short-lived *Gaceta de México y Noticias de la Nueva España* (six issues in 1722). The second *Gaceta de México* was published, with interruptions and a name change, from 1728 to 1742. A *Gazeta de Goathemala* was published from 1729 to 1731. A *Gazeta de Lima* was published bimonthly in 1743–1767. In 1768 the Mexican scientist José Antonio de Alzate y Ramírez published a few issues of *Diario Literario de México* before it was suppressed by the government. In 1787 he started another paper, emphasizing science and utilitarian matters, which quickly died. In 1788–1794 he published the monthly *Gazeta de Literatura de México*. The *Gazeta de México, compendio de noticias de Nueva España* was put out in 1784–1810. The first Mexican daily appeared in 1805, the *Diario de México*. The first daily in all Spanish America was the Peruvian *Diario de Lima* (1790–1793). Also in Lima appeared every three days in 1791–1795 the *Mercurio peruano de historia, literatura y noticias públicas*. Havana had two papers in the 1760s and one in the 1780s; then beginning in 1790 the *Papel Periódico*, which continued with changes of name until 1810. Papers were published in the 1790s and early in the nineteenth century at Bogotá, Quito, and Buenos Aires.

Such periodical publication was not very important before the 1780s, but it did represent an increase in communication with the world. Spanish America had existed in semi-isolation. News of otherwhere came slowly and was disseminated largely by word of mouth among the few people who cared. Some of the new periodicals had a rationalistic orientation and emphasized utilitarian subjects, though often only by implication. Although this material was quite mild before the 1790s, the government viewed it with trepidation. The big change came in a flood in the 1790s and early nineteenth century, with many new and more daring newspapers. The difference between the *Gazeta de Goathemala* of 1729–1731 and the *Gazeta de Guatemala* of 1797–1816 was that between two worlds.

Historical Works and Science

An explosion of Spanish intellectual energy resulted from observation of vast new lands and flora and fauna, the excitement of finding great Indian states, and the challenge of conversion to Christianity, a part of which involved intricate problems of Indian linguistics and ethnology. Much of this scholarly work was done in the sixteenth century, and most of the students and writers were peninsular Spaniards. Many of the authors were churchmen, some were soldiers, a few civil officials, and there were learned Indians and mestizos who put down the history and culture of their forebears as they had it from their own relatives and neighbors.

Some men set down what they saw during the conquest. The five great dispatches (*Relaciones*) of Cortés to the king in 1519–1526 began achieving publication in Europe in 1522. Gonzalo Fernández de Oviedo (1478–1557) was the first official chronicler of the Indies, which he visited a number of times. He published in 1526 a short account (*Sumario*) of the historical and natural scene in America. His detailed and valuable *General and Natural History of the Indies* was published in 1535–1559. Bartolomé de las Casas' polemical *Brief Relation of the Destruction of the Indies* we have noted was published in 1552. His huge *History of the Indies* remained in manuscript until published in six volumes in Spain in 1875–1879. It contains much data on things he observed or had testimony on from eyewitnesses.

Bernal Díaz, who went to America with Pedrarias and then to Mexico with Cortés, and later settled in Guatemala, in the 1560s wrote his *True History of the Conquest of Mexico*. This is not only a prime source for the conquest and for the early relations between Europeans and Indians, but a fascinating personal account of high adventure. Pedro Cieza de León went to the Indies from Spain in 1532 and remained until 1550, participating in the conquests of most of western South America and becoming an *encomendero*. The first part of his *Crónica del Perú* was published in Spain in 1553. He kept detailed records of his observations of the landscape, the Indians and their customs and traditions, and of the Spanish conquest. José de Acosta, a Jesuit, saw many parts of the Indies in the later sixteenth century, and in 1590 published in Spain his *Natural and Moral History of the Indies*, a valuable source on many aspects of Indian and European life and the interrelations of the cultures. Friar Bernardino de Sahagún (died 1590) lived many years in Mexico, studied Indian language and customs, and wrote extensively about Indian life. His *General History of Matters Concerning New Spain* was not published until the nineteenth century. It is a major source to modern anthropologists, ethnologists, archaeologists, and historians. Work of comparable quality was done by churchmen among the Maya of Yucatán. The dictionaries, grammars, and other works produced by these dedicated and learned churchmen constitute a remarkable body of information about long dead or still changing cultures.

The most famous of the early mestizo writers was Garcilaso de la Vega, known as El Inca, son of a conqueror of Peru and a noble Indian woman. The son learned much from his Indian relatives, the remnant of the old upper class used by the Spaniards as aids in governing and as concubines. In 1560 at the age of twenty he went to Spain and never returned to America. In Europe he composed his *Royal Commentaries of the Incas* (published 1609–1617), basing it not only on his recollections, but on chronicles of the conquest of the sort we have mentioned. It is a major source on the preconquest Inca culture and on the clash between it and Spanish culture. There were many other mestizo authors, working in both Spanish and the native tongues, sometimes writing the latter in the Roman alphabet according to systems worked out by the scholar-friars.

In later years, production of works on history and Indian culture declined, although some notable treatises were written. Some of the later authors were creole, but that group never did scholarly work in proportion to its numbers. The great legal scholars also were Spaniards. Not much scientific work was done in the seventeenth or most of the eighteenth century. To be sure, Spain was not noted for scientific study, either. The talent of Carlos de Sigüenza y Góngora (died 1700), a creole of Mexico, stands out the more because of the paucity of work in the field. In the eighteenth century, with the growth of interest in science, the Spanish government to a modest extent encouraged study and application in the field. It sent some scientific expeditions to America and took a few measures to try to improve technical training and applications. A very few creoles devoted enough time to science and such related technical subjects as medicine to achieve some eminence late in the eighteenth century. Francisco José Caldas of New Granada and José Hipólito Unanue of Peru are examples. Theirs was the last generation of the colonial era.[9]

Architecture, Art, Music

The greatest artistic achievement of the colonial period was in architecture. Spain had good architects and construction engineers, a tradition of craftsmanship in the building trades, and fine techniques in the fashioning of materials and decorations. Many Indians and *castas* were

trained in those functions. Although they occasionally brought to their work some touches of preconquest ornament, colonial architecture was European. Sometimes plans were sent from Europe, sometimes important designers went to the Indies, sometimes men on the scene did the layout, with much use of illustrations of famous structures in the Old World.

A notable aspect of architectural achievement resulted from the fact that many of the cities of Spanish America were given an appearance quite different from those of Spain, with a gridiron pattern of straight streets, and central and subordinate squares or plazas, unlike the seeming disorder that grew out of medieval patterns in the Old World. The gridiron plan was followed in America even before the crown directed it, apparently resulting from practical considerations of traffic flow, defense, and allocation of lots, plus possibly some concept of ideal urban arrangements better than, or at least different from, those of Spain. Most cities founded after the 1530s, excepting ports and mining camps, followed the model. Thus Philip II merely formalized an existing situation in his Discovery and Settlement Ordinances of 1573, which included articles on the forms of cities in America. Most of the new American towns came to display regular facades whose symmetry made the most of the sometimes monumental buildings on great plazas. The straight avenues connecting squares gave pleasing vistas. The town plan apparently stimulated architects and builders, who found it especially suited to the Italian humanist conception of urbanism in the Renaissance that was based on the classical work of Vitruvius. Before Mexico City was a century old, visitors praised its esthetic qualities. Walls surrounded only those few American towns that were exposed to attack.

Ecclesiastical structures were the most striking. Many thousands were built, an amazing number being of imposing size and artistic merit, some of the smaller jewels of their type, and many of the more routine in some measure praiseworthy in style and decoration. Churchmen as

---

[9] See Chapter 17 for the currents of interest such men represented.

soon as possible built noble temples of stone to replace the crude wood and thatch structures of the early years. The cathedral at Santo Domingo in Española was an imposing building by the mid-sixteenth century. Some of the early stone and stucco temples, such as the cathedral at Cuernavaca (begun in 1529 and built quickly), were given a simple fortresslike form, partly for defense in the still unpacified country. They had no aisles inside and little decoration, but were of such imposing height as to show the glory of God and the power of His church.

Some later churches were more elaborate, and much larger, perhaps with one or two towers, domes, and two or three entrances with carved stone facades set with statuary. In the most elaborate, the interior would have three aisles, marked by stately columns that soared to vaulted ceilings; they might have elaborate side chapels, in the nave high windows with stained glass, and marvelously carved wooden choir stalls, retables, and pulpits. The planning of such a great church was an intricate task, to be adjusted to many local factors, including the nature of the subsoil, the prevalence of earthquakes, and the qualities of the available stone. The plans of some were much altered over the many years they were in construction, and they became a blend, often very pleasing, of Renaissance and later styles. The first cathedral at Mexico City was begun in 1525 and used until the early seventeenth century, but long before then a new and much larger one was in construction. The immense labors began in the 1550s and continued until the new cathedral was put in use, unfinished, in 1626. The towers and dome were not completed until the very end of the colonial period.

There were large and sumptuous churches attached to monasteries in the countryside, serving not only the friars but the Indians of the villages. Many of great size now lie half-ruined in the fields, enclosing charming patios, where friars once inhabited cells, and dining halls and libraries now visited only by birds and tourists. Some of the archiepiscopal palaces, universities, and *colegios* of the church were handsome. Small

chapels for the use of ecclesiastics offered exquisite proportions, rich decoration in gold leaf and fine colored and glazed tiles, scrolls and intricate designs in plaster, even painted angels with all the spiritual appearance of pagan cupids. Quito, a moderate-sized town in the colonial period, remains today a treasure house of twenty beautiful churches, monasteries, and convents, mostly in the Baroque style. Many a smaller Spanish American town today boasts a church building far beyond its needs, lifting large colored domes toward the sun.

Many buildings of the civil government were imposing and pleasing in appearance. In the better ones the proportions were superb, the decoration plain and effective, usually with interior courtyards with fountains. Some buildings had covered walkways (*portales*) at ground level on the street side; and a plaza with such *portales* on two or three sides, and a great church on the other, was an imposing and pleasant sight—as some of them remain today. The palaces of viceroys and captains-general were in this style, and the seats of *cabildos*, the chambers of *audiencias*, and some other public buildings. Although the exteriors of the residences of the well-to-do were often plain, in other cases they rose somewhat above the limitations of the style, with large windows and heavy wooden shutters, small balconies with carved wooden or wrought-iron bars, and huge, carved wood and strap-hinged doors.

Some very fine sculptors and painters, especially of religious themes, arose in Spanish America, many of them Indians or mestizos. Especially fine work was done in Quito, where as early as 1552 Flemish friars were teaching arts and crafts. Wood carving also was practiced with great success, even at times with genius. Fine work was accomplished in jewelry making, silver plate, church ornaments, and all the luxury articles demanded by the rich, from cosmetic boxes and flasks to painted sedan chairs and coaches.

Drama we have mentioned in connection with recreation, but no notable work was composed in Spanish America. Sacred and profane music was much played, but great composers did not arise. Much poetry was composed but little of merit. Naturally the cultivated society of the larger towns of the seventeenth and eighteenth centuries would produce some persons with poetic leanings, but the environment was not kindly to literary ambition. It is more the wonder, then, that in Mexico appeared a lyric poet of real genius and finish, a creole woman who entered a convent and is known to us as Sor Juana Inés de la Cruz. In her convent she studied and wrote for years, having the use of a large library and the conversation of important figures of church, state, and private society. Her impressive intelligence, energy, and imagination led her into many fields. Her poems, some on the subject of sacred love, but the more notable flaming and unsurpassable poesy on profane love, went into six editions before 1700. Alas, she became involved in theological dispute, her superiors listened to complaints about her lack of attention to her vocation, and under pressure of the system and her own conscience she gave up her literary life, smothered her genius, and soon died during an epidemic.

13

Provincial and Regional Differentiation

Why is there an Argentina today? Why Chile, Mexico, and Colombia? Why not simply one Spanish American nation? The reason is that regional differentiation existed from the conquest and developed for three centuries. It was more marked than in English-speaking America, in an immensely larger territory. There were great differences in natural resources and in Indians suitable for labor. There were also locational advantages (or disadvantages) for defense or trade. Those three types of difference from place to place caused variation in many of the institutions emphasized in earlier chapters: class lines and socioracial distinctions; race mixture; forced and dependent labor; the great estate; the complex, but adjustable, governmental system; such economic institutions and practices as monopoly, high transport costs, contraband trade, local production and sale of handicrafts, mixtures of Indian and Spanish crops and agricultural methods, growth of herds of European animals, and the immense role of the church.

The variety of resources was sufficient to lead major provinces, sometimes called *reynos* (realms), to achieve considerable definition, much of it centering on the capitals, which were nodes for commercial and financial functions and magnets for people interested in intellectual or ecclesiastical training, edification, or prefer-

ment. The local awareness of differences, especially by creoles, became more pronounced with time. This awareness grew as a result of growth of attachment to a locality and its interests; economic changes of the eighteenth century that encouraged both localism and economic ambition generally; intellectual developments that led to a moderate increase in thought about local problems; and changes in the imperial system that stimulated local ambition. In this respect provincial differentiation was more than regionalism, becoming an incipient nationalism, a sentiment favorable to consideration of new political arrangements when events in Europe made such consideration necessary.[1] Although all ten of the Spanish American areas that were to become independent nations by the 1820s showed definition in the colonial era, each was large and varied enough to show also some subregionalism. Subregionalism was a factor in further fragmentation in the 1830s to a total of sixteen nations.[2]

a. The Antilles

A few Spaniards managed to survive in the islands in the cattle business and in small-scale

---

[1] See Chapter 17.
[2] No section is provided for the Floridas and Louisiana, as these areas were chiefly of interest for imperial foreign relations and defense.

agriculture and industry, especially sugar. Española, Jamaica, and Puerto Rico were never well developed. The small city of Santo Domingo, seat of an *audiencia* from 1511, suffered badly from raids by pirates and foreign navies in the seventeenth century. About 1680 it reportedly had only 2,977 inhabitants, including 1,300 slaves, many of the latter actually on nearby haciendas. The western third of the island was lost to France by treaty in 1697, and the French development of a profitable black-slave sugar culture contrasted with the poor Spanish colony. The population of the Spanish province of Santo Domingo in 1775 was only 152,640, including 30,000 slaves.

Jamaica was unprosperous when lost to the British in 1655. Britain proceeded to make Jamaica a rich sugar colony worked by black slaves. Puerto Rico never was prosperous. It received a small boost in the eighteenth century when Spain strengthened the fortifications at San Juan. The island had a population of only about 44,000 in 1765; after that it grew more rapidly, to over 100,000 by 1800. Its chief exports were sugar and hides.

Cuba's development was more notable, but it came late. After the mid-sixteenth century, Havana was a stopping point for the fleets returning to Europe, and late in the century Spain began to fortify it heavily. The city had only 60 *vecinos* in 1580 and 1,200 by 1630. The entire island— nearly eight hundred miles long and marvelously fertile—had only 171,620 people in 1774, after nearly three centuries of Spanish occupation. A great boom in the economy had begun in the 1760s, however, and by 1817 the population was 552,033.

Drastic changes resulted from the British capture of Havana in 1762.[3] Spain was relieved to get the island back in 1763 and made changes that transformed the sugar industry.[4] Sugar exports increased steadily after 1763 and no other

Cuban export approached its value. Tobacco exports seemed promising from the 1760s to the 1780s, but declined thereafter due to United States competition. Coffee exports were small before the end of the eighteenth century, when they gained somewhat from the ruin of coffee output in Haiti by the slave revolt and the migration to Cuba from there of experienced cultivators. No other crops were important exports, and subsistence agriculture was poorly organized, so that much food was imported, a usual concomitant of slave specialization on tropical plantations, because owners preferred to concentrate their slave hands on cash-crop production.

Concentration of resources also was evident in the growth of Havana, where the most important of the newly rich sugar *hacendados* lived and where government, finance, and commerce had their principal seat. The town reached some 48,000 by 1790, after several decades of steady growth, and 90,000 by 1817. This phenomenon of the "primate city," holding a high proportion of the important civil and ecclesiastical officials, the big merchants and owners of rural estates, and the major social and cultural institutions of the province, was a common factor in colonial Spanish America, and was to continue in the independent republics in the nineteenth century.

The importance of Cuba, and especially of Havana, was recognized in 1764 by making it a captaincy-general and attaching to it the newly acquired Louisiana country. In the same year the intendancy system was applied first in America to Cuba. Cuba's importance was further increased by the transfer in 1797 of the *audiencia* from Santo Domingo to Cuba's Puerto Príncipe. So increased political importance and great economic growth came with a rush to Cuba late in the colonial era. The sugar export business and a large black slave force differentiated it from most of Spanish America.

b. New Spain

New Spain was an empire in itself, as large as western and central Europe and comprising

---

[3] See Chapter 7, Section e.
[4] See Chapter 9 on slaves in Cuba, and Chapter 10 on the sugar industry.

many natural regions. The bulk of the population lived in the mountain valleys of central Mexico, from Oaxaca to Jalisco, generally at elevations of from 5,000 to 8,000 feet, with a pleasant climate, precisely where most of the Indians had lived before the conquest. There was a smaller concentration in the lowlands of Yucatán. Few people lived in the narrow coastal plains. A few Spaniards moved into more arid valleys north of central Mexico to mine silver and raise cattle. Very few went far beyond that to New Mexico, Texas, and upper California, and they were largely induced by government programs to meet threats of French, British, Russian, and United States competition. That strategic activity in the far north pushed the Spanish position beyond the capability of Mexico City or Madrid to control the occupied territory.

The central part of New Spain had 15 to 25 million Indians in 1519. In the mid-seventeenth century its population was about 1 million Indians, 125,000 Spaniards (peninsular and creole), and some 160,000 *castas*, mostly mestizos. In 1800 New Spain's population was 5.5 million: 2.5 million Indians, 1 million Spaniards (possibly 90 percent creole, many of them with some Indian ancestors), and two million *castas*. By then Mexico City had some 140,000 inhabitants, more than any city in the United States or any in Britain except London. New Spain had far and away the largest population of the realms of Spanish America.

Over this great realm Spain established authority and patterns that endured for three centuries. The viceroy had theoretical responsibility for the West Indies, the Floridas, and finally Louisiana, but that ordinarily did not extend in fact beyond defense and financial subsidy. After the 1560s, Central America was under a captaincy-general seated in Guatemala, and the viceroy of New Spain had no real power in that area either. The two huge *audiencias* of Mexico and Nueva Galicia (seated most of the time at Guadalajara) divided jurisdiction in New Spain. This division recognized that the realm was too large for detailed government from a single center, not only

because of the great distances but because there were regional differences in resources and needs. Despite this regionalism, the viceroyalty achieved enough definition and tradition so that it became one unified nation in 1821, at that time one of the largest countries in the world. In the nineteenth century, however, a continuing regionalism impeded full national integration.

New Spain's late colonial economic growth was spotty, affecting few people notably. The spectacular rise in silver output required big investment and contributed only modestly to development of the rest of the economy. Mexican agriculture had a miserable per capita value. Farm exports increased in the late colonial era, but silver remained about 75 to 80 percent of exports by value. Most of the rest was sugar and cochineal, both plagued by production and marketing problems.

A late surge of agricultural exports briefly quintupled their values. Unfortunately, the growth was due to temporarily favorable conditions. Furthermore, some 80 percent of the increase consisted of legal overseas exchange with Spain, and the rest was with other Spanish realms. Neither market was a sound basis for permanent growth of Mexican exports. The small exports of Mexican wheat toward the end of the colonial era could not stand up to world competition. Mexican maize was not exported. Cotton was little exploited, and United States producers offered unbeatable competition before Mexico became independent. In addition, the grazing industry was badly organized and inefficient, and its exports from Mexico were always small. The fabrication industries were small-scale. Textile making did not meet local demand and had difficulty competing with imports even of cheap stuffs, much less contesting markets abroad. No other industrial line offered promise of great wealth, lacking large domestic markets or much opportunity to ship abroad.

These realities were not so clear to creoles in New Spain. They were conscious of living in the largest, most populous, and richest Spanish realm in America. The size and resources of New Spain created regional pride and optimism, mostly latent rather than active. The Independence period after 1810 would show the existence of *Mexicanidad*—Mexican national sentiment. Long before 1810 Mexico had become differentiated from the other *reynos*.

c. Central America

Central America, a mountainous land with difficult communications, little precious metal, and in most areas a shortage of reliable Indian labor, held little attraction for Spaniards. In 1535 an *audiencia* was created at Panama for most of Central America. It was replaced in 1542 with the *Audiencia de los Confines*, seated at Gracias a Dios in present-day Honduras. Then the captaincy-general of Guatemala was created and moved in 1570 to Santiago de los Caballeros de Guatemala, functioning until Independence as a major realm (*reyno*) of America. It extended from Costa Rica through Chiapas (now in Mexico), with de facto exceptions around Belize and in Mosquitia, where Britain had claims.

Panama was a key to the defense of much of Spanish America and to the control of trade and bullion shipments between Peru and Europe. It again received its own *audiencia* in 1567, dependent on that of Lima, a position it retained for many years. Until 1592 the main Caribbean port was the village of Nombre de Dios, moribund except during the annual fair; thereafter, Portobelo replaced it.[5] Although the isthmian crossing was short and rose to less than three hundred feet above sea level, it was costly. Much cargo went from the Caribbean port a few miles by sea to the Chagres River, upriver by barge fifty miles to Cruces, where there were warehouses and mule pens, then by mule fifteen miles to the Pacific. The isthmus was hot, unhealthful, and lightly populated. Only its importance as a transit area kept a few Spaniards there. The permanent population of the unimpressive Pacific town of Panama in the mid-sixteenth century

was about 500 Spanish citizens (*vecinos*), which with families meant about 2,000 whites, plus several thousand blacks and mulattoes, slave and free. The population did not change much for two centuries thereafter. The great days of bullion and trade there were over long before the end of the colonial period, as Spain could not enforce the channeled trade ideal. The last *flota* went to Portobelo in 1741. The *audiencia* at Panama was abolished in 1751, and the area became a poorly regarded appendage of Bogotá.

Costa Rica was far from being the "rich coast" of its name. The few Spaniards lived in the highlands, and scarcely played a role in the life of the captaincy-general. Their tenuous connection with the sea and the long, rough land routes to Panama, Nicaragua, and Guatemala made for deep isolation. The Indians were intractable. The few Spaniards complained that they had to labor themselves. By 1800 Costa Rica had only some 65,000 population in twenty-one towns—nine of Spaniards and twelve of Indians.

Nicaragua was moderately better developed. It had sixteenth- and seventeenth-century exports of sugar, cattle, mules, cacao, tobacco, ship's stores. It built ships and had a useful port at Realejo. Both Indians and blacks labored in these enterprises. Some of its economy was destroyed in the eighteenth century by competition from other areas. Realejo was a target for corsairs, as was León, not many miles inland. Corsairs crossed the isthmus in boats over the big Lake of Nicaragua and down the San Juan River to the Caribbean. At the end of the eighteenth century the province held fewer than 70,000 persons, excluding the Indians and zambos on the Caribbean shore in the British-protected territory of the Mosquito King.

The territory of present-day Honduras usually had its capital at Comayagua, and much of the territory went by that name. It had only about 90,000 people at the end of the colonial period. A little silver was found, leaving rumors of riches. Then Honduras settled down to subsistence agriculture and some commercial grazing operations.

The province of Chiapa, today the southern-

---

[5] See Chapter 11 on the Portobelo fair.

most Mexican state of Chiapas, had about 100,-000 inhabitants, mostly Indians, at the end of the colonial era. It was not a critical factor in the history of the captaincy-general.

The small province of San Salvador was more densely populated. It had considerable exports of cacao in the sixteenth and seventeenth centuries and indigo in the eighteenth. This tended to give the area some definition, especially as the population grew rather substantially in the eighteenth and early nineteenth centuries. In 1807 the intendancy of San Salvador had a population of 165,278, assertedly made up of less than 3 percent whites, 43 percent Indians, and 54 percent mestizos. The town of San Salvador in 1810 had 616 Spaniards (peninsular and creole), 584 Indians, and 10,680 *pardos* (here meaning mestizos and mulattoes).[6]

The territory of Guatemala (about equal to New York State) was comparable in area to Nicaragua or Honduras, but it had more sedentary Indian labor. It also benefited from the presence of the top ecclesiastical and civil officials of the *reyno*, plus the chief intellectual institutions, including a university, the conventual houses, and the major merchants, with their access to the monopolistic system functioning through Sevilla and Cádiz. It had about 40 percent of the 1.2 million inhabitants of the captaincy-general at Independence in 1821. The town of Guatemala was sadly damaged by an earthquake in 1773 and abandoned for a new site, which had perhaps 25,000 inhabitants by 1800, many more than any other in the *reyno*.

By the eighteenth century Central America's cacao, shipbuilding and ship's stores, mules, hides, and cochineal enterprises had been destroyed or damaged by competition or other changed conditions. Indigo became the chief export, grown mostly in San Salvador and Guatemala, and hence there arose there larger markets for Nicaraguan and Honduran meat and hides. The indigo was sent through Guatemala City to

the Atlantic and Europe. Some of the hides also were exported.

The bigger cattlemen and indigo planters dominated the smaller, buying up their commodities and selling them goods obtained in Guatemala City. The big provincial cattlemen and indigo producers, however, in their turn were at the mercy of the major merchants at Guatemala City, who controlled credit and the markets abroad through the Sevilla/Cádiz monopoly, with which they were connected. Indigo production rose to a peak in the later 1780s and early 1790s, only to fall victim to wartime interruption of shipping and remain depressed until Independence. Only minor compensation could be found in tobacco and other crops. The *reyno* was a poor backwater. Its status did not impede the growth of regional sentiment; indeed, poverty possibly aggravated resentments among the provinces.

d. Peru

Peru became a viceroyalty in 1544 with its seat at Lima and jurisdiction in all Spanish South America except the extreme north of the continent, which was left under Santo Domingo. The usefulness of decentralization of authority was recognized by the creation of new *audiencias* (the Lima *audiencia* dated from 1542): Santa Fe de Bogotá, 1549; Charcas, or Upper Peru, 1559 (at La Plata, also called Chuquisaca, and after Independence Sucre); Quito, 1563; Santiago in Chile, 1609. More drastic division came with creation of two viceroyalties in the eighteenth century. New Granada (1717–1723, re-established 1739) included territory of the present republics of Venezuela, Panama, Colombia, and Ecuador. The Viceroyalty of La Plata (1776), with its seat at Buenos Aires, included Cuyo, Tucumán, Buenos Aires, Charcas (now Bolivia), Paraguay, and the Spanish claims in what is now Uruguay. The first three comprised much of the territory of the later Argentina. The transfer of Charcas especially pruned the public revenues available to Lima. Lima's authority was diluted further in 1777 when Chile was raised from a presidency to a captaincy-general, and in

---

[6] In some parts of Spanish America *pardo* meant only mulatto or at least a person of considerable black heritage.

1787 when an *audiencia* was established at Cuzco. By the late eighteenth century the Viceroyalty of Peru was but a shade of the original realm.

What are now Peru and Bolivia extended about 1,200 miles from the southern border of Quito to the northern parts of Chile and Tucumán. From east to west the extent varied from 250 to 400 miles from the Pacific to the eastern slopes of the Andes. The viceroyalty did not go into the rain forest beyond, which the Incas also had found impenetrable. The Peruvian coast was desert, scarcely habitable except in a few river valleys, where high-yield agriculture with irrigation had been practiced by Indian cultures and was continued by Spaniards with new commercial crops. The mountain valleys and plateaus where most of the Indians continued to live were higher than those of New Spain, so that possible crops were more limited.

Inca Peru's population of about 5 million fell quickly,[7] and other groups grew slowly. In 1800 Peru had a population of about 1 million, including 76,000 Spaniards (peninsular and creole), 244,000 mestizos, 40,000 black slaves, 40,000 free blacks and mulattoes, and 600,000 Indians. Thus at the end of the colonial era Peru had larger percentages of Indians and blacks, and smaller percentages of whites and mestizos, than New Spain. These figures lend support to the belief that Europeanization proceeded more rapidly in New Spain than in Peru. Lima had a population of possibly 25,000 in 1600 and over 50,000 in the 1790s, according to a contemporary account, including 17,000 Spaniards (peninsular and creole) and nearly 10,000 slaves. In 1810 it had 87,000. Potosí had about 120,000 inhabitants in the early seventeenth century, was down to 30,000 a century later, and was only a small town at the end of the colonial period.

Government worked about as in New Spain, although the *corregidores* of Indians in Peru may have been the worst in the Indies, a supposition founded in part on the famous report of Antonio de Ulloa and Jorge Juan, Spanish naval officers

who traveled in America in the 1730s. The report was so critical of conditions in Peru that the government in Spain hid it for years. The officers found a terrible tyranny of *corregidores* over Indians, with regard to *repartimiento* (*mita*) of labor and of goods, the tribute, and other matters. They also criticized other aspects of American life. When the report was first published, in England in the 1820s, it helped fix international opinion of the Spanish colonial system.

The chief export of Peru was silver. There was some long-distance shipment of such items as wine, olives, wheat, sugar, tobacco, and cotton, but seldom in large quantity. What is now Peru did not even supply the bulk of the needs of Upper Peru for American products; most of those came to the mining areas from the south from Tucumán and Cuyo in what is now Argentina. The legal system of European trade via Panama to Lima, to Upper Peru, to Tucumán, and east toward the Atlantic began to break down early. Lima in the seventeenth century progressively lost its hold on supply in Upper Peru and beyond. Goods flowed through Portuguese Colônia and Spanish Buenos Aires and Montevideo (in the eighteenth century) to the interior, some of them eventually to Upper Peru and even beyond to Cuzco and Lima. Silver flowed illegally in the other direction. Much of the contraband traffic in the seventeenth century was handled by Portuguese merchants, coming to Lima by way of Brazil, as has been noted. The later extension of licenses to *registros* to go round Cape Horn into the Pacific, and the extinction of the Sevilla/Cádiz monopoly, stimulated a modest increase in Peruvian maritime trade. That did little to alleviate general poverty in the heavily Indian province. The sizable elite at Lima was conscious of a greater Peruvian past, at least one basis for regional sentiment.

e. Quito

Quito (approximately present-day Ecuador) originally was attached to the government at Lima. It received its own *audiencia* in 1563, with jurisdiction including Popayán in the southern

---

[7] See Chapter 8.

mountains of present-day Colombia. When the Viceroyalty of New Granada was created in the first half of the eighteenth century, Quito was attached to Bogotá, as a presidency headed by the president of its own *audiencia* with considerable autonomy from Bogotá. Quito consisted of a Pacific coastal belt—tropical rain forest in the north, drier in the south; the mountains, where the bulk of the Indian population lived; and the Oriente or eastern slopes of the Andes and the lowlands of the Amazon basin, of little interest to Spain and only lightly held by the Jesuit mission province of Mainas.[8] The presidency (excluding Popayán) had at the end of the colonial era a population of about 800,000, most of them Indians and mestizos in the mountains. The coastal areas were lightly populated, with a considerable black element. The seat of government was San Francisco del Quito, in the mountains above 9,000 feet, nestling at the foot of the great volcano Pichincha. It had about 3,000 Spaniards early in the seventeenth century and a larger number of Indians and mestizos. It was surrounded by a large Indian village population. Most of the Indians lived at elevations of 7,000 to 10,000 feet. Guayaquil, a steamy and unhealthful little tropical town, lay in the low coastal plains, some distance up the broad Guayas River. It was the chief port of a poor and unpromising province. The elite in that province of Quito, however, as events were to prove, learned to think of it as their own.

f. New Granada

By 1549, when Santa Fe de Bogotá was given an *audiencia*, there were a number of small, scattered Spanish settlements in New Granada. It became a captaincy-general in 1569, and in the early eighteenth century a viceroyalty, with at least nominal jurisdiction over Venezuela, Panama, and Quito. Some parts of the Caribbean coastal area, however, were subject at times to Santo Domingo, and it has been noted that

---

[8] See Chapter 12, Section c, on Mainas.

Panama had its own *audiencia* till the mid-eighteenth century.

Some patches of the Caribbean lowlands were occupied by Spaniards, especially around Cartagena and Santa Marta. There were few Spaniards in the Pacific lowlands, even in the gold regions of Chocó, largely worked by slave and free blacks. The bulk of the population of New Granada proper (approximately Colombia of today) resided in the mountains, which extended north and south in three great ranges, enfolding isolated pockets of fertile and sun-blessed land. Spaniards, except for missionary friars, scarcely penetrated into the Amazon lowlands to the east. The Chibcha Indians of the Cundinamarca area around Bogotá were sedentary and pacific, providing labor and concubines. Most other Indians in New Granada were as intractable as those in southern Chile or northern Mexico.

The population of New Granada (excluding Venezuela, Panama, and Quito without Popayán) was about 1.5 million at the end of the colonial era, most of it in the mountains, although the province of Cartagena on the Caribbean had some 200,000. Whites were some 22 percent of the total, Indians about the same, blacks possibly 5 percent, and the other half of the population was of mixed racial heritage. The central and southern highlands were conspicuously white, Indian, and mestizo, while black heritage was especially strong in the western highlands and along the coasts. Bogotá had some 2,000 whites in 1600, and more Indians and mestizos. It grew modestly in its mountain (8,700 feet) isolation for the next two centuries, reaching some 20,000 in 1800. Cartagena, the great fortress port and commercial center, early in the seventeenth century had about 1,500 whites, and more blacks, mulattoes and mestizos. In 1777 a census gave its population as more than 13,000. Santa Marta on the Caribbean decayed quite early as Cartagena grew.

Transportation in New Granada was so dreadful as to be an insuperable barrier to many sorts of economic growth, as the nineteenth century would further demonstrate. The main route to

Bogotá was from the Caribbean via the Magdalena River, a hot, uncomfortable boat ride in its lower reaches, then interrupted by portages, and finally ended by mule back in the mountains, a slow total of 650 miles. Poor transport was more damaging to commodity trade than to mining. Gold output was of some consequence in the sixteenth and seventeenth centuries, but half of the colonial total was produced in the eighteenth. Although gold values were considerable, they were much less than those of the silver of New Spain or Peru and had less effect on the local economy.

There was tropical agriculture along the Caribbean, including sugar and indigo. During the seventeenth century the area suffered heavily from raiding by corsairs and foreign navies. It carried on contraband trade with the islands, especially British Jamaica. Isolated Popayán and Pasto, far to the south in the mountains, developed their own patterns of farming and stock raising. They bred mules and drove them as far south as Peru. But creoles in New Granada were under no illusion that they were prosperous, and their notable jealousies, resentments, and general parochialism were based in part on economic frustration. New Granada was an even better example of sectionalism or regionalism in the late colonial era than New Spain or Río de la Plata, as became painfully evident during and after the Independence period.

g. Venezuela

Venezuelan settlement was slow. The coastal areas offered little but pearling and salt. Cumaná and Coro, founded there in the 1520s, remained small. The attractive valleys of the coastal range were not settled until the 1550s and 1560s, when Valencia, Barquisimeto, and Caracas (at 3,000 feet, settled in 1567) were founded. Although the Indians proved difficult to subdue, their labor was used on small farms. In the southern plains (*llanos*) huge wild cattle herds built up, tended by mestizo cowboys (*llaneros*). The basin of the Orinoco to the south and the Gui-

ana Highlands to the east were explored but not settled. To the west in the high mountains marching toward New Granada small settlements were made. The heart of Venezuela in the northern coastal range faced toward the Caribbean rather than toward the difficult country surrounding it on other sides.

Through the seventeenth century Venezuela remained isolated and poor. It was under the *audiencia* of Santo Domingo well into the eighteenth century for virtually all but military purposes. In 1742 it was relieved of all dependence on the viceroy at Bogotá. It became a captaincy-general in 1777, and received its own *audiencia* (at Caracas) in 1786. The population at the end of the colonial period amounted to some 750,000, possibly half of mixed racial stock, 26 percent white (nearly all creole), 15 percent Indian, 8 percent black (some 60,000 slaves). The towns were small, except for Caracas, which had 40,000 inhabitants in 1800, with most of its growth having occurred in the eighteenth century.

Economic growth was slow until well into the eighteenth century. Venezuelan collaboration with contrabandists disturbed Spain. This, and the wish to develop the empire, led the Bourbons in 1728 to charter in Spain the Royal Guipuzcoan Company of Caracas to try monopolistic private exploitation, especially of cacao. The company found that the Venezuelan elite had to be bludgeoned into accepting the monopoly. The energetic Basques did so, while investing handsomely in the area. They cut down on Dutch influence, but could not stop all contraband. In a few years the company and the crown were making excellent profits, but the older residents were disgruntled. They had to sell their cacao to the company, which set prices low, and buy expensive imported goods from the same source. The company also insisted on pushing its own people into the public offices of Venezuela. Squabbles were followed by a serious uprising in 1749, headed by a well-to-do creole, Francisco de León. He received support from other creoles, including the *cabildo* of Caracas. With arms in their hands, they squeezed concessions from the government, which soon recanted and punished the rebels. The company was extinguished in the 1780s because the Bourbon reforms that to some extent freed economic life made its operations obsolete.[9]

Venezuela's cacao exports grew for a time in the eighteenth century. The province also enjoyed late colonial booms in cotton and indigo. Growth in the tobacco business proved to be temporary before the end of the colonial period. Only a small amount of sugar was exported. Coffee production and export began only at the very end of the colonial era. Mules and cattle products provided a modest export business. The creole elite exaggerated the opportunities for continued growth. That optimism was, nevertheless, a factor in the creole society into which Simón Bolívar was born late in the eighteenth century, and would play some role in his career as the Liberator.[10]

h. Chile

In Chile the Spaniards lived in the central valley, a series of narrow basins between the high Andes and the coastal range. The basins stretch in a narrow strip some 450 miles from the great desert of the north to the Bío-Bío River in the south, where the town of Concepción stood against the fierce Araucanians. The basins are only moderately high (Santiago's varies from 1,100 to 2,300 feet above sea level). They have a mild climate and excellent soil, renewed by silt washed down from the mountains.

Chile had an *audiencia* briefly in 1565–1573 at Concepción; then one permanently from 1609 at Santiago, including jurisdiction over the province of Cuyo, east of the Andes. The Cuyo territory was lost in 1776 to the Viceroyalty of La Plata. In 1778 Chile was raised from a presidency to a captaincy-general. In Cuyo, the towns of Mendoza and San Juan were founded from

---

[9] See Chapter 11, Section d, for more on cacao exports.
[10] See Chapter 11, Section d, on the growth and largely illusory nature of Venezuelan exports other than cacao in the colonial era; Chapter 11, Section e, on the Caracas Company.

Chile in 1561 and 1562. They were on a route from Chile to Tucumán and Peru that avoided the terrible desert in northern Chile and southern Peru. Mendoza was only about one hundred miles as the crow flies east of Santiago, via the 12,650-foot Uspallata Pass. San Juan was a hundred miles north of Mendoza. They were snow-fed oases in the southern and nearly rainless part of what is now Argentina's western Piedmont. Food crops and pasture were irrigated from streams that came out of the Andes. Cuyo was good country for vine culture and wine. From Chile via the Uspallata to Tucumán was more than 400 miles on the map, much more on the trail. From Tucumán to Lima was another 1,500. The route from Santiago to Buenos Aires via the Uspallata carried some contraband from Buenos Aires to Chile.

Chile was not attractive to Spaniards. The Indians were not only dangerous but difficult to turn to labor. The unending warfare with the Araucanians was a constant drain on resources. Small royal military forces were required during much of the colonial era, together with militia. Little precious metal was found. The population remained small, possibly no more than 100,000 (exclusive of uncontrolled Indians) as late as 1700. More rapid growth in the eighteenth century, to about 500,000 by 1800, presumably reflected economic improvement. *Mestizaje* proceeded about as thoroughly as anywhere in Spanish America, and racial distinctions became blurred, although class divisions remained strong. Santiago, founded in 1540, in 1657 had only 5,000 inhabitants, early in the eighteenth century possibly 12,000, and 40,000 in 1820.

The economy was largely agricultural and pastoral. Although it was one of the places where a form of encomienda lasted throughout the colonial era, much rural work was done by *inquilinos*, Indians and mestizos who were tied to the larger land holdings. Handicrafts, including textiles, were chiefly sold in the provincial market. Small amounts of food were packed to Upper Peru via the Uspallata, but the export traffic by sea to Lima was several times larger. The most important items in the latter exchange were Peruvian sugar and Chilean wheat. Chile also exported to Peru small quantities of hides, tanned leather, leather articles, tallow, dried fruits, olives, wine, forest products, meat, soap, copper articles, slaves that came from Buenos Aires for the Peruvian market, and gold. Combined exports and imports were worth only about 500,000 pesos a year at the beginning of the eighteenth century. The value increased to about 3 million pesos by 1800, and continued to climb intermittently during the wartime years that followed. Chile, as the smaller and poorer area, was dependent on Peru, and the merchants of the latter dominated the trade. Although the disparity in resources declined in the late colonial era, Chileans retained an exaggerated fear of the domination of Peru. Nevertheless, Chile's interests were recognized by permission for a *consulado*, created in 1795.

Some community of feeling was created among the Chilean elite by isolation, a compact settlement area, common poverty, jealousy of Peru, and military danger from the Araucanians and corsairs. The strength of that feeling was quickly demonstrated during the period of Independence.

i. Paraguay

Paraguay came under the distant *audiencia* of Charcas, but the governors at Asunción were much on their own. They had jurisdiction over Buenos Aires, after it was refounded in 1580 from Asunción, until in 1617 Buenos Aires and Tucumán received their own governors, equal with Asunción. Paraguay was a remote interior province, cut off from travel to the north and east by terrain, savage Indians, and the Portuguese. The original Spanish settlement in Paraguay, Asunción, made in 1537, was more than six hundred miles from the estuary on the map, and river navigation sometimes was difficult. It early traded south and west to Mendoza and over the Andes to Chile, and via Tucumán to the mountains of Upper Peru or Charcas. Paraguay also

traded south by the great river system to its Atlantic estuary and Buenos Aires, Colônia do Sacramento (from 1680), and Montevideo (from the 1720s). The area had little to trade but modest amounts of timber, tobacco, and mate, the invigorating local tea.

Paraguay was so poor that few Spaniards came, and the creole population was heavily Guaraní in physical heritage. The creoles naturally called themselves *españoles* and the crown settled the matter by asserting that the Paraguayan mestizos were Spaniards. This solved on a general basis what was done in individual cases all over the Spanish Indies. It did not, of course, eradicate class divisions. The total population subject to Asunción was never large. It was narrowed further by the grant to the Jesuits in 1607 of a large Indian mission area.[11] This grant was resented by the ruling elite at Asunción, who wanted to exploit the labor of the mission Indians, who numbered some 100,000 by the end of the seventeenth century. They also resented trade competition from the Jesuit Indian towns and the fact that it was aided by exemption from the sales tax and customs duties. After years of complaint about Jesuit "exploitation" of Indians, things came to a crisis in the early eighteenth century. The town council at Asunción represented the creole point of view, and the pro-Jesuit governor opposed their claims. The Asunción *encomenderos* persuaded the *audiencia* of Charcas to send a *visitador*, José Antequera, to look into the matter. Antequera sided with the *cabildo*, jailed the governor, and proceeded to act as governor himself in 1721–1726. When an Indian army came from the mission area, aided by pro-Jesuit Spaniards from Buenos Aires, Antequera led the local people into battle. The ensuing war went on intermittently for years. Antequera refused to obey orders from the viceroy at Lima to abandon his position. He was finally captured by armed forces sent from Buenos Aires and executed. Soon

---

[11] On the expulsion of the Jesuits in 1767, see Chapter 12, Section c; on defense and the Guaraní missions, see Chapter 7.

thereafter, the resentment and ambition of the Asunción elite was inflamed anew by Fernando Mompox, who with the elite declared self-government in Paraguay. This action was a *comunero* revolt on the model of that in Spain in the sixteenth century, not directed at Independence of the crown but at local control of affairs. It was, of course, as unacceptable to imperial authority as the sixteenth-century tumult in Spain. Finally, in 1735, the *comunero* revolt in Paraguay fell apart under a combination of military pressure and fears of threatened imperial reprisals. It had been largely a conflict over economic issues. Paraguay was one of the poorest of the provinces. What no one suspected was that it had developed a fiercely regional point of view.

j. Buenos Aires, Banda Oriental, and Río de la Plata

It has been seen that Tucumán and Cuyo were settled before Buenos Aires and were not under the latter's jurisdiction till 1776. What is now Argentina was thus first settled and governed from Chile, Charcas, and Paraguay. Unlike the Chilean settlement of Cuyo in the 1550s, the towns in the Tucumán area to the north were settled from Peru, except for Córdoba and Santa Fe to the east, founded from Paraguay. Each town was set up among small concentrations of Indians. Where the Indians were too intractable, there was no settlement—in the Gran Chaco to the north and the vast Pampas to the south. Spanish towns formed a great arc along the edge of the Andes, from Mendoza north to Tucumán just at the eastern edge of the mountains, then up into the ranges that continued into Upper Peru, where the towns of Jujuy and Salta sat in watered valleys. From Tucumán north Inca influence had been strong.

Just east of the mountains in the northern plain of what is now Argentina the first town was founded in 1553, Santiago del Estero. It was near the belligerent Indians of the Gran Chaco to the north, which impeded its development. The town of Tucumán was settled in 1565 after

two earlier failures; Salta in 1582; Rioja, 1591; Jujuy, 1593. Córdoba, far to the east of the mountains, was founded in 1573 from Paraguay. Córdoba's site was some wooded hills rising above the plain, occupied by Indians who provided the indispensable labor for a Spanish town. It became the largest and most important of all the northern settlements, prospering from its own production and from its position as a trade and communications center. Santa Fe, also founded in 1573 but from Asunción, was well to the east of Córdoba, in the good cattle country of the plains and on the route developed for traffic between Upper Peru and Europe and Africa. South of Córdoba and Santa Fe stretched the great Pampa, a sea of grassland, thinly sprinkled with warlike Indians. For the Spaniards it was a desert, and they avoided it, except to kill wild cattle, hunt salt, and chase Indians. The first Buenos Aires, on the edge of the Pampa and with its back to the sea, had existed only from 1537 until 1541, besieged by Indians. In 1541 the surviving settlers moved far upriver to Asunción.

The northern towns struggled for existence. The encomienda system was installed among the small Indian populations, and government efforts to eradicate encomienda were as unfruitful as in Chile and Paraguay. These poor Spanish settlements could not afford reformism. Warfare with unsubdued Indians was a severe drain. The few Spaniards produced numerous mestizo offspring, who became valuable workers and in a minority of cases acknowledged members of the Spanish family, hence creoles. *Mestizaje* by no means led to democratization. In fact, the elite became increasingly jealous of its position and insistent upon its status and prerogatives.

About 1600 the elite population ranged from a few hundred in Mendoza and a number of other towns to possibly 3,000 in Córdoba, with larger numbers of lower-class residents in the Spanish settlements. Outside the towns were village Indians, but no more than a few thousand for each Spanish town. In the mid-seventeenth century the entire area of present-day Argentina held possibly 250,000 uncontrolled Indians, a few thousand Indian laborers, and some 90,000 "others" (creoles, mestizos, blacks, mulattoes), nearly all in the northern towns. Those places gradually built trade with Upper Peru. They sent local wine, brandy, wheat, flour, corn, rice, sugar, dried fruit, rough textiles, leather articles, mules, tallow, and candles. They also, as time went on, passed along black slaves and manufactured goods coming from Europe and Africa. Córdoba was some four hundred miles northwest of Buenos Aires; Tucumán was five hundred miles farther, and Potosí another six hundred. No wonder luxury items brought from Europe for silver magnates were worth almost their weight in the metal! Much of the trade east of Tucumán went by huge oxcarts. Mules, which could not be bred at the great altitudes of Upper Peru, went by the thousand from Santa Fe and Córdoba, to be finally sold at the great fairs of Salta for use in Upper Peru.

Córdoba, part of Tucumán province, produced handicrafts, including textiles, food, cattle, and mules. Early in the seventeenth century it received a Jesuit university, the nearest to Paraguay and Buenos Aires. There may have been 15,000 encomienda Indians in the Córdoba area at that time. In 1618 it received a customs house to cut the contraband by then flowing from the Atlantic to Upper Peru. Cordobans were prosperous enough to have bought a number of black slaves. The town had a population of 5,000 in 1650 and possibly 8,000 a century later. Churches and religious orders multiplied, as did civil and ecclesiastical functionaries; buildings grew more elaborate; cobbled streets were laid. Still, it was a small town, much cut off from the world.

Buenos Aires was reestablished from Paraguay in 1580. It grew enough so that it was made a province in 1617, with its own governor, separate from Tucumán and Paraguay, but like them under the *audiencia* of far-off Charcas and the even more distant viceroy in Lima. The town itself had only about 3,000 inhabitants in 1650, reached 10,000 to 12,000 by 1750, 25,000 in 1780, and 40,000 to 50,000 in 1800. Buenos Aires was a Johnny-come-lately like Havana. The entire area

of present-day Argentina was still lightly populated at the end of the colonial era, with some 500,000 to 600,000. Well over half were creole and mestizo, the distinction having become increasingly blurred. Possibly 30 percent were Indian and 10 percent black and mulatto.

Cattle operators in the province of Buenos Aires made modest profits selling to the town market but met serious competition for hide and tallow exports from the Banda Oriental and Córdoba and Santa Fe. Merchants at Buenos Aires also had trouble competing for the attention of contrabandists. Officials often were allied with the Buenos Aires merchants' competitors. Transactions sometimes involved complex combinations of silver from Upper Peru, black slaves from Africa, European manufactures, hides from various places, and foodstuffs, wine, and rough manufactures from Tucumán and Cuyo. The vacillations in Spain's efforts to dry up contraband in the area have been noted.[12] Smuggling was aided by the existence of the Banda Oriental across the estuary from Buenos Aires. In that territory of present-day Uruguay great herds of wild cattle built up in the sixteenth and seventeenth centuries. Their attractiveness was limited because there was much the same to the west in what is now Argentina and northward in southern Brazil. Nevertheless, a few cowboy-adventurers came from both those places, fought off the belligerent Indians, and killed cattle and sold hides. It was unsettled territory when in 1680 the Portuguese founded Colônia do Sacramento there.[13]

The hide business in the province of Buenos Aires and the disputed Banda Oriental grew in the eighteenth century, but not remarkably until its closing decades. It was supplemented by growth in the salt- and pickled-meat business. The growth in the cattle industry was due not to Spanish enterprise but to increased demand in Europe and its colonies during the early decades

---

12 See Chapter 11, Section d, on illegal trade in the area.
13 See Chapter 7, Sections d and f, on Portuguese-Spanish rivalry in the area.

of the Industrial Revolution. By the 1770s those developments led to perception that cattle operations needed reorganization. Cattle had been treated as wild creatures, available to everyone. The municipalities did claim some control, but that amounted to little more than contracting for town supplies. For the hide trade, men went out into the unoccupied Pampa, killed cattle, shucked off the hide, and left the carcass. The unregulated slaughter became so great after mid-century that there were fears of serious depletion of the supply. Such indiscriminate killing, as well as the increased value of the industry, led enterprising men to wish to ensure their hold on profits. An essential move was to lay claim to ownership of herds, so that landownership came to have increasing value, and the accumulation of *estancias* (local equivalent of haciendas) accelerated. Another action by the landowners was to tie the previously nomadic gauchos to the *estancias* as cowboys and laborers. The gauchos were mostly mestizo, though some were partly black. They had lived on meat and *mate*, slaughtered a few cattle to sell the hides, fought Indians, and frequently engaged in banditry.

The new meat industry demanded larger-scale operations and heavier financing. The slaughter and treatment works were called *saladeros*. Some primitive ones were set up in Buenos Aires province and the Banda Oriental in the 1770s, and they grew more complex with time. A well-developed *saladero* late in the century was a group of sheds, corrals, butchering rooms with tables, heated cauldrons, warehouses, and sun-drying areas. It could handle cattle through all the processes of slaughter, cutting in strips, soaking in brine, drying in the sun, treating for pests, packing in salt layers in barrels, and shipping. It also made grease and tallow from fat and refuse of the bodies, used bones and scraps to feed the fires, exported the bone ash, made gelatin and oils from the hooves, and sold horns and horsehair. Although such elaborate operations scarcely were seen before the late colonial period, the earlier and simpler *saladeros* suggested that

the easygoing individualism and sloppy workmanship of the colonial period were about to end because a realistic vision of large profits made improvements necessary.

These developments played a role in the crown's attitude toward its territorial disputes with Portugal in the Plata area, which led to the treaties of 1750 and 1777.[14] The viceroyalty created at Buenos Aires in 1776 included Cuyo and Tucumán, plus the rest of present-day Argentina, Paraguay, Uruguay, and much of Bolivia. It was intended to help with the problems of contraband and territorial disagreement. Considerable military force was concentrated in the viceroyalty as the strategic importance of the area grew, to be available against not only the encroaching Portuguese and Brazilians but also the British invaders early in the nineteenth century.[15] In 1778–1782 the intendancy system was set up in the viceroyalty. In 1783 Buenos Aires was given its own *audiencia*, with jurisdiction in all the viceroyalty except Upper Peru, or Charcas.

At the very end of the colonial era the mines of Potosí were in decline, affecting their suppliers in Cuyo and Tucumán. The latter suffered from the effects of the imperial free trade system and wartime relaxation or disregard of regulations, which, together with increasing creole insistence on the right of completely free trade and viceregal permissiveness regarding contraband, meant that Brazilian and European, and even North American, commodities increasingly supplied Buenos Aires and Montevideo. Food and wine and manufactures from the interior provinces were being replaced by supplies from outside the legal system. The elite of Buenos Aires and Montevideo were naturally pleased. They had become as drastically different from New Spain and Peru economically in the late colonial period as had Cuba. But Buenos Aires would lead the way to Independence while Cuba became the "Ever Faithful Isle."

---

14 See Chapter 7, Section f.
15 See Chapter 18, Section c.

PART FOUR

Colonial Brazil

Colonial Brazil and Spanish America were similar with regard to the class system, oligarchic government, the influence of Roman Catholicism, slavery, popular attitudes toward Indians, metropolitan mercantilist aims but actual dependence on foreign goods and capital, the great estate, and the lack of incentive for good performance by slave or free workers and a consequent generally poor productivity. The differences, however, also need to be stressed. Brazil's Indians were far fewer than those of Spanish America, and all had relatively primitive cultures. Indian labor thus was less useful than in Spanish America, although the Portuguese hungered equally for it. Brazilians found scarcely any precious metal until the 1690s, although they searched tirelessly. The sugar export business in Brazil became important in the later sixteenth century and exercised a more profound influence thereafter than in Spanish America.

The principal centers of population were somewhat less dispersed than in Spanish America, both because the Portuguese area was smaller and because there seemed to be little use for much of Brazil. In European terms, of course, the territory was immense and the population widely dispersed. City life was less conspicuous in Brazil than in Spanish America, and intellectual institutions less developed, due partly to the more rural orientation of the elite and partly to the relative intellectual and financial poverty of Portugal. Black slaves came to constitute a much greater part of the total population in Brazil than in Spanish America; for that reason, and because the Indian population was smaller, the Portuguese sired a large mulatto population, as opposed to the huge mestizo population in most of mainland Spanish America. Finally, the distinctive Romance vernacular of Portugal set it off from Spanish America.

Historians disagree about the dominant themes of the colonial era in Brazil. Most consider the energy and persistence with which territory was explored, occupied, and defended to be of prime importance. The relatively few men and women of the colonial period laid the territorial base for the enormous Brazilian nation of today. Of nearly equal importance was the vast process of racial and cultural clash and only partial amalgamation that went on between Indian, European, and black African. The biological blending of white and black people in Brazil, begun on a large scale in the colonial era, continued thereafter as a major social phenomenon. Third, Portugal transferred to Brazil its version of the European class system, reinforced in America by the presence of Indians and especially blacks in a servile or dependent condition. A fourth major theme is economic development, largely agricultural and pastoral, heavily dominated by the great estate (*fazenda*). Another important theme is regional differentiation: the growth of regional attitudes, even loyalties, and some distaste for other regional groups. At the same time Brazilians developed an attachment—usually poorly expressed—to Brazil, as opposed to Portugal, and a somewhat better expressed distaste for peninsular Portuguese as opposed to Brazilians. In short, in three hundred years the Brazilians became a distinct group and grasped a vast new land.

14 Brazil: Territory and People

A few people of three races laid the basis for the gigantic Brazilian nation of later times. They did so by a massive intermingling of the racial stocks that peopled the colony against the ambitions of Spanish, French, and Dutch rivals; and by prodigious journeys into the heart of the continent. This activity, rather than the Line of Tordesillas or Spain's defensive efforts, set the limits of the colony. Everywhere they settled, in poor villages in the interior, mining camps, cattle ranches, or on rich sugar plantations near the coast, the Luso-Brazilians created a hierarchical and multi-racial society that was tough and enduring.[1]

a. The Land and the Indians

The Brazilians penetrated from the Atlantic westward to the mountains of Ecuador and ranged from the Amazon basin southward 2,000 miles to the Plata estuary. Theirs was an imperial domain of four natural regions. The vast lowland rain forest of tropical Amazonia was unimportant in colonial times. More useful were parts of the great Brazilian Highland, occupying much of the interior south of the Amazon basin. Its modest

elevations of a few thousand feet were enough to lower the temperature and humidity from those of the steamy coast. Some of it was excellently suited to agriculture even though some, especially in the northeast, was ridden with drought; some of its mountains were rich with gold and other minerals. A third region, the far south of Brazil, was subtropical or temperate lowland, some wooded, some grassy, merging into the plains of Uruguay, which Portugal coveted to carry it to the shores of the Plata estuary.

The most important parts of the colony long were stretches of the coast between 5° south latitude at the easternmost point of Brazil and 24° south near São Vicente (present Santos). The coastal plain between those latitudes was generally a narrow strip between the sea and the highland, sharply defined by a lofty escarpment. Parts of it were pleasant, warm, moist, fertile, especially suited to sugar culture, conveniently located with reference to trade abroad. Some of the most useful areas had natural harbors, and became the sites of colonial towns. Sometimes rivers gave good access to sugar lands for miles into the coastal belt, but they seldom permitted deep penetration, being turbulent as they fell out of the highland. To the north of the sugar belt the highland and escarpment petered out into tropic

---

[1] Lusitania was the Roman name for a province more or less corresponding to the later Portugal.

lowlands. It was a straight sea passage of some 1,000 miles from the eastern cape to the mouth of the Amazon, and Portuguese territory went beyond that to the boundaries of French Guiana. South of São Vicente the highland merged into lower elevations of temperate woods and plains. It was 750 miles by sea southward from São Vicente to the no-man's-land between Brazil's Rio Grande do Sul and the Spanish Banda Oriental del Uruguay.

The indigenous flora and fauna of Brazil were not significantly better or worse than those of Spanish America. The exotic plants and animals of tropical Amazonia excited much wonder but proved to be of little value. The variety, the immensity, and the beauty of the Brazilian landscape provoked rhapsodies from the beginning, and before long formed one of the bases of a growing identification with the natural environment.

When the Portuguese arrived in 1500, the Indians of Brazil numbered 1 to 3 million; the lower figure seems the more likely. Whatever the precise figure, the area was thinly populated. The Indians were scattered in small groups, all with relatively primitive cultures. They spoke many languages, but some—notably Tupí Guaraní—were related. The Tupí, numerous along the coast, were the first Indians the Portuguese met. Miscegenation with these Indians provided much of the population of the early colonial period.

The Tupí lived in thatched huts, cleared the forest, and planted crops—tobacco, maize, squash, beans, and manioc or cassava, from the rootstock of which a flour was made. They hunted, fished, and made fabrics, baskets, and pottery. They had animistic religious beliefs and what we might call medicine men. Tribal organization was not complex, and the units of population were small. They also made war with bows, clubs, spears, and blowguns—and sometimes ate captives. There was nothing in the numbers, possessions, labor organization, or technology of these Indians to impress Europeans with any great opportunity for exploitation.

b. The Early Colony

The strength of Portugal's maritime enterprise in the fifteenth and sixteenth centuries was a result of factors noted earlier:[2] the Lusitanian oceanic tradition and expertise; the seizure of outposts in the Azores, Madeira, the Cape Verde Islands, and Africa; the early achievement of a national dynastic state and an essential unity of national customs; the limited demographic, military, and economic resources of the European realm, but the excellent use that was made of its assets by a line of hardworking and commerce-minded kings, and by a nobility and church that participated enthusiastically in commercial enterprise; the rivalry of Spain and Portugal and the decisions taken to reduce competition and suspicion.

The great fleet of Pedro Alvares Cabral, bound for India, somehow veered so far to the west that it touched Brazil in April 1500. He thought it an island and so named it Ilha de Vera Cruz, claiming it for Portugal. There are assertions that Brazil was discovered earlier by Portuguese mariners and that Cabral went intentionally to secure this flank of the African route to India. Such claims are poorly supported with evidence, as are arguments for prior discovery of Brazil by Frenchmen. The Spaniards also asserted that Brazil had first been touched by its voyagers, including Columbus in 1498. Although Spaniards may well have "discovered" what later was the far north of Brazil, that did not affect the question of territorial jurisdiction. The eastward bulge of Brazil fell into the Portuguese sphere according to the agreement of Tordesillas, and Spain did not press a claim founded on discovery. The French made a considerable effort to secure a place in Brazil but depended on France's military strength, not on claims of discovery.

---

[2] See Chapter 2, Section b, on the resources and character of the Portuguese state and society; Chapter 3, Section a, on the reaction of Portugal to Columbus' discovery, and the Lines of Demarcation between Spain and Portugal overseas.

For several decades Portuguese, and other European, attention to Brazil was feeble. Very soon after the Cabral voyage, a company of merchants, headed by Fernando de Noronha, got crown license to cut and ship brazilwood, which gave a dye much prized for textiles. Other groups received licenses soon thereafter. They set up *feitorias* (factories—trading posts), as the Portuguese had done in Africa. These were all on the coast of Brazil, location depending on anchorage, supplies of wood, and the attitude of the Indians. They were camps, not towns—a small log stockade enclosing a few flimsy structures, with Indian shacks outside. In addition to the brazilwood traffic, these early traders exchanged trade goods for wild pepper, cotton, and a few other products. They also began the strange, fruitful, and sad Portuguese relationship with the Indians.

Other Europeans, especially Frenchmen, learned of the new trade and went to Brazil. They set up trading posts and entered the dyewood commerce. There were clashes between Portuguese and French traders and futile diplomatic exchanges between the Portuguese and French governments. Portugal supplied some naval patrols, but they were ineffective along the lengthy coast. Until 1530 Brazil had not been of much value to Portugal, except as potential guardian of the flank of the African route to India. The crown therefore invested no more than was necessary in the new western lands. Rather than neglectful, as is sometimes said, the policy was prudent for a government with quite limited resources.

By 1530, however, the crown had decided on colonization to secure the Portuguese position. A tiny fleet was sent under Martim Afonso de Souza, with some four hundred men. It made a long survey of the coast, attacked French settlements, tried to strengthen the Portuguese *feitorias*, and sent expeditions inland. In 1532 the expedition (Martim Afonso had returned to Europe) founded São Vicente (near present-day Santos) on the coast some two hundred miles

southwest of Guanabara Bay, where Rio de Janeiro later existed. Nearby, they also set up another tiny hut-cluster—Piratininga, predecessor of the later metropolis of São Paulo. Its site was above the escarpment that penned the coastal belt against the sea, not far inland on the great Brazilian Highland.

The expedition brought European seeds and animals, built log forts, set up town government, and made private land grants (*sesmarias*). It returned to Europe early in 1533, leaving behind the beginnings of the great estate system, a stronger sugar culture (which had started as early as 1521), and the beginnings of a cattle industry. At this date, to be sure, all this existed in such small quantity that the Portuguese hold on Brazil remained dubious.

The crown now was determined, however, to consolidate its hold on Brazil. Even before conclusion of the Martim Afonso expedition, the crown decided to extend to Brazil the donatary system used in its Atlantic islands. In 1534–1536 the king granted fifteen hereditary captaincies (*capitanias*) in Brazil to twelve grantees (*donatários*). The captaincies extended on the average some 250 miles along the coast, and carried rights indefinitely into the unknown interior, which of course ultimately ran through the Andes to the Pacific, where Pizarro just then was subduing the Incas. These mammoth hereditary holdings carried with them large political and economic powers. They often have been described as "feudal," which is useful as a suggestive description, so long as no exact analogy with medieval institutions is intended. The private captaincies also were "capitalistic," in that the holders invested money and hoped for profits. The *foral* (charter) of a hereditary captaincy detailed the roles of grantee and crown, made many provisions for demographic and economic development, and clearly reflected the class divisions of Portuguese society. This last is more important in understanding the history of colonial Brazil than speculation as to how much "feudalism" was contained in the grants. An interesting and realistic

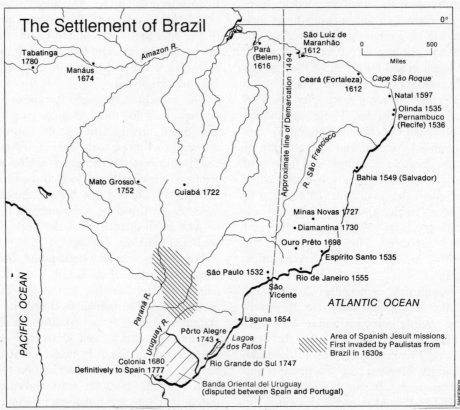

The Settlement of Brazil

provision of the charters was that foreign ships were permitted in the trade between Portugal and Brazil (but not elsewhere), subject to a 10 percent tax.

For various reasons (especially expense), most of the private captaincies were not populated or otherwise developed as the crown had specified. The hoped-for investment, attention, and colonists were not provided by the private holders. Two captaincies—Pernambuco in the north and São Vicente in the south—did succeed. These successes and the small amount done in other areas certainly justified the experiment. Pernambuco was held by Duarte Coelho, who handled his grant well. It was on the great eastward bulge of Brazil, handy to commerce with Europe and Africa. Its coastal plain had dyewood and, more important, excellent land and climate for sugar cane. Profits were soon being made. Most labor

in those early years was Indian and mestizo, since the Portuguese declined to engage regularly in manual labor, and black slaves were scarce for many years. São Vicente also made profits from sugar before the middle of the sixteenth century. By 1548 Brazil had sixteen settlements with an unimpressive but slowly growing economic basis and a small population, now apparently firmly fixed in permanent settlements, after half a century of sporadic Portuguese effort.

One of the weaknesses of the colony was the distance between the settlements. A voyage of more than 1,500 miles separated the small settlements in Pernambuco and São Vicente. The other feeble Portuguese settlements along the coast could scarcely defend themselves; instead, they sometimes consorted with the French, who continued to be active in the area. The crown therefore decided to modify the donatary system and to provide a central administration in America. Officials for that purpose arrived at Bahia in a fleet in March 1549: Thomé de Souza as governor-general, a chief treasurer (*provedor-mor*), and a chief justice (*ouvidor-geral*). The fleet also carried one thousand colonists, some with special skills, bringing the total population of the colony to about 3,500. The crown finally was making a sizable effort to develop and defend Brazil. It had bought the private captaincy of Bahia back from its holder to provide a base for the new government. The other privately held captaincies were to lose their governing powers in later years.

Thomé de Souza and his immediate successors as governor-general in the two decades after 1549 saw to the consolidation of the Portuguese hold on Brazil. By visits of inspection and by use of the new bureaucracy, they tied together the small coastal settlements, collected taxes, and secured cooperation for defense. They promoted the economy by distributing *sesmarias* (land grants) and by importing plants, animals, and workmen. They harried the French. The latter in 1555 mounted a serious threat when Admiral Nicholas Durand de Villegagnon set up France Antarctique on Guanabara Bay, clearly meant to be a strong, permanent settlement. Attacks by the Portuguese proved insufficient, so in 1565 they founded Rio de Janeiro nearby, and, using it as a base, drove out the French in 1567. That proved to be the last serious French menace, partly because France's multiplying internal troubles distracted its attention. In the late sixteenth century Frenchmen did trade with the Indians in far northern Brazil, and in 1612 began colonization in Maranhão there, but were expelled by Portuguese expeditions in 1614–1615.

The church aided in establishment of the new centralized system in Brazil. The crown held the patronage in America, as did the Spanish monarchs. The king defended the faith, and the church defended the monarchy. A bishopric was created for Brazil in 1551, seated at Salvador da Bahia, where the governor-general resided. With Thomé de Souza in 1549 had come six Jesuits,

led by Manoel da Nóbrega, one of the great personalities of Brazilian history. They were charged by the crown with bringing the Indians to the faith, something the earlier Franciscans in Brazil had done little about. This missionary effort often clashed with yet another of the endeavors of the early governors-general—the provision of labor for the struggling settlements.

c. The Portuguese and the Indians

In providing such labor, the Indians of Brazil for many years were of critical importance to the Portuguese.[3] The Tupí and most other groups of Indians in Brazil were culturally primitive compared with Incas or Aztecs, but it is misleading to dismiss them as "savages." They were people with complex beliefs and social structure. They had much to teach about the environment and their own methods of adaptation to it. The Portuguese learned to eat and dress in ways suitable to the resources and conditions of America. The hammock, that airy bed of the tropics, entranced many who first encountered it and who left us a record of their pleasure. The staple manioc, from which a flour was made, was widely serviceable, as were other native foods and Indian methods of growing and preparing them. The Indians provided a few products for trade. The Portuguese made use of Indian knowledge of travel routes as well as native canoes and paddlers.

They also made use of Indian women. There is much Brazilian literature celebrating (*a*) the sexuality of Portuguese males, (*b*) the unrestrained urges of adventurers and criminals among the early European residents, (*c*) the ease with which Portuguese bedded with dusky Indians because the former had known dark-skinned Muslims and Africans, and (*d*) the importance of the process in peopling a vacant land. This is mostly the dubious currency of popular speculation about sex. It is difficult to

---

[3] See Section f of this chapter on Indian slavery and the great *bandeiras* of São Paulo.

concede such factors much importance compared with the simple scarcity of other women in Brazil in the early decades. Race mixture was aided by the fact that many Indian women gave themselves freely to Portuguese men. Some of the provision of women to Portuguese was Indian custom, some a natural submission to apparently superior beings; both motives also operated in Spanish America.

Children of mixed Caucasian and Indian parentage were born at a high rate, and such *mamelucos* were a large part of the population nearly everywhere for some years until African slaves became important after the middle of the sixteenth century in the coastal areas. Portuguese who lived with the Indians and produced veritable battalions of a new type of Brazilian, like the famous Caramurú (Diogo Alvares), are known now as fathers of their country, who helped solve the great problem of exploiting an unpopulated wilderness. Indians remained important in some coastal and many interior areas long after that. Ultimately, the Indian genetic heritage was much diluted by the numbers of new Portuguese and Africans, by the sexual advantages of Portuguese males and *mamelucos* who had become part of the directing element in the new society, and by the cruelties of Indian slavery that reduced their numbers.

Labor was what the ruling element in Brazil chiefly wanted of Indians, precisely as in Spanish America. Most colonists were rough men faced with difficult problems of survival in a frontier wilderness. No more than other people did they enjoy living at the subsistence level. They saw a need for labor and a potential supply in the Indians; that was enough. Initial Indian willingness to help (in some cases) quickly turned to fear, anger, and flight. The Brazilians sometimes said that they only enslaved the Indians because they would work under no other system. This view of the sloth and general inferiority of the Indians was common. Mestizo Paulistas, who spoke Tupí themselves much of the time, were strongly of this view and were avid slave hunters. Like the primitive Indians in Spanish America, the Bra-

zilian Indians made relatively poor slaves, but the new lords of the land considered them better than none. Nor was this view held only among the cruder elite. It was shared by most of the few educated Portuguese and Brazilians who became part of the planter class and by most of the civil and ecclesiastical officials. They were convinced of its necessity for economic and strategic purposes, even its rightness in view of the need to control and Christianize the Indians. In any event it was inescapable, since no other policy could be enforced.

As in Spanish America, enslavement and other mistreatment of Indians was opposed by part of the regular clergy and in a rather legalistic and ineffective way by the crown. The latter certainly took seriously its duty to bring the Indians to the faith; it even spent money on doing so. Early royal decrees and other documents called for decent treatment of Indians. The kings also—as did Spanish monarchs—permitted enslavement under certain conditions (for example, refusal to submit to Portuguese rule, or cannibalism). The complicated and unenforceable rules were too much for Portuguese officials, including the *Mesa de Consciência e Ordens* (Board of Conscience and Orders) in Europe, which supposedly was a critically important religious voice on the issue.

Manoel da Nóbrega, one of the Jesuits who went to Bahia in 1549, led the effort to execute the crown's orders to Christianize the Indians. The Jesuits made the same decisions as missionaries in Spanish America: to gather the Indians together, so that they could be instructed, guided, taught new skills and habits of work, and protected from the Portuguese-Brazilian civil society. The Jesuits with great courage and energy learned native languages, lived in the wilderness, tried to fight off the incursions of slave hunters, keeping the Indians in isolation. The villages (*aldeias* or *reduções*) were as much hated by the slave raiders and planters of Brazil as the Spanish Jesuit missions of Paraguay by the civil society there. Inevitably the Portuguese Jesuits could not always protect their charges, nor could they bring all Indians into the *aldeias*. New Indian slaves were constantly taken and seldom survived to grow old in their captivity. The dedicated Jesuit José de Anchieta recorded in the late sixteenth century that slave raiders in Bahia had reduced the Indians under Jesuit care from 40,000 to 3,000. He estimated that 80,000 Indian slaves were taken to the area's plantations in six years but that they died off and were replaced with blacks.

The Jesuits protested time and again in many ways. Sometimes they railed against slaving in Brazil, but that was merely howling down a well. Their only hope, and we must judge it a slim one, was effective aid from the crown. The kings did issue declarations in the sixteenth and seventeenth centuries to try to reduce the taking of Indian slaves and to ameliorate the conditions of those enslaved. In 1605–1609 the Spanish king Philip II was also king of Portugal, and he declared that there could be no Indian slavery in Brazil, but planter protest in that colony forced him to retreat. General enforcement of fair treatment of the Indians really was impossible. Occasional fraternization—for example, elite attendance at the weddings of converted Indians—merely pointed up the general failure. The long Jesuit effort ended in 1759, in the time of Pombal's ministry, when the Jesuits were expelled from the Portuguese realms. One of the asserted reasons for the expulsion was the pitiful claim that the Jesuits had been a barrier to assimilation of Indians into society.

At about the same time, Portuguese legislation tried to guarantee the liberty and well-being of Indians. Apparently it did something to help what was left of the purely Indian population, chiefly in the north. Decrees in 1775–1778 secularized all mission villages. Prejudice and discrimination against Indians, however, were not to be contained simply by legislation. In any event, the Indians had either mostly retreated into the great forests of the Amazon or the wild west, died of abuse and disease, or become less and less detectable in the racial melting pot of colonial Brazil. Indian slavery and slaving did not quite end with the Pombaline legislation, but they were scarce thereafter. Abuse of Indians was not extinguished by emancipation, however, but continued as Brazilians moved into new areas of the interior.

d. The Black African in Brazil

The black African genetic strain in Brazil became much greater than the Indian. Indian labor was not very satisfactory and the number of Indians was too limited. The Portuguese, like the Spaniards, knew black slavery in Europe, and they also had participated in the European slave trade as suppliers from their African *feitorias*. By the mid-fifteenth century an average of some 2,500 slaves a year was taken from West Africa to Portugal. Again resembling Spain, the Portuguese conscience was little stirred by black slavery, whereas such treatment of Indians seemed iniquitous to a vocal few, especially in the church. But black slavery had a slow start in Brazil. A few slaves were brought from Portugal in the early years, but direct imports from Africa did not begin until the late 1530s. By 1585 black slaves were about 25 percent of the total "settled" population of 57,000 in Brazil. In 1700 black slaves were probably considerably more than 30 percent of the settled population. Possibly 3.5 million slaves reached Brazil from Africa from the middle of the sixteenth to the middle of the nineteenth centuries (importation continued long after Independence in 1822). The figures are much disputed. By one estimate, some 100,000 arrived in the sixteenth century, 600,000 in the seventeenth, 1.3 million in the eighteenth, 1.6 million in the nineteenth. In any event, this flood of black Africans may be compared with possibly 1 million Indians and the considerably smaller number of Portuguese who emigrated to Brazil in the colonial period.

The traffic was made easy by the relatively short voyage between Brazil and Africa and by Portuguese control of many African sources of supply. Brazilian products, notably tobacco, went to Africa in exchange for slaves. Other European nations also played a role in the traffic, directly and indirectly. Some of the trade was triangular or quadrangular between America, Europe, and Africa. The trade between Angola and Brazil was especially notable, but the slaves came from many parts of Africa and from many language and culture groups. There was a great variety of physical characteristics among the African groups, with shadings of skin pigmentation only one among many. As in Spanish America, slaveholders in Brazil developed views, based on experience as well as on prejudice, as to the qualities of Africans from various cultures; some were more desirable than others, either for skills or for reactions to slavery and to discipline.

For many years black slaves were found mainly in the coastal plain, especially in agriculture and associated processing industries, notably sugar. They performed a multitude of other tasks, on the agricultural estates (*fazendas*), in the sugar mills (*engenhos*), and in the towns. As cattle and other enterprises extended into the Brazilian Highland, some blacks were taken to work there. After 1695 many were carried to Minas Gerais and other interior areas to work in the newly discovered gold and diamond mines and at various tasks of field, shop, and household necessary for the new settlements there.

Eventually, at least a few black slaves could be found in all regions, but they were heavily concentrated in some places. Since they were expensive, large numbers were found only where economic activity repaid the investment in such labor. This included the areas of the coast that were heavily cultivated, the largest and most important being Maranhão, the Recôncavo of Bahia, and the area of Rio de Janeiro. It also meant certain mining areas in Minas Gerais, Goiás, and Mato Grosso. But both on the coast and in the interior there were places where the black population was sparse. Great areas of the interior were chiefly mestizo (*mameluco*), including many lands adjacent to the coast where black slaves were numerous. The far south of Santa Catarina and Rio Grande do Sul, settled relatively late, was heavily white, because of immigration by entire families from the Azores, be-

cause there were few Indians, and because investment in slaves did not pay there until the end of the colonial era when the *charque* (dried beef) business began to be important.

The Negro stock became massively mingled with the Caucasian and Indian. By the census of 1818 (margin of probable error unknown), Brazil had some 3.8 million people, including some 2 million classified as Negro slaves, nearly 600,000 free mulattoes or Negroes (probably mostly the former), about a millon whites (many of whom certainly had some black or Indian forebears). By that time the Indian population had declined to a few hundred thousand, many of whom lived far from the centers of population of Portuguese Brazil. In most places, race mixture, especially of white and black elements, was proceeding rapidly.

There is much dispute regarding Brazilian treatment of black slaves and free mulattoes and blacks. We will not repeat all the arguments and cautions presented on this issue for Spanish America,[4] much of which applies with little alteration to Brazil. Here we must note the long popular and scholarly tradition that celebrates a relative gentleness of Brazilian treatment of black slaves and free blacks and mulattoes. Recent studies have brought this tradition into serious question. For one thing, manumission of African slaves seems to have been rare in Brazil, so laws providing for it are considered of less interest than they formerly were. That a very large mulatto group of freemen came into existence is true but bears more directly on attitudes toward race than on slavery. Improved information seems to indicate that slave mortality in colonial Brazil was high. Black slaves possibly never averaged more than ten years of life after arrival in Brazil, and for some periods and places in the colonial era their life expectancy was five to seven years.

So far as slavery alone is concerned (that is, not including all aspects of race relations), these two factors seem of fundamental importance. Neither in terms of manumission nor of mor-

---

[4] See Chapters 8–9.

tality does there seem to have been more than a few percentage points of difference between the harsh treatment of black slaves by the colonial powers of America. What of punishments and labor discipline? In Brazil they sometimes were savage, nor did government edicts on more humane treatment have much effect. Most slaves were used for rough manual labor, and there is little disposition to claim that they were treated pleasantly. The minority of other slaves (for example, house servants, overseers, artisans let out by their owners to bring in income) probably was somewhat larger as a percentage than in other colonial areas and was better treated; but the size and quality of this "relief" have not been established. There is considerable evidence to show that many Brazilian slaves were ill fed and clothed, overworked, and harshly disciplined. Some of the testimony on better treatment of black slaves applies only to the nineteenth century after abolition of the legal slave trade, when higher prices for slaves forced some better treatment. Brazilians made no more effort to prepare slaves for another role in society than did the slave owners of other areas. If Brazilian slaves had somewhat more access to the comforts of Christianity—and the amount of the possible differential has not been established—it scarcely was a major difference. Finally, as an indirect comment on relative benignity, Brazilian owners had the usual fear of slave uprisings, which sometimes occurred, although as in all the Western Hemisphere, the owners underestimated their ability to control slave resistance.

Black slaves in Brazil used all the methods of resistance detailed for Spanish America. Flight was about as prevalent in one as the other. The attitude of slave owners toward runaways was notoriously harsh; slaves represented a big investment and a danger to the elite community. In 1755 a town council in Minas Gerais suggested that recaptured runaways have the Achilles tendon of one foot severed, so they could hobble to work but not flee. The viceroy condemned both the suggestion and the general misuse of slaves, but the affair hints strongly at the slave owner's attitude toward his slave property. In Brazil, settlements of runaways—and sometimes their descendants—were called *quilombos*. They were not a major drain on the slave population, but an expensive and sometimes fearsome annoyance. They blocked or made difficult the movements of the colonial society and made levies on their resources; they also encouraged slaves to hazard flight. The most famed *quilombo* and the longest-lived (much of the seventeenth century) was Palmares in the interior of Alagôas in the northeast. It may have had a population of 20,000. Palmares stood off many expeditions sent against it but finally was brought down, to remain a legendary monument to black rejection of the slave institution in Brazil.

e. Class and Caste

Much of what was said about class and caste for Spanish America can be applied to Brazil. The Portuguese brought the ideal of class division from Europe, even if it was a trifle less rigid than in Spain. It is true that wealth was not available as early and as lavishly in Portuguese as in Spanish America, and hence differences in styles of living were narrower at some times and places in Brazil. Furthermore, there had to be much rough-and-ready exchange and equality of sorts in Paulista *bandeiras*, just as in many circumstances in Spanish America. But when Paulistas acquired property or could claim leadership positions and services to the crown, they displayed the expectable thirst for honors, distinction, and privilege. It has been claimed that the fact that many *fazendeiros* lived more on their estates than did *hacendados* on theirs brought the former more into daily touch with the masses, and a vague fellow feeling or cordiality is imputed to this situation. Possibly, but the fact that *fazendeiros* showed great determination in pursuit of property at the expense of the lower class, in domination of local office, and in use of the militia for their own purposes seems more important. Portuguese and Spanish America were, in fact, alike in having very small upper classes, with most of the possessions, power, and privilege; enormous lower classes; and little "in between." Class distinction was set in Brazil by property, family background, office, and race. The ambition for distinction was as strong in Brazil as in Spanish America.

Racial differences increased social discrimination based on European models. White families certainly tried to find white husbands for their daughters. No one wanted to be called a black, which had too much connotation of slavery. Discrimination by law was stricter with persons of some black stock than with Indian-European mixtures, as in Spanish America. Sometimes in Brazil population estimates listed *brancos* (whites or so accepted), *pardos* (mulattoes), *pretos* (Negroes), and Indians. This left *mamelucos* (*mestiços*) to be put in with whites or mulattoes. Mulattoes, but not *mamelucos*, were denied the priesthood. A priest in the family, therefore, was a formal indication of the absence of Negro blood. The child of a Portuguese American father and an Indian mother could be accepted into his father's community as a *mameluco*, but he was considered Indian if he stayed in his mother's village. A mulatto might be free if recognized by his white father, but slave if left with his black slave mother. A stark example of differential prejudice occurred in 1771 when the viceroy of Brazil reduced the status of an Indian chief who sank "so low as to marry a Negress," thus "staining his blood."

It was clear in colonial Brazil, especially with the passage of time, that miscegenation was less frequent at the upper end of the social scale. We know also that there was considerable effort to marry or breed "up" in whiteness. The evidence, then, suggests a wary approach to the claim that it was easier for a person of color to rise in Portuguese than in Spanish America. If such a person was accepted into the elite, it was as a "white," whatever neighbors knew of his racial ancestry; and much evidence shows that such passage was related to the amount of skin pigmentation. Well-known is the story of the colonial Brazilian who "used to be a mulatto."

There is more to the first two parts than to the third of the famous remark that colonial Brazil was "a hell for blacks, a purgatory for whites, and a paradise for mulattoes." *Mulatas* were much sought as sexual partners, usually concubines, by elite males, as in Spanish America. Few of them derived much social profit from such associations, although they received such expensive gifts that the government (again as in Spanish America) tried to stop luxurious displays by *mulatas*—of course, with no success. Free mulattoes in Brazil were linked with blacks in legislation against the ownership and use of weapons, even though both racial groups were used for military purposes. There were rules against black or mulatto occupancy of high posts in church and state. Even though they were violated, the discriminatory attitude had effects both on bureaucratic staffing and on the general mind-set on color. Obsession with race was expressed in numerous terms for mixtures, with keenly felt pejorative gradations, and confusions that we find difficult to appreciate.[5]

Occupation in Brazil told a lot about status. Manual labor was associated with lower-class position, slavery, and an imputation of inferior race. A Portuguese immigrant, even though poor and lower-class, usually would not consent to be identified with those things. If he could not get into the army, or into the civil or ecclesiastical bureaucracies, he went into commerce. The Brazilian-born white (*mazombo*) considered it notorious that even poor Portuguese (*reinóis*) were taken into the monopolistic group of European-born merchants, to prey upon Brazilian society.[6]

Poor Brazilian freemen had limited opportunity. They certainly could not work their way into the rural aristocracy. The great estates were concentrated in a few hands. Some, notably in

---

[5] As in Spanish America, a term for a race mixture might have more than one possible meaning, depending on time, place, or context. *Mestiço* was used both for the male child of a black and a white, and for the son of an Indian and a white. *Caboclo* might be a mixture of white and Indian, a domesticated Indian, or simply a low-class person, usually of color. A *cafuso* was a mixture of Indian and black.

[6] See Chapter 16 on tension between *mazombos* and *reinóis*.

the sugar lands, were considerable economic enterprises with many types of structures, labor, and activities. They also were patriarchal social complexes, with numerous connections of the family occupying the great house (*casa grande*). The head of the clan dispensed financial rewards, tasks (if any), and justice (with the agreement of the civil authorities) to his attached sharecroppers or small farmers nearby, dependent on his processing and other facilities and his local power; and through overseers ran the short and brutish lives of his field hands occupying the *senzalas* (slave quarters). The old Brazilian claim is repeated even by Marxist historians, that long interdependence on such great estates made for more humane and friendly relationships between the master and most of the people dependent on him; that although there were aristocrats, they were not arrogant, because that was precluded by the indolent tone of Brazilian society. There is little to indicate significant operational effects from the "humanity" and indolence of the Brazilian estate owner.

There was an extreme lack of economic opportunity in colonial Brazil, some of it due to elite control of property and government. This, together with unwillingness to engage in some types of activity, created a large un- or underemployed population. Only a limited number of overseers was needed. There were few opportunities to become artisans, both because markets were limited and because some crafts were monopolized by slaves. It was difficult to get into the bureaucracy, especially if the man was too dark. The bureaucracy was much too small to absorb the population that lacked regular occupation. To go into law or medicine required money for some education in Brazil and the even greater expense of going to Portugal for professional training. There were a few opportunities in the church, even for poor boys including those of mixed blood, although the latter needed a special dispensation.

The result was that many people lived precariously in marginal enclaves or were more or less vagrant and sometimes intermittently criminal. There was much complaint about such elements, as in Spanish America and Europe. They made town life dangerous at times. In the rural areas some of them were taken into the private armies of great landowners who were active as local bosses and politico-governmental leaders. Also of low status in the countryside were most of the tenants (*agregados*) and plantation sharecroppers (*moradores dos enghenos*), who sometimes depended more on activity as flunkies and flatterers of the great estate owner than on agriculture. In any event, all these types made up the bulk of the free population, consisting of freed blacks and mulattoes, runaway slaves, unassimilated Indians, mixed bloods of all kinds, and some poor whites. The facts of class, of aristocratic dispensation, of slavery, of dependent and poorly paid labor, of proletarian hopelessness, were as prevalent in Portuguese as in Spanish America.

The existence at the end of the colonial period of 600,000 free blacks and mulattoes, 15 percent of the total population, suggested less absolute prejudice against black blood than in the slaveholding areas of English-speaking North America. In this, Brazil resembled Spanish America. Whether the difference of a few percentage points of that small total was highly significant or only of marginal interest long has been a matter for debate.

f. Territorial Expansion and Population Growth

Territorial Expansion

Territorial expansion for Brazilian historians, as for those of the United States, has been an heroic epic and an indispensable basis for national greatness. In both, the early settlers stayed near the Atlantic. Behind the little coastal settlements of early Brazil the interior loomed vast, mysterious, prowled by hostile Indians. *Entradas* were made, but no finds of precious metals or great groups of Indian laborers stimulated immigration from Portugal or led many people from the profits and safety of the coast to the perils of the wilderness. The few who roamed the interior often lived by capturing Indians to sell as slaves in the coastal settlements. Exploration moved outward eventually from each coastal settlement as pacification and eradication of Indians opened inland areas to cattle raising and trade. Trade routes grew as resources slowly were developed in the interior. Tiny settlements grew up in the hinterland at fords, route intersections, areas of meat supply, and other nodes. There were products of the interior to be collected— herbs, skins, fruits, the new cattle for meat and hides and tallow, and many other items, no single one of much value.

The Far North and Amazonia. In the far north, beyond the extreme eastward bulge of Brazil from about Cape São Roque along the coast which trends west and north, settlement was late, beginning in the late sixteenth century: Natal, 1599; Fortaleza, 1611; São Luís, 1614; and Belém, 1616, at the mouth of the Amazon. Much of this coast was subject to winds and currents that made sailing difficult to the east and south beyond the cape to the governor's seat at Salvador da Bahia. Communication with Portugal was easier, so in 1621 the state of Maranhão was separated from Brazil, and a governor seated at São Luís. The two states (*estados*) of Maranhão and Brazil remained separate until the 1770s.

In 1677 Maranhão was given a bishopric. It included much of the territory northwest of Cape São Roque. At the time of the establishment of São Luís de Maranhão, along all the great reach of coast from the cape to beyond the Amazon delta, there were only a couple hundred Portuguese in four tiny wooden forts and a few villages. Lack of population was to inhibit defense for decades. Even in 1700 there were only 2,000 in the Estado do Maranhão e Grão Pará. Fortunately, no large-scale foreign threats were mounted against it, although Portuguese and Brazilians had frequently to beat off small foreign encroachments. Although there were rumors

of riches in Amazonia, none were found. The north held little of value to Europeans. Its agricultural potential scarcely was touched before the eighteenth century. In 1737 the governor-general's seat was moved from São Luís to Belém at the mouth of the Amazon to improve defense of that entrance to the continent.

From these northern coastal settlements expeditions went into the interior, mostly from Belém. Some expeditions were sponsored by government; missionaries were active; there was a small amount of trading; and slavers rounded up Indians for the coastal plantations. Expeditions in the area were called *tropas* and often were fleets of canoes and boats, sometimes with Indian warriors, paddlers, and other laborers making up more than half the personnel. In the 1630s Pedro Teixeira went up the Amazon to Spanish Quito, establishing Portuguese claims to an immense territory, far beyond the Line of Tordesillas. Many other intrepid captains went into the area. Settlement in the interior of Amazonia came only slowly. The first in the far interior was a government fort, São José de Rio Negro, put up in 1669 near the present Manaus. Brazilian Paulistas occasionally came down the Amazon's southern tributaries to the sea at Belém. We have seen how the Spanish Jesuit Province of Mainas was penetrated in the eighteenth century by Brazilian *bandeirantes* in search of Indian slaves.[7]

The Northeast. From the coastal settlements of the bulge of Brazil south and west of Cape São Roque, the heart of plantation Brazil, *entradas* and scattered settlers penetrated the hinterland from Brazil's first important centers of population. This part of the *sertão* (backlands) today alone bears that term, but in the colonial era *sertão* was applied to all the interior. The *sertão* back of Bahia and Pernambuco was a hard and thorny land, subject to periodic droughts, into which moved cattle raisers, poor freemen, renegades, and petty traders, setting up ranches

---

[7] See Chapter 12, Section c.

and trading posts along the water courses. The *vaqueiros* (cowboys) were mostly Indians or mixed bloods, one of whose duties over the generations was battling the unsettled natives in the *sertão*. Cattle raising had penetrated two hundred miles from the coast by the early seventeenth century. Routes to the farther interior had been marked out and would be important when the gold rushes began at the end of the seventeenth century. Then, in the middle of the seventeenth century, life in the *sertão* inland from the territory between Olinda and Salvador da Bahia was affected powerfully by the massive Dutch intrusion.

The Bandeirantes of São Paulo. The most famous explorers of colonial Brazil were the Paulistas of the south. Their movement in the sixteenth century was limited by their small numbers. The town of São Paulo emerged only in 1562 from a combination of earlier tiny settlements. The Paulistas had virtually nothing to send out to the coast for export. The sixteenth century *bandeiras* did explore widely and reduced Indian capacity to interfere with movement. In the seventeenth century and first half of the eighteenth the *bandeiras* made many epic penetrations of unexplored territory and raids into Spanish-held areas, far beyond the Line of Tordesillas. Although the origin of their name is disputed, there is no doubt of the vigor of the *bandeirantes*, mainly Indian and *mameluco* (mixed Indian and Portuguese), driven to Indian slaving by the lack of other opportunities. Incidental to their main occupation was looking for gold. The *bandeiras* were made up of Paulistas, who generally shared in the profits of the venture, and usually a majority of nonsharing Indian warriors and Indian slave laborers. Sometimes considerable numbers of women went along; less often, animals were included, for food and carriage, although in the seventeenth century nearly everyone walked—often barefooted—and baggage (much of it food) was carried by porters.

Bandeiras often followed the watercourses, but canoes were little used until the eighteenth century, and then only in certain areas of the far west. In the eighteenth century, also, pack animals became more important. The *bandeiras* ranged from small groups to hordes of several thousand. The *bandeirantes* used homemade garments—rough cotton drawers and shirts, and big-brimmed hats; ate Indian dishes; spoke a version of Tupí-Guaraní. Their poverty and Indian-ness gave them the reputation in the coastal plantation areas of crude frontiersmen. So they were, and enjoyed their freedom from restrictions, from government supervision (although some *bandeiras* were government-sponsored), and the opportunity to claim lands and office as the reward of opening new territory. Distinctions between individuals obviously could not be as marked as in the more developed coastal areas, but the Paulista leaders cherished their authority and their own forms of distinction, and in later days their relatively simple patriarchal society easily slid into the general pattern of class privilege in Brazil. They were, of course, unaware that they were living a series of epics that were to form a conspicuous part of the nationalistic literature of the future nation, being compared by later writers to the Portuguese voyagers.

The *bandeirantes* harried the Guaraní missions of the Spanish Jesuits in Paraguay, in 1628–1632, many of them in territory that today is part of Brazil.[8] As the Jesuits retreated south with their charges, the *bandeiras* followed, into what is now far southern Brazil. The availability of the concentrations of Spanish mission Indians increased profits and stimulated Paulista interest in slaving. But by the middle of the seventeenth century the Spanish Jesuit mission Indians were too far off for effective raiding, and the plantations of coastal Brazil were less interested because of improvement in the supply of black African slaves. *Bandeiras* not only went slaving but often were sponsored by government to aid in warfare in areas far from São Paulo: for example, in the

---

[8] See Chapter 7, Section d.

northeast against Indians, the Dutch, and the African *quilombo* Palmares.

By the late seventeenth century *bandeiras* had ranged, at least occasionally, over much of the west, south, and east central part of Brazil. Their activity was altered in the 1690s by the discovery of large gold deposits in the Paulista area, in what soon became Minas Gerais. Paulistas then went farther west and in the early eighteenth century found gold in Goiás and Mato Grosso. This distant activity led Paulistas to take to the rivers and develop in the west a transportation system that was called the monsoon (*monção*), presumably so named because they departed during the rainy season of high water, in recollection of the monsoon rains of Portuguese experience in the Orient. Many of the far western needs, especially in Mato Grosso, were supplied by the canoe and dugout fleets, sometimes containing several hundred vessels. Some dugouts could carry several tons of cargo. The trip from São Paulo to Mato Grosso took up to five months and was arduous and dangerous because of navigational hazards and Indian attacks. The so-called "cycle of monsoons" lasted about a century, from the early eighteenth to the early nineteenth centuries, killed finally by the decline in gold production.

The Far South.   Expansion to the far south led to what is now southern Brazil and beyond that to Uruguay and the Plata estuary.[9] The rolling plains of Rio Grande do Sul merge into those of the Banda Oriental del Uruguay. Much of the southern expansion and defense effort was sponsored by the crown, but Paulistas were moving south in the late seventeenth and especially the eighteenth centuries into what became Santa Catarina, Paraná, and Rio Grande do Sul. In the last there grew up a gaucho life, based on cattle and horses, much like that in adjacent Spanish areas. Traffic in cattle hides and mules sustained Rio Grande do Sul, especially after a

herd trail was opened to São Paulo and Minas Gerais in the 1730s. Portuguese and Brazilian advances beyond the Line of Tordesillas finally were accepted and defined by the treaty of 1777, although Portugal gave up her claims along the Plata estuary. This settlement proved to be the decisive one, although Spain and Portugal fought over the Uruguay area for years thereafter, and their successor states, Brazil and Argentina, did not give up the struggle until 1828.

Brazil thus had expanded in three centuries from a fringe of villages along the coast to one of the greatest territorial agglomerations held by any nation on earth. The Luso-Brazilians had done it by ceaseless, aggressive movement, claim, settlement, defense. They overcame the theory of the demarcation agreement with Spain with irresistible fact, recognized as a new principle in the Treaty of Madrid (1750) between the two countries: *uti possidetis*, the fact of occupation, not agreement or claims. Although this treaty was annulled, the Treaty of San Ildefonso (1777) in essence retained the principle of *uti possidetis*. That principle also lay at the base of Brazilian territorial policy and diplomacy in the nineteenth century, which further pushed out the boundaries of Portuguese America at the expense of the surrounding independent states of Spanish America.

Population Growth and Location

By 1574 the sixteen towns of Brazil had about 3,000 full voting citizens (*vizinhos*), perhaps equivalent to some 15,000 whites, including families and others. About two-thirds of these lived near the coast in present-day Bahia and Pernambuco, that is, in the northeast. A decade later there were some 25,000 whites, 18,500 subdued Indians (of the 1 million or so in Brazil), and 14,500 Negroes. So by the mid-1580s settled Brazil was still a matter of only some 60,000 persons. Even in 1640 the settled population may have totaled only 200,000. It grew faster after the discovery of the mines in the 1690s. By 1776 it was possibly 1.9 million; some 2.85 million in 1798;

---

[9] On Portuguese and Spanish territorial struggles, see Chapter 7, Section f.

and 3.8 million in 1818, four years before Independence.[10]

About 1600 the settled population existed in six main nuclei, each containing little towns and agricultural clusters. They were Maranhão in the far north, Pernambuco and Bahia in the northeast, Rio de Janeiro well to the south, and Santos and São Paulo yet farther to the south and west of that. Most people still lived in a narrow fringe near the coast, even when they had moved up onto the highland. The mineral discoveries of the 1690s modified that distribution, and many people moved west and south in the eighteenth century. Although this was a great change in settlement patterns, it still did not ordinarily go more than two hundred miles from the Atlantic, because there were enough land and other resources for the small population without more penetration inland. In fact, in 1800 about 60 percent of the population (that is, 2 of 3 million) lived less than one hundred miles from the coast. The huge Amazon basin (1,158,300 square miles) in 1800 held only some 95,000 settled population, and 60,000 of that was in the settlements of the river delta.

Town life developed very slowly. In 1600 there were only three "cities," the largest being Bahia with 8,000 inhabitants, and fourteen towns. All except São Paulo were on the coast. Although towns developed more in the next two centuries and more were founded in the interior, Brazil remained even more rural than Spanish America. In 1806 the chief towns were Rio de Janeiro, 50,144; Bahia, 45,600; Recife, 30,000; São Luís de Maranhão, 22,000; São Paulo, 18,000. The total in these towns amounted to 165,000 out of the Brazilian population of 3 million. Even if Rio and Bahia were 50 percent larger, as some evidence suggests, the total urban population was small.

Even the population in the coastal belt and its immediate hinterland was far from continuous; rather, most of it was in a few concentrations, because much of the coast was unattractive for settlement. The far northeastern bulge from Cape Calcanhar past Recife to Maceió—about 350 straight sea miles—had possibly 20 percent of the coastal population in 1800 (that is, some 300,000). It was marked not only by good land, but by a chain of reefs that provided sheltered anchorage. Many small rivers gave access far enough to the interior to facilitate logging and export agriculture. Farther south was the Recôncavo district of Bahia, bordering All Saints Bay, about sixty miles long and thirty wide. The important town of Salvador was on this great bay. Rivers led inland. Possibly 100,000 of the coastal population lived there in 1800. From early colonial times this relatively small area had been the most heavily populated and the richest in Brazil. Because of this, and because for most of the colonial era it was the seat of the governors-general and viceroys, it had a great tradition and pride. Even farther to the south, the Rio de Janeiro area had a population concentration of about 170,000 by 1789, including possibly 50,000 in the city. This was a narrow coastal belt, the Baixada Fluminense. Guanabara Bay alone had a shoreline of eighty miles. The Baixada had a concentrated population from the middle of the sixteenth century.

Population was unevenly distributed in the interior as well as in the strip on and very near the coast. By 1800 possibly 65 percent of the total population lived in the captaincies of Minas Gerais, Bahia, Pernambuco, and Rio de Janeiro—that is, in three traditional centers of tropical culture and export on the coast and in the newer one based on the mines of Minas Gerais. This left only 35 percent of the population for an immense territory; even São Paulo, the next most populous captaincy, was very thinly inhabited. Amazonia, the far west, and the far south were barely sprinkled with residents.

By the end of the colonial era the white racial heritage of Brazil was almost entirely Portuguese. The often trumpeted tolerance of Portugal as compared with Spanish America had not extended to large foreign groups, nor were they much attracted to Brazil. A fair number of Por-

---

[10] For racial composition, see Section d of this chapter.

tuguese had been deportees, but their criminality, in the European juridical fashion of the day, often amounted to no more than thievery or a minor crime or indebtedness that social conditions made inevitable. Relative Portuguese tolerance did permit the emigration of a fair number of persons who were, or had been, of the Jewish faith. However interesting this might be from the social point of view, it was of no consequence racially. Portuguese immigration became especially brisk after the middle of the seventeenth century, chiefly because of Portuguese fiscal losses due to war (against the Dutch in America, and the Dutch and others in Europe and the Orient), and the loss of much of the Oriental trading empire to the Dutch. It was also stimulated by the gold and diamond strikes after the 1690s. The government in Portugal even began to fear for the depopulation of the European realm and tried, without success, to restrict emigration. One of the most striking things about Portuguese immigration to Brazil was that most of the immigrants settled in the towns, so that they had little influence upon the racial composition of most of the countryside.

g. The Dutch Intrusion

The Dutch mounted the single greatest threat to Luso-Brazilian growth in America. Their defeat after a difficult struggle stimulated Brazilian pride or nascent nationalism. The invasion resulted chiefly from European events. Philip II of Spain longed to unify the Peninsula. The two kingdoms had warred for centuries, and in recent times the royal families had intermarried. King Sebastian of Portugal (1557–1578) left his country two disastrous legacies: great expenditures of blood and treasure in adventures against the Muslims in Africa, where he was killed in battle; and a tangle of claimants to the throne. Philip of Spain was one claimant. He enriched his claim with bribery of Portuguese clergy and nobility and with armies. Portugal was too ex-

hausted by the recent debacle in Africa to put up much defense. Philip tried to consolidate his hold by promising Portugal virtual self-government and noninterference with its language, customs, and overseas trade.

He did not keep all these promises. For one thing, he had long fought the stubborn Dutch declaration of independence from his domains in the Low Countries. In pursuit of this, in 1594 he closed the port of Lisbon to Dutch merchants and seized some of their vessels. This was not only damaging in itself, but it interfered with the sizable Dutch traffic between Portugal and Brazil. This trade had been permitted by Portugal under certain rules of taxation and subject to clearance from a Portuguese port. The exchange of products and the Dutch profits from freightage had been considerable.

The Dutch retaliated in several ways that were dangerous for Portugal. They went to India and began reducing the Portuguese empire and trade position there, and before long they were also expanding in the Western Hemisphere. Early in the seventeenth century the new Dutch West India Company carried to the West Indies the remarkable Dutch business acumen and energy and their merchant and military-naval expertise. The company soon decided to take over part of Brazil. After some abortive attacks on Salvador in Bahia, the company was more successful in Pernambuco, where it took Recife in 1630. From there it extended its conquests till it had a hold on a coastal belt from northwest of Cape São Roque in Maranhão to about the mouth of the São Francisco River, some two hundred miles by sea to the south of Recife. They were then only three hundred miles from the center of Brazilian government at Salvador. It was a formidable challenge, rather rapidly mounted, that revealed the vulnerability of Brazil to well-organized and determined invasion.

The Dutch came to stay. Their West India Company was intelligent in its policies. Individuals were encouraged in various ways to invest and work in all activities but the slave trade, dye-woods, and munitions, which the company controlled. Sensible taxes and easy, plentiful credit aided development. Recife was much enlarged and improved. Dutch scholars studied the Brazilian tropics, its flora, fauna, climate, and resources.

But the great and seemingly successful days of the Dutch conquest, especially the regime of Jan Mauritz (1637–1644), were brief; after that, the Brazilian counterattack became progressively more dangerous to the Dutch position. The Brazilians never accepted the invaders, and their unremitting resistance and courage provided a brilliant illustration of the difficulty of dealing with a determined foe inhabiting a huge and virtually trackless wilderness where only he can live off the land and find his way. Guerrilla warfare periodically pecked at the Dutch position on the Atlantic fringe of the continent. Nor did Brazilians care about Portugal's temporizing with the Dutch after the Spanish union with Portugal was broken in 1640. The Portuguese of Europe and the Dutch were at one in their hatred of Spain, and could act with attention to grand policy. Brazilians cared nothing for such considerations (in fact, many did not know of their existence), only for destruction of the invader. Many of those wholly or partly of non-European race who fought the Dutch had been reared in a hard school as explorers and Indian fighters, accustomed to a spartan existence and violence, with few hostages to fortune in the form of possessions and elaborate family ties to weaken their resolution. It is difficult to imagine how the Dutch ever could have discouraged the attacks of such men.

In the mid-1640s the Brazilian resistance increased, and attained coordination under the governor-general at Salvador in Bahia. A big campaign began in 1645, involving leaders from Bahia and Pernambuco: *mazombos*, mulattoes, blacks, Indians, and Portuguese soldiers. It took several years of fighting. These attacks from the vast interior were coordinated with military and other aid to the Portuguese fighting the Dutch in Angola in Africa, where the Dutch were expelled. The pressure upon their position in Brazil was more than the Dutch West India Company could sustain. By 1648 it had nothing left but an enclave around the town of Recife and control of the sea. The Dutch finally surrendered in 1654, worn out by Portuguese naval action and the landward siege and isolated by the opening of the great naval wars between Britain and the Dutch, which overshadowed what little remained of their hopes for empire in Brazil.

The reconquest had been largely the work of Brazilians of various races from various parts of the country, even from far-off São Paulo. It was a victory over a renowned European power. It stimulated pride and probably some immeasurable sense of Brazilian-ness. No one can be sure of the spiritual results of such an effort, such a triumph, but historians agree that it was important. Brazilians today also look back on the great struggle with satisfaction as an expression of sustained courage and of Brazilian love of the land and determination to keep it their own.

15 Brazil: Government and the Economy

The government and economy of colonial Brazil did most of what they were meant to do. They promoted oligarchy and monopoly and guarded against disorder and famine. They saw justice through the eyes of the elite. They provided men, spirit, and weapons to smite the foreign foe. Much of that sounds like success, but, as always, judgment depends on the point of view. All the elite approved the systems insofar as they permitted the enlargement, enrichment, and defense of Brazil and protection of the system of class and caste. The Portuguese, on the other hand, were not so pleased that much of the land fell into the hands of the Brazilian-born, and the influence of those *mazombos* on government became heavy even though they did not hold the major imperial offices. No one remarked that as Brazil grew larger and stronger and a few Brazilians grew richer, institutions and attitudes grew more out of tune with developments in the most advanced countries. The governmental and economic systems performed great tasks, but they grew increasingly anachronistic. They were not preparing well for Brazil's future.

a. Government

The imperial bureaucracy, with the aid of the supporting and closely allied church, used a class system to rule the masses through an elite, while at the same time guarding royal power against elite pretensions. The crown believed that its colonies were in the nature of things subordinate to the metropolis and that the interest of the latter should be favored. It found, however, that the operation of government in Brazil diverged from theory, because the land was so diverse in its resources and needs, because both men and information were difficult to command over such great distances, because conditions kept changing, and because the Brazilian-born elite insisted on defining its own power to some extent. Like the *criollos* of Spanish America, the *mazombos* (Brazilian-born) were loyal subjects of the crown but modified the rules by inattention, misinterpretation, slow or no compliance, influence with officials who sometimes were allied with them economically or emotionally (even through marriage), petitions of redress, and coercion and bribery.

The king relied on a system of councils. He had, in addition, two Secretaries of State (one for a time was called the Minister of Navy and Overseas), but they were intermediaries rather than decision makers. Only after 1750 did colonial secretaries supplant the councils in influence. The Portuguese council system, unlike the Spanish, usually did not provide bodies dealing only with America. Instead, from 1550 to 1808 there were three councils that dealt with all colonial affairs in Asia, Africa, and America: the Treasury Council (*Conselho de Fazenda*, 1594–1641), the *Conselho da India e Conquistas Ultramarinas* (Council for India and Overseas Conquests, 1604–1614), and the Overseas Council (*Conselho Ultramarina*, 1642–1808). In addition, the Board of Conscience and Orders (*Mesa da Consciência e Ordens*, from 1532) handled various religious, moral, and church administration problems for Brazil. There was a Board of Justice (*Desembargo do Paço*) to supervise the judicial system for all the empire. Thus, there was no such concentration of function as in the Spanish *Consejo de Indias*. In the mode of the day, the Portuguese councils had what we would call a mixture of functions—administrative or executive, consultative, judicial, fiscal, commercial.

Although the governing apparatus in Portugal often tried to govern the metropolis and all the colonies by one set of standards, officials did take into account differences within the widespread empire. There was special legislation for Brazil, and officials in America had considerable leeway in interpreting law and policy to fit local reality. In any event, the frequent coupling of Brazil with the rest of the empire was of some benefit to the latter, in matters of trade and in providing posts in Africa and Asia for Brazilians. In its workings, the Portuguese system was not significantly better or worse than the Spanish.

It has been noted that in 1549 a governor-general was created for Brazil to centralize administration and to repair the deficiencies of the donatary experiment; and that Brazil was divided into two states early in the seventeenth century, an arrangement that endured until 1775. The governors-general had to contend with great problems of communications, a stubborn local elite, and competitors for power within the system of government. As in Spanish America, a weak chief executive might expect encroachment from all directions—from the church, military officials, judges, and the municipalities. Only three

governors-general before 1720 had the title of viceroy; thereafter all bore it. The governors-general and viceroys served limited terms, generally less than six years. They were appointed from among the Portuguese nobility and professional military. They were seated at Salvador da Bahia from 1549 to 1763, after that at Rio de Janeiro. The change reflected the growth of the south and the rise of conflict with Spain in the Paraguay and La Plata areas.

Brazil (both the territory governed from Salvador and the state of Maranhão) was divided into captaincies. There was a tendency to convert the private captaincies of the donatary system to royal status, by purchase or in other ways, beginning in 1548. Still, some new private captaincies were created thereafter as a means of developing areas. About 1700 there still were twelve hereditary captaincies in Brazil and Maranhão. In addition, there were both principal and subordinate captaincies: in 1800, eleven of the former and six of the latter.

The captaincies were headed by governors (with the additional title of captain), all royal appointees, and mostly Portuguese aristocrats or military men. Their actual subordination to the governors-general depended on distance, personalities, and other factors, including the encouragement by Portugal of direct communication by all officials and private citizens.

The magistrates were considered a critical part of the system, as they were in Spanish America, both for the administration of justice and as a check on the activities of governors-general and governors and the municipal councils. We have observed the arrival in 1549 with the Thomé de Souza expedition of the first *ouvidor geral* (chief justice). In 1609 Salvador received a high court (*relação*), with ten magistrates (*desembargadores*) and other staff. A second was created at Rio de Janeiro in 1751. Some time after creation of the first *relação*, inferior magistrates (*ouvidores*) were provided in the captaincies. After 1696 royal magistrates called *juezes de fora* were appointed for the towns.

Royal magistrates were carefully selected and

trained. They generally were not recruited from the nobility or the rural or urban proletariat, but from the gentry, merchant class, the military, and artisan families; many were the sons of magistrates. As in the Spanish service, magistrates owed their loyalty and positions directly to the crown, not to a class, and were trained professionals in public service all their lives. Most of the higher magistrates in Brazil were Portuguese, although a Brazilian was appointed to the Bahian *relação* as early as 1653, despite legislation prohibiting it (although the law provided that Brazilians could serve as magistrates in other parts of the empire). The crown tried to isolate magistrates from colonial society by limitations on residence and social relations but had no more success than the Spanish. Many incumbents used their elevated positions to improve their personal and family fortunes. Some became heavily involved in economic activities. Some married Brazilian women, against the law. They also became godparents in the elite Brazilian social structure. Some served as directors of the Holy Brotherhood of Mercy (*Misericordia*) with the cream of Brazilian society. All this probably strengthened the governmental system by improving the access of the colonial elite to decision makers. The Portuguese government, however, considered all these violations of regulations to be undesirable.

The fiscal system, a major crown concern, was headed in Brazil by a *provedor mor*, with subordinate *provedores* in the captaincies. The royal revenue system was complex. A tithe (*dízimo*) was levied on many products and a fifth (*quinto*) on minerals. The tithe on sugar was the main source of crown revenue, until the *quinto* took over first position after the gold discoveries of the 1690s. Customs on overseas traffic were collected at the seaports; internal customs were collected at key points of the roads and trails of the interior. There were excise taxes on selected commodities such as wine, tobacco, and salt. There were such crown monopolies as brazilwood, slaves, diamonds, tobacco, salt. The fisc also collected revenue from quitrents on crown property, legal fees, and other things. When all was insufficient, forced loans or gifts were exacted. Much of the revenue system was farmed out for a short term of years, in return for a fixed payment in advance to the treasury. The system bore heavily on the poor, as most tax systems do, but they had greater reasons for unhappiness than taxes. The propertied, of course, complained of taxes, and paid as little as they could, but they prospered.

Although the Brazilian-born received appointments to the bureaucracy, they were to the lower offices. The chief place in government of the Brazilian elite was at the municipal level, as in Spanish America. The town governments enjoyed more power than in Spanish America, however, partly because the royal government was weaker in Portuguese America. The *senado da câmara* (municipal council) in Brazilian towns was elected by a few men of property, known as *homens bons*, the equivalent of the *vecinos* of Spanish American towns. They chose justices of the peace, aldermen, and a public attorney. The council was presided over by a *juiz ordinário* (ordinary judge), elected by the other councillors, or by a *juiz de fora*, sent by the crown. The latter type became increasingly common, especially in important places, a part of the crown's effort to control the Brazilian-born.

The *senados da câmara* had jurisdiction over much rural land. They had many of the duties of the *cabildos* of Spanish America: judicial, police, and town functions in relation to transportation, sanitation, commerce, food supply, social welfare. A *senado's* income was much like that of the *cabildo's*, permitting essential, but far from lavish, services. *Senados* also had much influence over labor supply, prices, and other economic matters as they assumed powers belonging to imperial officials, a practice Lisbon often tried and failed to prevent. The role of the *senado* was in general greater and more nearly independent than its equivalent in Spanish America. The fact that the elite electors retained more control over membership of the councils than in Spanish

America, where sale and hereditary office undercut local power and interest in many cases, was an important reason. *Senados* claimed powers over the acts of higher officials on a greater scale than in Spanish America after the conquest period.

The *senados da câmara*, as centers of local feeling and interest, represented the *mazombos* in clashes with the *reinóis* (peninsulars). There were a great many clashes over Indian policy, with the towns especially determined to accept no restrictions on Indian slavery. Most importantly, the *senados* represented the small Brazilian upper class and especially the landed estate owners. Even though more merchants gained membership in the course of time, they could not much dilute the generally agricultural-pastoral orientation of the elite (and, indeed, sometimes shared it to some extent), nor did they desire reduction of the oligarchic character of the institution. There was, though rarely, a small influence in town councils by craft guilds, for example in Salvador for a time, but artisans were a minor factor in Brazilian society. Thus, the *senados da câmara* were more influential than the Spanish American *cabildos*, and equally oligarchic.

A part of the power of the elite at the local level in Brazil came from its control of a powerful militia force, unmatched in organization and use for politico-economic purposes by the militia of Spanish America. Both the militia and the *senado da câmara* were controlled by the local landholding elite (even in such a town as Salvador). Only three militia units were not officered by the landed aristocracy: the Henriques (free blacks), the *pardo* regiment (freemen of mixed race), and the Utéis regiment, formed in 1774 of merchants, mostly Portuguese-born. The chief figures of the little Brazilian oligarchy competed for leadership of militia units, which carried with it large judicial, economic, military, and administrative powers. The militia maintained order in the countryside; aided the royal judicial and customs officials; and acted unofficially to end minor disputes between landowners and their tenants, sharecroppers, and slaves.

The top militia rank was *capitão-mor* (equivalent to colonel). His power, as with other officials, tended to vary with the nearness and energy of other echelons of government, or the presence of regular army personnel. But the *capitão-mor* generally was a powerful, even a dreaded, figure. Often, in the vast but lightly populated spaces of Brazil, he became a strong local boss, *caudilho*. The *caudilhos* used the militia for their own personal and political purposes, which sometimes led to serious feuding between elite groups. Generally, they used the militia to support the wishes of the elite and to control lower-class turbulence, a constant fear of the oligarchs. There is some disagreement as to how much control the imperial system had over the militia, but there is little as to their great influence on local affairs. We have, then, a strong colonial tradition of military organization, and control of it by the local elite often for politicoeconomic purposes. This local *caudilhismo* of the colonial era was to carry over to independent Brazil in the control of local and state politics by the *coroneis* (colonels).

The imperial bureaucracy did try to control the militia, sometimes with regular army forces in Brazil. Brazilians served as officers and men in the regular army, but apparently below the grade of lieutenant-colonel. Brazilian army officers seldom came from the elite families, who preferred militia commissions because they were a road to influence and prestige. Regular officers had to perform socially demeaning duties, and training and performance requirements were higher for regulars, especially after the reform of the military code under Prussian guidance in 1767. Some rural militia units were put under regular army command. Often regular army personnel aided in the organization and training of militia units. Such measures did little to reduce the potential danger to the imperial system from the Brazilian-oriented militia. Fortunately for Portugal, Brazilian upper-class militia officers had no thought of separatism, and the ordinary soldiers accepted orders in military life as they did in civil, because they enjoyed the supplies, perquisites, and excitement of military service.

The Portuguese system endured more than three centuries in Brazil because the local elite supported the connection and the general tenor of socioeconomic arrangements, however much it insisted on its own interpretation of details. Critics judge that Portuguese institutions were poorly fitted to American conditions, badly defined, and sadly overlapping in function. They go on to claim that there was great mismanagement, disorder, delay in decision making, a poor system of justice, and too little investment in public facilities because the chief interest of the crown was in milking the colony. A more moderate view is that exploitation of colony by metropolis was the accepted theory of imperial powers at the time, that in any event much regulation was tempered with interpretation and disobedience, that many decisions satisfactory to the elite were made by them as local or minor officials and many more wholly or in part by unofficial and private action, and that large investment in infrastructure, as we would put it, was not common anywhere in the world at the time. As for the last, probably the Brazilian elite would not have cared for the higher taxation that such infrastructure would have required; it did not support much of it after Independence.

Complaint about the imperial system became acute at the end of the colonial period. Especially after 1815, there was an element of propaganda and exaggeration in Brazilian complaints, in a day when new conditions led to distaste for the Portuguese connection and when decision makers in Portugal blindly refused to recognize the necessity for accommodation.

b. The Economy of Colonial Brazil

The early bases of the Brazilian economy were much smaller and weaker than those of Spanish America. The Portuguese found no great accumulated Indian treasure or silver mines or populous cultures with established systems of regular labor. (*a*) The economy was dominated by the small elite, leaving little opportunity and low incomes for the proletariat, thus a lack of incentive. (*b*) The dominant unit of production was the large estate, usually (*c*) heavily dependent on slave labor, (*d*) characteristically concentrated on a single crop for export, so that (*e*) the dominant mode of production was externally oriented, dependent on distant markets, "colonial" in our present sense. (*f*) Agricultural exports were the most important, but commodities and their values fluctuated during the long colonial period. Most of the export production was near the coast, partly because of transport costs, partly because suitable land was found there. (*g*) Mineral production (gold and diamonds) began only in the 1690s, and petered out badly in something over half a century.

(*h*) A considerable livestock industry was developed, chiefly to serve the domestic market. As with agriculture, the large producer was dominant. (*i*) Although the total amount of artisan activity was large, it was small-scale, without leverage in the economy. (*j*) Transportation costs in the interior were high because of terrain and distance, barriers to river navigation, and lack of investment in roads for wheeled vehicles. The last scarcely existed. There was much porter traffic in the early years, after which pack animals (chiefly mules, though horses in some areas) became dominant. River traffic was relatively unimportant, though it played some spectacularly interesting roles in a few areas. (*k*) All the economy was marked by low productivity (as in much of the world), due not only to the poor skills and motivation of slaves or poorly compensated free labor, but to the elite's lack of interest in technology, even the simplest improvements of agricultural activity. (*l*) Portuguese mercantilist restrictions endeavored to regulate the economy, but their effects are debatable, compared to those of inescapable and unchangeable conditions of production and marketing. (*m*) The phrase "boom or bust" has been applied to the colonial economy of Brazil like a genetic weakness, but no fatal speculative psychology more virulent than the acquisitive lusts of Roman senators or English investors in the South Sea Company festered in Brazilian culture.

Agriculture

Agriculture dominated the economy, in terms of elite interest, income, and numbers of people involved. It had no competitor in the two centuries before the gold strikes of the 1690s, and that was a brief-lived phenomenon of limited influence. Stock raising and processing grew throughout the colonial era, but the money profits did not approach those of crop agriculture. Monopoly of ownership of the best land was only one of the elite's advantages. Many single grants (*sesmarias*) were 10,000 to 13,000 acres, and an owner could get more than one. Legislation to require actual use of land was not enforced. Some "nonuse" was really a part of the plantation system, dictated by the need for unexhausted soil and huge supplies of wood for fuel and other purposes. Oligarchic control and profits also were promoted by the labor system, by superior access to credit, and by elite influence in government. Additional matters of law, custom, and circumstance played a role in hindering a small holder or tenant or wage laborer from becoming a great estate owner.

Sugar production on the great estates was the heart of the Brazilian economy. Most of these estates were located in a few concentrations in the coastal belt from Pernambuco south to São Paulo, where soil, climate, and access to slaves and shipping were highly favorable. The European demand for sugar rose, and the price was attractive much of the time, so naturally the estate owners grew and processed sugar, and the crown encouraged them in many ways. The result was that Brazil provided most of Europe's sugar from the middle of the sixteenth to the middle of the seventeenth century, and substantial amounts the rest of the colonial period, even though other producers were cutting into the

market. By 1600 some 33,000 tons of sugar a year flowed from Brazil to Europe. By then it had financed in the colony the construction of mills and other edifices, and developed demand for supporting crafts, transportation, and commercial institutions and facilities, plus an improving life for the newly rich planters. During the colonial period, some 60 percent by value of all Brazil's exports was sugar. Sugar was of nearly overwhelming interest to the government and to the local elite, a situation somewhat paralleled by the role of silver in Spanish America, though the character and some of the effects of the two industries were quite different.

The biggest sugar estates not only grew cane but processed it. Only a large holder could afford the investment required for processing works of any size. These large enterprises were known as *engenhos* (the name of the mill), and their owners as *senhores de engenho*, the greatest magnates of the colony. Large ones might have several square miles of land of various sorts. The processing works included not only the grinding mill, but such other specialized operations as great boiling vats, and the purgery where the molasses was drawn off from the sugar. The estates also had many other buildings—the owner's house, slave quarters, stables, craft shops, and storage space. Sugar estates also produced rum and brandy, which had considerable markets in Brazil and as exchange for slaves in Africa. Sugar (both white and brown types) was packed in wooden chests, and their construction, packing, and transport were specialized tasks. Many animals were needed, especially oxen for the grinding mills and for hauling wood to fuel the cane-processing works. The nearly universal use of oxen for the mills was only one mark of the generally inefficient management of the Brazilian sugar business. This weakness did not matter so much during the first century of exports, but it became serious when foreign competitors came into production and when they adopted superior techniques. Waterpower was considerably more efficient for mills than oxen, but it was seldom used. In the captaincy of Pernambuco in 1777 there were 369 sugar mills, but only 6 used water-power.[1]

A big sugar estate was likely to have at least eighty slaves; very few had many more than that. Not only were slaves high-priced, but they did not live long, so that constant purchases were necessary. The bulk of the overseers and specialists on the sugar estates were former slaves. As for the cane, the *senhores de engenho* apparently grew the bulk of what they processed themselves, but considerable amounts (possibly on the order of a third of the total) came from tenants or freeholders, who were smaller producers, also using black slaves, who took their cane to the big mill. *Lavradores* were tenants on "contract *fazendas*," and some 30 to 50 percent of their processed sugar went in payment to the *senhor de engenho*. They had in addition to pay rent on the land they had from him. The freeholders, owning their land, could send their cane to any *engenho*, and retain title to about half of it, without additional deductions.[2]

After the middle of the seventeenth century, Caribbean sugar cut heavily into the Brazilian export market. The Dutch led in this effort, especially after expulsion from their conquests in Brazil. British and French Caribbean production became important also. Not only did Caribbean sugar provide a new source, but it also drove down the price. Brazil in the latter part of the seventeenth century was nearly ousted from the European sugar market, with considerable effects on many aspects of the Brazilian economy. There was a big revival of Brazilian sugar exports in the late eighteenth century as Caribbean troubles (especially the revolt in Haiti) hurt production there and as European demand increased and prices rose. The last two factors resulted from wealth coming from European industrial and commercial growth, population increases, and wartime demand. In the late eighteenth century the sugar revival was primarily of importance in the old plantation areas, but it also led to new or expanded cane cultivation in others.

The improved Brazilian sugar exports also owed something to belated efforts to improve the industry's structure. This late boom could not be sustained, as events soon demonstrated that Brazilian sugar could not compete in the international market with other producers, including late-blooming Cuba. The fact is that Brazil had been fortunate to face little competition in sugar exports in the late sixteenth and early seventeenth centuries.[3]

Despite difficulties, the Brazilian sugar business never ceased to be important. Even in periods of general decline of exports, there were years of countertrend. Also, sugar profits often were high, which provided a cushion for bad times. Sugar exports sometimes brought 60 percent net profit. Less than 2 percent of the value of sugar at the wharf went for the pay of the few wage laborers on the estates; services (including transportation) accounted for only 5 percent of that value; supplies (for example, wood, animals) for only 3 percent. Even after buying slaves and paying government levies, much was left to the planter, although it might not always be 60 percent. In addition, there was the considerable domestic market for sugar in Brazil, which remained when the export demand was soft. All in all, the economic, social, and governmental impact of the sugar magnates was heavy in the colonial era; they were, however, far from being all of Brazil, and many of the other Brazils could hardly be touched by their activities or influence.

---

[1] See Chapter 21, Section c, on the reasons for Brazil's technological backwardness.

[2] Sugar production and processing were more complex than we have indicated here. Some estate land was used for pasture, reserve wood lots, and food crops. Another large-scale sugar product was *rapadura* (sugar in cake form), which was commonly used by the lower classes of Brazil. Some of this was made not on the great estates but in small sugar plantations (*engenho de bagué*), common in areas of minor sugarcane production. There also were *engenhocas* (small *engenhos*) that specialized in making rum and brandy, often with molasses bought from the big estates.

[3] Much fluctuation occurred in world demand, prices, and Brazilian sugar exports, as might be expected over so long a period of time. For example, in 1640–1680 the price of black slaves doubled; in 1668–1688 sugar prices at Lisbon declined 41 percent.

Tobacco was a significant item in Brazilian exports before the end of the sixteenth century, and grew modestly in value thereafter. Although its value did not approach that of sugar, it was enough to be a motive in the Dutch invasion, to lead to a Portuguese royal tobacco monopoly, and to play a key role in the African slave trade. It was grown in many areas, but Bahian production was especially notable. The crop required much care but could be grown in small quantities without dependence on a large owner's processing works. These factors sometimes favored energetic and skilled small farmers, but most of the crop was in the hands of large proprietors, using black slaves.

Tobacco became important in the African slave trade in the seventeenth century, partly because of promotion by the Dutch West India Company. In mid-century the Portuguese crown created the royal tobacco monopoly. It brought sizable revenues to the crown at once, a century before Spain created a tobacco monopoly for its American possessions. In 1710 the crown received twice as much from the tobacco monopoly as from the royal fifth on gold. Tobacco exports remained more or less level during the eighteenth century, most going to Africa in the slave trade.

Cotton appeared late in the Brazilian export lists but for a short time was very valuable. The plant grew in preconquest Brazil but the Indians there did not use it. It was long used during the Portuguese colonial period, but for rough fabrics, and for many years fiber production was small-scale and not exported. The chief reason for lack of export was that European demand was small until late in the eighteenth century, when it shot up with the development of steam power, the mechanical loom, larger population, and increased ability to pay. The first export of Brazilian cotton was in the early 1760s, but it remained small for about twenty years. The new market began to affect Maranhão in the 1770s. That captaincy had suitable climatic conditions and, as one of the poorest in Brazil, needed a new enterprise. Many of the old sugar centers had too much rain or badly distributed rainfall

for cotton culture, but the crop spread in this late colonial period to many other areas; even far interior Goiás exported some cotton. Much more came from suitable lands in Pernambuco and Bahia, which at the same time retained their sugar production in the coastal area. Most Brazilian production of cotton was large-scale, using slave labor. It did not represent a lessening of the oligarchic character of Brazilian society.

Early in the nineteenth century, cotton accounted for 20 to 25 percent of the value of Brazil's exports. Brazil benefited from the cut in United States exports during the latter's diplomatic and military duel with Britain before and during the War of 1812. After that, in the few years before the Independence of Brazil in 1822, United States cotton exports drove Brazilian from the international market. The United States had some advantages in management, financing, location, shipping; but possibly its most important advantage was technological, and the reason is a complicated part of Luso-Brazilian social history. The United States cotton boom was tied directly to Eli Whitney's cotton gin of 1792. Brazil, instead of adopting the gin, clung to an antiquated, costly, slow method of removing cotton seed; the gin scarcely was used in Brazil by the end of the colonial era. To make themselves competitive with the United States in the international cotton market at that time would have required measures beyond the sociointellectual skills and financial capacity of Brazil or Portugal or any other country of the day.

Other agricultural exports were of small value. Wild cacao gathering in the Amazon was replaced by the beginnings of plantation culture, there and elsewhere in Brazil, in the late eighteenth century. Exports of cacao were modest in the colonial era. Some rice was cultivated for export, especially in Maranhão. Coffee production was barely beginning by the end of the colonial era; as a major export crop its history belongs to independent Brazil. Indigo cultivation was tried late in the eighteenth century, just in time to be ruined by the Asian competition that also undercut Spanish American indigo.

Food-crop production was sizable in total, but small-scale, inefficient, erratic, and of relatively little interest to the planter class or the government. Most food was grown either in subsistence patches, under all sorts of conditions of ownership or nonownership of land, with little if any surplus for sale; or in one of several fashions on the great *fazendas*. On the estates, manioc might be grown between sugarcane, or maize between cotton plants. Big cattlemen left food production to settlers attached to small sections of their *fazendas*. Some small landholders and tenant farmers grew food for the market, often doing their own work, or having one or two helpers. These men did not gain great fortunes or influence in the society. Manioc flour provided the "bread of the land," although maize was important in the more southerly parts of Brazil—from Minas Gerais south in the interior, but not so important along the coast till farther south. Beans and rice also were important food crops. Wheat in any quantity was only grown in the far south, where it was a staple element of diet; and small quantities were sent to other parts of Brazil. Green vegetables and fruit were little consumed and not significant commercial items.

Food production was organized for sale wherever in Brazil there was demand: in the mine zones of the interior, along major trade routes, and in the towns. It was, however, inefficient. Small farmers could not be expected to show interest in fertilization, irrigation, or careful soil preparation when those things did not interest the *fazendeiros*. The latter were not even much interested in preventing hunger in the towns, where shortages led to price increases and to crown measures to improve supply. The various government pressures on the estates to grow more food were met with flat noncompliance, because concentration on sugar profits was nearly absolute. Much of the land around the major coastal towns was in sugar production, so food growing was pushed far away or onto exhausted or otherwise underproductive soil. The crown was not prepared to try the drastic measures that would have been required to obtain effective

planter cooperation for supply of the towns. This was the same general attitude that we have observed in Spanish America.

Stock Raising

Stock raising was important in opening much of the country to exploration, especially the northeast and the far south. Cowpunchers also served valiantly as warriors against the Indians. Stockmen created trade and communication routes, sometimes over great distances. Some of the cattle drives in Brazil were longer than those later in the West of the United States. Also, where the stockmen went, they settled, controlled lawlessness, and integrated new territory into the colony.

Cattle were raised very early on the northeast coast, to supply food and to create oxen for sugar operations. As the number of cattle grew in the middle of the sixteenth century, their competition for good land in the coastal fringe persuaded both sugar planters and stockmen of the need for opening cattle lands in the interior. In later years, the government would issue legislation pushing cattle out of the Atlantic sugar fringe. An enormous area of some 386,100 square miles of the northeast *sertão* was penetrated by the cattlemen, moving into the interior from various coastal points, pushing on decade after decade. Their battles with the Indians in the northeast went on till the end of the seventeenth century. Ranches often grew when the proprietor sent one or two *vaqueiros* (cowboys) from the original rough headquarters about a day's ride into new territory, with a few cattle, to set up a new corral.

Much of the northeast was dry land with poor pasturage. Great reaches were needed for a few cattle, yet so vast was the region that by 1700 there were more than a million cattle thinly dotting the *sertão*. Long before, the São Francisco had become known as "the river of corrals." By that time the gold rush to the interior had begun, and it was said that a man could go more than 1,500 miles from the coast through the northeast *sertão* to the gold fields of Minas Gerais without ever sleeping out of doors. Many of those stops could be made at small holdings, but the *sertão* became dominated by great cattle *fazendas*. Finally, many of the proprietors were absentees, living in the coastal towns. Most of the workers were freemen, and a cattle outfit of some size could be worked with a dozen *vaqueiros*, though additional persons would be involved in operation of the ranching complex, including tenants on some of the better-watered lands, who grew crops for use on the *fazenda*.

Several features of life on the *fazendas*, such as the small use of slaves, have suggested an element of relative democracy in Brazilian society. Most *vaqueiros* were *mamelucos* or Indians, or had some Negro blood, and were freemen. Another argument is that the life-style at the master's quarters on a northeast cattle *fazenda* was not enormously elevated above that of the *vaqueiro*, although, as we have seen, many owners lived in town. It has seemed somewhat suggestive that major *vaqueiros* were paid with a portion of the calves, with which they might start their own enterprises. They did not, however, often become large proprietors. The cattle enterprises of the northeast *sertão* did not noticeably dilute the oligarchic tone and control system of colonial society; for one thing, the population was sparse and very isolated.

Northeastern cattle not only supplied food on the hoof to towns, coastal sugar plantations, and interior mining camps, but oxen were used in huge numbers at the *engenhos*, and some horses and mules were bred. The city of Bahía (Salvador) by the end of the colonial period needed 20,000 head of cattle annually. Then, and earlier, many of these were driven long distances from remote parts of the northeastern *sertão*, arriving scrawny and fatless at the end of the journey. Hides had a good market from early times and were exported from northeastern ports. A few areas produced significant quantities of dried salt beef. Most aspects of the northeastern cattle business were conducted at a simple technological level suited to the harsh environment. The enormous unfenced range with thin pasturage

invited cattle to go wild, and great efforts were made to keep them under control by corralling and taming at an early age. Supplemental feed was not to be thought of. The animals were not fit for dairy production and none was undertaken. They were too scrawny for tallow rendering. But the cattle products of the *sertão* played an important historic role and enjoyed a good market almost to the end of the colonial era, when they were sadly damaged by a particularly vicious series of the droughts to which the northeast was subject. At the same time the industry was facing growing competition from the much better cattle lands of the far south.

Another cattle area developed much later than that of the northeast in southern Minas Gerais in response to the great flow of population to the mines after the 1690s. The cattle were better because of finer pasture in a well-watered land, the use of supplemental bran-mash feeding, and wooden fencing from much better forests than in the scrubby northeast. Cheese was produced and sent as far as Rio de Janeiro. Swine for meat and sheep for wool were raised in the area, unlike the northeast. Another difference was that the cattle business in Minas depended on slave labor, partly because more specialized tasks made the investment sounder.

The great grassland of southern Brazil also supported a cattle industry. In the northern parts, cattle were carried from the port of São Vicente up into the highlands. The natural increase was rapid. Cattle were driven to the towns, including Rio de Janeiro at a considerable distance. Cattlemen very slowly made their way to the south, delayed by warfare with Indians and Spanish Jesuits. Well into the eighteenth century Rio Grande do Sul, at the southern extreme of present Brazil, became a land of great cattle *estancias* (as they were called there and in Argentina, rather than *fazendas*). The southern cowboy likewise was called *gaúcho*, not *vaqueiro*, and his clothes and work tools resembled those of the Pampas of the Spanish Plata area. Many of the cattle holdings of the far south were granted to veterans of the Indian and Spanish wars, to consolidate the Portuguese hold in the area. Some of them were enormous, and ownership became highly concentrated. For many years range products were cut off from the rest of Brazil by distance, but in 1733 the great overland route to Sorocaba was opened, and traffic grew, fed by demand at the mines to the north. Breeding of mules in the south for use in the north became lucrative. The annual stock fair at Sorocaba became a major affair. Then late in the eighteenth century Rio Grande do Sul benefited, as the Spanish Plata cattlemen did, by the spurting world demand for salt beef, *charque*, the first of which was shipped from Rio Grande do Sul about 1780. By 1793 it shipped 13,000 *arrobas*; about 1800 it sent out some 600,000, and what had been a remote, thinly populated, disputed frontier was on its way to becoming one of the most important areas of Brazil. Other livestock products of the far south were horses, cattle hides, and tallow. The differences in physical resources and historical development of the cattle industry in the far south from the industry in other parts of Brazil are illustrative of the enormous variety of the colony's natural and cultural environments. In the colonial period, as now, there were many Brazils.

Mining

The long search for gold by the Paulista *bandeirantes* finally, in the 1690s, led to the rich fields of Minas Gerais, some two hundred miles from the Atlantic. Beginning in 1695, gold production rose to an impressive peak in 1760, then tailed off rapidly. In the eighteenth century Brazil produced some 1,000 tons of gold, possibly 80 percent of world production during the period.[4] The gold was almost all taken by washing alluvial deposits, often in the fumbling manner of the equally inexperienced Spaniards in early

Española. This bonanza was especially opportune for Brazil and Portugal because of the already noted decline in sugar exports.

The gold (and later diamond) finds stimulated a remarkable surge of population from the coast to the interior, creating permanent settlements and markets and improving communications and transportation. It stimulated agricultural and pastoral output and handicrafts to serve the new population. In fact, change far outstripped government and private ability to adjust. A contemporary declared that in the mining areas commodity prices rose to twenty-five to fifty times normal. Men with gold would bid almost anything for scarce food or slaves. Some years passed before the situation began to stabilize, with local production and new mule tracks from Bahia and Rio de Janeiro bringing cattle from the northeast *sertão*, slaves, and manufactured goods.

Smuggling, tax evasion, and crimes of violence were rampant. Paulistas thought they owned the mineral area, and resented the outsiders—Brazilian and Portuguese—who swarmed into the interior and sometimes jumped Paulista claims. The Paulistas denigrated the newcomers as *emboabas*. The two groups fought a small War of the Emboabas in 1708–1709, with the Paulistas losing. Then the royal government established control in the area. Dissatisfaction remained, however, and in 1720 took the form of short-lived rebellion against a tax measure. Despite these troubles, the mining area developed, in recognition of which the government erected the captaincy of São Paulo and Minas Gerais in 1710, and in 1720 made the latter a separate captaincy. Minas Gerais was virtually unpopulated at the beginning of the gold rush. In fifteen years it had about 30,000 inhabitants; by 1800 some 500,000. Although gold production was much reduced by 1800, Minas Gerais had been transformed and was ready to play a great role in the life of independent Brazil. The gold search led farther west to Goiás, where strikes were made in 1725. It became a captaincy in 1744. Mato Grosso, also in the heart of the continent, yielded gold in 1718 and became a captaincy in 1748.

---

[4] Estimates of total production vary, as do estimates of the percentage of contraband and the money value of the gold. One estimate of the total value is some £130 million, which suggests a present-day purchasing-power value of several billion dollars.

The mines did not enrich Luso-Brazilians as much as they hoped. The flight from the coast had some unhappy economic consequences there for a time, with shortages of labor, capital, and management. The gold flow also contributed to general inflation in the Portuguese world. Crown authorities found collecting the royal fifth on gold production difficult. Much ingenuity was expended in profitable evasion. Gold was smuggled out of Minas Gerais and then out of Brazil. Notoriety has accrued to the activities of priests who carried illicit gold in hollow images of saints, but they could have accounted for but a fraction of the smuggling. The biggest drain was not gold smuggling, however, but payments to redress the Luso-Brazilian imbalance on the international market. Since the British were the biggest suppliers of Portugal and Brazil, the largest flow of gold went to them.

Diamonds were found in Minas Gerais in the late 1720s. Later, other fields were located in São Paulo, Goiás, and Bahia. The government tightly restricted access to, and activity in, the diamond areas. It also controlled marketing to sustain prices. The crown took over the diamond mines in 1771. Smuggling continued despite all precautions, some of them brutal. Production of diamonds in the colonial period came to some 3 million carats, representing a present-day purchasing power of several hundred million dollars.

Commerce and Mercantilism

Mercantilist restriction took a number of forms, but the effort to channel commerce was the most prominent. Brazil's production and overseas traffic were meant to enrich Portugal and especially the royal fisc, although some attention was paid to Brazilian needs. In the early years, especially before the forced union with Spain in 1580, trade policy was relatively unrestrictive, but the trade was small most of that time. Until 1591 foreign trade and ships properly cleared from Portuguese ports could go to Brazil and return Brazilian commodities to foreign ports if a return stop was made in Lisbon for another clearance. Legislation of 1591 and 1606 and other decrees tried to confine Brazilian trade to Portugal. The 1591 ban on foreign shipping in Brazilian ports was not abolished until 1808.

The Portuguese used annual convoys in 1649–1765,[5] with naval escort, partly to promote monopoly, but they were not very effective. Portuguese maritime resources were unequal to the task, and Luso-Brazilian and foreign commercial elements usually were not interested in cooperating with the convoy rules or the notion of confining traffic to the fleets. In any event, the convoys carried foreign goods that Portugal could not produce. Furthermore, wartime conditions required relaxations. Britain by treaty in 1654 received the right to send ships to Brazil provided they called at Portuguese ports on the outward and return voyages. Several treaties in the mid-seventeenth and early eighteenth centuries permitted a few Dutch and British merchants to reside in Brazil. The Portuguese crown disliked the concession, and it was inoperative by 1730. Actually, the concession did not much matter, since the trade did not depend on Britons resident in Brazil. British merchants at Lisbon and Oporto were allowed to operate merchant houses under their own names, unlike the situation in Sevilla and Cádiz, where they could only act through Spanish firms. The British firms in Portugal traded with Brazil via Portuguese firms operating there.

Portugal was a long way from achieving a trade monopoly. Contraband flourished. The reasons were much as in Spanish America: Portugal had insufficient capital, manufactures, or markets to control the Brazilian traffic. The long coastline made close patrolling impossible. But the main problem was that Portuguese officials and Brazilian buyers in large numbers disobeyed the regulations. Smuggling increased as time went on, and was very great in the eighteenth century, partly because of increase in Brazilian population

---

[5] Armed convoys shepherded merchant vessels to Brazil sporadically before the fleets were established, even in the sixteenth century.

and ability to pay, partly from production of gold and diamonds. It was encouraged by the high prices of many legally imported goods, which paid all the required government imposts and official freight charges. Statistics based on Brazilian complaints show cases where far more than half the value of legal goods coming in or going out went for such charges. The poor pay of customs officers and others encouraged bribery to evade the regulations.

Much contraband went to Brazil via Lisbon, for example, as hidden or mislabeled goods. In the coastal cities of Brazil, wholesale merchants and tradesmen dealt in illegal goods with the connivance of civil and military officers. Royal warships and private vessels chartered by the crown were exempt from search, which encouraged their personnel to smuggle. The trade between Asia and Brazil was subject to many restrictions and prohibitions, but they were evaded. Ships outward or homeward bound between Lisbon and India would stop in Brazil on trumped-up excuses of emergency repairs or sickness. The prices of illicit Oriental goods in Brazil often were as much as 40 percent under those imported by the official route through Lisbon. This traffic was sizable by the eighteenth century, because well-to-do Brazilians were able and anxious to buy Oriental luxury goods. The African trade also was riddled with contraband. Tobacco and gold went to posts in Africa, where they were exchanged for slaves and Asian and North European goods.

The crown did what it could to try to control this contraband. Sometimes it had the help of wholesale merchants in Brazil who suffered saturated markets or unmatchable competition. Informers were not very effective, because they were afraid to carry tales about prominent Brazilians or about crown officials conniving in the evasions. In addition, Brazilians generally detested such informers, much as Britons and British Americans did in certain periods of their history. In the interior, customs posts (*registros*) in the great hinterland watched for smugglers at river crossings, mountain passes, and other likely places. But they were few and the land was large; the posts were known and could be evaded. In addition, these puny stations in the wilderness could not attract personnel or offer pay that would stand up to bribery or coercion.

The amount of gold that made its way from Brazil to Britain is a telling measure of the hollowness of restrictive legislation and activity. British merchants profited not only because they had the bulk of the foreign trade with Portugal and Brazil via Lisbon; but because British ships also carried other foreign goods, thus earning carrier charges and commission or broker fees. This Luso-Brazilian trade of Britain was the easier for Portugal to bear in that Portugal was concerned for its own market in Britain, especially for wine. Portuguese wine enjoyed a tariff preference over French wines in Britain, especially by the Treaty of Methuen (1703), which also gave British woollens preference in the Portuguese realms.

An Englishman stated in 1732, "We are at least 2,000 English in Lisbon, and we very often have a hundred sail of English ships in this river." One estimate is that the annual flow of Luso-Brazilian gold into Britain during the first half of the eighteenth century was some £1–2 million, at a time when the annual production of the Brazilian mines was possibly £3–4 million. Of course, some gold came from Portugal's Asian and African sources, and some went to Britain only for reexport to other European centers. Probably, however, much of the gold going to Britain came from Brazil. Coins struck in mints at Bahia, Rio de Janeiro, and Ouro Prêto in Minas Gerais—and in Portugal—circulated widely in the West, including English-speaking North America.

Another destination for contraband from Brazil was Spanish America, though the value was less than the overseas illicit trade. Some of the smuggling to Spanish America received encouragement from the Portuguese crown. The contraband in slaves and other commodities from Brazil into the Plata area has been noted. Brazil received from Spanish areas silver from Upper Peru and in the late colonial era a flow of livestock, hides, and mules from the Plata area to Rio Grande do Sul. There was a small flow of contraband via the Amazon with Spanish Peru and Quito and a small late colonial flow between Mato Grosso and Upper Peru.

Another form of Portuguese restriction was on Brazilian manufacturing. Regulations aimed to keep colonial effort focused on production of raw materials and to prevent competition with goods shipped from Portugal. Vine culture was prohibited to protect the market for Portuguese wines. A variety of measures aimed at controlling or prohibiting crafts. Some fabrication, however, was encouraged: many types of crafts, shipbuilding, and the various aspects of sugar processing among them. The decreed barriers and expressed fears of competition reached a peak in 1785, although some manufacturing in Brazil still was permitted. Portuguese-manufactured exports to Brazil did increase some thereafter, but so did manufactures from other European countries, when wartime conditions allowed. English trade was usually permitted. Such restrictions on Brazilian fabrication probably had less effect on production than did problems of technology, entrepreneurship, managerial ability, capital, labor costs and skills, and marketing.

Other measures were taken to promote monopoly, often in the interest of the crown and Portugal. The crown decreed at different times its control of brazilwood, slavery, diamonds, tobacco, salt, and other commodities. Monopolistic trading companies were tried, and as in the case of Spanish America did not duplicate the success of French, British, and Dutch companies. Neither Portuguese nor Brazilians generally liked the companies. The *Companhia do Brasil* (1649–1721) did at least help defeat the Dutch in Brazil. The *Companhia Geral do Grão Pará e Maranhão* (1775–1778) helped develop the northern area that was short of population and investment capital.

Decreed—and sometimes enforced—restrictions did irritate Brazilians. Occasionally, their protests came in anticipation of damage—that is, they were sensitive to the issue. Over the years,

they built up for Portuguese economic policy a distaste which contained some exaggeration. Brazilian insistence on Indian slavery, despite crown restrictions, was deeply felt and had largely an economic basis. "Expulsion" of Jesuit protectors of Indians by *senados da câmara* showed a violent interest in the matter. In 1684 Manuel Beckman, a big landowner, headed a revolt aimed partly against Indian policy. Taxes also occasioned much protest. Competition between towns or areas or between Brazilians and *reinóis* also led to clashes that sometimes had some basis in economic policy. A prime source of conflict was the heavy Portuguese predominance in wholesale commerce. The largely European merchant monopolists charged high prices and were creditors of the Brazilian planter class. In the northeast, such conflicts of interest sometimes focused on Olinda, center of an agricultural elite, and nearby Recife, a commercial center, dominated by Portuguese. In 1710 the crown freed Recife from the governmental control of Olinda by making it a city, whereupon the agricultural elite took Recife by force of arms. This provoked the War of the Mascates (an unflattering term meaning peddler) in 1711. Although this was quickly settled by the government, Brazilian-Portuguese tension, partly over economic matters, continued. The tension did not, however, become crippling or highly dangerous.[6]

The Portuguese commercial predominance was in the later colonial era diluted by Brazilian participation as happened in Spanish America. Brazilian planters developed connections with commercial activity, and Portuguese merchants developed connections with the planter class. These connections were social (including matrimonial), economic, and governmental (especially in local affairs, including the militia). The Brazilian planter class came to exercise considerable influence on Portuguese economic policy and execution of law. The increasing intercon-

---

[6] See Chapters 16 and 22 for more on divisions in Brazil and the lack of much sentiment for Independence until just before the final crisis of 1822.

nections of Brazilian planters with merchants (both Brazilian and Portuguese) was one of the more important developments of the late colonial era.[7]

Portuguese trade with Brazil was more complex than we can detail here. It was affected by fluctuations in the prices of Portuguese olive oil and salt and by Portuguese currency debasements, as well as by factors noted in connection with the movements in demand and prices for Brazilian sugar and cotton and by the gold and diamond bonanza of the eighteenth century. But these complexities cannot obscure the fact that Brazilian trade depended heavily on sugar. The planters of Bahia wrote the crown in 1662, "Who says Brazil says sugar and more sugar."

Other Economic Activities

Export-oriented agriculture, commerce, gold and diamond mining, and stock raising enjoyed the socioeconomic support and attention of the Luso-Brazilian elite and government. Other economic activities were tolerated or mildly or sporadically encouraged. Their development sometimes was dwarfed, however, by weak support in the society: insufficient incentive to the individual, poor support from the elite, occasional interference by government to inhibit growth.

Many of the specialized artisan and service functions necessarily were less well developed in Portuguese than in Spanish America, because the population was less and towns fewer and smaller, and sometimes because the elite lacked interest. Guild organization was also weaker in Brazil, partly because of the smaller quantity of work, partly because of the wide use of slaves in the crafts which stunted the apprenticeship system. Free artisans owned some slaves to work in their shops. Some slaves in artisan work were *escravos de serviço*, hired out by their owners. The bulk of the free artisans in towns were mulattoes. Much craftsmanship occurred outside

the towns—on sugar and cattle *fazendas*, in villages, and in such specialized places as mule-train stops, country inns and supply points, shipyards, timber camps, fishing ports and camps, trading posts, missions, and fairs. There were some itinerant craftsmen.

Not all the colonial crafts will be detailed;[8] they have been sufficiently covered for Spanish America. Brazil's needs were much like the latter's, on a smaller scale. It had the same large demand for leather articles in "the age of leather," as a Brazilian historian called it. Much pottery and rush or basket work was needed for daily use. Fabrication of tile, brick, ceramics, glass, and the activity of the building trades were less developed than in Spanish America, although some fine building was done late in the colonial era. Some ironwork was done, notably in Minas Gerais, using local ores. Under the conditions of the colonial era, it could not have developed much more. Brazilians made shoes for draft animals, wheel rims, tools, hinges, decorative ironwork, and other items. Portugal interfered in order to protect the profits of merchants selling foreign ironware to Brazilians. At the end of the eighteenth century, this government attitude toward ironwork changed, and the industry was stimulated in a small way, but—as with the industry in many countries—found it difficult to stand up to British competition. A similar fate befell textile making. Small factories were created in the eighteenth century in Rio de Janeiro and Minas Gerais, but they aroused Portuguese fears, and a decree of 1785 killed most production, except sacking and rough cottons for slaves. Although this government restriction hurt production, how much could have been done to resist British textile imports is not clear. Portugal did not want to resist, and a few years later independent Brazil also found it inexpedient, economically and politically, to do so. The decree

---

[7] See Chapter 16, Section e, and Chapter 21.

[8] Additional Brazilian products included leather goods, soap, felt hats from sheep's wool, horse blankets, religious objects, gourd vessels, rope, and many others.

was revoked in 1808, but the competition of British textiles inhibited resuscitation of the Brazilian factories.

Extractive activities occupied some Brazilians, sometimes only sporadically. No single extractive activity was the source of large income. Forest products were gathered, especially in the Amazon. Wild *mate* was collected in southern Brazil, and some exported to Spanish Paraguay and the lower Plata provinces, where it was popular. Few Brazilians used *mate* tea. Some forest products entered trade, even overseas traffic, by chains of activity from gatherer to trader to shipper. Products of the forest included clove bark, cinnamon, Brazil nuts, sarsaparilla, wild cacao, turtles and their eggs. Wild animals were killed for the market. Timber was cut and sold for various uses, but it was subject to royal restrictions, as was salt production. Whaling off the Brazilian coast brought profits for a few years in the second half of the eighteenth century. It soon was mortally damaged by the arrival of British and English-American or United States whalers, who took the whales before they reached Brazilian waters. Brazilian whaling disappeared early in the nineteenth century, another victim of superior foreign enterprise and organization.

Little needs to be added to what has been said about service functions, credit, and internal commerce. Slaves took the place of the numerous free (but highly dependent) servants of most of Spanish America. Lawyers, physicians, and architects or master builders had limited scope for activity. Credit was even more limited than in Spanish America. Merchants (usually Portuguese) lent money to planters, as in Spanish America; but the much poorer Brazilian church could not play the role in lending that it did in the Spanish realms. Currency in circulation was limited, being exported to cover charges abroad. Much exchange was on a barter basis, since few people ever saw more than pitifully small amounts of currency. Many public levies and private dues were paid in kind. Domestic commerce (aside from the movements of export and import goods) was small-scale in most places. Food and other household items were the chief commodities exchanged. Trade in stock and animal products was large.

Transportation was a major constraint on the economy. Really epic feats were accomplished, but they took much time, the costs were high, and carrying capacity often was quite limited. The transportation business did stimulate food production and marketing at key points and the sale of lodgings, fuel, strong drink, and other commodities and services.

Although more use could be made of rivers than in Spanish America, most river traffic was in economically peripheral areas, especially Amazonia and the west of São Paulo, Goiás, and Mato Grosso. It was important to the small populations of those areas, and helped in the opening of Brazil and the consolidation of Portuguese control. Some dugout canoes were fifty feet long and could carry about five tons. They were propelled by poles or paddles, occasionally sails. Canoe freightage sometimes was 50 percent cheaper than mule carriage. It has been noted that the Paulista *bandeiras* often followed but did not travel on the rivers. Regular river traffic in the south central interior did not begin until the 1720s, and was the result of the opening of the west by gold hunters. One western canoe route led into the Paraná and Paraguay river systems and Spanish territory. Supplies for the gold fields of Mato Grosso went by the monsoon canoes. The "cycle of monsoons" died gradually in the early nineteenth century as the gold deposits petered out. In the most populous parts of Brazil the rivers were of limited use for transportation.

Most internal transport thus was by land. There was porter traffic, occasionally significant, but generally minor. Black porters were important in the early years of the gold rush, but most of their work was soon taken over by pack animals. Wheeled traffic was small except in a few localized cases. Difficult topography and lack of roads made vehicles impractical. Roads were really trails, and little work was done on them.

They often were very narrow, and in any case the mountain gradients were selected without thought for wheeled traffic. The first short carriage roads were built in the nineteenth century at the end of the colonial era. A few ox carts were used, mainly in the far southern plains. Sometimes persons of wealth were carried in hammocks or chairs slung on poles between mules.

Pack animals carried the bulk of the freight, horses in the north and mules in the center and south, with mules much more important, especially in the eighteenth century. The *tropeiro* was the owner of a string of pack mules, general supervisor of operations, and a merchant or trader, wealthy enough to lead caravans on horse-

back. He hired *arrieiros* or used slaves to drive and tend the animals and their loads. The mule trains became quite a large business in the eighteenth century, and many enterprises to serve them dotted the trails. As in Spanish America, the muleteers were a notably rough and thirsty lot.

The colonial economy of Brazil was formed by the opportunities offered in the Atlantic trading community and by a system of privilege that depended heavily on government support of great estates and poorly paid—often slave—labor. Both the privilege and the dependence on overseas markets would continue to dominate the new nation after 1822.

16 Brazil: Social Developments and Late Colonial Change

The upper class in Portuguese America enjoyed less town life and fewer cultural amenities than that of Spanish America. The effect was minor, however, because few of the upper class in either area were connoisseurs of art, music, literature, or science. Brazilian upper-class life did become somewhat more sophisticated in the eighteenth century, though still lacking the printing presses and universities that came early to Spanish America. Such cultural resources were not needed in Brazil in the eighteenth century to produce rising complaint against economic regulation by Portugal. That complaint was mildly spurred by a small stream of Brazilian "nativism" or nascent nationalism. Nativism and economic grievance were both bolstered and diversified by a continuing growth of regionalism, which by 1800 had created a Brazil of strong provincial interests and jealousies.

a. The Church and Religion

Although the church played about the same role as in Spanish America, in Brazil it was weaker and simpler, partly because it was poorer, partly because the church was less vigorous in Portugal than in Spain, so that missionary zeal and discipline and teaching were laxer in the Portuguese world. That was apparent in some-

what more toleration of Jews and in relative lack of interest in the Inquisition. Still, an upper-class man in the seventeenth or eighteenth century who married a woman of Jewish descent was barred, as were their descendants, from the priesthood or the imperial bureaucracy unless he obtained an exemption. This rule was not fully enforced, but it had some effect.[1]

Conventual houses conspicuously played a lesser role than in Spanish America in administration, landholding, money lending, and Indian indoctrination, protection, and government. One result was that the struggle between regular and secular clergy was less prominent than in Spanish America. The most often cited evidence of the lesser rigor of the Luso-Brazilian church is that church-state conflict was less important after Independence than it was in the Spanish American republics. That suggests more attachment to the church and its positions in Spanish than in Portuguese America.

None of this meant that Brazil was less Christian than Spanish America. Union of church and state was accepted by all in the Portuguese

---

[1] The same theoretical penalty attached to upper-class marriage with colored persons. Candidates for the priesthood were supposed to prove that their parents and grandparents were Old Christian, of "clean blood," free of Jewish, Muslim, or heretic taint.

realms. Royal patronage was firmly sustained. The number of regular clergy did grow slowly, together with Jesuit *aldeias* or villages of Indians in the great wilderness, and eventually sizable conventual houses of several orders in the towns. The episcopal organization of the secular church was gradually elaborated. An independent bishopric was set up in the mid-sixteenth century. In 1676 a papal bull made the bishop of Bahia the archbishop of Brazil, although for long the bishops of Pará and Maranhão in the north remained subject to the church in Lisbon. By the early eighteenth century, there were six episcopal dioceses in Brazil, subject to the archbishop at Bahia.

The elite at least attended to the formal side of Roman Catholicism. The towns held many ritual celebrations and processions. Public documents and functionaries constantly asserted the Catholicism of the realm. Money and labor were forthcoming for religious edifices. Bahia's churches and convents impressed many travelers in the eighteenth century. Some of the wealth of late colonial Minas Gerais was poured into religious buildings. The resident priests on the great *fazendas* of the sugar zones served religious needs, instructed the young, and inculcated obedience in the managerial staff and the manual workers. They apparently were undemanding pastors, and sometimes fathered children by slave or other lower-class women. It sometimes is asserted that the faith had less influence among the Brazilian than the Spanish American upper class, but that cannot be measured. Against the notion of significant religious difference between Portuguese and Spanish American elites, it may be asserted that there is little to choose between them with regard to forced Indian labor, black slavery, sexual permissiveness for upper-class men, and lack of brotherhood between elite and proletariat. Such similarities on important questions to which Christianity sometimes addressed itself render trivial the differences in formal worship and the other activity of the churches.

If the church made much less than perfect Christians of the elite, it did even less well with Indians, black slaves, and free men of color. The heroic efforts of the handful of Jesuits in Brazil among the primitive Indians were of no more permanent importance than those of frontier missionaries in Spanish America. The Jesuits learned Tupí-Guaraní and put it down in written form. This and their other efforts they carried out with devout dedication, but the Jesuit mission structure proved evanescent because of insistent slave raiding and because of the difficulty of permanently weaning the Indians from their own beliefs and social habits.

There was a greater potential opportunity among blacks and mulattoes, slave and free, but the task was gigantic and the church's resources limited. In any event, the elite of society would not have permitted the expenditure or the social risk required for thorough Christianization of the blacks, nor would the metropolitan government have tried to force it in the face of colonial objection. Such questions never arose in acute form. Not only were the clergy too few, but their dedication to the lower class was less than overwhelming. There was insistence on large marriage fees, for example, that was one minor factor contributing to the huge number of lower-class sexual partnerships that were irregular from the church's point of view. Some clerics were more interested in the lower classes for commercial than for spiritual reasons.

The most obvious and suggestive aspect of black religion was its syncretism—various combinations of pagan (especially African) religious beliefs and practices with Christian. This remains true in Brazil to the present. It had the effect, of course, of contributing to the gulf between blacks and whites, because the white elite regarded its formal adherence to the rites of the church as one of the marks of its superiority. Such discrimination also was practiced in the organization of the lay brotherhoods (*irmandades*), usually on a racial basis.[2] These were charitable and pious groups which did good

---

[2] The same strictures applied to regular as to secular clergy.

works: built chapels and hospices and put on celebrations. By the eighteenth century some had considerable wealth, partly from the bequests of members. The brotherhood of the Holy House of Mercy (*Santa Casa de Misericordia*) at Bahia cared for the needy and maintained hospitals.

Brazil, like Spanish America, was a Christian society. The elite sincerely believed it was. The lower class gradually was brought somewhat nearer to Catholicism. Church ideals and activity permeated life, sometimes weakly, sometimes strongly. However much the clergy found their mission in Brazil difficult, there is much evidence of respect for them in both upper and lower class. Brazilians at different times loved and ignored the church.

b. Family and Daily Life

The lower classes lived short and brutal lives as in much of the world. Brazil was unusual in the number that were slaves and in the amount of miscegenation that occurred. Not unusual, however, was the amount of lower-class disorder. It surely was not due chiefly to the fact that criminals (*degregados*) were sent from Portugal. They were a minority, some were only minor miscreants, and no one any longer believes that they left bad "seed" in their descendants. A few came from upper-class Portuguese families, but most were of less eminent origin. Some of the latter made their way into the elite in America, but more did not. Rather than looking for "naturally" turbulent stocks, it seems more reasonable to suppose that the violence of life in Brazil was a reflection of social conditions there. Family life and income were unsatisfactory. The coastal towns developed bad reputations for tropical heat and for the recurrence of several types of dangerous "fevers." Where life was cheap, many men were despised, lower-class life was a compound of discomfort and despair, and police power was inefficient, violence was bound to flourish. Brawling and homicide were certainly common, as were whoring and drunkenness.

There has been some exaggeration of the uniquely patriarchal character of the family life of the Brazilian elite. It needs to be remembered that in those centuries the powers of fathers and husbands were great in many lands. A Brazilian historian painted upper-class family life as "taciturn father, obedient wife, cowed children." There certainly were variations on this formula, however, and it was contradicted by another traditional belief—that upper-class boys were in many ways not severely restricted. Upper-class women in Brazil were more secluded than in Spanish America; in fact, Spanish Americans joked about the efforts of Brazilian husbands to keep their wives and daughters isolated. By proverb a virtuous woman left home three times: to be christened, wed, and buried. Their life was not as bad as that; they got out to mass and other religious celebrations. Some of this protectiveness was reflected in the numbers of girls put into convents in Brazil and Portugal. No one knows how much that "aggravated," as charged, the problems of bachelor immigrants in the gold fields in the eighteenth century.

There were fewer well-educated women in Brazil than in Spanish America, because in the latter more accompanied husbands taking up office in America and because urban social life was better developed in Spanish America. Upper-class Brazilians had windows on the world from the upper-floor balconies of their town houses. Living quarters for the family were high in the two- or three-story structures to get the tropical breezes. The women certainly were not very busy with household duties, since the children and everything else were taken care of by slaves. There were exceptional town houses with sixty slaves, but that large a staff could only be meant for show, although the inefficiency of slaves was notorious. From their balconies, the ladies could talk with friends and survey the life of the town, including the richly dressed *mulata* concubines and whores so much patronized by their husbands.

Bahia (Salvador) and Rio de Janeiro had spectacular sites on great bays with handsome and fragrant tropical foliage and hills with striking

Colonial Brazil

Small sugar mill just after Independence. From the late sixteenth century on, the sugar export industry was the mainstay of Brazil. Similar small mills, usually turned by oxen or mules, were common throughout Portuguese and Spanish America. *Library of Congress*

Litter borne by black slaves in Brazil, just about the time of Independence. All over Spanish as well as Portuguese America, upper-class people were carried by men or animals in litters, sedan chairs, and hammocks. A difficult terrain and lack of roads made wheeled traffic rare. *Library of Congress*

A government official goes out with his family. *Library of Congress*

Dom João VI, King of Portugal and
Brazil during the last years of the
colonial period.

A runaway slave is brought in from the back
country of Brazil.

Black slaves moving cargo on a wheeled handcart.
Library of Congress

Rio de Janeiro at the time of Independence.

locations for buildings and views over the sea. Bahia's business district lay on a strip of lowland by the harbor. The upper town on the heights was badly connected with the lower, by steep and narrow streets, chiefly traversed by porters and pack animals or by the sedan chairs of the upper class. It was no place for wheeled vehicles. The town finally had a windlass to crank up heavy loads. The upper town held the public buildings and the big houses of the rich. Rio de Janeiro was also on a narrow shore, dotted with hills and backed by mountains. At the shore was a great square, the Praça do Palacio, on which stood the viceregal palace. Most of the streets were narrow and winding in Brazilian towns, which did not adopt the rectilinear plan so distinctive of Spanish America.

It is argued that elite family life was especially formed by rural residence in the great house of the *fazenda*, with its complex relationships in an isolated setting. Even in the late colonial period, there were complaints by officials that the Brazilian upper class was inconveniently dispersed. Rural residence did increase an estate owner's interest in and opportunity to dominate local affairs in detail through the *senados da câmara* and the militia. But the effects of residence patterns of *fazendeiros*, as compared with Spanish American *hacendados*, on upper-class people is not clear, and they became more concentrated in towns with the passage of time, either as permanent residents or as long-term visitors to their town houses. They were prominent in the affairs of the coastal cities. Whether family ties among the elite were stronger in Brazil than in Spanish America is not certain. Family was important to the oligarchy because proper origins were a mark of upper-class position in both Iberian areas. In sum, rural life probably had little effect on oligarchic presumption and self-confidence as compared with the equally class-conscious and dictatorial town-oriented *hacendados* of Spanish America. The *fazendeiros* certainly were nearly all-powerful where their hold was strong. Free workers or tenants were highly dependent on the decisions and whims of the *fazendeiro*. Some of the sharecroppers (*obrigados*) were modestly more independent. In addition to economic, judicial, and physical power over his dependents, the patriarch also developed ties as a sponsor, patron and protector, as *padrinho* (godfather), and as *compadre* (coparent and sponsor of a child at baptism), thus establishing relations between members of the older generation and the new.

Two of the most prevalent conditions in Brazil were indolence and vagrancy, usually emphasized by colonial commentators in connection with the lower class, but sometimes noted of the elite as well. Such conditions were likely to exist in a society of servile and forced labor, small incentives to work, extreme social division and degradation, elite monopoly of property and governing power, and lack of much police or moral discipline. Scholars often ascribe these conditions also to the attitudes toward manual labor of the Indian, Portuguese, and African cultures. It must be agreed that traditional attitudes contributed to the lack of a strong ethic of work. Lack of incentive, however, must have been at least equally important. In Brazilian society, the exceptional energy of poor European immigrants was notorious among the local elite—as in Spanish America—and a source of resentment. In any event, officials and social critics in Portuguese America were as partial as their counterparts in Spanish America to condemnations of the "indolence" of the population, both common people and the upper class. What was missing, of course, was the perception that lethargy and vagrancy might have been reduced by a change in socioeconomic conditions.

c. Education and Intellectual Activity

Education and intellectual life were less developed in Portuguese than in Spanish America, largely the result of lesser wealth and population. Money, town life, and church teachers and investigators were in short supply compared with

Spanish America. Furthermore, the scholarly tradition of Portugal was weaker than that of Spain, so less intellectual stimulation could go from metropolis to colony through personnel, publications, or institutions. Many parts of Brazil long displayed the characteristics of a "frontier": rough, crude, violent, sometimes highly energetic, but not cultured. Most striking, possibly, was the lack of Brazilian universities or printing presses until the nineteenth century.[3] Thus, nothing existed like the rather critical Spanish American periodicals of the late colonial era or the infusion of new ideas in universities from Córdoba and Chuquisaca to Guatemala and Mexico.

Primary and secondary instruction was confined mostly to a small segment of the elite, although a few poor boys of promise were subsidized. The crown in 1721 urged local authorities in Minas Gerais to found a school in each town, and some made a modest effort. By the early nineteenth century there were four public primary schools in Rio de Janeiro, so small and weak that they scarcely affected the general state of illiteracy. The notable Jesuit educational effort was mostly confined to secondary schools, preparing men for church careers or for passage to the University of Coimbra in Portugal, for either ecclesiastical or civil studies. There was a school of military engineering at Bahia. By the early nineteenth century there were three secondary schools at Rio de Janeiro and some classes offered by government in a few classical subjects. This poor array of institutions was for boys, and few girls received more than rudimentary instruction.

Intellectual and esthetic activity outside the schools was also thinner than in Spanish America. Book collections of any size were rare in colonial Brazil, both symptom and cause of small attention to the life of the mind. The Jesuit college (secondary school and seminary) at Bahia

was unusual in having a library of 3,000 volumes at the end of the seventeenth century. Intellectual activity did increase somewhat in the eighteenth century when specialized investigatory and discussion groups were set up. For the first time in two and a half centuries intellectual questions more than faintly ruffled the surface of Brazilian upper-class life.[4]

Esthetic and artistic activity also developed modestly, especially in the eighteenth century. Even before then, popular "theatricals" were common, often in connection with religious activity. The first secular theater was set up at Bahia early in the eighteenth century but only operated a few years. Churches and other edifices were decorated by Portuguese and colonial sculptors, wood-carvers, painters, and smiths. Although critics differ sharply as to the quality of this work, it certainly represented a growing desire for and capacity to create pleasing effects and even beauty. A distinguished sculptor in Minas Gerais was the mulatto Francisco Antonio Lisbôa (died 1814), known as the Aleijadinho (the Little Cripple). In these and other ways, the increasingly town-oriented elite of Brazil was in 1800 far from the crude beginnings of the colony.

d. Provincial Differentiation

Another notable change that became more marked with time was provincial or regional differentiation. Some was based on natural differences of climate, topography, soils, vegetation, and subsurface resources. Then, as people made decisions about economic activity, those choices helped create diversity of institutions and attitudes. The regions developed differences of prosperity, habit, and outlook, aggravated by rivalries and disputes over crown policy and for government favor. Differentiation was often promoted by feeble communications between regions. Although the crown tried to centralize administration and fostered a common reverence for Portu-

---

[3] There was a press briefly at Recife in the early eighteenth century, but it was suppressed; the same fate befell a press set up at Rio de Janeiro some years later.

[4] See Section e of this chapter.

guese authority, it did not promote a sense of oneness or unity among the areas of Brazil—any more than Spain did in its American empire. All this created regional diversity that posed problems for the imperial administration and would present to independent Brazil its paramount task —preventing fragmentation along such lines of regional difference and interest.

The regions were, roughly, Amazonia, the northeast *sertão*, the sugar coast, the mining area of Minas Gerais, the territory of the Paulistas, the far west, and the far south.[5] But we are speaking not merely of natural regions but of groups of peoples, whose ideas were not uniform even within regions and which changed with time, happenstance, and opportunity. Nor did they always act in accordance with differences in resources or economic specialization. Usually, in fact, the most profound divisions existed not between regions, but between the small elite and the rest of the populace, between white and nonwhite, between slave and freeman, between American- and European-born, between town and country. Nevertheless, the potential developed during the colonial era for action on a regional basis. As has been noted, sometimes the elites of one captaincy—with administrative support there—demanded economic preference over other captaincies. Such rivalry was well resolved in the Brazilian colonial era, as in Spanish America, but in both cases erupted into action under the stresses of change to independent political status early in the nineteenth century.

e. Late Colonial Change

There was virtually no sentiment for Independence in colonial Brazil before 1800, but there, as in the Spanish realms, America was growing away from Europe, in customs, institutions, and attitudes. Brazil and Portugal had conflicting interests in some respects, and resentments and jealousies accumulated. These were in Brazil the bases upon which eventually, from 1816 to 1822,

would be grounded an enlarged sentiment for political change, even Independence, when conditions invited their expression.

The Government and the Economy

Government centralization and mercantilist protection for the metropolis were tightened in the late colonial era. Both tendencies notably were pushed by the Marquês de Pombal (Sebastião José de Carvalho e Melo), in 1750–1777 prime minister under King João I. Pombal was energetic, a man of firm opinions, a good representative of the "enlightened despotism" of his age in Europe. His predilection for firm government included regalism (support of crown against church) and took the form of expulsion of the Jesuits from the Portuguese realms. How much fear Pombal had of Jesuit activities and how much he acted out of his conception of prudence and proper government are not clear; in any event, in 1759 he ordered the expulsion. He certainly resented Jesuit resistance to parts of the Treaty of 1750 with Spain. There were only about six hundred Jesuits in Brazil, but they had been extraordinarily vigorous and intelligent in their activities, with special influence in Indian missions and in schools for the Brazilian elite. Pombal not only wanted the *aldeias* of Indians weakened or ruined, but he took other measures to try to integrate the small Indian population into Brazilian life: trying to get them to dress in the European mode, speak Portuguese, intermarry with whites, work at European trades.

Pombal insisted on centralization and otherwise strove to strengthen government administration. He increased Portuguese military strength in Brazil. He tried to restrict municipal powers, partly by reducing the privileges of the *capitães mores* (captains-major) who sometimes exercised dictatorial powers in the hinterland. Pombal's efforts did not really change the character of local government in the interior. More importantly, in 1772 he incorporated the state of Maranhão into Brazil, certainly a long formal step toward unification. He also ended all but one of the remain-

---

[5] See Chapter 14.

ing hereditary captaincies (it disappeared in 1791), so that all were under direct royal control. He also (1763) moved the seat of the viceroy from Bahia to Rio de Janeiro. One reason for the move was the growing strength of the central south—Minas Gerais and São Paulo—since the mining rushes had begun some three-quarters of a century before. Another reason was Pombal's desire to get agreement on southern boundaries with Spanish America. He pushed the principle of *uti possidetis*, recognition of the fact of enormous Luso-Brazilian expansion across the line of demarcation.

Pombal also tried to tighten the mercantilist system. He was committed to improving economic production in the realms, definitely sharing the new view of political economy of the great ministers of the contemporaneous Charles III of Spain. None of his measures was especially efficacious, and prosperity continued to depend largely on international factors. Pombal did nothing about the warnings issued even before his time by a few Portuguese officials, that while Brazil paid heavy duties on colonial commodities and other levies, it had become the most important part of the empire. They warned that this might lead colonials to reconsider the connection with Portugal. Although colonials did not do that, they had no reason to rejoice in economic policy after the time of Pombal. There was some discussion in Portugal of change in the system in the late eighteenth and early nineteenth centuries, but nothing of importance came of it. Crown revenues remained the chief interest of the imperial system.

Colonial resentment finally found new expression. A few Brazilians called flatly for changes in the mercantilist system. Brazilian-born, but Portuguese-educated, Bishop José Joaquim da Cunha de Azeredo Coutinho published in 1791 a memorial on sugar that opposed a new tax on the commodity. He also produced *An Economic Essay on the Commerce of Portugal and Its Colonies* (published 1794), that called for many changes. He condemned Portuguese economic policies, which he found shortsightedly milked

Brazil, instead of increasing production there. He declared that the salt monopoly not only drew money from Brazil but cut production there of salt fish, bacon, and other products, and he dramatized the problem of foreign trade by declaring that a handkerchief sent to Rio Grande do Sul cost more there than a local ox! In 1804 in a *Discurso sobre o Estado Atual das Minas do Brasil* he advocated renovation of mining methods. Other writers and speakers in the last years of the colonial era began to ask more freedom for the economy, both in foreign commerce and from taxation and controls on production. The municipal government of Bahia, early in the nineteenth century, just before the court fled to Brazil in 1807, collected the economic complaints of leading local men, some of whom indicated dissatisfaction with the economic system and interest in reduced regulation, together with what we would call development of infrastructure, such as roads, to help business. Such complaint was aggravated by intermittent damage to sugar exports by the great French wars that began in 1792, which sometimes interfered with shipping, and by continued competition from the Caribbean, although the wars of 1792–1815 generally stimulated Brazilian exports.

The Enlightenment in Brazil

Although intellectual life was feebler than in Spanish America, it increased late in the colonial era. The ideas of the eighteenth-century Enlightenment flowed to Brazil in some of the ways they went to Spanish America: in permitted or prohibited books, openly or in camouflage; with travelers from Europe to Brazil or in the other direction; with Portuguese officials and ecclesiastics sent to America; with foreign traders and mariners; with scientists and technicians and other specialists sent by the Portuguese crown; through literary, historical, and scientific societies in Portugal and Brazil. We have seen that the influence of the Enlightenment could not be spread by a Brazilian press or university; it was spread, however, by the University of Coimbra in Portugal, which a small stream of Brazilians attended. A few also attended other European universities. Some Portuguese officials at the end of the eighteenth and beginning of the nineteenth centuries specifically charged that Coimbra was inculcating advanced ideas in Brazilians.

The men of government in Portugal were themselves sometimes receptive to new ideas. More than twenty literary and historical academies and societies were founded in Portugal between 1650 and 1779. They all were aristocratic in tone and followed Italian rather than French models, but they did represent some expansion of Lusitanian interests. In the second half of the eighteenth century, French ideas slowly became more prominent in Portugal. The scientific side of the Enlightenment received recognition with the foundation (1779) of the *Academia Real das Sciencias.* In the first half of the eighteenth century, Freemasonry was established, a secret organization that favored at least some of the new ideas and a general attitude of rationalism. Membership became common in the army and upper class.

The Enlightenment in Brazil affected only a few, but they often had considerable influence. Freemasonry was there before the end of the eighteenth century, but its precise influence can never be known. The few Brazilian authors of the eighteenth century often showed the influence of the savants of the European Enlightenment. Libraries contained works of contemporary foreign authors. Claudio Manoel da Costa, a graduate in canon law from Coimbra, in the second half of the eighteenth century had a modest library of more than three hundred volumes in Villa Rica in Minas Gerais and some attachment to the notion of intellectual freedom, which he considered did not exist in that place. He wrote *Cartas chilenas,* on the model of the satirical *Lettres persanes* of Montesquieu, ridiculing the governor of Minas.

New organizations in Brazil, imitating those of Europe, especially Portugal, included the Brazilian Academy of the Forgotten (1724–1725) at Bahia, founded in imitation of the new Academy of History in Portugal. The colonial body was supported by the viceroy. It especially promoted Brazilian history and influenced Sebastião da Rocha Pitta, who later published (Lisbon, 1730) a famous *História da América Portuguesa.* Later (1759–1760) there was also at Bahia an Academy of the Reborn, which was suppressed by the governor, who suspected it of conspiracy. Its membership was representative of these late colonial organizations: forty active members (including twenty-one priests, five soldiers, a businessman, the rest officials) and seventy-six other members (thirty-four priests, one Frenchman, one Spaniard, and several Portuguese were included). At Rio de Janeiro there was an Academy of the Select in 1751–1752; an Academy of the Happy was founded in 1756; the *Academia Scientífica,* set up in 1771, became the *Sociedade Litteraria do Rio de Janeiro* in 1779. It finally was disbanded in 1794 by the viceroy, in the belief that it was "Jacobin," or radical on the new and infinitely alarming French revolutionary model. These societies were notable for some degree of interest in the latest European ideas and in Brazilian institutions and development and for a spirit of associationalism and discussion that had not existed earlier.

Contacts with new ideas were increased in some other ways in the late colonial era. The crown dispatched some 164 technicians and other specialists to America in the eighteenth century —not many, but providing leaven in the lump of colonial isolation. There always had been contact with foreign merchants and mariners, and that increased in the late colonial period. A new element at the end of the eighteenth century was Yankee ships, some of whose personnel were given to propagandizing the virtues of their own innovative society.

Brazilian "Nativism"

Nothing is more fascinating for a people than the roots of its sense of community. Brazilians of today are therefore much interested in those roots, and especially in those few Brazilians who in the late colonial era expressed stronger concern and affection for the beauties, promise, and other singularities of their environment. This can as well be called something like "incipient nationalism" as "nativism," except that scholars squabble over the phenomenon and the label. In any event, paeans to the Brazilian landscape and natural resources became tied to increasing complaint of Portuguese policies. It must be emphasized that the literary activity in which much of the evidence for this is found was produced and read by less than 1 percent of the population. Also, this was a literature of native pride, and to some extent of complaint, but it was not at all radical or revolutionary. To be sure, a few Portuguese perceived that it represented a potentially dangerous activity, even though there was no reason to suppose that society would be set aflame in the predictable future.

The ultimate roots of nativism go far back into the Brazilian experience. Even in the sixteenth century the lushness of vegetation, splendid prospects, and balmy air led to rhapsodies about "earthly paradise," as a Jesuit put it. Possibly its first literary monument is the *Dialogues of the Greatness of Brazil* (1618) by Ambrosio Fernandes Brandão, which not only celebrated the theme of the title, but criticized Portuguese who came to Brazil only to exploit it. In 1627 the Brazilian-born Friar Vicente do Salvador wrote a history praising Brazil's resources and potential. The Italian Jesuit who wrote as Andre João Antonil published in 1711 his *Culture and Opulence of Brazil*, which extravagantly lauded the wealth of the land. It was suppressed by the government as being too tempting to foreigners and apt to stimulate impudence in Brazilians. Rocha Pitta's *História* resounded with the wealth and virtues of Brazil, which he called a "vast region with favored terrain," where dawn and stars, waters and verdure made "an earthly paradise," that filled him with "love of my country." Other eighteenth-century historians pursued allied themes. Poets in the same century joined the chorus. Frei Manoel de Santa Maria

Itaparica's "Description of the Island of Itaparica" rhapsodized the natural and human environment. José Basílio da Gama (died 1795) in "O Uruguai" poeticized the Indians of the Jesuit missions who resisted Spanish and Portuguese domination, and romanticized the "immensity of space" and the "lavishness nature has produced." The "Caramurú" of Friar José de Santa Rita Durão praised the history and natural beauty of the land in a poem that became a classic. Finally, there is a link between the literature praising Brazil and the literature that concentrated more on studying its resources or problems, because the latter often led to praise of opportunities unrealized. All of this will be recognized as similar to what occurred in Spanish America, except that the element of love of nature was stronger in Brazil.

Some immeasurable influence must have been exercised also by the long rivalry between Brazilian and Portuguese.[6] The ungentle epithets applied to *reinóis* by *mazombos* indicated at least a small measure of fellow feeling on the part of the latter. There is considerable dispute, however, as to which groups of Brazilians were seriously affected by such antagonism, or if, indeed, it was sufficiently intense to be of fundamental importance before the last years of the colonial era.

The *Inconfidências*

All the things discussed in the preceding three sections helped produce a few *inconfidências*, or conspiracies, in the late colonial era: distaste for centralization and mercantilism; the ideas and attitudes of the Enlightenment, especially the tendency to analyze old structures and to look for "rational" change; the gradual accumulation of "nativism," of love of Brazil, and a generalized sense of alienation from Portugal. But those influences were weak in two ways: Some of them

---

[6] See Chapter 15, Section b, on the War of the Emboabas in 1708–1709 and the War of the Mascotes in 1710–1711.

affected very few Brazilians, and their influence was diffuse and unarticulated—a potential that had to be aroused, rather than a feeling that action was required. There were two good reasons for that. For one thing, the Brazilian elite sometimes did effectively make its complaints known by means of its considerable economic leverage, through public offices that it held or could influence, and by means of its general capacity to hamper execution of regulation and make other trouble. For another thing, the elite feared social change, especially anything that might have repercussions on the slave system or even lead to slave unrest.

The *Inconfidência Mineira* in Minas Gerais in 1788–1789 was a foolish little plot to end the Portuguese connection. The chief mover was Joaquim José da Silva Xavier, known to history by his nickname Tiradentes (Toothpuller). He was a failure in the Brazilian society, perennially disappointed and aggrieved. His business ventures failed. He sometimes pulled teeth. He entered the army at thirty-five in 1781 and could not rise above sublieutenant. A failure to get an army contract in 1788 rankled, and that year the disgruntled man of forty-three began to attack the governor of Minas Gerais, accusing him of preventing his advancement. Tiradentes and a few other men began talking about revolt against Portuguese tyranny, with especial knowledge that back taxes on gold, which were unpopular locally because gold production was declining, were about to be collected. Among the conspirators were several young men who had studied at European universities. They made some contribution to Tiradentes' ideas, but probably were not essential elements in his actions or beliefs.[7] The small group failed to stir the population against the government. Tiradentes went to Rio de Janeiro and in his heedless way spoke of revolt, even to strangers. Back in Minas Gerais, he

continued with the others in their poorly concealed discussions, fixed dates for the rising, and decided on banners and a program. The plotters were not even agreed on republicanism and abolition of slavery. Reports on the conspirators poured across the desk of the governor, and finally the arrests began in May 1789. The tiny, inept conspiracy was over, and no one came to its support, not even in Rio de Janeiro, where, Tiradentes had incorrectly told his fellows in Minas, unrest was ready to break into revolt. Tiradentes was tried at Rio de Janeiro while the others were tried in Minas. The trials took three years. Only Tiradentes was executed; some others were imprisoned and exiled. Of the five churchmen involved, three were sentenced to hang, but the sentences were reduced, and furthermore even their earlier sentences were kept secret.

Brazilian historians are in wide disagreement as to the importance of Tiradentes. Some find him very important, a martyred precursor of Independence; others think him of almost no consequence. The large Brazilian literature on the conspiracy shows that it had neither elite nor popular roots. Both groups were quiescent for many of the reasons the same groups were not stirring in revolt in Spanish America at the time: most of the elite were conservative, by no means in favor of revolution or social disorder; the popular classes were leaderless and generally apathetic toward public affairs. Those reactions certainly were illuminating. Also interesting was the fact that witnesses at the trials showed a fear of French "revolutionary" ideas, to which events in France and Haiti were giving a basis just at this time. But whatever the historians say, Brazilians are going to continue venerating the men of the *Inconfidência Mineira* as precursors of Independence.

A few men plotted national Independence in Rio de Janeiro in 1794 and were arrested. In 1798 an uprising occurred in Bahia, known as the Revolt of the Tailors. Most of the forty-nine conspirators that were arrested were mulatto freemen of the artisan class, so that theirs was unlike

---

[7] One was Joaquim José da Maia, who had studied at the University of Montpellier in France and had some communication in 1786 with Thomas Jefferson about Independence for Brazil. Jefferson had nothing to do with the Tiradentes conspiracy.

the upper-class conspiracies of Minas and Rio de Janeiro. The quickly suppressed *Inconfidência da Bahia* spoke for the grievances of blacks and in favor of liberty, equality, and fraternity, and republicanism.

None of the three *inconfidências* had enough support to indicate more than the bare beginnings of sentiment for independence, republican-ism, and abolitionism. The many complaints different groups of Brazilians had about government or other matters had by no means been transformed into demand for Independence. We will see that this attitude began to change under the great shocks of events in 1807 and thereafter.[8]

---

[8] See Chapter 21.

PART FIVE

The Independence of Latin America

The bases of Independence were laid in the hearts and minds of Latin Americans during the colonial era, but the developments that made consideration of Independence irresistible occurred in Europe early in the nineteenth century. The causes of Independence, therefore, fall into two parts: ultimate or underlying dissatisfactions of the colonial era that did not lead directly to demands for Independence, and immediate or precipitating causes. American dissatisfaction was a complex of economic, social, political, and intellectual factors, varying with individuals and difficult to judge. Although economic and political dissatisfaction among the creole elite did not lead to an Independence movement, it did create a self-consciousness and irritation that provided a base for consideration of new arrangements when crisis arose.

Creole dissatisfaction was increased by perception of opportunities for freer economic connections with Europe, and that perception was sharpened by British and French efforts to promote new ties. France and Britain needed better openings into Hispanic America as markets for larger-scale manufactures, sources of raw materials, freight for enlarged merchant marines, and arenas for expanded financial operations. The fate of the Hispanic world thus was bound up with struggle in the Atlantic basin for economic and political hegemony.

Striking events in the Atlantic world affected creole political opinion. The revolt of the English colonies in North America in 1775–1783 had some effect, as did the French Revolution that began in 1789. The innovations of the French Revolution soured some creoles on talk of change but stimulated a very few others to develop radical schemes. The events of the times did considerably increase economic dissatisfaction, because of new British efforts to breach the Spanish system—through Trinidad, captured in 1797; Havana, occupied in 1762–1763; and attacks on Buenos Aires and Montevideo in 1806–1807. Although the radical ideas and events abroad did not persuade many creoles of the desirability of Independence, they did radicalize (or sensitize) some of them to be readier to seize an opportunity for such action. That opportunity came with Napoleon's invasions of Portugal and Spain in 1807–1808. The Portuguese court fled to Brazil, and its presence there eventually created conditions that led to Independence in 1822. In Spain, Napoleon imprisoned the legitimate monarch and installed his brother Joseph Bonaparte on the throne. That led to a constitutional debate among resistance groups in Spain and creoles in America regarding governing arrangements for the overseas realms during the absence of the legitimate monarch. Without that debate and accompanying demands for action, changes in the political constitution of the empire might have come very soon in any event, because Charles IV and Ferdinand VII of Spain were quite capable of provoking demands for innovation by their own idiocies, unaided by pressures from Napoleon.

In Spanish America, although there was little demand for Independence before 1808, the constitutional crisis after that date revealed that enough vigorous innovators existed to make demands for change that were difficult to ignore. Self-appointed spokesmen turned quickly to political autonomy and even Independence. A constellation of dedicated, ambitious, and talented creole leaders quickly appeared to lead the fight for Independence. Many other creoles opposed that goal, while much of the lower class either was apathetic or served on either side with little sense of identification with their aims. But competition for the allegiance of the lower class that made up the enlisted men of the Wars for Independence (1810–1824) led creole leaders to offer them freedom for slaves, extinction of Indian forced labor, and other favors.

The shock of such innovation became commonplace. Republican constitutions were drafted, incorporating North American federalism, French egalitarianism, and other departures from the philosophy and institutions of the colonial era. Such measures created bitter division between liberal and conservative creoles, some expressed in loyalty to the crown, some in efforts to mold the new and independent society. Disagreement was the more bitter in that it occurred often in the midst of war, rebellion, and economic disorder and threatened ruin. From 1808 to the early 1820s, Spanish America went through one emotional and physical crisis after another. The old connection between colony and metropolis drowned in the blood of civil war and in the demands of newly proclaimed political institutions and their American managers. Life in America was profoundly changed by novel activity, and there were fears and hopes that more was to come.

The achievement of political independence was a less wrenching experience in Brazil than in Spanish America. Retaining the monarchy as the chief governmental institution helped confine the area of contention to certain elite interests. The lesser factionalism and warfare meant fewer opportunities for confusion, ambition, or desperate appeals for lower-class public action. The new government thus could concentrate effort upon control of the tendency toward regional fragmentation, securing for Brazil one of the largest national territories in human history.

The Independence of Latin America was a blow to political colonialism and to monarchism and a triumph for the principles of self-determination and of republicanism. It was, furthermore, a victory for creoles who wanted to increase connections with the North Atlantic world, especially Britain, over the supporters of the Spanish system of indirect dependence on the rest of Europe. Finally, Independence was a triumph of leadership and courage, and the deeds and dreams of the heroes of Independence are invoked today to sustain the drive of Latin America for a better society and for a stronger role in the world.

17 Late Colonial Bases for Spanish American Independence

Was Spanish America in a "prerevolutionary" condition before its War for Independence? No, because creoles did not contemplate Independence from Spain. Yes, in that creoles increasingly questioned old institutions and perceived the desirability of new arrangements. That at least forboded more challenge to the peninsular role in public policy. Such discontent might well cause serious strains under circumstances of novelty, danger, frustration, or uncertainty. Bourbon commercial and administrative reforms in the later eighteenth century quickened rather than quieted the strains. Creole ideas achieved better definition in actions by American *cabildos* and *consulados*. The new definition was chiefly a matter of interest and common sense but reinforced by a new spirit of analysis, which came from the rationalism of the Enlightenment that affected some creoles. The new critics questioned ancient verities, including Spanish discrimination against creoles and their interests. Creole restiveness increased with evidence of the incompetence of Charles IV (1788–1808), who turned affairs over to his wife's lover, the hated Godoy. Development of such a squalid and dangerous condition at the top of the imperial administration coincided with the catastrophic revolution and warfare that began in 1789 in France and spread over Europe. Those events increased creole misgivings about the weaknesses of Spain and its ability to protect and properly govern the American provinces. At the same time, the wars created irritating interruptions of trade, which sometimes brought new opportunities for exchange with foreigners. Those in turn increased creole desire for further relaxation of the restrictive system. Through all this, most creoles remained supporters of monarchy, the class system, and the connection with Spain. Their increased assertiveness was moderate, aimed at compromise within the system. The creole elite was little involved in the slightly increased number of tumults and conspiracies that occurred in America in the late colonial era. The new element was that some creoles were readier than their fathers had been to consider new arrangements, although very few thought in revolutionary terms.

a. The Enlightenment in the Spanish World

A mild intellectual ferment was stirred in the Spanish world by the work of the *philosophes* of the Enlightenment, who exalted reason over revelation and recorded wisdom from the past.[1] The new ideas had some influence in restricted

[1] See Chapter 12, Section d, on intellectual life and censorship during the colonial era as a whole.

circles in Spain in the first half of the eighteenth century but more thereafter. The ideas of such foreign radicals as Voltaire were disseminated by Spanish authors, after toning them down to suit Spanish orthodoxy. Such a careful critic was Father Jerónimo Feijóo (died 1764), who in many volumes condemned Spain's obscurantism and conservatism for the poor development of science there. He argued against Aristotle and scholasticism and for Cartesianism and rationalism.

Revisionists in Spain who approved of such ideas were moderate reformers, not revolutionaries or heretics. They often emphasized the scientific and technological aspects of the Enlightenment without thinking much of its philosophical and political sides or of the possibility that encouraging the former might foster the latter. Some of their reform propaganda was produced through the Economic Societies of Friends of the Country, some sixty of which were formed in Spain between 1775 and the dawn of the new century. They wanted to bring the Spanish world more into tune with the concert of European development. Gaspar de Jovellanos, a leading light of the Enlightenment in Spain, was active in the Spanish economic societies. In 1795 the Madrid Economic Society published Jovellanos' summary of its long-accumulating materials on the agrarian problem in a Spain of great civil and ecclesiastical estates and a poor peasantry. It condemned entail and mortmain and other burdens on agriculture. The recommendations of this dull and fact-ridden treatise would, if carried out, have revolutionized not only farming but the social arrangements and government of Spain.

The Inquisition quickly condemned Jovellanos' *Agrarian Law*, both because it attacked the church's landed position and because it might awaken people to the idea of equality of property rights. Those years of European revolution and war after 1789 were generally inimical to intellectual liberalism in Spain. Enlightened conservatives recoiled in horror from the French Revolution and turned against the Enlightenment—or at least hounded partisans of those aspects of

it they belatedly perceived as dangerous. The few members of the elite who remained faithful to the new ideas in some of their aspects were heavily outnumbered. Spain remained conservative and traditionalist, but it had transmitted many of the new ideas to America, and the colonists had derived others directly from the sources.

The new ideas penetrated Spanish America at an ever faster rate in the eighteenth century, first scientific and philosophical ideas, later sociopolitical. The scientific side of the Enlightenment came chiefly through Spain, where government encouraged it. For example, the Spanish Elhuyar brothers studied in Germany under official auspices, then organized government technological missions that did good work, especially in mining, in Peru and New Spain in the latter part of the eighteenth century. A number of other scientists went out from Europe during the same decades of the 1770s to the 1790s, under official auspices or as private citizens. Alexander von Humboldt, in Spanish America in 1799–1804, was the most famous, and his publications are a mine of information on the area.

Innovative political, philosophical, social, and legal ideas came most importantly in a moderate and disguised form, as in the works of Feijóo and various rationalistic "corrections" of scholasticism. Americans also derived such ideas directly by reading foreign—especially English and French—radical thinkers. Many later leaders of the revolutionary generation were infected with the rationalistic attitude and ideas while students in American *colegios* and universities. Although the curriculum there was essentially that of scholasticism, it had been diluted with massive injections of Newton, Descartes, and rationalism in general. The *colegios* and universities also became modestly infected with experimental science and even more with modern medical ideas and methods.

New ideas came to America with Spanish officials, ecclesiastics, merchants, and scientists and also with foreign travelers and residents in America. Frenchmen especially were influential in

America in the late colonial period, discussing radical and even revolutionary ideas. The Enlightenment was exported to America in Spanish periodicals. It was carried there by creoles who lived or traveled in Europe. A number of men who became prominent in the Independence years formed their taste for the new thought while abroad. Francisco de Miranda of Venezuela went to Spain in 1771; José Baquíjano of Peru arrived in Spain in 1773, and became acquainted with Jovellanos; Manuel Belgrano of Buenos Aires and Simón Rodríguez of Venezuela were in Spain in the 1780s; Bernardo O'Higgins of Chile was in England and Spain in the 1790s.

The new spirit was spread by the many new American periodicals that sprang up in the two decades before 1808.[2] The two or three that existed earlier had little influence; the late colonial papers had quite a lot. The scientific matter in the new periodicals alone was enough to bespeak the remaking of the culture of some of the upper class. They also contained discussion of economic matters and notable essays on sociointellectual questions. But perhaps more important than their subject matter was their critical attitude, however mild and even disguised in many cases. Nothing like it had existed before. Their relative cosmopolitanism increased creole dissatisfaction with the isolation of America. Some periodicals insisted that improvement of knowledge of their own areas was important, indicating a consciousness that information was not well developed on the subject, an implied criticism of Spanish policy. Focusing on local problems was bound to increase regionalism.

New ideas were also spread by formal and informal associations, almost unknown before the last decades of the colonial period. Social life and exchange of ideas had been heretofore rather closely confined to the home and educational institutions. The government had frowned on private associationalism, and was nervous at its appearance late in the eighteenth century. The

ostensibly literary group that included Antonio Nariño in Bogotá in the 1780s discussed new ideas, but it also flirted with treason.[3] At the same time Viceroy Flores in Mexico sponsored a salon for scientific and literary discussion that included some well-read creoles. Viceroy Revillagigedo in Mexico in 1790 on the one hand seemed to be a notorious friend of Frenchmen and on the other hoped to keep out cafes, where periodicals might be read and discussed. Cafes in Mexico nevertheless multiplied during the thirty remaining years of the colonial period. In Peru, the *Mercurio Peruano*, published by scientifically enlightened but socially conservative creoles, in the early 1790s expressed doubts about promiscuous public discussion. However, it also noted some use for cafes if properly conducted and found support in such luminaries of the Enlightenment as Newton and Leibnitz. The viceroy at Buenos Aires in 1802 found ominous changes in recent years in discussions "in cafes and outside."

Freemasonry in the latter part of the eighteenth century spread in Spanish America (as in Spain) among the elite, bringing its bias in favor of liberalism. Also liberal in some respects were the Economic Societies of Friends of the Country, which were exported from Spain to America. Fourteen were suggested in Spanish America in 1783–1819, and most of them were at least tentatively formed. One of their functions was as a conduit for the practical side of the Enlightenment through membership meetings, public discussions, prize contests, schools, and publications. The Economic Societies could attract patriotic conservatives, at least timidly experimental with regard to the economic-military state of the Spanish world, though unready to change the sociopolitical status quo; and moderate liberals whose patriotism was complicated by enthusiasm for rationalism, by a hankering for innovation, and by a desire to join what they thought was the parade of European progress.

---

[2] See Chapter 12.

[3] See Section c in the present chapter for more on this group.

The Enlightenment was the easier to spread because censorship, as in Spain, was somewhat relaxed, though it remained stricter than in the metropolis—as some creoles complained. It always was an annoyance, and at the end of the colonial period people were still prosecuted for owning prohibited books, though an ever larger amount of nominally forbidden reading matter was openly or surreptitiously imported. Foreign revolutionary documents seeped in from the rebelling British colonies and then from the United States after the 1770s, and from revolutionary France beginning in 1789. For years before the Spanish American Independence period began in 1808, Yankee ship captains propagandized for republicanism.

Thus, by the beginning of the French Revolution in 1789, the Enlightenment was influencing a few people in America as well as in Spain. The growing intellectual animation of some of the younger creoles could not be confined to "safe" channels. Speculative study in science, medicine, philosophy, and law led to affection for speculation and dubiety as techniques. Of course, the privileged class as a whole in America could no more be expected to embrace learning than that could be expected of similar groups elsewhere. Furthermore, even that minority of the elite that had swung over with some enthusiasm to part of the Enlightenment included many persons who had not examined the implications for their own position of such notions as the rational approach to government and the sociopolitical order. As in Spain, some of those fashionable partisans of new ideas found upon reflection, after 1789, that the new views were at bottom iniquitous, un-Catholic, and apt to turn things quite topsy-turvy.

b. The Bourbon Reforms

The Bourbons were cautious reformers. In the first half of the eighteenth century, more reform was tried for Spain than for America. A sizable effort for America did not begin until the 1760s. Experienced and intelligent men in Spain and overseas probed the problems of America and made reports, detailing possible solutions, even suggesting that the colonies might be lost unless changes were made. The Bourbons by no means ignored such advice; but as the administrators of an enormous enterprise they received many suggestions, often conflicting and often involving potentially dangerous clashes of interests. Such reports had to be weighed. There usually was no obviously clear path either to analysis or to action.

The reforms finally adopted did not strengthen the empire sufficiently to stave off its foes, external and internal. They were unequal to the task partly because Spanish concepts, information, and skills were less than adequate; partly because Spain's enemies interfered; partly because Spanish colonials were as difficult to please as were British colonials in North America. The Bourbon efforts certainly did not satisfy the creoles. Possibly they might have been more effective and more acceptable had not the French Revolution and its attendant wars commenced in 1789. There is nothing to suggest, however, that Spain under the incompetent Charles IV and Ferdinand VII would have shown sufficient statesmanship—or the creoles enough patience—to let the system long endure, or that the other powers would have permitted it—especially Britain, with its economic and territorial ambitions in Latin America. In any event, the history of the matter is that the French Revolution and the wars did occur. All sociopolitical systems must stand the shock of external forces, and at unexpected and inconvenient times, or go under.

Administrative reforms in the eighteenth century had only limited success, as was noted earlier of economic change.[4] New captaincies-general in Louisiana, Venezuela, Cuba, and Chile in the second half of the century did somewhat promote administrative efficiency and defense. The chief effort at improvement, however, was the intendancy system, introduced to America in 1764–

---

[4] See Chapter 11, Section d, on changes in overseas trade in the late colonial era.

1790. The intendants may have marginally improved administration. They had little to do, however, with what economic growth occurred. Most importantly, the intendants stimulated creole self-consciousness and complaint, although some of that would have happened even had the intendancy not been extended from Spain to America.

The wide powers of the intendants reached to the municipal level. They tried in some places to rouse *cabildos* from their torpor. In Peru the intendants even promoted freedom of choice in electing members of the *cabildos*. The creole town councillors responded happily to indications that someone thought they mattered. Rejuvenation sometimes took the form of efforts to stimulate the local economy, although town councils had no more funds than intendants for such purposes. In a few years the invigorated *cabildos* also turned to criticism of imperial institutions, to audacious governmental innovations (after 1808, mainly), and finally to Independence. No doubt many of these developments would have occurred, sooner or later, had the intendancy system not been extended to America, but they do suggest a kernel of sense in the old imperial belief that keeping the creoles powerless, quiet, and isolated was best.

The intendants played some role in the increase of public revenues in the second half of the eighteenth century in America. These revenues were especially necessary to Spain's large military efforts. Although creoles were not always pleased with new taxes and methods of administering them, they did desire Spanish victory, and made special contributions to war efforts. At the same time, they were interested in local affairs. It has been noted that the tobacco monopoly as a late colonial measure raised revenue but also tempers. First applied to Peru in 1752, it was extended to other areas over a period of decades, frequently causing trouble. Another "reform" was that the Bourbons tended to suppress private tax farming and to take the fiscal system into the crown's now more efficient grasp. Such efficiency in tax collection was not popular

with creoles. Nor was the expropriation in 1804–1809 of ecclesiastical property, which hit especially hard in New Spain, resulting in a rapid liquidation of private loans that hurt the creole elite.[5] These and other late colonial fiscal measures not only led to complaint and rioting, but they did something to stimulate that regionalism and heightened awareness of local as opposed to imperial interest that the crown had feared throughout the colonial period.

Church issues in the eighteenth century did not shake creole loyalty to the crown. Creoles had always supported the crown's policy of civil supremacy and efforts to control the numbers of the regular orders and their property. Creoles supported eighteenth-century efforts along those lines.[6] The expulsion of the Jesuits in 1767 was merely a more drastic effort. Creoles were happy to acquire Jesuit real estate. They regretted the loss of Jesuit teachers but not passionately. There was no question of much reducing the church's total role in society, so that conservative fears were not much aroused. Nor did the expelled Jesuits stir sympathy in Spanish America. Only a few of the exiles wrote open or disguised criticisms of the Spanish imperial system, and only two of those were flatly subversive. The more important was the creole Jesuit Juan Pablo Viscardo, who wrote a *Letter to the Spanish Americans*, which was not published until 1799 at Philadelphia. It inveighed against Spanish misrule, and called creoles to revolt for Independence. Copies reached creoles in Spanish America but had little effect.

The military "reforms" of the late eighteenth century did not much improve the effectiveness of the ground forces in America.[7] Their notable effect was to delight creoles with thousands of new appointments as officers. They were hungry for distinction, partly because they were virtually excluded from high posts in church and state. They also enjoyed the fact that the grades of

---

[5] See Chapter 18, Section b.
[6] See Chapter 12, Section c.
[7] See Chapter 7, Section b.

sergeant and up were given access to the military *fueros*. This was a privileged group (like the ecclesiastical and other types of *fueros*) typical of the corporative society of Spain and her colonies. The privileged and their families had access to military courts for many matters. They naturally tried to expand this jurisdiction (as did churchmen) to cover as many disputes and alleged misdeeds as possible, because the corporation tended to favor its own people.

Many officers in the expanded late colonial militia subsequently were leaders in the Independence movement. The creation of this military group was one of the most fateful steps taken by the Spanish government in the late colonial era, both for its own continuance and for the later history of independent Spanish America. It created a force and a corporative interest group that, given the character of Spanish American society, was for the next two centuries often to find it possible and inviting to play an important role in civil affairs.

c. American Politicoeconomic Attitudes

Old creole attitudes were in the late colonial era somewhat intensified or otherwise altered because of such new circumstances as wartime restrictions and opportunities, new revenue burdens, the intendant system, or radical ideas from the Enlightenment and revolutions in North America, Haiti, and France.

Creole-Peninsular Tension

The Bourbon administrative changes did not touch the creole objection to exclusion from the important offices of church and state, nor did they provide new or more direct creole input into the legislative process. Bolstering the efficiency of the tax system without increasing the creole role in planning taxes heightened the grievance of exclusion from office. Although there was an increase in appointments for creoles to American *audiencias* in the mid-eighteenth century, that

was quickly reversed after 1775. Nor did creole improvement of access to government decisions through marriage alliances with peninsular officials go far toward softening resentment of unfair appointment policies.

Although we cannot measure how much this motive of wish for high office affected creole attitudes, creoles surely had as much ambition for status and power as later colonial peoples who in the twentieth century complained about exclusion from high office and then made this complaint part of their demand for Independence. The Spanish American resentment was heightened by the legal fiction that creoles were equally eligible with peninsulars for office.[8] They were, in effect, being lied to, since the crown appointed few creoles. Resentment was aggravated in the 1760s and thereafter when almost no creole appointments were made to the new and powerful office of intendant. Every year resentment at exclusion from office was bound to grow because creoles far outnumbered peninsulars in America, were predominant in landholding, were prominent in town councils, and mingled freely on a social basis with peninsulars.

The creole desire for high office was tied to material benefits that flowed from position. At least as important, however, was a desire for titles and honors. That desire was evident throughout the colonial era in numberless squabbles over precedence. Creoles cared passionately about marching at the head of the *cabildo* contingent in the Corpus Christi procession or sitting near the viceroy in the cathedral to hear a solemn *Te Deum Laudamus*. Creoles also yearned for appointment to a Spanish military order of knighthood or to a captaincy in the militia. Purchase of a title of nobility was the goal of goals, but it was expensive. That gave an advantage to peninsulars, who made fortunes in commerce and money lending. Thus, of the fifty new titles of nobility granted (mostly for payment) in New Spain, more than half went to peninsulars.

---

[8] See Chapter 6, Section a, on the Spanish policy of reserving high office for peninsulars.

Many creoles and peninsulars commented on the creole resentment at exclusion from office. Sometimes peninsulars said that creoles were too lazy to exert themselves for anything but pleasure or public posts. But peninsulars also were afflicted with *empleomanía*—a raging passion for public office. The creole case certainly involved an issue of simple justice, as noted in the seventeenth-century *alternativa* struggle in Peru,[9] which involved denial to creoles of their proportionate share of monastic offices. The issue helped incubate creole group consciousness. Certainly creoles were fonder of *cabildo* office when it meant something in money or prestige than when it did not. That was reasonable behavior. When intendants stimulated some somnolent *cabildos* in the late colonial era, many creoles responded with enthusiasm and quickly demanded more authority. They also would have liked high office in the imperial administration.

The issue of office was made potentially more dangerous for Spain by a late colonial growth of regionalism, seen in tendencies to link local loyalties or interests into provincial webs. The Lima *cabildo*, for example, showed a tendency to speak for the creoles of all Peru. Other *cabildos* in capital cities did the same, sometimes with, sometimes without, support from the provincial towns, which usually had resentments that set them to some extent against the capital. Similar resentment was held by some small creole merchants against the larger Spanish merchants. The office issue also was linked to the growth of late colonial Americanism, that is, a sense of continental distinctness, partly due to common abuse suffered, but not so active that it could be termed a sense of unity. There certainly was an increase in objections to European assumptions of superiority over Americans. Well-known are the comments of Juan and Ulloa, in the mid-eighteenth century, that it was "sufficient to have been born in the Indies to hate Europeans" and of Alexander von Humboldt, at the beginning of the next century, that the most miserable and

uneducated European thought himself superior to whites born in the new continent, and that the latter preferred the "denomination of Americans to that of creoles."

So, late in the eighteenth century, the creoles spoke more and more of America, rather than of the Indies, and of themselves as Americans. And they railed at the notion that the colonial stock was or ought to be treated as inferior to that of Spain. The new *Gazeta de Guatemala* in 1797 printed a letter by "Guatemalófilo," declaring that such Europeans as Montesquieu, who asserted that intellectual merit could not exist in the "torrid" zone, simply were ignorant. The learned mestizo Espejo printed at Quito in 1792 a discourse in which he lamented that Europeans thought Americans ignorant and incapable of the sciences. The creole-directed *Mercurio Peruano* in the early 1790s defended local intellectual abilities against a Spanish competitor's description of Peruvians as "recently conquered savages." Creoles sneered at newly arrived Spanish "tenderfeet," often poor and miserly, far from dashing on horseback, unknowledgeable about American conditions, and all too often successful in business. The development of local and regional self-consciousness and its direction against outsiders led to increased complaint rather than disorder. There was, however, a small increase in disorder and rebellion.

Late Colonial Disorders and Rebellions

There were three types of late colonial disorders or plots to modify the system. First, some were similar to those of the sixteenth and seventeenth centuries, against a few conditions, and not aimed at general change. Second, some were at least in part the result of new Bourbon measures. Third, some included hope of radical change—even Independence—in the imperial system. The first type was not more numerous or dangerous than in earlier centuries. Of this type, the Paraguayan *comunero* rebels of the first half of the eighteenth century did not form part of a

---

[9] See Chapter 12, Section c.

peculiarly late colonial pattern,[10] nor did the Yucatecan Indian revolt of the 1760s or the Tupac Indian revolt of the 1780s in Peru.

Rebellion of Tupac Amaru. There were many Indian tumults in the colonial era in Peru, including fairly serious risings in 1742 and 1748, but none compared with the great rebellion of 1780–1783, the worst in the entire colonial period in Spanish America. It was led by José Gabriel Condorcanqui, a descendant of the Inca Tupac Amaru, who had been beheaded by the Spaniards in 1571. Condorcanqui was educated at a Jesuit school in Cuzco and bore the Spanish title of Marquis of Oropesa, which had been given the Inca line in the sixteenth century. As *curaca* in some Indian villages, he for some years opposed Spanish oppression of the Indians, which earned him the dislike of the *corregidores*. The Indians were also restive because in the 1770s in Peru one of the new-style Bourbon administrators, José Antonio de Areche, tried to collect taxes more efficiently. Condorcanqui finally seized a *corregidor* and executed him before the local Indian and mestizo population. He assumed the name Tupac and set out to correct abuses but not clearly to achieve Independence. He appealed to mestizos, zambos, and slaves. He also appealed to creoles to help destroy Europeans. Much of the Indian population caught fire and took up arms, mostly with homemade implements.

The creole and peninsular elite closed ranks, however, against a movement that took on the character of a race war. It also was a class conflict, because some Indians of the highest social and economic status in their own and the Spanish societies refused to recognize Condorcanqui as Inca. Tupac's horde was defeated, but only by great effort. He was taken prisoner. In May 1781 his tongue was torn out in the presence of his family and collaborators; his head and arms and legs were displayed in various towns that had supported him; his home was demolished and the site strewn with salt. Nevertheless, the Indians

continued the revolt, and atrocities multiplied on both sides. One Spanish town was massacred to the last soul. La Paz in Upper Peru was besieged twice, once for more than three months. After the revolt was put down by forces brought in from a wide area of South America, it broke out briefly the next year. The number of casualties in those years of rebellion is unknown, but the deaths alone were many thousands, most of them rebels.

The large but unsuccessful Tupac rebellion emphasized that during the colonial period control of Indians was so tight as to make serious revolt almost impossible, physically and psychologically. Furthermore, the Tupac outbreak not only did not spark general rebellion in nearby or distant parts of the empire, but had little effect in Peru in the next few years, except to solidify the elite further against the Indian, and to make the Indians indifferent in the coming wars of Independence. A royal order of 1781 began abolition in Peru of the *repartimiento* of goods, on the grounds that it was responsible for rebellion there. The hated *corregidores* were eliminated from Peru when in 1785 the intendant system was extended there, but that reform in the Spanish system had begun long before the Tupac rebellion. None of the Bourbon reforms much helped the Indians against their oppressors.

The few repercussions of the Tupac rebellion in other areas were notable for their feeble connections with the Indian masses; they occurred rather among disaffected creoles and mestizos. Of course, the Tupac rebellion showed in a form frightening to the elite the vast suppressed hatred of the proletariat for the social system. We cannot be sure what were the critical elements of leadership, immediate outrage, accumulated spleen, and frustration that triggered such an outburst.[11] We do know that they were exceptional. Probably leadership was the critical element. Such peasantries are not likely to produce

---

[10] See Chapter 13.

[11] See Chapter 19 for the Hidalgo revolt in Mexico, as dangerous as the Tupac uprising, but with connections with the Independence period.

leaders from their own village culture. Condor-canqui was not a simple villager. What was re-markable was that he did not identify himself with the dominant minority as peasants did when they moved into the ranks of the middle class. The defeat of the Tupac rebellion con-firmed the dominance of the elite and the virtu-ally hopeless subordination of the peasantry in the colonial era. The next century of life under the republics further confirmed that subordina-tion.

Other Disorders and Conspiracies. Some of the second type of disorder were totally or largely complaints against specific Bourbon taxes and administrative practices; others included various amounts of revolutionary goals—even Indepen-dence. There were a few that clearly were of the third type, entirely revolutionary in aim. A prob-lem thus exists in disentangling the motives in-volved in the disorders. Almost all this activity occurred in 1780 or thereafter. The major move-ments were fewer than a dozen in number; some of them were disposed of by the authorities with-out much difficulty, and they obviously did not spark general rebellion. From the 1750s on, there were protests against the new tobacco monopoly as it was installed in one realm after another. There were protests against other fiscal measures, such as the abolition of private farming of the sales tax. In 1767–1768, fiscal levies by the *visita-dor general*, Gálvez, caused disorders in Guana-juato in New Spain. Such levies in Chile in the 1770s led to rioting and rumors of rebellion, but a compromise was effected. All such fiscal prob-lems did not indicate rejection of the imperial system, but complaints that were easily adjust-able.

A series of conspiracies and disorders occurred in Peru and Upper Peru in 1780, before the Tu-pac rebellion began in November, and they dis-played some ambiguous sentiment for Indepen-dence from Spain. These were town affairs, largely creole-led with some *mestizo* support. They were mainly against specific fiscal abuses and were not revolutionary movements. A com-motion at La Paz was based in part on tax complaints, but it involved lampoons crying "death to the king." One at Arequipa was due primarily to fiscal complaints, some affecting the creole elite, some touching the Indians and *castas*. At least one lampoon there contained rev-olutionary sentiment against Spain and in favor of Independence. There were mob assaults on the new customs house. An affair of 1780 at Cuzco had conspiratorial roots going back several years. It involved creoles angry at the administra-tion of the customs levies and some individuals with revolutionary motives. One of the Cuzco lampoons showed influence from the recent com-motion at Arequipa. The Cuzco dissidents were put down with some executions. A bit later, a tumult at Cochabamba involved some secret and conspiratorial elements and produced lampoons that referred to the movements at La Paz, Are-quipa, and Cuzco and declared, "Long live the king and death to bad government." That cry had an ancient history in the tumults of Spanish America and was traditionally not subversive. It is difficult to know the mix of subversion and demand for change within the system in these affairs or to estimate how much disaffection was being expressed.

Also in 1780, a conspiracy was uncovered in Chile involving the "Three Antonios," two Frenchmen and a prominent creole who had lived in Europe and was familiar with French radical literature. They dreamed of republican government with free elections, a society with-out slaves or classes, and free trade with the world. That certainly was subversive, but it had no appeal to Chileans as a call to action and came to nothing.

In 1781 there was a serious tumult in New Granada. It was chiefly a protest against the new and hated Bourbon taxes, and the collection policies of a *visitador*, although it received some stimulus from the Tupac rebellion. It was led largely by creoles and enjoyed considerable mes-tizo support. It began in the province of Socorro, where Spanish officials were ousted, some anti-church sentiment displayed, and leaders elected to a junta. This often is called a *comunero*, after old Spanish tradition.[12] A horde of the protesters moved toward Bogotá to remove the governor. Apparently most *comunero* leaders wanted reform within the system, though they demanded a wide measure of self-government, participation in the administrative and legislative processes, and approval of their use of force against the government. The governor and *audiencia* sent the archbishop to treat with the rebels, who agreed to disperse in return for some changes in taxes and monopolies, erection of a militia, admission of creoles to public office, and popular confirmation of crown nominations for the governorship. After the rebels dispersed, the government jailed some of the leaders and used force to ferret out men with revolutionary plans. They did not find many, nor did the *comunero* commotion set the Indies afire.

The creole Antonio Nariño established a club at Bogotá in 1789 to discuss the ideas of the Enlightenment. In 1794 he printed on his private press a Spanish translation of the French "Declaration of the Rights of Man and of the Citizen." Although he made some effort to keep copies from the government, he did not succeed, and was soon in jail with ten others. The charges included improper criticism of the government, praising radical ideas originating in France and the United States, and planning revolution with foreign aid. Nariño was sentenced to ten years' imprisonment in Africa, but he escaped and went to France and England, trying to persuade officials to help free Spanish America. He went back to New Granada in 1797, made radical statements, was jailed, and declared he had seen the light, whereupon the viceroy granted him amnesty. The government in Spain disagreed and clapped Nariño into jail, where he remained until the Independence period began. Thus Nariño, one of the few proclaimed radicals in his province, accomplished little.

A handful of radicals, including Manuel Gual and José María España, wove a conspiracy in

Caracas in 1797. Both creoles and mestizos were involved, influenced by foreign ideas and events. Some of their ideas came from reading, some from contacts with the British, who had just occupied Trinidad and used the island to try to revolutionize next-door Venezuela. The Gual-España conspiracy produced documents and songs that celebrated Americans, the rights of man, the need for revolution, and an end to class division, with references to recent events in revolutionary France. The government discovered the plot and connected about ninety persons with it. Some were decapitated, drawn, and quartered. The propertied creoles of Venezuela showed no disposition to support this little plot. The creoles certainly were influenced to some extent by the slaughter and exile of the French planters of Haiti after the slave revolt had begun there in 1792; and by a black revolt at Coro in Venezuela in 1795. The population of the Coro district was more than half of African origin. A free black who supposedly had magical powers thought that France would aid in the extinction of slavery. Many free blacks, mulattoes, zambos, and Indians joined the uprising. A few whites were killed and some haciendas burned. But most whites held out until the militia arrived, and a bloody retaliation occurred. The Venezuelan upper class wanted to keep the aid of Spain against a change in the status or expectations of the lower classes.

Francisco de Miranda. Francisco de Miranda was the most famous of the so-called "precursors" of Independence. Born in Venezuela in 1750 of a Spanish father, Francisco was a creole, but not of the upper echelon. He went to Spain in 1771 and became an army officer. During his service he developed an interest in radical literature. He was transferred to the West Indies in 1780. Accused of smuggling and of treasonable activity, he fled to the United States in 1783. He was later exonerated by the Council of Castile. From 1783 he spent his life trying to promote the political independence of Spanish America.

---

[12] See Chapter 6, Section a.

That project took him to conversations with North Americans, Britons, and Frenchmen and to a large correspondence and friendship with men interested in Spanish American Independence, including creoles in exile or simply traveling abroad. Spending much of his time in England, he worked to encourage sentiment for Independence. We know that he had influence on individuals, but not how much. He knew such prominent creoles as Gual, Manuel de Salas and Bernardo O'Higgins of Chile, and the exiled Jesuit Juan Pablo Viscardo. The Spanish government worried about his influence, but there is little evidence to show that he had much with people in America.

In 1805, after more than twenty years of exile, Miranda visited the United States for a second time, disillusioned with Britain's policy of hinting at aid but delaying action to suit its interest. He had long been in touch with United States citizens who favored intervention to aid Spanish American Independence. He discussed his hopes with important persons in the United States in late 1805 and early 1806. He also prepared an expedition to invade Venezuela. The *Leander* sailed—in violation of American law[13]—in February 1806 with some two hundred volunteers. With two schooners chartered in Santo Domingo en route, it arrived on the Venezuelan coast in April 1806. Spanish vessels, forewarned, fired on *Leander*, which fled, and the other two vessels were captured. Miranda went to Barbados, where British Admiral Cochrane helped him. He landed in Venezuela again in August and captured the fort and town of Coro, but his call for an uprising met silence. The entire basis of Miranda's action was revealed to be quicksand. The population of Venezuela was not waiting for a call to support a political uprising. Miranda retreated

---

[13] There was much controversy and some legal activity in the United States and some diplomatic exchange as to whether the United States government had improperly aided or winked at the Miranda expedition. The Jefferson government contended that it had done nothing to encourage it. It was clear, however, that some individuals in the United States had aided the expedition.

to Trinidad, then to England in late 1807, and resumed discussions with the British government. The imperial crisis in Spain was to come the next year, and before long that would take Miranda back to Venezuela, where he again found that his long exile had left him out of touch with the people of his homeland.

Quieter but More Common Creole Aims

The creole elite were men of substance, conscious of their predominance in their localities. They naturally wanted to improve their economic and political position, but their style usually ran to quieter methods than raucous protest, public rioting, or violent interference with authority. They preferred representations, petitions, memorials, negotiations, compromise. Although they sometimes got involved in stronger action, they usually were not attracted to radical measures. Their quieter activity was more important than radical talk and tumult because it occurred everywhere and all the time, thus being continuously representative of the attitudes and aspirations of many prominent creoles. It is a better guide to the views of the creole elite than isolated attacks on customs warehouses, scattered lampoons, or the fuzzy schemes of individuals to oust Spanish authority.

All this does not mean that the great majority of creoles was united on all issues involved in discussions in the late colonial era or equally active in expressing complaints and hopes. Many had a general desire to improve their situation. Such hopes could be discussed easily when, as before 1808, there was little suggestion of their being accompanied by fundamental changes in government or social relationships. Such discussion was more difficult in 1808 and thereafter, because it became actually or potentially very divisive, obviously increasing the possibility of rather wrenching change.

Mariano Moreno is an interesting example of a creole whose active pursuit of change came only after the constitutional crisis began in 1808. He was born in 1778 of a Spanish father and creole mother and received his early education at a *colegio* in Buenos Aires. In 1800 he went to the university at Chuquisaca in Upper Peru, aiming for a career in the church. The university was a center of discussion of liberal ideas. Young Moreno read the writers of the Enlightenment and the older Spanish writers on popular sovereignty, became interested in the development of the new United States, and switched to the study of civil law. He returned to Buenos Aires, where he practiced law from 1805. Moreno was not active in the early radical seizures of authority there in 1806–1808, as he was dubious of some of the persons and ideas involved. Not until 1809 did he come out strongly for the economic interests of the *hacendados* of his area and against the Spanish monopolistic system.[14] Thereafter, he was a leading light of the creole patriot group. Although one can't call "typical" the details of Moreno's life to 1808 or the nature of his early reluctance to opt for radical activity, the generally slow development of his position certainly was representative of many other responsible creoles in the last years of the eighteenth and first years of the nineteenth centuries.

Irritation and frustration were the predominant creole attitudes of the late colonial era (about 1770–1807) toward the somewhat revised administrative and fiscal systems. Irritants included new taxes and monopolies and more efficient tax collection, plus American involvement in Spain's wars, especially since it was apparent that Spain could not give good protection to America or to maritime connections between the parts of the empire, and Spanish decisions often showed no regard for America. The creoles resented also the remaining effects of trade restriction and monopoly. This last resulted in frustration, because people normally resent with increased emotion remaining restrictions when some have been removed. Another cause of frustration was that increased trading with neutrals and enemies in wartime, together with rising

foreign demand, made the value of absolute free trade so obvious, especially in areas that had recently developed expanded agricultural and pastoral exports like Venezuela and La Plata. Even in quite remote places, like northern New Spain, some creoles with interests in selling their own or others' goods became irritated at the failure of Bourbon reforms to bring them the prosperity they thought their due. On the other hand, in some areas of manufacture, freer trade created a critical view, because those areas, such as Tucumán, lost American markets to the incoming foreign goods.

Much of the late colonial creole view was expressed by the *cabildos* and the new *consulados*. Heightened *cabildo* activity, in part stimulated by intendants, was one of the most important developments of the late colonial era. A few examples will illustrate it. The town of Trujillo in Peru in 1784 tried to improve the local economy by requesting a more adequate supply of black slaves and a ban on the import of Brazilian sugar into the Spanish realms. Thus the *cabildo*, dominated by local *hacendados* who grew sugar and other produce, spoke for American interests that at least some of the larger Spanish merchants in Lima opposed when they supported certain aspects of the restrictive system.

In 1793 the *cabildo* of Arequipa in Peru protested a royal order of 1789 that increased the local powers of military officers and reduced those of the *cabildo*. The order was supported by the intendant and in 1795 by the Council of the Indies. Also in 1793, the *cabildo* of Lima sent the learned creole José Baquíjano to Madrid to seek increased rights for the *cabildo* and also more creole representation in the *consulado* of Lima. So here was an instance in which creoles in the *cabildo* and the *consulado* could agree, which was not always the case. Baquíjano was also ordered to argue that at least one-third of the judges of the Peruvian *audiencias* should be creoles, serving, as the *cabildo* said, in the land of their birth. This demand surely was significant. Only a small part of these substantial demands

---

[14] See Chapter 19, Section e.

was granted, in 1802, and that partly because the *cabildo* greased the way with a sizable donation to the perpetually impecunious crown. The Peruvian *cabildos* certainly had become more self-confident and were increasing their pressure for power. Although this development was relatively quiet, it was of great potential significance because it involved the men who were the almost inevitable leaders of the community by reason of their possessions, family ties, education, and accustomed public activity. Many of them, including Baquíjano, were quite conservative on many issues, but they were dissatisfied with their place in the imperial system.

A final example is the *cabildo* at Concepción, Chile, which in 1794 called a *cabildo abierto* (open *cabildo*) of the sort that soon would be common during the Independence period.[15] This was a meeting of some scores of prominent citizens, that is, a gathering of the oligarchy to give weight to the decision and action contemplated by the town council. The open *cabildo* wrote the captain-general that a tax measure projected by the *audiencia* at Santiago was improper, both because the latter had not consulted the attorney of the *cabildo* at Concepción and because the *audiencia* favored the commerce of Santiago over that of Concepción. The appeal thus was for representation in the taxing process, which was often enjoyed indirectly during the colonial period in Spanish America by way of consultation; and against economic subordination to the capital city of Santiago, whose merchants and *cabildo* had been consulted about the projected tax. The *audiencia* in 1795 ordered the intendant of Concepción to call another *cabildo abierto* and condemn before those local oligarchs, in the name of the *audiencia*, their recent actions. The intendant also was to prevent future *cabildos abiertos* that had not received permission to meet from authority higher than the intendant—that is, from Santiago. This was another instance showing both the feistiness of a *cabildo* and division based on regionalism.

The multiplication of *consulados* in the 1790s also gave new focus to creole views. In combination with freer trade, this development increased opportunities for smaller merchants everywhere, including those in towns formerly heavily dominated by Lima and Mexico City. At Veracruz in 1793 a group of twenty-three merchants petitioned the *consulado* at Mexico City for extension of more of its functions to the port, including a more adequate commercial court system there. The Veracruz *consulado* was established soon thereafter. The Cartagena *consulado* was created in 1795. One of its effects was to intensify dispute between the merchants of the port and those of inland towns. Bogotá asked for its own *consulado* and had support from some other inland towns. Socorro was especially critical of what it called Cartagena's indifference to the needs of the hinterland. Socorro charged that rich merchants on the coast built carriage roads for their own convenience but would not expend funds on roads to the interior. The charge had some basis in fact, but the real problem was that no *consulado* in America had the resources even to scratch the surface of transportation needs. In many places a century would pass before roads were much improved.

Both these cases revealed some of the localism often detectable in the actions of late colonial *cabildos* and *consulados*. That can be interpreted either as a sort of nascent nationalism or as regionalism or both together. Regionalism might promote nationalism in the sense of united interest of all parts of a major realm, or it might promote a geographically narrower nationalism for one part of a realm. This complicated matter was to be important for the independent nations in the nineteenth and twentieth centuries. A final phenomenon must be stressed: the tendency of capital cities to claim predominance, or "natural" leadership, over other cities and areas. The Lima *cabildo* has been noted for doing this, with demands in connection with the *consulado* and

---

[15] See Chapter 6, Section b, on *cabildo abierto*.

the *audiencia*, institutions affecting the entire Viceroyalty of Peru. Buenos Aires was also given to similar assumption of leadership for all the realm of the Río de la Plata.

Some revealing expositions of creole economic aims were produced in the late colonial era. The well-educated authors knew the new political economy that was discussed in the Economic Societies of Friends of the Country in Spain and America and in the new American periodicals. They also knew the economic bases of the North American and French revolutions. The Bourbon economic reforms they considered inadequate. They were notably emancipated from parochialism and wanted to see their realms integrated into a wider economic system than just the Spanish empire.

Manuel de Salas was born at Santiago, Chile, into the creole elite, and studied at the university at Lima in the early 1770s. Back in Santiago, he was briefly a member of the *cabildo*, then in 1777–1784 was in Spain trying to obtain a government position, but failed. He returned to Chile a man of the Enlightenment but a responsible member of the elite. He had seen something of the world. He knew, and corresponded with, Manuel Belgrano, a creole of Buenos Aires with views much like his own. In 1795 the crown named Salas to a legal post with the new *consulado* of Santiago. In December 1795 he advised the executive committee of the *consulado* of the need to establish public education in arithmetic, geometry, and draftsmanship in order to promote the development of agriculture, industry, and commerce. In January 1796 he submitted his "Representation on the State of Agriculture, Industry, and Commerce in the Kingdom of Chile." He claimed therein that Chile had the resources to be rich and well populated but was neither and was plagued with idle hands. He thought that the way to improvement was through the widening of markets by free trade.

Salas wanted to establish an Economic Society of Friends of the Country on the model of those he had known in Spain; he did not succeed until 1821, after Independence. But he was talking

about societies and academies in the "Representation" of 1796. In another of his voluminous writings, a memorial of 1801, he called for societies to promote learning and the unity of classes, calling to his support the Spanish official and political economist Campomanes. Salas did manage to create at Santiago in 1797 an academy of arithmetic, geometry, and draftsmanship. He thus combined interests in marketing and production, which was typical of many of the creoles active in public affairs in the late colonial period.

Another such individual was Salas' correspondent Manuel Belgrano, born of a Spanish merchant father and a creole mother at Buenos Aires in 1770. He went to school in Buenos Aires, then studied law in Spain, where he was admitted to practice. He was in Spain in 1789, when, as he later wrote, the French Revolution and ideas of liberty, equality, security, and property "took firm hold on me." But they certainly did not make of him a social revolutionary. He was still in Spain in 1793 when he was appointed secretary to the new *consulado* of Buenos Aires. Back at Buenos Aires, he was displeased to find that the crown still favored peninsular Spaniards in the *consulado*. He recorded that those merchants knew little and cared less about the development of production in the area, one of their stated responsibilities. They were, he asserted, only interested in their own commercial profits, how to "buy for four and sell for eight." He quietly tried in 1794–1806 to promote his own ideas of development, with such little success that he wrote, "All foundered on the opposition of the government at Buenos Aires, Madrid, and the merchants who composed the *consulado*."

Francisco Arango y Parreño (1765–1837) was of the creole oligarchy in Cuba. He had a mind and education considerably above the average. He studied law in Spain and was the agent there of the *cabildo* of Havana. He returned to Cuba in 1792 and presented to the government his "Discourse on the Agriculture of Havana and Means of Improving It." It was full of economic ideas common among such Spanish writers as Campomanes and Jovellanos but directed to the problems of large landowners in Cuba. Arango noted Cuban difficulties as compared with the colonies of France, Britain, and Portugal: it was deficient in slaves and in technical equipment and knowledge; suffered from a stricter system of commercial and revenue control; and was oppressed by higher rates of interest. Arango, like most of the elite at Havana, favored economic freedom at least for their own operations. He quarreled with the crown's tobacco monopoly—as creoles in so many places did—and with the small tobacco growers, because they opposed the rapid development of sugar. He also quarreled with engineers of the royal navy, who claimed a monopoly for their own purposes of timber needed in sugar processing.

During his long and distinguished career, involving many public posts, Arango was concerned chiefly with political economy, in its practical rather than theoretical aspects, from the point of view of the *hacendado*. He did some work for the Havana Economic Society, which met first in 1793, but was more involved with the new *consulado*, erected in 1794, partly on his recommendation. He agreed with Economic Society objections to economic monopoly and restriction, but he did desire government intervention for the encouragement and development of growth, by which he meant sugar, and he opposed the demand of some society members for economic diversification in Cuba. Arango remained loyal to the connection with Spain, since that was the only practical course of action in Cuba; but it is easy to imagine him as a neighbor of Belgrano in Buenos Aires or Salas in Santiago supporting Independence.

Similar economic views to those of Salas, Belgrano, and Arango may be read in the records of *cabildos, consulados,* Economic Societies of Friends of the Country, and in the new American periodicals of the 1790s and early nineteenth century. The creole elite was responding with irritation, frustration, and hope, informed by its new knowledge of political economy. At the same time, it made a large error because of the limitations of that knowledge. Creoles were impressed by their perception of resources lying fallow, which was what José Baquíjano of Peru had in mind when he wrote in 1791 that the province's "immense territory forms a true desert." He thought it could be made to bloom rather easily. He and his class were overly persuaded of lost opportunities due to Spanish regulations. They minimized the influence of international economic conditions and the shortcomings of their own socioeconomic attitudes. The political economy of that day did not comprehend the enormous difficulties of economic development. So they were frustrated, but hopeful, alert for opportunity. It was about to be given them in very difficult forms by the French Revolution and Napoleon Bonaparte.

18 The French Revolution and Its Effects, 1789–1807

The fires of slave revolt in Haiti were lit by the French Revolution. The upheavals in France—first the cockades of the republic and then the eagles of Napoleon—weakened Spain and Portugal in 1789–1807 with war and maritime insecurity. In the case of Spain, this continued on a larger scale the damage done it by the great French-British contest for hegemony in the wars of 1756–1763 and 1775–1783.[1] The opportunities of the great wars led to British invasions of conquest in the Río de la Plata in 1806–1807. Although these events were not accompanied in Hispanic America by much demand for Independence, they created conditions that could have made such demands attractive. They increased doubts about the ability and willingness of Spain and Portugal to defend the old society and imperial systems against the Napoleonic juggernaut and British sea power. Two decades of unsettling events and rumors of worse charged the atmosphere in Hispanic America with a new excitement and apprehension.

a. The Revolt in Haiti

When the French Revolution began in 1789, Haiti held some 41,000 whites, mostly French,

living well from the export sugar economy; about 440,000 black slaves; and 26,000 free blacks and mulattoes. The new French government in 1789 invited its American colonies, including Haiti, to send delegates to the National Assembly. In 1790 the French National Convention declared the colonies integral parts of the French empire and authorized them to set up colonial assemblies. But this reformism was limited, and the French government continued to favor the rights of metropolitan France over the colonies.

In Haiti the whites were fearful of radicalism in France, and they had to struggle with the free colored people of Haiti for influence. The whites briefly had the best of the contest; then in 1791 the free coloreds (*gens de couleur*) provoked a slave rebellion. The huge majority of blacks rather easily seized power, and in the process many whites were killed and much property destroyed. The government in France favored Haitian blacks over whites and mulattoes and abolished the slave trade in 1793 and slavery in 1794. Orderly government had not been established when, in 1793, whites in southern Haiti invited in British troops (Britain and Spain were at war with France). Spanish, British, and Haitian armies fought in various parts of Haiti for the next few years. By now nearly all the whites were dead or in exile. Serious friction also had

---

[1] See Chapter 7, Section e.

appeared between mulattoes and blacks. The chief black leader was Toussaint L'Ouverture, a slave who had secured his freedom, become educated, and accumulated property. In 1798–1800 he and his chief lieutenant, Jean Jacques Dessalines, an ex-slave born in Africa, won a bloody struggle against armies led by mulattoes. By 1801 they had also conquered the Spanish part of the island.

Some of the white refugees had gone to Spanish America, intensifying fears of slave revolt among the upper class there. It was true that many upper-class Spanish Americans had no stake in slavery, and a few even favored emancipation, but the majority disliked the idea of insurrection from below and the disturbance of old relationships between classes.

A constitution was adopted in Haiti in 1801, providing for racial equality and making Toussaint president for life. In 1802 Napoleon's General Leclerc came from France with 20,000 troops to reestablish a great French position in America, hoping to include the Mississippi Valley, since Napoleon had reacquired Louisiana from Spain. Toussaint was tricked into submitting, then sent to France, where he soon died. Dessalines and Henri Christophe, also a black, took to the mountains and fought the French. It was a war of extermination, complicated by a British blockade of Haiti and of France. Numbers, terrain, and disease were too much for the French, who surrendered in November 1803. On January 1, 1804, Dessalines proclaimed the independence of Haiti, now confined to the western end of the island, because the French—and later the Spanish—controlled the rest. Dessalines was governor-general until he proclaimed himself emperor in 1806. He was soon killed trying to put down discontent and rebellion. In 1807–1820 the country was divided into a "State of Haiti" (in the north, under the dictatorship of Christophe) and the "Republic of Haiti" (in the south, under mulatto rule). In 1820, at Christophe's death, the president of the south, Jean Boyer, took over the north also. In 1822 the Spanish-speaking population of Santo Domingo revolted against Spain,

whereupon Boyer occupied that part of the island also. The two parts were ruled together until 1843. Rebellion and disorder in Haiti after 1791 were thus unsettling to some Spanish Americans, while others were attracted by its success in establishing an independent nation. They could have been attracted by nothing else, because Haiti quickly settled into a political pattern of violence and dictatorship and an economic pattern of subsistence farming and total absence of development.

b. Spain and the Wars, 1792–1808

The French Revolution began in 1789, and three years later there began in Europe what proved to be more than twenty years of warfare over republicanism and French efforts to achieve continental and possibly transoceanic hegemony. They were costly wars. Battle casualties tended to increase with the size of armies, better gunnery, and more forceful tactics. Navies were larger, and the British used theirs with a new decisiveness, both in new tactics of concentration and destruction in fleet engagements, and in enlarged and more effective blockades. In 1793–1795 Spain fought unsuccessfully in a coalition headed by Britain against revolutionary France. By treaty in 1795, France exchanged her conquests in the north of Spain for Santo Domingo (Spain finally got it back by treaty in 1814, only to lose it to rebels in 1822). This disastrous war was followed by an enforced alliance of Spain with France in 1796–1808. Spain thus inherited all France's multiplying enemies, especially Britain, which used its sea power to attack many Spanish positions and to expand its trade. In 1797 it seized Spanish Trinidad, a loss that proved permanent. It was also dangerous because it was a fine base for military action in the Western Hemisphere and a splendid door to smuggling and subversion in Venezuela. A principal military event in this period was the defeat of a French-Spanish fleet by the British at Cape St. Vincent, in Europe, in 1797, indicative of British naval superiority and of Spain's inability to protect her military, administrative, and commercial links with America.

Another consequence of the French alliance was that Napoleon forced Spain by a secret treaty in 1800 to retrocede the Louisiana territory to France, promising that further change would only be a return to Spain. He, of course, in 1803 sold it to the United States, in one of his typically amoral actions. This did, however, relieve Spain of a burden, since it had in any event more to defend than its resources permitted. In 1801 Spain agreed with Napoleon to detach Portugal from its ancient alliance with Britain. This move led to war between Spain and Portugal in 1801, a conflict Spain could have done without. The Treaty of Amiens in 1802, between Britain, France, and Spain, gave Minorca near home to Spain, but confirmed Britain's possession of the island of Trinidad.

This uneasy truce between Napoleon and Britain soon ended, and before long France forced Spain again to enter a war on its side. Within a few months (1805) a British fleet at Trafalgar ruined French-Spanish naval might. Napoleon turned to other methods to beat the British, with a "continental system" of blockade to keep British goods out of Europe. In 1807 he dragged Spain into a treaty to aid in partition of Portugal, to stop leakage of British goods through that country to continental buyers. The French commander Junot was in Lisbon by November 1807, aided by Spanish forces, but the British navy had conveyed the Portuguese court to Brazil. The next year Napoleon took over Spain.

The expense of the wars after 1792 drove Spain to various fiscal expedients. A drastic measure was application in 1805 to Mexico of the 1798 Law of Amortization for Spain. This law provided for liquidation (known as the *consolidación*) of church funds in favor of the state, and it required redemption of mortgages. Much property in the control of the church in Mexico came from pious bequests in the form of foundations, which the church managed by lending money to property owners on the security of their lands. Such mortgage loans were essential to the gen-

erally land-poor estate owners of America. They approved of and depended on the church's role as a lender. They were, therefore, shocked when, under the *consolidación*, some big estate owners could not pay off their debts and lost their lands. The effect was more drastic, however, with medium and small proprietors, who had fewer resources and more often had to sell property at unfavorable prices. The *consolidación*, in reducing church income, also angered churchmen, especially poorer lower clergy, who lived on interest on loaned capital. The outcry against the *consolidación* finally led to its suspension by the viceroy of New Spain in 1808 and by the supreme junta in Spain in 1809. But it had collected 12 million pesos and angered a large part of the upper class in Mexico, peninsular and creole, contributing to the view that Spain's foreign policy was damaging to America.

Under these unhappy circumstances of war and financial desperation, Spain was trying to carry forward the reforms instituted under Charles III. But exceptions to the trade laws had to be permitted, especially to neutrals in wartime. The exceptions naturally were pleasing to those creoles who wanted free trade with the world. Also, exceptions to the censorship rules were promoted by the position of France as an ally of Spain, and a number of Frenchmen in America led discussions of radical ideas. In any event, administration of regulations was difficult because Charles IV (1788–1808) was incompetent. Affairs were dominated by the queen's lover, Godoy, who was heartily despised by almost everyone except the cronies he installed in office, some of them in America. Everything seemed to conspire against poor Spain.

c. British Invasions of the Río de la Plata, 1806–1807

A British fleet and army took Buenos Aires in 1806, and the reaction of the local population was a violent and convincing demonstration of latent political and military energy merely waiting for employment and of repudiation of foreign domination. The British had been taking over the Dutch possessions in South Africa, because the Dutch had been incorporated into Napoleon's empire. Sir Home Popham, the naval commander in South Africa, had no orders to attack Spanish America, but he argued to the local commander in chief that their military forces should not stand idle, that Spain was an ally of the great enemy Bonaparte, and that influential circles in England had for some years been discussing the possibility of acquiring Spanish areas in America. Popham, himself, only recently in England had been discussing the subject with government and mercantile figures. Buenos Aires was valuable and near South Africa, thus an obvious target. Popham thought he knew that Spanish Americans longed for freedom from Spanish restrictions and would welcome foreign aid. So with only the permission of his local commander in South Africa, Popham sailed with a little army under General Beresford to attack the Plata area.

His first surprise was to find that Montevideo was too well fortified and defended for his force to attack. He sailed across the estuary to unprepared Buenos Aires, and almost without resistance took the city of some 50,000 with 1,600 men. Viceroy Sobremonte had expected nothing so quixotic as an attack on Buenos Aires while Montevideo lay threatening the invader's rear. He retreated inland to gather an army. The English occupation was well ordered, and the opportunity for expanded trade was obvious. The British offered freedom from Spanish restrictions and incorporation into the British system—that is, conquest. So the British received their second surprise: Whatever the local people thought about Spanish restrictions, they did not want to be ruled by Britons.

To meet the attacking British, Captain Santiago Liniers, a Frenchman in the Spanish naval service, put together a small army of some 2,000, made up of remnants of royal forces, plus local volunteers. This force assembled across the estuary around Colônia and Montevideo, then moved on Buenos Aires. At the same time, other leaders were organizing irregular cavalry among gauchos and other rural elements. They kept the British hemmed into Buenos Aires and would have made penetration of the countryside for any distance an expensive and hazardous enterprise. Finally, guerrillas were being organized in the city. When the Liniers force attacked the city, the activities of the urban guerrillas were decisive. Buenos Aires was laid out on the common Spanish American gridiron pattern, and the houses came flat to the streets with parapets on the roofs for snipers to hide behind. The position of lightly armed British troops in the streets was extremely dangerous. The British surrendered. A measure of the toughness of the local troops was the fact that Liniers had difficulty preventing a massacre of British prisoners.

In Britain, there was considerable ambivalence at news of Popham's unauthorized adventure, but news of his first success brought support and some euphoria about conquest of all Spanish America, although there were also doubts about widening military commitments while facing Napoleon. Within a few weeks the British had expeditions in preparation to reinforce Beresford and Popham, to conquer Chile, and to seize Mexico. The new commander in chief sent out to the Plata was General John Whitelocke, and he was saddled with the notion that *porteños* wanted to be British. Whitelocke took Montevideo. Unlucky Viceroy Sobremonte was there and again took flight. This second display of lightfootedness led the *cabildo* of Buenos Aires to declare Sobremonte deposed, an astonishing assumption of authority. The *cabildo* also conferred military authority on Liniers. Some months later, in 1807, Whitelocke ferried his army across the estuary and attacked Buenos Aires, only to be humiliatingly bested, badly chewed up in the streets of Buenos Aires, which Whitelocke previously had declared he would avoid. Whitelocke surrendered before he could be beaten, urged on by Liniers' statement that he could not control his men, but would let the British out safely if they surrendered quickly. Charles IV greeted the news by making the hero Liniers interim viceroy.

The *porteños*, aside from not wishing to be

conquered and made part of the British empire, had economic reasons for rejecting the British adventure. It quickly became clear that while the Spanish restrictive system would be ended, the British had their own imperial greed to satisfy. While some of the words of Popham and Beresford sounded eloquently of economic freedom, their actions said otherwise. They managed to capture the state treasure Viceroy Sobremonte had carried out of Buenos Aires, but the British refused to share it with the *cabildo* of Buenos Aires, instead shipping it to Britain as a prize of war. That certainly was no way to induce cooperation. *Porteños* promptly hid their money and proceeded to make more by selling supplies to the British, who had promised to accept prices fixed by the *cabildo*; instead, Popham pegged prices. Finally, some of the British mercantile people in the area plainly showed their support of favoritism to British interests. There thus was not much reason for people in the Plata area to favor the British intrusion, and there was no mystery about their resistance. What was interesting was the vigor of that resistance. Where was the supposed sloth of the creoles?

Following Whitelocke's capture of Montevideo, thousands of Britons, many of them merchants, hurried there. They were knowledgeable about the great economic growth of the area in recent decades. There were other Europeans and some people from the United States in this migration, only the bare beginning of what was to become a remarkable movement of population and capital to the area, especially to Buenos Aires and its hinterland. This promise of development came together with the heady local military success, required because of the military weakness of Spain, which could only be despised, and with the assumption of governing powers that the crown had in part confirmed. The creoles of

Buenos Aires had been given a great boost in self-confidence even before the imperial crisis began in 1808.

d. The View at the End of 1807

At the end of 1807 no rebellion was occurring in Spanish America. The great initiative of the creoles of Buenos Aires in deposing a viceroy was not seen as disloyal to the crown. Nothing like it happened elsewhere. The rash of little movements and protests in 1780 had not been followed by a pattern of repetition or continuation. Probably most worrisome to the crown was the spread of radical political ideas drawn from European literature and practice and some creole tendency to be more critical generally, but both those things seemed to be confined to rather restricted circles. The Gual and España conspiracy and the Miranda effort to raise rebellion in Venezuela with British help had found little support. Creoles had made clear in many ways that they did not want foreign rulers. They had given little sign of wishing to get rid of Spanish rule. There were grievances and considerable latent ambition among the creoles but not a very sharp sense of oppression. It has been stressed that the creole elite was conservative, having the prudent preference of wealthy and responsible people for pressure by petition and argument, bargaining and compromise. They did want attention to such grievances as commercial restrictions and insufficient access to office. Creoles were not cut off from the world; they knew about the North American, French, and Haitian revolutions. Those events had not ignited a flame of imitation in Spanish America, but they contributed to creole attitudes and knowledge in 1807 that had been undreamed of in 1707.

19 The Independence of Spanish America, 1808–1817

In 1808 the accustomed world began to crumble for Spanish Americans. The connection with Spain was disrupted by Napoleon. Creole reaction to that development produced bitter divisions. Arguments led to blows. The social compact of three centuries was shattered on a hundred battlefields.

a. The Process of Independence

Creoles suddenly were presented with opportunities and demands for decisions of a sort they had never encountered in three hundred years of colonial experience. Not that creoles never had made governmental decisions, but they usually did so either indirectly or in minor official positions. Now they could choose or refuse a direct role in imperial constitutional and operational policy, and some chose attitudes that led toward creation of independent governments, provoking warfare with opposing creole and peninsular elements. Even within the groups who favored Independence there was dispute that sometimes led to blows. So leaders had to learn to mold support while controlling an often armed opposition; both those processes required hard choices and often violence.

One reason for the difficulty and bitterness of choice was that the enlarged scope of political and governmental activity opened up vistas of social change. The view was sometimes only mistily seen, but at others horrifyingly clear to conservatives as radicals proposed measures that seemed to threaten the traditional social fabric, or as men from the lower orders grasped directly for the new military and political leadership. Such factors aroused factionalism based on fears for social and material privilege and on differences of philosophy or ideology, often mixed with a new and vaulting political ambition.

The most dynamic leadership role was naturally assumed in many cases by advocates of change. Some were men whose interest was narrowly focused on freer trade or political power, but many had a generalized wish to modernize various aspects of society, assuming that the creole upper class would control the process. They immediately began appealing to mestizos and lower orders of the society and sometimes found a response, although in many cases the *castas* and Indians preferred to support the Spanish cause or remain neutral, indifferent, or alienated. Some of the lower clergy, poor and of humble social background, became prominent in the patriot cause, like Hidalgo and Morelos of Mexico; but many were passive during the struggle. The upper clergy, on the other hand, strongly supported the Spanish cause. Even so strong an advocate of economic and administrative reform as Spanish Bishop Abad y Queipo of New Spain rejected the idea of a break with the mother country.

Among leaders friendly to change, there quickly appeared a type of nationalism, at the least a desire by local leaders to direct affairs without outside interference. Often the earliest display of this sentiment was in a town council. Very early there were cases where the town council of a provincial capital tried to speak for the entire province, something not unknown even earlier. This leadership ambition involved much personalism rather than love of country and had few roots among the general populace; it nevertheless was a type of nationalism. Spanish American leaders moved from a provincial orientation to nation building with a passion that quickly led to the creation of independent states and drove men into armies and to death to define and preserve the new fatherland (*patria*).

Each area concentrated on its own interests, with little communication with or interest in others. Distance and absorption in local problems reduced the possibility of common action. Such cooperation as developed proved short-lived, and generally succumbed to the desire of leaders to direct their own affairs without considering other areas.

The military struggle began at different times in the provinces of America. It was sporadic in many places and in many of little importance. Spanish military forces were small and highly concentrated. The loyalist side did have support, however, from a large part of the upper class, creole and Spanish. It often benefited also from the passivity of the lower classes or from their dislike of the creoles who had been their chief oppressors; thus some men of the lower class fought against Independence.

The military events of Independence fall into two periods: 1810–1817, when most forces fighting for Independence were badly battered; and 1817–1824, when the Spanish and loyalist creole forces were defeated. The loyalists were not "winning" up to 1817, however, because some areas

became virtually independent without fighting, and in general Spain's position was destroyed beyond mending. For 300 years it had depended on the loyalty of the elite and the quiescence of the masses, so that little military force was necessary. With that loyalty splintered, Spain's military problems became insuperable without help from other powers.

Some of the military campaigns of Independence were epics of daring and endurance. The territory was huge, the terrain often difficult. Most rebel leaders lacked military training and had to learn in the field. Most officers were creole, but a military career also became a new route out of lower-class misery. Irregular military forces sprang up on all sides, often made up of lower-class leaders and men who followed them as personalistic chiefs (*caudillos*), who could lead them to food, booty, excitement, and possibly a permanently improved position. Armies were small, with 6,000 in the field for a campaign rare. Sea power seldom was important on either side. Foreign arms, money, and men were important at times, but most activity was supported from American sources. Discipline was a serious problem, with amateur troops, often dragooned into the army, so there was much poor performance and desertion. There also were some splendid performances by lower-class troops. Their society certainly had accustomed them to violence, as threat or act, so that they were not squeamish about bloodshed. Performance also was secured by upper-class promises: freedom for black slaves,[1]

---

[1] Suggestions in 1810 and thereafter that the slave trade be suppressed, or that slaves be emancipated, existed in Spanish America not only because traders wanted to gain the support of blacks and mulattoes, but because in some areas slavery was not important, and some creoles opposed slavery as a barbaric anachronism. The many early suggestions included: the Caracas junta of 1810 prohibited the slave trade; Hidalgo in 1810 proclaimed the abolition of slavery; in 1811 the Venezuelan constitution prohibited the slave trade, Chilean patriots ended the slave trade and provided that black children henceforth would be born free, and a Mexican delegate at the Cortes of Cádiz advocated gradual emancipation; in 1813 Morelos in Mexico proclaimed abolition of slavery. Similar actions continued in succeeding years. See Chapter 23 on final abolition of slavery in Spanish America to the 1850s.

relief for Indians from burdens, a better life for all, immediate booty. The continuing social resentments of lower-class soldiers was one cause of frequent butcheries on or off the battlefield. But the killing of defenseless people was also ordered by upper-class leaders, out of hysteria, in retaliation for loyalist atrocities, or for tactical reasons.

A grave problem for Independence leaders was hastily contrived government, badly constituted and staffed for warfare, finance, supply, or communications. They were fortunate when such governments could do what was indispensable and even a part of what merely was highly desirable. Deficiencies were made up by military commanders, often by confiscations which spared neither rich nor poor. When that supply was insufficient, the military made and unmade civilian governments, which were too weak to stand against armed coercion. The military thus developed a contempt for civilians, which owed as much to military resentment of civilian indifference as it did to the needs and sufferings of the armies. The military, therefore, developed a taste for forcing solutions on society, and incidentally ensuring their own privileged status. That was one of the legacies of the Independence period.

b. Imperial Crisis in Spain, 1808–1814

When Portugal fell to the greatest military machine of the day, Napoleon Bonaparte's, its government fled to Brazil. Napoleon predictably rewarded Spain for permitting him to march through its territory by demanding more aid. Spain in 1807–1808 admittedly faced difficult choices; her misfortune was to face them with miserable leadership, so that the heroism of the populace was badly wasted. Division of counsel in Spain included not only doubts as to how to deal with Napoleon, but the ambition of Crown Prince Ferdinand to succeed to the throne. He corresponded with Napoleon, even complaining of the relations between his mother and Godoy! The government of Charles IV discussed flight to America, but the idea came to nothing be-

cause of irresolution and intrigue. In March 1808 Ferdinand's faction arrested Charles IV, and he abdicated because the army and the people rejected the despicable Charles and Godoy and did not yet know Prince Ferdinand. These royal maneuvers were succeeded by others equally squalid. Napoleon, the lion of his age, herded these two pathetic princelings to ill-concealed captivity in France, where he had them renounce their rights to the throne. In May 1808 he declared his brother Joseph Bonaparte king of Spain.

Some highly placed Spaniards collaborated with Napoleon, impressed or frightened by his reputation; but the ordinary Spaniard began in May 1808 to resist the French troops, heroically repudiating foreign domination. In July 1808 Joseph had to flee Madrid. Napoleon was forced to invest big forces in his Spanish enterprise, even to hold the cities and main lines of communications. Britain in August 1808 seized this golden opportunity by sending Wellesley with an army to the Peninsula, where for the next six years he provided supplies, bases, and military pressure, shoring up resistance to the French.

The constitutional situation in Spain was ambiguous. The Bonapartes proclaimed the legitimacy of their creation and assembled Spanish collaborators at Bayonne in June 1808, where they approved a charter that the captive government of Spain "accepted." Although its purpose was to support a Bonaparte on a throne in Spain, inevitably a frame of government prepared by Napoleon had some modern or liberal features (which he might not permit to be executed): taxation was much equalized, a Napoleonic measure that had for years struck terror to the hearts of the old regime in Europe; torture was abolished; the home was declared inviolable; feudal and ecclesiastical property rights were reduced. The Bayonne charter conceded seats in the Cortes to the ultramarine provinces, but fewer in terms of their population than for the European provinces. The charter was not acceptable to Spaniards or Americans, especially when coupled with a Napoleonic regime. Its provisions did appeal to some liberals, however, and that slightly increased pressures for change. But those pressures came also from many sources more important than the Bayonne charter.

Spanish resistance to the French was led by self-appointed leaders who formed *juntas*. The most important declared itself the Supreme Central and Governing Junta of Spain and the Indies (*Junta Suprema Central Gubernativa de España e Indias*), at Aranjuez, on September 25, 1808. It soon was forced south by French victories. In Sevilla in 1809 it declared America an integral part of the monarchy, but it also ordered that thirty-nine representatives to the *junta central* be elected for the provinces of Spain, while only nine were to come from the ultramarine (America, the Philippines) provinces. Thus was acceptance or "integration" (to use a term then employed) mingled with inferiority. Americans vigorously criticized this disparity.

Other striking actions quickly followed. In May 1809 the *junta central* approved the meeting of a Cortes or parliament, finally convoked for January 1, 1810. Thus, after nearly two years of crisis, the nearly defunct parliamentary tradition of Spain seemed to be revived. In January 1810, however, the French advance in Spain almost pushed the resistance government out of the Peninsula. The *junta central* moved to Cádiz on the coast, appointed a five-man Council of Regency (including one American member), and dissolved itself.

The events of those two years not only offered to Americans a bewildering variety of opportunities and choices, but at the end the French armies apparently had conquered Spain. The resistance governments were only paper constructions, about to be burned by Napoleon or carried in flight to the overseas provinces. Furthermore, the concessions to America by the irregular governments seemed insufficient to some colonials. There was special irritation at the five-man regency with only one American member, when America had more than half the population of the empire.

A Cortes seemed to some to be essential in the absence of a legitimate monarch, but the Council of Regency, a conservative body, delayed its election and inauguration. The delay reflected differences of viewpoint on methods of convocation and representation, to say nothing of the legality of a convocation by any agency but a legitimate monarch. The liberals of Spain welcomed it as a means of reform, while conservatives feared it; but the influence of radicals was briefly exaggerated because they were present in unusual numbers in and around the resistance governments. The Cortes that was agreed on included ultramarine seats, though not equal to Spain's. In fact, many American representatives were to be *suplentes*: Americans resident in Spain and selected there in the absence of word from American districts. It turned out, as might have been expected, that *suplentes* were not thought in America to represent their views and interests properly. The revived parliament finally began work at Cádiz on September 24, 1810.

On the second day of the Cortes, September 25, the American deputies asked for a declaration that the rights of Americans and peninsulars were equal. On October 15 a decree confirmed the doctrine—if not always the practice—of the *junta central* and regency that Spaniards in both hemispheres were part of a single nation with equal rights. On December 16, 1810, a committee of American deputies presented eleven propositions, including demands for free trade and for equal representation in the Cortes. The same month, the Cortes named a committee to draft a constitution, and in March 1812 a liberal charter was signed by 134 peninsular deputies and 51 Americans and Filipinos. The fount of all this activity, the irregular parliamentary body of 1810–1812, was known as the Extraordinary Cortes. It convoked an Ordinary Cortes for October 1, 1813. The actions of the later Cortes (to the 1820s) were of minor interest for America, being overshadowed by other developments.

The debates on the convocation of the Cortes included wrangles over American representation, a constitutional novelty. There was debate about the justice of such representation, the size and diversity of America, its various castes, the lack of good population statistics, and the shortness of time before the Cortes was to meet. Back of it all was Spanish fear of the size of the American population, and determination not to count for representation many of the non-Europeans. There is no way of knowing how Americans might have reacted to equal representation in the Cortes; they certainly scorned the failure to provide it. The American deputation at Cádiz made repeated efforts to get equality of representation. A delegate for Buenos Aires to the Extraordinary Cortes supported equality in a tract published at Cádiz in 1812, arguing that at the very least it was expedient in the light of the determination of many Americans not to recognize the legitimacy of the Cortes without it.

By the end of 1812, after four years of turmoil and new opportunity, some Americans simply had lost interest in the Spanish system, even as declared revised. The various actions of *junta central*, regency, and Cortes on the trade system and on such American social problems as black slavery and abuse of Indians had little effect in America, partly because they were ambiguous or did not go far enough or because they could not be implemented. The difficulty also included differences of opinion in America, where some reform measures were anathema to much of the elite. But most important was the fact that many Americans had lost interest in what Spanish agencies—especially irregular agencies without fair American representation—were doing.[2]

Ferdinand VII, in any event, soon ruined much of what was left of American interest in Spanish governmental institutions. He returned to Spain in 1814 with the defeat of Napoleon and swore to uphold the new constitutional sys-

tem that put so many restraints on his authority. He soon foreswore himself, and in a delirium of reaction decreed an end to all the liberal actions taken by the irregular governments since 1808. He reestablished absolutism where he could, and persecuted those who had supported constitutional monarchy and representative government. In 1815 he sent an army of 10,000 to crush the American rebels in Venezuela and New Granada. A military revolt in Spain in 1820 seemed to put an end to Ferdinand's five-year effort to return America to precisely its former condition of subservience. He felt compelled to swear again to accept the liberal Constitution of 1812 (and of course before long again foreswore himself). But by 1820 much of America was in fact independent, uninterested in whatever sort of imperial system Spain at the moment might seem to have adopted.

c. Initial Reactions in Spanish America, 1808–1810

The first Spanish American reactions were to repudiate Joseph Bonaparte, sympathize with the Spanish resistance, and declare for Ferdinand VII, labeled by some, in misplaced enthusiasm, *El Deseado* (The Longed For). Much of the government structure in America continued to function as it had during the crises of centuries. There was disgust with the performance of the Spanish Bourbons but even more fear that Spain would be conquered by France. Officials devoted much attention to extracting (without difficulty) oaths of loyalty to Spain and searching out subversives. But Spanish fears that Americans would succumb to the blandishments of French agents proved groundless. A few Americans were interested in French culture, but apparently nearly everyone abhorred the idea of French government, and many took seriously the official cry that *los afrancesados* (the frenchified) were an atheistic peril to the faith.

Some Americans did argue that French conquest of Spain destroyed the usefulness of the latter to America and posed the danger of an

---

[2] There is debate as to how much the Constitution of 1812 influenced Spanish Americans during the Independence period or thereafter. It vested sovereignty in the nation, and provided many controls on the powers of the monarch, an effective legislature, an equitable system of taxation under the Cortes, and abolition of torture and arbitrary arrest or search.

alien rule. Avoiding such an eventuality would require vigorous American action. Some argued thus from conviction, others to excuse changes in government. Even more of an invitation to discussion and innovation was the constitutional question. The American provinces always had been the property of the crown of Castile. It could be argued (or denied), with learned references to law, philosophy, and history, that America did not belong to the Spanish "nation."

There being no Castilian monarch in Spain, who was to supervise the territory of Castilian princes in America? The *junta central* and regency in Spain declared that Spanish subjects in America owed allegiance to them as the authorities ruling for the merely absent Ferdinand VII. Some Americans said that by ancient usage the American provinces were *reynos* (realms or kingdoms), even as Aragon and Castile, equally entitled to form juntas in time of emergency, rather than obliged to obey juntas formed in the peninsular *reynos*. The term *reyno* certainly was used for major areas in America, but in many respects they had not been treated over the centuries as equal to the European. Great resources of intellectual ingenuity, historical documentation, and interested sophistry in Spain and America went to "proving" what system of government was legitimate while the French ruled most of Spain and Ferdinand VII remained the guest of Napoleon. The tangle encouraged both confusion and innovation. The argument in America quickly became less legal and more political. More important than arguments from medieval Spanish precedents for popular sovereignty became the contradiction between the declaration of the *junta central* that the American provinces were an integral part of the Spanish monarchy and their grant to America of numerically inferior representation.

Developments in Spanish America varied in accordance with local conditions: creole and peninsular leadership; the strength of the royal military forces; the degree of alarm local events caused among the elite—for example, when there were open demands for autonomous political in-

stitutions, even a few for Independence, or scattered suggestions of republicanism, or discussion in a few cases of radical social change. In the midst of variety, however, some tendencies were clear. First, repudiation of the French. Second, argument as to whether to accept the authority of the *junta central* and regency, with acceptance generally prevailing in 1808–1809, although there was some support for American juntas. Thus, for about two years political development was vigorous but did not take obviously radical forms. Events in those two years, however, prepared for the more drastic decisions of 1810 and thereafter. Third, much of the discussion occurred in the *cabildos*, where creoles were predominant. Finally, beginning in 1810 there was a widespread movement for the creation of independent American juntas, ruling in the name of Ferdinand VII. From then on, actions for political autonomy and Independence developed rapidly. Here we are concerned with the American reaction in a period of just over two years in 1808–1809 and early 1810.

In most places early initiatives by creoles were chiefly innovative in proposing some increase of creole authority at the expense of peninsulars. But even suggestions for small changes aroused contention. Circumstances often suggested some innovation, largely because of the worrisome events in Europe. Peninsular actions, often in response to creole initiatives, frequently were channeled through *audiencias*, viceroys, or captains-general.

The creole elite in Mexico had a special grievance in the great liquidation of its mortgages by the war-pressed Spanish government in 1804 and thereafter.[3] That influenced the argument of the *cabildo* of Mexico City in 1808 that since there was no legitimate king in Spain, sovereignty should be exercised in New Spain by its governing bodies, including the *cabildo*, until they could turn it back to a proper Spanish monarch. The *audiencia* rejected not only the immediate expansion of creole and municipal authority, but

---

[3] See Chapter 18, Section b.

feared that it concealed a wish for Independence. There was some reason for this fear, since the *cabildo* certainly was anxious to expand its authority. It received aid and comfort from Viceroy Iturrigaray, a crony of Godoy's, who was concerned about his personal position in those parlous times, which were going to bring out the worst in a great many other people as well. Iturrigaray thought that Spain would certainly fall under the Napoleonic yoke. There was suspicion that he dreamed of himself as an independent king of Mexico. He agreed to the *cabildo's* scheme for a general junta, with provincial cities sending representatives. The *cabildo* communicated with other town councils, and the latter selected representatives. Thus, the Mexico City body claimed to lead the whole *reyno*, as it had in the past on a few occasions and as *cabildos* in other chief cities of Spanish America did at this time and later during the Independence period. There were a few precedents in the colonial centuries but not many. The imperial system had not encouraged such notions of primacy coupled with leadership for selected *cabildos* or indeed the idea of consultation among *cabildos*.

There was, then, a strong effort at political innovation by the creole elite. They were not otherwise radicals. Creole merchants, *hacendados*, and mine owners wanted more authority for themselves but not socioeconomic change. There were only a few vocal radicals in New Spain in 1808–1809, and they stimulated opposition rather than support. The radical priest Talamantes spread the notion that the junta might turn into a *congreso nacional* and Iturrigaray into a king. But the creoles of the *cabildo* opposed a national congress. They also opposed such other radical notions as popular suffrage, which a very few people advocated. The creole elite favored voting only by the traditional privileged class.

The junta met in August 1808, but accomplished little before there was a peninsular counterattack, supported by the *audiencia*, upper clergy, university, other prominent officials, and peninsulars in commerce. In September 1808 a few hundred armed Spaniards, many from commercial houses in Mexico City, imprisoned Iturrigaray in his palace. The *audiencia* soon sent him to Spain and installed Pedro de Garibay as viceroy. The peninsular-controlled government in New Spain recognized the *junta central* in Spain in March 1809. The peninsulars found Garibay too placid about creole disaffection and persuaded Spain to appoint (July 1809) Archbishop Lizana as viceroy. Finding Lizana also insufficiently vigorous, they had Spain replace him in May 1810 with an interim *audiencia* rule. Thereafter, the regency in Spain appointed a military officer as viceroy, and Francisco Xavier de Venegas arrived at Mexico City September 14, 1810, a bare two days before the volcanic Hidalgo rebellion began. It would drive moderate and conservative creoles and peninsulars together to oppose social revolution.

In the Captaincy-General of Guatemala news came from Mexico in August 1808 of the invasion of Spain. The captain-general called to his palace the members of the *audiencia*, ecclesiastical chapter, and town council, with the archbishop and a number of other administrative, ecclesiastical, commercial, treasury, and military dignitaries. This group repudiated the abdications of the Spanish throne, proclaimed loyalty to Ferdinand VII, and agreed to "continue upholding the laws hitherto in force, and maintain unity of action, for the sake of religion, peace, and good order." Other expressions of loyalty followed in succeeding months, most of them by the privileged corporations.

More radical initiatives occurred in Upper Peru and Quito. In May 1809 in Chuquisaca a junta was created on the model of those in Spain, to rule in the name of Ferdinand VII. In July at La Paz the *cabildo* assumed governing power, and some revolutionaries called for Independence. The viceroy of Peru quickly put down these movements. In Quito in August 1809 the *cabildo* created a junta to rule for Ferdinand. This move had various roots, but it was precipitated by creole-peninsular rivalry over elective office to the *cabildo*, which led to a serious polarization that erupted in almost hysterical charges and fears, including a rumor that peninsulars meant to exterminate the creole elite. Creoles then planned to act against what they called European treason that involved dealings with Napoleon. Some creoles said that Ferdinand VII was dead, others that the *junta central* in Spain was planning to give America to France. So events in Europe exaggerated tensions in America, encouraged rumor mongering, and created more fluid political conditions. Officials at Bogotá, to which Quito was subject, objected both to creation of the junta in Quito and to its rude ousting of royal officials. The Quito junta found itself without much support from other towns.

The viceroy in Bogotá called a meeting there of the *audiencia*, clergy, *cabildo*, royal officials, *hacendados*, and other notables. Its deliberations on the Quito situation aggravated tension between peninsulars and creoles in Bogotá. While measures were being taken against Quito, in October the viceroy learned of a creole plot in New Granada to seize him and set up an independent junta. Neither that plot nor the Quito rebellion could stand against the viceroy's troops and the continued loyalty or uncertainty of the creole elite. But such affairs certainly tended to open up political life.

Although there were somewhat similar reactions in 1808–1809 in other provinces, they are discussed later in connection with events in 1810 and thereafter. There was, however, one other type of activity in 1808–1809 and early 1810 that must be treated—elections. The *junta central's* call for selection in America of representatives to that body contributed to the opening up of political life, although only the *cabildos* participated in the election process. The American response was far from uniform, due to poor communications, varied interpretations, and deliberate delays. Mere knowledge of the invitation had some effect. The elections occurred in some areas, but not all those chosen went to Spain. No deputies elected in America arrived before the *junta central* dissolved at the end of 1809.

Elections to the *junta central* were finished in Puerto Rico and Bogotá by September 1809.

The little Villa de Socorro in New Granada provided instructions for the *reyno's* representative, suggesting removal of all restrictions on commerce, emancipation of slaves, new civil and criminal codes, extension of education (especially into the field of political economy), and hoping that the "ideas of humanity" would become diffused through society so as to assist the *junta central* in preparation of a new constitution. Peru chose a representative by October 1809, and the *cabildo* of Lima gave him instructions which demanded more power in Peru, declaring that the election marked the end of colonialism. The instructions also listed a formidable number of complaints against the administrative and economic systems. In Chile nearly all the *cabildos* took part in the election for the *junta central* at the end of 1809 and beginning of 1810, although the captain-general prevented such action in Santiago. The election took nine months in Guatemala, fifteen *cabildos* in Central America sending names to the capital, from which was selected a final slate of three, all members of the creole elite of Guatemala City. A girl pulled the name of one of the three from an urn in March 1810.

These and other events in 1808–1809 and early 1810 were preliminary to the Independence movement, stimulating discussion and arousing enthusiasm for change and fear of it. The new political animation would have made difficult a reconstruction of the old colonial system, even with wise and generous statesmanship in Spain, and even if radical decisions not been taken in several places in America in 1810. In the years after 1808 the Independence movement developed as a continuous process, with a series of sharp jumps upward in the scale of actual or desired innovation in 1810.

d. New Spain: Rebellion Contained

The creoles in New Spain, after the coup by peninsulars there in September 1808, generally turned to nonviolent discussion of their grievances, although some of it was seditious and conspiratorial. Groups of dissidents met and communicated with each other. The government was aware of much of this activity but expected no serious trouble. One group in central Mexico had members in the cities of Querétaro and Guanajuato and nearby villages. Prominent members, all creoles, included Ignacio Allende and Juan Aldama, who had experience in the militia; Miguel Domínguez, a former *corregidor* and textile manufacturer, and his wife; and Father Miguel Hidalgo y Costilla. They collected arms, tried to recruit men with military experience, and scheduled a revolt to begin in December 1810. The chief aim of the conspirators was creole predominance in government, but some were not certain whether a connection should be retained with Spain. The government, acting on reports from an informer, on September 13 began to arrest the leaders of the conspiracy. Allende and a few others eluded capture and on September 16, 1810, arrived at the village of Dolores, where Hidalgo was parish priest.

The creole priest of Dolores was little more interested in celibacy and other aspects of asceticism than many another who went into the church for lack of a better occupation. He did have so much interest in modern ideas that the Inquisition twice investigated him. He had been a teacher, head of a seminary, and priest in several parishes before 1804, when he was sent to Dolores, a backwater post for a man whose career had not prospered. By 1810 Hidalgo was in his forties. His parishioners at Dolores were Indians and mestizos. He interested himself in their economic problems, but his efforts to promote silk raising and wine production ran afoul of Spanish mercantilist rules. Hidalgo was a kindly, convivial, rather romantic man, who sympathized with the poor and resented the exclusion of creoles from high office.

At Dolores, the handful of creole conspirators faced a hard choice. In desperation, they accepted Hidalgo's suggestion that they switch from a movement based on creole dissatisfaction to an Indian uprising. Some leaders soon would regret it. Hidalgo's church bells summoned his parishioners, and he told them to take up arms against Spanish oppressors who were about to betray the Christian faith to the godless French. The famous *Grito* (Call) of Dolores was "Long Live Our Lady of Guadalupe! Death to bad government and to the Spaniards (*gachupines*)!" So the Indians, rallying to the Mexican Indian Virgin, seized what weapons were available— tools, clubs, stones—and set out to destroy their oppressors.

The horde swept through the villages, picking up members by the thousand, looting and killing. Allende and other creole leaders tried to control the lawlessness, but Hidalgo accepted it as the price of the whirlwind they had raised. The horde could be guided but scarcely controlled. It became clear to creole leaders that to the Indians and *castas* a *gachupín* was almost any member of the elite, creole or peninsular. The great mob went to the city of Guanajuato, a rich jewel of colonial culture, set among silver mines. The Spaniards of the city retreated into the thick-walled public granary, the Alhóndiga de Granaditas. Many of the city poor joined the peasant horde to batter down the doors of the granary at the end of September 1810, and hack to death five hundred upper-class men, women, and children, some of them creoles. The attackers lost 2,000 dead, but they were not counting costs. The town was sacked. Hidalgo, in command of the movement, left a creole government at Guanajuato, while he went west with a part of the force, and the rest went north to ravage the countryside and take the towns of Zacatecas and San Luís Potosí. All over Mexico self-appointed leaders were raising bands, sometimes using them to attack Spaniards, sometimes engaging in brigandage. Some leaders displayed a ferocious hatred of the upper class.

Hidalgo's horde may have included 80,000 men, women, and children, plus goats, cattle, mules, horses, burros, and all sorts of captured impedimenta. Just the daily levies on the countryside for food, drink, and fuel were the equivalent of a major plague of locusts. The city of Valladolid was taken without opposition, so there

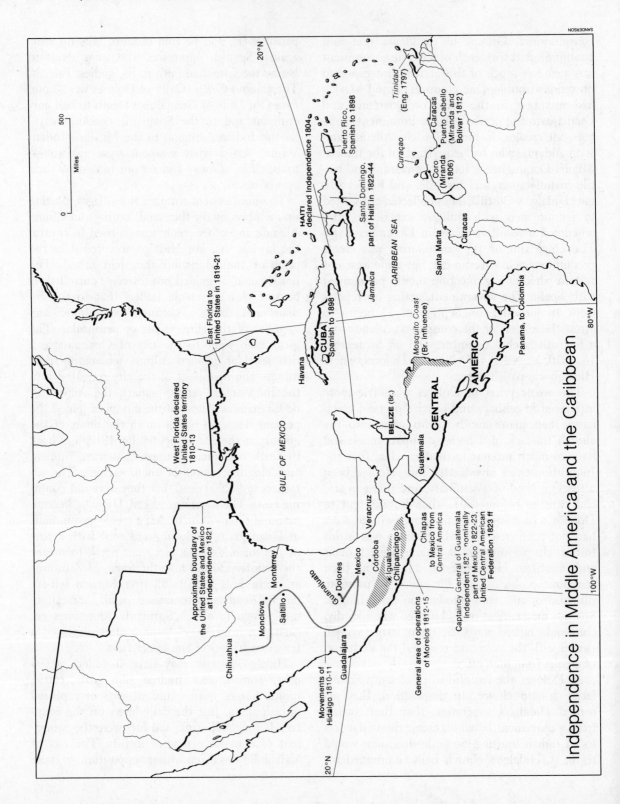

SANDERSON

Independence in Middle America and the Caribbean

500

Miles

0

20°N

Trinidad
(Eng. 1797)

Caracas
Puerto Cabello
(Miranda and
Bolívar 1812)

Curaçao

Coro
(Miranda
1806)

Santa Marta

Caracas

Puerto Rico,
Spanish to 1898

HAITI
declared Independence 1804

Santo Domingo,
part of Haiti in 1822–44

CARIBBEAN SEA

Panama, to Colombia

Jamaica

Coro, to Colombia

East Florida to
United States in 1819–21

CUBA
Spanish to 1898

Havana

Mosquito Coast
(Br. influence)

CENTRAL

AMERICA

West Florida declared
United States territory
1810–13

BELIZE (Br.)

GULF OF MEXICO

Guatemala

Approximate boundary of
the United States and Mexico
at Independence 1821

Veracruz

Chiapas
to Mexico from
Central America

Córdoba

Captaincy General of Guatemala
independent 1821 nominally
part of Mexico 1822–23,
United Central American
Federation 1823 ff

Iguala
Chilpancingo

Mexico

Guanajuato
Dolores

General area of operations
of Morelos 1812–15

Monterrey

Saltillo

Monclova

Chihuahua

Guadalajara

Movements of
Hidalgo 1810–11

100°W

20°N

80°W

was little looting, a prudent example followed by many towns. A few men were trained militia, but most were raw recruits from field and street. Hidalgo tried to organize and train them to fight, but time and resources were not available. He also tried to keep creole support by talking mildly of elected government and retention of a connection with Spain, but his distribution of land to Indians and the race war he headed made the appeal suspect. There were creoles, including some young intellectuals, who justified the bloodshed in the name of justice. The church, however, excommunicated the rebel leaders and preached obedience to the old regime.

Hidalgo marched across the mountains almost to Mexico City and drove from the field a royal army, at a loss to his own force of some 3,000 men. He then decided not to proceed toward Mexico City, possibly because he feared that his force would lose all cohesion during looting in the capital. Such dissolution might be fatal because the best royalist army, under General Calleja, was then marching from the north to protect the Valley of Mexico. Allende and other creole leaders wanted to move on the nearby capital. That course would have been best, but the rebellion almost certainly was doomed in any event. Mobs seldom do well against trained troops; even worse, the mobs tend to disintegrate with time and the accumulation of hardships and losses. Most critically, the Indians and *castas* depended not only on creole leadership but on creole acquiescence in their movement; instead, creoles were rushing to help crush the rebellion. It was significant that there was no sympathetic creole rebellion in Mexico City when Hidalgo's horde was within a few miles in October 1810.

Hidalgo withdrew to the north, losing his artillery and other equipment to the advancing Calleja. Allende refused to serve longer with Hidalgo and split off toward Guanajuato with a force. In late November 1810 General Calleja drove Allende from Guanajuato and took the city, to the accompaniment of atrocities on both sides. Hidalgo had gone farther to the northwest

and taken the city of Guadalajara, where he began organizing a government. He further alarmed creoles in December 1810 by decreeing the abolition of slavery and suspension of Indian tribute collection. Neither of these things was of critical importance to creoles, but preservation of the general pattern of predominance by the European elite was. The civil and race war now had become a complete horror. Allende had no choice but to rejoin Hidalgo at Guadalajara. In January 1811 Calleja with 6,000 trained men overwhelmed the Hidalgo horde, and its remnants fled north, with Allende again objecting to Hidalgo's rashness as a commander.

In 1811 the Spaniards in Mexico developed effective anti-insurgency methods. Furthermore, bad communications and regional jealousies badly hampered rebel bands. Most important, most cities were royalist. After the big hordes were dispersed, the task became easier, although Calleja complained that the insurrection was "Hydra-headed," and there was Spanish pessimism through 1812. Thereafter, much of Mexico was pacified until 1821. Essentially, the method was local defense based on the loyalist towns and haciendas. It was risky for the Spaniards to arm and train creole officers and lower-class soldiers, but they had little choice. Other measures were taken to prevent rebel interference with essential communications in central Mexico, and to police the towns. In Mexico City movements of citizens were severely restricted. A passport system in 1811 established better control of travelers and of Indian suppliers of the capital. Other towns used similar methods. Terror became a fixed policy. An extraordinary court in the capital summarily dealt with alleged subversives. All this put the lid on the Independence movement for several years, while many creoles feared social upheaval, but it did nothing to improve creole affection for peninsulars.

The disintegrating rebel hordes streamed north in early 1811, hoping to find refuge with groups in the United States interested in adventures in Mexico. The rebel leaders were captured, however, and their executions completed by midsummer 1811. Hidalgo's career as a revolutionary leader had lasted much less than a year. The movement, in fact, probably was a failure after its first two or three months. The skulls of Hidalgo and fellow rebels perched for a decade atop the granary of Guanajuato. The rulers of Mexico hoped that this display would sufficiently remind the upper class of the dangers of division.

Many rebel or bandit bands continued to fight. Ignacio Rayón created what he called a "supreme governmental junta" and swore to support Roman Catholicism and the Spanish king. Few such bands had more than symbolic importance. The most famous was that of José María Morelos y Pavón, a parish priest of humble origins, ex-student of Hidalgo, who in October 1810 "commissioned" Morelos to operate in southern Mexico. Morelos was a responsible, disciplined democrat, who opposed class distinction, the great estate system, the ecclesiastical *fuero*, compulsory church tithes, and much else of the old regime. He was a talented guerrilla leader, but he had insufficient support. At a representative assembly he gathered at Chilpancingo to draft a constitution in 1813, a number of radical measures were proclaimed: Independence, the abolition of slavery, torture, *alcabalas*, monopolies. Morelos called on the shades of Cuauhtémoc and other great men of the Indian past to reestablish the "Mexican" empire, scarcely a reassuring notion to creoles who identified with European culture. Another congress at Apatzingán in 1814 produced a constitution. But Morelos was taken prisoner and executed in 1815. He deservedly remains a great hero. By 1815–1816 the Mexican rebellion apparently had been so effectively crushed that it was possible to offer amnesty to some rebels.

The response to the *Grito de Dolores* was unpredictable, inexplicable. The bells of Hidalgo's church blew up a blaze of Indian social protest and race war that seemed to threaten the entire oligarchic structure built during three centuries. To state that it erupted from the profound Indian sense of grievance explains little. All Indians had that, but only the Tupac revolt in Peru in the 1780s had been comparable to the Hidalgo conflagration of 1810–1811. Medieval European peasants had such a sense of grievance, and their occasional wild outbursts were equally unpredictable. We can only conclude that something about the Hidalgo leadership was vital to the sudden disruption of ordinary Indian apathy and fear; that the aid of some creoles with military training helped; that general creole rejection of the rebellion took some weeks to accumulate; and that in the meantime the initial successes of the movement caused the lower classes to lose all sense of caution. It demonstrated that Indian revolts could not succeed, and that Indians were well advised not to try them.

During and after the Hidalgo rebellion, many creoles took part in elections that affected their attitudes toward public affairs. The regency's order for election to the Cortes was implemented in New Spain in 1810, with the *cabildos* in the fifteen provincial capitals naming slates from which delegates were drawn by lot. Eventually, fifteen men from New Spain were seated in the Cortes, although one did not arrive until August 1812. Thereafter, elections to the Cortes followed a formula in the Constitution of 1812 which favored powerful and active minorities. The process, begun in November 1812, was accompanied by complaints that only creoles were chosen. Only seven or eight Mexican deputies ever got to the sessions of the Cortes in Spain in 1813–1814.

By 1810 popular election of town councillors was dead in the major towns of Mexico; the office was hereditary or sold at auction. Then the Cortes of Cádiz adopted the measure of a Mexican deputy that provided for *cabildo* elections. This process moved slowly in Mexico, because communications were poor and because some Spaniards, including Viceroy Calleja, feared the results. In fact, although the men elected were creoles, they seldom were of a sort to frighten Spaniards, except that they thought creoles should run Mexico. The number of obviously qualified men was small in many towns, and they tended to fend off new men, so there was a tendency to perpetuate the same group in office. Arguments against this practice had little effect.

New Spain in 1810–1816 had suffered considerable violence and severe economic decay. Creoles and peninsulars were at first even more polarized, then driven together by fear, then further polarized by several new-type elections. Creole ambition was stimulated rather than dampened. News of fantastic events in Europe and Hispanic America poured into Mexico. The few liberal leaders with small bands in the mountains helped to keep alive the fervor of creole and mestizo liberals in the towns who could do little about their dreams in the face of the conservative predominance and police rigidity there.

e. La Plata: Creole Autonomy Without Warfare

Buenos Aires and an ill-defined hinterland became the earliest independent area of Spanish America. The essential bases of interest in that status were laid by the contraband traffic that exchanged black slaves and European goods for silver from Upper Peru and the products of the Plata cattle industry that expanded rapidly in the late eighteenth and early nineteenth centuries.[4] Traffic was impeded by the restrictive system, so that free trade increasingly seemed to creoles the great policy goal. Wartime conditions after 1793 weakened the Spanish restrictive system, both by foreign aggression and by Spanish need to bow to colonial necessity. Another potential threat to the system was stimulation of creole self-confidence and political sensitivity by their role in repulsing the British in 1806–1807, deposing Viceroy Sobremonte and imposing the hero Liniers as interim viceroy, and by the acceptance of those innovations by Spain. Then, in the crisis of 1808 local residents—creoles and peninsulars—again took the initiative and met relatively little resistance.

In La Plata the events of 1808–1809 stirred the same fears and discussion as elsewhere in Spanish America. An emissary of Napoleon arrived at Buenos Aires in August 1808, and not only made no converts to the Napoleonic regime in Spain, but raised fears of the Frenchman Liniers. The latter declared his loyalty to Spain, but some Spaniards and creoles wanted a junta to rule at Buenos Aires. Thus here, as in Mexico, Spanish conservatives proposed innovative political measures to preserve conservatism. Spain's position seemed to be served by the agitation to replace Liniers, which persuaded the *junta central* in Spain to put Admiral Cisneros in his place in 1809. Cisneros was ordered to support the exclusive rights of peninsular merchants. But the general trend of the times was in favor of the creoles of Buenos Aires. They exerted such pressure on Cisneros that he felt obliged to agree in November 1809 to virtually free trade, as had his predecessor Liniers. Conquered Spain was certainly in no position to serve the needs of America. A strong new voice of creole interest in 1809 was Mariano Moreno,[5] secretary of the *consulado*, who in September published a representation of the views of the local *hacendados* on the free export of their products. This important document revealed the strength of the American producers' point of view when presented by a man who was familiar with the new political economy and entirely free of any traditional affection for the Spanish system. At the same time other men were discussing the need for change. The underlying disaffection with the Spanish system among creoles was bubbling to the surface under unusual circumstances. There was even some talk of Independence. Equally obvious was the increasing polarization between pro-American and pro-Spanish parties.

Early in 1810 came the news of French victories in Spain that seemed to presage the end of the resistance movement and government there. This in La Plata, as in so many places in Spanish America, intensified the argument over the Amer-

---

[4] See Chapter 13, Section j.

[5] See Chapter 17, Section c, on Moreno's earlier career.

ican political posture. The *cabildo* of Buenos Aires tried to resolve the issue, but its deliberations were disturbed by creole military movements and by agitation in the streets, so that it called a wider meeting, a *cabildo abierto,* on May 25, 1810.[6] The *cabildo abierto* quickly ousted the viceroy and created a junta to rule in the name of Ferdinand VII. Moreno was representative of the radical view: that since Spain was deprived of legitimate authority, then reconstitution of the state fell to the people, from whom princes ultimately derived their authority. He drew this idea at least in part from Rousseau, though it also had medieval and modern precedents in Spanish literature and law. In addition, Moreno was like many men of his position in various parts of America: events and his judgment of Spain convinced him that no Spanish government would give equality to America, for all the talk on the subject.

Although the political action of May 1810 was somewhat ambiguous, the economic policy of the junta was not, thus reflecting the views of a constituency that was not sure what it wanted politically but was much surer of its economic aims. Buenos Aires (but not the provinces) was for much freer trade. The junta immediately removed prohibitions on trade with foreigners, and within weeks drastically cut export duties on commodities and restrictions on bullion shipments. It did continue some heavy duties on foreign imports, including 54 percent on British cottons. But although policy was somewhat mixed, on the whole it favored the position of creole cattlemen and merchants and did not please most Spaniards, including the supposedly liberal Cortes in Spain.

Innovative political dispute was promoted by the press in a detailed and frank fashion that had been impossible earlier. In 1810 the *Gazeta de Buenos Aires* was founded, and in it editors Mariano Moreno and rising politician Bernardo Monteagudo supported *porteño* views. By early

1811 the *Gazeta* was stating that the Spanish Cortes was illegal, composed of deputies from cities and provinces that had recognized Joseph Bonaparte, deputies who certainly had not delegated their power to anyone. It also stated that America could convoke such a Cortes of its own if it wished and that the Spanish body was conspicuously opposed to American equality.

The actions of May 25, 1810, are celebrated in Argentina as Independence Day, although formal declaration of Independence did not come until 1816. The territory of present Argentina was in fact self-governing from the earlier date. No fighting was necessary. Fighting did occur when Buenos Aires supported the thesis that all parts of the viceroyalty still owed it allegiance. That claim was repudiated successfully in Upper Peru, Paraguay, and the Banda Oriental del Uruguay. An army sent to Upper Peru won some victories in 1810 but was beaten by the royalists in 1811. The royalists then mounted an offensive against what is now northwestern Argentina, but were beaten by General Manuel Belgrano in September 1811. Later Argentine offensive efforts in the area failed.

Upper Peru was too distant and the terrain too difficult for Argentina to conquer in the face of strong royalist forces there. Upper Peru remained under royalist control for another decade, and finally became independent as Bolivia. By that time it appeared that even without royalist forces, Upper Peru would sooner or later have offered strong regional or nationalist opposition to domination from far-off Buenos Aires. On the other hand, the royalists could not successfuly invade Argentina from their mountain stronghold, although they tried to several times. They could not even subdue the area of Salta, immediately adjacent to Upper Peru, because most of the dominant ranching families of Salta were for Independence, and their gaucho militias generally gave a good account of themselves.

The Buenos Aires effort to subdue Paraguay quickly failed. Asunción refused the call of the Buenos Aires junta to send representatives there to assist it in governing the viceroyalty. The tra-

---

[6] See Chapter 6, Section b, on the *cabildo abierto* in the colonial period.

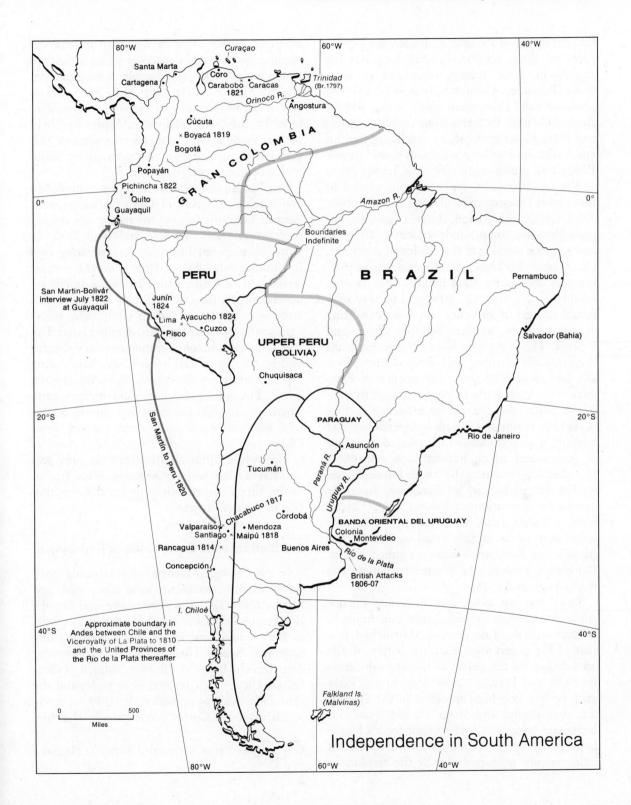

80°W

Santa Marta
Cartagena

Curaçao

Coro
Carabobo
1821
Caracas
Trinidad
(Br.1797)
Orinoco R.
Angostura

Cúcuta
× Boyacá 1819
Bogotá

G R A N   C O L O M B I A

Popayán

Pichincha 1822
× Quito
Guayaquil

0°

60°W

40°W

Amazon R.

Boundaries
Indefinite

0°

San Martín-Bolivár
interview July 1822
at Guayaquil

PERU

Junín
1824
×
Lima   Ayacucho 1824
• Pisco   • Cuzco

B R A Z I L

Pernambuco

Salvador (Bahia)

**UPPER PERU
(BOLIVIA)**

Chuquisaca

20°S

San Martín to Peru 1820

PARAGUAY

• Asunción

Tucumán

Rio de Janeiro

20°S

Parana R.

Uruguay R.

Chacabuco 1817

Valparaíso •   • Mendoza
Santiago × Maipú 1818
Rancagua 1814 ×

Córdoba

Buenos Aires

BANDA ORIENTAL DEL URUGUAY
Colonia •
Montevideo

Río de la Plata

Concepción •

British Attacks
1806-07

I. Chiloé

40°S

Approximate boundary in
Andes between Chile and the
Viceroyalty of La Plata to 1810
and the United Provinces of
the Rio de la Plata thereafter

Falkland Is.
(Malvinas)

0   500

Miles

Independence in South America

80°W

60°W

40°W

ditional dislike of Paraguayan leaders for Buenos Aires led them, for the moment, to prefer the regency in Spain. Buenos Aires sent an army under Belgrano, which was beaten in 1810 by peninsular and Paraguayan creole forces. Buenos Aires could offer Paraguay some economic gains, and it tried—for example, by suggesting that an end to the royal tobacco monopoly would permit Paraguayan producers to command higher prices at Buenos Aires. That and other ploys failed to move most Paraguayan creoles to support Buenos Aires. On the other hand, the new situation did push Paraguay toward Independence, partly by arousing one member of the *cabildo* of Asunción, Dr. Gaspar Rodríguez de Francia, against attempted domination from Buenos Aires. A revolutionary party of creoles grew, and in May 1811 forced transfer of authority to a junta consisting of the governor, another Spanish officer, and Francia. The party soon forced the governor off the junta. By October 1811 Buenos Aires virtually had recognized the independence of Paraguay. The creole party in the latter kept increasing its power, and Francia his influence, so that in 1813 a congress declared Independence and adopted a constitution which created a system of government which Francia soon controlled. For decades thereafter he single-mindedly defended the nationality of Paraguay, especially against the pretensions of Buenos Aires. The efforts of Buenos Aires in the nearby Banda Oriental were to be equally fruitless, though the struggle for domination went on much longer. Uruguayan existence as a separate nation was not assured until 1828.

There was one other area in which Buenos Aires or Argentina expended men and funds in military activity. José de San Martín had persuaded the government that the safety of the area demanded the defeat of the Spanish forces in Chile and Peru. A creole born in the Plata area, he had long been an officer in the Spanish armies in Europe and Africa. He left Spain as a lieutenant colonel in 1811 to fight for his homeland, going first to Britain, where his ideas on independence were nurtured by the revolution-

ary propagandist Miranda. San Martín became a member of Miranda's shadowy secret society, in which San Martín played a role at Buenos Aires and later in Chile. He returned to Buenos Aires in 1812, and at once was employed in military tasks by the creole regime. In September 1814 he was made army commander in place of Belgrano, thus replacing an amateur military leader with a thorough professional.

San Martín also persuaded the government to appoint him governor of Cuyo in the far west, because he wanted to use the region as a staging base for invasion of Chile and then Peru. In Cuyo he prepared his army, incorporating into it Chileans who fled in 1814 from the royalist reconquest of Chile, which had been briefly independent. In January 1817 San Martín led his army over the mountains to Chile. The subsequent military campaigns are detailed later. The Argentine government's enthusiasm for the plans of San Martín quickly cooled, and before long expenditures were refused and the army ordered home. The subsequent important military campaigns of San Martín depended mostly on his own determination, with great support from Chile.

Meanwhile, although after 1810 the provinces of what was to become Argentina were free of Spain, they disagreed violently on the organization of the new society.[7]

f. Other Areas of Quiescence or Repression

In the Captaincy-General of Guatemala small independence movements were suppressed, and from 1808 to 1821 the government and population responded rather calmly to the great events in Europe and America. Elite opinion generally supported Spain. There was, however, growing disagreement between the town council of Guatemala City, which favored freer trade, and the *consulado*, which opposed it. In 1810 six representatives to the Cortes were chosen by the chief

---

[7] See Chapter 24 on the political history of Argentina after 1810.

administrative districts. The instructions of the *cabildo* of Guatemala City to its deputy to the Cortes, adopted also by the other Central American deputies, were printed in Guatemala in 1811, a notable example of the way the press in many areas contributed to political development. The instructions—a severe indictment of Spanish government, law, and customs—asked for a constitution that would prevent despotism and for protection of the three sacred principles of property, liberty, and security. They also included a copy of the French Declaration of the Rights of Man and of the Citizen of 1794. That was remarkable for a generally moderate town council, dominated by men of property in an area little touched by rebellion. In 1813 in Guatemala an election to the reformed town council resulted in enlarged social representation, which conservatives found disturbing. The new council displayed some mildly liberal tendencies, clashing with the conservative Spanish administration of the captaincy-general. There was even in the area a small radical group that favored Independence. But many of the elite who supported some innovation remained conservative on most questions. Relatively passive, Central America awaited resolution of issues elsewhere.

In the Spanish Antilles, Santo Domingo was little disturbed by the idea of Independence from Spain and much disturbed by Spanish, French, British, and Haitian military forces. The small and poor population had no opportunity to develop an independent life. After years of upheaval, largely due to forces sent in from outside, the Spanish-speaking population in 1822 was forced by Haitian armies into a union of the island that lasted until 1844. Cuba and Puerto Rico were largely outside the stirring events of the Independence years. Spanish naval and other strength kept those islands loyal or quiescent.

In Quito and Peru, after the outbreaks of 1809, strong Spanish military forces controlled dissident opinion. The forces in Peru were strong enough not only to repulse the Buenos Aires invasion of Upper Peru and to hold down local dissidence, but to send men to Chile to defeat the early Independence movement there. Serious moves for Independence in Quito and Peru therefore awaited the arrival of armies from Chile and New Granada in the 1820s.

g. Warfare in Venezuela, New Granada, and Chile

Venezuela and New Granada

In Venezuela and New Granada warfare on an extensive scale began early and continued late, partly because of local leadership, partly because of the arrival of a Spanish army. News reached Venezuela in April 1810 of the French occupation of Sevilla and the flight of the *junta central*. As so often in those years in America, those events alarmed many of the elite (peninsular and creole) with the specter of French adventurism in America and the disappearance of effective connection with a legitimate Spanish government. After two years of discussion of the various crises in Spain, at least a few creoles were ready for innovation. The captain-general called a *cabildo abierto* to discuss the situation, and on April 19, 1810, it demonstrated how far some opinion had moved by ousting him and some other officials and creating a junta to rule for Ferdinand VII. Caracas also began to assume a leadership role for the entire province, as often happened with creoles in American capitals in the Independence years, by urging *cabildos* to form juntas and collaborate with Caracas. The response was spotty, not a good augur for the future. In fact, in Caracas and elsewhere, creoles were unsure of themselves and were divided as to what steps to take. They did know that lower-class cooperation would be needed for a real struggle with Spain, so they declared an end to Indian tribute and the African slave trade. Not only were those moves too radical for many creoles, but events quickly showed that they were not enough to overcome the dislike of the *castas* for creoles.

Simón Bolívar, then twenty-six, was among the radical creoles favoring Independence. Born into a wealthy family but orphaned young, Bolívar was educated by tutors in Venezuela and Europe. Married as a young man, he was soon widowed and never remarried. He was enamored of many of the ideas of the Enlightenment and the accomplishments of the revolutions in Britain's North American colonies and in France. On visits to Paris he not only confirmed his interest in modern ideas and free discussion, but at first admired Napoleon's deeds, though he later disliked his autocracy. Young Simón also enjoyed parties, salons, and dances in France, Italy, Spain, and later in America. He joined the Freemasons, a becoming and almost inevitable action by a young man of that time who wished to proclaim his modern outlook. His reading, travels, experience, and the radical ideas of his tutor Simón Rodríguez all induced in Bolívar, at least as early as 1805, a passion for freeing Venezuela from Spanish rule. His residence in Spain contributed to this attitude, for he visited the court and knew at first hand the relations between Godoy and the queen and the unlikable character of Crown Prince Ferdinand. He also experienced the slighting attitude of Spaniards toward colonials. In these general ideas Bolívar resembled a number of other prominent young men of the pre-Independence and Independence years, and like other creoles whose wealth was based on agricultural exports, he was attached to the "liberal" doctrine of free trade. Bolívar, however, had a uniquely volcanic personality, and the consuming passion for action and leadership that marked Napoleon. As an individual, Bolívar certainly was fully ready for Independence.

Meanwhile, the creole liberals and radicals were in trouble within a few months of creation of the junta in April 1810. Spain was able to send troops from Cuba and ships for a blockade. Division and confusion disrupted life in Venezuela. Bolívar was sent to London as head of a delegation to get British aid. He failed, since the British were interested in Spanish American Independence as useful to their own economy but cautious about complicating their military and diplomatic problems while facing Napoleon. Bo-

lívar did confer in England with Francisco Miranda, a native Venezuelan, former Spanish officer, and long-time revolution monger in exile,[8] and persuaded the sixty-year-old propagandist to return to Venezuela late in 1810. The young Bolívar and the aging Miranda found that the group in Venezuela claiming to rule for Ferdinand VII was merely marking time. Factionalism and disagreement, timidity and fear were crippling. Most of Venezuela was uncommitted to the pretensions of that group. Bolívar and Miranda helped push a call for a congress, which was elected by *cabildos*, and met in March 1811. On July 5, 1811, it declared Venezuela independent, the first such action in Spanish America by what could with some plausibility call itself a "national" body. It prepared and promulgated (December 1811) a constitution with federalist features, which signified both its liberalism and its inability to guess how divisive and usually unworkable that type of government would prove in Spanish America.

A number of other liberal measures were proclaimed but could not be enforced. While the government failed to capture the allegiance of much of the population, the economy decayed under blockade, disorder, an inflated currency, and the flight of Spanish capital. The expenses of the rebel government led it to issue paper money, which was known to be valueless, so that people resisted being required to accept it, considering that a form of confiscation and violation of property rights. Prices soared, which hurt everyone with a fixed income, including soldiers in the rebel or patriot forces. Meanwhile, the new government fought royalist armies and rebellions in its own shakily held territory.

Unhappy Venezuela was visited March 26, 1812, by an earthquake that killed some 20,000 in the Caracas area. Casualties were especially heavy among supporters of Independence from Spain. The loyalists, including the church hierarchy, used that fact to persuade the devout or

---

[8] See Chapter 14, Section c, on Miranda's earlier career as a precursor of Independence.

superstitious that action against Spain was impious, subject to divine punishment. There is no knowing the importance of the issue. Many members of the lower class were in any event inclined toward the loyalists. Many *pardos* (usually meaning mulattoes) with reason considered creoles their principal foes. Indians and blacks at first tended to see nothing for themselves in upper-class quarrels. They tried to stay out of them until they learned they could profit from participation, whereupon they enlisted with either side. In short, the Independence party— led by creoles—was in trouble with the lower class. In 1812 the creoles had that support in some places, including the Caracas area, but that was not enough.

In June 1812 the patriot army was thrashed at Puerto Cabello. Miranda, as commander in chief, signed a capitulation. There is controversy as to whether he showed cowardice, senility, compassion, or good sense. Probably he meant to resume the fight later, but Bolívar and others accused Miranda of treachery and turned him over to the Spaniards. He died in prison in Spain. Bolívar was allowed by the Spaniards to depart, both because they were grateful and because he did not seem important. The first Venezuelan republic had lasted about a year.

Bolívar, now twenty-nine, in December 1812 went with some other Venezuelans to Cartagena on the Caribbean coast of New Granada. Cartagena had in May 1810 established the first junta in New Granada to rule in the name of Ferdinand, after many parts of the *reyno* had been discussing the situation for two years, usually in not very radical terms. Not until the period from July 1 to December 31, 1810, had the liberal creole movement rolled through New Granada and swept out Spanish officials. The Bogotá *cabildo* created a junta in July 1810 that swore loyalty to Ferdinand VII and ousted royal officials. The Bogotá junta claimed predominance, and other areas resented and resisted the claim. Juntas were created in other towns, but some such movements failed as royalist military forces won at Panama, Popayán, and Santa Marta. The

difficult terrain of New Granada and old regional conflicts and suspicions made the realm a tangle of confusion and suspicion.

There were very real conflicts of economic as well as political interest. The port of Cartagena enjoyed a brisk trade within the Spanish system, as well as contraband activity, and interior towns objected to its economic policies. Cartagena, in turn, was only one of the numerous regional centers that objected to domination from Bogotá. In September 1810 both Cartagena and Bogotá suggested congresses of provincial delegates, the former on a federalist basis, the latter on a centralist. Thus began a fundamental struggle that occurred in such other areas as La Plata early in the Independence period. The congress of delegates met at Bogotá in December 1810. Present were both Camilo Torres, a radical spokesman of 1809, and Antonio Nariño, the old liberal whose advocacy of innovation went back to the 1780s.[9] Nariño favored centralized government under Bogotá's control; Torres, federalism. The congress broke up early in 1811 precisely on the issue of whether the junta of Bogotá or the congress of delegates from several provinces was the supreme authority in New Granada.

New Granada was both politically disordered and economically depressed when Bogotá issued a constitution in 1811, under which a president was named and legislative, financial, and military action undertaken. Nariño, although not president, was a dominant figure and the leader of centralist sentiment. Torres headed the federalist opposition. The government soon had to be reorganized, partly because of fears of Nariño's unabashed centralism, which he trumpeted in his own newspaper, another early example of the role the press and propaganda generally played in the Independence era. Nothing like that had been known in colonial times. The country simply fell into political parts. In 1811–1812 there were two assertedly "national" governments, the new one in 1812 at Bogotá being headed by Nariño as centralist leader, and another repre-

---

[9] See Chapter 14, Section c, on Nariño.

senting federalism in the provinces. Neither had much authority. Individual provinces and towns exercised independent powers and even engaged in economic warfare with tariffs and other methods.

Nariño failed in an effort at union by military means and had to consent to a congress of the United Provinces of New Granada, which met at Leiva in the fall of 1812. No agreement could be reached there, and the civil war continued. But Nariño was confined to a narrow central area, and royalist armies threatened from north and south. At this point in late 1812, Bolívar arrived, preceded by the reputation he had won in the wars in Venezuela. He joined forces with Cartagena, which was warring with royalist forces centered at nearby Santa Marta. Very soon Bolívar issued a statement to New Granadans in favor of centralist government, as a means of uniting against the Spaniards. It reflected his disillusion with the federalist element in the first Republic of Venezuela, and the development of a view that firm government was a necessity in Spanish America.

In late 1812 he led forces against royalists in New Granada and liberated Cúcuta, at the border of Venezuela. He was made a citizen of New Granada and a brigadier. He also managed to convince some important New Granadans of the importance of rooting Spanish forces out of Venezuela; even Camilo Torres and Antonio Nariño agreed. But much popular opinion in New Granada was more shortsighted and objected to use of money and men to fight in Venezuela. Bolívar did have aid from the New Granadan government and a combined force of Venezuelans and New Granadans when he invaded Venezuela in 1813. He issued a proclamation of "war to the death," authorizing the killing of all who actively supported the opposition. It was an effort to force fence sitters to take sides and to stimulate a sense of patriotism. George Washington had done much the same thing, although without declaring a war to the death. Bolívar's proclamation has been criticized as brutal, which says nothing about its possible value

as a tactic or about the brutalities being practiced by the royalist forces. In any event, the proclamation did little to increase the ferocity of a war in which butchery already had been committed on both sides. Bolívar's military effort carried him quickly to Caracas in August 1813. He founded the second Republic of Venezuela, was proclaimed Liberator, and in January 1814 was named dictator. By then it was becoming clear that he could not hold the country. The royalists were too strong. The *pardos* in the southern *llanos* or plains were still royalist, partly because they had been promised war booty and legal equality. They also had a talented Spanish leader, José Boves, who made of this fierce irregular cavalry from the cattle country a terror to the opposition. In a further indication of the violence of feeling during the conflict, Bolívar wrote from his military headquarters in October 1813 to the governor of Curaçao:

> The fierce Spaniard, spewed upon the shores of Colombia, proceeded to transform Nature's loveliest of territories into a vast and odious empire of cruelty and plunder. . . . Men and women, the aged and the young, their ears having been cropped off, were skinned alive and then cast into poisoned lakes or put to death by slow and agonizing methods. Nature was violated in its innocent beginnings when yet unborn babes were destroyed in the wombs of expectant mothers by blows or bayonets.

On February 8, 1814, Bolívar ordered commanders at La Guaira and Caracas to shoot all Spanish prisoners in jails and hospitals; more than eight hundred royalists were slain. More atrocities followed on both sides. In June Boves beat the patriots (as they called themselves) at La Puerta. On July 6 Bolívar evacuated Caracas, and much of the population fled with him in terror, harried by pursuing royalist forces. Bolívar again fled Venezuela, by sea, in September 1814, leaving his supporters to the mercies of the royalists. He had no choice, since he was neither quixotic nor romantic and saw no point in throwing away his life as a gesture. Besides, he was right in his belief in the importance of his leadership to the cause of Independence. He understood the nature of the terrible struggle in which he was engaged, the bitter social divisions and hatreds that he had not created, but that he in some part would learn to control, until their essential uncontrollability would nearly break that valorous heart.

Meanwhile, the political struggle had continued in New Granada, in the period historians call that of the *patria boba* (foolish fatherland), when men quarreled over regional influence and the structure of government—and personal ambition—while royalist forces threatened from all sides. Cundinamarca—central New Granada—in July 1813 declared independence from Spain, but would not agree with the Congress dominated by the other provinces and the federalist idea. A royal army was moving from the south, backed by the royalist strongholds in Quito and Peru. Nariño led a southern campaign against it, only to be captured and shipped to prison in Spain in 1814.

In late 1814, Bolívar, back from his defeat in Venezuela, was given a military command by the federalist Congress. He took Bogotá for the Congress in December, and it soon moved there. But disaster loomed. Ferdinand VII was on the throne of Spain and in rampant reaction. He sent an army under General Pablo Morillo to northern South America. Royalists in many places were encouraged to increase their efforts. New Granada was being reconquered. Bolívar fled to Jamaica. Many patriots despaired of victory and opted for collaboration, which meant the old Spanish system of viceroy and *audiencia* so far as Ferdinand VII was concerned. By 1816 the Congress was dissolved, many patriots had fled the area, and Morillo was spreading terror and death and confiscating property. His notion of pacification was the execution of such men as Dr. Camilo Torres and the scientist Francisco de Caldas. No wonder that although the terror made collaborators of the timid, it merely enraged others. It is misleading to assert that by 1816 Venezuela and New Granada were pacified; it is more to the point, as events proved, to state that the temporary tactical victories of the Span-

ish and loyalist American forces were used by them to convince their opponents further that only military methods would serve in argument with the antique Spanish colonial idea.

Chile

In Chile, as everywhere, much of the reaction to news from Spain reflected old divisions between creoles and peninsulars, which were intensified under the new circumstances after 1808 and especially 1810. The patriots (called "revolutionists" and less polite terms by the loyalists) came to believe that the Spanish resistance governments were unwilling to grant real equality to America. Creole political development was quiet for two years in Chile, from 1808 into 1810, although General García Carrasco, the captain-general, lacked political finesse. He capped other unpopular moves with illegal arrest of some conspirators in May 1810. Leading organizations and individuals protested. The general stuck to his guns, in part because of news of the May coup d'etat at Buenos Aires. Such bumbling brought him increased agitation, and led the Santiago *cabildo* to call a *cabildo abierto*, which met in an atmosphere of armed alert by creole and Spanish parties. The conservative Spanish *audiencia*, fearing rebellion, managed to get García Carrasco to resign.

His legal successor as captain-general was Brigadier Mateo de Toro Zambrano, Conde de la Conquista, a creole landowner and an octogenarian. Men arose to make impassioned pleas for Independence and republicanism. One wrote as "John, Lover of the Fatherland," this being a term applied in these years to areas all over Spanish America. The aged captain-general felt compelled to call a *cabildo abierto*, which some 350 men attended on September 18, 1810, and proceeded to create a junta, at least nominally loyal to Ferdinand VII. It was to rule until a national assembly could meet. The junta was rather conservative in composition. Many Chilean creoles were conservative people of property, and they feared retaliation by the viceroy's military forces in Peru. The junta was not then clearly seen as a move toward Independence, although events later proved that it was.

A Congress met in July 1811 and lasted until December. It elected another junta. Both junta and Congress began to proclaim liberal measures, including one favoring free trade and another calling for the gradual emancipation of black slaves. In the Congress, also, Santiago began to clash with the provinces, a common development in Spanish America in the Independence period. Prominent in those days was Juan Martínez de Rozas, a rich creole allied to important mercantile interests. During a long public career, he had been legal adviser to Ambrosio O'Higgins, intendant at Concepción. Rozas was of the group of late colonial creoles who favored innovation within the empire. He went to Santiago with General García Carrasco, when the latter became captain-general. Before long he abandoned the bumbling general and returned to Concepción. Soon he became a member of the first Chilean junta, named by the *cabildo abierto* of September 1810. In this and immediately subsequent governments—changing rapidly in Chile in those years—he supported a radical position for Independence, but also supported Concepción and the south against domination from Santiago. He was a good example of the wealthy, well-educated, moderate creole with considerable experience in government under the colonial regime, who was in many ways well prepared to play a prominent role in the stirring events after 1808.

Another creole who came to prominence at this time was Bernardo O'Higgins, illegitimate son of that Ambrosio O'Higgins who had been intendant of Concepción, later governor of Chile, a marquis, and viceroy of Peru. Bernardo was also the godson of Martínez de Rozas. But Bernardo suffered badly from his bastardy. His father barely acknowledged his existence, did not communicate with him, did not provide for him at his death. Bernardo did ultimately, with great difficulty, get title to some of his dead father's lands in southern Chile. The son was educated in part in Europe, where he naturally became acquainted with current liberal ideas. He knew the revolution monger Miranda in England. In 1802, aged twenty-four, he returned to Chile. He was in the first Congress, where he was a radical and favored Independence.

Another prominent leader was José Miguel Carrera, twenty-six when he returned to Chile in 1811 from a distinguished career in the Spanish army. He was a member of a rich and large creole family. His reputation and his family connections made him at once a leader, a radical. In December 1811 he used military force to dissolve the Congress and set himself in the control of government. Through 1812 and into 1813 he became the most important figure in government, at times a virtual dictator, ever ready to use force to gain his ends. O'Higgins did not care for Carrera, but for a time reluctantly supported him for the sake of unity in gaining Independence. Martínez de Rozas opposed the military dictatorship because it represented centralization at Santiago, and a threat to his own ambitions in the south. In the civil war that arose, Martínez de Rozas was captured by Carrera and sent into exile, where he died in 1813. Newspaper publication began in 1812, and the priest Camilo Henríquez in the *Aurora de Chile* carried on propaganda for the radical position. The new press contributed to political development and liberty and to factionalism and disorder. In fact, conditions were so disturbed that little could be done to alter institutions in Chile.

The Chilean government had continued to pay lip service to the Spanish connection, but few were fooled—certainly not the viceroy in Peru, who in March 1813 launched the long-feared counteroffensive against Chile. A small force was sent from Peru by sea to southern Chile, where it became largely Chilean by the addition of local loyalists, including peasants and Araucanian Indians. So the conflict was a civil war, and the *patria vieja* (old fatherland—the first Chilean republic) was destroyed not only by personalism and poor government but by a serious division in the population.

It also was destroyed by military inefficiency. The events in Chile were illustrative of much of the military side of the Independence period elsewhere, although there was more military experience in Chile than in many places because of the Indian frontier situation. There was a so-called line, or regular, army of about 1,900. The enlisted men were Chilean, as were most of the officers, though the senior grades generally were peninsular. This little force was poorly organized, trained, and equipped. The militia had a nominal strength of 16,000 and its personnel were nearly all Chilean. The command of militia units was given to the most prestigious landowners or well-to-do in the localities. The Chilean Independence forces thus inherited little in the way of professional military training or experience. When an infantry battalion was raised in 1811, the officers named were men prominent in civilian life. That was, of course, an old practice in the world, and common in the revolt of the British colonies of North America a few years earlier. The Irish military engineer MacKenna observed that in Chile the only requisite to becoming an officer was possession of a fancy uniform and a pair of buckles. A modern Chilean historian has called the early patriot forces there a horde. How could they have been otherwise?

With the beginning of the Spanish counteroffensive, O'Higgins turned to military activity and quickly became a major commander, learning as he practiced. Carrera, as military chief, could not stem the Spanish advance. For this reason, and because his arbitrary military rule had made him many enemies, he was ousted from his command, and O'Higgins was made chief commander in March 1814. He also became a member of the junta. But the junta gave way to a supreme director, a common recourse in such crises in Spanish America during Independence. The dictator was Francisco de Lastra, a creole who had served in the Spanish navy. In May 1814 he signed an agreement with the Spanish commander for an armistice. It did not please either side but kept the peace for a few months. O'Higgins kept his army extant and would not accept the armistice. More important, the viceroy in Lima did not accept it, ordered renewed hostilities, and demanded unconditional surrender. He also sent more troops. The long feud between the Carreras and O'Higgins was patched up briefly in face of the terrible threat of reconquest. At Rancagua, near Santiago, in October 1814, O'Higgins fought a bloody battle with the royal forces, while Carrera kept his troops back until it was too late. The Carreras and O'Higgins retreated east over the Andes to join San Martín in Cuyo in what is now Argentina, where Buenos Aires was supporting preparation of an army to invade Chile and Peru. The Spanish in Chile set about ensuring continued opposition by oppressive measures and by reestablishing the old colonial system. Guerrilla warfare against this in Chile continued the development, so well begun in 1811–1814, of physical destruction, factionalism and social hatred, and appeal to the military solution of problems. Eight years of wrangling, experiment, and warfare in Chile and elsewhere settled only one thing—the mystique of the old empire was dead. That was enough to ensure the eventual defeat of Spain.

20 The Final Phase of Independence, 1817–1825

Now the Spanish Americans went from triumph to triumph, dismembering the Spanish empire, following the United States in the defeat of European political control and in acceptance of the revolutionary principle of republicanism. The prospect of military victory enhanced the value of political control, stimulating ambition and faction, and aggravating into nationalistic xenophobia the localism or regionalism that had grown up in the colonial era. To the leaders the problems of finance and social order seemed ever more difficult, and often they decided that only authoritarian measures offered hope of temporary solution. The upheaval in this enormous area, which it seemed increasingly likely would win Independence, was followed most carefully abroad by Britain, which of all the best-developed powers stood to gain the most from exploitation of markets for industrial goods, capital, technological expertise, shipping, and marine insurance. Its sea power could decide the issue of European intervention in America. Its merchant ships served the likely markets of Spanish America during the war years and there met Yankee vessels equally eager to link the natural commodities of Spanish America with the manufactures of the North Atlantic.

a. From Low Tide to Victory

Although the patriot or Independence cause was at low tide in 1816 in terms of control of territory or armies, its true situation had been expressed a year before by Bolívar, when he wrote that the destiny of America was decided, because "the habit of obedience, [which was] the tie that bound her to Spain, has been severed." Too many Americans had lost respect for Spain's kings and statesmen and loathed connection with a country that proclaimed America's inferiority and tried to sustain sovereignty with guns. Even though the Independence movement had scarcely started in some places, and where it had was badly battered (except in Buenos Aires), that loss of respect for Spain was critical.

It was true that in some places Spanish victories brought an increase in loyalism, stimulated also by fears of the social reform that seemed to threaten when old verities and habits were disturbed. In addition, the return of Ferdinand VII to the throne in 1814, his restoration of absolutism and the old colonial regime, and the dispatch of the Morillo army to northern South America seemed ominous for the Independence movement. There also was much fear that Spain might get help from other conservative powers in Europe, now in rampant reaction after defeating Napoleon and, they hoped, republicanism. Finally, there was gloom among Spanish American rebels and optimism among loyalists in contemplation of the factionalism that weakened rebel efforts.

To suppose that in 1816 Spain "controlled" much of America would be misleading. Its hold was precarious and costly. In New Spain, Calleja, the chief architect of Spanish control, nearly despaired of establishing it and considered joining the cause of Independence himself. The Argentine exception to the generalization of "defeat" by 1816 was a very large exception indeed, and reconquest would have been difficult. How much control in Chile could the Spanish party be said to have with guerrilla warfare going on in 1814–1816? In addition, there were in Buenos Aires people who realized that if Spain could pacify all other areas, she then would be free to send forces to the Plata, so help was prepared for Independence forces in Chile and Peru.

Loyalist optimism and creole pessimism in 1816 must be tempered by noting what the Spaniards did with their victories. The savage repressions, the rigid reapplication of old colonial rules, in Chile, New Granada, and Venezuela in 1814–1816, or in New Spain even earlier, meant despair of return to rule by consent and reliance on naked force. Spanish power could not sustain such a method, even if the national leader had not been the incompetent Ferdinand VII. European conservative aid to Spain for its American problems never materialized, because the continental powers had but limited interest when there were so many costly tasks to pursue in a Europe threatened with republicanism; while the British were opposed, and their navy sat astride the line of communications with America. In January 1820 an army mutiny in Spain became an insurrection that forced Ferdinand again to swear to the Constitution of 1812. Americans paid little attention; it was too late for shallowly based liberalism in Spain to knit up the raveled fabric of empire. The conservative Concert of Europe sent armies into Spain in 1823 to put down radicalism, so that Ferdinand once again could foreswear himself and restore absolutism.

Many rebels had not given up in 1816 but had merely withdrawn to reorganize and fight another day. The very existence of these men ensured almost endless difficulty in establishing a Spanish control system that could be maintained at bearable cost. Many rebels were quite irreconcilable. They would not accept the old colonial system, with its discrimination against creoles and its attempts to stifle the American economy. They had experienced the exhilaration of political leadership and power, and they had learned that Americans could effectively organize and use military force.

What they needed now—and found difficult to acquire—was courage and persistence, better military organization and leadership, a certain modicum of supplies, and sufficient cooperation from the general population. George Washington had required much the same a third of a century earlier, and he too found it difficult to acquire. Spanish American leaders at least had some advantages: Spain was less powerful than Britain, and the terrain and distances of Spanish America made Spain's problem even more formidable than Britain's had been. The leadership was developed on the basis of experience in the earlier period and on the use of men with good military training, like San Martín and the small cadre of foreigners who fought in Venezuela, New Granada, Quito, Peru, and Chile in the last phase of Independence.

The greatest military exploits of the liberators naturally occurred in the final phase. The important role of leadership was illuminated by victory. That role came out of a social situation in which the personal qualities of commanders were important to the confidence or morale of unsophisticated common soldiers. Much the same could be said of the troops of Alexander the Great and Napoleon. In the modern age the functional equivalent is the enlisted man's belief in the national aims and the technical efficiency of the force in which he serves. In any event, much of the final victory in Spanish America was a matter of leadership. Some of this was sheer force of character and persistence; some was military skill; some was political decision, notably in persuading more of the lower class to fight for the creole cause and in finding money and supplies, either by cajoling or threatening civil government, or by seizure in the countryside.

b. Chile

The Chilean refugees who joined San Martín at Mendoza in Cuyo in 1814 carried with them their disagreements. Carrera tried to insist on his predominance but found San Martín unresponsive. The latter could not be browbeaten or flustered and could not in Argentina be treated to a sample of Carrera's method of military imposition, so Carrera departed. San Martín organized the Chileans into a reserve and made O'Higgins their commander and a general of the United Provinces of the Río de la Plata. San Martín prepared the attack on Peru through Chile with the care of a professional officer. There later was dispute as to some of his actions as a field commander, but his ability as an organizer and trainer of military forces was unquestionable.

At the beginning of 1817 the Army of the Andes, some 5,500 men, mostly infantry, went over the high mountain passes into Chile. On February 12 they beat the royalists at Chacabuco, near Santiago, with O'Higgins and the Chileans prominent in the victory. Although the Spaniards retained a strong position in southern Chile and won victories thereafter, Chacabuco proved the turning point of the war in Chile.

Patriots, both the sincere and the suddenly converted, celebrated the arrival of the victorious army. San Martín was offered political power by the Santiago open *cabildo*, but he preferred his military tasks, and he and O'Higgins had decided before leaving Cuyo that the Chilean would be leader in his own land. San Martín traveled back to Buenos Aires for orders. The rest of his career in America was to be marked by his lack of interest in the dual political-military role so

conspicuously played by men like O'Higgins and Bolívar. O'Higgins became supreme director of Chile and head of its army (not including San Martín's men). He was head of a state trying to act in a country where many men opposed it or were not fully committed and where ancient social divisions had been exacerbated by the destruction, carnage, pressures, and betrayals of years of civil war. Finding resources to pursue the campaigns against the royal forces in the south was difficult.

O'Higgins raised an army that was typical of the period. There was a big problem with discipline, and the troops required close supervision, which the officers often could not or would not provide. Uniforms were highly miscellaneous or absent. Sandals were more common than shoes, partly because new ones could be made from green hides in the field. Pay was low, half of it was held back for rations, and sometimes the rest was in arrears. The rations were often scanty and sometimes dreadful. A foreign observer said that the ills the men suffered were left "almost entirely to nature," which was what they were accustomed to in their civilian lives. Many soldiers were accompanied by *mestiza* wives or concubines, who prepared meals and built shelters and otherwise comforted them. The same sort of lower-class enlisted men served in the royalist forces.

The new state had scarcely more than declared Independence from Spain in February 1818 when its military advances in the south were wiped out by new troops sent from Peru. In March the royalists moved north under General Osorio, the same commander and the same movement that had defeated the patriots four years before. Also the same were the many Chileans who prepared to collaborate with the latest conquering army. Osorio beat O'Higgins badly at Cancha Rayada, near Santiago. Fortunately, San Martín had returned, and his leadership and troops were decisive in a great patriot victory at Maipú on May 5, 1818. Possibly 5,000 men were engaged on each side, a large battle for the Spanish American Wars of Independence. This was one occasion on which American troops performed magnificently. Some 2,000 royalist soldiers were killed, about as many were captured, and "only a ragged remnant escaped." Chilean Independence was secure, and the road to Peru lay open. A comment on the times was the fact that at Maipú fought freed blacks whom San Martín had brought from Argentina.

O'Higgins' rule lasted from 1817 to 1823. There was no congress, and O'Higgins resisted the rather strong demand for a more representative system. Something like a constitution was adopted and approved, as O'Higgins insisted, by a plebiscite—in which no one voted against it. O'Higgins considered that dictatorial rule was necessary in view of the disorder in the country, the needs of the expedition to Peru, and the great problem of changing Chilean society sufficiently to make it capable of self-government. This method of rule met increasing opposition, not lessened by the fact that until August 1820 O'Higgins had the support of San Martín. He also had the aid of the Logia Lautarina, a branch of Miranda's secret society, which San Martín had insisted on setting up as a means of knitting together leaders who were committed to Independence. They were expected to collaborate secretly not only on military matters, but on governmental, when members became civil officials. O'Higgins, a member, depended on the lodge. Understandably, many Chileans objected both to the method and to its Argentine connections.

They had plenty of other reasons for complaint. O'Higgins frequently interfered with the press and expressions of opinion. He used arbitrary means of trying to change Chilean social customs. His use of troops and summary courts to put down rural brigandage seemed to rural magnates part of an undesirable centralizing tendency. He used public funds lavishly to support the expedition being prepared for Peru. Many people did not have the strategic vision of O'Higgins and San Martín regarding the necessity of defeating Spanish forces that were not just over the horizon from their own doorsteps. Money

went for ships, equipment, and foreign officers, for a navy, not only to fight Spanish naval forces, but to carry the army to Peru, rather than to march through the great northern desert. All the naval cost was borne by Chile. Army support was Chilean, too, because Buenos Aires had ordered its men home and stopped financial aid. It too was following a doorstep-horizon policy. San Martín and many soldiers remained in Chile.

The military was much in evidence in Chile. O'Higgins used it directly, and he used it as a threat. There was no doubt of the need for military force against royalists and bandits; sometimes distinguishing between them was difficult. In the south royalists still had help from the local population and some from Araucanian Indians. The warfare in the area was barbaric, and for some years after 1819 generals Freire and Prieto struggled to end it. Not only was a brutalization process continuing among the general population, but military commanders were enlarging convictions and ambitions that centered on military solutions. In 1821 Prieto managed to defeat many of the southern royalists/bandits. He executed some, but pardoned others and incorporated them into the army. This happened in many places in Spanish America. It is not certain how much more inclined to the support of *caudillos* such elements were than other enlisted men, but they can scarcely have been more attached to constitutional government. In July 1818 a special agent of the United States wrote to the State Department, describing the militarization of Chile,

> The government itself is a completely military one. Everything is done by soldiers. Even for the execution of a thief . . . the soldiers are drawn out . . . and they fire upon the criminals. The Directoral Palace . . . is guarded and thronged with soldiers. In fine, all the cities resemble military barracks and the country more or less is covered with soldiers.

c. The Bolivarian States, 1817–1822

To a remarkable degree Simón Bolivar came to dominate military and civil affairs in what was

Independence

Miguel Hidalgo y Costilla, a well-educated and liberal Mexican priest, in 1810 led the warfare in Mexico for independence from Spain. Although the fighting began as a creole conspiracy, Hidalgo, in order to gain support, turned it into an Indian uprising, from which it evolved into a class war. The rebellion was savagely suppressed, but Mexico today celebrates its outset as Independence Day. *Organization of American States*

Simón Bolívar of Venezuela was a creole artistocrat who helped liberate large areas that later became six independent republics. The battles he led started in 1810 and did not end until 1825. *Organization of American States*

Bernardo O'Higgins was the foremost hero of Chilean Independence. His combination of military power and civil office created resentment in the upper class and prefigured the dictatorships of later decades. *Organization of American States*

José de San Martín, an Argentine with experience in the Spanish army, was a skillful military organizer and commander. He helped to protect Independence in Argentina and extend it to Chile and Peru. *Organization of American States*

Henri Christophe despotically forced laborers to build the Citadel, a huge fortress in Haiti. Its cost—in lives and money—illustrates one of the dilemmas of Independence: How much individual choice does a society require to function successfully? How much discipline? *Courtesy of the Haitian National Office of Tourism*

briefly the Republic of Colombia (called Gran Colombia by historians), including Venezuela, New Granada, Panama, and Quito. He had gone to Jamaica in 1815, as the royalists, aided by the army brought from Spain by General Morillo, took over Venezuela and most of New Granada. Bolívar stayed in Jamaica more than six months. One product of his exile was the Jamaican (sometimes called the "Prophetic") Letter, an important example of his many statements on political problems and philosophy. His political ideas and actions sometimes then and later were criticized as betraying an improper mingling with military factors and thus a sad contribution to the future of Spanish America. That view exaggerates his influence on the social environment, which he could manipulate in a limited number of ways but could not change. Like the other leaders of a time of political and military uncertainty and poor social communications, he depended heavily on personal relations. Bolívar was fortunate in being a man of great charm when he wished to be. He also was a remarkable speaker, a useful quality in such times. He was generous with funds when they could be found and went to great lengths to care for his men. They respected him because he was physically courageous. Finally, he was a man of boundless energy. He followed exhausting official labors with hours on the dance floor. This, and his numerous intrigues with women, might hurt him with a few leaders but not with the bulk of his men.

The Jamaican Letter stated Bolívar's hope for a free, powerful, and well-ordered Spanish America. He did, however, think that the Spanish heritage made development of political principles and skills difficult, because the people had been kept in a "purely passive" condition, and in "permanent infancy with regard to public affairs." He also revealed the beginnings of what would become his conviction that extreme paternalism or oligarchic government was needed. He opposed the federal system as too complex for Spanish American society. He supported a union of Venezuela and New Granada as "Colombia,"

with a government resembling that of England, but with an elected president, though he might serve a life term. Bolívar thus repudiated the monarchism some conservative Spanish Americans favored, but he favored rule by an elite. He indicated his supposition that uniting all Spanish America into one state or confederation would be nearly impossible, but he favored calling representatives of all areas to a congress at Panama. Many of these ideas were sustained by later events, although Spanish Americans did develop political principles and skills—but not always the ones Bolívar had in mind. Those that did emerge were often confined to small minorities as he had predicted.

Bolívar went to south Haiti, where President Pétion supported refugee Spanish American patriots. Pétion agreed to help Bolívar if the latter would emancipate the slaves. In March 1816 Bolívar sailed with some 250 officers and supplies for an army to be recruited in Venezuela. On his arrival, the Venezuelans understandably were not enthusiastic about a man with a handful of followers whose real dedication to their interests was impossible to judge, when strong royalist forces lurked just over the horizon. As the royalists approached, Bolívar decreed slavery abolished, and sailed back to Haiti. Now, however, he displayed the imagination that often marked his career: he determined to invade not the more heavily populated north of Venezuela, but to go up the great Orinoco River into the remote interior. With more help from Pétion, he did so in December 1816.

During the next three years, with Angostura (later Ciudad Bolívar) his headquarters after July 1817, he took some critical steps. (*a*) He recruited foreign aid, both men and supplies. (*b*) He made persistent efforts to get more aid from the lower class by promising a fair sociopolitical system, including abolition of slavery. (*c*) He kept up military action, but without enough success to promise final victory in Venezuela; still, merely to endure was a triumph. (*d*) He called a Congress and adopted a Constitution that offered a rallying point to creoles, including specific appeal to New Granada as well as Venezuela, and also a further appeal to the masses by providing for the abolition of slavery. And when all this seemed too slow or too little, (*e*) he adopted a daring new military strategy by invading New Granada out of the *llanos* of Venezuela.

One reason Bolívar endured in the backlands was that he induced José Antonio Páez to join him with his *llaneros*, horsemen of the plains, who were to be an important part of the military and civil history of Venezuela for years to come. Páez's men followed him as a *caudillo*, a chieftain who won, because he knew how to deal with them. He was not too strict about such trifles as looting, treatment of prisoners, and discipline generally. Furthermore, Páez was an epileptic, which was thought awesome and lucky. When Bolívar asked Páez's bodyguard, El Negro Primo, why he had earlier fought with the royalists, he said "Greed," meaning that to a man with nothing more than a shirt a bit of money and a sense of self-respect and achievement were more attractive than creeds. Fortunately for Bolívar, the royalists did little to inspire confidence in the *pardos* (mulattoes), who were a large part of the lower class in Venezuela. A high Spanish officer there in 1815 wrote the government in Spain that although the *castas* at the moment preferred the royalists, they might turn to the patriots, which could be dangerous considering the military experience they had been acquiring. He also noted that colored soldiers on both sides singled out whites for slaughter. He favored permitting more leeway to escape the infamy of African blood, especially through the systems existing for legally extinguishing it. But the crown opposed such a policy, and certainly the creole royalists were against it.

Aid from Europe was to be important. It began arriving in 1817. Some 3,000 to 5,000 paid foreign volunteers served in Venezuela and New Granada from 1817 to 1820. Most were English and Irish soldiers unemployed with the end of the Napoleonic wars. The maximum that served in any one of Bolívar's military campaigns was 1,200, but they constituted a substantial minority in the small armies of the time. Their knowledge, experience, and discipline under fire proved invaluable on a number of occasions. Inevitably, there was jealousy of these foreigners of the British Legion.

The three years of Bolívar's Orinoco campaign were difficult. The royalists were too strong for him to do much more than hold his own. He wrote in May 1818 that he had destroyed some 5,000 to 6,000 Spaniards and creole royalists, but that even more still were under arms. In August 1818 he decided to call a Congress as one way of prosecuting the struggle. It met at Angostura, in a remote and thinly populated land, in February 1819. Some delegates had been elected in towns, some chosen by soldiers. Bolívar told the Congress that he opposed one-man rule and favored free elections, popular sovereignty, republicanism, a government of powers divided among its branches, and the elimination of slavery and titles of nobility. But he opposed federal government, because there were great divisions between social groups in Venezuela, and the population lacked the "political virtue and moral rectitude" found in the United States, which used that system.

He held up the English system as a model in some respects. He wanted popular election of deputies to a lower house, but senators chosen by the Congress from among the leaders of Independence, after which the office would be hereditary. This system, he asserted, would make of the Senate a "bulwark of liberty." He favored a strong executive as a necessary ingredient in the struggle against the foes of the government and as a barrier to anarchy. In addition to the third, or judicial, power, he called for a fourth, the moral power (Areopagus), to act in the realms of education and civic purity, seeking to eliminate sloth and other social ills. He favored inclusion in the government of New Granada (including Quito), and there were some New Granadan delegates at the Congress. In August 1819 the Congress signed a provisional Constitution embodying much of the Bolivarian scheme, although the moral power was not adopted. It was put into an appendix to the document. The Congress in December 1819 proclaimed the union of Venezuela, New Granada, and Quito as the Republic of Colombia. The capital was to be at Cúcuta in New Granada, near the border with Venezuela. The Congress elected Bolívar president. All this set up a scheme to appeal to wide creole support and to gain the interest of some of the lower class. The latter, however, could find little to excite it in the Constitution and in any event was taking sides more on the basis of reactions to personalities, the supposed orientations of leaders and groups, and the actions of the latter in military campaigns and in the propaganda and promises directed to the popular classes. The Constitution did provide a focus for Bolívar's military and civil activities and was a clear exposition of his conviction of the need for firm rule by the creole minority.

Between Bolívar's opening address to the Congress of Angostura in February 1819 and its actions later in the year in adopting a Constitution, declaring the Republic of Colombia, and electing the Liberator as president, he invaded New Granada. It was a daring move and an epic march, out of the tropical lowlands of the Orinoco basin west into the high Andes to join the New Granadan patriots. At the Battle of Boyacá in August 1819 the patriots won a great victory, capturing 1,600 royalists. The viceroy immediately fled Bogotá. Various patriot forces took over most of the highland cities. In Venezuela, Spanish General Morillo recognized that this stroke possibly was decisive. Early in 1820, when the liberal rebellion occurred in Spain, the new government ordered Morillo to negotiate with the rebels on the basis of the Constitution of 1812. Few people in America now cared about that instrument. In November 1820 the representatives of Bolívar and Morillo signed a treaty establishing a six months' armistice, ending the barbarities of the war to the death pursued on both sides, and agreeing to negotiate a permanent peace. The agreement clearly was favorable to the waxing Independence cause. Morillo re-

turned to Spain. The patriots broke the armistice by attacking the royalists in Venezuela. In June 1821 Bolívar won a great victory at Carabobo, losing only some 200 of his 6,000 men, while the royalists lost some 40 percent of their force of 5,000, as dead, wounded, or captives. The war was over except for the expulsion of some coastal garrisons in 1823.

In early 1821 a constitutional convention at Cúcuta adopted a permanent Constitution in place of the 1819 instrument. The Constitution provided a union of Venezuela and New Granada but did not mention Quito. Some leaders expected, however, that Quito would become part of Colombia. The convention also elected Bolívar president, declared black children free at birth, and abolished Indian tribute. Although some obviously liberal actions were being taken, on the whole the actions and personnel of government were dedicated to the interests of men of property. Bolívar had relatively little time to spare for the routine of government, being preoccupied with plans for carrying the war to the royalists of Quito and Peru. He tended to leave affairs to the vice-president, Francisco de Paula Santander. In the field, Bolívar and his staff handled a large correspondence, mostly dealing with military affairs; but inescapably he often took actions that were essentially civil in nature without consulting the government or issued strong demands that the civil government resisted.

Money and supplies for the military inevitably caused clashes. The country had suffered grievous losses of life and property. The essentially agricultural and pastoral economy had been weakened. The colonial revenue system was disrupted. The politically active population was divided by regional jealousies that bad communications enhanced, and it lacked unity on such basic questions as the position of the church, centralism versus federalism, treatment of the lower classes, and war supplies or anything else that cost money. Bolívar was plagued by the lack of government funds and increasingly insistent on the use of taxation and forced loans. He sometimes showed favoritism for his military comrades and some disdain for men who had not fought for liberty. He strongly supported the distribution among his officers and men of public lands and properties sequestered from loyalists.

d. The Final Junction in Peru

General Sucre was sent from New Granada by sea with an army to liberate Quito, arriving at Guayaquil in May 1821. A year later he won a great victory over the royalists at Pichincha, in the high mountains near Quito. Meanwhile, Bolívar proceeded south by land with much difficulty due to the terrain and royalist resistance, by no means dead in the mountains of southern New Granada. He reached Quito on June 16, 1822, to find the area secure and incorporated into Colombia. Plans could now be made for the invasion of Peru.

In the meantime, in the fall of 1820, the expedition against Peru under San Martín sailed from Chile. In view of the weak maritime tradition and enterprise of Spanish America, it was not surprising that the new Chilean navy was commanded by cashiered British Admiral Thomas Cochrane, and that of its thirty-one officers only seven were Chilean. Crews were made up of foreign seamen and Chilean fishermen and day laborers. A foreigner said that in all Chile he had met not a dozen men who could distinguish between the mizzen chains and the spanker. Foreign naval leaders had to be used in other parts of Latin America during the Independence period. Vessels had to be seized or bought since Spanish American shipbuilding facilities were very limited.

The liberating army of 4,450 was about 60 percent Argentine, the rest Chilean. The Chilean contingent resigned or deserted rather rapidly, so that by December 1824 only about a hundred were in Peru. The soldiers believed, with reason, that Peruvians should die and otherwise pay for their own liberation as soon as possible. San Martín knew from the beginning that his army was too small to defeat the royalists in Peru. He carried supplies for the Peruvians he expected to recruit. For that reason the initial landing in September 1820 was at Pisco, some one hundred miles south of Lima. The expected joyful welcome did not materialize, although some lower-class recruits were obtained. Most creoles in Peru were either intensely conservative or prudent in the face of the strong royalist armies. Negotiations with the viceroy came to nothing. Although the news of the liberal revolt in Spain early in 1820 caused some restiveness among Peruvian creoles, it was too feeble to help the liberators. In the invading army murmurs began that San Martín was too timid. San Martín moved the army by sea and settled down north of Lima, spending months trying to persuade Peruvians to support the liberating army. Admiral Cochrane, blockading Callao, the port of Lima, urged more aggressive action.

Finally in mid-1821 San Martín marched on Lima. At his approach the royalist army withdrew, because of a food-supply problem in the city and because of the increasing strength of supporters of liberation. San Martín's policy seemed to achieve results, but some in his army either could not or would not see them. San Martín entered Lima in July 1821, declared the Independence of Peru, and became protector and head of the state. He controlled very little. The royalists had most of Peru and all of Upper Peru. San Martín's army did not grow, remaining much smaller than the royal forces. Despite or because of the prudence of his waiting policy, grumbling continued. Admiral Cochrane insisted that his naval personnel be paid, and when San Martín said payment was Chile's responsibility, Cochrane seized funds and sailed off on a raiding expedition into the Pacific. O'Higgins supported his action! He found that Chileans would not send more money or supplies to Peru, and even resisted expenditure on the campaign against the royalists in the southern part of their own country. That was expectable human behavior, and the equivalent occurred in a number of places in Spanish America during the Independence period.

Public opinion in Peru still did not turn

strongly to the support of the liberators, and by late 1821 San Martín and Bolívar (in Quito) were convinced that collaboration between their military forces was desirable. After an exchange of letters, San Martín went by sea in July 1822 to Guayaquil to confer with the Liberator. Their famous *entrevista* (interview) there always will be shrouded in some mystery because they held meetings without witnesses and their later comments were to some extent ambiguous and conflicting. They were men of quite different personality, style, and interest, but how much these differences contributed to the conflict at the meetings is not certain. Bolívar went out of his way to emphasize that Quito was part of the Republic of Colombia, but that issue probably was not important to San Martín. Such evidence as there is indicates that San Martín's expressed willingness to serve under Bolívar's command was met evasively by the latter. Critics of the Liberator sometimes put his reaction down to simple jealousy, but Bolívar's preference not to have so illustrious a subordinate in the volatile political conditions of the time may be called prudence. In addition, Bolívar's dream of creating a huge nation by additions to Colombia cannot be declared despicable merely because ambition was involved in it. Finally, San Martín's decision was influenced by his lack of stomach for the brickbats and calumnies of politics. He wrote at the time that he was weary of "being called a tyrant" and of the charge that his inclination to a monarchical government for America extended to a hope of becoming king.

San Martín resigned to the Peruvian Congress in September 1822. He went to Chile, where he stayed only briefly, the Chileans having long since indicated their distaste for him; then to an Argentina that also had little place for him; and in 1824 to Europe, where he lived until his death in 1850. Argentina later recognized him as a national hero.

His withdrawal from Peru left the way open for Bolívar to proceed against the royalists there. Bolívar found himself blocked by the refusal of the Colombian Congress to permit him to under-

take a new war. New Granada liked neither an absentee president nor a military commander who incessantly requested men and funds for distant wars. The republic was for many reasons in shaky condition. There was separatist sentiment in Venezuela. The news from Peru was no better: the Independence army and government in Lima bickered and decayed and lost skirmishes to the royalists. In February 1823 a military rising forced out the junta appointed by the Constituent Assembly and put in Colonel José de la Riva Agüero as president of the republic. On invitation of Riva Agüero, Bolívar sent troops from Quito under Sucre to try to prevent a total collapse of the patriot position. They were needed; in May 1823 a patriot army under Santa Cruz tried an invasion of Upper Peru and was badly defeated.

When Bolívar finally received permission from Bogotá to proceed and arrived at Lima in September 1823, he faced the same difficulties as San Martín. The Peruvian Congress made Bolívar dictator but did little else. Factionalism among Peruvian creoles was as instantly bitter as nearly everywhere in Spanish America. Inevitably, there was resentment and fear of the foreign army and the ambitions of Bolívar. Collecting recruits, supplies, and funds was endlessly difficult and time-consuming. The dissatisfied Argentine troops mutinied and let the royalists reoccupy Callao in February 1824. Bolívar had to evacuate Lima and retreat north to Trujillo. There in April he wrote to Sucre,

> Money is being collected from churches and individuals. . . . I have . . . ordered the sale of state properties, and we shall not hesitate to confiscate all the funds of the congregations and brotherhoods. With a few forced loans we shall have enough to cover expenses for some months more.

Gradually, the Independence forces accumulated men and money. The royalists were weakened by dissension. Most of America was independent; the royalist cause seemed hopeless to most. News that French armies had restored absolutism in Spain reached Upper Peru, and led General Olañeta to revolt against Viceroy La

Serna, who had been appointed by liberals in Spain. Bolívar pressed into the royalist strongholds in the high mountains and in August 1824 he and Sucre won a victory at Junín that marked the beginning of the end for the royalists, who evacuated Lima far down by the coast. Sucre, left in command in the mountains, in December 1824 destroyed the last substantial royal army at Ayacucho. Olañeta held out for a time, but his troops were deserting. The royalist garrison at Callao did not surrender until January 1826. Although the fighting had come late to Peruvians, they finally suffered a full measure of death, destruction, division, and general misery.

So ended Bolívar's heroic career as the Liberator of what became six Latin American republics. Already he had felt the rising wind of interest and faction that would follow him to the grave in the coming Age of the Caudillos.[1]

e. New Spain and Other Areas

Paraguay and present-day Argentina, as has been noted, were independent in fact from an early date. Uruguay was a bone of contention between Buenos Aires, Brazil, and the local population until it was recognized as an independent buffer state in 1828. Cuba and Puerto Rico remained Spanish, and Santo Domingo was forcibly made part of Haiti from 1822 to 1844. Panama, a part of the Viceroyalty of New Granada, joined Bolívar's new Republic of Gran Colombia in 1821. The Captaincy-General of Guatemala, comprising the rest of Central America, was quiet in 1808–1821, then declared Independence in 1821 under pressure of events in Mexico and Spain, rather than from a strong indigenous demand for a new state. Iturbide's Mexico failed in a brief effort to incorporate Guatemala.

The circumstances of the Mexican Independence achieved in 1821 were yet another varia-

tion of the inescapable themes of (*a*) imperfect agreement on goals at times when drastic decisions seemed necessary; and (*b*) fear—on the liberal side that a decision would not bring the modest amount of change it desired, and on the conservative side that the same decision would not preserve the continuity and privilege of the oligarchic society. In a community where most of the politically active were the prey of serious uncertainty and fear and had recent experience of fire and sword, bold adventurers found room for maneuver.

By 1820 New Spain had been nearly pacified for five years. The Independence movement had been confined to peripheral, primitive areas and to small expeditions penetrating from the United States.[2] The creole *guerrillero* Guadalupe Victoria had been driven into hiding. The mestizo Independence leader Vicente Guerrero had some 2,000 ragged men in the remote southern and western mountains. The last thing the upper class wanted was another Indian uprising, and it considered the proper preventive to be strong conservative government. It therefore observed with some dismay the events of 1820 in Spain, where a military mutiny led to a liberal revolution and reinstitution of the Constitution of 1812. Ferdinand VII dissipated whatever little respect remained for the crown by apologizing for annulling the Constitution in 1814 and declaring that the ancient absolutism was wrong. Press censorship was lifted, which alarmed conservatives in Mexico who favored a system of social repression. The rebels in Spain displayed some anticlericalism, which alarmed the hier-

---

[1] See Chapter 23, Section a, on the breakup of Bolívar's "Gran Colombia."

[2] United States interest in Mexico would become increasingly worrisome for Spain and independent Mexico. Francisco Javier Mina was an example of a self-proclaimed leader who used the United States as a base. He fled Spain after trying to oppose the restoration of absolutism under Ferdinand VII in 1814. He did some planning of Spanish American Independence in England, where the British encouraged a number of such figures. Then he went to the United States and found some supporters, sailed to Galveston and then farther south in Mexico, and tried to rouse the countryside. He was taken by the royalists in 1817 and executed.

archy and its conservative supporters in Mexico. Political prisoners were released in Spain, including some Mexican rebels. These and other measures that Mexican conservatives labeled with loathing as "liberal" led them to consider independence from Spain as now a possibly desirable thing. Protection of class and personal interest seemed to require sacrifice of the tie with Madrid.

The conservatives decided that the way to accomplish Independence was by creating a sympathetic force within the royal military in New Spain. They chose for the command Agustín de Iturbide, an unprincipled but energetic and shrewd creole adventurer, an officer who had fought against Hidalgo and other rebels in 1810 and following years. Iturbide showed spectacular greed in gouging the inhabitants of the areas of his military commands. The practice was not unusual at the time in Mexico, and private enterprise generally by military commanders had been common in Europe for centuries, but Iturbide went too far and was forced into retirement with his gains. In 1820 he accepted the scheme of the conservatives, and they persuaded the viceroy to give him an army to destroy Guerrero's rebel band in the south. In November 1820 Iturbide led his force out of Mexico City and proceeded to play the conservative game, but with variations aimed to his personal advantage.

He pretended to campaign against Guerrero, but found that any sustained effort to catch him would be costly and dangerous. Iturbide collected all the funds and men he could from the viceroy and the conservatives (including the church), and simply appropriated wealth—including that of merchant supporters—when that seemed convenient. He then invited Guerrero to join him in a movement to pacify Mexico on the basis of supremacy for Roman Catholicism, Independence—preferably with monarchy, and union or equality for all men—meaning, ostensibly, peninsulars, creoles, Indians, mestizos. These Three Guarantees of the Plan of Iguala, February 24, 1821, were issued by Iturbide with Guerrero at his side, promising grand and contradictory things to both liberals and conservatives: peace,

Independence, an end to the class system, conservative government.

The support of Vicente Guerrero brought in liberals, including rebels who had been driven into hiding by successful royalist military campaigns. Iturbide tried to recruit Viceroy Apodaca to the movement of the Three Guarantees, but the viceroy declared its leader an outlaw. He did not, however, try to proceed vigorously against Iturbide, which would have been difficult. Although many conservatives probably preferred to go back to the pre-1820 system of government, the situation was difficult for them. That Iturbide would damage their interests was not certain, and he was gaining much support. After a time, some royalist commanders went over to Iturbide, and no leadership appeared for a competing movement. Although some politically active Mexicans were not prepared to fight for the regime loyal to Madrid, they were not enthused about Iturbide either. A situation existed that was to be common in subsequent Latin American history: the correct course was not clear to people, in large measure because information was not available regarding Iturbide's plans and capabilities. Yet a decision apparently was likely to be made, and doing nothing was merely to acquiesce in whatever decision came. This is a common and agonizing dilemma for citizens in societies with such political cultures.

Viceroy Apodaca resigned in July 1821, and almost at the same time a new viceroy, O'Donojú, appointed by the Spanish liberals, arrived at Veracruz, where he was penned in at the port by supporters of Independence. There followed a conference between O'Donojú, Iturbide, and Santa Anna, commander of Veracruz, who was learning from the career of Iturbide how to manipulate Mexico. There followed (August 1821) the Treaty of Córdoba, by which O'Donojú agreed to an independent monarchy for Mexico, with Ferdinand VII promised first refusal of the post. Spain, however, rejected the agreement. Iturbide by then had so much support that in September 1821 he marched into Mexico City in the company of Vicente Guerrero and Guadalupe Victoria, to a hero's acclaim. It was all very human, with people grasping what seemed the best available solution in troubled times. It was all fuzzy hope and promise and lasted no time at all, because basic differences of view and interest had merely been buttered over with euphoria and ignorance of the character of the deliverer.

The largest, most populous, and richest realm of the empire thus became independent without the dreadful warfare required in Venezuela, New Granada, Quito, Peru, and Chile. By agreement or by gunfire, the empire was breaking up. In 1810 part of La Plata in fact became independent, in 1821 much of the rest of the empire was freed from Spanish rule, and in 1826 came the final blows in Peru, 334 years after Columbus established Spain's claims to America. What enormous changes during those centuries had been suffered by Europeans, Amerindians, and black Africans in Spanish America, making another sort of new world for their posterity after 1826.

21

The Independence of Brazil

Brazilian independence was a triumph of nationalism over a colonialism that tiny Portugal could not maintain once the Brazilians had determined to repudiate it in 1822. It also was a triumph for British policy, which maintained the ancient connection with Portugal while improving its economic position in an independent and promising Empire of Brazil.

a. The Court Moves to Brazil, 1808–1815

Dramatic changes occurred in Portugal and Brazil in 1807–1808 that led to increased Brazilian political sensitivity. Napoleon ordered Portugal to take various actions against the British, including closing ports to the latter's trade. Prince Regent João, ruling for his demented mother Maria I, would not meet all those demands, so Napoleon's General Junot invaded Portugal late in 1807. The Portuguese court resounded to the expectable counsels of despair and submission, but while confusion seemed to reign, João competently prepared for evacuation of court and imperial government to America. His was a formidable operation, physically and psychologically. The decision was eased by the urgings and promises of assistance of Lord Strangford, the British minister at Lisbon. In return for British help in transport and naval escort, João granted commercial concessions in Brazil. Surely the price was not too high for preservation of the empire, especially given Britain's long-time advantages in the Brazilian trade that did not depend on expanded legal permission to exploit. João's decision to choose flight and resistance over what some of the Portuguese elite argued would be a more comfortable collaboration seems the more courageous as compared with the antics of the contemporary Spanish Bourbons.

The move was a veritable migration of some 15,000 of the elite and powerful of Portugal and their satellite lackeys and hairdressers. The confusion in city and dockside as the French armies advanced never degenerated into panic. Mountains of personal, public, intellectual, and financial baggage were crammed into the great fleet. The larger part of the armada, including the royal family, dropped anchor in the great bay at Salvador da Bahia in January 1808, three centuries after Cabral had claimed Brazil for Portugal. The city enthusiastically welcomed the migrants. Reactions elsewhere in Brazil were much the same. Obviously those Brazilians who thought about such matters were loyal subjects of the crown, and they were pleased to have the center of power moved to America.

Very soon at Bahia João took an action that increased enthusiasm for the regime. He was confronted with arguments regarding the commercial policy of the empire during the crisis of war, occupation of Portugal by the French, and government in exile. Two partisans of freer trade were the governor of Bahia and the Brazilian political economist José de Silva Lisboa. João was doubtful, apparently either having no firm grasp of the problem, or trapped in ancient mercantilism and the political pressures of its partisans. But on January 28, 1808, he issued a declaration of freedom of trade, subject to tariff duties. The action was popular with prominent Brazilians. It seemed to its partisans an augury of good things to come from the move to Brazil. As the event proved, the removal of legal restrictions on trade helped stimulate it to some extent, but so did wartime conditions. Before long, other measures were announced to alter economic policy. Prohibitions on manufacturing were revoked by a decree of April 1, 1808. A Banco do Brasil was erected the same year in Rio de Janeiro, where the court settled permanently, and branches were set up at Salvador and São Paulo.

The Bank of Brazil was important as marking the beginning of an effort to provide modern technical and investment facilities. It had some value in aiding commercial transactions, receiving royal revenues and treasure, running the diamond monopoly, and issuing paper currency. The elite —especially the Portuguese—bought stock in the bank and deposited funds there. The institution did not, however, establish a sound banking system for Brazil. Its chief direct effects were on government operations. It pursued a policy of currency inflation—that is, issuance beyond revenues—that would often mark government financial policy during Brazil's independent history.

The financial developments contributed to the political education of Brazilians. Political attitudes also were affected by exciting intellectual changes wrought by the imperial government in Brazil. Intellectual and educational institutions were set up in a colony where they had been sleepy and sparse: naval and military academies (1808–1810); a National Museum and School of Fine Arts in 1808, as well as the beginnings of what became the Botanical Gardens; and before long schools of medicine in Rio de Janeiro and Bahia, the first public library, and courses in agriculture, commerce, and chemistry. Another important development was that printing presses began to function in an area where their absence had contributed to the general placidity, now reduced by so many developments. A newspaper, *Gazeta do Rio de Janeiro*, appeared in 1808. Bahia had a newspaper by 1811. All these developments were exciting and valuable from the Brazilian point of view; for the Portuguese, they merely duplicated what they had enjoyed in Europe, but had prohibited or neglected to establish in America.

At the same time, the imperial government was being set up, duplicating the structure that had existed in Lisbon, with some changes. More important than adjustments in the machinery was the presence of monarchy and bureaucracy in Brazil, giving to the Brazilian elite intimate and not always pleasing glimpses of its operations. Also unpleasant was the fact that the imperial bureaucracy remained staffed primarily with Portuguese. It was irritating that the Europeans had to be crammed into the existing public and private structures in Rio de Janeiro, and even more irritating that some of the Portuguese condescended to the Brazilian elite. João's wife Carlota, a Spanish princess, was especially contemptuous of provincials. That could be overlooked to some extent because she was arrogant and unpleasant with everyone, including her husband. At least it was pleasant that João was a pudgy, unformidable, gracious prince, who obviously enjoyed living in Brazil. So the wartime years, 1808–1815, seemed to demonstrate the viability of the imperial system, whether the center of government was in Europe or America. With the end of the European wars, however, the antagonisms within the system erupted into angry expression.

b. Portuguese versus Brazilians, 1815–1821

On December 16, 1815, João declared Brazil a kingdom, and it appeared as an ostensibly equal part of the newly styled "United Kingdoms of Portugal, Brazil, and the Algarves." [1] The change occurred as the end of the great French wars permitted European statesmen to turn more attention away from the consuming problem of containing the Napoleonic monster. Representatives of the victorious powers, and defeated but once-again monarchic France, tried to direct from Vienna a reconstruction of the old sociopolitical order. It seemed proper to them to return to the layered society of pre-1789, with a minimum of republicanism and equality and a maximum of monarchism and class privilege, all part of the preservation of "legitimacy," that god of the idolatry of the Concert of Europe. The men of Vienna viewed the presence in America of a European court as unseemly, unsettling, and innovative. They complained that making the colony a "kingdom" appeared to spread a gloss of legitimacy over the situation. When Maria I died in 1816, the regent became João VI, head of the new dual monarchy.

Prominent persons in Portugal loathed the arrangement and demanded return of court and government to Europe. Their demand was only natural; the Portuguese wanted the jobs, the power, the prestige, and the profits of the empire centered in Europe. João infuriated the European party by preferring to reside in Brazil. Portuguese insistence on renewed domination of the system understandably irritated Brazilians, who knew that Brazil was richer and more populous than Portugal. For this and other reasons, Brazilian views were more potent than previously. They had experienced at least a theoretical equality and wished to make it more effective, not give it up. They feared that return to the old-style

subordination would damage their international trade prospects and would also lead to unfavorable taxation. They enjoyed the new cultural institutions established so recently. The press had given them an instrument for more effective expression of their views, and for drumming up Brazilian opinion against Portugal throughout all the captaincies. The old colonial mold had been shattered, and the Portuguese could not put it together again. It was mildly ironic that the apparent eradication of Brazil's political inferiority by declaration of the dual monarchy occurred just as debate over it became a matter of critical concern. It was merely one more demonstration of the truism that theories unrelated to reality aggravate more problems than they resolve.

A rebellion in Recife in 1817 revealed how recent change in Brazil had altered some outlooks without changing the old antagonism between Portuguese and Brazilians. A few men were well aware of the nature of the contemporary world, and others had heard dimly of the ideas of the Enlightenment and the revolutions and wars in the United States, France, and Spanish America. Some of the elite in Pernambuco, of which Recife was capital, were elated at their big cotton profits made while United States exports fell before and during its War of 1812. Fearing new Portuguese economic restrictions, they conspired to create a northeastern republic. The rebels seized the governor of Pernambuco and sent him to Rio de Janeiro. They then erected a provisional government, which sent representatives to several countries for arms and other aid. They also solicited the aid of other Brazilian captaincies, with little success. The imperial armed forces destroyed the rebellion within a few months. The rebels had expressed egalitarianism, but never had a chance to put it to a test, and probably not much could have been imposed on the oligarchic society. Of most significance was not the indication of anti-Portuguese sentiment, but the fact that it found violent expression in only one province. Regional variations of opposition permitted the metropolis to crush rebellion easily.

The government in those years pursued old

---

[1] The last was a part of European Portugal.

Luso-Brazilian ambitions in the Plata area. Although it had definitively lost (treaty of 1777) Colônia do Sacramento, across the estuary from Buenos Aires, the *gaúchos* of growing Rio Grande do Sul rode without hindrance into Spanish-claimed territory in the Banda Oriental del Uruguay. Open warfare in 1801, an offshoot of European conflict, pushed the Brazilian border southward. In 1811 João sent troops into Uruguay, when that area and nearby Buenos Aires and other parts of present Argentina were rent with dissension. Britain soon persuaded João to withdraw, but he sent a force back in 1816, and in 1821 declared the Cisplatine Province (Uruguay) part of the Luso-Brazilian empire. All that cost money, and, as it turned out, did not permanently incorporate Uruguay into Brazil.

During all those years, while King João tarried in Brazil, pressures accumulated and positions hardened on the question of location of court and imperial government. Continual discussion invested the obvious material aspects of the issue with fiery overtones of pride, ambition, and lust to dominate. The question became acute with the republican outbursts of 1820 in Europe, and the swift armed reaction of the legitimists of the Concert of Europe. Spain, Portugal, Greece, and Italy rang to clashes of arms between republicans or constitutional monarchists on one side and partisans of the old absolutism on the other. Sometimes the struggle was complicated by nationalist fervor. Rebels in Portugal rose against the regency that ruled there while the king was in Brazil. They both hated the regency's connection with British policy and wanted the monarch and imperial government back in Europe. They also favored restrictions on monarchical power by adoption of a constitution. The rebels were able to force the regency to call a Côrtes, the parliament that had not met for more than a century. Brazilians were to choose sixty-seven delegates to the Côrtes, but Portugal was allotted one hundred. The Côrtes began its sessions in January 1821.

The Brazilian elite favored a constitution, but wanted the king to stay in America. Some Bra-

zilians favored "home rule" for Brazil, with separate constitutions for Portugal and America and union provided by the crown. Whichever residence João chose, there was a chance that the other part of the shakily dual monarchy might declare its independence. The Portuguese military in Brazil demanded that João return to Europe. Crown Prince Pedro urged that his father leave, at least in part because he wished to act in America either as regent or as an independent king. The British government favored João's return to Portugal. Finally, in February 1821, while the Côrtes in Portugal still was constructing a constitution, King João decided to return to Europe. Then, following this announcement, he lingered, and called to Rio de Janeiro Brazilian electors to choose deputies to the Lisbon Côrtes.

The electors met April 21, 1821, and proceeded to proclaim as a constitution for Brazil the liberal Spanish Constitution of 1812, which provided for an effective legislature and constitutional limits on the crown. They also demanded that the king remain in Brazil. The Brazilian elite had committed itself. On April 22, João accepted this Assembly's actions. On April 23 the Portuguese military in Brazil dispersed the Assembly and persuaded João to proclaim again the Portuguese Constitution. On April 24 João boarded a warship, and two days later sailed for Europe. The long years of indecision had ended, with apparent defeat for the Brazilian party. The contest, however, had scarcely begun.

c. Economy and Society, 1808–1822

World events in the early nineteenth century conspired to foster an economic optimism in Brazil that was in fact poorly based, depending on emphemeral external conditions. Some Brazilian exports that had been in serious decline in most of the last quarter of the eighteenth century enjoyed enlarged demand. Sugar exports boomed as civil war ruined Haitian output in the 1790s and naval war intermittently interrupted shipments from other Caribbean areas from 1792. With prices and demand up, the value of Brazilian sugar exports rose nearly 1,000 percent during the Napoleonic wars. Cotton exports from Brazil soared as United States shipments fell before and during its War of 1812 with Britain and as the British cotton textile industry mushroomed. Some other Brazilian exports benefited from wartime conditions that hurt other shippers. These were conditions independent of Portuguese policy and beyond Luso-Brazilian control. The increased trade of those years did not result from the free trade decree of 1808. The catastrophic decline from 1807 to 1808 in the Portuguese role in Brazilian shipping and supply came not from policy but simply from the French invasion of Portugal. Most Brazilian commodity exporters, of course, cared more for demand and prices than for the nationality of the merchants with whom they dealt and welcomed the increase of foreign ships at Rio de Janeiro from 90 in 1808 to 354 in 1820. Portuguese merchants established at Brazilian ports were not always so pleased.

Brazilian manufacturing, like Brazilian international traffic, was little affected by Regent João's decrees. His revocation of the prohibitions on manufacturing in 1808 brought no surge in production. The tiny textile and iron fabrication enterprises of Brazil grew little in succeeding years. There was no base for such a growth in a society short on capital and technical knowledge and lacking in sociopolitical support for manufacturing interests. Brazil's agricultural elite certainly would not supply the funds and leadership for such an effort. Steam engines were imported for sugar mills, but slowly; for many years the industry continued to display a serious technological lag. The bare beginnings of steam navigation in Brazil date from 1819, but its development within the country, and to and from foreign markets, was to be slow and heavily influenced by outside capital, technicians, and decision making. In short, the industrial age scarcely affected Brazil before Independence, except as it influenced the demand for and marketing of its agricultural exports. Of more impor-

tance to Brazil in 1815, when both the Napoleonic wars and the United States–British War of 1812 ended, was the reentry of the United States into the British cotton market and the renewed and increasing flood of sugar into world markets from Brazilian competitors, especially Cuba.

To regard João's decrees as "liberating" the Brazilian economy is thus misleading; to build a national economy is not so easy, as the development-oriented twentieth century has discovered at great cost. Neither is it helpful to call the 1810 Portuguese-British commercial treaty a "surrender" to the British and to Brazilian slave-owning agricultural exporters. The treaty set duties for British imports to Brazil at 15 percent, while those from Portugal paid 16 percent and other countries 20. It also permitted Britons to use their own courts at Brazilian and Portuguese ports. There were objections to the treaty, but João had little choice. Criticism then and thereafter centered on the advantages the treaty gave to Britain, rather than in analysis of reasonable alternatives. The offense was as much to nationalism and independence as to profits.[2]

The fact is that Britain long had enjoyed enormous advantages that no treaties were likely to affect much. Britain's big manufacturing plant, technological lead, managerial personnel, and her financial, merchant shipping, naval power, and marketing strength simply overwhelmed much of the world, in one way or another. Brushing this aside, some nationalist commentators today allege that the commercial treaty of 1810 began a fatal retreat from possible industrialization by "abandoning" the possibility of "protectionism." To speak of abandoning something that did not exist is unhistorical. Effective protection for industry could not exist in the Brazil of the late colonial era, or in the rest of the nineteenth century either. Where was the support for it to come

---

[2] The imperial government's agreement in 1817 that Britain could search slave ships and establish an Anglo-Brazilian admiralty court at Rio de Janeiro was another irksome admission of dependence on Britain.

from? Where was the capital to come from? Finally, would it have been rational to push hard for industrialization? A soundly based view today is that commodity-exporting countries hungry for the diversification, independence, and respect of industrial strength should foster their traditional exports in order to accumulate capital for the building of a better-rounded economy and society. That is, of course, as unhistorical and anachronistic an observation as the current grumbling about surrender to the British in 1810 and thereafter.

As in Spanish America, increasing population growth at the end of the colonial period has been taken to mean easier economic and social conditions. The important question is: How much improvement? The answer is, not much. The bulk of the population and most social structures were scarcely affected. A few more opportunities opened for entry into trades, services, production on the fringes or in support of the larger enterprises. Sometimes that is stated as growth in the "middle" class. Brazil's total population rose from about 2.97 million in 1798 to some 3.8 million by 1818. In that period, slaves increased from 1.5 million to 1.93 million, remaining about half the total population; it was even more a slave society than the United States. At the same time, colored freemen increased from a quarter to a half million, a sizable social and demographic phenomenon. Whites were stationary at about 1 million, a figure that it is difficult to interpret because it was a guess at social status that corresponded generally with a large Caucasian genetic heritage. Although these round figures need not be taken as gospel, they certainly meant that under then prevalent conditions in Brazil, the position of the slaveholding agricultural elite was being bolstered by continued slave imports and by growth of the free colored population, which could not resist the control and exactions of the upper class. There was nothing in demographic developments to suggest a trend favorable for investment in manufacturing or an expanded educational system to

serve it. Brazil was, and long thereafter remained, rural in terms of residence, occupations, attitudes. Rio de Janeiro had grown to more than 50,000 residents in 1800 and possibly 100,000 in 1822.

d. Final Steps to Independence, 1821–1822

Securing the return of the king to Portugal in April 1821 naturally seemed to Portuguese statesmen, centering in the Côrtes, evidence that they could reestablish their preeminence in the empire. They insisted that Brazil be restored to its colonial status. Portuguese, who divided into liberal and conservative positions on institutions in Europe, tended to agree that Brazil should be subordinate. In April the control of Rio de Janeiro over the captaincies was abolished, making them directly responsible to Lisbon. Pedro was ordered to Portugal, so he would not be available as an anti-European leader. Brazilians were declared ineligible for political and military office. Brazil was forbidden a university. The minority Brazilian delegates to the Côrtes, arriving in Lisbon in August 1821, were unable to stem this flood of political idiocy. The Brazilians in the Côrtes sometimes were treated abusively by their supposed colleagues of the Portuguese majority.

Brazilian resentment of these Portuguese actions was especially strong and effective in Rio de Janeiro, Minas Gerais, and São Paulo, where the landed aristocracy felt economically and politically abused and was advantageously located geographically to put pressure on the capital. These Brazilian magnates naturally focused on the regent Pedro as the leader of their resistance movement. João had advised Pedro of the likelihood of Brazilian secession, and recommended that his son head it himself rather than let Brazil escape control of the family. Pedro was then twenty-four. The defects of his temperament and education, which were to become so apparent later, at that time were of little consequence because the overwhelmingly paramount issue was defense against Portuguese pretensions, and Pedro willingly aided in that. But means of defense were limited, and Brazilian opinion was by no means united. João had carried with him a sizable treasury of cash and jewelry, as well as several thousand Portuguese, an exodus that pointed to the supposed shift in power back to Europe. The gutted Banco do Brasil failed in July 1821. Government revenues were small. Responding to the orders of the Côrtes, provincial and municipal juntas were created in some places, corresponded directly with Lisbon, and refused to support the government in Rio de Janeiro. European garrisons in the north and south kept the local situations doubtful.

Leaders in Rio de Janeiro, Minas Gerais, and São Paulo proceeded to demonstrate the determination and force that for more than a century thereafter often enabled them to dominate events in Brazil. Newspapers and pamphlets railed against the Côrtes. But the upper class contained a variety of opinions, and a period of consolidation of views obviously was needed. Some men favored the Côrtes; some disliked it as much for its liberal views on restriction of monarchical power as for its rabid colonialism; some had close family or business ties with Portuguese in Brazil or Europe; some leaned toward something like "home rule," with separate constitutions for Portugal and Brazil and union provided by a common monarch; there were even a few republicans. In addition to the worrisome problems of regional division and providing a sufficient financial base for resistance, Pedro's supporters feared a military test. Prudent men knew that trained and professionally officered European forces posed a problem for essentially amateur militia. Sober estate owners, heads of large families and enterprises, feared the loss of the coastal cities and production areas. They were feeling their way in fluid, uncertain, and potentially dangerous circumstances.

Rallying support around Pedro was essential for the resistance leaders. They used a variety of methods of persuasion and propaganda, in which the Freemasons played a role. A petition was sent from Rio de Janeiro to São Paulo and Minas Gerais to get support for Pedro's continued residence in Brazil, a matter that had assumed a great psychological as well as practical significance. On January 9, 1822, a committee presented the petition to Pedro, and he responded, "As it is for the good of all and the general felicity of the nation, say to the people that I will remain." This *Fico* (I Stay) was acclaimed as a declaration of freedom from Portuguese domination. It fixed Pedro in Brazilian affection and provided an acceptable head for an independent state if that step should become necessary. Nothing remotely comparable to Pedro's succession could occur in Spanish America, and it was a stroke of great good fortune for Brazil. It had nothing to do with differences between Portuguese and Spanish institutions and attitudes, but resulted from the fact that a reasonably intelligent, stable, and likable regent and monarch—João—fled to America (with British persuasion and help), whereas Charles IV and Ferdinand VII had none of those qualities (and lacked the British urging) and went to live in Napoleon's custody rather than carry their government to America. So the characters of individuals do sometimes make considerable difference in human history.

On January 11, 1822, the Portuguese military in Rio de Janeiro ordered Pedro to submit to the Côrtes or suffer a bombardment of the city. The Brazilian militia and populace flew to arms. Portuguese policies had not cowed Brazilian resistance leaders but intensified resentment to the point of accepting a test at arms. The Portuguese military commander observed the belligerent movement in the streets, and on January 12 moved his troops away from the city. A month later he took his force to Portugal.

Dom Pedro in February 1822 created a consultative Council of Ministers, made up of representatives of the provinces. By this time, discussion of Independence was common. In May Pedro declared that actions of the Portuguese Côrtes required his approval for application to Brazil. The same month he accepted from the

Rio de Janeiro city council the title of "perpetual and constitutional defender of Brazil." In August Pedro issued a series of proclamations that urged Brazilians to resist coercion, forbade landings of Portuguese troops without his permission, and sent a circular to the diplomatic corps stating that Brazil was almost ready to declare Independence.

Much of this action reflected the views of the outstanding member of the Council of Ministers, José Bonifácio de Andrada, a Paulista, student and professor at Coimbra, noted scientist and scholar, and long-time resident of Portugal, who returned to Brazil only in 1819. This distinguished and forceful man had come back to his native land just as it needed him. He went from São Paulo to Rio de Janeiro early in 1822 to support the demand of the resistance leaders that Pedro remain in America. He was a strong advocate of resisting the Portuguese policy of trying to fragment Brazil on the basis of regional jealousies and interests. Although José Bonifácio had great influence, and was made minister of the kingdom, the bulk of Pedro's advisers and bureaucracy remained Portuguese. Brazilians never ceased to be resentful and suspicious.

The declaration of Independence was a simple action by Pedro alone, so far as form was concerned, but in essence it resulted from the observable crystallization of opinion among a majority of the Brazilian elite. Pedro was traveling in São Paulo, building support, when letters reached him with the news that the Côrtes had revoked his acts and those of his Council and had declared his ministers traitors. He also re-

ceived advice in writing from his wife Leopoldina and from José Bonifácio that now was the time to respond with a declaration of complete Independence. So on September 7, 1822, beside the River Ypiranga, Pedro dramatically cried, "Independence or Death!" This Grito de Ypiranga sufficed. A majority of the Brazilian elite agreed. It had rejected Portuguese domination, while clinging to the monarchical form of government. These two policies, it believed, would protect free trade, meaning chiefly exchange with Britain; preserve the traditional social order against innovation; and, it hoped, permit unification of the many regions of Brazil. Even those Portuguese in Brazil and their local supporters, who preferred retention of the connection with Portugal, agreed with the general social orientation of the Independence group. Most of the populace was politically apathetic, isolated, or inert in a servile status. On December 1, 1822, Pedro I was crowned "constitutional emperor and perpetual defender of Brazil."

Fortunately Brazil needed few military heroics to defend itself from the feeble Portuguese response. The Brazilian elite was sufficiently united in its repudiation of the tie with Lisbon so that the tiny motherland had little room for maneuver among the ranks of the magnates of its vast colony. With a Portuguese prince on the scene who was acceptable to the local elite, no wrenching political debates were required. Thus, the transition to Independence was less disruptive than in much of Spanish America. That, it will be noted later, helped hold Portuguese America together, but its other effects were less obvious.

22 Afterword: The Legacy of Independence

The Heroes of Independence. The heroes of Independence were its greatest legacy: staunch San Martín leading his soldiers through the snows of the high Andes, noble Morelos fighting to the death as a *guerrillero*, the indomitable Bolívar in the battles of half a continent, and hundreds of other leaders from Argentina to Mexico pledging their lives and squandering their blood for a dream of freedom for America. They helped inspire and unite at least part of the citizenry during the long hard years of nation building thereafter. *El Día de la Independencia*—Independence Day—remains in Latin America a feast of patriotic enthusiasm, with the great men of the struggle for political liberty linked to the modern cry for an end to subservience to the developed world.

Continuity and Change in the Independence Years. Much of the colonial heritage continued beyond Independence and was little touched by that process; that is, continuity was more important than change. Hispanic American leaders did not transform society or wish to. The most important of the continuities was oligarchic rule. Although in Spanish America a few lower-class figures entered the elite, notably by the new politicomilitary route, they adopted the oligarchic attitudes and mode of governance. The fact of

rule by a small minority was not altered from colonial practice. Rule by the elites meant that they had the apparatus of the state to ensure continuation of social structures. The system of class, of privilege, of concentrated property holding, remained to channel the efforts—not very vigorous—of innovators. Private income and public expenditures were dedicated, as in the colonial era, to the interests of the small ruling minority. The bulk of the population ordinarily remained passive and diffident, a continuity of immense importance. In all this there was little to choose between Portuguese and Spanish America. There was, however, one conspicuous difference between them: Brazil retained the monarchical system, which helped ensure another difference —that Portuguese America was not fragmented during and after Independence as was Spanish America.

Leaders did deliberately bring about some changes, including initial efforts to incorporate the area fully into the international trading community. Other changes simply flowed unplanned from events, as did the invasion of Spanish American political life by military personnel and methods, which occurred as the latent *caudillismo* of the creole elite became active and virulent when freed of the restraints of the imperial administration. Finally, many things were un-

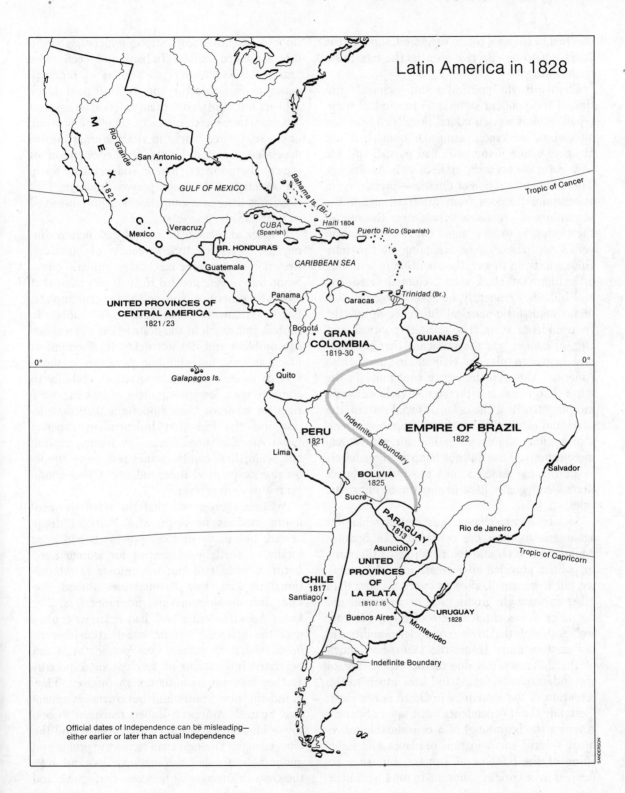

Latin America in 1828

Rio Grande

1821

San Antonio

M E X I C O

1821

GULF OF MEXICO

Mexico   Veracruz

Bahama Is. (Br.)

CUBA (Spanish)   Haiti 1804

Puerto Rico (Spanish)

Tropic of Cancer

BR. HONDURAS

Guatemala

CARIBBEAN SEA

UNITED PROVINCES OF CENTRAL AMERICA
1821/23

Panama

Caracas

Trinidad (Br.)

Bogotá

GRAN COLOMBIA
1819-30

GUIANAS

0°   0°

Galapagos Is.   Quito

PERU
1821

Lima

Indefinite Boundary

EMPIRE OF BRAZIL
1822

BOLIVIA
1825

Salvador

Sucre

PARAGUAY
1813

Rio de Janeiro

Asunción

Tropic of Capricorn

CHILE
1817
Santiago

UNITED PROVINCES OF LA PLATA
1810/16

Buenos Aires

URUGUAY
1828

Montevideo

Indefinite Boundary

Official dates of Independence can be misleading—
either earlier or later than actual Independence

SANDERSON

touched or changes barely suggested, some of the latter not to be effective even in the late twentieth century.

Change in the political realm included creation of independent states, and in most of them republicanism was an added novelty. There was an end to the creole-peninsular quarrel, if not at once, before many years had passed; and the new governments were staffed with Americans. There was enunciation of liberties—press, speech, association, freedom from arbitrary arrest; the beginnings of rancorous debate over the role of the church in society; argument over federalism versus centralism; some widening of the franchise, mostly in theory; the abolition or lessening of burdens on black slaves, colored freedmen, and Indians. Frequently, however, these developments made little practical difference during the Independence years. The greatest political novelty, of course, was the influence that the military began to play in civil affairs in Spanish America. Although this was a continuity in the sense that actual and threatened violence was a prominent part of the colonial social system, the overt and often illegal activity of Spanish American military officers in public life was a real discontinuity. That did not happen immediately in Portuguese America, but the military forces there were equally used in support of oligarchic rule.

Socioeconomic change was considerable but again less so than the continuity. In Spanish America the wars and the new role of the army in politics provided an increase in social mobility, but it was small, affected mestizos more than other subordinate groups, and in any event did not alter the essential system of oligarchic control. Although that source of social mobility did not exist in Brazil before the 1880s, how much of the difference was due to the experiences of the Independence period and how much to the retention of the monarchy in Brazil is not clear. Certainly the Independence years saw in Spanish America the beginnings of a considerable movement toward emancipation of slaves and lightening of the burdens of Indians, but they remained in essentially subordinate roles with little

hope of improvement. Strong upper-class prejudice remained against Indians and even more against blacks. Such creole leaders of Independence as San Martín and Bolívar used black soldiers but considered them inferior beings and a danger to the creole society. The lack of need, or desire, to free blacks in Brazil during the Independence period hinted at the retention of slavery there longer than in independent Spanish America. The event proved, however, that there was little or no superior benignity involved in the Spanish American actions.

Change also came by way of destruction during the Wars for Independence: of buildings, irrigation works, mine machinery, animals, crops. Some mines were flooded to such an extent that renovation became too costly to contemplate. Labor systems in some cases were badly disrupted. But much of the destruction was a short-run problem and did not delay development as much as such long-standing problems as shortages of capital, poor transportation, inability to compete with foreign suppliers, or lack of incentives for laborers. More important than destruction was the fact that Independence opened Latin America more directly to foreign capital; but again, that capital would not come simply because of political independence. Other conditions also were necessary.

Another change was that the restrictive economic systems of Spain and Portugal disappeared, but many of their provisions had been totally or partially ineffective for a long time. Latin America still had to compete in international markets, buy manufactures abroad, pay foreigners for shipping and insurance fees. The Latin American elites now had enlarged control over the financial system, but that neither relieved them of worries over public funds nor suggested innovations of much value, especially as they had no wish to tax themselves. They found the new armies and bureaucracies expensive. Spanish American leaders managed to borrow a bit abroad during the wars but found the charges high. The best road to private profits and public solvency lay through exports, and here there was a divergence between Portuguese and

Spanish America during the Independence years. Brazil was well integrated into the North Atlantic trading system as a satellite of Britain, while much of Spanish America had poor connections with Europe and the United States because of wartime damage and confusion, especially affecting mines and ports, and because of small or high-cost production of export agricultural crops.

The Independence years did not contribute much to differences between areas of Spanish America; those differences that existed either continued or altered in response to local conditions or international opportunities that had little to do with the process of Independence. Heavy fighting in Venezuela, Colombia, Ecuador, Bolivia, Peru, and Chile made those areas neither more nor less independent than the areas where there was little warfare. Nor did the amount or length of warfare in itself cause important differentiation between the political, governmental, or social systems of the Spanish American countries in later years. Lesser fighting in Argentina or Central America did not create such differences as there were between those areas and the Bolivarian lands. The retention of the Spanish connection in Mexico for years after Venezuela and New Granada were adopting constitutions did not in itself commit those three countries to different lines of development. If Independence had come to Venezuela or Colombia without warfare, surely the institutions of the new nations there would have been much as they were after the long wars. Finally, some of the changes begun or accelerated or suggested in the Independence years would have occurred, probably before too long, even if political independence had been delayed considerably beyond the 1820s.

The leaders of the Independence years acted in response to the social institutions and attitudes inherited from the colonial era, including those liberal ideas that came from the eighteenth-century Enlightenment. They responded also to the revolutions of North America and Europe in 1775–1815. Whatever they used, however—the Spanish Constitution of 1812, ancient Iberian notions of popular sovereignty, modern theories of federalism—was transformed to some extent by the American social environment and by the limitations of Latin America's opportunities in international economic life. The leaders of Independence used their heritage, under difficult conditions, to deal with immediate problems. They were "ready" for Independence in the sense that they had withdrawn the consent to rule from Europe on which the colonial system had been based, whatever their readiness for constructive action after dissolution of the ancient system. It was a matter of a few years only that the Independence leaders handled the instruments of government, the organization of political support, the proscription of foes, the collection of taxes, foreign capital and entrepreneurs, civic freedom, and education. Often what they did was revealing of the probable long-term attitudes of the elites, but this did not and could not commit their posterity to solutions of the problems of the new nations.

The View at Independence. Leaders in the new nations in the 1820s were both apprehensive and hopeful. Apprehension included fears of the conservative Concert of Europe and of Britain's great power and ambition, political and economic;[1] and the old terrors of lower-class turbulence, accentuated by the new political violence that arose during the Wars for Independence in Spanish America. Hope was based on enormous territories and the belief that they held unexploited resources that new arrangements would translate into great wealth. Contemplation of American control of political affairs was also pleasant. Not foreseen was how deeply and how long their complex colonial heritage would mold their adjustment after Independence. Nation building, development, and modernization are among the most difficult of human enterprises. In the 1820s Latin America's leaders had barely shouldered those great tasks.

---

[1] See Chapter 23, Section c, for the influence on Independence of the Concert of Europe, British policy and sea power, and the Monroe Doctrine.

PART SIX

Political Instability and Minimal Social Change (Independence to the 1880s)

Civilization or barbarism! That was the way Domingo Sarmiento of Argentina put the choice in the 1840s. Barbarism seemed to him and to observers in Europe and the United States to be dominant in much of Latin America. Little of what we call modernization had been possible in the years since Independence.* Political life consisted too much of factionalism, regional rivalry, military government, and civil war. The economies were nearly stagnant. Society remained frozen in class and caste, upper-class privilege, and peasant apathy.

Spanish Americans like Sarmiento found the roots of faction in the Spanish heritage, but that was a misleading simplification. Latin America did not "progress"—to use a popular nineteenth-century word—following Independence more slowly than the United States merely because of differences between their mother countries in the colonial era. What they had encountered in America made a difference, too. Spaniards in America found mountains of silver and millions of Indian workers, and Britons in America found neither. The colonial elites, reacting to these conditions, helped determine institutions as much as the mother countries did. Spanish Americans after Independence were the product of Spanish institutions but also of their own American environment. It was not understood in what complex ways the colonial heritage made change difficult in Spanish America. That was true also of Brazil, but there the peace of continued monarchism obscured the fact that socioeconomic structures were changing no more rapidly than in Spanish America.

Brazil and Spanish America lacked attitudes and institutions well suited to broad-gauge modernization, which required, at the least, a considerable interest in economic development other than in export agriculture, mining, and commerce specializing in imports. In Latin America the class system and the great

---

* See the Preface for varying definitions of modernization.

estate, defended by much of the elite as necessary to their privileges and comfort, impeded industrialization and other sorts of modernization. The developed nations of Europe, furthermore, especially Britain, preferred that Latin America remain a primary-commodity exporter, thus dependent or economically colonial. Europe thus reinforced a view that suited the Latin American elite. Acceptance of that role in the world economy ensured profits to the Latin American elite, and it involved few social changes that would threaten the oligarchic system— as rapid industrialization might have. Even more important was the fact that the commodities exported from Latin America had almost no market at home, so that no reasonable alternatives to export were available.

Yet some change, progress, development, or modernization was achieved. In the 1830s the Chilean elite eliminated unregulated *caudillismo* and created a stable governing system. In the 1850s Argentina emerged from disunity and terrible civil conflict to become a promising national polity. Mexico in the 1880s was apparently wrenched from factionalism by the centralizing dictator Díaz. The long and sometimes bloody quarrel over federalism in Latin America largely was settled in favor of centralism. The church issue had been thrashed almost to death and seemed finally destined for elimination as a serious matter.

In mid-century some countries achieved faster export growth. A revival of mining became prominent by the 1870s and 1880s. With profits from involvement in the international trading system came wider effects in manufacturing, railway and port development, commerce, and finance. Gains in the export economies had by the 1880s in some countries caused modest social changes and promised more. To be sure, class and privilege remained, sustained by ancient habits of unthinking domination and submission. But at least slavery and legal class lines were gone except in Brazil. Miscegenation continued at the massive rate attained by the eighteenth century, but people of mixed blood found that barriers to advancement barely weakened. Although Latin America remained rural in residence and outlook, urbanization was quickening by the 1880s. Illiteracy still was the rule, but economic gains and government decision permitted more support of public education. In Argentina education had proceeded far enough to suggest drastic alterations in social and other conditions if the process continued.

All these partial victories over formidable difficulties involved epics of dispute and even war. Promising as they were, however, they made the 1880s a dividing line in history more for what was promised than for what had been realized. The coming years were to show that the promise was both real and frustratingly incomplete.

23

Instability and Social Change to the 1880s

The world soon learned to shake its head at the Latin American nations, not understanding the dreadful complexity of their problems. Everything, from topography to the class structure to the international trading system, made improvement difficult. People of talent and courage went to their graves defeated by insuperable challenges.

a. Bolívar Plows the Sea in "Gran Colombia"

One of the defeated was the Liberator, Simón Bolívar. Anarchy was what General Bolívar saw about him at the moment of military triumph in Peru in 1825. La Plata and Chile were lacerated by the armies of chieftains who fought for loot and place. Bolívar feared that disorder there would encourage the royalists remaining in Peru, the desire of the Holy Alliance in Europe to restore America to Spain, and what he called the ambitions of Brazil. Bolívar, still president of Colombia despite his long absence in the south as a military commander, wrote his vice-president, Francisco de Paula Santander, that the "infection" of "popular revolts" might spread to Peru from the Plata. At the same time, Bolívar wrote his chief lieutenant, the young Venezuelan General Sucre, then in Upper Peru, that the financial condition of Peru and the army there "have me desperate." Peru found it could borrow from private bankers in Britain only on ruinous terms and refused them, remaining unable to meet its obligations. Bolívar had to write to Bogotá in May 1826 that Peru could not settle its debt to the Colombian government.

Still Bolívar lingered in Peru as dictator, although he knew the government was rotten with corruption, uncontrollable personal ambition, and a regionalism that threatened to tear it apart. The treasury was undernourished partly because the propertied class thought it should pay no taxes. It also thought that the foreigner Bolívar and his Colombian troops should leave. The Liberator stayed, however, because he hoped to build some sort of political union or alliance between Colombia and Peru. He persisted despite the statement in his Prophetic Letter of a decade ago that overcoming regional problems and forming large states in Spanish America would be difficult.[1] Possibly his change of heart stemmed partly from ambition; it also stemmed from fear of anarchy in small states with few resources. So he persisted although he could see that regional leaders were ready to du-

---

[1] See Chapter 20, Section c, on the Prophetic Letter and on the early history of "Gran Colombia," the name historians use to distinguish the republic that included Venezuela, Ecuador, Panama, and New Granada from the later republic that included only the last two.

plicate the wars that were raging in La Plata and Chile.

Finally, Bolívar had to bow to facts and leave Peru in 1826. Before going, however, he accepted the regional ambitions of leaders in Upper Peru to have a state separate from that governed from Lima, giving it his name and a constitution providing for a lifetime presidency. The constitution of Bolivia was another effort to hold off anarchy and was a signal to his enemies everywhere of the trend of his thinking. Bolívar consented to be chief executive of the new state, with Sucre as vice-president and actual administrator. Then Bolívar went north, leaving Sucre to face the Bolivian hatred of foreigners and Lima's rage at separation of Upper Peru from its rule.

Bolívar found resentment of himself as a Venezuelan foreigner when he returned to New Granada after an absence of four years. But he also found support. Some people welcomed his return because they were committed personally to his career; others thought he could provide more effective government than Santander, and New Granada and the other parts of "Gran Colombia" were suffering from ineffective government. As Bolívar moved north, towns granted him dictatorial powers, thus undercutting Santander and the Congress, and feeding rumors of Bolívar's dictatorial intentions. He stayed only briefly in Bogotá, acting unconstitutionally and arbitrarily, then hurried to Venezuela to try to put down secessionism led by his old military lieutenant Páez. He did not manage to do so, and he had to turn around and hurry back to New Granada to deal with dissension there. Santander, a moderate, was at the center of the plotting against Bolívar's rule, objecting to arbitrary government and especially the use of troops in civil affairs.

Bolívar's support in the Congress declined in 1827. The Congress called a constitutional assembly for 1828, but when it met at Ocaña, nothing could be decided because of disagreement over the issue of dictatorship. Bolívar persuaded the Congress to declare him dictator, but public opinion was against it, and his use of re-

pressive measures failed to quiet dissension. Bolívar's supporters and enemies were ready for civil war. To his other troubles was added the ruination of his unpopular design for a great confederation, to include Bolivia and Peru. Rebellion against Sucre in Bolivia in 1828 was encouraged by Peruvians. Sucre resigned and left the country, whereupon Bolívar insisted on war with Peru and went south to meet a Peruvian invasion of Colombia. He did not return to Bogotá until January 1830, and by that time Venezuela and Ecuador were breaking away from "Gran Colombia."

Bolívar was forced from the government. Dying of tuberculosis, he left Bogotá for exile in May 1830. He could see the great republic disintegrating around him. He had news of the assassination of his beloved Sucre, another of the great talents of the Independence generation destroyed by the factionalism and fanaticism of the times. In December, on the Caribbean coast, Bolívar died, bitterly believing, as he said, that "America is ungovernable. Those who have served the revolution have plowed the sea."

One can easily understand his disillusion, seeing so much of what he dreamed and fought for unachieved and himself reviled and repudiated. But, of course, people's hopes come true only if they do not ask too much. Independence, a very great thing, Bolívar had heroically and with remarkable persistence and skill helped to attain. The orderly society and political life he also wanted were simply unattainable within so few years. All Spanish America went through the same travail that led to Bolívar's cry about plowing the sea. Social conditions would permit nothing else.

b. Political Factionalism and Disorder

Factionalism and disorder were the most dramatically evident ingredients of Spanish American political life after Independence, whereas their role was muffled in Brazil by the monarchy. For Spanish America, disorder, tyranny, and violent solutions were enshrined in the term often given to the half century after Independence:

"Age of the *Caudillos*"—dictators who combined the talents of a military chieftain with those of a political boss.

The Spanish American upper class inherited from the colonial era a belief that it was entitled to what it desired, a tradition of violent solutions (threatened or executed), and an accustomed use of family ties to pursue advantage. Limited opportunities after Independence strengthened faction and violence, because control of government was more important for economic gain than in better-developed societies. The elite, joined by aggressive persons from the lower class, competed for privilege—tax advantages, franchises, tariffs, public salaries. Factionalism was potent because a sense of national community could not thrive together with strong attachment to class, family, region, and locality. Faction fed also on new fears of change, because liberals talked about "progress" and human perfectibility, which seemed to threaten the system of privilege.

The political culture that emerged during Independence and succeeding decades was not an aberration from some sanctified norm but a reflection of Latin American society. Nor was it a complete failure; decisions of value were made, and while there was disorder, it was not "anarchy." But Latin Americans of the time knew that achieving more orderly and productive political institutions was a serious problem. Economic development certainly would be difficult with too high a level of political disorder and inefficiency. On the other hand, while factionalism disrupted political life, it was largely an activity of the elite and left mostly undisturbed the underlying social structures. So, spectacular rivalry and a limited number of changes of policy affecting the elite caught the attention of observers, somewhat obscuring the continuity of much of Latin American life.

Class Structure, Privilege, Social Immobility

Possibly the most important continuity from colonial times was the system of privilege, although during Independence and thereafter it sustained several blows. In Spanish America republicanism replaced monarchy, and titles of nobility were abolished. Within a few decades little remained of legal discrimination against Indians, mestizos, and mulattoes. Between the 1820s and 1850s slavery was abolished in Spanish America. The practical effects of such action, however, were small because the upper class and the functional elites from the families of wealth and birth or from the new military institution opposed effective social change. They were more often moved by class allegiance than by a sense of duty to the recently proclaimed nation. The lower classes had so little reason for hope that they retained the apathy and diffidence that had marked their colonial condition.

Many interrelated colonial families retained property in the new nations. Some functioned as the elite in government and the professions, but they were joined during and after the Wars for Independence by rude military leaders of lower-class origins. The latter accepted the system of privilege and shared in division of public lands and the property of loyalists. The "reconstituted patriciate" guarded its influence with the consent of custom, the cement of class structure, and the personality and military force of the *caudillo*. Thus, the concept of social hierarchy and privilege continued, modified by the new conditions.

The most valuable property long remained in agricultural and pastoral enterprise, which encouraged retention of the traditional attitudes. Many estate owners, however, lived all or much of the time in town, as they had in the colonial period. Furthermore, agricultural and pastoral interests often were mixed with commercial ventures, and later with financial and industrial. The mixture of upper- and middle-class economic interests probably was more important than the clashes of such sectoral interests as agriculture, commerce, and manufacturing. Nevertheless, rural landlords often did not develop varied interests and usually resisted innovation. Furthermore, the avidity with which new men bought landed estates indicated their confidence in the socioeconomic importance of land, and provided new recruits for the support of privilege.

The privileged class emphasized its status by clothes, education, residence, servants, deportment, diet, carriages and fancy saddles, and by confining marriage to its own ranks or a few rich or powerful newcomers from the lower class. Some newcomers, often successful *caudillos*, were of mixed racial stock. Generally, however, Indian or black heritage made it difficult to rise, and downright racial prejudice was not dead. Even before the middle of the nineteenth century, some of the upper class complained that political and social life were being invaded by the lower class. Such events as the 1848 republican revolutions in Europe stimulated fears of democracy as the wave of the future. It was, however, a slow-moving wave. With slow economic growth, opportunities increased, and a "middle sector" grew between the acknowledged upper crust and the lower class. It had enlarged access to education and acquisition of elite habits, but not all the attitudes or roles of the historical bourgeoisie in Western Europe, which was more assertive of its role. The middle sectors in Latin America preferred to imitate and join the upper class rather than follow a separate path. In politics, a few middle-class individuals turned toward the left, but the bulk of the middle class was conservative on most issues, eager to improve political leverage by conventional measures.

There were concentrations of middle-class persons in commerce, finance, transportation, and manufacturing. But promotion of nonagricultural enterprise was not a class matter, as the older monied groups moved capital and supervisory energy to new fields. In any event, with economic growth and diversification, urbanization, and education, new groups (some rich, some barely out of poverty) somewhat altered the social mix. In the Buenos Aires of the 1880s, society was greatly transformed from that of a half century earlier, or that remaining in the provinces. Remoter areas felt small winds of change as the railroad came through, ex-peasants greased engines and sold passenger snacks, and more drummers from York and Lyons sold ribbons and hardware to country stores.

Social immobility remained propped up in the 1880s by the fact that most of the lower class lacked reason to emerge from its apathy and alienation. Although alienation was a mental or spiritual malady of the poor and put-upon, it also was a defense. It permitted the individual to compartmentalize his attitudes toward his social environment, not allowing connection in his mind of the parts, and thus avoiding the contradictions of his existence and improving his chances of not being overwhelmed by life. In this conception it has been said that alienation "makes men strong against the injuries of class." In this sense, also, the widespread drunkenness of the poor in nineteenth-century Latin America can be viewed as a defense or escape, a factor for survival.

What numbers were involved? A few in the upper class; not many more in the middle, though it grew considerably in some places by the 1880s; and most people still in the lower class after half a century of Independence. Of the 700,000 inhabitants of Venezuela in 1825, about 3.5 percent were upper class or rich bourgeoisie; possibly 7 percent were in middle groups (less rich and less well connected socially, but not laborers); some 81.5 percent in the free lower class; about 4 percent slaves; another 5 percent uncontrolled Indians. This was roughly representative of the size of the classes at Independence in most of Spanish America. There was a much larger slave component in Brazil. Truly, Latin America for decades after Independence was a society of class and privilege, of minority domination and popular submissiveness.

Violence and Personalism—*Caudillismo*

The privileged also guarded themselves with legislation and violence. Constitutions and laws declared the sanctity of property. The suffrage was restricted by literacy and property requirements. The burdens of taxation, trade levies, monopolies, franchises, and land law channeled income and opportunity from the poor to the rich. The class system ensured, of course, that the national bureaucracies were staffed with the cousins and other clients of the privileged. There were not enough places for the masses, and besides they were illiterate.

These weapons were bolstered with physical violence and menace, as in the colonial era: by economic exploitation, police and military brutality, and judicial decision. On the haciendas beatings and debt slavery continued from colonial times. The armies were filled with poor men simply seized for service. Forced labor gangs worked on coffee plantations and elsewhere even when it was illegal, for there was one law for the poor, another for the rich. If plebeians were allowed to meet the election requirements, it was to be herded to the polls, then to respond as ordered in the public balloting.

Violence occurred frequently in an entirely new way: for seizure of power and maintenance of "illegitimate" government. With extinction of the imperial system in Spanish America, the competition for power became naked, constant, and unpredictable. Seizure of power was a new and frightening element in the society and one that the old privileged class could not control, although it usually retained most of its privileges and property under the illegitimate governments of the *caudillos*. Brazil long was untroubled by the problem at the national level, because continuation of the monarchical system to 1889 prevented the dilution of the structure of authority that occurred in Spanish America. Monarchy helped prevent territorial fragmentation of Brazil. On the other hand, the *caudillismo* and military activity in politics and government in Brazil after 1889 suggested that the social factors that led to *caudillismo* in Spanish America were present also in Brazil, merely muffled by the monarchy in 1822–1889.

Caudillismo thus grew first out of necessities and opportunities as Spanish authority was destroyed and new regimes faltered. It did not re-

quire military experience to feel the temptation to seize power, though that doubtless made it easier to succumb. The Wars for Independence created military bands and leaders ready for expanded activity. Poor transportation encouraged local seizures of power and property because the reach of national authority was so uncertain. The opportunities for armed action were so plain that it would have occurred had Independence been achieved peaceably. *Caudillismo* did not, in fact, vary significantly with the amount of fighting for freedom from Spain. For one thing, *caudillismo* was fostered by the *personalismo* that had been so influential in the colonial period. Individuals depended on personal relationships for favor; everyone sought a *patrón*.

Unfortunately, the wars induced in some military leaders a contempt for civilians as cowards and profiteers; a conviction that soldiers deserved rewards for their sacrifices; and a conclusion that civilians could not govern the new nations. These wartime leaders commenced the process of forcibly making and unmaking governments, or of exerting military pressure upon them. José Miguel Carrera seized authority in Chile in 1811 and used force to maintain his rule. Bolívar, José de San Martín, and Bernardo O'Higgins received dictatorial powers and used the military for political purposes. Justifications offered for early grants or seizures of dictatorial powers included military danger, the difficulty of collecting resources, or the need to control subversion, defeatism, and factionalism. Before long the new constitutions began to include provision for the "state of siege" (*estado de sitio*), an institution that remained prominent in Latin America to the later years of the twentieth century. The state of siege provided for the suspension of constitutional guarantees (as free speech, press, and assembly) if the nation was threatened by serious internal disturbances. Necessary as the device might be in many circumstances in Latin America, it frequently was used simply or mainly for political purposes.

Another root of *caudillismo* was the emphasis in society on courage, a part of the *machismo* (masculine intrepidity or daring) that a later age fascinated with psychology would celebrate as an important source of violence in Latin America.[2]

Other motives for the creation of dictatorial regimes were personal ambition and greed, the more potent because opportunities in private enterprise were so limited. Desire for offices and public grants led to faction and violence, as did regional economic competition, and different policy needs as between export agriculture and entrepreneurs desirous of furthering manufacture with protective tariffs. So the volatility of politics often resulted from quarrels among elite factions. That, of course, offered opportunities to lower-class *caudillos*.

Some leaders soon concluded that social conditions made dictatorial government, or at least heavy paternalism, necessary. Most people lacked conceptions of representative government or protection of individual rights, and either accepted *caudillos* passively or joined their armies. On the other hand, the educated minority thought that the rules of the game did not include acceptance of defeat in elections, but permitted action to set the results aside, and often supported violent removal and creation of governments as a proper reaction to disorder or tyranny. So *caudillismo* was a practical answer to existing social problems, not a deviation from some norm suitable to the Rhineland or Nebraska.

Most *caudillos* came to power by violence, and they depended on force and personal magnetism or charisma. Many were military leaders. Even if they had not been to military academies, they lived by the sword. They kept the military happy with a fat slice of the public revenues. They also had to play military politics, because subordinate commanders could not be allowed to become too popular with their men or with the public. Such politics required potentially perilous juggling of commands, and trumped-up charges of misdeeds, followed by executions, exile, or prison.

In cases of regional commanders with local followings, the national *caudillo* had to decide whether to try to smash regional forces or set up a system of collaboration. Both methods had successes and failures. This extensive rule by force was far from militarism. Latin American society was about as little militarized as imaginable; it was violent, but undisciplined.

Nineteenth-century *caudillos* offered rich variety. Some were brutish chieftains of warrior clans; a few were cultivated; many were a combination of personal force, ruthlessness, and political shrewdness. With some of them *personalismo* became vain parading, titles fit for minor deities, obsequious flattery. Many used crude terrorism. Every nineteenth-century *caudillo* drove some of his fellow citizens into exile, and a few seemed intent on creating nothing but exiles, corpses, and slaves. A wild horseman like Facundo Quiroga of northwestern Argentina had the appetites and interests of a wilderness outlaw. Sarmiento judged him "a man imbued with the genius of barbarism," who made of "the law . . . a plaything in vile hands." Santa Anna was president of Mexico half a dozen times without revealing one redeeming feature, and mismanaged everything he touched. Melgarejo of Bolivia showed his mettle by drunkenly ordering soldiers to march off the roof of the national palace or be shot for disobedience. Diego Portales, a Chilean businessman, used military means to force his country into a political mold that would permit economic development. Portales was a national *caudillo*, Facundo a regional. Many national *caudillos* had to share power, in one way or another, with regional *caudillos*. The great size and poor transportation of some countries were factors in this regionalism.[3]

Caudillos kept power in as few hands as possible. They preferred weak or absent legislatures.

---

[2] *Machismo* has been ascribed to the European aristocratic tradition of courage, the alleged intensity of male Hispanic sexuality or obsession therewith, and a strong individualism in the Hispanic cultural tradition.

[3] Sometimes personalistic authority with a large element of violence at levels below the national is labeled *caciquismo*. We will speak of national and regional *caudillos* and local *caciques*, a term applied in some areas to arbitrary bosses at the city and what we would call the county levels.

Many of their aides were relatives, or *compadres*, linked by coparent ties.[4] Members of the inner group had to have property and income, or their loyalty weakened, and the necessity of paying off civil and military collaborators alone was enough to make *caudillos* avaricious. In addition, many *caudillos* had been poor boys, who hungered for personal possessions. There were few locally usable methods of chicanery and thievery that *caudillos* did not try. They were adept at manipulating the propertied class, which was eager to pay for government-created or protected monopolies and other privileges. Thus the *caudillo* struggled to keep his place, knowing that his manner of leaving it might be painful. It was a dangerous job, and ten years was a long term of survival.

Modernization did tend to make crude personalism by *caudillos* less acceptable, but it certainly did not guarantee such a change. Pressures for more thoughtful administration grew especially where economies improved and society became more complex. Another change was that better transportation and communications by the 1880s helped national *caudillos* establish more control over regional leaders. Those factors also meant, however, that in some cases the rigor of arbitrary national rule could be "improved." In the 1830s the Chilean elite replaced the battling of military chieftains with an effective civil government. In Argentina regional *caudillismo* prevented creation of national government until the 1850s, after which the old-style *caudillo* was submerged by the efforts of the upper class to create an oligarchic republic that would ensure the export profits so obviously beckoning. Even in countries that developed more slowly than Chile and Argentina the possibilities of modernization forced *caudillos* to adopt more sophisticated attitudes. In any event, complete rascals and brutes were the minority of *caudillos*. Many brought an order that some citizens preferred to the uncontrolled contention they displaced. They were praised for contributions to unity. Some *caudillos* ruined the local economies, but others charmed domestic and foreign investors and entrepreneurs with law and order. So Latin Americans have debated the role of the *caudillos*. Was the policy of Francia of Paraguay in isolating the country merely tyranny, or an element in a glorious campaign to prevent the absorption of the fatherland by giant Argentina and Brazil? Was Rosas merely a bloody despot or the lustrous father of Argentine nationalism? Should the brilliant economic achievements of Porfirio Díaz of Mexico be fluted above the death shrieks of civic freedom?

Regionalism

Regionalism continued rivalries from the colonial era, inevitable in an area of more than 8 million square miles, scattered population, and often difficult terrain. It retained its colonial roots in economic competition, poor communications, and in the tendency of capital cities to levy toll on the provinces. Regionalism was exaggerated during and after the Wars for Independence by replacement of the imperial system with weaker governments. It was aggravated when the wars sometimes eradicated all but local government or private rule by *hacendados*. Bolívar said that each such local center was a "little world" that he had to struggle to unite into a national whole. It was encouraged by the creation of regional armies. Regionalism also was encouraged by the new politics—ideas of freedom, elections, federalism.

Regionalism here simply means sizable differences of viewpoint from place to place that had notable effects on history. The largest "regions" were nations. Brazil managed to prevent extensive regionalism from splitting it into more than one nation. Buenos Aires failed to unite all the territories of the Viceroyalty of La Plata, and

---

[4] Established when a person, on the invitation of the parents, sponsors a child receiving a sacrament, especially baptism. The strength of the tie of *compadrazgo* thereby established between the natural parents and the godparents may vary from near zero to very strong. In some cases *compadrazgo* merely reaffirms old friendship; in others the parents hope that it will create significant new ties.

the results before the end of the 1820s were the republics of Argentina, Bolivia, Paraguay, and Uruguay. By 1826 there were ten independent states in Latin America—Mexico, Central America (later five nations), Colombia (later four nations), Peru, Bolivia, Chile, Haiti, Paraguay, La Plata, Brazil (at the moment including Uruguay). In 1830 there were thirteen nations— Uruguay became independent in 1828, and Colombia fell into three nations (Venezuela, Ecuador, and New Granada or Colombia). In 1844 there were eighteen Latin American nations— that year the Dominican Republic freed itself from Haiti; Central America had divided into five parts in the 1830s. There was no further division by the 1880s, and Cuba remained a Spanish colony.

Regionalism remained within the nations as finally constituted. The larger the territory, more difficult the terrain, and varied the resources, the more likely regionalism was to play a role in national affairs. It was strong in Argentina, Brazil, Mexico, and New Granada. Some provincials felt economically "colonial" to the capitals and threatened by their policies. Much of the quarreling over federalism and centralism was aggravated by regional rivalry. It was stimulated also by poor communications and by the culture of violence, which helped regional *caudillos* to use local sentiment to support their power. Regionalist sentiment was in turn diluted by parochialism or localism. Horizons were near and narrow. Such narrowness of outlook was not surprising for an Indian village on a mountain trail, but it also was true of larger places.

The politically important elements usually were concentrated in the regional or national capitals, which held the best educational facilities; the richest people and investment funds for private enterprise; and the dispensers of government funds and privileges. Commercial activity for cash was amazingly feeble in provincial towns compared with the national capitals. Such factors meant that although regionalism was important in politics, the national capitals enjoyed great advantages in contests for power; indeed, sometimes the capture of the national capital practically decided an issue.

Regionalism was weakened, or threatened, by developments that by the 1880s were influential in places in Latin America and could be expected to grow. Wherever the export economy gave or promised profits, national attention came to focus. Landowners, shippers, suppliers wanted assistance from the national government, which itself wanted to suck public revenue from exports. National governments had varied success in controlling areas of great export modernization. Sometimes the influence of regional *caudillos* was reduced, in others the new riches increased the power and pretensions of regional elites. One service that frequently was fortified in areas of export growth, and sometimes increased national control of regionalism, was transportation, especially railways, important in several areas by the 1880s. Railways reduced some types of regional economic complaint and increased national government military capabilities against regional insurgency.

Finally, the sentiment of nationalism before the 1880s increased enough in a few places to weaken regionalism. In some countries it was stimulated by such extraordinary experience as resistance to invasion or by pride in material and cultural achievements, clearly merited by the 1880s in Brazil, Argentina, and Chile. Nationalism became a more potent factor when education facilitated propagation of the idea, as occurred on a considerable scale by the 1880s in Argentina; and it was certain to happen elsewhere. The trend of development in Latin America, then, was away from regionalism and toward national integration, although by the 1880s' the latter still was feeble.

The Role of Doctrine

The role of political doctrine escalated in the Independence period when theories of government became tied to action groups competing for control of new regimes. Most people mixed theory with material interest, although there were some ideologues, for whom doctrine had value outweighing practical matters. Ideas played a role in initiating controversy, in shaping it, and in providing a sense of higher values that sometimes prevented issues from degenerating simply into contests for advantage.

Republicanism was a prime doctrinal issue.[5] As a revolutionary idea, suggesting popular representation and limitation of power, it lurked behind debates over constitutional monarchy, even if republicanism was not mentioned. Most creoles wanted no monarchic threat to their influence and thought of republicanism as something modern that people of reason must accept in place of the outworn social system that centered on monarchy. Bolívar continued to support republicanism even when his interpretation of it included a life-term presidency, a functional equivalent of monarchism. The republican idea helped keep alive the debate over popular participation in public affairs. Even tyrants found it expedient to give lip service to republicanism.

Most nineteenth-century doctrinal dispute was between liberals and conservatives, often organized into parties with those names. Doctrines to the left of liberalism, like anarchism and socialism, were only feebly disseminated in a few places in Latin America by the 1880s. Although conservatives thought some liberal ideas revolutionary, the two groups agreed on many issues. Liberal doctrine, as well as conservative, was the "class truth" of the propertied. Liberals were not egalitarians but held a nineteenth-century liberalism that focused on political freedoms and institutions, based on the eighteenth-century Enlightenment and expressed in the North American and French revolutions.

Although disputes were largely political in form, they had socioeconomic implications that

embittered debate. Conservatives thought that political leveling would bring socioeconomic egalitarianism, and thus feared a broad franchise, free elections, general eligibility for office, free speech, decentralized government (though they sometimes favored that), and general education. Conservative support of a broad role for the church, and a tie between it and government, also was in part a practical line in support of a political ally. Although there were fears of property division expressed in connection with political doctrine, socioeconomic issues generally were at one remove from debate; and, in fact, little economic or social change resulted by the 1880s from adoption of political reforms. There was an apparently direct attack on property in the liberal effort to abolish entail, but since its extinction did nothing to reduce the great estate system, it was reform only in theory. Liberals did tend to support greater tariff reduction and less government activity in the economy generally than conservatives. Economic difference was a significant source of friction between liberals and conservatives.

The role of doctrine, thus, represented an important discontinuity with the colonial era; but continuities of class and privilege, the common human competition for power, and the disinterest of most people in theory ensured that its role would be circumscribed by other considerations. It is an old argument, however, that fascination with theory has been a weak element in Latin America's political life. This notion cannot be attached to the chief executives, nearly all notably pragmatic. It is therefore argued that if zealous liberals (and later radicals) had been less doctrinaire, they might have attained more power! It also is claimed that the frequent change in Latin American constitutions and the detailed provisions for reform in some signify belief that doctrine can conquer where politics has failed. It merely shows, however, that ideas get into Latin American constitutions that decision makers will not implement. The explanation of the inclusion and the lack of implementa-

---

[5] In Brazil republicanism was much less of an issue than in Spanish America because of retention of the monarchical institution until 1889.

tion is not so simple as relative affection for theory.

c. Arbitrary but Feeble Government

Although government often was arbitrary, it engaged in only a narrow range of activities, and most of those were poorly executed.

Limited Functions, Programs, and Revenues

The upper class wanted a government of limited functions and expenditures, even though conservatives often wanted more than liberals. Governments did not tax great landholdings or landed income. Much public revenue came from levies on foreign trade, which tapped only a part of the national wealth, and oscillated in accordance with uncontrollable international factors. Public revenues thus were small and uncertain, insufficient for extensive activity. Early loans were secured abroad, but interest was high. Finally, financial administration was often inexpert and corrupt. That capital existed in Latin America that was not used for national development is true, but the politically dominant minority would not consider its mobilization for such purposes. Echelons of government below the national were even worse off financially, very dependent on the national capital for funds. One reason country towns were dirty and dull was that they could not afford to be anything else. Of the limited public funds, many went for military and police functions or jobs in the bureaucracy for members of the elite and their clients. Early Latin American governments had only limited programs of expenditures that were goal-oriented in national terms.

Revenues grew in later years with the export economies, and the somewhat more complex societies and expanded opportunities resulted in more ambitious government programs. By the 1870s and 1880s several governments had adopted development projects of some size— railways, ports, municipal improvements, education, support for immigration, arrangements for

public and private banking, even some promotion of manufacturing. But much investment in transportation and seaports came from foreign investment and from Latin American governments, paying in land and operating monopolies rather than in cash. Increased revenues did not always lead to happy results. Corruption and *empleomanía*—the lust for public office—drained off substantial sums.

Legislators came from the literate minority and generally ignored the needs of the lower class. In any event, the legislatures—and the courts—found it difficult to oppose executive fiat. To their great credit, some Latin Americans never abandoned hope of altering this unpalatable fact. Another problem of government was that citizens were disinclined to obey laws unless they suited their convenience, finding justification in the fact that government orders often were arbitrary or directed to class or personal rather than community interest. Often a local military commander or an isolated civil official concentrated in himself all authority and so misused it as to bring government into disrepute. Sometimes the great roadless hinterlands made enforcement difficult. As regime succeeded regime, after violence and orders and counterorders and new constitutions rained on the countryside, understandable mixtures of confusion, apathy, fear, and outrage affected obedience to law.

The deficiencies of government in the nineteenth century were apparent to all, and many were as prevalent in Brazil as in Spanish America. A large literature then and later explored the "failures" of government. It was popular among liberals in Spanish America for some years to ascribe "failure" to an outmoded Spanish heritage and a lack of "preparation" of colonials for independence. Such lack of preparation, however, might be ascribed to the poor and illiterate but only with difficulty to the upper class. Educated Spanish Americans understood political requirements as well as other people. The total social environment—the class structure, *latifundio*, economic underdevelopment, and the rest— made violence in public life inevitable. Spanish

Americans, before and after Independence, were as responsible for the social environment as was Spain.

The Federalist-Centralist Duel

The duel between federalism and centralism involved both doctrine and practice. In Brazil's monarchical system, to 1889, federalism took the form of opposition to the emperor's powers; later the issue was much as in Spanish America. Some Spanish American liberals thought of federalism as a modern or progressive device, carrying government to the localities, reducing the dangers of tyranny, helping guard against continuism in office and the imposition of candidates. To a few it also was gilded by its use in the United States, then admired by liberals. Support came also from observation of conditions in America and from traditional Spanish theory and practice. People with a strong concern for regional interest often supported federalism. Conservatives often tended to object to federalism, because they saw it as costly and requiring many expert personnel, and because they wanted centralized authority to guard against social and certain sorts of economic change. On the other hand, conservatives sometimes supported federalism as a safeguard against national action by liberals, and were for economic changes that benefited conservative interests.

Although the duel between the ideas was mixed with other problems, an amazing amount of argument dealt squarely with federalism. It was, however, losing support by mid-century, because the majority of leaders preferred strong government and considered it less likely to prevail under a federal system. Argentina and Mexico in the 1880s retained a strong theoretical attachment to federalism, but in practice it was different from federalism in the United States. In Brazil, with the fall of the monarchy in 1889, a federal republic was created, but the principle remained a bone of contention thereafter. In the rest of Latin America federalism was dead or dying.

Church and State

The place of the church in the new society caused bitter dispute in Spanish America but less in Brazil, where the colonial church had been weaker and where continuance of the monarchy after Independence permitted adjustment of most questions with minimal trouble. The church-state quarrel was founded on colonial objections to clerical privilege and property, on the hierarchy's support of the Spanish side during the Wars for Independence, and on practical and theoretical arguments in relation to the new governments.

Creoles generally began by protecting the privileged position of the church, although from the beginning some liberals favored equality of sects. The union of church and state was much loosened. After long debate, the *patronato* (most importantly, the power to appoint prelates) generally went back to the church. The Inquisition soon disappeared. Governments seized some church property during and after the Wars for Independence. There was frequent chipping at the church's educational role and its control of vital statistics and cemeteries. During the first half century the church was driven into a narrower and narrower field of activity, but some ties between church and state remained in most countries throughout the nineteenth century. Roman Catholicism retained a somewhat privileged position as compared with other sects.

The arguments over the church's position often were emotional because they were connected with sociopolitical issues. Liberals decried the church's activity as part of the conservative alliance in politics. Conservatives had a complex of fears of loss of privilege, social revolution, and immorality. The liberal attacks on the church were anticlerical, not antireligious, but ecclesiastics and conservative laymen made the charge of atheism. The attitude of the lower classes in this highly politicized debate is difficult to discern. Although much attached to their version of the faith, peasants had not been well served by the clergy. Some clerics were more interested

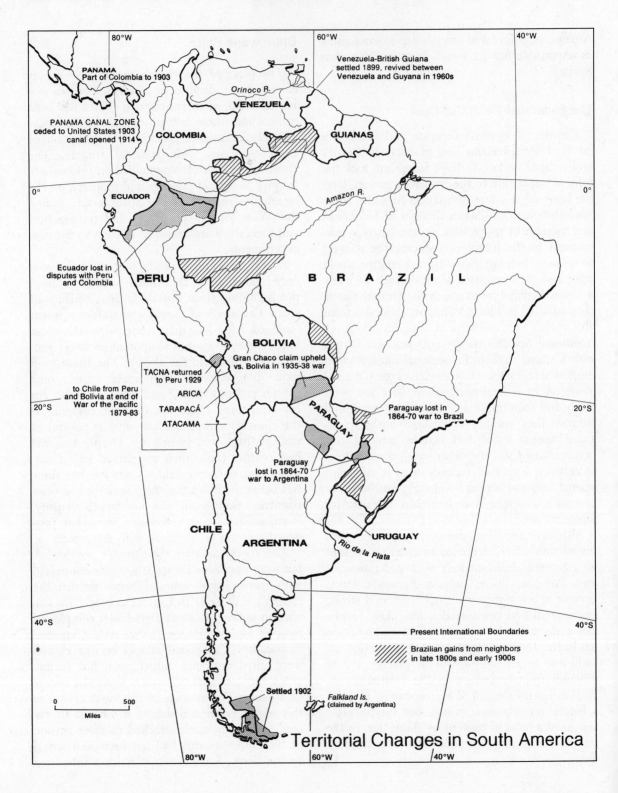

PANAMA
Part of Colombia to 1903

Venezuela-British Guiana
settled 1899, revived between
Venezuela and Guyana in 1960s

Orinoco R.

VENEZUELA

PANAMA CANAL ZONE
ceded to United States 1903
canal opened 1914

COLOMBIA

GUIANAS

Amazon R.

ECUADOR

0°   0°

Ecuador lost in
disputes with Peru
and Colombia

PERU

B R A Z I L

BOLIVIA

Gran Chaco claim upheld
vs. Bolivia in 1935-38 war

TACNA returned
to Peru 1929

ARICA

to Chile from Peru
and Bolivia at end of
War of the Pacific
1879-83

TARAPACÁ

ATACAMA

20°S   20°S

PARAGUAY

Paraguay lost in
1864-70 war to Brazil

Paraguay
lost in 1864-70
war to Argentina

URUGUAY

CHILE

Rio de la Plata

ARGENTINA

40°S   40°S

——— Present International Boundaries

////// Brazilian gains from neighbors
in late 1800s and early 1900s

0   500
Miles

Settled 1902

Falkland Is.
(claimed by Argentina)

Territorial Changes in South America

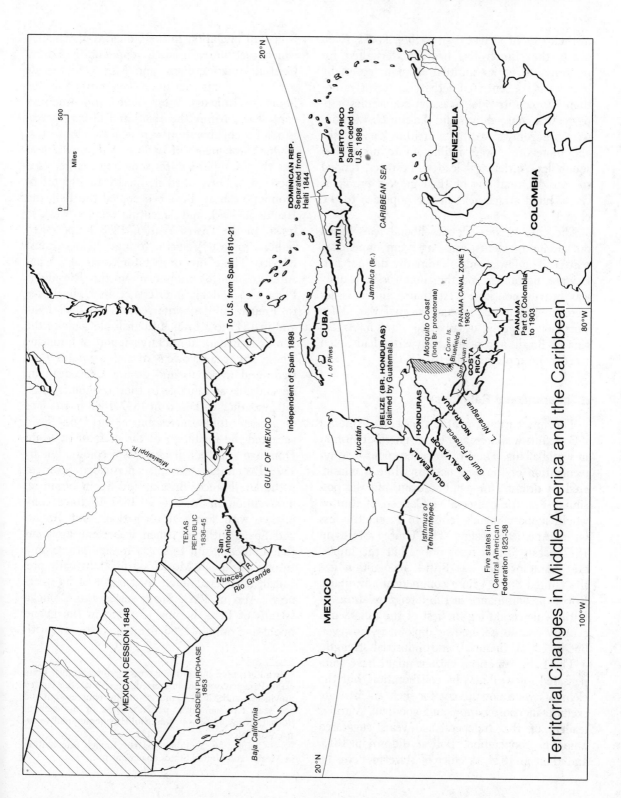

Territorial Changes in Middle America and the Caribbean

20°N

To U.S. from Spain 1810-21

DOMINICAN REP.
Separated from
Haiti 1844

PUERTO RICO
Spain ceded to
U.S. 1898

CARIBBEAN SEA

VENEZUELA

HAITI

CUBA

Independent of Spain 1898

Jamaica (Br.)

COLOMBIA

I. of Pines

Mosquito Coast
(long Br. protectorate)

PANAMA CANAL ZONE
1903-

BELIZE (BR. HONDURAS)
claimed by Guatemala

Corn Is.
Bluefields

PANAMA
Part of Colombia
to 1903

80°W

GULF OF MEXICO

Yucatán

HONDURAS

San Juan R.

COSTA
RICA

NICARAGUA

L. Nicaragua

GUATEMALA

EL SALVADOR

Gulf of Fonseca

Five states in
Central American
Federation 1823-38

TEXAS
REPUBLIC
1836-45

San
Antonio

Isthmus of
Tehuantepec

Mississippi R.

Nueces R.

Rio Grande

MEXICO

MEXICAN CESSION 1848

GADSDEN PURCHASE
1853

100°W

Baja California

20°N

Miles

500

0

in their ease or in fees than in their flocks. Even worse, the church was badly understaffed for performance of its spiritual mission, especially because it concentrated activity in towns rather than the countryside. Peasants sometimes supported the conservatives and the church, at times were antagonistic to the church and its priests, and more often were indifferent to upper-class squabbles. Anticlerical leaders, however, tended to consider that one of their gravest problems was a blind attachment of the populace to the church.

The church issue, despite liberal fears based on specific incidents, was largely an upper-class matter. The lower orders ordinarily did not participate in politics, and the church issue usually was heavily politicized. At times church issues were an important element in civil war. They were not, however, usually important in Argentina or Brazil, and nearly everywhere had much receded in importance by the 1880s.

d. International Relations

The international relations of Latin America reflected its weakness and the strength of Britain in world affairs. The British government held up recognition of the new nations while it considered its distaste for republicanism and the possibility that the conservative Concert of Europe would support Spain's refusal to accept the loss of its American realms. The United States in 1822 began formal recognition, but the important result of that was British recognition lest the United States gain a commercial advantage. British predominance in the foreign relations of Latin America during the rest of the nineteenth century was not secured by diplomacy, however, but by naval, financial, and industrial strength.

The Latin American nations might have compensated for weakness by collaboration, but the elements were not present for such an intricate exercise in coordination and goodwill. Various leaders of the Independence years suggested union or cooperation. Bolívar did so in 1815, and then in 1824, as chief of state in Peru, he

issued an invitation to the Congress of Panama, which met in 1826, with representatives from Central America, Peru, and Mexico.[6] It made some agreements that never were ratified by the home governments. Subsequent Latin American conferences before the 1880s and literary propaganda for collaboration were of little moment.

One consequence of Latin American weakness was that European states sometimes either used coercion or threatened it, mostly in support of economic claims. Britain occupied the Falkland Islands in 1833, and Argentina was too weak to resist. In the Pastry War of 1838 France used military force at Veracruz to press claims against Mexico. The efforts of dictator Rosas of Buenos Aires to control commerce in the Río de la Plata area and his interference in Uruguay led to French military intervention in 1838–1840, and in 1845 to a French-English blockade of the Río de la Plata and military support of Uruguay. These European powers wished to guard their trade and nationals and ensure Uruguayan independence as valuable to their economic interests, but they withdrew in 1847–1848 in the face of Rosas' stubborn resistance. In 1861 Spain accepted the invitation of the dictator of Santo Domingo and took it again as a colony, but by 1865 Dominican resistance persuaded Spain to withdraw. France, Britain, and Spain began an intervention in Mexico in 1862 to force compliance with financial obligations, but Britain and Spain withdrew when it became apparent that France meant to seat a foreign prince on a throne. Although Mexico's arms eventually prevailed, it suffered sorely as a result of its weakness.[7] Also in 1862, Spain seized the Chincha Islands of Peru, hoping to share in the guano boom and only in 1866 abandoned the war with

---

[6] Brazil accepted but did not send a representative; Francia of Paraguay was not interested; Argentina (the United Provinces) and Chile approved of the congress but did not send representatives, partly because of suspicion of Bolívar; Uruguay was at war; Bolivia's representative arrived too late.

[7] See Chapter 26, Section e, on the French intervention in Mexico and United States objections to it.

Peru and Chile that ensued.[8] Foreign pressures led Brazil in 1867 to open the Amazon River system to the world's merchant marines.

Although these affairs illustrated Latin American weakness, they also demonstrated that military activity in the area was apt to be expensive. The new states had some ability to resist. In addition, Britain was not keen about European territorial adventures in Latin America, and the possibility of intervention or pressure from the world's premier naval power exerted some restraint.

The United States' most important relations with Latin America involved projects for acquisition of territory. These mostly aimed at reaching the so-called continental boundaries: the acquisition of Florida, the western part by proclamation in 1811, the eastern by a treaty with Spain ratified in 1821; the acquisition of the Republic of Texas by declaration of the United States Congress in 1845, which brought on the Mexican War of 1846–1848, ending with transfer of territory from Mexico that became much of the present United States Southwest and Pacific Coast. There was also interest in acquiring Cuba or in forbidding its occupation by a stronger power than Spain, which led to various crises but no conclusion until the 1890s. The United States also showed interest in acquiring Santo Domingo in the 1860s and 1870s and even had the consent of one of that island nation's dictators, but the mood in the United States Senate was against it. Finally, United States interest in canal sites in the American isthmus led to a rivalry with Britain for control that seemed to threaten serious trouble until damped by the Clayton-Bulwer Treaty of 1850, by which the two nations agreed not to acquire exclusive rights to construct such a canal. That compromise lasted for half a century. Shortly before that (1846) the United States concluded a treaty with New Granada (Colombia), guaranteeing the latter's rights in its province of Panama, and receiving a concession to build a railway across the isthmus there.

---

[8] See Chapter 27, Section c.

In 1823 President Monroe told Congress that Europe should not colonize further in the Western Hemisphere. That statement caused little stir in Latin America, where it seemed of small use compared with British protection. Neither in the case of British occupation of the Falklands nor the British-French blockades of the Río de la Plata did the United States government perceive a violation of its vital interests. Even in the United States the principles of Monroe were not accepted as a "doctrine" until years later. Attachment to the idea was solidified by the French attempt to seat Maximilian in Mexico in the 1860s. The fall of Maximilian was mostly due, however, to the costliness of the adventure, resistance by the Juárez government and the Mexican people, France's multiplying problems in Europe, and also the end of the United States Civil War, which brought increased American pressure on France and more aid to Juárez. By the 1870s the Monroe Doctrine was well established as an American policy, but no important occasion for its aggressive use arose until the 1890s.

The weakness that permitted a number of humiliations of Latin American nations in their relations with the United States and Europe was not primarily in will and diplomatic techniques. The economic growth that was one requirement for strength as a foundation for more independent foreign policies could not be conjured out of the air. Another requirement was the creation of a sentiment of nationalism to support the sacrifices almost certain to be attendant upon resistance to great power pressures. Nationalism of sufficient intensity, however, required improved socioeconomic conditions for the bulk of the population—not only difficult to arrange but opposed by many leaders. It is true that sheer courage, as in Rosas' resistance to French and British military pressure, might be sufficient; but unaccompanied by other weapons it was not a dependable means of resistance.

Relations between the Latin American nations generally were peaceful. They had more important problems to solve with Europe and the United States. Their economic relations with each other were minimal. Most of them had ample territory for their scanty populations. Boundaries generally were set by accepting the *uti possidetis* of 1810—the supposed boundaries in that year of the Spanish American divisions governed by viceroys, captains-general, or presidents of *audiencias*. Although this left ambiguities, it caused little serious conflict. The greatest expansionism resulted from Brazil's claims against its neighbors.

Wars were rare. In 1839 Chile defeated the forces of Andrés Santa Cruz, who in 1836 had created a confederation of Bolivia and Peru. The War of the Pacific (1879–1883) resulted in a decisive Chilean victory over the same two neighbors and Chilean acquisition of rich mineral territories from them in what is now northern Chile. The war was quite simply a Chilean military reaction to Bolivian and Peruvian desire to resist Chilean economic hegemony in their national territories.[9] In another area, the Paraguayan War (1865–1870) was the result of the dementia of dictator Francisco Solano López of Paraguay, who fancied himself an American Napoleon. It is chiefly of interest for the extraordinary valor of the Guaraní Indian population of Paraguay and the military weakness and ineptitude shown by Brazil and Argentina, allied with Uruguay against little Paraguay.[10] The Latin American military systems were not organized, trained, and equipped to engage in any but the simplest combat; their chief functions were the preservation of internal order and a role in the political process. This weakness inevitably had effects upon Latin American international policy. It did not mean, however, that in the nineteenth century invading and holding substantial amounts of Latin American territory would have been easy, as the Maximilian fiasco in Mexico showed. Blockades and the occupation of ports were a very different thing from deep and prolonged penetrations by ground forces into hostile territory.

e. Economic Privilege and Colonialism

The privileged class had that freedom to trade with the world for which it had hungered in the late colonial era, convinced that removal of all theoretical as well as actual restrictions would enormously increase traffic and their profits. They exaggerated. Flexibility in the legal systems, plus contraband, had permitted exchange between colonial Hispanic America and the world. Gains from elimination of the Portuguese and Spanish profits and tax and supervisory systems were limited. Really large gains depended upon Latin American improvements in production of goods desired by buyers in the rest of the world, increases in world demand, and relations between the prices of Latin America's exports and imports. Specializing in raw material exports and needing European capital, markets, and manufactures, Latin American participation in the Atlantic trading community increased in the nineteenth century hand in hand with Latin American dependency or economic "colonialism." Complaint grew only slowly, but by the 1880s both economic and political objections to dependence had grown significantly.

Latin American economic development could not be like that of the United States because the societies were different. The British colonies had been started on modernization with more literacy, popular participation in economic and social affairs, and incentives to thrift, investment, hard work, and innovation. The British colonies and the succeeding United States were not distracted from agricultural and industrial development by silver mining. They had useful and profitable maritime enterprises. Finally, in the United States domestic financial operations were much stronger than in Latin America, because of colonial economic tradition and because of post-Independence capital accumulation, entrepreneurial enterprise, and encouragement of banking,

---

[9] See Chapter 27 on the Chilean wars.
[10] See Chapters 24–25 on the Paraguayan War.

insurance, and dealing in stocks and bonds.

The opportunities for large profit were scarce in the early years in Latin America. Much property had been destroyed, labor dispersed, the output of export crops interrupted, herds slaughtered. Capital had been drained and frightened by government exactions. Dubious currency circulated. In many countries economic activity was lethargic to the end of the century. In a few places the export economies soon began to pick up, became moderately prosperous by mid-century, and occasionally enjoyed spectacular growth by the 1880s. Mining was nearly smashed by the wars and not clearly on the road to recovery till the 1870s and 1880s. Manufacturing was as difficult to foster as in the colonial era, and for the same reasons, so that not until the 1870s and 1880s was there notable, though still modest, growth. How much Latin American slowness in economic diversification was due to dependence on the developed North Atlantic countries is not clear.[11] The largest merchants often were foreigners, as in the colonial era, although there were many Britons in place of peninsular Spaniards and Portuguese. But much commercial, small industrial, and transportation activity was in the hands of Latin Americans. Most people, however, remained subsistence farmers or agricultural workers for minimal compensation. The rich still used public authority, the class system, and actual or threatened violence to maintain their economic advantages. The landed estates grew like a whirlwind that seemed powerful enough to suck up all the national territories. Modernization or development was desired by only small groups, but it did occur fitfully, sometimes as an unplanned outgrowth of activities.

The Subsistence Economies

Lack of change in the huge subsistence economies of the colonial era was one of the great continuities. The rural poor scarcely could diminish because *latifundio* grew, and government responded to the aims of *hacendados*. Subsistence producers remained inefficient, for economic, technological, sociological, and psychological reasons. The poor had no incentive to improve productivity, and much of the exploiting class supposed that the most important labor factors were availability and low compensation. Hacienda terms for tenant farming or for worker use of garden plots resulted in sloppy cultivation. Export-oriented estates neglected food production. The small freehold farmer still was as unimportant as in the colonial era. None of those things changed because of Independence from Spain and Portugal, so that dual economic systems continued to exist, with large populations only feebly involved in the capitalistic system.[12]

Although black slaves were freed by mid-century in Spanish America and early laws relieved Indians of forced labor and tribute, the elite managed to continue using both at low levels of compensation. Even where large agricultural or pastoral exports arose, especially after mid-century, and compensation rose to attract immigrants, the compensation was not high. Some peasants and farm laborers were tied by debt to thieving hacienda stores. Much labor remained as in the colonial period forced or dependent, sometimes not even receiving money wages, and those received were tiny. The fact was that much labor was feudal rather than capitalistic. With little income, the lower class offered a poor market; but that did not concern producers of exports and their commercial and other allies, who were interested mainly in selling abroad. To the elites of Latin America in the nineteenth century, the system seemed rational for their own and for national development.

---

[11] See Chapter 24 on the evidence for this in nineteenth-century Argentina.

[12] Dependency theorists of the late twentieth century insist that small involvement in the monetary system indicates most importantly domination by it, but not everyone needs to agree with that emphasis; subsistence production and feudal relations dominated the local economies.

Internal Trade and Markets

Wholesale and large retail merchants were the most dynamic element in Latin American economic life during much of this period, reflecting the pettiness of most retail operations, the lack of a banking industry, the weakness of manufacturing, and the fact that producers of export commodities necessarily depended on the expertise and connections and credit of large export-import houses. Hacienda owners often were heavily in debt to merchants between marketing seasons. All of this merely continued conditions of the colonial era. Mining capitalists scarcely could keep above water for many years because of damage during the Wars for Independence. With the great rise of pastoral and agricultural exports after the mid-nineteenth century, large producers in that sector increased their profits, but of course commercial elements did too. Even the local wholesale merchants had a thin time of it immediately after the Wars for Independence, because foreign merchants had the same advantages in capital, expertise, and overseas connections that had aided Spanish and Portuguese merchants in colonial times. Foreign merchants married into prominent Latin American families and established connections with the landed aristocracy, just as had Spanish and Portuguese merchants in the colonial era. There were also many Latin Americans in large-scale commerce. Their numbers had increased in the later colonial era, and in the decades following Independence some new investment continued to flow from land to commerce.

As exports picked up, internal markets fattened only a trifle. The larger merchants continued to be most interested in domestic sales of imported goods, especially higher-priced items. The total size of the market economy was small in all Latin America even in the 1880s, especially if Argentina is left out. In many countries it was puny. A major provincial town in Mexico in the 1880s might have a chamber of commerce with only a few dozen members, mostly proprietors of grocery and hardware stores. Most processed foodstuffs, housewares, and clothing were made in the home or acquired through barter or in small local money exchanges from petty merchants, selling locally made and cheap imported wares. Sellers of candles and licorice could not save and buy pots and other fancier wares, amass more capital and establish wholesale firms, prosper further, and acquire haciendas.

The Export Economies

The biggest economic change came from export growth, based mainly on more demand for raw materials and food by a more populous and industrial Europe. The nineteenth-century trading system dwarfed all earlier systems, but Latin American commodities had to compete in price, quality, and delivery schedules with those from other areas. In the late colonial period that competition had been too much for some would-be exporters of wheat, cotton, and indigo in Latin America. Furthermore, Latin American nations competed with each other for international trade. Also important was the European capital that flowed in, at profitable interest rates, to finance some of the expanded production. It often was begged by Latin Americans, not thrust on them by imperialist leeches. Additionally, there was much land available, often in large holdings unburdened by heavy purchase costs or taxes. Finally, there was cheap labor, and the governments were prepared to help mobilize it. When local supplies were insufficient, the governments encouraged immigration.

Before the late 1850s Latin American exports were too small to push agriculture and stock raising far out of their colonial languor. Some percentage growths in the early decades were spectacular because the starting base was small. They were important to individuals, and provided revenues to half-starved governments. Argentine exports enjoyed growth before the 1850s, but it was much more important in the 1860s and 1870s, and the greatest expansion came in the 1880s and thereafter.

The history of Brazil's agricultural exports was similar, with large percentage increases in coffee shipments up to 1875, by which time it provided half the coffee in the world trading system. But the export growth that came thereafter in Brazil did much more for modernization. The value of Chilean exports in millions of gold pesos went from 68.4 in 1870 to 143.3 in 1883. The value of Mexican exports doubled between 1877 and 1900. On the other hand, some Latin American countries made slight contact with the world trading system by the mid-nineteenth century and still had only modest exports in the 1880s.

Much of the great estate complex in Latin America remained badly run or badly served by local conditions. Cotton generally could not compete with United States cotton in European markets; Brazil was glad to make temporary inroads in Britain during the United States Civil War. Sugar was grown in most Latin American countries, but they could not compete in world markets with producers in the Caribbean isles. Brazil, from having been at one time a great sugar shipper, after Independence could not compete in the international trade. Mexico, with great cattle haciendas, could not after Independence match Argentine triumphs in pastoral exports, because of higher costs due to transportation and poorer natural feed, plus political turmoil. The nineteenth century echoed to Latin American wails that great export riches were being neglected. The complainers underestimated the difficulties. The really excellent opportunities often were successfully exploited without urging. For the more difficult cases, providing the requisite capital, entrepreneurial skills, labor, and distribution was not easy.

The results of export growth were sometimes remarkable, both for good and for ill. (*a*) Profits in some cases became high before the 1880s, although the greatest came later. Some of the growth accrued to Latin Americans, but much had to be remitted abroad. At times in the 1880s annual remittances in gold from Argentina to Europe in the form of interest and profits may have equalled more than one-half of the value of a year's exports. Foreign governments and private bankers, shippers, suppliers, and merchants naturally insisted on a profit. (*b*) The export activity and income had wide subsidiary effects on the economy: other forms of production, distribution activities, banking, services, port development, railways, and shipping. (*c*) It also had important social effects. It paid for expanded educational and cultural facilities, and they seemed to many people an unarguable proof of the value of the system. It supported ostentatious expenditure by the rich. It contributed to corruption of government. In Argentina by the late 1880s profits in exports and in land speculation produced a near hysteria of greed. The Argentine society did benefit from the export boom, being better integrated than most in Latin America, the conditions of political competition more rational, and national government and policy better developed. There were people in Argentine government genuinely interested in modernization, admirers of British society and institutions or at least of the aristocratic element therein.

The export system fastened more securely on Latin America the great estate and monoculture, two major inheritances from colonial times. The elite gobbled huge territories from Indian communities, the church, and the public lands. They thus enlarged the material and psychological powers they had in the colonial era. Their concern for profits often was unaccompanied by interest in efficiency. Innovation was often suspect for production, although there were exceptions. It also was suspect in other realms because the *latifundio* gave influence to those who in the main were political and social reactionaries. On the hacienda their souls were about all non-owners could call their own. Life was routine, subordination was ground into the fiber of being: "Si, patrón," and hat in hand the peon, a humble and almost totally dependent client, awaited the decision of the overlord.

(*d*) Where there was an export boom, it affected public and private financial practices. Individuals borrowed funds to buy more land, and speculation sent property values up. In Argentina government credit policies were loose in order to foster this process, and it brought a financial crash late in the 1880s. Government at times also lowered the value of local currency in order to enable Europeans to buy American goods more easily. In the limited areas of feverish boom, optimism led to overinvestment not only in land, but in supplies and facilities; and to large expenditure on city and country mansions, carriages, and a riot of luxury.

(*e*) Finally, the export business kept Latin America dependent on Europe and on the vagaries of demand and price in international trade. The effects of lean years were made the worse by speculation and lack of thrift by the rich, and by the practice of tying government revenues to the export-import traffic. The acceptance of a "colonial" economic position, with concentration upon a few commodities for export—monoculture—meant that other forms of activity were less regarded, although they might not have been more developed even if exports had remained small. These two factors—dependence and skewing of development—were to be greatly accelerated and exaggerated after the 1880s. Both factors had, of course, existed in the area in the colonial era.[13]

Manufacturing

Manufacturing faced formidable difficulties. Export interests, which feared competition by manufacturing, dominated local capital and labor, and resisted adoption of effective tariffs or other protection for manufacturing. So, hopeful promoters of manufactures struggled with shortages of capital, partly due to the superior attractions of export agriculture and mining and the mercantile enterprise dependent on them. They also faced the cost of training workers; shortages of experienced managers; the cost of machinery; problems in obtaining and transporting raw ma-

terials; difficulties of distributing the finished product; and the very limiting factor that national markets for goods were small. Finally, they had to compete with more efficient and larger-scale producers abroad, who offered a product that enjoyed the esteem of Latin American buyers, whose prejudice against locally made goods endured to the late twentieth century. The fact that export producers and import merchants sometimes put money into manufacturing merely indicated that some opportunity existed in that sector; but most agriculturalists would not support expensive measures that would hurt exports or force consumption of local goods.

When manufacturing growth occurred in Latin America in the half century after Independence, it did so largely because local conditions permitted, although government protection sometimes helped. Public and private schemes to foster manufacturing usually came to little, especially in the early decades. Hopeful promoters sadly underestimated the difficulties of establishing industry. Some inherited from the colonial era the supposition that weak manufactures then were a result of Spanish and Portuguese restrictions. A book by Gregorio Funes of the United Provinces of La Plata (Argentina) in 1817 bewailed that influence in supplanting the small manufacturers of Tucumán, in the western interior, by imports from Europe. Argentines in later years complained that the process was accelerated because of a "failure" to control the greed of the littoral (eastern coastal) provinces, which preferred to sell and buy with Europe. In fact, the view of the littoral prevailed in the nineteenth century because Tucumán could supply but a fraction of the manufactures Buenos Aires needed and could not buy the littoral products. For the interior provinces to complain was reasonable, but the great exchange of European manufactures for Argentine pastoral products was due not to an unfortunate "decision" in Buenos Aires but to advantages possessed by Buenos Aires and industrial Europe. Industrial development was expensive and difficult, and likely markets tiny; export agricultural

---

[13] See Chapter 34, Section b, on the modern theory of dependence.

and pastoral development was cheaper and simpler, and the markets were immense.[14]

Manufacturing did increase, but even the larger factories in the 1880s were modest operations. Textile manufacturing and processing plants for agricultural and pastoral products were areas of early growth. Little foundries and plants were set up to provide replacement parts and repairs for pumps, streetcar and railway equipment, food processing works, steamships, and other parts of the industrial world that slowly invaded Latin America.

Mining

The mines of Latin America were in ruins as the new nations began their histories, but many people were anxious to restore their fabled riches. It proved difficult. Lucas Alamán in Mexico and Argentine Domingo F. Sarmiento, during his exile in Chile, were only two prominent Latin Americans who before mid-century tried unsuccessfully to make money in mining. Large-scale mining required capital, a scarce item in Latin America. European interest soon died as it became evident that sociopolitical conditions made profitable operation by foreigners difficult. Silver production in Mexico was almost dead, when in 1824 a British company took over the famous Real del Monte. It went bankrupt in 1849 due to shortages of capital and lack of flexibility by the British in meeting difficulties in the local environment. Some of the technological improvements introduced by foreign firms, like steam engines, were used more effectively by Latin American managers than by foreigners.

Not until mid-century did silver production in Peru and Mexico become significant again, and in Bolivia revival was even later. Development of industrial minerals had barely begun by the

1880s, although by then demand from the industrial nations and the richness of Latin American supplies—especially at first in Mexico, Peru, and Chile—were leading to expanded production. Much of the development waited for completion of railways from the sea to the mineral areas in the mountains.

Transportation

Transportation involved the other most important economic changes until the 1880s. A few streetcar lines were laid down in cities. Road building remained limited, and journey by coach was a jolting experience. Cart traffic in the interior scarcely changed from colonial times. Pack animals wended their slow way by the thousand. Porters trudged the mountain trails. Ocean shipping, on the other hand, greatly expanded, and service improved. Ports now were open without impediment to the merchant marines of the world. As transforming as free commerce was the coming of the steamship. Although a few called in Latin America in the 1820s and 1830s, regular service came later. The export-oriented governments expended great efforts to improve port facilities, sometimes by granting contracts and monopolies to foreign companies to build and operate piers and warehouses. Such expanded ports as Buenos Aires, Rio de Janeiro, and Valparaíso became centers of maritime activity far surpassing anything known in the colonial era.

Equally transforming by the 1880s, in fact or in prospect, was the railroad. Although railway enterprise had its bare beginnings in Latin America in the 1840s, it had little effect for decades. Much of the financing and construction was by foreigners at the price of high interest rates, land grants, operating monopolies, and other concessions. Usable track by the 1860s was negligible, but by 1890 the total was well over 15,000 miles, most of it in Argentina, Mexico, and Brazil. Clearly building would continue, with important effects on economic and social conditions.

---

[14] The so-called industrial advances of late colonial times in Latin America were merely the temporary results of enlargement of the markets of little handicraft activities, similar to those that all over the world were falling and continued to fall to the advantages of the new power-driven machinery.

The chief aim of railway building was to service export enterprise and the major cities—sometimes merely the capital. Many railways thus were laid down inland from a port to tap one of those needs. Few connecting lines were constructed in the interior; they would not directly serve the foreign traders, and the domestic money economy was so restricted, and most market areas so localized, that connecting lines were not attractive investments. In short, although there was "planning" in railway building, it was not our modern planning designed to promote integrated national development. Where the railways went by the 1880s, they provided a new type of employee, to build the lines, to operate the trains, to provide supporting supplies and services—roundhouse repairmen, parts manufacturers, cartage workers, porters, engineers. Railways also opened new possibilities in military transport, political maneuver and propaganda, entertainment, commerce, and urbanization.

Other Aspects of the Economies

Finance was especially weak in Latin America. Banking institutions—public or private—comparable to those of Europe did not exist at Independence. Banking expertise also was understandably in short supply, but Latin Americans learned the theory of banking before their societies could sustain strong financial institutions for them to manage. Lack of capital resources was but one of the difficulties; also important were ignorance and bad financial habits among the great estate owners and public policies that often made a shambles of orderly financial procedures. It was chimerical, of course, to expect financial sophistication from a sugar *fazendeiro* satisfied with his local barony or from a *caudillo* who had fought his way from rude beginnings to a national palace. Public and private banking did grow under the demands of export growth and recognition that public financial agonies would not disappear with inattention. Argentina, Brazil, Chile, and some other countries before the 1880s had some banking structures, and the

elite had produced a number of people with extensive understanding of the subject.

In the largest cities by the 1880s there had been a considerable growth of retail trade, professions, and service occupations. Smaller winds of change blew through the more bucolic republics, where coffee culture was under way and the international banana business was being organized by foreigners. Everywhere, local entrepreneurs were looking for opportunities; and traveling salesmen from overseas were hawking barbed wire, patent stoves, and metal tanks. All these changes, in Brazil and Argentina, less strongly in Ecuador and Guatemala, contributed to the modernization of the area. A part of it was artifacts and methods, but the most important thing was the increase in that desire for change that was a prelude to change itself.

The Latin American economy to the 1880s reflected the society. People adopted the ideas and courses of action available; they seized the obviously fattest opportunities. There seemed no alternative to export specialization. Probably to have refused it—if the possibility can be imagined—would have meant more poverty and dependence rather than less. Even if leaders had received magically the development aims of a later day, to have organized domestic resources much differently would have required knowledge and skills unavailable to the world at the time, and not entirely serviceable in the mid-twentieth century when large efforts were made to force modernization through technical aid. In any event, Illinois or Leeds could not be created by decree in Michoacán or Bahia. Latin America had to respond to the opportunities and pressures and misfortunes of modernization in its own way.

f. Social and Intellectual Conditions

Population, Race, and Class

Sparsely populated, Latin America grew only slowly in the nineteenth century. Slaveowners wanted new supplies from Africa, but large numbers were provided only to Brazil and Spanish Cuba and Puerto Rico. Most countries wanted immigrants from Europe, supposedly more industrious and amenable to civilization than Indians, blacks, and persons of mixed race. Immigration and colonization schemes in some places, including Guatemala and Mexico, had little success; others, especially in Argentina and Brazil, brought significant numbers from Europe. Europeans naturally went to those areas where economic opportunities were great enough to justify immigration to Latin America rather than to the United States. Of possibly 4 million European immigrants to Latin America from the 1820s to the late 1880s, more than 3 million went to Argentina, Brazil, and Uruguay; and the largest part of the remainder went from Spain to its colony of Cuba. Immigration jumped upward during the 1880s, ushering in the period of greatest flow.

The population of Latin America was about 20 million at Independence. By the late 1880s it was 60 million. Huge Brazil, with a mere 3.6 million in 1822, reached about 14 million in 1889. Mexico, the most populous Latin American nation at Independence, grew only from 5.8 million in 1805 to 9 million in 1870. The complex racial structure at Independence became more confused in some places, less so in others.[15] In Brazil large-scale miscegenation continued,

---

[15] Of some 17 million population in Spanish America about 1810, probably 2–3 million (10–20 percent) were white or predominantly white, the difficulty of the estimate indicating the confusion arising from miscegenation; possibly 50 percent was Indian; 4–6 percent largely black; 30 percent racial mixtures. More than 1 million blacks were carried to colonial Spanish America; in 1810 there were on the order of 775,000 in Spanish America, more than half of them in the Caribbean area, with the largest concentration in Cuba. Spanish America at the end of three colonial centuries had a smaller population than at the conquest, and it had an immensely more complicated genetic and cultural heritage. Brazil's population of 3.61 million in 1822 was more than half black and mulatto, and there were few pure-blooded Indians left, of an initially small (1–3 million) number. For comparison, the United States population in 1820 was 9.63 million, with some 18 percent black and mulatto and much less than 10 percent Indian or mestizo.

and slave imports from Africa did not end until the 1850s. In most countries the slave trade ended much earlier, because the demand was not great. In some Spanish American areas the black population was so small that the process of race mixture by the later nineteenth century had destroyed most evidence of African heritage. In Mexico and Peru blacks were overwhelmed by the Indian stock; in Argentina the assimilation of blacks resulted from large European immigration into an area where the population was relatively small and the Indian element less important than in many countries.

At Independence nearly all Latin Americans lived in a rural environment. The small towns and villages, ranging from a few families to several thousand persons, displayed few of the economic or social characteristics of urban life. Most places slept in profound physical and cultural isolation, only a bare handful of residents having much idea of the outside world. Slowly the towns grew, and transportation and communications improved, but by the 1880s much of the population was scarcely more urbanized than a half century earlier. A few cities enjoyed considerable growth, most notably Buenos Aires, which had 40,000 residents in 1800, possibly 100,000 in the early 1850s, and half a million in the later 1880s. By the 1880s urbanization in Latin America seemed likely to proceed at an accelerated pace.

In Spanish America legal discrimination against Indians, blacks, and persons of mixed racial heritage was eliminated during the half century following Independence, continuing a process begun during the Independence years. The upper class was ambivalent about the change. Practical considerations involved the need for enthusiastic soldiers and workers and damping the urge to rebellion. Modern social ideals favored legal equality. Arguments against liberalization were based on fears of ruin of the labor system, stimulation of lower-class political and social ambition, and incitement to race war. Bolívar displayed this ambivalence. He retained his love for his black wet-nurse and took blacks into the army both as a military necessity and as a deterrent to slave rebellion; on the other hand, in the increasing general pessimism of his later years he showed more dislike and fear for people of dark skin. His sister displayed the more simpleminded upper-class attitude when she wrote him in 1825 that Caracas was "uninhabitable because of the excesses and threats of domination by the people of color."

The abolition of Indian tribute removed a badge of that group's inferior status. The elaborate colonial designations of socioracial status generally lost the support of law and administration: for example, in 1822 the newly established government of Mexico ordered that parish registers abandon identification of Spaniards, Indians, mulattoes, and the like. Such practice, in any event, had been breaking down in the late colonial era.

Black and mulatto slavery was eliminated. In all the Latin American countries, even before full emancipation (some freed slaves in stages) the free black and mulatto population was increasing, as in the colonial era, by manumission, flight, children sired by slave men of free women.[16] Some ineffective but significant efforts at emancipation had been made during the Independence years.[17] Definitive abolition occurred in Argentina in 1813; Central America, 1824; Mexico, 1828; the rest of independent Spanish America by 1858; finally, Puerto Rico, 1873; Cuba, 1886; and Brazil, 1888.

Although moral views of slavery played a part in settlement of the issue, more important was the economic value of slavery to powerful groups in an area and the way the issue happened to get entangled in political rivalries. Estate owners in

Venezuela had their way in 1830 by putting through a manumission law that pretended to concede something to reform but which was a subterfuge for maintaining slavery. Slaves were especially numerous in the older plantation sections of Venezuela, devoted to cacao and sugar, and in the enterprises of the major merchants, and these groups dominated the government. When a coffee boom occurred in the 1830s, on lands farther back in the countryside, the estate owners there depended much more than the older *hacendados* on peon labor—Indian, mestizo, black, mulatto. Some of these free but dependent workers were blacks or mulattoes who had been freed by their owners during the last several decades and could find no other place in society. The coffee boom ended in the late 1830s, when the overextended growers fell victim to a drop in coffee prices. This disgruntled group formed the nucleus of the Liberal party which was organized at that time. They entered political conflict with the Conservatives, who centered on the traditional commercial elite and its agricultural allies. The abolition of slavery then became tied to the maneuvers of these two oligarchic groups. The definitive abolition law of 1854 was designed both to weaken the position of Conservatives and to attract support to the Liberals. In a similar way, in Brazil, abolition resulted not only from economic factors and from growing moral rejection of slavery, but from a tie between that issue and replacement of the monarchy with a republic.

These actions, together with repeated constitutional assertions of equality, were of value to nonwhites, but they found that freedom proclaimed in law had little effect on social, economic, and political prejudice and discrimination. That contradiction between theory and practice moved a liberal minority of the elite to protest. The bulk of the upper class, however, maintained the attitudes and, so far as possible, the practices of the colonial era. It remained intent on having a conveniently available and low-cost labor force. It used as denigrating labels socioracial terms that now had no standing in

---

[16] In Cuba by 1860 the proportion of free blacks and mulattoes to slaves was several times that in the United States.

[17] The Spanish Constitution of 1812 counted for American representation in the new imperial Cortes Indians but not men of African blood. The American representatives at Cádiz had tried to get blacks counted too, probably less out of a sense of racial justice than out of desire for preponderance in the Cortes. The decision, of course, drove blacks to the rebel cause.

law. *Indio* in the mouth of a *hacendado* set a man definitely in a lower order. The upper class continued its traditional disdain for manual labor, in America largely the lot of people with dark skins. There remained, then, a general view among the oligarchs that the lower orders were ignorant, lazy, thieving, illegitimate. Since they generally were nonwhite, the inference was that there was a causal connection. All this the upper class based on what it thought it observed and on what it knew of the past, and little experience or doctrine came to notice to contradict the comforting belief that the abject dark creatures of the lower orders were made of lesser material than their celestial selves. By the 1880s there were some positivists in Latin America, supposing themselves liberated by science into a realm of pure rationality, who decided that people of Indian and black stock were not good stuff for the building of modern nations. The many—for example, Bolívar and Sarmiento—who earlier expressed similar views at least did not seem as cold-blooded and pretentious.

Although socioracial prejudice and discrimination remained oppressive, some change occurred. Men of color rose by military means but were incorporated into the privileged class and did not affect the condition of the subordinate majority from which they escaped. A few lower-class men made their way in politics, although that was not easy. The somewhat expanded educational systems allowed a bit more lower-class entry to professional, intellectual, and journalistic careers. Economic opportunities very slowly increased for people of dark skin. These upward movements involved a small percentage of the lower class. A much larger phenomenon was the increase of miscegenation. It encountered even fewer barriers than in the colonial era, and then its progress had been rapid. The number of people who could "pass," aided either by marriage or by economic success, thus increased. The great mass of people of mixed genetic heritage, however, seemed to face little better prospects in the 1880s than in the 1830s. Their plight did not, however, lead to much conflict with a racial basis. Where

Indians and mestizos made some progress in politics, as in Mexico, they fought the elite as an oligarchy, not as a white racial group.

Imitation of Europe

The upper class in colonial times had imitated European ideas, styles, technology, culture in general. It used but did not admire such American items as hammocks and corn cakes. The list of prestigious American products did not expand much in the nineteenth century. In many respects the admiration for Europe increased, based on its new achievements, and on a wider Latin American upper-class acquaintance with countries other than Spain and Portugal through travel, reading, and the residence of Europeans in Latin America. Also influential was European—especially French—literature, which cemented an admiration founded on respect for European economic, political, scientific, and military glories. Interest was much weaker in the lesser achievements of the United States.

This phenomenon affected Latin American literature, education, dress, politics, government, and economic activity. Latin Americans adapted European norms to American conditions, with greater or lesser deliberate and inadvertent departures from the model. Mauro Fernández, who in the 1880s began his career as the great educational pioneer of Costa Rica, was a strong admirer of British institutions, habits, and attitudes. Admiration for Britain—or at least the oligarchy's role there—was strong among the *hacendados* of Argentina, and some statesmen there thought they were approaching the British rule of law and order. When new military systems were wanted in Latin America late in the nineteenth century, European advisers were acquired. Some cultivated Latin Americans were disappointed that Europeanization did not proceed more rapidly. Imitation even took the form of government subsidies to foreign opera and dance companies which played to nearly empty houses in the isolated mountain capital of Guatemala.

Imitation of the culture of better-developed lands thus was an aspect of modernization, of trying to bring Latin America somewhat nearer to what was thought to be the modern ideal. In the later nineteenth century some of this fascination with "progress" was loosely bound together with the ideas of Auguste Comte on the "scientific" or "positive" stage of human cultural evolution and thus was called positivism. It often was rather uncritical, and it included an element of denigration of the American that demonstrated how far the area was from possessing the nationalist spirit that before long would fiercely repudiate the foreign except as adapted to local institutions and psyches.

Education and Intellectual Life

Although educational practice generally conformed to the demands of elite dominance, it responded also to liberal doctrine, imitation of Europe, and the need for trained people. For several decades education made little progress because of conservative opposition and shortage of funds. Liberal leaders sometimes pursued the issue tenaciously, aware that liberal institutions in politics and government required an educated and prosperous citizenry. Bolívar often pointed to the illiteracy of the masses as a reason for their lack of interest in democratic government, and he favored, but could not finance, free public education. Latin America was more than 90 percent illiterate at Independence, and some forty years later, in the 1860s, the situation was little better. Then some impressive gains were realized or promised. Argentina was nearly 30 percent literate by 1870, and its gains thereafter were even more impressive. Chile also made progress. Somewhat more surprising, because not so obviously the result of prosperity, in the 1870s and 1880s Uruguay and Costa Rica expanded their lower schools. In these two cases early promise continued until they took their place among the more literate countries of the world. Most of Latin America made more modest beginnings in public instruction, but the

ideal of general education had been established and promised well for modernization.

The gains were somewhat misleading, however. Few of the children in the schools received more than a year or two of instruction, so many remained functional illiterates. There were almost no secondary schools, and those that existed were private. Few youngsters had the training, money, clothes, leisure, or desire to attend private secondary schools. The university structure of the colonial era had decayed during Independence, and was only weakly reestablished. Although by the 1880s some new investment had been made in higher education, it remained flimsy, performing best in the traditional specialties of law and the humanities.

Daily Life

Daily life is a convenient tag under which to list some conditions that need emphasis. (*a*) Popular income and opportunity were so generally inadequate that how most people lived and thought was narrowly restricted by what they could afford. Only the beginnings of expansion of popular income appeared by the 1880s, almost entirely in the cities. (*b*) As a consequence, achievement motivation was feeble, acceptance of misery commonplace. (*c*) The poor had no sense of social solidarity, no organization. Labor unions were barely beginning in the 1880s. The mutual aid societies that existed earlier among workers had limited functions. It was at least prophetic of the future that in a few places in the 1880s the doctrines of anarchism and scientific socialism found isolated voice in Latin America. (*d*) One aspect of misery was bad health. The poor suffered more from disease than the rich, partly because of the bad hygiene in their hovels, partly because of weakness due to malnutrition. By the 1880s scientific knowledge in the field of medicine had not advanced greatly over the colonial era, and what advances there were had been little translated into public health measures in Latin America and were little reflected in mortality rates. The slow rate of population increase was the best evidence of this. By the 1880s, however, some cities had been much improved from their condition in mid-century. They stank less of offal, had better lighting and water supplies, and had more paved streets. (*e*) Although improved police and fire protection were established in some cities, crime rates remained high. (*f*) The physical aspects of some of the larger cities were altered. Even in the 1850s in Brazil the arrival of regular steamship service brought to ports such new features as comphene lamps and macadam pavement. Toward the end of the period there was much imitation of nineteenth-century European—especially French—architecture. A few large department stores on the European model had been opened. The number of specialized shops had multiplied amazingly in cities like Rio de Janeiro and Buenos Aires, many of them selling almost exclusively such European wares as tools, books, machines, hardware, cloth, and furniture. (*g*) Life in the provincial towns was slower and

simpler, and ambitious young men increasingly fled them for the metropolis. Life in the villages, the great estates, and tenant farms hardly changed at all.

Latin American leaders in more than half a century of Independence had struggled, sometimes heroically, with various mixtures of conservatism and usually modest innovation. Pressures for modernization increased, powerfully in a few countries, much less in others, but seemed certain to become more potent in the years ahead. To many leaders in the 1880s "progress" seemed attainable without revolution. They thought the most favorable developments of the past half century could be repeated and multiplied everywhere, and that that would ensure attainment everywhere of a progress acknowledged by all. They did not sufficiently recognize the difficulties of repeating Argentina's experience in Guatemala or Ecuador or indefinitely continuing Argentine development, or coping politically with new definitions of progress, modernization, or social justice.

24

Argentina from Independence to the 1880s: The Price and Profits of Unity

War was the price of unity in Argentina, but the profits were fabulous. For weary decades, however, civil disorder seemed the permanent fate of the misnamed United Provinces of La Plata. The modernizing centralism of the educated minority, especially of the city of Buenos Aires, who first tried to organize the country, clashed with the conservative regionalism of the provinces. Brutal use of lower-class militias for public purposes and private profit poisoned interprovincial relationships. Warring provinces followed their *caudillos*, and an Argentine nation did not exist before the 1850s. Disorder and disunity depressed economic development for half a century. Then in 1852 the armies of provincial unity defeated the tyrant of Buenos Aires, Juan Manuel de Rosas. The capacity of that greatest province to spoil unification by insisting on domination was reduced. The Argentine nation began to emerge. The more violent types of *caudillismo* disappeared. The new national polity encouraged economic growth. By the 1880s the profits of unity were so great as to set Argentina off in triumph from the rest of Latin America. Solutions seemed to have been found to the problems of regionalism and disorder, and with that the formerly modest and spasmodic economic growth was replaced with continuous and transforming development and modernization.

a. Regionalism and Limited Economic Growth, 1810–1850s

The lack of political stability was like a wasting disease in the entire period to the 1850s. The hegemony of Rosas in Buenos Aires in the later years was not sufficiently extensive, either in territory or in its appeal to people's minds, to permit much improvement.

Failure of the Modernizing Centralists, 1810–1829

Buenos Aires could not forget its role as seat of the vast Viceroyalty of La Plata since its creation in 1776. At the same time, the elite of the city of 50,000 were excited by recent rapid growth of exports of hides and salted beef to meet the needs of an industrializing Europe and its colonies. Spain, especially in wartime after 1792, had been unable to restrict the growth of free trade in Buenos Aires, and creole affection for freedom naturally soared. Confidence in creole strength was boosted by the victories over British invaders in 1806–1807. This deflection outward of the interests of Buenos Aires tended to alienate it from its own hinterland. The internal provinces had been hurt by the decline of the silver mines of Potosí, in present-day Bolivia, which damaged the beef, mule, and other suppliers of the mining area in what is now northern and western Argentina. The latter area also was hurt by increasing imports of commodities from Brazil, Europe, and even North America to supply Buenos Aires and Montevideo, replacing the food, wine, and artisan manufactures of the interior. This economic situation widened a gulf between the interior and Buenos Aires that was wide enough for other reasons. The provinces had different customs, a considerable sense of historical autonomy before the rise of upstart Buenos Aires after 1776, and a natural desire to handle their own affairs without interference from outsiders. Some of the elite families in the interior had enjoyed a local predominance for generations.

The de facto independent governments at Buenos Aires after 1810 supported the thesis that all parts of the former viceroyalty still owed allegiance to the regime in Buenos Aires.[1] Armies sent against Upper Peru and Paraguay were defeated, partly by royalists, partly by local creoles who preferred to run their own affairs. The most expensive and politically debilitating warfare was over the Banda Oriental del Uruguay, where José Gervasio Artigas was a prominent early exponent of provincial autonomy of the sort the leaders in Buenos Aires found objectionable. In the Banda Oriental, the Uruguayan Artigas and Buenos Aires alternately fought Spaniards and loyalists, invading forces from Brazil, and each other. Montevideo changed hands several times. The last Spanish troops were defeated there in 1814, but the other contestants remained.[2]

Buenos Aires opposed Artigas' plan for autonomy for the Banda Oriental, partly because it

feared the principle in general and partly because it wanted to control competition by the port of Montevideo. Artigas developed close relations with the *caudillos* of Santa Fe and Entre Ríos, the upriver littoral provinces that would not accept the government trying to function at Buenos Aires.[3] Artigas was one of the pleasanter *caudillos*, and a visitor at this time found him a gracious figure, seated on an ox skull in a dirt-floored hut, dictating to secretaries, with couriers and their horses waiting outside to carry his messages through the nearly unpopulated countryside. One of the fathers of his country, his career exemplified the military might of the gaucho, and the corrosive effects of the determination of Buenos Aires to dominate.

There was also friction between provinces that did accept the government at Buenos Aires. Much of it was between conservatives or traditionalists and liberals or innovators. The latter, especially strong in the city of Buenos Aires, supported it and its province on the grounds that they possessed superior political, economic, and intellectual resources. This fed dissidence among other provincial leaders. That there was a regional basis for such dissidence was not surprising in so large a territory (present-day Argentina), throughout which there were only 700,000 people in 1820. Communications problems alone were enough to make effective government difficult. In addition, government revenues were inadequate and often went largely for military purposes.

The junta at Buenos Aires, whose secretary was Mariano Moreno, represented mercantile and pastoral interests who intended to pursue through free trade the export profits that they had been developing in recent decades. The junta removed prohibitions on trade with foreigners and cut export duties on commodities and restrictions on bullion shipments. It kept some duties on im-

---

[1] See Chapter 19, Section e, for creation of the government of 1810, the effective beginning of Argentine Independence.

[2] In a four-year war, the Brazilians defeated Artigas and Buenos Aires. In 1821 the Banda Oriental was proclaimed the Cisplatine Province of Portuguese Brazil, thus briefly fulfilling an ambition of more than two centuries; and the next year it became part of independent Brazil. The three-cornered war over Uruguay resumed in 1825–1828, after which Uruguay became definitively independent, partly because British policy favored such fragmentation.

---

[3] The littoral provinces were those with shore areas giving them connections with the sea. The upriver littoral provinces had only river ports, whereas Uruguay and Buenos Aires also had seaports.

The States of Argentina

ported manufactures, but protectionism was not an effective policy then. The handicrafts of the interior were less valuable than pastoral products and could not compete with imported manufactures, and the support for them was weaker than for the pastoral industry. Buenos Aires continued to levy tribute on the trade of the provinces by its control of customs receipts and navigation. This angered the upriver littoral provinces that exported pastoral products similar to those of Buenos Aires.

Moreno tried to fashion support through manipulation of the press and by force and threats, but his reach scarcely extended beyond the city. The junta persuaded interior towns to elect deputies, who began arriving by the end of 1810. The regional–federal dispute was thereby aggravated because the provincial delegates to the junta supported moves to reduce the power of Buenos Aires, partly by advocating a national congress. The provincial leaders got rid of Moreno by sending him on a foreign mission, on which he died.

Many of these early provincial leaders were civilian statesmen of considerable knowledge and experience, but their discussions of government theory tended to be rather unrealistic because at that moment in the provinces gaucho militias were being used by *estancieros*[4] and others to preserve order and pursue private business.

Dispute over government continued for two years in Buenos Aires. A triumvirate was tried, beginning in 1811, with Bernardino de Rivadavia, a convinced modernizer, its secretary. It promoted education, a free press, court reform; forbade the slave trade; improved the army with a general staff and better discipline. The triumvirate was soon ousted by military action, and in 1813 an assembly of provincial delegates met at Buenos Aires. It extended the vote to mestizos and Indians, and ended torture, the Inquisition, Indian forced labor, entail, and titles of nobility. Diplomatic missions were sent abroad. In the meantime, the provinces were running many of their own affairs, so that many supposedly "national" actions at Buenos Aires had but narrow effects.

By 1816 many were disillusioned with the government at a time when rebels were doing badly against royalists in other parts of Spanish America, and in Spain Ferdinand VII was trying to restore absolutism. Efforts to stabilize government at Buenos Aires had been hampered by military problems and expenditures, some due to fear of a Spanish expedition of reconquest, possibly building on royalist forces in surrounding areas. A big expense was arming San Martín's expedition for the invasion of Chile.[5]

Early in 1816 a constituent Congress met at Tucumán and declared independence from Spain. The most pressing need, however, was for an acceptable formula of government, and the Congress did not produce one. The odds were heavily against success because the upriver littoral provinces did not send delegates, and some representatives of the western interior provinces disliked the reformism and unitary (nonfederalist) doctrines of *porteño* leaders.[6] Some westerners, on the other hand, were most concerned about the rise of the wild gaucho militias and regional *caudillos*. Many Buenos Aires leaders feared both this popular violence and the trend to provincial autonomy. The climate of fear encouraged supporters of monarchism at Tucumán, including some enlightened people from Buenos Aires. To be sure, it was a limited, constitutional monarchism, which they meant to dominate, but it was a retreat from the high republican hopes of a few years earlier. San Martín, then preparing in nearby Cuyo for the invasion of Chile, supported the monarchic idea.

No monarchic suggestions were adopted; instead, the Congress continued the system of rule by a directory. But the search for a suitable prince continued, and news of that search soon further damaged the centralist idea that the interior identified with Buenos Aires. The effect of experience was evident in the Tucumán Congress's demand for "an end to revolution, a beginning to order." But it stimulated suspicion by naming as its director Juan M. de Pueyrredón, an antifederalist. His centralist doctrine was never accompanied by control over all the regional *caudillos*. The Congress moved to Buenos Aires, where it wrote a centralist constitution that was published at the end of 1819 and promptly rejected by the other provinces. A test at arms early in 1820 between the army of the directory and the littoral *caudillos* was won by the latter and ushered in what Argentines call the "Terrible Year Twenty," when violence reigned in the disunited provinces and the Banda Oriental appeared likely to fall permanently to the Luso-Brazilians.

In that year the leaders of the province of Buenos Aires turned away from national leadership. Representing the cattlemen of the interior of the province, they began to push the *cabildo* of the city farther into the background. Even though *estancieros* had residences and business

---

[4] Owners of *estancias*, the local equivalent of haciendas.
[5] See Chapter 19, Section e.

[6] *Porteño*: resident of the port—of Buenos Aires.

in town, their affairs in the countryside required more attention. New estates were being built in the Pampa. Ambitious men led their gaucho bands in driving back the Indians so they could accumulate land and curb cattle rustling. No effective effort was made to create small holdings, the expansion of the 1820s and thereafter continuing a colonial tradition of *latifundio* wherever it could be made to pay. It is true that in these early years there was no luxury in the countryside and necessarily a considerable camaraderie around the campfire, in the corral, and in Indian skirmishes. Juan Manuel de Rosas had to be able to outride and outfight his gauchos and he claimed that there was no aristocracy in the province and that the masses ruled. They did so only in the sense that no one could withstand the gaucho militias with money or class position alone. The *caudillos* were, however, far from egalitarian. Their accumulation of land was a conspicuous way in which they set themselves apart from their followers, and in the course of time that would greatly change social relationships. *Estancieros* seldom did much for the poor, even their own gaucho soldiers.

Despite heavy rural influence on some policies, the province of Buenos Aires also contained the city and educated liberal leaders dedicated to modernization. The provincial legislature met in the port. In the early 1820s Bernardino de Rivadavia and Manuel José García, in the administration of Governor Martín Rodríguez, had a vision of fiscal order, government-assisted economic development, social aid to the needy, expanded education, a wider franchise, control of the church, and broader landholding. Rivadavia, the dominant figure, one of the new generation of enlightened spirits in the late colonial era, remained thereafter a liberal and a centralist. Eminently a public-spirited man, he fought against the British in 1807, was secretary of the first triumvirate, and in 1813 went on a mission to Europe. In the provincial government, he continued the Spanish policy of government control of the church, which offended church partisans, who generally were conservative opponents of his other policies

also. He favored immigration from Europe but did not devise a practical way of securing land for the immigrants, although a land program (*emphyteusis*) became law for the province in 1822. It had inherited from Spain large public lands and added more by Indian wars. Under the new law some of this land was sold, but much had to be rented because the lands were security for foreign and domestic loans. Rivadavia hoped that *emphyteusis* would broaden landholding and encourage wheat culture. It did neither. The law did not limit the size of purchases or rentals, so that the wealthy added to their holdings without restraint. No law, however, could have prevented the growth of *latifundio*.

Rivadavia was too much the innovator for his time, and he lacked political talents. He was forced from office in 1824. During his absence in Europe, centralists got together an all-Argentine Congress in 1825. It declared the second Argentine Confederation, including the Banda Oriental, which led to war with Brazil. It chose Rivadavia president, a position he filled in parts of 1826 and 1827. The new central government passed unitarian measures, thereby reducing its always weak support in the provinces, while its revenues and popularity also were drained by the war with Brazil. Rivadavia, always the rational advocate of strong government, supported the idea of making the city of Buenos Aires into a federal district so its revenues could be used for less developed parts of the country. That idea would be adopted half a century later, but at the moment helped solidify the regional *caudillos* against the new regime while also turning much of Buenos Aires against it. Rivadavia was ousted in July 1827. Although the *unitarios* were not quite finished, the following decades were to belong to various types of federalism, which in fact meant regionalism, military tyranny, and leaders whose own bent and that of their clienteles were profoundly different from the cultivated liberalism and modernism of people like Moreno and Rivadavia.

The political forces revealed in the first twenty years remained much the same for decades thereafter: Buenos Aires against the other provinces; educated and liberal modernizers, especially in the city of Buenos Aires, supporting centralism against the conservative and federalist element generally; the large pastoral interest, supported by allied commercial groups, against other economic interests, so that agriculture and manufacturing were scarcely represented. The church had little independent power, but its conservative positions had support in the rural centers of federalism. The "military" was a potent interest group that participated in affairs, although most of it was an irregular and part-time force, and it was fragmented between national and provincial governments and even *caudillos* without a hold on office. More than just an interest group, men with arms and a disposition to use them were an omnipresent instrument that leaders constantly were tempted to use. The lower class played a role of considerable importance as soldiers and in town as spies and bullyboys, often manipulated by the educated. But the masses were not class-conscious and not demanding and followed leaders as chieftains or patrons, asking little in return. "Popular" armies did not mean leaders interested in popular needs and did not result in popular economic and social policies and institutions.

The "Federalist" Tyranny of Rosas, 1829–1852

Although Rosas' regime seemed a tyranny to liberals with an interest in modernization, to his followers it was a proper government and he was a popular figure. That was something his enemies had to learn at the expense of their intellectual prejudices. They could not topple him simply by calling him a barbarian. Rosas' federalism could not be found in texts on political theory; it meant just what he and his clientele wanted it to mean. The regime opposed all political and most social modernization, focusing its interest on pastoral exports. Dominating the area for more than two decades, Rosas' power and his narrow range of ideas and policies made achieving national unity or satisfactory socioeconomic progress impossible.

The Rise of Rosas, 1829–1835. Juan Manuel de Rosas was born into an upper-class Buenos Aires family in 1793. A man of courage and energy, he fought the British invasion as a lad and thereafter took to the rough life of the back country, virtually living on horseback, working and fighting alongside the gauchos, accepted by them as a leader. He acquired land, killed Indians to protect and extend his holdings, and was a pioneer in developing *saladeros* (meat-processing works). He was a nascent *caudillo*, of federalist persuasion, when the unitary party was taken over by military men after Rivadavia's fall. The unitarians commenced a savage warfare against the federalists. They proved no match for Rosas' gaucho horde, and he emerged from the civil strife of 1828–1829 as governor of the province of Buenos Aires by vote of the legislature in December 1829. In addition to his popularity with the gauchos, a United States diplomat noted in 1832 that Rosas was friendly with the old Spanish types who were "proud, bigoted, narrow-minded, and oppressive, hating all foreigners." These comments described Rosas well at the beginning of his remarkable public career.

As governor (1829–1832) Rosas displayed his repudiation of the modernizers of the city of Buenos Aires. He had little use for discussion with critics; for him, one was totally for or totally against Rosas. He was untiring in searching out enemies. These included *unitarios*, of course, and he was untroubled by the fact that his own brand of federalism included belief in the dominance of Buenos Aires. His foes therefore included federalists who believed in provincial equality. He also accumulated as opponents all who objected to tyranny. Even hints of disagreement Rosas smashed with confiscations of property, imprisonment, torture, murder; and exile or silence soon seemed the course of prudence. He justified his methods by appeals to the needs of the community, and the majority cried after him, "Death to the savage *unitarios!*" His color red became the ubiquitous pledge of solidarity, prudently displayed on breast and door and saddlebags. His wife, Doña Encarnación, also of an upper-class Buenos Aires family, was a worthy partner—shrewd, demagogic, and ruthless. They trumpeted his virtues and indispensability, reducing theory of government to one-man rule.

Rosas in those three years also showed the outline of his version of federalism: personal alliances with other *caudillos*, but with special privileges for Buenos Aires; and opposition to any leader who became too powerful. He supported a Federal Pact in 1831, an alliance with the governors of Entre Ríos and Santa Fe which gave Buenos Aires power to represent them all in international and some financial affairs. Also, with some good luck, Rosas managed to cut down the power of the nine-province Unitarian League put together in the interior provinces by General José María Paz. But Rosas had little time to pursue this or his other policies, because late in 1832 his term as governor ended. He had been granted dictatorial powers in a time of crisis, but now a majority of leaders refused to extend them into another term, so Rosas declined to serve again.

He went off to fight Indians for the province. Charles Darwin visited Rosas in the Pampas in 1833, finding him immensely popular with his men, extending the safe ranching area along the frontier, with little military posts of mounted soldiers living in pampas-grass huts. While he was thus engaged, Buenos Aires provincial leaders in the city were trying to cope with the political talents of Doña Encarnación. When some federalists supported the new governor in departures from Rosas' policies, the *Rosistas* denounced them as traitors to the unique leader. Doña Encarnación organized support among all elements of society. She put together the notorious *Mazorca* (Ear of Corn), an organization that engaged in everything from fund raising to spying and murder. She was adept at inciting mob violence and contrived disorders that toppled the governor from office. Continued agitation and sabotage disrupted the rule of the successor gov-

ernment. After long resistance to such a move, in April 1835 Buenos Aires leaders invited Rosas back with dictatorial powers of indefinite duration.

The Rosas Tyranny. His rule in 1835–1852 carried further the system of personal adulation and constant enunciation of party loyalty, with Rosas' picture paraded and prayers delivered for his preservation to the *patria*. The *Mazorca* widened its spying, denunciations, beatings, property seizures, and murders. Few could stand against such a relentless tyranny, hitting not only at their persons but at the safety, dignity, and livelihood of their families. His enemies competed in listing his crimes, one claiming he was responsible for 3,765 beheadings. Esteban Echeverría, in a contemporary story, *The Slaughterhouse*, so labelled Argentina, where the butchers condemned "as savage Unitarians . . . any man who was neither a cutthroat nor a crook."

Such diatribes slighted Rosas' ability and the depth of his support. He controlled the press and information and instruction generally. He had support from the foreign merchants of the city, whom he favored in a number of ways and who benefited from the funneling of trade and public revenues through the capital of the province. His support from the poor was the stronger for being grounded in emotion. He was admired for his *machismo* (male virility and courage) because he had slept on the ground with the gauchos, because he and Doña Encarnación treated blacks and mulattoes and others of the city poor as people worthy of consultation and collaboration, because he proclaimed a simple group of virtues and condemned complex foreign ideas and institutions, and because he provided opportunities to abuse persons of property and education. People supported his claim as defender of the faith against foreign-influenced liberal heretics. They saw nothing wrong with pictures of Rosas on church altars. They had no awareness that his policies were not improving the life of the ordinary person but inexorably concentrating landed property in a few hands. Those of the upper class who benefited from this process naturally tended to support Rosas. Many of them also shared his xenophobia and conservative religious and social views. They certainly shared his attachment to the enforced domination of the port of Buenos Aires.

Rosas had no interest in socioeconomic modernization. He was not an educator. He ended Rivadavia's immigration system, not caring about the kinds of development it implied and fearing the social and political consequences. He had little economic interest except in the unfettered export of pastoral products and the dominance of the commerce of Buenos Aires. He encouraged development of the great estates by ending *emphyteusis*, by urging acquisition by war of new lands along the Indian frontier, and by a policy of inflation that eased the cost of labor to the great landowners and helped their sales abroad. He helped them avoid taxes by levying duty on the provincial exports that came down the river system. By special taxes for calls at Montevideo or upriver Argentine ports he made sure that vessels used Buenos Aires. His was the typical revenue system of the nineteenth-century *caudillo*: tax foreign trade but not the great estates. The value of foreign trade rose from some 62 million pesos in 1829 to 292 million in 1849, but in some years it was drastically hit by Rosas' aggressive foreign policies. In any event the growth was far from remarkable given Argentine resources and the growth of European markets; it would be much larger in later years.

The "Federalism" of Rosas. There was contradiction between Rosas' denunciation of centralism and his despotic government in Buenos Aires and insistence on some powers over other provinces. But he did prefer to deal with other provinces on an individual basis and did not want to create a national government. His federalism was, furthermore, an expression of his repudiation of modernizing central government. He interfered in other provinces without desiring to run them along lines of national policy. He levied tolls on the interior provinces and committed them to drastic foreign policy initiatives, but that was far short of the national aims of Bernardino de Rivadavia. When some elements involved in the Littoral Pact of 1831 brought together a representative commission that favored calling a congress in 1832, Rosas would not permit it. He opposed all suggestions for the nationalization of trade policy and taxation. A national government might have pushed the idea of federalization of the city of Buenos Aires, so that its lush revenues might be used for the benefit of poorer provinces; Rosas preferred to keep them in his *patria chica*, little fatherland. Rosas at least did the service to centralism of linking his type of federalism with barbarism, so that even those who favored division between national and state government also supported a strong central government as necessary to modernization and a decent society.

Nationalistic Foreign Policy. Two views of Rosas' foreign policy have existed from his own times to today: defender of American rights against European aggression, or subverter of the national rights of Uruguay. There is some truth in both contentions. He had two aims in Uruguay: to control its economy and especially the trade of Montevideo; and to strike at exiles from his terror who fled to Uruguay. The exiles supported groups unfriendly to him in Uruguay, and together they intrigued with the upriver littoral provinces of Argentina. By the mid-1830s Rosas was supporting Uruguayan President Manuel Oribe, a conservative, while the liberals followed ex-president Fructuoso Rivera, who had the support of Rosas' *unitario* enemies in exile there.

Rosas recognized the value of good relations with Britain, which since 1810 had sent public and private capital to the Plata. Rivadavia had pledged Argentine public lands to secure a loan from Baring Brothers Bank of London. A treaty between Argentina and Britain in 1825 guaranteed to Britons exemption from military service and freedom of religion. Rosas accepted these agreements, and he reacted mildly to Britain's seizure of the Falkland Islands in 1833. The treaty privileges that reinforced Britain's natural strengths irked the French, but a series of efforts, including naval action, failed. Finally a French naval blockade was set up in 1838. Buenos Aires, dependent on the sea, even suffered shortages of firewood. But resistance was fierce to what a French journal said was an effort to civilize "the degenerate children of the Spanish heroes of the conquest."

The French allied themselves with the anti-Rosas Rivera forces in Uruguay, stirred up trouble in the littoral provinces, and seized the island of Martín García in the estuary, a key to Buenos Aires control of trade. The French found, however, that the complexities of local politics and their own lack of an army made a victory unlikely, so they signed an agreement with Rosas in 1840 that acknowledged French interests. Rosas, flatly stating that respect for Uruguayan independence depended on the needs of the Argentine Confederation, seemed stronger than ever. By late 1842 Oribe with Argentine help was besieging Montevideo. Almost half the population of the city was foreign, including Giuseppe Garibaldi, later the liberator of Italy, who had come from a career with republican rebels in southern Brazil. The struggle against Rosas thus took on overtones of an international crusade by liberalism against reaction. The British and French navies and marines were there and would not let Rosas' navy bombard the beleaguered city. In September 1845 the British and French proclaimed a blockade of Buenos Aires, as the only method they had of applying pressure. Their action hurt the trade of city and province and the ability of Buenos Aires to collect tolls on upriver traffic, which now flowed to Montevideo. The blockade dragged on for three years, with mixed results. It was costly to everyone concerned. The disorder and uncertainty inclined many people toward some novel solution. By 1850 anti-Rosas leaders at Montevideo let Rosas know that they now preferred to welcome Oribe rather than suffer domination by the French. Although again and again people in Buenos Aires and the upriver littoral had rallied against

the foreigner, directly or indirectly supporting Rosas, many were wearied of his belligerence and the contradictions in his policy.

The Fall of Rosas.   Rosas tumbled when his accumulating enemies were joined by Justo José de Urquiza, a great upriver *caudillo.* Certainly, Rosas' enemies in Buenos Aires and the exiles in various countries could not bring him down alone. Young poets and critics had formed organizations in the 1830s to protest the regime. Literary weapons were not effective against Rosas, however, and the critical Generation of 1837 went into exile. Some would return to distinguished careers in a new Argentina. Their literary output in Argentina, but especially in exile, often reflected European liberal ideas, and the work of such writers as Echeverría and Sarmiento spoke for modernization and Europeanization as against the creole brutishness of the Rosas regime.

Urquiza was governor of Entre Ríos and a *caudillo* whose army was a power in the upriver area. Experience finally had convinced him that the Rosas system was a failure, that what was needed was an effective national government involving the real collaboration of all the provinces. Various plans for development in Santa Fe and Entre Ríos had been ineffective. Men of influence rightly found a cause in political conditions. In the meantime, the wealth of Buenos Aires had been growing and was resented. When Rosas in early 1851 made his periodic gesture of resigning his office in Buenos Aires, expecting the leaders of all provinces to urge him to continue, Urquiza proclaimed Entre Ríos a sovereign federal province and canceled the powers it had given Buenos Aires. In May Urquiza signed an alliance with Brazil and Uruguay aimed at Rosas and his supporter Oribe in Uruguay. The ensuing war in Uruguay was won by Urquiza. In November 1851 Urquiza headed an allied army of 21,000 that included 4,000 Brazilians and Uruguayans.

The exiles came back to join the movement of liberation and integration. Domingo Sarmiento, Bartolomé Mitre, and others sailed from

Chile in September and were at Montevideo in December. Then all the way upriver, on a Brazilian warship, they saw signs of anti-Rosas feeling. His enemies, however, were by no means in perfect agreement. Sarmiento, put in charge of propaganda, clashed with Urquiza, who was much the more practical about the need for compromise. Sarmiento was hailed as a famous author, but Urquiza declared that torrents of words had not drowned Rosas.

When the armies met at Monte Caseros in February 1852 the battle was more a demonstration than a combat, with barely four hundred men killed on both sides. Rosas had lost long before the meeting, as he knew, having arranged a vessel for flight into exile. He had no more part in Argentine history, except that he left behind a heritage on which Argentines could not agree. Some consider him a misfortune; others celebrate his rule as standing for Argentine culture against corrupting influence, national unity against debilitating complexity, and independence of foreign domination. He remains for some Argentines a model of the strong-man rule they claim the country still needs.

Socioeconomic Growth to the 1850s

Argentine society remained essentially traditional in the 1850s. The small population grew slowly, from some 700,000 in 1820 to 1.5 million in 1869, with growth much faster after than before 1852. Immigration was only a trickle before Monte Caseros. The *estancieros* in the 1850s tried, without much success, private methods of enticing cheap labor from Europe. The anti-Rosas Alberdi was only one of the prominent exiles who declared that "to govern is to populate." It could not be done effectively before the fall of the tyrant, and the 1850s remained too disturbed to encourage much change. In 1860 only 5,000 immigrants arrived. Foreigners did have considerable impact in a few areas, as in sheep raising, and especially in various occupations in the city of Buenos Aires. Some 5,000 Britons, the largest foreign group, supported a clubhouse,

Protestant churches and schools, and an English-language newspaper. The Indian and black element remained prominent in Argentina. Nearly a quarter of the residents of the metropolis in the early 1850s were "colored."

The city of Buenos Aires from 1810 to 1850 grew from 50,000 to 90,000 and then much faster to 180,000 in 1869, but even then it retained some aspects of an overgrown village. Its buildings were low and undistinguished. The night watchman made the rounds of the narrow streets lit with horse-oil lamps. It had "not a single jetty, wharf, or pier," and ox carts went into the shallows to help with lighterage of the heavy water traffic. Laundresses spread clothes all over the waterfront. The lack of sewers contributed to periodic epidemics.

The other towns of the country were much smaller. Córdoba as late as 1869 had but 34,000 people. Rosario in 1854 had about 7,000. The population and wealth of Buenos Aires had put a great distance between it and the other provinces, which were largely rural, illiterate, poor, and parochial in outlook. Everywhere, including Buenos Aires city and province, most people knew little of public affairs, and participated only by obeying the orders of leaders who organized demonstrations or armies. They had no independent force in elections and the discussion of public issues. Social differentiation was increasing rather than declining, pushed by the growth of commercial fortunes and middle-class comfort in the metropolis and by the growth of *estancias* in the countryside.

The export cattle industry remained primitive in the 1850s, but change was under way.[7] Some fencing appeared by the 1840s, but broad technological change did not occur until after the 1850s. Cattle products remained predominant, accounting for 78 percent of export value in 1851, although a trend to sheep raising was apparent, often involving English, Irish, and Scottish investors and workers. The back country was so

---

[7] See Chapter 13, Section j, on the cattle business at Independence.

uninhabited that Indians still carried off cattle, and in the 1850s raided Argentine towns. There were flows of domestic and imported agricultural products, but the values were small. Wheat and flour were often imported. Manufacturing was puny. Merchants remained the most important part of the urban business community, and they were predominantly foreign, especially in Buenos Aires. Each province had a small group of entrepreneurs interested in modernization, but they had few resources. In Santa Fe in the 1850s they wanted steamships, railways, immigrants, new production, but the political condition of Argentina frustrated their hopes for foreign capital and labor.

The failure to solve the political problem in the 1850s meant continued economic stagnation for every area but Buenos Aires. The upriver provinces could not develop good connections with the Atlantic economy that was enriching Buenos Aires. They needed improved navigation aids and ports but could not afford them. They found that European investors and shippers would not put money into the interior. Trade wars between Buenos Aires and the upriver provinces merely showed that the former had all the advantages of position and established strength. By the end of the 1850s Argentina still was not a viable polity; it was poor; its small population was unlettered, unambitious, and unproductive. A small minority dreamed of unity and development, but in half a century had shown little aptitude for arranging either, or so it seemed; happily, appearances were deceiving, and the long period of depressing failure was revealed as preparation for amazing success.

New Efforts to Create a Nation, 1852–1862

For the next decade majority opinion in Buenos Aires still was unwilling to accept the Confederation. Urquiza was widely distrusted in the city. He tried to influence elections to the provincial assembly and led efforts to create a national government. This increased fears in Buenos Aires

and they increased more in May 1852 when a meeting of provincial governors agreed to the Pact of San Nicolás, making Urquiza provisional chief executive, condemning trade restrictions between provinces, and calling a constituent congress. Bartolomé Mitre of Buenos Aires opposed the San Nicolás agreement, and Urquiza drove him into exile. This clash embodied much of the problem of concord between Buenos Aires and the confederation, because Mitre was not among the most intransigent supporters of *porteño* regionalism. He wanted a strong national government, but the problem was that he thought Buenos Aires should lead it.

Mitre was born in Buenos Aires in 1821. He began his education in schools in the city and developed a permanent fondness for learning. The family were unitarian opponents of Rosas and lived in the 1830s at Montevideo, where Bartolomé went to the Military College, then served in the wars in Uruguay with the Rivera forces against the *Rosistas* of Argentina. He also pursued his intellectual interests and wrote for newspapers. He was forced out of Uruguay by Rivera's justified suspicion of some of the Argentine exiles. After some time in Bolivia, where he was a military officer and newspaper editor, Mitre went in 1848 to Chile, where he became a newspaper editor for his fellow Argentine exile Alberdi. After Monte Caseros in 1851, Mitre made his way as a leader in Buenos Aires because of his abilities and his opposition to Urquiza, rather than because of his nationalism, which offended many *porteños*. When Urquiza cut short Mitre's exile for opposing the San Nicolás agreement, he returned to lead the opposition to the moves of the Confederation to end the Buenos Aires domination of commerce in the Plata area. In September 1852 Buenos Aires took over full control of its own government, and the province supported it, although there still were differences of opinion in the community. A new provincial governor was elected, and Mitre became his minister of government and foreign affairs and also assumed command of the national guard, which was preparing to meet an attack by Urquiza.

That came early in 1853 with a blockade of the city by land and sea and bloody skirmishes in the suburbs. But Buenos Aires was too strong for the Confederation; it broke the blockade and maintained its independence.

While Buenos Aires was being blockaded by the Confederation, the latter was holding the constituent congress at Santa Fe, without Buenos Aires delegates. The Constitution of 1853 provided a federal republic but called for national unification and policies of economic development and social progress and gave strong powers to the president, including the right to "intervene" in the provinces under certain conditions. Although some of the language of the Constitution reflected that of the United States, the content and the attitudes of the delegates largely came out of reactions to their own experience. That was true of the famous *Bases and Points of Departure for the Political Organization of the Argentine Republic*, which the Argentine exile Juan Bautista Alberdi sent to the congress from Chile. He thought good government in Argentina required education and economic development, and he favored immigration for labor, technical expertise, and the moral-economic habits of Europeans. He prescribed economic and social modernization, through investment, improvement of communications, and instruction.

Urquiza was elected president under the new constitution, serving in the upriver capital of Paraná until 1859, when he was succeeded by Santiago Derquí. The Confederation government —without Buenos Aires an Argentine "nation" did not exist—had limited resources. In addition, Urquiza found his political power limited by regionalism and local *caudillismo*. He tried to overcome these problems, with a vision of nation building that transcended his beginnings as a regional chieftain. He tried to get foreign support, sending Alberdi to Europe; but public and private foreign interests preferred to keep a foot in each camp, and certainly were not going to abandon economic ties with Buenos Aires. The two governments sometimes uneasily collaborated on trade policy, sometimes clashed; but it was clear

that Buenos Aires would probably win tariff wars and other economic contests.

In Buenos Aires in the 1850s differences of opinion coalesced into two major groups. The majority were *Autonomistas*, for a narrow provincialism that owed something to hatred of Urquiza, but especially objected to giving up to a federal government customs receipts of the great port, the largest public revenue in Argentina. The other group, the *Nacionalistas*, later called Liberals, were for national union but mistrusted Urquiza as well as Mitre and Sarmiento. Mitre's views included an equitable commercial system for the Plata region, believing that the situation of Buenos Aires did not justify milking the provinces, and opposition to a constitution for the province on the grounds such a charter was only for sovereign nations. In short, Mitre was for a *patria grande*, but he had to move warily because many *porteños* favored a *patria chica* (little fatherland).

The *porteños* had a substantial basis for their willingness to go it alone. Even under the uneasy political conditions of the 1850s, the export production of the province and commerce of the city continued to grow. It seemed that under a system of national government the other provinces would be a drain on Buenos Aires rather than an asset. And the provinces, so the argument went, would introduce barbarous people and standards and habits into civilized Buenos Aires. There was reason to hope that Buenos Aires could continue to control the trade of the interior by force and agreement. The province of Buenos Aires was as large as some European countries, and great lands beyond the Indian frontier remained to be added.

All efforts of the government at Paraná failed to do much damage to Buenos Aires or aid the Confederation, and the future seemed to promise increasing advantage for the richest province. The Confederation government could not even meet its payrolls. So it decided to try full-scale war again. There had been much skirmishing in the 1850s, with much changing sides by officers and men, indicating confusion of issues and lack of commitment. Urquiza appeared with a numerically superior force, mostly cavalry, at Cepeda, on the plains north of Buenos Aires, in October 1859. Mitre, the Buenos Aires commander, decided that the tactical situation required withdrawal into the fortified city, which Urquiza's cavalry could not take. The two forces then made an agreement to end the war, largely on the basis of changes in the Constitution to meet *porteño* demands. The effect was merely to strengthen Buenos Aires. Urquiza withdrew his army. The Constitution was revised. But in the meantime Mitre had been elected governor of the province of Buenos Aires, and all the conflicts and suspicions of the two governments remained unresolved. New charges were made and punitive actions taken. War resumed, won by Mitre at Pavón in September 1861. The battle convinced many, including Urquiza, that the struggle to defeat Buenos Aires was hopeless, that union would have to be found in some other way. Following a series of negotiations, agreements, and elections, Mitre was chosen president, becoming the first man who clearly exercised executive authority over all the provinces. At last a national polity existed.

b. The New National Polity, 1860s–1880s

The administrations from 1862 into the 1880s strengthened the central government, sometimes using drastic methods, including the constitutionally sanctioned right of federal intervention in the provinces. Major leaders conducted politics largely on a personal basis, by compromise and agreement. The system was essentially oligarchic, run by the bosses of provincial cliques. Parties scarcely existed. The franchise was restricted and voters subject to fraud and intimidation, partly because balloting was public, partly because social relationships were such that a man voted by direction of his employer, *patrón*, or local magnate. Outgoing presidential administrations dominated the choice of the next chief executive because they controlled the electoral machinery and the armed forces.

The administrations supported some types of economic and social modernization. The great export pastoral industry was favored, and much of the growing wealth of the country went to the *estancieros* and their commercial and financial allies. Government efforts and subsidies led to feverish railway building, valuable to the entire country, but especially to producers for export. Government aid to immigration provided hands to work the estates. A portion of the new income was poured into the finest educational system in Latin America, the most conspicuous evidence of oligarchic progressivism. The political system, and the condition of the society, were a vast improvement over the earlier period, but as time went on its shortcomings made it seem increasingly unsatisfactory to a minority of dissident spirits.

Argentina was fortunate in the first two presidents of the united republic. Mitre (1862–1868) and Sarmiento (1868–1874) are often regarded as giants of the early national period who were succeeded by lesser men. They are identified with the heroic resistance to Rosas and to regionalism generally, and before and during their presidencies performed great services in establishing national unity and the national polity. Both men produced literary monuments to patriotism and the dream of Argentine greatness. Both had been poor, and their public careers were untainted in the public mind with personal pursuit of riches or with the apparent growth of materialistic motivation in public life that came after their administrations. Both men did, nevertheless, make big contributions to the growth of the oligarchy, through their policies of centralization and modernization.

Mitre—soldier, writer, statesman, and a model of honesty and morality—enjoyed great prestige and at times popularity. As president, he did not favor Buenos Aires in the exaggerated way his enemies in the provinces had predicted. He appointed provincials to his government. He spent some of the increasing public revenues from the nationalized customs and from higher tariffs on railway and immigration projects that ultimately would be valuable to all provinces. His handling of the currency and credit systems increased confidence at home and abroad. His government promoted the growth of cable and telegraph lines, streetcars, and the postal service. He used force against bandits and *caudillos* in the countryside. He was, thus, essentially a centralizer and modernizer. He was, however, unable to solve the national capital question. Although he favored federalization of the city of Buenos Aires, the opposition in the city and province was too strong, and it still disposed of much of the economic and demographic power of the republic.

Mitre aroused new opposition to his leadership by a belligerent policy toward Paraguay. That landlocked little country long had been a focus of the territorial and economic ambitions of Argentina and Brazil, but had defended itself with xenophobia, dictatorship, and military organization and ardor. In 1862 Francisco Solano López inherited primitive Paraguay from his dictator father and turned out to be not only autocratic in the Paraguayan tradition, but reckless, a quality his country scarcely could afford. He received from his father an army of 44,000 and proceeded to enlarge it. He had reason to fear his great neighbors Argentina and Brazil, but his dream was not only of defense, but of conquest. The excuse he seized for war was Brazilian and Argentine interference in the affairs of Uruguay, something they had been doing for decades. The unstable López managed to embroil his country in a conflict with Uruguay, Brazil, and Argentina.

Mitre, embracing the war effort and hoping for territorial gains, spent most of his time at the front. But the Paraguayan War (1865–1870) went on and on, so savage that far over half of all Paraguayan males died. Some men and boys fought because López killed the reluctant himself, but that did not explain the phenomenon. Some sense of community or of xenophobia helped give the Guaraní of Paraguay fanatical courage. In addition, the war dragged on because of the poor logistical capabilities of the allies and the unwillingness of Brazilian and Argentine leaders to accept the political consequences of a compromise or to give up hope of territorial conquest. The casualties and financial cost were unpopular in Argentina. Although public revenues increased, so did war expense, and Mitre contracted a loan with Baring Brothers of London. Inability to beat little Paraguay seemed to Argentines evidence of shameful mismanagement. Mitre's enemies denounced his actions as immoral and damaging to the country. The war embittered the second half of his administration, which ended in 1868, before Argentina acquired valuable lands in Misiones and the Chaco as a result of the costly conflict.

Mitre could not constitutionally succeed himself, and did not try to dictate his successor, a useful example to the new national political system. The candidacy of Sarmiento was supported by those who wanted a continuation of strong government and economic growth and who feared provincialism and *caudillismo*, identified with Urquiza, who was a candidate. Many of the same supporters also feared a third candidate, who represented the strictly *porteño* point of view, also unacceptable to centralists in most of the country.

Domingo Sarmiento was born in the northwest interior in 1811 in the small town of San Juan, of a poor creole family. Through books he became an admirer of the best that civilization had to offer, which contrasted sadly with his own environment. Observation of the antics of federalist *caudillos* turned him into a *unitario* while in his teens. He bore arms for his beliefs and suffered exile in Chile. Back in San Juan in 1835, he spent five years in political activity, school administration, newspaper editing, and literary studies; then was forced to flee again. By then his distaste for federalism and Rosas had broadened to include the entire Spanish heritage, and he preached in print the necessity of Argentine imitation of the institutions of modern Europe and North America. He served the Chilean government's Ministry of Education, visiting the United States and Europe in that connection in the 1840s. He pursued what was to be a longtime interest in the training methods of Horace Mann of Massachusetts. He produced literary works that had made him famous by the time he joined Urquiza in 1851. The next year this man of the provinces, with a vision of a unified and modern nation, entered the city of Buenos Aires for the first time. He could not get along with Urquiza and soon went back to San Juan. Back in Buenos Aires in 1855, he became chief of the provincial school department and held other posts, continuing to support Buenos Aires against the Confederation. In 1862 he returned to San Juan and was elected governor of the province, where he justified the use of the state of siege to fight barbarism, an argument rejected by some of his contemporaries and some of his posterity. In 1864–1868 he was Mitre's minister to the United States, and was elected chief executive during his absence.

Much of Sarmiento's support in the election and during his administration came from leaders in the interior, who wanted to share more in the growing prosperity and who could collaborate with men of like mind in Buenos Aires so long as the latter were not intransigent on the capital issue. Sarmiento and Mitre now became political enemies, both because of differences on issues and because of personal rivalry. Aside from this, Sarmiento followed Mitre in acting for the nation as a strong executive, using intervention where he thought necessary, and supporting the same economic growth. Sarmiento accelerated the educational advance of Mitre's administration, giving it much personal attention. He fought against compulsory religious (Roman Catholic) instruction in the public schools and was labeled atheistic, as he had been in earlier years. His commitment to education resulted in a doubling of enrollments in six years. He also continued to support the idea that European immigration would help eradicate the barbaric tendencies in Argentine life. His contribution to Argentine education was remarkable, but Sarmiento lived to wonder, after his presidency, why immigrants and education did not eliminate personalism and violence in politics. His critics said

that his own example was less than perfect, that he was a new kind of *caudillo*.

The election of 1874 demonstrated both the strength of the new national polity and the fact that fraudulent and violent electoral practices had not been eliminated. Sarmiento supported for the next term his minister of education, Nicolás Avellaneda, a representative of the leaders of the interior. So far had provincial views developed that Avellaneda even had support from people who had been partisans of Rosas and Urquiza and who now saw the value to themselves and their regions of the new national economic policies, so long as they were not dominated by Buenos Aires. Avellaneda also had support in Buenos Aires from the old *autonomista* group that long had fought against Mitre's *nacionalistas*. Mitre ran against Avellaneda and ascribed his predictable defeat to manipulation by the government. Mitre then led a revolt in favor of free elections. He also declared that dominance by Buenos Aires was necessary to prevent control of political life by "bastard leagues of political bosses," a doctrine that did not perfectly square with his comments on electoral fraud. After losing the civil war, Mitre was sentenced to exile by a military court, because as an officer he had violated his oath to the constitutional system, but President Avellaneda voided the sentence.

The Avellaneda administration (1874–1880) presided over a continuation of rapid economic growth, now expanding more into the interior, though much of the growth was still concentrated in the city and province of Buenos Aires. The government also removed one of the last barriers to exploitation of the country by sending Minister of War General Julio Roca in 1879–1880 with an army to round up the few thousand poor Indian survivors of the long frontier wars. He did so to the accompaniment of considerable cruelty and celebrations of the heroism of the "conqueror of the desert," an enthusiasm that made Roca eminently available for the presidency. Roca also was a suitable successor from Avellaneda's point of view, because he represented the political bosses of the interior.

The candidate of the Mitre group was Carlos Tejedor, governor of Buenos Aires. When he was defeated in the election, Tejedor began a revolt, partly because Avellaneda had made clear that he supported an immediate and permanent solution to the capital question, for which dozens of formulas had been offered over the decades. Although Tejedor had considerable support in the city, Mitre and Alberdi, two giants of the past, opposed the revolt. But when Avellaneda proposed to punish the rebels severely, Mitre joined Tejedor and became commander of the city's rebel forces. He managed to arrange a compromise. The legislature of the province of Buenos Aires was forced to agree to federalization of the city, thus consummating a policy that Mitre long had favored. He again had acted as a nationalist, while maintaining his ties with regionalist forces in Buenos Aires.

The city now was a federal district, capital of the nation, and the province of Buenos Aires had to build itself a new capital at La Plata. The long contest over the status of the metropolis was "won" by all who favored strong national government, control of politics by a minority, and economic growth by support of the export economy. The old tangle of passions that had been mingled with the capital question and regionalism now was overlaid with new issues. The great city now was a possession of all the provinces, capping the trend of several decades toward national unity. It did not reduce the importance of the city as a cultural, financial, and governmental center, but it did remove it as a support to the ambitions of the province of Buenos Aires in the arena of political division. In 1883 a congressional amnesty to all political offenders further promoted unity.

Roca continued the policies of his predecessors, but economic growth became more hectic, political corruption more blatant. In the 1880s the system of oligarchic government was called the *"unicato"* (one-party rule). A congressman wrote

in 1882 that Roca was a "Consul, who aims to hold undivided power, no doubt in order to be Caesar, at least for six years." The oligarchy believed in civilization and progress, embodied in political leadership by an elite, and expressed in orderly legislative and judicial processes. Roca at his inauguration called for "peace and administration," by which he meant no more armed revolts, but a better system of safe agreement among the important leaders of the country, and a continuation of successful socioeconomic policies. He seemed to some observers the worst representative to that time of the new politics of sheer materialism, although he did continue the immigration and education policies of previous administrations. A Law of Public Education (1884) provided for free and compulsory instruction. In the debate on the law, liberals who supported it claimed that the church still dreamed of predominance over temporal authority. One congressman declared that "the state of world civilization" supported the measure, as well as the urgent necessity of maintaining the sovereignty of the people. At the end of his administration, Roca confirmed the views of his critics by continuing the system of imposition, putting his brother-in-law, Miguel Juárez Celman, into the presidency for the term 1886–1892. That administration was to face an economic panic and a political crisis that suggested new directions in public life.

c. The Social Profits of Unity, 1860s–1880s

The new national polity was a factor in encouraging the most notable socioeconomic growth in Latin America. Population soared from 1.3 million in 1859 to 4 million in 1895. It was heavily concentrated in the province and city of Buenos Aires, continuing a process that had been going on for several decades. The metropolis reached half a million before 1890.

Much of the growth was due to immigration, even though many immigrants were *golondrinas*, "swallows" who flew back to Europe eventually with a little nest egg. In the 1860s there was an average annual net increase from immigration of 15,000; it was 30,000 each year in the 1870s, and rose sharply in the 1880s. Total entries were 109,000 in 1885; 121,000 in 1887; and 261,000 in 1889. In 1851–1890 a total of 1.74 million Europeans went to Argentina, an unmistakable tribute to the opportunity they perceived there. Spaniards and Italians accounted for about three-quarters of the immigrants.

Both private and public Argentine organizations encouraged the flow. Most of the immigrants paid their own passage. Some were brought over by railway companies to settle the lands the latter received from the government. A few days' free room and board were available at the Immigrant's Hotel in Buenos Aires. By the 1870s the government had an employment bureau in the Buenos Aires railway station, where requests for workers were received from all over Argentina. Many newcomers settled down in the city either at once, or after an unsatisfactory trial of life in the provinces. In the 1880s more than half the population of the metropolis was foreign-born. In 1895 a quarter of the national population was foreign-born, compared with less than 17 percent in 1869. Life in the countryside, dominated by the great estate, often proved hard for the poor immigrant. Large numbers went into Buenos Aires province, as tenant farmers, sharecroppers, laborers, truck farmers, sheep herdsmen; by the 1870s there were some 35,000 Irish sheepherders there. Some immigrants continued to go to a few upriver ports, and a few went into the interior of Santa Fe province, where the railway company was opening wheat culture to colonists. The flood of immigrants coincided with and contributed to the near extinction by the late 1880s of blacks and mulattoes as distinguishable groups. Indians declined both absolutely and relatively and became a small part of the national population. The proportion of mestizos declined, but remained a sizable element in much of the interior while being submerged in the city and province of Buenos Aires.

The work in these decades in communications and transportation wrought considerable change and promised more. Steam navigation by foreign shipping countries was a boon to a nation dependent on foreign trade. Really modern port works to match the vessels, however, were not built until the 1880s and thereafter, underscoring the fact that the great boom in trade came after 1890. Communications were revolutionized by the international cable and domestic telegraph. The actuality and the promise of the Argentine economy encouraged an earlier massive construction of such facilities than in the rest of Latin America. Even by 1875 the Argentine National Telegraph had sixty stations in the country, and a line went over the Andes to Chile. In a country much larger than those of Europe (except Russia), many economic, political, military, medical, and personal matters were handled via the telegraph, a great contribution to national integration. Tram (street railway) lines were begun in the towns, often by British investors, beginning in the late 1860s, a great asset in Buenos Aires, which was flowing into the countryside in all directions. Trams were horse-drawn through the 1880s.

The railways were immensely important, in fact and in prospect. There were only 1,500 miles of track in 1880. Although trackage rose quite rapidly thereafter, to 3,720 in 1886 and 5,580 in 1890, much of the greatest growth came later. The early lines were bothered by livestock on the unfenced range and by Indian attacks. Early financing and construction were disjointed and small-scale. Politicians, often allied with landowners, boosted construction costs by insisting on small construction concessions from which they squeezed profit. There were several track gauges. Service and rates were poor. The larger companies were British, and more interested in profit than in service. Despite these difficulties and the initially slow growth of the lines, leaders appreciated the potential of the railway. The railway line from Rosario, on the Paraná River, went west through the northern Pampa to Córdoba and beyond that by 1876 to Tucumán, at the edge of the mountains. Thus ended the ox-cart and wagon route that for three centuries had connected the Atlantic with Tucumán, beyond which traffic went by muleback to Upper Peru (Bolivia). The northern lines promoted wheat farming by immigrants in Santa Fe, and in the 1880s some wheat was sent by railway to be exported by ship. The railways opened better prospects to the pastoral products of the north and to the wine and sugar of the northwest, now in a better position to compete with the Brazilian sugar that went to Argentina by sea. The full effects of the railway were felt, however, only in the decades after 1890, when the system was much expanded and improved.

The heart of economic advance was in the great *estancias*. Old and new laws favored continuation of the process of concentration of ownership. The political and economic systems gave insuperable advantages to the wealthy and a few insiders. A comprehensive land law in 1876 provided for small holdings, but it also permitted colonizing companies, and that device was used to build *estancias*. Talk continued about the virtues of small holdings. A law of 1884 allowed homesteading, but in a southern grazing area only. The new lands acquired after the Paraguayan War and the last Indian campaign went into large holdings, to the accompaniment of speculation, favoritism, and chicanery. By the 1880s the best land had been taken up by private owners and either was in large holdings or soon would be.

Under various systems of tillage and remuneration, the *estancieros* reaped the major advantage of the growth of cultivated acreage, which rose by a factor of fifteen between 1872 and 1895. Especially in Buenos Aires province, where land was expensive, poor native Argentines and immigrants alike found that getting ahead as farmers or stock raisers was difficult. Some immigrants occupied *estancia* land as sharecroppers. Others became tenants, investing in equipment and buildings, plowing up the native sod, and planting alfalfa, all of which pleased *estancieros*. Some saved enough money to buy their own land,

often in another province. As European export markets brought new profits, *estancieros* also had the excitement of watching their fortunes grow because of the escalation of land values. Even in the 1860s it was said that people bought cheap land and some sheep, then went to sleep and got rich as the value of land rose eight to ten times in a few years.

In the 1860s Argentina began a growth with few parallels in economic history, for high rate and duration, extending to 1930, with only temporary setbacks during depressions. Growth was largely fueled by exports, which more than tripled in value between 1870 and 1890. So long as the world marketing system remained relatively free and expanding, Argentine specialization in primary export commodities seemed sensible. Exports were nearly all pastoral, although enough wheat shipments built up in the 1880s to suggest that agricultural exports had a good future. But till 1880 the traditional wool, hides, salted meat, tallow, hair, and bone together accounted for more than 90 percent of the value of shipments.

The jerked meat went mostly to feed slaves in Brazil and the West Indies in earlier years, but by the mid-nineteenth century that no longer was a growth item. Wool exports went up, however, because a richer and more populous Europe bought more for clothing and to supply the new rug-weaving machines that were providing floor coverings for an enormously expanding middle class. Expansion was evident in the province of Buenos Aires by the 1840s. In the 1850s sheep ranches radiated out from the city of Buenos Aires, pushing much of the cattle business farther inland. In the 1860s some sheep owners (many of them foreigners) had 20,000 to 100,000 head and were trying to improve their stock. By the late 1870s wool was about one-half the value of all exports, and cattle hides most of the rest. In the 1880s wool was 50 to 60 percent of the value of exports.

The modern meat business had its beginnings in Argentina in the 1880s, although shipments were not large until later. The industry's problems had engaged attention for some time. Europeans would not buy dried and salted meat. Meat extracts and juices were developed during the 1850s and had some sale in Europe, but it was a minor gain. Refrigeration was begun in the 1870s but took time to perfect and would not open large markets unless the grade of meat was improved. The Rural Society, organized in Argentina in 1866, spent many years promoting stock improvement and other forms of modernization of large-scale rural production. Breed improvement took time and money for fences, prize bulls, special pasture, and other items. The resulting beef brought higher prices than the lean animals sold to the *saladeros*. On-the-hoof shipments to Europe increased some. Freezing was a better solution, however, if it could be perfected. The techniques were worked out in Europe. The first modern meat-packing plant (*frigorífico*) was built in Argentina in 1882 by the British, but the full transformation did not come until the 1890s and thereafter. The frozen- and chilled-meat business depended heavily on British money in stock raising, meat processing, railways, and steamships, and most of the meat went to Britain, also.

There was some growth of smaller-scale stock raising and farming, although agricultural production generally was badly organized and operated, because of the great emphasis on pastoral activity, so that many people were still asserting that the Argentine land was not well suited to cultivation. Some immigrants went into truck farming near the towns, especially profitable around Buenos Aires, growing grains, fruit, vegetables, and providing milk and cheese. Such holdings usually were fenced with wire or hedges. Other immigrants found cheaper land in the upriver provinces of Santa Fe and Entre Ríos, where agricultural colonies grew up in the 1870s and 1880s and began to move wheat by rail for export.

The large export income of Argentina paid for a river of imports, not only of all manner of manufactured goods, including machinery, hardware, textiles, and luxuries, but books, art objects, foodstuffs and wine. The coming of the industrial age through imports was clear by the 1860s in advertisements for sewing machines, fence wire, mowing machines, steel plows, corn shellers, and steam engines and boilers. The commercial and financial operation of the country grew with foreign trade. Banking and insurance became well established by the 1870s, often run by foreigners, although older landed families were involved also, directly and indirectly. The construction industry was sizable in the city of Buenos Aires by mid-century, although the big boom did not come until the 1890s.

The metropolis, in fact, was by far the most dynamic marketing, financial, distribution, and manufacturing center in Argentina. It offered many opportunities to rough and skilled laborers, with some of the latter enjoying good pay. Foreign capital was essential in some of this growth and suffered little criticism. Argentines knew the problems of foreign ownership and profits and the cultural assimilation of immigrants, but those problems were unimportant compared with the great need of developing a poor and vacant land. Only later and richer generations would be able to afford elaboration of the themes of nationalization of the economy and culture. Furthermore, Argentina benefited from the enlarged economy. In the period 1810–1860 the growing foreign trade helped the growth of locally financed and controlled river and land commerce, storage facilities, salting works, agriculture, and other enterprises. "Neocolonialism" and "dependency" decreased in 1810–1860; if they increased after 1860, Argentina still derived much benefit from the enlarged economy.

The modern factory had not arrived. The considerable amount of fabrication in Buenos Aires by the 1880s was in small enterprises, often with but a handful of workers. There was much food processing (*saladeros*, the first *frigoríficos*, makers of chocolate products, crackers, beer); tobacco products were turned out, as well as many other such common items as soap and furniture. Fabrication enterprises often were owned and operated by immigrants. The government was not promoting fabrication, except indirectly by supporting transportation and banking operations. There was enough manufacturing so that an Argentine Industrial Club was founded in 1875. If Argentina was not a highly industrialized country in the 1880s, it had gone farther along that road than other Latin American countries and far enough so that more growth could reasonably be expected soon.

The attachment of the Argentine upper class to some forms of modernization had an admirable expression in heavy investment in education, mostly at the primary level. In 1850 only some 7 percent of school-age children were receiving instruction; in the Mitre administration (1862–1868) the percentage rose from 13 to 20 percent; by 1884 it was more than 38 percent. The cost —buildings, teacher training, salaries—was formidable. In 1871–1886 more than thirty teacher-training schools were opened. The result of these efforts was that by 1869 about a third of the population was literate, and by 1895 one-half. The deliberate speed of this transformation obviously meant that it would continue, and that Argentina would be one of the most literate countries in the world. Already in the 1890s, Argentines spoke pridefully of their civilization and thought it a national duty to improve its quality.

In the great metropolis in the 1890s literacy was much higher than in the provinces, and the higher culture of the country was also concentrated there, together with much of the wealth and power of the nation. The interior long had envied and resented this disparity, and it rankled that the city's share of population and wealth continued to grow. Furthermore, a new resentment arose as the metropolis increasingly drained from the provinces their brightest and most ambitious youth. Provincials, and some others as well, began to ascribe national deficiencies to the exaggerated size of the capital city.

After the 1870s Buenos Aires no longer could be described as an overgrown village. A yellow fever epidemic in the 1870s brought extension of the system of running water and the first efforts

to provide modern sewage disposal. In the 1880s the first stages were begun of the physical transformation that by the early twentieth century made Buenos Aires one of the world's great cities. One reason was the desire of the oligarchy to make Buenos Aires into a Paris of the New World. In 1880 the city still bore much of its colonial aspect, with low buildings, narrow, largely unpaved streets, and more tallow wicks than gas jets lighting the streets. Modern port works were begun in the late 1880s. The black and mulatto washerwomen were prohibited from their colorful activities along the shores of the estuary. Some buildings went up to the dizzying height of four stories. The city began to receive new broad avenues, better paving, and rebuilt and beautified plazas. It had restaurants, hotels, newspapers, Catholic and Protestant churches, upper- and middle-class clubs, and lower-class mutual aid societies, a notable number of brothels, and new *conventillos* or slums.

Much more than distance separated the polyglot capital from the great hinterland. The railways had little direct effect on most people in the provinces. There were no feeder lines to the main-line connections between major towns. There were no roads, either. Many rural dwellers lived not in villages but in isolated shacks or small hut-clusters. On the Pampa many dwellings were mud and straw *ranchos*. People lived in dirt, with limited diets and little hope. Country stores provided a bit of occasional diversion, with petty purchases, often of strong drink, and with gossip and fighting. A visitor to a village in 1891 recorded that it was an environment perfectly conducive to suicide. In this countryside the wild, free gaucho was gone. In 1866 he had been painted as a man whose face was blackened by the weather, with long, black, matted hair that hung to his shoulders and mingled with his beard, poncho, kerchief on head, a knife, and on his legs and feet the skin of the legs of a colt. Whatever his appearance, he was being tamed by changing conditions, becoming a peon. The gaucho was almost gone in the 1870s when José Fernández published his poem *Martín Fierro*, which helped create the cult of the gaucho in a country from which he had disappeared. The Argentina of the 1880s was a far cry from the country of Rosas. The countryman now was tied down to the tasks of the great estate in the new export economy.

d. The Crisis of 1888–1892

A financial panic in the late 1880s brought to a head complaints about the ruling oligarchy, because its policies so obviously were both unsound by conventional standards and worsened by favoritism and dishonesty. Roca in 1881–1884 briefly stabilized finances, but in the last two years of his administration returned to the old policy of government deficits, borrowing abroad, heavy emissions of paper money, and acceptance of the ensuing inflation of prices and decline in the international exchange value of the peso. This was carried further under Juárez Celman, who even went so far as to issue new currency secretly! With credit easy, speculation in land on mortgages went to crazy extremes. The government kept shoveling gold to Europe to pay for loans that covered its deficit spending. *Estancieros* did well because they received foreign currency for their exports; but everyone dependent on the large import commerce of Argentina was hurt, because they paid for imports with pesos that were being bled of value. The laborer was pinched because wages did not keep up with the cost of living.

Shipments of gold out of Argentina were 4.5 million gold pesos in 1888, but soared to 25 million in the first nine months of 1889. As the value of the peso plunged, gold value in pesos went from 158 in May to 233 in December 1889 and on to a high of 312 on April 12, 1890. The situation was worsened by the fact that it coincided with a worldwide panic. Credit virtually disappeared for private or public needs, at home or abroad. All creditors wanted repayment at due date without extensions, and big borrowers had been living on constant extensions of credit. Liquidations of holdings for cash began, values fell, bankruptcies multiplied. The government

suspended many of its operations, including public works construction, throwing laborers out of work and interfering with the lush profits contractors had been making and sharing with their friends in politics.

It was a classic case of an overextended economy, much of it closely tied to the world trading system. It was bound to have repercussions in Argentine politics simply because of anger at losses and expectable charges of mismanagement. The repercussions were heightened because economic disaster was linked with complaint about oligarchic rule, as evidence accumulated that not only incompetence and greed but thievery in high places was involved. There were also criticisms of the ties between the government and its supporters and foreign economic interests. These were based on many considerations, including an 1887 scheme by the Juárez government to lease public health works to a foreign enterprise. Even ex-president Roca, the very symbol of the ruling clique, objected to this proposal as an unacceptable alienation of national sovereignty. Liberals had good reason for broader objections to foreign influence in the economy.

In the late 1880s there were several groups prepared to act against the Juárez administration. (*a*) There were dissidents within the oligarchic group, which was organized loosely into the National Autonomist Party (P.A.N.), but more often was referred to as "The Regime," or similar names. Some dissidents in the P.A.N. had been unhappy with the ruling combination for years, serving it in one way or another without believing in its goals or methods. They had no hope of influence within the P.A.N. In addition, a few impeccably conservative P.A.N. leaders occasionally rocked the boat of consensus. Roca, now in the federal Senate, was in a sometimes uneasy alliance with Vice-President Pellegrini to serve their own ambitions and possibly get rid of Juárez Celman before he wrecked the country. The old hero Mitre, thundering in his *La Nación* against The Regime, was an undoubted supporter of many conservative policies, but he stood for more control of materialism and fraud in public life. He also was interested in being president again.

(*b*) There were would-be reformers who wanted a free and honest political system. They were middle class in being literate, not manual workers, and not directly involved in the *estanciero* export economy. They were men of the city with some education, not much concerned with economic questions, and chiefly ambitious to force a better place for themselves in the closed political system. Leandro Alem, Aristóbolo del Valle, and Hipólito Yrigoyen had worked for P.A.N., but found it inhospitable to new ideas. In the 1880s some of these dissidents were part of the small opposition in the national congress. They formed political clubs and discussion groups. Before the financial crisis of the late 1880s, their prospects did not look bright. They certainly could not speak for a large and coherent middle-class point of view, because that did not exist, although there were every year in the city more and more persons of education and property ready to discuss political change.[8]

(*c*) There were some Catholic political activists, chiefly men who had been roused by recently enacted anticlerical laws, especially the exclusion of religious instruction from public schools. As with many men in politics, they often acted out of several motives, in some cases a desire for a more democratic political system, which provided them with an issue in common with the middle-class reformers. The Catholic group was not a major factor in Argentine politics, but could enlarge its role by alliance with others.

(*d*) There were army officers willing to act against the regime. They included junior officers, graduates of the Military College established in 1870, who considered themselves better prepared and oriented to serve the country than either their commanders or the national political leaders. In the late 1880s they were being hurt by the inflation. Presumably some were not uninfluenced by the hope of arranging more rapid promotion for themselves. These officers founded a Lodge of 33, which they said was "to return the country to the Constitution and respect for the popular will." They finally chose as political leaders two senior officers who happened to be followers of Mitre and were uninterested in the ideals of the young officers. One interesting aspect of this military development that was possibly ominous for the future was the apparent demonstration that professionalization or modernization of the officers' corps by improved training would not automatically eradicate its taste for political activity.

Most Argentines did not participate or have a very active interest in the dissident groups, being busy with their private affairs or being ineligible to vote, like women or unnaturalized foreigners—this last affecting much of the middle class. Some men did not bother to vote because of oligarchic control of the machinery and intimidation during the public balloting. Labor interest in politics was small because it was not organized into unions, although anarchists and Marxist socialists were discussing organization in a small way in Argentina in the 1880s. Marxist socialist groups were formed in the metropolis, partly under the influence of German immigrants, and gave support to feeble early efforts to use the strike. They put on a little display for the first celebration, May 1, 1890, of the new world festival of labor decreed by European leftists in 1889. In the Argentina of 1890, however, industrial labor was of virtually no consequence in public affairs, although the economic growth of the country suggested that it might be in the future.

In 1889 various dissident groups met to discuss possible courses of action. Roca supporters did

[8] The size of the middle-class population of Buenos Aires in 1890 cannot be estimated with any certainty, since it depends on definition. Literacy might be taken as one gauge, but of course many literates were children, and many others too poor to qualify as middle class on economic grounds. Being foreign-born or in nonagricultural occupations were not necessary ingredients in middle classness, as sometimes is hinted. But education, and something better than a subsistence income, especially if nonagricultural, certainly were marks of the middle class. At any rate, the middle class had been growing steadily, and it had reasons for satisfaction and complaint.

not take part, being satisfied with their chances in the election of 1892. The eighty-year-old Mitre, however, was active. His *La Nación* in August 1889 declared that the youth of the country should be ashamed for having submitted to the oligarchic system; whereupon, on September 1 students held a protest meeting in the Jardín Florida that was attended by dissident leaders of several types, including Senator Aristóbulo del Valle, some Catholic leaders, and Leandro Alem, important among the middle-class reformers. This meeting created a Civic Union of Youth, with Alem as president of its executive council, to press for effective democracy. Alem was a man of the city middle class, then in his late forties, who had worked in politics in Buenos Aires for the conservative P.A.N., then tried several methods of developing an independent political base. He was a melancholy, introverted man, whose life had been a largely unsuccessful search for political influence, and whose career, social position, and personality were undistinguished from the point of view of the traditional politicians.

The next few months were spent in the political organization and agitation for which Alem and his nephew Hipólito Yrigoyen had considerable talent and experience, and which was helped by the fact that the national financial situation was going from bad to worse. An important rally was held in a ball court (*frontón*) on April 13, 1890, the day after gold had driven the peso to 312. Old Mitre spoke. Then the *Unión Cívica* was organized, with Alem as head of its executive committee, a move that drove Mitre out of the group for a time. A few days later the Lodge of 33 (now with sixty officer members, able to order some 1,500 troops into action) affiliated with the new organization. The two senior officers leading the young officers in the Lodge found their personal support of Mitre frustrated by his departure for Europe, so they flirted with the P.A.N. dissidents led by Roca, who hoped to capture the presidency in 1892. Thus, the new and untried Civic Union faced all sorts of problems.

Alem realized that they could not win an election, that military action was necessary, but he also feared military dictatorship and quarreled with the military leaders. Neither the military nor the civilian element in the conspiracy was strong enough, the organization was defective, and its plans were betrayed by a military officer. A small amount of fighting in July 1890 quickly ended with an agreement to persuade President Juárez to resign, an idea that many people favored by this time.[9] On August 6 a number of congressmen demanded that Juárez step down, which he did. Vice-President Pellegrini succeeded and at once named Roca minister of government. The oligarchy had consolidated its position by ousting the incompetent Juárez. Pellegrini and Roca proved capable of maintaining the system for years to come. How they were perceived by their effective constituency was demonstrated by one of Pellegrini's first acts: He called in a group of bankers and other wealthy men and told them to find 18 million pesos to straighten out the finances of the national government, and they quickly did so.

The next two years were even more revealing of the difficulties the reform group faced. Mitre came back to Argentina from Europe still anxious to be president. The Civic Union adopted him as its candidate, but some elements of that organization simply were incompatible. Alem continued, as he had in 1890, to speak for broad and honestly supervised political participation. The *Mitristas* considered him a radical. Mitre's followers were, whatever their personal ambitions and their disagreements with recent administrations on some matters, men of property and conservative views. They campaigned on a moderate platform, and even negotiated with Roca. The result was that the determined reformists, includ-

---

[9] It became an article of faith in some interpretations after the revolt of 1890 that it was critically damaged by Alem's losing his head during the fighting. There is no reason to believe, however, that the rebels had any chance of winning.

ing Alem, organized the *Unión Cívica Radical,* soon known as the Radical party.

All this effort by liberal and conservative dissidents failed in the election of 1892, for the government clique elected Luís Sáenz Peña without difficulty. How much the reform leaders could improve upon their unimpressive initial performance remained to be seen. There had been a financial crisis, but the regime and the country survived it handily. Rich Argentina had enormous resources, and European demand continued to grow. There was no overwhelming reason to suggest that the political crisis had not been surmounted also, although some conservatives feared that real revolutionary conflict had begun. There was, in fact, little reason for such fear, but the rapid pace of economic and social change in Argentina suggested that there would be rising demands for political and other sorts of modernization.

25 Oligarchy and Empire: Brazil from Independence to the 1880s

An accident of history helped make the huge Brazilian nation. There was available on the scene a prince with a clear claim to legitimacy, who favored unfettered commercial links with the Atlantic world and around whom the elite could rally.[1] Agreement on Pedro as head of an independent monarchy muted the expression of regional jealousies and ambitions enough so that Brazil escaped the territorial division that afflicted Spanish America. Two lesser gifts of the monarchy to Brazil were an absence until 1889 of unconstitutional changes of government or of military participation in politics. The absence of those phenomena did not mean, however, that Brazilian society lacked the conditions that created them in Spanish America but that the monarchy provided a focus for keeping them under control. After the fall of the monarchy in 1889 those conditions quickly asserted themselves, as Brazilian politics and government came more and more to resemble those then current in Spanish America. From 1822 to 1889 Brazilian political institutions were as oligarchic as in the colonial era, and social mobility, political awareness, and education increased less in monarchic Brazil than in republican Argentina and Chile. The monarchic system cannot be blamed, to be

sure, any more than republicanism in Spanish America for upper-class insistence on minimal social change and concentration on an export economy, which seemed to the upper class the only large opportunity available.

a. Pedro I, 1822–1831

The new nation under Pedro I was vast in territory but thinly populated. Many of its people, furthermore, had no interest in the fate of Brazil, being either black slaves or members of a poor lower class that had little hope of betterment. The economy was dominated by great estates whose owners were resistant to ideas of change in technology, organization, or labor management. These unpromising conditions in the new nation were not lightened by the fact that support for Pedro I was far from unanimous. Many Portuguese in Brazil resented the new state, because it divided the Portuguese world and threatened to replace their influence in America with that of Brazilians. Some Brazilians disliked Pedro because of his ties with Europe. His father was now king of Portugal, and Pedro might inherit that crown. Pedro kept many Portuguese around him, which irked Brazilians. A Brazilian minority disliked Pedro because it

---

[1] See Chapter 21 on Brazilian Independence.

wanted a republic. Some people did not care for Pedro as a person. Although he could be likable and had a sense of responsibility, he also could be imperious, and he had been badly reared and educated, so that both his knowledge and his self-discipline were defective. All these problems were complicated by old regional rivalries, based on economic differentiation and local ambition. Regional economies and social contrast were strengthened and integration retarded by poor internal communications and transport. The effect on national politics, however, was reduced by the ability of Rio de Janeiro to communicate easily by sea with key population and production centers on and near the coast.

Northern Brazil was dominated at Independence by troops, naval forces, and supporters of Portugal. Pedro hired Lord Thomas Cochrane, the experienced British naval officer who recently had served Chile for pay. The little Brazilian force that Cochrane put together helped expel the Portuguese military from America by early 1824. Since Portugal was weak, with its own resources it could do little. Brazilian forces put down a revolt in Recife in 1824 that was partly an expression of an old regionalism and that proclaimed a "Confederation of the Equator." Other reasons besides regionalism for interprovincial warfare were weak as compared with Spanish America, because arguing about an established system and its chief executive was less divisive than arguing about a new type of government and the ambitions of many individuals to become head of state.

Pedro's government could not feel safe so long as Portugal did not recognize its independence and Lisbon hoped for aid from the conservative European powers. Reports on Portuguese intrigues with the European powers raised the political tension in Brazil in 1822 and thereafter. The British, however, not only objected to such schemes, but wished Portugal to recognize Brazil's Independence. That desire was reinforced in 1824 when the United States became the first nation to recognize Pedro's regime. Britain, lest this result in commercial advantage for Yankees,

arranged Portugal's recognition of Brazilian Independence in 1825.

Meanwhile, a new government system was debated in Brazil, where Pedro was crowned emperor on December 1, 1822. His decision to remain so weakened the republicans that they turned to attempts to limit the powers of the crown. Some early maneuvers between factions on this issue took place in the Masonic order in Rio de Janeiro, of which Pedro was a member. Soon after his coronation, Pedro turned against the advocates of severely limited monarchy in that lodge and dissolved the society. Thus began Pedro's long-sustained defense of the royal prerogatives.

Pedro, responding to demand, called a constituent and legislative assembly for May 1823, ruling in the meantime by decree. He appointed ministers, including José Bonifácio de Andrada e Silva, a leader of the move for Independence and an able conservative. Conservatives, however, rejected José Bonifácio's desire to end the slave trade, while radicals detested his defense of strong executive powers as necessary to prevent such disorders as disfigured public affairs in Spanish America. José Bonifácio was not primarily responsible for the political crisis that soon developed; that was due, rather, to Pedro's determination to make personal decisions, in which he was encouraged by his Portuguese coterie.

The constituent assembly of a hundred prominent men was virtually ordered by Pedro to bring in a constitution to his liking, or he would reject it. Instead of doing so, the assembly determined to limit the emperor's powers. That was one issue that led Pedro to break with the influential Andrada brothers, who were willing to support him if he would compromise. José Bonifácio soon resigned and he and his brothers were part of the opposition in the assembly. Tension mounted in Rio de Janeiro, with both sides fearful and angry. Pedro in November 1823 led troops himself to dissolve the assembly. Six members were arrested, including the three Andradas, and sent into exile. This move had support among the Portuguese in Pedro's anti-Brazilian

States and Territories of Brazil

court and military establishment. The military put down an uprising in Pernambuco that favored the dismissed assembly.

The Brazilian elite was reconciled by Pedro's decision to name a committee of Brazilians to revise the assembly's work. The committee naturally reflected Pedro's distaste for the assembly's constitution and turned out a document that suited him. Approved by the oligarchic town councils of Brazil, it was promulgated in March 1824 and lasted until 1889. It provided a four-branch government, with the executive and the "moderating" branches reposing in the emperor, giving him potentially enormous power.[2]

This was the chief addition to the constitution the assembly had drafted. The emperor appointed presidents of provinces, ministers, bishops; could call or end a session of the legislature (General Assembly); had a veto of legislation that was difficult to overturn; and controlled papal pronouncements in Brazil. These conservative provisions were reinforced by a Senate of members appointed for life by the emperor from nominations by the small provincial electorates under a system of limited suffrage. Freedom and equality before the law were guaranteed, but of course that was significant primarily to the small propertied and politically active group. A number of liberal provisions included freedom of the press, religious liberty, and inviolability of the home. There was nothing in the Constitution to disgust the Brazilian oligarchy except the powers

---

[2] See Section e of this chapter on the use of moderating power by Pedro II.

given to the executive.[3] The powers of the crown, especially the fourth or moderating branch, never ceased to cause trouble.

The Portuguese issue caused continual suspicion of Pedro. In a secret provision of the 1825 treaty on Independence he agreed to pay his father, King João of Portugal, for the properties João had left in Brazil and to assume Portugal's debt to Britain. Revelation of these concessions brought criticism, as did the fact that Pedro had sent the treaty to the Assembly (joint session of Senate and Deputies) after he had ratified it, in violation of the Constitution and political good sense. The Portuguese issue flamed anew in 1826 when João died in Portugal and the regency there proclaimed Pedro king of Portugal. Brazilians with difficulty made clear to Pedro that they would not put up with his acceptance of the crown of Portugal unless he detached himself from Brazil. He did finally give up the Portuguese crown in favor of an infant daughter, though he tried to hedge the transaction with restrictions in order not to cut himself off entirely from European affairs. Although he was persuaded at the end of the 1820s to reduce his reliance on Portuguese advisers, he would not eliminate them. All this made Pedro's birth in Europe seem like a fatal flaw that could not be eradicated.

The economy did not prosper. The development that did occur was chiefly in the export sector, enjoying credit from British interests and consisting of a few growers of export commodities and the export and import merchants dependent on that traffic. The Brazilian-British trade fostered by treaty in 1810 was favored by a new treaty in 1827.[4] The special commercial privileges conceded Britain caused resentment in Brazil, as did the continuation of the right of British vessels to search slave ships in Brazilian waters.

Public revenues were small. The treasury was continually in difficulty and issued poorly backed currency that deteriorated in value. As in so many things, Pedro regarded the treasury as at the disposition of an uncheckable monarch and issued orders to it without authorization from the Assembly. The government's financial position and its general reputation were worsened by Pedro's long adventure in Uruguay. When Portuguese military forces withdrew from Uruguay in 1824, Pedro pursued the old Luso-Brazilian ambition by proclaiming it the Cisplatine Province of Brazil. Uruguayan patriots resisted with the aid of Argentines. Most Brazilians were not interested in far-off Uruguay; they resented the cost of the war in lives and money. When the conflict ended in 1828, however, with agreement to creation of an independent Uruguay as a buffer between Argentina and Brazil, that resolution was also unpopular in Brazil.

Pedro clashed with the parliament on other things. The parliament argued the basis of Pedro's right of patronage over the church. In addition, the Chamber of Deputies wanted the ministers—the operating cabinet or executive—to be responsible to it, whereas Pedro claimed the Constitution made the cabinet responsible to him, an extension of his own powers. They quarreled over appointments, especially for Pedro's Portuguese friends. When José Bonifácio returned from exile at the end of 1829, he managed to persuade Pedro to conciliate his opponents by appointing an all-Brazilian ministry. Pedro did not, however, give up his Portuguese friends, or reform his tendency to autocratic behavior.

All these clashes were aired in newspapers, now a well-established institution in Brazil, and generally unmolested in political discussion. Most papers were anti-Pedro. As they were reporting the antiabsolutist sentiment stimulated by the revolutions of 1830 in Europe, Pedro dis-

---

[3] Members of the Chamber of Deputies were elected for four-year terms. A Council of State advised the emperor. Roman Catholicism was made the official faith, although others were given some limited rights of worship. Religious questions ordinarily did not much disturb Brazilian affairs after 1822.

[4] See Chapter 21, Section c, on the 1810 treaty.

missed the ministry. He then tried to ensure the election to the Chamber of Deputies of a supporter in Minas Gerais, and his candidate was spurned by the electorate. By now Brazilians in the Assembly spoke of the hated Portuguese in Brazil as "traitors." Tempers were rising. On the night of March 13, 1831, Pedro's foes and adherents fought in the "night of the bottles," named for the missiles used. Disorders occurred in the provinces. The moderates and radicals in the opposition began coalescing, with encouragement from the army, whose officers had become more Brazilian during the war in Uruguay.

Pedro made a partial concession on March 20 by appointing a ministry of moderate Brazilians, but he did not consult the deputies, nor were the new ministers deputies, so that did not appease his enemies. On April 4 he dismissed that ministry on the grounds that it was not maintaining public order and named a ministry of aristocrats, which seemed further evidence of his absolutist tendencies. Disturbances increased in Rio de Janeiro. Radical *exaltados*, who had wanted a republic in 1822, called for one now. Pedro tried desperately to hang on but without making sufficient concessions, and all the army abandoned him by April 6. He abdicated and left on a British warship, taking all the wealth he could. The best that can be said of Pedro's nine-year reign is that it was preferable to the political confusion and often desperate military action of the first decade of independence in Spanish America. The most valuable heritage he left was his little son Pedro.

b. The Dependency of Pedro II, 1831–1840s

The political dependency of Pedro II extended from his accession at five, through a regency, to his coronation in 1841, and for several years thereafter as he more and more asserted his independence and mastery of Brazilian politics and government. Regencies during the minority of princes often have been disturbed periods. They cause uncertainties that encourage dissent and adventurism. In Brazil there were four regencies

in nine years. The situation encouraged regional defiance of the central government. It also caused disturbances in the capital city. Little Pedro had sometimes to be taken from his palace to a place of greater safety. The regents did see that Pedro received a thorough moral and intellectual preparation. He became a handsome, self-disciplined man of many interests, with a strong sense of duty to Brazil.

In the 1830s few Brazilians had a sense of nationalism. Only some of the politically active minority, possibly 10 percent of the population, was interested in holding the huge territory together. The active minority was divided, however, by a number of issues: Brazilians versus Portuguese, monarchists versus republicans, disagreement as to the extent of executive power, personal antipathies, and the issue of provincial power. The heart of that minority was the large landowner, whose interest and powers of obstruction had to be borne in mind by every government. The debate over provincial power became a principal issue between liberals and conservatives even before they adopted those labels in the late 1830s. The liberal interest in provincial power, as a way of fending off absolutism, had to contend with upper-class fear that social order required a strong central government; and recognition, even by some liberals, that regionalism might split the country into several independent states. The number of revolts in the 1830s and 1840s suggested that Brazil might develop something like the *caudillismo* of Spanish America.[5] Although many of the disturbances aimed at local autonomy rather than at independence, the largest rebellion proclaimed a separate republic. That was the Farroupilha (War of the Ragamuffins, the name relating to their rough frontier dress) of 1835–1845 in Rio Grande do Sul. That cattle country was far from Rio de Janeiro and lay along unpatrolled international boundaries,

---

[5] There were serious disturbances or rebellions in Maranhão in 1831–1832 and 1840; in Pernambuco in 1831–1835; in Amazonas in 1831–1833; in Ceará 1831–1834; in Pará 1832 and 1835–1847; in Bahia 1832–1835 and 1837.

great backlands in which the populations of several countries mingled and feuded with little concern for national authority. The authority of Rio de Janeiro was not established in the far south until near mid-century.

The weakness of the central government was evident throughout the 1830s and most of the 1840s in sparse revenues, a weak military establishment, and an instability in the upper reaches of the administration that the country could ill afford. Until the ex-emperor Pedro died in Portugal in 1834, the issue of his possible interference agitated politics. The issue of republicanism also frequently disturbed affairs, although on the whole the great men of the empire supported the monarchy as a practical necessity even when, in some cases, they would have preferred a republic. The liberal majority in the General Assembly defined regency powers narrowly, thus exalting the legislature. It named a permanent regency of moderates who supported constitutional monarchy. There still were partisans of absolutist monarchy, however, whose hopes were pinned to restoration of Pedro I, but that hope ended with his death, and the restorationists went into the combination that became the Conservative party. Finally, there were the *exaltados*, republicans, who would be a disturbing factor throughout the history of the empire but were not influential enough to control affairs.

The tension between the three points of view came to a head over the issue of Pedro's tutor, José Bonifácio de Andrada,[6] opposed by *moderados* in the lower house and defended by the Senate of life-time appointees and absolutist sentiment. The minister of justice, Diogo Feijó, a *moderado*, led an effort in July 1832 to turn the Chamber of Deputies into a national assembly to rewrite the Constitution and possibly eliminate the Senate, but the deputies themselves declined to support the scheme, thus

choosing orderly government rather than an increase in their own authority.

Absolutism was the target also of a grant of authority to the provinces, a way of diluting authority, done in 1834 by an *Acto Adicional* (Additional Act) amending the Constitution. It received authorization first from the electorate, then from the deputies, the Senate having been excluded from the process because it opposed the principle. All through this period the powers of Senate and Chamber were interpreted by political leaders to suit their convenience. Under the *Acto* the government appointed provincial presidents, the provinces could create elected legislatures in place of their appointed councils, and public schools (except universities) were put under the provinces. Other liberal measures were included in the *Acto*, including the abolition of entail, which in Brazil, as in Spanish America, was a symbolic blow by liberals at conservatism in general, but had no effect on the great estate system, which many liberal statesmen supported.[7]

The bestowal of widened powers on the provinces was important, however, and remained a vexed issue. Many *exaltados* strongly supported provincial power, although what they really wanted was a federal republic, that goal of so many liberals in Spanish America also. But Bernardo de Vasconcelos, one of the authors of the *Acto*, decided that it dissipated authority in a country already suffering from regionalism and that was one of his reasons for helping found the Conservative party in the late 1830s, hoping it could restore authority to the central government. The Liberal party also was founded in the late 1830s, so the absolutists, *moderados*, and *exaltados* went into the two parties that dominated politics thereafter. Around the same time, Vasconcelos worked to restrict the *Acto Adicional*. A law of 1841 did so, limiting the powers of provincial legislatures. This was, of course,

---

[6] José Bonifácio was that common phenomenon of politics, a man once celebrated as a liberal, who in his old age thought order (monarchism) more important than change. His distaste for republicanism was reinforced by what he knew of it in Spanish America.

[7] The *Acto* made some other changes: for instance, it turned the regency into a one-man elective office; and it abolished the Council of State, which conservatives had dominated.

the issue of "federal" versus central authority that so agitated affairs in Argentina also. The law of 1841 also restored the Council of State as an element in national executive strength.

The temporary nature of the regency came more and more to seem a major cause of ineffective government. Conservatives under the regency of liberal Feijó had one view and a different one when under the Araújo regency. Liberals in the late 1830s favored declaration of Pedro's majority as a way of returning to power. They promoted it with propaganda and political maneuvering, so that before long even Conservatives accepted the idea. A thoroughly unconstitutional series of maneuvers in the parliament finally resulted in a decision in July 1840 that Pedro was of age. The accession of the new emperor was popular; everyone was weary of the regency.

The early years of Pedro's rule were a time of transition: from initially disturbed conditions to the comparative peace of the long middle years of his tenure; from his immaturity at fifteen to his mastery of political conditions in the empire; and from the nearly stagnant economic situation of the first half of the nineteenth century to the brisk growth of later years. The Liberals, who had been out of the ministry for several years, were rewarded for putting over the majority of Pedro with a new ministry appointed in July 1840, headed by Antonio Carlos de Andrada. It dismissed provincial presidents and other officials to make room for Liberals. In 1841, when a new four-year Chamber of Deputies was elected, the ministry corrupted the process. There was a great protest and the ministry resigned, whereupon Pedro had Conservatives form a government. The teenage emperor was quickly exposed to political passions and corruption of the electoral process.

The Conservatives, as has been seen, then altered the *Acto Adicional*. In the same year they moved judicial powers from local to nationally controlled police, as another prop to the central government. Before the Liberal chamber could meet in 1842, the Conservative ministry per-

suaded Pedro to dissolve it on the grounds that it was corruptly chosen. The Liberals then raised rebellions in Minas Gerais and São Paulo that were put down. It was not that Brazilian politicians were much less willing than Spanish American to use violence in politics, but that continuity at the top of the system made it seem less likely to succeed.

The Liberals were in power again in 1844–1848 and used authority that they had objected to in the hands of Conservatives. In 1847 they created the presidency of the Council of Ministers, amounting to a prime minister, named by the emperor, which helped establish Pedro's authority over the ministries of his later years. When Pedro dismissed the Liberal ministry in 1849, the party promoted the Praieira revolt in Pernambuco, which so damaged the Liberal reputation that Pedro ruled with Conservative governments for more than a decade. Thus for many years the system depended on an uneasy balance between the emperor and various factions of the *fazendeiros*.

c. Social Conditions Under the Empire

The Brazilian population grew briskly from less than 4 million in 1822 to about 14 million in 1889. Most of it remained concentrated within a narrow belt near the Atlantic coast. Most of the gain was due to natural increase, though assisted by continued imports of black African slaves to the early 1850s and by a small number of European immigrants before that time and considerably more thereafter. The Indian element became less evident, remaining strongest in cattle areas and in the lightly populated hinterland and Amazonia. In 1822 it was supposed that half the population was black, about a quarter white, and the other quarter mixed and Indian. The census of 1890 claimed to show a big change, with the population 44 percent white, 15 percent Negro, 32 percent mulatto, and 9 percent Indian and mixtures with Indian. The figures reflected the large process of miscegenation and also the Brazilian practice of counting persons as white if their appearance and mode of life made that easy, rather than the practice in the United States of counting persons as other than white if any excuse to do so appeared.[8]

Slave imports were large. In 1838 some 46,000 were introduced. The numbers then declined as the British stepped up their antislavery efforts, and in 1840–45 the yearly importation was 20,000 or less (in 1841 "only" 10,000). Then, as the British became more determined and Brazilian slave owners anticipated extinction of the traffic, they imported some 150,000 in 1846–1850. The British pressure, aided by Brazilian government cooperation, then took effect, and the rate declined in 1850. The traffic ended during the next two years. An estimate of 1847 put slaves at 3.1 million out of a total population of 7.3 million. The census of 1871 showed 1.5 million slaves in a population of 9.9 million, a big decline, but still a large slave community. Slaves always were heavily concentrated in the old northeast and in the provinces of Rio de Janeiro and São Paulo.

European immigration was more important than in most of Latin America, though less so than in Argentina. Before mid-century immigration was small. The estate owners preferred to import slaves. The end of the slave trade in the 1850s stimulated interest in immigrant labor, coinciding as it did with an improvement in the export market for Brazilian commodities. The end of the slave trade also made Brazil seem a more attractive place to immigrants, and the flow quickened. It did not become large, however, until the 1880s: only 11,000 in 1881; about 28,000 a year in 1882–1886; 55,000 in 1887; and 132,000 in 1888, the year slavery was abolished. Total immigration to Brazil from 1822 to 1890 was some 900,000. Much of the quickened immigration was tied to the growth of coffee culture. Immigration schemes were developed whereby landowners paid the passage and initial

production costs of sharecroppers from Europe. Immigrant laborers and sharecroppers proved highly profitable to the great estate owners in the new coffee areas. Most of the immigrants after mid-century went to the south. Even before then, a small stream of Germans went south of São Paulo into Rio Grande do Sul, where there were some 60,000 of them by 1870.

Brazil was an overwhelmingly rural country. Rio de Janeiro had possibly 250,000 people by mid-century, and Bahia some 150,000; all other towns were much smaller. Urbanization quickened only slightly thereafter, although it became apparent that new economic opportunities were going to sustain at least a small trend away from the land. The town of São Paulo had little more than 30,000 in 1880, but it stood on the threshold of one of the greatest urban growths in modern times. Some drag on immigration was due to Brazil's bad reputation for dangerous diseases, especially on the tropical coast. Yellow fever and cholera epidemics were a constant fear. In mid-century there were no sewers in towns; slaves carried filth away in barrels. All ladies were said to have lice in their hair. Pedro II's sense of public responsibility and his interest in science led him to invite Louis Pasteur to Brazil to fight yellow fever. Although Pasteur did not go to Brazil, some minor progress was made in public health.

In a poor country dominated by a small planter aristocracy, little money was forthcoming for education, although there was more support and more expenditure for it than in the colonial era. The constitutional draft of 1823 had called for schools in each village and town and for public high schools; but the final Constitution of 1824 merely said that each citizen had a right to primary education. Furthermore, the Additional Act of 1834 gave control of primary and secondary education to the provinces, except in the city of Rio de Janeiro; and the provinces were conservative on education or any other social expenditure. As usual in Latin America, educational efforts were concentrated in the towns, especially in the capital city.

---

[8] All Brazilian population figures for the period are suspect. After the treaty with Britain on suppression of the slave trade, slave imports were handled so surreptitiously that estimates are especially chancy.

In 1871 in a population of some 10 million only 150,000 were receiving primary, and fewer than 10,000 secondary, instruction. In the later years of the empire an increasing interest in improving educational opportunities was a part of the mounting concern with reformism and modernization. Statesmen pointed to the poor shape of education in Brazil compared with more advanced nations. In 1882 Rui Barbosa reported to the Senate that the educational situation was abysmal as compared with the United States. The effects of this rising insistence on more educational effort were not great before the creation of the republic. Even at the end of the empire in 1889, in a population of over 13 million, primary instruction was reaching only 250,000 children.

Predictably, the governing elite did most for specialized education that would benefit its own class. An upper-class family sent the brightest son to law school, which trained for a career in the courts or legislative and executive government; the stupidest was sent into business, which was not admired; others might go into medicine, or the army, even the church. Such attitudes help explain the strong role played by foreigners in commerce and industry in Brazil. The first law schools were created in 1827. A polytechnic school was created in 1847, partly to turn out engineers. A school of mines was founded in 1856. Some small-scale developments were aimed at the improvement of general education. The imperial high school (later the Colegio Pedro II), founded in 1838, had as one purpose serving as a standard for all provincial secondary schools. The first normal schools to train teachers were set up in the 1830s. Foreign missionary schools had some influence in the later empire. Pedro II had a modern outlook on education, as in so many areas, but few resources, financial or political, to do much about it. He devoted time to promoting the importance of education and declared teaching the most important profession. The system of higher education in 1889 consisted of two faculties of medicine and surgery, two law schools, a school of mines, one of fine arts, a

conservatory of music, the polytechnical school, three military schools, and a naval school. In addition, the emperor gave modest support to libraries, archives, and museums. Thus there was some development of intellectual life in the period 1822–1889.

Consciousness of class divisions necessarily remained strong in Brazil under the empire. The lower class included on the order of 90 percent of the population. The small upper class controlled politics, the professions, intellectual life, the professional military, the militia, and the press. Outside the few cities the great estate owners dominated society so completely that no innovation decreed by Rio de Janeiro had much chance of implementation without their cooperation. Furthermore, this oligarchy, founded on agriculture, dominated the central government, directly and indirectly. Most of its great political leaders supported the monarchic system; even liberals like Joaquim Nabuco thought it preferable to the disorderly republican oligarchies in much of surrounding Spanish America. The bourgeoisie was small by any definition, and its wealthier, dynamic component in the larger towns even smaller. Many of the richer bourgeois, furthermore, were foreigners, especially until the later years of the empire, and thus cut off to some extent from the Brazilian landowning class. The growth of commercial, financial, and manufacturing activity in the later empire increased demand for power and policy changes to benefit nonagricultural interests, and that promised more modernization in future years.

Communication between the classes and the masses was a matter of patron-client relationships. A *fazendeiro* processing the cane of a tenant would take 50 to 80 percent. The plantation lent money in the surrounding country. The estate-owner class furnished an area's officials, military and militia officers, judges, physicians, and other men of training and influence. The growth of newspapers under the empire thus was important mostly for the mobilization of opinion among the politically active minority, although they sometimes were used to encourage popular participation in the towns in the form of demonstrations and even more violent actions. This was, however, a matter of occasional manipulation, and did not lead to the formation of populist parties. Freedom of the press, of which upper-class Brazilians properly were proud, existed for all the points of view of the politically active. This was far from "freedom" in terms of access to the media by all possible points of view. Communication among Brazilians was further restricted by the dreadful state of transportation, with railways barely begun in the late imperial era.

Under all these circumstances, nationalism was a sentiment confined to the few who defined it in terms of their conception of proper social arrangements. There was some nationalism shown in resentment of British economic predominance and a tendency to arrogance in diplomatic relations with Brazil. There was a continuation of the literary affection for the Brazilian scene that had begun in the colonial era and a very slow growth of sentiment for better national development as a patriotic necessity, a view that grew among professional military officers. It was, however, unimportant in the empire until its last years, and even then was poorly defined. National communication and integration scarcely were promoted by religious life, which remained bifurcated between the rather tepid orthodoxy of the upper class and all manner of combinations of Christian and African religious ideas and practices in the lower class. Although popular religious practices posed no threat to the social order, they did occasionally display a locally disturbing fanaticism. In the 1830s in the *sertão* (back country) of Pernambuco a movement begun by a self-proclaimed prophet dreamed of the New Jerusalem of King Sebastião, where the old would be young, the poor would be rich, and blacks and *mestiços* would become whites. Human sacrifices were made to hasten arrival of the millennium before government troops dispersed the members. Such

sects of frustration and despair could not become political movements in the absence of political self-consciousness among the poor; there was no class struggle in imperial Brazil.

d. The Economy Under the Empire

The economy of Brazil in the first half of the nineteenth century not only was poor, but it generally worsened until the 1840s. Lack of growth was due not to the commercial privileges given Britain but to international demand and competition, and to opinions, practices, and social structures in Brazil.[9] Development could not be simply legislated. Public and private capital were limited. The economy was almost entirely agricultural and pastoral, with the former predominating. Most persons working in agriculture were slaves, free laborers, or small subsistence farmers, with only a feeble class of moderate-sized farmers who made modest incomes, largely through contract and other arrangements with the *fazendeiros*. Farming was inefficient, because of primitive methods and lack of motive for innovation: among the great estate owners partly because of a traditional lack of interest in technical matters; among the masses, a lack of actual or perceived opportunity.

The export economy offered the main hope of profit, as the upper class perceived. Such profits were the chief source of investment capital, since foreign funds were limited by lack of enthusiasm abroad about Brazil's prospects. Unfortunately, the export economy was depressed, with cotton and rice markets captured by the United States and sugar by Cuba. Furthermore, the prices of Brazilian exports trended downward, while industrial import prices stayed up. The value of Brazil's exports in 1800–1850 grew on the average less than 1 percent a year, considerably less than population growth. Total export values were only about £4 to £6 million a year in that period, not

---

[9] See Chapter 21, Section c.

enough to exert important pressure for economic change in Brazil. Little change came before the 1840s and the greatest growth came after mid-century.

In 1849–1856 export value more than doubled. By 1866 the value of exports was some $150 million; by 1880, $220 million; in 1887, more than $300 million. Even though the dollar then represented much more purchasing power than it does now, the magnitudes even in the 1880s merely put Brazil on the threshold of important export income. Before 1860 the value of imports exceeded exports, and Brazil had to ship out funds in compensation.

Sugar exports, depressed in much of the late eighteenth century and revived during the great wars of 1792–1815, lost out to more efficient producers thereafter. The Brazilian industry was technologically backward. Cotton had even greater difficulty with international competition, except for a brief revival when United States shipments were interrupted by the Civil War there. Southern Brazil's cattle business was disrupted by its own civil war. By far the most important export growth was in coffee. In the 1820s it was the third export, after sugar and cotton; in the 1830s coffee became the leader. It was at first concentrated in the province of Rio de Janeiro, but by 1840 São Paulo was the biggest producer. Coffee development shifted the economic balance strongly toward the south, in turn creating divergencies of view and political ambition between southern men of property and the old aristocracy of the north, which was entrenched in political power. Although this process was well under way before the end of the empire, its greatest results came later, under the republic. Another result of the rise of coffee culture was to bolster the influence of *latifundismo* and monoculture and emphasize commercial export agriculture. That made for neglect of locally consumed food crops, either on the great *fazendas* or in smaller holdings. The worst form that neglect took was failure to attend to efficient systems of cultivation.

The dominant political class had little interest in diversification. Industrial, commercial, and financial pursuits remained feeble and heavily tied to the agricultural export sector, especially for investment capital. Privileges granted the British were not the chief reason for the lack of industrial growth. Markets were small in Brazil. Only the roughest homemade wares could compete with imports. The superior industrial development of the United States was due to larger internal markets, a greater interest in business by people with capital, and great profits from exports of agricultural commodities. Brazilian coffee production, after mid-century, was a major factor in demanding and financing the railways. It also helped expand manufacturing in the towns and paid for luxury items for the new urban rich and middle class. The coffee planter, too, experimented with European immigrant labor, while it was the sugar *fazendeiro* who clung to black slavery, although many coffee growers also kept slaves until abolition. The agricultural export sector would not, however, support strong measures to promote manufacturing. Protective measures were feeble under the empire, and applied to a few industries rather than to the sector in general.

Pedro II thought that Brazil should concentrate on agricultural and pastoral activity. He was not sympathetic toward the Baron of Mauá, the most prominent Brazilian entrepreneur in the later decades of the empire. Mauá's career in commerce, banking, shipping, and manufacturing certainly showed response to new opportunities, which he carried to bankruptcy. However, even if many more of Mauá's stamp had appeared and worked more cautiously, the economy probably would not have been altered much more rapidly. Other Brazilian entrepreneurs did appear, although much industry was owned and worked by foreigners. The economy did change some. Economic and political conditions would permit no more.

The cotton textile industry was the earliest manufacturing enterprise of consequence in Brazil, as in much of Latin America, and factories with textile machinery went up in a few places.

There was a sizable internal market for cheap cloth. The number of cotton mills increased from eleven in 1865 to forty-nine in 1885, but the big textile growth came thereafter. By 1889 the manufacture of such consumer goods as hats, candles, soap, and cigars did add up to an interest that scarcely had existed at the beginning of the empire, and it clearly was going to grow more. A transition to a more diversified economy was taking place.

Improved transport began to have an effect after mid-century. The first regular steamship service to Europe began in the early 1850s. Coastal steamship service was useful to the country, and steamships helped consolidate Brazil's hold in Amazonia. Mauá's steamship company on the great river was bought out in 1874 by British interests, an action representative of the difficulties Brazilians experienced in entering the industrial age and of the impact of British capital in nineteenth-century Latin America. Brazilians operated a shipbuilding industry and carried much coastal and river traffic, but the lucrative international trade was controlled by foreign, especially British, interests.

The value of other innovations was also clear to Brazilians, but the country could not afford to introduce them rapidly itself or provide much of a market for foreign investors in such systems. Early efforts were made to use telegraph and cable communications, but progress was slow. The first cable to Europe was finished in 1874. In 1889 Brazil had only about 11,000 miles of telegraph lines, valuable for governmental, personal, and business purposes, but far from adequate for so large a country. The same was true of road transport. The old dirt tracks did well enough for mules and carts, and paved surfaces were expensive. A few miles of macadam paving were laid down with the aid of imported steamrollers, beginning in the 1850s.

Although railroad building also began in the 1850s, there were fewer than 700 miles of track in 1870. About 1,400 miles were laid down in the 1870s, but the total in the country at the end of the empire was only 5,600 miles. Difficult topography created construction and financial difficulties. From Santos to the interior plateau of São Paulo, where coffee culture was growing, was a climb of 3,000 feet. This line was typical of railway construction in much of Latin America in the nineteenth century, running from a port into an area that supplied goods to it, either for local use or for export and bringing back imports. There was no economic incentive for building lateral lines connecting areas of Brazil in the interior; railways, like so much else, were tied to the international trading system, a part of Brazil's economic colonialism.

Commercial and financial activity were stimulated by export growth; there was even a notable quickening in the 1840s. Much of this activity was in the hands of foreigners. Banking was feeble until late in the empire. The Bank of Brazil that Regent João had created in the late colonial period (1808) and then looted on his departure for Portugal in 1821 was liquidated by the Brazilian legislature in 1829. For years thereafter there was no bank in the country. Credit was advanced for local purposes by *fazendeiros* and merchants. The few banks that were established by mid-century trebled in 1851–1858 as the economy improved. They often were badly run, however, and they sometimes abused their right of issuing paper money. After mid-century the flow of foreign capital to Brazil increased, and foreigners formed new banks and stock companies for commercial and industrial enterprise. The first foreign bank (the London and Brazilian) was established at Rio de Janeiro in 1862.

The economy in the second half of the imperial period was much more dynamic than in the first. Although change was spotty, confined to a few areas and a minority of the population, and the annual rate of innovation and growth was still not spectacular, the cumulative effects were sizable. There were productive forces and political interests in 1889 undreamed of in 1822. In the early years of the republic after 1889 economic development would accelerate appreciably, with ancillary effects on social institutions generally.

e. Maturity of Pedro II's Regime, 1850s–1889

The electoral system explains politics and government under Pedro II better than the publicized maneuvers of ministries. A few *fazendeiros* dominated elections. In mid-century they and their families totaled some 400,000 persons, on the order of 5 percent of the national population. A small income test for voting kept the franchise from most Brazilians. Even following the 1881 election reforms only some 142,000 citizens qualified as voters in a population of about 14 million. Many other things favored control by these few families: the dependence of others on them for economic and psychological reasons; tradition; their determination to rule; the passivity of the general population; the bad state of communications; and the dependence of the emperor on them to uphold and administer the realm, believing the common person not ready to play a role in the process. Finally, the local election committees were controlled and corrupted by the national government, with the general agreement of the local *fazendeiros*.

The local unit was the *município*, similar to a county in that it had a *sede* (seat), other towns, and countryside. The electoral committee in the *município* supervised the polls, the ballot counting, and announcement of the result. The committee was controlled by the *fazendeiro* faction then holding the ministry in Rio de Janeiro. Electors even gave blank ballots to the president of the province, who filled in the names. The system was backed with police and military force, so that the ministry faction could never lose. If the system did not produce the proper result, the minister of empire, who had jurisdiction over the presidents of provinces, could declare the election invalid and order a new one. Whatever *fazendeiro* group—Liberal or Conservative—at the *município* level was in control of the national government supported such moves; and the outs protested but basically approved the system.

After all, it faithfully represented the society of privilege. Ins and outs were of like mind on such fundamentals as taxation and social con-

trol. That control was preserved, as it always had been, with both economic and social coercion and with physical force and threats. *Fazendeiros* were accustomed from colonial times to raising private armies to chase slaves, guard against rebellion, or engage in feuds; and to officering the militia. In the early 1830s Minister of Justice Feijó created a national guard to control disorders, because the national army was unreliable. That unreliability was partly due to a price inflation that especially hit urban populations and was reflected in rebellions of army garrisons in the towns. The countryside was less affected by price changes. The government passed out commissions in the guard to its supporters.

At this time many an estate owner became a *coronel*, and the term *coroneis* (colonels) came to have political meaning in the provinces. In fact, the system merely sanctioned the long-time practice of *fazendeiros* in dominating their areas by force when necessary. The soldiers in the militia served not because of a rule issuing from Rio de Janeiro, but because in the isolated countryside nearly everyone was the client of a local magnate. It was usual, in fact, for two factions to compete with armed force for control of an area. Local rule by factions of magnates, often with actual or threatened violence, was not changed by Independence, nor by the shift from monarchy to republic in 1889. It would yield more to railways and other economic and technological change and to the growth of a new nationalist sentiment, notably in the national army, in later years, than to legislative debate. In the meantime, *coroneis*, provincial political bosses, in many ways set limits to what could be done in Brazil under the empire and in the first decades of the republic.

Both Conservatives and Liberals in the *fazendeiro* class, some of whom lived in town a good part of the time, were determined to preserve the union of the provinces, fearing the disunion and republicanism of Spanish America. The last violent move to gain local autonomy occurred in 1848; thereafter *fazendeiro* unionism was not threatened. Generally, these gentlemen leaders of government were in public life not for direct material gain, but for prestige, opportunity to serve and direct, excitement, and joy of power. The Liberals were in general for subordination of the executive to the legislature, for moderate autonomy for the provinces, and for progressive social and economic measures; the Conservatives for less of those things. There was little, in fact, that either group wanted to change. Proclamations on such things seldom meant much in practice, and the real contest was for office. These representatives of the landed upper class did not encounter much antagonism from urban groups until the last years of the empire, when its appearance marked an increase of pressures for modernization. The upper-class orientation of legislators and ministries was reflected in the press; there really was no debate about the unknown views of the popular classes.

Pedro used his great powers to alternate the factions in power, believing that the ability of a ministry to corrupt the electoral process was such that the "moderating power" given him by the Constitution must be used to enforce an alternation of views and men. Eleven times he appointed a new ministry and dissolved the deputies, often without any issue being involved except his belief in rotation. A new ministry saw to election of deputies of its own political coloration. Often the new ministers did not have seats in the Assembly at the time of the appointment, but in 1840–1881 only one minister was defeated for election while in office, which suggests the stranglehold of the ministry on elections. The ministry, in turn, was determined by Pedro, except for the two elections following an electoral reform in 1881, which is discussed later. Political leaders who were ousted naturally found this practice difficult to bear and railed against it; on the other hand, they were pleased with such action when it brought them back to power and unwilling to reform the local electoral system and thus remove Pedro's chief justification for so using his power. In fact, if there had not been an emperor with a moderating power permitting him to enforce rotation in office, Brazil might

have had the same tendency toward perpetuation of groups in power that marked the contemporary political scene in Spanish America, and armed revolts would have been necessary to break the pattern.

The Council of Ministers and the Senate were the chief bulwarks of the imperial power and generally resistant to change. The emperor appointed senators for life, generally men who agreed with him, though usually from the party controlling the ministry. The Senate's aloofness and conservatism were expressed in its nickname of Siberia. The council, chosen by the emperor, generally had ten members. He worked closely with it, and it nearly always was quite conservative. Both these centers of imperial power figured in a quarrel between Pedro and the Liberals in 1868, with the latter calling for an elective Senate with limited powers and transfer of the emperor's moderating power to the council. There is no doubt that the Liberals wanted to increase the powers of the legislature at the expense of the executive; there is much doubt whether that would have altered legislation much.

The executive had available the army, militia, and police forces, although their loyalties were often to local rather than national leaders. The emperor could create nonhereditary nobles, and that reward did something to increase the loyalty to the system of the 1,000 or so men thus honored. Court life was not ostentatious, since Pedro had no taste in that direction. Once a week he held an audience for the public, and even poor Indians and blacks came to present petitions. Another political aspect of Pedro's admirable character was his refusal to take offense at criticism, even at republican cries for an end to the monarchy.

Government financial resources were feeble before mid-century, so it was fortunate that government was conceived as performing few functions: foreign relations, internal order, and a very little economic or social development or regulation. Most expenditure went for internal order, the heavy expenditures of the Cisplatine War of the 1820s and the bigger cost of the Paraguayan War of the 1860s, and for the bureaucracy, which was swollen beyond the needs of the government by the imperative demands for salaries for the families, friends, and hangers-on of politicians. The financial ingenuity of imperial statesmen was modestly exercised by demands for port works and railways, but by little else of an economic nature. There were some small costs for education. Foreign affairs were not costly and, aside from the two wars, not very important. Brazil was not being menaced from outside, was in no condition or mood to try menacing anyone else, and had more than enough to occupy it internally.

The fiscal machinery of the early empire was so simple that there was little choice but to depend on customs duties. In the 1820s the government had to resort to foreign loans, and especially to the issuance of paper currency, whose volume more than doubled by 1830. For this and other reasons the international exchange value of the *milreis* declined, raising the cost of imports. Inflation was felt mostly by the urban population, including small tradesmen, public employees, clerks, and military men. The *fazendeiros* and their dependents were relatively little affected by the increase in import prices, and the decline in the value of the *milreis* made selling their exports easier. Other public revenues were mostly state levies on exports, and especially indirect national taxes, which bore heavily on the urban poor and middle class. The great estate owners permitted levies on exports as preferable to the likely alternatives. Finding other sources of revenue was difficult. In any event, the *fazendeiros* did not want to increase government activity or revenues much. The cost of collecting taxes in the interior was prohibitive. One tax gatherer sent to collect duty on hides in the *sertão* was sewn into a hide, with his head protruding, and shipped to the emperor with an impudent message. External loans were increased in 1831–1889 from £5 million to about £30 million, not an enormous sum, but in the state of Brazil's finances enough to make servicing it difficult. Central government revenues were about stationary in 1829–1843,

then improved as the population and economy grew in mid-century and thereafter. By 1888 they were nearly ten times what they had been in 1840, so government finance was moving in some sort of rhythm with the expansion of needs and demands.

Two events in the 1860s had a deep influence on politics. The first was that the quickening economy and the development of people of new outlook in the cities played a role in a Liberal victory in the election of 1860. This current of change ran through the rest of the history of the empire. It had little more than begun, however, when politics became dominated by the long, costly, and controversial Paraguayan War (1865–1870). One cause of the war was a demand by Brazilians for damages due to the chronic disorder in Uruguay. Such reparations became a political issue in Rio de Janeiro, so the government made demands on Uruguay. When Uruguay refused, Brazil decided to use troops, even though dictator López of Paraguay had warned that such action would upset the balance of power in the Plata. López had some reason to fear the territorial and commercial ambitions of his large neighbors, but he was also spoiling to use his swollen army on a career of conquest. When Brazil invaded Uruguay, López invaded Brazil and Argentina, and the war of Paraguay against Argentina, Brazil, and Uruguay began. Brazil could not afford a war but was driven by considerations of pride and political prestige, and a secret agreement with Argentina to partition Paraguay, which became public before the end of the war, and further divided Brazilian opinion on the conflict.[10]

Paraguayan forces were soon pushed out of Uruguay, and the war became a brutal siege and search-and-destroy operation against the entire population of Paraguay. When Humaitá, the Paraguayan fortress on the Paraguay River at a strategic point just north of its confluence with the Paraná, finally fell in July 1868 and Asunción

---

[10] See Chapter 24, Section b, for a discussion of Argentina and the war.

was taken, the war seemed virtually ended. López, however, got together more women, children, and graybeards, who continued the nation's heroic, astonishing, and suicidal resistance. It was difficult for Brazilians to be proud of the willingness of the allied forces to exterminate a good part of the population of little Paraguay or the little skill they showed in doing so. Brazil paid heavily with 50,000 dead, great expenditures, and much political acrimony. Ultimately, the most disturbing result of the war for Brazil was its stimulation of military esprit de corps, which finally helped induce a military interest in intervention in public affairs.

Although church issues seldom were important in Brazilian politics, Pedro suffered one notable series of controversies. It arose not because the church in Brazil was militant or the populace very pious. There was a generally relaxed attitude on the part of churchmen and faithful. Pedro, though scarcely a believer, went to mass and was not anticlerical. The Constitution was liberal for its time, permitting religious freedom although Roman Catholicism was the official faith. There were no conflicts pending with the church when, in 1864, Pedro refused, as was his constitutional right, to approve a papal encyclical forbidding Catholic membership in the Masonic order. The Masons in Brazil consisted of upper-class Catholics—even Pedro was a member—who engaged in charitable works and had some liberal ideas.[11] The Masons in Brazil were not as militant as some Masonic groups in Europe. The 1864 encyclical went unenforced in Brazil, without much comment; then in 1871 a priest delivered a Masonic-flavored sermon on the emancipation of slaves. The bishop of Rio de Janeiro disciplined him and ordered him to leave the Masonic order, but the priest refused, stating that the encyclical was not valid in Brazil. The bishop of Pernambuco denounced Masonry and the crown's right

of patronage, which was part of the Constitution. He also tried to purge Masons from religious brotherhoods (*irmandades*), which had a long history among laymen in Brazil. Other prominent churchmen got involved. In 1872 the Masonic lodges of Rio de Janeiro called all Masons to oppose the Brazilian episcopate. They were urged on by the viscount of Rio Branco, who was prime minister as well as grand master of the Masonic order in Brazil. It became a question of the government of Brazil against the church. Pedro II upheld regalism. A mission was sent to Rome. There was intense discussion all over Brazil. The government in 1875 granted amnesty to clerics it had imprisoned. Both supporters and opponents of the government actions thought that the crown had been weak. The dispute suggested the pent-up fury that discussion of the abolition of slavery could arouse in a Brazil that usually seemed politically placid.

f. Abolition and Republicanism

Abolition and republicanism came more and more to shape political life in Brazil, together with the economic changes that were helping destroy slavery and undermine support for the empire. Republicans and the antislavery movement both existed at Independence in 1822, but neither was of much consequence before the 1870s. Republicanism was a small current, its fate bound up with the growth of the antislavery campaign. The slavery question scarcely arose for many years after 1822, although a few people thought slavery dangerous, and some feeble efforts were made to send blacks to Africa. Much more important for decades was the slave-trade issue. *Fazendeiros* were determined to import more Africans, even though the treaty of 1826 with Britain required an end to the trade and a Brazilian law of 1831 so asserted. The law was massively disobeyed, and the *tumbeiros* (coffins) still brought blacks from Africa. A law of 1837 to improve enforcement was also ineffective. The British navy did what it could to intercept the traffic, making use of treaty right to search ships,

---

11 Masons had been prominent in the movement for Independence. Pedro I became a member in 1822. In the early empire even priests were members. After the European republican revolutions of 1848, papal objections to the Masons increased everywhere.

even in Brazilian waters, and to use joint Brazilian-British admiralty courts to try cases. This infringement of Brazil's sovereignty rankled. The British treaty ran out in 1845, but the British continued to act unilaterally,[12] with the result that Brazilian tempers rose, although they managed to increase imports of slaves, in anticipation of stoppage. More than 60,000 blacks were brought from Africa to Brazil in 1848 alone. Brazilian statesmen decided, however, that the trade would have to be ended. A Conservative ministry in 1850 put through a number of measures that soon killed off the traffic.

Even before the Civil War of 1861–1865 ended slavery in the United States, some Brazilians recognized that the institution was an anachronism. Although slavery had been abolished in the independent Spanish American states, in 1860 about half the Brazilian population was still slave. Brazil received criticism and sneers from all sides. Pedro II, a cultivated and humane man, knew this, and in the later 1860s urged action. All statesmen realized that nothing could be done rapidly, because the slave owners and their allies were too influential. By 1871, however, enough opinion had been mobilized, including some Conservatives, so that the Rio Branco Law of the Free Womb could be passed. After that, children born of slave mothers were free, although at the age of eight the former master could elect the labor of the child to age twenty-one or a payment from the government. This solution with compensation was acceptable to slaveholders. It meant, of course, that emancipation might be a long-drawn-out process, and, in fact, nearly all slave owners elected to use the services of children to age twenty-one.

Some abolitionists found the Rio Branco Law unacceptable, and it remained an issue before the government and the public; eventually it would bring down the empire. Demands for political change alone would not have brought a

crisis so soon. But the two issues tended to be linked. The Liberals, in the aftermath of their dismissal by Pedro in the late 1860s, issued a manifesto calling for reduction of executive authority—including abolition of the moderating power—and an end to slavery. The issue was given increased and constant prominence from 1878, when Joaquim Nabuco entered the Chamber of Deputies. An aristocrat and a cultivated and sensitive man, Nabuco saw slavery as an issue of conscience. When he found that the chamber would not pass legislation to end slavery more rapidly, he founded the Brazilian Antislavery Society and turned to extensive publicity, partly in the pages of *O Abolicionista*. The prominent abolitionists were people of conviction, but supporters of the reform to some extent followed economic interest. In Rio Grande do Sul, where slavery was relatively weak, the reform met little obstacle, but in areas that depended heavily on slavery, agricultural societies were formed to counteract the emancipation movement.

Nabuco had gone to the chamber in 1878 on a tide of Liberal electoral victory, which meant that Pedro had decided on another alternation of party. But Liberals had come to object to Pedro's use of his power. They pursued reform by the Saraiva Law of 1881, which provided direct elections in place of voting for electors who then chose the deputies. The indirect method was often adopted in Latin American countries for the purpose of reducing popular influence in politics and government. Popular influence in Brazil to 1881 had been drastically confined, in any case, by property qualifications, and the Saraiva Law also reduced these. It enfranchised naturalized citizens, non-Catholics, and freedmen, thus increasing the size of the electorate to admit what might be called some of the new middle class, but still leaving most men outside the voting pale, both by law and by their economic and social subordination. In this oligarchic society a paltry 142,000 voters acted for the 14 million inhabitants of Brazil. An electorate so small made it or the ballots relatively easy to manipulate, and a group so select on economic

---

[12] The Aberdeen slave-trade bill of 1845 gave British admiralty courts authority to deal with slaving cases in ways that flagrantly violated Brazilian sovereignty.

and social bases inevitably had little interest in the concerns of the bulk of the citizenry. The law also provided that both parties were to supervise elections and contained some other provisions to make the process fairer. Conservatives opposed the 1881 reform. Pedro favored it because he hoped it would appease some of the growing criticism of the entire system by discontented elements.

In the 1880s all the forces that were to destroy the empire came together, in one way or another, on the slavery issue. They were not enough, however. Nabuco was defeated for the legislature in 1882 because of his abolitionist activity. Political reformers knew that they had to destroy the dominance of the *fazendeiros*. For a short time the Saraiva Law had been applied fairly; then politicians had returned to the system of manipulation and corruption. Republicans were a clamorous minority of the politically active population. In the first decades of the empire they had their chief influence through support of "federalism," which meant dilution of the emperor's powers in favor of the provinces and the Chamber of Deputies. In 1870 they founded a Republican party and began to advocate both the abolition of the monarchy and many of the reforms the Liberal supporters of more limited monarchy wanted. A Republican manifesto in 1873 was signed by Prudente de Morais and Campos Sales, both later president. Republicans managed to elect federal deputies in 1876, but could not develop significant strength. They had some support among the new business elements and the intellectual class. Pedro bore the Republicans no ill will; tolerance was one of his engaging traits. The function of the minority Republicans was in propagandizing their alternative form of government for use when other groups had turned against the monarchy.

The slavery issue was a matter of intense national concern; republicanism was not. As time went on, more and more Liberals who wanted to reduce the emperor's powers joined the abolitionist movement as a way of damaging the *fazendeiros* who supported the royal prerogative.

Increasingly opinion veered toward immediate emancipation without compensation. As time went on there were fewer landowners strongly tied to slavery, partly because immigrant labor proved preferable on coffee *fazendas*. Urban areas generally supported abolition. By the mid-1880s it was clear that speedier emancipation of some sort probably could not be avoided much longer, but opponents in the Chamber of Deputies kept delaying it by offering compromise measures. Their tactics were the more useless because slavery was being eradicated on a provincial basis. In 1884 the provinces of Ceará and Amazonas abolished slavery, and municipalities in Rio Grande do Sul did the same. Slaves fled to free provinces. Furthermore, the old methods of preventing slave flight were breaking down. Even within the slave provinces bondsmen were roaming about and the machinery to return them to their masters was falling apart. There was popular interference with pursuit of runaways. The army asked to be relieved of the duty of chasing fugitive slaves. Nabuco in Parliament in 1887 appealed to the army to refuse to capture slaves. Young naval cadets were reprimanded for cheering Nabuco. Some big users of labor already had shifted to European immigrants under conditions of compensation that made them cheaper than slaves.[13]

In 1884 the Liberal party adopted abolition, an important gain for that goal. In the same year Nabuco ran again, as a Liberal, for the national legislature from his home province of Pernambuco, an old northeastern slave area, and on the sole issue of abolition. The campaign raised great excitement, and when the results favored his Conservative opponent, a mob reacted murderously against the election officials for suspected fraud. In a new election Nabuco won. Then the national legislature refused to accept that result,

---

[13] Violence by slaves and sympathizers made the system less attractive. In São Paulo immigrants served the *fazendeiros* better than slaves, and the slave population there fell from 28 to 19 percent of the population in 1854–1873.

but the Liberals soon elected Nabuco from another district. The abolition cause was creating unprecedented interest in public affairs. Nabuco's picture appeared on cigar and beer labels. But the Conservatives in 1886 abandoned the Saraiva free-election law and used the old methods to defeat Liberals, including Nabuco, who turned back then to reliance on propaganda.

The slave system that was the object of these efforts was not notably more kindly than in the United States,[14] except that manumission was somewhat easier in Brazil. The treatment of black slaves was harsh in both areas in law and practice in the nineteenth century: in both, the law defined the slave as a person and a thing; in both, the church gave little comfort to the black slave; in both, slaves were abused in many ways, and their lives were short and brutish. Possibly slaves were physically better treated in the United States in the nineteenth century than in Brazil, although slavery was an inhuman institution everywhere in America. The United States depended on slave breeding,[15] which required some care of slaves, whereas Brazil depended heavily on imports until the early 1850s. The imbalance of sexes among the Brazilian slave population caused sexual deprivation. Some other specific forms of mistreatment in Brazil were not duplicated in the United States.[16]

There was, however, an important difference between the two countries. Although *slaves* were feared in both, *blacks* were feared in the United States but not in Brazil. The difference was evident to some extent in colonial times, but it became more marked in the nineteenth century.

North Americans and Brazilians were equally fearful of slave revolts, although their incidence was not high in either area. North Americans were much more fearful, however, than Brazilians of the possible actions of free blacks and mulattoes. In the North American South there was more fear that free blacks and mulattoes would conspire with slaves. In neither area, in fact, did much of that occur. In Anglo-America there was more fear of sexual and economic activity by freedmen. Legal or attitudinal objections to miscegenation scarcely existed in Brazil. Significant also is the fact that in nineteenth-century Brazil a high proportion (possibly two-thirds in Bahia) of overseers, slave catchers, and slave dealers were black or mulatto.

In Brazil there was much less justification of slavery on grounds of an asserted biological inferiority of the black race. A French visitor in 1862 noted this difference in strong language, declaring that North Americans felt they had "to invent for the Negro a new original sin." The willingness of Brazilians to manumit slaves much more freely than in the United States was the result of not fearing free blacks in great numbers. There was little fear in Brazil of being "overwhelmed" by blacks partly because the poor white group, so strongly anti-Negro in the United States, was much smaller proportionately in Brazil. Manumission in Brazil was not, however, unlimited. Until 1871 there was no law compelling the master to permit the slave to buy freedom. But in Brazil there were none of the impediments to manumission that became embodied in state law in the United States, especially after 1830. There was not in Brazil, for example, anything like the requirement in the South of the United States that emancipated slaves remove to other states. To be sure, Brazilian manumission practice was not all designed to aid blacks. Some slaves were freed when they became ill, maimed, or old, to relieve the masters of the burden of their care. The number of slaves manumitted was, however, too large to make that an important reason. Free blacks and mulattoes were a higher proportion of those racial

---

[14] See Chapter 9 for a comparison of the English- and Portuguese-American systems in the colonial period.

[15] The United States was unique in history anywhere (including the ancient world) in its great reliance in the nineteenth century on slave breeding. In Brazil the internal slave trade did increase in the mid-nineteenth century when the slave trade from Africa finally was ended, and that resulted in considerable disruption of families in Brazil.

[16] For example, in Brazil the use of females as prostitutes and the use of iron or tin masks, usually to prevent the eating of dirt or the use of liquor.

groups in Brazil than in the United States at the end of the colonial period, and in the last years of slavery in the 1880s in Brazil, as compared with the 1850s in the United States. Even by 1872 there were in Brazil more than twice as many free blacks and mulattoes as slaves.

The reasons for these differences are much debated. They are said to lie in religion, general cultural attitudes (based on a number of supposed causative factors), and the experience of the Portuguese in the Middle Ages and early modern times with Muslims and black Africans. They are also said to stem from the fact that in the South of the United States there was a numerous nonaristocratic white population willing to grow food and perform artisan tasks, whereas in Portuguese America the lack of such a class and an aversion for manual labor made the use of free blacks and mulattoes more of an economic necessity. Distaste for the blacks on the part of poor and middle-class whites in the United States South also provided—for whatever reasons—a social dimension not found in Brazil. Even more difficult of solution is the problem of *how much* racial prejudice did exist in Brazil. It was less than in the United States, but how much less?

g. The Military

The army in the early years of the empire was small and had a bad reputation for boisterous behavior and insubordination. The national guard was created in part to act against army indiscipline. The performance and reputation of the army improved only slightly in mid-century. It remained small, without prestige. At the beginning of the Paraguayan War in 1865 it had only 15,000 men. The army played virtually no role in public affairs, and the imperial government was determined to keep the military subordinate to civil authority. Pedro II increasingly resisted having military officers as ministers of war, and between 1865 and 1889 only nine of thirty-eight were military men.

The Paraguayan War stimulated some changes in military attitudes that gradually became important. The war increased the size of the army, and reduction thereafter met military complaint. The fighting created among officers an increased awareness of public policy as it affected the prosecution of the difficult war, the public reputation of the military, the ability of officers to influence policy that affected them, and the general strength of the nation as reflected in its military establishment. The strains of witnessing death and disaster and the exhilaration of participating in victory increased the esprit de corps of officers, who hitherto had not engaged in events of such magnitude. In the decade of the 1870s the army remained loyal to the monarchy, but there was dissatisfaction with military expenditures and with Pedro's general lack of enthusiasm for the military institution.[17] Officers after the war did become somewhat more inclined to debate policy but did not create a problem until 1879. The Military School was founded in 1874, and new officers received there a stronger indoctrination than before in the importance of their role in national affairs. What happened in 1879 and thereafter made it evident that something profoundly important was going on within the officers' corps.

Rumors about the government's intentions with regard to the military had been current for some years. They related to a dispute over the right of military officers to discuss public affairs or to organize for such discussions. They created enough of a problem so that regulations in 1859 and 1878 prohibited officers from dealing with service matters in the newspapers or from criticizing their superiors. Early in 1879 military officers met to condemn a parliamentary bill to reduce the military establishment. Some officers said that it was part of a move to abolish the

---

[17] The interference of the Duke of Caxias, ex-commander in Paraguay, in the political process in the latter days of the war brought charges of military intervention, but it was a personal intervention, and the next decade did not see it translated into a general tendency among military officers.

army and justification for revolution. The problem of military rights to public debate arose again in 1883 and in acute form in 1886. In 1886, in separate incidents, a colonel and a lieutenant-colonel criticized the minister of war to the press. They were disciplined by the minister and then received wide and vociferous support from fellow officers.

In February 1887 Marshal Deodoro da Fonseca, most popular officer in the army, wrote the emperor that the government was wrong on this issue, invoked the pride and dignity of the military, and warned of a "storm" that would arise if such "injustice" was not corrected. Army garrisons were secretly declaring their support of Deodoro. The government retreated. Soon thereafter in 1887 some officers founded the Clube Militar and named Deodoro its president. The club immediately rang to talk of military honor and political methods of ensuring it. This institution remains today at the heart of discussion among officers of their role in the affairs of the nation. By 1887 the republican movement was appealing to the new military interest in politics, partly because officers increasingly came from an urban and middle-class background that inclined them to favor innovation and modernization. The combination would quickly bring down the monarchy. But even without the republican issue, clearly the military was going to play a much broader role in public affairs unless a way could be found to curb it.

h. The Fall of the Empire

Republican efforts to subvert the military were not important until 1887, although as early as 1871 a few Republicans discussed use of the military to end the empire. Other Republicans, however, opposed a military role in public life. In the early 1880s some Republicans supported the military position in the controversy over the right to criticize the government. In the 1887 debate over that question, the Republican effort to incite the military against the monarchy became intense. Republicans could see that they could not by themselves bring down the monarchy. The disintegration of slavery obviously was weakening Conservative support of the monarchy, and correspondingly increasing Republican hopes and activity. A Republican newspaper in November 1888 declared that the military contained "the only ones who know how to behave with true and praiseworthy solidarity." At the same time some Republicans tried to dispose of the danger of military dictatorship by stating that it could not happen in a federal Republican regime, a view scarcely borne out by Spanish American experience. By this time Republicans had converted a minority of army officers (the navy was more aristocratic and conservative), but senior officers remained loyal to the empire.

One source of politicization of the army was the Military School, where by 1888 Lieutenant-Colonel Benjamin Constant Botelho de Magalhães had spent some years as an instructor, partly in the official technical subjects, partly in an unofficial curriculum of his own devising. The former emphasized the importance of scientific reason and technical training. It in turn reinforced Constant's unofficial teaching, which was to some extent based on the positivism of Auguste Comte, and preached the need for a more rational ordering of society, and the superior ability of technically trained military officers to accomplish that as compared with the merely politically oriented traditional statesmen of the empire. All over Latin America a minority of civilians and military officers were imbibing this scientific or technocratic or positivist attitude, which inclined some of them toward a new justification of elitism by the talented and trained. Constant also promoted republicanism and abolition.

The year 1888 saw a continuation of republican propaganda in general and the special effort to turn the military against the monarchy, a series of new clashes between the military and the civil government, and the abolition of slavery. By early 1888 slavery was disintegrating, and all that remained was to decide the manner of official interment. The Conservative ministry in

May presented a measure for emancipation without compensation. It was passed by the Senate and Chamber of Deputies. On May 13 the Princess Regent signed it for her absent father Pedro II.

With this, many slaveholders at least temporarily abandoned the monarchical system. Most of them did not become Republicans, but in their anger they lost enthusiasm for the monarchy. During 1888 and 1889 that was important because it deprived the monarchy of what always had been its chief prop. The church was neither powerful enough nor well enough disposed toward Pedro to try to save the monarchy. Rising commercial, industrial, and financial elements often thought a republic might be of use to them. Pedro as an individual had respect but little affection from his subjects and was ill and aging. There was no pleasure in the thought of his daughter as the next monarch, because of her sex, her rumored subservience to the church, and her French husband.

In 1888 two more substantial clashes between government and the military occurred. One case had to do with the right of the police in Rio de Janeiro to arrest a naval officer out of uniform. There were military protest meetings and street clashes between military and police personnel. The opposition press backed the navy, and the government backed down. Later in the year the military in São Paulo clashed with the police, whereupon the Military Club in Rio de Janeiro supported the army, and the government again backed down. The military were dictating to the civil government and getting away with it.

In 1889 plans to overthrow the government were being developed within the military. Some officers wanted a republic, some merely wanted a new ministry more favorable to the military point of view. Rui Barbosa, who would be one of the great exponents of civilian predominance in later years, in 1889 used the press to promote the notion that the government was trying to weaken the military! This sort of activity by civilian politicians to incite the military to political action was a major contributing element to

the growth of such activity, just as it was in Argentina, as has been noted.

Benjamin Constant played a key role in persuading senior officers to overthrow the empire. He had spent years preparing for what proved to be the final crisis in 1889. The Military Club was a vehicle nicely suited to his aims, since in a secure atmosphere, in the capital of the country, it permitted him to influence important officers and to receive from them some sort of mandate to act in their name. At the Military Club on November 9, 1889, a group of officers instructed him to get a satisfactory agreement from the government or take drastic action. The latter was what he wanted. Although Constant met in the next few days with a number of officers and a few civilians, his critical conversations were with Marshal Deodoro, who finally accepted the thesis that the government was trying to destroy the army. It is difficult to believe that Deodoro was not also influenced by the evidence that his fellow officers were inclining to that belief and by the knowledge that his own influence depended on not departing too far from them. On November 14–15 various military forces moved against the government: the palace guards abandoned their posts; Marshal Floriano Peixoto, soon to be president of Brazil, refused the prime minister's order to attack military rebels. Deodoro on November 15 proclaimed a republic, possibly influenced in part by one of the many rumors that had fueled the entire movement— in this case one to the effect that an old enemy of Deodoro's would be made prime minister by the emperor.

The coup d'etat was purely military. It surprised nearly everyone, including Pedro II, who was at the nearby resort of Petrópolis. No one fought to preserve the empire or to protest military seizure of power. The tiny minority of politically active citizens was divided, without experience of coups d'etat and lacking much affection for Pedro II or the political machinery he had manipulated to prevent the complete domination of the oligarchy. The military of Brazil in 1889 turned out to be at the beginning of a long history—extending to our own day—of intervention in the political process. The monarchical institution had preserved the territorial heritage of Portuguese America; it had for some decades spared the country the considerable waste and violence that occurred in Spanish America as the result of efforts at violent change in government; it had not created conditions that would permanently ensure broad political participation and constitutional rule. What republican institutions could do about social, economic, and political modernization remained to be seen.

26 Mexico: The Struggle for Reform Until the 1880s

Everything went badly in Mexico. Not that reformers and modernizers were lacking, but they were frustrated by the great strength of *hacendados*, church, and army in conservative combination, undiluted by the new interests created by economic growth in Argentina and Brazil. Mexico suffered in extreme form all the bitter warfare between liberals and conservatives, so that political stability came later than in Argentina and Brazil, and then only on the equivocal basis of the long-term *caudillismo* of Porfirio Díaz. Important Mexican export growth was not achieved until the 1890s, decades later than in Argentina and Brazil. In addition, Mexico suffered two major foreign invasions, one from the United States, the other when conservatives invited French troops to win for their party what it could not gain for itself. Although Mexico suffered a terrible purging, some leaders remained faithful to a dream of unity and progress. One was a new man, unthinkable in the colonial society, the Zapotec Indian Benito Juárez, who came out of the mountains of Oaxaca to become the supreme figure of Mexican history, as revered as that other Indian hero, Cuauhtémoc, who tried to defend Tenochtitlán against the Spanish conquerors in the sixteenth century. Like the liberal cause, Juárez often was defeated, never vanquished. Frustrated in his larger aims during his lifetime, Juárez' spirit reemerged triumphant in the Great Revolution of the twentieth century.

a. The Political Culture

Mexico was as large as western and central Europe. The bulk of the population lived in the pleasant valleys of central Mexico, at elevations of 5,000 to 8,000 feet, and only small settlements existed in the far north, as far as San Francisco, Santa Fe, and San Antonio. It had been the largest, most populous, and richest realm of Spanish America, with a numerous well-to-do class of officials, ecclesiastics, hacienda owners, merchants, and mine owners. The creoles of this class, as in all Spanish America, wished to extend their authority, so when Napoleon invaded Spain in 1808, the town council of Mexico City favored local control of affairs until a legitimate king returned to Spain. The Spanish party in Mexico prevented such an innovation. A minority of creoles in various places then turned to conspiracy, but Hidalgo's class and race war in 1810–1811 drove most creoles into alliance with peninsular Spaniards.[1] Then in 1820 a liberal revolution in Spain made creoles consider Independence from Spain. This conservative movement for a

---

[1] See Chapter 19, Section d.

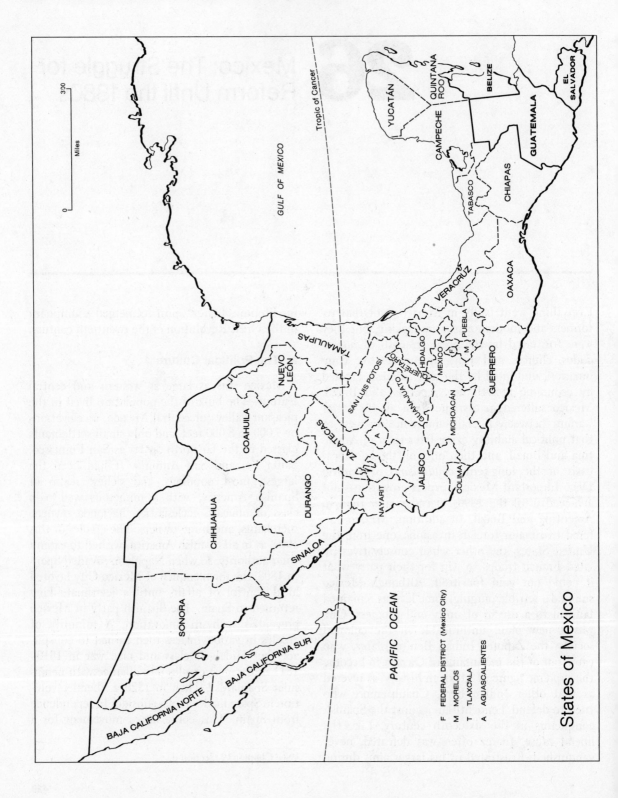

States of Mexico

F   FEDERAL DISTRICT (Mexico City)
M   MORELOS
T   TLAXCALA
A   AGUASCALIENTES

radical political change was managed in 1821 by creole Agustín Iturbide, with the support of a variety of liberal and conservative interests, including lower-class *guerrilleros* and some royalist military commanders. He even received the agreement of Viceroy O'Donojú to creation of an independent monarchy for Mexico, with Ferdinand VII promised first refusal of the post.

Spain did not accept that agreement of the summer of 1821, but by then Iturbide had so much support that in September he marched into Mexico City in the company of *guerrillero* leaders Vicente Guerrero and Guadalupe Victoria, to a hero's acclaim. It was all very human, all fuzzy hope and promise, with people grasping what seemed the best available solution in troubled times. It lasted no time at all, because differences of view and interest merely had been buttered over with proclamations and parades.

The political culture of independent Mexico was close to the model described in Chapter 23, without two variations present in Argentina and Brazil. In Mexico the hacienda system did not enjoy the export growth that affected the attitudes of great estate owners in Argentina and Brazil long before the 1880s, and the Mexican church was richer and stronger and more involved in public affairs.

Regionalism

The small educated and propertied minorities in Mexico had united to put down the Hidalgo revolt, but were divided on several issues. Economic conflict among the propertied was mainly on regional lines. *Hacendados* were often allied with merchants, both in business and in opposition to social change. Conflicts of agriculture and commerce with industry could not be great because the manufacturing interest that wanted protection was very small. Serious divisions in the socioeconomic elite occurred, however, when regions or states were pitted against each other, for economic or political reasons. Debate over tariff protection often involved regional interests. Some regional disputes came to extremes of fed-

eralist sentiment, civil war, even secessionism. Some regional or state *caudillos* were virtually independent, supported by their own armies. Considerable autonomy also existed at the municipal level,[2] where *caciques* or *jefes políticos*, supported by gangs, ran affairs with little interference. The huge and varied country was full of *patrias chicas*—little fatherlands.

Fragmentation was threatened not only by extreme federalists of the upper and middle classes but by anti-Mexican or antiwhite movements among Indians in areas where bringing government power to bear was difficult. Much of the northern frontier long was out of the control of Mexico City. Mexican filibusters joined Texans in schemes for secession. Far to the northwest the Yaquis rose in 1845–1846, and again late in the century. In far southern Mexico, the Zotzil Maya revolted in 1868 and were put down with difficulty. In the peninsula of Yucatán both upper-class federalism and lower-class rejection of any European rule kept the area often in turmoil and loosely attached to Mexico City.

Communications between Yucatán and central Mexico were difficult, and the ruling elite of Yucatán embraced federalism as the creed suitable to that fact and their ambition. A turn to centralism in the 1830s in Mexico City irked them, as did the end of protective tariffs, which hurt Campeche shipping and threatened Yucatecan sugar. In 1838–1840 a local revolt against centralism drove Mexican troops from Yucatán, and the Yucatecan upper class declared that the area would return to the republic only when federalism was restored. In 1842 Santa Anna sent an army from Mexico, and the Yucatecans defeated it.

Despite these actions, many upper-class Yucatecans doubted the wisdom of Independence. They offered to restore their allegiance and aid Mexico during the war with the United States that began in 1846. The offer came to naught

---

[2] The territorial influence of municipal officials in Mexico, as in all Latin America, extended far beyond the built-up urban area.

because the fear of the centuries—a class and race war—erupted in 1847. The class system was faithfully represented in the military in Yucatán. Officers of the militia were mostly of the upper class. The soldiers were Indians serving in straw hats, white cotton blouses and drawers to the calf, a belt for an ugly chopping machete and a drinking and eating gourd. Some had guns. In a skirmish between factions at the town of Valladolid in Yucatán, *indio* troops gave vent to their resentments with shouts of "Kill those who have shirts!", began an effort to exterminate Spaniards (whites), and raped and mutilated upper-class girls. The Caste War of Yucatán that followed was marked by atrocities on both sides. In the eastern part of Yucatán, to which the rebellion was confined, the lower class was restive because of labor and other changes due to new export agriculture (henequen, sugar), and because of old fury at civil taxes, church levies, forced labor on public works, and the debt peonage that prevented a man from changing residence or jobs without a certificate from his last employer.

The upper class faced financial ruin and possible death or exile. The terrible conflict left little thought for anything but fighting, and a phenomenal proportion of the men served in the field. Such issues as federalism were forgotten. The national government of Mexico could not help during the war with the United States, especially with the latter's navy blockading the coast. The Yucatecan government in despair offered Spain, Britain, and the United States political allegiance in return for aid in the Caste War. President Polk of the United States refused the territory and invoked the Monroe Doctrine to warn off European powers. The rebels after several years' fighting were driven into the deep forests. The worst was over by 1850, but the population of Yucatán had been reduced about 40 percent in four years.

A more dangerous regionalism, nearer the center of the country, was in Jalisco, northwest of the Valley of Mexico, where economic interests had conflicted with those of Mexico City even in colonial times. Jalisco had economic ties and ambitions in many northern states. It had ports on the Pacific and after Independence wished its own connection with the Atlantic, without the necessity of going through Mexico City and Veracruz. It resented the siphoning of money by taxes and other means to central Mexico. Federalism was an attractive doctrine for the leaders of Jalisco, centered at Guadalajara. Revolts and rumors of revolts were common there, including a notable effort in 1841 to resist the then strong centralist tide. The "Jalisco question" continued to worry governments in Mexico City during four decades thereafter. It was resolved partly because of subregionalism within the area of Guadalajara's ambition in the northwest, which Mexico City encouraged. The result was the creation of new states, partly taken from Jalisco—Sonora, Colima, Nayarit, Sinaloa—that drastically reduced Jalisco's influence. The quarrel came to a climax in the 1870s, when the *caudillo* Lozada used his troops in the name of liberalism to ask statehood for Nayarit. The national government (of the Liberal Lerdo de Tejada) supported Lozada, whereupon Jalisco, in 1874, rose against the fragmentation supported by Mexico City. Porfirio Díaz put down the rebellion and kept the area pacified thereafter.

Conservatives and Liberals

The politically active minority in Mexico quickly divided into Conservative and Liberal parties, on the basis of various mixtures of interest and doctrine. Although neither party was for much improvement in the political participation or socioeconomic condition of the lower class, both at times asked popular support: the Liberals by appeals to equality and justice against privilege; the Conservatives by calling for defense of the church and the faith against the godless. Neither party was well organized by present standards, and they had few funds; so not only their willingness but their ability to involve many persons was slight.

Liberals were of several types, mostly moderate. Liberalism was strong in provincial towns where opposition to the power of Mexico City found a natural home. Since Liberals opposed some of the old social privileges, they were attractive to men of the lower or lower middle classes who wished to improve their status. That led a Conservative to say of Liberals in the early 1830s that many were new to public affairs, and "unknown in good society," now required to "put on a dress coat . . . and gloves for the first time in their lives" to attend the opera. Liberals favored more freedom of speech and press, curbs on arbitrary arrest, relatively generous educational institutions, and what they considered enlightenment, progress, and modernization in general. They favored strong legislatures and fair elections. They seemed less liberal when they supported restrictions on voting rights and office holding, proscribed their enemies, and engineered coups d'etat. Some Liberals were for free economic enterprise and against state intervention in the economy, but others favored certain types of government aid. There was Liberal support for industrial protection, partly because it seemed a progressive activity compared with the colonial emphasis on mining, large-scale agriculture, and monopolistic commerce. There was a radical element in the Liberals, sometimes known as the *puros,* who stimulated Conservative fears. The reprisals of the latter drove moderate Liberals to extreme measures in retaliation, defense, or despair.

A notable exponent of liberalism was Luís Mora, who had a brief political career in the early 1830s, and thereafter was chiefly a publicist and literary figure. He favored eradication of the Spanish heritage of corporate privilege, especially the rights of church and military that gave them the protection of special courts and encouraged them to play dominant roles in public affairs. He favored confiscation of church property; an end to militarism; emphasis on science rather than religion; secular education for the masses— in short, that modernization then called progress, and against a social regime that he thought of as "feudal." Typically, however, Mora wanted full citizenship confined to property owners, who

he thought "as a rule alone have genuine civil virtues."

The Conservatives favored centralized government and an even more elitist approach. Many Conservatives favored modernization in terms of material progress, but differed from laissez-faire liberalism by wanting to achieve development by government action. Lucas Alamán (1792–1853) was a prominent exponent of their views, based on personal observation of the violence of the Hidalgo period and on detestation of social disorder. Alamán, trained as a mining engineer, was an admirer of British institutions and a notable historian. His conservatism was so blinding that he could condemn the influence of the Masonic lodges as invisible government, without fearing contradiction with his own preference for restricted access to decision making. As a member of the government of President Bustamante in 1832–1833, he displayed his willingness to use violent methods against the Liberal opposition, most notoriously in the execution of ex-President Guerrero. Alamán also believed in the importance of property rights and was interested in economic development, with strong participation by the state. He considered that the church was the only institution able to bind Mexicans together, and that the Spanish conquest of the Indians was the beginning of a civilizing process. Briefly back in government in the 1850s, Alamán's reactionary political views helped bring on the War of the Reform and the French Intervention.

The parties divided most bitterly over the church, which was a wealthy and influential interest group, with a comprehensive doctrinal position which supported the secular interests of the Conservatives and sometimes could be used to move the masses. Certain lines of conflict between Liberals and Conservatives over church issues were unavoidable, existing from the moment of Independence, but Mexicans then did not anticipate the bitterness that events would lend to such dispute. A considerable range of church-related disputes quickly evolved. Churchmen supported the Conservatives in so unspiritual a fashion that they drove Liberals to anti-clericalism.

The Military and the Government

The army was the group with the most political potential, so it was a focus of interest for both parties and for ambitious individuals who had no commitment to either. Military adventurers were encouraged by the weakness of other groups, by appeals from various interests for military aid, and by the small size of the politically active population. They also were encouraged by the poor economy, so that control of the public purse seemed the best road to fortune. The middle class, and notably lawyers, flocked to the bureaucracy and intrigued with military leaders to keep or install their factions at the public teat. The officers in the federal army were thoroughly politicized. Iturbide at Independence began the process of using military appointments as rewards and bribes; he could scarcely have avoided doing so, since he had little else to give, and officers so clearly were prepared to seize reward if it was not proffered.

The army was neither large nor efficient, so that its ability to control political affairs testified to social disorganization and apathy. It was top-heavy with officers. In Iturbide's day the Mexico City garrison had some 2,000 officers, 3,000 non-commissioned officers (NCOs), and 8,300 enlisted men, an early basis for calling an army with as many chiefs as Indians a "Mexican army." Many officers and NCOs were incompetent, badly educated, even illiterate. The force often changed drastically as *caudillos* raised irregular forces, led them to victory, and incorporated them into the federal army, while killing or expelling some of the former personnel. Another weakness was intermittent tension between white and mestizo or Indian officers.

The ranks were filled by pressing poor men into service, sometimes by raiding Indian villages and marching the men away in chains. The soldiers often were unpaid, and sometimes did their own foraging, partly because dishonest officers sold their rations. It was common for commanders to draw pay, rations, and equipment for men not on the rolls, pocketing the difference, with necessary tips to subordinates. The training of soldiers was sketchy, largely drill and elementary discipline. Often no arms or ammunition was available, and there was little instruction in their use. The progress of army units through the countryside—in peace or war—was enlivened by seizure of food, clothing, animals; and by accompanying crowds of wives and concubines, laden with pots and the boots and spare clothing of their men. Not only were the brutalized soldiers inclined to looting and rough treatment of the citizenry, but often the officers were unable or unwilling to restrain them. The booty and the excitement were, after all, the only compensation the men received.

The chief features of government were instability, irresponsibility, and lack of funds. In its first half century the Mexican republic averaged more than one chief executive a year. Governments shuttled in and out of office too rapidly to accomplish much, marked by ringing *pronunciamientos*, sharp constitutional debates, skirmishes at arms in town and country, proscriptions and vendettas and executions, and a shrieking absence of the spirit of compromise. Heads of finance seldom had time to do more than find their offices, aid in or resist the looting of public funds, and learn despair at the poverty of government resources. The expectation of imminent change in regime paralyzed initiative. Rebellion in states against governors mushroomed into national movements as leaders from other states rushed to call for a march on Mexico City. A nineteenth-century Mexican complained that such commotions were "incessant."

Much of the wealth of Mexico was difficult to tax for political or administrative reasons. The chief reliance was on import-export duties, which ran 80 to 90 percent of normal revenues. A foreign loan was first arranged in Britain in 1824. It gave Mexico less than 6 million pesos but saddled it with repayments of more than twice that. Loans thereafter also were on harsh terms.

In 1867 about 95 percent of the customs revenues were pledged to the repayment of debts. The condition of the country did not permit efficient collections. State and local governments, even individual officials, collected levies promiscuously. Smuggling cut the customs. So the government tried not only loans, but special taxes and downright confiscations, advances on taxes, refundings, paper currency, and other expedients.

As sad for Mexico was the use to which revenue was put. The cost of the military was considerably greater than in the late colonial era, and in some years took on the order of 90 percent of expenditures. Civilian officials had to put up with military influence on spending. Administration was often crippled by fanaticism, looting, uncertainty, and poor management, and it was observed that provincial officials were able to act like "petty sultans." Under these conditions, although only limited modernization could be attempted, enlightened Mexicans never ceased to fight for better conditions.

b. Factionalism and *Caudillismo,* 1821–1850s

The first third of a century was a maelstrom of factionalism and *caudillismo*. The Liberals generally dominated to 1834, then the Conservatives to the mid-1850s, insofar as any civilian group could dominate a Mexico in which Santa Anna and the army exercised decisive power.

The Generally Liberal Years to 1834

Iturbide inaugurated the country's independent political history by setting himself at the head of a junta of government, which saw to the convocation of a constituent Congress in 1822. It manipulated affairs to make him Emperor Agustín I.[3] He lasted ten mounths, as he quickly revealed himself a man lacking in judgment. As

opposition arose, he imprisoned congressmen, then replaced the Congress with a junta he could control. Regional leaders were restive, and beyond Iturbide's reach because the army was unpaid and thus disgruntled. When Iturbide sent General Santa Anna to oust the Spaniards remaining in the fortress of San Juan de Ulua in Veracruz harbor, Santa Anna instead conspired against Iturbide.[4] In February 1823 Santa Anna and some other generals, including the hero of Independence Guadalupe Victoria, issued the Plan of Casa Mata for a federal republic. Iturbide was by this time so bereft of supporters that he called back the Congress and offered to abdicate; instead, the Congress deposed him. He was exiled. In 1824 he returned to Mexico to try for power again but was captured and shot.

The Conservative Congress appointed a military triumvirate to run the country provisionally. Then in November 1823, a constituent Congress met, with a Liberal majority, and in October 1824 it adopted a liberal Constitution that provided for a three-branch national government and a federal system with elected governors and legislatures for the states. Liberalism was displayed also in abolition of the Inquisition and of torture, granting the public lands to the states rather than to the central government, prohibition of reelection of a president until after a four-year interval, and provision for a bicameral national legislature with one house representing the citizenry, the other the states. Less liberal were provisions making the Roman church the established faith with no mention of toleration for others and letting the state legislatures choose the national president and vice-president.

Revolutionary hero Guadalupe Victoria was elected president in 1824 and served out his term (1825–1829), the last elected president to do so for half a century. Victoria did not enrich himself from public funds, which also proved unusual for some decades; but members of his administration did. Politically naive and a poor

---

[3] On Central America's brief connection with Iturbide's Mexico, see Chapter 28.

[4] The Spaniards remained until 1825, cutting off the new Mexican government from revenue from commerce.

administrator, he could not cope with his Conservative enemies, including Vice-President Nicolás Bravo. Political factions polarized about two branches of Freemasonry. The York Rite was Liberal/federalist, and included President Victoria; the Scottish Rite was Conservative, calling for centralized government; it included Bravo. This contest was complicated by the competition of the United States and Britain for advantage in trade in Mexico. Joel Poinsett, the United States representative, was so flagrant in his support of the Yorkists and liberal republicanism that the Mexican government finally demanded his recall.

Vicente Guerrero, another hero of Independence and a *puro*, lost the election of 1828, when nine state legislatures voted for him and ten for his opponent. With the aid of Santa Anna and the liberal Indian General Juan Alvarez in the south, Guerrero took arms against this decision. He briefly became president, being deposed at the end of 1829 by Santa Anna, after the latter had enhanced his reputation by defeating a Spanish force that attempted a reconquest of Mexico at Tampico. Santa Anna handed power to the Conservative Vice-President Anastasio Bustamante. These were the opening moves of the long political career of Santa Anna, the leader above all others who proved able to manipulate the weaknesses of the political environment.

Santa Anna (1795–1876) was the son of a propertied family of the province of Veracruz. He entered the royal army at sixteen and fought against the Hidalgo rebels and on the frontiers of the colony and early republic with valor and ruthlessness. With Independence he perceived the uses of armed force in public affairs. A man of political talent, he could cajole, intimidate, dazzle, and seduce. He understood the weaknesses of individuals and of institutions. He was audacious when that served, patient or sly when that was more useful. He took credit for the good and evaded blame for the bad. He was untroubled by morals, affections, or scruples. He proclaimed his patriotism from the rooftops, metaphorically waving the leg he lost in his

country's service; and he served it badly and faithlessly, though at times with courage. He enticed the ambitious and the greedy, for his victories and talents led them to support the probable winner in the political wars. He cowed men of property by threats against their possessions and their families. He was president under one arrangement or another nine times, often abandoning Mexico City for the ease of his Clove Spike Hacienda in the pleasant lower altitudes near Jalapa in the state of Veracruz, where he bore neither the burdens nor the blame of administration.

Bustamante's Conservative government became unpopular because of its repressive measures against Liberals, and Santa Anna took advantage of it in a characteristic way. In 1831 the colonel commanding the Veracruz garrison was short in his accounts, so he asked Santa Anna for a loan, which he got on condition of rebelling against the government. The colonel put the proposition to his officers, who agreed. Seizure of the customs receipts at Veracruz gave the rebels an immediate attractiveness, so in 1832 Santa Anna was able to extinguish the Bustamante government. He soon contrived his own elevation as president, with the *puro* Valentín Gómez Farías as vice-president, then retreated to his hacienda. Santa Anna occasionally visited Mexico City to be president for a few days and test public opinion—then back to Jalapa.

Gómez Farías was in office only ten months in 1833–1834, pursuing a *puro* program. He attacked the *fueros*—special privileges—of the church and the military, declared state control of ecclesiastical appointment, secularized the California missions and their endowment funds, ended church control of education, permitted retraction of vows made by members of religious orders, made the tithes voluntary (hence uncollectable), and created state militias.

The Conservatives and the War with the United States, 1834–1850s

In early 1834 an outbreak of cholera in Mexico City weakened the Liberal position when priests declared that the godless actions of the government were the cause. In April Santa Anna took over the presidency again, dismissed Gómez Farías, became a dictator, and revoked the hated laws. He dissolved the Congress, and in an election a Conservative body was chosen, meeting in January 1835. It soon pushed Santa Anna into retirement—for Conservative as well as Liberal politicians preferred to govern without *caudillos*. The Congress decreed an end to the *puro* program, leading to regional uprisings that Santa Anna helped put down. Congress drafted the Seven Laws (known by Liberals as the Seven Plagues) that were promulgated in December 1836 as a new Constitution. The Seven Laws eliminated the federal system, making the states into departments dependent on the central administration, and put harsh property restrictions on the franchise and federal office holding under a system of indirect elections. They also created a Poder Conservador with power to oust the president, nullify laws, and override the courts.

During these early years of the Mexican republic, a dangerous transformation was occurring in its northern state of Texas. Spain had granted to North American Moses Austin, and Iturbide had confirmed to Stephen Austin in 1821, land and settlement rights in Texas. The grant was made to strengthen a lightly held border territory and to provide income to a country that badly needed it, from taxes and increased commercial activity, but not all Spaniards or Mexicans thought it a wise move. By 1830 there were 25,000 North Americans in Texas. Most immigrants came from the southern states, and some brought slaves. Their numbers, and their resistance to Mexican language and customs, alarmed Mexican leaders.

Even in the early 1820s Mexicans feared United States designs on their territory, and the British in Mexico encouraged them to look to them for protection. A revolt in Texas in 1826–1827 involved some North Americans with Cherokees in a scheme to divide the territory between a "Fredonian Republic" and the Indians. Although United States settlers in the Austin lands defeated the rebels, the British minister in Mex-

ico helped persuade leaders that the United States had inspired the Fredonian Revolt. Another source of friction in the 1820s was argument in the United States as to whether the boundary with Mexico was at the Sabine River, as specified in the treaty of 1821 between the United States and Spain, or farther south at some of the other rivers between the Sabine and the distant Rio Grande. Yet more worry for Mexico resulted from the westward movement of United States citizens beyond the Mississippi, where Missouri became a state in 1820. By 1822 a hide trade by sea began between New England and Mexican California. In 1825 the United States Congress authorized a commission to lay out a trail from St. Louis to Mexican Santa Fe.

These problems led Mexico to corrective measures for Texas. In 1826–1827 immigration orders tried to stem the flow of North Americans, requiring a declaration of allegiance to the Roman Catholic faith. Then in 1829 Mexico abolished slavery, unimportant in Mexico for a long time and in line with current liberal doctrine there. Mexico hoped it would discourage immigration into Texas, but it neither did that nor eradicated slavery in Texas. An 1830 colonization law encouraged Mexicans to move to Texas. Another Mexican measure in 1830 combined Texas with Coahuila, which gave the enlarged state a Mexican majority, keeping state government out of the hands of Yankees. Texans had to travel to far-off Saltillo to transact political and legal business in an atmosphere they could not dominate. The state legislature did pay some attention to the needs of North Americans in Texas, notably by making English a legal language.

Texans of United States origin probably could have lived quite comfortably if willing to assimilate to Mexican law and custom by giving up slavery, becoming bilingual, and accepting the Constitution and decisions of the central government. They might have brought cheap labor from central Mexico. On the other hand, they might have suffered inconvenience and some penalties for their Protestantism: that and their foreign birth made attainment of public office difficult. Furthermore, violence, arbitrariness, and corruption in the government inclined Texans to mistrust Mexico City. So they supported federalism and thought that protection for local rights was diluted by the combination of Texas with Coahuila. Still, even as disagreement increased, Texas in 1833 sent to Mexico City a delegation to declare that Texas was loyal, wanting only the powers of a state within a federal system. Two years later the federal system was abolished in Mexico, though not just because of the Texas issue.

A majority in Texas still opposed independence, but the issue was seized by leaders there who would not be governed by the views of a majority they thought could be made to change its mind. The leaders began a rebellion in 1835, and a constitutional convention in 1836 declared Texas independent. Mexicans considered, with reason, that the rebellion had been encouraged by public and private persons in the United States, and that an important motive in both Texas and the United States was the expectation of annexation to the northern republic. Some Mexicans suspected that President Andrew Jackson had conspired with Sam Houston, but no proof ever was found, although Jackson had tried to buy Texas before the declaration of independence and tried again thereafter.

Santa Anna, marching north with an army, ordered captured rebel leaders executed and black slaves freed. He was soon beaten and taken prisoner by the Texans under Sam Houston at the Battle of San Jacinto. Santa Anna promised Houston that he would confirm Texas independence and repeated the promise later to President Jackson in Washington. For those actions, Santa Anna was met with suspicion when he returned to Mexico late in 1836.

Jackson gave no official aid to the Texas rebels (or secessionists), but could not entirely prevent private aid. He refrained from proclaiming neutrality, which would have aided the Texans by giving them belligerent status. The chief factors, however, were that the military situation was stabilized by the difficulty of communication between central Mexico and Texas, and by divisions in the Mexican upper class; and that the annexation issue was stalled by conflict in the United States over the admission of new slave states. Because of the slavery issue, Jackson went only so far as to recognize the independence of Texas on March 1, 1837.

In Mexico, under the new Conservative Constitution Bustamante was elected president in 1837. The next year, when French forces occupied Veracruz in support of financial claims, Santa Anna ousted them, losing a leg, which revived his popularity.[5] In 1841 he led a revolt, and returned as head of government. Revenues were so depressed that pay vouchers were discounted up to 90 percent. Santa Anna squeezed what he could from church and *hacendados*, and they continued to support him. As always, he spent lavishly on his personal pleasure and sopped up the flattery of which he never tired. A constitutional change—the Bases Orgánicas of 1843—permitted him to be reelected in January 1844. But times were bad. Hungry mobs rioted. Statues of Santa Anna were mutilated. Army officers and others sniffed a coming change. Congress named a new president late in 1844, and Santa Anna fled for his life. The story runs that he was disguised but that some Indians recognized El Gordo—Fatso—by his wooden leg, and prepared to cook him with chiles as a giant *tamal* wrapped in leaves, but the local priest is supposed to have blocked this engaging scheme. Congress let Santa Anna go into exile, keep his property, and receive a general's half pay. He left in mid-1845, and was back the next year to fight against the United States.

Benito Juárez.   Politics was not all fraud and force in those decades. Although dialogue and participation were confined to a minority, they had expanded since the colonial era. The press was intermittently free. Education was expanded some and was freer and more varied. Some politi-

---

[5] This incident is known as the Pastry War because one of the French claimants was a restaurant owner in Mexico City.

cal opportunities did open to new people. At the end of the colonial era, in 1818, an orphaned Zapotec Indian boy of twelve left his shepherding and other farm tasks and moved to the little town of Oaxaca. He spoke no Spanish. Benito Juárez was befriended by a bookbinder for whom he worked, and who encouraged him to go to school. In 1821 he entered the local church seminary, not from desire to be a priest, but because no other way to further education was open. In 1827 the Liberals in the Oaxaca state legislature founded a Civil College, to which Juárez transferred the next year. The church declared that the college was full of heresy and sexual promiscuity and persuaded upper-class families to keep their sons out of it. In 1831 Juárez began practicing law and was elected an alderman. In 1833–1834 he was a Liberal member of the Oaxaca state legislature. He had a difficult time economically and socially in the little provincial capital. His European-style clothes could not hide his purely Indian ancestry, and his lowly origins were well known.

Still, he made a living, although his law practice was with the poor. He established a reputation for sobriety, honesty, good judgment, and industry. One of his cases illuminated several features of the environment. In 1834 he represented in ecclesiastical court some poor villagers complaining of an extortionate curate. The case probably was heard only because the Gómez Farías *puro* regime briefly was in power in Mexico City, and when it fell not only was the case terminated but the accused priest contrived the arrest of the villagers who had complained of his fees. When Juárez visited the prisoners, the local judge began an action against him as a vagrant. Juárez returned to Oaxaca and accused the judge in a state court, but the curate got a writ of arrest against Juárez on a charge of inciting people against the authorities. Juárez was in jail nine days, then released on bond. This ended an affair showing the role of ecclesiastical *fueros*, the corruption of the civil courts by politics, and the critical role of the church in the affairs of the time.

All through the 1830s and 1840s Juárez lived an industrious life of mild prominence in isolated Oaxaca. He showed no signs of radicalism, associating amicably with Conservatives. He married into a family of Spanish-Italian origin. He was named to the bench in 1841, elected in 1845 to the Conservative state legislature, and in 1846 after the national Liberal revolt was part of a triumvirate set up to run Oaxaca temporarily. He went to the national Congress in 1847, and later in the year became governor of Oaxaca, a position he held five years. Indians came down from the mountains to his inauguration with a petition saying, "You know what we need and you will give it to us, for you are good and will not forget that you are one of us." He could not do much because the state was poor. He got on well with the church, gave no sign that he favored social reforms, was a good administrator, and did what he could for education and road building, which he recognized as major problems. It was remarkable, and promising for the future, that an Indian should have risen so far, but when he left the governorship in 1852 no one could guess the grandeur the man was to achieve in the last twenty years of his life.

War with the United States. During this phase of Juárez's career Mexico suffered another disaster in connection with its northern territories. While the slavery controversy in the United States stalled the annexation of Texas, Mexico did not try a reconquest. Mexican nationalism was aroused, but it was difficult to get agreement on military measures. In the summer of 1844 the Mexican Congress defied Santa Anna's demands for money and a force of 30,000 men to use against Texas, fearing that he had other goals at least partially in view. Mexico warned, however, that annexation of Texas to the United States would bring war.

Mexico was supported by the British and French governments, which disliked and feared the growth of the United States. An independent Texas, possibly extending to the Pacific, seemed to them a providential restriction on that growth.

They recognized the independence of Texas and promoted trade with the new republic. They finally helped arrange a preliminary agreement between Texas and Mexico that provided for Texas to be independent and to agree not to become part of any country. Before it could be translated into a treaty, Texas received word that the United States Congress finally had voted annexation, so Texas agreed and repudiated the protocol with Mexico providing for independence by treaty.

The stalemate with the United States over the admission of Texas was broken because election results in November 1844 showed not only the slave South for Texas but also the West and parts of the middle states. President Tyler asked for and was given a joint resolution of Congress for annexation in March 1845. Mexico broke diplomatic relations later in that month. Texas voted approval of annexation and was officially admitted as a state December 29, 1845.

Mexico did not declare war even though it considered that it had ample cause, including the open interest of the United States in the acquisition of California. In 1842 U.S.N. Commodore Jones seized Monterey in Mexican California because he had a false report that war had begun between the two countries. United States citizens in mounting numbers used the trails to Santa Fe and California, although Mexico tried to keep them out. Mexico's action in 1845, nevertheless, was merely to move troops near what the United States claimed as the new border between the countries at the Rio Grande.

That border claim was one issue that made negotiations difficult. Mexico said that the Texas border was at the Nueces River, while the Texans (hence the United States) put it at the Rio Grande, some sixty miles south of the Nueces. Furthermore, the other western territories claimed by Mexico under the United States–Spain treaty of 1821, and threatened by the United States, made of the Texas annexation and boundary issues part of an enormous complex of possible disaster for Mexico. If there had not been threats to California and other western

territories, it would have been easier for Mexico to contemplate loss and negotiation on Texas annexation and its boundaries. It was difficult to do this when Polk considered that population movement to California ensured its incorporation into the United States as a "natural" area of expansion. He also thought Mexican claims weak and feared that Britain would seize California.

In October 1845 Polk received Mexican permission to send a commissioner to discuss the Texas boundary, but instead he sent John Slidell as minister, with instructions to get all the territory he could without payment and at least the Rio Grande border (which Mexico had been ready to accept earlier in 1845 for the Republic of Texas); buy whatever he could of the territory west to the Pacific; and get an agreement on damages claimed by United States citizens. Slidell reached Mexico City late in November 1845, and the Mexicans became aware of his ambitious instructions. General José Herrera had become president in early 1845, as Santa Anna went into exile, and Herrera refused to recognize Slidell as a minister because that would imply that no reason existed for Mexico to break off diplomatic relations, that is, that the Texas annexation was acceptable. He also feared that it would lead to a coup d'etat against himself. A coup did occur in any case in January 1846, and General Paredes succeeded Herrera and also refused to receive Slidell. Both Mexico and the United States have been accused of recklessness for not being willing to compromise on Slidell's status.

In January 1846 Polk ordered General Taylor into the disputed territory between the Nueces and the Rio Grande, which Texas claimed but did not occupy. The Mexican military forces were south of the Rio Grande and did not move north after Taylor's troops crossed the Nueces, even though he built a fort across the Rio Grande from Matamoros, Mexico. Meanwhile, Slidell returned to Washington and Polk began to draft a war message based on Mexico's "insult" to the United States by refusing to accept Slidell and its failure to meet United States damage claims. Before Polk could act, on April 23 President Paredes declared war, and on April 25 Mexican troops went north of the Rio Grande and attacked some of Taylor's forces in what Mexico claimed was its territory even if Texas was independent. There were casualties.

News of the fighting caused Polk to change his war message to emphasize that Mexico had invaded the United States. There is no way of satisfying all points of view on the question of whether Polk "provoked" the war by sending troops across the Nueces or merely acted in support of a belief that it was United States territory. In any event, he sensed correctly the temper of Congress and no doubt of a majority of the United States citizenry, which tended to unite during wartime, although there was opposition to the war.

The Mexicans did well against General Taylor in northeastern Mexico. In February 1847 he was only as far as Saltillo, where he met General Santa Anna in the Battle of Buena Vista. Taylor won a tactical victory but faced a difficult campaign down the high, semiarid plateaus. Polk turned to a plan by which the navy landed General Scott at Veracruz in March 1847. The Mexicans fought bravely, but with insufficiently equipped and trained soldiers. Scott was in Mexico City in September.

Events in the West demonstrated the drive of the United States government and private citizens in that direction and influenced the terms of the peace but did nothing to defeat Mexico. The United States army, navy, and irregular militia in several campaigns took Santa Fe, parts of Chihuahua, and California. The heart of its strength was far to the south of those lightly held areas.

In Mexico City leaders naturally were reluctant to agree to the drastic terms presented them, but they did want to get rid of the occupying army. So the Treaty of Guadalupe Hidalgo was signed in February 1848 and soon ratified. In July United States troops left Mexico. By the treaty, Texas independence was acknowledged; and Mexico ceded to the United States its claims to a huge territory between Texas and the Pacific,

which included all or parts of the later states of New Mexico, Arizona, Nevada, Utah, Colorado, and California.

Mexico had not been able to arrange a less drastic result by more practical policies because of factors of pride, patriotism, a sense of being in the right, and the fragility and frequent irresponsibility of political and governmental institutions. In the United States, a different sort of president might have proceeded more slowly, but he could not have stopped the movement of United States citizens into Texas, California, and the other lands Mexico could not exploit. That movement already was uncontrollable in 1845, three years before gold was found in California. Inevitably, since the territory west of Texas was ceded to the United States in toto, analysis of the parts of the cession has been of little interest, but the fact is that Mexican claims to Utah, Nevada, and Colorado were weaker than those to California, Texas, Arizona, and New Mexico, where it had better claims by reason of exploration and especially of settlement.

The movement of Taylor into northern Mexico in 1846 and the seizure of California brought the Liberals back to power in Mexico City, with Gómez Farías as president, and restoration of the federal Constitution of 1824. The Liberals brought Santa Anna back from exile, and he after the Battle of Buena Vista ousted Gómez Farías, who had been pursuing his anticlerical passion. The church had sent word to Santa Anna that it would finance his return to power. The lower-class mob in Mexico also again favored Santa Anna. After his defeat by Scott, however, Santa Anna was again exiled.

The tremendous blow of the territorial losses did not reconcile Liberals and Conservatives or change attitudes toward political methods. Mexican nationalism was too weak for such a result. Moderate administrations in 1848–1853 accomplished nothing, and were ended by a revolt in January 1853 that returned Conservatives to power. They at once brought Santa Anna back from exile, not because they trusted him, but because they thought only he could break the

Liberals and the federal ideal and ensure the privileged position of church, military, and *hacendados*. Lucas Alamán became a minister in the new government, clinging to the notion that only a monarchy could "save" Mexico. He died in June 1853 as Santa Anna began his usual shameless and extravagant administration. He was more despotic and expensive than ever, yet the Conservatives supported him because he followed some of their wishes. He quickly raised money by arranging the Gadsden Purchase with the United States. Also in 1853, he arrested Juárez and Melchor Ocampo, the great Liberal of Michoacán, and sent them into exile. Santa Anna assumed some of the trappings of monarchy, and considered importation of a foreign prince. Opposition arose on all sides, but Santa Anna held out until August 1855, when he went into exile—for the last time, as it proved.

At the time there was no way of knowing that this was more than just another change of regime. The years from Independence to the 1850s had seemed disastrous in all respects, but three momentous decisions slowly had been made: (*a*) that the issues now were firmly defined; (*b*) that disagreement on the issues was irremediable; and (*c*) that nearly intolerable conditions justified almost any sort of radical means to gain victory for one point of view or the other.

c. Socioeconomic Stagnation to the 1880s

Political disorder was an important factor in keeping the economy stagnant, and both factors impeded social development.

The Economy

Economic production in independent Mexico was for several decades less than in the late colonial era. Exports did not recover the value level of late colonial times until the 1860s. Many people testified that disorder frightened capital, like the congressman who said that it had "given the death blow to confidence, which is the basis of prosperity." Some Mexicans thought stagna-

tion was due to factionalism and bad policy alone, that their natural resources ensured prosperity with proper effort. Although there was merit in that view, it did underestimate Mexico's problems: the cost of better transportation, a better-trained and motivated labor force and competent managers, and competition from other producers of agricultural and pastoral commodities. Argentina and Brazil had some advantages over Mexico, and their export economies fueled growth earlier and faster.

Bad transportation and communications hurt Mexico more than Argentina and Brazil. Roads were so bad for wheeled traffic that trains of mules and burros continued to dominate most cargo routes, and the transport of bulky commodities was expensive. The result was that often good cropland only a few miles from markets was not worked because freightage would eat up the price of produce. Another result of freight costs was that the far north did much of its trading with the United States.

Railway building was slower than in Argentina. The first concession was made in 1837, but fewer than twenty miles of track existed in 1860. The Veracruz–Mexico City line finally was inaugurated in 1873, but it tapped only a small part of the country. In 1880 there still were only seven hundred miles of track in the republic. Much travel, therefore, still was by public stagecoaches that seldom covered more than a hundred miles in a day. They were uncomfortable and much harassed by brigands. Stagecoach companies kept blankets and clothing at their stops for passengers who were stripped by bandits in the wild reaches of Mexico that could not be patrolled.

Agriculture changed little. Maize remained the chief crop, but its production increased only enough to meet local population growth. Cotton culture also stagnated. When cotton sold for fifteen cents a pound in the United States, a Veracruz grower might spend nearly as much just to get a pound from the field to the buyer. Cotton production was encouraged by the Mexican government with import restrictions, but that drove domestic cotton to fifty cents a pound, while much cotton still had to be imported. Sugar might cost one cent a pound to produce, sell for less than that near the fields, and bring twenty-five cents in distant areas. Wheat at times sold for less than the cost of production. The transport and other problems kept agricultural/pastoral exports small, in the latter part of the period only some 15 percent of total Mexican exports.

One problem was that the large estates remained dominant in the countryside, but were often inefficient. The *hacendados* acquired more land partly to fend off competitors for labor and in commodity markets, but also because land gave social prestige. They acquired land from the church, the communal holdings of villages, and the public lands the state inherited from the Spanish government. Mexican national and state governments sold vacant public land (*terrenos baldíos*) because they were desperate for funds. Juárez, needing money to fight the French invaders, in 1863–1867 sold nearly 4.5 million acres of *terrenos baldíos* to individuals and companies at an average price of two and a half cents an acre.

Liberal governments after 1856 forced Indian villages to distribute their *ejidos* (communal lands) to the heads of families on the misguided theory that the program would create a class of industrious small farmers with a new sense of initiative. What it did was let *hacendados* buy the small plots from the poor owners. Some village lands were also incorporated into haciendas by fraudulent boundary manipulations or by declaring them part of state-owned *terrenos baldíos*. Church lands went to secular owners by a number of measures in the 1820s and thereafter, with the reform of the 1850s accelerating the process. The church lost most of its properties by 1872. The *hacendados* generally were Conservatives and firm Catholics, but they were happy to buy former church land.

Mining suffered disastrously during the wars for Independence, and gold and silver production recovered notably only by the 1840s. It attracted a small amount of foreign capital. By 1855 output was nearly that of the late eighteenth century; by 1868 it was back to that of 1808; and it grew somewhat more in the 1870s. It remained confined to silver and gold, and the total values were not large, although it did make up on the order of 85 percent of the country's exports. The modern boom in mining did not begin in Mexico, however, until the 1880s, when big foreign investment entered the industry.

The larger merchants of the cities, many of them foreigners, continued to dominate the business community, as wholesalers, retailers, and sometimes as money lenders. Their services in this last connection were far from adequate, and the country badly needed credit institutions. A special class of lenders to government (*agiotistas*) fomented political adventure rather than economic development. A government-created bank (Banco de Avío) to aid development operated briefly in the 1830s, but it was too weak to have much effect. The first regular banking institution was created in 1864, but the banking industry remained feeble for decades thereafter.

The merchants had a restricted clientele as wholesalers and as retailers to the small upper and middle classes, chiefly for imported goods. Veracruz continued to be the most important port, both because it was convenient for the best markets in the Valley of Mexico and because it was favored by the central government. Although there was much controversy about aiding other ports, by itself such aid could merely redistribute rather than increase trade. A limited number of imported items made their way to the urban and rural poor, but much of the consumption of that class came from homemade products. Those were sold, and sometimes exchanged by barter, in tiny shops, at fairs, or by peddlers. Mexico City had one unique system by which Indians brought goods—including flowers—into the city by canal. Much trade of all sorts was inhibited by internal imposts: *aduanas secas* (dry customs), state and local *alcabalas* (sales taxes), and other levies that sometimes bore little resemblance to their names. Taxes on the movement of goods were not so much a measure of preference in public finance as of simplicity and of desperation for funds.

At Independence Mexico barely had passed beyond the craft level in textiles and sugar. Optimists insisted, however, that the opportunity existed for large growth of industry. They were wrong. Capital was short; taxes were sometimes too high and of uncertain application, creating a climate almost intolerable to entrepreneurs; fuel, consisting of wood and charcoal, was scarce and expensive, even in mining operations; metalworking, for machinery repair or adjustment, was weak; industrial labor was expensive to train; the national market was small; transportation shortcomings were almost a sufficient barrier in themselves; and foreign competition was fierce, with ways of fending it off none too certain.

Ways of fending it off included tariff protection, but that proved of limited value. It was difficult to enforce and smuggling flourished. A notable protagonist of tariff protection for industry was Esteban Antuñano of Puebla, whose knowledge of the British economy proved of little value in nineteenth-century Mexico. Even some Liberals, who favored laissez-faire in theory, in practice wanted to exclude cheap foreign goods that hurt provincial manufacturers, especially in their home states. The regional interests in fabrication thought that less attention to the needs of Mexico City and of agriculture and commerce would permit industrial growth. They exaggerated the power of government and the ability of protection to foster industry in Mexico. Although some protection was provided, Mexico generally operated under a laissez-faire system, and the small efforts at protection had little result.

Modern manufacturing, therefore, grew little to the 1880s, much less than in Argentina and Brazil. Local, and sometimes ephemeral, spurts of modernization had little national effect, as in the case of Yucatán's henequen (sisal) industry. It imported foreign machinery in the 1830s, but the enterprise declined during the Caste War. By the late 1860s manufactures, aside from crafts products, possibly were worth 50 million pesos a year, not much on a per capita

basis. Power-driven factories were of consequence only in textiles. Establishments of various sizes and with some industrial features—machinery, sizable operations, labor specialization—were created in other lines of production but were not typical. Most output was in homes or small shops. In various areas there was sizable production of pottery, tiles, bricks, ironware, soap, oils, tobacco products, lumber, cheap paper, shoes, sugar, rum, brandy, wine, and alcoholic beverages made from the maguey plant. These were important to relatively few persons.

At the end of the colonial era, the most important industry, aside from mining and agricultural processing, was textiles, with possibly 60,000 employees. It was unmechanized, much was in tiny workshops, and the commercial industry was collapsing. The output was inferior in price and quality to foreign imports in grades of any fineness. There was considerable discussion of ways of promoting it, and the governments of independent Mexico quickly provided some protection against imports and permitted duty-free import of machinery, which began coming in about 1830. It had help from the Banco de Avío in the 1830s, which lent some 70 percent of its funds to the textile industry and only managed to give it a moderate boost. By 1845 mechanized cotton spinning and weaving mills employed about 9,000 workers, but the industry remained near that level for the next quarter of a century. Mexico tended to supply more than one-half of its textile needs from legal and smuggled imports. A foreign visitor wrote in 1846 that the cotton manufacture of Puebla existed only by tariff protection, selling goods at thirty cents a yard that cost only six cents in the United States.

Social Conditions

At Independence Mexico was the most populous country in Latin America, but in the nineteenth century it grew more slowly than Argentina and Brazil, from about 5.8 million in 1805 to 9 million in 1870. It also differed from Argentina and Brazil in attracting little immigration. Mexicans tried to encourage it, but Europeans saw better opportunities in more dynamic economies. Since few Europeans came and the small pool of blacks had been assimilated, the genetic makeup of the population remained strongly Indian. The population also remained heavily rural. Mexico City had more than 200,000 population in the 1870s, but no other city approached the capital in size. The port cities all were small, no more than towns, in sharp contrast with Argentina and Brazil.

The class system remained rigid, supported by minority control of access to office, property, and capital. The upper and middle classes, including several thousand foreigners in Mexico City, could afford to imitate European modes in dress, architecture, education, and intellectual life. The rest of the population lived at or near the subsistence level, and since there was little opportunity for improvement, there was no motive for effort and thrift. In the towns, especially Mexico City, the very poor (called *léperos*) often slept in doorways, and were notorious for their unappetizing appearance, persistent begging, and criminal activities. Mme. Calderón de la Barca in the 1840s was equally appalled in the cathedral by "the miserable *léperos* in rags" and a "floor so dirty that one kneels with a feeling of horror." But the privileged felt no horror at the fact that they offered to the proletariat little except drunkenness, pitifully inadequate private or public social assistance, and a milieu in which violence was prevalent and accepted.

Still, escape from the lower class was marginally easier than in the colonial era, aided by the new republican institutions of government and education. Juárez was an example, although he still met socioracial distaste for the Indian, an attitude that was a mixture of views on poverty, filth, vulgar behavior, bastardy, and traditional prejudice. Such views still were in effect supported by the church, although its own influence was weakening. Despite the slight opening of society under the early republic, a great gulf remained between the poor, illiterate wearers of

sandals and the propertied and educated wearers of shoes.

The educational system that helped lift Juárez was small because funds did not exist for more. The percentage of literacy barely climbed, and the country was approximately 90 percent illiterate in 1880. Education was somewhat freer and more varied than in the colonial era because of the reduction of church influence. Education beyond the secondary level, however, virtually disappeared. Secondary instruction received somewhat more attention. Dr. Gabino Barreda, beginning in 1867, helped design and administer a new system of public education, including a National Preparatory School, on the basis of secular scientism. Barreda had studied in Europe, and was influenced by the positivism of Auguste Comte, whose effects were noted in late nineteenth-century Brazil. This positivism Barreda and his collaborators imparted to young men of the ruling minority who would be influential in the Díaz government for many years, including José I. Limantour and Justo Sierra. Although President Juárez supported Barreda's work as a liberal program aimed at reducing church influence, it eventually became antiliberal in its emphasis on elite instruction, orderly progress without interference from popular elements, and distaste for some of the classical liberal political institutions.

Communications improved a bit during the half century because of the slight increase in literacy, because schools were somewhat freer, because speech was at least intermittently less restricted, and because newspaper publication grew. There was virtually no increased communication because of labor agitation or organization. A few talented writers published, but many of their products were bland and romantic, although a minority included some social criticism. J. J. Fernández de Lizardi inveighed against the old stigma on the manual arts. Juan Díaz Covarrubias (died 1859) in a novel *The Middle Class* sympathized with a poor orphan girl seduced by an aristocrat. Such material had no effect on social affairs. Both literature and the arts tended to be highly imitative of Europe, as was natural in so small a cultivated community where art patronage was not a tradition, earning a living by artistic effort was impossible, and the activity on the whole not highly honored.

Under all these circumstances of isolation, limited education, and contrasting outlooks, nationalist sentiment grew slowly. There were xenophobic eruptions connected with the wars over Texas and the French invasion. The few who favored national industry or objected to sale of the country's natural resources found little support. Even the politically active often thought as much of state loyalties as of national, while the Indian masses thought of themselves as citizens of their villages.

d. *La Reforma* and Civil War, 1854–1861

The accumulated Liberal disgust with the Conservative combination and Santa Anna's antics erupted in rebellion, proclaimed in Guerrero in the Plan de Ayutla (March 1, 1854), issued by the Indian *caudillo* Juan Alvarez, who had fought with Morelos for Independence and in every Liberal uprising thereafter, and by Ignacio Comonfort, a *moderado* and ex-bureaucrat. Alvarez was to be chief of state pending a constituent convention. Santa Anna took an army to Guerrero and found that in its mountains all advantages were with the *guerrilleros*. Thereafter he remained in central Mexico, menaced by a growing number of chieftains who declared for the Plan of Ayutla. Santos Degollado, a law professor of Jalisco, and young Porfirio Díaz of Oaxaca were among the dictator's accumulating enemies. Santa Anna clung to Mexico City, and the treasury, until August 1855, then went into exile.[6]

Meanwhile, Juárez made his way by sea from exile in the United States to Acapulco in Guerrero by July 1855. He became minister of justice

in the provisional government, which also included Melchor Ocampo, ex-governor of Michoacán. The two great Liberals had returned from exile determined to break the Conservative combination, which meant above all the church, with which both had clashed in their home states. Ocampo in 1851 was involved in Michoacán in a case where a curate refused burial to the body of a peon whose widow could not pay the interment fee. When sanitary reasons urged haste, the curate advised the poor woman to salt and eat the cadaver, or so the story ran. Ocampo paid the fees, and petitioned the state legislature to reform the system of parochial charges. The curate printed an attack on efforts to impoverish the clergy, which he said would lead to more weakening of the church, including freedom of worship and conscience, which had led to socialism in Europe and might lead "the hungry masses of Mexicans" to advocate equality of property. It was precisely this linkage between church and property and privilege that brought some Liberals finally to a radical attack on the combination of *hacendados*, army officers, and clerics.

At Cuernavaca, near the capital, a meeting of leaders, chaired by the aged Gómez Farías, chose Alvarez president, although some thought the illiterate Indian *guerrillero* unqualified for the post. On November 14, 1855, Alvarez entered Mexico City, where the propertied feared him as an Indian barbarian who might encourage the peons to revolt. The radical drift of opinion was indicated almost immediately when Alvarez proclaimed (November 22) the *Ley Juárez*, which abolished the ecclesiastical and military courts. The attack on the *fueros* of those privileged corporations was recognized as aiming at permanent disruption of the Conservative combination, and the latter shouted "Religión y fueros!" and prepared for war. The law made Juárez a national figure. But some Liberals were less ready for strong measures, including many *moderados* like Comonfort, fence sitters whose lack of spine had facilitated the antics of Santa Anna. Ocampo was forced from the government in December as too radical. At the same time Alvarez went

---

[6] He came back to Veracruz in the 1860s to join the Maximilian adventure, but was deported by the French. Allowed to return to Mexico in 1872, he died in poverty in 1876.

back to Guerrero, conscious of his lack of preparation for government and threatened by former supporters.

He left the government to Comonfort, who had doubts about the *Ley Juárez*, yet on January 25, 1856, had to proclaim another drastic measure, the *Ley Lerdo*, drafted by his minister of the treasury, Miguel Lerdo de Tejada. This law ended the property holding of all corporations, which meant chiefly the church and Indian villages, which from time out of mind had held communal lands—*ejidos*. The *Ley Lerdo* was to raise funds for government, strike a blow at the church, and create small Indian proprietors—a measure dear to Liberal theoreticians. Proceeds of church and village land sales were to go partly to the government. Some Indian uprisings occurred at once in protest, but many *ejidos* were sold. Later in the year the government amended the law to divide *ejidos* among villagers, but even when that was done, speculators bought the land from the new holders, and most ended in great estates. Much church land also became part of haciendas, though some sales were rigged to leave land in effective ecclesiastical possession. There simply was little support among the upper class for a small-farm system, and the opponents included lower-class figures who became generals and *caudillos*. This was partly preference for property concentration, but it also was bound up with a general fear of encouraging the pretensions of the masses.

Comonfort had to meet Liberal dissension, Conservative rebellion, Indian risings, and the knowledge that the clerics—especially friars—were inciting Conservatives to general revolt. Conservative bitterness was deepened by a constitutional convention that in February 1857 produced a new and more radical charter. As was common in Latin America, the government had ensured election to the convention of people it trusted. Most of the delegates were moderates, many of them lawyers, with a strong faith in words, or at least a compulsion to act as though they had such a faith in a society where they could not compete with the decisive weapons of

violence. The Constitution incorporated the Juárez and Lerdo laws, and included other measures intolerable to church and army. Apart from these provisions, it was far from a radical document.[7]

Administration of the oath of allegiance to the new Constitution began in the spring of 1857. Some bureaucrats relinquished their jobs rather than comply, a heavy sacrifice in a society where opportunities for the middle class were sparse. Clericals began to carry banners proclaiming "Long Live Religion! Death to Tolerance!"

Comonfort was elected president under the Constitution, and Juárez head of the Supreme Court, and first in line of succession, no vice-president being provided. Their terms hardly began when in December General Félix Zuloaga declared against the government, dissolved the Congress, and arrested Juárez. Comonfort at first cooperated with this movement, then changed his mind, released Juárez, tried unsuccessfully to raise armies, then went into exile in January 1858. Juárez made his way north to Querétaro, where seventy Liberal congressmen acknowledged his succession to the presidency. The Liberals were, however, in full disarray. As Juárez passed through one place, a witness recorded: "An Indian by the name of Juárez, who calls himself President of Mexico, has arrived in this city."

---

[7] Although it provided broad suffrage, an indirect system of elections would weaken popular influence, which abstentions in any event would make unimportant. A federal system was provided, but that would be subject to conditions in Mexico, as always. There were guarantees of freedom, if they could be enforced: press, speech, petition, assembly, and from forced labor or imprisonment for debt. The framers tried to restrict presidential powers, but it was not the language of the constitutions that made for dictatorship in Mexico. They abolished the Senate, which had been a center of Conservative strength, but the enforcement rather than the passage of laws was frequently the critical problem. There was impassioned debate over freedom of worship or an established church, which ended with no mention of either in the Constitution. It was a purely political document, normal for the time. No attention was paid to a radical delegate who favored effective redistribution of land, on the grounds that without an end to "the absurd economic system," it availed nothing to "proclaim abstract rights."

But he was harried by pursuing Conservative forces until he took ship on the Pacific coast.

The laws and Constitution of 1855–1857 were the radical culmination of decades of Liberal effort to establish equality before the law and control church and military intervention in the political process. It brought them the civil war that Comonfort feared. The War of the Reform, and the French Intervention as its extension, soaked the Mexican soil in blood, destroyed the Conservative party without ending conservatism, and gave the Liberals a seeming victory but few of its fruits.

The Conservatives had the advantages of a central position, the resources of the capital, most army officers, military equipment, the financial support of the church, and recognition by the European powers. They also had what some of them thought the advantage of European interest, possibly to put a European prince on a Mexican throne. They had another advantage in talented young Miguel Miramón, who soon replaced Zuloaga as commander. Some Indians fought for them and the faith, but others fought with the Liberals. Both sides in the War of the Reform acted barbarously at times. Prisoners frequently were shot. Liberals shot monks they caught bearing arms and priests who would not administer the sacraments to those they considered the enemies of Christ. Both sides called on the dark Virgin of Guadalupe, who had appeared so long ago to a humble Indian.

Juárez arrived by sea at Veracruz in May 1858, and that was the seat of his government for nearly three years. He was the greatest asset of the Liberal cause, although his collaborators there included such talented men as Miguel and Sebastián Lerdo de Tejada, Melchor Ocampo, and Guillermo Prieto. The area was Liberal, and the port commanded the important customs revenues and communications with other Mexican ports and with arms shippers abroad. But the town was small, uncomfortable, and dangerous. The least of the dangers was the muggy heat, and the greatest was disease, especially the terrible yellow fever. The last at least protected it from

highland armies, for Miramón came twice and was turned back in part by fever among his troops.

Although the Conservative armies did well at first, a Liberal tide turned out to be running in Mexico. Juárez bolstered this advantage with the Laws of the Reform, in 1859–1860. These confiscated without compensation all church property except the temples themselves; suppressed monasteries and gradually phased out nunneries; made marriage a civil contract; nationalized cemeteries; restricted public religious processions; and separated church and state. The measure on church land had little effect, since many estates of the church were gone before the war began, and Miramón sold more during the conflict, as did other chieftains on both sides. The movable property of churches was stripped by the armies.

Miramón's initial advantage was dissipated in 1860. The Liberals waxed; the Conservatives waned; and the former were in Mexico City in January 1861. Juárez was nominal head of a divided and impoverished people, apparently little advanced by forty years of factional strife. The Conservatives nursed their defeat, unvanquished. Continuing rebel military operations cost the government heavily. Raids came to the edge of Mexico City in the summer of 1861. Conservative guerrillas in Michoacán killed Ocampo and Degollado. Juárez, true to his principles, insisted on amnesty and free political debate. The result was factional abuse between and within parties. Many Liberal leaders did not care for the solemn, invariably black-suited, little Indian. The Congress that met in May 1861 included many radical orators, including Ignacio Altamirano, who would become a great literary figure. Anti-Juárez sentiment was rife. The country needed a united government, and it did not have one. It also desperately needed government revenues. National production had been mangled by the civil war. There was little more to be seized from the church, as the government was surprised to discover. An election in 1861 confirmed Juárez in the presidency, and he cut his own salary as a gesture. Most of the customs had been pledged on foreign debts. In July 1861 Juárez suspended service on those obligations. He really had no choice.[8] As was well known, unpaid soldiers were dangerous. Britain and France broke relations with Mexico. Mexico had many reasons for feeling strangled by foreigners. Worse was to come: six years of foreign invasion.

e. The French Intervention, 1862–1867

The foreign invasion of Mexico had roots in the Conservative longing for monarchy as a way of preventing modernization ("progress," Liberals called it). Some Mexican exiles in Paris in the 1850s tried to influence the French government in favor of intervention with that in view. The European powers wanted to collect their financial claims, including the unserviced loans and new claims arising from the fact that both sides in the War of the Reform had taken or damaged foreign property. Napoleon III's half-brother, the Comte de Morny, became a lobbyist for the claimants on the notorious Jecker bond issue. In 1859 Miramón's government had issued 15 million pesos' worth of bonds through the agency of Jecker, Torre and Company, receiving less than a million in cash. The Mexicans facilitated sale of the bonds by permitting merchants to use them in customs payments, appealing because they clearly would sell at a discount. With the Liberal victory, the bonds were worthless, and some claimants were Frenchmen. Napoleon made payment on the malodorous

bonds a condition of recognizing the Juárez government.

Napoleon's interest also was stimulated when Juárez ended debt service and Britain and Spain appeared ready to intervene. So in October 1861 France joined Spain and Britain in the London Convention: agreeing to take ports and some military points in Mexico, but not to acquire territory permanently or interfere with Mexico's choice of its form of government. Napoleon had decided, however, to garner some prestige abroad to cover the deficiencies of his domestic policies. He foolishly accepted the views of various relatives, officials, exiles, and lobbyists that the way to this dream was by carrying a monarch to the supposedly happily expectant Mexicans. The candidate decided upon was the eager Archduke Maximilian of Hapsburg. Napoleon III and Maximilian made a matchless case of the blind leading the blind.

The armed forces of the three powers were at Veracruz in January 1862. Spain and Britain withdrew when they found that Napoleon was bent on conquest. The French met one disappointment when there was no national uprising against the "tyranny" of Juárez, and a second when on January 25 the latter declared the invaders outlaws and Mexicans who aided them subject to execution. The French army made the difficult march to Puebla, where it found a Mexican army dug into a hill. The French commander on May 5, 1862, incautiously stormed the heights, and was defeated with a loss of more than a thousand men. This, the glorious Cinco de Mayo, and the earlier declaration that the French were pirates, might have warned a more intelligent man than Napoleon the Little. Nor had Napoleon or his generals much conception of Mexico's size (nearly four times that of France) or the difficulties of its terrain. Napoleon the Great might have given some hints based on his own disastrous experience in Spain. Napoleon III sent 30,000 more troops under General Forey, who was not ready to march inland until early 1863. Puebla heroically stood a siege of two months, eating rats and weeds

---

[8] While he was at Veracruz Juárez tried to raise money by selling to the United States transit rights in the Isthmus of Tehuantepec, an act of desperation that brought much criticism. The sale was provided for in the McLane-Ocampo Treaty of 1859, which permitted the United States to keep troops in a zone granted in perpetuity. The United States Senate rejected the treaty. Juárez had some reason to worry about possible United States intervention if he did not agree to the treaty. In 1861 the United States minister in Mexico suggested financial aid in return for mineral rights, but Juárez would not agree. The Mexican minister in Washington knew of some—minority—sentiment in the United States in favor of acquisition of all Mexico.

before it surrendered. Porfirio Díaz was one of the officers who escaped at the end. Only seventy miles away, on May 31, Juárez, his cabinet, and a ragtag army fled north from Mexico City, the president in his black suit and black carriage, once more a fugitive, but this time pursued by the modern army of a great power. Benito Juárez thought of dying but not of surrender.

In areas within reach of the French armies, Conservatives were briefly ecstatic, until Forey issued a guarantee to the existing owners of former ecclesiastical properties, some of whom were French citizens. The clergy threatened to close the churches. Forey said he would blow them open with artillery. The Conservatives were learning what in their fanaticism they would not anticipate—that the invaders came to serve their own purposes. Conservatives clung to their disastrous course, as they had clung to the unspeakable Santa Anna, convoking an assembly to offer a crown to the unknown Maximilian of Hapsburg.

Driven to the north by the French, Juárez had some comfort in United States recognition. Washington protested the French invasion, but was occupied with its Civil War. Union victories in 1863, however, improved supply lines to sections of Juarista coast, and put heart in the Mexican patriots. But Juárez was discovering again that patriotism in Mexico was often smothered by personal interest, even with the artillery caissons of the invader rumbling down the roads of the *patria*. Santiago Vidaurri, *caudillo* of the northeast, declared for Maximilian, and Juárez had to use scarce men and supplies in a regional civil war. Although many Conservatives took up arms in alliance with the French, the patriot *guerrilleros* also assembled. In the south indomitable Juan Alvarez, now seventy-four, declared: "Men of the coast! I, who have ever led you against tyrants, still live!" But French General Bazaine conquered the northeast by autumn 1864, and Juárez went far northwest to Paso del Norte (later Ciudad Juárez) on the Texas border, ready to pass again into exile in the United States.

The emperor Maximilian, in his early thirties, and his wife Carlotta, a Belgian princess, arrived at Veracruz in May 1864. He came with the assurance that Mexicans wanted him, for he had insisted on that, accepting a trumped-up plebiscite because he wanted to believe it. He also arrived with an exaggerated notion, shared with Napoleon III, of the riches of Mexico. The squalid little port of Veracruz was disillusioning; so was a letter he received there from Juárez, informing him that history would judge him a thief and a murderer. Not much better was the trip in a mule-drawn coach over the rough mountain road to Mexico City.

Maximilian soon discovered that many Mexicans hated all aspects of the invasion. He and Carlotta pathetically tried to identify themselves with the country by wearing *serapes* and eating *tortillas*. It was disappointing to discover that the Conservatives were less interested in good government than in their own positions. Maximilian shocked them by embracing Liberal measures. He also extracted large sums, sometimes forcefully, from clerics and *hacendados*. Although some abandoned him, most did not; and the Liberals were not impressed. Some Liberals did collaborate with the regime, from one reason of expediency or another, but most did not; it remained chiefly a Conservative treason. Maximilian despised the inefficiency and corruption of Mexican bureaucrats and the irresponsibility of his Mexican collaborators. He came from an orderly country, and wanted to make Mexican government and society function like those of Austria, an impossible dream. Maximilian was profoundly disappointed, but he insisted on pretending to others, and sometimes to himself, that he was not. He was incapable of hard realism and escaped into dreams, finding time to fuss about court etiquette and architecture when his problems called for unremitting toil. He liked to draft laws when action was needed. He was a poor judge of people and a bad executive. He was extravagant in a situation where there was not a peso to spare. He had some fuzzy ideals and unformed ideas about making the peasants happy, of which his defenders make much, but on the whole he was a weak lost soul, dependent on a French army that determined many of his policies but could not defeat the Juaristas. French soldiers hated the duty. It was dangerous to stray from the main roads, or to pursue simple pleasures among a people who wished them dead and were eager to contrive the same.

With the end of its Civil War in April 1865, the United States increased aid to Juárez. Napoleon III now could imagine the use in Mexico of the veteran troops of Grant and Sherman. He was appalled by the cost of his adventure. He knew that he had more urgent problems in connection with expansionist Prussia. He began to disengage himself in 1865. As Bazaine retreated, the Juaristas followed. Maximilian long considered but finally rejected abdication, and stayed to face nearly certain death. In March 1867 Bazaine left Veracruz with the last French soldiers. Maximilian was captured and shot in June. He had stayed partly out of a sense of duty to his supporters. Carlotta also wanted to cling to the throne. She went to Europe to plead with Napoleon and the Pope for aid, became deranged, and lived in that condition well into the twentieth century. She has seemed to some a symbol of romantic tragedy, of young love betrayed and broken. Juárez rejected pleas for mercy for Maximilian from exalted Europeans. He was not vindictive, merely just and realistic. A man who had come with arms in his hands and was responsible for thousands of Mexican deaths—even if others shared that responsibility—could not be told, "Go, and sin no more." Invasion, paid for with the blood of patriots, must not be dismissed as a peccadillo.

f. Factionalism and *Caudillismo*, 1867–1890s

After the defeat of the French and the Conservatives, Juárez and the other Liberal leaders wasted their opportunities in squabbling until Porfirio Díaz swept away all discussion with a dictatorship that lasted thirty-five years.

The Restored Republic, 1867–1876

What Mexicans call the Restored Republic relied on the old methods and for a decade repetitiously demonstrated their ineffectiveness. Juárez recognized in 1867 that Mexico needed peace and that it could be achieved only through strong government. He tried to provide it himself, and his actions led to charges of excessive ambition and betrayal of Liberal principles. He used traditional methods of electoral manipulation to secure his election in 1867 and 1871 and to try to secure friendly Congresses. The last was impossible, as members resented Juárez's efforts to strengthen the presidency. There was only minor objection to his lack of effort to enforce the Reform laws, however. The Liberals were split, as usual, while conservatism still lived although the Conservative party was dead. One of the gravest threats to peace and orderly government was the swollen army, which Juárez pared for reasons of principle and economy. Disgruntled, accustomed to action, unable to find opportunities for material advancement, these men were ever ready for action against the government.

Juárez also had the usual problem with the states and knew that his authority depended on voluntary cooperation. Public revenues remained small. A subsidy of a million pesos a year to finish the Veracruz–Mexico City railway ate up nearly 10 percent of the budget and met criticism as an extravagance as well as a giveaway to British interests. Discussion of new revenues from land taxes, even on uncultivated lands to encourage their use, met congressional refusal. As a result, although Juárez retained the interest in roads and schools of his days as governor of Oaxaca, he could do little about them.

He was not accepted in his lifetime as the eminent figure he became later. He was anathema to doctrinaire Liberals and a barrier to all the ambitious. Porfirio Díaz and Sebastián Lerdo de Tejada opposed his election in 1867 and again in 1871. In 1871 there were disorders in various places in protest, and Porfirio Díaz rose in rebellion with the cry of "No Reelection!" Juárez got emergency power from the Congress, pressed men into the army, and put down the rebellion, only to die in 1872.

His liberal legacy was neither immediately apparent nor usable. Mexico wanted development more than political reform. But Juárez had established for a later generation an ideal of steadfast patriotism and justice. No one believed that the supreme man of the law had robbed or betrayed his fellows, his nation, or his posterity. However Juárez's ambition be judged, he was a man of towering integrity, and the incidents of his life of service were the expression of a rare spirit. .

Lerdo de Tejada, head of the Supreme Court, finished the presidential term to 1876. He was intelligent, learned, arrogant, and a poor politician. He saw to incorporation into the Constitution of the Reform Laws of 1859 and enforcement of restrictions on the use of clerical garb in public and in religious processions, and inaugurated the Veracruz–Mexico City railway in 1873. In 1876 he was reelected, by the usual methods, and Porfirio Díaz had resort to the only means of ousting an administration candidate. His revolt proclaimed the idea of "Effective Suffrage! No Reelection!" Although Lerdo had strong support, Díaz gradually won. Díaz had some minor aid from the United States, where Lerdo, suspicious of ties with the north, had offended railway promoters. But it was individual and regional ambition and a fragmented political system that were too much for Lerdo, as for many a president before him. Díaz would change that.

Economic Change in the Early Porfiriato, 1876–1890s

Díaz began as a poor mestizo boy of Oaxaca (born 1830). He received little schooling. Serving in the army as a youth, he undertook a military career as a leader of irregular soldiers, first against Santa Anna, then for La Reforma, next against the French and their Conservative allies, and finally against Juárez and Lerdo. During those decades he also learned the realities of Mexican politics. He became the quintessential *caudillo*, with a rare feel for political tactics. He served as president in 1876–1880, gave lip service to no reelection by putting a friend in for the term 1880–1884, then returned to office for the next quarter century. The political methods that made this possible will be considered later.[9] Díaz brought political peace but not modernization in the sense of participation.

Economic modernization, of a sort, Díaz did promote. This became apparent in the 1880s. Although Díaz tried to keep economic change from affecting political and social institutions, in the long run he failed. For this reason, the economic changes he wrought seem now—though not to many living then—to suggest coming transformations, although their expression was long delayed. In 1910–1917 the imbalances and frustrations created by the Díaz regime, some due to economic change, would produce a social explosion without precedent in Latin American history.

Díaz established firm control of rebellion and banditry for the first time in the history of the republic, an essential contribution to economic development. A good credit rating abroad was assured by the early 1880s with settlement of the British debt at a figure that outraged some Mexicans, but seemed a necessity to the development-minded. Foreign investment quickened, especially from Britain and the United States, with emphasis on railways and mining. Probably in the absence of the Porfirian dictatorship the railways would have been built more slowly and with equal waste and profiteering and poor planning. Díaz at first was doubtful about railway building and canceled a Lerdo contract,[10] but he quickly changed his mind. The mere 360 miles of railway in 1876 became 6,876 in 1892. There were 1,000 miles of track for horse-drawn trams and 24,000 miles of telegraph lines.

---

[9] See Chapter 32.
[10] Díaz had in 1876 charged Lerdo with delivering Mexico into the hands of a British railway company, with a monopoly and high rates he said damaged the economy.

Many means were used to promote and regulate railways, some of them to protect users against the companies. The railroad law of 1880 made foreign corporations in Mexico subject to Mexican law. Although the Díaz government was determined to have the railways built rapidly and expected the foreign promoters to make big profits, it was aware of the dangers. Hundreds of concessions for lines were granted, most often with generous subsidies of money, notes on national lands, customs certificates, or guarantees of interest on capital for each kilometer of track laid. Many Mexicans profited from the building of the railways. The line up the central valleys was built in 1880–1884: 1,224 miles between Mexico City and Paso del Norte, across from El Paso, Texas. San Luís Potosí in the highlands was linked with the Atlantic port of Tampico in 1891. The short route to the eastern United States, through Monterrey to Laredo, was ready in 1888. Connections between Veracruz and Mexico City and Oaxaca were finished by 1892. Other lines were completed or begun. The importance of this rapid railway building for the economic, political, and social development of Mexico can hardly be exaggerated.

The modern mining industry began because of measures adopted by Díaz. In 1884 and 1892 laws modified the Roman/Spanish/Mexican thesis that subsoil rights are granted by the state and have no relationship to landownership. This change was congenial to the legal traditions of Britain and the United States and to the holders of capital with an interest in mining. The change in mining law, together with political stability, railways, and the reduction of banditry, brought money into the industry in the 1880s and thereafter. Industrial minerals for the first time assumed some importance alongside silver. Although mineral output still was not great in the 1880s, it seemed likely to grow rapidly thereafter.

Commerce, manufacturing, and banking benefited from all these developments. By the 1890s, a new economy was emerging with an enlarged middle class and a small industrial laboring group. Even the *hacendados* felt the breath of new opportunities for commercial operations. They shipped cotton by the new railways. But the haciendas changed in no other way, and the regime's protection of *latifundio* and peonage caused some of the pressure for change. Those pressures were accumulating in the 1890s. When they burst the shell of old institutions in 1910–1917, they would scald some of them mortally.

27 Chile: Stability and Growth, from Independence to the 1890s

Chile did something surprising. Nothing about its colonial experience or its performance in 1810–1830 suggested that it would be first in Spanish America to achieve a notable combination of political stability and economic development. After ten years of the squalid and generally unproductive *caudillismo* that befouled the early history of the rest of Spanish America, Chile abruptly changed course. It did so by tough conservative insistence on predominance over liberals and civilian predominance over the military. The shift was a triumph of leadership by one man, Diego Portales. Peace and effective government helped economic development, and that strengthened upper-class attachment to the system. Prosperity improved public revenues, and some went for schools, which contributed to an early growth of a stronger spirit of nationalism than in much of nineteenth-century Latin America. That helped with the appearance of the beginnings of popular participation in politics in Chile in the 1880s, a small start on the struggle against the society of privilege. Prosperity was increasingly tied to dependence on exports of a few commodities, chiefly mineral.

a. Autocratic Rule and Economic Growth, Independence to the 1860s

Chile was a poor colony, with little precious metal and only modest exports of agricultural

and pastoral products, although they increased in the eighteenth century, stimulating the economic ambitions of the elite. The whites and the small Indian population mixed more thoroughly than in most of Latin America, and racial distinctions became blurred. That did not, however, weaken class divisions. In 1810 creoles began forcing local rule, and proclaimed such liberal measures as free trade and gradual emancipation of black slaves.[1] Conservative and liberal creole groups formed, and regional differences assumed a more political character. Independence forces lost to conservatives aided by the Spanish administration in Peru, and the country suffered the creation of many military bands, some of them quickly habituated to robbery and promiscuous violence. In 1814 the patriot leader Bernardo O'Higgins had to retreat over the Andes to join Argentine General San Martín, commander of an army forming to invade Chile and Peru. In early 1817 San Martín's army crossed the high mountains into Chile, with O'Higgins commanding the Chilean troops. The allies beat the royalists at Chacabuco, and O'Higgins became supreme director of Chile and head of its army. In 1818 Independence was declared and a great victory over the royalists at Maipú secured it. What

---

[1] See Chapter 17 on Chile in the late colonial era; and Chapters 19–20 on its experience in the Independence period.

was not secured was agreement among the Chilean elite on political matters.

Establishment of Stable Government, Independence to the 1830s

O'Higgins thought agreement could not be obtained by discussion, and that the times did not permit prolonged confusion. So he ruled in 1817–1823 without a Congress, rejecting demands for a more representative system. Something like a constitution was adopted and O'Higgins had it "approved" by a plebiscite in which no one voted against it. O'Higgins thought dictatorial rule necessary in view of the disorder in the country, the needs of the expedition to Peru, and the great problem of changing Chilean society sufficiently to make it capable of self-government. This last argument for dictatorship was to be offered many times in Latin America in the next century and a half.

O'Higgins met increasing opposition, not lessened by his support of San Martín, until the latter sailed with the army to Peru in August 1820. O'Higgins had the aid of the *Logia Lautarina*, a secret society that San Martín had set up in Argentina to knit together leaders who were committed to Independence. They were expected to collaborate secretly on civilian and military matters. O'Higgins, a member, depended on the lodge when he returned to Chile. Understandably, many Chileans objected both to the method and to its Argentine connections.

The dictator had many good qualities, but tact and a spirit of compromise were not among them. He used the military in civilian affairs, directly and as a threat. He frequently interfered with the press and expressions of opinion. He used arbitrary means of trying to change Chilean social customs. His use of troops and summary courts to put down rural brigandage seemed to rural magnates part of a dangerous centralizing tendency. He used public funds lavishly to support the expedition being prepared for Peru; for ships, equipment, foreign officers, a navy with transports to carry the army around the great

northern desert. Many people lacked the vision of O'Higgins and San Martín on the necessity of defeating Spanish forces that were not visible from their own doorsteps, so expenditures seemed to them excessive.

There was much need of military force against royalists and bandits, sometimes difficult to distinguish. In the south, royalists still had help from the local population, and some from Araucanian Indians. The warfare in the area in 1819 and succeeding years was barbaric as Generals Freire and Prieto struggled to end it. Not only was a brutalization process continuing among the general population, but military commanders were building convictions and ambitions that centered on military solutions. In 1821 Prieto managed to defeat many of the southern royalist and bandit forces. He executed some, but pardoned others and incorporated them into the Independence army. This common practice in Spanish America sometimes was due to expediency, sometimes to ambition, but it never improved military attachment to constitutional government.

O'Higgins became unpopular not only because of military rule and high taxes but because of a tactless insistence on liberal measures. He offended with anticlerical acts, religious toleration, freedom of opinion, and a plan to abolish entail. His other liberal actions were much like what was done or suggested in other countries immediately after Independence was secured, and the conservative reaction resembled that in Argentina and Mexico to similar measures. The O'Higgins regime was toppled in 1823 by uprisings in which General Ramón Freire was prominent. O'Higgins, after more than a decade of service as soldier-statesman, was forced into exile, and never returned.

During the next few years Chile was as turbulent as any area in Latin America. Soldiers of the Independence movement, outlaws, Indians, lower-class figures with no other opportunity, used violence to seize or maintain rule or to take property. In the upper class there were conflicts between monarchists and republicans, between federalists and centralists, and between views on the church. In the 1820s military expenses swallowed most of the public revenues. The military was unreliable and often acted in response to bribes. This disorder was ended by a businessman, Diego Portales. In 1824 his company received the tobacco monopoly (*estanco*) from the government. It was unpopular and unworkable, so Portales almost at once began trying to get a favorable termination. His *estanquero* faction drew heavily on the more conservative part of the oligarchy, known as the *pelucones* (bigwigs), and Portales began to give the group a definition it had not had before. It was opposed by a more liberal group of the politically active minority, known as *pipiolos* (novices or tenderfeet). The views of these factions were much like those of the liberals and conservatives in the rest of Latin America, and in Chile they would finally become parties with those names.

Portales was a practical man, who wanted a stable system that would be good for private business and for the kind of national development he thought possible. He rejected monarchy and democracy, the latter as being unsuited to a population generally lacking, he thought, in civic virtue, that must be guided firmly by the few virtuous and enlightened citizens. When a civil war broke out in 1829 over an election, Portales became minister of war and with great energy and talent directed his faction to victory by 1830. Then he erected a conservative system that endured, with adjustments, until 1891.

His supreme and astonishing achievement was subordinating the military to civil government. In this accomplishment Portales followed the obvious course of centralizing authority over the military in the civil government at Santiago, to prevent the growth of satrapies under individual officers, which plagued Chile in the 1820s and much of Latin America throughout the nineteenth century. He executed many officers of the opposition in 1830, and thereafter handled officers with bribes, demotion, exile, and death. He tried to improve professional skills and attitudes by founding a military academy and hiring French and British instructors. An unsuccessful

army revolt in 1837 eliminated more unreliable officers. Portales also quickly put down banditry, partly by persuading municipalities to create police forces. He furthermore reduced the size of the army and put it under severe discipline, with the aid of regular pay and careful selection of officers. He organized militia units to serve as a makeweight against the army and required the upper class to support them.

That political feat, of course, was what made his other measures work: he persuaded the upper class to show a substantially united face and willingness to take up arms in favor of civil supremacy. In the beginning, it was largely a conservative policy. Liberals were purged from the army, and civilian liberals who objected to this or other measures were treated harshly. But some civilian liberals at once, and others soon, accepted the wisdom of controlling the military. Probably a majority of the politically active in all Hispanic America accepted that principle, but Portales made it effective. This early subordination of the military in Chile, unmatched elsewhere in Spanish America, removed one great source of rancor and instability from political and governmental affairs, reduced military expenditures and property damage, and contributed to a civic and financial atmosphere reassuring to business enterprise.

The second major part of Portales' system was conservative domination of office, which he secured by vigorous persecution of liberals. The system was fostered by the Constitution of 1833, which endured until 1925. It provided a president chosen indirectly and permitted immediate reelection, literacy and property qualification for participation in civic affairs, a centralized governmental system with no features of federalism, Roman Catholicism as the state religion with other sects not permitted to worship publicly. The government was given authority to use severe measures (for example, the state of siege) in case of emergencies. The Constitution was an unremarkable nineteenth-century conservative type.

The operation of the political-governmental system was quite remarkable. It was supported by an effective majority of the propertied and by the church. While it made ample use of the state of siege, it was blessedly free of the military adventurism so common in Mexico. Three elected presidents served two five-year terms each in 1831–1861,[2] a record without parallel in those years in the rest of Spanish America. One reason for this success was Portales' ability. Also, regionalism was weaker than in some countries, because of the small population and its concentration in the center, and the relative ease of getting at rebels in the north and south by sea. Another suggestion is that the fusion of the landed aristocracy and the mercantile class had gone so far by Independence that there was less tension between them than in other places. In any event, there was effective agreement among the majority of the upper class for many years, and *caudillismo* could not find a foothold.

Portales in 1836 insisted on a war with Peru and Bolivia, because Bolivian Andrés Santa Cruz had proclaimed them united. Portales (and some Argentine leaders) saw a threat in so large a combination. That interpretation was strengthened by the fact that Santa Cruz gave aid to rebel Chilean General Freire. There also was friction due to a tariff war involving Peruvian sugar and Chilean wheat. There was opposition to the war in Chile, aggravated by Portales' assumption of dictatorial powers under a state of siege, and his institution of what a Chilean historian has called a "reign of terror." An army faction seized Portales and he was killed in 1837 during the ensuing civil strife. Chile ultimately won the war of 1836–1839, and the federation of Peru and Bolivia was ended. The attitudes of nationalism and *realpolitik* in the Chilean policy were to be characteristic of its leaders in the nineteenth century.

The Rise of Liberalism, 1830s–1860s

Repression of liberals declined at the end of the 1830s, and in the 1840s liberals gained new

strength from intellectual developments. The lively intellectual activity at Santiago was made possible by the prosperity due at least in part to peace and stable government. European ideas were discussed. Newspapers promoted controversy. One intellectual critic was José V. Lastarria, an eloquent advocate of more democratic government. A more radical enemy of the system was Santiago Arcos, an intellectual socialist. Young Francisco Bilbao in the early 1840s expressed liberal views on the church and other questions and became a hero to rebellious youth. After being punished by the government, he went to Europe in 1844, where he imbibed more radical doctrine and witnessed the republican revolution of 1848 in France. He returned to Chile in 1850 and created a Society of Equality, which favored social change in a rather hazy way, with reason and love as governing principles. The organization attracted foes of the government and turned to politics, whereupon the authorities closed it. In 1851 the government prepared in the usual way to impose its candidate in an election. It used a state of siege, closed newspapers, and exiled liberals, including Lastarria. The resulting riots did not prevent the election of Conservative Manuel Montt, so the Liberal party (formed in 1849) tried a revolt and put up a bloody resistance before being subdued.

During Montt's administration in the 1850s the tension between Liberals and Conservatives escalated, due to a number of economic and religious issues. One great controversy concerned entail.[3] At Independence in Chile, as in all Latin America, some liberals considered this protection for great estates unjust, detrimental to agriculture, and a key prop of the old society. O'Higgins proposed the abolition of entail in 1818 but an upper-class outcry made him desist. The subject was debated on a number of occasions in the 1820s. The Constitution of 1828 abolished entails, and that was one reason for Conservative fervor in the civil war that brought them to power under the guidance of Portales. The Constitution of 1833 restored entail. There was not

---

[2] Joaquín Prieto, 1831–1841; Manuel Bulnes, 1841–1851; Manuel Montt, 1851–1861.

[3] See Chapter 23 on entail.

much discussion of entail thereafter until 1845, when it became one of the issues promoted by the growing liberal group and was pursued with passion thereafter, often in the newspapers. Bilbao wrote a diatribe against entail as contrary to the constitutional system. By the early 1850s public opinion had turned against entail, and it was abolished in laws of 1852 and 1857. Although the legislation was a defeat for Conservatives, it did not end concentrated landownership. Destroying *latifundio* in Latin America was extraordinarily difficult.

During all these years in Chile there had been the usual Latin American liberal criticism of an established church and its practices, but it was for long a minority view. Camilo Henríquez in the early 1820s asserted it in newspaper articles. The prevailing view, however, was more nearly that of Don Juan Egaña, a stern conservative, who thought that a single faith and church were needed to avoid not only disagreement and even civil war but a confusion that would lead to irreligion. Later, the privileged church came under renewed attack during the intellectual ferment of the 1840s. The wider use of newspapers and growing difficulty of muzzling opinion led to argument that freedom of religion was a condition necessary for "civilization" and for "progress," as a newspaper put it. Bilbao embraced the free-worship view, and the church declared him blasphemous and immoral. There had been argument for years over the constitutional prohibition on public worship by non-Catholics. Foreign Protestants at Valparaíso, many of them merchants, long came near to violating the prohibition. In the 1850s the Catholic archbishop said everyone knew that Protestants used a building for worship that had the appearance, illegally, of a church, and that was a danger to the credulous. Anticlericals replied with demands for change in the Constitution.

The quarrel split Conservatives. Some who wanted reform of the church and also curbs on presidential powers went into the Liberal party; other moderate Conservatives joined moderate Liberals in a new National party that supported the incumbent Montt; and a third group of Conservatives, reactionary in bent, angered by the end of entail and by the course of the church dispute, allied with the radical wing of the Liberals. This third group campaigned against the presidential candidate of the administration, so Montt took repressive measures. Revolts and other pressure of such magnitude resulted that Montt switched candidates, to José Joaquín Pérez, who was more acceptable to moderates, and he was elected in 1861.

This decision and others in the 1860s marked a considerable strengthening of the Liberal position and a softening of the repressive measures used in earlier decades. Early in the new administration the Radical party was established. Begun as a party of mining interests in the north, with support from regionalism there and in the south, it later attracted wider backing. Although it was liberal rather than radical, it was the leading group favoring less presidential power, a wider suffrage, and drastic church reform. In 1864 the Liberals won the congressional elections, and the first Radical was chosen. Since the 1840s political life had opened up considerably, although the system was still essentially oligarchic.

b. Economic and Social Development

The effective political system of Chile encouraged economic growth and paid for a superior educational system. Those developments contributed to an early surge of nationalist sentiment in Chile.

The Economy

The economic prospects of Chile at Independence appeared only fair. By good management, however, its elites did well in the following decades with the opportunities in commerce, agriculture, and especially mining. Chilean economic development was one of the most notable in Latin America and made possible Chile's strong foreign policies and better-than-average social development. It diversified the interests of the upper class and increased the size of the bourgeoisie, but scarcely affected the poor.

Government economic policy was a mixture of laissez-faire and intervention. Government operations and fiscal policies were favorable to business. Expenditures were scrutinized with a conservative eye. Taxes ordinarily were kept low. Import duties generally were 50 percent or more of total revenues, with export levies on metals a close second. Whereas in 1856 about 66 percent of government revenues came from levies on foreign trade, in 1897 it was 97 percent. Although that distribution was partly by Chilean decision, since import duties brought the most revenue, mining levies were nearly as important, and the total situation plainly was that of a monoculture.

Legislation generally aimed to further Chilean development without major outlays from the treasury. When Chilean capitalists declined to invest in such low-profit enterprises as railways and steamships, the government provided subsidies for foreign entrepreneurs. Where Chilean capital was avidly busy, notably in mining, the government supported it in various ways, even finally with a war of conquest. The question of foreign participation in the economy caused debate but was settled more on practical than theoretical bases, because Chile needed foreign technology and capital, especially with local money allowed to flow where it pleased. By the standards of the nineteenth century, foreign participation in Chile was not excessive, especially before the increased foreign role in mining late in the century. It is, however, a favorite Chilean leftist charge of the later twentieth century that capitalist-oriented Chileans of the nineteenth made inferior, foreign-dominated development decisions.

Protectionist measures helped only a few lines of fabrication.[4] Protectionism was diluted or defeated by contraband, by preference for better or cheaper foreign goods, and in many cases by the obvious inability of Chile to provide the needed capital, markets, or expertise. The elite would not support the expense of thoroughgoing protectionism.[5] In 1843 such protection as existed was loosened, to the advantage of imports. And as the century went on, laissez-faire sentiment in Chile grew considerably, with disastrous effects upon Chilean mining interests. Manufactures grew steadily but modestly in a country that had only 2.5 million inhabitants at the end of the century. In 1883 the government sponsored a national association of manufacturers. By then many sorts of food processing and textile and clothing manufacture were of some consequence, and mining and transportation activities required semi-industrial foundries for the modification and repair of equipment.

Mineral income was the key to Chilean growth. Opportunities leapt to the eye and created great enthusiasm. Chileans and foreigners ran to the mines of the north in the hope of fortune, and some found it. As early as 1820 there was argument about foreign participation, even in shipping out copper and supplying the mining camps, which were in an inhospitable desert. By 1840 Chile was a major producer of copper and mined silver and gold. Coal from the southern mines went to local steamships and railways in midcentury. By 1864 about 70 percent of the value of Chilean exports came from mineral products; it was more than 78 percent in 1881. The industry used some foreign technicians and methods but mainly Chilean capital. Copper was usually the leading Chilean export from the 1830s to 1880, though in some years silver took

---

[4] In 1824 a special tax concession was designed to help nationals and foreigners establish factories for several lines, including hemp, linen, and copper.

[5] There was considerable debate in Chile in the 1850s over classical free trade theories, and local people indicated that they understood that such policy worked better for highly industrialized nations than for underdeveloped Chile. The fact remained, however, that Chilean government and private resources severely limited the amount of planned development that could be indulged in. There was constant support for certain sorts of government intervention, but it was to support Chilean private enterprise. Its sinews were robust but small and its aims realistic.

first place. In the 1870s Chilean copper met serious foreign competition. Although it still supplied 38 percent of the copper in world markets in 1876, it was falling off rapidly and did not come back until the twentieth century.

Nitrates were worked for fertilizer in the northern desert as early as 1830. In the 1860s they also were used in nitroglycerin and smokeless powder. In the 1880s nitrates were the most important source of government revenue, having surpassed copper. Much of the fabulous nitrate lode lay in Peru and Bolivia, and there Chilean investment grew rapidly in the 1860s and 1870s. The nitrate industry was dominated by Chilean capital and workers, who not only exploited the deposits, but built roads, railways, and ports. British and German interests were also at work. In addition to nitrates and iodine, silver and guano were exploited in the north. Peru and Bolivia feared that they were losing control of some of their most valuable national territories. Many controversies arose over taxes and other regulations. The result was the War of the Pacific (1879–1883), discussed later, by which Chile acquired jurisdiction over much of the territory. The mining industry as a whole was large enough by the 1890s to have created in the north a new regional interest that objected to Santiago power and policy, as well as an industrial proletariat that was about to inject a new force into politics.

Agriculture in Chile remained in the hands of large holders. The great estate owners were a part of the conservative combination. Tax and other policy favored their operations. There was, however, a considerable turnover in estate ownership in the 1870s and thereafter. Some of the new holders came from commerce and mining. Many of the great owners lived in Santiago, and their fortunes and their children became much mixed with fortunes from mining and commerce. The fact remains, however, that the diversification of elite economic interests was of no value to the rural poor. The *inquilinos* were peasants tied materially and psychologically to the *fundos* (estates often smaller than great haciendas, a word that dwindled in usage in Chile). The

inquilino condition was as miserable as that of peons in Mexico. Rural labor, tenants, and small holders had a thin time of it. In time, there was some replacement of *inquilinos* with wage labor, and *inquilinos* moved to town, to complicate social problems there. German colonists in the south did better, but they were few in number. There was a boom in wheat and other exports to California in the 1850s and 1860s, but it soon met unmatchable competition. Before that happened, Chile built some of the best flour mills in the world. Some owners continued to make money in agriculture, for the growing Chilean cities and the tens of thousands of people living in the desert mining areas ensured demand.

Although the mercantile community of Chile was small at Independence and the merchant marine tiny, there were ambitious people in the field, and some had capital from prominent families; also, some foreign merchants, mainly from Britain and the United States, went to Chile. A free trade decree in 1811 by the new independent government improved opportunities for foreigners, primarily to encourage them to bring in arms for the contest with Spain. But some Chileans even that early objected to competing foreigners. In 1819 the O'Higgins government decreed against foreigners in coastal trade or retail selling, but it had to grant exceptions. This gap between desire and fact aborted many measures of economic nationalism in nineteenth-century Latin America. Many foreign merchants became Chileanized, in some cases by marrying local women. As in other places, some of them engaged in other activities, as banking, mining, agriculture.

The economy benefited from the introduction of steam navigation and railways. Steamships were a godsend to a land at the ends of the earth, and Chile adopted them promptly upon their effective development in Europe and North America. As in the case of new flour-milling techniques, Chileans acted quickly when technology could be made to pay in the environment. In this case, the first risks were assigned to William Wheelwright of Massachusetts, who received a franchise in 1835. His vessels arrived in 1840, but the company lost money until the end of the decade, when the discovery of gold in California helped the shipping business. When Wheelwright's monopoly ran out in 1850, Congress, listening to local entrepreneurs, ended the exclusive privilege. It did, however, continue subsidies to shipping companies, one of the forms of intervention that the Chilean elite approved and could afford without large taxes. Commercial activity continued to grow, and was the source of a number of fortunes.

In 1845 Wheelwright asked the government for a railway contract. His request caused debate, some of it dubious of foreign participation, but it had considerable support from capitalists in Chile and passed in 1849. Henry Meiggs, another North American, went to Chile in 1855 and built bridges and railways. The government granted subsidies of various sorts, including land, as in all Latin America. The lines were short, and in the typical Latin American pattern ran from ports to areas of traffic inland, without lateral connections. This pattern was especially inviting in such a long, narrow country, with gaps between inhabited sections, so that north-south transportation was best handled by sea. Railway lines inland to the northern mines were a vast improvement over pack mules. Wheelwright opened a railway of some fifty miles between the Copiapó mines and the sea in 1851. The railway from Santiago to its port, Valparaíso, opened in 1863. Other railways, streetcar lines, and the telegraph were laid down.

Social Developments

Chile had a small population in a country larger than France—not much over half a million at Independence, about 1.5 million in the mid-nineteenth century, and 2.5 million at its end. The bulk of the people lived in the central valley, with smaller numbers in the northern mining desert and the forested middle south. The Araucanian Indians were confined to the south, with a situation of frontier warfare, and peace was not arranged until the 1880s on the basis of creating "reservations" for them. Gradual emancipation of the few black slaves was provided by Congress in 1811, and full abolition in 1823. The black element soon was assimilated. There was little immigration from Europe. With the population increasingly homogeneous, racial differences were less a cause of tension than in most Latin American countries. Residence was heavily rural, but after mid-century a stronger trend toward town dwelling set in. Santiago was by far the largest city, with 48,000 in 1830, and 100,000 in 1860.

Chileans were highly class-conscious, and social mobility was limited by that as well as by the system of privilege in economic life. Although the well-to-do differed to some extent, as on church questions, they were generally fused on social matters. With time, diversification in the upper class did weaken this fusion; prosperity created a larger middle class that was not part of the ruling combination, and education created intellectuals who objected to what they considered the exaggerated situation of class and privilege.

Only about 3,000 of the 200,000 school-age children attended schools in the 1840s; consequently, most people were illiterate. There was demand for improvement, especially by Liberals, but also among some Conservatives. In the 1840s the pressure for more schooling became important. In 1842 a normal school for training teachers was created at Santiago. The Argentine exile Domingo Sarmiento performed excellent service as its chief. A Pole, Ignacio Domoyko, in the 1840s contributed to modernization of the secondary-school curriculum. In 1842 the University of Chile was established, with the Venezuelan Andrés Bello as the first rector. Although it grew only slowly, before the end of the century it put Chile in the forefront of Latin American intellectual development.

The upsurge of interest in intellectual matters in the 1840s was helped by somewhat lessened repression by government, although both civil and ecclesiastical officials continued on occasion to try to control the increasing liveliness of discussion. Newspapers had multiplied, and by 1842 two of them were dailies. Foreigners helped to bring in the most recent concepts and technologies. The intellectual life of the Chilean educated minority became more sophisticated after mid-century. Cities became larger and received improvements of function and appearance. Elegance and learning became not only more prevalent but more honored. Educated Chileans desired both the fruits and the reputation of civilization and progress, two words they often used. Thus, the idea of modernization grew, together with some of its manifestations.

Nationalism grew faster in Chile than elsewhere in Latin America, encouraged by upper-class agreement on many aspects of public policy and by economic success, and less inhibited by regionalism than in most countries. Nationalism was expressed in and increased by two foreign wars, one undertaken against Peru and Bolivia precisely because they were seen as planning a combination potentially dangerous to Chile, and one fought to acquire economic resources from the same two countries. Nationalism was also promoted by superior communications, which were facilitated by the compact settlement pattern; by an educational system that before the end of the nineteenth century produced a considerable increase in literacy; and by more freedom of the press and discussion in general than in most of Latin America. If nationalistic sentiment was strongest among the elites, at least they devoted much thought and effort to the future of their country, which they naturally tended to connect with improvement of their own fortunes. The Chilean elites by the end of the century, like those of Argentina, had good reason to believe that they had done well.

c. Growing Diversity, 1860s–1890s

The intensification of political debate in the 1840s and 1850s continued thereafter, with growing effects upon legislation and upon political organization. The Liberals increased their strength. The new Radical party remained small.[6]

In 1873 the Liberal-Conservative coalition disintegrated, and President Errázuriz formed his regime upon a new Liberal Alliance of Liberals, Radicals, and Nationals, who agreed in a general way on religious reforms and other measures that they considered progressive. The struggles of the 1860s–1880s between and within the oligarchic groups that controlled Chilean society had several important results. They produced decisions on the role of the church and education that would affect politics and social development. They sharpened the debate on presidential power and the centralization of authority in Santiago. They contributed in at least a small way to general politicization.

The controversies of those years may be divided into the "religious" and the governmental. After a Liberal victory in congressional elections in 1864, the legislature took up the church question and all the old arguments were rehashed, to the accompaniment of considerable public excitement. Liberals claimed to be good Catholics, but declared that the "liberty of cults" was a principle accepted in most civilized lands. The Conservatives had women fill the congressional galleries and shout "Viva la religión!" That point of view, however, had been undermined by changing public opinion, and the Congress in 1865 declared a reinterpretation of the constitution that approved both non-Catholic churches and private schools of religion for the children of dissenters.

All the other usual subjects of dispute were raised in Chile, but much of the contest at this

---

[6] Prominent in organization of the Radical party in 1861 were wealthy mining magnates of the north who were dissatisfied with policy and their lack of connections with the old families that controlled the government. The party attracted a heterogeneous group of impecunious dissidents, including intellectuals, some of them with connections with the upper class, and in any event parlor liberals not then concerned with winning a popular following for the party. In the early decades the Radical party favored free suffrage, reduction of presidential power, and public secular education. It would become more broadly based and important later. (See Chapter 33, Section a, and Chapter 40.)

point shifted to education, with the Conservatives gradually losing ground. In 1873 the minister of public instruction permitted the German Protestant colonists in the south to decline to have their secondary-school children take the religious instruction offered in the public schools. The next step was to excuse secondary-school graduates from university-entrance examination on religious (Catholic) questions. Measures in the 1870s and 1880s established non-Catholic rights in cemeteries, ended the church courts (1875), removed church control of family statistics, and made marriage a civil contract (1883). Some of the debates over these matters generated great emotion. Conservative politicians could see that each clerical redoubt taken by the opposition reduced their own force, and clericals knew that one relaxation of standards led to another. In a controversy over free competition for university instructorships, the Conservatives not only objected to accepting advocates of the new science as damaging to morals and religion, but wished to keep their monopoly of university patronage. Thus politics in an oligarchic but gradually diversifying society permitted wide freedom of discussion and legislative participation in decision making, and they took on increasing complexity.

Liberals also won victories on strictly governmental questions. In 1864 a congressional committee recommended constitutional reform on the grounds that since 1833 there had been too much rule under states of siege and other autocratic modes. A constitutional amendment in 1868 prohibited a president from serving two consecutive terms. This rule might help reduce *continuismo*, but to be really effective would have to be combined with control of electoral fraud. Public opinion would play some role, so that governmental action in 1872 promising almost complete freedom of the press was encouraging. Although only a minority was participating in politics, an environment providing that minority more freedom of action than in earlier and more repressive years was a mark of modernization.

There were other important decisions. In 1874 constitutional changes helped increase the responsibility of ministers to Congress. This move by no means insured the legislative branch against the common Latin American presidential predominance and arbitrary action, but, as the event proved, it was a signpost to such assurance in Chile. In 1884 legislation strengthened the protection of individuals against arrest by officials. Also in the early 1880s, laws permitted the Congress to pass constitutional reforms over presidential veto by a two-thirds vote, and a suffrage reform gave the vote to all literate males over twenty-five, thus eliminating the income requirement of the Constitution of 1833. Although all these changes during Liberal administrations were opening the political system modestly, it remained essentially oligarchic, and the Liberal governments continued to intervene in elections. Even the broadening of the franchise left most men and all women without the vote, and many of those with the right could only with difficulty be persuaded to use it, as has been noted was the case in other countries.

Partisan politics was shunted aside during 1879–1883 while Chile fought the War of the Pacific with Peru and Bolivia. Essentially, Chile went to war to protect the mining position its citizens had built up in the desert territories of its northern neighbors. The smashing Chilean military victory was a demonstration of the superior political and economic achievement of Chile since Independence. Both political leadership and economic strength were elements in the important improvement of the Chilean navy after an experience with Spanish aggression in the 1860s.[7] The quarrel with Bolivia and Peru over treatment of Chilean business became a war of conquest, and the material rewards to Chile were enormous in the acquisition of rich

---

[7] Chile objected to Spain's seizure of Peru's Chincha Islands in 1864, whereupon the local Spanish naval squadron demanded an apology at Valparaíso, and bombarded it when the demand was refused. Chile then built up its navy until in the late 1870s it was more powerful than that of the United States.

mineral territories.[8] The war stimulated Chilean nationalism, creating a constellation of heroes, and it fixed in the national consciousness the necessity of maintaining military strength against irredentist sentiment in Peru and Bolivia.

Soon after the war the political system of Chile suffered a major crisis in the administration of José Balmaceda (1886–1891). He was the first president chosen under the newly broadened suffrage rule. Balmaceda was a liberal, and the administration candidate in the election of 1886, supported by the majority of his own National party and a faction of the Radicals. It was a bitter election campaign, conducted in an atmosphere that suggested that more fragmentation of parties was imminent. The next year, indeed, a new Democratic party was created by dissident Radicals. Although the leaders were middle class, they began calling it "the political party of the working people." They found an issue in 1888 in a bill sponsored by the conservative National Agricultural Society (founded in 1869) to erect tariff barriers against Argentine beef. At the moment that meant stringy cattle driven over the mountains from western Argentina, but a railroad was under construction that would expose the backward meat industry of Chile to competition from the blooded stock of Argentina's eastern Pampas. Chilean cattle growers had no ex-

ports, and wanted to preserve their domestic market. The bill of 1888 was tied by the Democratic party to the oligarchy's inflationary policy of some years, which pressed hard on the lower middle class and the poor. The growing urban population (250,000 in Santiago) included many migrants from the countryside, and there was much unemployment. A minority of the capital's artisans, small merchants, and skilled workers had organized well over one hundred mutual aid societies, to which the Democratic party appealed in connection with the beef-tariff measure, claiming it would raise all food prices. The Democrats encouraged work stoppages by the mutualist societies in 1888. The tariff made an especially good issue because the Agricultural Society acted as a quasi-official agency of the government. It was the most powerful associational interest group in Chile. Most of its three-hundred-odd members owned large estates, and many also were involved in urban enterprises and served in high government and party offices.

The Democrats held a public rally on the issue at Santiago in July 1888. They also published a pamphlet declaring that the tariff would be "taking from the poor to give to the rich." Considerable debate ensued in the newspapers and elsewhere, some of it referring to the Democratic party charge that the lower class would be deprived of meat. The Agricultural Society demonstrated its unfitness for popular debate by declaring that the masses got along fine on beans and stew and in any case never had eaten much fresh meat, which probably was not good for them. Protests and strikes spread to other towns. Although the Democratic party, the mutual aid societies, and workers generally had no direct representation in government, Balmaceda persuaded the Agricultural Society to withdraw the bill.

The Democratic party at its convention in 1890 came out for an array of what then were thought radical measures: political democracy, industrial protection, labor legislation, equal rights for women, compulsory free education. It was the first mass-based party in Chile. For many

---

[8] Chile received Tarapacá from Peru and Antofagasta from Bolivia. The latter conquest left Bolivia without a seacoast. Chile also won occupation of the Peruvian provinces of Tacna and Arica for ten years, after which the local inhabitants were to decide their allegiance in a plebiscite. Disagreement on the plebiscite left Chile in possession for decades. In 1929 a United States arbitration gave Tacna to Peru and Arica to Chile. The historians of the three countries naturally view the war from different perspectives. Peruvians and Bolivians consider Chile an imperialist aggressor. Chileans believe that they had one reason for action in a secret alliance between Peru and Bolivia. They also say harsh things about the treatment of Chilean investors in the mining areas and have ascribed much of the difficulty to inferior governmental and social arrangements in Peru and Bolivia. The vigor of Chilean foreign policy in the nineteenth century was displayed also in the 1840s in claiming the Straits of Magellan and much of Patagonia. The latter could not be sustained against superior Argentine strength.

years it contributed to lower-class political consciousness, but could not exert much influence on government. Still, the campaign of 1888 against lowering the diet of the poor and the use of the strike showed that enough social change had come to Chile that more political change could not be too far behind.

d. The Civil War of 1891

Balmaceda was a wealthy landowner and a conservative modernizer but not much of a social reformer. He wanted a great increase in government action and expenditures for transportation, education, sanitation, waterworks, and other measures that most oligarchs considered in their total effect extravagant. To get funds for his aims Balmaceda proposed to nationalize the Tarapacá nitrate industry and railways, much of which now was in foreign hands.

His opposition had the majority in Congress, including many of his own party. That body had been for years gradually establishing its right to control the ministry by adverse vote, one way of reducing executive predominance and imposition of measures, so common in Latin America. Congressional use of this power in 1886–1890 inflicted thirteen ministries upon Balmaceda. Between this and congressional objection to his legislative proposals, little of his program was accomplished. Each side considered the other irresponsible. Balmaceda, a man of imperious temperament, finally claimed the right to choose his cabinet independently of congressional approval, thus defying the trend of opinion in recent years. In 1890 a special session of Congress failed to produce a budget, so Balmaceda declared that the appropriations measures of 1890 would apply until the Congress enacted new ones. Balmaceda also tried to nominate his successor, whereupon Congress passed an act making such nominations unconstitutional. But Balmaceda refused to sign it. It seemed an impasse, except that tempers now were ready for drastic measures.

The congressional opposition included many

of the richest and most influential men in Chile. They thought of themselves as the political establishment and Balmaceda a maverick. In November 1890 they asked General Baquedano, hero of the War of the Pacific, to head a coup and become president. He declined, and decided to stay neutral in the conflict, a position that Balmaceda did not argue because of the general's great popularity. The pattern of competition by civilian factions for support by military groups was all too familiar in other Latin American countries at the time. The congressional group turned to Naval Captain Jorge Montt in December, and he agreed to lead armed resistance if Balmaceda tried to govern without congressional collaboration beyond January 1, 1891. The heavily upper-class naval officers' corps supported this agreement. Balmaceda, aware of events, early in January ordered the fleet to leave Valparaíso, to get it away from rebel influence, but the congressional party heard of it and took over the fleet even before the sailing orders arrived.

The reasons for the bloody civil war that ensued have been much debated. By this time the Tarapacá nitrate fields were controlled by foreigners. Before the War of the Pacific, the strong Chilean position there had been operated under a monopoly. During the war a commission was set up by the government to plan the future of the industry in the area. The commission decided against continuation of the monopoly, partly because of strong sentiment in favor of laissez-faire and partly because of fear of the financial consequences if the Chilean government had to take over Peruvian government debts in the area. The result was that the Englishman John North bought up the Peruvian obligations cheaply and established a strong position in the industry. By 1884 Peruvian capital was eliminated, Chilean was down to 36 percent, British was up to 34 percent, and other European was 30 percent. The process continued thereafter, and brought much later criticism in Chile.[9] It

---

[9] Foreign capital controlled 85 percent of the industry in 1901.

could happen at the time because well-to-do Chileans believed in laissez-faire and were willing to collaborate with foreign capital. It was a Chilean decision, not a plot by foreigners. The same happened with foreign influence on the civil war of 1891: it was a minor factor, with Chileans acting largely out of their own deep-seated motivations. The insidious foreign influence idea is largely a fairly recent thesis, obviously stimulated by the xenophobic nationalism and anti-imperialism and anticolonialism and anticapitalism of the mid-twentieth century. Furthermore, Balmaceda's efforts to increase revenues from British operations in the nitrate area were continued by the victorious rebels.

It has been suggested that a strike of miners that was put down in 1890 by the government with considerable loss of life confirmed the workers in an anti-Balmaceda attitude, but they were not a major factor in politics in 1891, although they did serve in the congressional army recruited in the north. Balmaceda had proposed a national bank, which conservatives feared would lead to other moves that would hurt private bankers, but persons of property had other objections to Balmaceda as well. The major reason appears to be the one most advanced at the time: a constitutional crisis brought about by Balmaceda's assertion of freedom from congressional control. Latin Americans, though Chileans less than most, had a much harsher experience with this issue than North Americans, and it seemed to them important. This is not to say that congressional oligarchs had no class and personal interests mixed in their motivation; their manipulation of the government after their victory in the civil war abundantly showed that they did.

The rebels were at an initial disadvantage because most army officers supported Balmaceda. That support was due partly to service rivalry, in which the navy felt neglected, and to the less aristocratic connections of army officers. The congressional party had control of the sea. Although the navy was a force of only about 300 officers and 1,800 enlisted men at the beginning

of the war, it quickly expanded, seizing merchant vessels that were used to transport men, arms, and supplies to the insurgent stronghold in the north. There the rebels got financing from mining interests and deprived Balmaceda of important export levies. They were protected by the lack of land connections between the northern desert and central Chile. Some army officers did join the rebels, including Colonel Emil Körner, a German who had arrived in 1886 and set up the War Academy for the advanced instruction of officers. Some of his Chilean officer disciples joined him in the north, where he was the single most important military figure in preparing an army to fight the civil war.

Majority opinion was against Balmaceda, and he did not improve his popularity with the strong measures he took. Most of the 5,000-man army and 500-man coast artillery joined Balmaceda. The army quickly was increased to 32,000. It benefited from possession of a cartridge factory and an armory for military maintenance and repair, but the new troops were badly trained. The insurgents were ready to invade the south in late summer. They had smaller forces, but what they had were superior in quality, and in any case presidential forces tended to melt away because the enlisted men had no heart for the struggle. The bloody war ended in September. Balmaceda committed suicide.

The United States was almost alone among foreign countries in sympathizing with the presidential side. That was partly because Britain favored the congressional, rebel forces, and the United States minister to Chile was an anglophobe who sent anti-Balmaceda reports. In 1891 the Chilean ship *Itata* took on arms for the rebels off the Pacific coast of the United States, and Washington insisted that the *Itata* return from Chile with its cargo.[10] This helped embitter United States relations with Chile, which were poor in any event because of Washington's insistence

---

[10] In 1893 the United States Supreme Court declared that the *Itata* had not violated the neutrality laws of the United States, and ordered it returned to Chile.

on trying to mediate the recent War of the Pacific in spite of Chile's objections.

Captain Jorge Montt was elected president by all parties in October 1891, which was not surprising. An unexpected result of the war against presidential power was the establishment of a true parliamentary government in Chile. Insofar as this might be considered an advance for broader participation in decision making and a curb on presidential autocracy, it was modernization—except that in practice it proved too weak, and decades later a return to more presidential power seemed like modernization at that time. The parliamentary government of the 1890s proved as nationalistic on the British railway monopoly in Tarapacá as Balmaceda had

been, so apparently that sentiment was well established in Chilean life by that time.

Chile was with justice considered by outsiders in the 1890s a progressive country with a generally stable system of government. Its leaders had done well within the limits of their elitist notions of social arrangements. Some had opted for support of various reform measures, and their views would ensure a continuation of change, as would the existence of industrial mineral operations and the continued growth of manufactures. It was not possible then to see that the incipient workers' movement, with some intellectual support, was starting a history of important growth. In any event, some modernization had been achieved and more was promised.

28

Other Nations in the Nineteenth Century

The other nations of Latin America exhibited various mixes of the problems and attitudes discussed in Chapter 23. They were less successful by the 1890s than Argentina, Brazil, and Chile, although Uruguay and Costa Rica displayed some signs of what would later become notable social development. Cuba was a colony of Spain to 1898, and Panama a part of Colombia until 1903.[1] In all, natural and social resources were unfavorable for development, or the key to united effort could not be found. All were affected, but often weakly, by the international trading system, foreign investment, new technology, and the hope of change. All resounded at least softly to new ideas. All were much afflicted with violence in public life; *caudillismo*; strong class lines, often complicated by racial differences; lack of opportunity for common people and their generally apathetic acceptance of their lot. Many of the national histories, nevertheless, contained little epics of struggle for change. Pressures for modernization did build up over the years; change was slow, but society was not frozen.

a. Uruguay and Costa Rica

Scarcely a breath of modernization ruffled the surface of life in Uruguay and Costa Rica for decades, and even by the 1890s the winds of change did not seem strong to contemporary observers. Looking back, however, we see that both were in the beginning stages of transformation from the older Latin American "norms."

Uruguay

The colonial Banda Oriental (left shore) of the Uruguay River was of little consequence except as a strategic position at the Río de la Plata entrance to South America. Portugal and Spain, and their successors Brazil and Argentina, contested control of the area. Not until 1828 did Uruguay emerge as a permanently independent nation.[2] It had a tiny population of 60,000, with 14,000 of them in the capital and port of Monte-

---

[1] For the nineteenth-century history of Cuba and Panama, see Chapter 33, Sections d–e.

[2] In 1811–1820 José G. Artigas was the chief leader of Uruguayan forces for Independence. In 1825 Juan Lavalleja and "The Immortal Thirty-three" began what proved to be the final struggle, involving Argentina, Brazil, and Uruguayans. Britain served as mediator. Uruguay has remained a classic buffer state between two powerful and jealous neighbors.

video. Political life was disorderly for years, partly because of foreign intervention, partly because the sparse Uruguayan population of the back country was largely made up of gauchos accustomed to violence and unused to methods of patient industry.

A political polarization began early between conservatives and liberals, known as *Blancos* and *Colorados*, with the former representing landowners and clericals and enjoying Argentine dictator Rosas' support. The *Colorados* were strong in Montevideo. There was almost constant warfare from 1839 to 1852—Uruguayans call it The Great War—and for the last nine years of that Montevideo was besieged by the *Blanco*-Rosas forces, but aided in its defense by foreign naval forces and immigrants in the town. Although Rosas fell in 1852, and foreign intervention in Uruguay eased, the Brazilians still were interfering. López of Paraguay forced Uruguay into the 1865–1870 war, so not until the 1870s did Uruguay have a proper opportunity to handle its own destiny.[3]

The disorderly political situation improved only marginally after mid-century, but it was being undermined by socioeconomic changes that altered old institutional patterns without being highly visible. After the overthrow of Rosas in Argentina in 1852, conflict between Uruguayan *Colorados* and *Blancos* continued. Federalism was not an issue in so small a country. The church question was not prominent.[4] Arbitrary executive power, dishonest elections, and access to the public purse were the great issues. The system was oligarchic, run by persons of property and military chieftains. Government revenues were heavily siphoned to military and partisan purposes that made little contribution to the country, although in the latter part of the century this situation improved, notably in expenditures for education.

The liberal *Colorados* were far from egalitarian. They did benefit, however, from their somewhat more popular orientation, and gradually became dominant, although not strong enough to overwhelm the *Blancos*. In 1872, after a civil war, they made an agreement by which the *Blancos* accepted assured control over four of the fifteen departments into which the national territory was divided. This interesting device somewhat reduced violence, leaving the *Blanco* oligarchs safe in their own rural fiefdoms. But the presidency still was decided by fraud and force, and armed clashes between parties and factions continued. In 1897 there was a notable *Blanco* uprising against *Colorado* control of presidency and Congress. As a result, *Blanco* control was extended by agreement to six of the then existing nineteen departments, and the electoral system was put under the control of both parties, a measure that might fundamentally alter electoral practices, if it could be enforced, which was the critical issue.

No wonder there was little economic growth in Uruguay before the end of massive Argentine intervention in the early 1850s. Modest profits came from exports of hides and salted and dried meat. After mid-century the economy improved, remaining oriented toward the pastoral industry, almost Uruguay's only natural resource. It was controlled by great landowners. Uruguay's sheep increased from fewer than a million in 1852 to more than 18 million in 1900, cattle from 1.9 to 6.8 million. Exports continued to include such traditional items as salt meat, hides, wool, hair and bone, and such new items as meat extract, canned meat, live animals, and at the end of the century refrigerated meat. After mid-century proprietors installed fencing, windmills, better corrals and other facilities, and imported blooded

---

[3] Fructuoso Rivera (*Colorado*) and Manuel Oribe (*Blanco*) were the most prominent leaders of the years of warfare and foreign meddling. See Chapter 24 on Rosas and Uruguay; Chapters 24–25 on the Paraguayan War.
[4] The Roman Catholic church had a special position by the Constitution of 1829, but, as was common in Latin America, later liberal measures cut into it. In 1859 Franciscan convents were suppressed. In the 1880s the church lost control of cemeteries and vital statistics, and marriage became a civil contract. Even many *Blancos* came to consider church matters largely a question of private conscience.

Ancient Holdovers

Many things after Independence in Latin America changed very slowly.

A village scene in Marín, Yaracuy Province, Venezuela. Unpretentious as these houses are, they are better than some in Latin America today. The huge rural population has always been badly housed, fed, clothed, educated, and cared for medically. *Courtesy of Standard Oil Company of New Jersey*

In Nicaragua, a farmer and his oxen are passing a canal at the site of a hydroelectric project under construction in the 1960s. Oxen are still widely used for plowing and hauling. Primitive farming methods since Independence have kept agricultural yields low. *United Nations*

A *fazenda* in Minas Gerais, Brazil, in the 1860s. The great estate, employing scores of workers (count them), was the dominant economic unit in Latin America during the nineteenth century, and in some areas it remains so today. *Courtesy of Boston Public Library*

An Argentine gaucho in 1868. Cowboys were important in colonial Latin America. Often ruffians during their own lifetime, they are romanticized nowadays. *Courtesy of Hovey Collection, Library of Congress*

A public washing place at Taxco, Mexico, provides stone washboards and cold water. Even in modern times, many homes have lacked plumbing. *Courtesy of Delta Air Lines*

stock. The business benefited from steamship connections with Europe in mid-century; the 1,000 miles of railway built from the 1870s to the end of the century; the telegraph that came in the 1860s, and the telephone in the 1880s.

Montevideo skimmed off much of the export profit for taxes and handling and financing charges. The bustling city also had a thriving European import business, and developed small fabrication establishments. Although tariffs were used mainly for revenue, some protected a few lines of manufacture. Primitive labor organizations appeared in the 1890s, and José Batlle y Ordóñez, son of a former president, in 1895 came out for worker demands for a shorter workday. The government modernized the capital with port works, street railways, educational facilities, public buildings, sanitation, and streets. Much was financed by foreign loans, so that Uruguay was using 40 percent of its central government revenues in 1901 on foreign debt service. The expenditure could be justified on the grounds that other financing was not politically feasible.

One result of economic growth was immigration from Europe. It furthered racial homogeneity in Uruguay, which had few Indians. Europeans brought skills and knowledge and a habit of hard work. Many congregated in Montevideo and made it a center for modernization and of *Colorado* party strength. About 400,000 European immigrants went to Uruguay between Independence and the end of the nineteenth century, most of them after the attainment of more peaceful conditions and improving exports in mid-century. The total national population was some 400,000 in 1870, a notable increase over the figure at Independence; it was half a million early in the 1880s, and just over a million in 1908. Montevideo reached 100,000 early in the 1870s.

Most of the benefits of economic growth went to a few people: most to the rich, quite a lot to the growing middle class, some to the urban labor group, and little to the rural poor. Pressure for social reform in nineteenth-century Uruguay was ineffective, with a notable exception: begin-

ning in the 1870s, the elite agreed to considerable expenditures for education under the leadership of José P. Varela. The population of the metropolis, where the immigrants favored education, was important in this development, and most of the change occurred in the city. This brought Uruguay within sight of 50 percent literacy by the end of the century, a revolutionary step toward modernization. It established one foundation and one source of pressure for more change.

Other cultural developments in the city were of potential importance. A university was founded in 1849. Secondary schools grew modestly. Social and cultural organizations multiplied. A small literary production occurred. In 1900 José E. Rodó published *Ariel*, which expressed both the general Latin American fear of cultural domination by the expanding United States and an educated Uruguayan's distaste for an excess of materialism in local life. More influential than the small literary community were the newspapers that grew with wealth and literacy. In 1878 José Batlle y Ordóñez began his career in journalism, and in 1886 founded *El Día*, using it to promote his own political ambitions. No one could guess, when he became a national deputy in 1891 and a senator in 1898, that by 1903 he would be president and prepared to lead Uruguay into a program of modernization without parallel in Latin America at the time.

Costa Rica

Costa Rica at Independence was like Uruguay in being small and lightly populated, with some 60,000 citizens. It had only 243,000 in 1892. Unlike Uruguay, Costa Rica could not attract immigrants. It had less connection with the international trading system at Independence than Uruguay did, but developed it with exports of coffee and bananas. Landholding was less drastically concentrated than in Uruguay. Costa Rica had nothing like Montevideo in size, wealth, and pressures for modernization. It resembled Uruguay in having few Indians to complicate class lines or the development of nationalist sentiment.

Costa Rica was bucolic and very isolated, with most people dwelling in the pleasant central highlands. Connections with the hot coasts were poor until a railway link was established late in the nineteenth century.

In the colonial period, lacking many servile workers, minerals, or much trade, the few Spaniards who lived in Costa Rica necessarily worked the land themselves. There were differences in property holdings, and some families asserted their social eminence at Independence, but the situation was so different from the Latin American pattern that efforts have been made to find its source in the cultural origins of the population. Hardworking Galicians are said to account in part for industry and egalitarianism in Costa Rica, but there is no reason to believe that they were an important factor.[5] It was a place of unwanted near equality in property and relative social homogeneity because nothing else was feasible.

In nineteenth-century Costa Rica the few moderately prosperous families ran the government and set policies in their own interest. Land concentration in the highlands, however, did not become as exaggerated as in most of Latin America. The government before mid-century even participated in some fairly wide distribution of state land. The crops and labor system accounted for some of the relatively slow pace of growth of *latifundio*. The only cash crop of consequence before mid-century was coffee; there was no large servile labor class; and small holders could work part-time on larger holdings.

Armed contests were common, but Costa Rica did not have the savage *caudillismo* of many countries. When Colonel Tomás Guardia came to power in 1870 by a coup, he did so with the aid of the oligarchy; and when he soon broke with it, the results were a dictatorship and a new Constitution in 1871 that provided for strong executive authority. But Guardia reduced oligar-

chic power by confiscating some estates and exiling individuals, and he aided economic development. He did not, however, broaden political participation before his death in 1882.

The so-called "Rich Coast" at Independence was miserably poor, but it soon enjoyed new income from coffee exports, which began in the 1830s and remained the chief export throughout the century. Coffee exports were joined by bananas as a result of Guardia's invitation in the early 1870s to Henry Meiggs, a North American railway builder in Chile and Peru, to come to Costa Rica. Minor Cooper Keith, another Yankee businessman, took over Meiggs' interests there and in 1872 began planting bananas to provide traffic for his railway. Keith did not complete the narrow-gauge line from Puerto Limón to San José until 1891. In the meantime, he imported Jamaican blacks to work in the unhealthful Caribbean lowlands. The Costa Ricans of the mountain interior (*meseta central*) were willing to have blacks build the railway and work in lowland plantations, but not, as it proved, to allow them to move to the highlands.

The large-scale shipment of bananas from the American tropics to northern countries began from Jamaica in the 1870s. Keith made his first Costa Rican shipments to New Orleans in 1881; by 1890 he was exporting over one million bunches a year. In 1899 he combined some competing firms into the United Fruit Company, which at that time owned 10,000 acres in Costa Rica alone and was well on the way to becoming a giant enterprise in a number of countries, with plantations, railways, ships, wharves, and company towns.

Although by the end of the nineteenth century Costa Rica had two valuable exports, the subsistence agricultural sector was inefficient, the livestock industry poor, and manufacturing scarcely existed. Furthermore, the railway and the banana businesses were too strong for easy control by the Costa Rican government. Keith finally had a contract by which he funded the national debt and had monopoly rights on the railway and a big land subsidy. Bananas received tax exemption

---

[5] Basque origins for Chilean prosperity, and Jewish settlers for the exceptional development of the Antioquia area of Colombia are similarly unproven and unlikely assertions.

in the early years, a reasonable concession to get the industry started, but it proved difficult to end. Not until 1907 did even a low tax on bananas get through the legislative and executive branches, to the accompaniment of charges of coercion and bribery. Costa Rica was experiencing the pain of development by foreign capital and entrepreneurs, which made its economy dependent or colonial.

Toward the end of the century a great change in education began. For long it had been the privilege of a small propertied class. In the 1860s the country still was about 90 percent illiterate. Then in 1885 Mauro Fernández was named minister of finance, commerce, and education and put the country on the road to a transformation. Fernández was a well-educated lawyer, with some experience abroad and admiration for certain aspects of North American and European culture. In his educational work he was influenced by their practices and by those of Argentina. He himself visited the United States, sent representatives abroad, and imported Swiss educators. He concentrated educational authority in the hands of the ministry, to the indignation of the church. He emphasized primary instruction, breaking with the oligarchic preference for elite education by closing the scarcely functioning university in 1888. Fernández succeeded in making support for education a matter of patriotism. He was one of those fortunate men who lived (until 1905) to see a plan for social transformation for which he was heavily responsible becoming reality. Illiteracy was down to 69 percent in 1892. By the time Fernández died, his country was 60 percent literate, compared with 10 percent in his boyhood. It is not to detract from his achievement to point out that Costa Rican society had to be ready to support the new educational effort; it was not put across by force of arms. The necessary prelude to educational change, therefore, was a weakening of the oligarchic hold on society.

A sign of that weakening appeared in the 1880s, when President Bernardo Soto, who had supported the work of his minister Fernández, in 1889 held the first really fair election in the country's history, and his candidate lost. There were revolts and serious irregularities for several years thereafter, but in 1902 the system settled down to generally peaceful elections. Soon Costa Rica could boast that it was a democratic society, with "more teachers than soldiers."

b. Peru

Peruvians were not able to rejoice at the departure of the last foreign forces (Spanish and Colombian) until 1826. They then had to themselves a land of coastal desert and a mountainous interior, a heavily Indian population, a memory of silver wealth, but a recent history of economic decay. Nowhere was the social mold more rigid. The holders of the great estates remembered the great Tupac Amaru Indian uprising of the 1780s. Opportunities were sparse for the ambitious, and the country at once suffered a plague of military leaders who competed for access to power and the public trough.

Peru struggled to the 1840s with all its problems unsolved,[6] and then apparently a great opportunity arose. On the desert coast and islands were bird droppings—guano—that the ancient Indians used as fertilizer. Now it was needed for European fields. The first guano was shipped in the 1830s, but the boom began in the 1840s. To 1875 about 20 million tons of guano were shipped to a value of possibly $1 billion. Although the lack of exports and government revenues that helped cripple the country in its first years now was remedied, the "opportunity" this offered Peru existed only in an ideal sense. The socio-

---

[6] When the Venezuelan General Sucre was driven from Bolivia in 1828 by the local elite, Peru invaded Bolivia and ineffectively considered incorporating the territory. Peru later was part of Santa Cruz's Confederation of the Andes, defeated by Chile in the war of 1836–1839 (see Chapter 27). The church assiduously played politics in these early years in Peru, but the roles of federalism and regionalism were less than in Mexico, Colombia, or Argentina in the early years.

political culture had made poor use of Peru's slender resources before the 1840s, and it did as badly with guano.

Guano was nationalized in 1842, and for years thereafter was consigned to foreign entrepreneurs in return for advance payments. The consignees could insist on low returns to Peru, so high profits went abroad. The system encouraged fiscal irresponsibility in Peruvian government. Peruvians knew its defects. A writer in 1860 noted the worsening of the balance of payments because of the temptation to increase imports with funds that came so easily. Changes in the system in 1869 foundered in part because the guano market became depressed by competition from nitrates. The guano bonanza financed only a minimum of public and private improvement in Peru. It did help with the railway building that was important to modern exploitation of the mines of the interior.

Ramón Castilla, one of the better presidents, could do little about guano wastage or other problems. A shrewd and energetic mestizo (called *cholo* in Peru), Castilla lived by military-political activity in the early republic, achieved the presidency by arms in 1844–1845 and again in 1855–1862. A poorly educated man, liked by the lower classes because he resembled them in race and manners, Castilla had a sense of national responsibility, even some notion of economic development. An excellent politician, he used coercion, conciliation, reform, and economic development to force and seduce support or acquiescence. He considered the military an indispensable force for order in a violent society. In his second administration he decreed the end of Indian tribute and immediate emancipation of slaves with compensation to the owners. Although these were actions compatible with modernization, slavery was no longer important, and the end of tribute lowered government revenues. More importantly, with no tribute to pay, the Indians, when not burdened with forced labor under various disguises, cut production and withdrew even more into isolation from the rest of society.

The use of violence in public life proved one of Peru's most intractable problems. The Constitution of 1856 included congressional control of military promotions. A more radical suggestion in the constitutional assembly to prohibit permanent armies and deny executive office to soldiers had been defeated. Castilla disliked the reduction of his control over the military, and a civil war by conservatives changed it back in a new Constitution in 1860. Then more than a decade later Manuel Pardo, founding father of the *Civilista* party, was the first civilian and the first nonadministration candidate to be elected (for the term 1872–1876). He had to fight a military faction, however, that tried to prevent his inauguration. He had aid from a mob that butchered some military men, but mobs did not usually do well against soldiers.

Pardo reduced the army to 2,500 men, which left many soldiers dangerously unemployed, and he tried to reduce the influence of the army by building up a civilian national guard, a device often tried in Latin America. His reduction of the army was not only politically perilous, but foolhardy in view of the fact that nitrate nationalization was offending Chileans in the industry on Peruvian soil. Pardo had to contend with military risings and conspiracy that were encouraged by civilians, in the common Latin American manner. In the election of 1876 the *Civilista* candidate, who won, was an army general acceptable to both *Civilistas* and moderate military men. The opposition candidate was an admiral. It scarcely could be claimed that military influence in public affairs was being reduced!

Caudillismo continued to be the rule after Pardo's administration. Its value certainly was not evident in the disastrous War of the Pacific (1879–1883), by which Peru lost its southern nitrate areas to Chile.[7] The *Civilistas* came to power again in 1895 under Nicolás Piérola, but only after a bloody civil war. So a man with progressive ideas again had tried for power by violence, perceiving it the only route to the presi-

---

[7] See Chapter 27.

dency. Piérola, knowing he could not eliminate the military, hoped to tame it by better training and by turning it to tasks of national construction. He made the military school one of the best sources of instruction in the country. He imported a French military mission in 1896. His administration installed a system of national conscription, but before long the army was seizing Indians in the same old way. Still, there was a change in the later nineteenth century.

Unhappily, the change was not entirely for the better. A Peruvian historian put it optimistically that after 1895 winning power with improvised forces was more difficult and it was more important to subvert army garrisons. Also, some tacit or expressed public support was increasingly necessary. Thus the country was no longer prey to roving bands as before mid-century, certainly a gain; but civilian cooperation in regular army political action was scarcely a happy substitute. The new system could be seen, for example, when President Billinghurst was ousted in 1914 by a military rising encouraged by the *Civilistas*, and including the chief of the general staff, Oscar Benavides, and a young captain Luís Sánchez Cerro, both of whom would be prominent in politics for years thereafter. The *Civilistas* had not really reduced the role of actual and threatened violence in public affairs.

The *civilismo* of the 1870s and thereafter received support from new business interests, intellectuals, and others influenced by positivist ideas. They favored "progress," under elite leadership. Pardo was representative of new ideas and interests, trying to modify—not extirpate—the older oligarchic pattern. Some of the new men were for expanded government activity. The shock of the War of the Pacific not only contributed to that idea, but to birth of a few suggestions that alterations in the basic society were needed. The Piérola administration of 1895–1899 and subsequent *Civilista* administrations often are dubbed a turning point of sorts, as representing an increase in middle-class influence and concern for the masses, but the increase was small. Piérola was an aristocrat with a bent for arbitrary gov-

ernment; and though the poor found him sympathetic, the title of "democratic *caudillo*" sometimes given him is misleading. The modest development of progressive ideas, together with an equally modest array of institutional changes, indicated movement toward broader participation in politics, but it was slow.

There were efforts to alter politics by changing the law, usually ineffective. The Constitution of 1860 (the country's fifteenth) prohibited the immediate reelection of a president, as had earlier charters, but that had no effect on executive predominance. Peruvians were among the more ingenious Latin Americans in constructing constitutional and electoral systems to sustain oligarchy. The Constitution of 1860 provided electoral colleges in each department to screen the choice of officials from too much "popular" influence, even from the very limited electorate, in elections that were, in any event, fraudulently conducted. When a law in 1896 eliminated the electoral colleges and provided for direct voting, the effect was small. There was no secret ballot, so landowners and other employers and patrons continued to supervise their employees and clients at the polls. Office holding and voting were much restricted by property and literacy qualifications. Although the number of registered voters gradually increased, many did not join parties or vote. Parties were run by tight little groups. Toward the end of the nineteenth century a politician said that all members of any given party in Peru would fit in a railway car. The slow reduction of the church's position contributed to liberal strength, but it did not broaden participation.[8]

---

[8] The constitutions of 1856 and 1860, although they differed on some matters, agreed on abolition of state collection of church tithes and on elimination of ecclesiastical and military *fueros*. That was a gain for the construction of a national system, and for the liberal element, but had nothing to do with broader participation. The first *Civilista* president, in the 1870s, suffered the enmity of both the church and the military. He met the usual church objections to broader state participation in education. The church gradually lost that, and many other, arguments. At the end of the century marriage was made a civil contract. Although separation of church and state was argued, it was not enacted.

Civilistas from 1895 to 1919 managed only small improvements in electoral conditions.

Governments after the mid-nineteenth century made somewhat more effective efforts to improve the economy. They also improved public facilities, principally in the towns. But government efforts were restricted by small public revenues. Peru suffered the usual determination of elites not to tax themselves. By 1889 the foreign debt was about $225 million, while government revenues were under $35 million, too little for the army and other regular costs of a simple administration. An agreement of that year canceled much of the foreign debt in return for concession to the Peruvian Corporation, composed of English bondholders, of a monopoly of Peru's state railways and other privileges. The president had great difficulty forcing these concessions to foreigners through the Congress, and the implementation and theory of the arrangement caused criticism for years. Nationalist complaint also was directed at the concession of a French company controlling the docks at Callao from 1887 to 1929.

Transportation was so poor that some thought that a solution would be a panacea, whereas Peru had many other economic problems. Funds and concessions went to a few favored routes. By 1893 the Peruvian Corporation had extended the central railway from the port of Callao into the mountains as far as La Oroya, in a mineral-rich district, and in the next decade to Cerro de Pasco, in another mineral area. Early in the twentieth century North American investors at Cerro de Pasco began to exploit the great copper deposits and before World War I were a target of nationalist complaints. Foreigners also came into Peru late in the nineteenth century in search of petroleum. In 1889 the London and Pacific Petroleum Company got a concession, which went to Standard of New Jersey in the 1920s. In the early twentieth century there began a long dispute over the fact that the London company was exploiting more than its contract permitted.

Agricultural exports increased in the late nineteenth and early twentieth centuries, as large-scale sugar and cotton plantations were developed in the irrigated river valleys of the coastal desert. There was little power-driven industry before the twentieth century, and mainly in minerals and food processing. There were power looms as early as 1847, but the cotton textile business was small until World War I. Government policy provided little protection for industry. All these developments did create some new wealth, points of view, pressure on government, and a small industrial labor group.

Artisan mutualist societies appeared in the 1880s, promoting such uncontroversial measures as night schools. Toward the end of the century there were a few socialists and anarchists in Peru. Modern labor organization began in a small way in 1904, and before long began to use strikes. President Guillermo Billinghurst (elected 1912), a conservative who favored aid to labor to forestall the growth of radicalism, gave some support to labor organization, the eight-hour-day movement, and obligatory collective bargaining. José Pardo as president in 1915–1919 pushed through legislation regulating child and female labor but found it difficult to enforce. In January 1919 he faced a three-day general strike by workers who had been hurt by the depression at the end of World War I. The army broke up the movement, but later that year socialist and workers' parties were preaching the doctrine of class struggle. Industrial labor was becoming a force at least mildly to be reckoned with.

The population reached 2.7 million in 1876, growing almost entirely by natural increase. Lima by 1903 was a small city of 140,000. Its growth included internal migration, but the flood of country people to town was still in the future. The economic and social condition of the population generally had improved little since Independence. Despite a number of efforts to expand education, the country was about 90 percent illiterate. Social mobility had only fractionally increased.

The intellectual community, largely consisting of a few writers and the fewer than 2,000 university students and their part-time professors, became considerably more lively in the two decades before World War I. More thought was given by intellectuals and a few politicians to the possible better use of the predominantly Indian lower classes. Manuel González Prada (died 1918) preached the need to destroy all old institutions and reconstruct society on the basis of the Indian masses. Although his immediate influence was small, he would be a posthumous prophet to future reform leaders. The university reform movement of 1918 in Argentina spread at once to Lima, where the students not only demanded a new organization and curriculum for higher education but supported the workers in the general strike of January 1919. By the end of World War I, then, modernization had not penetrated very deeply into Peru, but it appeared likely to continue. Its growth was to prove agonizingly slow and indeterminate.[9]

Leaders in Peru, as in Chile, had accepted opportunities to increase ties with the Atlantic economic community, exporting raw materials and importing manufactures, capital, and technological expertise. Peruvians had done less well than Chileans, however, in using those opportunities to strengthen the society. That suggested that the consequences of economic colonialism or dependence varied with local conditions and the quality of leadership, and were not absolutes that automatically and fatally poisoned the life of underdeveloped countries. Peruvians in the late nineteenth century certainly thought Chile had been better run than their own country.

c. Colombia

When the "Gran Colombia" of Bolívar's dream broke in 1830 into the republics of Venezuela, Ecuador, and Colombia,[10] the last included Panama. Colombia (sometimes in the nineteenth century called by its colonial name, New Granada) was not only more than twice the size of France but was broken by geography, climate,

and local interest into pockets of potential separatist sentiment. Isolation of mountain valley and of coast backed by marsh and forest helped make of federalism in Colombia something like a religious faith, and people slew each other to set up or tear down that idol. There were not many of them—under 2 million in 1843 and 5 million in 1912, mostly living in the mountains, with small concentrations in the Caribbean lowlands, and few on the Pacific coast or in the lowlands of Amazonia.

Colombia was poor in 1830 and poor in 1900, although modest improvement appeared late in the nineteenth century and continued into the early twentieth. Roads scarcely existed. A water route from the Caribbean coast up the Magdalena River required costly portages. Steamboats, used on the rivers by mid-century, brought only marginal improvement. A mere 660 miles of railway were built by 1911. Great estates held much of the best land. Manufacturing scarcely existed. The few efforts at protection of industry had little effect, and as in much of Latin America effective beginnings of protection began during World War I.

There was a modest amount of gold and emerald production. The growth of highland coffee production for export was the most promising economic development of the nineteenth century, but it remained small in volume. All the commodity exports of the country were worth little more than $1 million in 1832, and only $23 million in 1911. Shortly before World War I, however, Colombia's prospects improved, with rising demand for coffee and bananas and with the introduction of modern mining technology. Profits from exports were highly concentrated in a few regions and hands. With government revenues heavily tied to exports, military and bureaucratic expenses left little for socioeconomic development.

Social immobility was as exaggerated in Colombia as anywhere in Latin America. Class differences were exacerbated by race, a large part of the population being Indian, black, or of mixed heritage. The Colombian elite strongly

---

[9] See Chapter 33, Section e, on Peru after World War I.
[10] See Chapter 23, Section a.

resisted entrance into its ranks. In 1900 the educational system still offered but a tiny doorway to change, and about 80 percent of the populace was illiterate. The upper class honored cultural excellence and produced enough men of intellectual distinction, nearly all in the humanities, so that before the turn of the century Colombians felt justified in calling Bogotá the Athens of America.

Members of the Liberal and Conservative parties in the nineteenth century devoted intense effort to politics, not sparing their blood in defense of belief and party. Federalism and regionalism were expressed in many constitutional changes. The struggle over the interlocked issues was unusually bitter in Colombia, but as was common in Latin America the centralist idea prevailed before the end of the nineteenth century. The church quarrel also was savage. The church faction was stronger there than in most countries, and such attrition of ecclesiastical positions as occurred was slower. A Constitution in 1863 separated church and state but did not settle the question.

Colombians claim that parties there were more sincere about principle than in most of Latin America, but that is unmeasurable and its practical value doubtful. The parties were virtually unstructured and heavily influenced by *personalismo*. Colombians point out that they did not submit to long-term *caudillos*, but that did not seem to improve political or other development. The many short-term presidencies meant a lack of continuity that was damaging. Most elections were fraudulent. The country had its full share of civil warfare, coups d'etat, conspiracies, and short-term and regional *caudillismo*. For sheer factional ferocity and bloodshed the Colombians had no superiors in Latin America.

The Liberals in the 1880s were reduced to a subordinate position by President Rafael Núñez. He was yet another progressive or radical who decided that order was more important than reform. He became a Liberal president in 1880–1882, but as chief executive in 1884–1894, Núñez helped found a Nationalist party, which combined with the Conservatives and Independents (moderate Liberals) to support him. The Constitution of 1886 (which lasted until 1936) made the states into departments in a centralized system with their officials dependent on the president; gave the church protection (though not the official creed) as essential to social order; and made education a Catholic-based activity. The proclerical charter was reinforced in 1888 by a concordat with the papacy that gave the church many of its old privileges, including compulsory religious teaching in schools and universities.

Núñez was a talented leader, but he could not destroy Liberal objections to his system. Not long after he died in 1894, divisions in the Conservative party became serious. In 1899 the Liberals rose against what they considered unprogressive policies and against what certainly was fraudulent exclusion from office. The result was the worst civil war (1899–1902) in the country's history. The damage in bitterness and property loss and disordered public finance was immense.

Then in 1903 Colombia lost the province of Panama. It had been a locale of regional conspiracy for autonomy or independence. Separated by impassable country from land connection with the rest of Colombia, Panama's leaders coveted full control of transisthmian travel. By a treaty in 1846 (ratified 1848) the United States had received transit rights in the isthmus from Colombia (New Granada at the time), in return for a guarantee of its sovereignty there. The concern of New Granada was with British expansion from the nearby Mosquito shore of Central America. The isthmian railway that went into operation in 1855 gave Panama the advantage over the Nicaragua route. A few years later a French company began to dig a Panama canal but went bankrupt. The United States in 1903 helped Panama become independent and received from it the Canal Zone.[11]

Political conditions in Colombia then began to improve. An arbitrary Conservative president,

---

[11] See Chapter 33, Section e, for the independence of Panama.

Rafael Reyes, was forced to resign in 1909 because of disgust with his methods, combined with nationalist objections to his willingness to accept a small payment from the United States for recognition of Panama's independence. A law for minority representation in the congress and the cabinet went into effect in 1909. This small contribution to broader political participation somewhat quieted the worst features of factionalism. Voting still was confined to a few, and electoral conditions were corrupt. The reduction in political warfare coincided with a slightly accelerated socioeconomic growth, which suggested that increased pressures for modernization would have some effect. Not until the 1920s, however, did these become evident in new form.

d. Venezuela

Venezuela at Independence held fewer than a million persons in a territory nearly twice that of France, and fewer than 3 million in 1917. Most lived in the low mountain chain near the coast from Caracas west to the Colombian border. Caracas was only seven miles from the Caribbean, at an elevation of 3,100 feet. Great estates dominated rural life. There was money to be made in exports, but far from enough to transform the country. Competing in cattle products with North America and Argentina, in coffee with Brazil, in sugar with Cuba, or cotton with the United States was not easy.

Much of the early political history of Venezuela was dominated by José Antonio Páez and the brothers Monagas. Páez, a hero of the Wars for Independence, was an uncultivated cowboy (*llanero*, for the *llanos* or plains south of the mountains), but a shrewd and strong man of good intentions. Venezuela was on the whole fortunate in his domination during much of 1830–1846. He was a typical lower-class *caudillo*. He impressed his *llaneros* with his strength and valor and his victory in battle, and they followed him blindly. Páez was clever enough to manipulate the upper class, but he was "captured" by

them to some extent, as were many lower-class *caudillos*, needing them as administrators, developing a fondness for their social habits, and accepting many of their prescriptions for public policy. The usual liberal-conservative divisions quickly developed.

Páez had the inevitable problems with political violence, and rivals finally triumphed over the old *caudillo* in the 1840s, when José T. Monagas and a brother took over the presidency and held it by force and fraud for fifteen years.[12] In 1870 Antonio Guzmán Blanco seized power and held it for nearly two decades. He was an extravagant despot who promoted some economic development and modernization because it contributed to his comfort and profit. Although he was less obnoxious than many a *caudillo* in Latin America, the country benefited little from his rule, unless harsh measures against political disorder may be counted a gain, surely doubtful in view of his lack of concern for an increase in political participation or in social progress. A man of upper-middle-class origins, Guzmán Blanco was an interesting example of the educated *caudillo* who in essence perpetuated oligarchic privilege while making clever use of the masses to intimidate people of property—all this, of course, without rewarding the mob except with a bit of loot, a few jobs, and the psychic satisfaction of venting their frustration in violence.

Guzmán Blanco did not hold the presidency all the years from 1870 to 1889. In the style of many another, he preferred to devote some time periodically to his amusements. During an absence in France, his puppet in Caracas in 1889 asserted his independence. Local *caciques* enlarged their armies and fought for promotion to national *caudillo*. In 1892 General Joaquín Crespo attained that position, retaining it to 1898. He is remembered because in his time Venezuela and Britain revived their boundary

---

[12] Páez was back in the presidency in 1861–1863 and lived into the 1870s, but most of his influence was gone by the late 1840s.

dispute in the light of rumors of gold in the wilderness of Guiana. The issue was settled by insistence from the Cleveland administration in Washington that it be arbitrated and that Britain comply because "the United States is practically sovereign on this continent, and its fiat is law." Thus began a great expansion of United States claims to influence in Latin America that would leap in 1898 to Cuba and Puerto Rico and soon to other places, alarming and angering the nations of the area.

Juan Vicente Gómez took over the government in 1909, and ran the country as though he owned it. Despotic and ruthless, ignorant and shrewd, he was a disaster for Venezuela. To list the few things that he did not completely botch as indications that he could have been worse is idle. He could not entirely hold back modernization and the wish for more of it, but he inhibited good use of the petroleum revenues that poured into the country for fifteen years before his death in 1935. In many ways, Venezuela did not emerge from the nineteenth century until that year.

e. Ecuador

Ecuador at Independence had a population of under a million, most of it Indian or mestizo, living in the mountains. Fewer people, including some of black stock, resided in the coastal lowlands, and almost none in the Amazonian lowland of Ecuador's Oriente. Social disorganization, poverty of resources, difficulties of terrain and climate were as severe in Ecuador as anywhere in Latin America. Little advance was made toward modernization in the nineteenth century. Politics was disorderly, for the familiar reasons. An increasingly bitter regional rivalry grew up between Quito in the highlands and Guayaquil on the coast.

From 1830, when Ecuador split off from Gran Colombia, until 1860 the politics, government, and economy were those of the less successful

Latin American nations in those years.[13] In 1860 Gabriel García Moreno came to power by arms. He was a dedicated Conservative and a convinced proclerical. An educated and courageous man, he fought for his beliefs for years before achieving national power. He dominated the years to 1875, mostly as president himself. He believed that only the Catholic faith could bring decent government and development, and embedded that conviction in constitutions in 1861 and 1869, and in a concordat with Rome in 1863. He made Roman Catholicism the state religion, and only Catholics were allowed to be citizens, while the church had its own courts. Finally, in 1873, the Congress dedicated Ecuador to the Sacred Heart of Jesus, and it seemed to Liberals that theocracy could go no further. García Moreno was an intelligent sponsor of efficient administration and economic growth, and his draconian methods of keeping the peace assisted this to some extent. García Moreno's anachronistic regime depended almost entirely on his own will and ability, and when he was assassinated in 1875 the country's political life returned to its previous condition.

Liberals and Conservatives hacked at each other for the next two decades, with the former gradually gaining strength. Eloy Alfaro in 1895–1912 led the Liberals to predominance. He pursued the usual Liberal anticlerical line, even eliminating the Roman Catholic church as the state faith in a new constitution (the twelfth) in 1906. Such an action still could bring hot protest from Conservatives, and Alfaro eventually was killed by a proclerical mob. Generally, party conflict continued to be a matter of personal ambition and private profit. A few changes percolated into the country without affecting

---

[13] For some years after 1830 the chief leaders were General Juan José Flores and Vicente Rocafuerte, the former with his chief base in the highlands, the latter centered in Guayaquil. Sometimes they cozily took turns in the presidency. Flores was a Conservative, Rocafuerte a Liberal, but the labels covered factionalism more than ideas except on a few issues.

most of the population or the basic political system. The Indians continued to live in the high mountains, on poor land, subject to a variety of abuses by government and landlords.

A railway was begun in the late nineteenth century and early in the twentieth went into operation from near Guayaquil to Quito. During all the nineteenth and the early twentieth century the economy was one of the worst in Latin America. A small export business existed in a few tropical agricultural products and "Panama" hats. There was a small cacao export boom in the late nineteenth and early twentieth centuries. A little consumer-goods industry gradually was established. By the 1930s there was enough economic activity so that the middle class was slightly larger than a century earlier. Education had been expanded but remained poor and confined to the few. There was a trifling amount of labor organization. The country was too weak even to defend the national territory in the eastern lowlands. In 1904 Ecuador lost territory by agreement with Brazil and in 1916 to Colombia. Peruvian claims and encroachments were a constant threat, accelerated greatly in 1941 with aggressive military action that led in 1942 to great losses of territory by Ecuador.

f. Bolivia

Chuquisaca in the high mountains of Upper Peru had important local administrative power during the colonial era, and the elite there in 1825 insisted on the creation of Bolivia as a state separate from that ruled from Lima. A second basis for separate government was the difficulty of communications from Argentina and Peru, both of which nursed ambitions to rule Upper Peru. Bolívar acquiesced in Upper Peru's desire for Independence, and gave the new nation his name and a Constitution providing for a life-time presidency, a post he accepted for himself, with General Sucre as vice-president. Bolívar returned to Lima, leaving Sucre to face the local resentment of foreigners. The unpaid Colombian troops in Bolivia rioted at the end of 1827 and

early in 1828. Peruvian troops invaded, and neither Colombians nor Bolivians fought hard against them. Bolívar had long since left Peru for Colombia. Sucre resigned in August 1828 and left the country to local leadership.

The new country had a population of some 1 million, mostly poor Indians. Communication and transportation problems were dreadful. In a national territory more than twice that of France, most of the population lived in the high mountains, and virtually none in the lowlands of the east, where the boundaries with Paraguay and Brazil were undefined, or in the desert lands of the Pacific coast. The little towns, perched at great altitudes, were among the most isolated in the world. The first capital, Sucre, the colonial Chuquisaca, was nearly as inaccessible as Lhasa in Tibet. La Paz, which took over most of the functions of capital city late in the nineteenth century, sat in a great hollow of the mountains at 12,000 feet, an altitude that left the few visitors gasping for breath. The great days of silver mining were long past, and the industry remained in the doldrums to the end of the century. The Indians tilled the thin soils at the great heights under the domination of the small elite, which maintained its position throughout the century with constant changes in its ranks resulting from military skirmishes for loot and power that threw up new men from below.

Bolivia could maintain its independence but it could not create an effective polity or economy. Andrés Santa Cruz seized power in 1829, and created a confederation with Peru, which Chile destroyed. Santa Cruz ruled the country by force and with some competence for a decade; thereafter, the regimes usually were short-lived. Understandably the country could not defend its Pacific coast territories and their valuable nitrates against Chile in the War of the Pacific.[14] There also was territorial loss in the lowlands east of the mountains. In 1903, after considerable controversy and some violence, Brazil and Bolivia

---

14 See Chapter 27 on the Santa Cruz confederation and the War of the Pacific.

signed a treaty by which Bolivia gave up her claim to much of the isolated Acre territory, where Brazilian rubber hunters had penetrated.[15]

The usual conflicts between liberals and conservatives were in Bolivia of little consequence, in an environment of the most unrelieved and unstable *caudillismo.* Finally, in the very late nineteenth and early twentieth centuries, some small changes occurred. Steamships appeared on huge Lake Titicaca, eventually improving communications from Bolivia through Peru by rail to the Pacific. Beginnings were made on railways in Bolivia. A line by 1912 linked it with its old port of Arica,[16] by then part of Chile, which helped the development of mining in the Bolivian mountains. Economic and social change were exceedingly small, however, during the first century of the Bolivian republic. In the 1920s the biggest change began with an increase of foreign capital in mining; that finally would be important in generating reform sentiment that would permanently alter attitudes in the country toward the middle of the twentieth century. But until then Bolivia truly was what one of her writers early in the twentieth century said was a "sick" nation and people.

g. Paraguay

Political modernization did not touch Paraguay in the nineteenth century, nor more than a breath of economic and social change. Poor at Independence, Paraguay remained poor, a land of subsistence farmers who could exist without much effort in a benign climate, with small exports of cattle products, yerba mate, and quebracho. One of the smaller Latin American republics, located in the heart of the South American continent, with ill-defined boundaries at Independence, all its territory was in the lowlands. There were a few hundred thousand Paraguayans at Independence, nearly all mestizos of heavily Guaraní Indian stock. Few immigrants arrived. The population was about half a million in 1865, and only a million in the 1930s. A target of the ambitions of its neighbors Brazil and Argentina, Paraguay remained independent partly as a buffer area, partly because of the valor and sense of community of its people against outsiders, and partly because its highly authoritarian rulers successfully mobilized its resources for defense.

Argentine pretensions in Paraguay were spurned in 1810 and thereafter.[17] From the declaration of Independence in 1811, the country was dominated until 1840 by Dr. José Gaspar Rodríguez de Francia, almost all of that time as dictator-president. A man learned in theology and law, Francia's principles of government were absolute independence and absolute despotism. He feared foreign interference with Paraguay to the extent of permitting few relations between his country and the world. The legend arose that few entered and none left, but not even so complete a tyrant as Francia could manage that. He ruled with a passionate attachment to his homeland, demanding that people work as he did; and killing, jailing, breaking, exiling those who questioned him.

At Francia's death, Carlos A. López won the fight for power and ruled the country from 1841 to 1862. López gave up isolation and ran Paraguay as his personal estate, from which he serviced the few cronies needed to help him manage it. He was one of the most supreme of the *El Supremos* of the age of *caudillos.* He prepared his son Francisco Solano López to succeed him, partly by making him a general at eighteen. The second López was a drunk, twisted with Napoleonic ambitions, who led Paraguay into the terrible war of 1865–1870.[18] For the brave Guaraní

---

[15] Bolivia's original territorial claims of about 850,000 square miles ultimately were cut to about half that as its neighbors made good competing claims.
[16] The Arica railway was built by Chile under terms of a 1904 treaty by which Bolivia surrendered her claims to the lost province of Tarapacá. Bolivia also received an indemnity and use of Arica as a free port. That did not satisfy Bolivia permanently, however, and in later years the issue of the Pacific was revived.

---

[17] See Chapters 19 and 24.
[18] See Chapters 24–25.

the Paraguayan War was a true holocaust—the population of half a million was halved, and most of the survivors were women. The country also lost much national territory. Fortunately for Paraguay, the Brazilians killed the demented López.

Paraguay after the war remained disorderly, poor, and apparently without prospects. The labels of Conservative and Liberal were used, with little meaning. Small exports of pastoral, agricultural, and forest products profited a few. A little foreign capital, especially Argentine, arrived. Steamships and the telegraph and other modern technology came in modest quantity, without much affecting life in bucolic Paraguay. Steamboats operated in the rivers in the mid-nineteenth century. In the second decade of the twentieth century a railway was completed from Asunción to Encarnación on the Paraná River, where it connected with an Argentine line. A few cultural institutions—newspapers, schools—served the elite. But even in the mid-twentieth century Paraguay was a land of the poor, apathetically accepting rule by dictators.

h. Central America: The Failure of Union

After declaring Independence in 1821, upper-class leaders agreed to a connection with what seemed the comforting conservatism of Iturbide's Mexican monarchy; when that collapsed, the Central Americans in 1823 created a republic, the United Provinces of Central America. Except for Chiapas, which chose to attach itself to Mexico, it included the territories of the colonial Captaincy-General of Guatemala: Costa Rica, Nicaragua, Honduras, El Salvador, and Guatemala. The population, heavily Indian and mestizo, was about 1.2 million, much of it in Guatemala. Communications were primitive, the economy wretched. The small exports of the colonial period generally lost ground following Independence. Only in Costa Rica did coffee give sizable new income before mid-century. It became important later in El Salvador and Guate-

mala, aided by opening in 1855 of the Panama Railway, which brought west coast ports nearer markets in Europe and the United States.

There was much regional jealousy between the local elites; with Independence came new opportunities to express it. That rivalry was complicated by the usual division into Liberal and Conservative camps, with frequent resort to violence. Out of the early fighting emerged Francisco Morazán as Liberal dictator, hated by Conservatives and the church. Congress abolished religious orders, disestablished the church, proclaimed religious freedom, took some church property, and did a little for education. There was much political warfare, over church issues, provincial rivalries, and the tendency of Guatemala to assume a dominance based on its greater resources and its ancient role as capital. The union broke down in the later 1830s as leaders in the provinces successfully used force to establish independence.

Rivalry between the United States and Britain in the 1840s for influence in Central America led to new schemes for union, but they came to nothing, partly because of the opposition of Rafael Carrera, a Conservative dictator of Guatemala until his death in the 1860s. Justo Rufino Barrios, chief political figure in Guatemala from 1871 to 1885, interfered in neighboring states in support of liberalism, as Carrera had done for conservatism. Barrios was an intelligent and convinced advocate of modernization. He thought that the little Central American states should unite their human and natural resources in an assault on backwardness. In 1885 he declared the necessity of union, set out with an army to achieve it, and was killed at the outset. Regional jealousies, fear of Guatemala, distaste for Barrios' liberalism, and the virtual impossibility of conquest by the weak forces of Guatemala in roadless Central America made the effort chimerical.

Liberal José Santos Zelaya, the dominant figure in Nicaragua from 1893 to 1909 and influential in some of the other states at times, in 1894 incorporated into the regular government the Mosquito shore reservation that a treaty of 1860 made a British protectorate.[19] A British naval blockade of the Pacific port of Corinto during the ensuing crisis revived Central American unionist sentiment. A loose confederation of Honduras, Nicaragua, and El Salvador was created in 1895 and died in 1898. In 1899 Guatemalan students began a movement to promote Central American sentiment for union. In 1902 Zelaya persuaded all the states but Guatemala to agree to establish a regional tribunal to settle disputes. It could not be immediately effective because conservative dictator Estrada Cabrera of Guatemala opposed Zelaya. At this point the United States began to concern itself in detail with schemes for Central American arbitration, mediation, cooperation, and union; all of which were mixed with Washington's interests in naval bases, canal routes, protection for investments, and the need to promote political "stability," for its presumed virtue as a shield against attacks on the new Panama Canal Zone after 1903.[20]

Guatemala

Central America's most populous state held scarcely more than a million persons, mostly Indians, in the 1860s, and fewer than two million in 1900. *Latifundios* with few commercial possibilities, and subsistence farms with even less, occupied nearly all the population. From the 1820s to the 1860s cochineal and a little indigo were almost the only exports, and they could make no headway against international competition and the development of synthetic dyes. Coffee was not an export crop of importance in Guatemala until the 1870s, after which it grew considerably, paying for a modest amount of modernization in the country.

Local resources, institutional patterns, and in-

ternational markets and competition did not permit more development. A few Guatemalans thought the answer was hardworking European immigrants with special skills, but colonization schemes failed. The schemes were the badly conceived products of Guatemalan positivism that the same Liberal interest in progress tried with conspicuous lack of success in some other Latin American countries. The fundamental labor policy of Liberals in Guatemala in the late nineteenth and early twentieth centuries was to force Indians to work cheaply on the expanding coffee *fincas* by drastically reducing Indian communal lands, thus forcing them to seek wage labor. That policy was reinforced with laws on vagrancy and debt. So coffee exports integrated Guatemala more into the world economy, increasing *latifundio* primarily as a method of mobilizing labor. Indians in Guatemala were more exploited than they had been in the colonial era.

The Liberals' interest in "modernization" also focused on railways, essential to large-scale exports as opposed to the small-scale exporters of the area from the sixteenth to the mid-nineteenth centuries. So innovating administrations with limited revenues, by encouraging foreign capital, managed in the last quarter of the nineteenth century some limited construction of railways, telegraph and telephone systems, and electric power.

Guatemala endured many years of dictatorial rule. Rafael Carrera was an illiterate Indian learning to be a *caudillo* when in 1837 a cholera epidemic came to Guatemala. Clerics cried that Liberals and foreigners were poisoning the water. So Carrera led the pious Indians against the Liberals, terminating whatever little chance the Central American republic still had to endure. Carrera was Conservative chieftain of the country from 1838 to 1865, adored by those of his race as the savior of religion against what they were told was the atheism of the Liberals. Carrera was a ruthless *caudillo*, supported by Conservatives of the elite who despised him but preferred his

---

[19] On Mosquitia in the colonial era see Chapter 7, Section d.
[20] See Chapter 44, Section c, for Central American unionism since the early twentieth century; on Panama in the nineteenth century, see Chapter 33, Section e; on Costa Rica, see Section a of this chapter.

rule to that of Liberals of their own class. Justo Rufino Barrios, dominant in Guatemala in 1871–1885, was an educated Liberal, strongly favorable to economic development, education, and other modernization. He also was a severe dictator who thought nothing else would serve in his society. His actions against the church helped to reduce permanently its importance in public life. Manuel Estrada Cabrera was a "civilian" dictator from 1898 to 1920. Corrupt, without social conscience, he was ruthless and feared by all. He did have the virtue, from the Conservative point of view, of presiding over a time of export prosperity, using some revenues for the promotion of business, and insisting on absolute obedience by labor, especially the Indians who worked the coffee *fincas*, without any nonsense about adequate compensation. If Guatemala was not quite as backward by the 1930s as in the 1830s, a full century of history had meant pitifully little to the country.

El Salvador

Little El Salvador had at Independence only about a quarter of a million inhabitants, mostly mestizos, to use its fertile volcanic soil. Exports, led by indigo, were weak for more than half a century. Coffee shipments improved this situation from the 1880s. By the 1920s the country was fairly prosperous by Central American standards, which were low. The population, mostly rural and illiterate, reached a million before the turn of the century. As late as 1916 the capital and largest town, San Salvador, held only 65,000 persons. Even the usually optimistic Pan American Union noted in 1933 that the distinction was sharp between the upper class and the lower, and that the middle class was "negligible." During most of those years of minimal development, politics was marked by the squabbling of local chieftains, often complicated by involvement in intrigues and warfare with neighboring states. In the first third of the twentieth century political conditions slightly improved, partly in response to the growth of coffee income. Much of the

profit went to a few families, who played a heavy role in public affairs. Coffee money paid for a modest diversification of the economy and a few of the amenities of contemporary technology.

Honduras

Honduras was the most unfortunate of the Central American states. Its central position and weakness put it in the middle of many intrigues and wars. Its politics displayed the worst features of primitive and unstable *caudillismo*. No exports of consequence existed for many decades. It had a subsistence economy, a population of barely over a million by the 1930s, poor communications, and almost no social services. The capital of Tegucigalpa was a country town of 40,000 as late as 1938. At the end of the nineteenth century the international fruit business came to the isolated coast, and the large-scale shipment of bananas began from Honduras in 1899. In the next few decades it became an extreme example of foreign corporate influence in Latin America, the epitome of the "banana republic." Honduran politicians welcomed foreign capital, and in an environment nearly devoid of economic opportunity scrambled to give it favors. This laid the basis for growing insistence by reformers that the fundamental needs of the country were being neglected in the interest of outside forces. But the weakness of Honduran institutions was even more to blame than the strength of the foreign corporations for this result.

Nicaragua

The census of 1890 found only 375,000 Nicaraguans, most of them poor mestizos, with a small concentration of people of African heritage on the Caribbean. The bulk of the population lived in the hot lowlands near the Pacific coast, leaving the mountains and the Caribbean coast thinly populated. In the middle of the nineteenth century Nicaragua derived some income from travelers who went up the San Juan River to the Nicaraguan lakes, thence by boat and animal power to the Pacific. Before long, however, the Panama Railway (completed 1855) killed this traffic. No exports of importance existed until late in the century, when coffee and bananas provided slightly expanded income. A few other unprocessed commodities brought small amounts of foreign exchange. Warfare between Conservatives and Liberals tempted a filibuster from the United States, William Walker, to adventure in Nicaragua in the 1850s. Although briefly a power in the little country, he soon fell to local enemies, United States and British pressures, and the enmity of Commodore Vanderbilt, who had operations in the area. Apart from Walker's exotic activities, the violent alternations in power of local chieftains were lacking in surprises—or constructive results either. Most of the first third of the twentieth century was dominated by persistent United States intervention in Nicaragua's affairs, an activity that contributed little to the country's modernization.[21]

i. Haiti and the Dominican Republic

Haiti and the Dominican Republic (sometimes called Santo Domingo after its capital city), sharing a beautiful island, made little progress toward modernization in the nineteenth and early twentieth centuries. Haiti from 1822 to 1844 despotically ruled larger but less populous Santo Domingo, provoking fears among the Dominican elite that the black element in the local population would be increased permanently. The result was a legacy of distrust between Haiti and the Dominican Republic that endures today.

Haiti

Most of the half million people in Haiti were black ex-slaves,[22] and most of them wanted only to be left in peace as free subsistence farmers, a life favored by nature, which permitted easily built huts, a minimum of clothing, and food from tropical garden patches supplemented with fruits and chickens and pigs. The new peasants had no strong desire for more possessions or for public facilities or interest in the fate of the nation. Men of ambition had almost no outlet for their energies except government, since economic opportunity scarcely existed. Leaders dragooned peasants into armed bands and savagely competed for power and access to the meager public revenues. Obviously the only economic hope of the country was continuation of export agriculture, mainly sugar. It was badly damaged by the wars and by the distaste of ex-slaves for regular wage labor when life was possible without submission to such discipline. A few early leaders held commercial sugar culture together by harsh means that improved little on the French slave system. That course was taken by the illiterate ex-slave Christophe, the despotic ruler of the north from 1808 to 1820. Alexandre Pétion, an educated mulatto, ruled in the south from 1808 to 1818 and took a less authoritarian course that included parceling of land, whereupon commercial sugar production rapidly dwindled. He was succeeded in 1818 by Jean Boyer, another mulatto, who took over the north also at Christophe's death in 1820, conquered Santo Domingo in 1822, and ruled the entire island until deposed by a Haitian rebellion in 1843. The economy continued to worsen and some trifling coffee exports were almost the only source of foreign exchange.

The early heavy influence of urban mulattoes in government was reduced drastically in 1843 as class conflict with a racial aspect became more intense. From 1843 until the United States intervention began in 1915, government usually was dominated by blacks, though they used educated mulattoes in the bureaucracy. The subsistence economy yielded but poor returns to the rulers of Haiti, many of whom were brutal tyrants, rapidly succeeding each other with frequently frightful violence. Most Haitians spoke *créole*, a mixture of French and African elements that the

---

[21] See Chapter 44, Section c, for Nicaragua and the other Central American republics in recent years.
[22] See Chapter 18, Section a, on Haitian Independence and early government; Chapter 44, Section e, on Haiti in recent years.

small cultural elite scorned. The latter also emphasized its Catholicism, while the folk put its faith in voodoo, only marginally affected by Christianity, but a full-bodied and satisfying religion based largely on African elements. The cultural elite also clung to education, European clothing, and an ideal of cultivated life generally. The elite existed on government jobs or in the tiny business enterprises of the republic. In the late nineteenth century a few French and German merchants in Haiti stimulated modest growth of sugar and coffee culture, but in general foreign capital would not go in to struggle with irresponsible governments and an untried labor force when so many better opportunities existed elsewhere in the world, including the Caribbean. Money was found—some being borrowed abroad —in the late nineteenth and early twentieth centuries for a bare beginning of railway, telegraph, and telephone construction, and improvement of dock facilities, which did not affect the back country, where nearly all Haitians lived.

The Dominican Republic

Santo Domingo had been a poor and sparsely populated province in colonial times. As the Dominican Republic it suffered from disturbed international conditions for many years. Napoleon's defeated army in Haiti retreated to Santo Domingo in 1804 and remained in control there until a local rebellion threw it out in 1808. The Dominicans asked for British protection, which lasted until 1814, when the territory became again a Spanish colony at the defeat of Napoleon in Europe. A local rebellion in 1821 cast off ties with Spain but also encouraged Boyer of Haiti to conquer the territory in 1822.

In the years of forced union up to 1844 Santo Domingo's scanty exports declined. Juan Pablo Duarte, chief hero of the Independence movement in 1843–44, ushered the country into an unpromising future. For years thereafter the population was so small and the economy so weak that fear of Haiti and personal aims led some leaders to favor connections—even annexation—with Spain, France, Britain, and the United States. Attacks by Haiti's Faustin Soulouque (1847–1859) seemed especially dangerous. Spain returned in 1861 by invitation of *caudillo* Pedro Santana, largely motivated by his desire to maintain a prominent position in the local cutthroat politics. Spain in 1865 withdrew for a variety of reasons from an unpromising territory. Feelers to the United States from Dominican leaders in the 1860s and 1870s intrigued President Grant and a few others but foundered on an essentially antiexpansionist attitude in the United States Congress.

Internal affairs improved little in the next few decades. The sugar export business grew some. The first big steam-driven sugar mill opened in 1874. More fateful for the little republic were foreign borrowings that led to intervention. In 1904 President Theodore Roosevelt of the United States insisted that foreign control of the customs of Santo Domingo was necessary to ensure payment on foreign debts, to reduce the likelihood of European intervention, and to establish the orderly conditions that he declared the United States and civilization required in the area.[23] The United States control of customs

---

[23] Ulises Heureaux, an extravagant despot who ran the country from 1882 to 1899, piled up debt abroad. Some of the European debt was bought by United States citizens, who organized the Santo Domingo Development Corporation in the United States, lent Heureaux more money, and received control of the customs. The total amount of the country's foreign debts early in the twentieth century was only $32 million, two-thirds of it held in Europe. The debts in this case of intervention—as in others the powers were involved in during the nineteenth and early twentieth centuries—were much smaller than claims in the mid-twentieth century that roused much less violent response. The probability of European intervention in the Dominican Republic was difficult to judge in Washington, to say nothing of its likely danger to United States strategic positions. Some North Americans had an exaggerated notion of the profits to be made by Latin American investment; some others merely were interested in windfall profits from small operations that they did not hesitate to identify as of major importance to the United States.

pleased foreign creditors but not Dominican leaders, who remained as disorderly as ever. So in 1916 President Woodrow Wilson began a military intervention to fend off imagined danger from German activities and to improve internal aspects of Dominican culture. The military intervention was abandoned in 1924, and the fiscal intervention later, both having been counterproductive, or even, according to critics, disastrous.[24]

[24] On the Dominican Republic in recent years, see Chapter 44, Section f.

PART SEVEN

Acceleration of Socioeconomic Development, 1880s–1930s

The winds of change blew more strongly in the half century from the 1880s to the 1930s. In a few places—notably Argentina and Uruguay—they seemed to blow away completely the barbarism of Sarmiento's fears and to assure civilization or modernization. In those most advanced of Latin America's countries, hopefully showing the future of others, great export profits were plowed into education, transportation, public health, and other public services and infrastructure. Corruption of the electoral processes declined. Participation in political life broadened. The role of the military in public affairs dwindled. In Uruguay a broad system of social insurance was installed. Of course, even Argentina and Uruguay had problems; modernization was not so accelerated that it could overcome all of Latin America's traditional barriers to change.

In the other countries those barriers remained stronger, except in Costa Rica, where a transformation to literacy and orderly government occurred. Chile achieved literacy and considerable political participation. In Brazil great export income and some industrial growth aroused among a minority a nationalist ambition that was frustrated by the fragmentation of power in the federal republic dominated by coffee *fazendeiros*. In such less-developed lands as Bolivia and Honduras new income from foreign tin and banana ventures proved corrupting as well as modernizing and roused nationalist minorities. Mexico had an astounding revolutionary experience in 1910–1917, from which it emerged deeply changed. In Latin America as a whole, conservative and moderate elements remained in control. Although the Depression that began in 1930 saw an increase in military activity in politics, a rise in nationalist fervor, and some growth of interest in leftism, their importance could scarcely be gauged. It did seem likely, however, that demand for more drastic change would grow unless the challenge of modernization—growth and justice—was met more forcefully.

PART SEVEN

Acceleration of Socioeconomic Development, 1880s–1930s

29

Accelerated Development, 1880s–1930s

There was great export growth, but its uncontrollable oscillations led to nationalist demands for diversification to reduce dependence. Such demands led to somewhat expanded government activity in the economic realm. The new wealth paid for expansion of education systems, several of them remarkably. It also paid for public health measures that raised the rate of population growth. With industry came the beginnings of modern labor organization in the 1880s. Early in the twentieth century labor forced some modest social legislation. The doctrines of anarchism, socialism, and communism came to play a small but growing role among industrial workers and political theorists and leaders. The breaking down of communications barriers by better transport, the telephone, literacy, radios, and the cinema helped to spread these and other new ideas. All these changes affected the organization and aims of political parties. New parties, especially, supported broader participation, notably by the middle class, and more liberal legislation. Appeals for lower-class support became more prominent, although its income remained low, and it retained the diffidence ingrained by the traditional class system. The new parties sometimes secured fairer electoral laws and practices and broader roles for the legislatures. The depth and permanence of such gains, however, remained suspect because

political activity by the military by no means disappeared. One of the most important developments of the half century in Latin America was the growth of nationalism, a force that might be usable to root out the traditional barriers to modernization. That nationalism received a boost from the policy of intervention and penetration pursued by the government and private interests in the United States in the 1890s and thereafter.

a. International Relations

United States interventionism comprised one of four major factors in the international relations of Latin America. The United States expanded as it grew into a major economic power and began to translate that into naval force and international strategic doctrine. In the 1890s it began to implement a policy of political and economic intervention and penetration in the Caribbean. United States investment, notably in Cuba and Mexico, grew swiftly in the two or three decades before World War I. United States trade replaced much of Europe's during the war and retained some of it thereafter. United States manufacturers established branch factories as far away as Argentina early in the twentieth century. New United States power and doctrine led to abolition (1901) of the canal treaty of 1850 with Britain, and the latter agreed to United States control of the Panama route. The United States established military bases in Puerto Rico and Cuba. Washington took a persistent interest in what it called political stability and "civilization" in the Caribbean. Political pressures and military expeditions to influence local activity followed on a larger scale than the British had undertaken during their years of hegemony. It also stimulated lively Latin American fears of United States intentions.

In the second place, general world developments reduced Latin America's already feeble capability for mounting independent foreign policies. The growing size and complexity of manufacturing, financial institutions, transportation and communications, and military systems increased the advantages of the developed nations. The celerity with which the new steam-propelled navy of the United States disposed of Spanish power in 1898 and fanned out over the Caribbean demonstrated the speed with which things now could occur. The digging of the Panama Canal showed the gulf between the industrial and financial superpowers and the poorly developed nations. The tanks and submarines of World War I, the airplanes that came to open up mountainous Colombia and Bolivia in the 1920s, and the automotive vehicles, chemicals, and medicines sold to Latin America all showed how increasingly dependent the area was on the science, technology, and economic force of the developed world.

The third development was that the export economies tied Latin America more closely to the international trading system and market fluctuations that Latin American countries did not control. Each specialized in one or a few exports, which increased their vulnerability to world developments. The monocultural export economies poured out rivers of coffee, wheat, wool, bananas, meat, sugar, copper, and other commodities. Till World War I the expansion of exports usually dominated foreign relations, except in Mexico during the Revolution after 1910, and in the

Caribbean areas of United States intervention. Then during World War I interruptions of both exports and imports caused dislocations and fears in Latin America, stimulated distaste for economic colonialism, and enlarged desire for diversification. During the 1920s some exports advanced again, and some areas received large foreign investment, but weak spots in international economic relations persisted. Then the Depression that began in 1930 dealt an even heavier blow to the export economies than the war had. The severe decline of prices and demand was made worse by economic nationalism in the developed countries. The larger Latin American countries for the first time mounted sizable programs for development of their economies on a broader basis than exports, chiefly through industrialization. Those programs, however, long had limited effects, so Latin America remained to a high degree dependent on commodity exports.

The final major factor was that the cited developments did little to improve collaboration between Latin American countries. They still had their chief international economic relations with the world outside, so economic collaboration within Latin America had no basis in circumstances, and changing those circumstances seemed too difficult for serious thought. Faced with their individual weakness and the limited value of united action, the Latin American nations searched for international agreements that would give them the protection they could not provide from their own resources. From 1889 they sought it in the Pan American Union, but found the United States determined to use that institution primarily for its own purposes. Latin American demands for changes in the Pan American Union had little effect until the 1930s.

The international Hague Conventions of the late nineteenth and early twentieth centuries raised Latin American hopes for protection by agreement. The conventions on the peaceful settlement of disputes turned out to depend entirely on the willingness of the great powers to cooperate, and so were of little value to Latin America. Then Latin America from 1919 hoped for such protection by international agreement through the League of Nations and again was disappointed. During the 1880s–1930s period Latin American statesmen tried to get international attention for doctrines they propounded for their own defense, especially in favor of the juridical equality of states and guarantees against intervention in the internal affairs of other nations. None of those efforts to find doctrinal or institutional defense was effective. Latin American weakness was made frighteningly clear by the remarkable series of interventions by the United States in the Caribbean area between 1894 and 1934; by the course and nature of World War I—the complex and expensive weapons and training and organizational systems, the submarine warfare on commerce; and by the alarming ideologies and military methods of European fascism and Japanese expansionism in the 1920s and 1930s.

Other international developments included Brazil's successes in boundary negotiations with its neighbors, solidifying its position as one of the largest national territories on earth. Also important were the freeing of Cuba from Spain in 1898 and the separation of the Republic of Panama from Colombia in 1903, bringing the number of independent Latin American nations to twenty. Third, Mexico's great Revolution of 1910–1917 created dangerous friction with the United States, but never quite led to a catastrophic clash. Fourth, Argentina, Brazil, and Chile for a time were thought of as the ABC Powers, which was expressive of their superior development, as well as of some disposition on their part to engage in diplomatic and military rivalry and expressions of leadership on the traditional model of Europe. That did not have serious effects on international relations in the area, because of suspicions and rivalries among the three nations and because they were afflicted with many internal problems of greater moment than maneuvering for serious diplomatic or strategic hegemony. In addition, there was some doubt about how the United States would react to a serious rival imperialism in the hemisphere.

b. The Old and the New in Economic Life

Optimism outran economic performance. There was a rather unfocused belief that the limited innovation being adopted eventually would improve most of the huge and poverty-stricken traditional part of the economy. There was as yet little concern that otherwise, demands would increase for radically different methods of change.

Interpretations of Modernization

The new economic developments that became manifest before the 1880s continued thereafter, but without nearly extinguishing older patterns. Nor was it clear how much the new was socially desirable as opposed to merely pleasing to individuals. That is, how much of the economic growth could be labeled "modernization" in the sense of national development? Many Latin Americans considered a part of the modern economy their giant haciendas and plantations that turned out exports of beef, mutton, wool, wheat, coffee, bananas, sugar, sisal, and their big mines sending to the world silver, lead, tin, copper, zinc. In size those enterprises were modern as opposed to small traditional ventures. In some, however, productivity was low, so not all were in that sense modern. They aided modernization by generating large amounts of foreign exchange. They were modern when they called into being subsidiary processing, financial, transportation, repair, and other enterprises, and demanded workers and managers with complex education or training. But many of them employed large numbers of workers at low wages, whose social condition scarcely surpassed that of a century earlier. Argentine *estancias*, for example, became larger, used wire fencing and better pastures, bought good breeding stock, controlled pests—all of which was modern and contributed to profits. But they also often used more land rather than using old land better and kept nearly as heavy a hand as earlier on laborers and tenants.

Modernization of another sort occurred where conditions of work created new attitudes, as at some mines and factories by the turn of the century, where concentrated work forces and contact with socialist, anarchosyndicalist, and other ideas led to discussion, organization, even to a few strikes. Insofar as new job patterns drew people out of the isolation of rural life, modernization was promoted, even if it did not at once include much improvement in compensation or other conditions of life. In some countries, most notably Argentina, occupational patterns were much altered by economic diversification in the first decades of the twentieth century. Tradition, then, in the period from the 1880s to the 1930s was being more rapidly diluted than in the previous half century, but much of it remained. Development of production and markets, together with social decisions as to expenditures, made Uruguay and Argentina by the 1930s in some ways quite modern and well developed, even if less so than Sweden and France.

Latifundio remained through the 1930s as exaggerated as ever, except in Mexico, where the Great Revolution that began in 1910 commenced the process of breaking up the great estates. Much public and private land there was redistributed, often to communal holdings (*ejidos*). Land reform in Mexico helped destroy the old role of the *hacendados* in national life, and it inclined peasants to support the new regime; it did not, however, end private ownership and profit making in agriculture, or even all large estates. The *ejidos*, especially beloved of idealists and theory-oriented reformers, were undercapitalized, and for this and other reasons performed less well as producers than individually owned agricultural and pastoral lands.[1] In any event, Mexico was not joined in drastic redistribution of landownership until after World War II.

Weak motivation for achievement, low outputs, and poor compensation remained common in Latin America, reflecting the slowness of social and economic modernization. The elite was reluctant to perceive advantage to itself in en-

couraging popular effort by permitting higher incomes. Technological levels remained especially low in rural areas, many of which in the 1930s had essentially the production and distribution systems of the colonial era. Although railways and roads and demand opened new areas, many remained in which most goods were produced and consumed within small market regions, only feebly connected with the wider world.

Exports

Some parts of Latin America, however, greatly increased their involvement in the world economy from the 1880s to World War I. Even smaller nations that scarcely had exported in the 1880s now became dependent on shipments and recipients of import benefits. Honduras and some other countries became part of the international banana business, organized by Britons and North Americans. The coffee shipments of such small countries as Guatemala and Costa Rica increased impressively. In Cuba the sugar export enterprise became enormous, much invaded by United States money and corporate methods and tied to United States economic policy. Mineral exports from Peru, Chile, and Bolivia provided income and made them ever more dependent on the international system.

The export business in Argentina led to such euphoria and speculative excess by a private economy and a government that was heavily influenced by great estate owners that a financial crisis in the late 1880s and early 1890s briefly shook the oligarchs. The crisis led to creation of the Radical party, the first important Latin American party with some populist doctrine and considerable popular support. But Argentina emerged from the crisis to plunge into even more feverish growth, based largely on exports. Brazil's coffee exports grew rapidly, and provided capital for some diversification of the economy. In Mexico, exports multiplied tenfold during the dictatorship of Porfirio Díaz (1876–1911), and that helped speed an expansion of the railways and of the economy generally. It was done by attracting

---

[1] See Chapter 39 for analysis of this complex matter in recent Mexican history.

foreign investment with a ruthless law-and-order regime and all manner of concessions. Those two policies led to charges that Díaz sold the national patrimony to foreigners and had more interest in profits than in people.

As exports grew in Latin America, so did economic colonialism or dependence.[2] On the other hand, exports provided capital that might be used for economic diversification and the reduction of dependence. Some of the export income was, in fact, usefully employed by the 1930s for economic and social development. Much was wasted, however, because private greed was relatively little restrained to that time by populist political organizations or by developmental philosophy connected with national aspirations and protection of national sovereignty. The production and sale of export commodities was necessary for Latin American development, but so were theories and political organization and governmental structures that would permit optimum use of the income. Government intervention in the economies was relatively limited before the 1930s, then became much larger, stimulated by the disastrous world Depression which killed Latin American affection for dependence on exports. Between 1929 and 1932 the value of the area's exports fell about two-thirds.

Internal Trade and Manufacturing

Internal trade in the Latin American countries picked up with export growth. It also benefited from increased population. Of critical importance was continued railway construction, much more effective after than before the 1880s. Modern road building also began, though much later. Argentina and Mexico in the 1930s began serious efforts to extend paved roads; clearly the automo-

tive age ultimately would bring great changes to all of Latin America.

Manufacturing, which had barely begun in the middle of the nineteenth century, and still was small in the 1880s, grew more significantly thereafter, although Latin America was far from a highly industrialized area by the 1930s. Argentina went farthest in developing manufacturing and other nonagricultural pursuits. By the 1930s more than half its gainfully employed citizens were outside the agricultural/pastoral complex.

In Latin America most manufacturing plants were small; many that were listed in industrial censuses as factories had only a dozen workers. Nearly all turned out consumer goods. Heavy industry was tiny in the 1930s. A Latin American steel industry scarcely existed. Although the first modern integrated mill went into operation soon after the turn of the century (in Mexico), basic iron and steel production in Latin America grew slowly until the 1940s. Motor vehicles were assembled in the 1920s in several countries with parts shipped from North America and Europe, but their manufacture from locally made components was scarcely dreamed of in Latin America by the 1930s.

There were other developments of importance. For one thing, the availability of foreign loans and investment increased with the economic capacity of Latin America. Some countries contracted loans beyond their ability to repay, sometimes encouraged by private bankers and governments abroad, which Latin American critics condemned as a new, or at least a growing, type of imperialism. Foreign investment in Latin America in 1914 was about $8.5 billion, of which some 80 percent was in Argentina, Brazil, and Mexico, with Britain the chief lender, especially in railways. Between World Wars I and II the United States supplanted Britain as chief lender, investing $4–5 billion, of which about half went to government entities in 1921–1931, and by the early 1930s was mostly in default, another victim of the great Depression.

Another important development was that private and public financial institutions in some

---

[2] See Chapter 34, Section b, for the post–World War II theory of dependence, making the attitudes of the propertied class in Latin America part of a world capitalist web, unbreakable except by structural changes, probably by revolution. But the propertied class by the 1930s was changing its attitude toward dependence under the influence of nationalism.

Latin American countries grew stronger. They developed expertise that enabled them to handle their economic affairs better. That expertise tied into an increasing support for economic nationalism and for closer regulation of private enterprise. Also important was the fact that with the increasing complexity of economic life, especially in the growing cities, occupational specialization burgeoned: clerical workers multiplied in public and private bureaucracies; the growing middle class hired more servants; taxicab drivers and workers on city streetcars increased; growing expenditures for education included more teachers; more professionals were needed. By the 1930s, however, there was a surplus of certain types of professional people, especially those trained in law, who were unsatisfied with the opportunities they found in society.

Growing modernization, urbanization, and export profits increased Latin American concern with business activity and aims. Cities became more European, losing more of their colonial habits and appearance. Modern organization of business began in the 1870s with creation of the Mexico City Chamber of Commerce. Many other organizations of merchants, manufacturers, bankers, stock raisers, and exporters followed. By the 1930s the Latin American nations contained hundreds of these organizations. Some had great influence not only among the producers but with government. Their point of view certainly had more influence on government decision making than that of organized labor.

c. Social Developments

Population and Living Conditions

Earlier population growth had been modest, but now it accelerated, and by the 1930s and 1940s was one of the most important of all modern Latin American social developments. In 1850 Latin America had about 33 million inhabitants, by 1900 it was 60 to 65 million, and for 1930 the figure was well over 100 million. Much of the explanation of the change was a decreased death rate due to better public health measures. Immigration—nearly all European—provided considerable increments only to the populations of Uruguay, Cuba, Argentina, and Brazil. The rural population remained a large percentage of the total, although drastically reduced in a few countries. Argentina and Uruguay, the most advanced nations in many ways, by the 1930s were nearly as urban as rural, presumably prefiguring a similar evolution in the rest of Latin America. Miscegenation continued on a large scale.

Incomes for the majority of families improved little, if at all, a natural result of the persistence of the great estate, the feebleness of organized labor, lack of incentives, poor technological conditions, and the continued hold of the propertied class on politics and government. The most conspicuous change was a considerable growth of the middle class—that is, people neither very rich nor ordinary industrial or agricultural workers or peasants. Some of the small minority of highly specialized industrial workers were well enough paid so that from many points of view they could be considered middle class. In many countries the real incomes of peasants declined, for example, in Mexico under the Porfiriato of 1876–1911. Although material conditions were not much improved for most Mexicans by the 1930s, many of the common folk had at least some new optimism for the future. Many people were better off in Argentina as the result of enormous economic growth, some increase in better-paying occupations, and some enlargement of social expenditures by government. A very large group in Argentina had a satisfactory diet, access to education, and essentially middle-class expectations for themselves and especially for their children. In Uruguay not only economic growth but a system of social insurance brought material and spiritual benefits in the twentieth century to much of the population in the greater Montevideo area. Modernization through urbanization in Latin America, however, left millions of people living miserably in the poor wards of the growing cities. In the megalopolis that Buenos Aires had become by the 1930s, huge mansions patterned on those of the *faubourges* of Paris peered across the city at foul slums.

Class and Privilege

In the better-developed countries the growth of economic activity complicated the system of privilege. Much of the old exclusivism remained. The specific tie with the great estate was, however, weakened with the growth of other forms of enterprise. Strains within the wealthier part of the community resulted: for example, between manufacturers who wanted protection and agricultural exporters who preferred free trade. They competed for political eminence and for control of public policy. At the same time, old fortunes that originally were based on the land continued to move at least in part into new opportunities in mining, industry, commerce, and finance. New fortunes made in those fields were put in part into agricultural and pastoral enterprise. In short, with the rich and the upper middle class, the differences between sectors of the economy usually were less important than their common interest in control of the society in general—labor systems, credit policy, taxation. The middle class may have been a fourth or a third of the population of Argentina by 1930. If it was 10 percent of the Mexican population, it included a million people. The Latin American middle classes, although clashing at times and on some matters with the rich, tended to identify with them, support them, and hope to join their ranks. The course of economic and political development, therefore, in some ways increased the capabilities of the propertied to control the poor.

Social rigidities continued of considerable importance. Families that considered themselves of the uppermost class remained resistant to acceptance of newcomers. Some practiced racial discrimination in their choice of marriage partners, though that factor scarcely can be separated from the social factors involved. Class lines and family ties remained important in business activity in many instances, even though counterproductive economically. Class lines were drawn

in admissions to and promotions in the military services and in professional schools, though they now had to be implemented by subterfuge. Improved opportunity meant, of course, that more people made their way upward socially because of economic success. Mobility became easier as opportunities opened outside the export agricultural sector dominated by the great estate.

Although the racial aspect of social immobility by no means disappeared, the identification of citizens by race met growing objection due to the increase of nationalism, popular participation in politics, and egalitarian political and social theory. Mexico and Brazil by the 1930s had made racial identification illegal, which did not, of course, entirely dispose of prejudice and discrimination. By then some Latin Americans had developed the thesis that race prejudice and discrimination in the area historically and actually were less unjust and debilitating than in Anglo-America. Gilberto Freyre of Brazil expounded that view in the 1930s in his *Masters and the Slaves*. To some extent that Latin American attitude was a response to United States aggressiveness, to some extent it represented increased pride in Hispanic history and society. Not long after the 1930s this optimism was to be considerably diluted by a more sober examination of the realities of race attitudes in Latin America.

The area remained so much one of class lines and privilege, still bolstered by an oligarchic political system and by actual and threatened violence, that signs of its reduction received great attention. The old system certainly was reduced but far from eradicated. Apathy among the very poor remained a prime aspect of the social scene. Much had happened to reduce apathy, and more improvements were apt to occur, but it clearly was not likely to disappear rapidly or easily.

Communications and Education

Developments in communications and education were among the most important trends of the half century, both for what they accom-

The Old and the New

As important changes came to Latin America, much that was old remained.

An Indian *lechera* (milk woman) of Lima at work during the 1950s.

Courtyard of Posada Belém in Antigua, Guatemala. Originally a convent, it is now a hotel. Such conversions of old structures for tourist uses are common in Latin America. *Courtesy of United Fruit Company*

The *casa grande* (great house) of an Argentine *estancia,* mid-twentieth century. Here a hundred years ago may have stood a mud hut on the treeless pampa. This luxurious dwelling indicates the vast profits that have funneled into the pampa in exchange for pastoral-agricultural produce shipped to Europe. *Courtesy of Moore McCormack Lines*

Sugar cane cutters have been a common sight in Latin America since colonial times. Nowadays cutting machines are sometimes used—but they may be socially undesirable in areas with high unemployment. *Peter Menzel*

Oxen are still being used in the sugar industry in Costa Rica. But the carts have pneumatic tires and are unloaded by a mechanical crane. *Courtesy of United Nations*

A contemporary market scene at Pisac in the mountains of Peru. *Peter Menzel*

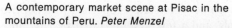

plished and for what they promised. The most obvious change was in the absolute and relative number of literate people. They had been few in almost all Latin American countries to the 1880s, but in the next half century nearly every country experienced considerable change and contemplated more. In a few—Argentina, Uruguay, Costa Rica, Chile—notable progress was made. Uruguay was 50 percent literate early in the twentieth century, and by 1930 it and Argentina were three-quarters literate. Most of the rest of Latin America was heavily illiterate (over 80 percent) at the turn of the nineteenth century, but in many cases they improved in the twentieth. The growing acceptance of education as a necessary function of the state became before 1930 one of the obvious bases for further modernization of attitudes and institutions. The expanded primary instruction systems, it was true, often were weak. Many of the literates listed by government censuses had so little schooling—often one to three years—that they were functionally illiterate.

Secondary and higher instruction also were expanded but remained quite small before 1930, essentially reserved to an elite from well-to-do families. Many specialized training schools were created in hairdressing, welding, accountancy, stenography—to serve the more complex society. Some were state supported, others private schools, and a few were operated by large industrial enterprises for their workers. Education remained highly concentrated in the towns. The countryside remained poorly developed in this as in other ways, because of both the problem of expense and the political pressures for such differentiation: great estate owners did not want their workers highly educated; the leaders of conservative parties preferred ignorant voters in the back country. Opposition groups were better able to organize pressure for schools in towns than among the dispersed and suspicious peasants and agricultural laborers.

A modest expansion in higher education included some modernization of curriculum. Most of the universities, however, remained poorly

funded and staffed and neglectful of the great shifts in interest and methodology in the great universities of Europe and North America. Argentina developed the best Latin American university system, with its chief strengths in the humanities, law, and medicine. The University Reform Movement emerged in Argentina as a well-publicized phenomenon in 1918. It promoted an end to political interference by the state in university affairs, a broadened and modernized curriculum, and government of the university by faculty, students, and alumni. The movement achieved a great part of those goals in Argentina and spread quickly to the rest of Latin America. It led to establishment of the dogma of "university autonomy"—freedom from supervision or interference by other authorities. It contributed also to student organizations, and to activity in public affairs by those organizations. The universities became centers of opposition to economic colonialism and foreign domination of Latin American affairs. The effects of university politicization promised to be increasingly important after 1930. The pedagogical and scholarly or scientific benefits of the reform were less evident.

Communication was promoted by expansion of newspaper, magazine, and book publishing, all of which had been feeble before the 1880s. The press generally remained highly partisan. The reading public for books was so small that most Latin American authors could not live from their writings alone. The coming of motion pictures and radio in this period promoted communication and common aims and values. A radio in a country bar brought the world in some of its aspects to literates and illiterates alike. Motion pictures long before the 1930s were being shown in open air theaters in tropical ports, on the sides of gypsy vans, and in crumbling halls of mud brick in mountain Indian villages.

Railways grew even more than before 1880. Argentina, with the largest system, had only 2,800 miles in 1885, but 21,000 in 1914. Seaborne communications and travel improved. Roads were expanded, and buses began not only to carry city residents but to bring to market peasants with their livestock and sacks of onions and squash, all packed into the seats, aisles, bumpers, and roof. Airplanes dramatically improved communications in the mountainous interiors of some countries. Voluntary associationalism increased. Business organizations have been noted; there also were YMCAs, Italian-Argentine associations, Spanish-Cuban clubs, and others.

The growth of nationalist sentiment improved the incentive to communication. The new populist parties depended on communications to make their appeal. But improved communications and transportation could only slowly break down inherited values and attitudes. Even when institutions changed their names and forms and ostensible functions, often the underlying values and attitudes of the people did not undergo great transformation. Organized university students and leaders of radical parties discovered that they could not easily communicate their ideas to peasants or industrial workers with sufficient intensity to move them to collaborative action with the propagandists or would-be organizers. Imported "modern" institutions often did not reflect popular value orientations. That was one major reason why continuity was so important in Latin America and why change proceeded so slowly and differentially.

d. The Old and the New in Politics

Federalism and regionalism continued to diminish. Many economic, communications and transportation, and doctrinal developments were working for centralization in much of the world, including Latin America. Federalism by the 1930s was scarcely a large issue any longer except in Argentina, Brazil, and Mexico, and even in those countries the power of the central governments increased. Central power notably increased during the crises of the 1930s, partly through the adoption of wider government intervention in economic and social life. Vargas in Brazil, for example, in that decade considerably reduced the powers of the states. Regionalism, of

course, continued to exist in all countries, based on differences of economic interest and on perceived differences of attitude and ambition. During this period regionalism began to suffer severe shocks from growing nationalist sentiment, which supported much of the centralization that occurred.

The church issue continued to decline in importance. By the 1930s it seldom was of consequence in politics in Argentina or Brazil, and anticlericalism came out of the Mexican Revolution as a strongly dominant point of view. Other old issues remained important without achieving all that reformers wanted. The drive for a broader vote continued to make gains in law, but somewhat lesser gains in fact. Declaring more citizens eligible to vote did not always persuade them that doing so was worthwhile, especially when electoral corruption continued. The secret ballot was adopted everywhere, but politicians proved equal to the challenge. Ballot counting still was frequently fraudulent, and cancellation of elections by fiat occurred. Still, the number of political participants did increase, and the larger size of the electorate complicated the role of political leaders. The old liberal plea for more effective legislatures kept its appeal and made rather sizable gains in Argentina, Uruguay, Chile, and Costa Rica; but the overall pattern of executive predominance left the issue a common one in political combat.

The use of violence and illegitimate action in terminating or installing national regimes remained an outstanding feature of political life. None of the considerable changes in society generally or in military institutions specifically seemed to diminish or much threaten the military role in public affairs. There were predictions that it inevitably would diminish with wider education, better communications, more popular political participation, and adoption of social legislation. Such reduction did not occur except in two apparently unambiguous cases—Costa Rica and Uruguay—and in several where apparently some progress was achieved in reducing such activity, notably in Argentina. Events were to prove that the success in all those instances tended to disintegrate under pressure.

"Professionalization" of the military by providing soldiers with better training, equipment, and pay did not turn them either from their corporate interest or from willingness to exercise the role in public affairs so obviously open to them, to which they were so often urged by civilian politicians. Nor did changes in social aspirations, or in the social origins of officers, seem to alter much the military's perception of its role. To be sure, details of policy and action were adjusted to fit new circumstances, but the fundamental fact of intervention remained unchanged. Better military education and the growth of nationalism combined to give officers a more elevated conception of their intervention in public affairs but did not reduce their willingness to intervene. Regional *caudillismo* or *caciquismo* was reduced by improved communications and transportation. The cruder sorts of nineteenth-century banditti and political brokers at the head of armed bands found it difficult to operate or develop wide influence. The crisis of the Depression of the 1930s increased military intervention in public affairs. Finally, United States policy at times seemed to favor conservative regimes, including military dictatorships, as promising some sort of "stability" that would be useful to United States strategic and economic policy and to United States private business interests in the area.

Persons of property led the resistance to effective extension of the franchise, fair elections, strong legislatures, and control of military intervention. They did, however, in some circumstances support all those things. They retained considerable capacity to influence the political behavior of their economic dependents. Professional officers tended to support the views of the well-to-do, both out of distaste for change generally and for what it might do to their position, and because of dislike for populist or radical doctrine.

Deep-seated conservatism and a tendency to violence in politics meant that new issues and participants faced formidable barriers. Liberal doctrine was widely adopted in advanced circles in the late nineteenth and early twentieth centuries. Some parts of it were acceptable to persons of wealth; some other parts, only to more adventurous spirits. Some of the latter were from the middle class, and their reformism seldom extended to support of really radical measures. Some Social Darwinists, positivists, and fascists were elitists, who used what they considered modern, and even scientific, ideas to support rule by the elect few. Other doctrine also was used. Anarchism began to fade as the twentieth century advanced. Socialism made a contribution in many ways, acknowledged and unacknowledged, persuading many political leaders that it offered at least part of the road to justice, national development, and political power. Socialist parties did not do well, however, during the half century. That of Argentina had considerable success, but could not capture national power; that of Chile developed some influence. Communist parties, founded just before and after 1920, offered ideas, organization, and leadership to a tiny minority. Communists often had to operate underground. All the leftist groups were led by men of middle-class origins.

The most important new political organizations during the half century were reform groups that appealed to local attitudes and concentrated on local issues, using foreign doctrine but concealing its origins, accommodating it to American reality. The Radical Civic Union of Argentina, formed in the 1890s, was the first important indigenous party with a populist component. Even though its leadership and policies were middle class, it received considerable support from working men. José Batlle y Ordóñez transformed the *Colorado* party of Uruguay early in the twentieth century into a supporter of economic and social reform. The leaders of the Mexican Revolution in the 1920s formalized their organization in the National Revolutionary Party, which in the 1930s had an organization stressing national echelons of peasants, industrial workers, and other groups. However much the element of reformism in the Mexican party may be argued, its size, programs, and appeals to the public made it different from the traditional parties of Latin America. Víctor Raúl Haya de la Torre in 1924 began organization of the American Popular Revolutionary Alliance (APRA) to bring together the workers of Peru against the control of the oligarchy and its military allies. Other efforts to create broadly based parties with a populist appeal began by the 1930s in other countries.

All this certainly portended increased political pressures on the old regime of privilege. But conservative parties continued to operate, though often with reduced effect. Equally important were personalistic parties, vehicles for individuals, which continued to be created and to have great success, often backed by military force. The increased pressures for innovation were not sufficient to root this element out of political life. It turned out that personalist presidents and parties could gain wide support from some poorer citizens and that they did not automatically earn active rejection by others: that is, they could play at promising economic and social gains on the one hand and on the other count on public apathy. In the 1930s leaders showed that they could successfully make use of the growing nationalist sentiment, either for economic growth or for independence, sometimes expressed as distaste for the United States. So great was the disillusion of many Latin Americans with political leaders that sometimes obviously dictatorial figures were supported because of their socioeconomic promises as readily as leaders who also promised political equality and justice.

By the 1930s many of the issues of politics were obviously changing, especially in the direction of economic and social modernization. New leaders had arisen to exploit those issues. What was not clear was how the political and governmental systems would be altered. Organized students in a few instances helped precipitate political change, but generally they were a minor political element. A much larger group, the industrial workers, remained largely unorganized; and even when gathered in syndicates, they

were closely controlled by government. Peasants scarcely had a role in politics. General political apathy remained a major reason for conservative and military control and manipulation. Conservatives could not resist—sometimes did not want to resist—all demands for change, but they powerfully molded the timing and the characteristics of change.

e. The Old and the New in Government

Much of the old tradition in government remained, with modifications. Corruption and inefficiency were little touched. That inertia no doubt resulted partly from habit, but also from the poor pay of civil servants, lack of job security, poor training, inefficient organization, poor equipment and procedures, the concept of public office as a source of profit rather than of service, and the society of privilege. "External administration" was an inherent part of the system, requiring petitioners to government, even for relatively routine documents, to coordinate government activity themselves, passing out tips to get action. Despite these weaknesses, some aspects of government operations were modernized: for example, the handling of public electric power projects and irrigation works. As the bureaucracies grew with population and new conceptions of government function, their enlarged ranks were organized by government leaders to support their political fortunes. The bureaucracy became more conspicuous as an interest group. There was much practice, also, by government of open and concealed monopolies, in-group franchises, use of dummy contractors, and similar devices that were more highly polished in such centers of political virtue as Paris, France, and Albany, New York.

The continued subservience of many national legislatures has been noted. On the whole, Latin America somewhat improved the position of such bodies between the 1880s and 1930s, but the experience of the latter decade scarcely was encouraging. The legislature of Mexico remained a nullity; Vargas reduced that of Brazil nearly to impotence; and the Argentine Congress in the 1930s labored in the shadow of a conservative regime with minority support, kept in power by force and fraud. Even when the legislatures of the half century managed some independence of the presidents, they managed precious little independence of the oligarchic interest groups.

The most important government change was broadening social and economic functions, as was happening in much of the world. Little of this occurred in Latin America until after World War I. A small amount came earlier, with elite support of transportation, manufacturing, and some other enterprises. The sheer complexity of the more modern parts of the economy and of life in big cities required some expansion of government regulating and support activity. Some resulted from the economic nationalism that began at the end of the nineteenth century and grew to a crescendo in the 1930s. Furthermore, social legislation slowly was extended. In Uruguay government functions were greatly expanded before the 1930s, by government participation in the economy and by operation of a big social insurance system. Argentina, Brazil, and Mexico considerably enlarged their government operations before the 1930s, and much more during that decade. Chile, badly hurt by the decline in mineral export income during the Depression, created a government development corporation. All of this prefigured a government expansion in Latin America that was to continue with great acceleration during and after World War II. The trend to greater economic and social activity by government was in some of its aspects supported by the old privileged groups, but often opposed, especially when they could not control its details. It met relatively little opposition from the popular classes because they never had much opportunity to benefit from private economic activity and had no traditional attachment to private business as a form of activity superior to that of the public sector. The Depression speeded changes that were coming in any event. Government became widely involved in industrialization programs, tariff protection, exchange controls,

regulation of organized labor, all of which had small beginnings before the 1930s. In the 1920s and 1930s the study of economics began to assume greater importance as the profession became more and more an essential part of government activity.

The increase of government functions, tied as it often was to national goals or programs, encouraged the central governments to reach more often and efficiently into the provinces. The new methods of communications and transportation facilitated this outreach. Such centralization of power could be accounted gain or loss depending on how it was used. Although expanded government functions required more funds, Latin America was slow to modernize its public revenue system. Till World War II import duties provided from one-third to one-half of government revenues in the area. Even relatively well-developed Argentina received about 40 percent of federal revenues from import duties as late as 1935. Income taxes scarcely existed in most countries. Property taxes remained exceedingly low. Taxation bore heavily on the poor, through such things as sales taxes and license fees. The propertied not only were lightly taxed, but notoriously evaded payment. One barrier to large social expenditures, thus, was the simple fact that public revenues were low in Latin America. The lightness and the inequity of Latin American revenue systems were among the least modern of the area's institutional patterns.

f. Continuity and Change from Independence to the 1930s

Continuity and change were both important in the first century of Latin America's independent history, the former little disturbed to the 1880s, much more thereafter. In the later nineteenth century and early twentieth, isolation, parochialism, apathy, class rigidity, and oligarchic control were weakened but far from eradicated. The elites were slow to root out the remnants of feudalism or to push cultural and social integration.

Education was not expanded enough, and there was too little emphasis on science and technical studies. Too much agriculture remained primitive, a drag on the entire society. There was resistance to industrial development via such policies as protective tariffs and other subsidies.

That lack of change was partly due to insufficient development of nationalism, which would demand expulsion of more foreign economic threats. Nevertheless, clearly a new Latin America slowly was emerging, although its partisans had to fight their way against the old society.

The struggle for material and moral modernization gained in organization and support, however slowly, and in several countries remarkable, almost revolutionary, changes occurred. Change was obviously accelerating, and would continue. It might be most marked in Buenos Aires and Rio de Janeiro, but it inevitably would stimulate to some extent Tegucigalpa and Asunción, peasants as well as stevedores and college professors. One could only guess at the beginning of the 1930s that the future would be neither quiet nor easy.

30 The Amazing Argentine, 1890s–1930s

The term "the amazing Argentine" was used long ago to describe the country's development in the later nineteenth and early twentieth centuries. It seemed to have found the key to modernization. It became one of the great trading countries of the world and one of the most literate, best fed, orderly, and hardworking. But the praise that Argentina received and the pride felt by its elite were accompanied by protests that the vast new wealth was not efficiently or equitably used for economic, social, and political development. The Radical and Socialist parties roused the middle and working classes with demands for justice and captured the allegiance of the majority of voters and finally the national government. As aspects of modernization were partially achieved, the citizenry enlarged its aims, and traditional elites and much of the great middle class peered aghast into an abyss of endless agitation for change. With much of the material aim of modernization attained or apparently within reach, its spiritual or social aspects were the more fervently embraced. The conservatives struck back with military intervention. The best-developed Latin American nation entered the phase of sociopolitical contest earlier begun in better-developed European countries and at the same time and in some ways more successfully in Uruguay.

a. Economic and Social Development

Economic growth in Argentina from the 1890s to World War I fulfilled the bright promise of the preceding decades. After some difficulties during the war, growth went on at a high rate. Much of it was directly or indirectly due to what became a mammoth export sector, and that and foreign investment tied Argentina ever more closely to foreign partners. The wealth that poured into the country went heavily to a rich minority, but large amounts went also to a much enlarged middle class. Although the urban and rural wage earner and small independent or tenant farmers did less well in terms of money income, the condition of some of them improved markedly as compared with much of the world. Argentine society by most measures became the most modern in Latin America and more modern than all but about a dozen countries in North America and Western Europe and Japan.

Immigration and Urbanization

The society continued to benefit economically from rapid population growth, much of it from immigration. Total population went from 3.9 million in 1895 to nearly 8 million in 1914 and 11.2 million in 1930. Argentina's one million square miles were still lightly peopled compared with Europe or the United States. Europe sent to Argentina in the 1890s more than 300,000 immigrants, over 1 million in the first decade of the twentieth century, fewer in the next ten years; but in 1810–1914 about 3 million immigrants had entered Argentina, and nearly a million more arrived in 1921–1930. Then in 1930 the great Depression led to Argentine restrictive measures, and one of the most formative processes of its modern history was drastically altered.

Argentina had 31 percent foreign-born in 1930, twice the percentage that ever occurred in the United States. Most immigrants went to the city and province of Buenos Aires, which helped give those two areas 46 percent of the national population in 1914. At the same time, a slight majority of the city population was foreign-born. A much smaller number of immigrants went to some of the agricultural areas of the northern littoral and to Córdoba and the far west. Many went to the metropolitan area because of the difficulties the great estate system posed to poor newcomers. Thus, a high proportion of them went into industrial, commercial, and service occupations. When they went to the countryside, it was to agricultural rather than pastoral activity, the latter being dominated by the native-born upper class. The bulk of the immigrants were Italians and Spaniards, the former predominating in the late nineteenth century, and Spanish immigrants overtaking the Italian in the twentieth. One of the results of European immigration was that the once conspicuous mulatto population was assimilated and obvious mestizos became rarer, except in the far northwest. Argentines began to refer to their "pure" European blood in such a manner as to irritate some other Latin Americans.

The distribution of population reflected modernization of the economy: the proportion of urban dwellers increased from 25 percent in 1869 to 37 percent in 1895 and 53 percent in 1914. For the first time a Latin American country—Argentina—had less than half its population in rural areas. Although the urban definition of Argentine censuses included areas with cultural affinities with rural life, the trends were clear and remarkably rapid and continued after 1914. Another feature of population distribution was that the city of Buenos Aires continued to grow faster than the rest of the country. It had somewhat more than 500,000 in 1889, and in 1914 the metropolitan area had 2.03 million, or 25 percent of the national population, and it maintained a percentage of about that order thereafter. Other cities enjoyed rapid growth, though it came later than in Buenos Aires, and they started from such small bases that none was very large before World War I. Rosario grew from 40,000 to 220,-000 in 1880–1914. Tucumán, the largest city in the far west, had fewer than 100,000 in 1914. The far interior (beyond the littoral and the Pampas) long remained retarded in economic and demographic growth. The interior population did not migrate to the littoral cities in significant numbers until the twentieth century. These demographic changes had important implications for many processes, including the ease and nature of political organization and appeals and the allocation of federal government funds for economic and social infrastructure, from street paving to educational facilities.

The Transport Revolution

Before the 1890s the transport revolution had been well begun in Argentina, especially through the building of railways and the development of refrigerated ships, but most of the expansion and effects were felt in that decade and later. New port works benefited Buenos Aires and some other littoral cities. They came to use large amounts of labor, modern transport, materials-handling machinery, and storage facilities. Rosario was transformed after 1902 into a modern grain port under contract with a French company that received a forty-year monopoly of the installations it built, an example of the usefulness of European capital to Argentina. Unfortunately, the high profits made by the company also illustrated the lack of care taken to protect Argentine interests. Early in the twentieth century electric trolleys were replacing horse-drawn cars, especially useful in huge Buenos Aires, whose expansion was outward rather than upward. A British-built subway opened in the metropolis in 1914. Motor vehicles were imported more rapidly into Argentina than into the rest of Latin America, but road building was neglected before 1930, so autos had restricted usefulness. Airlines went into operation in the 1920s but were not important until after 1930.

Railway mileage went from 2,800 in 1885 to 10,000 miles in 1900 and 21,000 in 1914, concentrated largely in parts of the northern half of the country, where population and economic production promised returns on investment. Expansion into less profitable areas required much more use of Argentine—largely public—capital than the older lines, largely laid down with British and some French capital. In 1914 British concerns owned and operated over 70 percent of the railway mileage. The concentration of foreign capital in the most profitable lines in the Pampas, together with other problems of their financial and operating policies, brought laws to control the railways. Legislation in 1907 provided more government regulation of the private lines. The total national railway mileage was about 31,000 in 1939. A line reached the Bolivian border in the far north in 1908; a line reached Chile in 1910. Railway building largely ended before 1930.

These railways were immensely important to national economic development. Before 1930 that meant largely big pastoral and agricultural interests—producers, distributors, processors, shippers, and the important commercial interest and its financial and other allies in the cities of the littoral. Although they helped some other producers of the remote interior, they hurt some by facilitating imports of competing goods. Since the aim was to connect export-producing areas with ports, few feeder lines were built, so that most rural dwellers were left as isolated as before the lines were constructed, because roads scarcely existed before the 1930s. This pattern of railway construction was typical of Latin America. Argentina quickly received the nearest approach to an adequate network, but it was only an approach.

The Surging Economy

Changes were wrought by huge increases in the value of exports, by diversification of commodities shipped, and by expansion of production to wider areas of the republic. Long before 1930 Argentina had become one of the ten greatest trading nations in the world. Export value went from 100 million gold pesos in 1890 to more than 150 million in 1900 and 390 million in 1910. Foreign trade constituted a large share of national income: about 30 percent in 1914. Meat packing, railways, grain elevators, and other aspects of the export and import business were heavily funded by British interests, which had $1.5 million invested in Argentina by 1910. Most of the exports continued to be agricultural and pastoral from holdings that remained highly concentrated in ownership. Investigations during those years in Argentina showed that the concentration of landownership was becoming ever more drastic. Some 78 percent of all land in 1914 was in holdings of 2,500 acres or more, and a good number were immensely larger, including nearly five hundred of 60,000 acres and more each. Some land, especially in the province of Buenos Aires, became so valuable that the owners had no incentive to sell off parcels.

Two especially important changes occurred in the export business. One was that agricultural products, notably wheat, became important. From the 1880s much of the Pampas was quickly converted from pastoral production to agriculture—to wheat, maize, and beef-fattening pastures. Grain exports had been practically nil in 1880 but reached 238,000 tons in 1887 and several million by the turn of the century, and in 1904–1905 wheat exports began to top meat exports in value. Argentina had become a major world supplier of wheat. Already by the 1890s the growth of Argentine wheat exports worried competing interests in the United States.

The second great change was in the meat export industry from the 1880s: from salt meat to live animals to frozen meat. In 1887 nearly half of all meat exports still were salt beef, but by 1907 scarcely any salt beef was shipped. In the interim, frozen exports increased, and live-animal shipments soared briefly late in the nineteenth century. Live-animal shipments soon were eliminated by improvements in refrigeration and by English prohibition of such shipments in 1900 because of fear of hoof-and-mouth disease. Frozen beef shipments went from very little in the middle 1890s to more than half the value of all meat exports in 1907. Thereafter, continued improvements in refrigeration techniques permitted shipment of chilled beef, which was more palatable and brought better prices. The sheep business in Argentina early in the twentieth century was being altered by declining European markets and the new agricultural and beef enterprise, which pushed sheep farther into the peripheral areas of the country.

The economy was neither all thriving nor all closely tied to agricultural and pastoral exports, although those exports were heavily dominant as measured by profitability and influence on public policy. Although much commercial and financial activity was tied to exports, some was not. There had to be much fabrication, commerce, and service activity in a city the size of Buenos Aires. Most of it was by individuals, family workshops, or small plants. There were large plants in meat packing, tanning, and flour milling, but most "manufacturing" establishments had fewer than a dozen workers. In 1895 a census listed 22,204 industrial plants, but they employed fewer than 150,000 persons. In 1914 there were 48,779 such enterprises, but only half were classified as factories. Foodstuffs still were by far the largest category of such fabrication. But until 1930 most manufactured goods were imported. Just before World War I about 40 percent of all goods (including agricultural) were imported, and there was not much change in that until the 1930s.

These beginnings of manufacturing in the early twentieth century accounted for only about 14 percent of national production. A slow continued increase included branch plants of foreign companies. Automotive assembly, for example, began in 1916. Industrial growth did not owe much to national policy. Protective tariffs on manufactures before the Depression began in 1930 had little effect except on a few lines singled out for special attention. Import duties were largely for revenue and accounted for 65 percent of federal funds in 1890. World War I, however, did considerably increase protectionist sentiment. Interruption of supply from abroad made more local fabrication necessary, and some of it proved to be permanent.

Textile manufacturing, especially, expanded steadily from World War I through the 1920s, and a number of other consumer goods industries did well. Sugar and wine making increased, helped by the new railways and by government protection. Small foundries and metalworking shops became quite numerous, since there was a great demand for their services in replacement, repair, or modification of modern wares. Heavy industry, however, did not exist, so that Argentina seemed in some ways more dependent than ever on the better-developed countries, as some nationalists pointed out before 1930. Splendid basic commodity exports, and an extensive light industrial plant, had brought Argentina far out of the depths of underdevelopment; it was only natural that her nationalists should wish for more.

Social Changes

Although some of the new wealth trickled down to a sizable part of the population, income distribution was most uneven, especially in the *campo*, dominated by the great estate and a traditional paternalism. There was somewhat better distribution in Buenos Aires, especially to the expanding middle class, in all its ramifications from the small retail merchant to the prosperous commercial, professional, and industrial elements. Wage earners were, however, the great majority of the metropolitan population, and their situation improved only slowly. An element in this was the feebleness of the organized labor movement, so that workers did not have much political influence, and governments did little to help them, even supporting the organized employers in their resistance to worker demands. One problem of labor organization was that many workers were foreigners and passive in an alien environment. Another problem was that organization began under anarchist and socialist leadership, resulting in emphasis on social doctrine, political objectives, and direct action methods—especially general strikes—that frightened the employing class and the political elite and failed to bring enough benefits to the workers to make them militant. Only a small proportion of workers joined unions (*sindicatos*). In the 1920s union membership did not even keep pace with the growth of the industrial labor force. Furthermore, union members gave poor support in dues, strikes, or demonstrations. An appeal to labor was a part of the doctrine of the Radical party, but it provided little help in legislation. The Socialist party was more sincere in its interest in labor, but its minority position limited its accomplishments. The growth of the middle class and industrial labor did, nevertheless, alter hopes and demands in Argentina and could be expected to do so yet more powerfully after 1930.

The striking improvements in education that began before 1890 continued thereafter. National literacy reached 46 percent in 1895 and more than 60 percent by 1914, and it remained heavily concentrated in the cities. In 1914 in the city of Buenos Aires 80 percent of the school-age children received instruction, in the province of Buenos Aires 61 percent, in the province of Salta only 48 percent. Clearly, the urban middle class and industrial labor benefited most from the expanded system of primary instruction and the rural workers least. The decision of 1884 to eliminate the church from primary education was adhered to throughout this period, and complaint against it was feeble. Secondary instruction was little expanded before 1930 and was largely used by the small minority preparing for the universities and professional schools.

There was more development of higher education in Argentina before World War I than in the rest of Latin America. Most of the institutions were professional (law, medicine, engineering) schools in the old tradition. The University of Buenos Aires added a Faculty of Philosophy and Letters in the 1890s, and the new University of La Plata (founded 1906) put some added emphasis on science. Some work of distinction in legal and other humanistic fields was done. In 1925 there were fewer than 20,000 students enrolled in five universities and eighteen other postsecondary institutions. Dissatisfaction with the system grew in the early twentieth century. It was too small, basically serving the upper class. It suffered government interference with intellectual and pedagogical issues. There was resistance to new ideas. There was insufficient funding, one result being part-time instructors, often badly prepared for instructional duties, and only intermittently available for consultation. The system was weak in modern science and the new social studies. Research was not adequately encouraged.

These complaints with the university system became connected with political protest, and with the conviction among some of the younger generation that the material achievements of Argentina entitled her to a more modern cultural environment. Such views culminated in the "University Reform Movement" that began in 1918 at the University of Córdoba and spread rapidly through Latin America. Results included university "autonomy," removing institutions from direct intervention by government (including military and police), and giving great decision-making powers to organized faculty and students. Members of the new middle class could more easily break the conservative monopoly of university administration and teaching and promote a new curriculum. Unfortunately, the fact that the reform increased political activity in the autonomous universities impeded improvement in education and research, although that by-product became most apparent after 1930.

Communication among Argentines was being stimulated not only by education, but by expansion of newspaper, magazine, and book publishing, and of the railways to carry the print throughout the republic. In the 1920s radio further improved communications. With the growth of the educated community came an increased demand for recognition of intellectual activity as a specialized and valuable class of endeavor. The number of persons devoting their attention to national questions greatly increased. Many of them displayed nationalism of one variety or another. Socialists by the time of World War I proclaimed fervid nationalism. There was resentment of the huge British stake in the economy. Some of the Generation of Eighty (those whose careers began about 1880) were in the 1890s and early twentieth century demanding less subservience to European modes and more emphasis on what was genuinely Argentine. It was suggested that the dictator Rosas should be reinterpreted as a strong voice of authentic native determination not to submit to foreign domination and as an example of the firm leadership needed to guarantee Argentine strength in a world of dissolving standards.[1]

By the time of the celebration of the centenary of Independence in 1910 these nationalist voices were quite strong. The nineteenth-century poem about the gaucho Martín Fierro had become a national passion, and the cult of the gaucho appealed to nostalgia, nationalism, and love of the picturesque, after the gaucho culture had disappeared and was no longer a threat to modernization. Ricardo Rojas' *La Argentinidad* (1916) was one of many celebrations of the country's virtues and also expressive of the fears of dilution or domination by foreign cultures and economies. José Ingenieros was a widely read

author who thought the "whiteness" and cultural achievements of Argentina entitled her to leadership in Latin America. By the 1920s a marvelous variety of nationalist literature and organizations had appeared. There even were rightist nationalists praising European fascism and quoting with approval from Henry Ford's *Dearborn Independent* passages of the spurious anti-Semitic tract "Protocols of the Elders of Zion." The huge public school system taught nationalism in its history texts, which the extreme nationalists thought tepid. There was increasing complaint that immigrants did not become citizens and that they retained too much of their European culture. Nationalist literature and sentiment were paralleled by or reflected in some political activity and legislation, but most of that effect came after 1930.

The superior economic and social development of Argentina by the late nineteenth century was causing changes in the class structure, especially in the city of Buenos Aires, and especially by enlargement of the middle class. In the metropolis in 1890–1914 the middle class may have increased from 15 to 30 percent of the total. Whatever definition of middle class is adopted, it certainly grew considerably from the 1890s to 1930. The oligarchy was wealthier than ever, a small minority of probably less than 1 percent of the total population. Although they retained their great landed holdings, long before 1930 much of their wealth was in industries, commerce, and finance. When they lost the presidency to the "middle-class" Radical party in 1916, it turned out that the rich retained enough political force to guard and expand their holdings by friendly legislation and administration. The oligarchy had many ties of interest with various of the directors of the Radical party, some of whom were wealthy men. People of property were more unified than fragmented by socioeconomic change in Argentina in this period. Tension between economic sectors had not yet become acute, and the propertied generally agreed on policy on such matters as taxation and labor.

---

[1] Adolfo Saldías published a "revindication" of Rosas in the 1880s, and the idea never died thereafter.

Persons of the middle class achieved considerable income and education. They were much more active citizens than the proletariat, and their interest was reflected in their achievement of political power. They did not, however, constitute a coherent and self-conscious group in the sense of desiring to control the country in some middle-class interest. Instead, they were largely intent on improvement of their status, generally in the direction of the small upper class. This concern probably was the reason for the declining birth rate of the middle class in Argentina. They supported modernization, but were far from a politically innovative group. A large recent literature has rather deplored this attitude, sometimes ascribing Argentina's ills to middle-class materialism and want of political resolution. Possibly the general unwillingness of the middle class to develop much interest in labor is more to the point. Manual labor in Argentina as a whole remained by far the predominant occupation. Outside of towns there was virtually no middle class by any definition. Not only was the rural lower class large, but it was isolated from the influences that in the cities stirred at least a few workers either to upward striving or to militance. Great as the changes were in Latin America's best-developed country from the 1890s to 1930, the pressures for modernization still were localized. Social mobility had increased, but much rigidity remained.

b. Challenge to the Oligarchic Polity, 1892–1912

Socioeconomic development in Argentina led by the 1890s to demands for political change, but the economic and political elites feared and resisted reform.

The Conservative Governments

The old conservatives continued to control the Argentine political and governmental systems from 1892 to 1912, presiding over and assuming the credit for the great material and social improvements in the country. During most of those two decades, Roca and Pellegrini continued as powerful members of the political elite, supporting the policies already laid down that encouraged foreign investment, exports from the great *estancias*, immigration, education, better transportation, modernization of the city of Buenos Aires, and a corrupt polity to ensure their continuance in power. Measured by crude material growth, and some sorts of social improvement, especially education, the administrations were successful, as the conservative leaders believed.

The attitude generally was one of laissez-faire, which meant that there was little government aid for groups (like manufacturers) that wanted help against the dominant export economy or for the poorest part of the population in either town or country. Most government measures supported the economic order that its directors thought should continue forever. Social assistance from public sources, aside from education, was thin and paternalistic, while private charity was quite inadequate. The governments were slow to respond to the needs of the new urban working class, although a small amount of social legislation benefiting labor was passed in the early twentieth century. A Department of Labor was created in 1907 with its jurisdiction limited to the Federal District and the National Territories. Unions were permitted to exist, but subjected to considerable police supervision. All this was, of course, traditional in Argentina, and prosperity, for all its differential distribution, blunted the edge of discontent.

Argentine pride, ambition, and nationalism were evident in the conduct of foreign relations, although the country had sufficient problems and opportunities internally so that they consumed most of the energy and interest of leaders. The armed forces, one factor in international policy, were considerably enlarged and modernized under the conservative governments after 1890. The long boundary controversy with Chile was settled in 1902. On the whole, Argentine statesmen were satisfied with their ties with Europe and with the improved strength economic development had given them to support their ancient rivalry with Brazil. Argentina was not in a position to take a strong line with Europe, on which it was highly dependent. It had little interest in the far-off United States, except that as time wore on, Argentine leaders developed an animus against United States intervention in the Caribbean area.

As a weak nation, Argentina long had wished protection against intervention from abroad. In the later nineteenth century Argentine Carlos Calvo published the thesis that foreign governments should not use force to collect private debts. Argentine statesmen—and other Latin Americans—tried to promote this and related doctrines at the first Conference of American States, Washington (1889), and at the second, Mexico City (1901), with the United States resisting. In 1902 Argentine Foreign Minister Luís M. Drago, in a note to the United States, restated the Calvo Doctrine in slightly different terms, retaining the prohibition on foreign intervention. Such concern for the protection of sovereignty remained a mark of Argentine diplomacy in later years. The conservatives also expressed their nationalism regarding the petroleum that was discovered near Comodoro Rivadavia in 1907, by creating state reserves. That move was not incompatible with free enterprise but, as events proved, ultimately led to state trol of the petroleum industry.

The presidents of the period were unremarkable, save for Roca, whose second administration (1898–1904) was the epitome of bossism, oligarchy, and chicanery.[2] Such men were not given to self-doubts, so analysis of methods and goals was not characteristic of their regimes. There were some conservatives, nevertheless, who considered that there was an unfortunate contradiction between the wonders the Argentine system had wrought in economic and social realms and the corrupt political order. Probably this conclusion of a minority of the political elite was based more on pride than on guilt. These were prosperous, self-assured men, in some cases admirers of what they thought they understood of upper-class activity in the political and governing systems of England. They believed in a rule of law, with important decisions being made by the oligarchs in executive office, the legislature, and on the bench. They were liberals in some senses but not democrats; they thought that they were the proper rulers of Argentina; and that common people were incapable of handling public affairs properly. Votes were regularly sold. There were men who made a business of getting citizenship for immigrants and then conducting them in groups to the polls to vote as ordered. In the cities hired bullies assaulted polling places to ensure a proper result. In the countryside the oligarchs were so firmly in control that chicanery scarcely was necessary.

The concerned members of the elite, however, kept thinking that there ought to be a way of ensuring rule by the few without displaying to the gaze of Argentines and the wider world a political process that led the opposition to shout fraud and even to engage in armed revolt, declaring it the only way to defeat the machine. A few in this minority of the elite even inclined to political reforms that were almost certain to threaten or eliminate their control of government; if they had been willing to think of that likelihood more closely, they might have been less attached to such change. Ex-President Pellegrini, just before his death in 1906, told the Congress that the frequency of rebellion and forcible suppression finally had convinced him that the price of peace was political reform.

The Campaign Against Electoral Corruption

The new political groups organized in the 1890s, most importantly the Radical and Socialist parties, put constant pressure on the conservative system. The Radicals continued nominally under the leadership of Alem from the founda-

---

[2] Luís Sáenz Peña resigned in 1895, and his vice-president finished the term. Roca imposed Manuel Quintana for the term 1904–1910, but he died in office and his vice-president succeeded.

tion of the UCR in 1892 until he committed suicide in 1896. That was the act of a moody and unstable man, embittered by the fact that his nephew, Hipólito Yrigoyen, was taking over leadership of the party. Yrigoyen's insistence on one-man rule of the party early drove out such talented liberal leaders as Aristóbulo del Valle, Lisandro de la Torre, and Juan B. Justo.

Yrigoyen ultimately became a remarkably successful political leader, and much of that success was due precisely to the intense focus upon him personally. Although that was offensive to men who stressed issues, it aroused many Argentines to support of the party because they had faith in Yrigoyen. Yrigoyen was born in 1852; he was just ten years younger than his uncle Alem. He went through secondary school and began but did not finish work on a law degree. He grew up in the Argentina of the oligarchic era of peace and prosperity and limited and fraudulent elections. He worked for a time for the conservative P.A.N. In 1878 he was elected to the Buenos Aires legislature as a member of the Republican party. Then in the 1880s Yrigoyen and Alem looked for ways to build an independent political force. Yrigoyen held several unimportant jobs, never was prosperous, and had little interest in property. He spent some time as a teacher in a private school. His cultural equipment was not elaborate, and some of his efforts to be profound brought snickers from his detractors, even when he was president of the republic. His method of public expression was turgid, ambiguous, and high-sounding; to his enemies it was pretentious and ignorant; to the true believer it was idealistic and sincere.

The fact was that many people felt sure that Yrigoyen was not interested in personal wealth, that for him the campaign to clean up the electoral system was a crusade, and that it would redound to the benefit of common people. Yrigoyen did not need to spell out programs to get across the impression of sincerity and dedication; what his foes and rivals found windy generalities were enough to make him the greatest figure in Argentine politics. He lived frugally and gave of his small earnings to charity. His manner was solemn, and his conversation and speeches had a tone of moralism that helped convince many followers that he was a saintlike man. His critics, on the contrary, found him dreamy, impractical, imprecise, and called him "the Apostle." He was an able practical politician, reared in the vote-buying and violence-ridden ward (*barrio*) politics of Buenos Aires. He knew machine politics in all of its aspects: what it could do, how hard it was to oppose it. So he built his own machine.

The ingredients of the Radical party were complex and contradictory, and its expressed policies ill defined, except for opposition to the conservative clique and the corrupt political system. That opposition, however, had diverse bases. Yrigoyen's own motivation was obscure. He certainly wanted a fairer electoral system, but it was difficult to know how to weight that goal against his fascination with political power. He was a dictator within his own party, and as president of the republic he was sometimes arbitrary and arrogant in the use of authority. He was a practicing democrat in the sense that he was without social pretension, but that had little effect on his policies as president. He gave generously of his own small funds to the poor, but had little interest in their condition as a social phenomenon that might engage the attention of public agencies.

On the other hand, there were leaders in the Radical party who had precisely that interest in legislation for the underprivileged poor. And a great many ordinary citizens supported Yrigoyen and the Radicals because of a generalized supposition that the party would be of use to them. The Radical party also attracted men with political ambition who had no hope of penetrating the inner ranks of the P.A.N., because they lacked the money or social position to make them attractive to the clique. Although new men constantly were entering the political and economic elites of Argentina, their groups remained small. There were many men, especially in the city of Buenos Aires, with the temperament or the education that led them to believe that they deserved a chance to make a greater contribution in public affairs. Some of these men also were partisans of a broadened political system on grounds of principle; others thought the distribution of property and income unjustly skewed; others thought such deficiencies stood in the way of building a greater and sounder Argentina.

Increasingly, in the 1890s and thereafter, there were lawyers not engaged in serving the regime in business, office, or on the bench who wanted a political alternative. The universities were charged with being little more than factories to spew out advocates who could not find an adequate position in society. Then there were men of property who wanted changes in the economic policies of the government, especially to divert subsidy and direct expenditures from support of the agricultural/pastoral export industry to support of their own activities. A good many interests wanted government aid. Manufacturing was the most obvious example (mining, lumbering, sugar were others), and easy to understand: it wanted to depart from the free-trade, commodity-export system and install whatever government controls and expenditures were necessary to promote domestic manufacturing. Such ambitious economic groups could claim that the traditional system of public aid to the economy was enriching a minority at the expense of balanced growth and independence. That argument appealed to intellectuals who joined the Radical party. With such disparate elements supporting the party, no wonder its following quickly became large, or that constructing a program to fit all needs was a problem.

The Socialist party also became a large dissident organization. It was formed in 1894 by Juan B. Justo, who liked neither the leadership methods of Yrigoyen nor his policy interests. Justo, a physician, was an example of the intellectual in politics in Latin America, where they have been notably prominent in leftist and labor groups. He helped give the party the theoretical cast that was one of its weaknesses. It began

publishing a newspaper, *Vanguardia,* in 1894, an action indicating the new role that argument and persuasion were to play in the political process of a literate Argentina. The Socialists also encouraged foreign-born workers to become citizens and engage in politics. While the party sometimes attracted a large vote, its leaders often found communication with the rank and file difficult, although they pursued genuinely populistic objectives with more consistency than Radical leaders. The Socialists were handicapped in not being able to penetrate the provinces because of the control of regional bosses, the lack of an adequate supporting element of industrial labor and intellectuals there, and inability to deal with a scattered population that had no conception of socialist doctrine or labor organization. The party was handicapped everywhere by its inability to attract the middle-class element that sustained the Radicals.

The Radicals and Socialists would have been glad to come to power by election, but the conservative clique would not permit it. The Radicals organized demonstrations in the summer of 1893. Then, in September, they tried armed uprisings, which were quickly contained. Alem, Yrigoyen, and some other Radical leaders were jailed. Alem favored another revolt, but Yrigoyen opposed it. Lisandro de la Torre later said that Yrigoyen took that position simply to destroy Alem, even at the expense of the revolution. At that point President Luís Sáenz Peña formed a Radical cabinet but soon found that it had disturbing plans for investigation of past conservative governments, and he dismissed it. In the election of 1898 the influential Radical leader Bernardo de Irigoyen wanted to collaborate with other dissident elements to prevent the imposition of Roca for a new term, but Hipólito Yrigoyen successfully opposed it, and forced out of the party a number of its more liberal and promising leaders, including Lisandro de la Torre. The latter declared on leaving the party that Hipólito had deliberately sabotaged the revolutionary plans of 1892 and 1893. De la Torre thereafter concentrated on a Progressive Democratic party that he organized in his home state of Santa Fe. It demanded a fairer political system, but lacked much influence.

Yrigoyen in 1905 made his only serious effort at armed revolt. It was a complete failure. Although there was a conspiratorial element in the army, the government had been modernizing military equipment and training for years, fearing just such rebellion, and in 1905 the army firmly supported the government. Yrigoyen was briefly jailed, but the government did not take drastic retaliatory measures. It was kept on the alert, however, by continued violence by dissidents. Anarchists had been using terrorist tactics for several years, so that in 1902 a Law of Residence authorized the deportation of revolutionaries. In 1905 a Catalan extremist tried to shoot President Quintana. In 1909 the Buenos Aires chief of police was killed in the streets by a bomb thrown by a Russian anarchist. The ruling clique was in no danger, however. It intervened in three provinces in 1907, three in 1909, and one in 1910. The president called an extraordinary session of Congress for November 1907 to deal with the budget prepared by the administration; when he met strong opposition, he closed the Congress by decree and adopted for 1908 the 1907 budget by executive order. With such methods, the government usually had its way, though such high-handedness occasionally brought objections from members of the ruling elite. Pellegrini, embittered by quarrels within the elite, in 1905 wrote:

> In our country political power rests in the government, which does not permit the existence of any committees or parties which might limit this power.... Senators and deputies are not representatives of the people of the provinces but of the governors, to whom they owe obedience, and on whom they depend for reelection.

After the fiasco of 1905, Yrigoyen adopted the tactic of nonparticipation in the electoral process, to emphasize its corruption. The Radicals put out propaganda excoriating the system. Yrigoyen spent much of his time talking to followers in his modest shuttered house in Buenos Aires that came to be called "the Cave" for its dim interior and the isolation of the conversations there. He has been faulted for defective organization of the party in those years, but there was little use for an elaborate structure until the electoral system was operated fairly or another revolt tried. The Socialists were developing their organization in the metropolis and in 1904 managed to elect Dr. Alfredo Palacios as a national deputy. He immediately began introducing populistic legislation in the Congress. He got a bill passed in 1907 regulating the labor of women and minors, giving minimum wages, and safeguarding worker health. The coverage was small, however, and most of his legislative suggestions failed to pass. The conservative government thus supported a modest amount of social legislation, some of it before Palacios appeared in the Congress.

In 1910 the conservatives imposed Roque Sáenz Peña as president of Argentina. He was an eminent member of the political elite, a distinguished lawyer, who had served the country well as a soldier and diplomat. He had enjoyed strong support for the presidency in 1892, partly because he seemed more liberal than the old-line bosses of the country. For that reason, the bosses distrusted him, and put forward his father, Luís, as more malleable, and Roque withdrew from the competition. It is supposed that this experience of some two decades earlier had reinforced in Roque Sáenz Peña a disposition to dislike the system of bossism, force, and fraud, which it has been noted came to be the view of even such a prominent political manipulator as Pellegrini. Any disposition to prefer fairer elections must have been reinforced by the national experience since 1892 with revolts, however feeble; abstention from elections as a protest; terrorism by anarchists; demonstrations and manifestos of all sorts by dissident individuals and groups; the use of federal intervention in the provinces and states of siege to continue the *unicato* (one-man rule) that concentrated authority in the president; and the continuing upgrading of the armed forces, sometimes used for political purposes, to keep down opponents of the ruling clique.

When during his campaign for the presidency Roque Sáenz Peña promised electoral reform, his promises were taken as the usual preelection rhetoric. They were not, however, and Sáenz Peña said at the beginning of his administration (October 1910) that he wanted minorities represented and would guarantee their rights. How much this was a desire for justice and how much a sensible desire to defuse dissidence and the danger of revolt is not clear. Soon after the election, Sáenz Peña asked Yrigoyen to let Radicals participate in elections, but Yrigoyen said that awaited proof of an honest electoral system. The president also offered Radicals four ministries, together with a promise of the secret ballot and honest elections; but Yrigoyen did not care to collaborate with the administration.

In 1911 Sáenz Peña sent a proposal for electoral reform to the Congress. It provided for males over eighteen an obligatory, free, and secret vote. It also provided that the party that got a plurality would receive two-thirds of the seats in the Chamber of Deputies, and the party with the second largest vote would get the other one-third—in other words, a type of guaranteed minority representation. There was strong conservative opposition, with the usual assertion that the populace was not ready for such responsibility. The president used his formidable power and influence to pressure legislators into passing the reform. It was widely believed that the electoral reform of 1912 would be subverted by conservatives through force and fraud. As it turned out, the reform marked a turning point in Argentine politics.

c. The Radical Party and Modest Reform, 1912–1928

Although the conservatives finally permitted the moderate reformers to gain political power, the new men in the Radical party made poor use of their opportunity. Their unwillingness to do much for working people opened the door to more leftist doctrine, and led to the description of the Radicals as a "Light That Failed."

Results of the Electoral Reform, 1912–1916

With the electoral reform of 1912 the Radical party resumed participation in the political process. Radicals and Socialists in the next few years won some municipal, state, and federal offices. The number of voters increased now that participation was more meaningful. Many more men who did not belong to the old clique ran for office. The conservatives were alarmed, and many were willing to emasculate the new electoral law. They were restrained both by indications that such action might meet serious rebellion and by the powers of the presidency, which had been such a prominent part of their own control. Roque Sáenz Peña supported the new law until he fell ill in 1913. Vice-President Victorino de la Plaza, who took over for the rest of the term,[3] was another of the minority of elite statesmen who admired the English respect for the rule of law. He enforced the electoral reform.

Yrigoyen doubted that he would be allowed to win the presidency for the term 1916–1922. The Radicals nominated him to the accompaniment of great emotion, both in the party convention and in the streets of Buenos Aires. He then refused the nomination on the grounds that the great struggle had been for political morality and not for office. He allowed himself to be persuaded to run, but did not campaign. Regardless of how sincerity and calculation were mixed in this performance, Yrigoyen possibly did better by not campaigning. His character and presumed objectives were well known. The conservatives retained much strength in the interior provinces, where there had been less economic and social change than in the littoral. They also were entrenched in the province of Buenos Aires. The Radicals had support among the middle class of a number of cities and in some areas where there were substantial numbers of small independent

---

[3] Sáenz Peña died in 1914.

or tenant farmers. Yrigoyen received a majority of the popular vote, but not a majority of the electors. A group of dissident Radicals from Santa Fe controlled the deciding votes, and finally supported Yrigoyen, so that he won by one electoral vote. The Radicals did not win control of the Chamber of Deputies, however, and elected only one member of the Senate, which was chosen by the provincial governments. The party gained control of only three provincial governments.

Still, it had the presidency. The crowds in the streets of Buenos Aires for Yrigoyen's inauguration in 1916 were joyous. There was a sense that a millennium had been reached. Yrigoyen had said little about policy for his administration. He was known to be for honest elections, which meant new men in office; and the party was for "regeneration," which presumably meant new policies. As Yrigoyen came from the inauguration ceremony, the crowd took the horses from his carriage and pulled it themselves through the rejoicing city. Women threw flowers from balconies on the hope of a new and better if not-too-well-defined Argentina. Sad to say, only fourteen years later ladies would be throwing flowers from balconies to soldiers marching through the streets to remove Yrigoyen from office.

The Administration of Yrigoyen, 1916–1922

That Yrigoyen as president from 1916 to 1922 did not "do" much is a misleading and unhistorical judgment. True, he preferred not to have a set program, and resisted efforts to persuade him to announce such aims. That was partly a lack of interest, partly a belief that politically he was better off without a program. Yrigoyen was above all a politician; he had spent his life organizing, persuading, conspiring. And he did have a political program: to entrench the Radicals as firmly as possible. He had only a limited understanding of cultural, social, or economic development, but he had some ideas on these subjects, and did a modest amount to pursue

them. Most governments in the world at that time were not accustomed or geared to big action programs.

Yrigoyen was not under great pressure for economic or social innovation. The Radical party included defectors from the conservatives and a great many middle-class leaders interested primarily either in their personal positions or in modest tinkering with what seemed a high-performance system. Middle-class leaders in government and private life certainly were not interested in costly social programs. The Radical party was not proletarian in leadership, ideas, or aims; it received some lower-class support out of a generalized supposition that Yrigoyen would be better than the conservatives. Even if Yrigoyen suddenly had revealed a burning interest in social reform, how much he could have accomplished in that direction is doubtful.

Yrigoyen's firmest views and actions were political, and his administration often has been criticized for concentration on control and office rather than on social issues. That was quite traditional, so that the great victory of 1916 was politically only a limited break with the past. Yrigoyen introduced new men but scarcely altered the terms of political combat and objectives. Then in his mid-sixties, Yrigoyen continued in the *Casa Rosada* the political habits he had developed over the long years of defeat. He preferred to talk to individuals or small groups. He was a dogged rather than brilliant tactician. He occasionally supplemented his obstinacy and moralistic observations with considerable personal charm. He had the politician's habit of leaving his visitors with the impression that he agreed with them; the more acute simply found that they could not fathom his views at all. This enigmatic quality was not just that of the jovial politician; Yrigoyen was genuinely secretive. He retained during his presidency his lack of personal ostentation and his habit of describing his aims in generalized but very uplifting terms, even to the extent of referring to his "apostolate." His foes might sneer at him, but it was acceptable to many Argentines.

The conservatives could not like Yrigoyen, even when they discovered that he would not remake Argentina overnight. They were disturbed by the extensive, if ambiguous, talk of reforms and justice for common people. Yrigoyen offended with his informality. Conservatives considered that he showed an unfortunate affinity for the lower class. He was friendly with his bootblack. They found that he "damaged" the international prestige of Argentina by wearing carpet slippers while receiving an ambassador. Petty report and innuendo were but expressions of the fears of the old elite that new men and manners portended new policy.

Yrigoyen used the presidential power to promote the Radical party, following the view that "reparation" of the administration called for maximum replacement of conservatives. His most notorious move toward this objective was the use twenty times of the constitutional power of intervention in the provinces, in flagrant contradiction of his long-time proclamation of the need for a just political system. He could, of course, argue that most of the state governors and legislatures had been fraudulently elected, but that merely stated that the end justified the means. In addition to damaging the moral basis of the Radical appeal, such action tended to centralize authority in the federal government, a trend that was being slowly furthered by the growth of its activity in economic and social fields. He also promoted a personal type of centralization by demanding of his political and governmental subordinates what has been called "a loyalty bordering on the sycophantic"—that is, he liked to be surrounded by toadies. He also has been accused of organizational and other excesses in politics that increased "hatred" between Argentines, but surely the economic and social policies of his and earlier and later administrations had more to do with that than political rivalries.

Yrigoyen used the military in such a way as to suggest that he was not concerned that military force had been an important element in corruption of the political system in the past. He used military and police forces during interventions in the provinces. He appointed army officers to executive positions in the government petroleum agency *Yacimientos Petrolíferos Fiscales* (Y.P.F.). Yrigoyen's actions irritated some army officers, and they approached Marcelo T. de Alvear, as Yrigoyen's likely successor in 1922, for assurance that as president he would keep the army out of political activities, and that he would bring military equipment up-to-date. Officers were not agreed, however, on their political function, and some were interested in military activity in connection with petroleum and other industries of prime military concern. The very division of opinion over such matters was a contribution to politicization of the military. Possibly the most important contribution, however, was the "professionalization" of the military from the late nineteenth century, through better doctrine, organization, training, and equipment. German military missions before World War I were especially influential in that development. It stimulated pride, esprit de corps, and self-conscious examination of the function of the military establishment. The broader education of officers had an important effect on the military's view of its roles. Officers came to appreciate better the relationships between military power and political, social, and economic institutions. They also knew more about the history of military influence in public affairs, in Latin America and elsewhere, including, later on, Mussolini's fascist regime in Italy.

There was little about the administration to alarm the economic elite. Yrigoyen's middle-class supporters did not want to disturb the export economy. They merely wished to alter details—for example, land rents—and attain more power and prestige in society. The administration promoted a land reform that touched unimportant parts of the national territory and had little effect. It did not alter the credit and tax systems. The role of foreign capital was not diminished. The economy still boomed during much of the administration and on precisely the traditional bases. The university reform that the administration supported was more a political than a social move on its part.[4]

The weakness of organized labor was scarcely altered, although the administration sponsored a small amount of legislation to aid workers. Yrigoyen was the first president actively to arbitrate disputes between labor and management. The government protected labor against strikebreaking. That protection, however, went by the board with the labor unrest toward the end of World War I. Strikers multiplied because of inflation and stepped up labor organization efforts, some of it by anarchists and communists. Employer resistance included a campaign to identify labor organization with foreign radicalism. Violence and tension excited public opinion. In January 1919 a strike in Buenos Aires quickly escalated from local skirmishing with police to widespread sympathy strikes, then to general street fighting. Violence also occurred in Rosario. Yrigoyen's previous moderation toward labor disappeared. He used troops to restore order, and became identified by some workingmen as a strikebreaker himself. He jailed some labor leaders and deported others. In 1921, also, when employers' associations used professional strikebreakers to start battles, Yrigoyen supported the associations. In Argentina, as in most of Latin America, business and employers' associations—notably chambers of commerce and industry—organized effectively and attained considerable prestige and influence long before labor syndicates.

Yrigoyen's administration displayed a nationalism that reflected the growth of that sentiment in Argentina. He continued the policy of neutrality in World War I that most Argentines favored, even though there was considerable sentiment in favor of France, cultural home of many upper-class Argentines, and Britain, Argentina's great trading partner, also admired by some conservatives for its political and governmental systems. Neutralism for Yrigoyen was a form of

nationalism, a concentration on Argentine problems, a rejection of outside pressures. He even tried to promote neutralism in other parts of Latin America during the war. The charges that he was pro-German have no substance; he was pro-Argentine. After the war his administration took Argentina into the League of Nations, but soon largely withdrew because Argentine suggestions were not adopted there. In such actions Yrigoyen had the support of most Argentines.

His economic nationalism aroused less interest because most of it was rhetoric of the sort that had been heard for years about foreign enterprise in Argentina. He said in 1920 that he would not "alienate an ounce of the public treasure" or "cede an iota of the absolute dominion of the State" over national resources. He thought that the state should have greater authority over "industrial enterprises that provide public services." He was sincere in such beliefs but had little opportunity to translate them into action. He did take one action that ultimately would seem significant. Petroleum exploration and exploitation had begun earlier in the century, and that had led to some federal action in the national interest, as has been noted. Yrigoyen carried this further by creation in 1922 of Y.P.F., a state agency with supervisory functions over foreign activity and exploitation powers of its own. Although Y.P.F. was not immediately important, it became later not only a critical agency, but a symbol of Argentine control of its natural resources and of economic nationalism generally.

The Socialists jeered at the failure of the Radicals to pursue strongly their declared aims of social justice and economic nationalism. The Socialists, as has been noted, developed great strength in the city of Buenos Aires. There was a small split after the Russian Revolution of 1917, and in January 1918 dissident Socialists formed the International Socialist party, which changed its name to the Communist Party of Argentina in December 1920, when it joined the Third International. The old Socialist party in Argentina after the electoral reform of 1912 worked to get the reform extended to the muni-

---

[4] See Section b of this chapter.

cipal council of the federal district. The government of the federal district was headed by an executive (*intendente*) appointed by the president of Argentina, but the elected council had considerable power. It traditionally was chosen by a narrow electorate of taxpayers, with only 14,497 registered in 1911 in the huge city. The electoral reform was extended to the Buenos Aires council in 1917, with the result that in the council elections of October 1918 there were 141,897 votes cast. Thereafter the Radicals generally were in control of the council, although Socialist members occasionally outnumbered them. The changed composition of the council brought new issues. In 1926 an ordinance was passed establishing an eight-hour day and forty-four-hour week for municipal workers and for the workers of employers under contract to the municipal government. The council also concerned itself with improving the streets, sewage, and other facilities of poor areas of the city, often on the request of ward associations. So broader political participation was important at other levels besides that of the office of president of the republic.

The most acrimonious debates in the city council were on transportation. There were two electric streetcar companies, the larger being Anglo-Argentine Tramways (AATC), founded in 1876. It not only had some two-thirds of the streetcars, but in 1914 opened the only subway. By 1924 the two companies were carrying 648 million passengers a year. The foreign company resisted demands for extension of its lines and improved equipment to meet expanding needs, claiming that Argentine authorities would not permit realistic fares. Critics in Argentina declared that the company gave poor service while making exorbitant profits which went out of the country. These were important economic and emotional issues for the common people. The upper class did not ride streetcars; indeed, they sneered at Yrigoyen for using them. In 1919 the companies asked a raise in fare from ten to twelve centavos, to cover higher costs of equipment and electricity and a new pension fund.

The Radicals in the Buenos Aires council passed the raise, to the accompaniment of jeers from the Socialist minority at the supposedly nationalistic Radical party's previous strictures on the remittance of profits abroad. Through the 1920s the Radicals on the council tended to support the AATC, whereas the Socialists tried to probe conflicts of interest between public officials and foreign companies, the effects of unregulated monopoly, and the real cost of transportation services. Fares in Buenos Aires, in fact, remained quite low in the 1920s.

President Alvear, 1922–1928

Alvear came from the wealthy conservative class as one of that minority that had a few liberal ideas, meaning largely an attachment to political liberalism but little concern for socioeconomic questions. Yrigoyen picked him as a suitable front for his own continued domination of government. As so often happens, the new president declined to follow Yrigoyen's advice. A split developed between Yrigoyen supporters and Alvear men, the latter calling themselves Antipersonalist Radicals. That was, of course, a development reminiscent of Yrigoyen's unwillingness to put up with rivals during the earlier history of the party. The quarrel did not take the form of division on doctrine. Although there was much division within the party, it did not solidify into right and left wings. Continuing prosperity had something to do with that.

Alvear's administration was not conspicuously more conservative than Yrigoyen's, although it sometimes is so described. Some conservatives and army officers certainly considered Yrigoyen more radical, and feared his return in 1928. Alvear left the export economy undisturbed, foreign capital untouched, labor virtually unorganized, social legislation only slightly extended, nationalistic sentiment little deepened, with little effect on government. Argentina "merely" continued to enjoy the best economic and social development in Latin America under the established laissez-faire system. The Socialists were far from militant and even supported the export economy, requesting some adjustments in consumer prices and other details. The continued enlargement of the middle class and of the literate group would, of course, play a role in any future crisis that occurred. Political participation continued to broaden. The 1.19 million registered citizens in 1916, of whom about three-quarters of a million cast votes, in 1926 became 1.8 million registered and 1.2 million voting. The province of San Juan in 1927 permitted women to vote on an equal basis with men, an example of how pressure for a reform could have effects on the state level in Argentina, even though federalism generally was a weaker force there than in the United States.

For the next presidential term the Antipersonalist Radicals tried to oppose the candidacy of Yrigoyen. Some leading conservatives and army officers discussed the possibility of preventing a new term for Yrigoyen. None of these groups could contend with the old man's remarkable hold on the citizenry, and they were unwilling to act illegally. Yrigoyen announced his candidacy only at the last moment and then did not campaign; a living legend does not need to. He was now seventy-six years old, and his age became an issue during the campaign. Enemies asserted that he was ninety. Most people did not care how old he was. Yrigoyen received two-thirds of the popular vote, an astonishing total, and an even larger proportion of the electoral vote. The decision proved a disaster both for the voters and for Yrigoyen.

d. The Crises of 1928–1930

After his second inauguration, it quickly became evident that Yrigoyen was in no condition physically or mentally to head the government. His secrecy and jealousy of power in others led both to inactivity and to spasms of poorly considered decision making. Yrigoyen never had been a good administrator, and now graft, favoritism, and bad management were accentuated by his almost complete inability to supervise

affairs. Intervention in the provinces was even more notorious than in his first administration. Then in 1929 came the world Depression to make more nearly unbearable so poor a national leader.

All sorts of interests made known their conviction that a change was required. In December 1929 an attempt was made to assassinate Yrigoyen. In March 1930 the Radical party suffered a severe electoral defeat in the city of Buenos Aires. There were protests and demonstrations, worsening in August and early September 1930. There was a serious riot with bloodshed on September 4, 1930. The next day onetime Socialist deputy to Congress and now dean of the Buenos Aires Law School Dr. Alfredo Palacios demanded that Yrigoyen resign. By that time the government was fearful that it might not be able to depend on the armed forces to defend it.

One man who raised such doubts by his activities was General José Uriburu. As a young officer in the early 1890s he had taken part in the military movement against President Juárez Celman. Although in the succeeding four decades the military had not been interfering in the political process except on orders by the presidents, including Yrigoyen, Uriburu had developed a strong belief in military activity in public affairs. He thought the country needed unity, order, strong government, and no dissent—a classic military view. Uriburu apparently was sincere in this opinion, and possibly also in his view that only he could effectively head such a new order. Although he knew of current domestic and foreign doctrine in support of such a disciplined society, he also knew of the tradition of Rosas. Finally, Uriburu's long military career had probably reinforced a temperamental distaste for political turmoil and what seemed to him as a commander a dangerous and inefficient uncertainty at the helm of the state.

Uriburu conveyed his ideas to various people, some of them quite prominent, including both civilians and military officers. The convinced talked to others in turn. In the manner of such conspiracies in Latin America, the principal effort was to convince military commanders either to join the movement or not to resist it. If a commander agreed, his enlisted men would obey orders. In some cases, civilian conspirators tried to persuade military officers. Such widespread discussion of conspiracy could not be kept secret; the government learned of much of it, and Uriburu went into hiding.

He had conceived the idea of starting a coup with a march by the cadets of the military school from their installation outside Buenos Aires into the city. There are several ways of viewing this exploitation of very young men scarcely able to form independent ideas of the nature of such action, when they were hearing conflicting notions of where the path of true patriotism ran. They did march into the city on September 6, 1930, to the acclaim of happy throngs. There was almost no resistance. Although only a minority of officers was pledged to act in the coup, an even smaller minority felt obliged to defend the government. Units that had not joined the movement previously on September 6 fell in line, with almost no exceptions. The presidential guard regiment accepted the coup. There was no military ideology involved in all this, merely a general notion that Yrigoyen had not used

the armed forces well, and that the country desperately needed a new president.

The coup d'etat of 1930 did not seem at this time to be of long-term significance; it took care of an immediate problem. As it turned out, it became linked with continuing military participation and interest in public affairs that would peak in the military regime of 1943 and in constant military activity in politics for thirty years thereafter, and with a great increase of economic nationalism in Argentina in the 1930s. In 1930, however, these possibilities were not anticipated. The coup could be supported or accepted with complaisance by nearly everyone. Radicals did not know that the result would be a return of conservative-controlled political fraud and violence. Oligarchs supposed that the coup might help both the economic situation and their minority political position. Events proved that four decades of Radical effort would be frustrated by conservatives combining with the military, then by military efforts to run the country alone, partly by exploiting new issues of social justice and nationalism. If the Radicals had made any political advance in 1916–1930, aside from somewhat broadened participation, it was not enough to ensure adherence to constitutional procedures.

31

Brazil: Strains of Regionalism and Export Specialization, 1880s–1930s

Modernization proceeded in Brazil under the Old Republic (1889–1930), yet seemed to critics less than resources could support. The country generally was managed in the interest of the great coffee *fazendeiros*, though with growing minority collaboration by commercial, financial, and industrial interests. It was a laissez-faire system, with governments doing little to direct the economy. Even if the elite had wanted to scrap laissez-faire, doing so would have been difficult under the federalist government adopted for the republic. There was severe fragmentation of political activity, government authority and revenues, and community attention to problems. Federalism was given a special twist by concentration of people and economic resources in São Paulo and Minas Gerais, which permitted domination of the presidency by those states. The dangers of feeble integration intensified the tendency of the military to think themselves the guardians of the national fate. That military interest threatened to dominate politics in the early years of the republic; and although it was expressed less openly in succeeding years, it remained strong beneath the surface of affairs. One form it took was a frustrated nationalism, especially in the 1920s and early 1930s, that demanded military action to level barriers to quicker progress. That military interest in faster change coincided with

the growth of new civilian economic and social points of view, some of them nationalistic in character, and with irritation among politicians with the São Paulo–Minas Gerais political axis. Accumulated changes and frustrations produced in 1930 a politicomilitary movement that put Getúlio Vargas into office and turned Brazil toward more rapid development, modernization, and integration.

a. The Military Presidents, 1889–1894

Military men headed the governmental system during the first five years of the Old Republic, claiming that only the military institution was capable of holding the country together without a shattering factional and provincial dispute. The transition to a federal republic was accomplished smoothly, with a declaration (November 16, 1889) by Deodoro. He acted as president until an election could be held, ruling by decree, sometimes illiberally in the manner of a military autocrat. His cabinet was largely civilian, including the distinguished jurist Rui Barbosa as minister of finance; but it also included Colonel Benjamin Constant and an admiral as heads of the military ministries, suggesting that Pedro II's preference for civilians in those posts had been repudiated. The personnel strength of the army promptly was raised 60 percent, justifiable on the grounds that the 13,000 before the coup were too few for protection against dissatisfied elements, egged on by monarchists. The increase certainly was pleasing to the military, as was a 50 percent increase in officer pay. In addition, army officers became governors of half the states. Military influence had grown with the change of regime; the question was how it would develop in the long run.

A number of problems were handled reasonably well. The ex-royal family was hustled into exile. Recognition soon came from most foreign governments. Deodoro decreed the separation of church and state, later incorporated in a new Constitution and approved by the church itself. In December 1889 Deodoro appointed a commission to draft the Constitution. Its work was reviewed by the government, then by an elected Constitutional Assembly that included a number of military members, to which civilians objected. The Constitution was promulgated in February 1891. It created a federal republic, with sufficient powers to the states so that critics predicted the sort of disastrous fragmentation of authority that had occurred in the early empire. The states had the right to levy export duties and to maintain militias. On the other hand, the central government had large powers, including the right of intervention in the states. Furthermore, the Constitution would not by itself determine the way government worked; that would depend on the balance of forces in Brazil. Involvement of people in the political process was limited by confining the vote to the literate.

Election of a president and vice-president by the constituent Congress in early 1891 was dominated by fear of the army, some of whose officers had been discussing the need for a dictatorship. Civilians generally preferred not to have a military president, but election of one seemed prudent in order to fend off the possibility of violent military reaction. Since Deodoro had been quarreling with the Congress, it punished him by naming him president with fewer votes than it gave Marshal Floriano Peixoto for vice-president.

When Deodoro had difficulties with clashes of points of view in his government, Benjamin Constant suggested that he become a dictator. One of the president's problems was such intense military interference with public affairs that he complained to Constant in his role as minister of war. More important was Deodoro's inability to adjust to the ordinary process of give-and-take with a legislature, and he sometimes acted with a brusqueness that suggested a longing for return to the discipline of military administration. These irritations were rasping enough that in May 1890 he threatened to resign. Finally, on November 3, 1891, Deodoro dissolved the Congress and declared a state of siege, claiming that danger from monarchic plots required an end to bickering. There was opposition to this move not only by civilian politicians but by elements in the navy, jealous of the army and somewhat monarchical in leanings.

In the meantime, Floriano functioned less as vice-president of the republic than as a conspirator to succeed to the presidency. A cold man known as "the Sphinx," he was part of a plot, including other military officers, to supplant Deodoro. The latter ordered the arrest of the plotters, but one of them, Admiral Custódio de Melo, persuaded the navy to support the rebels, and Deodoro resigned. So the first president fell to a military conspiracy.

Floriano was equally notable for his decisiveness and his lack of interest in political principle —except the principle of firm government. He was known as "the iron marshal." He simply refused to submit the presidency to a new election as the Constitution seemed to require, helping establish a new tradition of military proprietorship over interpretation of that document. He not only put in military men as heads of the ministries of war and navy, but selected prominent plotters against Deodoro, including Admiral Custódio. He replaced pro-Deodoro state governors with pro-Floriano military officers. Protests mounted, with Rui Barbosa prominent in the opposition. Military objections to Floriano's actions the new president disposed of with summary punishment. Such arbitrary—"strong" was the word his supporters used—government drew not only protest, however, but praise. In Brazil, as in Argentina, there were those who thought the great problems of the country could only be resolved by a single firm hand and voice.

Floriano had a major problem with political turmoil in Rio Grande do Sul. Some principle was involved in wrangling there, but it also was a contest for control of the state. The "Federalists" had some monarchist traditions, and wished to oust the regime of Júlio de Castilhos, president (governor) of the state, who was more in sympathy with the new central government. Floriano naturally supported Castilhos. In 1893 this rivalry became warfare. Floriano's control of the country was threatened even more later in 1893, when in September, Admiral Custódio de Melo, resigning as minister of the navy, again led a naval revolt. This again was due to navy jealousy of the army and to monarchism in the navy. In December the rebels received the support of Admiral Luís Felipe Saldanha da Gama, head of the Naval Academy, and a man of great prestige. Foreign governments, however, would not recognize the belligerency of the naval rebels and thus did not accept their efforts to blockade Rio de Janeiro. The United States Navy even positioned vessels to impede the use of rebel navy guns against the capital city. The rebels received little support throughout the country, while Floriano was energetic in opposing them. The strong civilian regimes of São Paulo and Minas Gerais were notably firm in supporting Floriano. A few hundred rebels fled by sea to Argentina, and some then joined the anti-Castilhos forces in Rio Grande do Sul, but Floriano put the rebellion down ruthlessly.

Floriano was viewed by Brazilians in two very different ways: one group favored centralized power, and celebrated his victory over regionalism; another feared centralization, especially under a military regime. Such a regime on a permanent basis was unlikely, because the military did not have the tradition, doctrine, or trained personnel for such an effort. For decades after Floriano's time those factors would be insufficiently present to induce the military to take over the government, although they increased sufficiently to make the development ever more plausible. Furthermore, in the mid-1890s the great landowners and their allies in business retained formidable influence over local and state elections. To control their dissatisfaction with continued military rule would have required a prolonged effort. Other economic interests either were allied with export agriculture, or were too feeble to contest its predominance seriously. São Paulo leaders informed Rio that they meant to continue their "autonomist" tradition. They also quickly expanded the small state police unit into a semimilitary force that had 3,000 men by 1893. Such determination, combined with armed forces, in São Paulo and Minas Gerais posed a problem of fragmented power that the national military was not yet ready to confront.

Traditional political leaders generally had refrained from supporting the rebels of 1893 or had actively supported the central government. The leaders of São Paulo, the strongest state, had actively supported Floriano's efforts. They declared their intention of supporting the system as laid down in the Constitution, arranged the aid of civilian politicians in other states, and in March 1894 helped elect ex-governor of São Paulo, Prudente de Morais, as president. He was inaugurated in November. The government thus returned to the great estate owners, and especially to the coffee export sector, and there it remained until 1930.

b. Economic and Social Developments

There was a critical growth in the modern sector of Brazilian society under the Old Republic. It remained smaller than the traditional society, but the modern sector became strong enough to assume a much more dynamic character, ensuring continuing strong pressure for change.

Population and Labor

Population growth quickened in the 1890s and thereafter. The national total was 14.3 million in 1890, 30.6 million in 1920, and 42 million in 1936. In the 1890s Brazil grew at a slightly slower rate than the United States, but in 1900–1920 it had the advantage by 79 to 39 percent. In the half century 1890–1940 Brazil increased 192 percent and the United States 52 percent. The bulk of this growth came from a high birthrate and lowered deathrate, although immigration improved even on its record pace in the 1880s. About 1 million immigrants arrived from 1886 to 1895, and nearly 2.5 million in 1896–1925. In the entire period 1886–1935 about 4 million immigrants arrived. More than half the newcomers were Italian and Portuguese. Important as these immigrants were to Brazil, they were a much smaller percentage of the population than in Argentina or the United States. In Brazil in 1920 about 5 percent of the population was foreign-born, compared with 13 percent in the United States. The immigration flow was cut drastically in Brazil by restrictions during the Depression years of the 1930s.[1]

Population growth was greatest in the south. Movement westward remained small and the great heart of the continent little inhabited. The southern growth was due to superior economic conditions, which attracted nearly all the immigrants to the country and caused internal migration in that direction. Of the foreign-born in 1920, more than one-half were in the state of São Paulo and very few north of Minas Gerais. The state of São Paulo, which had 837,000 persons in 1872, went to 1.38 million in 1890 and 6 million by 1930. Although the proportion of people living in towns increased, Brazil remained one of the most rural countries in the world. The urban growth of the future was prefigured, however, in the spectacular rise of the city of

São Paulo, from 35,000 in 1883 to 239,000 in 1900, 579,000 in 1920, and more than a million by the mid-1930s. By 1930 Brazil was no longer plagued by the *falta de braços*—lack of hands—that so long had marked one of the lightly populated countries of the world. With a much enlarged and somewhat more urban population, it was developing an economic base supportive of the growing sense of nationalism among its leaders. Demographic growth was to become one of their aims.

Although people of black and mixed racial heritage[2] and European immigrants encountered prejudice, there was optimism in the Old Republic about Brazil's ability to assimilate all stocks into one Brazilian type. With the end of slavery and the economy growing, social mobility increased somewhat, although freed slaves received no more help than in the United States after emancipation there. Some writers denied that racial prejudice existed in Brazil. A later generation was to say, however, that the intellectuals of the 1920s and 1930s exaggerated the extent of mobility and the supposed weakness of prejudice. The optimism of the Old Republic was reflected in census figures that showed "assimilation" into the white group, which reflected both fact and hope.[3] Before World War I some voices were raised about the problem of assimilating immigrants, many of them congregated in groups that preserved the culture of the old country. Imperfect assimilation caused increased concern during World War I and during the 1930s, when Hitler talked of the obligations of German blood to the Third Reich. Those fears proved to have little substance in Brazil but contributed to the growth of nationalist sentiment.

Levels of living remained low. Per capita income in 1930 was about forty-three dollars, when it was six hundred dollars in the United States. Since a few rich and the growing middle class

---

[1] Only about 600,000 immigrants came in 1822–1885. Of the 4.6 million immigrants in 1820–1937, Italians were 32.6 percent, Portuguese 30.3 percent, Spaniards 12.9 percent, Germans 4.9 percent, Japanese 3.9 percent.

[2] See Chapter 25, Section c, on their supposed percentages of the population in 1890.

[3] See Chapter 38, Section a, on racial prejudice and discrimination in recent decades.

lived well, obviously most Brazilians had virtually no money income. The miserable condition of the huge rural population was reflected in its faith in local prophets and hunger for miraculous intervention. Some of this was an outgrowth of poor health. When in 1889 the Host being offered a poor woman at Joaseiro, a hamlet in the back country of Ceará, turned to blood, it created a local cult that brought pilgrims from far and wide, hoping for cures.

The new industrial laborers were not pampered. In São Paulo in 1920 they were paid about sixty cents a day, probably no more than rural day laborers and less than coffee *colonos* (sharecroppers). Furthermore, about a quarter of the industrial workers were under eighteen, and whole families had to work to stay alive. At the same time manufacturers were insisting that labor was well paid, although inefficient and lazy. Workers had virtually no protection by organization or legislation. By 1907 there were two anarchist weeklies in São Paulo, and some socialist publications. During World War I inflation and food scarcities increased labor unrest. Unions grew modestly in size and militance. The number of strikes rose, and there were general strikes in 1917 and 1919. Such activity had been slowly growing for years, especially among European immigrant groups. Anarchism was stronger than Marxism, but neither was very important, except as a possible portent of the future. A number of groups merged in 1916 to form the Brazilian Socialist party. A few middle-class figures took a mild interest in the problems of industrial labor. The chief reaction of the employer class was to attack the labor movement with spying, blacklists, and strikebreakers. Industrial labor organizations before 1930 were of little consequence, save as an indication of what was to come. There was no organization among rural laborers.

There was almost no social legislation before World War I. Beginning in 1917, some minor aid was granted for accidents on the job. The first important labor act was passed in January 1919 and provided only modest accident compensation, later extended to cover occupational disease. In 1923 railway workers were granted aid for old age and infirmity, with their widows and orphans given some assistance; the measures were extended to dock workers in 1926. These government measures did not cover many workers or provide large benefits and often were not enforced. There was a minor amount of paternalistic aid by private firms. On the whole, however, employers were tough. Industrialist Francisco Matarazzo in 1928 declared that the result of the "liberal" labor policies of Brazilian employers was that workers remained inefficient.

Political appeal to labor was unimportant because industrial workers were few and poorly organized and had little support among the politically active part of the population. The *civilista* campaigns of 1910 and 1918 in São Paulo did include rhetorical appeals to workers, indicating recognition of change but having no influence on events. More noteworthy was an appeal by Bernardes as a presidential candidate in 1922 to labor organizations as a possible counter to the army, which was antagonistic to him. Soon thereafter, as president, he created a National Labor Council to advise government on labor problems. He saw to the organization of pension funds for the railway workers. Then he lost interest in labor in 1924 during the São Paulo rebellion, since unions seemed more likely to cooperate with the army than to oppose it. The fact was, of course, that labor was not yet a very useful ally in politics, and it usually was regarded by politicians only at election time. The labor question had, at any rate, arisen, and a fair estimate was that it would become more important in the future, one aspect of the effects of modernization.

The Economy

The Brazilian economy still was dominated by agriculture and the great estate (*fazenda*). Other forms of activity did challenge agriculture more than under the empire, with a considerable participation by immigrants. The south as a whole was the area of great economic growth, led by São Paulo. The old northeast in general suffered economic malaise, but there were pockets of growth. Even in the *sertão* merchants arose to compete for power with *fazendeiros*. By 1930 the modern sector of the economy was enormously more complex than it had been in 1889.

Fazenda dominance was aided by the fact that public lands passed from the empire to the states in the Old Republic, and the *fazendeiros* controlled the states. By 1920, 10 percent of the proprietors held more than three-quarters of surveyed land (omitting much without value) in estates averaging some 5,000 acres. Even in São Paulo, where such factors as industrialization gradually broke up estates, in the early 1930s more than 60 percent of agricultural land was controlled by 7 percent of the owners.

Exports continued the focus of interest. There was a short and spectacular rubber boom, from the late nineteenth century to a peak in 1912, followed by a precipitous slide to near extinction. Coffee was still the most important export, and millions of coffee trees were set out in east central Brazil, especially São Paulo. As late as 1924–1933 coffee was 71 percent of the value of Brazilian exports, but its dominance declined before the end of the 1930s. To the beginning of World War I most coffee went to Europe, thereafter to the United States. So important an enterprise naturally was influential with the federal and some state governments. São Paulo began to subsidize coffee growers by 1906; that is, government reduced the risk of coffee operations by levying on other taxpayers. Such aid—often called valorization—essentially was required by periodic overexpansion; so in 1912 the federal government prohibited further planting of coffee trees, and took other measures to slow expansion. Such action had little effect. In 1921 the government bought almost a third of the coffee crop. Thereafter, valorization was shifted to a semi-private Coffee Institute, financed by foreign loans and the state-owned Banco do Estado de São Paulo. In 1928 it bought 16 million bags of coffee. Coffee prices broke in the spring of 1929

and declining revenues from that source became a factor in the destruction of the Old Republic.

Coffee specialization was of doubtful value to agriculture generally. As usual, one-crop estates paid little attention to food production. *Colonos* were obliged to grow only coffee, so they had to buy other food at *fazenda* stores. Laborers and tenants did not enjoy increased income. Coffee cultivation and picking remained largely hand operations, so their productivity did not improve. Mechanization came to the *fazendas* in transportation, processing, and commercial operations, the benefits of which were confined to owners and their business allies.

Coffee specialization was one reason why so little attention was given to agricultural diversification or productivity. One effort was made, however, when import duties on rice were raised in the early twentieth century and so stimulated production that by World War I imports no longer were necessary. Most food crops, however, were badly cultivated, and a vast rural population remained near the subsistence level. There were some efficient small farmers, notably in the south, often among German settlers, many of whom specialized in grain. But even many grain farmers, in Brazil as a whole, still cultivated with a hoe and with poor results.

Manufacturing increased in the Old Republic, with much capital coming from coffee profits, mercantile enterprise, and from foreign sources. Importers also sometimes went into manufacturing because they had the expertise, contracts, credit, and distribution channels. Coffee profits not only were invested in manufacturing but provided the funds for the economic and social infrastructure (railways, ports, hydroelectric power, schools) it needed.

Industry was stimulated by economic and population growth but also by World War I, partly because of difficulty in obtaining supplies from abroad but even more because of the growth of an export market, especially for Brazilian textiles. The new opportunities were most spectacularly exploited by Francisco Matarazzo, who arrived in Brazil from Italy in 1881. He opened a small-town store, become a hog dealer, turned to lard rendering because of the high price of imported lard, moved into the importing business, then to flour milling, then a cotton mill to make flour sacking with pretty printing for the farm women who used the sacks for dresses, and on to many other enterprises.

Manufacturing was limited by the low purchasing power of Brazilians, so that the census of 1920 showed only 275,000 industrial workers, not many in a population of 30 million. The best opportunities were with bulky and low-value common items of consumption, made of local materials, which could undersell imports.[4] In 1920 more than 40 percent of the value of industrial production was in the manufacture of foodstuffs, and cotton textiles accounted for a sizable part of the rest. The old cotton-textile industry had so far expanded that in the 1920s imports of cottons were declining, and some Brazilian textiles were 50 percent cheaper than imports. The industry was helped by new tariff protection, which in earlier years saddled Brazilians with high prices for the protected goods.

Although tariff protection was not the chief reason for the growth of Brazilian industry, it helped. Protectionism as an attitude and a policy was complex. The *fazendeiros* who controlled government on the whole opposed protection, objecting to the high prices charged in Brazil by "coddled" industries. They also complained that the new industry drew labor from agriculture. The older agricultural elite of São Paulo sneered at the upstart immigrant manufacturers and their pretensions. There was a prejudice against Brazilian manufactures on the grounds that they must necessarily be inferior to· the established brands of the industrial powers. On the other hand, although *fazendeiros* preferred tariffs for revenue, they did permit some for protection. That ambivalence may be seen in the career of President Campos Salles (1898–1902), who charged that industry drew labor from agricul-

ture and that many manufactures were "artificial," while more protection was enacted during his administration.

The planters insisted on using the import levy as a chief source of federal revenue because they disliked other possibilities even more; they were not going to tax their land or their incomes. Their revenue tariffs, however, sometimes were high enough to give some protective effect, and they had no method of correcting for that result. The protection that sometimes was deliberately arranged for a specific industry was allowed because export agriculture did not see it as a general threat or because of ties between coffee money and manufacturing interests. That sort of special protection even extended in 1910 to a new bathtub factory in Rio Grande do Sul. Manufacturers also were sometimes aided by exemptions from the federal import levies in the case of machinery they needed for their operations. But the general revenue-oriented tariff of 1900 remained until 1934, when general protectionism finally was adopted. Manufacturers under the Old Republic benefited from the fact that state taxes came generally from export levies, so that they were not subject to much state tax and often managed to evade that.

Manufacturing by the 1920s was large enough, and its prospects so bright, that for the first time its leaders began to show some cohesiveness. All through the history of the Old Republic they preferred not to irritate the planter group, but in the 1920s some signs appeared that a serious clash might be on the way. Even when prices for some protected commodities went down and the argument was made that tariffs therefore could be lowered, doing so proved politically impossible. A long-term effort in this regard was made after World War I, but the Congress postponed and defeated it, and in 1929 even raised some duties on textiles.

Industrial growth under the Old Republic displayed several other notable features. Much of it was concentrated in the state of São Paulo, which by 1920 surpassed Rio de Janeiro as the country's chief industrial center. The average annual value of the state's industrial output in

[4] For example, construction materials of wood, clay, glass; plumbing fixtures; bottles; beverages; shoes; boilers; coarse textiles; flour; pots; hats; cement.

the late 1920s was eight times what it was just before World War I. Such growth indicated that the hegemony of the state's agricultural elite was likely to be threatened soon. Prominent in manufacturing in the city of São Paulo were new men, foreign-born or the sons of immigrants. Another type of important foreigner was the manager of the branch factories from abroad, which in the 1920s were turning out light bulbs, household appliances, transformers, and many other items. Finally, an important aspect of manufacturing development was that there was still almost no heavy industry. The metallurgical industry was small, for example, although Brazil was known to have large deposits of high-grade iron ore. Furthermore, nearly all the new technology of the age came as imports. These conditions troubled nationalists.

The Old Republic was like the empire in depending heavily on foreign investment and loans. In 1890–1934 federal, state, and municipal governments received about $1.7 billion in external loans. Foreign capital poured into the São Paulo coffee industry. By 1913 only two Brazilian firms ranked among the fifteen largest exporters from Santos. United States private capital—much of it in utilities and branch manufacturing plants—grew in Brazil from $50 million in 1918 to $550 million in 1930, when it was second only to British investment. In time, this dependence was challenged by local enterprise and nationalist pressures. Minas Gerais interests were anxious for development of heavy industry by foreign capital, but the nationalism of Governor Bernardes and others would not permit it in the dominating form demanded by the syndicate represented by Percival Farquhar.[5]

In 1921 federal exchange control diverted to Brazilian institutions the profit on exchange transactions. Brazilian-owned banks, insurance companies, and other financial institutions began a considerable growth. Hope of greater gains was induced by perception of the larger national market due to population growth and the increase in the number of persons with incomes above

the subsistence level. The market did remain small, however, partly from the high price of local manufactures. Some of it was due to inefficiency in production, but some was due to interstate duties, a form of federalism that nationalists came more and more to deplore. It was due also to poor transportation, which the Old Republic did little to improve. The defective railway system was allowed to deteriorate, except where exporters found it important, and only expanded modestly from the 5,600 miles in operation in 1889. Road building was not then a national priority.[6] Such deficiencies of policy, plus distaste for foreign influence in the economy, and frustration that great resources were not being developed more rapidly put economic development on the agenda of the nationalists of the 1920s, though only in a general way.

Education, Communications, and Nationalism

Development of a widespread sentiment of nationalism depended on education, but the planter aristocracy was not interested in general instruction. In 1920 only 22 percent of children of primary-school age were enrolled, with the highest state figure in São Paulo, and even that less than 40 percent. The city of Rio de Janeiro, as always, was more modernized than the rest of the country, with 65 percent of its primary-age children in school. With so weak a school system, Brazil could not expect to be more literate than the 30 percent showed by the 1920 census.

The elite kept secondary schools largely private, beyond the purses of the poor, who therefore could not prepare for the entrance examinations to the higher institutions of learning. Although industrialists in São Paulo before the 1930s were not even much interested in technical training for their own operations, preferring to depend on trained immigrants or institutions

---

[5] See Section c of this chapter.

[6] Auto roads were encouraged by the federal government in the late 1920s, prefiguring a policy that would become very important in later years.

abroad, the state did somewhat expand professional and technical schools. Law remained the most popular profession, but as early as the 1890s engineering instruction was receiving increased attention, and medical instruction expanded.

Communication was being improved slowly by telegraph and telephone networks, and then in the 1920s by radio, motion pictures, and air transport. The railroad improved the integration of a few backcountry communities with the coast. Rural *coroneis*—political bosses—of the planter class increasingly depended on or collaborated with *bachareis*, who came with professional degrees from major cities. The latter favored various sorts of modernization. When they became federal deputies, they disliked being known as the representatives of "hick" communities. These rather weak additions to the communications process were scarcely reinforced by social legislation, which was too feeble under the Old Republic to contribute to national fellowship.

Nationalism was promoted chiefly by an intellectual and artistic minority and a few political figures. Artistic nationalism had some roots in the empire, and grew stronger under the Old Republic, but before 1930 it was far from the overwhelming phenomenon it was to become later. The historian João Capistrano de Abreu was already in the 1890s celebrating the development of a new culture in the interior of Brazil. *Os Sertões* (1902)[7] by Euclides da Cunha became a monument of nationalist literature, dealing with the peculiarly Brazilian life of the backlands of the northeast and with the great variations in landscape and human habits in a country of magnificent extent.[8] Another example of the new spirit early in the twentieth century was Afonso Celso's *Porque Me Ufano do Meu País* (Why I Am Proud of My Country), praising its natural resources and beauties and the excellent qualities of a population too little regarded by

the world. Some artistic nationalism took the form of self-assertive innovation, often using Brazilian themes. A prominent expression of this was the Modern Art Week in February 1922 in São Paulo, with emphasis on the Brazilian environment. The young Heitor Villa-Lobos conducted his compositions on folk themes, using indigenous instruments. Writers were demanding a national rather than imitative literature. Gilberto Freyre was engaged in studies that led to his famous treatise *The Masters and the Slaves* (1934), celebrating Brazil's combination of races and cultures.

Politicians were paying somewhat more attention to nationalistic and other new issues. Many of the artistic crowd played some role in innovative politics. A few military nationalists made radical demands and engaged in equally radical actions. Thus, by 1930 at least a minority of Brazilians was much more self-conscious about the need for action to plan a national future than had been the case in 1889.

c. Politics and Government in the Old Republic

After the military chieftains Deodoro and Floriano in 1889–1894, all but one of Brazil's chief executives until 1930 were civilians, although that by no means meant extinction of military influence in public affairs. None of the administrations stands out for superlative achievement.[9]

---

[7] Translated as *Rebellion in the Backlands*.
[8] See Section c of this chapter on the political implications of this work.

[9] There were nine four-year terms in 1894–1930, and eleven chief executives, two having succeeded on the death of the president. The administrations: Prudente José de Morais (1894–1898), of São Paulo; Manoel Ferraz de Campos Sales (1898–1902), of São Paulo; Francisco de Paula Rodrigues Alves (1902–1906), of São Paulo; the administration of 1906–1910 was split between Affonso Penna, of Minas Gerais, who died in office, and Nilo Peçanha, of the state of Rio de Janeiro; Hermes da Fonseca (1910–1914), of Rio Grande do Sul; Venseclau Brás (1914–1918), of Minas Gerais; Rodrigues Alves was inaugurated for a second term in 1918, and died in 1919, so a new election was required, and Epitácio Pessoa, of Paraíba, was elected president for 1919–1922; Artur Bernardes (1922–1926), of Minas Gerais; Washington Luís Pereira de Souza (1926–1930), of São Paulo.

Much essential and valuable activity occurred, but some of it now seems contrary to later accepted notions of the proper direction of development. Such views could not become dominant, however, until the older interests and methods had demonstrated their inadequacy and in so doing called into being sufficient opposition to force change.

Provincial Bases of Politics and Government

State machines dominated politics under the Old Republic as politicians had preferred under the empire. Parties were conveniences for state machines without influence outside the state. The few efforts at political integration were temporary coalitions of bosses. National parties could not exist because nationalist sentiment was too weak to bring them forth as a means of integration and faster growth in service of the entire community, and because the states had so much traditional power at the local level and received so much state-level power under the new federal Constitution. The states had great powers over their own economic and fiscal policy, levying international tariff duties, controlling public lands, setting immigration policy, contracting foreign loans, controlling their educational systems. They even had their own armed forces. The militias of São Paulo and Minas Gerais sometimes far outnumbered national troops stationed within their borders.

Within these powerful states small minorities dominated affairs as under the empire. The grass roots power of state machines still lay in *coronelismo*. The *coroneis* still came largely from the landed aristocracy, and some harbored monarchist yearnings. The state political machine left them almost complete freedom to fight out their rivalries at the level of the *município* (well over 1,000 in the country), demanding only that the winning faction support the state bosses on state- and national-level issues. Ex-President Campos Sales wrote in 1908 that Brazilian politics was run by many "*caudilhos,* all equally sovereign." Control of the *municípios* meant control of pa-

tronage, police power, contracts, routes for transportation lines, and many other valuable matters, as well as access to promotion to state and national office. At the *município* level and in its subdivisions were police forces, local courts, schools, records of vital statistics, post offices. Only at that level were most citizens touched by government. The *coroneis* of the Old Republic kept their subjects on a short leash with fraud, intimidation, and violence. They were aided by the fact that the literacy requirement for voting eliminated most people. Before 1930 votes cast never were more than 4 percent of the total population. In the election of 1919 a vote of 300,000 was mustered out of a population of 26 million. In 1922 only about 1 percent of the total population cast ballots. Even eligible voters mostly felt that there was no point in exercising the right.

Coronelismo rested on great distances, poor communications, and the alienation of many of the poor. The importance of these conditions was reflected in the career in the early years of the republic of a popular religious leader known as "the Counselor" (*O Conselheiro*). Over the years in the *sertão* of the northeast he developed a reputation as a wandering saint and miracle worker. He preached that happiness would come with the end of the world in 1899, and convinced some poor people that they could build a new Jerusalem in the *sertão* of Bahia on an old *fazenda* named Canudos. He disturbed the government of the republic by his belief that the emperor had enjoyed divine right, which it was feared would encourage monarchist plots. Equally disturbing, the settlement at Canudos refused to acknowledge its tax and other obligations to the new republic. Canudos survived three official efforts to subdue it by force of arms. The fourth expedition brought overwhelming strength to bear in a remote corner of the vast republic to smash a tiny pocket of popular dissidence. Such folk religion as that of Canudos, often with overtones of actual or potential political heterodoxy, was common in Brazil.

Joaseiro in the *sertão* of Ceará has been noted in connection with the controversy over miracle cures. The priest there, Padre Cícero, ultimately became involved in the ambitions of people at Joaseiro to break it off from its *município*, making it the seat of a new one. That campaign succeeded. Although Cícero long insisted that his championing of the miracles in his village had no political significance, *coroneis* of the *sertão* of Ceará were convinced that he was heading a political movement. The difficulty with Canudos in the later 1890s heightened concern over Joaseiro. The national hierarchy of the church had condemned *O Conselheiro*, and they refused to accept the miracles of Joaseiro. A newspaper in nearby Pernambuco said Father Cícero was a danger to public order and linked him with Canudos and a need to control superstition as the road to "anarchy." The controversy over Cícero flared again in the early twentieth century when factions vying for control of the state began using violence on a considerable scale. Cícero's enemies accused him of organizing the backcountry bandits of the state of Ceará. National politicians, and even the national government, became involved in events at Fortaleza, the capital of Ceará, in 1911–1912, but they ordinarily could not go below that level to such *municípios* as Joaseiro. So Joaseiro and Canudos illustrated the weakness of national authority in Brazil.

On national matters, most notably the selection of a president of the republic, the state political bosses engaged in bargaining and typically settled the succession before the election. Inevitably, the most powerful states—and especially São Paulo and Minas Gerais—had the greatest influence. The bosses of the weaker states did what they could to secure advantage—offices, honors, contracts, legislation—within the bargaining system, but their opportunities were restricted by their weakness, by the dangers and difficulties of alliances between small states, and by the fact that Minas Gerais and São Paulo usually collaborated in alternating the presidency between themselves. In 1890–1930 all but two presidents were from those states. Rio Grande do Sul was a rising and ambitious state that found some leverage in this bargaining system, but even in 1930 found that it could secure the presidency only through physical force.

Still other factors accounted for acquiescence in the system of provincial power. Industry in São Paulo did not contest it but supported the candidates put up by the dominant planter group, rather than entering a contest it could not win. Industry received its reward in the generally probusiness policy that both groups favored, and in such specific measures as control of labor organizers and "agitators." The system also was protected by the concentration of federal power in the hands of the president, reinforced by the tendency under the Old Republic to rule under a state of seige in moments of tension. No check on the system of bosses was offered by the Congress, since it was selected by them. Finally, the provincially oriented system was in effect supported by the national military, despite the doubts of individual officers.

There was little call for more popular participation. A few voices spoke up in Ceará in 1911–1912, when for a few weeks the petty bourgeoisie and urban labor of Fortaleza rioted because of objections to the state political machine and police shooting of a child. The riots helped overthrow the governor. The riots coincided with political demands by the rising higher bourgeoisie of Fortaleza, and thus in a general way suggested how economic growth must affect politics in the long run. As it turned out, the popular classes of Fortaleza did not repeat this role again under the Old Republic. Nevertheless, urban elements were becoming potentially more of a threat to the essentially agrarian *coroneis*, bulwarks of the provincial system.

The injustices and insufficiencies of the system were not apparent to many people in the 1890s. By the early 1920s there was more disaffection, and such leftists as Assis Brasil and Luís Carlos Prestes were distributing propaganda, though not with much success. A few people became interested in European fascism, including some prominent industrialists in São Paulo. Francisco Matarazzo sighed for Mussolini's system of "patriotic discipline." Nationalism spread a bit more in politics, even in the small state parties. After World War I some small nationalistic parties were formed, mostly in Rio de Janeiro and São Paulo. One in Rio de Janeiro was the National Social Action, which advocated transfer of capital from coast to interior; nationalization of commerce; retention of profits in Brazil; a stronger federal government; a national capital in the interior. Interestingly, it did not demand industrialization or the preservation of natural resources, measures that were soon to be prominent in nationalist programs. Nationalism in the 1920s in these little parties, as in artistic movements and the military, was still relatively weak and unformed; its slow growth, however, in diverse forms suggested that it would develop as in other parts of the world.

President Campos Sales (1898–1902) accepted the system of collaboration between state bosses, especially under the tutelage of his own state of São Paulo and neighboring Minas Gerais. Rio Grande do Sul offered competition, but only once captured the presidency after the terms of Deodoro and Floriano. For some years after their time, Rio Grande do Sul was represented at the national level by Pinheiro Machado, who in the national Congress was a master at building voting alliances. He played an important role in the surprising election of 1910, when the system faced a severe test. It came in such a form that much of the contest was stated in terms of civilian versus military influence in government, but it also was a contest between the alliance of civilian state machines and the military against all those who wanted a broader and more open method of making political decisions.

In the campaign of 1910, one of the political allies of President Affonso Penna declared that Brazil had progressed beyond the need for military men in public office, whereupon Minister of War Marshal Hermes da Fonseca resigned in protest and became a candidate for president. Pinheiro Machado at first favored Rui Barbosa for president. A caucus of congressmen showed them closely divided between Rui and Hermes

da Fonseca, nephew of Deodoro, who was supported by an officers' corps aroused by recent criticism of its abilities. The political leaders settled on Hermes partly on the grounds that Rui's abilities were too intellectual. Pinheiro Machado helped his friend and fellow *gaúcho* Hermes to the presidency, with the usual control of small electorates by the state machines.

Distaste for the dictated candidate of the administration included disappointment, dislike of the corrupt politics represented by Pinheiro Machado, and objections to a military man. The opposition was strong enough to hold the first democratically elected nominating convention in the country's history. It chose Rui Barbosa as candidate of a *Civilista* party. Rui made an unprecedented campaign tour, condemning the oligarchic political system and what he called the menace of military rule. Rui was a man of great talents who had served Brazil well at home and abroad. At the Second Hague Conference in 1907 his abilities had won Brazil international acclaim. In his unprecedented campaign of 1910, Rui not only accepted the hopeless task of defeating the alliance of bosses and federal government control of the electoral system, but he appealed directly to the electorate in a vigorous campaign, an unheard-of thing to that time in Brazil. He also denounced the restricted political system generally. The administration candidate won, as always, but Rui's reputation and oratorical powers brought him 30 percent of the manipulated vote of less than half a million in a country with a population of 22 million. The result suggested that the right kind of leader and program might draw even more support, especially in the growing towns, where there was less subservience to the state bosses than in the countryside.

In President Hermes da Fonseca's term (1910–1914) Pinheiro Machado created what he called the *Partido Republicano Conservadora*, although it was not a party (*partido*) but a temporary alliance of state machines. Pinheiro played factional politics in many states, which shifted control and alliances without changing the nature of the system. He inevitably created many enemies, especially in Minas Gerais and São Paulo, which was fatal to his own hopes of the presidency. Those two states supported for the term 1914–1918 Hermes' vice-president Venseclau Brás. Pinheiro tried to put over ex-President Campos Sales. When the latter died, he tried unsuccessfully to make a deal with Rui Barbosa, who refused to abandon his principle for the sake of a chance at the presidency. Early in the administration of Venseclau Brás, Pinheiro was assassinated by a man who declared that he meant it as a blow at tyranny.

With Pinheiro's death his alliance system collapsed, and Minas Gerais and São Paulo continued their dominance without his disturbing activities. In 1919 they made more explicit their policy of alternating the presidency. The presidents they provided did, however, need to consider the importance to their administrations and to coming elections of the various state bosses, including Antonio Borges de Medeiros, long governor of Rio Grande do Sul, who continued to play an active role in national affairs. President Bernardes (1922–1926) helped reduce the control of Borges de Medeiro in his own state by supporting other elements in Rio Grande do Sul. So long as factionalism and regionalism took such forms, promoting national integration was difficult.

The Military and Public Affairs

The military insubordination over essentially civilian issues that was observed under Marshals Deodoro and Floriano in 1889–1894 also occurred occasionally in 1895–1930. Although the military did not take over public affairs again, it frequently disturbed them and was recognized as a threat to tranquillity. Civilian politicians solicited its aid. Some military activity was at least well motivated, whatever might be thought of the methods selected for attaining goals. The view grew among the military that Brazilian strength must be promoted on more rational

grounds and with purer instruments than traditional politicians. That attitude was not simply positivism, idealism, or technocracy, though all were present in the officers' corps and among civilian politicians as well. Military education became more sophisticated and increasingly tied to new currents of domestic and foreign thought.

It has been noted that military personnel were increased immediately after the revolution of 1889. Civilian politicians did not care for that growth because it was expensive, and many feared military influence. President Prudente de Morais, who succeeded Marshal Peixoto in 1894, worked hard to use factionalism in the armed forces to consolidate civilian rule. He could not get a reduction below 28,000 in the authorized strength of the army, but he contrived to reduce actual personnel to 16,500. That was much less important than his failure to cut actual officer strength, which stayed at 3,352, against 1,516 authorized. All he could do was stave off suggested increases in the number of officers. Furthermore, the most he considered prudent to do about war ministers was to choose generals apparently favorable to civilian predominance. His successors had similar problems with the military force. One of their failures was evident in the fact that by 1908 Brazil was ordering dreadnaught-type warships from Britain, an expensive and prestigious war vehicle not clearly justified by Brazilian need.

Prudente bravely sustained a clash with the military over the Canudos affair. After the defeat of the third expedition against the settlement in the backlands, the Military Club sent a committee to consult with the government on the series of disasters that reflected so sadly on military competence. Some officers charged wildly that Prudente's purpose was to destroy the military. In November 1897 a soldier fired at Prudente and killed the war minister, giving Prudente plausible grounds for declaring a state of siege. He also incited mobs to attack newspapers that had criticized the government and ordered the Military Club closed. This last astonishing order remained in effect until well into the next administration.

The election of 1910 has been described; at that time many military officers were aroused by the charge of impropriety or incapacity aimed at Marshal Hermes da Fonseca's candidacy. That sympathy did not prevent the marshal as president from suffering a number of revolts and disorders. Hermes' election encouraged more participation in politics by military officers. Four became governors of states. Officers garrisoned in the states often were involved in political maneuvering. Some turned against the state machines that had put Hermes in office. They allied with civilians to oust the bosses in Pará, Bahia, and Pernambuco. They called these actions *salvações* (rescues) and the newly imposed military governors *salvadores*. Some of the motive for such action was to forestall Pinheiro Machado, who planned to use the old state machines to foster his own ambitions for the presidency. All aspects of the Hermes administration were so unsatisfactory that it scarcely increased enthusiasm for another military president. At the end of his term, Hermes went into voluntary exile in Europe.

There was some trouble with military dissenters in the next few years, and it flared especially when Pessoa became president in 1919 and named civilians as ministers of war and marine. Military opinion was hardening on that issue, one disturbing sign for the balance between civilian and military influence in public affairs. Then the usual caucus of party leaders nominated for the presidential term beginning in 1922 Artur Bernardes of Minas Gerais. Soon after, ex-President Nilo Peçanha joined a dissident group that included some military men and offered himself as an opposition candidate. Hermes, just back from Europe, was president of the Military Club and took an interest in the election in favor of Peçanha. In November 1921 a Rio de Janeiro newspaper published a letter, by implication from the pen of Bernardes, that strongly criticized the military. The Peçanha

camp gave it wide publicity, but the Bernardes group proved it a forgery. Then Hermes demanded, successfully, that the election results be judged by a "Court of Honor" rather than by the Congress, as provided by the Constitution. Bernardes won in any event, after this dramatic military intervention in the political process.

Hermes took the result with ill grace. Soon after the election there was a political battle in Pernambuco between two factions, and Hermes telegraphed the military commandant of the area to act in accordance with the dictates of his conscience—that is, if necessary, against the orders of the president of the republic and the minister of war. The latter sent Hermes a message of censure; Hermes returned it in pieces, yet another act of defiance. By this time there was a nationwide conspiracy, with military and civilian participants, to prevent the inauguration of President-elect Bernardes. Some conspirators advocated a coup d'etat to seat Hermes as chief executive. President Pessoa and Hermes exchanged messages on the Pernambuco affair, then Hermes was arrested and imprisoned in the summer of 1922.

Shortly thereafter, in July 1922, some younger officers among the military conspirators began a revolt at Fort Igrejinha in the Copacabana section of Rio de Janeiro. Government troops surrounded the rebel position, but eighteen of the young officers chose to march out onto the beach, where most of them were killed. The "Eighteen of Copacabana" became a symbol for patriotic youth. One of the survivors, Eduardo Gomes, lived to become a top air force officer and a candidate for the presidency. The young officers had thought that the condition of the country required drastic change, especially reduction of regionalism and promotion of national integration. They had no detailed program. They became celebrated within and without the military as idealists, martyrs to love of the fatherland. The Copacabana revolt became known as the first of such actions by the *tenentes* (lieutenants). Men of that rank had, of course, revolted before; the new *tenentes* were a nationalistic breed that believed in political activism. The term came to stand not just for lieutenants, but for nationalistic and activist junior officers generally, and even for a general military attitude of dissatisfaction and of willingness to sacrifice for national greatness.

Bernardes was inaugurated later in 1922, knowing he was disliked by the military. He was a nationalist, a partisan of private enterprise, and an important man in the traditional civilian political system. He had a great deal of trouble with dissidence and used extraordinary powers to try to control it. In 1924 he seemed to face a sea of foes, but in fact each group was small, their actions were poorly coordinated, and they received little support. There were six military revolts in that year, the most important beginning in São Paulo on the July anniversary of the Copacabana affair of two years before. The young officer rebels in São Paulo were soon forced to retreat and disperse.

The affair was significant not because it accomplished much immediately, but because it helped precipitate revolts in five other states later in 1924, because it was a further demonstration of the malaise of younger officers, and because of the Prestes Column. Captain Luís Carlos Prestes supported the Paulista rebellion, then fled west with a few companions, joining fugitives from other revolts, together with revolutionaries and adventurers. The 1,000 or so members of the Prestes Column wandered thousands of miles for two years in the wild backcountry, trying to generate interest in revolution. It failed, but when its members fled into exile before government pursuers, they had established the beginnings of a legend: that revolt and courage, with participation by the professional military, could shake, and hopefully remake, the old regime. Prestes became head of the Brazilian Communist party. Three of his companions in the Column were important national figures in a few years: Juarez Távora, Osvaldo Cordeiro de Farias, and João Lins de Barros. The *tenentes* of 1922 and 1924 were hailed by some not as in-subordinate but as idealistic and courageous foes of an outmoded and oppressive system.

Some Policy Areas

The governments of the Old Republic had great success in defining the national boundaries on generous terms in agreements with the surrounding smaller and weaker nations. Territorially, Brazil was a giant among the world's countries. Size ensured some of the bases for the drive toward national greatness that came to possess at least a few spirits before 1930. One territorial decision was an arbitral award by President Grover Cleveland of the United States in 1895, giving the territory in Misiones, disputed with Argentina, to Brazil. That award provided one basis for another important development in Brazil's foreign relations, because it created enthusiasm for the United States in Brazil. In addition, the United States and Brazil were untroubled by economic conflicts, and the former became the greatest buyer of Brazilian coffee. The balance of trade favored Brazil. Also, Rio de Janeiro did not feel menaced or outraged by expanded United States activities in the Caribbean after 1895. A spirit of goodwill and even of collaboration between the two countries was solidified during the foreign ministry of the Baron of Rio Branco (1902–1912). These generally cordial relations between the giants of the Western Hemisphere were to be more important than the frequent antagonism between Washington and Buenos Aires.

It was a matter of some moment that it was not politically feasible to do much national planning, because most politically active citizens still believed that the best method of using Brazil's export profits was by private decision. The result, as already noted, was that the notion of a general policy of industrialization had few advocates. Even the military nationalists of the 1920s had no detailed views on economics, and were not yet adamantly against foreign capital. Nevertheless, the coming face of economic nationalism was visible under the Old Republic in discussion of a national steel industry. Little existed in Brazil before 1946. Small furnaces using local ore and scrap made iron and steel in several places. The little industry had some tariff protection. Creating a larger industry presented formidable problems of investment, improved transport, and the use of the defective local or expensive imported coal. Every president of the republic from 1909 tried to find solutions to the problems of steel production.

The idea became tied to the plans of United States promoter Percival Farquhar, who adopted an idea that had been discussed for some years—to export Minas Gerais iron ore in return for capital to build a steel industry. In 1919 Farquhar discussed his plan with President Pessoa, and in 1920 Pessoa signed the Itabira Contract to implement it. By that time British, United States, German, and Belgian interests controlled most of the best iron ore deposits in Minas Gerais. The Itabira Iron Ore Company was to build a railway and a steel mill with a monopoly to ship iron ore to Europe and the United States and bring back coking coal. The $80 million capital investment envisaged by the company was large for the time. There was strong support for the scheme in some political and industrial circles, but not enough in Minas Gerais, where Governor Artur Bernardes and his associates thought it too ambitious and a threat to Brazilian control of the economy. Since Minas Gerais had to approve the agreement, Bernardes was able to block it. Bernardes, in a political career covering 1904–1952, including the presidency in 1922–1926, was an outstanding example of the new nationalism in Brazil.

Farquhar offered concessions but not enough to placate the nationalists, who feared that the steel companies in the developed countries really did not want to build competing plants in Brazil. No doubt they were right; what the foreign companies wanted was Brazilian iron ore and manganese. They were willing, however, to build some sort of steel mill. While the Farquhar plan hung fire, Bernardes became president of Brazil,

and in that post in 1924 proposed that the government subsidize some small steel plants, improve railways to serve them, and intensify use of national coal supplies. The scheme was not implemented. The political support to mobilize the capital internally was not present. Finally, in 1928, Farquhar renegotiated his contract, surrendering some rights in return for being excused from financing a steel mill. But this was not executed because Brazil still could not mobilize the capital to build a steel industry. The Vargas administration would take up the problem again in the 1930s and bring it to a nationalist solution in a day when such policies were better supported.

The government's revenues were insufficient to finance heavy industry. Public finance depended on foreign trade: the states taxed exports of raw materials and the federal government taxed imports. The planter class prevented the imposition of unpalatable alternatives and kept government expenditures at relatively low levels. Expenditures did increase some, however, because the population grew. Even a modest amount of modernization was expensive, the bureaucracy was expanded to provide jobs as well as services, and the military required funds to carry out its functions and to maintain the sort of force its pride demanded. Federal revenues rose from $87 million in 1900 to $257 million in 1920, generally coming some 70 percent from import duties. It never was enough. Under the Old Republic, as under the empire, public expenditures generally outran revenues, and the deficiencies were made up by foreign investment, borrowing, and currency emissions. The frequent accompaniment to such policy was inflation, which much of the planter class found preferable to taxation of its own property or income. All during the Old Republic statesmen struggled with the problem of the foreign debt, while borrowing all the time. Eight times as much was owed externally in 1933 as in 1889. To be sure, some of this represented real wealth erected or brought into the country, but that did not relieve the pressure on the treasury.

President Campos Sales (1898–1902) made a notable effort to improve European confidence by controlling expenditures. One of the greatest failures of the unhappy administration of Hermes da Fonseca (1910–1914) was in finance, involving efforts to sustain the coffee and rubber interests, increases in paper currency, and borrowing abroad. Then in 1920–1923 there was an especially high inflation, when the amount of currency in circulation, the cost of living, and the price of foreign exchange all doubled. Some of the *tenentes* of President Bernardes' time (1922–1926) not only were hurt personally by inflation but saw it as a principal aspect of a planter system of fraud and manipulation. Bernardes responded by adopting a hard-money policy, reducing currency in circulation. He received support from some propertied elements that always favored a stable currency. His move toward deflation was in this instance softened for São Paulo coffee planters by loans from the state's Coffee Institute. The federal government borrowed money many times with which to hold coffee from world markets till prices rose. Even the *fazendeiros* favored by this policy called the coffee warehouses "cemeteries." Other interests, like manufacturing, that were not in control of government, suffered more. All sorts of economic strains, with at least potential political consequences, were the inevitable accompaniment of the government's fiscal policies.

Fiscal problems would have been even greater had the dominant planter group permitted much expenditure for social purposes or for economic diversification. They blocked such projects at local, state, and federal levels. They resisted much expenditure for education, as noted; had no concern for land redistribution or other schemes for the improvement of rural poverty; and even refused to do much about transportation. Long-range planning for the last was badly needed. Government efforts under the Old Republic were useful but far short of the immense transportation needs of the country. As in so many areas, neither the economic nor the social implications of inadequate transportation had

been fully grasped, not even by nationalists. On the other hand, the Old Republic did rather well in promoting public health and to a modest extent the convenience and attractiveness of city life. It could do so because the cost was relatively light and because it was of immediate interest to the planter aristocracy. Rio de Janeiro especially was remade from the early years of the republic. Dr. Oswaldo Cruz, who had studied in France, had great success in eradicating yellow fever and smallpox. The government drained swamps and compelled vaccination. The results of the new measures were astonishing in Brazilian cities, where pestilence had been a notorious hazard.

d. The Election and Coup d'Etat of 1930

Washington Luís (1926–1930), a Paulista, was the last president of the Old Republic. The provincially based system was destroyed at the end of his administration because of its accumulating enemies, the impact of the Depression that for Brazil began in 1929, the ambitions and talents of a new generation of civilian and military politicians, and Washington Luís' own decision not to recognize that it was the turn of Minas Gerais to name a president. He named another Paulista, Governor Júlio Prestes, to carry on the policies of the outgoing administration.

The result was that the Mineiro hopeful, Governor Antônio Carlos Ribeiro de Andrada, joined Rio Grande do Sul politicians Borges de Medeiros and Governor Getúlio Vargas in what was called the "Liberal Alliance." They agreed to try to persuade President Washington Luís to support Antônio Carlos for president and a Rio-grandense for vice-president; if that failed, Borges or Vargas would be the presidential candidate of the alliance. When the alliance failed to move Washington Luís from his decision to impose Júlio Prestes, Vargas was nominated by the alliance. Since an incumbent president had every advantage of force and manipulation in seating his choice, the only hope of the dissidents was conspiracy. Preparations for revolt were carried out on a considerable scale before the election. Oswaldo Aranha of Rio Grande do Sul was the leading figure in these moves, which included conversations with many civilian and military figures, including some of the exiled *tenentes*. Collection of arms also was part of the preparation. Such processes were facilitated by Brazilian tradition; the great size of the country and the poor transport system, which impeded countermeasures; the great powers of the states, so that Rio Grande do Sul could protect itself to some extent; and by differences of opinion in the national military establishment and doubts as to how much energy it would show if ordered to move against dissident comrades.

Vargas was cautious. He acted as though he might be willing to accept a compromise by an agreement with Júlio Prestes whereby the latter did not campaign in Rio Grande do Sul and Vargas campaigned personally only in that state. Possibly Vargas had some hope of winning, though that is difficult to believe; what everyone learned of his political acumen later indicates that he preferred to wait for a clearly favorable opportunity to act in whatever manner then seemed likely to be useful. He aided the preparations for revolt to some extent. His partisans did not try to prevent the election of March 1, 1930, and at first merely cried fraud at a result that could not have surprised them: Getúlio lost by 1.1 million to 1.9 million. The large Vargas vote might be considered a stirring demonstration of national interest and of support for the "liberal" or "reform" candidate; on the other hand, it showed the continued control of the electoral machinery by the incumbent group, and especially its unshaken grip outside the larger cities. At the end of May the administration demonstrated its intention of giving no quarter when the Congress refused to seat opposition deputies elected from Minas Gerais and from Paraíba, home state of Vargas' running mate for vice-president, João Pessoa.

Then in July 1930 Pessoa was assassinated. The conspirators charged that the slaying was arranged by the administration, and the charge, an additional complaint against the old political system, was widely believed. Vargas, who was largely unknown to Brazilians, by now seemed to several groups the only hope of reform. He had promised amnesty to the rebels of the 1920s, a fairer electoral system, social legislation, and rapid economic development. Urban groups interested in what they conceived of as modernization had supported Vargas in the election. They included nationalists of various sorts, economic interests stifled by the dominance of export agricultural policies, and all the politically ambitious who found competition with the entrenched oligarchic system of control difficult.

The govenment knew of preparations for an uprising. The citizenry, suffering from the great Depression, heard many rumors and was in a state of expectation when on October 3, 1930, the rebellion began. Rebel military forces fanned out from Minas Gerais, Paraíba, and Rio Grande do Sul. Uncommitted officers joined them, which, in the usual fashion of Latin American rebellions, meant that the enlisted men did, too. The role of the *tenentes* was emphasized by leadership of the Paraíba rebels by Juarez Távora, veteran of the Prestes Column. What went on for the next three weeks was a process of maneuver, persuasion, bargaining. It became clear that the administration had little support. Essentially, the military abandoned the government and thus settled the matter. Their decision was influenced, however, by perception of considerable civilian support for the coup. In this sense, then, changes in the economy and society and demands for modernization were responsible for the military decision. The actual mechanism of the coup was a military matter, as in 1889.

In Rio de Janeiro the military ousted the government and proclaimed a ruling junta of three military officers on October 24. Vargas was far away in Rio Grande do Sul. During a slow movement north to the national capital, he rallied support. The reaction to the coup and his accession as provisional president—accomplished in Rio de Janeiro on October 31—showed that the Old Republic had outlived its usefulness. The coup showed, as so often in Latin American history, that replacing an entrenched regime was difficult except by violence.

No one knew how Vargas would interpret his declared intentions or how much he would be affected by existing dissatisfaction with conditions in Brazil. Critics felt that the country's great potential had not resulted in the degree of modernization to be found in Argentina, Uruguay, or Chile. The country only awaited new leadership to embark on a more self-conscious and wider-ranging course of development. No one could guess that Vargas would remain in office fifteen years, longer than most of the dictators in the Spanish America at which Brazilians long had sneered.

32 Mexico: Tyranny Brings a Great Revolution, 1880s–1934

Violence seemed a badge of Mexican character before the 1880s. The country's history had been a riot of *caudillismo*, civil war, and foreign intervention. Porfirio Díaz then became the most dramatically successful Latin American tyrant in the Age of the Caudillos. The last two decades of the Porfiriato brought spectacular economic growth but at heavy cost in political and social repression. That cost was repudiated in 1910–1917 in a hurricane of revolution unprecedented in Latin America's history. It destroyed so much that the ground it cleared for a new day in Mexico was not readily visible. That new day dawned rather slowly, so that the achievements of 1918–1933 were underrated. It was no wonder, however, that the new leaders of Mexico required some time to remake politics, develop the dream of Mexican nationalism and integration, and commence a policy of economic development that thereafter would permit a sustained growth equal to that of Argentina in earlier times.

a. The Porfirian System

Under Díaz, power was at last effectively organized and used. The potential benefits of such rule by chieftain were freedom from debilitating civil strife, unity against foreign pressures, and an order appealing to investment capital and the spirit of business enterprise. All were achieved by the Diazpotism; and it seemed worth the price to the elites in Mexico and to foreign business and government. A later Mexican generation would say that the price was excessive.

Politics and Government

Díaz took over the government in 1876 and was driven into exile in 1911. He ruled by force of arms, supplemented with shrewd use of bargaining, bribery, threats, and corruption, all on a highly personal basis, untroubled by a party organization or by complex political ideas. He made bows to constitutionalism, for example, by providing a stand-in for president in 1880–1884. After Díaz's return to the presidency in 1884, the Constitution was altered to permit immediate reelection, then a bit later to allow unlimited succession. He put up dummy opponents, claiming that real elections occurred. All of this was merely inexpensive window dressing: in fact, his regime was well characterized as one of *pan o palo*—bread or the club.

Díaz knew the limitations of his instruments. The army of 20,000 and the federal *Guardia Rural* (*Rurales*) of about 3,000 could not closely police a country more than three times the size of France. The main use of the army was to suggest to Díaz's allies the advisability of collaboration. Díaz took great care to keep the army officers satisfied. The notorious *Rurales* had a hard way with suspected bandits that much reduced that ancient occupation in Mexico. Within this system, Díaz was the first chief of several regional *caudillos* with their own armies and political and economic satellites, insulated from Mexico City by distance. The railways increased Díaz's coercive powers in the regional centers, but he could not reach back into the bailiwicks of the small town *caciques* (*jefes políticos*), which even the regional *caudillos* found it did not pay to try to control in detail. This system worked much as *coronelismo* did in Brazil, for the same reasons.[1]

Collaboration gave the regional chieftains access to rewards that bolstered their local positions: appointments in the growing federal bureaucracy; consideration for public works; a share in contracts; the prestige of titles and association with the great in the capital; freedom from inspection of local practices or objections to local tyranny; and the aid of the central government against local enemies. Díaz savagely mangled opposition political groups; they had no right to exist. He corrupted the middle class with positions in a bureaucracy that grew 900 percent, the alternatives being penury, persecution, exile, even death.

The economic elite supported the regime because it understood their needs. Commerce, manufacturing, investment, and big agriculture were well identified with the dictatorship and with its indifference toward the social and economic problems of common people. Although the church accepted the regime because Díaz restricted it less than the *juaristas* had, it only modestly improved an economic position that had been badly damaged by the latter.

Effective protest was not permitted in the Porfiriato. To the few of the educated who resisted, Díaz denied effective influence in speech or print. Publication was his whore, the schools his tool, the courts his creature, and labor organization a criminal offense.

Within this system grew up in the 1890s a group known as the *científicos*—scientists. The name came from the positivism that has been noted in several Latin American countries: a compound of the ideas of Auguste Comte and other intellectuals; disgust for certain features of the American social environment, and especially the lower classes; a dream of development and "progress"; and a conviction of their own worthiness for rule. The *científicos* in Mexico were a small elite, with its core in the federal government. They accepted the political methods of Díaz, but knew he did not understand the economic development in which their greatest interest lay. Díaz, for his part, allowed the *científicos* much authority outside the realm of politics. They were technicians, not an element in *caudillismo*, which was a political system. Díaz would not permit the *científicos* to act like a party, and their dreams and plans for power after his passing were restricted by that fact. The most important restriction on their political dreams, however, was that they were incapable of providing the sort of tough, militarily based leadership that Díaz's successor surely would need.

The most prominent *científico* was José Ives Limantour, who became minister of finance in the early 1890s, and was for nearly two decades the epitome of the financial successes of the mature regime. He helped establish the foreign credit of Mexico, partly by balancing the federal budget, partly by a reputation for ability, responsibility, and probity. He helped make Mexico safe for business. He presided over the largest growth in the federal revenues under Díaz, from about 15 million pesos to 110 million. That still was low, however, by the standards of the better-developed countries. Reform of the regressive and primitive public revenue system might have been of more permanent value to the country than foreign investment, but it was politically impossible.

---

[1] See Chapter 31, Section c.

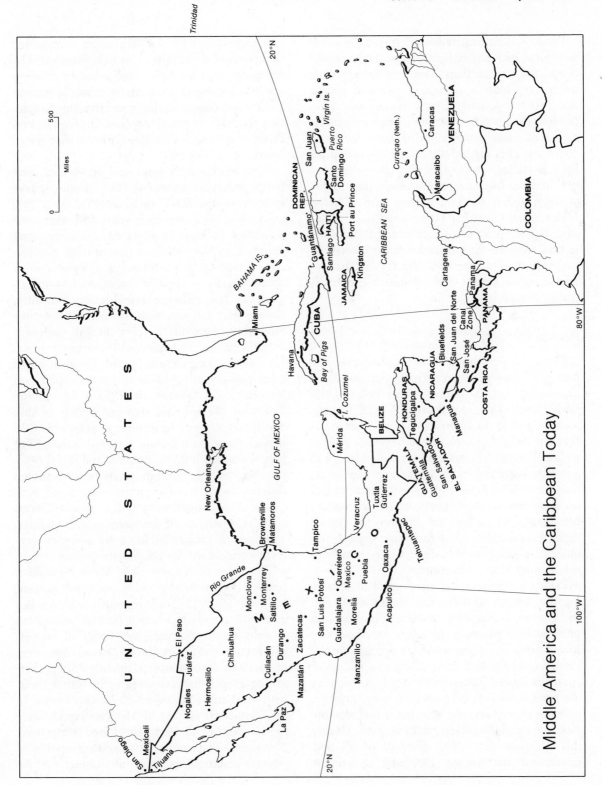

Middle America and the Caribbean Today

Limantour and his fellows despised the crude stealing of such earlier figures as Santa Anna, but considered proper their own enrichment from inside knowledge, government pay and perquisites, contracts, and private investment. They thought the liberalism of earlier years a misapplication of ideas suited only to more-developed countries. They viewed the notion of popular political participation as chimerical, given the primitive state of Mexican society. They knew themselves qualified to lead Mexico into a better future, especially when Díaz should have passed from the scene, an event increasingly anticipated as time went on. As it turned out, the *científicos'* understanding of their own country was shallow, and men of classes they despised eventually turned them out.

Porfirian Society

Economic growth under the Porfiriato was the best since Independence. Production increased an average 3 percent annually from 1895 to 1910, far better than the record in 1821–1894. But the regime held to an interpretation of laissez-faire that encouraged growth of the hacienda system, at the expense of the general rural populace, and a narrow industrial, mineral, and commercial expansion, for the benefit of the entrepreneur and his government allies. There was little concern for the general welfare. In addition, the system depended on inducement to foreign capital that quickly resulted in the alienation of much of the resource base of the country.

Private investment was encouraged by balancing the budget, servicing the foreign debt, and the control of banditry, political disorder, and promiscuous government levies on business. More than $2 billion worth of foreign capital came in, nearly half from Europe, a bit more from the United States. With this sum, huge for the time, foreigners dominated mining, utilities, industry, commerce, and they had a considerable stake in agricultural and pastoral land. During the Porfiriato more than one-half of all new investment was foreign. Domestic investment

also increased, but the local elite complained that some of its opportunities were preempted by foreigners, and *hacendados* objected to development as a cause of a scarcity of labor. It became a common charge during and after the Revolution that the economic structure during the Porfiriato was oriented outside with no thought of the needs of Mexico.

Port works were improved, telephone and telegraph service extended. The railway system grew from the 6,872 miles in 1892 to 12,000 miles by 1910; by then rails connected all states but Tabasco. Capital for the railways came mainly from the Mexican government and foreign private sources. There was apprehension about foreign—especially United States—investment in the railways, but Mexico had little choice. The railways were essential to any significant increase in the tiny modern sector of manufacturing. They reduced the price of cotton for mills. Manufactures could be distributed more cheaply, as could labor and foodstuffs and imports of all varieties. In 1877 a mill in the Valley of Mexico paid sixty-one dollars to ship cheap cotton goods to nearby Querétaro; in 1910 it paid about three dollars! Railways reduced not only economic but also political and social isolation. In 1908 Limantour created the National Railways, with over 50 percent government ownership of the stock of a system that included about 60 percent of trackage in the country. That was a nationalist move by a regime generally condemned for lack of nationalism.

The value of foreign trade, about 50 million pesos annually in the 1870s, grew 900 percent from 1877 to 1910. Trade benefited from a policy of retaining a silver peso that declined in relation to gold, raising the price to Mexico of imports and interest payments abroad but making prices of Mexican exports more attractive. Much of resulting export flow consisted of increased traffic with the United States, which Mexico feared. In 1877 nearly 60 percent of Mexican exports were to Europe, but in 1901 the United States took 82 percent. The country remained an exporter of primary commodities, much at the mercy of international conditions, but there was some change in the items shipped. Although minerals, especially silver, continued for years to account for about three-quarters of all exports, the industrial metals and agricultural items increased their role. In 1904, for the first time, precious metals accounted for less than one-half of export value. Agricultural and pastoral exports went from a mere 7 million pesos to over 100 million. But the poor cost and quality of Mexico's agricultural/pastoral products made competition in the international market difficult. As for imports, food had to be brought into a country that had idle land and hands, luxuries flowed to the elite, and many of the industrial imports went to foreign companies.

The mining industry obviously offered the country a great opportunity, and the government took sensible measures to seize it. It has been noted that rapid mineral growth began in the 1880s, aided by legislation in 1884 and 1892.[2] In 1886 the Ministry of Development, as the price of government aid to mining, insisted that the industry reduce its costs through improved technology to a level compatible with world prices. Smelting plants for industrial minerals were built from the early 1890s. The modern coal industry began in the mid-1880s.

Petroleum refineries were built in the 1890s, before Mexican petroleum production began in 1901. Ownership of the new mineral industry was concentrated in a few, largely foreign, hands, and much of the profit flowed abroad. Furthermore, the mineral industry was not a heavy employer of labor.

Manufacturing grew considerably in the last two decades of the regime, but remained a small part of the national economy. In 1911 fewer than 11 percent of workers were in manufacturing, compared with 64 percent in agriculture. In fields of new manufacture, only a small part of national demand was satisfied, and large imports continued. Furthermore, Mexican goods were high priced. Manufacturing experience in

1900–1910 suggested that further growth would be difficult. The most impressive growth was in cheap textiles, but for all grades of textiles as much was imported as was produced at home.

Agriculture and grazing continued to absorb the attention of most Mexicans but gave few of them more than a bare subsistence. The concentration of landownership increased, and became more obnoxious as considerable tracts fell into foreign hands. By 1894 there was no limit to the amount of public land an individual could acquire, much of it at an average of less than four cents an acre for land that was worth at least two dollars. By 1910 no more than 3 percent of the population owned any land, most of it in haciendas rather than one-family farms (*ranchos*). Free village lands were increasingly alienated, often simply seized. Millions of Mexicans lived as peons on haciendas, or as "free" villagers had to work at least part-time on haciendas to keep alive. One hacienda in Zacatecas had nearly 2 million acres, another in Durango over a million, three in Colima claimed a third of the state. Luís Terrazas in Chihuahua owned haciendas totaling nearly 5 million acres.

This concentration was not accompanied by good production practices. Much land was idle. Technology was poor. Total agricultural production in 1877–1907 went up only 21 percent and population nearly 40 percent. Agriculture paid increasing attention to industrial crops as opposed to food. It also slightly increased food exports when domestic consumption per capita was declining. Although the number of cattle increased, more went to export; slaughter for domestic consumption did not keep up with population. In 1890–1910 meat prices rose 50 percent. Cattle export was limited, however, by inefficiency, and meat quality was poor. Mexican animals provided about half the meat per head of Argentine stock. The sheep population declined, Mexican wool being too poor for export, and its mutton unable to compete with the big world producers. In nearly every economic sector Mexico had terrible problems that the Porfiriato had not begun to solve.

---

[2] See Chapter 26, Section g.

The population of Mexico grew to 15 million in 1910, about 80 percent of them living in places of less than 2,500 population. In 1900 there were only six cities over 50,000. The lack of urbanism partly explained the absence of cohesive nationalism. Mexico remained a land of isolated villagers, with vision no wider than that of the *patria chica*—little fatherland—of the local community. Almost no immigrants arrived in Mexico, although the *científicos* wanted to replace Indians with hardworking Europeans, not appreciating that Indians would work harder with proper incentive. The class system remained rigid. Fewer than 2 percent of the population were members of the controlling upper classes, possibly 8 percent were middle class (with some surplus income and opportunity to save), and more than 90 percent were in the lower or popular classes.

The low popular income and consumption declined during the Porfiriato. Men in debt peonage on haciendas or tied to factory stores bequeathed their debts and their bondage to their children. The *rurales* saw that the peons kept their noses to their furrows, making flight difficult. Criminal syndicalism laws made industrial labor organization dangerous. From the 1870s a small amount of labor organization was attempted. Troops were used against strikers, with the result that there were not many labor disorders. Still, strikes increased slightly, and industrial management and labor developed distinct attitudes, which brought a new element into Mexican life, even if on only a small scale.

Social services scarcely existed, aside from education. Public health was dreadful, and the high deathrate notorious. In 1895 life expectancy in Mexico City was on the order of half that in major European cities; in 1910 it was thirty years for Mexico as a whole compared with fifty in the United States. Surcease from misery was provided by plentiful drink, with some hacienda owners specializing in the production of cheap intoxicants from the maguey plant. Mexico City in 1900 had 1,300 *cantinas* (cheap bars), compared with 51 in 1864. The commoner had no

reason to work hard, nor reason, either, to revere the institutions established by the elite. On the other hand, lower-class people knew that protest was dangerous, so they did the only thing possible—remained sullen and apathetic.

The elite still contrived to subordinate educational expenditures to things they thought more important. A disproportionate share of what there was went to upper-class instruction. The elite still feared general education, but a mark of some change was that they became more reluctant to say so in public. When some intellectuals who collaborated with the Díaz regime poured their energies into education, they equated it with nationalism and patriotism, and funds were found for it. By the end of the Porfiriato about 30 percent of the school-age children were receiving instruction, compared with 3 percent in 1821; illiteracy was down to about 80 percent by 1910, compared with possibly 99 percent in 1821. There was a sharp rise in primary school enrollment in 1906–1910, from 738,000 to 889,000.

Thus, although Mexico remained a heavily illiterate country, some change did occur. It was the more important because of the increase in the secular and nationalistic component in instruction, in public and church schools. In 1889 a congress on education formulated a program for promoting nationalism, through obligatory primary education, civic instruction, and national language training; and it wanted to help incorporate the Indian into the Western society, alleging that his reputation for intellectual inferiority was undeserved. The minister of education declared that the schools should be used to create a "true national unity." Soon thereafter, another minister of education, the famed Justo Sierra, wanted to "realize the religion of the motherland in the soul of the child," to create "the civic religion, the religion which unites and unifies." In 1910 Sierra founded the National University, which he said would "nationalize learning, . . . Mexicanize knowledge."

Nationalism was also celebrated in learned publications. Manuel Orozco y Berra directed the monumental *Diccionario de historia y geografía* that honored Mexican culture; and his *Geografía de las lenguas indígenas* and his *Historia antigua de México* increased awareness of the unique Mexican cultural heritage. Also important to the growth of critical thought and discussion was the increasing number of newspapers, their circulation improved by railways and their content by educational progress and the telegraph. Improvements in communications, therefore, laid much of the basis for the coming era of revolutionary change. A number of Mexicans were generating ideas that either would directly undermine the Porfirian system or would inspire new-style leaders to make the effort. Finally, it should be noted that although Mexican government and capital were in alliance with foreign capital, a number of the Mexican elite wished and hoped to reduce dependence. Nationalistic resentment of economic colonialism was a common phenomenon in Latin America, even though it was difficult to translate into policy.

The Coming of the Revolution

Mexico did not appear to be in a prerevolutionary condition in the last years of the Porfiriato. To the developed world, Mexico never had seemed more stable and prosperous. Marxists expected revolution in industrial, not peasant, countries. Díaz kept off balance each potential rival within the system. The peasants were quiet. Organized labor was puny. Labor disorders at the mines of Cananea and the textile mills of Orizaba in 1906–1907 were put down brutally, without much increasing opposition to the regime.

There were only a few thousand dissidents trying to promote organization for change. They were a mixed lot, jealous of each other, unable to agree on strategy. Some were intellectuals. There were a few anarchists and socialists. They issued illegal newspapers, pamphlets, and broadsides. In 1900 they helped create a new Liberal party. Liberal clubs were formed in various places. In 1906 some leaders of the tiny party called for revolution, a declaration that found little echo.

Andrés and Ricardo Flores Magón were anarchist labor leaders in this group, hounded by the regime, and finally driven into exile in the United States. They, and most other dissidents, were middle-class figures, and they did not much involve peasants and industrial laborers in their activity.

There was even one upper-class figure calling for moderate change. Francisco Madero was born in 1873 into a rich Coahuila family and received the education of his class in Mexico, Europe, and the United States. He returned home with an interest in the welfare of the lower class, although it was a generalized paternalism with little grounding in the realities of Mexican society and politics or much thought of the detailed needs of the poor. He was interested in free elections, a rarity among the rich in Mexico. His family and associates worried about his views for a time, but it soon appeared that they were causing scarcely a ripple of interest outside the small group of middle-class dissenters. Madero seemed unlikely to offer effective leadership in Mexico. He was a short, slender man and mild in manner in a society that put a premium on male vigor and strength. He was a teetotaler where heavy drinking was common. In Europe he had become an adherent of spiritualism, scarcely likely to appeal to many Mexicans. But Madero developed influence because of his evident sincerity, goodness, and courage and persistence. He became one of the most prominent of the antiadministration speakers and organizers in the last decade of the Porfiriato.

Díaz, apparently having no cause for worry, in 1908 granted an interview for foreign consumption to an American journalist, James Creelman, and told him that he was retiring in 1910 and welcomed the creation of a political opposition. This self-serving lie was printed in *Pearson's Magazine*, then reprinted in Mexico where few people can have believed that Díaz meant what he said. Madero, however, seized on it as an excuse to intensify his mildly antiadministration activities. He soon published a slender volume entitled *The Presidential Succession in 1910*, in which he trumpeted that old Mexican cry that Díaz once had used himself: Effective Suffrage and No Reelection. He also called for the formation of a democratic party. Madero and a few supporters began organizing Democratic Clubs, which early in 1910 nominated Madero for the presidency.

Díaz found none of this alarming, but as a precaution in June 1910 imprisoned Madero. Shortly thereafter, Díaz was reelected without difficulty. Madero went into exile in Texas, where in October he issued the Plan of San Luís Potosí, calling for a fair electoral system; correction of abuses relating to land titles, including those of Indians; and a rebellion to begin November 20. On that day Madero rode from Texas into his native state of Coahuila, discovered that no revolution had begun, and rode back into Texas. His cry had not gone unheeded, but it was difficult for people to decide how and when to act, especially in view of the probability of strong reaction from federal forces. The result was that rebellion began on a local basis in different places at different times.

For some time the only dangerous pressure on the Díaz regime was exerted by Pascual Orozco and Pancho Villa in the northern state of Chihuahua. They began with a handful of followers, mostly on horseback, as was natural in a grazing area of great distances and widely scattered settlements. Villa, who eventually became the more important, was a man of the lower class, unlettered, at odds with the law, with enormous energy and volcanic emotions, recklessly valorous, a truly remarkable popular leader and director of irregular cavalry. Orozco and Villa and many others of the north were not peasants, not focused on problems of village land, but often cowboys—*vaqueros*—who turned easily to brawling and marauding in a good cause. They swept up the smaller, isolated communities of the state, and the loot and excitement of success brought them more followers. They then could seize control of parts of the long rail line from central Mexico through the state of Chihuahua to the United States border, on which the *federales* depended.

Various dissident groups put pressure on Mexico City, and each took its toll of confidence, attention, supplies, and soldiers committed or held in reserve. In the state of Morelos, just fifty miles from the capital, over a range of mountains to the south, great sugar haciendas near Cuernavaca and Cuáutla had for centuries taken land from Indian villages and drawn on them for labor. The villagers in the first decade of the twentieth century were fighting what seemed likely to be their last battle to preserve what remained of their lands. In 1909 at the village of Anenecuilco a new president of the village council was elected in the person of Emiliano Zapata, then thirty. He had a bit of land of his own and some income from horse and mule breeding. He was known as a man of independent mind and deep resentment of the ruling system. By the summer of 1910 Zapata had decided that the recourse to law so often tried was not going to work, and he had his neighbors arm themselves and seize the land they claimed. By the end of 1910 Zapata was making rulings on land disputes in various nearby areas, often dividing hacienda lands. Zapata said that he was not in revolt as a *maderista*, but merely dividing fields that belonged to the local people.

The spread of this popular movement of land seizure was due largely to government weakness caused by the disastrous experience of the federal army in Chihuahua. By early 1911 a few bands in Morelos were openly in revolt, looting, burning records, and in March Zapata declared himself for the Plan of San Luís Potosí and in rebellion against the government. Madero had just reentered Mexico and gone to Chihuahua, where the *villistas* were pressing an offensive against the *federales*. For months the Morelos men had been organizing militarily. Now they began to fight, and Zapata quickly established himself as a leader of unusual talent.

He and Villa were alike in being lower-class figures who could expect nothing under the old regime. Their talents came to light only because of revolution. Each was a man of energy, determination, courage, capacity to inspire loyalty, and generally excellent judgment in military affairs. Villa was mercurial, mostly driven by a simple urge to dominate, endure, enjoy. His social outlook consisted of little more than a distaste for the old society, for "pantywaists" generally, and in favor of his own friends and supporters. Zapata, on the other hand, was a man of rare concentration of purpose: He wanted to secure the village farmer in his land. His view of Mexican affairs scarcely went further than that, although he understood the usefulness of some cooperation to destroy the federal armies. Villa and Zapata were a part of the coming of the Revolution, the destruction of the Díaz administration, the war thereafter, but they were too simple to make acceptable rulers of a new Mexico. Yet they were as strong, talented, interesting figures as any lower-class leaders ever thrown up by events in the history of the Old World.

In early 1911 the Díaz regime talked of reform, but it was too late. On May 11 Villa and Orozco stormed Ciudad Juárez. On May 21 the Treaty of Juárez between the *maderistas* and the federal government provided for the resignation of Díaz; for installing Francisco de la Barra, a man of the old regime, as provisional president until an election was held; and disbandment of the revolutionary forces. It was widely supposed that Madero soon would be president. No one realized that the forces of Villa and Zapata could not be effectively disbanded, and that yet other revolutionary forces would arise in new areas; in short, that the Revolution scarcely had begun.

b. The Revolution, 1911–1917

The Mexican Revolution developed spasmodically, as new leaders in the huge country contested bloodily for dominance and as the shibboleths of the emerging national movement took form.

Madero: The Hesitant Revolution, November 1911–February 1913

Madero was elected president in October and inaugurated in November. The Revolution was hesitant in his time because men were trying to decide what needed to be done. There was no ideology or accepted program for change, rather much confusion and clashing opinion and fear. Madero was hesitant about reform, and he retained unreliable elements in the government. He faced much ill will, jealousy, and uncertainty with weak military, financial, technical, and bureaucratic instruments. By now some state legislatures were passing radical measures. That alarmed conservatives, still strong in many towns and especially the capital, where reformers openly discussed social change. The federal army, which was nearly intact, was officered by men theoretically loyal to the government in office, but in fact chiefly interested in their individual and corporate fates, which they identified with retention of some version of the old regime.

Violence was inevitable, given the division of opinion and interest and the weakness of government. Even when armed bands dispersed, reassembly was a simple matter. All over the vast country some individuals who had not yet borne arms were shaken from their passivity and caution, perceiving the possibility of improved status, and were ready to fight.

Madero scarcely took the oath of office before he faced armed rebellion by General Bernardo Reyes, long the satrap of the northeast. It was quickly quashed and Reyes imprisoned. Also in November, Zapata proclaimed his Plan of Ayala, repudiating Madero as supporting "*científicos, hacendados,* and *caciques.*" Zapata called for the direct distribution of land to the poor. For conservatives that confirmed the impossibility of compromise with any reform element; for Madero it confirmed the necessity of creating traditional governmental forms before attempting reform and his view that Zapata could not understand the need for orderly procedure.

The two men had conferred, with Madero trying to convince the peasant leader that the new administration would carry out land and other reforms, but insisting that only the central government, not revolutionary armed bands, could adjudicate land titles. Zapata considered that too slow, and a scheme to aid landowners. Zapata, therefore, continued to support forcible land seizures and Madero to protest them. During the rest of his tenure, Madero was at war with Zapata.

Liberals thought Madero too conservative, and conservatives thought him radical. The fact that the government had little money and limited authority created situations of disappointment and fear. Madero knew that his enemies were conspiring; but he was trusting and compassionate, opposed to large-scale purges. It was a time of much discussion, conjecture, rumor, agitation. Some violent physical changes had occurred in the provinces, beyond the control of the central government. Reformers were discussing the integration of the Indian into the general life of the nation, the distribution of land, changes in education. Labor organization and strikes increased. All this occurred in a new atmosphere of free discussion, stimulating to young reformers but disturbing to conservatives. In the Chamber of Deputies, the press, and informal discussion groups, new people talked of a new Mexico. At the same time, vilification, damaging rumor, and panic mongering were common. The press was irresponsible and corrupt, and much of it was conservative. The government did try to control it by subsidies, but later revolutionary regimes would use stronger measures.

Pascual Orozco, now military commander in Chihuahua, rebelled in February 1912. Madero sent Victoriano Huerta, a competent veteran of the Díaz army, who defeated Orozco by July, although in the process Huerta and Madero became distrustful of each other. Then in October Madero put down a small barracks rising at Veracruz, led by General Félix Díaz, nephew of the former dictator. Díaz and Reyes were imprisoned in Mexico City. Some of Madero's advisers, including his brother and close collaborator, the practical Gustavo Madero, advised him that charity toward rebels in Mexico was dangerous. Madero was too compassionate a man to survive in the brutal world of Mexican politics.

As was expectable, Reyes and Díaz found ways to conspire together, and to negotiate with officers of the federal army, including Huerta. In February 1913 they were released by officers in the conspiracy. There followed a period in which the rebels and Madero's forces, usually managed by Huerta, exchanged artillery fire in Mexico City, to create confusion and provide a cover for their conspiracy. The disruption of city life hardened the views of another of Madero's enemies, the United States ambassador, Henry Lane Wilson, a conservative who thought Madero a weakling and a dangerous radical. During this Decena Trágica (February 9–18, 1913) Wilson's improper intervention in Mexican affairs and his biased reporting to Washington made him one of the worst envoys in the history of his country. Henry Wilson suggested to Madero that the latter resign, as the best "solution" to the disorder. He permitted Huerta and Félix Díaz to use the embassy for discussion of how to depose the president of Mexico.

The rebels and Huerta made an agreement, known to Mexicans as the "Pact of the Embassy." They then murdered Gustavo Madero, whose toughness had been one of his brother's shields. Without revealing the murder to the president, Huerta persuaded him and his vice-president, José M. Pino Suárez, to resign on promise of free passage into exile. Congress accepted the resignations, the minister of foreign relations automatically succeeded to the presidency and resigned within the hour, so that Huerta as next minister in line became the "legal" president. Four days later Madero and Pino Suárez were murdered by Huerta men. Mexicans understandably assigned H. L. Wilson some blame for the murder of Madero. But Huerta and such reactionaries as Félix Díaz were nearly as unaware as Wilson that the old Mexico was dead. The signs had not been entirely clear during the two years since the fighting began against the Porfiriato. The murder of Madero made them clearer, loosing angers, fears, and ambitions that barely had been tapped before. Although Madero did not function well in Mexican politics, he succeeded magnificently in focusing attention on the need for some increase of political participation and some attention to social problems. As a decent man, martyr to the need for modernization, he continued to serve after death as an inspiration to his posterity.

The War Against Huerta, 1913–1914

Huerta lasted just a year and a half (February 1913 to July 1914), although he had the old federal army, the support of the wealthy and most state governors and the Catholic party, and the favor of foreign business and the European powers. Huerta's foes hated him for his conservatism, his brutal character, and above all the murder of Madero. Huerta also had the enmity of the new (from March 1913) United States president Woodrow Wilson, who disliked not only murder but dictatorship and unconstitutional changes of regime.

Of the many forces ranged against Huerta in Mexico, the most important were Zapata, just south of the capital; Villa in Chihuahua; a new group of revolutionary leaders in Sonora in the far northwest; and Venustiano Carranza in the northeast. Huerta thus faced more important revolutionary forces than had risen to end the Díaz regime. More Mexicans were becoming involved in public affairs, partly because of the accumulation of discussion of change, but also because of outrage at the murder of Madero. His death caused a dispersion of intellectuals from Mexico City to join the anti-Huerta forces. The intellectuals did something to increase awareness among the military chiefs of the arguments for social reform.

The fighting was savage. Huerta's seizure of power began a large-scale military struggle that went on for nearly three years. The violence and brutality of Mexican life that went back to the colonial era prepared most participants in the Revolution to accept violent death and mistreatment almost as commonplace. The shooting of

military prisoners was not considered remarkable. Slaughters of civilians were unhappily frequent. Wartime brought out the worst in some individuals, like Villa's monstrous friend General Rodolfo Fierro, "the Butcher of Ojinaga," who gleefully killed people with his own hand. The reportage, memoirs, song, and legend of the Great Revolution abound in *hacendados* incinerated in their homes, men shot to make their wives and daughters more easily available to warriors, others executed out of hand in moments of rage.

Carranza, governor of Coahuila, had been a senator under the Díaz regime. In March 1913 he issued the Plan of Guadalupe, declaring himself first chief of the Constitutionalist Army, a shrewd title suggesting attachment to effective suffrage and no reelection. His photographs showed a fifty-four-year-old graybeard of serious mien. His numerous detractors found him pompous. He certainly wanted to be president, but so did some of his critics. His views on Mexico amounted to little more than improved administration and fairer elections—things that were certainly needed. He disliked the idea of socioeconomic reform. Not surprisingly, his personality and conservatism did not appeal to his contemporaries or to later historians. But Carranza was honest, energetic, intelligent, and persevering.

In central Mexico, Huerta's efforts to crush Zapata failed and only made the latter more radical. Zapata now had with him a few of the fugitives from Mexico City, including Antonio Díaz Soto y Gama, an anarchist who became a major spokesman for agrarianism. In the north, Villa took up arms again, recognizing Carranza as leader of the movement against Huerta. Villa quickly swept up nearly all the big and roadless state, his famous cavalry assembling from mountain and plain. In the fall of 1913 he took the cities on the railway. Now the women—*soldaderas*—who appeared with his army in so many photographs, joined their men on the trains, feeding and otherwise comforting them, and occasionally aiding in combat. By early 1914 Villa was ready to fan out east and west, as well as continue south toward Mexico City. Carranza regarded him with disapproval for his independent ways.

In Sonora anti-Huerta forces quickly became dominant, led by Adolfo de la Huerta, Alvaro Obregón, Plutarco E. Calles, and others who became important figures in the Revolution. Obregón was a middle-class farmer who had fought against Orozco in 1912. He displayed an extraordinary talent for military affairs. Within a few months in 1913 he had control of most of Sonora and began penetration of Sinaloa to the south. The legislature of Sonora recognized Carranza as first chief. In September 1913 Carranza went from the northeast to far-off Sonora, where the war against Huerta was going so much better than in the northeast.

All anti-Huerta forces were both aided and irritated by President Woodrow Wilson's persistent efforts to influence Mexican affairs. Wilson's interest was focused on political issues that he thought of as defining "decent government." He was an ex-professor of North American and English constitutional and legal institutions. He did not understand how different the experience and the society of Mexico were from those of his own country. When Mexican practice deviated from the norms he approved, he wished to instruct and punish until improvement occurred. It was not surprising, then, that his policy initiatives badly served both Mexico and the United States.

Wilson refused to recognize the Huerta regime and tried to get him to resign. He supposed that his efforts would be popular with Huerta's enemies and was irritated when he discovered that Carranza was a strong nationalist, suspicious of North Americans bearing gifts. Wilson did permit arms to flow to the Constitutionalists (as the *carrancistas* were called). Then in April 1914 he seized the port of Veracruz. The events that led to this began at the oil port of Tampico, where a few United States sailors were detained briefly by Huerta forces, then released with apologies. Just at that time Washington heard of a munitions ship en route to supply Huerta, and Wilson seized the excuse of the Tampico inci-

dent to order Veracruz occupied. The results were: Mexicans were killed by United States forces; Huerta got the munitions from the ship by a simple maneuver; Carranza denounced the United States action, further enflaming Wilson against what he thought of as Carranza's obstinacy; and Wilson had a Mexican city that he did not want. It finally was evacuated in November 1914, long after Huerta had fled Mexico.

In May 1914 Carranza was so worried about Villa's success that he ordered him to leave his central position and move east, hopefully eliminating him from what was becoming a race to Mexico City. Villa did not want to go, and eventually returned to the central line of march. Carranza forces in the north and northeast cut Villa off from coal for his locomotives—effectively stalling him—and from supplies coming by sea to Tampico. So Carranza and Obregón were in the capital in August, before Villa. The war against Huerta was ended. Carranza thought he should be permitted to direct things from that point. The military commanders had other ideas.

Obregón/Carranza versus Villa, 1914–1916

Mexican leadership was badly fragmented in the summer of 1914 when Carranza and Obregón occupied Mexico City. The *zapatista* Army of the South held positions within the Valley of Mexico, demanded justice for the underprivileged, and declared that the *carrancistas* were not true revolutionaries. Carranza sent emissaries to Cuernavaca, where they met a *zapatista* demand for adoption of the Plan of Ayala for land distribution. Carranza not only rejected that, but the simplicity that concentrated on land titles almost to the exclusion of other issues. He followed Madero in treating Zapata as a rebel.

There was trouble between factions in distant Sonora, so Obregón went north to solicit Villa's aid there. During negotiations marked by mutual suspicion, the two generals at least agreed that Carranza was not to head the government! The mercurial Villa and solemn Carranza always had clashed, and now Villa condemned the first chief's rule by decree and refusal to call a congress. Carranza had convened a convention of selected leaders for October 1 at Mexico City, but Villa and Obregón informed him that the omission of *zapatista* delegates would have to be rectified. Carranza replied by cutting the railway between Mexico City and Chihuahua, whereupon Villa withdrew recognition of him as first chief, and began moving troops south; in addition, he nearly had Obregón executed. Obregón was gaining a good insight into the character of the Chihuahua *caudillo*. More negotiations among leaders at this time in 1914 led to the summoning of a convention for October 10 at Aguascalientes. When Carranza's convention met on October 1 in the capital, the assembled generals recognized that the meeting was unimportant and most of them made their way north to the Aguascalientes Convention. Carranza seemed to be abandoned.

The Revolutionary Convention at Aguascalientes was made up largely of military delegates, in the majority Constitutionalists, but not now representing Carranza. The delegates waited while a special invitation went to the suspicious *zapatistas* in Morelos, who then sent a delegation that included Antonio Díaz Soto y Gama, who treated the soldiers of the Revolution to the voice of radicalism, chiefly on land reform. This was the first national forum that discussed social change. After nearly four years of turmoil, some of the great reform issues began to assume a prominence that would permit clearer discussion of the aims of the Revolution. But practical military and political issues were what concerned most of the delegates. Obregón at Aguascalientes said flatly that the men who had fought in the Revolution would decide the fate of the country. Events showed that there was much truth in his declaration, although the generals could not escape entirely the influence of new dreams of innovation and justice.

The *zapatistas* and *villistas* at the Convention tended to collaborate, which alarmed Obregón as much as the intransigent behavior of the More-los *agraristas*. The Convention agreed on the resignations of Carranza and Villa, and on November 6 declared as provisional president of Mexico General Eulalio Gutiérrez, who was attractive because he lacked passionate enemies. Obregón was willing to support Gutiérrez, but not when the Convention's president appointed Villa his military commander. So Obregón rejoined Carranza, believing that Villa could not be controlled by civilians, a judgment at once vindicated by events. Some other generals also preferred to stay with Carranza, but his army had to evacuate Mexico City late in November 1914. Since neither Villa nor Carranza would resign, as the compromisers wished, war was the only answer.

Villa's "Army of the North" became the "Army of the Convention," and Pancho the white knight of constitutionalism, an impossible role for him to sustain. He did not, in fact, pay much attention to the Convention government but did as he pleased. The intellectuals in the government—including young José Vasconcelos —who pinned their hopes on the Convention because it represented civil government could see that it was the prisoner of Villa's troops. When in January 1915 General Gutiérrez and the rest of his "government" fled the *villistas*, Pancho merely appointed a new president.

He had been very slow about pursuing the apparently fading *carrancistas*; not until December was he in Mexico City. There was an historic meeting between the popular leaders Villa and Zapata. They agreed to collaborate, but they had little in common in temperament or in their vision of the future. They were alike in being repelled and perplexed by the multitude of issues better-educated and more sophisticated leaders insisted on discussing. In the stress of revolution, Mexico produced these remarkable sons, but neither could fully understand the requirements of collaboration with others. The cooperation of *villistas* and *zapatistas* was haphazard and ineffective.

The Carranza forces were damaged by their rejection of the Convention, which enemies said proved a lack of attachment to reform and decent government. Obregón and Carranza retreated east to the hot Gulf Coast and the port of Veracruz. Clearly, a political offensive was needed to revive support for Carranza. It was the more necessary because reform measures had been instituted at the state and local level, so that expectation of change was growing. Such state reforms included cancellation of debts and debt peonage, decrees for minimum wages, abolition of corporal punishment of servants, electoral reforms, efforts to improve education. So in December 1914 and January 1915 Carranza issued reform decrees, reluctantly, as urged by his civilian and military advisers. He promised return of village lands, fair taxation of real property, aid for rural and industrial workers, electoral and judicial reform, revision of the law codes, abolition of monopolies in natural resources, and a constitutional convention. Thus he increased the attractiveness of the *carrancistas*, especially when contrasted with the riotous conduct of the *villistas* in Mexico City.

Obregón, in the following military campaigns, solidified his reputation as the greatest soldier of the Revolution. He soon fought his way back into central Mexico, and in a great battle at Celaya in April 1915 broke the back of the Villa forces. Now the *carrancistas* could turn on Zapata, driving him into defensive positions in the mountains. By the fall of 1915 Villa was virtually confined to Chihuahua. When he attacked Sonora, Woodrow Wilson finally recognized the Carranza government in October and permitted transport of Constitutionalist troops to Sonora on United States railroads. In retaliation, Villa raided the United States, whereupon Woodrow Wilson sent General Pershing into Mexico with troops. They could not find Villa and infuriated the nationalistic Carranza.

By the spring of 1916 the *carrancistas* had the military situation in hand, although regional leaders retained forces that would be potentially dangerous for years. Villa and Zapata were reduced to impotence and some years later would be murdered. The old oligarchs retained considerable property, but had lost most of their political influence, as thousands of new leaders demanded political voice, honors, and material rewards. There had been five years of immensely disruptive warfare, requisition, looting, and both careless and wanton destruction. When the troops went home, wrote a contemporary novelist, they found that "the black trail of the incendiaries showed in the roofless houses" and that the people hated soldiers.

The Constitution of 1917 and the Hope of Social Reform

In 1916 it seemed to people of a reform disposition that little had been accomplished. Regional and local changes in property holding and declarations of principle on elections, the church, debt peonage, and other matters seemed precariously based. Already old conservatives were maneuvering to get back properties that had been seized, and the new revolutionary generals were staking out claims as a new species of *hacendado*. Carranza as first chief was trying to run the country by decree, and that seemed a denial of the revolutionary hope of just government by elected officials. The country was far from pacified. Villa and Zapata were at large and might combine with Félix Díaz, who headed a well-financed conservative movement, or with Manuel Peláez, the northeastern *caudillo* who squeezed lush revenues from the foreign petroleum producers, now in an ecstasy of profits during World War I, or with other armed bands, some of them but weakly attached to Carranza's regime. The country suffered food shortages, high prices, and a scarcity of acceptable currency.

These conditions, Carranza thought, made the first order of business the consolidation of military and political power, rather than social reform. He knew that this would be decided by military-political leaders rather than by broad popular opinion. As Azuela had a character say in his novel *Underdogs* in 1915, " 'What position does Carranza have? The truth is, I don't understand politics. . . . Look, don't ask me questions. I didn't go to school. . . . Just tell me, Do this or do that. . . .' " So Carranza, like Mexican leaders before and after him, tried to manipulate the small politically active population. When he decreed municipal elections for September 1916, he left procedures to the state governors he had appointed, after excluding from the new town posts men who had supported the enemies of the Constitutionalists or current military officers unless they resigned from the army before taking office. He took similar precautions in the October elections for a constitutional convention. But none of Carranza's maneuvers secured his personal position; he was supported only in default of better alternatives, because at the moment the chief leaders of the Revolution were more interested in consolidating the new regime than in starting a contest over political control.

The constitutional convention met at Querétaro from late November 1916 to January 1917, and produced a document not only fateful for Mexico but influential in much of Latin America. It was a convention of new men; it included no Porfirians. Both prominent military men and relatively obscure civilians were there and they held a considerable range of views. They were young men, few of them with higher education or professional backgrounds, mostly intensely Mexican in their interests, who fixed their attention on certain solutions to ancient problems so intently that they could be called principles or shibboleths of the Revolution. Their views were not structured, however, by any ideology more complex than belief in nationalism, justice, and a vague egalitarianism; there was nothing like positivism, anarchism, or Marxism cementing their ideas. Possibly the shibboleths of the Revolution were the stronger for being so firmly tied to the Mexican experience.

The convention at once showed its lack of interest in Carranza by not considering simple acceptance of the draft constitution he had provided. That was little different from the 1857 document of Juárez's time, and they agreed to incorporate the structure of government as laid

down then; but they went on from there to add drastically new and radical articles: restricting the church, giving a social definition to property, emphasizing education, providing organizational and social rights and benefits to industrial labor, and inserting much explicit nationalism on political and economic subjects. This represented the views of the majority of the delegates, although it once was argued that the radical nature of the Constitution of 1917 resulted from maneuvers by a radical minority. That analysis was based partly on the subsequent slow implementation of the constitutional provisions, which led to an assumption that the military men in the convention did not favor such radical measures. It now is recognized that many military delegates did favor the radical articles, while supposing that they could not in prudence be implemented immediately. To a certain class of critic such advocacy of revolutionary principles together with delayed action is hypocrisy and a denial of the revolutionary essence. The critics demanded drastic action at all times, but such a notion was foreign to nearly all leaders of the Mexican Revolution.

The new Constitution retained the old prohibitions on monastic orders and ecclesiastical courts but went beyond the anticlericalism of the nineteenth-century Liberals. New provisions prohibited the church from owning property, so that even the temples belonged to the state, and banned political activity by churchmen or criticism of the fundamental laws of the country, the government, or its personnel. It required that priests register with the state and let state legislatures set the maximum number of ministers for localities. The animus against the church was so strong that some delegates were willing to require a married clergy and abolition of oral confession.

With regard to land, the national government was given control of subsoil riches; agricultural estates were to be broken up and village lands restored; foreigners were not to own land within sixty miles of the frontiers or thirty of the seacoasts. Aliens acquiring land had to promise to abide by Mexican law and forgo appeals to their home governments. In education, there was to be lay instruction in all the schools through secondary (public or private) and in public higher education, which left religious instruction permissible only in private higher education. There were extensive provisions authorizing labor unions, the right to strike, employers' liability for accident and disease, minimum wages, time limits on labor, child labor, and many other matters.

These and other provisions codified the previously scattered dreams of the great Revolution. The military side of those years—the heroism, suffering, and triumph—had provided a limitless pool of recollection—of history—for the strengthening of Mexican national feeling. Already popular song made them the years of the giants, and down the decades all would remember the martyrdom of Madero, the valor of Villa, and whisper that over the mountains of Morelos still could be seen riding a shadowy and gigantic Zapata calling his people to die on their feet rather than live on their knees. Now the Constitution set down a program for the future, a magnificent prospect of modernization and justice that served as a guide for the next half century.

Following the instructions of the convention, Carranza set the conditions for elections; he was chosen for president without opposition, and inaugurated with the new Congress in May 1917. Whether the whirlwind that had swept Mexico since 1910 would be succeeded by a viable new political and social system remained to be seen. Neither in Mexico nor abroad was there much supposition that the Porfirian system would return; on the other hand, there was much doubt as to what might replace it. Mexicans were of many minds as to how to proceed. Foreigners were stunned by the prolonged ferocity of the upheaval in Mexico. That attitude was enhanced by the Bolshevik Revolution of November 1917 in Russia and subsequent events there, and supporters of the status quo wondered what was needed to prevent what they feared might be a general world collapse into social revolution.

c. Consolidation of the Revolution, 1917–1934

The presidents of Mexico from 1917 to 1934 invested most of their attention and other resources in what seemed to them the inescapable priorities: maintaining order and organizing political power. They did something, however, to promote agrarian reform, education, public health, organized labor, dignity for Indians, and a sense of Mexican nationalism. For critics then and now the political emphasis meant "corruption," new types of *caudillismo* and oligarchy, and too little economic and social change. Viewed as political consolidators, however, Obregón and Calles were successful; and Portes Gil, as president, agrarian leader, and political manager, was as clearly a new type of nationalistic and pragmatic modernizer. These men passed on to Cárdenas in 1934 a political system more reliable than they enjoyed themselves at the end of the Revolution. Thus the consolidators laid a base for the great progress of the Cárdenas years.

President Carranza: Conservatism and *Continuismo*, 1917–1920

Carranza as president is remembered mainly for his lack of belief in the desirability of attempting much reform, and for his violation of the shibboleth of effective suffrage and no reelection by trying to impose a successor. That is not entirely fair, since his rivals and successors displayed those tendencies in some measure; but some of them were at least convincing supporters of parts of the new principles of reform. In addition, Carranza's freedom of action was badly restricted. Public revenues were meager. The economy was in worse condition than before the Revolution, and remained depressed in 1917–1920, except for petroleum production by the foreign companies. All echelons of government had difficulty preserving order. A strong radical socialist movement in Tabasco kept that state in turmoil. Other states rocked with banditry, armed clashes between political factions, and financial scandals. Much money went to buy the loyalty or quiescence of chieftains and their hungry retainers. Satisfying the cry for gain after the long strife of Revolution was a task almost more terrible than war.

Although the chief danger to the administration was from leaders of the Revolution, it had other foes. Mexican commercial, manufacturing, and mining elements disliked the regime, as did the old *hacendado* class. Then there was the church, whose hierarchy adopted an intransigent attitude, declaring that the constitutional articles affecting the church could not be accepted. No opposition group was formidable alone, but combinations could be serious. Finally, there was fear of action by the United States, where some groups condemned the effects of the radical Constitution on property and the church.

It was, in any event, a new Mexico. The church's position was weaker than it had been during the century since Independence. State governments used the new Constitution to restrict the church yet further. Another part of the new Mexico was the extinction of peonage, and the promise—however difficult to implement—that the largely Indian peasants would be integrated into the national community. Labor organization was encouraged. In 1918 the Regional Confederation of Mexican Workers (CROM) was formed as a prop of the regime, with Luís Morones as general secretary. Hereafter organized labor would be part of the government political combination, and labor bosses would serve their political masters more than the members of the syndicates. Strikes increased, to the dismay of businessmen, even though Carranza tried to control such militance.

Carranza preferred not to depend on those he considered rivals for influence. One much feared source of opposition was removed in 1919 when Zapata was assassinated. *Zapatistas*, however, were given important positions in Morelos and elsewhere, so that source of support for agrarian reform did not disappear. Another source of

concern to Carranza at least removed himself from Mexico City when Obregón resigned from the cabinet because he thought the president cared too little for his views. Obregón went home to Sonora, and in July 1919 announced his candidacy for the election of 1920. Carranza retaliated by putting forward an obscure candidate he obviously meant to impose through his control of the electoral machinery. It thus could be claimed in Mexico in 1919–1920 that Carranza was betraying the Revolution.

Carranza made moves against Obregón's personal safety, and shifted federal troops into Sonora. Governor Adolfo de la Huerta and his chief of state militia, General Plutarco Calles, who had also recently resigned from the cabinet, prepared for hostilities. The Sonorans in April 1920 issued the Plan of Agua Prieta for a provisional government named by the Congress to serve until a fair election could be held. Major leaders throughout Mexico announced for the Plan. Carranza fled toward Veracruz early in May and was murdered. Congress later that month named Adolfo de la Huerta provisional president. He and his minister of war and marine, General Calles, pacified the country. They even persuaded Pancho Villa to accept a hacienda and abandon the political wars. They supervised Obregón's election in September and his inauguration in November 1920. At that moment, the prospects for political peace seemed dubious.

President Obregón, Pragmatist, 1920–1924

Although Obregón was accounted more radical than Carranza, he was above all a pragmatist. He would not push reform rapidly because of lack of funds, fear of damage to production, and belief that his chief problems were preservation of order and collaboration among the forces that had won the Revolution. He thought embezzlement in government and in government-connected enterprise was unavoidable, the alternative being increased conspiracy and rebellion. Obregón attended to civilian as well as military support, receiving strong labor support from the CROM in his bid for the presidency and then later favoring the agrarian party.

The consolidation that Obregón preferred was threatened by the United States, which refused to recognize him as president. Its aim was a guarantee against application to United States–owned property of some articles of the Constitution. Obregón resisted, because he was a nationalist and because knuckling under to Washington would damage him politically. The issues included claims of United States citizens on the public debt and for damages to persons and property, plus the new constitutional annulment of foreign titles to public lands acquired after 1876 and the provision that subsoil property belonged to the state, to be let out on special concession, the law during most of Spanish and independent Mexican history. Carranza had taxed United States–owned oil properties in a way deemed objectionable and also had tried to force North Americans to apply for Mexican drilling permits.

Obregón promised that he would not act against United States–owned properties. Washington demanded a treaty guarantee. Obregón had his Supreme Court rule on oil cases in 1921–1922 that if the owners had erected drilling equipment or performed other "positive acts" before the Constitution of 1917 went into effect, their property rights were guaranteed and they did not need drilling permits. That ruling was also unacceptable to Washington. Finally, the contestants agreed to the Bucareli Conferences, at Mexico City, in May–August 1923. There Mexico agreed to limit seizures of land for *ejidos* —communal farms—and the United States to accept bonds rather than cash as compensation for expropriated agricultural lands. They agreed on mixed commissions to set the terms of specific claims. Mexico reiterated a view expressed earlier that the mineral provisions of the Constitution would not be applied retroactively. Mexico agreed informally to continue the policy of "positive acts," a verbal agreement known as the "Extra-Official Pact." With this truce, the petro-

leum operators felt a little assured, Mexican leaders put off their nationalist campaign against foreign companies until a more propitious moment, and Washington in August 1923 recognized the Obregón administration.

Only a few months later Obregón had to meet the serious de la Huerta revolt. Dissidents, needing a leader with a national name and with qualities that could be proclaimed superior to those of Obregón, settled on Adolfo de la Huerta, who had experience as president, governor, and as diplomat and cabinet member under Obregón. His negotiations in the United States had convinced conservative Mexicans that he was better —more conservative—than Obregón. His supporters emphasized that he was a civilian, but his rebellion depended, in fact, on his military collaborators. The enthusiasm of conservatives within and without Mexico for de la Huerta depended partly on the fact that Obregón had picked Calles as his successor, and they thought Calles a radical. De la Huerta certainly was more conservative on property issues than Calles. De la Huerta, suffering from presidential itch, thought Obregón undervalued his advice and services. He decided that the Bucareli Conferences had sold Mexico's sovereignty to the United States. But with all his ambition and pique, de la Huerta hesitated about rebellion. He was urged on by a motley collection of conservative civilian capitalists and politicians and regional *caudillos* and army generals, some of them disgruntled, some merely hungry, many of them reckless. Finally they virtually dragged de la Huerta into the rebellion, which began in December 1923.

A conspiracy of such magnitude could not be kept secret, and Obregón had been working for months to counter it. That was the workaday function of a Latin American leader under the traditional conditions of endemic violence and weak social and political organization. Before December 1923 Obregón had suppressed smaller rebellions. The de la Huerta generals controlled a sizable part of the federal army but were badly scattered throughout the national territory. Obregón had tight control of his resources, whereas the rebels were so uncoordinated and so mistrustful of each other that the effort would have seemed ludicrous in a more orderly society. United States businessmen in Mexico found de la Huerta more to their taste than Obregón and Calles, but Washington supported the government, especially by refusing aid to the rebels and by pressing them not to levy on foreign concerns.

The rebellion pointed up the conservatism of the opposition to Obregón. However slowly he pursued reforms, he did favor them, unlike the *hacendados* supporting de la Huerta. Peasants and labor supported the administration. Obregón efficiently destroyed the rebels by May 1924. His victory gave Obregón new opportunities to realign the army. Even before the rebellion he had commenced reducing it, and he had usually kept generals out of his cabinet and from state governorships, although critics found them distressingly evident in other public and private positions. With the rebellion, Obregón further reshuffled the officers' corps, with executions, resignations, and reassignments. After the rebellion the dominant clique had an improved hold on the country and more leeway to consider other than political and military issues.

Calles as President and *Jefe Máximo*, 1924–1934

President Calles (1924–1928) used the same methods of reward and pressure with the military and political chieftains that he helped carry out as Obregón's minister of *gobernación* (law enforcement). He continued gradually to increase control of the national army, furthering a policy that before long would become a cornerstone of the official system. Military expenditures, nevertheless, still siphoned off a significant part of the budget. Another of his political policies was heavy reliance on organized labor, and especially the CROM, whose czar, Luís Morones, became minister of industry. Morones continued to accumulate an unsavory reputation for corruption, for subservience to employers rather than care

for workers, and for the strong-arm methods of his *Grupo Acción*. Calles' reliance on labor became offensive to *agraristas*, and reinforced their support of Obregón.

Calles' social policy generally is judged to have been conservative, but he did expand education and health programs somewhat, and during his administration began the campaign that resulted in the first federal labor law. His economic policies encouraged business interests. He used government authority and funds to improve banking and to commence public works in road building and irrigation. He distributed much more land under the new constitutional provisions than Obregón had, but that has been obscured in historical works by his later repudiation of that shibboleth of the Revolution and by the great distributions of later years.

One issue on which Calles was "revolutionary" in Mexican terms was the church. Since 1917 the national governments had done little to implement the anticlerical provisions of the Constitution, even though the Mexican hierarchy maintained a defiant attitude. The central government winked at church schools, the use of clerical garb, unregistered priests, foreign ecclesiastics, and public religious ceremonies, although drastic action was taken at state and local levels. With the inauguration of Calles the church's fears increased, because he was known to be more anticlerical than Obregón. In February 1926 a newspaper printed a statement by Archbishop José Mora del Río that repeated the hierarchy's 1917 declaration that it would "disavow and combat" the offending parts of the Constitution. Calles then took strong action in support of the old Liberal thesis, confirmed by the Revolution, that the church must confine itself to a spiritual role defined by the state.

He exiled foreign priests and nuns, closed clerical schools, insisted on the constitutional requirement that priests register with the government, and encouraged the states to restrict the church further. The church refused to permit the registration and appealed to its supporters, some of whom were well-to-do conservatives on economic and social as well as religious matters and some peasants merely blindly following their pastors. In an atmosphere of crisis, the church declared an interdict—suspension of clerical services—to begin at the end of July. The interdict in the Middle Ages sometimes brought the faithful to the support of the church and civil governors to their knees, but sometimes it entirely failed to do so. In Mexico in the 1920s, a majority of citizens turned out to be indifferent to the withholding of priestly ministrations, either because they were accustomed to the Mexican church's neglect of its duties or because they in general supported the aims of the new Constitution. In any event, an interdict was an odd, a clearly anachronistic, weapon for the church to be brandishing in the twentieth century.

The rebellion took its worst form in the creation of small armies that fought under the banner of "Christ the King," giving the rebels their names of *Cristeros*. They were localized in parts of west central Mexico. The hierarchy officially was against the armed action, but it was widely believed that priests fought with the *guerrilleros*. Support involved a tangle of conservative religious, political, and economic ideas, and local hatred for federal soldiers. Brutal acts were committed by both sides. The government from the beginning of the Cristero Rebellion put the churches under committees of citizens to keep them open for worship, and for much of the populace that was enough. The armed revolt was not extensive enough to threaten the government, but it posed the possibility that adventurers would join for their own purposes.

There was only small-scale fighting after the summer of 1927, but that and doctrinal differences kept the issue inflamed. Washington was concerned because some Catholics in the United States insisted that the situation required mediation or intervention. That was one reason President Coolidge sent Dwight Morrow as ambassador in 1927. He was an effective representative because he obviously was interested in the Mexicans and their culture. They responded to a representative of the great power to the north who did not condescend to them but assumed that their points of view deserved attention. Morrow helped bring both sides to the point of compromise in 1928, and the issues finally were settled, or tacitly forgotten, with Vatican approval, in mid-1929, and clerical services were resumed. The church had lost the contest. Also losers were the peasant rebels who, supposing they were fighting for Christ the King, finally hung by their necks to telegraph poles, slack in rough cotton shirts and drawers and sandaled feet, suffering as so many of their kind down the centuries for issues they scarcely understood.

Some members of the North American hierarchy and other official or self-appointed spokesmen continued to encourage the supposition that the church and the faith in Mexico were in danger of destruction. They found little echo in the majority of Catholics or non-Catholics in the United States, where enemies of Mexico's economic policies tried to use the religious issue to promote intervention. But Morrow worked to smooth over both issues, and we now know that the Washington administrations of the 1920s and 1930s had no intention of intervening.

The Assassination of Obregón. Obregón and Calles agreed to put the former into office again and forced through Congress a constitutional amendment permitting it. That posed the possibility of a long Sonora dynasty with two *caudillos*. To make certain of Obregón's election in 1928, Calles used draconian methods. No opposition figure was brave or optimistic enough to come into the open after two generals were shot for objecting to the imposition. But the scheme came to naught when Obregón was elected, then assassinated in July, before his inauguration, by a Catholic fanatic. There were cries that the church was back of the assassination, but apparently that was not the case. There also was belief that Calles' men, including organized labor with its notorious *Grupo Acción*, had engineered the deed to keep its faction in power and the *obregonistas* and *agraristas* out.

For weeks the possibility of large-scale violence

seemed high, and small disorders did occur. If Calles had imposed himself, or a close colleague —especially Morones—the *obregonistas*, including many military men, would have taken up arms. Calles made conciliatory moves, including rearrangement of the cabinet, with one new appointee, Emilio Portes Gil, a young *agrarista* politician from Tamaulipas, as minister of government. Most importantly, Calles made a decision on the presidency in which his own interest and that of the country coincided. His chance of winning a civil war was problematical, and he might find himself with a badly disrupted and uncooperative country. So on September 1, when the Congress assembled, he informed it that Obregón should be the last *caudillo*, that thereafter laws and institutions rather than individuals should run Mexico, and that the Congress should choose a provisional president from among the *obregonistas*. Calles deserved credit for a valuable service, even though his subsequent actions indicated that he intended to rule from behind the scenes. A few days after the annual presidential message to Congress, in which this advice was given, Calles in person informed the generals that they should leave the decision to Congress. Although some of the generals were restive, they allowed Congress to elect Portes Gil to serve December 1, 1928 to February 1930, and to set November 1929 as the time for election of a regular president.

Jefe Máximo, *1929–1934*.   For five years Calles was the *jefe máximo*, or political boss, of Mexico. He understood the serious limitations on authority because the "revolutionary" group was a loose coalition, with the incumbent president furnishing the leadership, many of the rewards, and much of the muscle that kept it operative. Such an unstructured system left conditions so fluid that the possibility of successful rebellion invited conspiracy. So when Calles suggested a party structure, he knew that if it became effective, it would promote centralization of political power, and he expected to be the prime beneficiary. For a time, the new party did seem to

serve Calles' personal ends; but it also proved of value, ultimately, to reform leaders and to the nation. It was a workable innovation, its worth not dependent on Calles' motives in promoting it.

Calles and his supporters presented the idea in December 1928, and it was implemented in March 1929 in a convention. The delegates came from nearly all groups supporting the postrevolutionary regimes: the important military and civilian *caudillos, agraristas,* and organized labor. The Morones labor leaders were left out, because *agraristas* distrusted him and Calles did not want to push the issue. But much of the juice was shortly sucked from the Morones unions, and new ones became part of the party in the next few years. Not included in the convention were business groups, the old *hacendado* class, or groups with a religious interest or affiliation. The predominance of popular elements— with military backing—was reflective of the rearrangement of emphases by the victors in the Revolution. The great property interests and the church had lost ground in the public political arena. How much this loss had affected business's ability to influence government policy and legislation has remained a subject of debate ever since.

The leaders at the convention established the National Revolutionary Party (P.N.R.) as little more than a system of collaboration in certain methods of selecting and supporting candidates for public office. Of course, that might be of critical importance if it became effective, but at the time such a result seemed uncertain. The elements of the party—local political machines and interest groups—were to retain their identities, while collaborating with the machinery of the P.N.R. The leaders, and especially the regional bosses, meant to retain their independence. The fact that this independence turned out to be impossible made the new institution so important. Politicians, interest groups, and reformers proved ready for the change. President Portes Gil helped the party on its way by ordering national government employees to give the

P.N.R. seven days' pay a year. He helped it in other ways, establishing from the beginning the interpenetration of party and government that has been so important in recent decades.

The March 1929 convention also nominated for president Calles' choice, Pascual Ortiz Rubio, minister of government in the Portes Gil administration. But the convention was scarcely finished when some dissatisfied generals revolted, and gained civilian support. Calles became minister of war and by May defeated a movement that involved nearly a quarter of the army. Although much of the action was the classic maneuver and negotiation of Latin American revolts, and casualties were low, it emphasized the continuing problem of controlling the military and developing a dependable system of party collaboration.

In the election of November 1929 José Vasconcelos ran against Ortiz Rubio for the Anti-Reelectionists, inveighing against corruption, military government, and subservience to the United States. Vasconcelos as a young intellectual had served in the ineffectual convention government of 1914, which had been strangled by Pancho Villa. Vasconcelos later was a valuable minister of education in the Obregón administration. The official results gave Ortiz Rubio more than 1 million votes to 20,000 for Vasconcelos, and the latter went into exile, crying fraud. He spent many years thereafter, in Mexico and abroad, bitterly condemning political practice and public policy in his homeland. Conscious of his own intellectual abilities and convinced of his moral superiority, he could not reconcile himself to the fact that different qualities were required for achievement in the Mexican political environment.

Ortiz Rubio generally took orders from Calles, who spent much of his time at his pleasant villa in Cuernavaca. When the president's ineffectiveness—due in part to the world Depression—became harmful to Calles, the latter forced him to resign, and had Congress elect General Abelardo Rodríguez. That put yet another Sonoran

in the national palace, emphasizing the *continuismo* practiced by the *jefe máximo*.

Economic and Social Development to 1934

The economic and social achievements of 1917–1934 were part of the base upon which were erected the impressive gains after 1934. Some commentators stress the "revolutionary" elements in those years, and others the "conservative." Both can be found. The Revolution had reduced but not shattered the influence of the old propertied class. It was pushed farther from political decision making, although it continued to have influence on legislation and its implementation. Business circles muttered about the danger of bolshevism, but complained more about taxes, pressures on private landholding, disorder, inefficient public administration, state imposts on national trade, and the deplorable condition of the railways. But there was no effort to end private ownership. The only sizable increase of state ownership was in the communal farms—*ejidos*—and that did not interfere with the revival of private agriculture. The federal government was putting businessmen on government boards dealing with banking, railway rates, taxes, and other matters, so that critics of the system said that business complaints deliberately obscured its partnership with government.

In the 1920s, although a few people prospered, the average annual increase of output was under 2 percent. An improvement over the declining production of the years of Revolution, it was slower growth than in the late Porfiriato. Furthermore, with the Depression in 1930, production declined in Mexico, and in 1932 was lower than in 1910. Investment was one of the country's greatest problems: severely pruned during the Revolution, it recovered little before 1934. Capitalists at home and abroad were dubious about a disorderly and apparently radical land. The government did not begin public development investment until the mid-1920s, and then on a small scale. Although in 1933 production slowly began to climb, the Calles era ended on a note of economic pessimism.

To conservatives in Mexico and abroad, the new land policies were the clearest evidence of radicalism. To Mexican radicals, slow implementation of land distribution was the surest sign that the Revolution was in the hands of reactionaries. The fear of declining production was a major reason for cautious land distribution, but leaders also went slowly because it was a complicated matter, and because the concept stirred political opposition and alarmed capital. Nevertheless, by the 1930s about 20 million acres had been distributed to more than 4,000 villages with 2 million inhabitants. Carranza did little, Obregón more, Calles more yet, and Portes Gil during 1929 distributed more than in any previous year. This was not insignificant, even though more land remained in private hands than in the *ejidos*, and much of the *ejidal* land was poor. There was some effort to extend the role of small independent farmers, but opposition to them was strong because of memories that the effort under the Constitution of 1857 had led to further concentration in haciendas. It was held that only the inalienable *ejidos* could stand against the rapacity of latifundists.

Advocates of more distribution to *ejidos* were told that the *ejidal* production record was poor. It was, but the reasons for it were disputable.[3] The government provided inadequate capital and advice to the communities. In any event, some supporters of *ejidos* were less interested in their immediate economic performance than in moving toward proletarian government and socialist economics. But land distribution was stopped in 1930. Calles, for one, was convinced that it damaged production, both because the *ejidatarios* lacked incentive to work well and because it frightened out of agriculture persons with capital to pay for better production meth-

ods. This decision reinforced in the reform wing of the P.N.R. discontent with land policies after 1917.

In the mid-1920s and early 1930s the government created a few institutions with functions directly related to economic development. The Bank of Mexico was reestablished in 1925. Public works that ultimately were of great importance began in 1925 with creation of the Road Commission and the National Commission on Irrigation. The government established the National Agricultural and Stock Bank (1926) and the National Bank for Urban and Public Works Mortgages (1933). There was a modest increase of interest in national economic planning. Calles told Congress in 1928 that the time had come for "a program based on calculation." The government created a series of bodies that discussed the value of national planning: the National Economic Council (1928), a National Planning Commission that was approved in the National Planning Law of 1930, and a National Economic Council in 1933. All these public activities, especially those in banking, irrigation, and highway building, both increased the government's capacity to intervene in the economy and aided private enterprise. Both results exactly represented government policy from then to the 1970s: foster private enterprise while increasing government regulation and participation.

Although the government failed to bring the foreign petroleum companies under control, it did build national support for efforts to do so. Calles did not accept the Bucareli agreements of 1923 as the last word on the issue, and in late 1925 demanded that the petroleum companies exchange their titles for fifty-year leases. In the United States a minority cried for intervention. Negotiation failed to settle the matter, and that was one question that led to Dwight Morrow's appointment as ambassador late in 1927. He was an able negotiator on the petroleum as well as the church issue, even though he was identified with the North American big business and banking that Mexicans feared. In November 1927 the

---

[3] See Chapter 39, Sections a and d, for a discussion of this issue.

Supreme Court, on President Calles' orders, interpreted petroleum legislation in favor of the companies, and in 1928 Congress modified the law to the same effect. In the meantime, there had been changes in Mexican petroleum production. It grew enormously in the second decade of the twentieth century. In 1921 Mexico accounted for nearly 25 percent of world output. Then Mexican production declined in the 1920s, from about 200 million barrels in 1921 to only 33 million in 1932. The decline was partly the result of the world Depression but also of company concentration on other areas because of problems with Mexico over ultimate title, taxes, labor rights, and pay rates. The Mexican government was determined not only to assert its views and to align the industry according to national needs, but it believed that the production methods being used were damaging to the oil fields.

A remarkable social change wrought by the Revolution was in the national view of the Indian, who had been denigrated by most of the upper and middle class. The Revolution, in emphasizing the needs of common people and the resources of a revitalized nation, necessarily honored the rights and capabilities of people who were heavily Indian in bloodstock, and many of whom lived in a village culture impregnated with Indian and partially Indian artifacts, institutions, and habits of mind. The intellectuals and artists of the post-Revolution years glorified the culture of the preconquest Indians. Cuauhtémoc, who led the last Aztec resistance to Cortés at Tenochtitlán, became a national hero, while Cortés and the conquerors were condemned as exploiters. The archaeological record of ancient Indian achievement now was regarded as a great national heritage. Enthusiasts argued for encouragement of the native languages, methods of production, and other traits. *Indigenismo* became a cult, and some of its devotees believed that it would remain a major part of the revolutionary heritage. There was, however, some faddism and dilettantism in the movement. It did not eradicate prejudice against villagers among city dwellers, nor did its praise of indigenous culture cut interest in Western goods and culture. It did help the construction of nationalism, of archaeology and anthropology, and of a somewhat kindlier attitude toward village Indians.

Enthusiasts for modernization rested many of their hopes on education. Since much of the Porfirian educational system was destroyed in the Revolution, increasing the percentage of school-age children receiving instruction from 20 to 40 percent in 1924–1930 was a considerable achievement. Although the schools seldom could give more than rudimentary instruction for a year or so, the enthusiasm, commitment, and sense of experiment and community building that went into many of the efforts often were remarkable. Education for all was accepted as a shibboleth of the Revolution.

José Vasconcelos as minister of education under Obregón helped establish the infectious new educational spirit. A striking effort was directed to rural areas, which during the previous history of Mexico scarcely had known schools. Now when a rural school was called "the House of the People," it coupled egalitarianism with patriotism. Vasconcelos persuaded students of the higher schools in town to go into the villages as missionaries of the new national education. That had effects far beyond instruction in letters and reckoning. They organized community support, persuaded people to put up simple school buildings, and directly and indirectly taught Mexican nationalism. Many rural schools had affiliated programs: basketball, chicken raising, school gardens, adult education, vaccination campaigns, road building, community baths, bringing in the telegraph or telephone. Most of the rural teachers had little or no preparation, and partly to compensate for this the Vasconcelos administration developed cultural missions, which spent some weeks in a succession of villages, dispensing the advice of such personnel as nurses, agronomists, and teacher-training specialists. The spirit of this work shines in the 1928 report of an outgoing school committee in a small rural community. The report said the committee had "brought their grain of sand to the civilizing work" and "the sacred task" of education. It recounted their small deeds—a chicken coop, a lamp for the night school—and told the new committee that "the nation will honor you" for outdoing what had been done before.

There was exaggerated fear that the new federal school system was teaching Marxism and intended to introduce dangerous material on sexual matters, and there were some enthusiasts within and without the educational establishment who had such interests. In the early 1930s the archbishop of Mexico ordered Catholic parents not to send their children to lay secondary schools. Discussions of the value of sex education in the schools just at that time led to rumors that it had been instituted without notification. The government, in fact, had few funds for secondary schools, and parents with money, and often with political influence, insisted on using private, including church, institutions. There was even less money for higher education, which in the essentially preindustrial Mexico of the 1920s still could emphasize humanistic studies and law. The Latin American university reform movement had repercussions in Mexico, and in 1929 the government gave the national university partial autonomy. It became completely independent in 1934.

Labor organization was a social gain of those years, even though the leadership, as so often in Latin America, responded as much to government direction, which sometimes favored management, as to the needs of workers. At least now Constitution and government acknowledged that labor had rights. In the 1920s the CROM claimed nearly a million members, but not nearly that many were active in union affairs. Business interests claimed that the new syndicates and federations prepared the way for bolshevism. There were 310 important work stoppages in 1921. Then the federal government adopted a policy of compelling agreement, often on terms favorable to management, although labor made some gains. There were only five major strikes in 1929. For some years the labor law was

made by the states, and management complained that its variety was a burden. But when in 1925 serious discussion began of a federal labor law, management voiced fear of centralization. What it really cared about, of course, was an effective voice in setting the conditions of labor. The federal government understood that, and let discussion drag on for years. Such procrastination became typical of the method of the new rulers of Mexico—to give opposing interests time to vent their views and sufficient attention to permit some feeling of access to the legislative process.

The Federal Labor Law, finally promulgated in 1931, was a milestone on the road to implementation of the Constitution. Organized business made a concerted effort to get a favorable law. A new national Employers Association was founded by conservative businessmen from Nuevo León expressly for that purpose. Much of business, however, preferred not to become too closely identified with the notoriously right-wing and regionally oriented men of Monterrey in Nuevo León. The law of 1931 required employers to join in collective contracts with unions on request, prohibited lockouts, legalized the closed shop, restricted the right of employers to discharge workers, provided for government boards of conciliation and arbitration, provided for dismissal wages for workers fired without just cause and for pay for workers on strike legally. In the early 1930s labor organizational work was stimulated by the determination of PNR leaders to punish Morones. One new organization, created in 1932 by young Vicente Lombardo Toledano, was the General Confederation of Workers and Peasants. Lombardo Toledano was one of the new and more radical labor leaders who supported the reform program of the left wing of the PNR.

Many political, diplomatic, economic, and social developments directly or indirectly promoted national communication. There was much discussion and publication on many subjects, especially in Mexico City. Although the dominant political figures, and especially the presidents, thought prudence required that reform be gradual, there were lesser political figures, together with leaders in agrarian and labor interest groups, and artistic and intellectual circles, who were moved by what they considered the revolutionary spirit. So 1917–1934 does not come clear solely in statistics but must be seen also as a time of excitement, of dreams of a brave new world, of dedication to the spirit of the epic Revolution. Graft, corrupt politics, military arrogance, lack of funds for rapid social change could not quench the new spirit abroad in the land.

Although federal and state governments did interfere with publication, most such interference came on immediately pressing political issues and scarcely affected general debate. Nor did it affect the ferment in artistic and intellectual circles. The government supported the activities of a remarkable galaxy of artists, of whom Diego Rivera, José Orozco, and David A. Siqueiros were only among the more prominent. Much of their work was plastered on public buildings, so that its overtly "revolutionary" content was greatly in evidence. The work often was spectacular in color and form and violent or didactic in content. Popular themes were Mexican nationalism, xenophobia (often directed at the United States), the culture of the pre-Columbian Indians, the dignity of modern peasants, anticlericalism, communal effort, and Marxism triumphant over capitalism. The fame of the great muralists added something to the clamor for change in Mexico, although they had little influence in politics, and probably the common people scarcely looked at the astounding paintings that surrounded them.

The Six-Year Plan and an Election, 1933–1934

In the early 1930s there were accumulating grievances against the bossism of Calles, a feeling that his indifference to reform was betrayal of the Revolution, and concern that the world Depression required more dynamic leadership in

Mexico. The PNR was increasing its influence as members found it a useful forum and mechanism for coalition. In 1932 it was strengthened by abolition of the regional and local parties that had entered into the combination and by creation of more elaborate PNR machinery. Calles, aware of party restiveness, supported the adoption of a Six-Year Plan at the PNR convention in December 1933. That appealed to the advocates of increased government activity, who recently had displayed some interest in planning. It appealed also to the minority that was attached to Marxist ideas and to the larger number of political activists who had a general distaste for private enterprise.

The discussions of national planning in 1928–1933 had laid a base for discussion of the Six-Year Plan. It resembled the National Planning Law of 1930 in generality, lack of cohesion, and conception of a plan as a banner unfurled rather than as a technical instrument. It called for economic nationalism, a cooperative system, social justice (especially through agrarian reform), education, labor protection, irrigation, better transport, and improvements in production. It usually did not discuss matters in quantitative terms, but stated that it would be executed by the president with the party's cooperation. The plan really just imparted the framers' wish for economic development and justice. The discussion of issues was helpful in establishing the sociopolitical preconditions for self-sustained economic development, to use a terminology not then in existence.

President Rodríguez supported the Six-Year Plan, and put the government machinery behind the presidential nominee chosen by the convention, Lázaro Cárdenas of Michoacán. Cárdenas had fought in the Revolution and thereafter supported Obregón and Calles. He was head of the PNR briefly in the early 1930s and served in the cabinet. As governor of Michoacán he built a reputation as a member of the left wing of the PNR, but like his contemporary Franklin Roosevelt, he did not reveal before he became president the extent of his willingness to innovate. He spent more effort on his campaign, through wide travels and on the radio, than had previously been the practice, and that strategy later would be seen as an early indication of his intention to move the party's programs more toward the needs of the proletariat. In July 1934 Cárdenas was overwhelmingly chosen in a quiet election. No one dreamed that the frustrated aims of reformers were about to receive passionate reaffirmation from as great a leader as Benito Juárez.

33 Changes in Other Countries, 1890s–1930s

The trend of modernization was evident in those decades in Uruguay, Chile, Costa Rica, and Cuba. All four, furthermore, were heavily dependent on exports and hard hit by the world Depression of the 1930s. Their distaste for dependence or economic colonialism increased, and they reacted with doses of nationalism. Change was remarkable in Uruguay in terms of both social and political modernization, but most of the benefits accrued to the city population and to the *latifundistas*, leaving the rural proletariat little changed. Chile, with a larger and more complex society, became something of a Latin American pioneer in the development of labor organization and leftist political activity, but welfarism and political participation were less developed than in Uruguay, and the rural poor equally little touched. The promise of Costa Rican change in the late nineteenth and early twentieth centuries became by the 1930s a pattern of the politics of bargaining and compromise—by an active minority, with violence definitely subordinated—while literacy and egalitarianism, though limited, became better developed than in most of Latin America. Cuba became independent of Spain, strongly tied to the United States, and able to use a large income from exporting sugar for local consumption and some developmental purposes. Among the other twelve coun-

tries, Colombia and Peru felt the strongest pressures for modernization. The other ten republics bowed in lesser degree to the winds of change.

a. Chile

From Independence to the 1890s Chile had made one of the most successful Latin American adjustments to nineteenth-century problems, by reason of uninterrupted control by a substantially unified upper class. But Chile in the 1890s still was dominated by the old parties; labor organization had barely begun; industrialization was scanty and not a prominent object of public policy; and pressure for social legislation was feeble. The country was enjoying, however, the fruits of its conquests in the War of the Pacific and its superior political and educational systems. By World War I Chile was recognized as one of the ABC (Argentina, Brazil, Chile) "powers," which at least was a measure of its success in Latin American terms. By the 1930s the Socialist and Communist parties played a conspicuous role. Though still small minority groups, they united with the Radical party to elect a Radical to the presidency. By the 1930s the organized labor movement was firmly imbedded and more nearly independent of government control than in most of Latin America. Industry grew and in the 1920s began to benefit from a nationalist drive toward diversification and lessened dependence that received support from public funds. Social legislation of many types was passed, although the implementation was scanty. The dynamism displayed by Chilean society in those decades seemed to promise well for the future.

The Society

Population grew from about 2.8 million in 1889 to 4.7 million by 1938, with a quickening in the 1930s. Urbanization accelerated. By the late 1930s about 43 percent of the population lived in towns of more than 5,000 persons. Santiago, with a population of 330,00 in 1907, was a metropolis of over 800,000 by the late 1930s.

The great estates still controlled the countryside. In 1925 in the central provinces the 5,300 *fundos* of 494 acres and more had 89 percent of the farm land and the 76,000 other properties divided the rest. The peons—*inquilinos* in Chile—were poor, illiterate, subservient, allowed to use a bit of land on the *fundo* without hope of gaining their own. Small farmers lived with the fact that national financial policy and local credit were controlled by the oligarchy. The owners of *fundos*, especially through their control of the Senate, virtually had veto power over tax legislation. The *fundos* and small farms of Chile were still able to feed the country, even if prices were somewhat inflated by tariff protection. That capacity, however, was soon to end.

Nitrate exports continued important before and during World War I, were hurt by synthetics thereafter, then rose in the late 1920s from 1.5 to 3 million tons. Copper had waned late in the nineteenth century, due to foreign competition, then early in the twentieth was revived by new technology. Large United States mining interests acquired holdings, building a monopoly position that later was called the *Gran Minería*. Iron ore production began to fall under foreign control, as Bethlehem Steel in 1913 acquired a concession. Then in the 1930s mineral

exports were shattered by the great Depression. Chile's total exports fell from $473 million in 1929 to $274 million in 1930, with disastrous social and political effects. Then in 1932–1937 improving demand and government promotion raised export values more than 300 percent. But tempers were rising against dependence on mineral exports, their domination by foreign investors, and the fact that they were not large employers. Critics said that the *fundo* and the foreign monopolist smothered hopes of development in the national interest. Such views were not dominant in the 1930s, but they were stronger than in the 1890s; they soon would echo in every corner of Chile.

Industrial growth was modest, though more notable than in most of Latin America. The 1930 census showed that 33 percent of the gainfully employed were in industry, mining, and transport and communications. Aside from mineral operations and transportation, industrial growth centered in consumer goods, construction, and operations in support of them. By 1900 some plants employed 250 to 600 persons, notably foundries, machine shops, and operations in sugar, brewing, tobacco, and textiles. There were smaller plants in other lines. Some industries received tariff protection early in the twentieth century. This mild support, which went well back into the early days of the republic, was supplemented in the later 1920s by a new emphasis on government-propelled industrialization, under the nationalistic dictator Ibáñez. That policy received impetus from the great Depression, a landmark being creation in 1939 of the state's Chilean Development Corporation (CORFO). A great growth of government participation in the economy had begun.

Inflation, partly due to protective tariffs, has been noted as a problem with political aspects in the 1890s and early 1900s. It led in 1905 to a flare-up of protest, propaganda against large landowners, and a "Red Week" of riots in Santiago in which more than 300 people were killed. The riots involved armed aristocrats and lower-class mobs of stone throwers in a display of class war-

South America Today

International Boundaries

fare. The nitrate boom of World War I brought profits to some, but inflation of prices continued to hurt laborers. By 1919 protests against inflated food prices also included demands by intellectuals for agrarian reform to improve productivity and government price controls. The large foreign borrowing of the 1920s was useful for investment in infrastructure and other aspects of economic development, but it also contributed to inflation. By the 1930s there also was pressure on prices from government payments to the growing bureaucracy and the social security system. The oligarchic political elite in the 1920s began to take measures to control or subsidize food prices, a decision that enhanced the stability of the system.

The growing industrial population at the mines and in the cities increased its demands. It has been noted that labor organization began in the late nineteenth century with mutual aid societies and with anarchist influence, as in all Latin America. A struggle began between Marxists and anarchists and the influence of the former greatly increased in the twentieth century. Luís Recabarren, a labor organizer at the end of the nineteenth century, became a socialist and fought for Marxist influence in labor. Strikes in the 1890s, including the first general strike in 1890, signaled a new era. In 1905 worker protests in Santiago against exclusion of Argentine meat led to disorder. A 1907 miners' strike cost workers' lives. From 1911 to 1920 there were about three hundred strikes. In 1908 the Chilean Workers Federation was formed as a conservative employers' organization, but it turned militant, calling for the abolition of capitalism by the time of World War I. In 1919 it affiliated with the international communist union movement. Recabarren organized the Socialist Workers party in 1912, and the Communist party in 1920. Although labor organizations enrolled but a minority of workers, their direct pressures and political party support brought laws in 1924–1925 for such benefits as low-cost housing and insurance against sickness, disability, and old age. The Social Fund created to administer the sys-

tem was inadequate, but represented recognition of public responsibility for welfare.

Although labor organization and leftist political groups met much opposition from the old elites, they had more independence from government in Chile than in most of Latin America. They made notable advances with creation of the General Confederation of Labor in 1931 and the Socialist party in 1933. The communists and socialists were competing to control the labor confederation. Those leftist parties were minorities but better placed in a relatively open political system with more working-class participation than in most of Latin America.

In all this period, however, class lines and oligarchic control remained prominent features of the social landscape. New mineral, industrial, commercial, and financial fortunes, and a large growth of the middle class, created strains within the privileged minority, but the *fronda* (aristocratic branch, a common term in Chile) was well united on many issues.

Political discussion was promoted by good communications. The ruling element continued to support one of the better educational efforts in Latin America, especially in the towns, and literacy reached 56 percent in 1931, although little more than half the school-age children were receiving instruction. *Inquilinos* and rural laborers not only remained largely illiterate but scarcely participated in national life. *Rotos* (the broken or uprooted) increasingly moved from country to town, where they lacked influence. There was improvement of urban facilities, with electric streetcars, auto buses, sewage, lighting; and for a small minority mansions, theaters, museums, and improved secondary and higher education. Toward the end of the period the University of Chile achieved the autonomy that was the main goal of the Latin American student movement. All this and the accumulation of fine furnishings, clubs, beach resorts, and other amenities of culture and prosperity gave the upper and some of the middle class a pride in the achievements of the society that had a substantial basis.

The Parliamentary Republic to 1920

After the civil war of 1891,[1] the triumphant conservative foes of presidential power created a parliamentary system. It endured until a new Constitution was promulgated in 1925. Few fine words are lavished upon Chile's Parliamentary Republic. It tipped authority in favor of Congress, making the cabinet subject to the continuing approval of the legislature. In 1892–1925 there were more than 120 cabinets, an average of nearly four a year. It also encouraged a party fragmentation that was occurring in response to social change. The four major parties up to the 1890s became seven in that decade and more were added in the late 1920s and the 1930s.

The congressmen permitted only minor innovations by legislation. Although most of their active constituents agreed, some of the economic elite in nonagricultural activities wanted changes, as they had during the violence in 1891. They still resented the influence and proagricultural policies of the older families who owned *fundos*. Such differences among the economic elite should not be exaggerated, however, because *fundo* money had moved into other lines of endeavor, either through investment diversification or younger members' desire for new careers. Both this mingling of lines of investment and the general interest of the propertied in cautious socioeconomic policies gave the elites a common set of beliefs.

Control by the leaders of the parliamentary system was aided by the fact that few of the eligible literate males thought voting worthwhile. In the election of 1915, for example, only about 5 percent of the population was registered to vote, and a fifth of those did not cast ballots, so some 75,000 votes in a population of 3.5 million made the decision. Nevertheless, the larger, more urban, less agriculturally oriented population was being sensitized by instruction in school and by labor organizers and the leaders of small new leftist political parties. The working classes of Santiago in 1905 seized control of much of the

city for two days in violent protest against their weak access to the governmental and political processes in a time of rising prices. Possibly two hundred workers were killed as the government reestablished order. Other violence and strikes have been noted, indicating the likelihood that political changes would be attempted. The ruling elite made some concessions. The Congress passed the first workmen's compensation law (1916), an employment liability law (1917), and a railway retirement act (1919). Although the provisions of those acts were not generous, pressure for more was sure to follow. These developments were reflected in the 1918 congressional elections, when a Liberal Alliance that included Radicals, Liberals, and Democrats was successful enough to suggest a turning point in political affairs.

Arturo Alessandri, 1920–1924

Only two years later, in the presidential election of 1920, occurred what at the time seemed almost a revolution. In the second decade of the century, Arturo Alessandri, son of an Italian immigrant, changed from a conservative corporation lawyer into an ambitious leader of the dissatisfied. In 1912 he was elected senator from the mining district of Tarapacá, representative of a regional interest, and a friend of industrial labor. In 1920 he was presidential candidate of the Liberal Alliance, including the Radical and Democratic parties. The National Union put up Luís Barros Borgoño, a landowner of the old elite. His support included the Conservative and much of the old Liberal parties.

Alessandri's platform alarmed the old regime: state control of banks and insurance, rights for labor and its organizations, government control of nitrates, social legislation, and separation of church and state (to appeal to the anticlerical Radicals). Also alarming was his pioneering use of extensive campaigning, including appeal to a large segment of the population. He was a vigorous and dramatic man, known as the "Lion of Tarapacá," who aroused enthusiasm among classes that heretofore had paid little attention

---

[1] See Chapter 27, Section c.

to politics. Although Alessandri's chief electoral support came from the middle sectors, he seemed a rabble rouser to the old regime, especially when unemployment during the depression following World War I caused strikes and disorders, some of which had an element of support for Alessandri's candidacy. Miners' strikes shut down the railways and led to imposition of a state of siege.

Alessandri's biggest problem was that the rural oligarchy still could vote its clients as a bloc. The result was close. The Conservatives controlling the Congress selected a "Court of Honor" to study the returns. It reluctantly confirmed a narrow Alessandri victory, fearing disorder if it did not. He was inaugurated in December 1920. In March 1921 congressional elections gave the Liberal Alliance a majority in the Chamber of Deputies but left the Senate in Conservative hands. Alessandri asked for reform legislation: employment insurance, an income tax and higher land taxes, government control of banks and insurance, better living conditions for the popular classes, and an end to the Parliamentary Republic with restoration of presidential powers. His suggestions received little support in the Senate in the next few years. In 1924 it even refused to approve the next budget if an income tax was made a part of it. Alessandri turned to an effort to get new men elected to the legislature.

He not only campaigned for congressional supporters in 1924, but used force to corrupt the electoral process, which brought the Liberal Alliance a majority in both houses. Then the new legislators caused trouble by attending to their own compensation. There was nothing necessarily disruptive about that. The Constitution did not provide for pay for national legislators, because in 1833 the oligarchs who wrote the Constitution assumed that they would monopolize Congress. By the 1920s, however, men were elected who needed help if they were to serve properly. The Congress voted itself expense money, which was sensible; unfortunately, Congress was not sensible enough to pay attention also to the needs of other public servants. Army

officers, for example, suffered from inflation, and were angered that their problem was ignored. Anger at the Congress was increased also by its inability to agree on Alessandri's reform measures.

Even before the 1920s there were indications of growing interest in politics by military officers. Early in the twentieth century Chilean army officers founded a secret *Liga Militar* that was enough disturbed by the ineffectiveness of the parliamentary system to discuss a coup. A secret *Liga Naval* in 1912 discussed reform and a possible coup. A military conspiracy in 1919 was broken by government action. Such restiveness was in part the result of improving the education of officers, which increased their interest in national needs.

In 1924 a secret society of civilians and military called TEA (Tenacity, Enthusiasm, Abnegation) conspired against the government. At the same time, military officers in the Santiago area discussed their compensation problem, aware of recent political interventions by officers in other countries. On September 2–3 junior officers in the Senate gallery during debates on congressional salaries expressed their disapproval. On September 5 officers urged Alessandri to veto the congressional pay bill, and a military junta began to direct army political activity. By this time General Luís Altamirano headed the military group. The president did veto the pay bill. The Congress quickly voted higher military compensation and social insurance and labor reforms that Alessandri had been asking and which the protesting military officers favored. At this point Alessandri discovered that the military junta meant to remain in existence, so he resigned on September 8 in protest against a threat to the Constitution and his own powers. He soon left the country.

Dictatorship and Military Intervention, 1924–1931

A military junta headed by General Altamirano took over the executive branch and on September 11, 1924, closed the Congress. It appointed a ministry of civilians. All this happened without much protest in Chile. On January 22, 1925, another military coup put in a more radical junta, headed by two officers, Carlos Ibáñez and Marmaduke Grove, who were to be important in politics for some years. Ibáñez, a man in his forties, may have acted because his career was not progressing well; if such was the case, it illustrated one of the evils of military intrusion in public affairs. Grove turned out to have some fuzzy reform ideas and a talent for political showmanship. Communication with Alessandri abroad brought the reply that he would return only with reestablishment of civilian government, military withdrawal from politics, and preparation of a new Constitution. In response to this, on January 27 a new junta, headed by a civilian, was created to govern until Alessandri's return.

Alessandri was back in control of the government in March. A new Constitution of 1925 was adopted, which made certain that Congress could not depose ministers by censure and that the Congress would not have quite the stranglehold on the nation's finances that had contributed to the clash in Balmaceda's time. The Constitution also separated church and state, limited private property rights where necessary for community welfare, and turned the election of the president over to direct vote. Otherwise, Alessandri's return to power was not a success. Some worker enthusiasm for him disappeared when he met a strike in the nitrate mines with troops, and some workers were killed. Even more disturbing, Minister of War Ibáñez was promoting his own political ambitions, and Alessandri thought that he should resign. Unable to force Ibáñez out, Alessandri resigned himself in October 1925 and for a second time went into exile in Mussolini's fascist Italy, a choice of residence that critics deplored.

The military had subjected the political system to a faster and more irregular series of changes than it had known for nearly a century. Nor was it finished. Civilian Luís Borgoño took over as president, while the parties agreed on a rapid and illegal method of electing Emiliano

Figueroa president for a term beginning in December 1925. Workers protested this procedure with a two-day general strike that so disrupted economic life that the government declared a fifteen-day state of siege. A Congress had been elected in November, but it soon appeared that government revolved around Ibáñez, who continued as war minister, then added the posts of minister of government and vice-president. He ultimately forced Figueroa out in May 1927 and had himself "elected" president in an irregular procedure in which he received nearly all the votes, having no opponent. He set up an authoritarian regime, violating the guarantee of free speech and jailing and exiling labor leaders, conservatives, and other opponents. That regime continued until 1931. Some commentators gloss over his dictatorship because of his efforts at socioeconomic modernization. In any event, he often is regarded as the earliest Latin American practitioner of "national socialism" in its right-wing sense, or of "authoritarian reformism" or "democratic Caesarism."

Ibáñez believed in an active government making large expenditures. He built transportation and power facilities, urban services, and education. He spent considerable sums on the armed forces, both to modernize them and to keep them satisfied. Little of his activity had much direct bearing on agriculture. It was an expensive administration, and Ibáñez paid for his programs with foreign loans and investment in mining, especially from the United States, rather than trying the dangerous method of revising the tax system. At the time, many moderate reformers agreed with the scholar who said the Ibáñez regime was a "revolution that swept away the power of the oligarchy . . . and put government in the hands of the people." That was an exaggeration, because Ibáñez neither turned government over to the people nor found a way permanently to improve the economy or the social system. He did increase support for government participation, stimulate the spirit of nationalism, and increase the national debt.

With the beginning of the world Depression in 1929, loans dried up and export income withered. By 1931 a large part of government revenue went to debt service. In 1930 Ibáñez tried a government monopoly of sales (but not ownership) in nitrates as a way to hold up prices, but the Compañía de Salitre de Chile (COSACH) was unable to control world production and marketing. Ibáñez's larger problem was that people who were hurt by loss of jobs and reduced public services naturally blamed him for their troubles. On July 26, 1931, he resigned under pressure from strikes and protest movements, involving workers, students, and even physicians and lawyers.

There followed more than a year of unstable government reminiscent of 1924–1927. The Senate named an interim president and set elections for October. Before they took place, there was a naval mutiny in September protesting conditions in the service. Communists exploited the affair, increasing fears that order was breaking down. In October a Conservative, Juan Montero, defeated Alessandri for the presidency. He took office in December and presided over six months of turbulence, until ousted in June 1932 by a military-civilian coup led by Colonel Marmaduke Grove and Carlos Dávila, a civilian. Dávila was for economic growth through government participation but with retention of private enterprise. Grove was a non-Marxist with some socialistic ideas and the notion that he should be running the country. They dissolved the Congress and declared a "socialist republic," which in fact never existed. They decreed reforms they could not enforce or pay for in a country wracked by disorder. A military coup in September was soon succeeded (October 1932) by a presidential election in which Grove ran second to Alessandri.[2]

Alessandri Again, 1932–1938

Alessandri was elected by the half of the literate males who bothered to vote. Now he represented the center parties, having come to believe that reform was less important than social peace. His administration was authoritarian. He harassed his political opponents, especially socialists and communists. He offended the Radicals by preferring to give office to Conservatives and Liberals. He permitted in 1933–1935 a so-called Republican Militia that declared itself the enemy of dictatorship. It seemed, however, to be mostly concerned about leftism and was itself accused of fascism. Alessandri protected it for a time against army disapproval. He did not have a great deal of trouble with labor until 1936, but then strikes became widespread. Alessandri gave the army control of the railways, proclaimed a state of siege, dismissed Congress, and banished labor leaders. In the congressional elections of 1937 Alessandri used government power against "subversives." Such actions brought into being a strong center-left movement against the administration. A different sort of suppression, but indicative of the disorder of the 1930s in Chile, was the smashing of the little Nazi rising of 1938, led by a native German fascist and ever-hopeful Carlos Ibáñez.

Economic policy was conventional, directed by Minister of Finance Gustavo Ross, who became for the leftist opposition a symbol of return to oligarchic domination. Ross believed that what was good for private enterprise was good for Chile. Under his guidance, exports rose from 290 million pesos in 1932 to 948 million in 1937, and nationalists were pleased by abolition of COSACH, which they connected with foreign control. Some of the economic improvement was channeled to social security measures, and employment improved slightly; on the other hand, the cost of living rose, and many Chileans remained in a precarious social condition, which the left hoped would bolster its political prospects.

The Popular Front, 1936–1938

The idea of a popular front was promoted by the 1935 decision of the Soviet Union's Comintern that communist parties throughout the world

---

[2] Alessandri got 183,744 votes from center groups, including Radicals and the left of the Liberals; Grove, the Socialist, 60,261; Rodríguez, Conservative, 45,267; Zañartu, Agrarian and many Liberals, 42,273; Lafferte, Communist, 4,621.

should collaborate with leftist and center parties against the menace of fascism. The most famous popular fronts were formed in Spain and France. Both the Communist party and the Radicals of Chile claim to have initiated the front there. In any event, it was furthered by Alessandri's repressive actions in 1936. The Communists made a major contribution to the idea by bringing in the Radicals, essentially a center party, though with a wing considerably to the left of Alessandri. The Radical party in early 1936, praising the popular front idea, declared that the party recognized the "battle of the classes," favored "proletarian revindication," and "justice and liberty" for the humble. These goals did not make it Marxist, as some conservatives claimed. There was not only Radical party dissatisfaction with Alessandri's policies, but it was ambitious to elect a president of its own, and the Communists agreed to promote that. The Chilean Popular Front came into existence in 1936 as an alliance of the Radicals, Communists, Socialists, Democrats, Democratic Socialists, and the new Confederation of Chilean Workers (C.T.Ch.). It was a powerful center-left combination against the right, but inherently unstable.

Congressional elections in 1937 made the Front seem more attractive to major elements in it: the Radicals because their 19 percent of the vote was the lowest since 1912; the Socialists and Communists because their 11 and 4 percent, respectively, represented a big increase. All the Front groups accounted for about 40 percent of the vote in the 1937 election. It was, therefore, with much optimism that in April 1938 a National Convention of the Left met, with delegates assigned thus: Radicals, 400; Socialists, 300; Communists, 160; Democráticos, 120; C.T.Ch., 120. The Socialist Grove had enough support to prevent a decision but finally withdrew, and the convention nominated the Radical Pedro Aguirre Cerda. He was a wealthy man, not of the left wing of the Radicals, and originally had opposed their collaboration in the Front. In 1922 as a senator he had introduced a bill authorizing expropriation or purchase of land to be sold for one-family farms. In 1929 in exile he wrote a book, *The Agrarian Problem*. His ideas on agrarian reform may have been sound, but they were middle class, not leftist.

The Popular Front put on a vigorous campaign, aided by the fact that the administration conservatives nominated Gustavo Ross, which gave the impression that they rejected any thought of innovation. Aguirre Cerda barely squeaked out a victory, although the Front upped its percentage of the total vote to 50.6. The Popular Front victory was hailed as a great surge forward for the left. That was an exaggeration. Much of Aguirre's support was middle class, and he was far from a leftist himself. Clearly striking, however, was a great increase in the vote—nearly half a million men cast ballots. Political mobilization or activism certainly surged upward in 1938. The left had increased its role in national politics, and the fallout would be felt in every future campaign, although its full effects would not shake the country for another thirty years.

b. Uruguay: Batlle and the Great Transformation, 1903–1930

Uruguay, it has been noted, benefited in the nineteenth century from large European immigration, educational development, and promising growth of exports. By 1900, however, there was little indication of the economic, social, and political transformation that occurred during the following decades. Much of the astonishing change was due to the political genius of José Batlle y Ordóñez. Born in 1856 of a distinguished family, he received a good education, and the liberal ideas and associations of his university days remained important to the end of his life. In 1886 he opened the newspaper *El Día* and made it, like other Uruguayan newspapers, into a highly partisan journal, mouthpiece of Batlle's ideas and ambitions until his death in 1929. He early adopted the view of many educated Latin Americans that progress depended primarily on eradication of political violence and *caudillismo*. No Latin American achieved so much of this goal as José Batlle y Ordóñez. He did it by persistent attention to practical politics, with the aim of creating a party strong enough to insist on what he wanted. Batlle was an idealist whose feet were firmly planted in reality.

The nation he set out to transform was small: only 1 million people in 1902, in a territory slightly larger than England and Scotland. Its economy was heavily dominated by pastoral exports, shipped from great estates through the port of Montevideo, whose 300,000 people included most of the important people of the republic, even the important ranchers when in residence in their town houses. In this small society all the leading figures were acquainted, and ran the republic without admitting much advice from the populace. The *Blanco,* or Nationalist, party had modified its resort to violence—without giving up its arms—by accepting virtual autonomy in six of the nineteen departments into which the supposedly centralized republic was divided.[3] The *Colorados*—Batlle's party—were somewhat more progressive than the *Blancos,* but generally willing to govern by making deals with the opposition. They were badly divided and primarily concerned with patronage and personal privilege rather than the welfare of the country. Batlle decided that the progress that had been made since the early days of almost constant politicomilitary brawling was not enough. He set out to change his own party, and irked many of its leaders by his insistence. His position in the *Colorados* was not assured when he was elected president by a narrow margin in 1903 by the Congress, a handful of politicians in a country where a not much bigger handful of the literate males voted for the legislators.

One of Batlle's convictions was that he had to end the cozy habit of buying off the opposition with autonomy in part of the departments and with positions in the government so that they would not revolt. The Nationalists were led by

General Aparicio Saravia, an upper-class but uncultivated gaucho with a fabulous history in the political warfare of the nineteenth century. When Batlle began to appoint *Colorados* in the Nationalist departments, Saravia saw his action not only as a political but as a military threat and prepared to revolt. The Nationalists demanded even greater autonomy in "their" departments, while Saravia prepared his gaucho army. Batlle strengthened the national army, which the Nationalists considered a provocation. Although even today there is some debate as to which side was responsible for the war, the predominant view is that Batlle stood for sensible government and modernization and that Saravia was merely a dinosaur left over from a social age that needed to be buried. As much as anything, the cause was the Nationalists' hostility to Batlle's purposes and their fear that he meant to carry them out.

The war lasted eight months and involved heavy casualties. It was not simply a war between Montevideo and the interior, since men from both were in the two armies, including ranchers, university students, and even divided families. Nor was it a class war. Rather, it was a war between parties and political systems, even if only Batlle and his closest colleagues were fully aware of his aims. The Nationalists got military supplies from Brazil and Argentina, which bordered their positions in northern and western Uruguay. President Roca of Argentina and others in his country favored the Nationalists, and Batlle became blunt in his demands that Argentines cease interfering in Uruguayan affairs. When Batlle was losing, some Argentines said that he should agree to mediation to end suffering. Batlle said that if he were forced to mediate, he would try to bring the United States into the process, something the Argentines did not relish. Batlle also had to resist the demands of well-to-do groups and other peace mongers in his own country that he owed it to profits and humanity to end the fighting with a negotiated peace. Batlle insisted on complete victory, on much the same grounds as Abraham Lincoln during another Civil War,

---

[3] See Chapter 28, Section a. Both parties had considerable representation in both city and *campo,* although the *Colorados* were especially strong in Montevideo.

and he was similarly criticized by the small-minded and pusillanimous for what they called his "implacability."

With the end of the war, Batlle insisted on maintaining the strength, loyalty, and efficiency of the army, a policy which the Nationalists naturally condemned as provocative, the attitude of the *caudillo* toward the modernizer who stood for such iniquities as political decision by ballot rather than bullet. Batlle was even accused of militarizing Uruguay, when the exact opposite was to be one of his greatest achievements. Batlle also ended the system of assured control of some departments by Nationalists, which they, of course, recognized as threatening their state within the state, with its lines into Argentina and Brazil. Batlle also insisted on government by *Colorados*, ending not all the Nationalists' patronage but their ability to hamstring decision making at the top. He accompanied these policies with a few suggestions for socioeconomic change that gave him a reputation among conservatives as a dangerous radical. Finally, he imposed his will, through his friends, on the *Colorado* party. His power was based on political skill, not on interest group support: the rich and middle classes were dubious about him; the lower class was unorganized.

Batlle was tolerable to many conservatives for several reasons. For one thing, his political skill and determination were so formidable that to stand in his way required resolution. For another, he was a careful administrator and conservative on finances, even during the war. Also, he was interested in developing the economy through private business (as well as through public enterprise) and wanted foreign capital, but preferred to control it in the national interest. When, immediately after the war, Saravia's family and others prepared for armed combat again, the Rural Association and the Manufacturers' Association warned that they were against a revolt. Finally, although Batlle insisted on national government control of the departments, he did not interfere with socioeconomic domination of the countryside by the great estate owners.

Not many of Batlle's numerous ideas for change were enacted into law in his administration of 1903–1907. Some were not even introduced into the legislature but promoted in the pages of *El Día*. He did, however, propose enough innovations so that his enemies spoke of a "veritable rain of projects." The most important things he did were to fasten the control of the *Colorados* on the country and his leadership on the party. He had a genius and indefatigable appetite for political maneuver. He was the example par excellence of that rare breed: the true reformer and complete political professional in one. He put men he could rely on every place he could and was a sound judge of his fellows. For president Batlle picked university rector Claudio Williman, leaving him in charge in 1907–1911, while he himself toured Europe. Batlle was especially impressed with the orderly prosperity of Switzerland, thinking it largely due to its collegiate executive. When he went back to Uruguay just before the next election, to be president again (as generally expected), Batlle carried with him the notion that if the executive power of Uruguay were put in a committee, *caudillismo* would be yet more submerged, and peace and well-being would follow.

The accomplishments of Batlle are not to be found merely in his administrations of 1903–1907 and 1911–1915, but in his influence between terms and in the years thereafter to his death in 1929. He retained enormous influence, which he used constantly as a party leader, proprietor of *El Día*, and as a government official. He was elected president of the national administrative council in 1920 and in 1926. The influence of *batllismo* can be treated as political, governmental, economic, and social. In the political and governmental realms, the *Colorados* remained the dominant party throughout Batlle's lifetime and long thereafter. Elections were fair, the press free, and the army apolitical. The government constantly added functions, which led to a notable increase in the bureaucracy. In 1913 Batlle resumed a plan earlier announced for constitutional reform, to include the collegiate executive.

It met strong objection and became part of a new Constitution only in 1917. It went into effect in 1919, as a compromise dividing executive powers between the president and a National Council of Administration. The new Constitution also ended the old system of congressional election of the president and submitted the choice directly to the voters. It provided the secret ballot and made registration obligatory. It established a system of proportional representation, similar to the reform in Argentina, whereby the first and second parties in the vote received, respectively, two-thirds and one-third of the seats in the Congress and in the administrative council. These changes, together with growth of schools and freedom for parties and interest groups, including organized labor, soon led to a great increase in popular participation in the political process. It was representative, however, of Batlle's caution that he did not much tamper with the old tax system, leaving the country heavily dependent on indirect taxes and customs levies and notably deficient in income taxes or imposts on land. This, of course, avoided tension with the *hacendados* and other well-to-do, who affected great shock at even the modest increases in their taxes that were suggested.

Uruguay prospered in those years. The pastoral industry became even more dominant, while agriculture grew slowly and much of it remained primitive. Agricultural products accounted for only 10 percent of the value of exports in 1938. Pastoral exports boomed. Sheep had been fewer than 1 million in the mid-nineteenth century, but reached 19 million in 1900 and 26 million by 1908, their peak population. Cattle went from fewer than 2 million in the mid-nineteenth century to over 8 million in 1908, near the peak of their number in Uruguay to the present. In 1903–1907 there was a great increase in the number of pedigreed sheep and cattle, further indicating investment in the pastoral industry. Big ships coming for Uruguay's exports still had to be handled by lighter at Montevideo in 1902, but a French company was building modern docks.

Free trade grew from 5 million pesos in 1902 to 72 million in 1907 and continued upward to World War I. The first modern meat-packing and refrigeration plant—*frigorífico*—opened operations in 1904. Wool, however, rather than meat remained the most important export. These developments considerably increased the value of land, which was mostly kept in large holdings and lightly taxed. When Batlle in 1904 proposed a tiny rise in the land tax, the Nationalists were perturbed less by the immediate impact—insignificant—than by the president's statement that society, not landowners, was responsible for rises in land values. This idea, that Batlle got partly from single-taxer Henry George, he did not try to carry out.

Industry grew modestly, with some tariff protection, although tariffs were largely for revenue. In 1931, at the beginning of the Depression, the country adopted stronger industrial promotion measures, together with many Latin American countries. But Uruguay did not have the resources or markets to establish much industry.

Although Batlle's friends doubted that he knew anything about economics, he did know that he disliked foreigners sending profits out of the country. He made foreign trolley and railroad companies build ahead of traffic to meet coming needs, thus avoiding one problem that plagued Buenos Aires. In his first administration he supported nationalization and expansion of the Montevideo municipal electric power system. In his second administration he expanded the state monopoly of electric power to the rest of the country. The nationalization of the British-owned railroads was begun in this period but not completed until 1948. From 1915 on, the government was involved in chemical production. In 1916 a state corporation was formed to manage the port of Montevideo. In 1928 a government meat-packing plant was set up as a yardstick to ensure decent prices to stock raisers. In 1911 the Bank of the Republic was converted into a state enterprise. In 1912 a State Mortgage Bank was created; also a State Insurance Bank, which competed with the private industry, with various advantages including tax exemptions. The notion of

New Technology and Production

Some aspects of economic modernization were especially obvious, even dramatic.

The day the first electric streetcar started operating in São Paulo, Brazil—May 7, 1900. Replacement of the old horse-drawn vehicles was badly needed in such rapidly growing cities.

Steamboats on Río Magdalena, Colombia, in recent years. This area is one of those where the steamship has been very important to internal traffic. International shipping has, of course, greatly affected all of Latin America. *Organization of American States*

On a banana plantation run by the United Fruit Company in Honduras, the crop is protected by plastic bags. Even so poor a country has some modern elements. *Peter Menzel*

A big mining operation in the bleak mountains of Mexico. The grim shacks of the miners and their families on the slope have their counterparts in other countries —Peru, Bolivia, Chile. *Courtesy of National Railways of Mexico*

batllistas that state enterprise was a way of gaining freedom from foreign domination was one reason for the founding of some costly public enterprise.[4]

Changes in the social realm had by the 1930s made Uruguay into what many people considered the most progressive nation in Latin America. Literacy went from about 46 percent in 1900 to 55 percent in 1907 and continued upward thereafter. It was much higher in Montevideo than in the countryside until the 1920s, when the first serious effort at rural education began. Freedom of speech was respected. Organized labor was protected and grew from almost nothing in 1900 to a sturdy condition by the late 1930s. Batlle's *El Día* defended socialist "agitators" and strikes. In his first administration Batlle advocated shorter work hours, time off for expectant mothers, and accident insurance. The eight-hour day was granted in 1915. Insurance for accidents, retirement, and old age was a fact by the 1930s, and this social security system especially set Uruguay off from most of Latin America. Neither social security nor education, however, extended much beyond Montevideo. Batlle and his successors modernized the metropolis, and left later generations to worry about the *campo*.

El Día in Batlle's first administration supported complete separation of church and state as part of an eventual constitutional reform, and it appeared in the Constitution of 1917. Batlle was so anticlerical that at one point during his presidency he declared that there was a church plot against the government. The church in Uruguay, however, had about as little influence as in any country of Latin America.

By the 1930s the population of the country was over 2 million and Montevideo a metropolis

of 700,000. Population growth was slow, both because of a low birthrate and because of immigration lag in the late nineteenth and early twentieth centuries. Although only 8,000 immigrants came in 1902, in the next twenty-eight years net average annual immigration was 15,000, a considerable number, although far from the floods going into Argentina. Immigration was virtually eliminated after 1930, when the Depression led to restrictions.

The world Depression of the 1930s had a devastating effect on the little export-oriented country. Shipments fell to as low as 20 percent of their former value. *Blanco* leader Alberto de Herrera planned a coup, but before he could act President Gabriel Terra in 1933 decided that the economic crisis required him to overturn the governmental system with the aid of the military. He dissolved Congress and the executive council. Terra declared that the country could not be governed in an emergency with divided executive powers, so he had a constitutional convention abolish the council. The Constitution of 1934 also made voting compulsory for both sexes (women got the vote in 1932), and included the social benefits incorporated in the 1917 Constitution and later legislation. Terra extended his presidency to 1938 by vote of the constituent assembly. His authoritarian tendencies were mild, not much affecting the system of free politics and government that had been established. The partial *colegiado* was restored in the next administration. Terra's actions were a reminder, however, that the real test of a system comes in times of stress.

In the later 1930s the economy recovered somewhat. Impressive political and social modernization and relatively high levels of living came partly because the small and compact and homogeneous population had good communications that permitted development of a sense of common purpose. It was not strange that foreigners called Uruguay the Switzerland of America. Montevideo deserved such a title, and few knew that another nation lay beyond the city.

---

[4] In 1931 the government created ANCAP (National Administration of Combustibles, Alcohol, and Cement), and in 1937 it completed a modern refinery and went on to enlarge operations. In 1937 the state opened a fishing enterprise, involving boats, an ice plant, and door-to-door delivery. This does not exhaust the list of state regulation and activity in the economy.

c. Costa Rica

The social change that began so quietly before the 1890s in Costa Rica became marked thereafter. The precise character of the social and economic elements involved in the change have been argued for years. Export income from coffee and bananas continued to provide a modest but regular public and private revenue that was better used than in much of Latin America, if only because so little went to military purposes and so much to education. The country remained heavily agricultural, and an unusually large number of persons owned land. The fact was, however, that many of the landholdings were *minifundios,* too small to support a family decently, so that the owners worked part-time in town or for larger landholders. The banana business contributed nothing to egalitarianism, small landholding, or the income of most Costa Ricans. Although the coffee growth that began in the 1830s benefited mainly a small group, more coffee was grown on small and medium holdings than in most of Latin America.

A mark of Costa Rican differentiation was a higher proportion of people in the middle class by the 1930s than in most Latin American countries. Much of what constituted middle-classness in Costa Rica was a matter of education, attitude, aspiration, and relative lack of class consciousness rather than of differences of property. As literacy continued to grow after the 1890s, it increased awareness that material aspiration was not being well met by achievement. Incomes and material existence were modest by the 1930s, even though better than in such places as Guatemala or Bolivia. In 1927 more than 60 percent of the work force still was in agriculture and only 8 percent in industry. There was pressure on resources due to rapid population growth, from some 60,000 in 1821 to 472,000 in 1927. A notable fall in the deathrate began in the 1930s. The effects of this population growth were accentuated by the fact that people were concentrated in a part of the *meseta central,* the central highlands, and much national territory was poorly used or idle.

The literacy rate by the 1930s was higher than in any Latin American nations but Argentina, Uruguay, and Chile, and Costa Ricans were noting with pride that they had more schoolteachers than soldiers. Still, the little land of the *Ticos* was far from a paradise, and they were becoming increasingly aware of it. The fact was that disparities of wealth began increasing in the 1890s, and socioeconomic problems were less well handled than political.

After the 1890s there was less violence in politics in Costa Rica than in most places in Latin America. Presidents generally served out their four-year terms. Freedom of speech, assembly, and the press were good by Latin American standards. Parties and nominations still were handled by the oligarchy, and fraud and some unconstitutional actions occurred in elections. This is not to deny the progress, but to explain that lack of participation was so great that in the 1920s and 1930s it became a part of a new cry for reform.

There was a rebellion in 1918 by War Minister Federico Tinoco Granados, but he soon resigned because he received little support. From then until the 1940s the results of elections generally were well accepted with little discussion of unconstitutional seizures. But opinion forming in favor of reform was strongly evident in the 1920s in General Jorge Volio's Reform party. In 1930 the Communist party was organized as the *Bloque de Obreros y Campesinos* (Workers and Peasants Bloc) by Manuel Mora Valverde, a twenty-year-old law student. It operated throughout the 1930s, frightening some of the upper class. On the whole, however, it was accepted as a domestic reform group and sometimes referred to under the label of *comunismo criollo* (creole communism). In 1934 the communists organized a strike in the banana zone that won some wage concessions for the workers. The violence involved in the strike upset the oligarchy, and in the presidential campaign of 1935–1936 León

Cortés Castro, candidate of the National Republican party, made the communists the main issue as alien and against the family, religion, and Costa Rica's historical ideas. At this time the National Republican party was given a firmer structure, so that it did not entirely disappear between elections. That was another sign of movement in the political process, the ephemeral nature of political parties being one of their principal stigmata in Latin America, especially before the 1930s.

Some recognition of the need for change was given in 1924 with erection of the National Bank of Insurance (after 1948 the National Institute of Insurance) with a monopoly on each type of insurance as it became capable of handling it. This was designed not only to provide lower rates, but to keep the insurance business inside Costa Rica, so it indicated both social progressiveness and nationalism. The insurance business was late developing in Latin America generally, and Costa Rica was rather early in turning to this measure for combatting economic colonialism. Modernization also was evident in the establishment in 1933 of a minimum wage and in congressional criticism in 1934 of United Fruit Company labor practices in the coastal banana zones. By the time Rafael Calderón Guardia was elected president by the National Republican party for the term 1940–1944, the country was ready for a greatly expanded discussion of the deficiencies of Costa Rican society. His administration became a dividing point in the history of the country, but it built upon changes from the 1890s to the 1930s.

d. Cuba to the 1930s: The "Independent" Protectorate

Spain retained Cuba as a colony because it could concentrate military forces there and because well-to-do Cubans preferred a connection with conservative Spain, partly to protect black slavery. Possibly a million Africans were carried to Cuba during its history, more than half of them in the nineteenth century. By 1817 the colored population outnumbered the white. Final eradication of slavery did not occur until 1886. During all those years a considerable stream of Spanish immigration flowed to Cuba.

The most important economic development was the growth of export sugar. Shipments went from 50,000 tons in 1820 to 726,000 in 1870 and continued upward thereafter, reaching 1 million in 1894. Mechanization of the sugar industry began in the 1820s in Cuba, increasing capital requirements, but many plantations remained small until the 1880s, when the great *centrales* began to change the industry into one dominated by a few giant enterprises. Since the 1790s there had been discussion of the relative merits of monoculture and diversification, but nothing stopped the consolidation of the great sugar estates.

The Problem of Independence to 1898

Until the mid-nineteenth century, Cuban agitation for independence was weak. Then a rebellion in Spain in 1868 against the miserable regime of Isabella II sparked a Cuban revolt for independence, which became the great Ten Years' War that went on savagely until 1878. Cuban exiles in the United States raised men and supplies to send to the rebels. Spain at the end of the rebellion promised amnesty, government reform, and emancipation of the slaves, but did not perform well in any of those areas. Exiles in the United States plotted more rebellion. One was Jose Martí, who became a revolutionary in his teens in Cuba. A journalist in the United States, he wrote with idealism and eloquence of Cuban freedom. His nationalism sometimes took the form of warnings about the United States, as in 1891: "The scorn of our formidable neighbor, who does not know us, is the greatest danger for our America," meaning that a lack of respect might lead to intervention. When a great rebellion began in Cuba in 1895, with aid from Martí and fellow exiles in the

United States, he went to his homeland to serve, and was killed. He became the most honored of all Cuba's sons and a herald of nationalism throughout Latin America.

The rebels destroyed crops and buildings. The Spaniards set up concentration camps (*reconcentrados*), pushing people into restricted areas so they could not aid the rebels. There was much suffering in the *reconcentrados*, which seemed to North Americans warfare against women and children. Opinion turned strongly against Spain. Some statesmen, businessmen, and church missionaries also welcomed the possibility of exerting United States strength for a variety of strategic, political, economic, moral, and religious purposes. United States investment in Cuba had grown in recent years. Washington kept prodding Spain to make concessions to the rebels. General "Butcher" Weyler of concentration camp notoriety was recalled in 1897, but by that time the issues of Spanish cruelty and tyranny had become deeply entangled in United States opinion.

It was a serious political issue for President McKinley, with some people insisting that he could negotiate a settlement, others declaring that he was permitting atrocities on the nation's doorstep. Congress pushed for recognition of the belligerency of the rebels. All sorts of negotiations and exchanges of views occurred between Madrid and Washington. The final efforts of the United States early in 1898 to persuade Spain to make concessions in Cuba always will be argued about. Spain finally agreed to nearly everything McKinley asked. It did so slowly, however, and after so many proofs of unreliability that McKinley took the ground that the promises were unworthy of trust. He also faced the problem that independence, which Spain had not promised, now was the only thing that would satisfy either the rebels in Cuba or many interested parties in the United States. So in April 1898 he asked Congress for a declaration of war.

The Cuban rebels had inflicted severe damage on Spain by that time and would have preferred to finish the war with only logistical aid from the United States. That was politically impossible in Washington, which was under pressure to grapple directly with a problem now thought worthy of war. The Spanish forces proved weak and the war soon was over, though not before frictions had arisen between Cuban and North American military personnel. The peace treaty gave independence to Cuba.

The Protectorate of 1898–1934: Political Aspects

Important individuals in the United States wanted to do well by the Cubans and by United States economic and strategic interests, believing those things compatible. We cannot know what mixtures of conviction, ignorance, cynicism, and naiveté were involved in each case. Some intelligent and responsible United States citizens thought that Cubans needed guidance. A temporary military government was set up. It disarmed the revolutionists, after some acrimonious differences of opinion, distributed aid, helped the public services, and provided a structure until a Cuban system could be erected. One considerable service was eradication of yellow fever, by carrying out work based on the discovery of the Cuban Carlos Finlay that it was transmitted by mosquitoes.

The Cubans selected a constitutional convention and early in 1901 produced a document. It appeared that European cynics who did not believe United States self-denying declarations were about to be disappointed, but as it turned out they were half-right: independence was permitted, but with strings attached. The Cuban constitutional assembly was presented with demands known as the Platt Amendment, which made of Cuba a protectorate by limiting its powers over treaties and its own finances and giving the United States the right to intervene in Cuba to preserve its independence or to maintain an "adequate" government. It also pledged naval stations to the United States and stipulated that the status of the Isle of Pines had yet to be determined.[5] Under protest, the Cubans put those provisions into the Constitution, and later into a treaty in 1903.

Politics fell at once into the hands of the leaders of the fight for independence. Tomás Estrada Palma was elected president for the term 1902–1906 and reelected for the next in a fraudulent proceeding. The regime was soon threatened by revolt, leading Estrada Palma to appeal to the United States. President Roosevelt sent William Howard Taft to persuade the factions to agree. That failing, Roosevelt sent Charles Magoon to serve as president, which he did until an election in 1909 seated José M. Gómez, a general in the independence struggle. Although Magoon was an honest and reasonably able man, Cuban historians understandably condemn the intervention. Those who accuse him, however, of inventing for Cubans the padding of public payrolls overlook the fact that Spaniards and Spanish Americans had excelled at such practices for centuries.

A fraudulent election in 1917 caused a revolt, and United States troops were landed. In 1921 Woodrow Wilson forced on Cuba an "advisor," General Enoch Crowder, who sedulously fought graft in the Cuban bureaucracy. It was not difficult to find (nor unknown in the United States). Such actions by the United States only briefly and locally affected Cuban practices. Some of the motivation for intervention was laudable, but it also was supported by economic groups in the United States whose chief interest was not in public administration. Both the fact of Crowder's intervention and the existence of a United States business interest in it became subjects for Cuban complaint. That was not diminished when Crowder was made ambassador to Cuba.

The administration of Gerardo Machado (1925–1933) showed the futility of intermittent supervision of Cuban administration, when the underlying attitude of Cuban leaders toward government remained unchanged. Machado was corrupt, wasteful, and brutal. The slowness of United States interest groups or government to react against Machado's dictatorship increased Cuban resentment of tutelage. It remains today one of the chief items in the Cuban communist condemnation of the protectorate. When sugar prices fell with the coming of the Depression in 1929–1930 and economic distress added to other objections to Machado, armed groups including students and professors began trying to overthrow him. Machado was increasingly brutal in his countermeasures. Now the United States declined to intervene and was accused of protecting tyranny by inaction. The fact was that government in Washington had been backing away from intervention in Latin America for several years but did not yet properly appreciate that an intrusive power will be accused of intervention whether it acts or not. The best defense is not to be there.

The new president, Franklin Roosevelt, in May 1933 sent Sumner Welles to try to force a change. The dissidents became more active. There was a general strike in August. Then the army turned on Machado, and he fled. Cubans had ousted the dictator themselves, with no more than minor United States criticism of Machado. After a brief provisional presidency, in September some young radicals met at the main army base outside Havana with representatives of the enlisted men of the army, dominated by Sergeant Fulgencio Batista. The latter, who had been preparing his organization for some time, proceeded to oust nearly all the important officers of the army and put in his own friends. This group took over Havana, and a group of five leftists assumed authority and named Batista a colonel and chief of the army. Welles is said to have been "stunned" by this development and called on Washington to intervene with troops, but Roosevelt decided against it. As it turned out, Batista

---

[5] Although Cuba was obligated to permit the United States to annex four naval stations, only two were taken, as leaseholds, and one of those was returned in 1912, leaving Guantánamo the sole United States enclave on the island. An agreement giving Cuba the Isle of Pines was concluded almost at once, but intrigues by speculators in the United States held up ratification until 1925, although it was administered as Cuban territory during all those years.

did not represent the rise of radical enlisted men in Latin American military politics. He merely happened to be a sergeant with the attitudes of an officer, and when he attained the latter eminence, acted like other Latin American military politicians. He was not followed by a wave of ambitious sergeants, because enlisted men of Batista's knowledge, ability, drive, and good luck are rare.

By September 10, 1933, the civilian aspect of government was in the hands of one member of the junta, Dr. Ramón Grau San Martín, physician and professor, long an idol of leftist university students. He proclaimed a socialist revolution. Washington refused to recognize him and stationed naval vessels off the coast. Urged by Washington, Batista ousted Grau in January 1934. Batista then quickly offered successive puppet presidents, and Washington recognized the second, apparently because the United States government simply wanted to regularize relations and because consideration of Grau, who inexplicably had caused fear along the Potomac, was no longer necessary. In May 1934 Cuba signed a treaty abrogating the Platt Amendment. The formal protectorate was ended.

The Protectorate: Economic and Social Aspects

The United States presence was not merely political but was accompanied by economic and social pressure and even "intervention." United States investment increased during World War I, replacing European as the dominant foreign element. It went from some $50 million in 1895 to $200 million by 1906, $265 million at the end of World War I, $1.24 billion in 1924, and $1.5 billion by 1929. It was heavy in sugar mills, less so in cane growing. As the *centrales* became larger and more efficient, they came to dominate the *colonos* (small growers), who had to sell to the nearest *central*. American-owned mills produced only 15 percent of Cuban sugar in 1906, but nearly one-half in 1920, and about three-quarters in 1928. Heavy United States invest-

ment was also made in electric power, telecommunications, and transportation. United States banks became important in financing the Cuban government.

Commercial relationships were set by reciprocal trade treaties. That of 1903 gave Cuban sugar a 20 percent preferential reduction in United States tariffs, while various United States exports to Cuba received 20 to 40 percent reductions in Cuban tariffs. This system greatly increased commerce between the two countries. The United States became Cuba's best sugar market, while United States exports to Cuba increased from $27 million in 1897 to $200 million in 1914. Adjustments in the system required constant negotiation. Although a part of the purpose was to assure a market for Cuban sugar, also involved were United States exports to Cuba and the interests of beet and cane growers in the continental United States, Hawaii, and the Philippine Islands. The pressures on the United States government were largely of United States origin, and Cuba was tied to a system on which it exerted little influence. Relatively high-cost sugar growers in the United States fought for tariff and other measures to help them compete. Refiners were split between those who used domestic sugar, those who imported Cuban raw (unrefined) sugar, and those who (by the 1920s) refined sugar in Cuba. The issue became so complicated that sections of a corporate conglomerate sometimes made conflicting demands on Washington.

The complexities and oscillations of the system led to United States efforts in the 1930s to stabilize it on a new basis. The Reciprocal Trade Agreement of 1934 reduced the duty on Cuban sugar and some other exports, and Cuba made concessions to the United States, including more privileges for United States exports to Cuba. In separate actions at the same time, the Cubans raised duties against Japanese goods that competed with United States manufactures in Cuba. Also in 1934, the Jones-Costigan Act set up a system for allotting portions of annual United States sugar requirements to domestic and foreign producers. Cuba's quota was 28 percent of the United States sugar market for 1934. This system, with subsequent modifications, also included levies on sugar to provide subsidies for high-cost domestic producers. That raised the price to North American consumers and gave low-cost Cuban producers a bonus over the world market price. The arrangement endured for the next quarter century, perpetuating the special relationship that had grown up since the reciprocal trade agreement of 1903.

Nationalist objection to the United States presence grew in the 1920s. Tourism brought sizable income to Cuba, but also North American habits, thought possibly corrupting to morals or to the Hispanic culture. Gangsters from the United States developed connections with gambling and prostitution in Cuba, but scarcely needed to teach those entertainments to the local boys. North American advertising, movies, and female dress were but a few of the pervading signs of Yankee influence. Cubans found it pleasant to play on the Florida Gold Coast. Prohibition across the narrow straits brought rum runners to Cuba; it also persuaded Cubans to ply the trade in the other direction. For nationalists, the dynamic and aggressive Yankees had to be controlled for spiritual as well as political and economic reasons.

Many aspects of Cuban life, however, were entirely or mostly the result of factors unrelated to the United States presence or intervention. The population grew rapidly, partly due to United States sanitary aid, from 1.57 million in 1899 to nearly 4 million in 1931. It also grew because Spaniards continued to pour into Cuba: 723,381 in 1903–1933, although many eventually returned to Spain. Class lines continued to be strictly drawn by property and education and to some extent by race. All these conditions went far back into Cuban history, although United States influence may have marginally increased race prejudice. Persons of considerable African heritage were at least one-third of the population.

The concentration of land and property also went far back into the Cuban past, and only an acceleration could be assigned in part to United States influence. Poor remuneration of labor remained a constant of Cuban life, inherited from the past. The Cuban elite were joined by United States business interests that fought organized labor. Education was considerably expanded, and the United States approved, however much business concerns battled against taxes.

Concentration on sugar exports had been a passion with the Cuban elite since the later eighteenth century. It merely was exaggerated by the influx of Yankee dollars and influence on government. "Rich as a Cuban" became a common saying, and the affluent used much of their income for sumptuous living, a taste known in the Spanish world before 1898. The oscillations of the international sugar market were beyond the control of either the United States or Cuba. The price reached 22.5 cents a pound in 1918, then collapsed soon after the war. It was at a low of 1.6 cents a pound at one point in the 1920s. Cuban sugar production reached 3 million tons in 1915 and 4 million in 1918, when it made up 89 percent of exports, compared with 54 percent in 1909. The *zafra* (harvest) was 5 million tons in 1929. Cuba was an extreme case of monoculture and dependence on exporting a single commodity. Exports brought in $434 million in 1924, but only $80 million in 1932, during the great Depression, which had a drastic effect on most aspects of Cuban life, including the capacity of government to act. No wonder, then, that Cuban nationalists deplored sugar specialization, and exaggerated United States responsibility for it. Still, the Cuban elite specialized in sugar as latifundists did in coffee in Brazil, wool in Uruguay, and cattle and wheat in Argentina.

The advocates of diversification made little more headway against the mania for sugar than they had in the late eighteenth and the nineteenth centuries in Cuba. Even Machado had some interest in diversification, and a law of 1927 had his approval in providing some protection for agricultural diversification both to cut down food imports and to stimulate industrialization. But little of that nature occurred during the period of the protectorate, and only partly because of United States opposition. Even if a great effort had been made, it is not clear what could have been accomplished and when, as the experience of Castro's Cuba after 1959 would demonstrate.

In any event, such effort required strong political organization, and Cuba did not have that. The feebleness of political structures was only partly due to direct and indirect United States interference. The political culture resembled that of most of Latin America: inefficient and corrupt bureaucracies, narrowly based taxation and heavy dependence on foreign trade levies, feeble parties strongly marked by personalism and aiming largely at the control of office and milking the fisc, fraudulent elections, frequent use of violence in public life, and restricted participation in the political process. Those things ordinarily were not in Latin America much due to North American influence.

Cuban governmental policy and electoral results were affected by United States pressures and intervention. The American Chamber of Commerce in Havana helped draft tax laws. North American statesmen suggested what qualities Cuban presidential candidates should have. General Crowder's notion of improvement in Cuban politics was more cooperation with United States interests. On the other hand, much policy in Cuba represented the wishes of the Cuban upper and middle classes, which closely resembled those of other countries. It was suggested that the United States preference for soldiers of the wars for independence as presidents distorted the nation's political development. That criticism ignored the generals' own ambitions and support, as well as the role of the military in the rest of Latin America. The generals certainly formed personalistic political groups and showed assiduity in padding the public payrolls, both Latin American specialties. A small army gradually came into existence. It was much increased in the time of Machado in the late 1920s, and he used it as dictator-presidents did in other Latin American countries. One promising influence for change arose in the 1920s when university students forced academic reforms on the government. Students and professors began demanding change, including termination of United States tutelage.

e. Other Nations of Latin America

The other nations of Latin America by the 1930s showed varying degrees of change that signified some pressure for modernization. There was more astir in Colombia and Peru than in the others among this group of thirteen republics.

Colombia

Colombia in the second decade of the twentieth century was relatively at peace after the factional wars of the nineteenth century, with a conservative-dominated political system and an economy showing signs of expansion on the earlier miserable structure.[6] In the second and third decades of the twentieth century there was continued development of banana and coffee exports, a small but growing foreign-financed petroleum output, and some growth of light industry. A gusher of foreign investment almost inundated Colombia in the 1920s, standing at nearly $400 million by the end of 1929, with three-quarters from the United States. Foreign trade also had fueled prosperity and change, rising from 63 million pesos in 1913 to 260 million in 1928. Between 1925 and 1929 total production increased at an excellent annual average of more than 7 percent, with much investment in public works and transportation, financed by the coffee boom and foreign loans. A steady rise in coffee prices in the 1920s encouraged expansion of the crop. Some new funds found their way into electric power, city streets, light industry, highways, river and harbor work, health and sanitation measures, and other useful activity. On the other hand, there was criticism of planning for national de-

---

[6] See Chapter 28.

velopment and of waste and graft in what was attempted.

The changing economy began to undermine old social and political arrangements and to bring what a Colombian called "the crisis of the traditional order." The trend to cash-crop farming increased the dependence of *campesinos* on international and national market factors. Population growth from 1912 to 1929 was the highest in history, with an increase from about 5 million to nearly 8 million. There also was more movement to urban areas. Squatters on public and private land became troublesome. These factors contributed to violence in rural areas in the late 1920s and early 1930s. Industrial labor was stirring, also. Workers for the United States–owned Tropic Oil Company struck three times in the 1920s, being forcibly suppressed in 1927. A banana strike in 1928 in the Atlantic coast plantations of United Fruit was put down by the army with copious bloodshed.

A few young men after World War I were influenced by the Mexican and Russian revolutions and other movements for drastic change in the world. Leftism and reformism became more popular with some of the middle class. Some were members of the reformist wing of the Liberal party. Rafael Uribe Uribe, a hero of the great war of 1899–1902, as early as 1913 said the Liberal party must socialize or perish, meaning adopt wider state intervention in the social and economic realms. The Liberal convention in 1922 declared for social justice. At the same time, some conservatives were adopting European fascist ideas. Although the pressures for change were not impressive by 1930, they soon would increase dramatically the demand for modernization. The Liberals returned to the presidency in 1930 and during the next decade proposed economic, social, and political changes that brought policy debate at last to a level approximating that in the Latin American countries that had responded most in an earlier period to the demand for modernization.[7]

Peru

President Augusto Leguía of Peru in his second administration, 1919–1930, pursued some modernization, ruling as a dictator while making gestures toward more political participation. He gave special attention to economic development, with emphasis on encouraging foreign enterprise. He invested in transportation and other public works, and modestly in education. The social situation scarcely changed, although the university students and miscellaneous intellectuals who were noted demanding reforms in the second decade of the twentieth century continued to do so in the 1920s and 1930s.[8] González Prada had disciples in José Carlos Mariátegui (died 1930) and Víctor Raúl Haya de la Torre (born 1895), both of whom relied heavily on Marxist ideas. The latter, and some other student leaders, were exiled in 1922 for opposition to Leguía's conservative and dictatorial rule.

Haya de la Torre, traveling abroad and taking reform ideas from many sources, was an outstanding example of the popular "intellectual" with political ambitions that was becoming increasingly common in Latin America. In 1924 in Mexico he declared creation of the American Popular Revolutionary Alliance (APRA). It was supposed to have the continent-wide appeal indicated by its name but never was of consequence outside Peru. *Aprista* doctrine was anti-imperialist and generally anticapitalist. It demanded an end to the endemic ills of the Latin American political culture. APRA soon attracted considerable support in Peru, including intellectuals and students and some others from the middle class, labor leaders and workers, and some peasants. The communists did not like APRA because it represented competition for allegiance on the left. Peruvian conservatives simply called APRA communist. It was the first of the modern noncommunist leftist parties in Latin America that achieved a wide following.

In Peru, although APRA provided new pressure for change, it had to fight for an effective

---

[7] See Chapter 42, Section a, on Colombia since the 1930s.

[8] See Chapter 28, Section b.

voice. A variety of grievances and the beginnings of the great Depression brought Leguía down in 1930 by an armed revolt led by Colonel Luís Sánchez Cerro. A mestizo who was not popular with the old elite, Sánchez Cerro ran for the presidency on a reform platform. A new electoral law for the first time established the secret ballot, eliminated property qualifications, and gave the vote to literate males over twenty-one. Even so, the election of October 1931 involved but a small part of the population. Sánchez Cerro received 152,000 votes to Haya de la Torre's 106,000, in a fair election. Sánchez Cerro had much popular support among the rural citizenry, and the old elite preferred him to the Marxist-oriented APRA. By now the right-wing conservatives were invaded by European fascist ideas, so that they favored corporatism and joined with it the old Spanish contempt for everything Indian.

APRA had competition from the communists in the labor movement, but it did very well with the middle class, including students, and with the unorganized urban proletariat. After the 1931 election APRA talked openly of rebellion. A constituent assembly had been elected at the same time as the president. After its meetings began in December 1931, the *aprista* delegates pursued a policy of obstruction, so in January 1932 President Sánchez Cerro arrested them. He now ruled under a state of siege and fought a savage war with the *apristas*. APRA resorted to the violence that would thereafter remain in some people's minds (including the military) a reason for not trusting the party. *Apristas* wounded Sánchez Cerro in an attempt at assassination. In July 1932 *apristas*, with the collaboration of some military personnel, took the Trujillo army garrison after heavy fighting, and armed the local population. Government forces defeated the rebellion in a few days, but the APRA leaders before retreating murdered and mutilated some sixty imprisoned military officers and enlisted men. The army in retaliation executed many citizens of the area (estimates ran as high as 6,000).

APRA had traveled fast, showing much imagination in its organization and appeal. It used an effective cell organization and telling propaganda.

It shaved APRA on the sides of llamas and put campaign slogans into the Quechua language. But it could not match the guns of the conservative-oriented army, which relentlessly pursued party members. Haya de la Torre was jailed and misused. Messages from all over the world asked the government to release him. He had made of his party an international symbol of the demand for justice and of revolt against tyranny.

The assassination of Sánchez Cerro in 1933 changed nothing for APRA. Army Marshal Oscar Benavides, president in 1933–1939, sent Haya into exile and kept a tight lid on APRA activity. An election in 1936 showed continued *aprista* strength so Benavides canceled the vote. Fear among the oligarchy of the continuing *aprista* hold on the lower class as well as intellectuals and middle-class reformers became an obsession. The military hated APRA, blaming it for army deaths in disorders and by assassination. It turned out that conservatives and military officers could hold off APRA until late in the twentieth century, but its existence and activity increasingly complicated the task of resisting social and political modernization, partly because APRA's example encouraged other groups to speak out.

Panama

The changes that came to Panama were separation from Colombia and construction of the canal. Although these brought some new money and opportunities, most of them were sopped up by a small elite. The government in the center of the country had little hold on the extremities to east and west. Independence was achieved in 1903 because the United States finally decided on the Panama route for the canal. The decision was based on the short passage across the Isthmus of Panama; astutely fomented fears in the United States that volcanoes and earthquakes made the Nicaragua route dangerous; clever peddling of the nearly worthless French Canal Company's concession by Philippe Bunau-Varilla, who made a fortune from the transaction; the impatience of President Theodore Roosevelt to get on with the digging someplace; and the weakness of Colombia. Bunau-Varilla and fellow conspirators in Panama declared independence, and the United States recognized it immediately and blocked attempted Colombian military action. Bunau-Varilla became Panama's representative in the United States and negotiated posthaste a treaty for a Canal Zone and protectorate. The ten-mile-wide zone was granted in perpetuity to the United States to use "as if it were sovereign." The United States also could take over, occupy, or police parts of Panama when it thought that necessary. What Panama got was $10 million, an annual payment of $250,000, commercial benefits flowing from the canal (opened in 1914), and a position of dependence on the United States.

Life in the little republic was marked by poverty and violence. Frequently in the early years the United States intervened to control disorder. Inevitably, the national police and a few political leaders ran the country, largely in the interest of a handful of prominent families. The population in the central cities was poor, mostly of mixed racial stock, illiterate, and easily manipulated. The United States position in the Canal Zone became part of the general Latin American complaint of Yankee intervention and imperialism. By the 1930s a few leaders in Panama were using nationalism and anti–United States views as political ammunition. In later years that cry would grow much stronger.

Changes in the other ten republics were so meager by the 1930s that their history after the late nineteenth or early twentieth century is resumed in later chapters, with emphasis on recent decades.[9] There were a few signs of change in institutions or attitudes that would suggest more pressure for modernization, but they were too feeble to illuminate the trends established more clearly in other countries from the 1890s to the 1930s.

___

[9] Venezuela in Chapter 42, Section b; in Chapter 44, Bolivia, Ecuador, Guatemala, Honduras, El Salvador, Nicaragua, Paraguay, Haiti, the Dominican Republic.

PART EIGHT

The Struggle for National Development Since the 1930s

Since the 1930s Latin America has suffered the classic nightmare of the ever-enticing but ever-elusive goal. The economies grew but not enough to satisfy increasing demand for social improvement. Desire for modernization increased and stimulated disagreement on its definition and ways to manage change. Intermittent increase in political participation often seemed to leaders merely to complicate the problem of modernization. Frustration increased the attraction of radical solutions, rightist or leftist, usually with a considerable reduction in political participation.

Where there was broadened political participation, it gained intensity from the rising influence of ideologically oriented parties and other groups. A new intensity came also from a tendency, heightened by international developments, to put issues in terms of national crisis. World War II, even more than World War I and the great Depression, showed leaders the perils of weakness and dependence, and the cold war reinforced the lesson. Such developments gave thrust to demands for economic growth and diversification, dramatized by use of the new ideas and tools of economic planning after World War II. Thus, political passion received new fuel from announced national goals and from the frustration resulting from failure to achieve them.

Moderate reformism seemed the wave of the future in the 1940s and 1950s. Its partisans, unfortunately, never handled economic and social problems so successfully as to stifle disaffection. Their hold always was doubtful on the rapidly growing middle class, which feared expensive populist measures. Industrial labor had no reason to be enthusiastic about moderate reformers and in any event was poorly organized and had little independent power in politics. Moderate reformers scarcely grappled with the difficult problem of organizing firm support among the poor. A few did manage it, however, notably the APRA in Peru, Perón in Argentina, and the PRI in Mexico. The moderate reformers at least had little to fear from the old socialists and communists, who seldom managed to gain the allegiance of much of the electorate. Moderate reformers did have to fear the old right and new left.

In the 1940s and 1950s it was possible to believe that the old right was diminishing, especially because a small decline occurred in military activity in public life, and it could be argued that changed social conditions would cause that decline to continue. Such a view became impossible, however, in the 1960s and 1970s, as military interference in politics became more pervasive than at any time since the Age of the Caudillos a century earlier. One reason was that the military had a traditional sympathy with the conservative point of view. Another reason was that the military continued to hear pleas from civilian groups for their aid, support, and even seizure of government. Also, there was military fear of subversives, some of them trained in communist Cuba. Small but violent guerrilla bands and urban terrorists aroused alarm in the 1960s and 1970s. Finally, in military and other conservative circles after the 1930s the idea of modernization grew while doubts arose as to its definition in political terms. Political questions were even sometimes regarded with an indifference or impatience reminiscent of the positivists of earlier times. Following World War II, and especially in the 1960s and 1970s, a new corporatism arose that favored economic growth as the goal of goals, as the essence of modernization. Its partisans, who included some military officers, businessmen, journalists, and technocrats (especially economists and engineers), were uninterested in broadened political participation as a goal, meaning that they also were indifferent to social justice except as it was tied to economic growth and optimum political control. What was occurring was a strengthening of technologically oriented attitudes among the elites that was more potent than the "demystification of authority" that led some rebellious elements—for example, among youth and intellectuals—to rail against the traditional oligarchic polity of Latin America.

Military men who inclined to this view continued to state that the military corps was the ultimate interpreter of the national fate, but they said more: That developmentalism was a tool of national greatness and that they knew how to apply it. Observers did not know what to make of that idea in the 1960s. In some new military regimes it seemed camouflage for traditional conservatism and pursuit of military power. In others it seemed to be accompanied by some species of interest in socialism. As time wore on into the 1970s nationalism became more clearly the strongest element in the new military view. Many military men simply welcomed a role in creating national strength through economic development. Doubts increased that ideological factors—other than nationalism—were important in military thinking. Military interveners benefited from the fact that the rising fury of the claims of groups competing to direct the national destiny compelled some citizens to choose, as they thought, more security at the price of less freedom. Repugnant as the continued political vitality of the Latin American military was to partisans of representative government, it seemed to parallel developments in other parts of the world.

The growth of this corporatism certainly reduced belief in the notion that modernization of production must bring political democracy. It had indeed tended to do so for a time, but clearly in the 1960s and 1970s it did not. That disillusionment led some analysts to contend that the sequence of events was "modernization without social change," which was an exaggeration. Improvement of production was likely to bring some social change or the promise or threat or increased likelihood of it. Even relentlessly "developmentalist" regimes in the 1960s and 1970s favored some sorts of social service activity.

Moderate reformers had also to fear the new left, including the rural and urban *guerrilleros* and terrorists. Less violent leftists pushed the view that the entire policy of economic growth for its own sake was mistaken, a disastrous imitation of the history of older developed countries. They wanted stress on a more equitable distribution of income, even at the price of slower growth. Numbers of Marxists, partial Marxists, and non-Marxists took up this view, which aimed at alteration of social and economic structures, as a prelude to their version of just and effective modernization. Agrarian reform, including changes of landownership—with or without division of units—was a central demand of the proponents of structural change. Only communist Cuba, however, carried out a massive change of rural landownership as part of a general structural change in society. That example increased the fears of conservatives and moderates.

Thus, the rage for economic growth continued, but the dream of a modernization including broad and free political participation, and popular design of social institutions, seemed to become more nebulous. It could be hoped that moderate and civilian reform parties would become predominant again, but it seemed possible that for some time they might be squeezed between extremists of the right and left.

34 Since the 1930s

Upheaval and placidity. Change and continuity. The twinning of the century before 1930 continued,[1] and although upheaval and change were gaining, they were far from triumphant. The contest over the political management of change and continuity was affected not only by rising national consciousness, but by irritation with dependence on the industrialized world and an explosive population growth and movement to the cities. The stress of development efforts tended to compress the definition of modernization simply to improved control over the physical and social environment, with weakened attention to popular participation in decision making. Such a concept was equally workable by capitalist or socialist, democratic or authoritarian regimes under various conditions. In any event, government participation in economic and social affairs grew and grew and grew. That was an aspect of modernization as inescapable in Buenos Aires and Managua as in Chicago and Gettysburg.

a. International Relations

In international affairs Latin America became more aggressive in stating its views, but since

words by themselves brought few gains, they chiefly increased frustration. Resentment rose against all foreign business and investment, especially that of the United States, although it generally was acknowledged that such elements were useful if properly controlled. Attempts were also made to reduce dependence by increasing Latin American economic collaboration, but those efforts had little effect, adding further to frustration and nationalism. Resentment of economic dependence increased Latin America's political objections to United States efforts to pull Latin America into the cold war and to supervise and spy on its internal affairs in order to prevent the growth of communism.

World War II

The massive United States intervention in the Caribbean area that began in the 1890s seemed by the mid-1920s not worth the cost of political recriminations at home and abroad. An edging away from intervention in the late 1920s and early 1930s was dramatized in 1933 by President Franklin Roosevelt's announcement of the Good Neighbor Policy. That soon was incorporated in inter-American agreements. In December 1933 at the Seventh International Conference of

---

[1] See Chapters 23 and 29 for discussion of the balance of change and continuity in the 1820s–1930s.

American States, the United States accepted a Convention on the Rights and Duties of States that included nonintervention, the juridical equality of states, and a pledge not to use recognition as a political weapon. Latin America long had sought such an agreement, and now it seemed that a new day had dawned in inter-American relations. That view was reinforced in 1934 when the United States abandoned its treaty rights making Cuba a protectorate and took the same action with regard to Panama in 1936 (ratified 1939).

These actions lessened suspicion of the United States and helped it secure agreements with Latin America on defense against the menace of militaristic fascism abroad. A Special Inter-American Conference for the Maintenance of Peace, held at the end of 1936 on the suggestion of the United States, agreed to consultation when the peace of the Americas was imperiled. In 1938 the Eighth International Conference of American States reaffirmed the consultation system and provided for meetings of foreign ministers to implement it. The United States wanted a collective security system, but Argentina led the successful opposition to that. When World War II began in September 1939, Washington asked for a foreign ministers' meeting, which at Panama in September–October declared the neutrality of the Western Hemisphere nations and a neutral zone averaging three hundred miles in width into the seas of the hemisphere, and resolved on economic cooperation. Soon thereafter, following the fall of France in early 1940, United States military forces were given transit and base rights in many Latin American republics. When the United States entered the war in December 1941, nine Caribbean nations declared war on the Axis the same month. Then, at a meeting in Rio de Janeiro in January 1942, the foreign ministers recommended breaking relations with the Axis; agreed to controls on sabotage, espionage, and subversion; and set up an Inter-American Defense Board. Mexico entered the war in May 1942, Brazil in August; all the others eventually followed.

The Latin American war effort involved the supply of raw materials, antisubmarine warfare, surveillance against espionage and sabotage, and provision of base facilities, supplies, and guards to United States forces in Latin America. Such collaboration was what United States military officials wanted rather than combat troops.[2] The United States, for its part, agreed to give economic assistance to Latin America through several agencies.

All this represented a great enlargement of the strategic or military function of the inter-American system as compared with World War I. Partly it was the result of Latin American perception of danger from expansionist fascism, but it also was made possible by United States renunciation of intervention. Thus, there was some Latin American hope of permanently improved relations with the United States, although doubters were not sure that the formal renunciation of intervention would hold up to the pressure of events. Furthermore, the war itself was unsettling to Latin America in emphasizing that Washington's interests were global and its attachment to a "special relationship" with Latin America a matter of show rather than substance. Latin America also was upset by wartime shortages of imported goods, which again emphasized its dependence on industrial supplies from abroad. These experiences increased Latin American nationalism, and that was for the area the great result of the war.

The Role of the Organization of American States

Latin America's view of the Pan American Union before the mid-1930s was dominated by resentment of Washington's control of its machinery, and by Yankee interventions in Latin America, subjects which the United States kept

---

[2] Combat troops were supplied only by Brazil—a reinforced division on the Italian front. Mexico had a small air squadron in the Asiatic theater of operations at the end of the war.

off the agenda of Pan American meetings from the 1890s to the 1920s. The improved collaboration after 1933 had not eliminated all Latin American suspicion by the time of the Inter-American Conference on the Problems of War and Peace, at Chapultepec in Mexico, February–March 1945. The Latins wanted the inter-American organization to be autonomous within the United Nations, which was under discussion elsewhere as a replacement for the League of Nations. In pursuit of this goal the Chapultepec delegates proposed to reorganize the hemisphere body, permit debate on the political issues Washington had been excluding, and adopt procedures that would dilute the formal—nothing could dilute the actual—influence of the United States. Latin America also wanted to involve the United States in economic development, but the latter refused. That refusal rankled and never was accepted by Latin America.

Argentina had been excluded from the conference because it had not cooperated in the war effort. The Latin Americans at Chapultepec, however, successfully pressed the United States to forgive Argentina, whereupon the latter in March 1945 accepted the acts of the conference and declared war on the Axis, thus qualifying for the United Nations meeting at San Francisco in April 1945. The Soviet Union objected that its admission was to reward the collaborators of fascism. Some citizens of the United States held the same view, but for Latin American leaders the question was neither strategy nor ideology, but protecting one of their own from outside dictation. This deeply defensive fear of subordination, dependence, or intervention continued to dominate Latin American international relations after the war, especially its attitudes toward the United States.

At Bogotá in March–April 1948 the hemisphere nations agreed to the Charter of the Organization of American States (OAS), putting the system on a treaty basis. The new charter give it expanded functions, and ended North American control of the formal machinery. The activity of the OAS since then has been marked

by increased discussion of economic development, with modest results, and resentment of the scale of United States aid; frequent United States insistence on OAS stands against communist dangers in the hemisphere, which Latin America usually preferred to handle outside the OAS; and by Latin American reluctance to use the OAS for collective action against rightist—often military —governments. Such weaknesses in the OAS, as in the Pan American Union before it, led to judgments that it was irretrievably dominated by the United States; of some use as a tension- or ego-relieving forum; capable sometimes of helping settle minor political issues; and useful in promoting uniform systems of commercial documentation, student exchanges, sanitary measures, and a modest amount of economic cooperation and development. Few people wanted to abolish the OAS, but many refused to take it seriously.[3]

Latin American Communism and the Cold War

United States policy for Latin America after World War II included much calculation of communist threats there. In the 1930s Washington had been mildly concerned about the problem. This concern grew with the sudden revelation in 1945–1948 of solid support in elections for Communist party candidates—newly legalized—in Brazil and Chile. The fact that those parties promptly were driven underground did not erase the suspicion that their support had not disappeared. This seeming communist strength was the more worrisome to Washington because just then the cold war began between the communist and noncommunist worlds. In 1947 the United States mounted the Truman Doctrine and the Marshall Plan to meet communism in Europe with arms and aid for economic reconstruction. United States policy also

---

[3] An amendment to its charter in 1970 made an annual General Assembly the supreme organ in place of the Inter-American Conference. Other changes emphasized economic development.

came to favor Latin American leaders who took a hard line against communists.

The United States adopted programs to strengthen Latin American military capabilities against internal or external communism. At the end of World War II there was an abortive effort to make uniform the military systems of the hemisphere. When the Latin Americans demurred, the United States pursued the idea on a bilateral basis, concluding military treaties with a number of states, which received United States military assistance and accepted roles in defense of the hemisphere.[4] The treaties were attractive to Latin American military forces, but stirred nationalistic opposition, and were rejected in some countries. United States military attachés and training missions—unknown in Latin America before World War II, when Europeans held the field—spent some of their effort on antisubversive activity in gathering information and disseminating anticommunist points of view. The United States supplied military hardware at low prices, partly to preempt the field and make Latin America dependent on United States suppliers and technical experts. There were joint exercises of the United States and Latin American navies. Many Latin Americans took orientation and training courses at United States military and police schools in the Panama Canal Zone and the United States. Washington made a strong effort during the Korean War, which began in 1950, to induce Latin America to send combat forces, but only Colombia did so.

---

[4] Also aimed at hemisphere defense was the Rio Treaty, produced in August 1947 by the Inter-American Conference for the Maintenance of Peace and Security. This Inter-American Treaty of Reciprocal Assistance created a permanent defense alliance. All states ratified by 1951. Each state was to help meet an armed attack on another from within or without the hemisphere. In cases of other sorts of aggression than armed attack, the Council of the OAS meets as Organ of Consultation while the Meeting of Ministers of Foreign Affairs is being convoked to take over that duty. The Organ of Consultation can vote such things as military action, a rupture in foreign relations, or economic sanctions. All decisions but those to use armed force are binding by a two-thirds vote of the nations.

Latin America considered that its great problems of modernization made it impossible for it to take up global political burdens.

United States embassies in Latin America directed open and covert information-seeking agents, and conducted counterespionage and other operations, often against local communists. Latin Americans declared that this was often interference in the area's internal affairs. There was a further, more extravagant charge, that it was part of a North American aim to curb Latin American economic development and independence. All the United States pressures and other activities relating to leftist subversion led to Latin American assertions that the United States was paranoid about the communist issue. Latin Americans further declared that they best understood how to deal with local communism and that analyses and recommendations out of Washington often were wrongheaded. Latin Americans charged that Roosevelt's good-neighborliness and the nonintervention treaties were being undermined. In the late 1940s and early 1950s oceans of angry words were uttered and printed on communist-related issues.

In 1954 Latin American fears grew when the United States decided that the danger of communism in Guatemala outweighed the value of Latin American approval of United States restraint. An effort at reduction of the oligarchic system in Guatemala that began in 1944, in 1950–1954 turned left under President Arbenz, with communists prominently collaborating. There was disagreement in the United States as to whether there was a serious threat either of communism or of peril to the United States. Latin Americans said there was neither, and resented Washington's emphasis on communism while Latin America claimed that aid for economic development was the prime issue for the inter-American system. In 1954 Guatemalan exiles in Honduras, with United States aid, helped topple Arbenz. Latin Americans claimed that the incident showed that the United States viewed all drastic reform as communist. Some North Americans agreed, but others held that

Latin Americans lacked serious world responsibilities or understanding, in effect depended on the United States military umbrella, and would not worry about communism because it was politically expedient not to do so.[5]

Then, in January 1959, Fidel Castro assumed power in Cuba after a civil war ousted anti-communist dictator Batista. This generally was welcomed in the United States, but the two countries soon fell into bickering for reasons that always will be disputed. Castro turned to dictatorial socialism. By one theory, he was forced to it by a lack of understanding and aid from the United States; by another, Castro moved left, and wanted a break with Washington to help rivet his strong-arm rule and dictate revision of Cuban society. Agrarian reform and confiscations of United States–owned property, a refusal to hold elections, and purges of opponents were among the acts excoriated in the United States in 1959. Castro said the Yankees meddled in Cuban affairs and camouflaged a reactionary fixation on business interests with fictions about communism.

Whether Castro ran or the United States pushed him toward the Communist Bloc, that is where he went. In 1960 he signed trade agreements with the Soviet Union and began receiving Soviet arms. During the next two years, United States–Cuban relations went from bad to worse, with exchanges of charges in the OAS and the UN, a break in diplomatic relations, a mismanaged United States–supported invasion of Cuba by exiles at the Bay of Pigs (April 1961), OAS sanctions against Castro in January 1962, and a crisis over Soviet missiles in Cuba in October 1962 that brought the world to the edge of nuclear war. During all of this Latin America had responded rather reluctantly to United States pressures for OAS sanctions against Cuba. By 1963–1964, however, Latin American governments were increasingly angered by Castro's subversion in their countries, and in July 1964 increased sanctions against Cuba. The decline after that of Castro's efforts to spread revolution encouraged Latin Americans to move back toward their traditional objections to interference in the internal affairs of nations. The ability of the United States to sustain Latin American pressures on Cuba soon diminished.[6]

In April 1965 a revolt in the Dominican Republic brought reports to Washington that communists might take over. President Lyndon Johnson quickly threw 20,000 military personnel into the island, avoiding the feeble action of Kennedy four years earlier at the Bay of Pigs, garnering instead charges of precipitate action and overkill. Justified or not, his action was a violation of the Charter of the OAS, and unacceptable for other reasons to much of Latin America, which reacted angrily. At the beginning of May a meeting of consultation of delegates of hemisphere foreign ministers at Washington received a United States request that an inter-American peace force be set up for the Dominican Republic. It carried, but over considerable opposition. The force was created at the end of May, with a Brazilian commander and forces from the United States, Brazil, and four small Latin American nations. All five of those Latin American states were ruled by their military forces, a fact that was used to sustain a charge that reaction rather than anticommunism was the name of the game. Johnson tried to get the OAS to go yet further by asking it to form a permanent force to deal with future communist threats. The OAS would not even consider the matter. The United States was fortunate to have been able to arrange the force for the Dominican Republic.[7]

The next crisis over the communist issue involved Chile, where since the 1930s the Socialist and Communist parties, and Marxist doctrine among workers, students, and intellectuals, had

---

[5] See Chapter 44, Section c, for more on the intervention in Guatemala.

[6] See Chapter 40 for more on Castro's Cuba and the United States.
[7] See Chapter 44, Section f, on the Dominican intervention of 1965.

been stronger than in most of Latin America. That strength developed in a country with free speech and an effective legislature. In 1970 Salvador Allende was elected president with only a bit over one-third of the vote, as candidate of a leftist coalition. He pushed socialization of the economy at a pace that critics declared was unjustified by his minority support. His actions included attacks on United States business enterprises, long important in Chile. At least one United States company, International Telephone and Telegraph (ITT), later was shown to have worked for the overthrow of Allende.

Allende's efforts to socialize Chile provoked angry accusations on all sides of brutality, espionage, invasions of sovereignty, and dictatorial aspiration. They also led to violence, in some measure encouraged by United States government funds. More important, however, were strong Chilean objections to the regime that were the result of local conditions rather than United States actions. A military group seized the government, and Allende died in the process. As in the Guatemalan and Cuban cases, the role of the United States (chiefly the CIA and private corporations) always will be disputed. Condemnation of United States actions was especially bitter because the Chilean military set up a brutal dictatorship that was widely condemned for violations of human rights for years after its formation in 1973.[8]

In the late 1970s it was not clear where United States policy on communism in Latin America might move. Castro's inability to mount successful revolutions in other countries had reduced concern in the United States and Latin America. Partly for that reason, the policy of isolating Cuba was falling apart. Washington's policy may even have strengthened Castro by stiffening the morale of Cubans and by increasing Soviet willingness to support him. The Latin American nations, furthermore, were anxious for whatever economic advantages could be gained

by resumption of relations. Also, to have relations with many communist states but not with Cuba seemed to them inconsistent and vindictive. Finally, they never had liked isolation of one of their number.

If the policy of isolation was not a complete failure, it had been only of short-lived and limited value. The real and alleged misdeeds of ITT and the CIA were under fire. The United States Congress was trying to establish enlarged control over foreign policy, and in 1975–1976 would not let the executive department interfere in the Angolan civil war in Africa. So when Cuba late in 1975 sent troops there to aid the leftist group, Washington merely said that it disapproved. No one could guess how the United States might react if another threat of communist government arose in the Western Hemisphere.

United States–Latin American Collaboration for Development

Latin America before World War II was uneasy about its poverty and its dependence within the world economic system. It did not demand, however, that the United States help improve its socioeconomic condition. That demand came with the war, especially by the impulse the war gave to nationalism. The United States gave Latin America some aid during the conflict and promised more.[9] After the war, however, most United States efforts abroad were directed to Europe and Asia as a means of shoring up the free world against communism.[10] Sour jokes were made in Latin America that the way to get

---

[8] See Chapter 40 for more on the United States and Chile.

[9] In 1940 the capital of the Export-Import Bank was increased so loans to Latin America could be expanded. Lend-lease shipments of military supplies to Latin America during the war amounted to $425 million, mostly to Brazil. From 1942 technical aid was provided through the Institute of Inter-American Affairs. The United States agreed to supply industrial goods that could not be obtained from Europe. Special agreements were made to aid in the economic development of Brazil and Mexico, especially in steel in the former and railways in the latter.

[10] In 1946–1959 only some 2 percent of United States foreign aid went to Latin America.

United States aid was to invent a communist danger.

The United States told Latin Americans to encourage private foreign investment. Latin Americans insisted that government-to-government aid was needed, that United States private investment took out excessive profits, went into lines unimportant to national development, and was controlled by foreigners uninterested in Latin American goals. At the inter-American meeting at Mexico City in February–March 1945 the United States refused to discuss general economic aid. At the Rio Conference of 1947 Washington promised to discuss economic development at the Ninth Inter-American Conference, Bogotá (1948), but at the latter stated that enough capital was available through the Export-Import Bank, the World Bank, and private sources. The Latin Americans wanted something like the Marshall Plan, then pouring vast sums from the United States to the Old World. The Bogotá Conference shunted the matter to a separate meeting for later in 1948, but the United States blocked that for several years.

As the argument continued, Washington somewhat increased technical aid and repayable loans for development.[11] United States loans from public funds required that Latin Americans use them for purchases from United States suppliers. That seemed reasonable to North American congressmen but not to Latin Americans. A meeting of finance ministers of the OAS countries took place at Rio de Janeiro in 1954. The United States adhered to its positions, and Latin Americans protested. An OAS economic conference at Buenos Aires in 1957 had much the same result, including a refusal by the United States to agree to an inter-American development bank.

Then a shocking thing happened in 1958. Vice-President Nixon, on a tour of Latin America, was badly received in several places. A riot in Caracas threatened his safety, partly because Venezuelan authorities gave him poor protection. The North American public finally had some notion of the depth of Latin American resentment, long known in the State Department and among academic specialists. Soon after the Nixon affair, President Juscelino Kubitschek of Brazil, in May and June 1958, suggested to President Eisenhower the value of an "Operation Pan-America" to "battle against the festering sore of underdevelopment," with much more United States aid.[12] In Washington in September 1958 the United States went along with a meeting of the hemisphere's foreign ministers that decided that the OAS should prepare a program for economic and social development. The United States had modified its policy.

What happened in 1958 was that the information on Latin American dissatisfaction was considered more seriously, which meant that the president had been persuaded. It was decided that Latin American strategic and anticommunist cooperation, and defusing leftist arguments in Latin America, required additional attention and money from the United States. Then in 1959–1960 Fidel Castro took over and transformed Cuba, and fixed the gaze of the United States on Latin America with unprecedented firmness. Washington supported measures to curb expansion of the Cuban revolution to other countries, and Latin Americans wryly noted that attacks on a United States vice-president and the fear of communism in Cuba did more to change United

---

[11] Under the Mutual Security Act of 1951, "Point Four" agreements were made by June 1953 with all Latin American governments except Argentina. Much technical assistance—for example, in education and health—under various programs was channeled through *servicios*, an administrative device theoretically jointly run by Latin and North Americans, typically imbedded in a Latin American ministry. It was supposed to handle funds for material things and to improve the administrative culture of the Latin American government by an example of efficiency and honesty. Very little change by example was accomplished. *Servicio* methods were ignored by the local bureaucracy except insofar as they had to be understood to be circumvented. Administrative reform, of course, depended heavily on overall social change, something no puny *servicio* could achieve.

[12] See Chapter 38, Section b, for doubt that Kubitschek's own policies were ideally suited to Brazilian socioeconomic development.

States policy than mountains of technical argument and humanitarian appeal. Of course they did. Latin American governments responded in the same way to immediate pressures and allocated resources in accordance with political realities and changing views of alternatives.

The policy change was in full flow in 1960. In July President Eisenhower said the United States would cooperate in a socioeconomic development program for Latin America. He recommended and Congress authorized $500 million to establish an inter-American social development fund. In September 1960 the OAS agreed to a United States proposal for the program of social development. To receive aid, nations were required to follow sound economic policies and eliminate obstructions to economic and social progress, a portent of United States conditions that was not taken seriously. In October the Inter-American Development Bank went into operation. It was part of the OAS program for development that the September 1958 meeting in Washington had charged the organization to draft. The United States provided nearly one-half of the initial $1 billion capital of the bank. Latin Americans were pleased that borrowers were not required to use loans for purchases from the United States.

This policy change received the blessing of the new president, John Kennedy, in January 1961, and he called it an Alliance for Progress. It was to be a ten-year plan, with $1 billion in United States aid the first year. A meeting at Punta del Este, Uruguay, in August 1961 approved the alliance in detail. The nations agreed to a remarkable array of political, economic, and social reforms: promotion of democratic institutions, tax reform, educational and agrarian reform, private enterprise; controls on inflation; better distribution of income; improved health; and more. All was to be put into comprehensive national plans. The aim was self-sustaining economies within ten years by at least an average 2.5 percent gain per capita in production a year, which meant more than 5 percent gross because of rapid population growth. The United States

was to provide a "major part" (undefined) of the minimum of $20 billion said to be necessary (an underestimate) from all external (to Latin America) sources. The amounts of external funds to come from international lending agencies, and from private and public sources in the United States, Western Europe, and Japan, were not spelled out. The Latin American contribution was not closely specified. There was room for endless dispute, and it occurred.

The alliance raised hopes that could not be fulfilled because neither Latin America nor the United States would take the risks or make the sacrifices required. For a short time rosy verbiage covered the alliance, although knowledgeable people knew that it was unlikely to accomplish much except sharpen the urge to develop. Soon the common question was, "Why has the alliance failed?" A popular Latin American answer was United States red tape and lack of understanding of Latin American problems. As a corrective, in 1963 the Inter-American Committee for the Alliance for Progress was created to increase Latin American control. It had little effect. The scale of new investment would permit no more than marginal effects. United States public funds in the alliance amounted to only about 5 percent of total annual investment in Latin America. Much of the United States input was in repayable loans. By 1968 the United States had paid out $5.8 billion and Latin America had repaid $2.8 billion. The United States Congress early became disillusioned with the program and with the endless Latin American complaint and within a few years was cutting alliance funds. The amount for fiscal year 1969 was down to $336 million.[13]

Occasionally Latin Americans conceded that much of the problem lay in their own institutions. They found tax reform politically unpalatable, as who does not. Agrarian reform was slow, being another politically sensitive issue. Improvement of Latin American bureaucracies

---

[13] Total United States aid to Latin America from 1961 to 1968 was $9.9 billion, of which less than $1 billion was military.

was a task for heroes. Controlling inflation often took more political courage than could be mustered. Political instability interfered with development efforts and administration of the alliance. Latin America in the first seven years of the alliance (1961–1967) averaged an annual growth of gross national product (GNP) of 4.5 percent, but only 1.5 percent per capita. By the 1970s the alliance was dead.

While the alliance dwindled, Latin America turned to other demands on the United States. It exerted pressure through diplomatic channels and by continued expressions of hostility. A trip by Senator Robert Kennedy to Latin America in 1965 met an unfriendly reception. A much-touted Nelson Rockefeller mission to Latin America in 1969 to examine the "problem" and devise policy for Washington was not well received. Those citizens of the United States who called such reactions simply the work of Latin American "subversive" elements were either ignorant or trying to deceive.

One demand was larger United States contributions to the capital of the Inter-American Development Bank, whose operations became greatly enlarged in the 1970s. Latin America continued a long-time demand that the United States admit more Latin American goods and arrange a "better" relation between their prices and the industrial exports of the United States. Latin American spokesmen put such suggestions into a 1969 "Consensus of Viña del Mar" that the Inter-American Economic and Social Council gave serious attention. It asked the United States to reduce profits by aiding Latin America, to end "tied loans" which had to be used in the United States, and it blamed Washington for the widening of the "economic, scientific, and technological gap" between the two areas. That did not prevent the United States Senate from further reducing foreign aid in 1971. The administration also increased protectionism. In the next few years Washington occasionally made conciliatory moves, but little changed. Latin America still hoped for concessions from the United States but also searched for help from Latin American collaboration and from discussions with the rest of the Third World of underdeveloped nations.

Inter–Latin American Collaboration

Schemes for Latin American economic collaboration were of no consequence before the 1950s and of limited value thereafter. Increasing nationalism and economic sophistication were the chief reasons for interest. The Alliance for Progress favored Latin American economic collaboration, and the alliance's shortcomings pushed Latin America even more toward regional integration as a panacea. The OAS and the Economic Commission for Latin America (ECLA) of the UN provided technical aid and convenient arenas for collaborative discussion. The obvious bases of hope were (a) the creation of a larger market; and (b) provision of markets, capital, raw materials, and technical personnel to permit creation of productive facilities—especially heavy and highly technical industries—that the individual countries did not possess. The aims were greater Latin American economic and social development and greater independence from the pressures and accidents of a dependent position.

The Central American Common Market (CACM) was created in 1960 to develop a free-trade area and common tariffs with the outside world and to agree on industrial specialization for specified states of the five-nation system, since often there was no capital or market for competing enterprises. Such aims encountered nationalistic rivalry, and the future of CACM was problematical in the later 1970s.[14]

The Latin American Free Trade Association (LAFTA) was set up in 1961 by Argentina, Brazil, Mexico, Chile, Peru, Paraguay, and Uruguay and later joined by Venezuela, Colombia, and Ecuador. It was to establish a free-trade area by agreement, but doing so proved difficult. The great differences in the size, resources, and state of development of the Latin American nations made collaboration strained, because the stronger

---

[14] See Chapter 44, Section c, for more on CACM.

nations did not abandon their ambitions and refused to make sacrifices for the weaker. Trade still was heavily with the rest of the world in the late 1970s.

The United States expressed approval of CACM and LAFTA but had little effect on their meager development. Their failure was acknowledged in 1969 by the signing of an Andean Subregional Integration Agreement by Bolivia, Chile, Colombia, Ecuador, and Peru to aid the area within LAFTA with regional collaboration of various sorts. The Andean Group by the late 1970s was still struggling to get off the ground. No one knew if more could be expected from the Latin American Economic System (SELA), organized in 1975 by the twenty Latin American republics and several former colonial areas in the Caribbean. Although faster economic growth and greater independence were the fundamental aims, as in the other organizations, SELA emphasized the defense of raw material prices, the creation of regional multinational companies, and control of non-SELA transnational corporations. Inevitably, some Latin American pronouncements on SELA made it sound like an organization antagonistic to the United States. Although Brazil joined SELA, it also agreed in 1976 to what was described as an "unprecedented" bilateral accord with the United States and "assured" the latter of its opposition to international cartels by raw materials producers aimed at the industrial nations. The United States and Brazil were suffering from the price rises decreed by the Organization of Petroleum Exporting Countries (OPEC), of which Venezuela and Ecuador were members. At the same time the administration in Washington endorsed a new international coffee price that would greatly benefit Brazil. It was a fair guess that SELA would not revolutionize Latin American economic development or efforts at integration.

Other International Problems

The basic United States political interest in keeping Latin America from going communist was allied with the hope of aid in controlling espionage; concern about a Soviet presence in Cuba, including nuclear submarines at bases there;[15] and a desire to maintain a strong position around the Panama Canal.[16] The United States also was concerned about guerrilla activity and terrorism in Latin America, which might lead to undesirable political developments and disturb economic conditions. Furthermore, United States diplomatic and military personnel and private citizens were kidnapped and murdered.[17] Such atrocities created pressures in the United States for retaliation and pressures in Latin America to deal with the terrorists in order to avoid such retaliation.

A continuing puzzle was what attitude the United States should take toward unconstitutional changes of government. Latin America usually favored the traditional diplomatic practice of recognition for whatever regime controlled a country, regardless of the way it came to power or its political coloration. Frequently, however, groups in Latin America demanded that the United States refuse to recognize regimes simply on the grounds of unconstitutional seizure of power, especially with objections to military coups d'etat that were denounced as reactionary. Such Latin American demands were supported by some opinion in the United States as necessary for the defense of democracy. President Kennedy in 1962 briefly tried such a policy but soon found it impractical because other nations followed the traditional rule of recognition.[18]

There was the puzzle of how to deal with anti-Yankeeism, which resulted from real clashes of interest and belief, fear of United States power, and nationalistic exaggerations of the latter's actions and interest. The objections to

---

[15] See Chapter 43, Section c, on this problem.

[16] See Chapter 44, Section c.

[17] For example, United States Ambassador John Mein, killed in Guatemala in 1968; Ambassador Elbrick, kidnapped in Rio de Janeiro in 1969 and held for ransom; and see Chapter 41, Section a, on a case in Uruguay.

[18] See Chapter 36, Section c, for the effort applied to Argentina, and Chapter 42, Section c, to Peru.

political and military intervention continued from an earlier day, and fears of economic domination grew after World War II. The emphases in Latin American complaint about the United States fluctuated with the problems and with fashions in political invective. Popular objects of condemnation in the 1960s and 1970s were the CIA; aid to "gorillas" (Latin American military); charges for United States science and technology; and the allegedly general iniquities of "transnational" corporations, plus their special crimes in corrupting the political process in Latin America. The last was a matter of great interest in the 1970s, as investigations in the United States revealed payments by corporations to foreign officials to gain contracts or other favors. Venezuela declared that it had ferreted out such payments in connection with petroleum. Honduras had the aid of United States courts in identifying such bribes to a local official by a United States banana company.[19]

Much of the political problem of relations was due to the difficulty of satisfying the United States and Latin America at the same time. Each had to balance the glory of not bending to demands against the costs of possible retaliation. Latin America faced a problem in that it was not of prime strategic importance, although the United States generally refrained from emphasizing the fact. Latin Americans, nevertheless, knew that was one reason they were "neglected" by Washington. Frequent charges of neglect resulted in efforts by the United States to refute the charge without changing policy. So "fact-finding" and "goodwill" missions to the south by North Americans often were judged cheap and useful. Usually, however, they meant next to nothing, except that ordinarily Latin America lacked the means to force substantial changes in United States policy. A trip by Secretary of State Kissinger to several Latin American nations in

early 1976 was an example of the assertion that "new attention" was being given to Latin America. Mr. Kissinger had rather a chilly reception.

It was obvious that many of the so-called political issues troubling the international relations of Latin America were at least in part economic. Latin American leaders were under great pressure to improve the quality of life and especially to prevent its degradation by foreigners. Certain types of foreign operations long had been special targets, like transportation, power enterprises, and petroleum and mineral activities that took out "nonrenewable" natural resources. Pressures in such areas by the post–World War II period were pushing foreign investment from such fields more into manufacturing, and even there Latin Americans demanded more control of ownership and of decision making. Expropriations of foreign-owned property had occurred before the 1930s, but disturbed international relations more thereafter. The United States after World War II accepted such expropriations—reluctantly—if adequate and prompt compensation was forthcoming; lacking that, various forms of retaliation were used. A notable instance was the Hickenlooper Amendment, first enacted in 1962 because of actions by Brazilian state governments against United States–owned companies. A later version (1967) required the president to suspend aid to governments that expropriated the property of United States citizens, or took some other forms of punitive action, without proper steps for compensation.[20]

Fishing rights became an issue. In 1947 Chile and Peru claimed sea rights for two hundred miles from their coasts, as compared with the United States claim of three miles of territorial jurisdiction and nine miles' control over fishing. Other nations later expounded the two-hundred-mile rule. The Latin American nations seized foreign-owned—especially United States—fishing boats within those limits unless they had bought licenses and otherwise complied with local claims.

---

[19] See Chapter 44, Section c. In January 1976 United Brands Company consented without admitting guilt to federal charges that it agreed to pay $2.5 million in bribes to Honduran officials in exchange for a lower export tax on bananas.

[20] See Chapter 42, Section c, on difficulties of applying this in Peru.

Latin Americans united on the issue and received much support from the rest of the underdeveloped world. United States opposition to the two-hundred-mile limit failed, and by the later 1970s the United States Congress adopted the two-hundred-mile fishing limit itself, partly because of foreign fishing near United States coasts.

One hope of Latin America was to diversify economic relations so as to avoid heavy dependence on a single trading partner. With the great growth of the Japanese economy after World War II, Latin America had some success in pursuing investment capital and raw materials markets there. Trade with Europe continued but a new worry arose when the European Economic Community began to discriminate in favor of European or African producers.[21] Trade with communist and Third World countries was pursued but without great success. Then in the 1970s hope of better terms of trade increased with the dependence of the industrial nations on imported raw materials. A huge advantage was won by agreement among petroleum producers and distributors. Although most of Latin America imported petroleum, it tended to support the world petroleum cartel for a time; but by the later 1970s such support had declined in such heavy importing countries as Brazil. Whether similar cartels could win advantage for other basic commodities—sugar, coffee, copper —remained in doubt in the late 1970s.

The human rights issue that had engaged some hemisphere attention since World War II received greater attention in the late 1960s and 1970s, partly because of terrorism and counterterrorism. It seemed to some people a problem of greatly enlarged proportions with the surge of the new corporatism that put most of Latin America under authoritarian governments. Some people held that strong methods were required against terrorists; others, that strength need not be accompanied by cruelty.

International protest at improper imprisonment for political offenses, torture, and other

violations of human rights was increased by publicity given in the 1970s to United States governmental and corporate political and military activities abroad. There was an exaggeration of the old charge that United States "support" of military regimes was a major element in their access to power and their autocratic actions thereafter. Such charges escalated with the overthrow of the leftist government in Chile in 1973. Most governments in Latin America did not participate in the human rights campaign, but rather were the recipients of accusations. In the United States, however, by 1975 there were strong pressures in Congress to discipline Latin American governments that violated human rights. In 1977 the new Carter administration embraced the human rights cause, publicized a list of countries violating such rights, and withdrew arms and other security aid from some of them. Five Latin American nations (Argentina, Brazil, Uruguay, Guatemala, and El Salvador) quickly renounced military assistance from Washington, and condemned interference in their internal affairs. It remained to be seen whether Washington would be able to withstand this traditional Latin American complaint, when, as seemed likely, most of Latin America and the rest of the world would not strongly follow the North American lead.

b. The Development Fury

Economic development became a passion, even a fury, that threatened to devour all other issues. In the sacred name of national development traditional liberties of speech, person, and government could be sacrificed to dictatorships of right or left with some hope of considerable popular support.

The Planning of Development

In the 1930s and 1940s government planning and direction of national economies increased throughout the world. In Latin America the Depression of the 1930s reduced belief in the old economic order; more leaders embraced change,

---

[21] See Chapter 36, Section a, for this practice as it affected exports of Argentine beef.

and the goals of economic development became more enmeshed in politics and tied to the social developments that might be financed by economic growth. National independence and power were perceived as tied to planning. Modernization thus was linked to national strategies. The development concept came to permeate patriotism and politics.

The new concepts and tools of economic planning were promoted by the United Nations, and especially its Economic Commission for Latin America, where the Argentine economist Raúl Prebisch after World War II developed ideas and data to support the theory that Latin America required development methods different from those used in North America and Europe. The OAS also promoted planning after World War II, and the Alliance for Progress gave a boost to planning.

Although propertied groups in Latin America generally disliked comprehensive government planning, a political party that resisted too strongly the claims for economic and social planning was likely to be labeled reactionary. That point of view grew markedly after World War II. Intellectuals were both convinced that the method was proper and pleased with the supposition that they would be important in the planning process. Military officers came to see national planning as a way to improve national strength and as a method of increasing their own contribution to the process. Military staffs, schools, and special agencies in the 1930s and thereafter studied problems of industrialization and the exploitation of natural resources.

Working people were willing to let government manage the future, since they had no emotional ties to business enterprise and no hopes of rising to managerial or ownership levels. Even some private enterprise groups—notably in manufacturing—favored government planning when it promoted their interests, or when it might spur general growth and reduce economic dependence, even when they feared state invasion of the private sector. Thus, plans and promises about national socioeconomic development tended to gobble up other issues. Furthermore, the fate of economic development plans became so critical an issue that governments constantly stepped in to use public resources to aid the process. The result was an escalating public role in economic life. Huge enterprises in petroleum, transportation, electric power, steel became either public enterprises or partially owned or directed by the state.

Ambiguous Results

Analysts disagreed on economic activity in Latin America. Pessimists stressed that growth rates often were low, and many people remained near the subsistence level and involved in "semifeudal" labor and production systems. Optimists emphasized that much economic and social infrastructure was built, economies diversified, the will to improve stimulated. The average annual growth per capita of Latin American production, however, was not impressive, although high compared with developing countries in Africa and Asia, largely because developments before the 1930s had prepared economic, social and political infrastructure. Even when growth was adequate or better,[22] many critics either ignored the growth or asserted that it was not used for productive purposes. In 1973 Brazil and Mexico were twelfth and thirteenth respectively in the world in total production. But each of them produced only about as much as Spain or East Germany, so they were far from being well developed.[23] Much of Latin America was a poverty area.[24]

---

[22] For example, an annual average (UN figures) of 5.8 percent in 1965–1970, and 6.1, 7.5, and 8.5 percent in 1971, 1972, 1973, respectively.

[23] World Bank figures, showing total national GNP in billions of dollars: United States, 976.8; Soviet Union, 497; Japan, 197.2; West Germany, France, United Kingdom, China, Italy, Canada, each 78.1; India, 52.19; Poland, 39.4; Brazil, 35.4; Mexico, 33.0; Spain, 32.4; East Germany, 32.3.

[24] By UN figures in 1974 some Latin American countries were well above the recommended daily caloric intake of 2,300; some were near that figure or below. Haiti, the poorest nation in the hemisphere, was estimated at 1,730, El Salvador at 1,930, Honduras at 2,140. In comparison, Bangladesh was 1,840 and Sudan, 2,160.

Improved skills and achievement motivation came to only a minority. There was much variation in the productivity of industrial workers, often a favored group in terms of wages and social services, although those were kept low in many cases by government control of labor relations. Pay in Latin American auto factories in 1974 was about one-third that in Japanese or West European plants. The low productivity of rural folk was a major drag on the economy. Governments preferred not to put scarce funds in peasant farming. Land distribution programs were often small or the new holders given little aid or incentive. It was argued that it was less important to change landholding than to industrialize agriculture, pushing population into other occupations, but of course, other occupations were insufficient, and unemployment and underemployment a terrible weakness in the society.

Mexico broke up many great estates after the Revolution of 1910–1917, although others were not divided until the 1930s, and disguised *latifundios* survived thereafter. Argentina remained a land of great estates. In the 1940s some 2,000 individual and corporate landlords in Argentina owned about 20 percent of the land area. This included much of the most desirable land: for example, in the province of Buenos Aires 320 families owned 39 percent of the land, and a mere 50 of those families held half of that. In the next three or four decades little was done to disturb this concentration of landholding in Argentina. After 1959 Castro expropriated the great estates of Cuba, and turned them into large state farms. Wide distribution of land occurred in Bolivia in the 1950s but, without investment in technology, seldom helped output. Several other countries struggled with limited success to change landholding patterns—notably Venezuela, Peru, Chile; in many others, including giant Brazil, *latifundio* continued a major problem. But Brazil in the 1970s showed that with proper incentives huge increases in agricultural production were possible without land distribution.[25]

Income distribution remained heavily tilted toward the wealthy and middle-income groups.[26] There was only slow growth of support for higher popular income to create markets for protected national industries, even though it was appreciated that the small size of internal markets hindered industrialization. The middle class grew slowly as a percentage of the population, but it did grow. It generally opposed revolutionary change and supported many kinds of dynamic economic policy. Its influence, concentrated in metropolitan centers, was greater than that of the urban or rural poor. Those very poor, living near the subsistence level, still were at least half the Latin American population in the later 1970s. In the 1950s and thereafter Latin Americans spoke increasingly of their poorer populations as "internal colonies" of the wealthy segment of the population. Their situation was not enviable, even though it sometimes was better than indicated by statistics on money income, because of social assistance in education, medical aid, and government food programs; or money or products that did not enter into records from home industries, trade and services, or food grown for home consumption.

Although exports declined as a percentage of production,[27] primary commodity export earnings remained critical for the purchase of foreign goods. Export growth generally did not meet Latin American hopes, and was less than in some other parts of the world. Sometimes Latin American governments, in the rush for industrialization, neglected the export commodity production that was needed to help in that process. They complained that Latin America suffered from a worsening of the terms of trade—the relation between the prices of their raw material exports and their industrial imports—although this was

---

[25] See Chapter 38, Section e.

[26] An ECLA study of 1967 showed that in Argentina, Brazil, and Mexico the top 10 percent of the population in income received 40 percent of the national total, and the bottom 40 percent received less than 15 percent.

[27] In some Latin American countries exports as a percentage of national production were many times the percentage in the United States, where the internal market was proportionately immensely stronger.

a much-vexed question.[28] They suffered competition from other areas of the world in such commodities as coffee, copper, cacao, and tin. In the mid-1970s they hoped to improve the terms of trade as export producers tried to combine more effectively to set prices. At the same time, however, much of Latin America was bled by the world petroleum-exporting cartel. Latin America as a whole in the middle and late 1970s had large deficits in its foreign trade, although that was partly because of large imports to promote industrialization. Shortages of raw materials in the industrialized countries suggested that Latin America's primary commodities would enjoy a good market for the foreseeable future.

Efforts were made, especially after World War II, to increase export earnings by reducing foreign profits in the exploitation of such products as petroleum in Venezuela and copper in Chile. Ecuador and Peru tried to maximize new fishmeal income by pushing foreign fishermen beyond a two-hundred-mile limit. Argentina, Brazil, and Mexico after World War II, and especially in the 1960s and 1970s, tried to develop export markets for their manufactures. The percentage of manufactures in Mexican and Brazilian exports grew steadily in the late 1960s and the 1970s. They tried, without much success, to make acceptance of their manufactures a condition of smooth diplomatic relations and toleration of foreign capital. Still, Latin America was far from a major exporter of manufactures in the late 1970s.

Foreign investment as a percentage of the total declined as economies developed, but it continued to be critically important for diversification. Private investment from the United States was especially important after World War II, and went increasingly to manufactures.[29] All foreign investment, however, encountered mounting nationalist opposition. Some foreign corporations accepted a minority ownership position as a way of muffling attacks. Despite nationalist attacks on foreign capital, nearly all Latin American regimes wanted as much as possible. With the development of the aggressive OPEC oil cartel in 1973 and the huge increases in oil prices, Latin America joined the rest of the developing world in increasing its foreign borrowing. Brazil alone owed $28 billion abroad by 1977. Another target of the 1960s and 1970s was the cost of foreign technology (machinery, patent and license fees), and the supposed unsuitability of much of it for Latin American conditions.

Price inflation in those decades affected investment and other economic activity, but it often was declared a necessary means of forcing economic development. In the 1950s alone in ten Latin American nations prices rose more than 50 percent and in a few of them by as much as 1,000 percent. In the 1960s Latin America's inflation was the worst of the world's major areas.

Economic diversification accelerated. Although there was argument as to whether it was worth the cost, most governments pursued it. The numbers of nonagricultural workers increased, as did the percentage of national product derived from such activity. Argentina, leading the way, had fewer than half of its workers in agricultural/pastoral activities by the 1930s. The shift followed in other countries. Not all of this represented modernization of the economy; some of the numerous new service workers in the cities after mid-century made little contribution to national production.

A basic steel industry scarcely existed before the 1940s, when a series of new mills increased output and laid the basis for much new indus-

---

[28] Legions of competent economists have for decades argued the question without arriving at any clear conclusion except that many Latin Americans complain more of the history of the terms of trade than the data will sustain clearly.

[29] Estimated foreign investment in Latin America by the end of 1914 was $8.5 billion, including $3.7 billion from Britain, $1.7 billion United States, and $1.2 billion France; in 1939 the total was $9 billion, including $4 billion Britain, $3.5 billion United States. The total in 1939 was less than that of 1914 in terms of purchasing power. Direct investment by the United States in manufacturing enterprise in Latin America reached $7 billion by the end of 1956. Total United States investment in Latin America was $12 billion by 1969.

trial activity.[30] Motor vehicle assembly using foreign-made parts was replaced from the late 1950s by manufacture of components. In 1959 Latin America produced fewer than 180,000 units; in 1973 it was ten times that. The chemical industry grew enormously after World War II. Manufacture expanded into new fields, from electric refrigerators, toasters, and washers, to roller bearings and fine pharmaceuticals. Chain stores, discount houses, and supermarkets had great success after World War II, despite predictions that they were alien to Latin culture. The construction industry became a giant in the major countries. The great ICA engineering and construction consortium in Mexico was by the 1960s working in many countries. The old economy of peddlers and hoe farmers still affected too large a part of Latin America, but it also held a large modern sector, much of it in a few countries. Manufacturing production in 1974 was 78 percent in Brazil, Mexico, and Argentina.

Great improvements in transportation were a vital aspect of modernization. New airlines and pipelines were important, but the greatest impact was from highways, which worked even more change than the railways had earlier. Latin American roads were poor until the 1930s, when several countries began big building programs. In the following decades long-time visitors to Latin America were astounded by the changes wrought by roads and motor vehicles.

Disagreements on Methods of Growth

Decisions on policy were in the hands of *políticos* rather than *técnicos* (economists and engineers). But politicians were divided on economic policy and often harried by xenophobic nationalists. Some issues engaged especially passionate debate after World War II: (*a*) The relative importance of agriculture and industry and how much effort each needed. (*b*) A fair and sound distribution between profits (used for investment) and wages (used to buy the products of

the new industry). It was argued that production increases were not enough when they left many people on the margin of the modern society. "Marginality" became a popular conception. Partisans of income redistribution said that the splendor of public edifices, superhighways, luxury apartments, banks, and hotels, made a sad contrast with the poverty of the countryside and city slums.

Foes of prevailing policies tried to arouse a feeling among the populace not only of their poverty, which they were aware of, but of their relative position in society, which they usually did not feel in a way that was usable by politicians, although efforts to arouse class feeling had some effects during these decades. In the 1960s and 1970s it was increasingly said that it was important to get more equal distribution of incomes, even at the price of slower overall growth. Raúl Prebisch, saying so in 1972, warned that it would take great political conflict to make the structural changes required to aid the 40 percent of Latin Americans who lived "at the margin of economic opportunity." In 1974 a foe of the Brazilian military government, which was pushing production growth with very uneven income distribution, protested the "marginalization" of much of the population.

(*c*) There was debate on inflation, which afflicted much of Latin America. Many groups were against it, but each wished others to sacrifice to control it. (*d*) There was debate as to the proper economic role of government. Although the public sector greatly increased its control and regulatory functions, and also became total or part owner of much productive enterprise, the economies remained dominated by private initiative, except in communist Cuba. Socialization of the means of production proceeded slowly enough so that it appeared that a strong private sector would remain in most countries for the foreseeable future.

The "Dependency" Theorists

Another debate was over dependency theory, a post–World War II reformulation of old so-

---

[30] Latin American production of steel ingots was 3.5 million tons in 1957, about half of area needs; 8.2 million tons in 1965; 17 million in 1972.

cialist argument with what the *dependistas* claimed were critical additions. Dependence—the old "economic colonialism"—was declared subservience not only to the world capitalist system but to an internal elite—the "national bourgeoisie"—collaborating with foreign capitalism. Emphasis on the importance of the decision-making control of the national bourgeoisie carried with it the insistence that internal reform or deep structural change—meaning socialism, in fact—was necessary before trying to reduce dependence on the world. The reason was essentially that the developed countries now were so strong that underdeveloped lands could not break out of dependence under the leadership of the national bourgeoisie, thus could not duplicate the earlier histories of the developed countries, even if the new national bourgeoisies had not been the subservient collaborators of world capitalism. All of this, they asserted, made it absurd to believe in the "diffusionist" idea of Latin American development, with reliance on foreign capital and local leaders of capitalist stripe, for nothing they ever would do could be of aid to the majority of the Latin American population.

The dependency literature was useful in emphasizing the strong and sometimes reprehensible role of world capitalism in Latin America. On the other hand, it was long on theory and weak on empirical data, given to moralizing and the quotation of holy writ, expert at ignoring inconvenient facts, and resolute in ignoring critics. (*a*) It dismissed the not inconsiderable signs of Latin American economic progress as not "fundamental," and denied that the area had available strategies by which dependence could be significantly reduced. Nationalizations of petroleum, iron ore, and copper, for example, were said to be ineffective unless part of total socialist programs. *Dependistas* either ignored the nationalist economic aims of the new corporatist regimes in Latin America or simply declared that they were window dressing or could not work because such regimes were merely part of the local and international capitalist combinations. *Dependistas* obviously were not going to consider the possibility that the new alliance in Latin

America of capitalist elements, technocrats, the military, and assorted nationalists might deliver enough socioeconomic development to spoil socialist hopes for many years. (*b*) Dependency theorists obscured the foreign investment picture by not making it clear that less than 10 percent of total investment in Latin America in the 1970s was foreign; instead, they harped on the ability of that small percentage to exert leverage because of its strategic position. The leverage argument certainly had some validity, but not enough to justify inadequate attention to the size of foreign investment. Furthermore, *dependistas* simply would not look in detail at the arguments presented for some positive effects from foreign investment. (*c*) *Dependista* assumptions of a monolithic bourgeoisie in Latin America were misleading. The national bourgeoisies were divided, with some elements increasingly nationalistic and inclined to stand against foreign interests in some ways. In fact, *dependistas* were not much interested in determining exactly what the national bourgeoisies believed in or how they acted, which was curious since so much of dependency theory depended on the bourgeois elements being self-conscious actors in defense of their own interests and those of foreign capitalism. (*d*) As one would expect, *dependistas* accepted the thesis that the terms of trade have historically generally been unfavorable to Latin America, which, as noted, was not clearly demonstrable.

Many other *dependista* ideas and omissions were dubious. They assigned sociopolitical arrangements just to the socialist version of class conflict and to their notion of dependence, whereas there were mountains of evidence to suggest that aspects of dominance in the Hispanic world have roots in old human urges to secure privilege by violence. But that interpretation of violence in human affairs does not square with Marxist doctrine. It also is interesting that *dependistas* betray no concern about dependency relationships between communist countries, where they surely exist. *Dependistas* let us believe that if Latin America becomes socialist, all problems of international trade will disappear, which surely would surprise communist China

Urban Life

The rapid growth of population and migration to the cities, especially after World War II, have posed great problems in Latin America.

Below—In Caracas, Venezuela the homes of the city's poor people sprawl up a hillside. *Peter Menzel*

Below—Slums like this one in Buenos Aires, Argentina have burgeoned everywhere in central cities or peripheral shack towns. *Peter Menzel*

In Quito, Ecuador some aspects of modern times
—transportation, good medical care—blend com-
patibly with traditional tile roofs and step-streets.
Peter Menzel

Caracas from a different viewpoint. Gleaming
skyscrapers in the great new cities contrast with
the aptly named *villas miserias* (misery towns)
and *ciudades perdidas* (lost cities). *Peter Menzel*

and Poland, whose economic relations with the Soviet Union have not been uniformly pleasing to them. Whatever the weaknesses of dependency theory, however, it remained a possible rallying point for new political combinations when the regimes in power in Latin America ran into difficulties with their economic development plans.

That new theory and methods were needed was suggested by the experiences of Argentina and Uruguay. The former had by the early twentieth century become the greatest success story in Latin America and by the 1930s one of the best-developed countries in the world. After the 1930s, however, Argentina began to stumble, and for some forty years its growth was minimal, a sad case of arrested development. Uruguay, also a great political, social, and economic success story for some decades in the twentieth century, began to stumble in the 1950s, plagued with soft markets for its wool exports, by the inefficiency of its large government economic operations, and by the generosity of its social insurance system. It was difficult to prove that either Uruguay or Argentina had run into trouble primarily because of international factors, and it could not be demonstrated that the errors of their elites were the result primarily of collaboration with foreign capitalist interests. *Dependistas*, of course, asserted that those were primary sources of crisis.

c. The Population Explosion and Urbanization

Huge population growth wrought great change in Latin America. It was not the result of immigration,[31] which was tightly controlled and relatively unimportant after the 1930s, but of a decline in the deathrate, mostly by better sanitation, epidemic control, and other public health measures. At least that element of modernization was achieved. More babies and mothers lived, and to much riper years. The Argentine deathrate by the 1950s was comparable with that of the United States. Latin America's annual population growth averaged 1.8 percent in 1920–1930, then steadily rose to 2.7 percent in 1950–1960. The UN in 1952 stated that in the preceding half century the top population increases in the world were 251 percent in Argentina, 231 percent in Cuba, 217 percent in Colombia, and 191 percent in Brazil. With life expectancy higher, the United Nations year after year reported Latin America as the area of highest population growth in the world, not an entirely enviable distinction. Its population was little more than 30 million in 1850, but 104 million in 1930, 158 million in 1950, 200 million in 1960, something more than 300 million in the late 1970s, and was expected to reach at least 600 million by the year 2000. Brazil by the late 1970s was the sixth most populous nation in the world and Mexico was fourteenth. Half the population of the area was in Brazil and Mexico; and they, plus Colombia and Argentina, held nearly 70 percent of Latin America's people.

Urban growth accelerated in the 1920s and 1930s, and virtually went out of control thereafter. By 1950 about 40 percent of the population was urban; by the late 1970s the figure was about 60 percent. Long before then several countries were predominantly urban. Argentina was 60 percent urban by 1933. By the late 1960s town dwellers were 80 percent in Uruguay, 73.17 percent in Argentina, 68.8 percent in Chile, 67.4 percent in Venezuela, and about half the population in Mexico and Colombia. Much of the growth went to the major cities. Until 1930 only Buenos Aires had a million people, but by 1950 there were nine Latin American cities with more than that, and by 1976 there were nineteen. By then several metropolitan areas were among the largest in the world, led by Mexico City with 12 million and projected to have 30 million by the year 2000 if the rate of growth continued!

Such runaway growth in scores of places nearly swamped all institutions and facilities. Where could the new urban poor—often migrants from

---

[31] In the century before World War II, over 12 million immigrants arrived in Latin America, although some of them did not stay. Some 6–7 million went to Argentina and most of the rest to southern Brazil; about 5 million were Italian; more than 4 million, Spanish; and over 2 million, Portuguese.

the countryside—lay their heads? Public housing could not begin to keep up with the need. The old slums could not contain them. So they built within or on the edges of cities shantytowns of waste lumber, flattened cans, and adobe. These mushrooms of improvisation went by various names, two of the most expressive being Argentina's *villas miserias* (misery towns) and Mexico's *ciudades perdidas* (lost cities). By the 1970s an estimated 45 million Latin Americans lived in such shantytowns. The most striking characteristics of these poorest of the urban poor was their stoical acceptance of suffering and their energetic search for work to reduce their misery by whatever trifling amount.

Urban growth put terrible strains not only on housing but on transportation, education, food supply, electric power, medical facilities, and other services. As the population became younger, a smaller proportion of adult workers had to produce for the young. These problems led to attention to birth control after World War II, and especially in the 1960s and 1970s, although popular ignorance and differences of opinion posed tactical problems for politicians. Some ecclesiastics, especially younger men, promoted contraceptive methods. On the other hand, some lay leaders argued that larger population was needed for economic development and assertion of sovereignty over the national territory. Some clearly thought of large population as a goal of nationalism. In any event, efforts at control were feeble as of the late 1970s. Some people claimed that the difficulty of promoting contraception among poor illiterates showed that the problem was linked with economic and social development. That contention gained color from the fact that modernized Uruguay and Argentina had low population growth. But if population control had to wait for reduction of poverty, it might be a long wait.

d. Communications and Education

The need for improved communications increased sharply during and after the 1930s, due to the new populist element in politics and the emphasis on national development. Much of what leaders said to their enlarging active constituencies was couched in nationalist terms: the *patria* needed educated people to staff the new industries; social justice was an aspect of patriotism; economic independence was linked to national greatness. Foreign petroleum operations proved to be one of the easiest nationalist issues to exploit. Expropriation of foreign petroleum properties in Mexico in 1938 evoked much enthusiasm. Brazil in the 1950s echoed to cries of "O petroleo e nosso" (the petroleum is ours), as nationalists used popular emotion to put across a state monopoly of the industry, despite Brazil's small production and the sacrifices involved in keeping out foreign petroleum capital. Perón in Argentina in the 1940s and 1950s was adept at the use of electronically amplified oratory with a high content of nationalism, directed at times against the oligarchy and foreigners. Castro in Cuba in the 1960s and 1970s used television to make his leadership appear necessary to the attainment of justice, a better life, and independence and power for the fatherland.

Scores of coups d'etat in Latin American countries included among initial steps the seizure of communications centers. Captured radio stations broadcast assurance that the outgoing criminal regime had been routed, that all should cooperate with the new order of equity and national fulfillment. Many Latin American governments had taken over telegraph and telephone service before 1930; in later decades many made state enterprises of radio and television. Newspapers continued to suffer much government interference, and were often highly partisan vehicles of individual or party points of view. The issue of freedom of the press frequently was an important one between groups contending for control of public authority. Rightist and leftist dictatorships were prone to censorship and intimidation of the media, and some centrist regimes also took drastic action, declaring that media irresponsibility was a danger to public order. Freedom of the press notably diminished in the 1960s and 1970s.

The larger populist content of politics made governments pay more attention to education; this, together with population growth, made that an ever-greater charge on the public revenues. Some progress was made in reducing illiteracy. The United Nations put Latin American literacy at 57.8 percent in 1950, 66.1 in 1960, and 76 in 1972, but such statistics, coming from the reporting countries, were inflated, and they obscured the fact that many presumed literates were only marginally so, because of poor and short-term instruction. There were great variations between countries; over 90 percent literacy in Argentina, 60 to 70 percent in Mexico, and less than 50 percent in several countries. The size of the problem was seen in the 1974 estimate that of Latin America's 56 million primary school-age children, 14 million were not in school.

Secondary and higher education were available to few before 1930. After that, secondary instruction was greatly enlarged in a few countries, but in the 1970s only about 25 percent of Latin Americans of high-school age received any instruction. Higher education at universities, technical institutes, and professional schools expanded a great deal but enrolled only a small percentage of the potential clientele. New "university cities" replaced many of the old university buildings scattered in downtown sites. In the 1930s and thereafter students increasingly acted in national political affairs, often in opposition to dictatorial government or in favor of economic and social reform. Deficiencies in Latin American society naturally induced university students to protest, and their protest on a political level distracted them from the intellectual and professional pursuits that could make another sort of contribution to solving national problems. It was a matter for individual judgment whether faculty and students were making the "proper" decisions on priority of effort. Although the universities became heavily politicized, in some a majority of students were passive, centrist, or conservative. The concept of the autonomous university, an area not to be invaded administratively or physically by the government, sometimes led to student use of university enclaves as subversive centers. When university groups took the initiative to try to induce political change, governments regarded the institutions as more political than pedagogical and were unwilling to create for them conditions in which they might better serve their instructional and research functions. So for both reasons—shortages of funds and concentration on political matters—most universities remained poor as judged by Western European or North American standards.

Improved communications reduced parochialism. The traditional, colonial, or village life dwindled with its crafts, costumes, and dances. Europeanization or modernization, and homogenization or nationalism, accelerated. Sometimes the shedding of old routine was accompanied by an increase of optimism, even among rural migrants to the great slums of the cities. The readiness of lower-class elements to exchange hopelessness and apathy for optimism was seen in their response to some populist leaders. Perón of Argentina in 1944–1954 aroused groups previously inactive in politics. Castro after 1959 showed a remarkable ability to replace popular alienation with enthusiasm. On the other hand, many regimes so disappointed the general population that it remained sunk in disillusion and nonparticipation; alienation among the poor still was a large-scale phenomenon. Alienation, or a less drastic indifference to the society, was thought by many observers to augur ill for defense against radical leaders and groups of the right and left. The church played only a minor role in alleviating such alienation or the low levels of living that helped cause it. Hierarchy and radical priests became more sensitive to social injustice, but people's hopes were mostly fastened to political ideas and organizations or government activity.

Class and race lines were for the first time subjected to close scholarly study. It was found that the accepted upper class enjoyed considerable but declining advantages. It provided a smaller percentage than formerly of the elites, made up of the individuals who were the leaders and decision makers in politics, the professions, business, education, religion, and the arts. Also evident was the fact that the upper class shared with the middle classes provision of nearly all the functional elites, because education was essential to leadership, and ties of family and friendship were useful and often essential to such activity. Since the middle class generally shared the attitudes and goals of the upper class, the social effects of middle-class capture of the elites were restricted.

Latin America also for the first time probed deeply into the phenomena of race prejudice and discrimination. The general tendency of studies was to concede that earlier generalizations on Latin American racial bias had been optimistic; there was quite a lot of it in the area, however camouflaged. Recognition of prejudice led to efforts by some governments—for example, in Cuba, Mexico, Peru, Brazil—to reduce prejudice against racial or cultural groups. The success of such efforts was difficult to judge. In parts of Latin America, however, the "mulatto escape hatch" continued to reduce racial tension somewhat; that is, mulattoes were to some extent a self-conscious group and to some extent served to integrate the society. There was, on the other hand, some bitter dissent to the effect that this was more appearance than reality.

The great Hispanic artistic tradition had a considerable efflorescence in Latin America after the 1930s. In part it stemmed from the creation of a larger leisure class of performers and consumers; in part it was response to a nationalistic desire for esthetic achievement to equal the growing sense of local social worth. A number of figures in music, painting, and architecture received international acclaim. Literary achievement was increasingly recognized. By the early twentieth century several literary figures had sufficient stature to have merited Nobel prizes in a later period; then in mid-century the area did receive two Nobel awards in literature and one in physiology. Improved social conditions and continuing concern for the Latin American future seemed likely to ensure an even greater artistic and intellectual contribution to the world in years to come.

e. The Political Culture

Political life took on new intensity as leaders increasingly used nationalism to mobilize opinion, while that nationalistic support forced leaders to proclaim goals of vast extent. At the same time, an increased ideological component in political life made for extremism. From the 1930s to the 1950s a politics of moderation seemed to have a future; in the 1960s and 1970s moderation was nearly overwhelmed by radicals of the right and left.

Increasing but Intermittent Participation

Increasing participation or invitation to participate in the political process worked changes in political styles and programs, if less in performance by governments. Increased participation by no means guaranteed rapid changes in income distribution. Votes—sometimes made compulsory—went to illiterates, women, and eighteen-year-olds. With millions of people involved, organization and appeal had to embrace more views. Leaders became adept at the use of radio and television. Military dictators of Bolivia and Peru in the 1960s cavorted on the hustings in knitted Indian stocking caps as everyone strove for the common touch. But since the performance of politicians in office was often disappointing, it led to heavy abstention from voting as unrewarding. Abstention also was used to protest electoral fraud or the proscription of parties. Wide mobilization did not occur in all countries. In Guatemala and Honduras, for example, the politically active were on the order of 10 percent of the population, others being effectively excluded by illiteracy, apathy, isolation, or fear.

Even where the populist element in politics increased, it sometimes was more an enlarged appeal for support by offering benefits than a pledge of popular participation in the decision-making process. Fidel Castro after achieving power declared that he knew the people's wishes, and that they wanted him to interpret them without debilitating reference to elections or legislatures. Probably there was some truth in this. New military regimes coming to power in Brazil and Peru in the 1960s made broad appeals for popular support, talked grandly of ruling for the people, but were quite autocratic. They received varying popular support, waxing and waning with economic and social conditions. Willingness to accept authoritarianism as the price of socioeconomic advance appeared in popular support of ex-dictators who assumed a populist stance, like Vargas of Brazil and Odría of Peru. Laboring men who supported Perón from the 1940s to the 1970s were not concerned about his views on representative government. The third of the electorate in Chile that in the 1960s and 1970s supported the Socialist-Communist coalition was concerned more with socioeconomic than political issues. The Latin American middle class was more concerned about representative government, although it wanted to interpret it in its own interest, and sometimes supported authoritarian regimes to fight a perceived threat from the left.

Interest Groups and Parties

Interest groups grew as society became better educated and organized and as communications improved. (*a*) Organized businessmen and property owners had influence in the later nineteenth century and increased it in the early decades of the twentieth. After the 1930s chambers of commerce and industry increasingly clamored for attention. While their role in politics declined, they often improved their access to the legislative process. Development-minded regimes might adopt business advice but perceived that it had little appeal in popular politics. (*b*) Organized labor from the 1930s grew in size, but much of it remained under government domination. Its influence often was greater in politics than in the legislative process. (*c*) The rural poor remained generally unorganized, their influence weak in politics and legislation. In Mexico and Cuba, where they were well organized, *campesinos* were under government tutelage and lacked

independent political power. (*d*) Although student organizations grew in influence, their ability to initiate or manage events varied widely. Students generally lacked good relations with organized labor. At times students precipitated or played prominent roles in political episodes; at others, their activity was counterproductive. Student influence generally was nationalist and reformist or leftist. There was some tendency to exaggerate the leftism of students, partly because nonleftist students were less well organized and active.

(*e*) The church's role as an interest group was by the 1930s reduced by the secularization and anticlericalism of society. As a spiritual force the church occasionally could focus attention on selected issues, especially if other groups were concerned or the climate of political opinion was fevered. Radical priests working with industrial laborers and peasants and liberal prelates spoke out for social justice and against violations of human rights. (*f*) The growing public bureaucracies were interest groups and tended to support incumbents to ensure their own jobs. (*g*) Intellectuals tended to reformist or revolutionary points of view but were an unorganized "public" rather than an interest group.

The political parties were interest groups, some of the personalist parties being little else, and the more complex parties a great deal more. Somewhat reformist parties of the center and left continued to be important—the Radicals of Argentina and the APRA of Peru. New parties included Democratic Action in Venezuela, the Peronists of Argentina, and the ruling party of Mexico, all dedicated to some sort of innovation. Christian democratic doctrine found organization after World War II, notably in Chile and Venezuela. Marxist parties multiplied, although membership in most countries was small. The old Soviet-inspired communist movement competed with Maoist and Fidelista varieties. Communists began to make big electoral gains in Brazil and Chile in the 1940s when abruptly cut off by repression. Castro's declaration for communism in the early 1960s was a triumph for Marxism. The election (with about one-third of the vote) in 1970 of Allende (a Socialist, running with Communist support) as president of Chile was a further gain for Marxism, at least temporarily canceled in 1973 by a military coup.

After a century and a half of political independence, the Latin Americans were sophisticated practitioners of the art of politics. They produced battalions of dedicated political organizers and hopeful leaders and legions of eloquent and passionate orators. Political parties sometimes were corrupt or led by demagogues, but many were effective organizers and brokers of power, and some were conduits for demands for innovation. Few leaders of parties or interest groups could forget, however, Latin America's tradition of violence in public life or the role of the military establishment.

The military continued to be an interest group, and some of its political actions were at least partially aimed at improving pay or perquisites, funds for installations or equipment, assignment or promotion patterns, or the general position of the military institution against degradation by changes in society. It often acted on the supposition that it was arbiter of constitutional rectitude and guardian of the national destiny, as was evident before 1930 in Brazil and Argentina. That attitude grew in Latin America in the 1930s and thereafter, partly because of the growth of nationalist sentiment in society at large, partly because of its enhancement in the military services. Increasing numbers of officers received training that included economic, social, and political considerations of a strategic nature that gave them a more detailed interest in national development. Their contemplated and actual interventions in public life became based more upon this concern for the nation's future.

Military influence on politics and government leaped to every eye in cases of coup d'etat, but most influence was less visible. The military often vetoed political candidates by making clear that it would not recognize their election. Parties asked military men to run for office under their banners. The military constantly was solicited

for advice on political and governmental questions, including legislation and its implementation. Officers were appointed to civilian posts in government. Civilian leaders asked military officers to oust governments from office, and others begged them not to let that happen. The professional military of Latin America were courted, petted, damned, bribed, but seldom ignored. Hopes that they would be reduced in influence by the growth of the middle class, increased labor organization, intellectual protests, and other social changes occasionally seemed justified by prolonged civilian rule. Uruguay, Costa Rica, and Chile for some years seemed to exemplify the reduction, almost the extinction, of military influence in public affairs. Alas, evidence accumulated that the political role of the military was waxing rather than waning.

Violence and Illegitimacy

There was no decline in the importance of violence in effecting changes in government. The fact that it often succeeded was a common justification and motivation. The argument that corruption of the electoral process justified violence was still made: that only violence could achieve a return to constitutionalism. That argument appeared in earlier decades in connection with the term "revolution," meaning no more than a change of public officials. From the 1930s, however, there was more talk of violent overturns to effect fundamental changes in the social order—veritable revolution. It was argued that gradualism and ameliorative change were a muddle strategy that did not work, that so much of the old social dispensation remained that sharp structural transformation was needed to disrupt stratification systems and create new attitudes.

Much, but by no means all, of such argument came from increasing interest in Marxist theory and practice. The leftist attitude among a considerable segment of the educated population in Latin America puzzled some North American observers, who could not understand that for some people living under authoritarian regimes in Latin America, "leftism" meant simply resistance to authority and to the old oligarchic society supporting it. Revolutionaries were sustained by their conviction that they, uniquely, knew how to cast corruption from society and build it better. The Marxist position after World War II was complicated by divisions in the communist world. Latin Americans who adhered to the Soviet position abandoned revolution in favor of other methods. New revolutionary groups were formed, often with Maoist orientation. The dramatic victory of Castro in Cuba gave a boost to the revolutionary position in the 1960s. The ousting of the Allende leftist government in Chile in 1973 by a military coup—with probable majority popular support—gave another argument to the partisans of violence that it was the only way to destroy the old regime.

Although much of the political violence resembled that of earlier times, something new was *La Violencia* in Colombia, a mixture of political factionalism, revolutionary reformism, proletarian alienation, and rural banditry. From the mid-1940s, for more then two decades, large areas of Colombia suffered disorder, and parts of them were outside the effective control of government. This terrifying experience was not duplicated elsewhere in Latin America. More widespread was the development in several countries, mostly after Castro's victory in Cuba, of rural guerrilla bands. Such bands had existed earlier, also, but although they then often had some political purposes, they were not partisans of social revolution. The bands of the second half of the twentieth century were not large, but they sometimes proved difficult to disperse, and their raids, sabotage, kidnapping, and other violent tactics induced considerable fear. An effort to demonstrate the inability of governments to preserve basic order was, indeed, one of their objectives. Despite some aid from Castro's Cuba, these bands generally were a nuisance rather than a major danger.

In the late 1960s and the 1970s, as the limitations of the rural bands became clear—and the

disinterest of the peasants in supporting them was a large part of it—revolutionary groups turned to urban terrorism. In large cities members were less exposed or detectable than in the countryside. The bands received more support in the cities, where the populace was politically more active and where people of reformist or revolutionary views mostly resided. In the cities the bands were near the centers of power, which they could seize, damage, or threaten. They had the advantage of tight organization and good communications, the ability to appropriate money and arms easily, and access to important persons to kidnap, menace, and murder. Assassination, kidnapping, terroristic bombing, sabotage proved unnerving in a number of countries, notably in relatively well-developed Uruguay and Argentina. Even as revolutionaries asserted that their violence was the result of violent, repressive systems, their own violence bred more violence. Repressive measures against terrorist organizations in many cases proved adequate to contain, if not eliminate, them. Whether or not the new terrorism on balance induced reform by creating fear among conservatives or moderates was difficult to judge.

Leftist political threats—violent and nonviolent—led to new and apparently stronger alliances of moderates and conservatives, with a strong military element, that in the 1960s and 1970s established authoritarian regimes in fifteen of the twenty Latin American republics. With a leftist totalitarian regime in Cuba, only Costa Rica, Venezuela, Colombia, and Mexico remained in the late 1970s with regimes that fell somewhat out of the authoritarian/totalitarian pattern. The fifteen regimes that exemplified the "new corporatism" stifled traditional liberal political institutions and pursued what they often called "national revolutions." The military, economic, political, bureaucratic, professional, journalistic, and technocratic elites had increased their communication and sense of solidarity in support of developmentalism and nationalism and against leftist political and economic measures. Thus, changing conditions in the later twentieth century increased the traditional elite-manipulated authoritarianism of Latin America, with police and military power an essential element in it. This technocratic or corporative or neopositivist (or fascist, according to some enemies) combination often tended to blame organized labor and populist politicians for developmental failures. It was a political phenomenon paralleled by developments in other parts of the world in modern times.[32] It had some root in old Iberic-Catholic tradition, also in the political practice of Latin America for a century and a half, and finally it was a response to the pressures of modernization. Those pressures created imperative political needs, and heightened the perception of economic subordination to the developed nations, so was in part a conservative or rightist response to "dependency."

f. The Changing Role of Government

The notable increase of government functions observable by the 1930s continued rapidly thereafter. Latin Americans more and more lived in administered societies. State planning agencies multiplied, especially in the 1960s and 1970s. The economic roles of government embraced regulation and supervision and a growing direct participation by the state. In Mexico by the late

---

[32] For example, similar conservative combinations in the Soviet Union, Germany, and Japan had promoted modernization of economies and of some social institutions—like education, medicine, workers' compensation—but paid only fitful attention to political modernization in the sense of broad participation and free speech. In many countries among the elites modernization consisted of economic development in a setting of nationalism, with the economic good taking precedence over the development of political participation when the two seemed incompatible. That was clear in both capitalist and communist countries. Although the corporative combination could be condemned for collaboration with private enterprise, at the same time it increased regulation of the private sector and direct public activity in production and distribution.

1960s there were over four hundred decentralized bodies and enterprises run or partially owned by the government, with budgets that exceeded those of the ministries. In Argentina the "military factories" had an important role in production. State petroleum enterprises became giant operations in several countries. By the late 1970s most Latin Americans lived under a government that provided at least one-third, and sometimes more than one-half, of annual investment, and it tended to increase its influence at the expense of private local investment and foreign capital. Immensely increased social services dealt with education, medicine, housing, accident insurance, and pensions. Nearly all social legislation was the product of the 1930s and thereafter. If social security in the 1970s scarcely touched the half of the population in the countryside, its reach in the cities steadily lengthened.

Communication and transportation networks were built, owned, or supervised by government. The public sector share of the electric power industry became very large. All these expanded economic and social functions required bureaucracies. Government was ever more concerned with problems of organization, administration, training, coordination, and mobilization and use of technical personnel. Despite justified complaints of government inefficiency, many of the new functions were handled reasonably well. Retarded economic and social development were due more to politically difficult policy decisions than to bureaucratic bungling. In most of Latin America military expenditure did not keep pace with production, so that was a decreasing burden. The military systems might be more than Latin Americans could afford, as often was charged, but they certainly were not heavily armed by world standards, except in the case of communist Cuba.

Public revenues had to be increased to finance all this activity. Latin America was, however, still a low-tax area, because people with money never had been compelled to contribute heavily for public purposes. A low level of taxation, therefore, was some indication of underdevelopment, of slow modernization. Latin American governments understandably moved with caution in increasing tax rates. At the end of World War II the proportion of national income taken in taxation by the central governments of Latin America was on the order of 10 percent or less, compared with over 20 percent in most of Western Europe. But the trend was upward in Latin America, although there was much variation among the countries. In Ecuador the proportion of national production consumed by government increased from less than 8 percent in the early 1950s to 17 percent a decade later, and in the same years in Venezuela from 16 to some 25 percent.

Such increases could not be achieved without reducing the traditional heavy reliance on export and import duties and excise taxes. In the 1930s the percentage of public revenues from levies on exports and imports still was 35 percent for Argentina and 82 percent for Haiti. The trend toward new tax sources thereafter may be remarked for Peru, where from 1947 to 1960 the proportion of direct taxes increased from 24 to 38 percent. Direct income taxes on individuals and corporations were increased gradually in Latin American countries, although by the mid-1970s Latin American personal income taxes were lower than in the United States or Western Europe.

A Latin American president of 1900 translated into the 1970s would be dismayed by the new complexity of his task, by the size and number of pressure groups, by the intricacy of economic and financial policy, by the insolence (as he might think) of labor and university students, and by the mass of legislation ground out since the first year of the century. On the other hand, he would be charmed with the swollen size of the bureaucracy and expanded functions of his administration, enchanted with the luxuriance of the new receipts, and stimulated (possibly a bit appalled also) by the demands of a more self-conscious and ambitious national sentiment. He would be surprised by the constant debate on the role of government, on the effectiveness of public as opposed to private activity, which has been noted in connection with economic development and political life. In 1900 that controversy, and the socialist doctrine and intense nationalism that underlay the debate, were in only a formative stage. In the 1970s government was big and certain to grow bigger; how big remained to be seen.

Argentina: The Most Developed Nation Falters, 1930s–1955

The best-developed Latin American nation faltered on the road to modernization, to the dismay of its own citizens and outside observers. Conservatives ruled by fraud and violence in the 1930s. The participating military, after some years of mulling the possibility of increasing their role, in 1943 seized power. Charismatic Colonel Juan Domingo Perón soon erected a political system based on greatly increased labor organization and participation in politics, social benefits for the workers, and intensified nationalism. The extension of political participation and of social legislation was resisted by the propertied classes and disliked by some military officers, and those reactions would remain powerful factors into the 1970s. The economy grew and was diversified in the 1930s and 1940s, but Perón's policies caused an economic stagnation by 1950 that endured into the 1970s. Perón's dream of a vastly more powerful Argentina foundered on his economic errors, especially abuse of the great agricultural/pastoral export industry to serve his political machine and a passion for industrialization. Nevertheless, when the military ousted Perón in 1955, Argentina remained more nearly modernized than the acknowledged Third World countries, and there seemed no reason why it should not develop its tremendous potential further. No one realized how difficult that would be.

a. The Conservative Republic of 1930–1943

The political performance of the conservatives from 1930 to 1943 was as little conducive to unity as that of the Radicals from 1916 to 1930. The Radicals were rudely thrown from the presidency in 1930 by a military coup that the country accepted without a murmur; the conservatives were similarly treated, with the same lack of popular reaction, in 1943. Both coups were executed by the military, but in the earlier case they returned to the background of public life. In 1943 they took over the government lock, stock, and barrel.

The Provisional Government of 1930–1932

The rebels agreed to General Uriburu as provisional head of state, and two days after the coup he and his ministers took the oath to respect the Constitution so recently fractured. Uriburu said they hoped soon to return to regular elections. Although most ministers in his government were civilians, the regime endured only by support of the armed forces. It used the state of siege, imprisonment, deportation of foreign labor leaders or agitators, and torture to such an extent that Uriburu lost most of the goodwill he originally enjoyed. Uriburu not only ruled by decree, but suggested that such methods be made permanent. He favored a corporative or fascist organization, partly under the influence of foreign ideas, although Uriburu's general orientation was Argentine. He was of the old upper class, a long-time professional soldier in the Argentine environment, an observer of the inadequacies of political and governmental institutions there, a nationalist anxious to strengthen his country. His civilian and military partisans organized a paramilitary force from nationalist elements. This Civic Legion Uriburu legalized by decree in May 1931 as a reserve for the armed forces. It soon had some 10,000 members, who received training from the army. The legion had a militarized youth section. All this was reminiscent of fascist organization in Europe. Uriburu claimed the legion was apolitical.

On the whole, however, Argentines did not want Uriburu running the government. His plans for constitutional change were well known, and although he had promised not to act illegally, obviously little reliance could be put on his respect for tradition. His claims to stand for national development under elitist leadership did not suit the ambitions of party leaders or the principles of constitutionalists. Additionally, Uriburu did not carry the armed forces. The military in 1930–1931 showed a factionalism that in some ways paralleled that of civilian political groups, complicated by the personal and institutional ambitions of the military. Those two years, therefore, contributed to the politicization of the military, which constantly discussed—in ways largely hidden from the public—problems of national development. The chief unifying elements were nationalism and distaste for the Radical party. Some military factionalism took the form of rivalry for offices in the *Círculo Militar*, an organization of active and retired officers of all services.

In April 1931 Uriburu permitted an election in Buenos Aires. His followers lost, and the Radicals did well, so Uriburu voided the election. By now the would-be dictator was discouraged and ill. In November 1931 a national election was won by General Agustín Justo, who had emerged as the strongest figure in the professional military. He ran for a combination of National Democrats (conservatives), Antipersonalist Radicals, and Independent Socialists. Justo scarcely could lose, since the Uriburu government disqualified the Radical candidate, ex-President Alvear. The Radical party then returned to its earlier policy of abstention from elections, although individual Radicals voted for Lisandro de la Torre of the Progressive Democratic party. Justo won by over 100,000 votes in a total of 1 million, not impressive when no Radical candidate was running. Elected vice-president was Julio A. Roca, representative of the oligarchy that his father, a two-time president, had so well served.

The Fraudulent Political System, 1932–1943

Fraud and coercion were the hallmarks of the conservatives' political system as they returned to power after fourteen years of Radical administrations. They maintained themselves partly by suppressing the Radical majority, partly by the sort of coalition tactics used in the 1931 election. They used the same formula in the election of 1937, but Justo then found he had to use massive corruption and violence to elect the candidate of the coalition—the *Concordancia*. Then, in the administration of 1938–1943, after a brief flurry of effort at honesty in elections, the *Concordancia* returned to blatantly dictatorial tactics. There were no triumphs in other spheres to make *Concordancia* political corruption more palatable, and Radical dissatisfaction grew alongside some conservative distaste, and a little-observed growth of military disgust with the entire system.

Justo was a conservative nationalist. He believed in elitist rule, a stronger and more independent Argentina, and working within the established framework of economic and social relationships. His most pressing problem was the drastic decline in the price of Argentine exports. Some relief was gained by raising export volume, but clearly a reduction of dependence on imports would be a better answer. Diversifying production to accomplish that took time, however, and meanwhile a terrible threat arose. Britain, Argentina's best customer, considered buying its grains and meat from its dominions ("Imperial Preference") rather than from Argentina. Justo averted that disaster with the Roca-Runciman Pact of 1933 (renewed in 1936), by which Argentina agreed to buy British industrial goods and guaranteed the profits of British-controlled enterprise in Argentina in return for British purchases of Argentine commodities. Nationalists in Argentina railed against the agreement as a sellout, but most Argentine leaders favored it. Even supporters of the pact, however, resented Argentine dependence on Britain. The dependence on foreigners appeared also in the fact that in 1935 nearly half the industrial capital in Argentina came or was controlled from abroad. Many international industrial giants—including a number from the United States—produced in branch plants in Argentina.

Identification of Justo and the *Concordancia* with foreign interests was dramatized by some other events. Widely publicized congressional investigations of the meat business in the 1930s showed corrupt connivance between foreign meat-packing companies and Argentine private enterprise and government. There was another scandal about a government effort to extend the contract of the French company that had for decades reaped rich profits from its monopoly of Rosario's port. There was criticism of the government for bowing to the British streetcar company's demand that *colectivos*, little Argentine buses, be banned. The government thought the action necessary to ensure continuation of the Roca-Runciman system; nationalists charged that foreign interests were preferred to Argentine need.

The Justo government was, in fact, not unduly subservient to foreigners, but prudently nationalist. It took many steps to promote manufacturing, including protective tariffs, exchange control operations, and government participation in enterprises. The old piecemeal protection of industry became a broad program. In 1935–1941 the number of industrial workers increased over 50 percent, and the gross value of manufactures almost doubled. The industrial labor force was about 500,000 in 1935, and 1.8 million in 1947. There was parallel growth in commerce, finance, professions, and services. In the mid-1930s more than half the gainfully employed workers and more than half the value of national production came from nonagricultural/pastoral activity. This economic modernization—and the social development financed by it—vividly showed the great distance Argentina had traveled from its feeble origins; it also set it off from most of Latin America.

The slow shift from small workshops to real factories continued, so that in 1939 there were forty-three plants with over 1,000 workers each. Most manufacturing enterprises, however, still had fewer than one hundred employees, partly because heavy industry scarcely existed. In 1939 about half of the value of Argentine industrial production was in domestically consumed foods and textiles, so diversification had a long way to go. But Argentina was almost self-sufficient in some goods by that time.

Argentine industrial growth was based in part on an excellent supply of raw materials. By the end of the 1930s over 70 percent by value of the raw materials for Argentine industry were domestic. Foreign capital still was important in industry, some of it in foreign branch plants, but there was a gradual shift to native capital, so that by the end of the 1930s industrial capacity in Argentina was 60 to 65 percent domestic. Argentina, thus, was by no means "owned" or totally dependent on foreign capital and materials, although the amount of that dependence remained large, and much was in costly heavy industrial imports. Foreign holdings also were important because some of them were in such critical fields as power, meat packing, and transportation.

Nationalism played a role in the decision that the Depression made advisable reversal of the long-time policy of open immigration. In 1935 only 17,350 immigrants arrived in the country.

This before long reduced the problem of cultural integration that had worried nationalists since late in the nineteenth century. At the same time, urbanization continued, with increasing numbers of rural laborers from the interior moving to the eastern cities. By 1940 only about 25 percent of the population remained on farms or in communities of 1,000 or less. Furthermore, industrialization was not improving the economic balance between regions: by the mid-1940s 80 percent of industrial employment was in a few cities on or near the coast.

Justo began a highway building program in 1932. Before long the British complained that this damaged the British-owned railways, and thus was contrary to the aim of the Roca-Runciman Pact. Highway building continued. Railway expansion was slow after 1930. The basic system had been built, and British companies controlled 70 percent of it. Argentines complained that the companies made too much money and offered poor service. The companies retorted that restrictions on earnings hindered investment in improved service. This sort of argument was going on in underdeveloped and developing countries all over the world. The Justo government also gave nationalistic support to Y.P.F., the state petroleum agency. Justo also presided over the beginnings of a real national income tax, which would eventually help to reduce the traditional heavy reliance on import duties and to raise the enlarged sums of money needed by governments accepting new responsibilities. The Justo administration suppressed provincial and municipal consumption taxes that often impeded internal trade. There were new government agencies for regulation of meat, cereals, wine, and milk products. Extreme nationalists wanted even more state participation in the economy.

General Justo as president had a mixed record with regard to the military. He nearly doubled military expenditures but did not delude himself that political discussion had stopped in the armed forces. His surveillance system to monitor such activity revealed a conspiracy, led by Colonel Juan Bautista Molina, an admirer of Hitler,

with ideas on restructuring Argentine society and government. Justo broke up the conspiracy with officer transfers. He later approved Molina's promotion to brigadier general, however, and in 1937 he did not prevent Molina's election as president of the *Círculo Militar*. Whether Justo's forbearance indicated prudence or partial sympathy, it did not seem to promise a reduction of political extremism in the military establishment.

The *Concordancia* ticket imposed on the country for the term 1938–1944 consisted of Antipersonalist Radical Roberto M. Ortiz and ultraconservative Ramón S. Castillo. Although Ortiz was a wealthy lawyer acceptable to Justo, he believed in free elections, like those conservatives of earlier years who desired to bring political practice into consonance with their vision of the country's general state of civilization. In 1938–1940 President Ortiz intervened in the provinces to ensure free elections, with the result that the *Concordancia* of National Democrats and Antipersonalist Radicals in 1941 had less than half the members of the Chamber of Deputies, although it still easily dominated the Senate, whose members were elected by the provincial legislatures. This activity by Ortiz infuriated *Concordancia* leaders. They also disliked the creation in June 1940 of *Acción Argentina*, a group that opposed the Axis and defended democracy in Argentina but was crippled because the Radicals would not support it. *Concordancia* leaders were relieved when illness in July 1940 forced Ortiz to release his powers to Vice-President Castillo, and Ortiz was not an important factor again before his death in 1942. The accession of the reactionary Castillo was hard luck for Argentina. But possibly no civilian president would have been able to restrain the growth of military ambition, especially as stimulated by another stroke of bad fortune, World War II.

The elevation of Castillo alarmed many people, with good reason, as it turned out. His administration was marked by the growing domination of foreign affairs issues due to World War II, a continuing fragmentation and emotionalization of political opinion, an increase in ultranationalist sentiment, and Castillo's determination to preserve rule by the minority conservative National Democrats.

The diplomatic, strategic, and economic implications of World War II were frightening and aggravated all existing divisions of opinion. Threats from the war and from the inflamed condition of Argentine discord provided the Castillo government with excuses for drastic action. Much of the debate over foreign affairs had roots in Argentine tradition: the tendency toward isolation, so marked during World War I; traditional fears of Brazil, which international crisis heightened; old ambitions in Bolivia, Paraguay, and Uruguay, which international upheaval might further; close ties with Europe, especially Britain, which by now had serious critics. There was a more recent tendency to resist the pretensions of the United States to leadership in the hemisphere. Such views affected Argentine attitudes toward the rise of totalitarianism in Europe in the 1920s and 1930s, and toward United States initiatives from the mid-1930s for an inter-American security system. Argentina at the Inter-American Conference on Peace and Security at Buenos Aires in December 1936 led the opposition to Washington's desire for strong collaboration against menace from outside of the hemisphere, so there was agreement only to consult on problems of non-American aggression against the hemisphere. Argentina objected that a United States plan to lease destroyers to Brazil in 1937 would upset the balance of power in South America. When Britain in 1938 bowed to Hitler at Munich, the United States proposed a defensive alliance of American nations; again Argentine opposition limited agreement to consultation.

After World War II began in 1939, the United States for a year and a half increased aid to the anti-Axis belligerents and promoted defense measures within the inter-American system. Argentina stiffened its neutrality, and elements within and without the government showed sympathy for the Axis, which increased Washington's animosity toward Buenos Aires. Some Argentine sympathy for the Axis was based on belief in 1939–1941 that it would win the war and that the United States would not defend Latin America south of the bulge of Brazil. Some Argentine military were pro-Axis or protofascist, but most simply wanted to follow the winning side and admired the successes and the sociopolitical systems of Germany and Italy. Castillo was not pro-Axis, just anxious to skirt foreign danger and outmaneuver his critics.

By the time of Pearl Harbor (December 1941) Argentina was beset by fears and dislocations due to the war and by rumors of rightist and leftist conspiracy against the government. At the meeting of foreign ministers at Rio de Janeiro in January 1942 Argentina successfully insisted that diplomatic ruptures with the Axis should be left to each state.[1] The Castillo government then declined to break relations with the Axis. As other Latin American nations did so and many declared war, Argentina became isolated. This frightened and infuriated some Argentine leaders. When the United States granted lend-lease military equipment to its ally Brazil, the Argentine military reacted with rage and obstinacy. When the United States accused Argentina of aiding Axis agents and the Argentine Congress produced evidence to sustain the charge, the Castillo government stubbornly rejected it and declined to reform its habits.

The debate in Argentina over the war was not as important as the debate over internal policy, but it made the latter more bitter. There was a sense that immense changes were occurring in the world, making it essential for Argentina to act to ensure her future. Castillo greeted Pearl Harbor as a reason to declare a state of siege, and he operated thereafter under this suspension of constitutional guarantees. That aided him in an effort to control the political and electoral systems before the presidential election set for November 1943. His aim was to impose a complete conservative, a more radical course than that followed by the *Concordancia* in the elec-

----

[1] See Chapter 34, Section a.

tions of 1931 and 1937. He used arbitrary power to beat down opposition. He knew, however, that some elements in the military opposed his government. In November 1942 he was compelled to put in a new minister of war, General Pedro Ramírez, who was acceptable to the extremist faction in the army. In January 1943 ex-President General Justo died. He had wanted to be president again and might have been a restraining influence or rallying point for reasonable elements in the *Concordancia* and in the armed forces.

Castillo chose as his conservative candidate Robustiano Patrón Costas, a wealthy sugar landowner and industrialist. Sugar was a protected crop, so that his money came from the equivalent of a tax on ordinary Argentines to keep out cheaper foreign sugar. Furthermore, the sugar plantations and mills of the northwest were notorious for their miserable labor practices. The choice demonstrated Castillo's lack of capacity for political maneuver in a country of many and often bitter divisions and an expectation of some sophistication in balancing conflicting forces. By mid-1943 the country was in a highly nervous state, aware of foreign criticism and fearful of retaliation, battered by the suspension of constitutional guarantees and by intervention in the provinces, railed at by extremists, and worried by rumors of conspiracy and coup d'etat.

We cannot know precisely what political solutions the Argentine people preferred in 1930–1943, since elections were corrupt. In addition, women and large numbers of the laboring class did not vote. Some conservatives supported Castillo's methods in the belief that Patrón Costas would favor their interests. The Radicals could hope to return to power if fair elections were held and if they could find an attractive candidate. They had some interest in running General Pedro Ramírez. That choice exposed their weakness as a party of men rather than principles, but they had reason to believe they were a majority party, if only they could detach the military from corrupting the electoral process. The Socialists were willing to collaborate with the Radicals

against Castillo, but the Radicals preferred to try to find a solution on their own.

The uncertainties and the violence and threats of more to come encouraged discussion of extremist solutions. Much of this was of rightist coloration, strongly nationalist in belief and aspiration. The growth of nationalism for several decades in Argentina has been noted. In the 1930s it received infusions from fascism and nazism in Italy, Germany, and Spain, which stimulated demands for more "discipline" to ensure the national destiny. The old praise of dictator Rosas was reinforced by cries that later presidents had surrendered the economy to foreigners. Thus, the cosmopolitan society produced and supported men who could devote their talents and passions to social analysis and propaganda for panaceas to which they gave shrill voice. These pamphleteers, poets, historians, and ideologues could do little by themselves, but they helped prepare some people for new policies, even for modifications in the governing structure.

The critical development in that direction went on within the armed forces. Military nationalism was growing. Officers increasingly believed that they should play a larger role in shaping public policy in a greater Argentina. Justo's economic nationalism encouraged the view that active government was required. Resentment of foreign economic influence stirred military passion. Events in Europe increased sentiment in favor of a disciplined and hierarchical society. These ideas often were expressed in speeches and publications, but at places and in journals not likely to come to the attention of many Argentines. Some observers in Argentina and outside in the years before 1943 declared that political action by the armed forces was contrary to Argentine tradition, that the 1930 coup was an aberration from a tradition of seventy or eighty years of civilian government. They thus ignored the intense violence of 1810–1852, the use of force for years after 1852 in the quarrel over the status of Buenos Aires, and various dubious uses of military force by governments and officers in the long years between federalization of the city of Buenos Aires and 1930. They also did not take account of what was happening after 1930.

The Coup of 1943

Rumors multiplied in early 1943, one of them that General Ramírez would run for president for the Radicals. The newspapers on June 1 carried Ramírez' denial. Military officers engaged feverishly in discussions. They were badly divided. On the whole, the navy was less inclined toward jettisoning the constitutional system than the army, and the latter contained many points of view in addition to that of the extremist GOU (Group of United Officers). When the decision was made to oust the government, virtually all the military cooperated or acquiesced. Troop movements began in the dark of the morning of June 4.[2] There was even less resistance than the small amount offered in 1930. For some hours there was great confusion, as the government held some installations and the rebels others. The public knew that Castillo had been ousted, but not who or what would replace him.

That the leaders of this purely military movement intended to hold power for some time quickly became clear; the action was not simply against an immediate situation but was also directed to a perceived need for fundamental change in the political and governmental systems. The coup (*golpe*) and the fact that the military thereafter remained openly and massively active in public affairs have led to many efforts to explain the reasons for this drastic interruption of the long effort to sustain constitutional and representative government.

These explanations involve analysis of what had been happening to opinion in the community at large, within the military establishment,

and the interactions between the two. No doubt, if the political and governmental systems had functioned with less discord and more attention to compromise and observance of law and had given clearer evidence of a capacity to promote continued Argentine development and strength, the military would have been less tempted to intervene. That does not tell us, of course, why those systems did not so function. To assign the failure to the rapacity of the larger economic interests and their political spokesmen is too simple. Such an explanation leaves the puzzle of the inept performance of the Radicals, who, although conservative on socioeconomic issues, were not quite as indifferent to innovation as the rightists. Possibly a failure of leadership let the Radicals concentrate on political office and spoils rather than national development in all of its senses. Assigning the blame to lack of unity in the middle class, by this time possibly 40 percent of the population, is common. Factions in the middle class, in turn, are often ascribed to conflicting economic interests or merely to an excess of materialism. Even Argentines argue the reasons for their political failures.

Whatever the reasons, a group of military officers was convinced that Castillo and his probable successor were inadequate to national needs. They also thought that Argentina had a great future that was being jeopardized. Their belief reflected conventional military interest in national strength and prestige, but it was also based on consideration of economic matters that earlier generations of officers had less inducement to study. The leaders of the *golpe* were convinced, furthermore, that the military was the proper institution to direct the country's destiny in place of the discredited traditional politicians. Here there was some foreign influence, especially from fascist Europe, but the theory was also reminiscent of nineteenth-century positivism. Very likely most officers did not want to govern permanently but were excited at the prospect of a greater role for the armed forces, with more opportunities for individual advancement and for directing the aggrandizement of the fatherland. The leaders

---

[2] As in virtually all cases of Latin American military activity in public affairs, only officers exerted initiative, and enlisted men obeyed orders. To be sure, the attitudes of enlisted men somewhat affected the character of their obedience.

of the *golpe*, members of the GOU, lacked plans for what to do with the opportunity they seized, but certainly had some vision of themselves as innovators and modernizers.

b. The Rise of Perón, 1943–1946

Many people hoped that the change marked the end of uncertainty and the beginning of new economic growth. The Argentine Supreme Court on June 7 recognized General Pedro Ramírez as head of a de facto government, which the United States and other nations promptly recognized. Ramírez dissolved the Congress, ruled by decree, began to intervene in the provinces, and canceled the scheduled presidential election. Members of the government were rightists, even admirers of fascism, and most moderate views were squeezed out of the cabinet by replacements, until October 1943. In the early days of the regime there was some spouting of anti-Semitism, race superiority, the necessity of rule by the strong, and other fascistic notions. They soon were either modified or camouflaged, and the military settled down to considering affairs from an Argentine rightist point of view, including possible territorial expansion.

The regime took a pro-Axis stance by interfering with the activities of those who favored the Allies, aiding pro-Axis publications and propaganda by German agents, and even permitting the supply of maritime information to German U-boats. Some Argentine military officers thought that the Axis would win. Some officers simply admired Axis achievements and disliked British economic influence in Argentina. In any event, the regime resisted adjustment to the likelihood of Axis defeat.

That was partly obstinacy in response to pressure from abroad. The Allied powers protested Argentine pro-Axis policies, with little effect. When the regime in August 1943 suggested that the United States arm Argentina as it was arming Brazil, Secretary of State Cordell Hull replied coldly that such aid went to allies. Washington also took the view that the Argentine regime was constructing a system modeled on those of the fascist states and for that reason constituted part of the "enemy." Finally, pressures by the Allies led the Ramírez government in January 1944 to break relations with Germany and Japan. In February the predominant officers' group replaced Ramírez with his vice-president General Edelmiro Farrell, thus pushing the blame onto an individual and opening the way to a change of policy. The military government, however, did not declare war on Japan and Germany until March 27, 1945, when the fighting was nearly over.[3]

Free speech was not an ideal of the military. Government newspapers were set up with privileges to help them drown critical organs. Many devices of harassment, including violence and threats, were used to intimidate editors. Dissent in general was discouraged by spying, denunciation, threats, and physical coercion. There were enough arbitrary arrests and other violent acts to cow many people into silence. The voice of disagreement also was muffled in the educational system, and glorification of the regime became the goal. In October 1943 a notorious antidemocratic novelist, Gustavo Martínez Zuviría (Hugo Wast), was made minister of justice and public instruction. The generals restored religious education in public schools, violating a rule that dated to 1884 and was widely supported. Interventors were appointed to run the universities, whereupon students struck on the grounds that the appointees were fascists. On October 28, 1943, Martínez Zuviría began closing universities. The conflict between liberal students and the regime was never resolved.

The regime at once received support from rabid nationalists, from business elements that thought leftism was being contained, and from a strong element in the church, enchanted with the new educational policy. Persons of property who supported the regime in the early days sometimes changed their minds as the tyranny developed, but some supported it or acquiesced until

---

[3] See Chapter 34, Section a.

policies, years later, came to seem damaging to large economic interests. The church position also would change in later years. In 1943, and for some time thereafter, however, both those groups contributed to the strength of the military position.

Opposition to the regime appeared quickly. Many Argentines believed in elections, a congress, and provincial governments, but now there was a government that possibly meant to eliminate them. Not since Rosas, before 1852, had there been such a threat to a civil society. In October 1943 a group of distinguished Argentines petitioned the government for a return to democratic processes and cooperation with other American nations in the war. The regime took reprisals against them. Opposition began to go underground. Many Argentines, however, still were not convinced of the need to fight the regime. At least a few of them must have been somewhat disturbed by the decree of New Year's Day 1944 dissolving all political parties as fraudulent and corrupt.

There was an intense power struggle within the military after the coup of 1943. With the seizure of national authority, officers became inflamed by the immensity of the prizes involved. The chief figures competed for top military appointments, which grew in number as the government raised military expenditures and the size of the armed forces; for posts in the government; and for political clout within military factions. The last did not correspond with military rank, but with the ability of officers to use the classic skills of political leaders.

Colonel Juan Domingo Perón of the GOU had those skills. He was a man of middle-class origins, in his late forties, a graduate of the military academy. He participated in the Uriburu coup against Yrigoyen in 1930. He had a reputation as athlete and scholar. On duty in Europe, he was impressed with the methods that led to totalitarian achievements in Germany, Italy, and Spain. He had more varied interests and abilities than the run-of-the-mill officer, a wider ambition, and a brilliant personality that was of some use

in conventional military life but of maximum value in a politicized military force or in general politics.

In two years Perón made great progress, as under secretary of war and then head of that ministry, as head of the department of labor, and as vice-president when his faction of the military replaced Ramírez with Farrell as president. Perón's work in the war ministry was important in building officer support, especially by influencing appointments, putting in key posts a faction that depended on his continued importance to ensure their own positions. This was ordinary army politics, but his activity in the labor field was entirely novel. The regime from the beginning tried to control labor and gain influence with workers, but had little success and aroused resentment by ham-handed tactics. Then in October 1943 Under Secretary of War Perón asked for the labor department, which he then had upgraded to the Ministry of Labor and Welfare, a remarkable move because labor had little influence in Argentina and lacked prestige in the class-conscious officer corps. What Perón saw was that most laborers were not union members, were not courted for political purposes, often did not participate in the political process, had poor incomes, and presumably could be organized as a political force as they were in Europe. Perón accomplished that feat through organization, exhortation, promises, and improvement of conditions of work. His methods were thorough, imaginative, and immensely effective. He increased the number of organized workers by five or six times. He found about 10 percent of the labor force organized in 1943; it was 60 percent (4 million workers) organized by 1951.

That task required great effort and ruthlessness. Perón was building a personal machine, so he threw out or neutralized old labor leaders. Some leaders were happy to collaborate, partly because of the opportunity to organize the workers who never had been in syndicates. The rapid result could not have been achieved without the aid of government funds and personnel. Perón even included some of the rural labor force, although that was more difficult to organize than urban groups. Gangs of toughs were used to cow and manhandle union opponents and protesting employers and organized business. Perón promised labor not only better working conditions but a more honorable place under the Argentine sun. He had a talent for popular oratory, sparking belief and enthusiasm. Much of it was due to his appealing personality—he was a large, handsome, very male (*muy macho*) person—and his excellent delivery of speeches (with the aid of amplifiers and radio). He had a sure feel for what would rouse the worker: cupidity, assured care, fear that gains would be taken away, and identification with a cause and leader. One notable oratorical ploy was identifying himself with all shirtless men (*descamisados*), doffing his jacket during speeches, thus separating himself from the generations of Argentine statesmen who thought politics was for the *gente decente*, socially acceptable men of education and sufficient wealth to dress "properly." He also used the term "oligarchy" to describe those responsible, as he claimed, for corruption of the political system.

Such efforts might have brought Perón support under any circumstances, but their great success depended on government decrees mandating higher wages, Christmas and other bonuses, rent control, price freezes, and on the *Peronista* mobs that were used to help enforce them. Perón also had control of a social security system, which he expanded to confer another class of aid, including health benefits, on laboring men and their families. Men, and their wives, flocked to the Peronist camp. Perón had an organization that he could use for political purposes, although for a time he disclaimed that intention. Few people can have believed him. The use he made of mobs to intimidate and destroy was daunting to civilians and suggested to his military enemies caution in the use of force against Perón.

Argentina was reaping great profits from exports to the anti-Axis powers, and at the same time restriction of manufactured imports stimulated Argentine industrial production. Not so

pleasant for the traditional economic elite were moves by the regime to increase government control of and participation in the economy. In April 1944 it created an Industrial Credit Bank and declared some private grain elevators public utilities and expropriated them. In February 1945 Vice-President Perón was confirmed as coordinator of all economic and social policy. This reinforcement of his powers followed closely on a January 1945 decree that provided greater authority for the government, including restrictions on the press, prohibition of lockouts and strikes, and a ban on any action that might hurt industrial production.

Propertied Argentines became dissatisfied with dictatorship and the expanded government role in society. They realized that Argentina must adjust to a fascist defeat in the war. This restiveness was encouraged when in May 1945 the United States named Spruille Braden ambassador to Argentina, after Argentina in March agreed to enter the war. Braden, from May to September 1945, followed his orders to praise representative government, without directly criticizing the Argentine regime. The target was obvious, however, so Perón claimed interference in Argentine affairs. Braden was certainly popular with anti-Perón elements in Argentina and encouraged their efforts. In June 1945 associations of commerce and industry issued a manifesto against Perón. When the government on August 6 lifted the state of siege that had been in force nearly four years, it quickly discovered that many people wanted to return to constitutional government. Demands for change multiplied, and in mid-September Perón informed the army that politicians and capitalists were trying to weaken military support of the government and even proposing foreign intervention.

On September 19 there was a big demonstration in Buenos Aires, including a "March for the Constitution and Freedom," that involved many men prominent in Argentine life who wanted an end to dictatorship. There was great excitement during the next few days and hope of concessions. There were none. On September

25 the government began action against a plot at Córdoba, and arrests included the presidents of the Argentine Industrial Union and the Buenos Aires Stock Exchange and the rectors of five universities. On September 26 the government reimposed the state of siege. Critical newspapers were harassed by the police. On October 5 the government broke up student sit-down strikes at several universities, and arrested some 1,500 at the University of Buenos Aires alone.

All these actions encouraged Perón's enemies in the military to force him on October 9 to resign from the government. But the next day Perón, orating outside the Ministry of Labor, announced that he had signed a decree granting workers raises and shares in profits. He urged workers to remain united under his leadership, and they cried "Perón for president!" The speech was broadcast over the official state radio network, and all other stations were obliged to air it. In other words, Perón retained friends in high places, including President Farrell, who appointed pro-Perón General Avalos as war minister. Then Farrell and Avalos reluctantly agreed to a demand that Perón be detained, on October 13, but Avalos announced that he was not under arrest, only being protected from his enemies.

Meanwhile, Perón's mistress, Eva Duarte, rallied his labor legions. It took several days to get them moving in numbers, but they increasingly showed serious intent as they marched about the city crying "liberty" for Perón. The police and military conspicuously did not interfere with them. On October 15 labor activity intensified, with extensive rioting and damage to property in central Buenos Aires. By October 17 the city was paralyzed, and still the police and army did not interfere. Perón's partisans in the military were in the ascendant; he was released; and on October 1 Peronists were put in command of the government under President Farrell.

Perón had been too much for his opposition. The large anti-Perón civilian element was not well organized; it certainly was not ready to battle in the streets with the *Peronistas*. Employer groups that hated Perón's labor policies

not only did little to woo workers, but even refused, in some cases, to pay for the holiday he had decreed for October 12, Day of the Race, a celebration of Hispanic culture. Above all, Perón's military foes did not try force against his worker groups. The demands for Perón's return by enormous crowds, with insistence that they were prepared to fight, alarmed the military. They knew they could disperse the mobs, but feared defection among the enlisted men, resistance by Peronist officers, and such a blood bath as would lead to a continuing civil war that might sweep the traditional military forces away or leave them permanently dishonored in the eyes of Argentines.

After this victory, Perón doffed his uniform, identified himself with reform through the electoral process, and ran for president. He set up a Labor party and continued his drive to control all labor. Late in October 1945 leaders of independent unions protested that the labor ministry was campaigning for Perón as president and interfering with their activities. That was serious for those unions, because under the state of siege they needed police permission for meetings, and in its absence had to work secretly. In December the government aided Perón by decreeing a national wage raise of 10 to 25 percent, plus an extra month's pay at the end of the year. He also had an organization to attract votes from the Radical party. In November he was endorsed in a collective pastoral letter by the Argentine bishops, telling Catholics not to vote for candidates favoring separation of church and state or secular education, thus ruling out the Radical party candidate.

The opposition formed a National Union of Radicals, Socialists, Progressive Democrats, and Communists. It thus did not include the conservative *Concordancia*'s National Democrats and Antipersonalist Radicals. The National Union nominated a Radical for president. His campaign was hampered by the government, but that was not a major factor in the result. The opposition equated Perón's methods with those of fascist tyrants, but that was an easily recognized exaggeration. Smiling Juan Domingo, with his civilian clothes and his raises in pay, had no such aura of brutality as Hitler or Mussolini.

Exaggeration was not confined to Perón's domestic foes. Some elements in the United States contemplated his possible election with distaste and fury. That reaction to dictatorial government, feeble aid during the war, and nasty Argentine jibes at the United States was understandable. Less understandable was determination to use strong methods against Perón, without similar action against equally objectionable regimes. That element of vendetta was expressed two weeks before the February 1946 election in a State Department Blue Book designed to help defeat Perón. It presented "incontrovertible evidence" that Argentine officials, including Perón, "were so seriously compromised" with the Nazis during the war that they could not be trusted by the United States thereafter. That was direct interference in Argentine political affairs. Perón promptly said that a vote for his opponent was a vote for Spruille Braden, now assistant secretary of state for Latin American affairs. The Blue Book probably helped rather than hurt Perón at home, and it brought him sympathy, and the United States censure, throughout Latin America.

The state of siege in Argentina was raised for forty-eight hours for the balloting. Argentines and the many foreign observers in the country agreed that the vote and the count were fair, with 1.48 million to 1.22 million in favor of Perón, a handsome victory considering how much of the traditional ruling element was against him. To uninvolved observers he seemed nearly as popular as Rosas a century earlier and more attractive. With support by a solid majority, in a country with many economic and social assets, Perón seemed blessed with opportunity.

c. Political and Diplomatic Peronism

Perón as president (1946–1955) accomplished much less than he hoped, the usual fate of

leaders, but his influence was felt, for good or ill, for decades. He deserves credit for his successes and only partial blame for his failures. His contemporaries recognized as much when, twenty years after driving him from power, they invited him back; no one better had risen in the interim. At least he was a man of size, and people became weary of midgets.

Politics

There were six main ingredients in Perón's political system. (*a*) Adulation of himself as *El Líder.* (*b*) Organized labor as the heart of a majority Peronist party that controlled Congress, a form of modernization by broadened participation. (*c*) Social modernization in the gains showered on the working man and his family. (*d*) Heavy-handed influence exerted on the media and the intellectual and educational spheres. (*e*) A politicized military as a favored institution, but Perón tried to balance it with his labor legions and with the Federal Police, and he juggled assignments in favor of officers who supported him. (*f*) Nationalism as justification of all actions.

Perón fostered national integration by focusing attention on simple rationales for policies, in the process sometimes corrupting the ideal of community or national good. He called for national unity as vital to Argentine safety and greatness in a dangerous world and hindered that unity by dictatorial actions. He justified redistribution of income by railing at the *oligarquía* but did little to damage their position, while alienating them and inducing a slowdown of economic effort. He expended rhetoric on a national and independent foreign policy that left so little result that one wonders how much of it was sincere and how much mere puffery. His use of nationalism as a justification for his economic policies contributed to the difficulty of countering idiocies with rational argument.

The dependence of the movement on the leader was a ubiquitous theme. Perón, and often Eva, beamed in a thousand confident poses, on horseback and skis, in tweeds and uniform, in newsreels, on magazine covers, in the government newspapers, and on numberless posters. The party bore his magic name. The workers sang "We are the Peronista boys (*muchachos*)." Signs endlessly reminded "Perón Cumple" (delivers the goods). Perón married Eva immediately after she helped him surmount the crisis of October 1945. She sang her husband's praises with gooey ardor, not hesitating to compare him with Jesus. Intellectual members of the cult took up the old claim that Rosas, bloody tyrant of a century earlier, represented the authentic Argentine strain, now happily revived by Perón.[4] Eva and the other faithful proposed Juan Domingo for the Nobel Peace Prize, celebrating his "Third Position" bridge between the antagonists of the cold war. Alas, the cult appealed only to Argentines.

Eva—Evita, little Eve, as she was affectionately known—in her more restricted way was as remarkable a leader as Perón. She was a passionate orator, able to inflame worker grievance against the oligarchs (a word she used). It helped that the workers knew she had been a poor girl. Eva was the more believable because the old elite snubbed her and told dirty stories about her, so that she reacted with effective rage and vindictiveness. She was strikingly handsome, though her enemies affected not to see it. The poor did not resent her new riches, her clothes and furs, but saw her as a *cenicienta* (cinderella) to whose transformation they could thrill. She told them, in fact, that the Perón program would give them what she had attained. She was intelligent and adaptable. The old aristocrats sneered at her as overdressed in the early days, but she learned to be as sleekly expensive looking as the ladies of the old cattle fortunes. So omnipresent was she in the Peronist system that some people ascribed to her much of her husband's success, slighting his original conception, organizing force, and indis-

pensable manipulation of the armed forces. She was not popular with the military gentlemen, who were stuffy in their social attitudes, *macho* (masculine, with what we would call more than a hint of male chauvinism) in both the military and the Hispanic traditions, and thought her representative of the worst of the populistic "demagoguery" of Peronism.

Perón kept the faithful happy with material and spiritual benefits. Until 1949 wages rose in response to government decree, sustained by a good export market for several years in war-torn Europe. The popular sector naturally responded with enthusiasm. In addition to wages, the state provided enlarged social benefits. Evita dispensed much of this through the Eva Perón Foundation, financed by the government and by "voluntary" contributions by business firms, other organizations, and individuals. Eva's huge operation aided education, health, and public housing, partly through construction programs, but also through services. It sold cheap food and other goods. Evita received streams of poor petitioners, and dispensed gifts of medicine, goods, money, jobs in the swelling state bureaucracy, and spiritual sustenance. No wonder she was called by such terms as "The Lady of Hope."

Much of the attachment of the laboring class to Peronism must be understood in this connection. It was political—that is, emotional or spiritual. The gratitude of the poor for improved health care, for example, was intense. That was something that not all middle-class leaders and voters in Latin America adequately appreciated. Some of the same reaction resulted from Perón's program of low-cost vacations at resorts. Luxury hotels at Mar del Plata, beach playground of the rich, were converted to popular use. It was too smug to dismiss such programs as "bread and circuses," even though Perón may have been insincere in aiding the workers. They responded with affection and a new sense of their own worth. Many must have been moved by a need in the impersonal urban environment to belong to something, to have a sense of involvement and identification. The importance of this reaction

---

[4] See Chapter 30, Section a, for turn-of-the-century praise of Rosas. That point of view enjoyed a revival in the 1930s.

was not smirched by Perón's maunderings about his social system as *Justicialismo.*

Perón depended heavily for support on reaction to his economic aims and achievements. An end to degrading dependence was the refrain, to the extent of incautiously promising never to accept foreign loans. Heavy and high-priced exports in the immediate postwar years sustained this euphoria. The pot of gold accumulated in wartime Britain Perón squandered on the acquisition of foreign enterprise, notably railways. Everyone could thrill at this blow to colonialism. Previously, Perón declared, governments had not properly planned for the economic independence and prosperity of the fatherland. He published an ambitious Five-Year Plan, to the accompaniment of thunderous self-advertising claims of a national victory.

The railway deal did not aid the economy. Another burden was military expense, which in the early years of the Perón presidency ran on the order of 30 percent of government funds. Military officers held positions in the administration and had some influence on economic development planning both in doctrine and through administration of the military industries. Early in 1949 signs of strain in the system appeared. Inflation led newspaper typographers to strike when their own union officers and the government resisted demands for a 25 percent pay raise. After 1949 there were few economic gains to prop up Perón's political position. His reactions to economic difficulty included more political reform, an inflationary expansion of credit, and a move toward restraining labor demands while encouraging investing and ownership elements in Argentina and abroad.

The Peronist party never engulfed the society, either by its numbers or by elimination of opposition. It did become large enough to dominate the government for a decade. In the 1946 election the Peronists won in all but one province, gaining control of Congress and of most provincial and municipal offices. The chief opposition, the Radical party, was reduced to about one-third of the Chamber of Deputies, much less in the Senate. A new constitution (1949) provided for much government participation in the economy, social assistance, rights for labor, and woman suffrage; and it permitted the president to succeed himself immediately. Evita organized the *Partido Peronista Femenino*, with herself as president, and it became a part of the *Movimiento Peronista*. In the elections of 1951 more women than men registered, and they cast ballots in larger proportions than male registrants and were more strongly for Perón.

The campaign for the election of November 1951 was for some time dominated by Evita's candidacy for the vice-presidency. In August Perón and Evita at a rally of workers agreed to run on a joint ticket. The crowd shouted "Perón fulfills! Evita dignifies!" Airplanes overhead wrote their names in smoke. But she was not nominated because of army objections. It had protested her activities before, and in 1949 came near to making them an issue. Now the officers took a strong stand, partly in rejection of the idea of a female commander in chief, partly against the unsuccessful economic policies of the administration and its political activities within the armed forces. Evita stated on radio that she preferred her old battle station as plain Comrade Evita. There was a rumor that the entire affair was staged to keep the opposition off balance.

The opposition was, in any event, off balance as the result of a 1951 electoral bill providing direct election of the president, and prohibiting the sort of party coalition that Perón's opposition used in 1946. The Radicals nominated Ricardo Balbín. He had for years courageously defied the Peronist law of *desacato* (disrespect), under which opponents of the regime were jailed and harassed for quite innocuous remarks. Perón declared himself winner of the election with a large majority. The campaign and balloting processes were so unfair that no reliance could be put on the figures.

Perón was not willing simply to trust to the electoral process. He used violence and threats. Argentina was not, however, a thoroughgoing police state. To compare it with Nazi Germany or a communist regime is an exaggeration. The opposition operated openly, even in Congress, though impeded by unfair and sometimes brutal tactics by the government and Peronist mobs. The Supreme Court was purged after a 1946 chamber vote of 107 Peronists for and 47 opposition deputies against the impeachment of justices. There was much interference with the media and with freedom of speech generally. The gradual extinction of independent newspapers was completed in 1951 with seizure of the famed conservative journal *La Prensa*. University faculties and administrations were overloaded with incompetent and anti-intellectual Peronists. Students, dismissed professors, and supporters of Argentine intellectual achievement never ceased their protest. Opposition deputies in the chamber spoke eloquently against the teaching of fascist ideology and subservience to Perón.

The problems of the Radical and Socialist parties were worsened by factionalism. The Radicals responded to their losses with some efforts at more liberal doctrine and with more promises to the laboring class, but could not make the offer credible. In the Chamber of Deputies the Radicals reacted to the bludgeon tactics of the Peronist majority in various ways, none successful. The Socialists failed to convince the workers of Perón's demagoguery. The Peronists were not immune to factionalism, but Perón used his great prestige and power to pull the party together when local leaders squabbled. It was an unhappy period for the old parties. Perón not only had great power, but he was too acute for the opposition.

Diplomacy

Posturing on international issues aided Perón internally by distracting attention from domestic problems. His chief policy aims were as follows: economic independence; international prestige; leadership for Argentina; resistance to tutelage or suggestion by the United States; promotion of the Peronist sociopolitical system; advertising of his notion of a Third Position between capital-

ism and socialism in the cold war; and at least limited territorial aggrandizement. He in fact pretended to be more venturesome than he was. His personal dynamism tended to inflate the importance of what he said. The possibilities open to him, however, were limited. There was little more than publicity value in his noisy claim to Britain's Falkland (Malvinas) Islands or the claim he staked out in Antarctica. He objected to friendly Uruguayan reception of exiles from his regime, but did little about it, knowing that there was a limit to what Brazil would permit there. He dabbled in economic pressures and political intrigue in Paraguay and Bolivia, as Argentine administrations had for a century and a half, but again was restrained by Brazil's interests. Possibly Perón was as aware as the military analysts of the great powers that the Argentine military logistical system scarcely could sustain operations beyond the country's borders.

He dreamed of a system of collaboration between Latin American nations under Argentine leadership, but it came to nothing. Some people thought this was the aim of his several bilateral economic agreements, but they accomplished nothing. He especially irritated other Latin American nations by the labor attachés he sent to his embassies. The attachés were notorious for heavy-handed propaganda activities, and for collaboration with local labor leaders. It was charged that Perón was promoting coups d'etat in Latin America to set up regimes similar to his own. He created an international labor organization, known by its acronym ATLAS. It attracted few members. All his efforts to export Peronism failed.

Perón asserted that between the capitalist system of exploitation and the communist system of Russia there was no fundamental difference, but that he had built a better social order, occupying a "third position" both in socioeconomic terms and in the diplomacy of the cold war. He was ready to act as the peace maker of mankind. His followers said that this increased the country's prestige. The reason for the popularity of the policy, of course, was that it was isolationist.

Argentines were no more anxious to be involved in the cold war than World War I or II.

Argentine speeches and newspaper articles and cartoons continued to abuse the United States. North American business interests, however, were uninterested in Perón's political coloration and were willing to do business with Nazis who appeared on the United States blacklist in the Blue Book. After the Blue Book fiasco, in fact, Washington decided that promotion of economic relations and of hemisphere cooperation was more important than Perón's irritating stances. In 1950 the United States Export-Import Bank granted Perón a "credit." The flurry of concern over Argentine fascism during World War II was, therefore, soon replaced with a policy of business as usual.

d. Economic Peronism

Perón's most damaging errors were economic, and in the end they brought him down. He directed increased shares of national income to the military and to wages and social services for workers. He greatly enlarged public sector participation in the economy. He repatriated foreign investment with nationalist fervor, heedless of economic good sense. His nationalism included a mania for industrial growth without insight into its relationship to the total economy and with overconfidence in the ability of the government to direct it. His misunderstanding of the importance of the pastoral/agricultural sector was so total as now to seem willful blindness. Nevertheless, he did somewhat aid diversification. His greatest socioeconomic contribution, however, was better distribution of income to the working class, with implications not only for justice and politics, but for expanded purchasing power for support of national industries.

Repatriation of resources was a nationalist goal of such apparent simplicity that many Argentines thought it beyond argument. It was observed in an earlier chapter that distaste for foreign enterprise in Argentina was fairly prominent by the end of the nineteenth century, was

fed by nationalist writers in the early twentieth century and exaggerated by the Depression of the 1930s and World War II. In the 1940s it flowered all over Latin America, as a passion and a panacea. The fact that the foreign share of the economy had been declining since World War I did not reduce the flowering in Argentina. Between 1943 and 1955, under a variety of terms, including purchase and confiscation, Argentina repatriated some banks, insurance companies, meat packing firms, telephone companies, gasworks, electric enterprises, streetcar lines, railroads. For such purposes went much of the $1.7 billion worth of foreign exchange Argentina built up abroad during World War II. The largest purchase was the British railways, greatest symbol of foreign economic domination. The British were willing to sell because profits under government regulation had been low for some time. Argentina paid a high price, especially given the run-down condition of the railways. As usual, however, Perón's decision was more rational in political than economic terms.

Perón's economic nationalism combined with his taste for statism. Most Argentinized enterprises were made state operations. His first Five-Year Plan was published with his usual ballyhoo. The thrust of the plan was toward industrialization, through construction of infrastructure and subsidies and other aids to manufacturing. Major attention went to fuels, electric power, and steel. Perón was at some pains to declare that the plan was not totalitarian, but "constructive democracy." It did not deliver all the economy into the hands of the state; unfortunately, it also did not provide effective coordination between the public and private sectors. In 1947 Perón began to retreat, calling the plan merely a general statement of intent. A second Five-Year Plan was published in the 1950s, with more attention to agriculture than in the first but not enough to rescue it from the depression partly induced by exaggerated industrialism.

Much of the Perón economic operation was dedicated to milking the great agricultural/pastoral sector. The most notorious of many devices was IAPI (*Instituto Argentino Para Intercambio* —Argentine Institute for Exchange). Agricultural producers had to sell commodities at low prices to IAPI, and it exported them at higher. It worked for several years, until Europe's production recovered so as to depend less on Argentine food and until Argentine producers rebelled against the control of their profits by IAPI. The producers curtailed their efforts, and output declined. Agricultural commodities were 94 percent of the value of Argentine exports in 1921–1944, but declined after World War II as planters reduced acreage. Before the war Argentina supplied about 40 percent of the world's export grains; in 1946–1947 the percentage was only 15. Thus began the process of decapitalization of the huge export sector: land, equipment, herds, drainage, corrals, a host of things were allowed to deteriorate since investment did not pay. Food available for export was also cut by the fact that workers had more money and spent much of it for meat, and by droughts in the 1949–1950 and 1951–1952 seasons.

Although the decline in exports restricted Argentine ability to pay for machinery and raw materials needed for industry, that sector did grow rapidly. The United Nations reported that Argentine industrial expansion of 61 percent in 1943–1950 led the world. By the end of the Perón regime almost all consumer goods were being produced in Argentina. More than a million workers were in industrial occupations. Workers in services increased sharply. Argentina moved farther and farther away from the old agricultural republic.

Export sales, however, did not develop. Furthermore, little progress was made in the heavy industrial sector. Steel output rose only slightly. Imports of coal and petroleum products still were heavy. In 1955 petroleum products ate up 20 percent of Argentina's foreign exchange. Electric power production increased 45 percent from 1946 to 1951, but barely kept up with demand. The railway system deteriorated, and was a burden on the treasury as it became a dumping ground of political appointees. Adequate rates could not be charged without political repercussions. Little was done for the inadequate highway system. The state airlines were expanded but required heavy subsidies. An enlarged merchant marine, however, saved some of the traditionally heavy payment to foreign shipping lines. Many of the larger manufacturing companies continued to make money, but inflation, taxes, state-mandated wage raises, and social security levies made things difficult for small enterprises. By the 1950s many people in the middle class saw their standard of living being reduced. Owners and managers in industry became strongly anti-Perón.

Moreover, as compared with many countries in the world, in Perón's Argentina capital formation as a whole was low, a major reason for the fact that by 1953 total national production actually was declining. Even before then, Perón and his critics quarreled about the state of the economy. They did not agree, for example, on the rate of inflation, or how it should be described. Perón liked to cite peso rises in per capita income, so that in May 1952 he boasted that the average was up 71 percent; his critics retorted that if adjusted for price rises, the real increase was 14 percent.

Another reason for this unhappy state of affairs in the most advanced economy of Latin America was that the Peronist governmental system was one of the most expensive in the world. In possibly no other country were government costs so high or detracting more from capital formation. In 1949 Argentina was ranked among the world's highest-tax countries. Much of the increase was new indirect taxation, including very heavy social security levies. Not only were the services generous, but the retirement age was set at a low fifty-five. Much of Argentine taxation was regressive and bore heavily on the poor. Direct taxes on individual and corporate incomes were low. The bureaucracy grew rapidly and was inefficient and corrupt. In 1948 a federal judge ordered the arrest for fraud against the government of the coordinator of the Five-Year Plan, the head of Perón's bodyguard, and the vice-president of the government's Bank of Industrial Credit.

Perón became more conservative economically after his reelection in 1951. He was less generous with wage raises and tried to tie them to gains in productivity. He made concessions, including higher prices, to agriculture. Argentines, premier shippers and eaters of meat, had to endure official "beefless days." Perón even modified his war on foreign capital and tried to entice it into the country. The greatest monument of Argentine economic nationalism, the oil agency YPF, was to receive aid from international oil companies. Negotiations began with Standard Oil of California in 1953, and a contract was signed in 1955. None of Perón's moves had much effect on an economy that had been badly handled for a decade and needed extensive rehabilitation. Nor could he easily alter a system of government expenditure that had built up new vested interests that opposed cuts in the bureaucracy and an end to inflation.

Thus, although Perón did not ruin the Argentine economy, as is sometimes charged, he did sadly damage it. The government spent beyond its means, resorting to deficit financing and price inflation. There was underinvestment in productive facilities, with government driven by political goals and the private sector fearful of public policy. Labor—or at least labor leaders—favored inflation with annual wage raises. Higher wages were useful in extending the domestic market, but inefficient manufacturers were sheltered by the protection against foreign competition. Perón's use of economic policy for political purposes left important interest groups without perception of a purpose for collaboration rather than conflict, and conflict would be one of the chief heritages of the Perón regime.

e. The Fall of Perón

Widespread repudiation of Perón's leadership did not occur until 1955. The popular classes were disgruntled but not rebellious. Perón's ability to deal with labor was damaged by Evita's death in July 1952; on the other hand, her passing removed an irritant to the military. A great outpouring of grief at Eva's death culminated in

an effort to have her canonized by the church. The next year, in April 1953, Perón demonstrated his continuing hold on his street legions by having them burn the Buenos Aires Jockey Club, haven of the rich hierarchy or oligarchy—Perón used both as terms of opprobrium—that he feared was intriguing against him, especially with military officers. This act was a warning both to wealth and to the military that there were millions of Argentines willing to use violence to sustain Perón.

Only the military, police, and *Peronista* mobs showed important potential for deciding events by violence. The rich and the middle class displayed little readiness to use force through their cattle societies, trade associations, or political parties. Although there was speculation that Perón's favored Federal Police of 15,000 men in the capital might play an independent role against the armed forces, that never was likely. The organization, training, and equipment of the Federal Police made them no match for the military. The Federal Police might provide, however, some stiffening to the *Peronista* street fighters, increasing the likelihood that the military in a showdown might have to kill considerable numbers of civilians, which they were reluctant to do. Perón did not try to create an armed popular militia, although there were reports that he might. The military would not have liked such a move, as Perón knew. Perón in his last years continued to play politics within the armed forces, struggling to keep men partial to him in important posts. That always was a problem not only because the military resisted dictated personnel policies but because Perón could not always be sure how much an officer's personal inclinations might be canceled by institutional pressures. Military opposition to Perón did increase in his last years, but most officers either favored him or were reluctant to support a coup d'etat.

Many groups of officers, especially after 1949, more or less seriously discussed a change in the presidency, or at least military dictation of policies. A small military effort at revolt in September 1951 was suppressed by Peronist officers, and military men were warned against joining the movement by actions of Peronist street demonstrators. The military was so badly divided and unsure of the desirability of acting against Perón that officers were unready to move in force until the time in 1954 when he unnecessarily complicated his position by attacking the church. Military action against Perón in 1955 and against Peronists thereafter has obscured the fact that the officer corps gave him heavy support for years and almost to the end was reluctant to oust him.

The accumulating complaint rained on Perón by the opposition political parties, rebellious students, military factions, labor leaders, and business interests must have been a major reason for his fear that an additional voice of protest could not be tolerated. In 1954 he detected such a threat in the church. After 1951 the church was clearly not so comfortable as formerly with Perón as an ally. Perón and Evita were not conventional churchgoers. They cut into the church's traditional charitable functions, taught a Peronist worship in the schools, and organized women for political purposes. The last was worrisome because the church depended heavily on the support of women. It did not like the moves to canonize Evita. But the church was not mounting a campaign against Perón, so the reasoning behind Perón's radical actions against it remains a mystery. Prominent explanations are the identification of some church elements with a small Christian Socialist group, some church criticism of Peronist policies, a fear that the church might serve as a unifying focus for the complaints against Perón, and a collapse of Perón's political judgment under pressure. We are virtually driven to the last explanation, since none of the others appears to later analysis to have offered much of a threat.

His uneasiness became near hysteria only in November 1954; between then and the middle of the next year he conducted a remarkably foolish offensive against the church. In November he objected to church encouragement of dissident labor and student elements. He probably would have caused no trouble by such objections, since Argentines for decades generally had preferred that the church maintain a low political profile.

Perón then declared that he would legalize divorce and license prostitutes. There was no substantial demand for either, yet he forced them through Congress. When there were protests, Perón retaliated by dismissing priests who were teaching in public schools. There were street clashes over the issue, some at churches. In May 1955 Perón ordered Congress to disestablish the church, although the mild form of establishment that had existed since 1853 seldom had occasioned serious controversy. On June 11 in Buenos Aires there was a large demonstration by pro-church elements. Perón deported two papal delegates and had the police and mobs sack the residences of priests. He seemed intent on committing political suicide. On June 16 the Pope excommunicated all government authorities in Argentina who used violence against the church, by some interpretations including Perón.

Long ago, Perón had lost much respect by his silly war with the church. The reaction was strong in the armed forces, where discussion of public affairs was the chief order of business in 1955. In June a military revolt, including aerial bombing of Buenos Aires, was put down by loyalist military forces. Clashes in the streets occurred. There were renewed reports that Perón would arm the workers. Perón declared that his forces would kill five enemies for each Peronist slain. In the midst of great confusion, Perón hung on for three more months. Then on September 16, 1955, military revolts began at several points in Argentina. Conflicting claims and demands were published and went out over the air. Airplanes made menacing sorties over the capital city. The navy radioed a threat to shell the city. On September 21 the military commanders in the capital area went over to the rebellion, and their men, as usual, obeyed their orders. The civilians of the metropolis understandably did not go out to face naval guns, military aircraft, and tanks. There was virtually no resistance. When the military abandoned Perón, he was finished. He fled to Paraguay. A military junta took over the government. How much this would resemble the military *golpes* of 1930 and 1943 remained to be seen.

36 Argentina: Political Instability and Economic Stagnation Since 1955

After Perón's fall, Argentina struggled to reestablish economic growth and failed. It sought political order and failed. It saw its weight in international affairs diminish. Its reputation as the leader of Latin American modernization dwindled. The engorged state apparatus ate up revenues and gave back shoddy services. The working classes that Perón had aroused and organized remained united, demanding their share of the Argentine inheritance. The military and propertied classes could not agree on the role and income of the popular classes. The officers corps, enthroned as the major factor in politics and government, heaved in dissension over the Peronist issue. Military officers alternately ran the country and stewed while civilians tried to do so. So hapless were the efforts of 1955–1973 that in the latter year old Juan Domingo Perón was invited to return as president. With his death in 1974, his widow carried on as *presidenta*, to a rising chorus of dissent and violence. In 1976 the military ousted her and installed another general as dictator, as seemed to be the modern tradition.

a. Economic and Social Development

The performance of the economy pleased no one, although Argentina remained richer than most countries in the world. Overall growth was slow, but accumulated socioeconomic capital still gave Argentina in 1971 a per capita GNP of $1,230, first in Latin America and twenty-seventh in the world.[1] In the mid-1970s, each Argentine ate 240 pounds of beef a year, twice the intake in the United States. International experts calculated in 1958 that with proper policies Argentina could increase its GNP by 77 percent in a decade, but by the late 1970s it had achieved only a fraction of that.

There was hesitation at home and abroad about investment, because political instability sapped confidence in the continuity of policy. Minister of the Economy Alsogaray, an advocate of free enterprise, in 1962 declared, "It is impossible to bring in foreign capital under the permanent threat of revolution." There were dismaying policy oscillations. How could business respect military regimes that in one year (1970–1971) elaborated seven conflicting economic programs?[2] For years foreign bankers and busi-

---

[1] World Bank figures. The United States at $5,160 was first; the Soviet Union at $1,400 was twenty-third; Venezuela was second in Latin America at $1,060; Mexico, $700; Brazil, $460; Bolivia, $190, was next to last in Latin America; India was $110.

[2] The question was asked by a Mexican government publication, savoring the political stability of Mexico, the

nessmen said that what Argentina needed was an economic policy that lasted more than three years. But such stability was difficult to arrange when the propertied class and wage earners could not agree on the relationships among wages, profits, and investment.

The financial situation usually was poor. The government overspent revenues, resorting to foreign borrowing and easy credit that increased the supply of money and drove down its value. What the Argentines called the "hippopotamus" (inflation) raised prices an average of 30 percent a year between 1955 and 1967, 40 percent in 1971, and more in 1972, when the International Monetary Fund called Argentine inflation the worst in the world. Government could not withstand demands for pay and price increases from labor, the military, and business. Some of the inflation was the result of agreements on prices and wages between employers and trade union leaders. The inflation got entirely out of hand in the 1970s, and by 1975–1976 was running at a rate of more than 300 percent a year.

Deficits in government accounts were due in part to costly social services, large military expenditures, and a civil service that totaled some 400,-000 personnel by the mid-1960s. Great sums also went into the growing public sector of the economy. The small beginnings of the 1930s, expanded by Perón, now became an empire in oil, gas, electric power, telecommunications, banking, railways, shipping, airlines, ports, steel, and other manufactures. By the 1960s some 600,000 persons were employed in government-owned and -controlled enterprises. Some were badly run and cost large subsidies above their revenues. Although the military supported free enterprise, which remained larger than the public sector, they also favored a public role out of nationalist fervor, plus a taste for the authority and pay that

went with their appointments to government enterprises.

Foreign investment to finance growth and reduce balance-of-payments problems was recommended to Argentina by domestic and foreign experts, but leaders were driven by pressures that blocked creation of a good climate for foreign capital. Leaders could not even satisfy Argentine investors, who at times had more liquid capital abroad than in the country. So the government borrowed abroad, and by the end of 1964 Argentina had the third largest external debt among the world's developing countries, after India and Brazil. In 1975 alone the foreign debt grew $1 billion, to a total of more than $10 billion. Critics said payment on the debt was a major cause of the economic malaise; government defended it in terms of improvement of productive facilities.

The root of much policy was nationalist desire to reduce dependence. That goal supported high tariffs, protecting some industries in an inefficiency that imposed high prices on consumers. Nationalists claimed that was a temporary price that must be paid for extermination of colonialism. Foreign capital in Argentina met pounding adverse publicity. It extended to distaste for advice from the International Monetary Fund, the World Bank, or the United States government, offered as the price of financial assistance. Such advice was said to be unsuited to Argentine conditions. Foreign-owned public utilities received floods of criticism, and the government so restricted them that they resisted making further investment.

The warmest focus of nationalist ambition was the petroleum industry, controlled since Yrigoyen's time by the government oil entity YPF. State control became costly with a widening gap between production and demand. In 1940 Argentina imported 43 percent of its requirements for petroleum products; in 1950, 67.5 percent; in 1957, 68.4 percent. In 1957 petroleum cost $270 million, 21 percent of all Argentine imports. In that year, an Argentine who stated that foreign petroleum investment was in the national in-

---

continuity of its policies, and an economic growth after World War II far superior to Argentina's. Of course, in all these things Mexico had been inferior to Argentina before the 1930s, as the Argentines generously pointed out at that time.

terest was accused of wanting to "sell out his country."

The next year President Frondizi put through Congress a law giving foreign petroleum companies contracts for specified profits, without ownership rights. That did not still nationalist clamor, however, even when production skyrocketed. Argentina imported only 35 percent of petroleum requirements in 1960 and 10 to 15 percent in 1961. When Frondizi was ousted by the military, in March 1962, pressures to change the petroleum system damaged production. In 1963 an investigating board stated that the Frondizi government had acted illegally, and new President Illía could now easily cancel the contracts. Although a compensation and renegotiation controversy dragged on, the companies were not ousted. When the military took over again in 1966, they continued the contract operations. At the end of 1974, YPF, by then Argentina's largest enterprise, was producing about 85 percent of the country's needs, but a third of it came from foreign contract companies there. The YPF director declared in 1974 that it was "the flag of the fatherland, the expression of our sovereignty."

Imbalances in international commodity exchange caused anguish, partly because of the passion for industrialization, which required an inflow of raw materials and machinery; partly because of low beef and wheat production for export, as incentive was cut by government levies and controls. In 1974 the National Grain Board was the only legal buyer of crops, and like Perón's earlier IAPI often paid less than the world price. One result was a black market. Lack of incentive also caused underinvestment, so that productivity declined. Pastures went to thistles. Equipment aged. Low meat export also was the result of high domestic consumption. As the urban population grew to about 80 percent of the total by 1975, politicians satisfied it with low meat prices by cutting the profits of the dwindling rural population. Although per capita exports remained high by world standards, they were much less than Argentina's productive capability and world demand seemed to justify. In 1974 agricultural/pastoral shipments were 70

percent of Argentine exports of $3.8 billion, but the Argentine share of world trade had been declining for years. Many experts declared that the agricultural/pastoral industry, which produced 90 percent of the foreign exchange of the country, could be greatly expanded. But rather than do something effective about exports, the government tinkered periodically with exchange controls.

Transportation and electric power deficiencies were bottlenecks to efficient performance. Merchant marine and port charges were costly, partly because of bureaucratic inefficiency and union featherbedding. Highway development and air transportation were neglected for years after Perón's fall. The government railways were the single largest source of government deficits, and gave poor service. Efforts at reform, including reductions in personnel, brought strikes. Estimates in 1962 were that the railways used twice the employees to handle half the freight of the period just before nationalization in the 1940s. In the 1970s the government was still seeking a solution.

Modernization in the sense of diversification proceeded. In 1969 production was 14.1 percent in agriculture and mining, 39.3 in industry and construction, and 46.9 percent in services. Iron and steel and automotive production were notable examples of a move into heavy industry. In 1957, when Mexico and Brazil had large basic iron and steel production, Argentina had only one small producer of pig iron, the Military Factories, although it did have a large metal fabricating industry. An iron-and-steel-producing complex at San Nicolás, begun by Perón in 1952, came into production in 1960, and production increased steadily thereafter. An automotive industry was created at the end of the 1950s by forcing foreign companies to replace imported with nationally produced components. By 1973 automotive vehicle production was well over 300,000 units. The increase in motor vehicles was coupled with highway construction. Argentina's intellectual and economic strength permitted Perón in the early 1950s to begin an atomic research program. The country in 1975 put into operation the first nuclear power plant in Latin America, using a German reactor and Argentine uranium. In 1977 Argentina signed an agreement to build a research nuclear reactor in Peru. In the nuclear field, as in many other manufacturing fields, government participation continued to increase after Perón's fall in 1955. By the 1970s government ownership and regulation of industry was an important part of the "corporative" alliance between private enterprise, the military, nationalists, and many technocrats and professional people.

Argentina's population growth remained slow.[3] Brazil and Mexico rapidly drew away from Argentina in total population, and Colombia apparently would equal it before 1980. The low growth rate was probably related to an urban way of life and high standard of living. By the 1970s greater Buenos Aires had a population of 8 million, and Rosario and Córdoba were near a million each. The federal district and the province of Buenos Aires had more than 40 percent of the 25 million inhabitants in the mid-1970s, a demographic imbalance that eased problems of control for authoritarian governments.

Argentines still had the highest level of living in Latin America. Although wages were low, so were prices, especially for government-controlled foodstuffs. Much of the population was middle class in its point of view and expectations. Even many laborers wore jackets and ties in public and hoped to see a son in the professions, including the military officers corps.

Housing in the burgeoning cities was inadequate. The shanty settlements called "misery towns" (*villas miserias*) in and around all major cities held over a million persons by the 1970s. Most shanty dwellers were employed, cooperated in community affairs, and were optimistic, not alienated. The alienated seemed not to have increased significantly among the poor.

Observers in Argentina worried that the citizen in the street was too materialistic, too attached

to ease, too apt to go to the beach in a time of political crisis. They claimed this attitude was shown by a waning inclination to work hard and by absenteeism, both of which hurt productivity, partly because of a 1974 law protecting workers from dismissal and providing payment of wages during illness. This unsurprising interest in material things no doubt was the reason most Peronist laborers were moderate in their views, except in times of great excitement. Workers had been politicized but generally not radicalized. They were self-conscious and militant, but mainly about Peronism, social legislation, and their unions. Many unions provided hospitals, physicians, dentists, low-cost vacation resorts, and aid in housing. The large middle class and the more conservative part of the laboring class were a barrier to violent social revolution.

The cultural level of Argentina remained high, with more than 90 percent of the population literate in the mid-1970s.[4] The citizen in the street was assailed by political argument and forced to give some attention to political violence from both right and left. The moderately reformist Socialist party remained strong in Buenos Aires. Solutions more extreme than it offered came to public notice, from terrorists, Marxists, and idealistic or revolutionary university students. The universities had been expanded in the 1940s and thereafter, but the great university reform of 1918 never brought the country an outstanding system. Quality was damaged by persistent political activity by students and faculty, and by intermittent government controls or even purges for political reasons. Although leftism in the universities created considerable alienation from society among the largely middle-class student body, moderates, passives, and conservatives probably were a majority, but less organized and active. University students and graduates had one complaint: the shortage of opportunities they considered appropriate to their training. That led

[3] At 1.5 percent a year, it was less than one-half the growth rate of Mexico and several other Latin American countries.

[4] In 1970 Argentina, with a population of 20.5 million, had 238,615 university students; 924,806 in secondary school, representing a huge percentage increase in recent decades; and 3.6 million in primary.

to a "brain drain," especially to the United States. Another complaint was the result of legal authorization of Catholic universities by President Frondizi. Critics condemned that as encouragement of conservatism. They also complained that the superior discipline and instruction at Catholic institutions, due to their lack of proper political spirit, made them improper competition for the state institutions! The politicization of educational views could scarcely go further.

Although many small political groups existed in Argentina, the chief division was between wealthy, middle-class, and military groups on the one hand, and on the other the Peronists. But the situation was more complicated than that. The middle class was in turn divided, especially between factions of the Radical party. The military were fragmented in many ways, but chiefly between those who wished to take a hard line against Peronism and leftism and those who were more willing to compromise. The fact that much of the opposition also disliked Peronism enhanced military influence. The propertied and the military tended—erroneously—to equate Peronism with Marxism. Many Argentines were committed to private initiative, often of an old-fashioned antilabor variety.

The Peronists were divided between conservatives and radicals, between those for and against Perón's return, and between the old-line labor leaders and the professional people and middle-class figures, including leftists, who were attracted by a movement that retained a hold on 25 to 35 percent of the electorate. The Socialist party was split and remained of significance chiefly in the federal district. The communists were a minor group. The church returned to its generally passive role in public affairs.[5] Propertied interests largely survived Perón and returned to their old

concerns, often promoted through powerful business associations. Their position after 1955 was complicated by the growth of the public sector of the economy, which gave the government more power to channel their activity.

Violence took the familiar forms of military pressures and threats against the civil government, coups d'etat, states of siege, politically inspired intervention in the provinces, street demonstrations, and student sit-ins. In the late 1960s and 1970s it also took the form of rural guerrilla activity and urban terrorism. Argentine intellectuals endlessly wondered what factionalism and violence indicated about the national culture. Their speculation came to little more than a vague identification of insufficient community spirit. Social theory did not permit useful comparison of factionalism in Argentina and other countries. Possibly factionalism was reason for optimism, indicating that debate over social arrangements was not cut off by a police state or by an ignorant and apathetic peasantry. Surely political participation was as widespread—if intermittently repressed—as ever in the country's history.

b. The Military Government of 1955–1958

The military regime declared that it favored "rule by law" and then governed under a state of siege until 1957. General Eduardo Lonardi headed the government briefly, mixing conciliation with coercion to the satisfaction of neither moderates nor extremists in the military. The hard-liners wanted to eradicate Peronism. Lonardi tried strong measures against organized labor, but they merely angered workers. He moved to rescue the floundering economy by calling in the eminent Argentine economist Raúl Prebisch, whose report at the end of October 1955 was pessimistic. The sad state of the economy and the belligerence of the Peronists brought a military coup on November 13 and General Pedro Aramburu as provisional president.

Aramburu led the hard-liners against Peronism. The *Peronista* party was outlawed, Peronist officials dismissed, and Peronist doctrine and per-

---

[5] In the 1960s and 1970s revolutionary priests appeared, some even believing in violence. On the other hand, some "Christian socialism" in Argentina was tied to Vatican doctrine favoring brotherhood and repudiation of class struggle. In the 1960s an organization called *Ateneo* attracted well-to-do Catholics with a mixture of piety and reaction that seemed similar to the rightist Opus Dei of Spain.

sonnel removed from the educational system. At the same time, the press was given considerable liberty. *La Prensa* was restored to its owners in 1956. Other types of property confiscated by the Perón regime were also restored. But Aramburu had no more success than Lonardi with harassment of organized labor. Peronists objected to efforts to restrict wage raises. Efforts to round up Peronist leaders in 1956 led to violence. Pro-Perón slogans blossomed on walls. Entrenched Peronist party officials and trade union leaders resisted threats to their power and perquisites. The rank and file had achieved a self-confidence and militance that would not shrivel with persecution.

The military decided to turn the problem back to civilians. In anticipation, the Radical party (UCR), still the largest in the country, held a nominating convention in November 1956. It then had two major factions, the *Unionistas*, who were strongly anti-Perón, and the *Intransigentes*, more flexible on the Peronist issue. Although this division affected the convention, the main issue was a personal rivalry. The convention nominated the Intransigent Arturo Frondizi, whereupon Ricardo Balbín of the same faction split off a part of the Intransigent Radicals (UCRI) and combined them with the *Unionistas* as the Popular Radicals (UCR del Pueblo—UCRP) and opposed Frondizi. In 1952 Balbín and Frondizi had been, respectively, candidates for president and vice-president of the republic for the united UCR.

The UCR split continued in the July 1957 election for a constituent assembly. Of the 208 seats in the assembly, the UCRP received 77, and the UCRI 73. More than a quarter of the votes in the election (2.06 million of 7.98 million) were cast blank, most of them by members of the outlawed Peronist party, demonstrating its huge size and determination. The military and other parties could deplore it, but it was a stubborn fact. The twenty-odd minor parties had relatively little support. The constituent assembly returned the country to the Constitution of 1853.

In February 1958 ordinary national elections were held. Frondizi, UCRI candidate, was a pro-

fessor of economics, of conventional views before a chance at the presidency opened to him. Then he called for programs similar to those of Perón: social justice, state intervention in the economy, elimination of oligarchic monopoly, overall planning, complete nationalization of petroleum and some other industries, war on foreign interests in the Argentine economy. His enemies in the UCR called him a demagogue and a leftist. Since Balbín and the UCRP would not support Frondizi, he needed votes from other groups, and found them among ultranationalists and in the Perón camp. Frondizi received 4.37 million votes, and probably nearly 2 million of them were Peronist. Balbín won 2.68 million. UCRI candidates won control of Congress and of most states. The election generally was accepted as showing the great hold that Peronist ideas had in the country. So, after more than two years of anti-Peronism directed by a military government, Peronists still seemed necessary to achievement of the presidency in an open election.

The economic policies of the military government of 1955–1958 were not successful. Its ideas were moderate, acceptable to the traditional economic elites more than to Peronists, the Marxist left, or the rightist nationalists. It did make some concessions to all those groups, on political rather than economic grounds. It somewhat reduced intervention in the economy. It continued Perón's late policy of wooing foreign investment but not his concessions to foreigners in petroleum. It tried to pare the bloated bureaucracy, but found doing so politically expensive. It renounced Perón's second Five-Year Plan and depended on improvisation—as Perón had done in fact. All aspects of the economy were in poor condition. So the floundering military regime of 1955–1958 bequeathed to Frondizi the same array of problems it had encountered at the fall of Perón.

c. Civilian Presidents While the Military Hover, 1958–1966

From 1958 to 1966 the military permitted three civilian presidents, but hovered over them with advice, demands, and threats. The officers corps squabbled over national policy, divided between hard-liners who opposed Perón and often favored military government, and moderates who were for civilian presidents, elected legislatures, and some sort of accord with Peronism. Frondizi endured four years, increasingly subject to military pressures, and was finally ousted in 1962. José Guido, president of the Senate, succeeded to the presidency and was a mere mouthpiece of the military for eighteen months. Arturo Illía was elected president in 1963, tried with little success to act independently of the military, and was ousted by them in 1966. During those nine years the problems of economic stagnation and Peronist demands were as difficult as ever. Military interference was not the only reason for the failure of the governments; but the officers stood waiting to take over when they judged conditions intolerable, a possibility that scarcely built confidence in government officials, party managers, directors of business enterprise, or managers of capital in other countries.

President Frondizi was inaugurated in May 1958 and quickly repudiated some of the nationalist doctrines he had been spouting. He declared that Argentina must pare expenditures and increase investment. Even more adventuresome, in 1958 he signed contracts with foreign (especially United States) petroleum companies, infuriating nationalists of every stripe. When the policy became a remarkable economic success, the nationalists merely said that the price was too high. Frondizi also stimulated industry and neglected agriculture in the Argentine pattern of recent years. Much industrial expansion was fueled by $400 million in United States public credits and another $400 million in private foreign investment (about half of it from the United States). Increases in output, however, were modest compared with industrial growth in Brazil and Mexico during the same years.

Support for financial stabilization from the United States and the International Monetary Fund brought criticism from leftists and nationalists. Labor complained that Frondizi's policies saddled them with low wages and high prices.

In the first half of 1958 there were 620 strikes. Under pressure from the military, Frondizi tried to coerce dissident elements. The Justicialist (Peronist) party protested pressures on the real income of workers. It also claimed that the agreement for the election of 1958 had included a Frondizi promise to legalize the party and permit Perón to return. The military would permit neither. The Socialists and the UCRP, both anti-Perón, also condemned the stabilization plan. Although military hard-liners clamored for Frondizi's replacement, his military supporters permitted him in June 1959 to reorganize the cabinet on a basis of monetary stabilization and planned economic development, which was the price of United States aid. The most important new official was Minister of the Economy Alvaro Alsogaray, an advocate of more free enterprise.

Distaste for Frondizi found expression in elections in March 1960: 2.04 million votes for UCRP, 1.77 million for Frondizi's UCRI, and 2.07 million blank, mostly by the outlawed Peronists. This proof of Peronist discipline irritated military hard-liners, and they increased pressure on Frondizi. His administration existed in a state of perpetual crisis. Before long, the military had another source of irritation in Frondizi's reluctance to alienate the left further by declaring against Fidel Castro. In March 1961 he suggested himself as mediator between Castro and Washington. His offer was interpreted as a bid for leftist support in the elections of 1962. The military reacted strongly and forced out two foreign ministers who implemented Frondizi's policy of amity with Cuba. One crisis was precipitated in March 1961 by the resignation of Army Commander in Chief General Carlos Toranzo Montero. Newspapers published his letter to the defense minister criticizing the government for leftism. Also made public (April 1) was a letter from Admiral Rojas (one of the 1955 rebels against Perón) making the same charge. The complexity, uncertainty, fear, and unremitting pressure of such a crisis, when the military divided and made demands on the civilian president, could scarcely be appreciated by citizens of countries with different traditions. The result was that on April 23 Frondizi requested the resignation of Minister of the Economy Alsogaray, whose unpopular austerity policies also were repudiated by military critics.

Frondizi tried to block the United States–inspired OAS conference to discuss action against Castro. When it was scheduled for Punta del Este in February 1962, Frondizi declared that expulsion of Cuba from the OAS would violate the principle of nonintervention and that reactionaries in the United States fostered rebellion in Latin America against governments that tried to act in their own interest. The military would have approved this nationalism if it had not been connected with leftism. As it was, they delivered an ultimatum to Frondizi, and in February 1962 he broke relations with Cuba.

This contest was linked to the struggle over domestic affairs, and the participants had an eye on the congressional and local elections of March 18, 1962. Frondizi let the Peronists take part with their own candidates for the first time since 1955, hoping that he had charmed some of them into the UCRI, which would reduce his dangerous and humiliating subservience to military demands. That hope died under an avalanche of Peronist ballots. They led all parties, with 35 percent of a total vote of some 9 million. The UCRI had 28 percent, the UCRP 22 percent, smaller groups 15 percent. Peronists won 5 governorships (including Buenos Aires), many provincial offices, and a big bloc in the new Congress, only a part of whose seats had been at stake. The new Chamber of Deputies would consist of UCRI, 77; UCRP, 59; Justicialist Front, 44; other, 12.

The military forced Frondizi to annul the elections won by Peronists in six provinces. Succeeding days were tense. The military feverishly debated whether, or under what conditions, to leave Frondizi as president. The Peronists launched an only partially effective general strike. The UCRI tried again for collaboration with the UCRP. Together they represented half the citizenry, essentially the middle class. The UCRP not only refused to cooperate but joined the chorus from

other quarters against the so-called antinationalist economic policies of Frondizi. The military decided against Frondizi and tried to get him to resign. He refused. So on March 29, 1962, the military occupied key points in Buenos Aires and imprisoned Frondizi. The next day they installed the man next in line for the presidency according to the Constitution, Senate President José Guido.

The armed forces once again had determined the fate of an administration, even though the Peronists had the support of about a third of the electorate, controlled at least half the 3 million members of organized labor, and could count on the support of more for some purposes. The military, of course, had much support from persons of property; and they had means of physical coercion and threat that society could combat but not control. The military also benefited from the fact that Frondizi had rendered himself odious to many Argentines.

Frondizi's fall presented the United States with a problem. A stronger Argentine policy against Castro was welcome in Washington, but the Kennedy government was declaring a commitment to civilian regimes in Latin America and a distaste for coups d'etat. The new Alliance for Progress celebrated democratic institutions, and made economic and administrative reforms a condition of United States aid. Washington had granted Frondizi economic assistance; and much United States capital—especially in petroleum and motor vehicles—recently had entered the country. Washington had praised Frondizi's conservative economic policies as a model for Latin America. So the election of March 18 could be interpreted in part as a repudiation of the United States position in Argentina. Furthermore, a report soon circulated that the annulling of the election was the result of pressure from the United States. In mid-April Washington decided to recognize the new government in Argentina and at once was attacked at home and abroad for supporting military government.

Guido was a feeble presence from March 1962 to October 12, 1963, while the military paraded its factions and used him to issue decrees. As political bickering mounted, the economy sagged. In April Alsogaray was brought back as minister of the economy. Since his ouster a year before, four heads of that ministry had come and gone. In the summer of 1963 unemployment led to labor violence. Military factionalism and irresponsibility reached ludicrous depths. The most important contest still was over Peronism, with moderates and hard-liners now known as blues and reds, and often divided into subfactions. There also was a neutralist or Nasserite group of leftist or Third Position nationalists in the officer corps. There were tensions among the three armed services. Individual prestige and position were important factors, as assignments, retirements, pay, even personal safety were involved in the military rivalry. Conspiracies were hatched constantly; crazy abortive rebellions were common; rumor inspired fear and preventive action. The civilian population tended to react to this unsettling environment with either apathy or despair, although some leaders fished in troubled waters for advantage. The Peronists aggressively demanded their congressional seats won in the election of March 1962, and the return of Perón. But Peronism was divided. The new professionals and leftists in the movement were clashing with the older and conservative labor leaders. Andrés Framini, head of the textile workers and Peronist governor-elect of the province of Buenos Aires in the annulled elections, declared that the government's false charges that Peronists were communists would not stop the class struggle or prevent an uprising if that was the only way to achieve justice.

The military settled the election issue by having Guido cancel the vote of 1962 in toto. In May Congress was forced into recess; it was dissolved in September. All twenty-two provinces were put under federal rule. In July the government issued a hard-line plan for elections for 1963 that included a ban on the Peronist and Communist parties. It was not strong enough for some officers, and they followed General Toranzo Montero in a rebellion on August 8 that demanded no concessions to Peronists and no

elections earlier than October 1963. Although the rebellion lost, for a time it seemed likely to cause civil war. The situation remained volatile for weeks. Then, on September 18, 1962, the anti–Toranzo Montero moderates, led by General Juan Onganía, revolted and took over the government, with some bloodshed in this purely military quarrel. The Onganía blues or moderates claimed the move was necessary to prevent erection of a military dictatorship. Onganía became commander in chief of the army. It appeared that there would be an election in 1963 and that the Peronists would be allowed to participate. That did happen, but it often seemed that it might not. How primitive and easy to understand the military moves of 1930 seemed by now.[6]

The national mood was gloomy at election

---

[6] The military factionalism in Argentina between September 1, 1962, and the election of July 1963 may be taken as a model of such events in recent Latin American history, remembering that they are in fact often more complex and confusing than appears here. The moderates and hard-liners both were nationalist, anti-Perón, anti-Communist; they differed on whether and when to have elections and how to treat Peronists. In December the military forced the resignation of Minister of the Economy Alsogaray. On December 12 an air force revolt was crushed. In January 1963 the three military ministers stepped up attacks on Peronists, fearing they were arranging collaboration with the UCRI. In March 1963 there was a serious crisis over plans for the election, the division being on how strictly to control the Peronists. By this time the moderates were split, and one group wanted to make General Aramburu president. The navy was pushing the 1962 red faction plan for a "democratic dictatorship"—that is, no election. On April 2 there was a hardline (red) military rebellion, mainly by the navy, but including now retired army General Toranzo Montero. It wanted "democratic dictatorship." After two days of fighting, an uneasy truce was patched up. In April 1963 Minister of Government General Rauch was arresting prominent men as Marxist-Leninists if they were members of the Frigerista group of Frondizi supporters. The latter still was a prisoner of the armed forces, but there were fears that his organization retained too much strength. In May Rauch demanded that not only Frondizi supporters but Peronist sympathizers in the government be purged. This hard-line demand brought on a crisis, which moderate Onganía dominated, replacing Rauch with a general of the neutralist nationalist faction of the army. The supporters of the election, now set for July, still had a shaky hold on the government. Many people doubted that the balloting would occur.

time in July 1963. The result gave no comfort
to Argentines who longed for unity. The largest
popular vote, but a mere 27 percent of the total,
went to Arturo Illía for the UCRP. The electoral college later in July chose Illía, a provincial physician, long opposed to Perón, with little
following. He was inaugurated in October, and in
November redeemed his campaign promise to
cancel the foreign petroleum contracts. Soon the
cost of petroleum imports began to climb again.
Illía's nationalist fervor also took the form of a
break with the World Bank and the International Monetary Fund, on the common Latin
American line that their loans perpetuated imperialist control. But he soon had to sue the IMF
for aid. The labor confederation (CGT) in May
and June 1964 implemented a "battle plan" to
improve the lot of workers by occupation of factories and public buildings. Some employers were
held as hostages. Tension continued during the
rest of the year. In 1965 it was clear that the
economic policies of the government had failed;
the financial situation was nearly desperate.

Illía did no better with political affairs. The
UCRP of the president was claiming to have
reduced Peronist intransigence. He had made
wage and other concessions to labor, bidding for
voters' support. In the March 1965 congressional
elections, the *Unión Popular*, chief Peronist party,
was allowed to offer candidates, and won about
a third of the vote, more than Illía's UCRP. The
Unión Popular used this demonstration of support to demand again the return of Perón. In
October 1965 he sent his third wife, Isabelita, to
Argentina to reunite competing Peronist groups.
The military became increasingly disturbed by
this issue, and it sharpened other tensions between Illía and the armed forces. The latter considered that Illía's inability to control the rising
cost of living was increasing the strength of
Peronismo and *Fidelismo* in the laboring class.
Anti-Peronism in the military was increased by
signs of the beginnings of collaboration between
students and workers. Late in 1965 Illía appointed a war minister reputed to have Peronist
sympathies, and Onganía resigned as chief of the

armed forces. Nothing improved in the next six
months, and in June 1966 a junta of the three
armed service chiefs took over, declaring that
Illía had presided over anarchy and ruined the
economy. It named General Onganía provisional
president. A system of economic growth and a
satisfactory method of controlling the Peronists
seemed forever to elude the military.

d. Military Governments Again, 1966–1973

Again the Argentine people accepted military
imposition. The reaction of some citizens was
relief, out of disgust with the Illía regime, or fear
of Peronist and Marxist extremism, or because
Onganía was one of the more moderate officers.
It became evident that some of the military had
wearied of civilians generally. Onganía spoke of
military rule for five or ten years. He issued a
"Statute of National Revolution" which authorized decree government. Use of the term "revolution" was a ploy increasingly resorted to by military regimes in Latin America in the 1960s and
1970s and involved varying mixes of conviction
of the value of firm military rule and need for
social change. It was difficult to judge the sincerity of the expressions of military "revolutionary" regimes. Onganía spoke of the need for
change in values. He also sent Congress home
and prohibited political party activity.

The familiar round of efforts to deal with the
economy began. In general, Onganía favored free
enterprise, though he did not want to dismantle
the government's regulatory agencies and production enterprises. He favored concessions to labor,
but wanted to keep labor out of politics. In
August 1966 he began to yield to labor demands
for wage raises to meet the inflation. In 1967 the
regime issued a law again authorizing concessions
to foreign petroleum companies. None of the
economic measures of Onganía worked well
enough to pacify the country. Conservatives objected to the continual growth of state participation in the economy.

The issues of Marxism, communism, and subversion still seemed to some people an indis-

soluble whole. Conservatives, the middle-class members of the UCR factions, and many military men who approved of Onganía's anticommunism felt that way. In July 1966 the government made an anticommunist move by seizing the universities and ending student participation in university government. A September 1967 law in effect permitted harassment of anyone who had ideas of a "leftist" flavor. The government tried to keep students out of politics and spoke of "criminal elements" in the centers of higher learning. Students reacted violently against the Onganía administration.

Peronists also opposed the regime, despite Onganía's early efforts to pacify them. He permitted Isabelita to live in Argentina in late 1966 and early 1967 while she tried to unite the Peronists. Her presence irritated Onganía's supporters. They were better pleased when in February 1967 he hardened his labor policy, though that worked no better than at any other time since 1955. By 1968 opposition tactics were a national issue as kidnapping and murder for political purposes increased.[7] Although most victims were Argentines, enough foreign businessmen were involved that an exodus began.[8] Kidnappings were undertaken to gain money for subversive groups, to bring the government into disrepute, and for revenge. Some violence was declared justified on the grounds of police brutality and torture. In 1970 ex-President Aramburu was kidnapped by Peronists, and later found murdered. Clashes occurred in many cities. The greatest damage was psychological. Political and journalistic rhetoric tended to be inflated by disorder and murder. In Córdoba university students and organized labor began to explore mutual interests. At the end of May 1969 dissidents, especially students and organized labor, joined in protests against the wage and educational policies of the military government. Huge crowds demonstrated, destroyed property, and fought with the police. Middle-class individuals joined in protest against military rule. The great outburst of passion and violence soon was being called the *Cordobazo*, in imitation of the famous riots at Bogotá, Colombia, in 1948.[9]

Onganía thereafter had continual trouble with his military fellows. In June 1970, frustrated and divided, alarmed at the scale of violence in the country, the military replaced Onganía with General Roberto Levingston at a moment when the city of Córdoba was paralyzed by strikes against the government. Levingston was subordinate to a junta of the heads of the three military services. The new regime tried to stem the violence by courting labor and Peronist leaders. It did not work. In March 1971 Córdoba erupted again. The military disagreed on what measures to take, and there was yet another brief and frightening division of the armed forces. Levingston was ousted and General Alejandro Lanusse took over.

Although there seemed no end to the presidential musical chairs, something new was about to occur. Lanusse as provisional president after March 1971 headed a military faction that despaired of peace without Peronist participation. He promised elections with Peronist candidates, and a "great national agreement." Late in 1971 he announced elections for March 1973. Lanusse encouraged a coalition of parties, but the major groups went their own way. In early 1972 Lanusse recognized the legitimacy of the *Justicialista* party. He invited Perón to return, and the old leader finally came from Spain in November 1972, tried to knit his party together, endorsed Dr. Héctor Cámpora for the presidency, and left Argentina again in December.

All through 1971 and 1972 the economy was unsatisfactory. Violence continued in 1972. The president of the Italian-owned Fiat automotive

---

[7] Probably a small amount of criminality was involved in some kidnappings, but efforts to push that thesis only distracted from the critical political aspects of the problem.
[8] Their families were sent away first. Few foreign executives in high-level posts remained by 1975. Some foreign diplomats were also victimized.

---

[9] See Chapter 42, Section a, on the *bogotazo*.

industries was kidnapped, and when Lanusse refused to deal with the terrorists, the man was killed. A commanding general of an army corps was assassinated in reprisal for his antiguerrilla activities. An army-run prison was raided by revolutionaries who freed political prisoners and made the military look foolish. Leftists and rightists engaged in murder and countermurder. Some conservatives and moderates came to feel more than ever that Peronism was equivalent to communism. Marchers in Córdoba sang the Peronist anthem while carrying banners for Ché Guevara. Some Argentine Marxists thought of Perón as a social reformer with whom they could work. Some Peronist leaders also favored at least a temporary collaboration with Marxists. Perón was about to return and reveal his views on these dreams of alliance.

e. Another Peronist Regime, 1973–1976

In elections on March 11, 1973, Dr. Cámpora of the Justicialist Front ran with the slogan "Cámpora to the Government! Perón to Power." He had support from many elements, because Peronism now seemed the best hope of national unity, the winning ticket, and Cámpora promised rewards on all sides. The government declared him winner with a "virtual" majority. The old anti-Peronist Radical Ricardo Balbín received 22 percent of the vote. Peronists did well in elections to the national and provincial legislatures. Cámpora was inaugurated in May 1973, and proceeded to try to heal the divisions in the movement, chiefly by favoring the left. In June he proposed a sweeping economic program, with emphasis on redistribution of income in favor of the popular classes.

Also in June, Perón, now seventy-seven, returned to strife-torn Argentina. It soon appeared that he did not support Cámpora's leftist measures. In a few weeks he forced Cámpora and his vice-president to resign, a move approved by the armed forces. New elections were set for September 23. Perón reorganized the Justicialist movement along more conservative lines. He insisted that his wife, a known conservative, be his running mate. In the election Perón and Perón received nearly 62 percent of the vote.

That same month the tiny but violent People's Revolutionary Army was outlawed, a move urged upon Perón by the military, partly because of recent assassinations of military officers. Perón moved steadily to the right, interfering with leftist publications and meetings. In February and March 1974 centrists and rightists in Córdoba province battled with leftists, and Perón confirmed his turn away from the left by naming a moderate Peronist as federal interventor of the province. Also in March 1974 there was a spectacular ransom payment of $14 million to guerrillas of the People's Revolutionary Army by the Exxon Corporation for an executive kidnapped in late 1973 and kept in a "people's jail." The disorders of that month led Balbín, the Radical leader, to declare that Argentina was a "sick country," and stability a remote hope. That seemed to be the case when Perón died in July 1974.

María Estela (known as Isabel and Isabelita), a woman of middle-class Argentine family, succeeded to the presidency at the age of forty-three, with nearly twenty years' experience of Peronist political ideas and maneuvering. She received pledges of support by the military and most political parties to complete the term that ran to 1977. Apparently, even a woman was preferable to another election; besides, to the military and the propertied classes conservative Peronism now seemed preferable to many other political groups.

The economy worsened under Isabel. Her administration nudged petroleum policy toward total state control again, but did not eliminate foreign activity. By this time Argentina had made enough progress so that it was accounting for more than 80 percent of its needs for crude oil and refining nearly all that in government plants. Still, the required imports in 1973 became much more costly as the oil exporting nations abruptly raised their prices. Isabel found no answers to the familiar economic problems of the country. Inflation ran at an annual rate of more than 300 percent in 1975–1976. There were big government deficits and poor exports of meat, partly because of exclusionary moves by the European Common Market.

La Presidenta followed her husband's political leads. The Peróns had reinforced Juan Domingo's initial moves against leftism in the universities. Here also, some of the unlovelier aspects of "pacification" were evident. Cámpora had appointed leftists to university positions, and in the usual fashion of political activity in Argentina they proceeded to weed out opposing professors, as Perón years before had stuffed the universities with rightists. The leftists also insisted on an "open-admissions" policy, a move devoted as much to politics as to education. Juan Domingo's Congress had countered with a law of March 1974 allowing him to appoint conservative rectors and giving the latter wide powers in the nineteen state universities. It also forbade political activity in the universities. Isabel began to implement the law in September 1974 against a background of violence by both major factions in the universities. Some of the new rectors began spouting fascism. The politicized university continued to contribute at least as much to the national debate on social organization as to pedagogy, science, and scholarship.

Isabel continued interference with the press, especially with leftist journals. In the campaign against terrorism, Isabel could count on the aid of most of the armed forces and police. Some progress was made at first, although politically inspired murders and kidnappings continued at a rate of several hundred a year. In November 1974, after a high police official and his wife were killed by Peronist guerrillas, Isabel declared a state of siege. Enemies of the government claimed that it did not act against right-wing terrorism, especially by the Argentine Anti-Communist Alliance, whose members sometimes posed as plainclothes police to murder leftists. Leftist murders of military officers apparently

boomeranged and increased military support for Isabel.[10] But all through 1975 violence escalated, and possibly 900 persons were killed by rightist and leftist extremists. There were frequent rumors of a military coup in 1975–1976, but military officers were badly divided. Isabelita clung to power, although there were incessant cries for her resignation or impeachment. Labor and capital were as unable as ever to agree to an accommodation.

f. The Military Again, Since 1976

In March 1976 the military seized the government, arresting Isabel, who was still imprisoned in 1977, threatened with trial for alleged misdeeds. A military junta was headed by commander in chief of the army General Jorge Videla. A military moderate, he declared that he favored return to democratic government, when subversion had been controlled and the labor movement converted to a nonpolitical status. Political parties were suspended, labor unions put under military control, and military courts received jurisdiction over crimes classified as subversive (including labor sabotage and strikes).

Videla's first priority activity was a relentless campaign against leftist terrorists of the Peronist Montoneros and the Marxist People's Revolutionary Army. Those two groups had an estimated 5,000 activists in tiny cells that were difficult to find in a nation of 1 million square miles, 24 million people, and several large cities. Videla used his military and police forces so vigorously (opponents said brutally) that in 1976 an estimated 1,300 political deaths occurred, mostly leftist. The campaign was aided by right-wing terrorists who were not molested by government

---

[10] In 1974 the armed forces had about 140,000 personnel, and a budget of $480 million, or $20 per capita, possibly twice the per capita cost of the military in Brazil. In both countries financial support of the military was larger than budget figures showed, for various reasons: for example, military personnel in state economic enterprises and other government positions, including police forces.

forces. The leftists continued with bombings and other violence, but were so severely harassed that they gave up the direct assaults on government positions (including army posts) that they had tried in 1975. In addition to known political deaths, some hundreds (or a few thousand) people were missing, some no doubt seized by terrorists, but most thought to be detained by the government. Officials refused to give information on those secretly detained, and international criticism became embarrassing to the Videla government. When United States military aid to Argentina was reduced in 1977 because of violations of human rights, the Argentine government charged Washington with interfering in its internal affairs.

Liberalization of government policies was opposed by a group of military hard-liners that wanted even stronger measures against the left. The seriousness of the split depended in part on the success of the antiterrorist campaign, and partly on Videla's hopes of straightening out the economy. In 1976 Argentina's inflation of 350 percent was the worst in the world. The military regime made some progress in bringing government expenditures into line with revenues and stemming the expansion of the currency. It even cut some workers from the payroll of the bloated state railways. Inflation in 1977 apparently might be reduced to "only" about 100 percent. Recovery was aided by a sharp increase in harvests and exports in 1976–1977, partly because of higher prices conceded to producers. Still, by mid-1977 neither the antiterrorist nor the economic campaign was certain of success, so military division would likely remain.

The most modernized Latin American society had spent decades trying to work out a synthesis between warring elements in order to permit further progress. The major immediate question seemed to be whether the military again would turn government over to civilians or would remain to direct one of Latin America's new-style corporatist regimes.

37

Brazil: Vargas and the New Nationalism, 1930–1945

Nationalism smothered regionalism in Brazil in 1930–1945. It was premeditated—by Getúlio Vargas, the military, and civilian nationalists. The state oligarchies, notably in São Paulo, resisted with arms in their hands, but they lost the war and the military and spiritual basis for fighting another day. Nationalism was used to subdue old interests and preferences, becoming a justification for integration—spiritual, political, governmental, and economic—and repudiation of the regionalism of the empire and Old Republic. Governmental authority was not only centralized, but much broadened into economic and social realms. The hegemony of the agricultural export interest was broken, for economic modernization was the prime goal of Vargas and the military, and they thought of political power in terms of that objective rather than of broadening political participation. They injected the government heavily into planning and operating the economy. It turned out that the nationalists of 1930–1945 represented views that were to find increasing support in succeeding decades and be fully dominant in the 1960s and 1970s.

a. The Centralizing Politics of Vargas

Vargas (1883–1954) was one of the most talented political leaders in the history of Latin America. The unusual length of his tenure as chief executive (nineteen years) was one measure of his influence. His career was notable, also, in that he endured rather by superb political maneuver than by force, although he used the latter. Much of the time he was a dictator, ruling by decree, but he did not establish a police state, and his forgiveness of enemies was legendary. He was an innovative pragmatist. During his first period as chief executive (1930–1945), he accelerated growth of the spirit of nationalism and promoted integration, broke the power of the states to compete with the federal government, increased the size and functions of the federal government, and gave impetus to industrialization and the hope of economic independence. He took the tendencies and institutions that existed in Brazilian society and by his talent and longevity intensified the influence of those of which he approved. His first administration was praised for its promotion of modernization, integration, and growth, and condemned for authoritarianism and minimal concern for common people. He was, inevitably, much admired and equally detested.

Getúlio was forty-seven when he became chief executive of Brazil, having been born into a propertied family of cattle raisers in Rio Grande do Sul. He attended the military academy, served briefly as an officer, went into law, and gave his most intense interest to the lively politics of his native state and of the nation. Political boss Borges de Medeiros promoted his career, which in 1924 led to the federal Chamber of Deputies, where Vargas was chief of the Gáucho delegation. In 1926 President Washington Luís named him minister of finance, not because Vargas knew the subject but to conciliate Borges de Medeiros, who favored conventional financial policies for the country. Before long Borges had Vargas elected governor of Rio Grande do Sul. In that position Getúlio displayed a talent for compromise, conciliation, and the melding of diverse political elements. During his considerable career before 1930 Getúlio made the acquaintance of many of the leaders of Brazil, and especially worked and cemented alliances with fellow *Riograndenses*, both civilians and military men, who were to be his collaborators later at the national level. Getúlio went to Rio de Janeiro as chief of state in full maturity, a man of experience, from an important state, with the right family background and connections. He was not supposed to be in any way remarkable. Some people thought him a plodding and indecisive figure. Understanding him took some time.

Although Vargas developed various plans in response to circumstances, from the beginning he meant to reduce the power of the states and to use a strengthened central government to promote national objectives. He had support from various groups, including military men, not least the nationalistic younger officers or *tenentes*. Some of the latter were just back from exile and had a reputation among the propertied class for radicalism. Vargas never delivered himself wholly into any political camp, but he used the *tenentes* enough so that his enemies in the early years sneered at the regime as *o partido dos tenentes*. The officers organized a *Clube 3 de Octubre*, which in its expression of views on civil affairs resembled many other military groups in modern Latin America. It demanded innovation flavored with nationalism, and favored military men as directors of such activity. But Getúlio listened to

everyone, placidly smoking cigars and seeming, by silence, to agree. The naive supposed him unable to act decisively, whereas he was waiting to cut the ground from under opponents, dangerous rivals, or disturbing elements, when he had maneuvered them into weakened positions.

For all his maneuvering, Vargas could not obscure his determination to reduce the state political machines and governments. He made some early moves to try to incorporate the state military forces into the federal establishment, but for some years was unable to go far. The mere interest was enough to alarm the old regime, the "liberal constitutionalists," who wished to retain the state-oriented system. State bosses, furthermore, had some allies among professional military officers from their states. More alarming was Vargas' decision at the beginning of his provisional presidency to eliminate the state legislatures (and the national Congress) and to appoint interventors to most states in place of the governors. A decree of November 11, 1930, gave the executive discretionary powers, combining his functions with the legislative power and suspending constitutional guarantees until a constituent assembly met. The interventors became the most prominent symbol and operating force of the new centralization. Many were young military officers, openly anxious to root out the old system. They had power to control actions not only by the state government but at the municipal level. Through the interventors, and his own power of appointment to a federal bureaucracy that grew as Vargas added to its functions, the provisional president—the dictator—purged the bureaucracies of much of the old political element, a ruthless blow at its centers of strength.

To the critical post of interventor in the state of São Paulo, Vargas appointed João Alberto Lins de Barros, a *tenente* who had been with the Prestes Column, thus in the popular mind identified with leftism. The fiercely regionalist *Paulistas*, dominated by big planters and industrialists, resented this appointment as imposition without regard for their views, interference with civilian rule, and as intrusion into state affairs of a radical. Although in July 1931 Vargas replaced João Alberto with a *Paulista* civilian, the state leaders were not appeased, aware of Getúlio's general intentions. Such awareness, and accompanying fear and resentment, accumulated throughout Brazil, often expressed in demands for the restoration of constitutional government. There were conspiracies in the key states of São Paulo, Minas Gerais, and Rio Grande do Sul, and in others, and communication among the groups. Vargas knew not only of the disaffection and demands for constitutional government, but specifically of the conspiracies. He made a conciliatory move in February 1932 by proclaiming a new electoral code, and then announced that an election for a constituent assembly would be held in May 1933. Neither the *tenentes* nor the liberal constitutionalists were pleased, the former claiming that only authoritarian government could oust the old regime and open the way for nationalist development, the latter not trusting Getúlio.

The conspiracy was strongest in São Paulo, Minas Gerais, and Rio Grande do Sul. If it could bring into an alliance their major political leaders, the state armed forces, and some of the national military stationed or originating in the states, it would pose a possibly insurmountable problem for Vargas. He naturally did his best to prevent it. He named as minister of war General Espíritu Santo Cardoso, candidate for the post of the *tenentes*, which helped keep the majority of the army loyal. Dissatisfaction among people in the weaker states about domination by rich and arrogant São Paulo also helped Vargas. That the rebel leaders Borges de Medeiros in Rio Grande do Sul and former president Bernardes in Minas Gerais were identified not only with states' rights (although Bernardes was a strong nationalist, of sorts, on economic issues), but with the old corrupt politics and lack of social vision also helped. The leadership in Minas Gerais was split on the issue of rebellion, and in the end gave little support to the movement. There was, however, a dangerous test of strength developing for Vargas, and some of his early collaborators in Rio de Janeiro went back to their states, even to his home state of Rio Grande do Sul, to join the movement against him.

Then Getúlio had a stroke of luck, though he himself had something to do with forcing it, when in July 1932 São Paulo began the rebellion without waiting for proper preparation in that state, or enough accumulation of support, arms, and coordination of plans with Minas Gerais and Rio Grande do Sul. If they had waited longer, of course, Vargas' preparations might have outstripped them. The *Paulistas* had good arguments about the suppression of constitutional liberties, and had the support of the old political machine in the state, including ousted office holders, although they could not expect support outside the state for their complaint that they provided a third of the federal revenues but that most of it was spent in other states. Even in São Paulo the movement was largely based in the middle class and wealthier groups. Workers were indifferent to a movement that did not seem to offer them anything. Even so, São Paulo had a state militia and police forces and some national army elements, plus 200,000 volunteers who came forward. Nothing like that number of men could be used in combat for lack of arms and training personnel, although the considerable treasury and industrial plant of the state bought and made munitions even before the fighting began.

The civil war was decided when São Paulo failed to receive help from other states, and when the national military largely supported the central government. It nevertheless went on for two months, with numerous casualties. Vargas demonstrated his political talent by granting amnesty to all rebels and having the federal government assume the indebtedness incurred by São Paulo in connection with the rebellion. Such action tended to defuse the charges that he meant to establish a tyranny or at least to suggest that his type of centralization was not dangerous to individuals.

Vargas also reduced complaint by announcing that the election would be held as scheduled. It was conducted under a 1932 Electoral Code providing that some delegates be elected by employers' groups, a corporatist measure that reminded observers of Italian fascism. Under the freedom provided for the election, political activity increased. The Communist party was active. In 1932 a right-wing party, the *Ação Integralista*, was formed, complete with fascist-style shirts, salutes, symbols, and doctrine. The right-left political battles of Europe seemed to be shaping up in Brazil. On the whole, Vargas welcomed the appearance of those groups, because they permitted more manipulation of organized forces against each other and offered opportunities to distract the attention of the public and conventional politicians from his own moves. Meanwhile, in preparation for the constituent assembly that had been elected, a preliminary commission worked on a draft constitution, and Vargas did his best to see that it agreed with his ideas. The document that resulted, and was accepted with changes by the assembly in 1934, did not satisfy Vargas, but it did not much handicap his centralizing aims. It included some corporate representation, though that was not an important aspect of the Constitution. It returned essentially to the federal structure of the Constitution of 1891, but it gave the government socioeconomic powers along the lines that Vargas had been developing during the last four years: for example, over the organization, pay, and treatment of industrial labor.

The constituent assembly became the Chamber of Deputies, approved the acts of the past four years by provisional President Vargas, and elected him president for a full term, finding that his provisional presidency escaped the new Constitution's ban on immediate reelection. In 1934–1937 Vargas continued to promote the economy under federal guidelines and to extend more attention to the workingman. He also made preparations to perpetuate himself in office. Although the freer political situation under the Constitution sometimes hampered him, it

also was helpful. When *tenentes* ran for state and national office under the new Constitution, many lost, because Vargas never wanted any group to become too important politically. He tried to pursue further the aim of nationalizing the state police and militias, but although some progress was made, the problem remained, and he conspicuously could not control the 20,000-man force of Rio Grande do Sul.

Vargas' maneuvers in another direction also brought him partial success. The *Integralistas* of the right and the communists of the left continued competing and fighting, sometimes in the streets. The disorder, especially when connected with what was known of similar battles in Europe, inclined some of the middle class to believe that a strong government by Vargas might be preferable to intensified radical conflict under a weaker if freer system. Vargas encouraged that point of view. The communists organized a popular front (*Aliança Nacional Libertadora*, National Liberation Alliance—ANL), with Communist party leader Luís Carlos Prestes as its honorary chief. The ANL spoke for socialist and nationalist measures and could appeal to a number of non-Communist elements.

In July 1935, when Prestes called for a revolution in favor of the ANL, Vargas had it outlawed and its leaders arrested. The Chamber of Deputies responded to the cry of a red peril and granted Vargas emergency powers. The peril seemed even more real in November 1935 when Communists stimulated revolutionary mutinies in the armed forces. These actions apparently were not very dangerous and may have been precipitated by government agents, but Vargas used them effectively to strengthen fear of communist violence. The Congress extended and strengthened Vargas' powers, including declaration of a state of siege. Many leftists were arrested, including Luís Carlos Prestes. All these measures, of course, increased Vargas' ability not only to deal with the left but to bring emergency power to bear against any group he chose. In September 1936 he secured creation of a National Security Tribunal to provide military justice during a state of war and internal disorder—that is, a special body to handle political offenses.

The situation late in 1936 was repression of the left, which led the right to believe that Vargas favored the rise of the *Integralistas* to power; constitutional prohibition on Vargas' being a candidate in the presidential elections of 1937 and no open indication on his part that he would try to circumvent it; and continued objection by the old state political leaders to the policy of centralization of authority in Rio de Janeiro. All elements in state politics, including *tenentes* where they now held elective office, took part in negotiations for the presidency, much as under the Old Republic. Vargas kept track of these negotiations and used them to his advantage. Armando de Salles of São Paulo had the support of his own state and Rio Grande do Sul. Vargas let it seem that he backed the candidacy of *tenente* José Américo of Paraíba, who apparently might receive the support of all other states but São Paulo and Rio Grande do Sul. The *Integralistas* still were hopeful, and nominated their leader Plinio Salgado. Vargas continued to act as though he would permit the election to occur, but also negotiated with leaders throughout the country, and intervened in several states to put his supporters in power. Some leaders had believed all along that Vargas meant to prolong his presidency; by mid-1937 many more were convinced.

Vargas had been not only cementing support among civilian groups but encouraging the view of military leaders that only he as chief executive, with a strong system of centralized government, could assure adequate national controls, especially their longed-for subordination of state military units to the national armed forces. He had Generals Dutra and Goes Monteiro, as war minister and army chief of staff, in strong support of these views. They were juggling military assignments in preparation for a coup d'etat. The press speculated about a possible coup, and people involved in planning it denied the possibility. One member of the administration conspiracy, Francisco Campos, the minister of justice, com-

posed an authoritarian constitution. By early fall 1937 Vargas was pushing leaders in the states to abandon José Américo and suggesting that the São Paulo candidate also was unsuitable. That left Vargas. In September the government claimed discovery of a conspiracy for the violent establishment of a communist regime. The Congress gave Vargas powers under a state of war.

A few weeks later the army began incorporating the state militias of Rio Grande do Sul, São Paulo, and Pernambuco into the federal military, and those states found it impossible to resist in the current conditions of public fear and national military determination. Now most of the state governments fell in line, backing Vargas' plan to continue in power. Even the governor of São Paulo abandoned the candidacy of the *Paulista* Armando. The *Integralistas* accepted the plan, supposing it meant the promotion of fascism. The proposed new constitution might be so interpreted, and Plinio Salgado had read it; so had a number of other military and civilian leaders during the negotiations for support of the coup. Much maneuvering could be kept from the public because press censorship was in force under the condition of emergency, but at least general information on most important developments was given to political leaders, except those the administration considered it useless to approach. Even they inevitably received some information. José Américo became more leftist in his pronouncements as his candidacy collapsed, and thus merely reinforced the arguments for strong government under Getúlio.

On November 10 the coup took place. There was no resistance. The Congress was closed by armed force. Nearly all state governors supported the change or acquiesced. Vargas used that new instrument of national integration, the radio, to celebrate his action against subversives and in favor of national unity and economic development. The Constitution of 1937 was promulgated, establishing the New State (*Estado Novo*). It declared that the president would rule by decree until a national legislature met, that all legislative bodies were dissolved, that the president would set dates for elections, but that a state of emergency existed. The remaining state militias became part of the national army. Interventors, responsible to the president, permanently replaced governors of states. There were no guarantees for the individual. Labor union activity was restricted. A department of propaganda was given control of public communications. It was stated that these great powers would be directed to development of the economy and social welfare.

This charter for dictatorship was supplemented on December 2 by a decree abolishing political parties, a shock to the *Integralistas*, who were optimistic that some fascist features of the document betokened affection for them. Their unhappiness led to conspiracy, which on the night of May 10, 1938, erupted in a weird attack on Guanabara Palace. A few hundred *Integralistas*, including an army lieutenant, were held off by Vargas and a handful of supporters, while the army and police unaccountably did not come to their aid for several hours. The attempt, for all its splendid opportunity, failed, and led to many arrests and other actions against the *Integralistas*. Before long Plinio Salgado went into exile. Luís Carlos Prestes was in jail. Both left and right were bottled up. The beginning of World War II in September 1939 provided an excellent additional excuse for government by decree. Vargas was relatively safe in power until the end of the war in 1945.

What has been said about Vargas the politician emphasized the use of force. The military was important in carrying him to power in 1930, in putting down the rebellion of 1932, in establishing the *Estado Novo*, in smashing the Communists and *Integralistas*, and in destroying the independent state militias. But in each case Vargas' political preparations were equally important, and much more intricate than indicated here. He was a master of the art, interminably involved in discussions—promising, bargaining, hinting, nudging, forever searching for those combinations of forces controlled by individuals that were essential in a political environment in

which power was much fragmented, and in the hands of an experienced and sophisticated political class, civilian and military. Creation of the *Estado Novo* by no means ended that tradition.

b. The Activist Government of Vargas

Getúlio loved power, but he also used it abundantly for economic and social purposes. This was the trait that made him attractive to many elements in the society, not his dumpy figure, colorless public personality, or genius for intrigue. He greatly increased the role of government, something that was going on all over Latin America—and the world—at the time. The constitutions of 1934 and 1937 reflected the enlarging definition of the functions of the state, and specifically of the central government. The charter of 1934 gave the federal government control of public health and regulation of labor, natural resources, and public lands. The 1937 ghost Constitution made provision, among many other things, for a definition of property in terms of the general welfare. There seemed to be no end to Vargas' ambition to modernize Brazil by means of government action. It was claimed that the volume of his decree law surpassed that of Nazi Germany. Development and regulatory bodies sprouted by the score from this activist philosophy: national councils of petroleum, railroads, mines and metallurgy, immigration and colonization, labor, textbooks, and even a national commission of sports.

All this required people, and the bureaucracy mushroomed, creating another source of support for Vargas. The civil servants were organized to serve the regime. The D.A.S.P. (Administrative Department), created in 1937, was supposed to have as one of its functions improvement of the public service, but its effects were minimal. It was, however, a step in the right direction. The Brazilian—and Spanish American—administrative tradition of nepotism, low pay, and graft was not to be altered rapidly, especially as the money was not available for high pay, and bureaucracies were heavily overstaffed for political and even humanitarian reasons.

Vargas made more progress in the almost equally difficult field of public finance, where favoritism toward the wealthy generally, especially big landowners, was traditional. Since adoption of the Constitution of 1891 states not only had levied taxes on imports, but had unconstitutionally put duties on interstate shipment of goods. The constitutions of 1934 and 1937 limited export duties, and the 1937 document prohibited interference with the internal circulation of goods. Such changes could only be applied gradually because the states depended on such imposts. Rio Grande do Sul was an extreme case in 1937 in deriving 60 percent of its public revenues from export levies. Vargas moved to reduce the dependence of the federal government on import duties, which accounted for 31 percent of federal income in 1937, while the government was getting less than 10 percent of its revenue from income taxes at a time when the United States received 56 percent of federal revenues from income taxes. In Brazil, as elsewhere, the effort to establish a modernized tax system was only beginning; forty years later a military government in Brazil still was struggling with the problem.

The interest of the Vargas regime in the economy was for some time dominated by the disastrous decline in Brazil's world trade in 1929–1932. Coffee prices fell from about twenty-five to less than eight cents a pound. Thereafter, coffee prices stayed low but were compensated by an increased volume of exports. This experience reinforced the distaste of all nationalists for Brazil's dependent economic position. Many devices were adopted for economic aid and regulation. Transportation, power, and technical education were improved. The growth in manufacturing continued to be concentrated in the south, especially São Paulo. Most of it was still consumer goods, but the government promoted heavy industry. In 1942 it bought out the British Itabira Iron Company. Cement production from 1930 to 1940 went from 87,000 to 700,000 tons. Such achievements required mobilization of large amounts of capital, technical expertise, and raw materials—including fuels.

The wood and charcoal still much used in Brazilian transportation and industry were for some uses inefficient and expensive. Brazilian coal, moreover, was low quality. The Vargas government in 1931 required that imported coal be used in mixture with Brazilian. Most petroleum products also were imported. Nationalists claimed that Brazil floated on a sea of petroleum and wanted the industry nationalized. But oil exploration was expensive and proceeded slowly. Nationalist pressure led the government in 1938 to found the National Petroleum Council to search for and exploit petroleum. Its immediate influence was small, but as in so many areas the Vargas administration was important in developing an agenda for the future, in setting new goals and helping define positions on the ways in which they might be realized.

The regime made great progress toward a steel industry. It has been seen that discussions of the subject in the 1920s were indecisive. Nationalists would not let foreign private enterprise build the industry, and the government was not ready either conceptually or financially to handle the matter. The debate over solutions continued for a decade under Vargas before the beginning of World War II brought Brazil an opportunity. The United States government began to prepare for possible involvement as a belligerent. One need was the use of Brazilian bases for naval vessels and for airplanes making the short ocean hop to Africa. The major price Vargas exacted for leasing bases to the United States was aid in construction of a steel plant. He thus on the one hand offended against nationalism by agreeing to lease bases but on the other got help for construction of one of the basic elements in national strength and independence. The nationalist side of his achievement was reinforced by the decision to handle the new venture through a state enterprise, the National Steel Company, founded in 1941. It had public and private capital, but since Brazilian private enterprise was not much interested in putting money into it, most of the investment was from the Brazilian and United

States governments. The huge iron and steel complex was not finished until the end of the war, when it at a stroke tripled the national steel-making capacity. It was an important accomplishment because of its size, the role it would play in other industries, the boost it gave to confidence and ambition in government and private enterprise in Brazil, and its role as the first large direct participation of the government in productive enterprise, something that would grow vastly in succeeding decades.

Vargas also broke new ground with social legislation. As in the economic field, his contribution was as much in asserting a wider responsibility as in his material accomplishments. Some useful work was begun in health and education. At the beginning of his tenure he created a new Ministry of Education and Public Health, and put at the head of it Francisco Campos, later author of the authoritarian Constitution of 1937. The new nationalism demanded a larger cadre of sound and technically prepared citizens. Developments in those areas were identified with the national need, with modernization, with patriotism.

Labor, especially industrial labor, was also a target of initiatives. A Ministry of Labor was created in 1930, which initiated decrees protecting the right of union organization and of collective bargaining. Both the unions and the bargaining process, however, were very much under government supervision. Although the Constitution of 1934 guaranteed the right to strike, that of 1937 forbade it. The government had no intention of letting organized labor build independent power and intervened in the process of wage settlement; before long it had fashioned a system of state-controlled minimum wages. The state also controlled the relations between labor and employers through a new system of labor courts. Under such a system labor leaders were more a part of government than representative of the union rank and file. The government meant to keep wages low, with the Constitution of 1937 helpfully recognizing that both strikes and lockouts were "incompatible with the superior interests of national production."

Labor was, however, the recipient of paternalistic aid in the form of nonmonetary compensation. The small amount of government social aid that existed in the 1920s was considerably expanded: pensions, benefits for job-related accidents and health hazards, food distribution. Hours of labor were regulated, paid vacations decreed, maternity benefits established. Barriers were put in the way of dismissal of workers. Labor was favored by immigration restrictions and by a limitation of alien workers to one-third of a factory crew. These things applied, however, to only a small percentage of the population, that in the cities, and even there many of the lower class were excluded from benefits. The favored group was more active politically than the rest of the lower class, and it was grateful to Vargas for its improved position. The system would get larger after Vargas, but retain the characteristics he gave it: strong government controls; a policy of low wages, supplemented with fringe benefits, many of them provided by the state; and application to only a small industrial and bureaucratic elite in urban areas.

The regime made other contributions to nationalism. The Constitution of 1937 banned foreign ownership of newspapers. The long-standing suspicion of the enclaves speaking languages other than Portuguese brought action during World War II to integrate them into the national culture.

At the same time, intellectuals were celebrating nationalist themes and the glories of the Portuguese tongue in its American form. Equally nationalist was Vargas' foreign policy, although it owed nothing to fascism (as some observers speculated). Vargas had little interest in other countries or in ideology. His trade agreements with Nazi Germany were for him merely a not very successful economic measure; and his refusal to condemn the actions of Germany and Italy simple prudence when the powers that were the targets of their preparations could not certainly protect themselves, much less Brazil.

The coming of World War II made it easier for United States policy makers to sink their disquiet about half-understood aspects of Brazilian life in the need to concentrate on better-understood strategic necessities. It also became easier for Vargas to offer visible, if inconsequential, "evidence" of his doctrinal purity.[1] Relations became closer in 1938–1939, with agreements on credits for Brazil and exchanges of visits by military personnel. When the United States entered the war in December 1941, accord between the two countries was well advanced, and Vargas undoubtedly judged that he had picked the winning side. In August 1942 Brazil became a belligerent.

The effects of the war on Brazil were considerable. It received aid from the United States, including the critical agreement on the Volta Redonda steel works. Manufactures were stimulated, including exports, shipments of cotton textiles being especially gratifying to a regime so dedicated to industrialization. Effort was made to mobilize resources and production, something that was easier than it would have been before Vargas' centralization and expansion of the federal government. The Commission for Defense of the National Economy was created in 1939. It controlled imports and exports and in general stimulated production. The National Defense Board was established in March 1942.

The Brazilian navy engaged in antisubmarine warfare. The United States was granted base rights and the use of Brazilian military and other personnel to help guard them. Headquarters of

the South Atlantic Wing of the United States Air Transport Command moved from British Guiana to Natal, Brazil, which became a center for flying aircraft across the South Atlantic to the European theater of operations. The United States Fifth Fleet was based at Recife. Brazil raised a reinforced infantry division as an expeditionary force. It was trained and equipped by the United States, arriving in Italy in July 1944. Military leaders in Brazil were enormously proud of the Expeditionary Force, and the veterans of that effort thereafter were prominent in military and civil affairs. Civilian as well as military leaders were stimulated by this taste of activity at the center of world affairs.

c. The Fall of Vargas

Vargas knew that the end of the war would bring demands for changes of government. Even so old a collaborator as Oswaldo Aranha thought it was time to end the dictatorship; so did some military leaders, including Goes Monteiro, another man who had helped seat Vargas in 1930. There was widespread support for elections, some of it from the press, which was trying to throw off censorship in early 1945. In May 1945 Vargas announced a presidential election for December 2 and elections for governors and state legislatures for May 1946. The big issues then became (*a*) Who would the candidates be? and (*b*) Would Vargas permit fair—or any—elections? One candidate was Eduardo Gomes of the air force, a surviving hero of the *tenente* revolt of 1922. He suggested that Vargas resign and let the Supreme Court handle the government and the elections.

There were widespread doubts that the election would occur. The suspicions of the anti-Vargas forces were well founded, as his actions kept suggesting. He had agents creating a force that finally became the Brazilian Labor party (PTB), the prop of his later years. His supporters also formed the Social Democratic party (PSD), and it pushed the candidacy of General Dutra. Vargas probably considered him unlikely

---

[1] Disquiet in the United States about Brazil included worry in intellectual circles about "regressions" from democracy that ignored the shortcomings of the Old Republic. There was a North American business fear that Vargas' nationalism was inimical to its aims for a free international exchange of goods (except in cases where business preferred protection). Minister of Government and Justice Francisco Campos, author of the Constitution of 1937 (much criticized in the United States), published a book favoring strong government and denouncing the weakness of democratic regimes. Vargas had Campos "clarify" this by statements to the press. In 1942 Campos was removed from the government. These moves were greeted pontifically in some quarters in the United States as signs of change in the Vargas regime; in fact, Brazil responded to United States opinions only for tactical reasons.

to become a strong political figure in his own right. That candidacy also had support from a strong military group that wanted Vargas to step down. The strongest anti-Vargas elements, including many of the old state politicians, created the Democratic National Union (UDN).

Vargas did not pretend that his support for Dutra was unshakable, and that knowledge and Getúlio's well-deserved reputation for political skill and trickery bred suspicion. One of his suggestions was that Goes Monteiro become a candidate. Probably that was designed to split the army leaders, who were under pressure from Dutra to guarantee the electoral process. Goes did not agree to the suggestion that he run. One of the most disquieting of Vargas' maneuvers was organization of the laborers whose support he had gained with new social legislation. Their demonstrations centered on the demand "*Queremos Getúlio*" ("We Want Getúlio"), so they were labeled *Queremistas*. Not only did this campaign prefigure the later use of the PTB by Vargas and his heirs, but he injected into it some of the xenophobic ultranationalism that he was to help enlarge in Brazil. In September 1945 United States Ambassador Berle expressed confidence that the elections would be held, and the *Queremistas* shouted that he had "intervened" in Brazilian affairs.

Vargas' maneuvers in October 1945 made even clearer his efforts to manipulate the electoral process. He tried to divide the military by shuffling commands, but only succeeded in hardening military determination to see him go. The military commanders finally asked War Minister Goes Monteiro to take command of the armed forces to ensure public order. Goes established military control of communications, put troops around the presidential palace, and demanded that Vargas resign. Vargas did so, and went home to Rio Grande do Sul. By decision of the military leaders, Supreme Court Justice José Linhares was sworn in as interim president on October 30, 1945. The long Vargas regime was over, but he had set the country firmly on a course toward national integration and modernization. How those things would be defined in the Brazilian environment of the future remained to be seen.

38

Brazil: Nationalism and Economic Development Since World War II

Brazil a world power—that was the dream by the 1970s. At least it was a dream of some Brazilians, including military officers who ran the country. It was based on the huge territory (fifth in the world) and natural resources of Brazil and on a population growth that carried it past Japan, to a total exceeded only by China, India, the Soviet Union, the United States, and Indonesia. It was based also on economic growth in Brazil after World War II. The new centralized nationalism made convulsive efforts to modernize Brazil through industrialization, with much less attention to agricultural development, social reform, and improved political participation. Brazil became an extreme case of unbalanced modernization. A huge traditional socioeconomic sector existed while a large modern community developed. Change and continuity both were so strong that the stresses and contradictions that are found in all societies became acute in Brazil.

The traditional military, political, and economic elites remained in control of the country, their performance circumscribed by two new factors. For one thing, a real national political party system was established, dominated by a small group of power brokers and the propertied. It neither satisfied popular dissatisfactions nor calmed factionalism among the elite. The second new factor was that all governments trembled to constant judgment of the state of the economy, magnified by new media of communications, interpreted variously and shrilly by a variety of idealists, nationalists, leftists, rightists, capitalists and socialists, and highly vocal and much involved officers of the armed forces. The military took an intense interest in the party political system and in economic development, both because of their conception of duty and patriotism, and because of the civilian leaders' invitation to do so. They became convinced that civilian politicians could not ensure order, properly develop the economy, or prevent leftist subversion. So in 1964 the military seized national power. In their view, as Brazil acquired the economic sinews of a great power, hence the concomitant military potential, it would be able to improve social conditions on a schedule consonant with those overriding aims. This view was held by dominant political groups in many parts of the world. It included patriotism, ambition, the urge to create, and a frustration and envy that might be expressed in the complaint that "a giant should be respected."

a. Social Development Since the 1930s

Although explosive population growth created problems, many leaders considered it desirable for strategic and economic reasons. In 1975, however, for the first time a high official publicly suggested the desirability of birth control. The population was 27.4 million in 1920, 41.1 million in 1940, 51.9 million in 1950, 93.2 million in 1970, and an estimated 113 million in 1977.[1] Improved sanitation, public health facilities, and antibiotics, especially after the 1930s, were the chief reasons for the lowered death rate. Life expectancy at the beginning of the twentieth century was under forty, but reached fifty-five in the 1960s. There were, nevertheless, much malnutrition and other health problems among the poor of Brazil in the late 1970s. One population problem, the integration of immigrants, declined with government restriction of immigration in the 1930s. Although there was some revival of immigration after World War II, with about 873,000 entries from 1944 to 1970, that was small in view of the greatly enlarged population, and it tapered off decidedly after the military government took over in 1964. Long before then, the problem of assimilation was receding rapidly.[2]

There were other important demographic developments. First, urbanization increased, especially after World War I. From 1920 to 1940 cities and towns grew about three times as fast as total population, and from 1940 to 1970 about twice as fast. The population of the largest cities skyrocketed. In 1970 over 30 percent of total population was in 115 cities of 50,000 population and up, compared with 22 percent in the 68 cities of that size in 1960. The city of São Paulo surpassed Rio de Janeiro, going from 575,000 in 1920 to 5.97 million in 1970 and considerably more in the metropolitan area. The urbanization

process occurred everywhere, but was especially prominent in the south and east, where industrialization was most rapid. Second, internal migration increased, and it continued to move south and to some extent west, following the best job opportunities or vacant land. Third, the proportion of workers in comparison with the nonworking young declined, a source of strain in the society. Finally, racial mixture continued on a large scale. The 1950 census asserted that the population was some 62 percent white, over 26 percent brown, nearly 11 percent black, and less than 1 percent yellow. It is impossible to suppose these figures anything but guesses, and they probably tell us as much about Brazilian desire to define people as white as about race mixture.

After 1930 Brazil made great efforts to improve education, mostly through federal government action. Whereas the Constitution of 1891 gave education to the states, that of 1934 transferred it to the federal government. Illiteracy declined from possibly 60 percent in 1920 to less than 40 percent in 1970. Since the population was increasing, the absolute number of illiterates increased from 17 to 30 million in that period. Illiteracy remained much higher in rural than urban areas and higher in the north than the south. By 1970 illiteracy in some rural areas was on the order of 80 percent, but in some cities only 20 percent.

As in much of Latin America, most children got no more than three years of instruction. Even that meant a huge increase in school facilities. Between 1940 and 1970 the number of students enrolled in primary classes in Brazil went up from 3 to 12 million. Secondary instruction grew even faster than primary, rising from about 200,000 in 1940 to 4 million in 1970, with much of the increase coming under the military governments after 1964. That growth was in part a reflection of new emphasis on terminal secondary instruction in technical, commercial, and professional subjects that began in Vargas' time. From 1932 to 1947 vocational education enrollment went from 120,000 to over 600,000. The government and private enterprise cooperated in many

---

[1] In 1890–1940 Brazil's population increased 192 percent, that of the United States 52 percent. In the early 1970s Brazil's population was growing at an annual average of 2.9 percent, compared with 2.2 percent in India, 1.6 percent in Argentina, and 1.1 in Japan.
[2] The assimilation problem caused alarm in the 1930s and during World War II, but proved almost groundless. In 1939 a campaign was mounted to assimilate foreigners. It included schools to teach the Portuguese language and Brazilian history in foreign-language areas. Foreign languages were forbidden in public offices and in the military.

of these training programs in the Vargas years and thereafter, turning out people to serve the new economy.

Whereas in 1920 there were only two universities in Brazil (plus some professional schools), and only five in the mid-1940s, by 1970 there were about sixty. Enrollments went up between 1940 and 1964 from 20,000 to 144,000, and increased much more from 1964 to 1970, under the military regime, to 430,000. The slow growth had been due partly to cost but also to the old elitist concept, expressed in insufficient public secondary schools preparing for university careers, and the difficulty of the entrance examinations for the limited university spaces. Modernization after World War II took the form of not only expanded facilities, but better paid faculties and greater emphasis on scientific, technical, and managerial and commercial subjects.

Expanded literacy and the growth of the number of persons with more than the bare minimum of instruction naturally affected intellectual life. The artistic and literary communities increasingly flourished. Popular journalism reached more people, although both the government and the private press often purveyed highly slanted information. Political commentary and charges and countercharges in the partisan press often became almost frenzied. Newspapers, radio, and finally television helped give a new populist dimension to factionalism. Vargas accepted radio as an instrument of politics and used it to build support for his programs and points of view. Motion pictures by the 1930s also were giving Brazilians a vision of new possibilities, building new desires.

Acting on this perception of novelty and opportunity became easier because transportation improved. At the beginning of the 1930s many areas still depended on pack animals and horse carts. Highway building then became a government measure for development and integration, although not on a large scale until the 1950s. Already by Vargas' time, however, the new transport and communications were as important as

nationalist doctrine in destroying the hold of the *coroneis* over small towns and countryside. The building of the new national capital at Brasília in the 1950s was accompanied by much road building between there and the coast. The military government in the 1970s began a project to build a highway in the Amazon area from the sea to Peru. As roads came into use, the number of motor vehicles increased, from very few in the 1920s to about 3 million in the early 1970s. Trucking and busses greatly improved travel and freight transport and assisted large-scale internal migration. The importance of auto transport finally was reflected in the construction of an automotive industry in the 1960s and 1970s. The small railway system received, during these decades, only limited, selective attention. Commercial aviation, with its beginnings in the 1920s, became a large enterprise.

Most people who moved to town remained manual workers. Moving up to the expanding government bureaucracy or to the professions or business was difficult because of lack of education, capital, and proper family connections. The middle class did grow larger, however, and more complex and supported the sort of economic development most Brazilian administrators favored. Lower-class migrants to town were not notably restive. They had been no better off materially in the countryside. Some of them did find opportunities in town, and that hope was invigorating. Many benefited from the better medical care sometimes available from the 1930s. The cities offered more entertainment. If many in the city were afflicted with more loneliness and insecurity than when surrounded with relatives in the country, where they often could also cling to some aid from their local patron (*patrão*), others adjusted well to life in the city slums. The gleaming new capital at Brasília had on its outskirts a big slum community of toilers not provided for by the planners. The enlarged city proletariat did offer a clientele to leaders who could rouse them to new points of view. When that began happening on a wider scale in the early 1960s, the military took over the government.

At least the city dweller in manual, service, and clerical positions encountered little racial discrimination in job allocation. Racial prejudice affected his chances of promotion, however, and it affected his social life, though in ways that the Brazilians themselves were slow to admit openly. After the 1930s there was much opposition in Brazil to racial prejudice and discrimination. Nevertheless, the families of old wealth continued to intermarry, avoiding racial mixture. The middle class conspicuously discriminated against persons of mixed racial heritage who aspired to the better positions in the military, civil government, and business. The older view that such discrimination was only against the poor and uneducated was replaced by recognition that it also had elements of racial bias. Studies of middle-class views and behavior showed wide acceptance of casual relations between whites and blacks and mulattoes but strong objections to miscegenation, although the same people avoided open expression of prejudice and actions that would create racial tension.

Racial tension was muted by the fact that much of the population was of mixed genetic heritage, and the process of mixture continued without letup among the poor majority; by a considerable traditional tolerance in the Lusitanian culture; and by a nationalist temper that stressed fraternity. But it was a wry carnival song that said, "Since your color isn't catching, mulatto girl, let's make love." A woman in a *favela* (slum) wrote in her diary in the late 1950s: "I wrote plays and showed them to directors, who said, 'It's a shame you're black,' forgetting that I adore my black skin and my kinky hair. If reincarnation exists, I want to come back black." A study in a small place near Salvador in the 1940s identified four classes: the white aristocracy with *fazendas*, who lived part of the year in the big city; a local upper class, which included all the whites in the small town, plus many mulattoes and blacks, and was the most conservative

class; the local middle class, which contained the largest number of persons who were improving their social position, by wealth or by marrying up, a process that was easier for the light-skinned than the darker; and the local lower class. Although a black could not be a member of the aristocracy, he could have easy relations with it, so in that sense no racial problem existed. In all Brazil there were a number (nine in some places) of commonly used racial categories, indicating that the difference between mixtures was considered important. There was no simple classification of blacks against whites as in the United States.

Labor organization, as has been noted, was feeble before the 1930s. Vargas established a ministry of labor and issued floods of labor legislation and social measures largely designed to serve industrial workers. The Constitution of 1937 contained extensive material on labor. Vargas' government set up an elaborate system for minimum wages and labor disputes. The rights of organization, bargaining, and the strike were recognized. All this activity helped labor some, but it remained under government control, and government policy from the 1930s to the 1970s was to keep wages low. Furthermore, much industry remained unorganized; fewer than half a million were in syndicates in the late 1940s. The Vargas government set up pensions, which some private industries had instituted in the 1920s. In Getúlio's first regime some 3 million workers came to be covered by a variety of funds. By the 1950s some 15 million workers, civil servants, military men, and their families had some sort of coverage. The favored bureaucrats and military personnel were props of the incumbent regime, as was common in all Latin America. By the late 1940s in Brazil charges for social legislation amounted to over 20 percent of payrolls. In addition, such groups received special medical attention, access to public housing, and payment for weekly rest days and public holidays. Such benefits went to a small proportion of the Brazilian population, but those people were organized and strategically placed and useful in politics and other forms of decision making.

b. Economic Developments, 1930s–1960s

Vargas gave new impetus to development and centered nationalistic policies in the federal government. Industrial growth became especially notable after World War II, with the government increasingly involved. By 1962 state firms accounted for 36 percent of Brazil's electricity-generating capacity, and their role was increasing. Although total economic growth was erratic, it outpaced the increase in population, though not by much until the late 1960s. Efforts were made to integrate the economic regions, mainly through highway building, especially from the 1950s.

The deficit financing, excessive imports, and easy credit policies that so long had characterized Brazil continued, sometimes in exaggerated form. After World War II inflation often was a major problem. Income distribution favored the rich over the poor even more than in earlier years, and more than half the population remained near the subsistence level. At the same time, the middle-income groups grew, so that at least in absolute numbers the modern society grew year by year. Growth continued, however, to be much greater in the south than in the depressed northeast or in the great interior of Amazonia and the west, where average income in the 1960s was about one-fifth that of the southern population.

As Vargas stepped down in 1945, three-quarters of the economically active Brazilians were in agricultural and pastoral activities; in the next three decades the proportion only slowly declined. Many people in this huge traditional sector contributed little to production. The technological level of agriculture was notoriously low, and acted as a drag on the entire economy. The problem of improving agriculture and stock raising was so big that the many efforts to help— some with United States aid after World War II—had limited impact. Brazilians understood the value of a massive attack on the problem, but elected—as did many countries—to go at development in another way. They did little about the great estate system, one of the barriers to improved cultivation. A law of 1931 encouraged the states to promote small farming; another, in 1941, established national agricultural colonies under the Ministry of Agriculture. The effects of such efforts were small. More development of efficient small holdings came from unassisted private activity. Small immigrant farmers, many of them German, in the southern states used superior techniques to achieve decent incomes from small and medium-sized farms. Truck farming around big cities was profitable on small, well-run holdings. Brazil was a major producer of sugar, cotton, rice, cattle, manioc, beans, and maize but usually could not compete in world markets. Cotton did enjoy a revival as an export from Brazil in the 1940s, but it was less important thereafter.

The country remained highly dependent on income from exports, which was critical for imports of fuels and machinery. One change in exports was a decline in the importance of coffee. In 1929–1932 the value of Brazil's foreign trade fell 67 percent, and exports alone were down some 75 percent, with coffee bearing the brunt of the decline. The Vargas government tried to keep down production in order to raise prices, but that strategy did not work. Coffee prices remained low all through the 1930s, but Brazil's volume of coffee exports increased, compensating for the price level. But coffee dominance was done, not only in exports but in government. In 1924–1933 coffee was over 70 percent of the value of exports; by 1938, only 45 percent, and the trend continued downward. After World War II coffee enjoyed some years of high prices, which led again to overexpansion in Brazil. But production was increasing in other parts of Latin America and in Africa, so that by the late 1950s there was serious world overproduction. The export problem was altered by a continued Brazilian shift to more diversified exports, so that by the late 1960s coffee was only about 30 percent of the value of exports.

Industrial growth in Brazil encompassed much of the dream of affluence, independence, and national greatness and power of the country's leaders. After 1930 collaboration between government and private industry became progressively more intimate. Capital continued to shift from agriculture to other forms of activity, including manufacturing. The great private financial and production groups—like the Matarrazo—continued to be typical, as in much of Latin America. Government aid came in many forms—subsidies, loans, guarantees of interest on invested capital. Foreign investment continued to play a conspicuous role in industrial development. After 1939 much refugee capital went to Brazil. From the 1950s mixed government-private industrial enterprises became more prominent. As industry grew, so did protective devices. Selective high protective tariffs dated from as early as 1890; from the 1930s they became more pervasive.

Industrialization made the propertied classes more nationalistic, because industrial complexities and investment costs required more government aid than export agriculture. Industrialization also aroused the interest of the military in economic growth, especially from the 1930s. Earlier, a few military officers supported the nationalist position on the Itabira Iron Company controversy.[3] The *tenentes* of the 1920s were only vaguely nationalist on economic questions. Under Vargas a few military officers became profound students of economic matters. That interest continued, and the views of the military specialists influenced the officer corps generally. They strongly favored the development of the Volta Redonda steel complex during World War II. Many problems of development came under the purview of the military scholars, and they fed their views into government circles and the officer corps. It became an article of faith that not only did Brazil have great resources—that belief was old—but that they could be developed quickly with proper resolution, including central direction, and that the old supervisory role of the military in national affairs now resided in important measure in its overview of economic policy. They developed a detailed vision of Brazil as a world power with an immense population and a high rate of economic growth.

At the beginning of the Vargas regime in 1930 Brazil was a minor manufacturer, without a clear prospect of industrial power. The picture changed drastically thereafter. Between 1920 and 1970 the industrial labor force expanded 700 percent, much faster than the population growth. In the 1940s the value of Brazilian industrial production came to surpass that of agricultural/pastoral.[4] That was, unfortunately, not only a measure of industrial growth, but of agricultural backwardness. The national market remained small because popular purchasing power was low.[5] Nevertheless, it was a considerable achievement that by the end of World War II Brazil was entirely or nearly self-sufficient in a number of categories of light manufactures; and heavy industry was soon to follow. Already by 1960 the new national steel industry was producing 2 million tons a year, a growth of far more than 100 percent in a decade.

Vargas' aim for industry in 1930–1945 was embodied in his wartime declaration that Brazil was no longer "essentially agricultural" and was finished with exporting raw materials and importing manufactures. General Dutra (1946–1951) believed that he could reduce Vargas' interventionism, but when private enterprise seemed unable to generate growth, he stepped up government intervention in the later 1940s. Imports were restricted for items that did not contribute to growth, and the state pushed economic plan-

---

[3] See Chapter 31, Section a.

[4] Between 1915 and the 1940s production by value was about 30 percent industrial and 70 percent agricultural/pastoral; for 1935–1945 industrial production accounted for more than half.

[5] One measure of this: In 1939 per capita consumption of iron and steel in Brazil was about 20 pounds, when it was 320 in France and 850 in the United States. By such a measure, modernization had a long way to go in Brazil.

ning and the creation of infrastructure needed by private industry. In 1948 the government inaugurated the SALTE five-year plan for state investment in sectors needed for a rounded economy but into which private capital did not sufficiently flow: transportation, electric power, petroleum, public health, and some aspects of the agricultural/pastoral sector. The census of 1950 showed that there had been great growth in the 1940s, especially in industry.

Growth continued in the 1950s, and was notably hectic during the Kubitschek years (1956–1961). Kubitschek decided to nationalize (or Brazilianize) the automotive industry by requiring the foreign companies assembling vehicles in Brazil to switch to progressively greater use of Brazilian-made components. Output in 1957 was only some 30,000 vehicles; in 1958 it passed 60,000; by 1964 it was over 100,000. Already by 1960, 1,220 plants were turning out components for the auto factories, and it was claimed that Brazil saved $300 million a year on vehicles that otherwise would be imported.

The composition of the industrial sector altered greatly. From the late nineteenth century, food processing and textile and clothing production had been dominant, as was common in developing countries. In 1940 they accounted for about two-thirds of the value of national industrial production, but in 1950 the proportion was down to about half the total; in 1960 it was 40 percent and continued down thereafter.

Fuel was especially difficult. Brazil's low-grade coal was mined in greater quantities over the years, and Vargas spurred national use by requiring that it be mixed with the higher-grade imported coal. Coal production went from a mere 13,000 tons in 1913 to a million by 1939. But coal resources were so poor (and petroleum so scarce) that in 1939 some 80 percent of all electric power was produced by hydroelectric plants. In 1934 a waterpower code was published. All hydraulic energy was made part of the national patrimony as inalienable property, requiring for most uses state concessions. In 1939 a National Council of Hydraulic and Electrical Energy was established to administer the code and supervise exploitation. The interest of the government in hydroelectric development continued thereafter, and some enormous projects were carried out. The Vargas administration established a National Petroleum Council in 1938, and it searched for petroleum to supplement the small Brazilian output, but little was found. By the early 1950s Brazil paid about $250 million annually for imports of petroleum products, and petroleum supply was called the nation's greatest problem. The need was increasing 10 percent a year. It became a nationalistic issue and resulted in creation in 1953 of a state monopoly, Petrobrás, after a wracking national debate.[6] Petrobrás built up the national refining and distribution system, but had little luck finding petroleum, so that the bill for imports kept rising.

For all the continuing problems of Brazilian economic development, the nation's leaders felt that they were solvable. They joined the Mexican governments of the 1940s–1960s in resisting the argument that great redistribution of income would be beneficial, preferring to favor profits over wages, thus the accumulation of capital for investment in productive facilities and infrastructure rather than more rapid expansion of purchasing power and amelioration of popular social ills. The economic and moral implications of such decisions met divided response in Brazil.

c. The Parties and the Military, 1945–1961

During these years of great economic and social change, Brazil for the first time had a national political party system. The number of voters increased—to nearly 6 million in 1945, because more men were literate, and literate women now also were enfranchised. The major parties, however, were run by the traditional political leadership, although more lip service was given to popular measures in campaigning. The PSD, which backed Dutra in 1945, was made up

---

[6] See Section c of this chapter.

of propertied interests. The UDN, which backed Gomes in 1945, differed chiefly in its dislike of Vargas and the *Estado Novo*. It sometimes was described as liberal-constitutionalist, which obscured the fact that its socioeconomic vision resembled the PSD's except on the question of centralized power. Both PSD and UDN were conservative on social legislation and income distribution. The PTB ostensibly was populist, but for some years it served as a personal vehicle for Vargas. Although he received voting allegiance because of his populist appeal, PTB office holders did little about popular measures.[7]

After Vargas' death in 1954, Goulart accepted a leftward swing for the PTB and met with some popular enthusiasm. When it became quite marked, however, the military took over the government in 1964. Before then, the PSD and UDN together usually controlled more than one-half the votes, so that strongly populist measures could not carry the national legislature even when proposed. During all those years the Communist party was an alternative, but often an illegal one.

The military did not abandon their interest in public affairs with the installation of General Dutra. During the next twenty-one years they continued to hold many offices in the civilian bureaucracy, expressed strong views on economic planning, quarreled over international issues, and insisted on large expenditures for the armed services. Many public issues became involved in factional struggles within the Military Club. The election of the club president was sometimes heated, followed in the public press, and related by all to national politics and government policy. Everyone knew that military leaders were consulted by politicians. The return of Vargas to the presidency by the election of 1950 stimulated military concern with politics, and the course of his administration in 1951–1954 increased it. There was sharp military division over Getúlio's past identification with dictatorship; over the

populism he now affected, which some officers thought could only lead to social disorder; and over the graft and inefficiency which the military since the late years of the empire had tended to think inseparable from civilian rule. Vargas finally was ordered out of office by the military and chose to commit suicide. The military thereafter was frequently at the heart of national political affairs and took over the government entirely in 1964.

The politics of Brazil in those twenty-one years were sophisticated and complex. A partisan and often violent press played a lively role in affairs. None of the three major parties ordinarily was able to get a majority of the national vote, so that the tactics of bargaining and coalition constituted an important dimension of the system. Although the state governments now had much less power than under the Old Republic, the parties were organized on a state basis, and state governors and other important leaders were involved in the bargaining on presidential candidates. The way to the presidency was still through the state capitals. The division of support was such that the voters were apt to elect a president and vice-president of different parties. It also meant that a president's party could not give him control of the Congress. These conditions, combined with the great economic and social problems facing the country, led to fears that representative government in Brazil was too divisive and not sufficiently able to make necessary hard decisions. Military officers deplored what they thought the temporizing and demagoguery in the system; on the other hand, many officers were involved heavily in civilian politics, even hankering for the presidency, contributing to the divisions and decisions that occurred during 1945–1961.

Dutra and the Return of Vargas, 1946–1954

General Dutra was a colorless president, but his years were significant for the growth of the new party system, a new era of participation and

---

[7] See Section c of Chapter 37 on the foundation of these parties.

discussion, but one from which it soon was decided to exclude communists; and for continuation of many of the trends in policy begun or given larger national importance by Vargas. It soon was seen that much of the Vargas legacy represented almost inescapable answers to Brazilian problems and demands. Dutra took office January 31, 1946. In September a new Constitution was promulgated, which repeated much of the social content of the *Estado Novo*. But under the new Constitution, and Dutra's interpretation of it, the press, the parties, and the legislatures were free.

The Communist party was allowed to operate in the atmosphere of liberalism and optimism in Brazil at the end of the war against fascism and the termination of Vargas' long dictatorship. The party immediately attracted considerable support. Luís Carlos Prestes was elected federal senator in 1945, and the Communists also elected fourteen national deputies. In the elections of 1947 the Communists made further gains. Prestes was declaring in public that Brazilian Communists would fight for the Soviet Union in a war between the two countries. In 1947–1948 the national legislature declared the Communist party illegal as a foreign conspiracy inimical to Brazil's republican institutions. The debate on the issue was prolonged and lively, but Communists clearly had only a limited following. Communists were ejected from elective offices to which they had been chosen. Protests from the Soviet Union led Brazil in 1947 to break diplomatic relations, which had been reestablished only the year before.

In the economic and political fields, the experience of the Dutra administration was a preview of much that would happen under succeeding presidents: argument over the amount of state intervention but a decision finally to increase it; a nagging inflation that constantly threatened to get out of hand; charges of graft and poor administration, including excessive expansion of the bureaucracy; much growth of private enterprise, fueled by continued inflows of foreign capital; controversy over the effects of policy on popular income, which in fact declined;

and intermittent flares of antiforeign sentiment—especially directed against the United States—on the grounds that foreign companies were making excessive profits. There also was complaint that Perón's Argentina, so long at odds with the United States, received a loan while negotiations for similar aid to Brazil were stalled.

Vargas' numerous enemies did nothing effective to prevent his return. He served in the national Senate, using it as one forum to build a new coalition. In the presidential election of October 1950 he ran for the PTB but had confederates and allies in all strata of Brazilian life. He now combined his reputation as a mover and shaker with support of representative government and emphasis on his interest in the poorer classes. He ran as a friend of the people, and the recollection of him as a dictator was politically ineffective, even when the anti-Vargas forces again tried to identify him with Perón. Vargas faulted the Dutra administration for not controlling an inflation that bore heavily on the poor, called for nationalization of petroleum and minerals, and declared that the country was stagnating and that he could get it moving again. He carried on a vigorous campaign, and the number of volunteers who appeared to aid him was a measure of his appeal.

His opponents were Air Brigadier Eduardo Gomes, survivor of the 1922 Copacabana revolt, as UDN candidate; and Cristiano Machado for the PSD, who promised to carry on the Dutra five-year plan. More of the same was not what many of Brazil's voters wanted. Getúlio received almost half the votes with 3.84 million. Many came from the PSD, which he had helped found, and which contained a strong nationalist element. Nationalists considered his opponents advocates of feeble and old-fashioned government. Vargas also had support from a more popular element—much of which could not vote—that preferred state action under an ex-dictator to what they considered do-nothing policies under "constitutionalists." That attitude also appeared in other Latin American countries in the years after World War II. As important as this tendency was the inability of the majority anti-Vargas elements to combine to promote their less nationalistic policies and more moderate government intervention in the economy. The vote for vice-president was more divided than that for chief executive, confirming Getúlio's election as a personal endorsement. He was inaugurated in January 1951, together with a Congress dominated by men unsympathetic to his record and his declared aims.

Getúlio's new administration inescapably faced the same problems as Dutra's. In both, some sectors of the economy—especially the industrial—grew notably. But currency inflation, excessive imports, heavy government expenditures, and some weaknesses in export markets created a weak financial situation, a combination of factors that. often afflicted Brazil between 1945 and 1964. Accumulation of indebtedness and decline in the international exchange value of the *cruzeiro* led to efforts to reduce imports and curb expenditures. Such "austerity" measures brought cries of pain from many quarters. They were the louder when austerity was the result of demands by foreign public or private agencies as a condition for credits. Ultranationalists inveighed against the United States, the International Monetary Fund, and the World Bank, as dedicated to theories that kept developing countries in a colonial condition. The growth of this view was an increasing temptation to political leaders in Brazil.

The key nationalist debate on petroleum came to a climax during this administration. Little oil had been found, and the scale of effort had been modest because of objections to activity by foreign petroleum companies. By the 1950s the cost of imported petroleum products threatened to become unmanageable. Brazil paid not only for imports of crude but for refining, since the national industry was small. Foreign companies also profited by control of distribution in Brazil. The ultranationalists claimed that foreign companies conspired to prevent petroleum development in Brazil, and that in any event the industry should be owned by nationals. The cry "*O petróleo e nosso*" ("The petroleum is ours") resounded throughout the land, mobilizing much opinion,

and indicating that often apathetic citizens would respond to some questions for emotional or political or spiritual reasons, that materialism was by no means the only approach to popular politics. Still, some Brazilians disagreed with the ultranationalists, but the issue was settled by a compromise that favored the latter. Petrobrás was created (1953) as a mixed public-private corporation, with a monopoly over much of the petroleum industry, notably exploration and the production of crude. The opposition to the ultranationalists—and it included a section of the military—had argued that foreign capital was needed and managed to preserve for it a role in distribution and processing, including petrochemicals.

The relations between military and civilian politics and the effects on both of nationalist issues were displayed in divisions in the *Clube Militar*. To this old institution, with its plush headquarters in Rio de Janeiro, belonged military officers of all services, on active duty or detached (for example, in the federal bureaucracy) or in retirement. It had a tradition of continual interest, and intermittent involvement, in the nonservice affairs of the nation. In 1950, the early days of the Korean War, a pro-Communist editor (a junior officer) of the club's *Revista* published an article calling the United States the imperialistic, warmongering instigator of the conflict, and accusing it of using biological warfare. At this time the United Nations had declared its support for South Korea against the invading North Koreans and Chinese Communists, and the United States, as the chief combat prop of the UN position, was trying to persuade other nations to provide troops. Ultranationalists in Brazil opposed Brazilian involvement. The first issue in connection with the *Revista* article was whether to reprimand the editor for committing the club to an anti–United States position. That issue soon was nearly forgotten, as the dispute moved to the independence of Brazilian foreign policy, military attitudes toward communism, and the meaning of the constitutional guarantee of a free press. It became entangled in an election to the club presidency. The officers' corps became polarized from general to lieutenant. The public press avidly followed the club election. The fact that the moderate, more pro–United States candidate won the election was less significant than the public interest in the views of military officers.

The creation of Petrobrás did nothing to appease Vargas' critics or to alleviate economic ills. Vargas blamed continued inflation on foreign companies and United States conditions for aid. In early 1954 workers rioted for better pay. Vargas' protégé in the PTB, fellow Gaúcho João Goulart, as minister of labor not only proposed big raises in the minimum wage but was friendly with radical unionists, including Communists. The military again stirred to rumors that Vargas wanted a Peronist-style party, and it grumbled at graft and inefficiency in the administration, with the suggestion that Vargas' age (sixty-seven at inauguration) prevented proper supervision. Early in 1954 some officers presented a "Colonels' Manifesto" to the minister of war. It complained of the erosion of military pay under inflation, and various faults in the administration. Vargas dismissed Goulart, but he continued to show inability or unwillingness to stem inflation and adhered to a strategy of building support with the popular classes. All these events were excitedly, often irresponsibly, reported by the lively Brazilian press. No one was livelier than Carlos Lacerda, editor of the capital's *Tribuna da Imprensa*, a strident critic of the administration who demanded that Vargas must go. Military men and civil political leaders were discussing possible courses of action.

Then in August 1954 something occurred that the military considered inexcusable. A gunman fired at and wounded Carlos Lacerda and killed an air force major with him, the latter presumably by accident. The accident was precisely the sort the military were unwilling to accept. Lacerda declared in his paper that the Vargas regime was responsible. The military refused to leave the matter to the government, but conducted an intensive examination of its own, tracing the murder to Vargas' bodyguard and possibly to the president's brother Benjamin, who had

a long and unsavory career in Getúlio's service. Military and civilian leaders were in a state of great excitement. A military delegation took the evidence to Vargas, and demanded that he resign. Rather than do so, Vargas committed suicide on August 24, 1954, leaving documents assigning his problems to the machinations of "international economic and financial groups."[8] This charge was useful to nationalist groups generally, and especially to Vargas' presumed political heir, João Goulart. Both leftist and rightist nationalists were eager to repeat the accusation. The Petrobrás fight had illustrated the willingness of those otherwise antithetical groups to collaborate on nationalist issues as a means of flaying more moderate elements.

Military Support of Civilian Government, 1954–1960

Vice-president João Café Filho (John Coffee, Jr.), who succeeded to the presidency, had only a weak political base. He had to resign in 1954 because of a heart attack. Carlos Luz, president of the Chamber of Deputies, took over as provisional president. All the period from the death of Vargas to October 1955 was dominated by maneuvering for the presidential election of that date. The PSD candidate was the governor of Minas Gerais, Juscelino Kubitschek. He received the support of the Vargas element in that party, offering them nationalism and rapid economic growth. The PTB also supported Kubitschek, although it ran Goulart as vice-president against the PSD candidate for that office. The UDN candidate was General Juarez Távora, one-time *tenente* and long-time figure of eminence in Brazilian affairs. The military were unhappy, lest Kubitschek follow the Vargas pattern, especially as coupled with Goulart. There was so much talk of military intervention that a Military Constitutionalist Movement was created to oppose such

---

[8] There is some doubt about the authenticity of one of the notes, but that did not affect the political results of their disclosure.

interference. Kubitschek won the election with only 36 percent of the vote, but the PTB did better for Goulart, who received 40 percent for vice-president.

Some anti-Vargas leaders still were determined to block Kubitschek. A group in UDN, a hopelessly minority party of conservative views, was of this opinion. Provisional president Luz favored such action. Several months of fantastic political intrigue followed the election, with efforts to discredit Kubitschek and Goulart with wild charges and worse rumors, even forged documents. The armed forces were badly divided as to whether Kubitschek should be inaugurated. The country followed much of this through the press. Provisional president Luz and ambitious publisher Lacerda tried to organize a coup but were prevented by Minister of War General Teixeira Lott and had to go briefly into exile. The Congress obeyed the prompting of the army and named vice-president of the Senate Nereu Ramos as provisional president of the republic. The army also prevented Café Filho from returning to the presidency as he wished. In addition, the army, led by War Minister Lott, had the Congress vote for imposition of a state of siege.

Under these bizarre circumstances Kubitschek was inaugurated in January 1956, while some people feared that the political system was unworkable. Kubitschek had been a good governor of Minas Gerais, approved by the propertied classes for his sound management and probity. As president, he displayed a striking ability to cajole, charm, and pressure Congress into giving him support. It seemed to indicate that successful collaboration between the two branches of government was possible, although it depended on the presence of a chief executive of unusual political ability, and most presidents could not be expected to have it.

Kubitschek acted as though he meant his campaign slogan of "Fifty Years' Progress in Five" He not only was uninterested in curbing inflation but increased deficit financing and endured higher inflation to pursue his idea of development. In pursuit of industrial growth, which

often seemed the whole of his economic interest, he appeared oblivious to Brazil's other great problems, including low agricultural productivity and low levels of living and purchasing power among the popular classes. He adopted an extreme version of the view that the conventional wisdom on debt and inflation in the older developed countries did not apply to Brazil, which must accept radically unbalanced growth to escape from the dependent and agriculturally oriented trap into which it had fallen. Many industrialists and their allies in other parts of the economy supported that view out of self-interest when the government offered benefits, although they disapproved of the state-participation ideas of advocates of forced-draught industrialization.[9]

Kubitschek's policies tripled the foreign debt. They led to worker unrest as wages lagged behind prices. Rising inflation added to the historic poverty of the northeast, which resulted in a Peasant League movement led by Francisco Julião that some people claimed was communist. That suggested to the propertied classes and the military a heightened possibility of the old nightmare of a peasant rebellion, led by communists or Goulart and the PTB, or both. Debt and inflation rose so high that the situation seemed about to get out of hand, but it never did, even when the cost of living went up nearly 40 percent in one year. People were not in a revolutionary mood. Kubitschek pursued his predecessors' policy of palliating the financial crunch with infusions of foreign money. When private investment was not enough, application was made abroad for public funds. In 1959, however, Brazilian government requests for credits from the United States Export-Import Bank and the International Monetary Fund were refused except on the condition that conventional financial policies be adopted.

The reaction of the Kubitschek government was instructive: its policies were more important to it than foreign loans. The argument that Bra-

[9] See Section b of this chapter on Kubitschek and the automotive industry.

zilian methods were superior in Brazil's environment was for the moment apparently fully dominant. The nationalists exulted in the refusal to knuckle under to what was called an international conspiracy to milk the underdeveloped countries. In Brazil as in Argentina, by this time such arguments had become difficult to resist. Most people paid little attention to the technical arguments of the forever squabbling economists. The political aspects of the debate seemed to show the continued importance of emotional or spiritual issues in human affairs. Both left and right made nationalist arguments, hoping to be the political beneficiaries of their implementation.

Kubitschek aggravated his financial problems by deciding to implement an old dream of Brazilian developmentalists and nationalists: putting the national capital in the interior, thus hopefully promoting a new period of economic growth and a "march to the west." The idea went back to the 1820s, and had been incorporated in the Constitution of 1891. Brasília began to rise six hundred miles northwest of Rio de Janeiro in the state of Goiás in what critics called the wilderness. The area had little population and only primitive connections with the rest of Brazil. Critics said that the country could not afford the expenditure. The direct cost was stated as $1 billion, but it was impossible to calculate. It required new transportation links and productive facilities. Kubitschek said that things of the spirit were superior to other considerations, and that in any event he had faith that the new capital would spur development in the great interior. The project did stimulate nationalism considerably. Its boldness was exhilarating. The design, by talented Brazilian architects, planners, and artists, quickened pride. As time passed the cost in money seemed less important, and Kubitschek was remembered as director of the great enterprise.

There was much tension in Brazil by the election year 1960. Kubitschek was leaving office with the national finances as troubled as ever. There was wide disgust with politicians as tools

of specialized interests, even thieves. This malady was perceived to run through municipal, state, and federal politics and government. The beneficiary of the mood of revulsion against corruption, and against the strains of the inflationary system, was Janio Quadros, known as an honest public servant. He campaigned with a broom as a sign of his determination to sweep the rascals from office.

Janio appealed to conservatives on the basis of his good relations with businessmen as mayor of the city and governor of the state of São Paulo. He promised to control inflation and government spending. But he also reached for nationalist and leftist support by promising policies that were unpalatable to conservatives. The divisions of party were such in Brazil that a successful candidate for president almost had to take such positions. The same thing was true in other countries in the world, but not all had politically active military forces waiting to pounce on what they viewed as mistakes. Janio's major political asset was his lack of identification with a party during his career in São Paulo. In 1960 the conservative UDN backed him, but Janio made it clear that he was not its man. He emphasized his independence in other ways, notably by visiting Castro's Cuba to show a lack of subservience to the United States.

Janio's chief opponent was Marshal Teixeira Lott, who had helped oust Vargas and later had directed military seizure of governing authority to insure the inauguration of Kubitschek. Lott was the administration, PSD, candidate, although his support from Kubitschek was tepid. Both the Communists and Julião of the Peasants Leagues supported Lott, for long-term tactical reasons, not out of affection for his generally conservative views. Lott ran on the memory of Vargas and the program of ultranationalism, but it was not enough. When Jânio won with nearly half the vote, his victory was considered a repudiation of the old politics, but no one was sure what else it meant about the attitudes of the electorate. Once again the curious electoral system coupled the president with a vice-president who did not share his views—Goulart of the PTB.

Quadros as president was a disaster. He proved so poor a politician, so bent on achieving his wishes by simple declarations, that megalomania was suggested to explain his conduct. He must have known that Brazilian presidents had to play politics every waking hour, that cooperation from the divided Congress could be had only by the sort of unremitting effort expended by Kubitschek. But Janio did not make the effort. If it was not miscalculation due to mania, Janio must have been simply overwhelmed by his admittedly difficult task.

The two principal issues facing him, the economy and the orientation of foreign relations, were intertwined. Foreign debt and currency inflation might, as usual, be reduced by foreign loans, but lenders were apt to demand better management in Brazil. Such advice was unacceptable to nationalists. Janio appeased them by demonstrating independence of United States policies, notably in relations with communist countries. He would not join the Washington-led campaign against Fidel Castro of Cuba and even decorated Che Guevara when the latter visited Brazil. In many ways Janio made clear his independent position in the cold war. While this was popular with Brazilian nationalists, including some military men, it caused apprehension in other quarters that were concerned about leftism. Presumably, Janio's largely rhetorical stances on foreign affairs would have been of little interest had he been able to improve economic conditions. He managed to get through Congress some austerity measures which required sacrifice from various groups, but he could by no means get all he wanted. That failure was not entirely offset by a United States decision to join with the International Monetary Fund in a $2 billion program of financial aid to Brazil (June 1961). The Kennedy administration had decided that Janio's financial orthodoxy was more important than his independent foreign policy. In a few months Quadros had alarmed or infuriated many military men, much of business, and many politicians. Carlos Lacerda, who had supported his election, now demanded his removal.

Quadros astonished everyone in August 1961 by submitting his resignation to Congress, presumably in the belief that an outpouring of support would compel it to reject the resignation and comply more with his wishes. Probably he supposed that the propertied classes that dominated the Congress would not want to see Vice-president Goulart succeed to power and that the military would agree. Quadros miscalculated. Apparently he was without important supporters by this time. To traditional politicians he seemed unreliable, uncontrollable, too much given to investigation of corruption and determined on a radical financial stabilization program. The military and the Congress promptly collaborated: the former "protected" Janio so that he could play no further role in politics; the latter accepted his resignation and named Pascoal Ranieri Mazilli, president of the Chamber of Deputies, as provisional president of the republic, in the absence of Goulart on a mission to Communist China. Janio left the country, largely unmourned, a man who had misjudged his constituency.

d. Military Wonder About Civilian Government, 1961–1964

For two and a half years, from August 1961 to March 1964, the military tried to decide if, and on what terms, to permit civilian government to continue under João Goulart. Although Goulart's character and record were notably sleazy, there was more to the problem than that because some military officers long had been dubious about the entire system. The military establishment was far from united, but crystallization of a majority view was promoted by several developments since the great crisis of the 1930s. Fears of populism and leftism were now greater, and experience in other countries suggested that once a leftist regime was established, it was difficult to alter. Fears of incompetent and corrupt government were also greater, both because of recent

Brazilian experience, and because of economic accomplishments since the 1930s which made inferior handling of growth seem less tolerable. In addition, government authority was now more important, with expanded functions, more revenues, and more effective techniques. Also, there was a much larger middle class, which had economic and technical interests that required rational government; it could be hurt by repeated political crises that diluted authority or made it uncertain and disturbed public order. Finally, all decisions involved more emotion and seemed more fraught with community portent because of the growth of nationalist sentiment. The political issue so agitated the country that other important matters that cried out for attention often were neglected.

The ministers of the three military departments (all military men, in accordance with recent custom) stated that Goulart could not be president because of his communist affiliations. The Congress declined to vote him from office, although it had taken similar action against others in the crisis after Vargas' death. Civilian politicians were in a strong position because they knew of the divisions in the military. There were, to be sure, civilians who favored ousting Goulart, but doing so depended on a military decision. Once again the military feared creation of a Peronist-style regime by the heirs of Vargas. Although Perón was now in exile from Argentina, the aftermath of his rule was far from reassuring to the Brazilian military. In addition to fears of leftism, they did not want a militant labor movement competing with them for power. The immediate issue, Goulart's return, was rather speedily resolved early in September when Congress passed a constitutional amendment establishing a parliamentary system, conferring many of the president's powers on a prime minister responsible to the Congress. Goulart accepted this, and returned to Brazil.

Goulart after his return spent much of his effort campaigning against the parliamentary system. He had support. The system was contrary to Brazilian tradition, and many people found it contrary to common sense in the environment. There was too little collaboration between president and Congress; the parliamentary system might make the situation worse. It took Goulart a year to put across the idea of a national plebiscite, but when it was held in January 1963, it overwhelmingly returned to the president his traditional powers. That was the only success of importance that Goulart enjoyed.

For the next year Goulart did nothing well but make enemies. An effort to get United States aid again met with a demand that he control inflation. He could not do so, partly because special interests—including the military—wanted other groups to sacrifice first. Inflation was 70 percent in 1963 and still increasing at the end of the year. A decline in economic production that had begun under Quadros continued under Goulart. A 1960 census had shown production value up 100 percent in the 1950s; but in 1960–1964 growth slowed and then ceased. In 1963 industrial output was stationary. Industrial unemployment mounted. Much of the turndown was the result of a rejection of Brazil by owners and managers of capital. Foreign public and private investment dried up, and Brazilian private capital fled the country. The situation was the expectable result of a refusal to curb expenditures and control inflation, plus the growth of ultranationalist demands for tight control of foreign profits or even expropriation of foreign holdings. In August 1962 the Congress approved limitation of the remittance abroad of profits earned by foreign companies in Brazil. When the United States ambassador warned that some types of regulation of foreign investment would harm Brazil, he was criticized there for "interference" in its domestic affairs. No relief resulted from a United States decision in 1963 to provide a credit of some $400 million, because Goulart would not meet the usual requirement that the government reform financial practices.

Brazilians were being driven to a decision as to whether they would adhere to conventional capitalistic notions of finance, collaborating with foreign bankers and corporations and with the

International Monetary Fund and the World Bank, encouraging rather than coercing domestic investors, or go further with policies bound to alienate those elements even more. Although Brazilians were arguing the economics of the choice, the matter was becoming political, to be settled by power in one form or another. Politically active Brazilians more and more saw the economic question as tied to the political: as a choice between leftism and something else, the latter conceived in several styles. For all the nationalist cries of foreign intervention, choice was to be made by Brazilians; foreign agents were not necessary to instruct Brazilians on the issues in the contest for control of the economy and the polity.

Goulart proposed two startling measures: division of the great landed estates and extension of the franchise to illiterates and to enlisted men in the armed forces. He could not get them through the hostile Congress. The agrarian measure seemed to some the more dangerous because violence in the countryside was increasing and obviously was organized, some of it reportedly by communists. The issue of votes for enlisted men Goulart audaciously supported by sympathizing with some mutineers who claimed that it was a major reason for their disobedience. Few things could have shaken military officers more. By early 1964 the country was in a fever of disagreement, suspicion, and conspiracy.

Whether Goulart might still have saved his office by any means is impossible to guess, but clearly, by turning abruptly farther to the left at this point, he solidified the military and many propertied groups against any more compromise. They feared the connections of Luís Carlos Prestes and of Francisco Julião, leader of the Peasant Leagues in northeast Brazil, with communist Cuba. Goulart was an amiable and weak man who was harried beyond his strength and understanding by the violent political atmosphere of Brazil. He listened to Leonel Brizola, his brother-in-law, who was governor of Rio Grande do Sul. Brizola, like Goulart, was a wealthy man. He probably opposed any income

distribution that would touch his own, but he was ambitious. He had been making a name for himself by violently nationalist speeches and acts. In February 1962 his state administration expropriated the ITT system there. He was driving for the presidency as a radical leader, presumably supposing that he could prevent the movement from falling into the hands of the communists. What Goulart saw was that he himself was in danger, and the only option seemed to be reliance on extremists and popular elements. Goulart knew that the military were conspiring against him. He and the men in his now clearly defined leftist political base deluded themselves into believing that the traditional political leaders of Brazil could be defeated by violence and intimidation. By that time, in early 1964, inflation was running at an annual rate of 144 percent.

In March 1964 Goulart began a campaign to overturn Brazil's traditional minority political system with one founded on activity by the general population. He accepted advice from communist chief Luís Carlos Prestes on this endeavor. It began March 13 with a popular meeting in Rio de Janeiro, at which Brizola demanded election of a constituent assembly, and Goulart signed decrees nationalizing private oil refineries and making various types of land subject to expropriation. He asserted his intention of decreeing votes for illiterates and enlisted men and other reforms and declared that such changes were necessary to construct a just society. This public activity in the presence of his popular constituency convinced some of his enemies that he would seize dictatorial power and use it to establish some form of socialism.

Before long, sailors in Rio de Janeiro demonstrated in favor of Goulart and refused to obey military orders to disperse. Goulart granted them amnesty—that is, said that he would define military discipline. Although workers did not respond in any numbers to a call for a general strike in favor of Goulart on March 30, the effort further convinced military men that Goulart meant to use labor cadres in setting up his dictatorship. On the same day, Goulart incited non-commissioned officers to disobey their officers in his support. The next day the military took over the government. The populace did not take to the barricades. Goulart had miscalculated. He went into exile.

e. The Military Regime Since 1964

It turned out that the military officers were ready to do without civilian government indefinitely. It also turned out that many important civilian elements were ready to collaborate in what was the first of a new breed of "corporatist" regimes in Latin America. Most poor Brazilians accepted the regime with the apathy they had displayed during most of the country's history. Leftist elements proved quite unable to challenge the regime. Military specialists and civilian technicians and businessmen fashioned economic policies that produced striking gains, which critics said exacted an exorbitant price in popular misery and authoritarian government. The regime's system of control, however, and the magnitude of its deeds and plans for the national future seemed likely to ensure its power for some time to come.

Politics and Government

The ministers of the three military departments declared themselves a Supreme Revolutionary Command. Appropriation of the label "revolutionary" started a trend among the Latin American military that confused many observers. On April 9 the junta issued an Institutional Act amending the Constitution to permit the executive to use the state of siege without congressional approval and dismiss legislatures at any level, and to permit the Congress to elect a president of the republic. On April 11 the Congress chose Field Marshal Humberto Castello Branco, a chief military architect of the coup. At that time some military officers wanted to run the government only long enough to get the

economy advancing, but others meant to manage the country indefinitely.

The regime declared its power to seize subversives and suspend their civil rights. Arrests were not numerous, but they had an extra aspect of ill omen because of the prominence of some of those seized. It suggested a military determination to dramatize its power. They declared suspended for ten years the political rights of ex-presidents Kubitschek, Quadros, and Goulart, only the last of whom could with any plausibility be labeled subversive. Several hundred other people also were proscribed, including some members of Congress, governors, labor leaders, intellectuals, and military officers. The civil service was purged of foes of the regime. Other institutions were closed or altered to bolster the regime. Congressional efforts to resist such measures were ineffectual.

In elections in 1965 several opposition candidates were elected, including two governors. Although "hard-line" officers wanted to annul the elections, that was not done; but in October 1965 a Second Institutional Act was issued, providing dissolution of political parties, election of the president and state governors by national and state legislatures respectively, packing of the Supreme Court by enlargement, and executive power to continue depriving citizens of their civil rights. In place of the previous political parties, the regime formed ARENA (the *Aliança Renovadora Nacional*) as its vehicle, and an opposition party dubbed MDB (*Movimento Democrático Brasileiro*), surely an example of "double-think."

General Artur da Costa e Silva, more nearly a hard-liner than Castello Branco, was selected by Congress in 1966 for the term to begin in March 1967. When protests against the regime arose in 1967–68, the influence of the military hard-liners increased. Congress, the Supreme Court, students, urban guerrillas, and others tried to exert pressure for dilution of the dictatorship. It included not only authoritarian government, but considerable press censorship and military support of the formation of "death squads" of off-duty policemen to kill people they defined as terrorists. Reports of abuse of political prisoners multiplied. Churchmen protested. The hard-liners responded in December 1968 with the Fifth Institutional Act, which disbanded the federal and state legislatures, suspended the Constitution, and imposed censorship (applied at times earlier). More persons were deprived of their civil rights.

When Costa e Silva suffered a stroke in August 1969, the ministers of the military departments (all officers) took power, ignoring the civilian vice-president. They picked General Emilio Garrastazú Médici for president and an admiral for vice-president and had Congress rubber-stamp the decision. Elections in November 1970 returned big ARENA majorities in federal and state legislatures. By this time the military benefited from an economic boom that overshadowed political issues. Real wages finally were rising, and the regime was channeling more funds into social measures. Médici occasionally spoke of return to more popular political institutions, but the hard-liners prevailed, sometimes saying that such a change awaited evidence that "personalism" and subversion had been purged from political life. Denunciation by Archbishop Helder Câmara of torture by government security forces embarrassed the regime. During 1970, among other repressive acts, ten of Brazil's finest scientists were dismissed from the Oswaldo Cruz Institute and deprived of their civil rights as "subversive and enemies of the regime." Even what was by then being called an economic miracle did not reconcile everyone to authoritarian government.

Médici was succeeded in March 1974 by General Ernesto Geisel, chosen by the military and named president by an electoral college formed of federal deputies and senators and representatives of state assemblies. The MDB's "official" opposition party candidate got 76 of the 497 votes and told the press that the procedure was a farce. Geisel declared that a return to civilian government required great economic and social changes that would alter the mentality of the citizenry.

On the other hand, Geisel spoke of a national consensus on a just and prosperous state, and a gradual return to democracy. The general-presidents before him had made similar statements. Geisel did make an effort. The freest campaigning in a decade was allowed for two months before the November 1974 elections for legislatures, presumably in the hope of quieting criticism of the regime. Instead, it brought an upsurge of opposition activity and votes. The government, amid rumors that it would cancel the elections, accepted the opposition capture of many of the national and state legislature seats that were at stake. Government forces in some states did imprison militant opposition leaders. Although the state and national legislatures had limited power, larger opposition forces therein could ask questions. But when the new legislators tried to investigate political prisoners and the use of torture, the government began an antisubversive drive early in 1975, and before long Geisel said that communist infiltration of Brazilian institutions made a freer political system impossible.

Repression continued, and in November 1976 the National Conference of Bishops condemned excessive security measures and the injustice of government land policies. The opposition in Congress early in 1977 blocked passage of a government bill as a protest against authoritarian rule, whereupon on April 1 Geisel dissolved Congress. Then on April 14 he decreed measures to prevent civilian critics from gaining power by election. He set up staggered and indirect elections for president, governors, and the federal legislature. Such measures removed all hope of political liberalization under Geisel and all doubt that there would be another military president after him.

The regime had discovered that people might agree to concentrated power in time of perceived political or economic peril, but as conditions improved, they demanded relaxation of controls.

The generals seemed to have no idea how to live with a free opposition. The result was that the military regime received a barrage of criticism from the left, from intellectual and artistic figures, and from political leaders unwilling to collaborate with the dictatorship. On the other hand, the regime had strong support from much of private enterprise; many professional people and technicians, including some with impressive intellectual credentials; many people in journalism; much of the middle class; and assorted nationalists of the center and right. Organized labor included but a part of the industrial workers of Brazil and was controlled by government, so it was not a focus of opposition. Although opinion and publication were interfered with, intermittently considerable criticism of the regime was permitted. The corporatist state was authoritarian but it was far from the totalitarianism of communist Cuba. The regime claimed to have saved the country from disorder and radicalism, but the countercharge was that whatever the merits of such an argument, the price of military tyranny was unacceptable.

International criticism of violations of human rights in Brazil did not appear to shake the regime and permitted it to emphasize its nationalism and independence of outside influence. A variety of foreign condemnations of human rights in Brazil culminated in criticism in early 1977 by the United States Department of State.[10] Brazil at once terminated all military aid from the United States and in succeeding weeks objected to interference by Washington in Brazil's internal affairs. Even opposition figures in Brazil echoed that complaint.

Economic and Social Developments

During its first three years the military regime had to revise the administration and national policies. That meant economies to be imposed

on others rather than themselves. The laborer was hard pressed by the austerity process, but military pay sharply increased. On the the other hand, total military expenditures were not raised conspicuously. Brazil in the mid-1970s still had only something more than 200,000 men in the armed forces and was spending only half as much per capita on military purposes as Argentina. Minimum wages were held down, government subsidies of bread and gasoline cut, credit tightened, tax collections improved, government expenditures better supervised. Such measures lowered inflation and improved the climate for domestic and foreign private investment.

The regime adopted "monetary correction" or "indexing," by which many things (like wages, rents, interest, taxes) were adjusted in accordance with price rises. It had the effect, as administered, of guaranteeing a real rate of return on investment, but it also cut real wages. Such a system was only possible without widespread trouble with labor because most workers were unorganized, and those in unions were dominated by the government. The regime also encouraged foreign capital by diluting certain types of nationalism. All this found favor abroad, and in 1965 brought the government nearly $1 billion in aid from the United States, the IMF, the World Bank, and foreign private banks. United States sponsorship of this aid was influenced by the fact that Brazil in May 1964 broke relations with communist Cuba and in 1965 supported with Brazilian troops the United States military intervention in the Dominican Republic. So cooperation with United States interventionism could be added by critics of the regime to its sins of dictatorship and economic favoritism.

Economic policy followed many trends set or suggested in earlier administrations, but now they were established more firmly, and were less subject than formerly to political change. There was more state planning and regulation and ownership, although the bulk of the economy remained private. But about one-half of investment was by the state, much of it in high-risk projects considered important for national devel-

---

[10] See Chapter 34, Section a, on the human rights issue in Latin America generally.

opment, including agriculture. The great state enterprises attracted good managerial talent with excellent compensation and opportunities for responsible achievement. Private enterprise criticized much of this development, but its anguish was nicely buttered over with profits. The biggest company in Brazil in the 1970s was Petrobrás, and its enterprises at home and abroad were reminiscent of the state petroleum company in Italy. In 1971, of the top twenty-five enterprises in Brazil, measured by assets, seventeen were government firms. Brazilian state enterprise dominated steel, mining, petroleum, energy, and some transportation. Together with tax regulation, tariffs, exchange controls, credit regulation, and other measures, the state had potent leverage in the economy. A popular defense of state enterprise was that it prevented dominance of sectors by multinational corporations.

By 1969 annual national production growth was up to nearly 10 percent and it kept about that high level for the next five years. From 1964 to 1974 Brazil's GNP rose 56 percent, far outpacing world growth. Total production, however, still was far from that of the developed countries. In the early 1970s Brazil's production per capita was only $460, which put it fiftieth in the world and far behind Argentina, in twenty-seventh place at $1,230.[11] In 1974 the economy began to falter, partly because of the great increase in petroleum prices, partly because of internal factors. Inflation increased, deficits mounted, the foreign debt soared, both for petroleum and for raw materials and machinery for the immense industrialization program. By 1976 about 40 percent of foreign exchange went to service the foreign debt, which was the largest in the developing world, about $28 billion by

1977.[12] National production slowed down to the 5 to 6 percent range. It was widely suggested that the Brazilian "miracle" was ended.

Aside from sheer growth, the regime claimed —with some justification—to be achieving diversification, independence, and integration at an accelerated rate. It had an ambitious transportation policy, which was useful to the country, although some of it was badly planned and costly. It even included the manufacture of light planes, and by the mid-1970s Brazil was turning out about six hundred a year. The great new highways were useful for commerce, but they did not counter the continuing differential growth of the southern part of the republic. Migrants still moved south to operate at least on the fringes of the modern economy. The opening of the interior was chiefly of advantage to large operations.

An example of diversification and modernization that captured the popular imagination was motor vehicle production, with output passing 900,000 units in 1975, and they were 100 percent of Brazilian components. Brazil by the 1970s exported automotive products and put pressure on its world trading partners to buy them. It expected to become one of the greatest automotive producers in the world, with vast resources of metal and with great pools of low-cost labor. In the 1970s on the new Brazilian cars nationalistic fervor took the form of bumper stickers proclaiming, "Brazil, Love It or Leave It."

The military regime was especially successful with exports, developing volume, variety of products, and diversifying markets, with the share going to the United States declining and that to Europe increasing. Export sales rose in 1969–1973 from $2.5 billion to $6.7 billion (much of it due to price inflation), and with the agricultural share down. The total list of export products went to some two hundred, including many manufactured goods. Exports of manufactures

---

[11] Although such figures (World Bank) must be used with caution, they are suggestive. The United States per capita figure was $5,160, first in the world, and it put the relationship between United States and Brazilian per capita production just about where it had been in the 1930s—that is, Brazil had neither gained nor lost in that comparison. The figures for the 1970s showed the Soviet Union with $1,400, Bolivia with $190, India with $110.

[12] The ratio of foreign debt to national production was 23 percent, which was much less than in the United States at times in the nineteenth century.

quintupled in 1969–1973. In 1974 exports of automotive products reached $250 million. But the foreign trade picture was altered drastically by two events: the great rise in petroleum prices in 1973 and the coming into production of great new agricultural crops in Brazil at a time when prices for them were high.

Brazil still was importing about 75 percent of its petroleum requirements when the OPEC escalated world prices. The cost of petroleum imports to Brazil was about $1 billion in 1973; in 1974 it was $3 billion, a quarter of all the country's imports; and in 1976 petroleum imports cost $3.8 billion. This would have made the balance-of-payments problem unmanageable except for the fact that world prices for Brazil's agricultural exports also rose, and the military regime had planned for it. Soybean exports rose from only $70 million in 1970 to approximately $3 billion in 1977! Some other new agricultural exports rose sharply. At the same time, coffee prices leapt upward. In 1976 coffee export earnings more than doubled, from less than $1 billion to $2.3 billion, although the volume of such exports was up only 7 percent. This leap was partly because of the rise in world price, but also because the government quintupled the export tax on coffee in 1976–1977. By that time coffee again accounted for 40 percent of Brazilian exports, despite the fact that the total value of exports multiplied five to six times in a decade. Brazilian sugar and cattle exports also increased. By 1977 it was also clear that Brazil was the world's second largest exporter of agricultural/pastoral products, following the United States. This achievement was magnificent, even though critics had a basis for their complaint that it was done by encouraging large private producers, and it did little directly to improve Brazilian nutritional levels or the incomes of small farmers or laborers.

Although agricultural exports compensated for petroleum imports, the balance of payments could be controlled only by drastic tightening of imports of raw materials and machinery for industry. To deal with this problem, the government began in 1975 to try to bring foreign petroleum capital back into Brazil, to explore on a risk basis. The conditions offered, however, were not good enough to appeal much to the private petroleum giants, and whether Brazilian nationalism would permit the generals to offer much more generous terms remained to be seen. The government also decided that nuclear power was a necessary part of a solution of the energy problem; in addition, Argentina led Brazil in the field, which Brasília found unacceptable. In 1975 a deal was made with West Germany for up to eight nuclear reactors and uranium enrichment and processing plants, to a total value of at least $5 billion. The United States took the view that the uranium processing system agreed to would provide Brazil with a technology usable for making nuclear explosives and thus was undesirable. Washington offered United States technology and fuel supplies that would not produce weapons-grade material. Brazil retorted that United States efforts to block the accord was interference with Brazil's internal affairs, an effort to prevent it from becoming a great power, and a ploy to keep a United States monopoly on nuclear sales to the world. Brazil noted that the United States could not guarantee to keep up deliveries of fuel, so that it was only prudent of Brazil to wish to use its own uranium as it pleased. Since this controversy occurred simultaneously with Washington's comments on human rights in Brazil, the combined effect was to persuade many Brazilians that the United States stood in the way of Brazil's efforts to achieve a higher place in the world's esteem. As an editorial in São Paulo stated in 1977, "If others can have it, it is not morally just for us not to have the bomb."

Critics complained that the great industrial growth had been of little benefit to the general population. By the census of 1971, 65 percent of the economically active had a monthly income of $60 or less, and only 1 percent received $350 or more. Apparently the gap between the poor and others was widening. The very rich got richer. The moderately well-off continued to grow in numbers: the "middle class," defined to include everyone from the better-paid factory and clerical workers through small merchants to medium-sized manufacturers and including some bureaucrats, intellectuals, and military officers. The poorest part of the population, near the subsistence level, was being reduced as a proportion of the total, but only very slowly, and its level of living changed little. Enemies of the regime said the concept of national development was a cover for unrestrained channeling of profits to a privileged few. An opposition leader in 1974 said, "We are saturated with promises. The Brazilian economic miracle has not reached the people." A finance minister retorted that more equitable distribution would hurt growth and "end up by leaving the nation dividing the misery more equally." Whatever one might think of the economics of that statement, its political ineptness and its apparent absence of compassion seemed too much in accord with the general aspect of the regime of generals and technocrats.

There were some social gains. Health care expanded. The percentage of public expenditures going for education increased. The regime claimed spectacular inroads upon illiteracy. As might be expected, it emphasized the technical rather than the moral or spiritual side of education; and it used political criteria in determining some educational policies, including the hiring and firing of university professors.

In the 1930s–1970s Brazil changed enormously. There was a great growth of the spirit of nationalism, a more integrated community was created through better communications and transportation and education, the economy was enlarged and diversified, a centralized governmental system of some efficiency was created, and the regionalism of the past probably forever shattered. At the same time, a huge and generally undemanding population made little contribution to economic, social, or political development. Apparently, that submerged class would remain large for many years to come. In the mid-1970s it was estimated that more than half the workers had a money income of less than $200 a year.

The actual or seeming improvements wrought by the military regime after 1964 did not still opposition, but many Brazilians plainly supported or acquiesced in the role the military had assumed. Brazil failed to develop interest groups and political parties with sufficient following and discipline to run the country with the stability and efficiency required to fend off military intervention. The military seemed to be attached to their new role in government. They certainly were determined to make Brazil a great power. They said so, and so did civilian nationalists. Both considered the national resources equal to anything. They opposed population control, dreaming of a nation of more than 200 million before the end of the century, linking that with the need for a larger economic base. The sheer size of Brazil, together with the regime's success in achieving certain types and concentrations of modernization, made the model of military direction appealing to some Spanish Americans. Some of Brazil's neighbors, however, felt "as if they were in bed with an elephant." [13]

----

[13] On Brazil and Bolivia see Chapter 44, Section a; on Brazil and Paraguay see Chapter 44, section d.

Mexico puzzled and infuriated many observers at home and abroad. The fury with which its achievements and failures were debated by left and right suggested that it had built a workable synthesis irritating to both extremes. The system also was unacceptable to traditional liberals in Mexico and abroad, unhappy with order and progress on the basis of a one-party dictatorship. The fact that the party preferred managed consensus to coercion did not make it more acceptable to critics. It achieved economic growth almost without parallel in the world and a sizable rise in the percentage of Mexicans with more than subsistence income and with "middle-class" (or modern) tastes and attitudes. But Mexico remained a land of great social contrasts or dualisms, with a large proletariat only on the margins of the modern society. It built a big system of social assistance, especially medical aid and state-supported food prices, but it did not reach everyone or solve all problems. It enormously enhanced the confidence of Mexicans in their ability to fashion an acceptable future. But many citizens remained outside that arena of hope. Were the gains so meager, in view of the incomes of the rich and the continuing misery of the numerous poor, as to call for rejection? Was the new system rightist or leftist, or both? Or were those terms misleading in describing the

synthesis in Mexico? Had the Revolution "matured" by perfecting the tools of modernization or by abandoning interest in fundamental change? The argument over Mexican modernization posed the issues as well as anywhere in Latin America.

a. Cárdenas Reaffirms the Revolution, 1934–1940

Cárdenas "reaffirmed" and promoted the shibboleths of the Revolution of 1910–1917, magnificently identifying himself with innovation, justice, egalitarianism, nationalism, and agrarian reform. Like his contemporary in the United States, President Franklin D. Roosevelt, Cárdenas was much loved and much hated, and like Roosevelt the effect of his administration is still debated. For conservatives he was simply a socialist, but he certainly did not destroy private enterprise in Mexico. The traditional "line" of leftist defenders of Mexico's Revolution is that Cárdenas reaffirmed that Revolution and his successors foully betrayed it, so that 1940 is the great dividing point in recent Mexican history. Marxists consider that the Mexican Revolution of 1910–1917 was merely a bourgeois readjustment and the Cárdenas administration more of the same, so that no transition or dividing point of importance occurred. A moderate view is that Cárdenas was more pragmatic and less revolutionary than his admirers and detractors believed. While he reaffirmed the shibboleths of the Revolution, he strengthened the political and economic systems in ways that permitted private enterprise to grow side by side with an expanding state apparatus that was used for both social and economic reform.

Politics

Cárdenas' political activity scarcely seems revolutionary now. His first task was to secure his authority against Calles; without that he could not act strongly as chief of state. Cárdenas' powers as president gave him great leverage to attach men to his camp. He also played astutely on party factionalism. He appointed as minister of agriculture Tomás Garrido Canabal, longtime anticlerical chieftain of Tabasco; then in 1935, as part of a move against Calles, replaced Garrido with another *caudillo*, General Saturnino Cedillo of San Luís Potosí. At the same time, he put Portes Gil in as head of the PNR, to continue reduction of *callismo*. Then Cárdenas jettisoned Portes Gil, a potential rival because of his agrarian connections. Cárdenas not only reduced *callismo* by dismissals from office but by shutting down *callista*-run gambling and prostitution. Calles fought back with anticlerical disturbances and criticism of Cárdenas' softness on strikes, but both those efforts told against Calles. By 1935 Cárdenas could remake the cabinet on a completely anti-*callista* basis.

Cárdenas strengthened his position with a great deal more than conventional politics. Much support came from his policies favoring peasants and labor, which were so alarming to *callista* politicians and the economic elite. Cárdenas earned popular affection by his unpretentiousness and warm human sympathy. He refused to live in elaborate Chapultepec Castle. He continued the populism of his campaign by incessant travel in which he dressed informally and talked with peasants and workers. He encouraged

petitions from ordinary citizens. He was quite sincere in his reformism but carefully used it for political advantage. In fact, he continued the pragmatic politics of Obregón and Calles, merely coupling them with much more economic and social reform. That way he could call Calles a reactionary and finally a fascist, linking him with the little Gold Shirt organization in Mexico. Finally, in April 1936, he forced Calles and labor leader Morones into exile.

Cárdenas remade the PNR into the PRM (Party of the Mexican Revolution) in 1938, giving it a functional structure of labor, peasant, military, and popular sectors. The small military sector was meant to give officers a formal role that would reduce their interest in dissidence. That precaution was soon judged unnecessary, and the military sector was dropped. Cárdenas did keep the army satisfied even while continuing the reduction of military expenditures that Calles had managed in his period of dominance. The popular sector was merely outlined in Cárdenas' time, and did not become effective until 1943. Most of the million members of the PRM in 1938 belonged to Lombardo Toledano's labor confederation (CTM) and to a new peasants' confederation (CNC).

The party became less an alliance of regional chiefs and more a machinery for the vocalizing of aims and the parceling of rewards. It also provided better mobilization of support for the government. It became ever more clearly a system by which many of the important voices in Mexico were herded within the party, and accepted (however reluctantly) final decisions arrived at there. Cárdenas was careful to balance the forces in his huge new supporting mechanism. He kept an eye on Lombardo Toledano's CTM, which became by far the most important labor organization in the country, so that Morones' CROM receded still further in influence.

Organization of the PRM was accompanied by declarations in favor of democratic government and the aim of achieving revolutionary socialism. The latter was not pleasing to organized business, which was outside the party. It was unhappy with the 1936 law on chambers of commerce and industry that converted membership into a legal obligation, declared that the chambers were to collaborate with the state, and that they had a "public character." The law also gave the government some controls over the chambers, including their membership and jurisdiction. Although neither Cárdenas nor his successors used the chambers law to try to control organized business closely, it did somewhat increase the state's capacity to exert influence on private enterprise.

Cárdenas was firmly in political control of Mexico. A revolt in San Luís Potosí in 1938 by shrunken local strong man Cedillo, with *callista* and other conservative support, was put down. It proved to be the end of a tradition of more than a century in Mexico. Henceforth, the only person resembling a *caudillo* would be the president of the republic and head of the party, two highly bureaucratized and prudent institutions that had nothing in common with the old *caudillismo.* State bosses were not able to consider seriously the use of military force against the central government. The federal military firmly supported a system that worked.

Economic and Social Policies

Cárdenas did much to expand government activities and to make a dynamic role for the public sector a settled policy of the party. His most potent arguments for that were its contributions to national independence, economic and social modernization, and reaffirmation of the Revolution. He created institutions that became important to intervention in the economy, including the following that still existed in the 1970s: the National Bank of Ejidal Credit; *Nacional Financiera*, the development bank; the National Bank of Foreign Trade; the Federal Electricity Commission; and PEMEX, the national petroleum monopoly. They proved to be valuable instruments in the long run, but did not play much role in Cárdenas' own administration. Although his government created or expanded various sta-

tistical or economic study agencies, economics was not a strong point with Cárdenas or sophisticated plans a feature of his administration. Cárdenas' style rather was expressed in a scornful party statement in 1937 on contemporary quibbling as to whether the Six-Year Plan deserved the name.

Cárdenas became indissolubly identified with an acceleration of land distribution, especially to *ejidos*, communal farms. He thus became loved —and hated—as a friend of the peasants. That was what he intended. Nothing is more consonant with Cárdenas' historical reputation than the photographs showing him standing in fields surrounded by peasants. When people say that he reaffirmed the Revolution, they mean this program especially. Cárdenas distributed 50 million acres to *ejidos*, nearly three times the distribution of 1917–1933. The gain in *ejidatarios* was about 770,000 persons, compared with 754,000 in 1917–1933, so by the end of the Cárdenas term there were about 1.5 million communal farmers.

Cárdenas no doubt was sincere in giving first priority to the needs of peasants, but what he thought about the long-term role of agriculture in Mexico is uncertain. Cárdenas made at least as much contribution to industrial as to agricultural growth, in both the short and the long run. During his administration industrial growth was greater than agricultural. Nor did the regime foster socialism, although the idea was much discussed in Mexico in the 1930s. The reaffirmed Revolution, in fact, developed and implemented doctrine in ways not very pleasing to international ideologists. Much of the reaffirmation involved extension of state intervention in the economy, but it fell far short of an effort to socialize the means of production. The railways were nationalized in 1937 and turned over to the workers for operation, an experiment that was not a success and had to be abandoned. That and other interventions helped create a balance-of-payments problem, frightened foreign capital, required deficit financing, caused inflation, and did little to improve peasant levels of living.

Cárdenas' policies, however, did help double domestic investment, partly because he increased confidence in the future. It is a fact that after Cárdenas the national economy sprang from the material and spiritual accomplishments of his administration into a period of rapid and self-sustained growth. Although the succeeding administration had the advantage of wartime demand for Mexican products, the same leap could not have been made from the institutions and public temper of 1933. A part of the change in both institutions and public temper related to confidence in the ability of Mexico to achieve growth; a part related to the notion that growth could be attained with internal resources, ownership, and management; and a part related to enthusiasm for the notion that government action was a serviceable instrument for the increase of the national product and for its more equitable distribution. Cárdenas, in sum, performed that service of widening demand for change which is a prelude to change itself.

Possibly Cárdenas' greatest achievement, then, was the promotion of the sense of national community and purpose. Between his emphasis on the peasant and his own Tarascan Indian heritage, he seemed the embodiment of all the fighters for integration of the Indian into national life that the revolutionary painters were displaying on the walls of Mexico. Although the government sometimes interfered with the press, Cárdenas also encouraged the expression of all sorts of ideas and especially those of the left. How much this encouragement expressed leftism in Cárdenas and how much it was political tactics is impossible to say. Enemies of the administration certainly exaggerated what they called its bolshevism. They deplored the grant of asylum in 1937 to Leon Trotsky, though that celebrated communist probably had as much chance of influence under Stalin as in Mexico. Cárdenas was a friend of education, and literacy continued to climb. His support of a socialist element in public instruction went along with a strong nationalistic content in the curriculum, and the schools and universities turned out many more members of the national party than of leftist groups. When Cárdenas welcomed leftist refugees from Franco's fascist Spain, conservatives shuddered, but the Spaniards turned out to be excellent citizens.

Cárdenas' nationalism and his identification with justice for the little man received their most dramatic expression in the termination of the long petroleum controversy. The situation continued to be one of a depressed industry, dominated by foreign companies that held to the agreements of the 1920s exempting them from some provisions of the Constitution. The militant CTM now urged the workers to press for higher compensation. The government backed the workers. Although Cárdenas wanted a compromise, the companies were intransigent and put him in a position where to accept dictation would be political madness. In March 1938 he proclaimed nationalization of all the property of the foreign petroleum companies. The move caused a surge of Mexican nationalism and Cárdenas probably was more strongly backed than any president in Mexican history. No one cared about the probable immediate losses in petroleum production and revenues. The public reaction showed the immense integrating power of the spirit of nationalism.

Many interpretations insist that after Cárdenas' reaffirmation of the Revolution, a great swing to the right occurred. Partly this idea arose because Cárdenas was an extraordinarily effective president in the sense that matters most—giving spiritual guidance to his people—and his successor was conventional and conservative and lacked an inspirational personality. Partly the thesis rested on overemphasis on the tone or style of Cárdenas' leadership instead of on his actions. Admirers tended to make him the foe of politics as a system of control, which he was not; a supporter of socialism, which he did little to further; a seeker for humanistic simplicity and justice, especially in a rural environment, against the subtleties and corruptions of modern urban and industrial life. It has been observed, however, that Cárdenas strengthened the one-party system, aided private enterprise, did not much alter the distribution of income, and presided over an economy in which industry grew more than agriculture. It is as meaningful to point to

Cárdenas as having helped prepare for the great upsurge of party control and private economic growth as to assign the great change to a new conservatism in the next administration. The Mexican environment and international affairs probably fixed most developments after 1940 as much as the ideological coloration of the likely candidates for president in 1940. In any event, Cárdenas did not dictate his successor, and the nominee was Minister of War General Manuel Avila Camacho, not at all the sort of person one would imagine Cárdenas wanting to carry on his policies.

b. Politics and Government After Cárdenas

For decades after Cárdenas Mexican politics was dominated without difficulty by the official party, and the presidents it elected guided a huge expansion of the state apparatus. They said that one-party dominance and proliferation of government functions ensured the continuation of the Revolution.

One-Party Dominance

If the old saw was correct that "happy the country with little history," Mexican political history after Cárdenas was jolly. The official party elected presidents for six-year terms, as well as nearly all governors, federal and state legislators, and mayors. The presidents were centrists, party men, administrators, conciliators, seldom exciting.[1] The relative conservatism or liberalism of the various presidents in retrospect seems inconsequential. Critics interpreted the lack of political drama as the enforced quiet of political repression. Admirers thought it the most effective combination of performance and participation in Latin America.

The PRM in 1945 was reorganized into the Institutional Revolutionary Party (PRI), a name

that suggested to leftists the abandonment of revolution. It now had peasant, industrial worker, and popular sectors. The last, provided for but not created in Cárdenas' time, was founded in 1943 as the National Confederation of Popular Organizations (CNOP). It included organizations of small businessmen, clerical workers, and civil servants, including teachers. An important element in CNOP was the FSTSE (government workers federation), with hundreds of thousands of members by the 1960s. The CNOP grew faster in numbers and influence than the other sectors, and critics saw in its relatively high-income and upwardly mobile membership the "bourgeois" orientation of the party after Cárdenas. It could also be regarded as emphasis on modern rather than traditional elements in Mexican society.

The PRI had 4 million members in the functional interest associations that made up the party by the early 1960s, and it continued to grow. Although the military lacked representation in the party, it remained active in government, which the officer corps firmly supported. Big business still was not represented in the party; there would be no political profit in that for a party that claimed a popular revolutionary orientation. But big business was allowed to help determine policy and legislation on matters of interest to private enterprise. The latter was not, however, heavily in politics in the sense of nominating and electing officials and administering the national party and dispensing patronage, though no one doubted that it had some influence on nominations and appointments. The church also was left outside the party, being largely isolated from politics by law, party wish, and public sentiment.

There naturally were differences of view in a party so large and heterogeneous, and a system in which discipline was not strongly enforced on some activities. There was a rough division between the dominant element that favored increased production, especially industrial, financed by enforced savings that pressed lower-income groups; and a left wing that emphasized income redistribution in favor of common people and more attention to labor and the small farmer and

---

[1] General Manuel Avila Camacho (1940–1946), Miguel Alemán (1946–1952), Adolfo Ruíz Cortines (1952–1958), Adolfo López Mateos (1958–1964), Gustavo Díaz Ordaz (1964–1970).

less to merchants and industrialists. It was difficult for outsiders to know the importance of this division; some observers thought it deep and critical; others suspected that some well-publicized differences of opinion between party leaders were exaggerated for the purpose of relieving political pressures through debate. Cárdenas, after his presidency, often appeared as a spokesman of the leftist or reform wing of the PRI.

The PRI was pragmatic rather than ideological, although it constantly stressed certain principles—nationalism, the improvement of the material condition of everyone, social and economic justice, the ongoing Revolution, and broad action by the central government to achieve its aims. The rather neutral or centrist presidents of Mexico tried to keep all elements reasonably content in a large party of diversified interests, regional jealousies, and wide philosophical range.[2]

A major reason for PRI strength was organization. Party domination of organized labor, for example, was so firm as to infuriate critics. Leftists cried that the party policy on labor served the entrepreneurial class; rightists complained that it permitted the laboring person no choice. But there was much more than organization to PRI's success. It depended also on the evident achievements of the administrations it installed; on generosity in welcoming new leaders into the fold; on attention to the needs of most of the country's many organized interest groups, within and without the party; and on the overwhelming publicity the government gave to the country's social and economic progress. Critics said that it also was due to the political apathy and low economic and social expectations of much of the population and to the political ineptitude of the elements opposed to the PRI. In any event, all those policies and conditions rendered relatively unimportant the use of government coercive power in the interests of the party. Critics

claimed, however, that not only was there more physical coercion than most people realized, but that insofar as the system operated peacefully, it demonstrated a corruption of national morale.

PRI was criticized for other reasons, also. Party direction was centralized in Mexico City. In the states, party officials and important members often felt that they were not sufficiently consulted, especially on nominations, although usually the party directorate did involve them to some extent. Rather than join the small opposition parties, PRI dissidents usually preferred to focus on the issue of free nominations of PRI candidates. Another criticism of PRI was that it permitted local bosses or *caciques* to carry on graft and even reigns of terror, whereas a freer political system, with more opposition candidates in a position to drive out incumbents, would help correct that old abuse in Mexican life. PRI also received criticism when in state elections citizens became sufficiently aroused to vote in large numbers against PRI, but the ballot count failed to reflect the dissidence.

Opposition parties were small. They seldom won elections. Their failures were so conspicuous that at times the federal government subsidized them to help make a show of real electoral contest. The most significant opposition party was the National Action (PAN), organized in 1939. It had the reputation of being a big business and church-oriented party, but that was partly due to propaganda by PRI and the left and partly to some coincidence between its views and those of conservatives in Mexico. It was better described as a Christian Socialist party, but it could not use such a name in anticlerical Mexico. Sometimes PAN sincerely advocated more socioeconomic reform than PRI was willing to undertake. PAN never captured as much as 20 percent of the national vote, and usually much less. It did at times do much better in elections for federal legislators and for state and local officers.

Leftist opposition suffered from PRI's identification with revolution, from the government's programs of social assistance and its considerable success in economic development, from the great government and party advantages in propaganda

---

[2] Organized labor and peasants struggled for favor and power in the PRI, and produced dissidence within the sectors that party and government leaders had to restrain and referee.

and communications, and, as the leftist opposition emphasized, from the unremitting vigilance of the national security forces.[3] PRI's hold was especially firm in the countryside, and its opposition strongest in the cities and among the more modernized part of the population rather than among the proletariat. PAN essentially was a middle-class party. PRI control of the *campesino* (peasant) vote would be difficult to shake. The continuing strength of PRI was bolstered by its interpenetration with government. Observers wondered where the one began and the other ended. All that was certain was that PRI officialdom and high government officials were important and that much decision making occurred outside the visible apparatus of the party, as in many countries. That included unofficial inputs to decision making by private enterprise. In any event, no one disputed the overriding power of the president of the republic, who possessed almost unquestioned authority throughout all echelons of the elaborate hierarchies of the PRI and the government. Thus, the centralization of party decision making in the presidency (as over nominations to any office in which he cared to intervene), coupled with the one-party system, made the pressure to conformity all but irresistible.

The wonder was not that arbitrary or ill-advised actions occurred but that they did not happen more often. PRI was not used to create a police state. It was disliked for its monopoly of power, and a freer electoral process surely would reduce PRI domination of office. But it might be able to accommodate to greater competition. It was a flexible institution, a fact sometimes obscured by its opposition to free nominations and its insistence on overwhelming the opposition. In

any event, so long as the governments it elected kept the economy moving, it probably could hope to maintain a strong position. Much of the middle class, heavy beneficiaries of the PRI system, disliked the party, but appreciated the peace and prosperity it presided over.

The Government Since 1940

Enormous growth of government in Mexico followed world trends in modernization by the addition of economic and social functions, aided by a remarkable record in reducing the military share of public expenditures. By the 1960s only some 10 percent of the federal budget went to defense; by the 1970s, less than 5 percent, and there were only some 70,000 persons in the armed forces of a country with 60 million citizens. By that time over half of government funds went to economic development and much of the rest to social services.

That was a major reason for the political success of PRI, whose leaders said they were erecting a "mixed" system of capitalism and socialism. Left and right argued as to whether one ingredient was too prominent in the mixture. Private enterprise grumbled at much of what government attempted, but many people in workshop and field did not. Much of government action was to their benefit, and they had no philosophical scruples against state socioeconomic activity. Popular mistrust of government in Mexico traditionally focused on the local boss, regional military barracks, or the tax gatherer. When the distant federal government began to distribute blessings, it increased the belief of the peasant that justice lay with the ultimate *patrón* in the presidential palace, if only a way could be found through his screen of underlings or if he came out into the fields as Cárdenas had done.

Government was not modernized by increasing the power of the legislature. The president originated most legislation, and Congress rubber-stamped it. The courts continued to be ineffective as interpreters of the constitutionality of legislation and executive action. The executive

[3] The Popular Socialist Party (PPS), with which leftist labor leader V. Lombardo Toledano was identified, was small, sometimes subsidized by PRI, and sometimes supported its candidates. Although Lombardo was driven out of the official party during World War II because of his Marxism, he was tolerated by PRI as a tame radical. The Communist party was very small. PARM (Authentic Party of the Mexican Revolution) was a tiny group of veterans of the Revolution, kept alive by PRI's desire to have opposition to point to.

budget was accepted virtually without discussion. There was no question of congressional disapproval of presidential nominations. The states became yet more subservient to the central government. Although decision making thus was highly centralized in the presidency, both physical necessity and sound practice required consultation with a variety of party, government, and private interests. The leaders of Mexico generally were prudent managers.

Many decentralized or semi-independent agencies were created, some four hundred by the 1960s. Some had income from the production and distribution of goods and services, and borrowed abroad, like the big petroleum corporation (PEMEX) and the Federal Electricity Commission. They and the regular ministries dealt with regional and local development, banking and other financial operations, social assistance, cultural development, and scientific investigation. The intricacies of the state apparatus led to many efforts to improve operations and supervision. Government agencies handled constantly more complex tasks, despite continuing assertions of inefficiency and graft. Some excellent people were recruited to the public service, increasingly attractive to those desirous of prestige and an opportunity to participate in the development of the country.

Achievement by government agencies benefited from political continuity, public order, and careful handling of public finance.[4] Mexico did not suffer as much as most of Latin America from problems of inflation, balance of payments, and foreign debt. The regime in 1940–1954 did let the value of the peso decline, to aid foreign trade and capital accumulation, but inflation was less than in much of Latin America. Then in 1954 Mexico adopted a policy of low inflation that gave the country until the early 1970s one of the lowest cost-of-living increase rates in the world, averaging about 5 percent a year.

Education was one area of large growth of public activity. Another was provision of low-priced necessities to the public on an enormous scale. A third area emerged in 1943 when an important promise of the Revolution was redeemed with passage of a social security law. Another large social effort was begun by the government in the early 1970s, with replacement of older and modest efforts at public housing with a National Workers Housing Institute (INFONAVIT), supported by worker and employer contributions.

International policies after 1940 were rational and nationalistic. Relations with the United States became relatively harmonious, although Mexican presidents found it politically valuable to stress problems with Washington, because favorable solutions met such satisfaction in Mexico. The 1938 expropriation of foreign petroleum properties and other financial claims were settled easily. Mexican collaboration during World War II was appreciated by the United States. There was persistent complaint in Mexico, however, that the United States exploited the *braceros*, legal and illegal Mexican laborers in the United States. It was a problem for Mexico's government because, although it had to try to protect *braceros*, it wanted them to have jobs and to send money to Mexico. A new socioeconomic factor in relations between the two countries was tourism, as year after year the flood of *gringos* to Acapulco and other havens swelled.

A much remarked element in Mexican foreign policy was that it was proliberal, especially on matters of conscience or in opposition to dictatorship or tyranny. So far as public statements went, they were chiefly opposed to right-wing

---

[4] One reason international confidence remained high in Mexico was that it modernized its tax structure somewhat. In one period of tax reform, 1961–1963, the number of persons and corporations paying taxes rose from 700,000 to 4 million. The proportion of federal revenue from the income tax rose from 7.5 percent in 1939 to 24 percent in 1951 and higher thereafter. The federal budget increased nearly 1,000 percent from 1947 to 1963. Tax collections of 105 billion pesos in 1975 were three times the amount collected in 1971. The gap between the weight of taxation in Mexico and better-developed lands was narrowing, although the Mexican government issued soothing statements to minimize the fact. The government also ensured the stability of the large private banking system.

tyranny, so that communist dictator Castro was acceptable but the military who overthrew Allende in Chile were not. Although there was some ordinary political hypocrisy in this, the Mexican international stance was on the whole genuinely liberal. It was pro-UN and pro-OAS. It supported moves to improve world political relations. On the other hand, Mexico was most concerned with bolstering its international economic ties. The drive to export was a key element in efforts at development and modernization, and leading lights of government and private enterprise toured the world on that mission.

c. Developmentalism in the 1940s–1960s

In raw growth the Mexican economy achieved as much of a "miracle" as any in the world. It averaged about 6 percent a year from the 1940s to the 1960s. Poor years brought cries that growth was stalled, the Mexican model bankrupt unless fundamental changes in policy were adopted. They proved not to be necessary; instead, government correctives revived growth and faith in the regime's ability to march toward modernization.

The regime focused heavily on investment, either directly, as through the huge development bank, *Nacional Financiera*; or by granting tax exemptions, import favors, and other inducements to selected forms of enterprise. It so much emphasized capital ventures that critics said it lacked interest in human beings. The government retorted that the growth of the economy depended on the high investment rate. The public share of investment long fluctuated around 40 percent. When it went to nearly 55 percent during an economic slowdown in 1962, private enterprise feared and leftists hoped it portended a drive toward socialism. But the public share of investment receded again, because the government wished heavy private participation. Everyone was pleased that at 10 percent the foreign share of total national investment was no longer dangerously high as in pre-Revolution days. Not

thought so pleasant, however, was the fact that 80 percent of foreign investment was held in the United States in the 1970s. There were also complaints that foreign investment was too concentrated in certain fields.

There was strong support for nationalization of some forms of economic activity, either through expropriation (uncommon) or by Mexicanization (purchase by nationals). Mexicanization increasingly became a campaign to compel foreign interests to sell controlling shares, and it was required in several fields.

The government's economic functions came to reside in a maze of regulatory, supervisory, and production agencies. Government participation in wholly or partially owned enterprises increased year by year. Steel was only one vital industry in which the government carved out a large ownership role. By the 1970s the railways and petroleum had been state enterprises for over a generation. After creation of the Federal Electricity Commission in the 1930s, the government pushed the growth of public electric power at the expense of private, until in 1960 nearly all the remaining private electric industry was happy to sell out to the state. Most telephone operations were in the 1960s and 1970s added to the state apparatus, as the telegraph was earlier. Much of radio and television fell into the public sector or was heavily regulated. The state took over the production of basic petrochemicals and fertilizers, with notable involvement in other areas. The government role in finance became large, involving some thirty public credit institutions, including the well-run central (*Banco de México*) and development (*Nacional Financiera*) banks.

Government and party controlled the *ejidos* and the conditions and compensation of industrial labor. The state had power by the reservation to it of subsoil resources, which it let out on concession. It had great leverage through the pricing policies of such state enterprises as PEMEX and the Federal Electricity Commission; and through activity in the field of credit, which exerted pressure on private financial institutions; by control of transportation development and policies. Furthermore, there were enterprises in which government and private funds were so mixed as to create ambiguity.

Despite these advances by the public sector, private enterprise retained control of the bulk of the economy. In the 1970s it was dominant in manufacturing; banking and insurance; commerce, including both merchandising and the important tourist and travel complex; other services and professions; and other substantial activities, including trucking and interurban busing. Private activities were aided by heavy public investment in infrastructure (transportation, power, communications, education, irrigation). Some private concerns became quite large, notably in manufacturing, but also in distribution, as supermarkets and discount stores proliferated. Mexicans took to Sears and *supermercados*, but the private sector also still contained many small industries or handicrafts and commercial enterprises. Their existence in the tens of thousands in the 1970s was one mark of the economic gulf between Mexico and the highly developed countries.

Manufacturing grew most rapidly. An undeveloped country in the 1930s, Mexico became a semi-industrialized nation. Much of the growth was the result of government encouragement, always to the accompaniment of criticism that resources should be channeled to agriculture, industrial wages, or social agencies. Increasing stress was laid on efficiency. By the mid-1950s an increasing number of people in big business and government called productivity gains and quality standards Mexico's greatest needs. By the 1960s Mexico was nearly self-sufficient in consumer goods and making great efforts to build heavy industry. During those decades there was a striking decline in the value of production in agriculture, stock raising, and mining as proportions of total national output. As the modern sector of the economy matured, workers increased rapidly in service occupations. As industrial production grew, interest developed in purchasing power for the internal market, which

provided an argument for higher wages that employers resisted bitterly and pressure for installment buying that everyone favored.

Although the most casual observation identified many miserably poor country folk, dirt-floored *jacales* (shacks), cultivation with plow oxen or hoes, Mexico was an outstanding example of a developing country that paid much attention to agriculture, rather than ignoring or abusing it by rushing into industrialization willy-nilly. The government did not solve the problem of poverty among the country folk, but it did increase total national agricultural production, which sometimes was in balance for many crops, despite large population growth. The key fault, by one view, was investment in modernization in private agriculture rather than in the populous *ejidos*, whose low productivity made many *ejidatarios* marginal members of the society. It was argued on the one hand that more public funds should be poured into their technology and on the other that noncommunal holdings necessarily were more efficient. Communal landholding had been an emotional issue since the Revolution, and especially since the time of Cárdenas. For some Mexicans, the *ejido* and the Revolution were almost identical, often for social or political as well as economic reasons. The three presidents between 1941 and 1958 distributed about 29 million acres of land, compared with 20 million in the single Cárdenas administration; and the administrations in 1959–1970 distributed large amounts. By the mid-1970s there were more than 23,000 *ejidos*, with about half the cultivable land in the country. But many landless peasants hoped for new distributions, and leaders told them it was their birthright under the Revolution. "Parachutists" (*paracaidistas*) sporadically descended on private land and squatted, with emotional response from the owners and from critics of government.

It was infuriating to critics that the modern—they often said capitalist or bourgeois—sector of the economy was so profitable. Its representational organizations—chambers of commerce and industry—were highly visible, defenders of business and what critics thought a retreat from socialism. Commentators argued as to whether the chambers were more notable for an antigovernment attitude or for collaboration with government—much like a similar dispute in the United States. The manufacturers group grew briskly, built handsome headquarters, and considered themselves in the forefront of modernization. The Mexican Bankers Association, founded in 1928, was but a minor factor for some years. It received a boost with the virtual elimination of foreign branch banking by law in 1934. Then during World War II banking began a rapid growth that in succeeding years peppered the country with glass and aluminum branches. Presidents of Mexico attended the annual bankers convention. A leftist journal stated in the 1960s that such meetings flaunted the identification of "the powerful bourgeoisie" and the "Hamiltonian [sic] bureaucracy."

The government lavished attention on exports but never found enough to feed its appetite for imports. It helped that from the 1940s tourism, the "industry without chimneys," grew rapidly, so that by 1961 it was the single most valuable earner of foreign exchange. Merchandise exports grew impressively and were diversified into more agricultural fields and into manufactures. Minerals never recovered their place after the Revolution, being 25 percent of exports in 1960, compared with more than 50 percent before 1910. Mineral production tended to stagnate after 1940, partly due to government policy, which inhibited investment in the privately owned industry. In the later 1960s and the 1970s the minerals industry was pushed into Mexicanization, and often into the hands of the state.

d. Nationalism and Social Development After Cárdenas

The surging economy of Mexico paid for considerable social modernization. The population grew more rapidly, from an average 1.7 percent a year in the 1930s to 3.1 percent in the 1940s and 3.4 in the 1960s. At that rate, it doubled in twenty years. There were 19.6 million Mexicans in 1940, 48.3 million in 1970, an estimated 63 million in 1976. The total was expected to reach 100 million by 1990. By the 1970s life expectancy was well over sixty years. With half the population fifteen years of age and less, the burden on workers and public facilities was heavy. Luís Echeverría as a candidate in 1970, and early in his presidential term, opposed birth control, then changed to advocate "family planning" as the Mexican way. A National Council on Population and other agencies tried, with modest results, to popularize smaller families. The middle class clearly reduced the size of its families. Control was not welcome to all statesmen, who still thought population growth desirable for national strength and development.

Growth was accompanied by urbanization, as people moved to town seeking better lives. Mexico City had 1.5 million inhabitants in 1940; in the later 1970s the metropolitan area had 12 million, one of the great urban agglomerations of the world. Guadalajara and Monterrey each had well over 1 million. The exodus of rural population to cities was altering the traditional Mexico of a sea of peasants ruled by a thin crust of town residents, although in 1970 nearly 20 million people lived in localities with under 2,500 inhabitants each, and a Mexican town of that size boasted few urban amenities.

The chief effort of the Mexican Social Security Institute (IMSS), created in 1943, and a counterpart for public workers (ISSSTE) was in medicine, and their numerous hospitals and clinics fixed more than anything else the impression in the popular mind of the value of government activity. Coverage gradually grew, and by the 1970s was slowly being extended to rural residents. In 1970–1975 the number of persons receiving some social security benefits increased from 12 to 19 million. Among their other functions was the construction of vacation centers. That built by IMSS at Oaxtepec, in a warm valley near Mexico City, was a fairyland of apartments, swimming pools, gardens, and a great golden dome that seemed to symbolize the interest of government in the well-being of common people.

Private enterprise was sour about social security as socialistic, but reconciled by government policies of discouraging strikes and favoring profits and investment rather than wages. When threats to the total system seemed to occur, as with strikes in 1958–1959, the government took strong measures against labor insurgence, which were approved by conservatives and condemned by the liberal and leftist opposition. Regular increases in minimum wages were a settled part of the system, with much negotiation involving government, labor, and organized business. Much of this program seemed to critics paternalistic, and certainly organized labor was controlled by government and party. When a new labor law in 1970 increased labor rights, business objections were muted. Private enterprise also managed to accept with minimal objections the profit-sharing section in the Constitution, when the government decided to implement it in the early 1960s. It did not damage business or notably enrich workers, and critics of the regime said that it was merely cosmetic reform.

The efforts of IMSS and ISSSTE in the field of recreation were paralleled by actions of all echelons of government in providing sport facilities. The federal government also kept the prices of cinemas low. Public policies on bus and railway fares and on gasoline prices encouraged recreational and other personal travel. Another aid to the poorer population was the supply and prices of popular necessities. Such operations were small before Cárdenas; then, beginning in 1938, new agencies were created to carry out enlarged activities. Those were merged in the early 1960s into CONASUPO (National Popular Subsistence Corporation). Other government agencies, including official banks, aided in this field. Their intervention in the economy on behalf of the poor included crop purchases, controls on exports and imports, price fixing, *tianguis* (farmers' markets) in city streets and parks, government retail stores (CONASUPERS). All of this obviously was of political value to govern-

ment and party. The reach of such activity by the 1970s was very long. Anyone could buy groceries and other items in a CONASUPER in a convenient location. CONASUPO silos and warehouses for crops dotted the countryside. Organized merchants fought these gigantic operations, although their opposition somewhat softened with time, partly because business built new sales lines with such profitable items as electric refrigerators, washers, cleaners, and television sets.

The condition of popular income was much debated. There certainly was much poverty in a country where the average per capita income in the mid-1970s was about $800, even though that did not include all contributions to levels of living from social security and other public services, or tips, unreported service activities, and widespread moonlighting. The middle class did increase somewhat as a proportion of the population. Arguments on these matters, with and without statistics, were common but inconclusive. One study in the 1950s described the population as 2.3 percent upper class, 14.8 percent middle class, and 83.3 percent popular class; whereas another put it at 5 percent upper, 30 percent middle, 20 percent transitional between popular and middle, and 45 percent popular class. Another type of imbalance that caused concern was that the Valley of Mexico in 1974 had nearly 30 percent of national industry, 43 percent of all commercial sales, and 36 percent of total production.

The improvements in income and in education increased the size of the population with middle-class life-styles, attitudes, and expectations. It also was the case that the poor were not very demanding, which might result from either optimism or apathy. Differences between social groups still were marked, despite a large increase in social mobility. At one extreme as a social group were Indians who lived in the traditional manner. The percentage of those speaking only Indian languages was down to less than 4 percent of the population by the 1950s, but another 9 percent spoke both Spanish and an Indian tongue, so that on the order of 15 percent of the population lived in villages according to the old modes. The persistence of pockets of the traditional life was shown in the rise from 1940 to 1970 of those speaking only an Indian tongue from 2.44 to 3.15 million. But as country folk moved to town, they put off sandals and donned shoes, and they supplemented their corn cakes (*tortillas*) with wheat rolls and bread. The government celebrated the glories of the Indian past and the abilities of people of Indian stock, but it also enumerated the population that wore shoes and ate wheat products. Its personnel were convinced modernizers who wanted to compete with the industrialized powers on their own terms.

A big effort was made in education, but keeping up with the problem was difficult. From 1910 to 1970 the percentage of Mexicans exposed to at least a minimum of literacy training increased from 10 to 15 to about 70 percent. The 1970 census showed about 35 percent illiteracy. In that year average schooling was less than three years (compared with about ten in Western Europe). In 1960 some 5 million of nearly 8 million school-age children received instruction. Public education remained predominant, and the state supervised the curriculum, materials, and methods of private schools. The old complaints of Catholics and conservatives about atheistic and leftist content in the schools erupted anew in the 1960s with creation of a federal program of free textbooks. Catholic and private enterprise complaints about the content of the texts put those groups in the politically weak position of opposing something that was badly needed in Mexico and confirmed their ineptitude in a populistic environment.

Although secondary, preparatory, and higher education increased, Mexico could not make the percentage gains of Argentina or Uruguay, partly because the latter two had higher per capita incomes, partly because their population growth was much slower. Mexico broadened the curriculum in more advanced instruction, with emphasis on commercial courses and some technical fields, like engineering and medicine. Huge numbers of auditors, accountants, and secretaries were turned

out. By 1961 there were 165,000 enrolled in higher education; by the mid-1970s there were that many at the National University (UNAM) in Mexico City alone, and 450,000 in all universities. UNAM long handled much of the higher education in the country, together with the National Polytechnic Institute, also in the capital. After World War II, however, state universities were expanded. By 1961 UNAM only had a third of Mexican university students. In the 1960s and 1970s especially, the growth of state universities was pushed. The University of Nuevo León grew 300 percent in 1971–1976, to an enrollment of 60,000.

There was cultural enrichment due to education, improved income, better communications, and reduction of apathy and increase of achievement motivation. The position of women improved. They gained the vote, entered government, and went to work in many new occupations, all of which had some liberating effect. Old attitudes remained strong, however, favoring a restricted role for women in the upper and middle classes. In those classes birth control became widely practiced after World War II. In the 1970s President Echeverría associated himself with a movement for equal rights for women, still much discriminated against in Mexico. Women began widening criticism of the ancient *machismo* that made them chiefly sex objects and mothers.

All these things contributed to better national communications and the spirit of nationalism. The latter was expressed and promoted also in literature and the arts. Octavio Paz and Carlos Fuentes became international literary figures, as did the historians connected with the Colegio de Mexico, notably Silvio Zavala and Daniel Cosío Villegas. Mexican painting continued to attract interest, and especially the work of the master Rufino Tamayo. These artistic achievements received especial attention in the United States because of the many tourists from that country to Mexico, who also created a vogue for the varied and colorful popular crafts products of traditional Mexico. Mexicans periodically expressed fears of intellectual domination by the United

States, even through such homely but popular exports as the movies *Earthquake* and *Jaws*.

The audience for reading materials increased. In the 1960s and 1970s the popularity of television grew by leaps and bounds. There was wide freedom to discuss, protest, and petition without fear of arbitrary arrest or physical coercion, except on the far margins to right and left. There was, however, coercion of opinion by threat of political, bureaucratic, legal, and economic retaliation. The media were heavily influenced by government, PRI, and conservative private interests. Still, there was sufficient variety of opinion, some of it published, so that government and party considered lavish outlays to uphold their own views before the public to be advisable. The PAN, organized business, and Catholic groups certainly had abundant opportunity to express their views. The superior communications of the establishment were by no means chiefly due to coercion or chicanery. In fact, the viability of the Mexican sociopolitical system was explicable in part as a triumph of communications and the mobilization of influence by the PRI and government. Certainly, no aspect of the activity of the establishment was more galling to the opposition than the ability of the former to maintain a workable national consensus with a minimum of the violent frictions so necessary to the hopes of the latter.

e. Strains in the System, 1940s–1960s

Although great gains were made in the thirty years after 1940, there were strains in the system, especially from restrictions on political participation and problems of economic growth and distribution. None of the strains proved crippling, but some people feared and others hoped that they would be.

Dictatorship and Unbalanced Economic Growth

Objections to income distribution patterns caused dissatisfaction of various sorts, some of it within the PRI. Until 1954 there were prob-

lems with inflation; then that largely disappeared until the 1970s. The growth of the public economic sector constantly irritated and frequently alarmed private capital and led to investment slowdowns and flights of capital. Economic complaints often sparked protest against the one-party-dominant political system, most of them localized and easily controllable. Occasionally protests got so out of hand that the president had the Congress declare—as the Constitution permitted—that government powers had disintegrated in a state; it then dismissed the governor and appointed a new man. Sometimes police power against disorder was invoked under the Law of Social Dissolution, an antisedition measure. A much discussed instance occurred in the late 1950s, when Demetrio Vallejo, a leftist railway union leader, promoted secession from the PRI's labor juggernaut, the CTM. Vallejo called a strike in 1959. It began to affect the economy, and President López Mateos put the strike down with troops. Vallejo was imprisoned for sedition, together with famous painter David A. Siqueiros, a communist participant in the strike movement. For many years critics of the regime pointed to these actions as representative of its policies.

A series of indications of strain and dissent occurred in the early 1960s. In March 1961 a communist-oriented international congress was held in Mexico City with Cárdenas a delegate. It produced much denunciation of the United States and of foreign economic interests in Latin America in general. As a result, a leftist front was formed in Mexico, the Movement for National Liberation (MLN). It received impetus from the April 1961 United States–supported invasion of communist Cuba. In May 1961 Cárdenas said he had withdrawn from the PRI and appealed to peasants for support for greater social reform. He continued in 1962 to be active in MLN and advocated more revolution for Mexico, but he also kept a position in government and praised some of its actions. Then in January 1963 antigovernment elements in Mexico created the Independent Peasant Central (CCI), to compete with the PRI's large National Peasants Confederation (CNC). CCI demanded faster and more effective land reform. Cárdenas gave CCI his blessing.

These radical initiatives in the early 1960s, together with the government's apparent sympathy with Castro's Cuba, led to an erosion of confidence in business circles; domestic and foreign investment declined, and production dropped. The PRI directorate and the government hastened to reassure private enterprise and moved to reinforce their political position. MLN thereupon decided not to take the long-rumored step of becoming a political party and not to create a formal connection with the CCI, even though in early 1964 Cárdenas appeared to be spearheading an effort to push the country to the left by supporting MLN and CCI. But economic growth had returned, MLN and CCI did not grow, and the PRI was promising to take care of peasant problems. Finally, in May 1964 Cárdenas came out for the PRI candidate for president in the July elections. Lombardo Toledano already had pledged support for the PRI candidate by the PPS. Fighting PRI was a tough proposition.

The recurring complaint about centralization of PRI authority in Mexico City was embraced in 1965 by a new young head of PRI, Carlos A. Madrazo. He supported the cause of free nominations for PRI candidates, and was fired by the old guard for his pains. He reappeared on the national scene in 1968 with an effort to build a following for liberalization of political practice, whether within or without the PRI. Leaders of the PRI exerted great and effective pressure to isolate Madrazo politically. Such pressures on potential schismatics to stay within the party were so great that only the desperate or the fully idealistic were likely to break away.

There were recurring complaints that PRI stole elections in a variety of ways. A notable instance was in Yucatán, a poor state with ancient grievances against Mexico City. In 1967 PAN scored a rare victory by electing Víctor Correa Rachó as mayor of Mérida, the state capital. He inevitably clashed with the PRI administration in the state, and the quarrel grew worse in the election year 1969. The governor tried to take control of the police in Mérida, and there were incidents of violence involving PRI and PAN members. A general strike called by PAN closed most business in Mérida on June 11 and seemed to indicate wide support for the party. The state government arrested some PAN officials in July. The approach of the gubernatorial election of November 23 increased the tension. The PRI candidate won, but there were many charges of fraud and claims that a majority of the Yucatecan people preferred the PAN candidate.

Another series of objections to PRI electoral practices occurred in the big, prosperous northwestern state of Sonora in 1967. A group of PRI leaders in the state objected to Mexico City's nominee for governor, partly because he was so incorruptible that he would not be malleable! But they also protested against centralization of party power. The issue came to demands for the resignation of the incumbent governor, who supported the nomination, wide strikes and agitation by students with considerable destruction of property, and finally gun battles. Federal troops were used to restore order. The PRI nominee was elected. Sometimes such affairs did result in more care about consulting local views in the future because the PRI always retained a certain amount of flexibility. It made concessions to dampen dissent. In 1964 a new arrangement gave to minority parties extra national deputies on a formula calculated on their percentage of the national vote. And this formula was made somewhat more generous in 1972. Also in 1972, all parties were given a role in administering the electoral process, and the minimum age for holding office as federal deputy or senator was lowered. Critics called these merely cosmetic moves. Most people appeared to be uninterested or disillusioned, but the PRI must have made some capital out of its concessions.

The Explosion of 1968

Critics claimed that outbreaks of violent protest showed repression and dissatisfaction. So they did, but such protests were not numerous for so populous and varied a country. Much the most serious disorder in years occurred in 1968 in Mexico City. It began in late July as fighting between high school students that was interrupted by police, allegedly acting brutally. Clashes continued, becoming wider and more violent. Federal troops intervened. Considerable property was destroyed, traffic disrupted, hundreds of people injured, more than a thousand arrested, and at least one killed. The city was alive with rumors that many more students had been killed and their bodies hidden. University students and faculty denounced police and military brutality. Furthermore, the protest movement demanded a variety of reforms.

On August 1 some 20,000 National University (UNAM) students and professors, led by the rector, made a peaceful protest march. On August 5 a new demonstration involved 30,000 students of UNAM and the National Polytechnic Institute, old rivals. A student National Strike Council was formed. Its demands included dismissal of policemen and soldiers responsible for alleged improper actions, abolition of the riot police, freedom for imprisoned students, and removal from the penal code of the articles on sedition under which Vallejo and Siqueiros had been imprisoned. During the rest of August higher and preparatory education in Mexico was seriously interrupted. Massive demonstrations were held. Students appealed to industrial workers and peasants for support, claiming theirs was a movement for constitutional government.

Public opinion was badly divided, with some belief that arbitrary government needed to be curbed and some that the demonstrators included foreign agitators and Mexicans of nonstudent status. The government alleged an effort to create panic and force cancellation of the forthcoming Olympic Games. The fact that no compromise could be found in August or the first half of September indicated a serious polarization of views between government and students. Then on September 18 the army occupied UNAM, arresting many students and professors. President Díaz Ordaz claimed that university buildings were being used for improper political purposes.

Serious clashes occurred on following days; then both sides made conciliatory moves and on September 30 the troops left the university.

The worst clash was yet to come. On the night of October 2–3, at Tlatelolco in the central city, where a student rally was being held in a plaza, troops opened fire. The government stated that they did so to counter sniper attacks from the surrounding apartment buildings. Witnesses both supported and denied that sniping. Whatever the provocation or lack thereof, the affair left dozens dead, hundreds wounded, and 1,500 in jail. The government announced that it would use enough force to guarantee the security of the Olympic Games, and they were held toward the end of October without interference but with the students still on strike. The whole thing guttered out, leaving widespread conviction that the government had handled things badly. The president took unprecedented abuse in public, even strong criticism from the usually respectful press. But students had not aroused the middle class, industrial workers, or the peasants. Tlatelolco remained a burning issue thereafter mostly with intellectuals.

f. Echeverría (1970–1976) and Thereafter

Luís Echeverría was the minister of government in charge of suppressing the 1968 student movement, so his selection as PRI candidate for the term 1970–1976 scarcely enchanted reformers. Many of his actions as president seemed more liberal than his reputation, but they irritated conservatives without convincing reformers. One of his first acts was to free some two hundred students who were still in prison for the 1968 disturbances. That did not, however, bring Echeverría the trust of the university community, and demonstrations continued throughout his administration. Another Echeverría practice was rhetorical attack on private enterprise, which he charged with egotism, selfishness, and betrayal of Mexico's national needs. He did not, however, much interfere with private enterprise, except indirectly by continuing expansion of the public sector.

He talked sweepingly about income redistribution and other aid for the poor, but his actions were conventional. Probably a quarter of the working-age population remained unemployed or underemployed, and illegal immigrants flowed to the United States to find work. At the end of Echeverría's administration some 40 percent of the population still was involved in agriculture and accounted for but 10 percent of the value of national production. In 1976 the Bank of Mexico estimated that 93 percent of the country folk lived in poverty because only 7 percent of them used modern production methods. Social services Echeverría did somewhat extend, but much of his heavy public expenditure went to industrial expansion, which created few jobs. Everyone suffered from higher prices charged by government monopolies for gasoline, electricity, and telephone service. A new public housing program was useful but reached only a part of the population.

Echeverría talked of democratization of the PRI, but there were few signs of it. He encouraged more controversial material in the media, and that was greeted with enthusiasm by figures in the journalistic and intellectual worlds and by reform politicians. Moderates and conservatives felt that leftist publication increased enormously. They exaggerated, in part because the leftist and other reform sentiment surfaced in *Excélsior* of Mexico City, the country's greatest daily. But in 1976 Echeverría reacted to what he considered excessive criticism in *Excélsior* and encouraged its employees (it was a cooperative) to oust the proleftist editor and his supporters. After that, the government tried to impede foundation by the ousted *Excélsior* group of a new leftist political weekly.

During the first half of the Echeverría administration economic growth continued as before, with income distribution little changed, peaking with an excellent increase in the GNP of 7.6 percent in 1973. After that, all was downhill, and growth in 1976 was only 3.2 percent, probably not equal to population increase, because of the imbalances and fears caused by the decision (or

neglect) that permitted a serious overheating of the economy. The administration insisted on spending far more than its revenues. Part of this money was put into expanded public services, part into economic expansion, especially in industry, much of it state-owned or directed. An enormous steel complex was merely the most expensive of such projects. The deficit problem was handled in part by great increases of the currency in circulation.

Foreign indebtedness also was greatly increased. Imports were permitted to rise to levels far above exports, partly for materials for industrial operation or expansion. The foreign debt reached more than $20 billion, and debt services required $4 billion a year. Higher taxes and increased fees for government services and products were insufficient to handle the problem but irritated much of the citizenry. Price inflation crept upward and then raced ahead in the second half of the administration to levels of 20 to 30 percent annually, destroying Mexico's twenty-year immunity from that common Latin American malady. At the same time, food production did not increase enough to meet population rises, and food imports shocked—possibly unnecessarily—a public that had been taught to believe that the food problem was solved.[5] It also lent ammunition to the large body of critics of the system that felt strongly about the *ejidal*—communal—sector of agriculture. *Ejidos* had about 60 percent of the cropland but were chiefly confined to subsistence agriculture. Criticism of neglect of the *ejidos* was a further reason for doubting Echeverría's credibility as a reformer.

Although the financial policies of the administration obviously made currency devaluation inevitable, when it was adopted in August 1976, it

---

[5] For Mexicans without much knowledge of economics, maize is the symbol of well-being. Therefore, imports of maize, almost regardless of amounts, generate fears. In January–October 1976, however, all cereal imports amounted to $131 million, which was only 2 percent of all imports to Mexico; and all food imports amounted to 2–5 percent of total imports. It was heavy imports for industry that were disturbing the Mexican economy.

unloosed a fury of fear and criticism. The peso fell from 12.5 to more than 20 to the dollar. The proud claim of price and currency stability that Mexico had been able to make for two decades was ruined. For political purposes, it did not matter that devaluation should help curtail imports, foster exports, and encourage tourism to Mexico and discourage Mexican tourism abroad. Even before the devaluation, investment was drying up, and capital was fleeing Mexico; with the devaluation, the process accelerated.

Worrisome as the financial situation was, the Echeverría administration's economic policies had useful aspects. Production facilities were expanded, making the industrial sector both larger and more complex. Many people were pleased by nationalistic laws to expand control over resources and profits. New efforts were made to curb multinational corporations. Echeverría identified himself with the effort, and he had much company. In 1972 an institute was created to monitor licensing and patent fees on foreign technology, a move that also had wide support. In 1973 a law required that all future foreign direct investment be limited to 49 percent participation in an enterprise and that Mexicans have executive positions in proportion to Mexican ownership. That move naturally was popular also. A sensible and courageous decision was made to permit PEMEX greatly to raise prices for petroleum products. The middle class grumbled but continued to drive its cars. The price increases meant that PEMEX accumulated large sums that it poured into exploration and other development work. The results soon were evident in enormous new proved oil fields. Mexico began to export petroleum again for the first time in years, at the prices decreed by the world petroleum cartel. The size of its newly proved fields was such as to suggest the possibility of export revenues of some $5 billion by the early 1980s. That was a stroke of great good fortune for Mexico, although it intensified the debate between those who wanted to sell the petroleum to develop the society and those who wanted to conserve it for future generations.

Echeverría's populist rhetoric on the condition of Mexican society was accompanied by a strenuous campaign in favor of socioeconomic reform in the world. As early as April 1972 he deplored a growing imbalance between rich and poor countries and called for a restructuring of the world economic system. He pursued the theme in many forums, with extensive travels abroad, clearly bidding for leadership of the Third World. Some of his critics at home complained of the expense of this effort and said it also detracted from his attention to pressing domestic problems. It also was suggested that much of the effort was due to a wish to gain for himself the Nobel Peace Prize or the post of secretary-general of the United Nations. He claimed major credit for the idea adopted by the UN General Assembly in December 1974 as the Charter of Economic Rights and Duties of States. His desire for the UN post became clearer late in his administration, and he pressed for support from Third World countries. Finally, in October 1976, he openly declared his candidacy, but failed to secure the post.

The state of the economy and Echeverría's criticisms of private enterprise at home and of the policies of the industrialized nations irritated business and government elements in the United States. Exaggerated reports of his radicalism led a group of conservatives in Congress to send President Ford a letter charging that Mexico was being prepared for a communist takeover. Although the State Department was not fond of Echeverría, it dismissed this effusion as irrational and ignorant. Another source of friction with the United States arose when Mexico voted for a UN resolution equating Zionism with racism. Jews in the United States boycotted Mexico's tourist centers. That, together with a few instances of violence against United States citizens in Mexico, reduced tourist income. Some Mexicans charged a conspiracy in the United States to damage the Mexican economy.

Such exaggeration became common in the last months of the Echeverría administration. Rumors circulated that he meant either to head a coup to continue himself in office, contrary to Mexican tradition of some years, or to maintain a big influence in the following administration, also contrary to Mexican tradition. The devaluation of August 1976, and the subsequent weakness of the peso, intensified rumors. Merchants on the United States side of the border were alarmed when their sales to Mexicans fell off drastically because the peso now bought so much less. The press in the United States often could not seem to put Mexican events in focus. It seized on a few instances of violence to suggested that "chaos" impended. The term "hysteria" also was printed with little basis. Inflated language became even more common when on November 19, eleven days before the end of his term, Echeverría expropriated some rich farmlands from private Mexican holders, saying they violated constitutional restrictions on the size of holdings. The lands were ordered distributed to landless peasants, who were waiting on the borders of the seized lands. The rumor at once was that Echeverría meant to encourage squatters (parachutists) to take over much more private land. A hullaballoo arose among partisans of private enterprise in Mexico and the United States. It did seem a radical action for Echeverría to take at the end of his administration, and it increased fears that he meant to remain a power in the land.

The fears soon were proved merely sound and fury. José López Portillo was inaugurated December 1, 1976, and Echeverría and his supporters receded abruptly into the obscurity of all completed administrations in Mexico. López had been chosen in a July election for which the PAN declined to nominate a candidate, reiterating its old charge that PRI did not permit free campaigns and elections. López at once undertook a policy of conciliation and economic stabilization. He opened no windows to the left, as some people hoped Echeverría had. López effectively reassured private enterprise and Washington of his political and economic moderation. The United States government, bankers in the United States and Europe, and the International Monetary Fund, even before López' inauguration, showed readiness to aid Mexico financially, on the assurance that it would control expenditures, debt, and inflation. López early in 1977 told a joint session of the United States Congress that he esteemed his northern neighbor, but that it would have to give more help to Mexico or the problem of movement of poor immigrants across the border might become even more nearly uncontrollable. He knew that the United States hoped to obtain large quantities of petroleum from the new Mexican fields. If he managed to restore the confidence of private enterprise, and if the economic growth rate returned to the level of most years since 1940, probably Echeverría would seem only another episode of adjustment like several others in the years since Cárdenas.

g. Is the Mexican Revolution Dead?

There was no revolution in 1910–1917, by one interpretation, merely a bourgeois reshuffle. Another idea was that revolution did occur in those years, was reaffirmed under Cárdenas in 1934–1940, but was dead from the latter date, betrayed by the coercion and corruption of a one-party political system and by a capitalistic economic order that permitted exaggerated inequality rather than pursuing a drastic redistribution to the popular classes. By the 1970s some critics called the PRI regime neo-Porfirista. For some critics, revolution meant only some sort of socialist order, which they declared historically inevitable.

By another interpretation, the veritable Revolution did provide discontinuity and new basic patterns and orientations that could not have evolved out of the rigidities of the Díaz system. The new elements included domestic rather than foreign capital investment; redirection of public expenditures toward basic development; change in the institutional framework making for a widening range of production; and considerable adoption of social and technical innovation. The claim was that a new and dynamic Mexico continued the Revolution, with one of the finest economic growth records in the world since World War II and great gains in education, health, and many other aspects of public and private activity. It was even thought that the persistence of capitalistic achievement in the country's economic evolution was as useful as socialism or the landholding traditions of peasant communities.

In any event, even some men of leftist persuasion believed that a seizure of power by the left was almost unthinkable, that the nationalist bureaucratic state was strong enough to prevent it.

Besides, the issue was not just what the Revolution of 1910–1917 intended or accomplished, but what Mexico needed in the late twentieth century. To compare it with the political conditions and relative socioeconomic stagnation of Porfirian Mexico was misleading, for injustice and inefficiency and poor integration certainly had been greatly lessened. The Revolution belonged to the Mexicans, and they would decide whether it was continuing, moribund, or defunct and what roles the concepts of revolution and evolution should play in the process of modernization.

40 The Struggle for Modernization and Justice in Chile

Left and right tugged at the fabric of Chile and split it down the center. Before that happened, there was much optimism about Chilean devotion to modernization by evolution. From the late 1930s until 1973 it did well with regard to political participation, free speech, fair electoral processes, and confinement of the military to professional duties. These achievements came despite notable party fragmentation, a politics of bargaining and coalition and of minority presidents, as well as a disquietingly rapid population growth and migration to the cities, a persistently elevated inflation, a bad balance-of-payments problem, and the frustrated expectations of an educated population with high hopes but a low average level of living. There was also a considerable conservative manipulation of the media as well as the use of economic advantages in the electoral process, especially among the rural poor.

Centrist governments from the 1930s to 1970 had limited success with socioeconomic problems and were increasingly condemned for insensitivity to popular needs and excessive collaboration with foreign capital. Thus the devil of domestic greed was linked oratorically with the devil of foreign exploitation. That linkage was celebrated in 1970–1973 in the efforts of a minority Marxist administration to remake society, and the vio-

lence of those efforts and the opposition to them polarized Chile and split it down the center. The military seized control of the country, probably with the support of a majority of Chileans. So died the legend of unbreakable Chilean attachment to representative government.

The shock of Chilean events contributed to a widespread unease about Latin America, increased by recent military interventions in public affairs in Uruguay, Argentina, Brazil, and other countries. Would Chilean modernization continue? If so, on an evolutionary or revolutionary basis? Under constitutional republicanism and representative government, or under a rightist or leftist authoritarian regime? How long would the military dictatorship last? What role had the United States played in the overthrow of Allende? For several years after the coup there were impassioned allegations that the division in Chile was manufactured in Washington until the absurdity of so sweeping a charge became manifest. Chile lived in the world, much influenced by international market and capital factors, as well as by attempted manipulation by the governments of the United States and the Communist countries. Its fate, however, lay largely in the attitudes and decisions of its own people. No one in the later 1970s could fathom

714

the shape of things to come in Chile, but for the moment it appeared that the military would either rule or heavily influence government.

a. Dissolution of the Popular Front, 1938–1941

The Popular Front that elected a Radical as president of Chile in 1938 predictably did not last long. It was important mainly because it suggested a future increase in the political leverage of the left. President Aguirre Cerda and most of the Radicals were uninterested in much social change, and the Congress was controlled by opponents of the Popular Front. The administration stressed industrialization rather than social reform. It created in 1939 an important state development corporation (CORFO). There were wartime problems to trouble the country, including interruption of trade. It also had to face the disruptive changes in leftist attitudes toward the war that depended on policy shifts in the Soviet Union. The result was a rift in the Radicals in 1940 when a prominent leader of the party, Juan Antonio Ríos, charged that the Communist party was under the direction of Moscow, a matter that people often decided without much reference to facts.

There were tensions within the left, too. The Communists and Socialists resumed their rivalry. Leftist cohesion changed, also, when the Radicals gave most government posts to their own people, partly because Radicals thought that Marxists would use their position in the coalition to improve their political leverage permanently. The government ordered the Communists and Socialists to cease trying to unionize peasants, an activity that infuriated and frightened conservatives. Antileftist fears were increased by the congressional elections of 1941, with the vote going 21 percent to the Radicals, 20 percent to the Socialists and allied groups, and 12 percent to the Communists, up from 4 percent in 1937 and the greatest gain for any party. Of course, the election also showed that the center and right (including most of the Radicals) still had the allegiance of most voters. By that time the Communists and Socialists had stopped cooperating, and the Popular Front died with Aguirre in 1941.

Voter support of the leftist component in the front soon diminished and took some time to rebuild. The Radical party was the largest immediate beneficiary of the front, electing the next two presidents. Its policies as revealed in 1938–1941 were moderate and nationalist: in favor of economic development with state aid and against great changes in social insurance or redistribution of income. That would be the posture of administrations for many years thereafter.

b. The Economy and the Society Since the 1930s

The population mushroomed during 1940–1975 from 5 to 11 million. The large proportion of youngsters put pressure on the provision of public services, jobs, and commodities. Urbanization accelerated. Migrants poured into town. Santiago developed great *poblaciones callampas*, communities of squatters' shacks. Possibly half the population was urban in 1940; it was more nearly three-quarters so in the 1970s. The capital city's population went from about 800,000 in 1938 to 2.9 million in 1970.[1]

The export sector continued to dominate the economy. Copper was king again. United States–owned companies had 85 percent of copper production, and shipments ran on the order of 80 percent of Chile's exports. Although copper provided a high percentage of public revenues and of foreign exchange, it was lightly taxed to 1925, when the levy was upped a little to 12 percent of profits; it rose to 18 percent in the 1930s, 33 percent in the early 1940s, 60 percent in 1953, and to expropriation of the companies' holdings in the 1970s. The foreign companies—the *Gran Minería*—sometimes were reluctant to make the

---

[1] The second city, Valparaíso, had only 289,000 in 1970. Chile was one of those Latin American countries (Argentina, Uruguay, Venezuela) where a "primate" city had a large proportion of the national population.

investment necessary to increase production, being uncertain of their treatment in Chile. Chileans' desire for more foreign investment in copper and increased production increased their resentment of dependence on foreigners.

Government-aided industrialization continued, much of it after 1939 with the help of CORFO, whose activity was often in support of the private sector. In the early 1940s the government created a state electric enterprise (ENDESA), which steadily replaced private enterprise. In 1950 a National Petroleum Enterprise (ENAP) gave the state control of the industry. The Huachipato steel works, partly financed by the United States Export-Import Bank, partly by Chilean public and private capital, began production in 1950, a monument to the "steel mill complex" that afflicted developing nations.[2]

Some industrialization was pursued as much from desire for "independence" as proof that it would improve the material condition of Chileans. Protectionism often fostered high prices. The average annual rate of industrial expansion in 1941–1946 was a respectable 11 percent; then it fell, the easiest substitution of imports with home production having been established. The problems of modernization in a small and only partly developed country with a small internal market and limited human and capital resources led to Chilean talk of economic collaboration with Argentina in the 1940s and 1950s, but it came to nothing. It led later to Chilean participation in the Latin American Common Market and the Andean Group.[3]

The inability of its agriculture to feed Chile became a key source of strain. Still dominated by the *fundo* owners, the sector increasingly could not cope with demand. Agricultural productivity was low and much land underused, common aspects of *latifundismo*. Possibly more small farms would have helped, since some of them were more efficient than the *fundos*. The government, however, not only was unwilling to take on the thorny problem of land division but was not prepared to give as sustained attention to agriculture as to manufacturing and mining. Imports of food were a heavy burden on foreign exchange: as much as $100 million annually by the late 1950s, $150 million by the late 1960s, $444 million in 1972, by which time Chile imported more than a quarter of its food. Long before then the government subsidized the price to the consumer, with further effects on the treasury and prices.

A belief spread widely that Chilean resources in land were not the problem.[4] Some thought the answer was eradication of the *fundo*; others favored improvement of the poor technological level on *fundos* by government action. UN experts in 1952 pointed out that lack of incentive to produce was partly the result of government protection of the *fundo's* domestic market with tariffs, import quotas, and compensatory trade agreements, plus government policies that caused farmers to switch production around to take advantage of shifting benefits, rather than encouraging them to raise output. As in the case of the agricultural/pastoral industry of Argentina under Perón, the problem was not simply a matter of ending *latifundio*. Allende, the Marxist president of 1970–1973, began destroying *fundos*. He thus damaged production; whether his action would have helped the production problem in the long run cannot be known.

Government financial policy was the most important contributor to a problem of price inflation that oscillated between nagging worry and crisis. A part of it was borrowing abroad. Ibáñez

---

[2] By the 1970s Chile was producing more than 600,000 tons of crude steel annually, which under a system of strong nationalistic protection provided metal for a variety of subsidized fabrication enterprises.

[3] See Chapter 37, Section a. In 1972 Chile sent 12 percent of its exports to LAFTA countries and bought 20 percent of its imports from them. That was not going to become an immediate solution to its problems.

[4] Considerably larger than France, Chile is 2,600 miles long and nowhere more than 120 wide. Much territory is difficult to farm—desert in the north and mountains in many places—but some estimates claim that it could feed twice its present population.

borrowed a lot in the late 1920s, and borrowing continued thereafter. The United States government poured loans into CORFO's development activities. The foreign debt in 1958–1961 went from $569 million to $1 billion. By the 1970s Chile had one of the world's highest per capita foreign debts, and servicing it ate up much of the public revenue. Chile also shipped money out for imported food, machinery, and raw materials for industry, and in payments for foreign technology and remittances by foreign corporations. Regardless of the amounts sent out (and they were disputed) or the value of the original foreign investment, Chileans came to resent this contribution to their financial problems and neocolonial status.

Another contribution to inflation was the inadequate and regressive tax structure, which increased the necessity of borrowing or printing currency. In 1951 only some 4 percent of government revenue came from direct taxes. Another contribution to inflation was the adjustment of government wages to an index of the cost of living. Since the bureaucracy constantly grew as the government added functions, the middle sectors depended heavily on it as a source of employment, and politicians knew them to be highly active at the polls, the burden was sizable. Social security, including pensions, also was costly. The luxury-importing class sent out foreign exchange for goods from abroad, and the government would not cut this trade off any more than it would drain off upper-level purchasing power through taxation.

Most years from 1940 to the 1970s saw considerable, sometimes staggering, inflation of prices. A cost of living index that stood at 204 in 1945 was 1,550 in 1951; prices rose 59 percent in 1953, 80 percent in 1955, and the problem remained acute thereafter. The persistent need for adjustments in prices and pay made personal and institutional life difficult.

Chileans remained dedicated to education. The country was some 80 percent literate by 1960 but did not improve thereafter. Higher education became more extensive and sophisticated,

with important effects on national life as better analyses of problems were available. Although it had an elite university system, a larger proportion of Chileans attended than in some European countries. Cultural achievement was recognized by Nobel prizes in poetry to Gabriela Mistral (1949) and Pablo Neruda (1971). The admirable devotion of Chileans to free speech remained undiluted throughout all but the last years of this period, so intellectuals had ample opportunity to influence affairs. Their motive was bolstered by the fact that economic failures left highly educated persons with poor outlets for their talents. As in all Latin America, many university people and other intellectuals became interested in leftist prescriptions for problems.

Free speech and association were also beneficial to the labor movement, whose strength increased. Socialists and Communists still competed for influence with workers. In 1953 a new labor central—CUTCH—was created. The militance of Chilean labor would be a factor in the great contests of the 1960s and 1970s.

Per capita income was low, less than $600 early in the 1970s. As in so many Latin American countries, the middle class increased, so the poorest part of the population shrank slightly but was about as badly off as ever. Chile for years was described as essentially middle class, obscuring the fact that on the order of a third of the population could not possibly lay claim to that status.[5] The social security system was extended but left many people untouched. Health indicators, as well as economic measures, were only moderately good by Latin American standards, but the superior political and intellectual development of the country gave the impression, even to some Chileans, that they were more modernized than they were. The fact that expectations were quite high in Chile meant that frustrations also were high. After the 1950s poor Chileans were en-

---

[5] Many commentators put the proletariat at half or more of the population, a few as low as a quarter. Chile certainly had one of the stronger middle groups in Latin America, however it was defined.

couraged, to some extent by the Christian Democrats and more by the Socialists and Communists, to articulate a sense of ill-usage. The middle-class ideal, which long had clashed to some extent with the oligarchic mystique in Chile, although often submissive to the latter, was now challenged by proletarianism and by Marxist theory and organization for class conflict. Chile's literacy and open political system gave it such good communications that debate and conflict were bound to be intense. In fact, voter allegiance to parties and ideas was quite uniform geographically, nor were they as much dependent on class status as might have been expected. The recent history of Chile suggested to many observers that compromise could be achieved without great violence. They were wrong.

c. The Administrations, 1942–1958

President Aguirre resigned due to poor health in 1941. Two more moderate Radicals were elected for the terms 1942–1946 and 1946–1952.[6] Ex-President Ibáñez won the term 1952–1958 as an apolitical candidate promising pie in the sky. The electoral system was quite fair. Women received the vote in 1949. Although voters were a small percentage of the national population, they represented more activism than was apparent because women could not be counted before 1949 nor illiterates and those too young to participate, which was half the population by shortly after mid-century. On one occasion in the 1940s about 400,000 voted in a national population of some 5 million, large enough to indicate that mobilization politics was a part of the system in Chile. Politics was marked by much activity by organized interest groups: labor, business, big agriculture, civil servants, students.

Elections were dominated by the multiparty system, in which none had the support of a majority of the electorate. Bargaining, compromise,

and sometimes coalition were necessary, and final selection of the president fell to Congress, which always chose the man with the highest total. In those circumstances, the Socialist and Communist parties had more leverage than would have been the case in a two-party or a one-party-dominant (like Mexico) system. For some years after the breakup of the Popular Front, however, leftist leverage declined. There was bitter competition for labor allegiance. That competition was muted in the 1940s by a severe fall in Socialist support, which reached a low of merely 2.5 percent of voters in 1946; whereas the Communists received 18 percent of the national vote in the municipal elections of 1947. The Communist party operated under handicaps in 1948–1958 when it was illegal, but it did operate.

The administrations of 1942–1958 generally permitted free speech, made heavy expenditures for education, and supported an elaborate, but inadequately funded, institutional setup for social assistance. The Commissariat for Food and Prices wrestled with the cost of living; the Housing Administration did what little it could afford; the Workers' Insurance Fund and other agencies provided some aid. All the administrations permitted labor organizations, had greater or lesser trouble with strikes, and rather frequently used limited states of siege and police power to preserve order and keep up production. Labor often said that the governments were trying to restrict its influence.

Sometimes labor disorders were violent. In 1946 there was a serious clash over poor living conditions. For a year the northern miners had been restless. The government accused some unions of going beyond the legal right to strike, so it canceled the unions' status and confiscated their property. The left and the Radicals (some of whom were not leftists) protested. The Confederation of Labor called a general strike and public meeting for Santiago, January 20, 1946. It became a riot involving the police. As a result there were cabinet resignations, and the president put the commander of the navy at the head of the cabinet to maintain order in the country,

---

[6] Respectively, Juan Antonio Ríos, who died in office, and Gabriel González Videla.

and the chief of the air force in charge of the ministry of public works, which controlled communications. A state of siege was declared for sixty days. The Confederation of Labor asked not only cancellation of such measures but appointment of a left-wing civilian cabinet and recognition of the right of peasants to organize. Before it was over, the Confederation of Labor had split into Communist and Socialist groups. This series of events may stand as an example of similar affairs that occurred in subsequent years. The general strike and the state of siege were especially prominent phenomena in following decades.

The administrations in 1942–1958 tried and failed to get control of the country's socioeconomic problems. There was much government support for action to develop the economy, but also much disagreement between the centrists in control and the left outside as to who should benefit. Five problems by themselves would have been enough to frustrate any regime: the inadequate tax structure; the deficit in food production; large fixed expense for social service and for a growing foreign debt; a rapidly growing population; and a constantly heavy inflation. The administrations would not fight for fundamental changes in taxation or in the system of agricultural estates.

Juan Antonio Ríos was a wealthy man and a moderate Radical. The opposition in 1942 was provided by Ibáñez, now running for the conservatives, and thought a fascist by some voters as a former military man, dictator in the 1920s, and part of a Nazi conspiracy in the 1930s. Ríos won by a plurality. He was centrist, nationalist, proindustry, and anticommunist and showed all those characteristics in a number of ways. He died before his term was up.[7]

---

[7] Ríos kept neutralist Chile uncommitted in World War II until January 1943, when United States pressures led him to break diplomatic relations with the Axis. Chile, like Argentina, felt that its location permitted less protection from the United States and more exposure to Axis raids; also, it feared subversion by Chileans of German stock in the south.

Gabriel González Videla won the term 1946–1952 for the Radicals. He was considered to the left of Ríos, but no leftist stance was noticeable in his administration. The Communists did give him their vote in the election, and he rewarded them with three seats in the cabinet. González fired them after five months, charging that they promoted their own purposes rather than those of the administration. Strikes in 1947 led to a state of siege. The Communists said the strikes resulted from the failures of the administration. Conservative newspapers carried on an anti-Communist campaign. González announced discovery of a Communist plan to sabotage the economy, attack the United States, and impede continental defense. He arrested some Communist leaders. By now the United States was a big factor in Communist propaganda as tension between the United States and the Soviet Union mounted. Such a line often found sympathy among non-Marxist nationalists in Chile. In December 1947 Senator Pablo Neruda, a world-famous poet and a Communist, published articles abroad saying González had betrayed the workers and sold out to the United States in order to get financial aid. González and his supporters began a campaign to outlaw the Communist party. Politics was heavily dominated by the issue for some time, and all the arguments were aired that Brazilians were using on the same issue simultaneously. The Chilean Communist party was outlawed by congressional act in the fall of 1948. Communists were stricken from the electoral lists, elected and appointed officials ousted or harassed, and leaders deported.

The nationalism and economic development ideas of González were similar to those of his immediate predecessors. He pushed economic development by finishing the Huachipato steel plant that Ríos had initiated and by accepting technical aid from the UN to improve monetary and fiscal methods. That the administrative technology of Chile was not equal to that of the best developed countries is true, but some Chileans understood such methods. The problem was that effective use of them required unpopular training and enforcement measures and even worse disruptions and sacrifices. González wanted to load the blame for innovation onto a foreign group, as well as the failure if that occurred. The Leland Mission was in Chile in 1949–1950, and gave the "austerity" advice that technicians in the UN, IMF, World Bank, and various governments of developed nations were beginning to shower on Latin America. The mission recommended such theoretically useful measures as a wage-price freeze and income tax data open to public inspection. Such things could not get much support in Chile. Everyone wanted others to sacrifice first and most. People of modest income believed that austerity would be manipulated by a well-to-do minority to fall heavily on others. The UN mission's recommendations were not carried out.

By the 1952 election, although there was much disillusion among voters, they listened hopefully to seventy-five-year-old Carlos Ibáñez, who campaigned against all parties as a self-proclaimed honest administrator who would get things moving. He declared himself a nationalist, free from foreign influence, labeling recent Radical administrations as subservient to Washington. The Communists, Socialists, and National Democrats allied in a People's Front, and Ibáñez received a large vote from the right and center because of fear of the left. He also got the votes of women and many people of modest means, who hoped that he could do something about the cost and shortage of food, as all the candidates promised. For the first time large numbers of rural workers and tenant farmers, voting for Ibáñez, repulsed the choice of the estate owners. Although Ibáñez received only a plurality, he scored a notable victory over the conservative candidate.

President Ibáñez had nothing to offer but his taste for authority. He generally supported centrist or conservative policies; the cost of living went up at an annual average of well over 50 percent, faster than wages and salaries; agricultural production was stagnant; he had constant trouble with labor and used repressive measures. He began trying to find a way to hold back exports of copper to wait for high prices, a strategy which was difficult to carry out, and to try to lower burdens on the foreign-held *Gran Minería*, whose production was expensive in world terms. His economic policy had or was imputed to have some relationship with the economic consultants Klein and Saks, whom he hired in the United States. When some of their austerity recommendations were tried, and bit into people's incomes, a minor revolution broke out in Santiago in April 1957. It began with students ostensibly protesting increased bus fares, common enough in Latin America, then turned into rioting that police and soldiers fought for several days. Possibly fifty were killed, but rumor put the number much higher. Long before the end of its term, the Ibáñez administration was a failure.

d. Jorge Alessandri for the Right, 1958–1964

In 1958 the old Conservatives and Liberals managed to elect, with 31.6 percent of the vote, Jorge Alessandri, son of the former president, a businessman and avowed partisan of free enterprise. Second with 28.9 percent was Salvador Allende, Socialist candidate of FRAP, a new leftist front formed in 1956. Third with 20.7 percent was Eduardo Frei for the new Christian Democrats (PDC). Further back was a Radical candidate. This fragmentation, which had been so common, was to disappear by the next presidential election, as the pressures for polarization reached a critical level.

Alessandri tried a conventional free enterprise solution to problems. Neither FRAP nor PDC wanted that, and they represented more than half the voters. Alessandri was blamed for lack of resolution, but it was difficult to see how more of that quality would have helped him against his potent opposition and the difficult problems of the country, which in no case could be much ameliorated in a period of six years. Of course, to get a viable program in train in such a period would have been possible with goodwill and patience in the electorate, but although Alessandri had that at first, he did not long enjoy it. Many Chileans felt that hope had been too long deferred and wanted drastic action. Alessandri's enemies said he merely wanted to serve up more of the austerity recipes of Klein and Saks and the IMF. He tried to balance public revenue and expenditures and to control the decline in value of the currency, but the pressures were too much for him. He tried to improve the copper situation by getting the foreign companies to increase investments, but his opponents now wanted more than that from the industry. He pushed a modest land reform that no one took seriously. He scarcely touched the tax system. The foreign debt kept going up and foreign exchange reserves down, and a flight of capital occurred. With his failures in the economic sphere, the important issue became political: Who would come after him?

The Communist party had been legalized again in 1958 at the end of the Ibáñez administration, and it and the Socialist and the Christian Democratic parties were busy during the Alessandri years. All political participation was aided by a 1958 change in electoral procedures, providing a single ballot supplied by the state, instead of the old party ballots that had permitted landlords to see how their clients voted. In the municipal elections of 1960 voter support continued strong for Alessandri's Conservative, Liberal, and Radical parties of the right center. After that, voter impatience became evident. In the 1961 congressional elections FRAP and PDC gained. Although the administration parties retained control of both houses of Congress, they were shaken and after the election created a Democratic Front. The municipal elections of 1963 revealed severe voter disillusion. There was a record abstention of registered voters. When the 2.07 million votes were counted, PDC emerged the chief gainer. That may have happened partly because the religious aspect of Christian Democrat doctrine appealed to women voters. PDC had become the single strongest party in the country, taking votes both from the administration Democratic Front parties and

from those of the leftist FRAP coalition. Although the centrist-right vote fell to 47.2 percent from 53.2 in 1961, it could scarcely be called feeble.

About a year later, in March 1964, a further leap away from the center-right was revealed in a special congressional election in Curicó province. It was 90 percent rural and a traditional Conservative party stronghold. But both FRAP and PDC had been making inroads into the rural electorate before, and in Curicó occurred what Allende of FRAP called a "veritable earthquake." FRAP took 39.2 percent of the vote, PDC 27.7, the center and right parties only 32.5. The Democratic Front disbanded, as Liberals and Conservatives rushed toward the Christian Democrats to help repel the advance of Marxism. Political mobilization now had reached into the last refuge of the traditional elites: the countryside, where for so long they made peasants, tenants, laborers, dependent small farmers, and village dwellers vote as ordered. The presidential election of 1964 would be the most important since 1920.

e. The Ambiguous Christian Democrats, 1964–1970

The Christian Democratic party had its beginnings in the 1930s in a youth organization of the Conservative party that included university students of progressive Catholic views. It became an independent body in 1938 as the *Falange Nacional,* unrelated to the fascist Falange of Franco's Spain. When it later changed to the Christian Democratic party, it imitated similar parties in Europe. Such parties based much of their policy on papal pronouncements on the social problems of modern times and on liberal Catholic lay thinkers. They declared the need for great social change, for the humanization of industrial society. They emphasized cooperation by individuals in the community rather than class conflict, not only in political activity but in the industrial firm. They offered it as an alternative to undiluted capitalism (which did not, in fact, exist) or communism (which did not exist undiluted either).

Christian Democratic parties were quite varied and attracted different sorts of leaders and supporters. The PDC of Chile included kindly Roman Catholics who wanted to humanize society patiently and non-Marxist leftists who wanted to make revolutionary changes at once. It also had some unavoidable identification with Catholic big business groups that displayed a paternalism that worker groups found objectionable. Marxist critics saw Christian Democracy as a rightist subterfuge that took advantage of the piety of the credulous; and besides, it was dangerous competition—supposing society was humanized, where would that leave Marxist utopianism? At the other extreme, reactionary capitalists with old-fashioned religious views looked on Christian Democracy as a whited sepulchre, faith—and free enterprise—sullied by the communist beast.

PDC in its campaign tried to identify FRAP and Allende with communism. That charge was damaging because many Chileans thought communism worse than socialism, as a proven doctrine of despotism tied to an international apparatus. Frei, the PDC standard-bearer, promised sweeping changes, including great gains for the popular classes; increased state activity, but less than FRAP proposed; and retention of democracy in what he called a "Revolution in Liberty," implying slavery under Marxist rule. His specific proposals included: reforms in the electoral system to include elimination of the literacy requirement; drastic changes in agriculture to include some expropriations of poorly used land, unionization of peasants, improvements in productivity in a generally free enterprise setting; more control of copper, with nationalization if the companies would not cooperate; industrial development; more equitable taxation; more public housing; and trade with communist countries. FRAP called for considerably more drastic state intervention in the economy.

The election of 1964 was quiet and fair, as the world had come to expect in Chile. The amaz-

ing result was that Frei was the first president of Chile in the twentieth century to get a majority of the vote in an election in which nearly all those registered voted. The citizenry was fully aroused. Frei received 56.1 percent (1.4 million), Allende 38.9 percent, and the Radical candidate 5 percent. Frei did well in rural districts, worker areas, and even with miners. Many supporters of FRAP in recent years obviously were not convinced Marxists but people who wanted change even if that could only be had through Marxist leadership. Frei also drew support from the right. And he took 63 percent of the votes of women.

Frei was an able and attractive person, another in the long line of capable men chosen president of Chile. Much of his political problem was linked to his performance in dealing with the socioeconomic ills of the country. That performance was a failure in the sense that it did not much affect the economy immediately or draw much praise. Possibly it was unreasonable to expect him to do much more than he did in six years, but the ordinary citizen must think in years rather than decades. The immediate results in the agrarian sector were small. Output did not increase, and large food imports still were necessary. Rural wages went up, but prices rose as much. Although a progressive new land act was passed in 1967, it had little effect during the administration. Possibly in time the Christian Democratic agrarian program would have had important results, but it did not have time.

The administration's actions on the critical copper issue also brought little immediate advantage to Chile. The heart of Frei's policy was "Chileanization," similar to the Mexican policy that has been noted. The United States–owned giants agreed. The plan was complex, involving purchase of varying amounts in the companies over time, partial government ownership of some mines, state participation in operations, and a doubling of copper production by 1970, partly by reinvestment of the sums paid the companies for part ownership. Frei got voters to increase his partisans in Congress, so that the Chileanization plan could be approved there in November 1965.

Many miners' organizations and Marxists declared that more concessions should have been demanded. The process of Chileanization had gone a long way by the end of the Frei administration. The doubling of copper production did not occur, and the value of increases would depend on world market conditions. Chile did benefit in Frei's time from a great rise in the world price of copper.

Inflation was kept lower than in Chile's worst years, but was still on average more than 20 percent a year. Education, housing, medical aid, and pensions received about all the attention the budget could afford, but that was no solace to people who thought they deserved more. A good many housing units were built, but the need was beyond the available funds. Frei did raise taxes some. Property taxes were doubled; that still left them low, but brought screams of anguish from the well-to-do. Labor considered that it gained little from the administration, and the latter sometimes used strong methods to control work stoppages and maintain production. It helped promote peasant unions. It encouraged and subsidized modestly another mass organization, Popular Promotion—neighborhood groups that helped with education, utility needs, child care, home sewing, and other common family problems. But support fell away from the Christian Democrats, and disagreement increased within the party. Some people considered that the biggest failure of the Christian Democrats was in the field of public relations: they could not drown out the Marxist criticism of everything they did, isolate the suicidally stupid reactionaries, or keep their own ranks unified.

The great electoral triumph that made possible passage of the copper plan occurred in the congressional elections of March 1965, with PDC increasing its membership in the 147-member Chamber of Deputies from 23 to 82, and in the 45-member Senate from 12 to 21. That turned out to be the high tide of its electoral support. PDC lost ground in the 1967 and 1969 municipal elections and in the 1969 congressional contest lost its majority in the Deputies. The right

quickly recovered from the fright that led it to give some support to the PDC in 1964 and returned to intransigent objection to change. The rightist National party talked about the need for a military government. Conflict in the PDC came increasingly from a militant left wing that suggested noncapitalist development of the country. In July 1967 populist and anti-Frei elements were elected to control of the PDC party apparatus, but Frei regained control the next year. Another reason for Christian Democratic gloom was that the Constitution prohibited a second successive term for Frei, and no other member of the party approached his popularity.

f. Marxist Salvador Allende, 1970–1973

Radomiro Tomic became the nominee of most Christian Democrats for the presidential election of 1970. He was a leader of its left wing, and one of his proposals was complete nationalization of copper, which Frei had also supported at the end of his term. That issue—as we have seen with petroleum in Argentina and Brazil—now was completely politicized. Distaste for foreign—especially United States—influence in the country was high. Leftist groups were angered by persistent United States enmity for the left. In Jorge Alessandri's time, in the first years of the Alliance for Progress in the early 1960s, the United States channeled more aid per capita to Chile than to any other Latin American country. Washington openly preferred Frei in the election of 1964—as the Soviet Union, Cuba, and some other countries preferred Allende. Tempers were further frayed by the 1965 revelation that the United States Army had a Project Camelot ready to study the predictability of social revolution in developing countries by using North American and Chilean scholars in Chile. Sinister motives were imputed to the project.

An effort was made to identify Christian Democracy with support of, and Marxism with rejection of, imperialism. Camelot was not helpful to non-Marxist reformism in Chile. Leftists said that their defeat in 1964 was partly the result of

United States interference; in 1965, when the United States intervention in the Dominican Republic was turned into an OAS action, some Chileans demanded that Chile pull out of the organization. United States policies had become a major issue in Chilean politics.

Allende, for a coalition called Popular Unity (UP—Communists, Socialists, and Radicals), rang all the changes on Frei's supposed subservience to Washington. He declared that the PDC socioeconomic failures were indicative of Christian Democrat emphasis on production rather than redistribution, both wrong-headed and "proof" that the worker did not come first in their thinking. The National (Liberals and Conservatives) party ran Jorge Alessandri. A splinter PDC candidate also appeared. In a vote of nearly 3 million, Allende received 36.3 percent,[8] Alessandri 34.9, Tomic 27.8. The Congress selected Allende in the traditional fashion, and he was inaugurated in November 1970. The country still seemed sadly divided. Furthermore, by the end of the Frei administration Chile had begun to experience some of the terrorist activity that Argentina and other countries suffered. A divided country possibly would invite more violence and find decision on methods of either prevention or control difficult.

Salvador Allende was a physician by training, a socialist by conviction, and a politician by choice and long experience. He had been a young cabinet minister in the Popular Front government of the 1930s and since then prominent in Socialist party politics and the national Congress. The Socialist party in Chile was different from those in many countries in including Trotskyite and Maoist communists and being more in favor of violence than the Chilean Communist party. Allende was a strong nationalist, concerned with improving the strength of his country and the well-being of the citizenry. He thought that

those aims could be achieved only by socialization of the economy, which he said would have to be done by stages, thus rejecting for Chile the method used by his friend Fidel Castro, communist dictator of Cuba. Allende said that neither socialism nor communism was a creed for despotism—which raised doubts about either his candor or his understanding of the nature of communist regimes. He often declared his devotion to the system of open politics and representative government, of which he long had been a part, and the belief that each country must develop the political institutions proper to its needs and culture. On the other hand, Allende was prominent in the Havana-based guerrilla front O.L.A.S. (Organization of Latin American Solidarity) and supported Latin American guerrilla movements as proper instruments for change under certain conditions. Of course, Frei, too, had publicly endorsed that view during his presidency, when driven to express an opinion by the leftist opposition. The ambiguity of Allende's opinions resided in many statements made over the years: for example, that Chilean economic dependence could be broken only by revolutionary means. There was no reason to doubt the sincerity of his many eloquent pleas for better diet and health care and a life of dignity for the poor.

The election of Allende provoked a panic among some of the well-to-do, with a run on the banks and a scramble for airline space to flee the country. The great majority who remained soon considered that the attitude of the administration toward private property justified fears that it would not be protected. The agrarian reform that had begun modestly under Jorge Alessandri and been expanded modestly under Frei was pushed with a speed that took no account of immediate economic consequences, one of which was a decline in production that helped push up imports of food. Within two years most farms of more than two hundred acres had been expropriated and turned into state-controlled cooperatives. This precipitous process was accom-

---

[8] Less than the 38.9 percent he received in 1964 or the 42 percent received in the 1969 congressional elections by the Communist, Socialist, and Radical parties.

panied by land seizures, sometimes organized by leftist groups, including the MIR (Leftist Revolutionary Movement), before the Agrarian Reform Institute had intervened in properties. Opponents of the regime considered that probably what was desired was irreversible radicalization of the rural population rather than solution of the national production problem; that a minority was using revolutionary, unconstitutional means of preventing the majority from effectively expressing its will.

By the end of its first year the administration had nationalized or bought control of copper, coal, steel, 60 percent of the private banks, a number of manufacturing enterprises, and the largest publishing house. The regime expanded socialization in the next two years, including much of the wholesale distributing system. The nationalization of copper was especially instructive. The PDC supported it, although it preferred that the industry go under a cooperative system rather than state socialism. The administration stated that the great copper companies owed so much in back taxes that no compensation was due them for expropriation. That view was popular in the underdeveloped world, bolstered with the opinion that foreign corporate giants usually extracted their investment in a few years and thereafter were largely exploiters.

All this activity was well supported in Chile. In fact, by the late 1960s even much of the industrial and agrarian elite favored nationalization of copper. The country had greatly improved its bargaining position with regard to the foreign copper companies, because of stronger national agreement, because of Chile's greater technical, economic, and diplomatic expertise than earlier, and because of the companies' huge and vulnerable investment in the country. Chile had not escaped entirely from dependency, but it had much reduced it and had done so before the Marxist administration was elected in 1970. Now it had open to it more control of dependency not only via socialism but via manipulation by the traditional elites, informed by

strengthened nationalism and technique. Such a door out of dependency had been opened by traditional elites in other Latin American countries.

The Allende administration was hurt by runaway inflation. It was 100 percent in Allende's first year; the IMF said that in 1972 it was the worst in the world, at over 160 percent; thereafter it rose by mid-1973 to an annual rate of well over 300 percent. At the same time the administration increased the wages and benefits of the poorest part of the population. They needed the increase, but it did not help inflation. Foreign exchange reserves almost disappeared. Imports were severely restricted. The country suffered shortages. The black market grew. Smuggling increased. In February 1973 the Agriculture Ministry announced that food imports for the year would cost $450 million, an enormous portion of the budget. So nationalization of the *Gran Minería* did not compensate for other economic losses. In fact, a large world decline in copper prices seriously depressed export values in 1970–1972. Since the foreign debt situation of Chile was worse than ever and private investment capital had dried up, international lending agencies became more important, and they had doubts about Allende.

Allende supplemented the notion that the foreign copper companies were only exploitive with the charge that the United States government supported the copper and other United States–owned corporations in Chile by bringing pressure on international lending agencies. He told the UN in December 1972 that Chile was a victim of "serious aggression" initiated by United States corporations, banking interests, and government agencies, which were trying to cut Chile off from the world, paralyze its trade, and deny it foreign financing. Extensive investigation in later years left the importance of United States financial pressures in 1970–1973 in doubt. A considerable, but far from all-out or fully effective, effort was made to put a credit squeeze on Chile. The United States cut its public aid and tried to discourage private investment. In fact, however, considerable aid continued to Chile from the United States Agency for International Development (USAID) and international banks; the IMF made an export loan; the Inter-American Development Bank made two new loans to private universities; there were some credits from United States banks; and considerable other aid from Europe and Latin America offset lessened United States aid. United States demands that Chile pay its foreign debt on schedule were abandoned in April 1972, when Washington accepted a European rescheduling of the debt that enabled Chile to contract new loans in Europe. In fact, Allende managed to increase the Chilean national debt by $800 million. United States demands that the copper companies be compensated failed, for Chile paid very little on its United States debts after 1971. The United States Senate discovered that the International Telephone and Telegraph company (ITT) had suggested to the Nixon administration actions against Allende, but they were not adopted. The investigation also revealed that United States business generally was not eager for economic warfare with Chile.

The investigations did reveal, however, that in 1963–1973 the Central Intelligence Agency (CIA) spent about $13.4 million on covert operations in Chile. Some $8 million went for electoral propaganda, especially in 1964 and 1970, with the largest amount going to the Christian Democrats, who were opposed by Allende and the left. There was a small-scale ($200,000) effort to promote a military coup in 1970 to prevent the inauguration of President-elect Allende. Various anti-Allende groups received money thereafter. There was much discussion of additional interference that came to nothing, partly because of disagreements in the United States government. The magnitude and effects of all these financial and political efforts always will be disputed, as will the parallel intelligence, political, and subversive activities of the Soviet Union in Chile. There is no question that the United States interfered in the affairs of a freely elected

Chilean government. Whether Soviet activities, or other considerations, justified that obviously is arguable. Marxist and other "dependency" theorists claim that the capitalist world order fatally squeezed Allende, not so much as part of a conspiracy as the inevitable consequence of their urge to dominate. Those who reject the charge contend that Allende would have had a great deal of room to maneuver, economically and politically, if he had not insisted on extremist policies, that his nationalism alone insured him much support.

During those years, in the Chilean cities a process of property seizure went on that had begun before Allende's time—and was known in various Latin American countries. The poor, including the lower middle class, were encouraged and organized to squat on vacant private or public lands and build shacks, invade empty structures and turn them into apartments, or even on occasion take over private dwellings. Middle-class property owners formed armed vigilante groups to protect their residential and business property. Lower-class groups also were armed.

Much of what Allende did was under the ample presidential powers common to Latin American constitutions. When he required congressional sanction, he ran into the opposition majority. Allende found this problem so irksome that in 1971 he expressed interest in an earlier Socialist scheme for a constitutional amendment to substitute for the bicameral legislature an assembly of the people. In 1972 he submitted the amendment, and the Congress rejected it, whereupon Allende threatened to take the issue to a popular plebiscite. He never carried out that suggestion, but it convinced some people that he would bend the constitutional system to suit his needs.

Local elections in April 1971 saw FRAP parties carrying their percentage of the vote to 49.7. In December 1971, the first large-scale demonstrations against the administration occurred, with a women's march in Santiago to protest shortages and high prices. Elections in 1971–1972 for university rectorships went to opponents of the government parties, although leftists remained in control of the student federations. In May 1972 the PDC did better in federation of labor (CUTCH) elections than the FRAP had expected. In the face of these signs of life in the opposition, Allende also had trouble inside his administration, one issue being whether there should be official action to stop the activities of MIR.

By August 1972 the country was almost in an uproar, and rumors of all sorts flew on the mounting winds of hate. Allende declared that he was horrified to hear talk of civil war. Possibly he was sincere, but he could not or would not calm the country. In late August most of Chile's 136,000 stores closed for one day to protest the administration's economic policies. There followed three weeks of tension as the middle class protested home seizures and other grievances. In September Allende denounced a "Plan September" that he said meant to depose his government by creating so much violence that the military would intervene. He forced into retirement a general who was rumored to be involved in antigovernment plots.

In October and November huge protests against the government occurred. They centered on a dispute between the Confederation of Truck Owners and the government over various changes in policy the owners wanted. They feared that their days as small entrepreneurs were numbered. Crowds of middle-class women again took to the streets, banging on pots to protest living conditions. The economy depended heavily on trucks. A state of siege was imposed in most of central Chile. Truck owners and drivers blockaded roads. There were arrests. Small businessmen and private farmers went on sympathy strike. The affair became nationwide, and the state of siege was widened. The strike was joined by private banks, pilots on national airlines, and others. The five opposition parties endorsed the strikes and said the economic mess was the result of government actions.

The opposition thought the government was acting unconstitutionally; the government coali-

tion thought that the opposition was trying to provoke trouble to bring down the government unconstitutionally. Suspicion fed on suspicion. Considerable class hatred obviously existed. One opposition demand was that military men be taken into the administration, to increase confidence in its adherence to the Constitution. Government forces thought the intent exactly the opposite—to bring in the military to subvert the Constitution against the freely elected president. Allende, nevertheless, brought the military commanders briefly into the cabinet until the strike crisis passed.

In a highly charged atmosphere the contending parties approached the congressional elections of March 1973. The leftist UP took 43.4 percent of the vote, a considerable increase over its total in the presidential year 1970, and increased its representation in Congress. Although a new Democratic Confederation (CODE) of PDC and the National party had 54.7 percent of the vote, there were fears that it might lose its majority in the future. The left later claimed that this fear drove the opposition to unconstitutional action.

From April to July there was a serious strike of copper workers wanting wage boosts. At the end of June 1973 there was a small attempt at an army coup. On July 26 the 40,000 members of the truck owners' confederation again struck, one grievance being an inability to get spare parts or new vehicles. The truckers were supported by associations of lawyers, physicians, architects, social workers, nurses, dentists, retailers, journalists, pharmacists, bank workers, private school teachers—in short, much of the middle class. In the early days of the strike Allende tried to make a settlement with PDC. He was opposed by MIR on the left and by the rightist Fatherland and Liberty terrorists, who avowedly wanted to bring Allende down. Terrorist activities in Chile occurred by the score. By August 8 Allende felt compelled to announce that he would bring into the administration members of the armed forces to end a "state of sedition." The huge labor confederation demonstrated its solidarity with the government. On August 22 the general heading the Defense Ministry resigned, to be replaced by his friend General Augusto Pinochet. The navy said it discovered subversive movements among enlisted men. By now Allende was fearful of military control, so he tried to reshuffle military command appointments to guard against it, but some of them were circumvented by the military. The strike went on into September with no end in sight and with the economic situation going from bad to worse.[9]

Military officers were discussing the desirability of taking independent political action. Although the Chilean military were described as apolitical and Chileans were proud of the substantial truth in that, it was known that military intervention recently had come to other Latin American lands with strong traditions of civilian government. The military on September 11, 1973, took over key installations. Allende refused a military demand that he resign, declaring on radio that he would resist with his life. Tanks and planes attacked the national palace. A military junta announced that Allende had committed suicide and quickly buried him. There was sporadic fighting, and an estimated 500 to 2,000 persons died on the day of the coup and in the weeks immediately following.[10] Thus, 60,000 trained men with weapons took control of the nation of 10 million, possibly with the support of a majority of the citizenry.

Who killed democracy in Chile? (*a*) Well-to-do Chileans by not making enough concessions to alleviate misery. (*b*) All the opposition forces to Allende by insisting that he was subverting the constitutional system but refusing to wait till they could replace him in the presidency by the ballot or by mustering the two-thirds in Congress required for impeachment. The courts, Congress, and considerable freedom of speech existed to the end of the Allende regime, despite threats or assaults against them. (*c*) The Allende government and its supporters by pushing socialization against the objections of the majority. They pushed it not only by constitutional means but by at best injudicious exercise of the president's wide constitutional powers and by violent actions by nonofficial and official organizations. They helped kill the constitutional system also by a variety of actions and statements, and by a connection with revolutionary organizations and ideologies. The latter suggested they meant to alter the economy so drastically that the opposition would find changing it back difficult, if such should be its wish when it again came into control of the executive branch. There was bitter disagreement in the world as to the character of the Allende regime.[11]

Foreign interference was but a minor factor in the division of Chile into warring blocs, although capitalist and communist countries had directly and indirectly influenced Chilean politics for years. Division grew almost entirely out of local conditions. The Chilean military considered that the Allende government was subverting the Constitution and promoting mutiny in the armed forces. They also disliked the existence of armed action groups among industrial workers. They decided that civil disorder and economic breakdown were at nearly intolerable levels. Chilean military officers made their decision without significant reference to the opinion of foreigners, although United States actions and attitudes suggested to anti-Allende officers that the United States would sympathize with a coup, and almost certainly raised some expectation of aid. No evidence has been found, however, that the

---

[9] There long were reports that the United States heavily subsidized the truckers' strikes in 1972–1973, but investigation showed that almost nothing was spent by the United States for those strikes.

[10] Some estimates are higher.

[11] Intellectuals and academics in the United States tended to find no fault in the Allende regime. The AFL-CIO, on the other hand, produced some powerful condemnations of Allende as favoring totalitarian government rather than democratic socialism, asserting that his labor policies showed that.

United States played a direct role in the 1973 coup.[12]

g. The Military Regime Since 1973

The military erected a despotism. The legislature and political parties were suspended. Leftist publications were banned and others censored. The junta arrested thousands of persons for political "crimes." There were wide accusations that the regime tortured prisoners. Some disappeared without a trace. Military courts were used to try both civilian and military personnel, and for some time they did their work in secret. Some persons were executed after such procedures. Some Marxists were forced to emigrate. Pursuit of the regime's enemies took the usual forms: roundups, arrests, states of siege, curfew, interference in all sorts of processes. These actions were attested to as fact by well-known bodies.[13] When the regime realized how much foreign distaste its methods aroused, it claimed that benignity lurked under necessary surgery. It did not, however, repudiate its declared intent of running the country for an extended period.

The military government did not try to put everything back as it was before Allende, so state activity in the economy remained important. In 1975 government spending accounted for nearly half of Chilean output. It did return to private

initiative many commercial and industrial businesses appropriated under Allende. The nationalization of copper was allowed to stand, but the military pledged compensation to the companies. Copper income was hurt by low world prices. The government did not try to repudiate the dismantling of the *fundo* system. It did try to force the cooperatives to improve production by threatening to return their land to private ownership if they did not perform well. It also tried to improve agricultural production by ending most subsidization of prices. Production recovered some from the dismal state it had fallen into during the last year of the Allende regime, when farm output declined about 25 percent. Most of these policies contributed to the continuation of inflation, although the regime reduced it some. Huge imports of food and petroleum products took more than half the copper earnings in 1974, and payment on the foreign debt consumed much of the rest. But Chile received financial aid from the developed free market countries and their international financial agencies. Nevertheless, the situation for ordinary Chileans worsened in 1975–1976 as the regime resorted to drastic curtailment of government expenditures to try to get control of finances. By 1977 there were signs of improvement of government finance, but it was too soon to be sure how the economy would develop.

Reports out of Chile—even a Gallup poll in 1975—suggested that a majority tolerated the military regime; presumably most preferred an open political system if it could be had without another polarization accompanied by violence. Chile seemed a sad case of the radicals of right and left preventing moderates from governing. Hopefully, the long demonstrated ability of Chileans to accommodate deep divisions again would express itself, permitting more socioeconomic and political modernization in the sense of a broadening of participation, but recent events in Chile, in Latin America generally, and in the rest of the world made it seem doubtful.

[12] Congressional investigations in Washington looked for it assiduously. The *New York Times,* no friend to the military junta, by March 1975 conceded that the overthrow of Allende was the result of decisions by Chileans, "acting for reasons of their own."

[13] In 1974 the government was condemned, after investigation, by the UN General Assembly, the OAS Inter-American Commission on Human Rights, and the Catholic hierarchy in Chile. In June 1976 and May 1977 the OAS commission again charged the regime with violations of human rights. In early 1977 the UN Human Rights Commission stated that torture still was a regular practice in Chile. The United States government in 1975 and thereafter eliminated military aid to Chile because of its violation of human rights.

41

Uruguay and Costa Rica: Two Cases of Latin American Democracy

Uruguay and Costa Rica long had been in the forefront of modernization in Latin America. After World War II both showed the strain of sustaining it in the face of adversity. Uruguay, which had been called a "modern utopia" for its democratic politics and enlightened social legislation, ran into stormy economic weather in the 1960s. The welfare state was so strained that demands for its modification grew. Economic pressures on constitutional republicanism caused it to be modified in the 1970s, and the Uruguayan military took over a prominent role in public affairs. Whether the reduction of popular political participation would be accompanied by gains in socioeconomic modernization remained to be seen. Costa Rica, unlike Uruguay, continued generally faithful to representative government and broadened political participation, but it too felt strains from insufficient social and economic progress.

a. Uruguay: Trouble in the Welfare State

The deservedly admired Uruguayan system did not carry the country to the modernization enjoyed in Switzerland, to which it had been compared. Pastoral exports would not sustain that much, and they began to diminish by the 1950s

and 1960s. Political friction increased. Critics on the left thought more socialism and an agrarian reform were required; critics on the right wanted to overhaul the large public sector of the economy to make it more productive, prune and improve the inflated state bureaucracy, and reduce the lush welfare system. Dissatisfaction led in 1958 to the first *Blanco* (Nationalist) president in ninety-three years. Continued financial stress led to rising violence. Finally, in 1972, the military became openly active in favor of conventional economic policies and a hard line on dissidence, and in 1973 it became the dominant factor in public affairs. Where the military would take one of the more modernized countries in Latin America no one could predict.

World War II and Its Aftermath

After Terra's flirtation with stronger government during the Depression of the 1930s,[1] the Uruguayan system returned to its previous condition, except for another brief interruption in 1942. That was the result of the opinion of President Alfredo Baldomir, expressed in 1940,

---

[1] See Chapter 33, Section b.

that a "careless, misguided, and unenlightened legislature" left him no choice but to ask for revision of the Constitution. He especially disliked the provision of the Terra Constitution of 1934 that gave the minority (that is, the second) party one-third of the cabinet and one-half of the Senate. These provisions were fully consonant with the *batllista*, and popular, fear of the executive power. The Congress was refusing to pass some of Baldomir's suggested legislation, and the *Blancos* in the Senate especially were resisting his policy of collaboration with inter-American measures for continental defense. The Senate also refused to discuss his suggestion for constitutional change. He dismissed the *Blanco* cabinet members, and when the Senate voted censure of the president, in February 1942, he used the army to close it and ousted the *Blancos* from the National Administrative Council that he had recently reconstituted. He did permit the scheduled elections in November 1942, which selected a president and legislature and agreed to alter the Constitution to get rid of that aspect of minority representation that Baldomir disliked.

The events of 1942 had not altered the basic system of government, nor had they changed the attachment of Uruguayans to a strong legislature. Nevertheless, in 1946 the voters defeated a proposal to create a full-fledged collegiate executive, that dream of Batlle's that had been tried only in diluted form but that always had supporters. In 1951, however, the proposal was on the ballot again and it passed. Now Uruguay had a collegiate executive of nine members, with six from the party with the largest vote and three from the second largest, and the chairmanship rotating among the members of the majority group. Although this official was called the "president," in fact the authority of the executive branch had been much fragmented. Uruguayans were enormously proud of the innovation, and foreign observers pointed to it as the answer to excessive executive authority in Latin America. That evaluation, of course, put the cart before the horse, since Uruguayans first reduced executive authority and then set up the collegiate executive.

The Uruguayan political system by 1951 operated under arrangements by which the two major parties not only were assured of the offices but were permitted to divide into factions without the divisions accruing to the advantage of third parties. The *Colorados* and *Blancos* were allowed factions that could run separate and competing candidates for the offices. But when an election was ended, all *Colorado* votes were totaled and all *Blanco*; then the one with the higher total (of all its factions) got two-thirds of the National Council of Administration and of the Congress, the places being assigned to the party's top vote getters in the election, and the other third of the seats went to the second party. This system helped promote Uruguayan participation in the political process, but it also fragmented responsibility by making party discipline difficult. It also entrenched two parties in control and relieved them of much necessity of worrying about the demands of other parties.

During World War II a nasty dispute arose in Uruguay between the more conservative Nationalists, led by Alberto de Herrera, and the *Colorado* administrations. Herrera admired European fascism and the Argentine military regime that came to power in 1943. He also bore a strong animus against the United States and Britain, so that collaboration with inter-American defense measures smacked to him of subservience to Washington and an inclination toward the anti-Axis powers. Then, after the United States entered the war, in December 1941, the Uruguayan government cooperated in inter-American defense measures yet more actively, breaking relations with the Axis in January 1942. In the meantime, in 1940 a Uruguayan professor had conducted an investigation of local Nazis and turned his findings over to the Congress. The result was the arrest of some Uruguayan fascists, which led to objections from the Nationalists (*Blancos*). All this, of course, figured in Baldomir's conflict with the Senate in 1942.

After June 1943 the Uruguayan government accepted refugees from the military government in Argentina and would not knuckle to pressure to cease. Perón cut off supplies and tourists and even ordinary travel to Uruguay. All that naturally caused the Uruguayan government to depend more heavily on ties with the United States as a defense against possibly stronger Argentine actions. In 1953 Uruguay ratified a mutual security pact with the United States but only after a long debate, with Herrera and his *Blancos* rabid against it.

The Uruguayan economy did well during World War II, and problems that grew immediately thereafter were submerged by an export boom during the Korean War of 1950–1953. There was knowledge that certain aspects of production and national finance could become troublesome, but there was no sense of urgency. Uruguayans continued to be the healthiest and best educated, fed, housed, and pensioned in Latin America, and by most standards in the world, after a handful of the best-developed nations. They were confident that the proven superiority of their system would permit whatever adjustments might be necessary.

They were wrong. There was inadequate appreciation that protected industry was costly; the bureaucracy swollen and not too efficient; the welfare system perilously near the limit of Uruguay's ability to support it without increases in production or taxation; productivity in the private sector was declining; domestic consumption was high (Uruguayans were among the greatest meat eaters in the world) and other factors cutting into and threatening necessary exports; the foreign debt constantly climbing; and government deficits chronic. There had, of course, been signs that this small nation with limited resources and much dependence on the vagaries of international demand might abruptly find itself in trouble. The nation had discovered as much in full measure in the early 1930s, but recovery later in the decade dulled the edge of recollection. By the end of 1942 the government faced severe financial

problems, as income scarcely sufficed to pay interest on the heavy foreign debt and also carry the social services and state-owned economic enterprises. Some of the latter were running in the red, partly because pricing and wage policies were set on political grounds. But again, exports picked up and aid came from the United States.

By 1950 worry seemed quite unnecessary, as Korean War demand made wool exports, especially to the United States, thrive. The few years that situation lasted were delightful, but in 1953 the United States Treasury determined that Uruguay's multiple exchange controls operated so as to subsidize its wool exports, which constituted unfair competition under United States law, and required imposition of compensatory duties. Uruguayans affected astonishment that so "unfair" a decision could be made. At the same time, Perón's interruption of the important Argentine tourist traffic to Uruguayan beaches and casinos cut into revenues. In 1954 Uruguay began to suffer higher rates of inflation, and they continued, while government deficits occurred yearly. The world price and demand for wool declined. The government tried to keep wages down as an anti-inflationary measure, and wage earners pressed for full compensation for rising prices. The result was that government stated, as it had since the early 1950s, that it would prevent strikes against the state, which meant a large (possibly 20 percent) part of the work force, if the state-owned enterprises were included. But for some years a stringent policy toward workers—other than briefly—was not adopted. In the open Uruguayan political system such an austerity policy was difficult to pursue.

The severe economic strains of the later 1950s so worked upon the electorate that in 1958 it voted the *Blancos* into power for the first time in ninety-three years. During the campaign everyone seemed agreed that inflation was the overriding problem. The *Colorados* essentially said: Don't let the *Blancos* take away the best system in Latin America. The voters decided that the *Blanco* insistence that they could control the inflation deserved a trial. In any event, many *Colorado* leaders were as identified with the special interests of the well-to-do as the *Blancos*.

Uruguayan Society

The way the Uruguayans arranged their society permitted one of the better and fairer life-styles in the world. Their achievement was limited by natural resources, the world economic system in which they were heavily involved, and the decisions they made about allocation of income and conditions of work and investment. In the first place, Uruguay's per capita export values declined from $94 before World War II to $60 in 1960–1961, with some recovery to $70 in 1965, but still an unsatisfactory figure in the mid-1970s.[2] The critical export sector was both helped and hurt by policy decisions. The size and value of exports were bound to oscillate for a number of reasons, some of them uncontrollable in the Río de la Plata, such as the weather and the decision of the European Economic Community to close out many overseas suppliers. The numbers of sheep and cattle remained stationary, but they were numerous, and the numbers were no more important than the cost of production, quality, and amount made available for export. Productivity was not sufficiently increased in the export enterprise, quality was too low, and much meat was kept for domestic consumption.[3] Wool and meat were the heart of the export enterprise, and other exports relatively unimportant.

The fact that export income often was insufficient to support everything the country thought it needed could be handled by cutting needs as well as by upping exports. Uruguay, however, would not accept such a scheme. Efforts at control met resistance. Smuggling of imports (and exports) has been a sizable problem. A country where the consumer had an active role in the political process was abstemious only under the compulsion of immediate peril.

Equally dismaying, after the mid-1950s government studies showed declines in per capita real income, productivity, and national production. For some time, however, people were not hurt enough to be willing to accept austerity programs. Cattle and sheep production could have been improved, but incentives given to the big producers brought political complaints about their profits. Agricultural production and exports were encouraged by subsidies, but that was speculative and expensive. Agricultural growth was low, as was investment, and technology was poor. A third of the land belonged to 1 percent of the landowners, and 75 percent owned a mere 8.5 percent. Uruguayan soils were not optimal for crop production. Public funds were poured into support of low prices for certain essentials of the local diet, a practice that could be attacked or defended. There was a tendency to meet the problem of unemployment by adding to the public payroll. By the early 1960s about 21 percent of the work force was in the public sector (bureaucracy and productive entities of the state).

Industrial production was fostered by many devices. The aims were reduction of foreign domination, some independence of foreign sources of supply, provision of employment, hopefully more control over prices. None of these motives was irrational or hopeless of attainment, depending on scope and many factors of execution. In a small country of limited market with few natural resources and little capital, not surprisingly many of the industries turned out a high-cost product, and many types of fabrication could not be established at all. Much subsidy and profit to special interests were involved in import substitution as a national policy.[4] The growth of overall

---

[2] In 1950 Uruguay reached its peak of exports per capita in terms of value.

[3] In 1961 the United States Embassy at Montevideo pointed out that Uruguay once had exported more than half her pastoral/agricultural production, but that the export share had declined to 30 percent.

---

[4] A system of multiple exchange rates long subsidized meat and industrial production at the expense of wool, with restrictive effects on the latter.

industrial production was 8.5 percent from 1945 to 1954, but as the plausible lines were exhausted, it fell off badly. Much more industrial growth was going to be difficult.

The state itself engaged in production but accounted for only a minor part of industrial output. Rates on publicly owned transportation and for public power, however, were set low, and thus were subsidized by other sectors of the economy. An interesting effect of government production occurred in meat packing. The state plant was given a monopoly of the domestic market, which kept growing, leaving the foreign companies a declining amount from the stable national cattle population. Swift and Armour complained that this situation and other problems kept them from making a profit. Finally, they announced withdrawal from the country. The government did not believe them until they pulled out in 1957.

Financial decisions had to be taken in support of the policies decided on. These tended to be inflationary for a number of reasons.[5] The government permitted the private banks to inflate credit generously. The big social welfare system, public payroll, and red ink in state enterprises often were met by deficit financing and heavy borrowing abroad.[6] The tax system was kept unprogressive and quite light. There was no mystery about any of these things, but Uruguayans did not react effectively. It was observed that they did not accept the dictum understood by such modern and high-tax countries as Norway that "charity is expensive."

The social security system provided coverage to a high proportion of the urban population, with pensions after twenty-five to thirty years of employment. The life of the worker was geared to the expectation of retirement income. By the late 1950s, however, the various funds were unable to meet the full obligation. By 1961 payments were only 80 percent of what was due. Additionally, attainment of paid retirement status no longer depended just on fulfilling the legal requirements, but on getting acceptance from the bureaucracy. A person who received payment only months after it legally was due was fortunate; waits of over a year were common. No one wanted to abolish the pension system, but there was much discussion of improvement of the amounts and the administration.

Uruguay developed the lowest population growth rate in Latin America, usually taken to correlate with satisfactory socioeconomic conditions. It was the result of a combination of a low birthrate and one of the lowest deathrates in the world. Life expectancy at birth went to seventy years for women and sixty-four for men. Evidently, Uruguayans enjoyed the good life. By the early 1970s there were 3 million Uruguayans and about half of them lived in greater Montevideo. Literacy climbed to more than 90 percent (87 percent even in rural areas). There was a great expansion of secondary and technical education, which increased fourfold from 1940 to 1960 alone. The university population was less impressive on a per capita basis than in Argentina, but still one of the best in Latin America.

Blanco Administrations: The Mixture as Before, 1959–1967

The *Blanco* or Nationalist party government elected in 1958 was installed in March 1959. It had called for control of inflation and improved management of government. By agreeing to the sort of stabilization and austerity being demanded all over Latin America by the developed countries and the international lending agencies that they controlled, the government obtained credits. The agreement included a sound money policy pursued with balanced budgets, credit controls, and improvements in the balance of payments. The *Colorados* and smaller leftist groups called

---

[5] The average annual increase in prices until the mid-1950s was 5.4 percent, but in 1955–1961 it went to 16.4 percent, and after that increased by leaps and bounds until it went up 100 percent in 1965 alone. The ingredients in the inflationary process varied from time to time.

[6] The foreign debt was $490 million by 1963 and went up a great deal thereafter.

this subservience to foreigners. The government installed the country's first, quite modest income tax in 1961. It developed a ten-year plan as part of the new Alliance for Progress, which met more charges of foreign interference. In 1961 it expelled the Cuban ambassador and a Soviet diplomat on grounds of subversive activities in Uruguay. To some critics this seemed mostly evidence of conservatism and eagerness to please the United States. None of these policies had much effect.

Voter confidence in the new broom fell off in the election of 1962, but the Nationalists retained their majority position for another four years, by a bare 24,000 votes of the more than a million cast. By now the Nationalists were signaling their frustration with increased bickering among themselves. The government declared that the economy had been running downhill for years, which was no comfort to the citizenry when the administration tried to keep wage increases below the rise in the cost of living. In 1963 the government agreed with the IMF to drop subsidies for domestic bus fares and milk and various export levies. That move was condemned in Uruguay as helpful to exporters and hard on common people, but the administration wanted IMF credits to support the peso. In 1963–1966 the economic situation generally worsened with foreign trade imbalances and inflation.

In 1965 the government defaulted on some of its payments. It sent a delegation to Washington to apply to the World Bank, the IMF, the Inter-American Development Bank, and the Inter-American Committee on the Alliance of Progress. It learned that the price of aid was more change in policy. With some difficulty, the Nationalists agreed among themselves on a new program of austerity and stabilization with restriction of imports, increase of exports, and control of wages. They tried to implement this program with control of strikes and instituted the first state of siege in years. It did not stop the striking, so arrests were made, and the armed forces operated public services. With 88 percent inflation in 1965 none of this could be popular;

nor was it in 1966, even though there was an increase of exports.

So a *Colorado* was elected again, with 50 percent of the vote—retired General Oscar Gestido. Furthermore, Batlle's dream of a collegiate executive system, first tried in modified form after 1919 and in its full vigor from 1951, was terminated by the voters, so Gestido had full executive powers again. The leftist coalition FIDEL received less than 6 percent of the vote[7] and the Christian Democrats 3 percent. The electorate was not turning away from the old parties. Very soon Gestido decided that he needed more power to deal with what he said were the prime problems of poor government and economic selfishness, so in October 1967 he declared a state of siege. That suspension of constitutional guarantees of freedom still was in effect when Gestido died in December, and was succeeded by Vice-President Jorge Pacheco Areco.

Violence from Right and Left, 1960s–1972

From 1967 on, Uruguay suffered a continuing economic crisis, leftist subversion and terrorism, and escalating military action in public affairs. Pacheco (1967–1972) was a conservative *Colorado*. The economy remained troubled in his administration, with the cost of living generally climbing steeply. Exports were forced up and imports down, intermittently, but such policies were difficult to maintain. When the government tried to keep wages below price increases, almost unceasing strikes occurred. Some welfare costs were pruned. Unemployment was high. The foreign debt rose.

It seemed to public and private workers that the government, run by conservative men of property, wanted them to bear the cost of stabilization. Promotion of exports brought profits to a privileged few. There were charges of corruption

---

[7] FIDEL: *Frente Izquierda de Libertad* (Left Front for Liberty), the Communist party, the university-based communist youth movement, and some sympathetic labor unions.

in government and between officials and private enterprise. Pacheco used the state of siege and other strong measures against workers most of the time. He imprisoned some striking bank employees in 1968 and sent some to military detention camps. His interference with the press led to congressional suggestions that he be impeached. He raised the state of siege briefly in 1969, then reinstated it. He mobilized strikers into the army, and when Congress said such an act was unconstitutional, the army intimidated it into changing its opinion.

Not only organized labor led the government toward violent methods. There also was concern with a leftist terrorist group, the Tupamaros, also known as the National Liberation Front. It was formed in 1964, one of the small revolutionary bands created in Latin America in the wake of Castro's victory in Cuba. The Tupamaros operated in Montevideo. At first they impressed some observers as rather romantic young idealists, striking blows for freedom and the downtrodden. They occasionally used the proceeds of their robberies to aid the poor. In the late 1960s they turned to terrorism. Partisans justified their bombings, kidnappings, and murders as a response to police brutality and as the only method of destroying a corrupt system that used force against the common people. Critics of the Tupamaros thought that conditions in Uruguay did not justify such anarchic pursuit of the views of a small minority.

The Tupamaros wanted to disrupt society and increase friction, to shake confidence in "bourgeois" rule. Some even argued that if they could provoke foreign intervention (for example, from the military regime in Brazil), it eventually would help bring down the old regime in Uruguay. Not even the conventional communists in Uruguay agreed on the prudence of such tactics. To accomplish such objectives the Tupamaros probably had 2,000 to 5,000 members, not all active at the same time. Some of them came from the privileged class, but they had little support among their families. Tupamaros claimed to believe that they could create a mass move-

ment, but there was little sign of any. In 1967 they blew up radio stations, robbed banks, stole weapons, organized strikes and riots. In August 1968 they kidnapped the president of the state electric and telephone service, a friend of President Pacheco, but released him unharmed with the statement that the safety of public officials depended on how the government conducted itself. So radical an announcement made it easier for people to form firm views on the Tupamaros.

In 1970 the Tupamaros kidnapped a Brazilian diplomat and two United States citizens. One of the latter was D. Mitrione, a public safety specialist (police instructor) lent to Uruguay. When he was murdered, some observers in Latin America and the United States said that such a person should not have been sent to Uruguay, a view that other observers found sad or infuriating. For twenty days in August 1970 some 10,000 troops and police combed the capital, and by December, 180 Tupamaros were in jail. The Congress wanted to appease the movement, but Pacheco supported the military in their determination to shatter the Tupamaros. Also indicative of Pacheco's troubles with the Congress was that in November 1970 it overrode many of his item vetoes of planned expenditures, more than tripling the anticipated budget deficit. As in many countries, legislators were under pressure from constituents not to cut off funds that would help them in the short run.

Military Dominance Since 1972

Through 1971 Uruguay still suffered economic depression, public violence, friction within government, and increased military activity in public affairs. In the 1971 election the *Colorados* barely won over the *Blancos*. More arresting was the fact that a Broad Front (*Frente Amplio*) of leftists—chiefly Communists, Socialists, and Christian Democrats—ran a retired general for president and took 18 percent of the vote, nearly doubling the support for those parties. By the time Juan Bordaberry, a conservative *Colorado* and big landowner, was inaugurated in March

1972, some military men were talking about a coup.

Politics and Government.   The army harried the Tupamaros so successfully that terrorist operations dwindled. Critics said it did so with unnecessary brutality. During 1971, the military became ever freer with advice. Officers arrested the prominent *Colorado* congressman Jorge Batlle for "insults" to the military honor. In February 1973 the armed forces compelled Bordaberry to make changes in the defense ministry and navy command, using tanks and troops and radio speeches as threats. They demanded redistribution of land and wealth, an end to corruption, harsher anticommunist measures, and a new National Security Council (COSENA) in which the military were to play a large role, directing government policy outside the traditional structure. Bordaberry agreed, but Congress would not. While that dispute festered, the armed forces demanded in May that the Senate lift the parliamentary immunity of a leftist member so he could be tried by court-martial for links with the Tupamaros. The upshot of those disputes was that Bordaberry and the military in June closed the Congress and dissolved all municipal councils. Representative government, which had been dying for several years, thus expired.

Although the military often seemed merely another group bent on using strong-arm methods, sometimes they hinted at more. The suggestion of February on redistribution of wealth was accompanied by some others of a populist flavor. In July 1973 the military declared it was subordinate to civil authority, a curious view of its activities. Some leftists, however, still talked as though the military might turn out to be a people's army. They distinguished between "good" military regimes (that in Peru was admired) and bad (as in Brazil), so the objection was to "nonrevolutionary" military activity in public affairs. This hope of revolutionary developments in the Uruguayan military was supported by the differences of opinion known to exist among officers.

That hope was damped in October 1973 when the military arrested the rector and other university officials for permitting Marxist agitation. The military remained in control of the university and claimed to find caches of weapons and subversive literature, possessions of "autonomous" universities that had been found in many countries of Latin America. In December the government outlawed the Communist and Socialist parties and some student groups. In the summer of 1974 the military was put in control of the major state-owned enterprises, including the communications and transportation systems, which much increased their hold on the country. At the same time, they forced Bordaberry to create an Economic and Social Council, through which they could advise him, to work with the older COSENA, which they dominated.

By then the military grip was tight, with suspension of the old political process, censorship, the purge of the educational system of alleged Marxists, and continuing political arrests of Tupamaros, communists, and others. In 1975–1976 Bordaberry and the military disagreed on how to manage the dictatorship, with the result that in June 1976 the military forced Bordaberry out and created a National Council that selected Aparicio Méndez as new president of the republic.

The use of violence by government increased. The armed forces grew from about 12,000 to 25,000 with enough attendant expense to put pressure on the budget.[8] Large numbers of known or suspected Tupamaros were imprisoned, along with increased numbers of other dissidents and Marxists. These activities became a subject of international discussion. There was much speculation as to the number of political prisoners in Uruguay; Amnesty International in 1976 alleged 6,000. Public agencies were charged with torture. People were said simply to disappear, into jails or into graves. In the United States reports of these activities led in September 1976 to a con-

---

[8] There were also about 20,000 men in police forces, which, as in most of Latin America, were controlled by the army.

gressional ban on military aid to Uruguay, which Montevideo said would give comfort to communists. In November 1976 the UN High Commission for Refugees asked Montevideo how Uruguayan exiles abducted in Argentina turned up in Uruguayan jails. It was believed that the military governments in Argentina and Uruguay were collaborating in pursuit of leftist and other dissidents. Those governments declared collaboration was sensible and was what communist governments did in harrying their enemies. Then in February 1977 the United States secretary of state publicly chastised Uruguay for human rights violations, whereupon Montevideo accused Washington of intervening in Uruguay's internal affairs. Such an exchange was a far cry from the days when North Americans called Uruguay the Switzerland of South America.

The Military and the Economy. The military addressed itself to economic developmentalism in much the same way as other military governments in Latin America. It relied heavily on well-trained civilian technicians and on the collaboration of private enterprise. Its efforts understandably brought little immediate improvement; such long continued ills could not be cured overnight. It used conventional methods of curbing expenditures, trying to hold down prices (and wages), and fostering exports while restricting imports. Policy included promotion of exports into nontraditional lines and reduction of protectionism to stimulate efficiency in Uruguayan production. Efforts were hampered by the great increase in world petroleum prices, which in 1974 required Uruguay to use some 40 percent of its foreign exchange for imports of petroleum products. Traditional exports were hurt by the 1974 decision of the European Economic Community to restrict meat imports. But at last in the first half of 1976 Uruguay achieved a favorable balance in exports for the first time in years. Whether this swallow would be followed by many more remained to be seen, and how working people would respond to the new control

measures, even though unemployment was at least temporarily reduced, was equally uncertain.

So another Latin American nation, under economic pressure and after turmoil and violence, seemed to fall firmly to a combination of military men, conservative but sometimes competent economic interests, and technocrats. Free speech, representative government, civil rights, and an effective role for organized labor received short shrift. Leftists were strongly suppressed. The process in Uruguay was a shock to all who hoped for the growth of political participation in Latin America, and for leftists who hoped that social turmoil would bring their type of dictatorship.

b. Costa Rica Since the 1940s

Costa Rica after 1940[9] improved its reliance on modernization by the politics of discussion and compromise, especially by involving more people in the process. The country was blessed with a relatively homogeneous population, which contributed to much better than average national communications, together with literacy, a compact settlement pattern, freedom of discussion, and poverty less grinding than in many lands. Costa Rica faced sizable problems, with possibly the highest population growth rate in the world, heavy dependence on agricultural exports, and small resources for the development of the national economy. Given its record for many decades, however, it seemed to promise well for modernization by evolution rather than revolution.

Economic and Social Conditions

The population in the 1970s remained overwhelmingly rural and agricultural. The population growth rate was phenomenally high. In the 1970s, Costa Rica had one of the lowest death-rates in the world. With only 60,000 inhabitants at Independence, Costa Rica reached nearly

---

[9] See Chapter 33, Section c, on Costa Rica in the 1890s–1930s.

900,000 in 1953 and 1.7 million by 1970. The attachment of the country to education stood up well to this pressure. Literacy was about 80 percent by the 1960s. Defects in the system were that more than half the population never went beyond the third grade; only 5 percent of the children finished high school; and university facilities were limited. Defenders said that high literacy made for good national communications; detractors stated that the system perpetuated elitism.

The degree of social mobility in Costa Rica was much argued. It was a society in which "only" money stood in the way of mobility, but economic opportunities were limited in number and by family favoritism. Persons of property had the largest decision-making powers, and naturally such things as the tax and educational systems favored their continued privileges. Even pessimists conceded that communications between classes in Costa Rica had been improving, with the result that more people became articulate about their needs and turned to politics to try to satisfy them. Their effort was facilitated by freedom of speech and by recognition of the rights of organized labor.[10]

Exports of coffee and bananas continued to be of prime importance, and Costa Rica enjoyed the greatest per capita exports in Central America, though not high by Argentine standards.[11] While coffee was the dominant export, there was some export diversification, which with the rather large number of small growers were social and economic strengths in Costa Rica. President Figueres made an especial effort, beginning with a higher tariff in 1954, to encourage light industry, which forced prices up so much that some people turned to inferior but cheaper Costa

Rican goods produced by handicraft methods.

The governments, especially from the 1950s, greatly increased public supervision and participation in the economy. Although the government role was most useful to persons of considerable property, some of it aided a wider spectrum of the population: credit from government banking operations helped with farm seed, equipment, and marketing; there was improvement of roads, telecommunications, and public electric power. Social insurance did a bit to improve purchasing power, but the small national market remained a barrier to some developments. A big program of public electric power began in 1949 with formation of the Instituto Costarricense de Electricidad, and power became relatively cheap and widely used. Although family income was low, it was high compared with countries such as Bolivia and the rest of Central America. Still, there was truth in the comment on the legend of equitable land distribution in Costa Rica that "What is well distributed is poverty."

Politics and Government Until the Civil War of 1948

The agitation of the 1930s had created an enlarged demand for change to improve Costa Rican life. Dr. Rafael A. Calderón Guardia was elected for the presidential term 1940–1944, having convinced many people that he favored change. He was the candidate of the National Republican party, founded in 1932, and moderately liberal for that time. Calderón won with a huge majority, as his fellow National Republican, the incumbent President León Cortés Castro, resorted to fraud, justifying it on the grounds that the opposition was supported by the communists.

It turned out that Calderón meant to carry out his campaign pledges. Politics became a matter of *calderonistas* and others. Former President Cortés in 1941 formed a Democratic party, because Calderón's National Republican regime was too radical for him. Much of the elite was alienated when Calderón collaborated with communist leader Manuel Mora Valverde to put over

---

[10] Labor unions were unimportant before the 1930s, when their beginnings were especially due to the Communist party. They became strongest on the coasts. Those founded in the *meseta* in the 1930s long were weak, but became stronger in recent years.

[11] Costa Rica's exports averaged $20 million in the Depression years 1929–1937. Later increases were matched by population growth.

reform legislation. But when the communists in 1943 changed their name from the *Bloque* to *Vanguardia Popular,* some Costa Ricans still thought of it as *comunismo criollo,* untied to international communism. In the midst of these developments, in February 1942 José Figueres in a radio speech attacked the president's policies and especially his growing relations with the communists. Although Figueres was not an important leader, Calderón was stung by the stridency of the criticism, and took the unusual step of forcing Figueres into exile. It had been a quarter century since a Costa Rican had been treated thus, and it began the Figueres legend.

Calderón encouraged the use of idle land and gave aid to small farmers with land distribution and rural credit, pushed a program of low-cost housing, established a social security system, and formed a national university. The Constitution was amended to include social guarantees, a social function for property, and support for the growth of cooperatives and the right of labor to bargain collectively. The elite hated the Labor Code of 1943, since it not only encouraged labor organization but provided for mandatory bargaining and special labor courts. Though the well-to-do generally turned from Calderón, he was not anticapitalist but a moderate reformer, influenced by modern papal doctrine on social reform and convinced that progressive persons of wealth must support evolutionary change or risk revolution.

The National Republicans elected for the 1944–1948 term Teodoro Picado and sent a large majority to the national legislature. The Popular Vanguard used strong-arm tactics in support of the administration and elected four members of the legislature itself. Picado's policies were *calderonista,* and enemies of the National Republicans looked forward bleakly to the probability of Calderón's candidacy in 1948. In that year the opposition began to unite. It also began using terrorist tactics, which it could claim had been initiated by the communists in 1944. The communists also received increased criticism when the cold war began, and their enemies claimed that they supported the Soviet Union against the democratic states.

The new social legislation was costly and required an expensive bureaucracy. Picado pushed through a modest income tax, long opposed by the well-to-do. Two new parties were created. The National Union party was conservative, dominated by Otilio Ulate, publisher of *Diario de Costa Rica,* foe of a *calderonismo* he linked with communism, partly because *Vanguardia Popular* now had several members of the legislature and some rather prominent members in the executive branch. The other new party was the Social Democratic, formed in 1945 by fusion of several groups. They comprised intellectuals who favored socioeconomic development by the state but did not care for Calderón, and *Acción Demócrata,* a splinter of the Democratic party, which had a strong interest in electoral reform and included supporters of José (Pepe) Figueres.

Figueres was born in Costa Rica in 1906 of Spanish parents. After secondary school, he went to the United States and lived by his own efforts for four years. Returning to Costa Rica, Figueres built up a plantation in an underdeveloped area, calling it "The Endless Battle" (*La Lucha Sin Fin*), which exactly described his attitude toward life. After his expulsion by Calderón he was a celebrity, endlessly energetic in promoting himself while in exile and on his return in 1944. A short, lean, feisty man, Figueres was an excellent speaker, with a talent for dramatization and a born politician's willingness to use a multitude of avenues to build support.

The opposition coalition held a nominating convention in February 1947, including representatives of such conservative groups as the Chamber of Agriculture, the Chamber of Commerce, the Coffee Growers Association, and the private banks; there also were more liberal representatives, among them Social Democrats and students. Figueres was a candidate, but the nomination went to Otilio Ulate. Some of the people back of Ulate were willing to arrange a compromise with the *calderonistas,* but the Social Democrats would not hear of it. They gained support when in October 1947 communist Mora declared adherence to the Comintern and attacked the position of the United States in the cold war. He thus intensified conservative fears of Calderón's return to office.

There was much excitement in Costa Rica in the last weeks before the 1948 election. The opposition said that the *caudillo civil* Calderón would return to office through electoral fraud, but it also knew that Calderón had wide support. Figueres prepared to seize power by persuading leftist President Arévalo of Guatemala to promise him the arsenal of the so-called "Caribbean Legion," a handful of men who in 1947 participated in Cuba in an abortive scheme to overthrow rightist dictator Trujillo of the Dominican Republic.[12] With the collapse of the Cuban enterprise, its arms went to Arévalo. Figueres, on his part, pledged to battle dictatorship in the Caribbean. So now Figueres was going to use reputedly leftist arms to fight a reform leader of Costa Rica, condemning the latter for communism. One result was that Figueres himself was shortly accused of communism, and the issue became hopelessly confused.

The election of February 1948 in Costa Rica was a nightmare of technical inefficiency by the Electoral Tribunal. It could not cope with the fact and charges of fraud on both sides and was subjected to great pressure. It turned in a report on an unfinished canvass that showed Ulate ahead. The unsatisfactory report went to the Congress for confirmation, but the *calderonistas* were not disposed to accept it on the grounds that the Tribunal was in the majority hostile to them. So the National Republican and Popular Vanguard representatives in Congress annulled the election, said a new one could not be held because the machinery needed revision, and declared Calderón elected. Figueres could now ensure himself *ulatista* support for direct action. On March 1, 1948, he began what he called the War of National Liberation at *La Lucha Sin Fin.*

Most of the troops at his farm were Costa Ricans, but some of the training was by foreigners from the so-called Caribbean Legion. A Dominican became Figueres' chief of staff, and the arms from Cuba by way of Guatemala were important. The government called the revolt rightist; Figueres said it was socialist. The latter's largely conservative supporters accepted this statement only as a tactic; their objections to it soon would appear. The international press interpreted the war as having implications far beyond the little republic. Somoza, the rightist dictator in next-door Nicaragua, wanted to help Calderón, because he feared the Caribbean Legion would hit him next. Communist Mora was against such help on the grounds that Somoza was a puppet of the United States.

Figueres on April 17 stated that he was anticommunist. On April 18, after seven weeks of conflict, a cease-fire was reached. Picado wanted to avoid adding to the 2,000 or so deaths attributable to the civil war. The agreement offered decent guarantees to both sides. On April 24 Figueres entered San José with his army.

Politics and Government Since 1948

Figueres persuaded Ulate to acquiesce in an eighteen-month rule by junta under Figueres' direction, during which a constitutional assembly would be elected. Figueres used that period to violate the agreement with Picado for a compromise peace. He thinned the leadership of the National Republicans and Popular Vanguard by removing them from public posts, by imprisonment, exile, and confiscation of property, using special courts from which there was no appeal. The junta outlawed the Communist party. By decree it also nationalized most banking and extracted a 10 percent forced contribution from private capital. These acts shocked and alienated many who had supported the revolt against the *calderonistas*; it fixed Figueres in their minds as anticapitalist.

With only minority support, the junta could do no more. It prepared a draft for a new Consti-

---

[12] See Chapter 43, Section b, on Fidel Castro and that scheme.

tution, providing an extension of state activity, but in the December 1948 election to the constituent assembly the Social Democrats polled less than 10 percent of the 82,000 votes. The constituent assembly would not even discuss the junta's draft, and instead simply modified the Constitution of 1871. One change put absolute control of elections in a Supreme Electoral Tribunal, and gave the vote to all men and women at age twenty. Figueres also lost support because of resentment at his use of Caribbean exiles in his army and revelations about his commitment with regard to fighting dictatorship in other countries. He was reduced to leadership of the small National Liberation group (PLN).

Ulate took over as president in November 1949, with the legislature heavily dominated by his National Union party. The *calderonista* social reforms were not abandoned but not extended. Economic growth was managed conservatively, with balanced budgets. Reformers said that these policies were part of an anachronistic ideal from a past that should be buried, and that modernization and justice required public expenditure, even if that meant deficits. Figueres in 1952 organized his movement into the PLN party, appealing for wide support for faster economic growth, more social programs, wider participation in the political process, and reduction of "an intolerable level of misery." During the presidential campaign of 1952–1953, it became apparent that Figueres had heavy support, that most people did not care about balancing the budget. Figueres won by a huge majority, and under a system of proportional representation the PLN got two-thirds of the seats in the Legislative Assembly.

Figueres in his 1953–1958 term seemed radical to conservatives. He made large expenditures on social and economic programs, some of which aided the poor, some the wealthy. He pushed the development of semiautonomous government agencies and public action generally. The largest new agency was a Housing Institute. He also doubled the income tax, which still left it low by European standards. Costa Rica, in the common Latin American fashion, remained heavily dependent on foreign trade levies. Figueres raised minimum wages, but not by much. He barely began a land reform. The fact was that Costa Rica could not afford large programs. Nor did Figueres wish to destroy capitalism. In common with liberal reformers in other Latin American countries, he favored a mixed system. His nationalism found expression in 1954 in a protective tariff that was immediately of more value to a few well-to-do manufacturers than to consumers, because it pushed up prices. Figueres spoke out against special concessions for foreign investment in Costa Rica and increased the government share of United Fruit Company income, but without running the risk of driving the company from the country. Costa Rica was surviving nicely as he left office in 1958.[13] He had established the PLN as the dominant party, and since then it has held the Congress and sometimes the presidency. The National Union party put in Mario Echandi for 1958–1962, partly because of a small split in the PLN. In 1962–1966 the president was PLN member Francisco Orlich. In 1966 the opposition barely seated José Trejos for the term to 1970. Figueres was president again in 1970–1974. The term for 1974–1978 went to Daniel Odúber, also of PLN, but Figueres and Odúber soon were feuding about the role in Costa Rica of United States financier Robert Vesco, sought by law enforcement officials in his homeland, who fled to Costa Rica in 1972. There he was protected against extradition by local leaders. Both Figueres and Odúber were charged with financial involvement with Vesco.

By 1963 some 10 percent of the working force was on the public payroll, including the semiautonomous government agencies, which by the late 1960s were spending about half of government funds. The big commitment to education

---

[13] In January 1955 Figueres faced a small invasion of *calderonistas* from Nicaragua, although by that time they had little support in Costa Rica. The OAS quickly put its peace-keeping machinery into operation to be sure that the rightist Somozas of Nicaragua did no more to disturb conditions in Costa Rica.

contributed many of the public employees. The government was involved in hospitals, electric power, manufacturing, commerce, the railway to the Pacific, banking, the Costa Rican international airline, housing, and national planning. It controlled the only insurance company and the only petroleum refinery, and monopolized all alcoholic beverages except beer. From the early 1960s on, it was in agriculture, especially through the National Institute of Land and Colonization, which slowly parceled land and gave some help with marketing.

The country held to regular elections. The Supreme Tribunal of Elections created by the 1949 Constitution made Costa Rica's elections among the most honest in the world, supervised by an agency out of the control of the government and parties. In 1959 voting was made compulsory, which increased participation, though more in urban than in rural areas. Between 1953 and 1970 the number of those voting rose from 197,000 to 537,000, and the percentage of the registered actually balloting went from 67 to 80. The presidents were less arbitrary and more subject to legislative check than in most of Latin America. The army was abolished in 1948.

How should this modernization be judged? At one extreme were those who said that the enlarged bureaucracy was important chiefly as a source of income to the privileged class; education was elitist; political party leadership was confined to the oligarchy; the remarkably elaborate set of political institutions, both formal and informal, tended to perpetuate inequality; poverty was widespread; and broader participation in politics and government, plus some income redistribution, surely would be beneficial. At the other extreme were those who said that Costa Rica had competitive electoral processes and a meaningful legislature that would help solve its admittedly difficult economic problems. So for little Costa Rica, as for huge Argentina and Mexico—and the United States—commentators split between those who emphasized what had been accomplished and those who stressed what remained to be done.

42 Accelerated Change in Colombia, Venezuela, and Peru

In recent years there has been notable acceleration of change—some of it unambiguous modernization—in Colombia, Venezuela, and Peru. Modernization in Colombia accelerated in the 1920s and 1930s and suffered violence and dictatorship in the 1940s and 1950s; thereafter its moderate modernizing elites struggled to maintain domination of popular discontent. Venezuelan change barely began in 1935–1945, briefly accelerated in 1945–1948, was in many respects retarded by renewed military dictatorship in 1948–1958, and thereafter proceeded under moderate reform regimes. There were growing pressures for modernization in Peru from the 1930s, but the propertied and the military were resistant. A "National Revolution" by the military since 1968 has provided a mixture of modernization, repression, and confusion. Development in all three countries remained a mixture of contradictions.

a. Colombia Since the 1930s

Events in the 1930s in Colombia confirmed the accumulation of significant pressures for modernization. In subsequent decades, however, dispute over the terms of adjustment displayed much of the factional violence of Colombia's nineteenth-century history. Improvements in public health led to a rapid increase in population, and various developments, including improved transportation, caused urbanization. One of the better records of economic growth in Latin America scarcely could cope with the demographic explosion and the rise in expectations. Colombia became one of the most tension-ridden battlegrounds between the doctrines of modernization by evolution and by revolution.

The Liberals Return to Power, 1930–1946

After being kept for decades in the political wilderness by Conservative fraud and force,[1] the Liberals returned to power in 1930. In part their victory was the result of socioeconomic change from World War I through the 1920s. Good exports and foreign investment and loans financed public improvements and an expansion of light industry. They stimulated labor organization. Workers struck in the oil fields and at the banana plantations in the 1920s and met strong government repressive measures. A few peasants began to react to population pressure and commercialization of agriculture, especially in the coffee areas, with illegal land seizures. A few of the

---

[1] See Chapter 33, Section e.

younger Liberal party politicians talked about more public activity to improve economic and social conditions.

The great Depression hit hard in Colombia, heavily dependent on coffee exports. That, together with the accumulated Liberal demands for a fair election, and momentary disarray in Conservative ranks, permitted Liberal Enrique Olaya Herrera to win the term 1930–1934. There followed in turn after peaceful elections other Liberals: Alfonso López (1934–1938 and 1942–1945), Eduardo Santos (1938–1942), and Alberto Lleras Camargo, after López' resignation, to fill out the term from August 1945 to August 1946. All were well-to-do men of the elite. This succession of elections after a century of frequent irregularities and considerable violence resulted in unduly optimistic claims of political "maturity." Events soon proved that peaceful succession of administrations had not been institutionalized.

Innovation under Olaya was so mild that a few Liberals, led by Jorge Eliécer Gaitán, formed a Revolutionary Leftist National Union, but it disintegrated for lack of support. López, however, was an innovator. In 1936 he eliminated the literacy and property qualifications required to vote for the president and the lower house of the national legislature. He eliminated from the Constitution mention of the church as the religion of the nation to cut its influence. López believed in wider use of government power to stimulate the economy and carry out some social reform. Parts of his economic program were designed to reduce the dependence of the country on foreign markets, loans, and supplies. He stimulated growth through credit, a road-building program, and aid to industry. He got money for his programs by new taxes, including the first effective (though low) income tax. He increased educational expenditures. Law 200 of 1936 tried to unravel the tangle of rural land titles, while promoting the idea that landownership carried with it an obligation to use the soil. He promoted the organization of labor, guarantee of its rights, and legislation on working conditions and social assistance. Possibly most dismaying to conservatives was the constitutional change that permitted expropriation of private property in the public interest.

López was a moderate reformer, a man of wealth, who believed that modernization was possible without rapid change in the traditional system, especially under his ideal of leadership sometimes called "Athenian democracy." His economic policies were chiefly of benefit to the wealthy and the growing middle class, the latter representing some recruitment from the poor. The Liberals became established with the voters as the majority party. Conservatives were dismayed both at the populistic and, they thought, socialistic policies of the Liberals and at their own apparently irreversible conversion to a minority status. The López program, therefore, stirred Colombian politics, and it raised debate over government activity and social legislation to a new level, because not even many Conservatives thereafter considered that obliterating all that López had done would be feasible. It affected politics in another way in that the gap between apparent aim and accomplishment stimulated some leaders to call for yet more drastic innovation.

Santos was more moderate than López. By the time of the election of 1942 at the end of Santos' term, Liberals were badly divided over modernization. López in his second administration faced a hostile Congress of Liberals and Conservatives. Wartime inflation made more evident the fact that rapid population growth, the continued misery of the rural poor, and low wages for the slowly increasing number of industrial workers spelled out an unchanged social condition. The larger middle class wanted faster improvement of its condition. The Conservatives were convinced, and some Liberals shared the view, that more innovation was not needed. There were disagreements in Colombia between supporters of the war against Hitler in Europe and reactionaries who feared that change was dissolving the role of religion and the old elites and that corporatism like that of Franco would raise the dikes against socialist inundation. López met such a torrent of opposition that he resigned, and Alberto Lleras

Camargo as provisional president finished out his term.

Lleras Camargo, a fair-minded and attractive moderate, conceived that his best contribution was to conduct a coalition government of moderate Liberals and Conservatives and not participate in the electoral contest. The Liberals nominated moderate Gabriel Turbay, whereupon Liberal Jose Eliécer Gaitán ran independently. Gaitán has been noted in earlier years as being in the left wing of the party. He was a man of humble origin who had reached eminence economically and politically, not an easy feat in class-conscious Colombia. But more unusual were Gaitán's appeal to the poor and attacks on the oligarchy. He had some support from Liberals who thought of him primarily in terms of innovation that could preserve the system from violent change. Although the two Liberal candidates together had a majority of the vote in 1946, the electoral system gave the victory to the man with the single largest count: Conservative Mariano Ospina Pérez, with some 565,000. Turbay had 441,000, Gaitán 358,000. Some Gaitán supporters demanded war, but he counseled patience until the election of 1950. Nobody in 1946 knew that before 1950 Gaitán would be in a martyr's grave and the country writhing under disorders as dreadful as any in the nineteenth century.

Conservative Reaction, Violence, Dictatorship, 1946–1957

Ospina appointed a Liberal and Conservative "unity" cabinet, but without *gaitanistas*. Gaitán energetically increased his following, and his position was improved by the death of Turbay, leaving Gaitán nominally the party leader. The Liberals in Congress, however, would not pass legislation Gaitán proposed, which whipped up the resentment of his supporters. Gaitán was increasing his attacks on the old political system, stating that there were "two Colombias," one of which monopolized privilege and power. He was

a passionate speaker, pouring out such slogans as "I am not a man, I am a people." His specific suggestions were not so radical, but his method and emphasis stimulated class feeling against the elite in both parties.

On April 9, 1948, Gaitán was murdered. In the belief that his political enemies had done away with him, his enraged supporters in Bogotá burned and killed. Several thousand people were slain, and large property damage occurred. It was not planned; there was no conspiracy. But various groups immediately claimed that rightists, communists, or someone else had prepared the "black Friday" of the *bogotazo*—a new word that came to stand for fears or hopes of revolution—although the magnitude of the outburst in the city was no more remarkable than the ability of the government to contain it.

It was not so easy to contain the violence that spread rapidly through the country. Ospina at first aggravated it by using the disorders as an excuse to undercut the Liberals. Hence, some of the fighting in the provinces was between Liberal and Conservative groups. In April 1949 the government removed Liberal departmental governors and began a strong program of suppressing "bandits," some of whom at that time were simply disaffected Liberals. The Liberal members of the cabinet resigned in May. Ospina forced out more Liberal officials and discriminated against them in the armed forces. In the June 1949 congressional elections, Liberals won a majority, which passed a law advancing the date of the presidential election from June 1950 to November 1949. Ospina vetoed it.

On June 24, 1949, Laureano Gómez came back from Franco's Spain, giving the fascist salute, calling Liberals communists, and running for president. He declared his disgust with the legislative and judicial systems as constituted. Gómez as early as 1937 had praised the Spanish Falange as the defender of Christian civilization. In the 1940s his newspaper *El Siglo* supported fascist-style "revolution," praised the Axis and damned its enemies, especially Anglo-Saxons, supposedly wanting domination under a "false liberalism and masonic atheistic democracy." When Colombia backed the Allies, Gómez said that López was "selling out to the rapists of Panama."

Politics had descended into the pit of blind faction. Congress frequently was in an uproar. It became clear that Ospina was corrupting the electoral process. He used the police and army to threaten and beat Liberals. When Congress threatened to impeach him, he dissolved it, declared a state of siege, dismissed the state legislatures and municipal councils, prohibited public meetings, and censored the press and radio. He continued to batter the Liberals in the provinces with violence, and many were killed or jailed. They withdrew their candidate for the presidency, so that on November 27, 1949, Gómez received all but fourteen of the more than 1 million votes cast. He was inaugurated in August 1950.

Gómez' right-wing repressions induced some of the important Liberal leaders to seek safety in exile in 1951. In September 1951, mobs, which Liberals thought were made up of Conservative government employees, burned Liberal party headquarters, two Liberal newspaper plants, and the homes of two leaders. Gómez later that year went into semiretirement after a heart attack. His extremism caused a split in his own party. Ospina led the moderates. In April 1953 Gómez emerged from retirement to use repression against the *ospinistas*. Violence was continuing in the countryside. The army had been stimulated by the experience of fighting in the United Nations forces against the communists in Korea,[2] and now officers were plotting with *ospinistas* to get rid of Gómez. Gómez tried to head that off by arresting the chief of staff, General Gustavo Rojas Pinilla, but the military would not permit it. Instead, in June 1953 Rojas took over the

government, to the jubilation of all except *laureanistas*.

Rojas offered an amnesty, and some guerrillas took advantage of it, but by late 1953 *La Violencia* was increasing again and it became worse in following years. Rojas freed the press in October, but he soon showed that he could not bear criticism and interfered with its operations. He brought together a Constituent Assembly, packed with his supporters. In 1954 the Assembly elected Rojas for the term 1954–1958. He kept the state of siege that had been in force since 1949. By 1955 it was clear that he wanted to set up a personal dictatorship, but he was inept at politics, and his support was shaky, even in the armed forces.

Alberto Lleras Camargo became head of the Liberals early in 1956 and discussed cooperation with the Conservatives. As a result, he visited Laureano Gómez in Spain, where in July 1956 those two unlikely collaborators agreed, in the Pact of Benidorm, to get rid of Rojas. That agreement pushed Rojas into yet more political ineptitudes. An accumulation of enmities and protests finally led the military, on May 10, 1957, to force Rojas to resign.

La Violencia

What Colombians came to call simply "The Violence" began in the countryside with the murder of Gaitán. It involved government-inspired or -conducted actions against Liberals, and Liberal guerrilla actions against both the government and Conservatives. For some time the motivation was heavily political. The scale of operations was increased by government action in mid-1949 in anticipation of a presidential election that the Conservatives were determined to win. The warfare did not have class-conscious goals, was not peasant versus great landowner; it was Conservative versus Liberal in the tradition of the wars of the nineteenth century, in which there was a large hereditary element of antipathy between parties that enjoyed adherence all up

---

[2] Colombia was the only Latin American nation to take such action. The motivation cannot be fixed precisely, but outstanding attachment to either the United Nations or the United States certainly was not involved.

and down the social scale. Some participants no doubt had economic motivation, some consciously or unconsciously wanted to relieve frustrations and some felt a simple desire to engage in exciting affairs. As time went on, especially when the Conservatives drew back from the policy of assigning all blame for the violence to Liberals and from the practice of trying to push the Liberal elite out of privileged positions, the nonpolitical motives predominated.

Possibly 20,000 to 30,000 operated in the guerrilla bands at the peak of *La Violencia*. Estimates of total deaths attributable directly to the violence ran upward from 100,000 and the wounded were left uncalculated. Property damage was high.[3] Most of the activity was in the central highlands. The many efforts to control the violence between 1949 and 1957 had limited effect, but after the creation of the National Front in 1958 the scale of activity declined. There was some reduction in 1958–1959; deaths were down to about 2,400 in 1962 and continued downward to only 544 in 1965. Some groups of bandits and murderers were so committed to the life that it was unlikely that such activity could be completely eradicated, and some of it, of course, had always existed.

Most of the combatants and leaders were rural folk. A few lived at times in virtually self-contained communities, called "republics" in Colombia, and they engaged chiefly in defensive action. Two had existed before 1948, and one of those was a communist enclave dating to the 1930s. In the difficult mountains of Colombia, attacks on such "republics" or on roving guerrilla bands were expensive for the government and danger-

ous for troops. Local people were not sympathetic toward the central government or the army and police, who often abused them, and they feared to give information against or withhold supplies from guerrillas. Some of the latter came to be made up of totally alienated and brutalized individuals who would, on occasion, butcher all the men, women, and children of a settlement.

Much Colombian effort was poured into attempts to probe the roots of *La Violencia*. Certainly it was not a communist movement, nor was it directed toward revolution, although a few leaders talked of that. Poor social conditions in many rural areas and pressures of population, plus tensions due to economic change, could make people restive or uncooperative. Land seizures sometimes were an outcome of violence. The notorious inability and unwillingness of the courts to punish captured guerrillas did something to keep their careers flourishing. Youngsters who witnessed atrocities were socialized to violence and entered the career as a natural action. The governments after 1958 not only paid attention to trying to understand the roots of *La Violencia*, but they tried to pull them up with reforms. Before the older guerrilla activity had been quite eradicated, urban terrorism began in Colombia in the early 1960s, and new types of small and clearly revolutionary bands with an important urban component were created in the countryside.

The National Front

The agreement in Spain in July 1956 between Gómez and Lleras Camargo became complicated after the fall of Rojas in 1957 by a split between moderate (*ospinista*) and right-wing (*laureanista*) Conservatives. Lleras had to go again to Spain, where in July 1957 he and Gómez agreed to the Declaration of Sitges. By this, the parties were to alternate in the presidency (*alternación*), share offices of all sorts (*paridad*—parity), and have a constitutional system in which a two-thirds vote in Congress was necessary for all but

---

[3] Most estimates on *La Violencia* are suspect. Figures on deaths go up to 300,000. Although those on property damage are unreliable, a total of several hundred million dollars does not seem implausible. Such a figure is highly misleading, however, in that much of the property lost was at least in part homemade and could be replaced from cheap or free local materials and the expenditure of the "worthless" time of an underemployed population. The wealth of the coffee fields and the great cities grew all through the years of *La Violencia*.

procedural matters. A plebiscite on December 1, 1957, overwhelmingly approved this remarkable arrangement. Liberal Lleras Camargo became the first National Front president. The system was to run sixteen years, and the last chief executive to be a Conservative.

Lleras Camargo served from 1958 to 1962; Conservative Guillermo León Valencia from 1962 to 1966; Liberal Carlos Lleras Restrepo, 1966–1970; Conservative Misael Pastrana, 1970–1974. The first chief executive elected after the agreement on the presidency lapsed was Liberal Alfonso López Michelsen, for the term 1974–1978. The system of parity in other offices was to last through his term. All these presidents were men of the ruling elite, intensely anxious about economic development, moderate about social reform.

Social and Economic Conditions

In the half century from World War I to the 1970s, the Colombian elite used revenues from coffee exports and foreign investment and credits to embellish their lives and modernize the country, aims that were not entirely compatible. At the beginning of the period, Colombia was one of the more isolated, underdeveloped, and apparently unpromising of the Latin American republics. In the next half century it became better integrated, with improved connections with the world, dotted with large and in some ways modern cities—one of the most populous of the twenty republics, with access to large quantities of foreign exchange, a large educational plant and considerable intellectual community, and an industrial establishment of some size, although its ambition had so far outrun its opportunities. With all this accomplishment went much failure, as attested by a huge and miserable lower class.

Although Colombia had a national territory twice the size of France and many natural resources, problems of terrain and social management made development difficult. Colombia developed an acute population growth problem,

going from fewer than 6 million inhabitants in 1918 to 8.7 million in 1938, 15 million in 1963, and an estimated 24 million in the mid-1970s. By 1958 more than 40 percent of the population was under fifteen years of age. The problem was complicated by a rush to the cities, although roughly half of Colombians still lived in a rural environment. By the mid-1970s Colombia had four cities near or over the 1 million mark, and Bogotá had gone from 330,000 in 1938 to 2.5 million.

Economic growth and the system of allocation of its benefits were not able to care well for many Colombians. The middle class grew, but so did the poor. Public housing efforts in the cities could not keep up with the growth of shantytowns. Although public health and education facilities were strained, by 1976 there were 1.4 million social security contributors who with their families received health care. Colombia claimed to have reached more than 60 percent literacy, but that figure was doubtful. The university system—public and private—flowered, with many new establishments that, critics said, confirmed the elitist orientation of education. The universities also became centers of discussion of national politics.

Colombia's recent economic history had been characterized by, first, good overall growth. It was largely based on coffee exports, access to foreign funds, and close attention by private and public managers drawn from the elite. Growth was rapid in the 1920s, somewhat slower from 1930 to 1945 in times of Depression and war, and quite rapid from 1945 to 1954, largely due to high coffee prices; performance has been mixed but favorable since then.[4] *La Violencia* scarcely touched coffee output. Second, dependence on a

---

[4] Growth averaged in Colombia 7.3 percent in 1920–1929; less than that in 1930–1945, with one five-year low of 2.2 percent a year; 1945–1955 was much better; 1956–1958 was down to 2.4 percent yearly. Ups and downs since then show the resilience of the economy, responding to the care of its managers. In some years of the 1970s growth was 6 to 7 percent, an excellent performance.

single crop still accounted for half its exports in the 1970s.[5] The third characteristic was an increase in manufacturing.[6] But many enterprises were small, and much industry depended on imports of machinery, parts, and raw materials; so it was a heavily protected, high-cost operation in a limited area. The Colombian elite kept industry largely in the hands of nationals, believing that they could build a viable industrial establishment. At the same time agriculture was neglected. Per capita production of food crops often stagnated or declined. Food imports increased. The *latifundios* remained and were seriously underproductive. The *minifundios* were wretchedly worked. Although land reform was discussed in the 1930s, little was done before the government in 1961 set up INCORA (Colombian Institute for Agrarian Reform). It had largely a political motivation—fear of Castro-style dreams among the peasantry. INCORA's work was limited in scale, to the enemies of the elite an example of cosmetic reform. A 1971 census showed that 4 percent of landowners held two-thirds of the land and most farmers eked out an existence on *minifundios*.

Fourth, the small size of the national market was in part a function of low popular incomes, less than $300 per capita, putting Colombia far below Mexico and even farther below Uruguay and Argentina. Fifth, much infrastructure was built that would aid further development. The transport system remained dreadful until the 1930s, when a notable road-building program began. A railway from the central highlands to the Caribbean opened in 1961. It not only improved the important route (heretofore mostly by river) from the Caribbean to Bogotá, but tied together such major cities as Bucaramanga, Me-

dellín, and Bogotá that previously had been indirectly or not at all connected by rail. Thus Colombia finally achieved something that had come to Argentina and Mexico well over half a century earlier.

Sixth, elite control and planning were superior to that in many Latin American countries. Many of the upper class took an active part in business and politics. Their political control was sufficient so that the country suffered little from military interference in public affairs. The elite took into its ranks the most talented of the growing middle class. Planning and decision making were marked by ability to recuperate from mistakes and unavoidable setbacks. Recurrent budget deficits and imbalances in international payments were compensated for by lower public outlays, import controls, new taxes and improved collections, and increases in international credits. The Colombian elite had no Latin American superiors in the art of persuading developed countries and international agencies to advance credits.[7] Such policies did not prevent inflation but kept it from the runaway levels that disturbed some Latin Amer-

---

[5] For example, exports in 1973 totaled $1.24 billion, of which 48 percent was coffee. Higher coffee prices pushed total exports to $1.5 billion in 1975. As recently as 1972 exports had totaled only $743 million.

[6] It was less than 8 percent of national production in 1925, nearly 15 percent in 1950, over 17 percent in 1959, and manufacturing and transportation were about 27 percent of production in 1973.

---

[7] Colombia received a flood of loans from the United States in the 1920s. After World War II high coffee prices for some years reduced the importance of credits; in the later 1950s they became more important. Colombia proved adept at arranging for the stretching out of its commercial arrears and other payments. Colombia was quick to take advantage of the Alliance for Progress. The theoretical beauties of its planning structure and development jargon seduced United States aid authorities to make Colombia the "showcase" of the Alliance, recipient of special largesse. The United States soon regretted both the decision and the phrase, because promised reforms in Colombia did not materialize. It was not so much that Colombians overpromised as that North Americans naively expected miracles. United States economic aid to Colombia in 1962–1968 totaled $732 million. By 1969 United States Senator Fulbright was denouncing the concentration of effort in Colombia, citing statistics to demonstrate that many of the aims of the Alliance were not being attained. Long before, Colombians had moved to reduce their reliance on the United States, persuading the World Bank to sponsor a Consultative Group of European countries and international agencies to provide credits to Colombia. In 1969 this group provided $328 million, and in 1973 another $310 million. In 1972 Colombia received about $500 million of financial aid from all foreign sources.

ican countries. The Colombian elite in the 1970s pursued a policy of Colombian control of economic enterprise, a part of which was the "Colombianizing" of firms and a part of which was refusal to accept more United States government aid.

The Political Dimension Since 1957

The Conservative and Liberal parties under the Popular Front quickly became fragmented, on personal and doctrinal grounds. Moderate *llerista* Liberals and Conservative *ospinistas* supported the front; right-wing Conservative *laureanistas* and left-wing Liberal members of the Liberal Revolutionary Movement (MRL) of Alfonso López Michelsen opposed the front. The factions also wished to control government patronage, which by the 1950s had become an important matter for the middle-class members of the parties.

Divisions in Congress were aggravated by the requirement that legislation receive a two-thirds vote. Presidential programs were held up by irresponsible actions in the Congress, and the presidents sometimes resorted to legislation by decree. Strikes, demonstrations, and riots occurred rather frequently and sometimes were met with states of siege. In 1966 President Lleras Restrepo even sent troops into the supposedly "autonomous" precincts of the National University.

The prevalence of urban terrorism beginning in the early 1960s also made such methods seem necessary. In that decade, too, there arose a new type of rural guerrilla group, dedicated to overturn of the society by revolution. In 1965 the People's United Front was created, with Father Camilo Torres as principal leader. He was an upper-class ex-priest and sociologist, a former chaplain at the National University—one of the radical priests of Colombia who worked for improvement of the lot of the poor. Late in 1965 Torres joined the ELN (Army of National Liberation), a Castroite organization. Early in 1966 he was killed, gun in hand, by elements of the national army. The ELN remained in existence, together with other small revolutionary groups, engaging in sporadic terrorist acts, but the fear that they would have wide influence subsided.

A more serious threat to the front parties was mounted by General Gustavo Rojas Pinilla. The ex-dictator returned to Colombia from exile, and in 1960 organized ANAPO (*Alianza Nacional Popular*—National Popular Alliance). It assumed a strong populist stance, using the term "oligarchs" for its enemies, and asserting a tie of reformism between the masses and the military. It captured some seats in the Congress and in departmental assemblies. In 1964 elections ANAPO benefited from a sharp rise in the cost of living, with Rojas declaring that he would not so abuse the common people. ANAPO's percentage of the vote soared, drawn mostly from Conservatives. ANAPO seats in the lower house rose from six to twenty-seven. Even more disquieting to the front was the turnout of only 26 percent of the eligible voters,[8] a sign of popular disillusionment with the system. In elections in 1966 and 1968 ANAPO did well, while most eligibles abstained from voting.

In the presidential election of 1970 ANAPO made a bigger effort, running Rojas. Conservative Misael Pastrana won for the front by only 60,000 votes. ANAPO gained in Congress, the departmental assemblies, and the municipal councils. It did best in the cities, following a common pattern in recent times for dissident parties in Latin America. Some concession to fear of change was involved in the government decision in 1970 to create a National Peasants Association, which in the next few years seemed to foment somewhat more political activity among the *campesinos*. The threat of ANAPO soon faded, however, partly because of Rojas' age and illness. His daughter María Eugenia took over. In 1972 elections the front regained control from ANAPO of nearly all the municipal councils and depart-

---

[8] Women received the vote in 1954. Many lower-class migrants to the cities did not participate because of the difficulty of reregistering in their new districts.

mental assemblies, with only 30 percent of the voters participating. In the presidential election of April 1974 Liberal Alfonso López Michelsen took more than 80 percent of the vote; a Conservative came in second, and María Eugenia Rojas was a distant third, with less than 10 percent of the vote. The traditional parties had buried the opposition. The dissatisfied in Colombia were not radicalized and were not participating.

There was, however, much dissatisfaction. President López took office pledged to revamp traditional social relationships, but pleased neither reformers and the poor nor the upper-class constituency from which he came. He took the position that land division was not a panacea; development of production in all aspects of the economy was better. He did nothing to alter traditional patterns of income distribution. Violence, including guerrilla activity, strikes, and demonstrations at the universities, continued into 1977. The administration frequently imposed a state of siege, while pushing development of the modern part of the economy, a common combination in contemporary Latin America.

b. Recent History of Venezuela

Little modernization came to Venezuela in the nineteenth and early twentieth centuries;[9] certainly, the long brutal dictatorship of Juan Vicente Gómez (1909–1935) permitted none by broader participation in the political process.

The Beginnings of Change, 1920s–1948

Petroleum transformed Venezuela. Foreign companies began to ship out significant quantities in the 1920s.[10] Although Gómez ran Venezuela like a private ranch, he could not spend all

---

[9] See Chapter 28, Section d, on Venezuela from Independence to the 1920s.
[10] Although Gómez showed some shrewdness in trying to maximize Venezuela's profits from petroleum, his primitive efforts are of little interest today.

his new river of income on the army, mistresses, or the pastoral activity in which his old mountain clansman's heart delighted. His relatives and other collaborators helped push for various public works and private conveniences: modern highways, electric power, and the like.

The spectacle of the oil bonanza being managed by the old barbarian intensified the rage of opponents who despised him for numerous excellent reasons. He survived many attempts at assassination and rebellion. Each batch of executions, jailings, and exiles increased the roster of those dedicated to his overthrow. Student opposition led him to close the Central University at Caracas from 1912 to 1923. When it reopened, students resumed opposition and were persecuted. Younger army officers became disillusioned with the regime. An uprising in 1928 of junior officers, students, and a few young people of the middle class was put down. Many dissidents lived in exile from 1928 to 1935. Among the young rebels of the 1920s who became exiles were Rómulo Betancourt, Jóvito Villalba, and Raúl Leoni, all to be famous later.

Gómez died in 1935. For the next ten years the government was headed by two army officers as president: Eleázar López Contreras (1935–1940) and Isaías Medina Angarita (1941–1945). Though neither tried to emulate Gómez and political and social life were much loosened, dissidents identified the generals with the old tradition. One group formed the *Acción Democrática* (Democratic Action—AD) in 1941, on the basis of some earlier post-Gómez organizations, with the student federation formed in the 1920s and labor elements that improved their position after 1935. When Medina seemed likely to impose another military president, some younger army officers engineered a coup that was joined by AD in October 1945.

A provisional military and civilian government soon was dominated by AD and its leader Rómulo Betancourt. The latter was born in 1908 of middle-class parentage. After involvement in the university movement of the 1920s, he was jailed, then went into exile until Gómez' death. He briefly became a communist. Back in Venezuela in the post-Gómez years, he was accused of conspiracy and fled abroad again. He returned in 1941 to become one of the founding fathers of AD, and after the 1945 coup he led AD in an effort to modernize Venezuela in a hurry. A new electoral law gave everyone over twenty-one the vote, even illiterates, and provided for the direct election of the president in a country where it always had been done by the Congress. Politics blossomed. Two new parties, COPEI and URD, were formed. Organized labor was encouraged, and its first national confederation appeared in 1947. The Communist party, created in 1931, disliked AD's competition for labor's allegiance, and some church elements were irritated by its attempts to favor nondenominational over church schools. AD also increased the government's share of the income of the private foreign oil companies. Betancourt tried to reassure private enterprise that confiscation was not contemplated, but it was suspicious. Some action was taken to promote agrarian reform. Great expansion in education and other social reform was discussed and a small amount of action initiated.

Opposition formed, as business, landowners, the church, and the army feared what might come next. In December 1947, AD received more than 70 percent of the votes for its presidential candidate, Rómulo Gallegos, one of Venezuela's great literary figures. He was inaugurated in February 1948 and overthrown only ten months later.

Military Regression, 1948–1958

Army officers, some of them participants in the coup of 1945, hatched a conspiracy against the AD government, fearful that the role of the military was being compromised by new political and labor organizations, and aware that many conservative elements within and without Venezuela would support extinction of a regime that seemed determined to overturn old agreements on property. The military took over in November 1948 without difficulty, claiming, as they did for the

next decade, that they were saving the country from communism. Betancourt in later years stated that AD had made a mistake in going so fast, underestimating the fear it inspired.

From 1948 until January 1958 the military moved in a dreadful progression from the merely deplorable to the despicable. The regime outlawed AD and harried its members viciously. Rule by decree, censorship, imprisonment, and torture earned for the gang an international reputation for right-wing brutality. Colonel Marcos Pérez Jiménez, leader of the regime in its later years, represented the worst features of military interference in the political process. Finally, the regime had ranged against it AD, URD, COPEI, the church, and the Communist party (earlier courted by the military), plus all who suffered from inflation, protective tariffs, and fiscal mismanagement, and even some army officers. In January 1958, with defection by some of the military, civilian strikes, and riots, Pérez Jiménez recognized his repudiation and went into exile.[11]

A Rush to Modernize Since 1958

The military clung to power for a time following the fall of Pérez Jiménez, trying to convince voters that its moderate element wanted modernization and decent government. Admiral Wolfgang Larrazábal ran for president on the URD ticket in December 1958, but the AD elected Betancourt. Inaugurated in February

---

[11] In May 1958 Vice-President Richard Nixon passed through Caracas on what was meant to be a goodwill trip, but was spat upon and otherwise abused, while the Venezuelan authorities were conspicuously lax about protecting him. It was an expression of Venezuelan objections to United States "support" of Pérez Jiménez and the general posture of Washington's Latin American policy. For one thing, Pérez Jiménez had received the United States Legion of Merit, which critics insisted was an unnecessary commendation of a murderer. Unnecessary it no doubt was, but it scarcely proved great affection for the military regime, although some North Americans did think it good for business, anticommunist activity, and that evanescent quality "stability." Still, the regime was not primarily the work of Washington, or of United States business, but of an ancient pattern of military violence with support from the oligarchy in Venezuela.

1959, he was the first of an unbroken series of moderate reform presidents since then. Thus Venezuela, a country with a dreadful political history, installed open competition and fair elections.

It was not easy. Betancourt faced an early threat from Rafael Trujillo, tyrant of the nearby Dominican Republic, who could not bear the criticisms the AD had been issuing of his regime since the 1940s. Betancourt was of the postwar crop of liberal *políticos* who spoke out against right-wing despotism in Latin America. He was a friend of José Figueres of Costa Rica, supposedly intimate with the so-called Caribbean Legion that had tried to oust Trujillo at the end of the war.[12] Trujillo, in turn, tried to identify Figueres and Betancourt with communism. More than that, he sent assassins who nearly killed Betancourt in June 1960. That led the OAS in August to condemn Trujillo's government and order suspension of diplomatic relations and the arms trade with the Dominican Republic.

The moderate modernizers in Venezuela also faced subversion from the left. *Acción Democrática* had helped Castro gain power in Cuba, but Betancourt soon reacted against Castro's efforts to export revolution. There was serious difference of opinion in Venezuela. In 1960 some leftists, including students, split from AD and formed the MIR (Leftist Revolutionary Movement). In November 1960 URD left the coalition with AD and COPEI because of Betancourt's attitude toward Castro. In the same year a militant faction of the Communist party set up the Armed Forces for National Liberation (FALN), which began terrorist activities, aided by members of Congress from the Communist party and the MIR.

In 1961 Betancourt supported OAS suspension of Cuba from the inter-American system and broke relations with Havana. In 1962 another group split off from AD and created the *Grupo ARS* to promote faster reform, and the govern-

ment banned the Communist party and MIR. In mid-1963 the FALN killed five national guards, and in September and October the government made many arrests of leftists, including members of Congress. The Federation of Students at the Caracas university, controlled by leftists, appealed for armed action to protest the arrests. Rumors were numerous that repressive measures were in response to military insistence, which critics of the government thought reprehensible, preferring a mild attitude toward terrorism. For this and other reasons Betancourt had to spend much time bribing and cajoling the military, although he still faced conspiracies and uprisings. He also faced for the next year an intensified leftist effort to bring down his government. In November 1963 a cache of Cuban arms was discovered on a beach by government forces. A charge was carried to the OAS that these were meant for the FALN, and the OAS supported the charge and voted sanctions against Cuba. There was no question about the matter. Havana radio praised the FALN and attacked Betancourt. Castro was at the height of his euphoria, bent on carrying revolution throughout Latin America, with Venezuela the prime target. Leftists in Venezuela kept up the pressure of sabotage and ordered voters to abstain in the December 1963 election.

Leftist terrorism failed. More than 90 percent of eligible voters in December 1963 went to the polls and elected another AD president. The courage of Betancourt and his colleagues bore up the fainthearted who preferred appeasement. It turned out that most Venezuelans did not think that scattered murders, kidnappings, and sabotage showed that the regime was unable to govern. *Campesinos* supported AD and would not aid *guerrilleros*. It sank into the consciousness of the most timid that organizations such as FALN were only a few hundred weak, and that mischief was worked more upon the nerves of Venezuelans than upon the physical structure of society. Terrorist groups continued to operate in the later 1960s and 1970s, but the terror now resided

---

[12] See Chapter 41, Section b.

in their acts rather than in the minds of the public.[13]

A continuing battle with leftists centered around the universities and especially the Central University of Caracas. It may be taken as an example of such conflicts in many Latin American countries in recent years. University students understandably supported reform, but the basis of such support was much obscured by persistent, clever, and often violent leftist distortion of student opinion through the use of minority leadership tactics. In the Central University of Caracas student opinion appeared more leftist than it was. But in the manner of students everywhere, strong government action was likely to bring student unity over given issues even though disagreement generally was profound between leftist and moderate students. The Central University, in the common Latin American mode, enjoyed "autonomy"; it was self-governing and off limits to police, troops, and government officials. Armed terrorists used it as a refuge. In December 1966 President Leoni, on suspending some constitutional guarantees because of terrorism that he stated was directed from Havana, declared that the university should not be a "state within a state." Henceforth, he announced, the university would "continue to enjoy self-rule in educational and administrative matters," but with regard to public order it would be subject to the legal procedures "which are the same for all citizens and institutions."

He had by no means settled the touchy issue. After several days of student violence in November 1969, President Caldera ordered armed forces to search the university for arms and explosives,

and some were found. In 1970 a law was passed to end leftist control of the universities, depriving them of autonomy and providing for government controls. Violent protests from students, supported by many faculty, led to closing the Central University for two years in 1970–1972. Neither leftist students nor the terrorist groups had ceased operations by the late 1970s, but government control methods seemed to be more effective and better accepted by the public than previously.

After 1958 politics was dominated by three centrist parties: AD, COPEI, and URD. Enemies on the left called them variously reactionary, capitalist, and bourgeois; the far right called them anticapitalist, even socialist. All were nationalist and favored gradual reformism. All appealed to a broad spectrum of the electorate. The leadership came from the educated middle class. AD was the strongest, though intermittently troubled by serious factionalism. It was weakest in Caracas. COPEI (its long name was meaningless) was organized in 1946 upon Catholic youth foundations. Its early rather conservative orientation became softened with more liberal doctrine and a broader appeal, although it remained the most "conservative" of the three major parties and counted as a Christian Democratic party. URD (again, the name was meaningless) was organized during the AD period in 1945–1948 as the personal vehicle of Jóvito Villalba and survived as an alternative for ambitious centrist leaders.

Betancourt won the term 1959–1964 for AD with nearly half the votes. Raúl Leoni won for AD in 1964, but with only 33 percent, while COPEI had 20, and five candidates split the rest. The compulsory electoral law brought out up to 90 percent of eligible voters. Ambitious AD leaders split the party in 1968, permitting Rafael Caldera, founder of COPEI, to win with 29 percent of the vote. Carlos Andrés Pérez won for AD in 1973 with nearly half the vote. When Pérez was inaugurated in March 1974, the system had endured severe shocks for fifteen years

---

[13] There were enough terrorist acts in 1966–1967 so that the government twice instituted the state of siege. In May 1967 government forces arrested on a beach a landing party of Cuban and Venezuelan *guerrilleros*. The Communist party of Cuba admitted support for the landing and said it would continue to aid Venezuelan revolutionaries. Venezuela charged Cuba before the OAS with subversion; the OAS substantiated the charge, but would do little about it. Venezuela carried the matter to the UN, with the predictable lack of useful result.

and had many achievements to its credit, but there was no knowing how firmly rooted it was in Venezuelan society. .

Although it was the overall performance of the administrations that won popular support, agricultural reform and petroleum policy were outstanding. Agrarian measures had little impact before a law of 1960 set up the National Agrarian Institute. Rural misery stimulated migration to the city, and poor production required increasing food imports—from $10 million in 1938 to $133 million a year by the late 1950s. In 1955 agriculture employed 42 percent of the economically active population but contributed only 7 percent of the value of national production. At the same time less than 2 percent of landowners held 75 percent of the land under cultivation. Venezuela displayed the classic Latin American stigmata of poor agricultural technology among most of the farmers,[14] a *latifundio* system with all its shortcomings, and a monocultural situation that concentrated national policy and efforts upon a single commodity—petroleum.

In its agrarian policy after 1960 the AD initially had a strong political motivation, wishing to win support and hoping to curb the rural migration to town; with time, however, economic aims received increasing attention. The law of 1960 provided for expropriation with compensation of private holdings over 370 acres, but much distribution was from public lands. One group thought of agrarian change largely in terms of production, often of the industrialization of farming; another was partly concerned with social goals, either approving the small freehold or the large communal farm as superior life-styles or arguing their potential efficiency under different public policies. All sorts of ideological clouds hung over such disputes.

The reform included aid to prevent creation of

more poverty-stricken *minifundios*. By the early 1970s about 150,000 farmers (and their families) had been resettled on 11 million acres, mostly in what amounted to cooperatives (some 800 of them), *asentamientos campesinos* (peasant settlements). Far more than half a million persons were involved in the agrarian reform, a considerable proportion of the national population. Unfortunately, much of the distributed land was poor, and many small farmers had to work part-time for large owners. Production often was low and the reasons much debated. Agricultural production in Venezuela did increase in the 1960s, and food imports declined, although they remained sizable. By 1970 the country was about 90 percent self-sufficient in food, some traditional imports had ceased, and new agricultural items were exported, an excellent achievement, as the UN noted. But it was not enough, and in 1975 the country imported more than $1 billion of foodstuffs, nearly 20 percent of total imports. One effect of the agrarian reform was attachment of the rural population to the political system, especially to AD, a result as galling to critics on the left in Venezuela as the similar result of the *ejidal* program to the leftists of Mexico.

Petroleum revenues provided a gigantic resource. Commercial production began toward the end of World War I, and by the late 1920s Venezuela was for a time the greatest petroleum exporter in the world; as late as 1951 it was the leading exporter; in 1971 it was fifth world producer and a top exporter. This tremendous enterprise was the work of foreign companies, operating in long-term concessions. Petroleum came to provide more than 90 percent of the country's exports and on the order of 70 percent of public revenues, an exaggerated case of the common Latin American dependence on foreign capital and exports.

Even Gómez tried rather feebly to protect his country's interests against the great foreign oil concerns. The general-presidents of 1935–1945 somewhat increased income from the companies. AD in 1945–1948 did many things to make better

---

[14] Venezuela had many subsistence plots called *conucos*, worked by *conuqueros*. These nomad farmers use the slash-and-burn method, often on steep slopes, that rapidly has depleted fertility in a number of areas in Latin America.

use of oil revenues for national development, including establishment of a fifty-fifty split on profits. The conservative military regime of 1948–1958 did not do much to try to secure more concessions from the companies, but it endlessly claimed to be "sowing" the petroleum revenues to the benefit of the country. With the fall of Pérez Jiménez in 1958, the profit split quickly was upped to sixty-forty, and perception of opportunity, plus political competition, thereafter led inexorably toward nationalization of petroleum, which Mexico had achieved in 1938 and Brazil in the 1950s.

Various pressures in the 1970s culminated in nationalization of the entire petroleum industry on January 1, 1976. The foreign companies agreed to compensation sums far below their earlier demands. The argument that they were "losing" exploitation rights that should have run to 1983 was no longer acceptable to the underdeveloped world. The companies adjusted to a future in which they would receive much reduced income from service contracts for helping to operate portions of the industry. Combined with nationalization in 1975 of the holdings of the foreign iron ore companies, the Venezuelan government gained control of 92 percent of its foreign exchange resources and provided yet another demonstration of the ability of Latin Americans to enlarge local control of resources by legislation rather than revolution.

In 1973–1974 Venezuela, as a member of the OPEC (Organization of Petroleum Exporting Countries), greatly increased petroleum prices. Petroleum revenues were $2.4 billion in 1969, $4.7 billion in 1973, and $11.5 billion in 1974. President Pérez assured other Latin American nations that this was a triumph for all underdeveloped nations and that Venezuela would use the new revenues to help get better prices for Latin American commodities that were discriminated against by the industrialized states in international markets. It turned out that he meant to spend less on that than other Latin American nations had hoped.

These events of recent decades occurred in a nation with a territory equal to the combined areas of France, Italy, and Switzerland. The population was small but growing fast. There were only 3.36 million Venezuelans in 1936; then the increase leaped dramatically upward until it was well over 3 percent annually by the 1950s, mostly the result of improved health. By the late 1960s Venezuela had one of the lowest deathrates in the world, and by the mid-1970s life expectancy at birth was nearly sixty-seven years. The population was nearly 13 million by 1977. At the same time mass migration to the city changed the country from some two-thirds rural in the 1930s to two-thirds urban in the 1970s. Caracas went from 203,000 in 1939 to a metropolitan area population of over 2 million in the mid-1970s.

With all its advantages, Venezuela could not provide jobs for such a flood of new citizens. The country's production in the 1960s and 1970s grew on an average of some 5 percent a year and at twice that rate in the industrial sector. The development of consumer-goods production was pursued with heavy government protection, much inefficiency, and high prices. Machinery, spare parts, and raw materials were imported for the factories, with assurances that in time they would make Venezuela free. The government also put great resources into the creation of heavy industry.

There were large expenditures for infrastructure, the results of which were not immediately apparent in the national economy. Transportation was modernized. Electric power output grew from half a million kilowatts in 1949 to more than 16 million in 1974. Heroic efforts were made in education. Improvement began with the death of Gómez in 1935. More than 60 percent literacy was reached by 1960 and 90 percent in the 1970s. School enrollment went up 74 percent from 1958 to 1968 alone, mostly in public schools; and technical education on the secondary level grew even faster, while university students increased by 16,000 to more than 50,000. These three areas of transportation, electric power, and education were in themselves enough to transform the nation.

The government involvement in industrialization included an array of new instruments: the Ministry of Development, the Venezuelan Development Corporation (CVF), and the Central Office of Coordination and Planning (CORDIPLAN). There was much consultation between the public and private sectors, and the latter remained large and influential. Ownership control of certain lines of activity was reserved to Venezuelans. The government participated in many areas: banking, transportation, food distribution, some production in agriculture and manufacturing, and communications. All this was supported by a national budget much greater than in most of Latin America. In 1938, at $106 million, it was three times that of Peru; it was $1.6 billion in 1949 and $14.6 billion in 1974.

The most spectacular of all development endeavors was in Guayana in the resource-rich interior of the east, which had enormous amounts of iron ore and petroleum, plus gold, bauxite, and other minerals.[15] A steel plant was started there in the late 1950s. In 1960 the government set up the Venezuelan Corporation of Guayana (CVG) to manage a plan for development of the area. Ciudad Guayana was founded in 1961 and grew to a city of 300,000, served by large cargo ships coming up the Orinoco from the Atlantic. Hydroelectric power, aluminum production, and iron and gold mining were but a part of the activity on this fabulous frontier. By 1977 the steel industry turned out more than 1 million tons annually and expansion under construction would push output to 5 million tons by the mid-1980s. Although Venezuela hoped to become a major exporter of steel products, for some years domestic demand would consume output. Venezuelan economic and social developments were encouraging, but there was considerable debate

as to whether the pace of modernization was satisfactory.[16]

c. Peru in Recent Years

Modernization was slow in Peru until the 1930s; then the American Popular Revolutionary Alliance (APRA) created more pressure for change. The military and the oligarchy strongly resisted populist political forces into the 1960s, and kept the lid on demands for drastic social and economic change. Then in 1968 the military took charge of the political system and coupled repressive government with economic nationalism and some fundamental socioeconomic change, notably agrarian reform in favor of the rural Indians.

The Problem of APRA, 1936–1948

The mass-based, but middle-class–led, APRA in the 1920s and early 1930s gained adherents but was kept from power by the traditional civilian and military elites.[17] It was nationalist, vaguely

---

[15] For fifteen years before the mid-1970s, United States steel companies shipped some 300 million tons of iron ore from Venezuela; then President Pérez nationalized their mining concessions.

[16] The cost of living was high, but the government supported prices on such items as bread, sugar, and eggs, and control of inflation was better than in most of Latin America. The OAS noted that from 1955 to 1965 the rise in the cost of living in Venezuela was one of the lower ones in Latin America, even a bit lower than Mexico's and much better than in Argentina, Brazil, and Chile, where it was a major problem. There was much criticism of the huge shantytowns of *ranchos* on the hills of Caracas, but the fact was that Venezuela had one of the most comprehensive public housing programs in Latin America; the problem simply was too great for easy solution. There were large government health, sanitation, and nutrition programs. Social security benefits went back to 1944 but were low for many years until much increased in the 1960s. In 1967 a new social security law added to the coverage insured workers had for medical aid and physical disability, giving for the first time old age pensions and death benefits to survivors. Some government workers were incorporated into the system. Although coverage was limited, it was growing.

[17] APRA was a pioneer noncommunist leftist or reform party with a mass base, but the term *"aprista*-style" party was less meaningful as time went on and parties of broad appeal in Latin America assumed a variety of characteristics. See Chapter 33, Section e, on Peru in the twentieth century to 1936.

socialist, in favor of incorporating the Indian and mestizo masses into the mainstream of national life. The military objected to APRA's aims and disliked it because *apristas* were courageous activists, willing to use violence, in which some military officers died. APRA's leaders, including Haya de la Torre, were at times savagely handled, and the party was outlawed from 1931 to 1945. During the late 1930s and World War II APRA gained influence through political activity. Haya de la Torre did modify his anti-Yankeeism in the face of the more abhorrent Axis threat. He had no opportunity to exercise direct power under dictatorial President (and army marshal) Oscar Benavides in 1933–1939 or conservative Manuel Prado in 1939–1945.

In 1945 the old elite permitted a fairly free election. APRA understood that it would not be allowed to elect Haya de la Torre, so it called itself the People's party (*Partido del Pueblo*) and joined a coalition to elect conservative José Bustamante. During the campaign, *apristas* were active and obviously popular, a disturbing event to traditional political elements, and more so when *apristas* won a majority in the lower house of Congress and half of the Senate. Before long, they received three seats in the cabinet. Apparently, they at last had their opportunity.

Judgment of what they did with that opportunity depended somewhat on one's point of view. They sponsored much reform legislation. They were active in organized labor, and the demands of unions alarmed the economic elite. The conservatives declared that APRA used its new position to undermine the government. The conservative claim that APRA meant to use violent methods assertedly was confirmed by the murder in January 1947 of a prominent rightist publisher, although the facts of the case have always been uncertain. To the accompaniment of disorders, tension increased until a naval mutiny was attempted in October 1948. The military and conservatives said it was fomented by APRA, and apparently the latter had a hand in it. The APRA argument was that the old regime would not give new men and ideas a fair opportunity,

even when they clearly had majority support, and that experience showed no reliance could be placed on adherence to the Constitution by the traditional rulers of Peru. As the country vibrated to rumors that had everyone on edge, Bustamante outlawed the People's party. The military wanted more drastic measures and soon ousted Bustamante and took over themselves. Once again violence had been used to "solve" the problem of APRA.

Civil-Military Tensions, 1948–1968

For the next eight years General Manuel Odría dominated government, from 1950 to 1956 as president by virtual self-appointment. Odría as president maintained the forms of a democracy, but the Congress had little authority. APRA remained illegal, under constitutional provisions barring "international" political parties.[18] The administration promoted those measures of economic development, sometimes with nationalistic overtones, that were being adopted all over Latin America. Economic promotion was aided by the fact that officers of the armed forces now received advanced instruction (as in Brazil, Argentina, and other countries) in strategic subjects that included the economic bases of national strength. They were interested in certain types of modernization. Peru continued to derive income from plantation cotton and sugar and from the international mining companies. Industry grew some; even a steel enterprise was started. There was, however, no modernization of politics in the sense of broader participation, and economically and socially the great mass of Indian and mestizo poor scarcely was in communication with the rest of the nation. Odría permitted an election in 1956, and APRA helped elect its old enemy Manuel Prado for the term 1956–1962 and put some of its own members in the Congress.

---

[18] Odría agreed in 1955 to give women the vote, presumably because they were thought to be more conservative than men.

The Prado years saw a continuation of established trends without solutions that satisfied dissidents. He restored the legal status of APRA but soon found that he could not depend on it for support. Economic growth was better than in much of Latin America, with sizable exports and good foreign investment, but Peru remained a very poor country in terms of per capita income. Under Prado demands for agrarian and other reforms became louder but even in modest forms could not always be pushed through the Congress, where even APRA was acting, according to the leftist interpretation, like a conservative party. A great search for new oil deposits was being carried on by foreign companies, and nationalist sentiment was rising for more state control of all aspects of the industry. The expansion of national planning under impetus of the Alliance for Progress did nothing to convince nationalists or leftists that an adequate start was being made on the basic changes they thought necessary.

The electorate seemed ready in 1962 to give the country a new-style administration. Haya had tuned up the potent APRA machine, which irked the military. Ex-dictator and general Manuel Odría was back and put together a *Unión Nacional Odriista,* a confusing mixture of appeal to the masses and connections with his old conservative allies. Also running was Fernando Belaúnde Terry, who had appeared out of the blue in 1956 with a quickly hatched up Popular Action party (PAP) and almost won the election, thus indicating wide dissatisfaction with the old choices. Belaúnde was from a family with a great name and tradition in Peruvian life. Dean of the National School of Architecture, he had a pleasing personality, a dramatic oratorical ability, and an idealistic dream for his country. He advocated economic development, as who did not, and many sorts of reform, including actions to incorporate the Indian into the national life, the old cry of the *Apristas.* He was received enthusiastically by many middle-class and professional groups and was unusual among politicians in having some appeal among students.

Haya de la Torre received the largest vote, but less than the one-third required for election. Belaúnde was second. The Congress had to choose between the top two vote getters. Haya de la Torre failed in an attempt to make a deal with Belaúnde; then Haya and Odría agreed to give the latter the presidency and APRA control of the cabinet. The army scotched that arrangement on July 18, 1962, by ousting President Prado, dismissing Congress, declaring a state of siege, and announcing a new election for June 9, 1963. President Kennedy of the United States made a brief effort to discourage unconstitutional changes in government in Latin America by refusing to recognize the military regime. When he received little support from Latin American governments, Kennedy abandoned the effort. As had been demonstrated often before, not all Latin American governments responded automatically to pressures from Washington.

The junta was repressive and inept, but it permitted the 1963 election, by which Belaúnde received 39 percent of the vote, Haya de la Torre 34, and Odría 26. So the military had what they thought they wanted: almost anyone but Haya de la Torre. Not too long afterwards, they decided that what they really wanted was to run the country directly themselves, as many people had suspected and feared for some time.

Belaúnde faced formidable problems in 1963–1968, one being control of Congress by APRA and the Odría party. There was abundant opportunity for clashes between president and Congress, because Belaúnde's style was "action." His critics said that he acted for action's sake, that he was impulsive and ignorant, with an architect's fuzzy notion of "design" brought to a national scene unsuited to it. Belaúnde tirelessly traversed the country, promoting his ideas in his attractive way. Insofar as he increased awareness of national needs, that was a service itself. It did not improve his political support. His loose Popular Action party, plus collaboration with the small Christian Democratic party, was an inadequate base.

On the agrarian reform issue Belaúnde never

succeeded in pacifying either the conservative opposition or the leftist demand for a drastic solution. The matter seemed to be becoming acute in the early 1960s, with peasant invasions of great estates and some evidence of orchestration by Peruvian leftists and support from Castro's Cuba. The guerrilla activity Belaúnde downplayed for some time, insisting that it was small-scale, but finally in 1964 he declared that he opposed whatever communist activity might be involved in it. In 1965–1966 he permitted the army to pursue the guerrillas, and it virtually destroyed the movement. At the same time, in 1964, Belaúnde put through the Congress an agrarian reform law. Conservatives thought it radical; leftists, timid. It did not contemplate expropriation of large estates if they were well run.

Belaúnde also had to deal with the potentially explosive issue of foreign, especially petroleum, capital. It had been a political issue intermittently for many years, worsening in the 1950s and early 1960s. Legislation was passed to permit foreign oil activity only on a concession basis, and Peruvian profits from such operations slowly increased. Even so, they could not still the controversy because the International Petroleum Company (IPC), a subsidiary of Standard of New Jersey, had a valid contract giving it ownership of subsurface resources, entered into (by an earlier company) before the Constitution had reserved such resources to the state. Prado's administration in 1960 put through a plan, acceptable to IPC, for gradual nationalization of IPC, but nationalists wanted it done at once. The debate was heated by cries of *"Beltrán al paredón!"* (Beltrán to the wall!) that echoed the *fidelista* roar in Cuba for the liquidation of opponents, in this case Prado's premier. Before Belaúnde's inauguration, the United States Congress passed the Hickenlooper Amendment (1962), cutting aid to countries that expropriated United States–owned property without prompt and adequate compensation. Peruvian nationalists said it was a form of coercion and even intervention; in the United States it was argued that

it merely tried to establish reasonable norms in contractual relationships.

Belaúnde at the beginning of his administration had a bitter disagreement with IPC. He wanted the company to accept a thirty-year concession and a sixty-forty split in net profits, proposing that it be nationalized if it would not agree. The company was adamant, so the Peruvian Congress declared that IPC did not own outright the La Brea–Pariñas field it had claimed to own since 1922. Disagreement existed also as to the value of IPC holdings. Belaúnde revived an earlier suggestion that IPC owed large amounts of back taxes. Finally, in August 1968, Belaúnde and IPC agreed to an operating concession in place of the old claim to absolute and perpetual ownership and to forgiveness of the tax "debt."

Belaúnde also met extremist criticism from right and left with regard to the economy generally. Although Peruvian exports were at high levels, Belaúnde's public works policies and large military expenditures had pushed the government by 1966 into deficit financing and the country into a quickening inflation. The situation worsened in 1967–1968 and contributed to political instability. By mid-1968 prices were rising at an annual rate of 150 percent. Belaúnde had five cabinets in the year following devaluation of the *sol* in September 1967. Both Belaúnde's PAP and Odría's party began to split. There were rumors of military intervention. Only APRA retained its structure and seemed likely to benefit from the situation. No doubt that was one reason why the military in October 1968 seized the government, although it claimed that intervention was needed to bring to a satisfactory conclusion the petroleum issue and to move forward with other pressing national problems.

The Military's "National Revolution" Since 1968

The Peruvian military made clear that they believed the Peruvian political system had not performed well, no doubt encouraged by similar military judgments in other Latin American countries. Officers came to national government not to adjust and repair and pacify but to stay. General Juan Velasco Alvarado, president of the junta, ruled without a Congress. He and his fellows declared that they headed a "national revolution" in the people's interest, that it was nationalistic and progressive, even socialistic, but not communistic, and that it aimed at more "human" government. The regime began interfering with the press almost at once, but it backed off, receiving credit for good intentions, and did not destroy freedom of the press until 1974. Statements were issued to the effect that the military dictatorship might last a long time, although Velasco in 1971 said they aimed ultimately at "participatory democracy." Another general in 1974 stated that the armed forces would remain until civilian groups were "ideologically equipped" to take over. Over the years other equally ambiguous hints were aired.

Many Peruvians and outside observers overlooked the authoritarian features because of what they considered the sanitary nature of socioeconomic policy. Within a week of the coup, the regime expropriated most of IPC's property. That move was popular in Peru. The military handled the issue astutely. They upped the estimate of IPC's debt in back taxes to $690 million, which meant that Peru could deduct compensation for IPC property out of the asserted debt and claim a balance due. The legal issues involved were intricate, of no interest to most people, and by now irrelevant; the issue was a political one. The regime survived a flurry of retaliation by the United States government and a fleeting fear among foreign investors. By 1970 it was making new agreements with foreign companies for petroleum exploitation. Soon United States companies were back in the business, under contracts with PETROPERU, the government oil agency. The military deserved the credit it received from Peruvians for a masterly performance. Unfortunately, not much oil was found. Peru still had an oil deficit, and by 1975 the foreign companies were pulling out.

The military did equally well with other nationalistic measures. The Cerro de Pasco Corporation, W. R. Grace, and others were expropriated with compensation in a series of moves that briefly shook private investors, but the latter came surging back to pour more money into mineral and other enterprises. The military continued support for the Peruvian claim to control of fisheries in a two-hundred-mile band of sea off their coast. The claim had grown out of the rise of the fish-meal industry in the late 1950s. The cool Humboldt Current from Antarctica brought to the west coast of South America vast quantities of anchovies which were eaten by sea birds, which then defecated *guano* on the dry coast and adjacent islands; a century earlier Peruvians sold the *guano* to Europe.[19] In the 1950s the Peruvians discovered they could sell fish meal (and some oil) for animal feed and fertilizer. It quickly became a huge industry, built with great skill by Peru. By 1963 Peru passed Japan as the world's greatest fishing nation. Fish meal came to account for over 40 percent of Peru's exports. But fishermen from several nations went to the Humboldt Current on the supposition that it was a common heritage of all people, so long as they stayed outside the ancient three-mile limit. Peru, Ecuador, Chile, and soon many other nations argued that the three-mile limit was obsolete, that two hundred miles was more reasonable from the point of view of their development, and they proceeded to seize foreign fishing vessels within that area. The military regime naturally received support for adhering to this policy.[20]

The military regime handled the agrarian reform problem with such vigor and imagination as to leave the opposition confused. When the military took over, about 2 percent of the population owned 90 percent of the productive land. By 1975 the government expropriated—often with compensation—on the order of 11 million acres, turning much of it into farm cooperatives supervised by military officers and elected assem-

[19] See Chapter 28, Section b.
[20] See Chapter 34, Section a.

blies. The program affected nearly a million people, and parts of it were so well managed that in some cases production was not damaged. On the other hand, part of agriculture continued to do poorly. The reform did quickly shatter the ancient hold of the *latifundio* (individual and corporate) in Peru. It did not, however, take care of half the subsistence farmers of Peru. Some of the successful cooperatives made so much money that the members resisted suggestions that they sacrifice to aid their less fortunate brethren. They also were accused of exploiting laborers hired from outside the cooperatives. Finally, they rejected progovernment slates in electing cooperative assemblies. How the military would resolve that bundle of problems remained to be seen.

The military presided over a country more than twice the size of France[21] with a rapidly growing population that went from 7 million in 1940 to some 15 million in the mid-1970s. It suffered the common Latin American rush to the city. As early as 1960 some 400,000 persons, mostly migrants from the Indian highlands, lived in *barriadas* (shack towns) that ringed Lima. Metropolitan Lima, with its *barriadas*, grew from 1.4 million in 1961 to 2.9 million in 1973, posing problems that might make any government despair. Although the government made sizable efforts in education and claimed more than 60 percent literacy, some of those were functionally illiterate. Much of the population was badly housed. Although the regime emphasized incorporation of the Indian into the national life, serious problems remained of language and of race and class prejudice. The money income of most Peruvians was small; even the official per

capita average in the 1970s was said to be under $300.

After World War II Peru often achieved a higher economic growth rate than much of Latin America. Export growth was good and better diversified than in many countries, with important shipments of cotton, sugar, fish meal, and copper and other metals. The military regime did not do so well with food production. What it clearly did was greatly increase state participation in the economy, but without eliminating private enterprise. There was much doubt as to the regime's intentions with regard to the latter.

Despite those doubts, the regime did not arouse the fears domestically or internationally that the Allende government did in neighboring Chile. The United States government took some actions against the regime, but no such interruption of foreign investment occurred as in the case of Chile. In 1972 Peru received huge refinancing aid from United States banks. In 1973 the United States government ended its pressure on international lending agencies, and the World Bank lent half a billion dollars to Peru for development. In 1974 a Peru–United States agreement awarded compensation to eleven companies whose properties had been expropriated. The government remained authoritarian, but leftists and others clung to their approving attitude, both because of the help the generals were giving the peasants and the thumping they gave corporations based in the industrialized nations, and because of their dismay at the growth in other Latin American nations of military governments they liked less.

In 1974–1975 there occurred a series of events that tested yet further the affection of observers for the Peruvian military. In 1969 the regime had interfered with the press, but it drew back from drastic action. Interference during the next five years was weak enough so that there was brave prediction that the military love for free discussion compensated for its distaste for conventional representative government. Then in 1974 General Velasco took over most publications on the grounds that they were "counterrevolutionary"

---

21 The boundary with Ecuador was not satisfactory to the latter. Peru occupied large areas in the lowlands east of Ecuador, possibly rich in petroleum, which Ecuador considered its own. The historical materials on the boundaries were so contradictory and ambiguous as to permit various interpretations. After military clashes in the early 1940s, a negotiated settlement was made in 1942, giving Peru most of the disputed territory. The pact was guaranteed by Argentina, Brazil, Chile and the United States. The Ecuadorans soon repudiated the agreement, and there were flareups of demands and border skirmishing.

and served foreign interests. Although the new publicly owned newspapers were said to serve such interest groups as peasants, professionals, and industrial labor, the government kept them on short rein. Predictably, many partisans of rapid change throughout the hemisphere clung to the view that, although despotic government generally was bad, in some cases eggs had to be broken to make properly sanctified omelets. The "Peruvian model," as the jargon went, was worth a little sacrifice.

General Velasco developed a strong military opposition as his policies damaged the country's financial condition, and in September 1975 he was ousted by the moderate majority of officers in favor of General Francisco Morales Bermúdez. Morales turned to more encouragement of private enterprise, which was not pleasing to those who hoped that the "revolutionary" military was committed to socialism. Foreign and domestic business interests were pleased, however.

But continuing financial troubles led Morales to use control of the press, the state of siege, and other repressive measures. The regime was committed to heavy expenditures for social services, payment for nationalized properties, industrialization in high-cost and protected enterprises, and consumer subsidies. Those burdens were worsened by the fact that world prices declined for copper, sugar, fish meal, and other Peruvian exports. The government persistently spent more than its revenues, while the foreign debt by the end of 1976 was $5 billion, a huge sum for Peru. Foreign lenders stated that "austerity" was the price of more loans. But the military services insisted on continuing imports of expensive weaponry. Morales did apply some austerity to laborers, while raising wages for the military and police. The natural result was popular unrest. In July 1977 strikes led to killings by government forces. Organized labor and the military government were at odds, a far cry from the "military-popular" alliance of a few years earlier. The so-called Peruvian model had lost its luster.

So the regime, trying to recapture some popular support, declared in late July 1977 that a constitutional assembly would be elected in 1978 and a civilian government would be chosen in 1980. That stimulated activity by APRA and Popular Action, but it remained to be seen whether they could act effectively. In the nine years of the military government they never had agreed on common political action. As in most Latin American countries, party leaders usually were more interested in their own careers than in national problems, even unconstitutional and authoritarian government.

Peru had achieved a measure of "controlled" change, some of it clearly modernization, under a military regime that was considered bourgeois by the left and leftist by the right. Possibly "developmental authoritarian nationalism" was as good a label for it as any. The role of the government in the economy had greatly increased. The military appeared determined to exercise an important, even a dominant, role. It seemed unlikely that international socialism or international capitalism would be allowed to control the new Peru. Possibly the most important "dependency" would be on domestic military authoritarianism.

43 The Cuban Hurricane

The Castro communist hurricane struck without warning and devastated the confidence of experts who thought they could predict Latin American events. It occurred in one of the more modernized Latin American nations, so the fear and the hope arose that it might occur in any other. Oceans of verbiage were spilled—by left and right and by United States intelligence services—trying to explain what had happened and whether and where it could happen again. Certainly, dissatisfaction in Cuba was due to poor performance by the political and economic elites in 1898–1958. According to one view, that might be partially explained and excused by the handicaps of inexperience and the curtailment of choices during the United States protectorate until 1933.[1] The excuse was less plausible, however, for the years after 1933, when Cubans had more leeway to determine political institutions and public policy (except in the view of Marxists). In any event, it was a key failure of the elites that, although Cuba became well-off materially by Latin American standards, it failed to give the numerous poor citizens confidence in a better future.

Cuba was so mismanaged by the elites as to make relatively easy the conquest of power by a political genius, Fidel Castro, who swept away

the old society like a hurricane, making of the new Cuba a socialist economy and a communist despotism. That political genius was the force that seems to explain best the astonishing transformation in Cuba, and the speed of its conversion. Compared with those processes, the much argued question of United States "responsibility" is a minor matter. Castro's astounding success suggested the leadership of a man of unusual quality, but also a weakness in Latin American society even greater than suspected, since he imposed communism on Cuba with less outside help than had accompanied other communist conquests since 1917. It may be, however, that his success was counterproductive for communism in Latin America generally. It alerted the traditional elites, including the military, and it sensitized the United States to the possibility of similar transformations. By the late 1970s no other leftist dictatorships existed in Latin America, whereas rightist dictatorial regimes predominated in the area.

a. Failure of the Elites, 1930s–1950s

Much of the mismanagement lay in the large role played by that talented manipulator Fulgencio Batista. He ran the country through seven successive puppet heads of state from 1933 to

---

[1] See Chapter 33, Section d.

Politics and Nationalism

The new communications media, growing nationalist sentiment, broadened social welfare measures, new weapons in the hands of governments often dominated by the traditionally important military element, and pressures from the cold war—all have affected political activity in recent decades.

Juan Perón of Argentina, shown below with his wife Eva, depended heavily on the microphone—and on military force. Fidel Castro of Cuba (above), caught in a typical oratorical stance, uses the same props to power. *Courtesy of Wide World Photos*

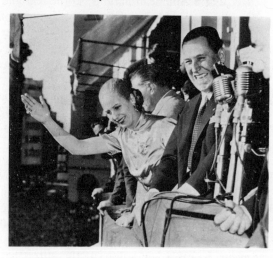

Colombian guerrillas in the 1960s. Rural violence and urban terror have sometimes been rather serious problems in Latin America, especially in the 1960s and 1970s. Many of the participants are very young. *Courtesy of United Press International*

Cold war international competition, linked with the drive to nationalism, has influenced events in Cuba. In 1962, Soviet-built military equipment paraded through Havana. *Courtesy of Wide World Photos*

President Truman as the Statue of Liberty holding up a lynched black. Such bitter anti-United States propaganda has been widely distributed; this particular cartoon emanated from the Argentine General Confederation of Labor in 1952 during the Perón dictatorship.

The library of the National University of Mexico, a tribute to the new spirit of national pride and commitment to education. The mosaic by Juan O'Gorman depicts Mexican cultural history since pre-Columbian times. *Courtesy of American Airlines*

1940, then took over the presidency himself from 1940 to 1944. Batista permitted the election over his own choice in 1944 of Ramón Grau San Martín, the professor who had seemed so radical to Washington in 1933. Seldom was promise of reform more shattered by timidity and incompetence. His successor, Carlos Prío Socorrás, proceeded to establish an even less enviable record in 1948–1952. In 1952 Batista seized the government without difficulty and established a dictatorship. There simply was insufficient organization of vital reform elements during the years 1933–1958, so that government fell to shoddy plunderers and meaningful opposition to extremist groups; while the middle class and the rich either participated in the carnival or acquiesced, and men and women in the street and the field despaired of the political system.

Batista, through control of the military and police, kept in hand an instrument of coercion that played a key role in his career. He had political ability, however, and used a big smile, bribery, public expenditures, favors, even social improvements to gain some reputation as a statesman. In 1933–1944 many kind things were said about him that were forgotten in 1952–1958. He even to a small extent promoted economic nationalism and diversification. That, and social expenditures, necessitated increases in the bureaucracy, and the middle class was happy to find openings in its traditional refuge.

Government and politics in 1933–1958 were stagnant and rotten. There were four major political groups: the Cuban Revolutionary party (PCR, known as the *Auténticos*—authentic revolutionaries), the Batista clique and coalitions, the conservatives (consisting of several parties), and the Popular Socialists (Communists). Party programs were the playthings of the ambitious and greedy. When the *Auténticos*—created by Grau San Martín in 1934—achieved power in 1944–1952, all they authenticated was their lack of principle. Graft was so prevalent in 1933–1958 as to make Cuban administration a mockery. Much of the lush revenue from sugar went into the pockets of individuals in or on the fringes of government. Tax rates were high by Latin American standards but not enforced. Immense graft led Eduardo Chibás in 1946 to break off from the *Auténticos* and form the *Ortodoxos*, and the latter briefly seemed to offer a refuge for honest people.

A feature of Cuban politics was *pistolerismo*. The revolutionary bands that formed against Machado continued after his fall, many merely the instruments of cliques bent on power and loot. Some of their activity was to control illegal income, some to achieve key positions in the bureaucracy. Assassinations and shoot-outs were common. No rational and progressive political system could develop beside such gangsterism, encouraged by a lack of organized public objection and by lack of faith in the administrations. Student organizations were almost entirely given over to politics and violence, justified by participants as the only means of dealing with a hopelessly corrupt political culture.

The Communist party had considerable success. Founded in 1925, it became important in the 1930s. It built a strong base in organized labor, an element favored by Batista in the 1930s. In 1939 the communists organized the Cuban Confederation of Labor (CTC), which claimed a membership of hundreds of thousands. The party also was active in propaganda, with a newspaper and radio station. Party militants may have numbered as many as 150,000 in the mid-1940s. Batista cultivated the left from time to time. The Communist party had been outlawed under Machado from 1925 to 1933, was legalized in the first Batista period in 1938, then outlawed in his second regime in 1953. Havana became well known as a major center of international communism in Latin America.

The Cuban economy was one of the richest in Latin America but heavily dependent on sugar and on the connection with the United States, and its growth generally was slow in 1933–1958. There had been a rapid growth of per capita income in the decades from independence to the

1920s, when it was one of the highest in Latin America: about $200 per capita, compared with $600 in the United States. In the 1950s Cuban income per capita was some $500, very high for Latin America, but population growth prevented much per capita improvement.

Export income, more than 80 percent from sugar, was high for Latin America, going from $186 million in 1937 to $427 million in 1944, then to $746 million in 1947, and oscillating considerably thereafter. In the 1950s world overproduction ordinarily confined the Cuban sugar crop to 5 to 6 million tons. About half of it continued to go to the United States under the quota system, with the premium above world prices, which in effect had to be spent for imports from the United States. The world sugar picture, together with increasingly strong Cuban regulation, halted United States investment in the industry. Cubans bought back much of it. They owned only 22 percent in 1939, nearly 50 percent in 1949, and by the late 1950s more than 60 percent. By that time Cuba held the third largest concentration of United States investments in Latin America, although its rate of increase was slow. United States investment in Cuba was slightly over $1 billion, only a quarter of it in sugar and the largest block in public utilities.

Cubans did something to diversify their agriculture and increase industry. Some agricultural changes of note occurred in the 1950s, but food still was imported. The industrial plant was fifth in size in Latin America (after Brazil, Argentina, Mexico, and Chile), although mostly in sugar and food processing. Cuban-protected manufactures were expensive due to the limited market, the need to import materials, and high labor charges.

A distressing feature of the economy was high unemployment and underemployment, as in many other Latin American countries. The sugar industry used much seasonal labor. Landownership was heavily concentrated. Caloric intake and health conditions were good for Latin America.

The population was more urban than in most Latin American countries, and the educational picture was better. Adult literacy was 60 percent by the end of the 1920s, and increased a bit more in the late 1940s and early 1950s, but drastic improvements in that or in the quality of education apparently were not going to occur. The labor confederation claimed over a million members, but many were not active. There were relatively few strikes, since government tended to meet wage demands, and pay was high by Latin American standards. The government protected industrial workers from dismissal. Social insurance was provided only to bureaucrats and organized labor, with low benefits. Many pension plans were in existence by the 1950s, although they were far from ideal.

A World Bank report in 1951 noted the excessive reliance of Cuba on sugar and on the United States for foreign trade and investment capital. It also suggested more industrialization and variety in agriculture. But those recommendations were difficult to carry out because people in sugar (increasingly Cubans) resisted agricultural change, and enlargement of protected manufactures competing with imports from the United States implied the likelihood of retaliation against the sugar quota. In any event, such changes in a small country with limited expertise and a small market would be difficult, as other Latin American nations had discovered and as Fidel Castro would learn after 1959. The anti–United States view has been that Washington critically constricted Cuban alternatives; another view is that it curtailed them to some extent but that the Cuban government and private enterprise made poor use of the considerable alternatives that were available.

b. The War Against Batista, 1953–1958

When Batista seized power in 1952, Fidel Castro was a lawyer in his mid-twenties. Of middle-class family, Fidel's chief interest from student days was in politics. He was a participant in what later was called the Caribbean Legion, preparing in Cuba to attack Trujillo of the Dominican Republic in 1947.[2] He was a delegate to a student anti-imperialist meeting at Bogotá at the time of the *bogotazo* of 1948. After graduation as a lawyer, he chiefly occupied himself with the *Ortodoxo* party until Batista's coup, which he at once determined to oppose by force.

On July 26, 1953, Fidel led a band of nearly two hundred students, ex-students, and workers against the Moncada barracks at Santiago de Cuba. The attack failed and most participants were captured. At his trial, Castro delivered a speech later widely distributed under the title of its conclusion, "History Will Absolve Me," condemning the injustices of Cuban life and promising a return to the Constitution of 1940. He was released in a general amnesty in 1955. By then, his 26th of July Movement was being formed. Fidel moved to Mexico to join his brother Raúl, a veteran of the Moncada adventure and a Marxist. Also there were Che Guevara, a Marxist of Argentine origin, and a few other exiles. In December 1956 a group of eighty-two sailed in a launch from Mexico to eastern Cuba. All but a dozen were taken by Batista's forces. Fidel, Raúl, Che and the few others made their way to the difficult terrain of the Sierra Maestra.

There they slowly built strength, gathered arms, including some from abroad, and improved communications with 26th of July groups elsewhere and with other anti-Batista elements. For some time urban groups, especially in Havana, were more of a problem for Batista than the few guerrillas in the Sierra Maestra. By no means all the urban rebels were affiliated with the 26th of July Movement. One student group in March 1957 attacked the national palace and penetrated near Batista himself. Liaison between Castro and groups in Havana gradually improved. The Communists long refused to cooperate in the rebellion, that being Moscow policy. As late as April

1958, when Castro proclaimed an islandwide general strike, he seemed to have little hold on Havana; the strike failed there partly because of Communist noncooperation. In the summer of 1958 a loose agreement was achieved between Castro and various anti-Batista groups. The Civilian Revolutionary Front was created with José Miró Cardona as coordinating secretary-general. Miró Cardona was head of the Havana Bar Association and an internationally respected lawyer. He was representative of the middle-class business, intellectual, and professional support for the rebellion. In February 1958 more than forty civic, religious, and professional groups signed a public statement declaring that elections should not be held during a civil war and would be fraudulent under the suspension of constitutional guarantees imposed by Batista. Just after that statement, Miró Cardona told the press that Castro's rebellion deserved support and that Batista should give way to a "regime of neutrality." The Communists were not part of the Civilian Revolutionary Front, but just after its formation they came to an agreement with Castro.

All this time, since December 1956, Batista was using savage methods against the rebellion and losing prestige as a result. Castro was improving his reputation by his heroic effort and by the sympathetic publicity he received from foreign journalists, some of whom visited him in his refuge in the Sierra Maestra. The United States contributed somewhat to Batista's loss of support, both by its policies and by reason of intense propaganda by pro-Castro elements that tied Cuba's problems to North American intervention over the years. A part of Washington's problem was that so many important elements in and near the national government had a fetish about "stability" and automatically feared any change in regime that suggested even mild uncertainty. Batista also had some United States support because he had in his latest regime adopted a strongly anticommunist stand. It was charged that United States military aid to the

---

[2] See Chapter 41, Section b, on the Caribbean Legion and Central America.

Cuban government was used against progressive elements in the island. The United States ambassador until May 14, 1957, Arthur Gardner, was notoriously pro-Batista. His replacement, Earl Smith, arrived in Cuba in July with instructions to show impartiality in Cuba's internal affairs. Critics of Washington's policy declared, however, that impartiality was in fact support for Batista. On March 14, 1958, the United States put an embargo on arms shipments to Cuba, and critics said that would not restore to life the young men already slaughtered by North American guns in the hands of *batistianos*. By then many influential men in Washington chiefly hoped that the Cubans would arrive at some solution that would remove the pressure.

Under the Constitution Batista could not succeed himself as president, and he decided it was not politic to try. He scheduled an election for June 1958, found that conditions did not seem to favor it, and postponed it to November. Castro's declared policy became to prevent the election as a travesty on democracy, serving only the ends of the dictatorship. He threatened punishment, even death, to candidates and other participants in the election. By this time, a large part of the population had abandoned Batista. Economic production and the movement of goods and persons were seriously disrupted. The men of the Sierra Maestra had come down into the plains and opened "second fronts." Army officers saw that either their forces would be defeated or they would simply melt away, so they abandoned Batista. He fled the country on the last day of 1958.

c. The Revolution Threatened, 1959–1961

The Castro contingent in the victory over Batista said it would carry out a "real" revolution but it was careful how it said so, since it faced potential opposition in the Cuban propertied class and in the United States. That opposition soon arose, but the enemies of the regime did not show much perceptiveness in analyzing Castro's

strength or much skill or courage in trying to bring him down. Castro, on the other hand, brilliantly sold himself to the bulk of the population, isolated his local foes, and so confused the government of the United States that its measures against him ranged from the simply ineffective to the ludicrous.

Isolation of the Middle Class

The government set up at Havana in January 1959 consisted mainly of moderate civilians, with Dr. Manuel Urrutia as president, José Miró Cardona as prime minister, and Castro as commander in chief of the armed forces. Since it quickly became clear that Castro had no notion of consulting his colleagues, Miró Cardona resigned in February, as he said, "to end the duality of powers," and Castro became premier. During the early months, critics said that nothing was done properly because Fidel lacked experience and a plan of action. Probably, however, he had a clear plan in the sense of meaning to keep things sufficiently in his hands and fluid— even ambiguous—so that he could consolidate his hold on power. He certainly accomplished that.

Many characteristics of the new regime became apparent within a few months and made the middle classes uneasy. First, it said it would carry out a "real" revolution, achieving social justice and decent government, including alterations in the rules on property. Second, rule by decree was declared necessary, without congress or elections, to prepare for "real" democracy and representative government. Third, a new revolutionary army was used for political purposes. Fourth, dissident views were discouraged and denounced. Fifth, the regime objected to suggestions that its orientation was communist, but its middle-class collaborators increasingly considered that such an orientation was evident. Sixth, it meant to spread revolution by interference in the internal affairs of other Latin American nations: some leaders in those countries, including former supporters of Castro, denounced that effort in 1959.[3] Seventh, the United States evinced a growing distaste for the regime, which Castro declared amounted to intervention in Cuban affairs. The highly nationalistic regime demanded independence of foreign influence, including the relations between the Cuban bourgeoisie and United States corporate interests. Still, those sources of uneasiness existed in forms that permitted various interpretations, for Castro moved cautiously at first, and his timid enemies seized on excuses for inaction.

Castro's use of actual and threatened force in domestic affairs provoked great anxiety among the middle class. Raúl Castro ran the regular armed forces—purged of *batistianos*. They were supported by a large civilian militia. Military force always stood behind Castro's actions, as everyone knew. There were not going to be elections or a congress soon, as he frankly stated. Parties were prohibited, although the Communist party was in fact allowed to operate. Control and intimidation of the media began at once and grew progressively stricter. A program of indoctrination commenced, which put pressures on people who objected to aspects of the new regime. Soon, a generation gap appeared in the middle class, with some of the younger people welcoming the purge of the old corruption in Cuban life. Finally, Castro built a cult of personality unsurpassed in Latin American history.

Although most Cubans supported the early trials of *batistianos* by military courts, there was objection to the decision in March 1959 that the acquittal of forty-three airmen had been, as Castro said, a "grave error." Since Castro defined what was right and wrong, the airmen were retried. One of the bastions of the middle class, the organized bar of Cuba, protested. Many

other of Castro's actions and statements alarmed the lawyers and other members of the middle class. On February 2, 1959, he declared that he would transform Cuba in five years and that agrarian reform would be a principal base of that change. So fears grew in Cuba and outside that communist influence was at work. Raúl Castro and Che Guevara, top leaders of the 26th of July Movement, were thought to be communists. Chief of the favored newspaper *Hoy* was Carlos Rafael Rodríguez, a long-time prominent communist. Back from exile were such other prominent communists as Blas Roca and Lázaro Peña, labor czar of the 1930s and 1940s. Suggestions that the regime was communist appeared to infuriate Castro, who stated that such charges were made with ulterior motives. Once, in April 1959, however, he declared that in Cuba anticommunism was counterrevolutionary. Interpretations of Castro's interest in communism occupied analysts throughout the hemisphere, undeterred by reliable information on the subject.

Washington's actions for some time did little to aid the middle class in Cuba or to damage Castro, partly because a debate raged in the United States as to the character of the regime. Castro cleverly fostered the difference of opinion with a blend of criticism of the United States, declarations of dedication to democracy, and emphasis on his pursuit of social justice. Thus, not until he promulgated an agrarian reform law did opposition to him solidify. Castro had spoken of agrarian reform in the Sierra Maestra and later, in February 1959, said it would be the basis of a revolutionary transformation of Cuba. Not many people cared to object to reform that was needed in most of Latin America. In Washington in April Castro told the press that the next big stage of his revolution would be agrarian reform, including land expropriations, with organization of cooperatives rather than seizure of land by the government. Such statements provoked some uneasiness, nothing more.

Promulgation of the Agrarian Reform Law, on May 17, 1959, did much more; it convinced many

---

[3] In March José Figueres of Costa Rica, a moderate liberal who had sent aid to Castro in the Sierra Maestra, told him in Havana that Latin America would support the United States against the Soviet Union in a war. Castro replied that Figueres was no revolutionary and that Cuba would be neutral in a United States–Soviet conflict.

people of Castro's radical intentions. The law limited farm holdings to 999 acres and pastoral holdings to 3,333. Excess lands were to be expropriated, with compensation in twenty-year bonds not convertible into dollars. The value of the lands was that declared for taxes in 1958, which, as in all Latin America, was notoriously under market value. All shareholders in companies owning sugar lands had to be natives. In the future, foreigners would not be allowed to buy or inherit agricultural lands. Companies were given ninety days to comply. Small private holdings and cooperatives were to be created out of the expropriated lands. The law created a National Institute of Agrarian Reform (INRA), to be headed by Castro, who soon appointed as operating head of INRA A. Núñez Jiménez, a communist. The United States sent Castro a note stating doubts as to the adequacy of the compensation, but recognizing Cuba's right to expropriate and expressing sympathy for land reform.

The enemies of the regime increased their efforts, and Castro moved against them, on June 2, 1959, announcing discovery of a counterrevolutionary plot, chiefly among the middle class. Castro said it showed the continuation of United States support of Cuban reactionaries. A former president of the Cuban Senate criticized the agrarian reform on television and asked that a date be set for elections. The next day Castro dismissed five moderate ministers. On June 15 the regime's publication *Revolución* declared that if imperialist agents landed in Cuba, 6 million Cubans were ready to die in its defense. Also in June, the chief of the air force, Major Pedro Díaz Lanz, resigned on the grounds that communists were too influential in the military establishment. He fled to the United States. On July 2 Castro stated that Cuba would not accept interference by any nation or international body, the latter referring to the charge of the Dominican Republic before the OAS that it faced invasion organized by Cuba and Venezuela. Castro claimed that the resignation of Díaz Lanz was part of a plan to accuse Cuba improperly of communism. Shortly after this, Díaz Lanz testified

before a subcommittee of the United States Senate that Castro was a communist. That helped Castro's identification of his enemies in Cuba as collaborators with foreign interests.

On July 17 Minister of State Roa denounced the United States for conspiring with the Dominican Republic against Cuba. On that day Castro on television said he resigned the premiership and that President Urrutia had joined Díaz Lanz in a plan to defame the government and was against the revolution. Urrutia resigned, and Osvaldo Dorticós was named president. Huge rallies were held in Havana later in July, at which the multitudes, being asked by loudspeaker, roared that Castro should resume the premiership. He agreed to do so. At that rally, masses of country folk (*guajiros*) marched, waving machetes, past a reviewing stand that included Castro and Lázaro Cárdenas of Mexico. How could the middle-class politicians just forced from office compete with such a machine, the more potent in that Castro offered the ordinary Cuban a better life with what seemed to be complete sincerity? All Cubans had to do was accept his arrangements without question, and most seemed willing to do so.

In late July Castro said there would be no elections for four to five years. In August he claimed to have broken a conspiracy that included wealthy landowners unhappy with the expropriations. In September 1959 Major Huberto Matos, an old associate of Castro's, objecting to the influence of communists, resigned from the armed forces, and Castro jailed him as a traitor.[4] In December the Confederation of Cuban Workers withdrew from the free world regional labor organization (ORIT) on the grounds that it was an "agency of imperialism." The communists Raúl Castro and Che Guevara were given cabinet-level posts. The middle class, increasingly isolated and outmaneuvered, began a migration that would become one of the great movements of population in modern times.

---

[4] He was still in jail in 1977.

The Defeat of Washington, 1959–1961

From January to May 1959, before the agrarian reform decree, United States–Cuban diplomatic relations were cool. Neither government was enthusiastic about the other. Castro criticized what he called more than fifty years of United States intervention and charged that it was threatening to reduce the sugar quota to maintain Cuban subservience. Cubans had come to consider the system of arranged exchange of sugar for United States manufactures—even if the sugar price was above the world figure—a detestable badge of colonialism or dependence. Castro effectively excited this nationalist sentiment, which declared that the United States dominated not only the Cuban economy but its political life and its culture generally.

In April 1959, however, Castro acted pleasantly during a visit to the United States and UN headquarters in New York. Although it was "unofficial," at Castro's request he was received by the vice-president and secretary of state in Washington and received general offers of economic aid, which he declined. He told the press there that his heart was with the democracies, he was not a communist, and he opposed intervention by one country in the affairs of another. Most people were disposed to believe him.

Soon after his return to Cuba, however, the agrarian reform decree of May loosed an avalanche of debate in the United States and Latin America. There were cries that it meant a move toward communism and retorts that such views identified the ignorant and reactionary. Some critics thought that a radical turn was also indicated by an April invasion of Panama by a little group that included Cubans, June expeditions from Cuba of Dominican exiles against Trujillo's Dominican Republic, and Cuban support in July of invasions of Nicaragua by dissident elements. In August President Betancourt of Venezuela criticized Castro for controlling the press and not calling elections. In September Castro was at UN headquarters again, advocating neutralism in the cold war, working with the Asian-African

bloc. Also in September, Cuba agreed to sell 330,000 tons of sugar to the Soviet Union. In October the student organization at the University of Havana was put under an army officer; planes piloted by Cuban exiles flew from the United States to drop leaflets, and Castro said they bombed Havana and cane fields.

During the later months of 1959 the Castro regime became strident in criticism of the United States, charging that it meant to use force against Cuba. Although Washington thought the trend in Cuba ominous, it took little action, and some Latin Americans praised its "patience." The CIA as early as December 1959, however, was recruiting Cuban exiles. In January 1960 Washington protested the seizures of United States citizens' property, while reiterating that it sympathized with land reform. It claimed that Castro made insulting statements about the United States and ordered the ambassador home to Washington for consultations. There was speculation that more drastic action impended, including a request by the administration to the Congress for authority to change sugar quotas.

Events in Cuba in early 1960 increased suspicions in the United States that the regime was communist. The labor confederation was purged in favor of communist leadership. By the end of January, INRA had completed or begun intervention in 8 million acres of land. By February most private property in Cuba was tightly controlled by the government. Also in that month, Soviet First Deputy Premier Mikoyan concluded a pact with Cuba for a credit of $100 million to buy equipment in the Soviet Union, while the latter agreed to buy 5 million tons of sugar over a five-year period. Thus, the loss of United States capital, goods, and military support was taken care of. A debate went on in the United States as to whether Castro wanted a Soviet connection or had been driven to it by the United States. A parallel dispute was over the question of whether Cuban–United States negotiations were now impossible or whether the door was always open to whatever initiatives the United States had sufficient "imagination" to try.

Relations worsened as Cuba rapidly developed a socialist economy and communist polity. In March 1960 Castro denounced the Rio Pact of 1947, which bound Latin American republics and the United States to help each other against attack from outside the hemisphere. He declared, as he had before, that the OAS was dominated by the United States. Also in March 1960 Castro used strong language to claim that United States sabotage had caused the French vessel *La Coubre* to explode in Havana harbor while unloading munitions. Officials in the United States were weary of the unceasing barrage of abuse directed at the United States from Cuba. That same month President Eisenhower authorized the training of Cuban exiles for possible use against Castro.

In June 1960 Castro ordered United States–owned refineries in Cuba to process petroleum from Soviet tankers; when they refused, he seized the refineries with another argument that the United States was trying to dominate Cuba. Very shortly, in July, Eisenhower virtually ended Cuban sugar sales to the United States, which Castro had been accusing him of planning since early 1959. If that did not "drive"—as some people charged—Castro into the arms of the Soviet Union, it accelerated the process. Khrushchev threatened later in July to use rockets to protect Cuba. Then in August Castro expropriated major United States properties in Cuba, valued at some $1 billion. Washington in October embargoed most exports to Cuba. With Cuba now a factor in the cold war, relations between Havana and Washington were extremely bad when, in January 1961, Castro in an offensive manner demanded that the United States reduce its embassy to eleven persons. Eisenhower seized the order as a pretext to break off diplomatic relations.

One reason for Castro's belligerence was suspicion, and by late 1960 knowledge, of United States preparation for an armed attack on Cuba. The Eisenhower administration planned to aid refugees in mounting an expeditionary force. The new president, John Kennedy, in January 1961 continued this scheme. Both administrations wanted a cheap way of overturning Castro, preferably through refugee activity in which the United States would participate visibly only before the landings in Cuba and thus could claim not to have "intervened." The CIA guaranteed such a cheap scheme by developing the notion that Castro's popular support was weak, so that a small landing would lead to a large uprising. Most Latin American experts outside the government and many inside, however, thought Castro's support was strong. The Kennedy administration lost its nerve and decided that it would chop off its involvement short of the beaches in Cuba. It thus could and did claim no "direct" military involvement. It thus also gave insufficient support to the invasion, training the force in the United States and in Guatemala, ferrying it to Cuba, and abandoning the Cuban exiles as the United States dumped them ashore. Castro easily rounded up the 1,200 Cuban invaders at the Bay of Pigs in April 1961. He had arms from the Soviet Union, the support of most Cubans, and a carefully constructed system of political defense.

Such a stunning disaster spoiled Washington's stomach for drastic action. After that it confined itself to lesser—and ineffective—weapons. United States officials decided that they faced a nearly unsolvable problem: damned if they used great force against tiny Cuba, damned if they let communism grow on their doorstep. Cuba and the Soviet Union had outfaced the United States. What small damage Castro suffered after the Bay of Pigs resulted mainly from his policy of trying to revolutionize Latin America, which turned traditional ruling groups against him and toward collaboration with the United States against his regime.

d. Making the Revolution

Castro made use of the division and confusion of his enemies via armed force, spying, denunciation, and terror. He also made a new society by changing attitudes, by what he often called education. He was aided by wide popular acceptance, resulting from his heroic legend, his overwhelming charisma, and the fervor and apparent sincerity of his promises and dreams. He also had the good fortune to come to power after the defeat of the national army, which he completely transformed into his own instrument; there was no military group with ties to the old regime to mount a counterrevolution. Finally, Castro had brains and ideas, and he turned Cuba into a continuous experiment, with everyone encouraged to participate in the struggle (*lucha*) to set up utopia. This had enormous appeal for the young and for those of all ages who had been alienated, frustrated, or abused, as well as for Cubans who saw in the revolution the opportunity to improve the nation's life and reputation.

At the core of the ongoing revolution was the conception that all activity was political. Thus, creation of the revolutionary person, the supporter of the new regime and the new ideal, was not left to political rallies, pamphlets, or television performances but went on in the school, the field, and the factory. Wherever people congregated, worked, or played, they were expected to *participate* in revolutionary organizations—simply belonging was not enough. In addition to this participatory role in the definition, execution, and defense of the revolution, political indoctrination went on in other ways—in advertisements, in songs, at recreation spots, everywhere. The revolution was all-embracing and all-consuming.

The Campaign Against Illiteracy.

Education for the revolution, together with primary and advanced instruction, began in early 1959. In the fall of 1960 a new National Commission on Alphabetization set up a much more elaborate organization with ramifications throughout the society. At the same time Castro told the UN General Assembly that the all-out offensive against illiteracy now beginning would undo the work of domestic tyrants and foreign exploiters who had imposed on Cuba an educational system that discriminated against the lower class. Now all

would receive, he said, proper skills and civic education.

In 1961 a big effort was made to use students, at least thirteen years old, with six years of schooling, in Conrado Benítez Brigades for teaching. They received training and then went out to their work. By the end of August 1961 some 300,000 Cubans, including the Benítez Brigades, were working as reading teachers. More than a million of the population of 7 million played some role in the campaign as students or teachers. Others participated through mass organizations, aiding the immense publicity efforts in favor of the literacy army marching to crush the foes of the revolution. Effective use was made of testimonial letters to Castro from new literates, helping this huge revolutionary mobilization to create a sense of national community and purpose.

Not only did the campaign promote national solidarity and belief in the revolution and its leaders, but it promoted proletarianism and distaste for the old rich and the bourgeoisie. The campaign was marked by that spirit of experimentalism that Castro emphasized when he said, "The revolution itself is our greatest teacher." It was marked also by the idea that all activity is political in its origins and in its solutions. Furthermore, in promoting national revolutionary solidarity the campaign concentrated on the countryside. An effort was made to show urban dwellers the problems of rural life, with some implication that such "revolutionary" virtues as selflessness, social conscience, and industry were found especially in the countryside. Castro meant to keep a strong rural base.

Committees for Defense of the Revolution.

Important institutions were the Committees for Defense of the Revolution (CDRs), created in the fall of 1960. They made up a "system of collective vigilance," by which people in a small area (block, factory, farm) would monitor each other's beliefs and actions. Castro had been considering such an action at least since March 1960, when *La Coubre* exploded in Havana harbor, suggesting the need for civil defense against sabotage and counterrevolutionary terror, some of which was being carried out by Cuban enemies of the regime. The CDRs, following the revolutionary formula, not only kept an eye on people but also promoted all the programs of the regime.

In late 1960 and early 1961 the government strongly emphasized the defense task, declaring that a United States–backed invasion was coming. When it came in April 1961, the CDRs rounded up thousands of suspected counterrevolutionaries. By that time the CDR system had about 8,000 committees and 70,000 members. It was only one of the instruments of the regime that the CIA had underestimated in advising that Cubans would rise against Castro. With the quick defeat of the Bay of Pigs expedition, the CDR system was greatly expanded. By September 1964 it had 2 million members in some 110,-000 committees.

Schools of Revolutionary Instruction.   Important to consolidation of the revolution were the Schools of Revolutionary Instruction (EIRs), secretly prepared in the latter half of 1960. They were secret partly because the political elements supporting the revolution still had not been perfectly melded under Castro's leadership. The formal opening of the EIRs came in January 1961, and from then until their termination late in 1967 they labored for the "ideological formation of revolutionaries" and through them for the ideological formation of the population. They were experimental and ever changing, learning within the revolution like all the institutions of the regime, but they always taught the local version of Marxism-Leninism in elite schools. Their initiation came several months before Castro publicly stated that it was a socialist revolution he was leading and nearly a year before his declaration in December 1961 that he was a Marxist-Leninist.

Confining intensive communist ideological training to restricted schools was the result of belief in an elite-dominated authoritarianism and the supposition that too much ideological

discussion would be divisive in Cuba at that time. There was ideology, of course, in educational and other programs from early 1959, but it was more general and emphasized nationalism and anti-imperialism rather than overt Marxism. The EIR students were carefully selected and at first went to full-time boarding institutions. There were only about 10,000 students in EIRs at the end of 1962. The history of the schools was affected by political developments in Cuba. They underwent great change in 1963, when creation of the *Partido Unido de la Revolución Socialista de Cuba* (PURSC) consolidated the political elements of Castro's support. Before then, as Castro said, groups and individuals who opposed him had adherents in the EIRs, but from then on the country was firmly on the road to communist socialism, dominated beyond question by one man.

Personal and Party Dictatorship.   The government was authoritarian from the beginning with no elections or legislature. Castro was leader of a minority group, even among those who had fought against Batista. Although he had declared his allegiance to the old constitutional system, he chose to pursue whatever his objective may have been as a revolutionary, using force to isolate or destroy rivals for power. Since he never deviated from that method, one must be skeptical of suggestions that he would have preferred democratic socialism if his internal and external enemies had permitted it. Political activity directed against Castro or communism was immediately discouraged and before long forbidden. In 1961 Castro openly identified the regime as communist and in December publicly announced his Marxist faith. Somewhat later he said that he had held that faith in the Sierra Maestra but knew better than to announce it too soon.

The media were completely controlled. Intellectual life was closely girdled wherever social controversy was possible; complaints had to be uttered with caution, because Big Brother's multitudinous agents were listening. Dissidents were clapped into jail. In the late 1970s it was widely believed that there were at least 20,000 political prisoners in Cuba. Castro also got rid of potential enemies by emigration, much of it illegal before 1965, when he gave permission for massive departures, retaining the emigrants' property. Some of the émigrés of the late 1960s and the 1970s were middle-class and professional people who had welcomed the Castro regime for its reforms and aspirations but then found much that they disliked in the new Cuba. By the late 1970s more than 600,000 Cubans had left. An equivalent population loss for the United States—where most of them went—would have been 13 million.

After guaranteeing his leadership, Castro still had to face friction among the new elites: between the veterans of the Sierra Maestra and others; between old communists and new converts to the faith; between partisans of different sorts of communism; and between supporters of various strategies for economic development and other matters. Over the years, Castro broke or isolated all the groups and individuals who opposed or displeased him.

The Integrated Revolutionary Organizations (ORI) were created in early 1961, fusing the 26th of July Movement, the Popular Socialist party (PSP—communist), and some other elements. During the rest of 1961 and well into 1962 the PSP played a prominent role in trying to meld factions into a revolutionary body organized into cells. The poor results led Castro in March 1962 to denounce the ORI as ineffective, an organizational mess riddled with personalism. He made a point of condemning a prominent PSP leader, Aníbal Escalante, as ambitious and critical of the heroes of the Sierra Maestra. Declaring he would save Cuba from the tyranny of the ORI cell system, Castro purged the ORI and set it to preparing the way for PURSC. That was succeeded in 1965 by the Cuban Communist party (PCC), an elite group with possibly 125,000 members in the late 1970s. Fidel dominated the PCC, aided by a directorate packed with military officers. For several years after 1965 Castro seemed satisfied with his domination of

party and government, until in July 1974 he began experimental elections of delegates of "organs of people's power" at the municipal level. They were followed by a new Constitution, adopted by the first national congress of the PCC, approved by a popular plebiscite, and proclaimed in February 1976. It gave top power to the PCC; provided that the elected municipal Assemblies of Popular Power elect a National Assembly of Popular Power, which chose from its members a Council of State, whose president was the chief of state. The National Assembly also designated the members of a Council of Ministers, the actual executive under the new system. In November 1976 elections began for 10,725 municipal deputies to the 169 new municipal assemblies, with candidates proposed by the PCC and other mass organizations. Communist "popular democracy" in Cuba now had the sanction of "elections." No one expected that Castro's power would decline under the new system.

e. International Relations of Communist Cuba

Castro's power after the Bay of Pigs was little damaged by external enemies, but they—especially the United States—made exporting revolution to the rest of Latin America, as he tried do, difficult. Castro called the United States the chief enemy not only of Cuba but of humanity. Washington said that Castro was a tyrant and part of an international conspiracy to erect communist dictatorships. United States actions consisted mostly of maintaining an economic, travel, and diplomatic embargo, and trying to get cooperation from the reluctant OAS nations. The OAS Council on December 4, 1961, with considerable opposition expressed, called the Eighth Foreign Ministers Conference for Punta del Este (Uruguay) to consider charges against Cuba. On December 6 the United States charged to the Inter-American Peace Commission that Cuba was a bridgehead of Sino-Soviet imperialism and a base for subversion, and in early January 1962 it made other charges. When the foreign ministers met, January 22–31, 1962, the United States asked for a trade embargo and rupture of diplomatic relations, and the Latin Americans protested that those would be interference in the domestic affairs of Cuba. There finally was unanimous agreement that the Castro government was communist and aligned with the Soviet bloc and that the principles of communism were incompatible with those of the inter-American system. But six nations—including Argentina, Brazil, and Mexico—would not exclude Cuba from the OAS, arguing that exclusion would violate its charter; a bare two-thirds, as required by the Rio Treaty, voted to exclude the "present" government of Cuba from participation in the inter-American system. Sixteen nations voted to suspend trade with Cuba in implements of war. The four countries included Brazil and Mexico. Fourteen nations broke relations by February 7, 1962, and eventually all but Mexico did so.

That meeting, however, marked the end of important OAS efforts against Cuba as a general delinquent. There was action later on Castro's effort to export revolution, which alarmed many Latin American leaders. In 1963 Castro made a sizable effort to bring down the Venezuelan government, the sort of liberal and noncommunist regime that might achieve modernization without revolution.[5] In December 1963 the OAS confirmed that Cuba had sent arms to Venezuelan rebels. A foreign ministers' meeting in Washington, July 1964, condemned Cuba for aggression and intervention against Venezuela. It also achieved a binding fifteen-to-four vote to cut relations and end trade with Cuba, but that included a "no" by Mexico and an abstention by Argentina. It was a fair guess that continued support for sanctions on Cuba could not be counted on. The OAS sanctions, in any event, did not damage Castro at home or end his efforts to subvert Latin American governments. There was much training of guerrillas and saboteurs in

Cuba. The United States, for its part, provided extensive aid to Latin American governments in counterinsurgency tactics, military civic action programs, and other aspects of controlling subversion.

The installation in Cuba in 1962 of Soviet rockets may have been partly in response to what Moscow perceived as United States weakness in the Bay of Pigs performance; if so, it was soon disappointed. President Kennedy in October 1962 put a naval quarantine on Soviet military shipments to Cuba, demanded that rockets there be pulled out, asked the UN Security Council to act against a threat to peace, and asked the OAS to invoke the Rio Treaty of mutual support against aggression. Amid fears of nuclear war, Soviet Premier Nikita Khrushchev agreed to Soviet removal of offensive rockets, under UN verification. When Castro forbade the verification, the United States did not insist. Some Soviet equipment was withdrawn, but the total Soviet military presence in Cuba continued to grow. Kennedy's acceptance of this meant that the likelihood of United States armed intervention in Cuba receded yet further. By the 1970s the Soviet navy, including submarines, was using bases in Cuba.[6] No crisis resulted. Cuba and the Soviet Union had had their way. Although the OAS supported the United States during the 1962 missile crisis, by the 1970s it had lost that concern.

Cuba's relations with the communist world expanded rapidly. The critical connection was with the Soviet Union, from which Cuba got diplomatic, economic, and military support. As the costs became burdensome, the Soviet Union insisted that Cuba accept advice on technical, economic, and administrative questions. The Soviet Union also objected to Castro's view that communist advance in the Third World should be via violent subversion and armed action. Castro expressed scorn for the Soviet policy of slower subversion within the parliamentary system. After

---

[5] See Chapter 42, Section b.

[6] And the United States retained its base at Guantánamo, which was a major affront to the nationalistic pride that Castro had so successfully stimulated in Cubans.

1965 he broke with conservative communist parties in the rest of Latin America. Friction developed with the Soviet Union because Castro insisted on controlling the PCC and purged old-line communists in favor of his own cronies. His conception of government included a dominant role for the armed forces rather than for the party, thus departing from older Soviet doctrine. But neither Cuba nor the Soviet Union wished to break off the collaboration.

Most Cuban trade was with the communist countries, especially with the Soviet Union. In 1972 Cuba accepted full membership in the international Soviet economic system (COMECON). Long before then, the Soviet Union was providing Cuba with massive credits. In 1973 Castro was so desperate for funds that he pledged Cuba's minerals for a Soviet loan, but at the same time the Soviets granted a generous extension in the repayment terms of the 4 billion dollars owed by Cuba.

Castro turned from his abortive—indeed, counterproductive—efforts to revolutionize Latin America to a Third World leadership role. He made gestures of friendship toward North Vietnam, then at war with the United States. In January 1966 he was host to the First Solidarity Conference of the Peoples of Africa, Asia, and Latin America, which discussed plans of action against imperialism and colonialism. Some of its more enthusiastic programs for subversion and terror led the OAS to vote eighteen to nothing (Mexico and Chile abstaining) to condemn such moves to extend wars of "national liberation" to America. In July and August 1966 Cuba hosted the Fourth Latin American Students Congress, sponsored by the Prague-based Communist International Students Union. Delegates from thirty-seven countries decided how to arrange communist control of universities in Africa, Asia, and Latin America, and created an Organization of Latin American Students to support subversion. In July 1967 Cuba greeted the First Conference of the Latin American Solidarity Organization. Leftist delegates came from all Latin American

countries. Castroites told pro-Soviets that power could not be won by peaceful means.

Before the end of the 1960s, the Cuban international position seemed stabilized. Latin American statesmen had lost their fear of Castro. His ability to induce revolution outside Cuba seemed limited, and the appeal of his political and economic claims was lessened by observation of reality in Cuba. Latin American statesmen were under political pressure to recognize Castro, to show independence of United States policy, to give a hand to a fellow *latino*, and to see if there were trade profits to be made in Cuba, since other nations of the world traded there as they could. By the early 1970s there was increasing support for returning Cuba to inter-American activity. In July 1975 the OAS voted an end to compulsory restrictions on Cuba. Several Latin American nations had diplomatic or trade relations with Cuba, and more would obviously follow. Support for normal relations grew in the United States. That received a setback with Castro's dispatch in the early fall of 1975 of troops to aid the communist-supported group in the civil war in Angola. But President Carter in early 1977 removed restrictions on travel by Americans to Cuba, and talks began on a possible regularization of relations. Even organized baseball in the United States favored renewed relations. It seemed likely that Washington would decide that relations with communist Cuba were as sanitary as with Yugoslavia and the Soviet Union.

f. The Socialist Economy

Most Cuban property was quickly converted to state ownership, including the great sugar lands, which became state farms run by INRA. Even more quickly, there was an egalitarian redistribution of income and of access to commodities, services, and amenities. There also was a redistribution of state expenditures, with more spent on economic development and education and health, and also more on military and security functions and on government propaganda. Many of the changes were welcomed by the majority of Cubans because they increased personal comfort, security, and welfare and because they appealed to nationalistic pride. The changes gave people a stake in a system that reduced dissatisfaction based on envy or outrage at injustice. For these reasons, to point out that Cuba had been one of the better-developed countries of Latin America before 1959 was misleading, because much of that development had seemed to many Cubans the possession of a small minority. Cuba had been a country especially subject to cyclical unemployment and underemployment during the "dead season" of the annual sugar cycle. Reducing the effects of that process on individuals alone was a great boon to many people.

The regime tried to create a new pride in labor and apparently did reduce the old disdain for grubby toil. On the other hand, the regime complained that there were excessive absenteeism, loafing, and other noncommunist delinquency. Furthermore, the new attitude did not create universal enthusiasm for "volunteering" labor outside the regular job. Nonetheless, people were not encouraged to complain about such essentially forced labor. Castro, after a big failure in the promotion of greater effort in 1970–1971, declared that the country was not ready for true communism; he increased emphasis on rewards for good work and touted the importance of productivity.

The regime early tried to diversify the economy, especially into manufacturing, to satisfy one of the major complaints of dependency. It found, however, that industrialization was a costly and difficult process, and Castro had to acknowledge a poor decision and return to emphasis on specialization in sugar for export. Trying for more income from that source, he pressed for larger output, and found that there were limits to Cuba's ability to increase cane production. Even more dismaying was realization that sugar income depended mostly on international demand and prices for sugar—which were not controlled by either Cuba or the United States. The price

in the late 1960s was three cents a pound; in 1971 it was six to eight cents; in 1974 it spurted to sixty-five cents; but the price soon fell again, and in early 1977 was less than eight cents, which barely covered production costs.

Sugar production in communist Cuba generally remained at 4 to 6 million tons annually, as in pre-Castro days. The state-operated collective farms did not improve output. Year after year Castro drove bureaucrats and students to the *zafra* (harvest) and himself wielded a cane knife. In 1970–1971 a drastic national effort was made to produce 10 million tons. It achieved 8.5 million but in the process badly damaged the rest of the economy. In succeeding years production fell back to normal levels, but still accounted for 90 percent of Cuba's export earnings. Castro accepted the shortfall in 1970–1971 as a failure, and it played a role in the new emphasis on rewards for production efforts. It remained to be seen how much Castro could reduce Cuba's dependence on sugar, or even its dependence on a single buyer—now the Soviet Union rather than the United States.

In all his economic efforts Castro had considerable aid from the communist bloc, especially the Soviet Union. It provided technical advice, exchanged commodities with Cuba, lent it money, and in the late 1970s sold it petroleum at less than the increased cartel price. The Cuban economy depended on the Soviet Union as it once had on the United States. The Soviets took a good share of the cane crop, at guaranteed prices, which sometimes were above the world price and sometimes under it. The Soviets for years counseled a cautious economic policy, with emphasis on sugar exports until other sectors could be soundly altered. It thus encouraged Castro to develop his economic relations with noncommunist countries, which did increase but still depended in important measure on the international price of sugar. Castro also in the 1970s increased borrowing and credits from noncommunist Europe and Latin America. Throughout the 1960s, on the order of three-quarters of

Cuba's exports went to communist lands, but it managed to reduce that proportion some in the 1970s. A sizable straw in the wind was the development in 1974 of exchange of sugar for Argentine motor vehicles. Since some of the vehicles were made by United States subsidiaries in Argentina, Washington tried to stop the trade, but found it impossible to stand against Argentine protests.

It was not clear how well the Cuban socialist economy performed or what its future would be. The regime did not encourage study of Cuban production and was secretive about its performance. The economy obviously operated well enough to maintain a healthy population and large military and educational establishments—with some subsidy (possibly $1 billion a year) from the Soviet Union. Rationing of food and other goods had been severe, however, and 1976–1977 was one of the more rigorous periods, as the low price of sugar tightened belts. New restrictions had to be put on the purchase of imported goods. Certainly, the new economic system wrought no miracles of production. Fidel in the late 1970s sometimes emphasized the poverty of Cuba, saying that if Cubans needed to adjust to that, so be it. He powdered such pessimism with rejection of "consumerism" as a goal, a code word more appealing to intellectuals than to ordinary consumers. How production would develop in the future was not evident, except that it would be done according to some sort of communist rationale.

g. Life in the New Society

A number of aspects of the new society clearly were improvements. A big effort was made in formal education, mixed with massive doses of political indoctrination. Cuba became more than 90 percent literate, a great achievement, even though literacy was rather high before 1959. Furthermore, the system of technical and higher education was greatly enlarged, although of course some subjects could be studied only from a Marxist perspective. These great efforts transformed the social landscape. Cuba was even able to export technicians. More important, universal access to instruction, together with state ownership of much of the economy, meant that the ordinary Cuban had more opportunity in choosing a career than before the revolution. In addition, progress in that career was more dependent on one's own efforts—so long as one collaborated with the communist order.

Health care was greatly improved, for which the ordinary person was profoundly grateful. Between better distribution of food and good medical facilities, the population grew rapidly, reaching about 9.5 million in 1974. Most people were also pleased with the new policies on living quarters. Rents were kept very low, and considerable new housing was put up. The regime greatly extended the recreational facilities available to the populace, some of which were previously confined to the members of exclusive clubs. Another large effort was poured into combatting race prejudice and discrimination against blacks, long prevalent in Cuba. Apparently it had some success.

The condition of individual expression was not so rosy. As in all communist countries, thinkers were free so long as they stayed "within the revolution," as the solemn restriction went. When the regime punished a well-known poet and made him crawl, admitting his ideological error, some European intellectuals finally found a flaw in the regime. People were discouraged from pointing out shortcomings in the system or grumbling; and slave labor (called by pretty names), jails, even the firing squad awaited dissidents.

Most people, however, seemed pleased with the regime or at least modestly satisfied; they grumbled only moderately, and presumably would resist forcible efforts from outside to change the system. But there was no real way of knowing how happy Cubans were because their opportunities to testify were so restricted. What Cubans would say about adjustments in the system if free elections were permitted no one could know, except that the results surely would be displeasing sometimes to the communist leaders.

The country, of course, contained numerous zealots who believed that no shortcomings of importance could exist in the new Cuba, that any surviving problems would yield to effort. They believed that Cubans had more decision-making authority than the citizens of capitalist countries and that all important changes were thoroughly discussed at places of work, in mass organizations, and in media that were proletariat- rather than capitalist-oriented. Certainly most Cubans were proud of what they considered a new independence from external influence. That was a great part of Castro's hold on popular affection. In addition, Cubans (and foreign eulogists of the system) to some extent accepted the defects of one-man rule because Castro was genial, human, not avaricious, not bloodthirsty, interested in common people, even willing to admit mistakes to some extent. No one worried much about what his successor might be like.

The ten other countries of Latin America achieved less modernization. In Bolivia in 1952 a revolution brought notable changes, but modernization was slow thereafter. Ecuador in the 1970s gained some enlarged opportunity from petroleum development. The other eight countries, all small and poor, included several in which there were major United States interventions—Haiti, the Dominican Republic, Guatemala, Nicaragua, and Panama. Their histories showed how difficult it was to make intervention serve North American ends and that intervention did not notably promote modernization.

a. Bolivia: A Poor Land's Struggles Since 1952

Near Stagnation to Mid-Century

Bolivia's efforts after Independence exhibited the worst features of *caudillismo, latifundio,* class division complicated by race, dependence on foreign capital, miserable transportation, and brutal poverty.[1] The small, basically Indian population lived mostly in the mountains, less than half the area of the country. The Chaco War, lost to Paraguay in 1932–1935, cost territory. It also increased nationalism among a few middle-class figures and army officers. Chief targets of the nationalist modernizers were the oligarchic political system and foreign capital in tin mining, virtually the only source of foreign exchange.[2] The mining corporations and great estate owners collaborated in the restrictive political and labor systems.

In the late 1930s and the 1940s some army officers and new-style civilian political leaders tried unsuccessfully to change national institutions. There were beginnings of propaganda to promote national integration by appreciation of the strengths of the Indians and their ancient culture. Colonel David Toro took power by coup in 1936, talked vaguely of socialism, and expropriated Standard Oil properties (1937). He was ousted in 1937 by another officer, Germán Busch, whose brief tenure (to 1939) saw adoption of a Constitution (1938) that included nationalization of subsurface resources. In 1940 conservatives in the army put at the head of government General Enrique Peñaranda. He gained notoriety for an army massacre of miners at Catavi in

---

[1] See Chapter 28, Section f, on Bolivia from Independence to the 1920s.

[2] There was also resentment against Standard Oil of New Jersey, which in 1922 took over the petroleum concessions of some other oil companies.

December 1942. The Indian miners had recently been organized and sensitized by new leaders. They were armed and used dynamite with abandon. Living in the bare high mountains in barracks and huts, abused by foreign companies and their own government, subject to accident and lung disease, fortunate to live to the age of thirty, they formed by the 1940s a core of resistance to tyranny and injustice that the army feared.

Also in Peñaranda's years, the National Revolutionary Movement (MNR) was organized by Víctor Paz Estenssoro, Hernán Siles Zuazo, and other middle-class intellectuals, and a mixed bag of socialists, other leftists, and nationalists. In December 1943 MNR and a military group ousted Peñaranda and put in Major Gualberto Villaroel as president. The regime's brutal treatment of opponents made enemies, and the United States criticized it as pro-Axis and fascist. It was toppled by rioting in July 1946. The MNR was forced underground and bore for a time a rightist reputation because of its identification with Villaroel, although many MNR leaders inclined to a variety of leftist solutions. The old conservative combination ruled again from 1946–1952, but it had problems. The price of tin fell. The MNR rebuilt underground on a nationalist and leftist basis. One member, a Marxist but noncommunist ex-miner, Juan Lechín, made progress among the miners. In the fall of 1949 MNR tried a revolt that involved severe fighting and almost succeeded. In 1951 the government permitted MNR to run Paz in an election, but when MNR won 45 percent of the vote, the military took over the government.

The Civilian National Revolutionary Movement, 1952–1964

In 1952 the MNR rose again, with aid from the *carabineros* (national police), and defeated the army with considerable bloodshed. MNR ran the government in 1952–1964. Paz was president in 1952–1956 and 1960–1964, Siles Zuazo in 1956–1960. Leadership jealousies and differences of belief divided the party. Paz and Siles were of the moderate wing of MNR. The United States made a considerable investment in economic and technical aid and budgetary support to bolster Bolivian development and stability. That helped the MNR regimes, but stability was as little in evidence as ever, with constant financial crises, strikes, riots, kidnappings, states of siege, plots, and rumors of military coups.

The MNR tried to protect itself by reducing the army and talked of eliminating it or transforming it by confinement to such useful and purifying tasks as road building. Elimination was rejected because an army was needed for national defense and especially for internal security. Furthermore, MNR hoped it had neutralized the army by creation of popular militias, especially among peasants and miners, but the militia never became an effective military instrument.

The most striking change brought by the revolution was eradication of *latifundio*. In 1950, 1 percent of the landholders owned about half the land. Changing that situation was a goal of MNR, although some of its middle-class leaders rather feared a drastic land reform. In any event, peasants immediately began to seize the estates. The economic and political position of the feudalistic estate owners was destroyed, and the term *indio*, so long a badge of inferiority, was replaced with *campesino* (peasant).

Independence, land, and dignity for the rural population not only made a revolution in itself, but altered political conditions in favor of modernization. It did not, however, immediately improve production. In 1953–1954 agricultural output fell nearly 50 percent. Mountain farmers were encouraged to move to the more productive, largely unused eastern lowlands, but results were slow because of Indian conservatism and the cost of development. Leftist partisans of agrarian reform found little to comfort them, as many mountain cultivators remained conservative peasants and the new eastern farmers often turned bourgeois in their thinking.

The MNR found the mining problem unsolvable. In 1952 the properties of the foreign tin companies were turned into a state enterprise—

COMIBOL (Bolivian Mining Corporation). That move had no effect on world prices for tin. It made the high costs of Bolivian production even higher, because COMIBOL became a plaything for individual and group interests. The miners naturally wanted better compensation for their dangerous work, and politicians—like Lechín—who depended on miner support fought for their demands. Labor costs went up, with higher wages, social benefits, subsidized commissaries, and a riot of featherbedding. Production fell to half of prerevolution levels, with more workers. By 1963 tin still earned on the order of three-quarters of Bolivia's foreign exchange, but the government lost $600 on each ton exported. COMIBOL, running yearly deficits, was a millstone round the neck of MNR, government, and country.

The sizable United States effort to aid Bolivia (about $400 million by 1965) had results that were ambiguous in all but one respect: the acrimonious complaint it induced. Little industrialization was possible. YPFB, the state petroleum monopoly, let contracts to foreign companies, but revenues remained low. The financial condition of Bolivia became dreadful soon after the revolution of 1952. Inflation got out of hand. The *boliviano* fell to 14,000 to the dollar.

It was no criticism of MNR to point out that little social change could occur because the resources for it did not exist. No one knew how to state per capita income for Bolivia, but in 1961 one guess was under $100. Foodstuffs still were imported. Nevertheless, transportation, especially highways, was considerably improved, a change which contributed to development of the eastern lowlands, where the town of Santa Cruz grew from 15,000 to 60,000 between 1955 and 1963. The country had a population of about 5 million in the mid-1970s, up from 3 million in 1950. Some money was available for education, and it improved after 1952, but in the late 1970s Bolivia remained one of the most illiterate countries in Latin America. Health conditions continued poor, with life expectancy only forty-eight years. In such an environment, no wonder the universal suffrage introduced in 1954 had minimal effects.

The Military in Power Since 1964

The army in the late 1950s and the early 1960s was given important functions in the national development program. Its position improved also because centrist MNR leaders came to believe that it was needed to control radical political elements. The size of the force was increased. These developments strengthened an old military taste for public affairs that recently had been intensified by the new developmentalist doctrine it helped to implement. A serious increase of division in the MNR during Paz's administration of 1960–1964 encouraged the military to return to its old role of political manipulation. This came to a climax with Paz's decision to change the Constitution to prolong his rule.

In early 1964 the MNR nominated him for president, but the party split. Thereupon, the military forced Paz to accept General René Barrientos as his running mate. They were inaugurated in August 1964. Troubles with strikes, guerrillas, and an asserted plot to assassinate the president and vice-president brought a state of siege. In November a military coup installed Barrientos as president with General Alfredo Ovando, chief of the armed forces, as the power behind him. The military now were strongly nationalist and developmentalist, and claimed to be either revolutionary or popular. They faced the same problems as the MNR had in 1952–1964 and were nearly as divided in policy. Military factions allied with civilian parties.[3] Con-

---

[3] Barrientos was chief executive until killed in a plane crash in April 1969. His civilian vice-president succeeded, and General Ovando ran for the presidency, but in 1969 gave that up and simply seized it, stating that the country faced anarchy. This was said to be the 185th coup in the 144-year history of the republic. A struggle between the left and right in the military, with civilian offshoots, soon developed, and Ovando was forced out in October 1970. The somewhat more leftist General Juan Torres became president and enjoyed the support of miners and students. He set up a "People's Assembly" to replace the Congress.

servative President Hugo Banzer from his accession in 1971 used repressive methods to rule the country. His economic policies could be described as "nationalistic capitalism," somewhat on the model of many other contemporary military regimes in Latin America.

The other important developments after 1964 were economic. After small gains in the later 1960s, in the mid-1970s Bolivia began to enjoy considerable improvement. Agricultural production rose, and Santa Cruz, with a population of 150,000, was center of a real boom area. At last oil began to produce larger revenues. In the mid-1970s its price went up all over the world. Tin prices also improved. Total exports in 1974 were about $500 million, double the amount of 1973. The eastern oil and gas fields were of intense interest to Argentina and Brazil, who were also rivals for new iron mines in Bolivia. These gains did not eliminate the danger of internal explosion. A campaign against Castro-supported guerrillas in 1966–1967 liquidated them, and ended with the execution of Che Guevara, who had come from communist Cuba to try—with total failure—to persuade the peasants of Bolivia to take up arms. But the native ingredients remained for continued political warfare, within and without the armed forces, for Bolivia was so poor that it could only have reform or even "revolution at starvation level."

b. Ecuador

Ecuador for more than a century was one of the least modernized countries in Latin America.[4] It suffered great territorial losses to its stronger neighbors. Ecuador accepted a boundary treaty favorable to Peru in 1942, at the urging of Argentina, Brazil, Chile, and the United States. That left its territory in the Oriente, eastern lowlands, much reduced from its original claims. Denunciation of the 1942 accord became a habit of Ecuadorean politicians. In 1960 the president declared that the 1942 treaty was invalid; similar statements followed in later years.[5]

The old heart of Ecuador in the heavily Indian high mountains lost economic and demographic ground to the coast, centering on Guayaquil, which controlled much of the export agricultural economy. Improved public health increased the population growth rate to over 3 percent a year, and the total from some 3 million in 1940 to 7 million in the mid-1970s. Most Ecuadorans were of Indian or mixed racial stock in which Indian blood predominated, with contributions from white and black elements, the last being mostly in the Pacific coastal lowlands. Urbanization increased. Quito grew from 400,000 in the mid-1950s to over 500,000 in the mid-1970s, while Guayaquil went from 650,000 to more than 800,000.

Ecuador suffered the ills of poverty, *latifundio*, class and race division, and violence in public life. Between 1925 and 1948 there were nineteen administrations. The Constitution of 1967 was the seventeenth. When the junta of 1966 was ousted, that was the twelfth unscheduled change in administration since 1931. The brief administrations were corrupt and inefficient. After 1960 governments were somewhat more intelligent about economic policy, but frequently implemented it in an authoritarian manner. The political system improved only marginally, and the country remained an extreme case of minority control of politics. Parties were run by a handful of activists, often were impermanent, and usually less important than the evanescent coalitions in which they participated. Parties necessarily treated with military conspirators because the latter always were so busy and so frequently

---

Such presumed leftism led the more conservative military to replace him in August 1971 with Colonel Hugo Banzer, a firm anticommunist, who had the support of the conservative part of MNR and of the right-wing Falange of Bolivia.

[4] See Chapter 28, Section e, on Ecuador to the 1930s.

[5] The commission laying out the boundary had almost finished when Ecuador denounced the treaty, also objecting that in any event the line laid down did not follow the topographic principles set forth in the 1942 agreement.

upset administrations. Much of the political maneuvering involved the rivalry between Guayaquil and Quito; the former long had the advantage, but in the 1970s the new petroleum income began to strengthen Quito's position. Not only was that income controlled by the government in the highlands, but the petroleum went out by pipeline from the Oriente to the port of Esmeraldas, far north of Guayaquil.

Three completed civilian administrations in 1948–1960 raised hopes of permanent reduction of the military role in public life. Such was not to be. Military maneuvering in politics sometimes seemed the only interest of the officers' corps. Although in the 1950s and thereafter more officers accepted nationalist and developmentalist ideas, they did not reduce their interest in politics and government. Nationalism was used to forge support for programs, but also for simply personal political purposes. Nationalists objected to the grant during World War II of bases to the United States on the Ecuadorean mainland and in the Galápagos Islands. There was more national enthusiasm for the declaration in the 1950s of a two-hundred-mile oceanic jurisdiction for the fishing industry and the seizure of United States boats in the area.

An expert at using nationalist slogans was José María Velasco Ibarra, the archetype of the demagogue who, as he said himself, needs only a balcony to win the presidency. His ability to win votes by playing on emotions and promising the moon was testimony to the lack of popular confidence in the political system. Born into a prominent family, Velasco existed to be president, finding support among the urban poor, the alienated middle class, students, and all sorts of leaders of regional and splinter groups who wanted to ride to power with the proven champion. He won by election in 1933, 1952, 1960, 1968, and seized power in 1944. He finished one of those terms. His election in 1960 came after the three unprecedented completed administrations of civilian presidents. He promptly alienated moderates with a pro-Castro line, and labor and students by several foolish moves. Velasco

continued to vindicate his reputation as an excellent candidate and poor president. He was ousted in November 1961. The vice-president who succeeded him was a drunk, and was ousted by the military in 1963.

A military junta set out after communists and pro-Castro terrorist bands, declaring that it would not restore constitutional guarantees until it had those elements under control. When university students in early 1964 demonstrated against the regime, police were sent into the supposedly sacred university grounds. The junta said that professional agitators were at work among the students. The junta also declared that it would push such reforms as land distribution and changes in the tax administrative systems. Some of these promises no doubt were the result of conviction among officers; some very likely were in response to the demands of the Alliance for Progress. The military regime did not please the public, and after bloody rioting in March 1966 it resigned in favor of a civilian president. The latter soon resigned, to be replaced by a constituent assembly, which named another civilian president. After all this confusion, an election was held in 1968, and Velasco Ibarra won it. Things did seem to be going in circles.

Between financial problems and various demonstrations by dissatisfied groups, Velasco claimed before long that chaos impended. The military accepted that analysis and in June 1970 dissolved the Congress and permitted Velasco to rule by decree. Then in February 1972 it ousted Velasco, unhappy with budgetary deficits, inefficiency and corruption, and his encouragement of the left, including friendly chats with Castro during a visit of the latter to Ecuador in December 1971. Chief of state after 1972 was General Guillermo Rodríguez Lara, who took up his task with a claim to being nationalist and revolutionary. What his revolutionary principles were was not clear, although he occasionally criticized the "oligarchy." By 1975 the general was stating that there was no immediate prospect of a congress and that the regime would continue as long as was necessary to meet the goals of the military.

In January 1976 he was ousted and replaced by a military junta.

Economic development was slow. Exports totaled less than $100 million at the end of the 1950s, with bananas, coffee, and cacao accounting for nearly all of it. Bananas were half the value of shipments as late as 1971, when total exports were $218 million. Then a dramatic change occurred. A small amount of petroleum had been produced on the Pacific coast for some years. Under a petroleum law of 1971, foreign companies went into the Oriente, operating under a new Ecuadoran State Petroleum Corporation (CEPE). As petroleum from the Oriente flowed out, the country's exports went to $372 million in 1972, $550 million in 1973, and $900 million in 1974, when oil was three-quarters of the value of exports. Ecuador was a member of OPEC, benefiting from the cartel's pricing, but in 1974 Ecuador could not sell all its relatively high-cost oil. In that year CEPE bought 25 percent of the Texaco-Gulf petroleum consortium. The junta that took over in 1976 had a popular issue in the claim that Rodríguez Lara had mismanaged the petroleum industry. It also was on sound political ground later in 1976 when it forced Gulf Oil to sell its holdings, which gave CEPE 62 percent of the consortium of which Texaco was the surviving foreign partner.

The uses the government found for the new revenues had been spelled out in recent years by new planning institutions, some of them set up in response to the demands of the Alliance for Progress. An agricultural reform law went into operation in 1965. The first distributions were modest, but the pace quickened in the mid-1970s. A 1973 law declared that landowners had to put their holdings to productive use or sell them to the government for collective farms. The problem of agricultural production was far from solved, however, and the country still imported food products.

Other resources were limited. Industry was small. Capital was sparse. Men with money put it where the greatest profits were—for example, in commerce rather than agriculture. Raising and

collecting taxes was difficult in such an underdeveloped country. Although the school system grew, it probably did not keep up with population growth, and half the population was illiterate or nearly so. Higher education enrolled only 5,000 students in 1958, but by 1974 enrollment was up to 55,000. Many students were in law and other overcrowded fields, and advanced training with a scarcity of appropriate jobs led to dissatisfaction. Even with the best of efforts—and those seemed unlikely—Ecuador faced a long road to modernization.

c. Central America

Central American Union and United States Intervention

Early in the twentieth century the maneuvers between Central American states were politically explosive,[6] with Estrada Cabrera of Guatemala and Zelaya of Nicaragua often involved. They led to coups d'etat and warfare. The United States became especially concerned after 1903, when it received a canal grant from the new republic of Panama. Peace in Central America seemed important to the safety of the proposed canal. Out of conferences in 1906 came the International Central American Bureau, which opened in 1907 at Guatemala City and promoted unionism for a time, and a Pedagogical Institute set up at San José, Costa Rica. A peace conference at Washington in November and December 1907 agreed also on a Central American Court of Justice, which was set up for ten years at Cartago, Costa Rica, to judge cases affecting the peace of Central America.

These apparently promising actions failed to accomplish union or to bring peace. Interference of one state in the affairs of another did not cease. Then the system early in its history had to contend with United States intervention in Nicaragua (1909–1933),[7] which not only arrayed

---

[6] See Chapter 28, Section h, for efforts at Central American union in the nineteenth century.

[7] See the section on Nicaragua later in this chapter.

some Nicaraguan groups against others but produced an especially divisive issue in 1913. Representatives of Nicaragua and the United States signed a convention giving the latter the right in perpetuity to build a canal through Nicaragua (including the San Juan River it shared with Costa Rica), leases on the Corn Islands in the Caribbean, and a concession to build a naval base on the Gulf of Fonseca in the Pacific. Several Central American countries protested that they had rights in those areas. The same terms were incorporated in the Bryan-Chamorro Treaty, ratified by the United States Senate in 1916. Acrimony growing from the treaty was one reason the Central Americans permitted the lapse in 1918 of the ten-year mandate of the Central American system established by the Washington treaties, but the collapse was due largely to jealousies among the Central American states.

In December 1922 the Central American states responded to an invitation from Washington and there signed a treaty and other instruments providing for a new peace structure, including a Central American Tribunal. The agreement was in effect until 1934 but had little influence, partly because Central American attitudes toward any institution involving the United States were soured by the latter's continued involvement in Nicaraguan internal affairs. Thereafter, interest in union was largely a matter of a search for a new spirit of collaboration. That was furthered in the 1940s by the rise of liberal political regimes in several countries, notably Costa Rica and Guatemala, and by the emphasis a better-educated generation placed on collaboration to solve the problems of the region. In 1951 a meeting of the foreign ministers of the five states signed the Charter of San Salvador, establishing the Organization of Central American States (ODECA). In 1954 they formed a School of Public Administration at San José and in 1956 a Technical Institute at Guatemala City. Much discussion went on, with technical aid from the UN and OAS. The United States encouraged the project. In 1958–1960 the governments made preliminary trade agreements. A treaty of 1960

created the Central American Common Market (CACM).

The system set out to meld the resources and markets of the five little republics. They set up a Central American Bank. Those products that were granted a "national" character could circulate freely in the regional market. There inevitably was a big problem assigning such industries to the states. In time there were supposed to be a standard tariff, full mobility of labor and capital, and other uniformities. Trade among the countries increased considerably. But the easy decisions soon were used up, especially in industries that could do well in Central American conditions of limited purchasing power. Foreign capital came for those. The difficult problems remained in connection with activities that were expensive to start and difficult to maintain in Central America. All this was complicated by conflicting national interests and pride, and by regional trade imbalances. In 1969 the so-called "Soccer War" (it began with a riot at a match) occurred between El Salvador and Honduras. It was due to rising nationalism and to Honduran fears of Salvadoran seasonal laborers, some of whom settled down permanently and illegally in Honduras. Population pressure in tiny El Salvador seemed a threat to thinly peopled Honduras. After 1969 Honduras blockaded Salvadoran goods and CACM's activities dwindled. An increase in bilateral trade pacts in Central America in the 1970s suggested the possibility that CACM might not be revived.

Guatemala

After Estrada Cabrera's long tyranny ended in 1920, Guatemala generally continued its tradition of conservative authoritarian government[8] until a revolt brought a controversial leftist and innovating regime in 1944–1954. That government was, in turn, ended by revolt and a return to generally conservative control of the country.

---

[8] See Chapter 28, Section h, for Guatemala in the nineteenth century.

In a land the size of New York State, the 5 million people of the 1970s were mostly poor farmers, and more than half were Indians, retaining much of their traditional culture and scarcely participating in national affairs. Ownership of land was heavily concentrated. More than half the people were illiterate. The country long had been dependent on exports of coffee. Some modest economic and social improvements occurred, but the problems remained enormous.

The Estrada Cabrera tyranny of 1898–1920 was followed by a decade of the familiar political maneuvers of oligarchy and military; then military strongman Jorge Ubico ruled from 1931 until 1944, when he was ousted by a rebellion that included a considerable civilian reform element. Elections were held at the end of 1944 in an atmosphere of free speech and demand for thoroughgoing change. It was, however, an election in which only literate males voted. The most popular contestant for the presidency—and eventual winner—was Juan José Arévalo, long an exile from Ubico's regime. He sometimes summed up his ideas as "spiritual socialism." He coupled strong nationalism with idealism and reformism, appealing to his supporters, who were politically active urban dwellers. He received 85 percent of the vote in December 1944 and was inaugurated in March 1945, when a new Constitution also went into effect.

Arévalo's administration stimulated demand for change and free discussion looking to that end. The new atmosphere was accompanied by novel political stirrings. A labor confederation (CGT) was formed in 1944, with advice from the Marxist Vicente Lombardo Toledano of Mexico. Students and teachers also organized. The Communist party, founded secretly in 1947, came into the open in 1950 and won four seats in the assembly. Arévalo was not a communist, and the party was negligible during his administration, but the legend of his communism began in the United States. The United Fruit Company refused Arévalo's suggestion that it improve the wages of labor and asked help in Washington, where a senator charged that Arévalo was "communistically inclined." In 1948 opposition on the far right formed the *Partido de Unificación Anticomunista* (PUA), which received some sympathy from United States business interests.

Arévalo's administration moved slowly. It had small resources of money and trained personnel. The president's desire for change was reinforced by the new Constitution, which included much of the traditional Latin American liberal doctrine on freedom for the individual and representative government and also gave the vote to illiterate males and literate women. The Constitution prohibited great estates and permitted expropriation of land with compensation to the owners. Little was done about the agrarian problem, but a new program of educating Indians, using some of the devices employed for that purpose in Mexico, was begun. More immediately important were the establishment of the Guatemalan Social Security Institute (1946) and the passage of a new labor code (1947) for both industrial and agricultural workers, providing labor courts. An industrial development law, including incentives for domestic and foreign capital, was implemented (1948) with an *Instituto de Fomento de la Producción*, following the lead of other Latin American countries.

Although this was a centrist reform administration and its measures would not have been disturbing in the better-developed Latin American countries, it was strong medicine for Guatemala. Difference of opinion naturally extended to the army. The conservatives were in the ascendant as the next election approached, headed by Colonel Francisco Arana, chief of staff, the most important military man in the country and a popular figure. PUA backed him. Leader of the reform faction was Colonel Jacobo Arbenz, minister of defense. The issue was decided by the murder of Arana in July 1949. There was suspicion that the Arbenz group had contrived it. He was elected president by a big majority.

Arbenz was only thirty-seven. He bore some resentment against the old Guatemalan society because he was not well received in it. He turned to friendship with men of reform interests and became committed to change but was not a communist. In 1951–1954 Arbenz tried to carry out a basic restructuring of Guatemalan life, and in the process aroused passions among opponents at home, international business interests (largely North American) in the country, in the United States, and in other countries concerned for ideological, diplomatic, or strategic reasons. Little Guatemala became the focus of intense scrutiny.

The Arbenz program was nationalistic, bringing him support at home and in the rest of Latin America. Nationalism included a general demand to be left alone, and a specific program to compel foreign investors to pay more to operate in Guatemala—in taxes, wages, and other ways—and to accept the decisions of the Guatemalan courts and Congress without appeals to other governments. It is a fair guess that the United States might have accepted this nationalism had the communist issue not been involved. Nationalism and a desire to improve socioeconomic performance led the regime to move toward a social-function definition of property, not novel—or necessarily communistic—in the world of the 1950s. The wish to control property in the community interest often was coupled with denunciation of "imperialism," so that clearly foreign property especially was a target. Guatemala objected to the International Railways of Central America on the grounds that it was a foreign monopoly not interested in giving the sort of service the country required. It was expropriated in April 1953. The same objection was made to the electric power company.

The regime's social aims included plans for education and other fields, but the greatest controversy arose over the social security plan. It was neither novel in the world nor extensive as to Guatemalan coverage. Conservative taxpayers in Guatemala simply objected to paying for it, but critics there and in the United States also connected it with communism, partly because some important officials in the Social Security Institute were communists. Arbenz continued the Arévalo promotion of political participation, al-

though that did not extend to many people on an active basis, since the Arbenz government was authoritarian. Labor organization was pushed hard. Furthermore, it fell into the hands of communists, and they tried to oust the older independent labor leadership and substitute for it people loyal to the administration.

All these programs damaged the old dispensation but were not as worrisome as two other programs. One was an Agrarian Law, passed in June 1952, permitting expropriations. Rather than giving the land to peasants, the government leased it for long periods. In 1952–1954 over 1.2 million acres were expropriated, and use of it granted to some 55,000 persons, mostly family heads, so that possibly a quarter of a million persons were directly affected. The expropriated owners had little voice in the process, and were not permitted to appeal decisions to the courts effectively. Inevitably, there was resistance and emotional debate. Nothing could have more clearly threatened the old order. Furthermore, communists were in key positions in the land distribution system. Indians sometimes were encouraged simply to squat on *latifundios* before they had been distributed by the government.

The greatest landlord was the United Fruit Company, and in 1953 the government expropriated extensive United Fruit Company lands. This move came after a long campaign to force the company to improve pay and other conditions for its workers, who the company contended were better paid and cared for than most others in Guatemala. No doubt they were. Since Guatemalan law would not let the company take agrarian decisions to court, it appealed to the United States government to help it. For Guatemalan nationalists its doing so was typical of the "imperialist" attitude of foreign corporations that expected special privileges. Defenders of the company said it was an efficient and socially valuable enterprise in a badly run society, invited in under one set of rules and now faced with an arbitrary change in operating conditions.

The other problem was communism. Although the regime used communist collaborators and permitted or aided the party to expand its influence, hard-core party membership remained small. The fact that reform and communist growth occurred simultaneously suggested conspiracy to opponents of the regime. The cries of nationalists in Guatemala often were indistinguishable from those of communists because they advocated many of the same things, a common phenomenon in Latin America in recent years. That led critics to conclusions that were difficult to prove. By 1952 communists ran the General Confederation of Workers of Guatemala; by 1953 they were prominent in the National Peasants Confederation. Communists also were active in the formation of front groups, promoting ties with communists in other countries and conducting campaigns in the media, notably against United States interests and policy.

By 1954 the reform movement had outrun its active support. In a nonindustrial country, organized labor was puny. Middle-class intellectuals and bureaucrats who were dedicated to change were few in number. The huge peasant population was happy to be getting land, but it had no concept of national politics and would be difficult to use in an armed struggle for power, even if organized for that. Not many army officers were enthusiastic about sociopolitical modernization. The well-to-do in Guatemala remained a source of opposition. Opportunism and self-interest were traditional and expectable in the environment.

There were indications after World War II that the United States might modify its renunciation of intervention by categorizing action against communism as the right of self-defense. The determined reaction of the United States to the cold war was more than a straw in the wind. There was agitation over a number of developments in Latin America: election of communists to office in Brazil and Chile in the late 1940s; the "Caribbean Legion" that operated in Costa Rica; the communist-oriented Latin American Confederation of Labor headed by Lombardo Toledano of Mexico; the violent *bogotazo* of 1948 in Colombia. The United States action in

the Korean War in 1950 was an indication that a powerful current of opinion in the United States favored drastic action against the growth of communism abroad.

Guatemalans certainly had been subjected to a barrage of United States pressures that left no doubt that concern about communist influence was involved. The Arbenz government struck out with intemperate press attacks on the United States, which the State Department in January 1954 called a campaign of falsehoods. United States publications boiled with speculation about debate in Washington over the nature and extent of the menace in Guatemala. Congress, the presidency, the State Department, and the intelligence agencies were uncertain, and huge quantities of evidence, rumor, and speculation were processed. There was reason for disagreement among responsible men. Washington decided in late 1953 or early 1954 to aid a movement against Arbenz. Exiled Colonel Carlos Castillo Armas gathered a small force of fellow exiles in Honduras, which agreed with the United States to harbor them. The conservative Honduras government felt threatened by the Arbenz regime, which had encouraged agitation in the Honduran banana plantations. In early 1954 Castillo Armas issued appeals to Guatemalans to support him.

By this time the Arbenz regime was frightened. It turned toward increasingly brutal repressive measures in late 1953 and 1954. Arbenz was aware that the existence of the Castillo Armas force encouraged his enemies. He tried for support from other countries in March 1954 at an inter-American conference in Caracas. Foreign Minister Guillermo Toriello delighted many Latin Americans with a slashing attack on what he called the United States policy of "the big stick, tarnished dollar diplomacy, and the landing of the marines." He said the United States unjustly accused his government of being communist as part of a North American strategy of keeping Latin America in subjection.

In May 1954 Washington revealed that communist arms were en route to Guatemala by ship from Eastern Europe. Many people in authority in the United States considered that recent history and common sense suggested that such a shipment was a serious matter. That view was not, however, as widely acceptable in 1954 as a few years later after Castro created a large popular militia. Washington knew in 1954 that Guatemalan army officers did not favor such an organization. That army attitude, in fact, was what settled the matter. The arms were landed in May directly into the hands of the waiting Guatemalan army, which whisked them from reach of those members of the administration who were, in truth, discussing the creation of a popular militia. Castillo Armas' little band crossed into Guatemala and skirmished a bit, while Guatemalan army officers decided what course to pursue. The decision was to oust Arbenz. The United States ambassador participated in discussions between the army and Castillo Armas that soon put the latter in the presidency.

Guatemalan politics and policy veered to the right, although the experiment and institutions of 1944–1954 could not be totally obliterated. A new Constitution in 1956 recognized the social obligations of the government. The Communist party was outlawed. Interference with political activity became common again. The heads of state in the next two decades offered little of interest. Membership in labor unions fell from 107,000 in 1954 to 27,000 in 1955. The peasants generally remained quiescent. Although the Agrarian Law of 1952 was revoked and most of the land division was declared canceled, land reform could not be completely undone. Periodically in the next two decades efforts were made to aid the Indian cultivators. In 1956 a new Agrarian Law provided for a moderate amount of distribution. The social security system was left in place, as was the new system of industrial promotion. The government after 1957 permitted a considerable growth of new political parties.

The memory of the innovative period remained to sustain would-be reformers. Before long a few guerrillas roamed the mountains and terrorists struck in the towns. They were middle-class dissidents, not peasants. Rightist terror

gangs answered with atrocities, as in other Latin American countries. Guatemalan political leaders had by the 1960s and 1970s to respond somewhat more to demands for broader inputs into the system, but little modernization occurred. The United Fruit Company issue subsided. It gave up some land to small farmers. In 1957 a new contract upped the Guatemalan share of United Fruit profits to 30 percent.

After Castillo Armas' assassination in 1957, General Miguel Ydígoras, of Ubico days, was elected president. He was inaugurated in March 1958. He could satisfy neither conservatives nor reformers, and political tension was increased by guerrilla and terrorist activity. It was Ydígoras who agreed to the training in Guatemala of the Cuban exiles for the Bay of Pigs expedition. The Revolutionary party (PR) of Mario Méndez Montenegro grew, and some members split off in 1962 to support a return of Arévalo. The latter declared from exile that he was not a communist. So a debate ensued as to whether he could be believed. Arévalo went to Guatemala in March 1963. Ydígoras then was ousted by a group of the military headed by Colonel Enrique Peralta, minister of defense, with conservative civilian support. This coup closed the door on Arévalo and other reformers of the left. Peralta was promptly recognized by Washington.

There followed fifteen months of strong government. The left was repressed. In July 1964 a constituent assembly met, dominated by conservatives. Peralta refused to run in the election of March 1966, in which nearly half a million votes were cast. At least that type of participation had expanded. When the candidate of the PR, Mario Méndez Montenegro, was murdered, his brother Julio replaced him and won the election by a plurality over two military candidates. Rightist and leftist terrorism continued. In 1968 two United States military advisers and the ambassador were slain. In 1971 an estimated 959 persons were killed by such activity and 365 were kidnapped or disappeared. Intermittently, states of siege were used to try to control the violence. But Méndez Montenegro finished his term. The

1970 election was won by Colonel Carlos Arana Osorio for the National Liberation Movement, which favored firm rule but was not the farthest right group in the country. Arana Osorio pursued a tough policy on terrorism, and it seemed to help. He also nationalized the Central American Power Company. National control of resources long since had been favored by most elements in the country. Nationalism was stimulated, also, by a continuing claim for the incorporation of Belize (formerly British Honduras) into Guatemala.[9]

In 1974, for the first time in Guatemala's history, a third consecutive president was chosen in an orderly election. Brigadier Géneral Kjell Laugerud García won for the ruling National Coalition of the National Liberation Movement and the Institutional Democratic party. The continuing problem of modernization in a peasant country dominated by a conservative minority was illustrated when Lavgerud tolerated a growing Indian cooperative movement, whereupon rightists labeled cooperatives communist.

One of the most cheering notes in recent Guatemalan history occurred in 1967, when Miguel Angel Asturias received the Nobel Prize for literature for novels that depicted corruption and misery in his homeland. People of genius throughout Latin America were calling for a just society and independence of foreign domination.

El Salvador

Little El Salvador (about the size of Massachusetts) continued in the twentieth century the modest economic growth of the late nineteenth,[10] an agricultural country, heavily dependent on coffee exports, but with a growing range of other commodity shipments. The almost completely *mestizo* population totaled about 1 million in 1900 and 4 million in the mid-1970s. Given its

socioeconomic institutions, the country was overpopulated, and considerable numbers went into neighboring, sparsely populated Honduras, sometimes welcomed as laborers but resented as squatters. The country remained 60 percent rural in the 1970s. The capital San Salvador had only 65,000 inhabitants in 1916, but by the 1970s more than 350,000, and a considerably expanded middle class and industrial labor group.

Rule by a few wealthy families was usual from the late nineteenth century until 1931, when the country fell under General Maximiliano Hernández Martínez. Until 1944 it suffered a capricious tyranny, in which the oligarchy generally acquiesced, since Hernández was not challenging its socioeconomic predominance. Moderates in the army who objected to this primitive regime helped overthrow it in 1944, and after a revolt in 1948 were able to impose some mild reformism. That did not involve civilian presidents, however, and all after 1931 were army men. The moderate reform element created PRUD (the Revolutionary Party of Democratic Unification), appealing to a somewhat broader clientele than had been the practice previously. Some of the economic elite approved of this way of damping tension; besides, the reforms were cheap and shallow. PRUD put into power two military presidents between 1950 and 1960, Oscar Osorio and José M. Lemus. Lemus' very modest reforms seemed too much to some officers, especially in view of the communist takeover in Cuba and the development of leftist terrorism and guerrilla activity throughout Latin America, particularly in neighboring Guatemala. They ended the Lemus administration by coup in 1961. After 1962 the country was run by the PCN (Party of National Conciliation), a new alliance of officers and the economic elite.

After the 1940s the military and well-to-do were somewhat more sensitive to popular demands. The first social security legislation in 1949 and subsequent extension represented modernization, but coverage was small, both because of government decision and because the country was poor. Education was extended considerably

---

[9] On British settlement of Belize in the seventeenth century, see Chapter 7, Section d.

[10] See Chapter 28, Section h, on El Salvador in the nineteenth century.

after the 1940s, but the country remained about 50 percent illiterate. Nearly universal suffrage was attained (women received full voting rights in 1952), but the effects were muffled by the elitist political system, although electoral institutions and practices were better than in the past. Labor organization was legalized in 1951, and unions expanded, but their activity was restricted by government. There was economic growth and diversification after the 1950s, but most of its benefits went to a small minority. It was estimated that 8 percent of the population got 50 percent of the income at the beginning of the 1970s. The best land was held by a few owners, and foreign observers sometimes were misled by the fact that rather a large number of people owned property, but most parcels were small.

In 1976 the military officer occupying the presidency for the PCN, responding to pressure from reformers, announced a land reform that would include expropriation of estates. Reaction by big landowners and their allies in the military stalled the measure. In the February 1977 presidential election the victorious PCN nominee, General Carlos Romero, promised a strong anticommunist regime and was considered a hard-line conservative opposed to land reform. Cries of electoral fraud and demands for reform intensified after the election. The church was turning from its old alliance with the elites and sponsoring relief for the poor. Priests working with the peasants encouraged them to demand help, with the result that conservatives condemned the church. Several priests were killed and others deported. In March 1977 El Salvador rejected further United States military aid because it expected Washington to cut off such aid with denunciation of violations of human rights. In May 1977 the bishops of El Salvador accused the government of "persecution of the church" in the name of anticommunism. During those months rightist and leftist organizations were engaging in terrorism. President Romero, inaugurated July 1, contended that strong measures were needed to contain leftist guerrillas who engaged in murder. The prospects did not appear bright for economic modernization or for social and political justice in El Salvador.

Honduras

Honduras was one of the least developed countries in Latin America.[11] A population of only 2.6 million in the early 1970s, largely of mixed white, black, and Indian stock, thinly peopled an area the size of Pennsylvania. The economy was nearly all agricultural and pastoral, and most people were subsistence farmers or wage laborers. Honduras was commonly thought to have considerable resources (including minerals), but there were few signs that they would soon be exploited. Town development was meager, with some 300,000 dwellers in the largest city and capital, Tegucigalpa, but about three-quarters of the population rural. Communications were poor. Education was scanty and the country possibly 65 percent illiterate. The government depended heavily on customs duties, especially on bananas and coffee.

Honduras was still dominated by a tiny elite, including a few wealthy families and professional military officers. Violence in politics was the rule. There was a weak two-party system, but the parties meant little except a division in the contest for power and the public purse. The country struggled to improve its relations with the foreign banana companies, which put pressure on government and resisted suggestions that they increase their payments to the treasury or to workers. In the 1950s the Honduras government began to have some success in this effort. Some of the reason was not entirely welcome, as banana workers were organized, partly by communists from Guatemala. Increased revenue was pleasing, however. One change was that the fruit concerns turned more production over to small local growers and acted as distributors. The gains to Honduras from that change were not impressive. Enough recognition of the need to change oc-

---

[11] See Chapter 28, Section h, for Honduras in the nineteenth century.

curred so that in 1959 the elite finally agreed to accept a new and more liberal labor code.

In 1974 a group of young reform-minded officers began to press for changes in Honduras. In April 1975 they spearheaded the military ouster of chief of state General Oswaldo López, longtime strongman, on the charge that he had been involved in bribery by United Brands, successor to United Fruit Company. The company admitted that it had paid a bribe to secure a reduction of banana taxes. In 1975 more military men began to talk, in the familiar fashion of officers in recent years in Latin America, of a rule of five to ten years to lift the country from its backward condition. At the same time the army put down peasant unrest with some loss of life. A modernized Honduras could only be a distant dream.

Nicaragua

Nicaragua had suffered underdevelopment, disorder, and foreign intervention in the nineteenth century,[12] and those factors troubled it in the twentieth. Dictator José Santos Zelaya (1898–1909) was a Liberal party authoritarian. For several years he took actions against United States business interests because he resented the failure of his negotiations with the United States to build a canal through his country. Washington was concerned lest his nationalistic tendency to abuse foreigners lead to European intervention. United States banking and other interests wished to secure business in Nicaragua and made suggestions to the State Department. They fit in with the contemporary notion in Washington that it should teach Caribbean states how to run orderly elections and governments, including proper service on foreign debts. They also served United States views on defense of the approaches to the new Panama Canal. Most statesmen in Washington were less concerned with the small opportunities for profit in Nicaragua than with

disorder and possible intervention and defense of the canal. Some intelligent, experienced, highly responsible United States public figures floundered around in the Nicaraguan morass because they were unable to empathize with a culture different from their own. United States pressure persuaded his colleagues to push Zelaya out in 1909, and public rumor had it that Washington was behind the revolt. The United States was not to blame in that exact sense, but it had put itself in a stance that made such charges inevitable, and many Latin Americans considered that at the least the great power of the United States, coupled with a clear expression of preference, constituted a type of interference. Zelaya resigned partly because of United States opposition to him and became a hero for many Central Americans.

The United States continued with pressures and suggestions and in 1912 and thereafter used armed intervention. United States activity from then until 1933 was a fiasco of choosing presidential candidates in an environment Washington did not understand and supervising elections as though Kansas could be transplanted magically to the tropics. Even naval vessels cruising the coast were unnerving for a tiny state that could scarcely bear interruption of traffic from its few ports or resist landings by small parties of marines. Such evident possibilities also inevitably encouraged the opponents of the regime against which the United States Navy was demonstrating. In a poor country with a tradition of political activity by conspiracy, force, and fraud, and with few controls by public opinion, politicians naturally sometimes welcomed United States aid against their opponents. But none was fond of such intervention, and most disliked it. United States military action finally raised a guerrilla hero, Augusto Sandino, who in his remote refuges thrilled Latin Americans with his resistance. The intervention came to include troops, constitution writing, election supervision, judgment of the propriety of Nicaraguan actions, and other activities that North Americans were illfitted to understand in the local environment.

---

[12] For Nicaragua in the nineteenth century, see Chapter 28, Section h.

When the marines departed in 1933, Anastasio Somoza "inherited" Nicaragua. He was commander of the National Guard, trained as a constabulary by the United States in the naive hope that it would be less intrusive in politics than an "army." Somoza took over as president in 1937 and was *caudillo* until he was murdered in 1956. His family ran the country thereafter much like a private plantation. Son Luís was president until 1963. Then a puppet occupied the presidency up to 1967, when son Anastasio, Jr., took over and ran the country, whether in the presidential seat or not. Anastasio, Jr., trained at West Point, was careful always to command the armed forces. The Somozas could not do everything in a country with a population that grew from half a million at the beginning of the century to 2 million in the 1970s. They had a party (titled Liberal) and used it as one way of doling out favors to their clique. Somoza was resoundingly anticommunist, no doubt sincerely, but also with a gaze fixed on Washington.

Increasing income under the Somozas was divided most inequitably on a personalistic basis. The family owned a sizable part of the country. Much of its success in promoting growth was through encouragement of foreign investment and credits, a process facilitated by the "stability" of the political system, meaning few damaging disorders, docile labor, and an expectation that tax changes would not suddenly and deeply cut into profits. A National Bank of Nicaragua existed to stoke development, advancing credits to favored private enterprise, especially in agriculture, that made increasing export profits. Aid flowed in from the World Bank and from the United States technical assistance program. The regime built a modern system of roads, possibly its most lasting achievement. There was no question but that the Somozas knew how to run a plantation.

Opposition to the regime in the 1970s included some churchmen, and in 1972 the conservative archbishop condemned the corruption of the political process. A guerrilla movement, the *Frente Sandinista de la Liberación Nacional*,

began to grow, with peasant support. In December 1974 the guerrillas seized hostages from a party honoring the United States ambassador and extracted a ransom of $1 million. President Somoza harried the guerrillas under a state of siege. Early in 1977 the Catholic bishops of Nicaragua accused the government of using torture and summary executions of civilians, including peasants, in the antiguerrilla campaign. It was likely that the system of conservative dictatorship would endure for some time, but it faced more troubles than in the past.

Panama

Control of politics by the National Guard and a few civilian politicians, usually with ties to the tiny economic elite, continued to be the rule in Panama in the 1940s and thereafter.[13] Their activity was complicated by growing nationalism, especially for the reduction of United States privileges. In 1939 the United States ratified a treaty ending Panama's status as a protectorate, abandoning the right to police the central cities at times, to appropriate Panamanian land, and to intervene in national affairs. It also raised the annuity to $430,000 from $250,000. The United States received excellent cooperation from Panama during World War II, but at its end Panama demanded that bases granted on its soil be evacuated at once. The bad judgment of Washington in not responding rapidly contributed to ill feeling. In the postwar years demands for changes in United States policy became increasingly vociferous. They created enough pressure so that the United States agreed to a treaty change in 1955, increasing the annuity to $1.9 million, giving up some property held in the capital city, and giving Panama new tax rights over its citizens working in the zone. It also eliminated in the zone the old "gold" wages for North Americans and "silver" for Panamanians, which

---

[13] See Chapter 33, Section e, on Panama from 1903 to the 1930s.

were damaging both materially and spiritually to the latter. Immediately after this change, Egypt seized the Suez Canal, further stimulating Panamanian desire to eliminate the United States presence.

Although Panama received a sizable income from the Canal Zone—in sales and employment, notably—it thought it deserved more. It objected to the commissaries in the zone, where civilian statesiders bought imported instead of Panamanian goods. Panamanians demanded a part or all of the tolls paid by ships using the canal. They complained that North Americans showed prejudice against the heavily black population of Panama. They insisted that the zone was Panamanian territory, because even under a perpetual lease "residual sovereignty" remained with Panama. They demanded that the Panamanian flag fly with that of the United States in the zone. They wanted a highway bridge over the canal. Heated discussions and demonstrations occured in the 1950s. Defenders of the status quo were dismayed when President Eisenhower conceded that Panama retained residual sovereignty. President Kennedy in 1962 agreed that the Panamanian and United States flags should fly together in the zone.

The point was long passed when Panamanian politicians could stand against nationalist demands. Theirs was a poor country, and the United States or the canal represented the best visible hope of investment capital. In 1964 the accumulating tensions burst into violence. Some United States students in the zone tried to fly their flag alone. Panamanians insisted that theirs be displayed. Mobs went into the zone from Panama and were met by United States troops. Rioting went on for three days with some loss of life and considerable damage to United States property. President Chiari broke diplomatic relations with Washington and tried to get the OAS and UN to investigate what he called United States incitation of the violence.

After 1964 Panama and the United States negotiated fitfully. Statesmen in both countries were under pressure not to concede too much.

The United States flirted with one solution when President Johnson in December 1964 announced a commission to study routes for a new canal. Much speculation followed about Nicaraguan and Colombian routes. Panama thus was left to ponder what would happen if a competing waterway was built, fearing loss of the more than $165 million a year from trade, wages, and purchasing arising from zone operations. But the United States commission report in 1970 recommended that from a technical point of view it would be best to build a new canal near the present one.

Panamanian determination to force a drastic solution continued unabated, with the cry of "Sovereignty or Death!" Finally, in August 1977 the United States and Panama announced they had agreed "in principle" on a new treaty that would transfer the canal and the Canal Zone to Panama by the year 2000. When the treaty was drafted and ratified, the United States was to scale down quickly its military installations and personnel and cooperate militarily with the Panamanian National Guard in defense of the canal. The United States was to have a role in defense of the canal after expiration of the new treaty at the end of 1999, by a separate protocol as part of an agreement to maintain the "neutrality" of the canal and its accessibility for all nations. The United States annual money payment to Panama was to be increased, probably to about $60 million, and the United States was to provide some sort of economic development aid. Some groups in both Panama and the United States denounced the agreement as a "sellout," even before a treaty with precise language existed. There was enough opposition in the United States Senate so that it appeared unlikely it would make a decision before January 1978. There seemed to be considerable sentiment in the United States against so many "concessions" to Panama, but no one knew how strongly people felt about the issue. Supporters of the agreement made much of the argument that such terms were critically important to the general relations of the United States with Latin America. That certainly was a considerable exaggeration. All Latin American nations were more interested in other United States policies than the arrangements for Panama.[14]

Meanwhile, conditions in Panama improved only marginally. General Omar Torrijos seized power in 1968 and became a dictator. By the late 1970s he had little support outside the 10,-000-man armed forces. Living levels remained depressed. With a population of 1.5 million heavily concentrated in the central cities next to the canal, apparently limited natural resources, and little capital, Panama had problems aplenty. Exports remained small. Panama tried to improve income by taking over banana production from foreigners in the 1970s. That and some improvements in other sectors left Panamanians far from prosperous. As everywhere, the students and intellectuals demanded drastic change. Recent governments had shown increasing intelligence about national planning, but the limited resources of Panama made it likely that modernization would come only if the nationalist campaign for great sums of money from the United States succeeded, which was unlikely.

d. Paraguay

It has been observed that Paraguay was one of the least modernized countries in Latin America until the 1930s.[15] It retained claims to the Chaco Boreal, contested with Bolivia because of conflicting data from the colonial era. Bolivia wanted access by river to the Atlantic. Both countries wanted the petroleum rumored to be in the Chaco. Military moves occurred from time to time in the first decades of the twentieth century and skirmishes began in 1928. Paraguay claimed that Standard Oil, with a concession in Bolivia, was subsidizing Bolivian aggression; Bolivia claimed that Argentina and Britain were inciting Paraguay. War came in 1932 and con-

tinued to 1935. Bolivia had a larger population, but found it difficult to concentrate forces so far from its highland centers, and the soldiers were troubled by the lowland climate. Possibly 100,000 lives were lost. A treaty in 1938 gave Paraguay a territorial victory.

The Paraguayan population, mostly of Guaraní stock and often speaking the Indian tongue, inhabited a tropical lowland about the size of California. The population totaled half a million in 1865, then was halved by the Paraguayan War of 1865–1870. It reached 2 million in the 1960s and was expected to reach 3 million by 1980. It still was more than 60 percent rural in the 1970s. Asunción (385,000 in 1970) was the only city of any size.

Most Paraguayans were small subsistence farmers. Exports were low, as late as 1963 only $40 million. They were up to $170 million by 1974. Exports included meat, timber, oil seeds, tobacco, citrus fruits, quebracho extract, cotton, and yerba mate. Much of this exportation of raw materials traditionally was to Argentina, and nationals of that country long were the chief foreign investors in Paraguay. From the 1950s on, however, Brazilians were increasingly active as investors in Paraguay. They built roads into the country, collaborated in a big hydroelectric project, and otherwise developed connections that Argentines regarded sourly. The Paraguayan economy was so poor that it could sustain few social services even if the governments had much interest. Illiteracy was high, average annual income low, political participation near zero.

The generally authoritarian governmental system of the early decades continued. Higinio Morínigo in 1940–1948 was as despotic as his predecessors. There was autocratic rule and disorder from 1948 to 1954; then General Alfredo Stroessner seized power. His authoritarian regime still endured in the late 1970s. The church had protested the despotism: in 1972 it asked social justice; what it got was harassment by Stroessner. In 1975 it complained of the regime's corruption, dictatorship, and use of torture; Stroessner said there was communist influence in the church. It

---

[14] For example, on tariffs, government loans, private investment, costs of technology, commodity prices, human rights, military aid, guerrillas and urban terroists, coups d'etat.

[15] See Chapter 28, Section g.

was dangerous to criticize government in Paraguay, a country that in many ways remained in the nineteenth-century Age of the Caudillos.

e. Haiti

No miracle intervened after the first century of independent Haitian existence to rescue its people from misery.[16] What intervened instead was the United States, concerned that disorder in Haiti might lead to European intervention, danger to the Panama Canal, or damage to the small North American investment. By that time the United States had protectorates in Cuba and Panama and interventions under way in Santo Domingo and Nicaragua.

Well-developed nations understandably recoiled from the savagery of Haitian society. The United States in 1914–1915 at least four times requested special powers in Haiti, and the Haitian government refused. Simultaneously, United States warships nosed about the coasts of Haiti, while the armies of local chieftains tore at each other. Admiral William Caperton kept warning Vibrun Sam, the new chieftain in Port-au-Prince, against violence. That was as useless as ordering calm at sea. Sam did not control his environment; he merely wanted to endure in it. Another chieftain, Bobo, attacked Sam in Port-au-Prince in 1915, and not only were there casualties in the fighting, but prisoners were slaughtered, common in Haiti and not unknown in European history. Caperton landed marines in July 1915.

What caused the intervention? For some, the explanation must be commercial greed, business controlling the State Department. The evidence suggests, however, that Washington was moved most by strategic considerations, as in the case of Nicaragua, although to be sure strategy almost inevitably required some consideration of economic matters. The United States had an interest in a naval base at Môle St. Nicolas in Haiti that went back to the nineteenth century. By

1915 Washington at least wanted to be sure no other nation had such a base. The beginning of World War I seemed to some to raise a new menace of expansionism, a notion that was most effective if mentioned but not analyzed. A European power would be unlikely to acquire bases in the Caribbean during the war and even more unlikely to develop facilities. The United States was yet more unlikely to be unable to find ways to stop it. There were also the policeman and "civilizer" roles that had been promoted with reluctance by McKinley, with a mixture of irritation and enthusiasm by Theodore Roosevelt, with determination by Taft and now with rather myopic rectitude by Woodrow Wilson. To call the motives squalid is unjust, but the reasoning was sloppy and the methods adopted disastrously naive, as in the other interventions.

The United States kept armed forces in Haiti from 1915 until 1934. A few Haitians agreed, by treaty and otherwise, to United States arrangements, but the alien presence was uninvited and unwanted. The United States did some well-intentioned work in financing, policing, education, public health, and road building, all desperately needed in Haiti, all without effect on Haitian resentment of intrusion, and all without much permanent effect on Haitian socioeconomic problems. The illiterate and desperately poor Haitians did not and could not change their habits or attitudes in a few years, on the basis of a few activities by foreigners, without attack on the primitive economy. It became ever clearer, even to the dull and obstinate in Washington, that the protectorate was a burden without compensation. By the late 1920s disillusionment had set in. President Hoover began the process of withdrawal. Franklin Roosevelt had the last marines out in 1934. The financial mission lingered to 1941. What remained was the same old Haiti.

Haitians did not prosper in the decades after the marines departed. The country remained at least 90 percent illiterate, populated by a largely black peasantry of subsistence farmers. There was a puny income from driblets of exports, in-

---

[16] See Chapter 28, Section j, on Haiti in the nineteenth century.

termittent tourism, sale of charming primitive art, and the modest amounts that could be extracted from international organizations. The government was the prey of military factions and gangs of thugs. One can understand cruelty and corruption in public life in a society so violent that any moment may bring ruin, exile, death. That was not an expression of the character of Haitians, widely liked for their cheerful endurance of misery; it was the inevitable consequence of one of the worst social situations in the world. Nor did it improve. By the 1970s, some 5 million Haitians, with their number increasing, occupied a land about the size of Belgium, with a fraction of the latter's income. With too many people on too little land, eroded and badly used, Haiti was called an "environmental disaster" and a country without prospects.

In September 1957 physician François Duvalier became president-dictator. In 1971, a terrible fourteen years later, he died, still master of power in Haiti. An educated black, Duvalier displayed some of the animus between blacks and mulattoes that intermittently had influenced the fighting for public office. He also displayed a great capability for holding onto power in the obviously most feasible way—by terror. His force of strongmen, the *Tontons Macoutes* (bogeymen, in *créole*), spied, intimidated, and murdered for the continuation of the regime. Duvalier also promoted a reputation for occult powers, and "Papa Doc" came to be regarded with awe by the peasantry as an embodiment of spirits, in their voodoo belief. The tyranny and butchery in Haiti became an international scandal. The doctrine of nonintervention, strongly supported in Latin America, prevented much speculation on interference.

In John Kennedy's time, beginning in 1961, Duvalier's regime seemed out of step with the brave hopes of the Alliance for Progress then being launched. Also, there was fear of interference in Haiti from communist Cuba. Although the United States put pressure on Duvalier, he survived it handily. When Papa Doc died in 1971, he was succeeded by a young son, who endured

as a puppet "Little Doc" under control of the army.

Papa Doc during his lifetime and thereafter was often portrayed either as a joke, a bogeyman, or as a horror of some variety. Surely such approaches were unfair and naive. The *Tontons Macoutes* were no funnier than the voodoo religion, a quite serious faith, and without some understanding of the social bases of both institutions Haitians were a mystery to observers. Horror as a reaction to Haitian conditions too often took the form of condemnation. What the Haitians needed was pity, understanding, and help. Surely, poor Papa Doc was to be pitied, living in fear, without hope of security, only enduring from day to day, as his compatriots still do.

f. The Dominican Republic

After the United States intervention in the fiscal system of the Dominican Republic in 1904,[17] the country was made to pay on its foreign debt, but nothing else changed. Continued disorder led Wilson in 1916 to order a military intervention, with the same hope of improving political institutions and conditions of life generally that animated policy on Haiti. A constabulary was trained and armed; roads, sanitation, education improved; the budget balanced—as was then thought desirable regardless of the condition of society. The intervention was resented, and there were clashes, so after United States diplomat Sumner Welles supervised an election in 1924, the marines were withdrawn. In 1931 the head of the constabulary, Rafael Trujillo, took over the country. He ran it until 1961 as though he owned it.

Trujillo was a bloody tyrant. He thought having the friendship, if possible, and certainly not the enmity of the United States important. His encouragement of the export agricultural sector probably was sound policy. Many Dominicans benefited from improved employment, schools,

---

[17] See Chapter 28, Section j, on the Dominican Republic to 1904.

transportation, and housing; but he milked the country for his own use, spent lavishly on the military, and indulged in building projects of little value.

Trujillo's ties to the United States may be linked forever with the alleged statement of a president that "he is a sonofabitch, but our sonofabitch." Trujillo had connections with business interests in the United States, which he brought into the country. His business associates pled his case in Washington and other places. He supported United States diplomatic positions, in later years as a vociferous anticommunist, and he bought public relations, legal help, and lobbyists in the United States. He had spies in many countries. He was fertile in ploys to suggest beneficence, enlightenment, and other endearing qualities he conspicuously lacked. He had the Brooklyn Dodgers for spring training. It has been noted that in the 1940s he was a target of the "Caribbean Legion" that opposed rightist government. By the early 1960s Trujillo was an embarrassment to the United States, though he retained a few (presumably paid) defenders in North America.

Trujillo was assassinated in 1961,[18] but his gang hung on, although Washington persuaded some of them to leave. An election in December 1962 put Juan Bosch into the presidency. Bosch was a man long in exile from the Trujillo butchery, an idealistic intellectual without experience in affairs. His inauguration early in 1963 was greeted with some enthusiasm in intellectual circles in the United States. What was not sufficiently realized was that Bosch faced terrible problems. Although the Trujillo family was gone, most of their collaborators still were in the civi-

lian or military bureaucracies. The public could not be expected ordinarily to take strong action to support the government. Bosch made some efforts at reform. The conservatives said he was a leftist. He tried to punish them, and they removed him from the presidency in September 1963 and sent him into exile. Bosch was a lamb among wolves.

For the next year and a half the Dominican conservatives and Washington maneuvered inconclusively; then on April 24, 1965, a revolt began, with attacks on the army around the city of Santo Domingo. The apparent intention was to restore Bosch, although there is no knowing what the rebels might have done had they won. They distributed arms to civilians to help them. The "loyalists"—that is, the conservative army supporting the president it had installed—asked logistical support from the United States to help them protect United States citizens. Messages from the embassy in Santo Domingo to Washing did not perfectly clarify a situation that was confusing to all participants. The big difficulty was that the suggestion was made to sound worse by reference to Castroism. The Johnson administration on April 28 decided to land marines, announcing that they were to protect United States citizens.

The fighting in Santo Domingo certainly threatened the safety of foreigners. The trouble with the announcement was that so many people suspected—with reason, as it turned out—that Washington also had containment of communism in mind. There was resentment at what was thought to be subterfuge, as well as objection to deceit. That made difficult discussion of the important issue: Was there a threat of communism, and what did it mean to the United States? On April 29 the embassy in Santo Domingo put out a list of fifty-three communists with the rebel forces. The list turned out to be inaccurate and in any event did not demonstrate much of a threat by itself. The question of the "evidence" for communism among the rebels and how that could be shown to be a threat became a mess of contradiction, innuendo, and shoddy practice.

---

[18] Before and after 1961 it was asserted that the United States was "responsible" for the Trujillo regime, certainly an exaggeration. Dictatorship grew out of just those social conditions that had existed in the country since Independence and had produced the same result in many other Latin American countries. Trujillo sustained himself largely with blood and terror. It may be argued that the United States helped prolong his rule by private investment and government support or acquiescence.

By April 30 President Johnson realized he had a bear by the tail, and he made extraordinary efforts thereafter to extricate himself with as much hide as possible. Individuals and groups with passionate convictions on the subject had lined up on both sides, and the president was going to be hurt no matter what he did. He soon adopted the view that the intervention was to prevent the creation of another communist regime in the Western Hemisphere. Possibly there was a danger, but it was not "proved." Johnson decided not to take a chance, using the information and advice he had available.

He was somewhat more successful in an effort to shift responsibility to the OAS. Under much pressure, that organization on May 5 created an Inter-American Peace Force, but five states voted against it and another abstained. Johnson was fortunate in that Brazil was run at the time by a military regime that was strongly anticommunist and dependent on good economic relations with the United States. Brazil promptly supplied a commander for the Inter-American Peace Force and the largest non–United States contingent of troops. Judgments of the OAS action varied. Critics scoffed at it as a useless subterfuge, and Brazil's collaboration as merely the lockstep of a client state. Regarding the matter so simplistically surely was a dangerous error. Brazil had more than one-third of the territory and population of Latin America and not entirely ludicrous ambitions for world-power status. It was no flunky of Washington. It helped reduce the load on President Johnson to suit its own purposes. The anticommunism of the regime in Brazil is not "made in the USA."

The Johnson administration quickly recovered from its initial confusion, which had been caused by defective reporting from the Dominican Republic and by poor estimation of the effects of its first actions on some vocal elements in the United States. Possibly the majority of the United States public either supported the intervention or was not much interested; that is at least as good a guess as the supposition that a majority was much interested in the protests of critics of the Dominican policy. Able people in the administration were hustled to the Caribbean to try to sort out the mess. Almost at once some considered reinstalling Bosch a likely move. But there was objection in Washington to that, too. The United States finally decided on civilian Héctor García-Godoy, who had served with Bosch. He had to be crammed down the throats of the loyalist military, and the United States was able to do so. The loyalists were not reconciled, so the United States supported a move in January 1966 that forced military leaders on both the rebel and loyalist sides out of the country.

In June 1966 an election was held. Juan Balaguer, campaigning widely and promising reforms, won. He had to contend with his reputation as an old collaborator in the Trujillo regime, but he apparently was not hurt in the eyes of the rural population, which supported him strongly. They knew that under Trujillo one fled the country, collaborated, or died, and they recognized that Balaguer was no butcher. Furthermore, common people had benefited under the Trujillo regime and had been little bothered by the tyranny, which hit the opponents and active collaborators of the tyrant. Bosch had lost his support. He had shown bad judgment and weakness as an executive. He had not returned when the revolt began in April 1965. He did not campaign as Balaguer did. Balaguer was reelected in 1970 and 1974 for four-year terms and continued an administration that was mildly authoritarian and mildly paternalistic. It presided over considerable economic growth, especially of sugar exports, that depended heavily on foreign capital. The coming of OPEC petroleum prices, together with lowered sugar prices in the mid-1970s, wiped out recent gains in foreign trade. The prospects were not rosy for the 4.5 million poor citizens of the lovely Caribbean land which Columbus so long ago had found enchanting. The citizens of the Dominican Republic, like those of the Caribbean generally, looked at beauty and lived in poverty. Modernization had a dubious future in the area where Europeans had begun their expansion to America.

Afterword: Whither Latin America?

A Nobel laureate reminds us that "there is little warrant for the belief that we know the laws of history well enough to make projections of any great reliability." It follows from this that neither bland optimism nor black pessimism about Latin America can be based securely on fact. We can feel comfortable, however, with a few predictions. Wherever Latin America is going, it will remain a large part of the earth's surface, and presumably Brazil, Argentina, and Mexico will remain among the largest nations. It will retain its magnificent heritage of natural resources, in land, waters, climate, petroleum, and minerals: 8 million square miles of land stretching from the border of the United States to the edge of the Antarctic seas. For some time, at least, its population increase is likely to continue at the gallop, with Brazil and Mexico among the dozen most populous nations on earth.

The persistent development and modernization of Latin America during the difficulties of the century and a half since Independence surely promise continued effort, and some success, in dealing with intricate social problems. National sentiment and national integration have much improved, and increasingly result from planned programs. Planning will presumably continue to favor enlarged state activity, but possibly the private sector will remain large. We can scarcely guess at the mix and methods and schedules of national or international effort in the future. We can only be rather confident that the expanding efforts of Latin Americans in recent decades will wax rather than wane. For some observers, what matters is whether progress comes by an evolutionary process or by abrupt revolutionary change. Some seem to care only for lessened "dependence." For others, the critical question is economic production—developmentalism—however achieved. There are those who reduce judgment to a matter of social justice. Yet others think the ultimate test is whether Latin America has open or closed societies, democracy or autocracy. Latin Americans have a variety of views of the future, for

Who shall know the Promised Land
Before he has seen it?

Suggested Readings

Guides. Charles Griffin, ed., *Latin America: A Guide to Historical Literature* (Austin, Tex., 1971). *The Handbook of Latin American Studies* (Cambridge, Mass., 1936–1951; Gainesville, Fla., 1951ff.). R. A. Humphreys, *Latin American History: A Guide to the Literature in English* (New York, 1958). Preston E. James, *Geography of Latin America*, 4th ed. (New York, 1969).

Colonial Period

Spain and Portugal. A. O. Aldridge, ed., *The Ibero-American Enlightenment* (Chicago, 1971). R. Trevor Davies, *The Golden Century of Spain, 1501–1621* (New York, 1965); *Spain in Decline, 1621–1700* (London, 1957). B. W. Diffie, *Prelude to Empire: Portugal Overseas Before Henry the Navigator* (Lincoln, Neb., 1961). Antonio Domínguez Ortiz, *The Golden Age of Spain, 1516–1659*, tr. by James Casey (New York, 1971). John H. Elliott, *Imperial Spain, 1469–1716* (New York, 1964). Richard Herr, *The Eighteenth-Century Revolution in Spain* (Princeton, N.J., 1958). Harold Johnson, ed., *From Reconquest to Empire: The Iberian Background to Latin American History* (New York, 1970). H. V. Livermore, *A New History of Portugal* (Cambridge, 1966). John Lynch, *Spain Under the Hapsburgs*, 2 vols. (New York, 1964–1969). A. H. de Oliveira Marques, *History of Portugal*, 2 vols. (New York, 1972). Roger B. Merriman, *The Rise of the Spanish Empire in the Old World and the New*, 4 vols. (New York, 1918–1934). Charles E. Nowell, *A History of Portugal* (New York, 1952). Stanley G. Payne, *A History of Spain and Portugal*, 2 vols. (Madison, Wis., 1973).

Amerindians. Wendell C. Bennett and Junius B. Bird, *Andean Culture History*, 2d rev. ed. (New York, 1964; 1st published 1949). Ignacio Bernal, *Mexico Before Cortez: Art, History, Legend* (New York, 1963); *The Olmec World*, tr. by D. Heyden and F. Horcasitas (Berkeley, Calif., 1969). Woodrow Borah and Sherburne F. Cook, *The Aboriginal Population of Central Mexico on the Eve of the Spanish Conquest* (Berkeley, Calif., 1963). B. C. Brundage, *Empire of the Inca* (Norman, Okla., 1963); *A Rain of Darts: The Mexica Aztecs* (Austin, Tex., 1972). G. H. S. Bushnell, *Peru*, rev. ed. (London, 1963). Michael Coe, *The Maya* (New York, 1966); *Mexico* (New York, 1962). Harold E. Driver, ed., *The Americas on the Eve of Discovery* (Englewood Cliffs, N.J., 1964). Garcilaso de la Vega, *Royal Commentaries of the Incas and General History of Peru*, 2 vols., tr. by Harold V. Livermore (Austin, Tex., 1966). *Handbook of South*

American Indians, ed. J. H. Steward, 6 vols. (Washington, 1946–1950); *Handbook of Middle American Indians*, ed. by Robert Wauchope (Austin, Tex., 1964ff.). J. Alden Mason, *The Ancient Civilizations of Peru* (Baltimore, 1957). P. A. Means, *Ancient Civilizations of the Andes* (New York, 1931). Robert C. Padden, *The Humming Bird and the Hawk: Conquest and Sovereignty in the Valley of Mexico, 1503–1541* (Columbus, Ohio, 1967). Ralph Loveland Roys, *The Indian Background of Colonial Yucatan* (Norman, Okla., 1972; first ed. 1943). Ronald Spores, *The Mixtec Kings and Their People* (Norman, Okla., 1967). Francis B. Steck, *Motolinía's History of the Indians of New Spain* (Washington, 1951). Robert Wauchope, ed., *The Indian Background of Latin American History: The Maya, Aztec, Inca, and Their Predecessors* (New York, 1970). Eric Wolf, *Sons of the Shaking Earth* (Chicago, 1959).

Exploration, Conquest, Early Colonization. Germán Arciniegas, *America and the New World: The Life and Times of Amerigo Vespucci*, tr. by Harriet de Onís (New York, 1955); *The Knight of El Dorado: The Tale of Don Gonzalo Jiménez de Quesada and His Conquest of New Granada* (New York, 1942). Herbert E. Bolton, *Coronado: Knight of Pueblos and Plains* (Albuquerque, N. Mex., 1949). C. S. Braden, *Religious Aspects of the Conquest of Mexico* (Durham, N.C., 1930). *The Broken Spears: The Aztec Account of the Conquest of Mexico*, ed. by Miguel León-Portilla (Boston, 1961). J. B. Brebner, *The Explorers of North America, 1492–1806* (New York, 1933). Robert S. Chamberlain, *The Conquest and Colonization of Honduras, 1502–1550* (Washington, 1953); *The Conquest and Colonization of Yucatan, 1517–50* (Washington, 1948). *The Journal of Christopher Columbus*, tr. by Cecil Jane (New York, 1960). *Life of the Admiral Christopher Columbus by His Son Ferdinand*, ed. by Benjamin Keen (New Brunswick, N.J., 1958). *Five Letters of Cortés to the Emperor* (New York, 1962). *De Orbe Novo: The Eight Decades of Peter Martyr D'Anghera*,

2 vols., tr. by F. A. MacNutt (New York, 1912). Bernal Díaz del Castillo, *A True History of the Conquest of New Spain* (New York, 1958, and other editions). Troy S. Floyd, *The Columbus Dynasty in the Caribbean, 1492–1526* (Albuquerque, N. Mex., 1973). Lewis Hanke, *Bartolomé de las Casas* (The Hague, 1951); *The First Social Experiments in America* (Cambridge, 1935). John Hemming, *The Conquest of the Incas* (New York, 1970). James Lockhart, *The Men of Cajamarca: A Social and Biographical Study of the First Conquerors of Peru* (Austin, Tex., 1972). Francisco López de Gómara, *Cortés: The Life of the Conqueror by His Secretary*, tr. by L. B. Simpson (Berkeley, Calif., 1966). P. A. Means, *The Fall of the Inca Empire and the Spanish Rule in Peru, 1530–1780* (New York, 1932). S. E. Morison, *Admiral of the Ocean Sea: A Life of Christopher Columbus*, 2 vols. (Boston, 1942); *The European Discovery of America*, 2 vols. (New York, 1971–1974). Charles E. Nowell, *The Great Discoveries and the First Colonial Empires* (Ithaca, N.Y., 1954). J. H. Parry, *The Age of Reconnaissance, Discovery, Exploration, and Settlement*, 2d ed. (New York, 1969). W. H. Prescott, *History of the Conquest of Mexico*, 3 vols. (New York, 1843, and later editions); *History of the Conquest of Peru*, 2 vols. (New York, 1847). Pedro Pizarro, *Relation of the Discovery and Conquests of the Kingdoms of Peru*, 2 vols., ed. by P. A. Means (New York, 1922). Robert Ricard, *The Spiritual Conquest of Mexico*, tr. by L. B. Simpson (Berkeley, Calif., 1966). Kathleen Romoli, *Balboa of Darien: Discoverer of the Pacific* (New York, 1953). Carl O. Sauer, *The Early Spanish Main* (Berkeley, Calif., 1966). John Varner, *The Life and Times of Garcilaso de la Vega* (Austin, Tex., 1968). Henry R. Wagner, *The Rise of Fernando Cortés* (Los Angeles, 1944).

Government, Territorial Expansion, International Relations. A. S. Aiton, *Antonio de Mendoza* (Durham, N.C., 1927). John F. Bannon, *The Spanish Borderlands Frontier, 1513–1821* (New York, 1970). Harry Bernstein, *Origins of*

Inter-American Interest, 1700–1812 (Philadelphia, 1945). Bernard E. Bobb, *The Viceregency of Antonio María Bucareli in New Spain, 1771–1779* (Austin, Tex., 1962). H. E. Bolton, *The Spanish Borderlands* (New Haven, Conn., 1921). John R. Fisher, *Government and Society in Colonial Peru: The Intendant System, 1784–1814* (London, 1970). Lillian Estelle Fisher, *The Last Inca Revolt, 1780–83* (Norman, Okla., 1966). Henry Folmer, *Franco-Spanish Rivalry in North America, 1524–1763* (Glendale, Calif., 1953). Cornelis C. Goslinga, *The Dutch in the Caribbean and on the Wild Coast, 1580–1680* (Assen, The Netherlands, 1971). C. H. Haring, *The Buccaneers in the West Indies in the Seventeenth Century* (London, 1910); *The Spanish Empire in America*, rev. ed. (New York, 1952). Jorge Juan and Antonio de Ulloa, *A Voyage to South America*, 2 vols., tr. from the Spanish (London, 1806, and later editions). Magali Sarfatti Larson, *Spanish Bureaucratic Patrimonialism in America* (Berkeley, Calif., 1966). John Lynch, *Spanish Colonial Administration, 1782–1810: The Intendant System in the Viceroyalty of the Rio de la Plata* (London, 1958). James M. Manfredini, *The Political Role of the Count of Revillagigedo, Viceroy of New Spain, 1789–94* (New Brunswick, N.J., 1949). Lyle N. McAlister, *The "Fuero Militar" in New Spain, 1765–1800* (Gainesville, Fla., 1957). P. A. Means, *The Spanish Main: Focus of Envy, 1492–1700* (New York, 1935). John P. Moore, *The Cabildo in Peru Under the Hapsburgs* (Durham, N.C., 1954); *The Cabildo in Peru under the Bourbons* (Durham, N.C., 1966). Magnus Mörner, ed., *The Expulsion of the Jesuits from Latin America* (New York, 1965). A. P. Newton, *The European Nations in the West Indies, 1493–1688* (London, 1933). J. H. Parry, *The Audiencia of New Galicia in the Sixteenth Century* (Cambridge, 1948); *The Sale of Public Office in the Spanish Indies under the Hapsburgs* (Berkeley, Calif., 1953). John Phelan, *The Kingdom of Quito in the Seventeenth Century: Bureaucratic Politics in the Spanish Empire* (Madison, Wis., 1967). Philip Wayne Powell, *Soldiers, Indians and Silver* (Berkeley, Calif.,

1952). Herbert I. Priestley, *José de Gálvez: Visitor-General of New Spain, 1765–71* (Berkeley, Calif., 1916). Robert C. West, *The Mining Community in Northern New Spain: The Parral Mining District* (Berkeley, Calif., 1949). Robert S. Weddle, *Wilderness Manhunt: The Spanish Search for La Salle* (Austin, Tex., 1973). A. F. Zimmerman, *Francisco de Toledo: The Fifth Viceroy of Peru, 1569–81* (Caldwell, Idaho, 1938).

Race and Black Slavery.   Hubert H. S. Aimes, *The History of Slavery in Cuba, 1511–1868* (New York, 1967; 1st published 1907). David W. Cohen and Jack P. Greene, eds., *Neither Slave nor Free: The Freedmen of African Descent in the Slave Societies of the New World* (Baltimore, 1972). Philip D. Curtin, *The Atlantic Slave Trade: A Census* (Madison, Wis., 1969). David Brion Davis, *The Problem of Slavery in Western Culture* (Ithaca, N.Y., 1966). Eugene Genovese and Laura Foner, eds., *Slavery in the New World* (Englewood Cliffs, N.J., 1970). Lewis Hanke, *Aristotle and the American Indians: A Study in Race Prejudice in the Modern World* (Bloomington, Ind., 1970); *The Spanish Struggle for Justice in the Conquest of America* (Boston, 1965; 1st ed. 1959). Melville J. Herskovits, *The New World Negro* (Bloomington, Ind., 1966). Kenneth F. Kiple, *Blacks in Colonial Cuba, 1774–1899* (Gainesville, Fla., 1976). Herbert S. Klein, *Slavery in the Americas: A Comparative Study of Virginia and Cuba* (Chicago, 1967). Daniel Mannix and Malcolm Cowley, *Black Cargoes: A History of the Atlantic Slave Trade, 1518–1865* (New York, 1965; 1st ed. 1962). Magnus Mörner, *Race Mixture in the History of Latin America* (Boston, 1967). Henry Raup, *The Life and Writings of Bartolomé de Las Casas* (Albuquerque, N. Mex., 1967). Leslie B. Rout, Jr., *The African Experience in Spanish America: 1502 to the Present Day* (New York, 1976).

The Church.   P. J. Barth, *Franciscan Education and the Social Order in Spanish North*

America, 1502–1821 (Chicago, 1945). H. E. Bolton, *Rim of Christendom: A Biography of Eusebio Francisco Kino, Pacific Coast Pioneer* (New York, 1936). W. M. Farriss, *Crown and Clergy in Colonial Mexico, 1759–1821: The Crisis of Ecclesiastical Privilege* (London, 1968). Richard E. Greenleaf, *The Mexican Inquisition of the Seventeenth Century* (Albuquerque, N. Mex., 1969); ed., *The Roman Catholic Church in Colonial Latin America* (New York, 1971). Henry Charles Lea, *The Inquisition in the Spanish Dependencies* (New York, 1908). Francisco Morales, *Ethnic and Social Background of the Franciscan Friars in Seventeenth-Century Mexico* (Washington, 1973). Magnus Mörner, *The Political and Economic Activities of the Jesuits in the La Plata Region: The Hapsburg Era*, tr. by A. Read (Stockholm, 1953). J. F. Rippy and J. T. Nelson, *Crusaders of the Jungle* (Chapel Hill, N.C., 1936). Antonine Tibesar, *Franciscan Beginnings in Colonial Peru* (Washington, 1953).

Economic. P. J. Bakewell, *Silver Mining and Society in Colonial Mexico: Zacatecas, 1546–1700* (New York, 1971). W. J. Barrett, *The Sugar Hacienda of the Marqueses del Valle* (Minneapolis, 1970). Woodrow Borah, *Early Colonial Trade and Navigation between Mexico and Peru* (Berkeley, Calif., 1954); *New Spain's Century of Depression* (Berkeley, Calif., 1951); *Silk Raising in Colonial Mexico* (Berkeley, Calif., 1943). David Brading, *Miners and Merchants in Bourbon Mexico, 1763–1810* (New York, 1971). William Dusenberry, *The Mexican Mesta* (Urbana, Ill., 1963). Earl J. Hamilton, *American Treasure and the Price Revolution in Spain, 1501–1650* (Cambridge, 1934). Brian R. Hamnett, *Politics and Trade in Southern Mexico, 1750–1821* (Cambridge, 1971). C. H. Haring, *Trade and Navigation Between Spain and the Indies in the Time of the Hapsburgs* (Cambridge, 1918). Walter Howe, *The Mining Guild of New Spain and Its Tribunal General, 1770–1821* (Cambridge, 1949). R. D. Hussey, *The Caracas Company, 1728–84* (Cambridge, 1934).

Robert G. Keith, *Conquest and Agrarian Change: The Emergence of the Hacienda System in the Peruvian Coast* (Cambridge, 1976). Richard Pares, *The Trade Between North America and the West Indies Before the American Revolution* (London, 1956). Ruth Pike, *Enterprise and Adventure: The Genoese in Seville and the Opening of the New World* (Ithaca, N.Y., 1966). A. P. Whitaker, *The Huancavelica Mercury Mine* (Cambridge, 1941).

Social, Intellectual, Miscellaneous. C. R. Boxer, *Women in Iberian Expansion Overseas, 1415–1815: Some Facts, Fancies and Personalities* (New York, 1975). François Chevalier, *Land and Society in Colonial Mexico*, tr. by L. B. Simpson (Berkeley, Calif., 1963). Sherburne F. Cook and Woodrow Borah, *Essays in Population History: Mexico and the Caribbean*, vol. 1 (Berkeley, Calif., 1971). Donald B. Cooper, *Epidemic Disease in Mexico City, 1761–1813* (Austin, Tex., 1965). Lillian E. Fisher, *Champion of Reform: Manuel Abad y Queipo* (New York, 1971; 1st ed. 1955). Thomas Gage, *Travels in the New World* (Norman, Okla., 1958). Charles Gibson, *The Aztecs Under Spanish Rule: A History of the Indians of the Valley of Mexico* (Stanford, Calif., 1964); *Spain in America* (New York, 1966); *Tlaxcala in the Sixteenth Century* (New Haven, Conn., 1952). Lewis Hanke, *The Imperial City of Potosí* (The Hague, 1956). George Kubler and Martin Soria, *Art and Architecture in Spain and Portugal and Their American Dominions, 1500–1800* (Baltimore, 1959). John T. Lanning, *Academic Culture in the Spanish Colonies* (New York, 1940); *The University in the Kingdom of Guatemala* (Ithaca, N.Y., 1955). Irving A. Leonard, *Baroque Times in Old Mexico* (Ann Arbor, Mich., 1959); *Books of the Brave: Being an Account of Books and of Men in the Spanish Conquest and Settlement of the Sixteenth Century* (Cambridge, 1949); *Don Carlos de Sigüenza y Góngora* (Berkeley, Calif., 1929). James Lockhart, *Spanish Peru, 1532–1560: A Colonial Society* (Madison, Wis., 1968). Murdo J. MacLeod, *Spanish Cen-*

tral America: A Socio-Economic History, 1520–1720 (Berkeley, Calif., 1973). Bernard Moses, *Spanish Colonial Literature in South America* (New York, 1922). Clement G. Motten, *Mexican Silver and the Enlightenment* (Philadelphia, 1950). J. H. Parry and P. M. Sherlock, *A Short History of the West Indies* (London, 1956). Mariano Picón-Salas, *A Cultural History of Spanish America, from Conquest to Independence,* tr. by I. A. Leonard (Berkeley, Calif., 1962). G. M. Riley, *Fernando Córtes and the Marquesado in Morelos, 1522–47: A Case Study in the Socioeconomic Development of Sixteenth-Century Mexico* (Albuquerque, N. Mex., 1973). Robert J. Shafer, *The Economic Societies in the Spanish World, 1763–1821* (Syracuse, N.Y., 1958). L. B. Simpson, *The Encomienda in New Spain: The Beginning of Spanish Mexico* (Berkeley, Calif., 1950). William B. Taylor, *Landlord and Peasant in Colonial Oaxaca* (Stanford, Calif., 1972). A. C. Wilgus, ed., *Colonial Hispanic America* (Washington, 1936). Silvio Zavala, *New Viewpoints on the Spanish Colonization of America* (Philadelphia, 1943).

Brazil. Dauril Alden, *Royal Government in Colonial Brazil* (Berkeley, Calif., 1968). C. R. Boxer, *The Dutch in Brazil, 1624–54* (Oxford, 1957); *The Golden Age of Brazil, 1695–1750* (Berkeley, Calif., 1962); *The Portuguese Seaborne Empire, 1415–1825* (New York, 1969); *Portuguese Society in the Tropics: The Municipal Councils of Goa, Macao, Bahia, and Luanda, 1510–1800* (Madison, Wis., 1965); *Race Relations in the Portuguese Colonial Empire, 1415–1825* (Oxford, 1963); *Salvador de Sa and the Struggle for Brazil and Angola* (New York, 1953). Luís Edmundo da Costa, *Rio in the Time of the Viceroys,* tr. by D. H. Momsen (Rio de Janeiro, 1936). Carl Degler, *Neither Black nor White: Slavery and Race Relations in Brazil and the United States* (New York, 1971). H. E. S. Fisher, *The Portugal Trade: A Study of Anglo-Portuguese Commerce, 1700–70* (London, 1971); despite the title, Brazil plays a role. Gilberto Freyre, *The Masters and the Slaves,* tr. by S.

Putnam (New York, 1956). Mathias C. Kiemen, *The Indian Policy of Portugal in the Amazon Region, 1614–93* (Washington, 1954). Pero Magalhães de Gandavo, *The Histories of Brazil,* tr. by J. B. Stetson, Jr. (New York, 1922). Alexander Marchant, *From Barter to Slavery* (Baltimore, 1942). Richard M. Morse, ed., *The Bandeirantes: The Historical Role of the Brazilian Pathfinders* (New York, 1965). Caio Prado, Jr., *The Colonial Background of Modern Brazil,* tr. by S. Macedo (Berkeley, Calif., 1967). Edgar Prestage, *The Portuguese Pioneers* (London, 1933). Stuart B. Schwartz, *Sovereignty and Society in Colonial Brazil: The High Court of Bahia and its Judges, 1609–1751* (Berkeley, Calif., 1973). Robert Southey, *History of Brazil,* 3 vols. (London, 1810–1819). Arnold Wiznitzer, *Jews in Colonial Brazil* (New York, 1960).

Independence. Charles W. Arnade, *The Emergence of the Republic of Bolivia* (Gainesville, Fla., 1957). Thomas Blossom, *Nariño: Hero of Colombian Independence* (Tucson, Ariz., 1967). David Bushnell, ed., *The Liberator, Simón Bolívar: Man and Image* (New York, 1970). Stephen Clissold, *Bernardo O'Higgins and the Independence of Chile* (New York, 1969). Simon Collier, *Ideas and Politics of Chilean Independence, 1808–33* (London, 1967). Lilian E. Fisher, *The Background of the Revolution for Mexican Independence* (Boston, 1934). Richard Graham, *Independence in Latin America* (New York, 1972). Charles Griffin, *The United States and the Disruption of the Spanish Empire, 1810–22* (New York, 1937). Alfred Hasbrouck, *Foreign Legionaries in the Liberation of Spanish South America* (New York, 1967; 1st ed. 1927). R. A. Humphreys, *Liberation in South America, 1806–27: The Career of James Paroissien* (London, 1952); and John Lynch, eds., *The Origins of the Latin American Revolution, 1808–26* (New York, 1965). William W. Kaufmann, *British Policy and the Independence of Latin America, 1804–28* (New Haven, Conn., 1951). Benjamin Keen, *David Curtis DeForest and the Revolution of Buenos Aires* (New Haven, Conn.,

1947). Jay Kinsbruner, *Bernardo O'Higgins* (New York, 1968); *The Spanish American Independence Movement* (Hinsdale, Ill., 1973). Vicente Lecuna and Harold Bierck, *Selected Writings of Bolivar*, 2 vols. (New York, 1951). John Lynch, *The Spanish American Revolutions, 1808–26* (New York, 1973). Salvador de Madariaga, *Bolívar* (London, 1952). Gerhard Masur, *Simón Bolívar* (Albuquerque, N. Mex., 1969; 1st ed. 1948). J. C. J. Metford, *San Martín the Liberator* (London, 1950). Bernard Moses, *Spain's Declining Power in South America, 1730–1806* (Berkeley, Calif., 1919). Thomas Ott, *The Haitian Revolution, 1789–1804* (Knoxville, Tenn., 1973). J. F. Rippy, *Rivalry of the United States and Great Britain Over Latin America, 1808–30* (Baltimore, 1929). William S. Robertson, *France and Latin-American Independence* (Baltimore, 1939); *Iturbide of Mexico* (Durham, N.C., 1952); *The Life of Miranda*, 2 vols. (Chapel Hill, N.C., 1929); *Rise of the Spanish-American Republics as Told in the Lives of Their Liberators* (New York, 1918, and later editions). Ricardo Rojas, *San Martín, Knight of the Andes*, tr. by H. Brickell and C. Videla (New York, 1945). G. A. Sherwell, *Antonio José de Sucre* (Washington, 1924). Wilbert H. Timmons, *Morelos of Mexico, Priest, Soldier, Statesman* (El Paso, Texas, 1963). John Street, *Artigas and the Emancipation of Uruguay* (London, 1959). Joseph Thorning, *Miranda: World Citizen* (Gainesville, Fla., 1952). George F. Tyson, Jr., ed., *Toussaint L'Ouverture* (Englewood Cliffs, N.J., 1973). A. P. Whitaker, *The United States and the Independence of Latin America, 1800–30* (Baltimore, 1941).

Since Independence

Politics and Government. Robert J. Alexander, *Latin American Politics and Government* (New York, 1965); *Prophets of the Revolution: Profiles of Latin American Leaders* (New York, 1962). Charles W. Anderson, *Politics and Economic Change in Latin America: The Governing of Restless Nations* (Princeton, N.J., 1967). Ronald Chilcotte and Joel Edelstein, eds., *Latin America: The Struggle with Dependency and Beyond* (Cambridge, 1974). H. E. Davis, ed., *Government and Politics in Latin America* (New York, 1958). Alexander T. Edelmann, *Latin American Government and Politics: The Dynamics of a Revolutionary Society* (Homewood, Ill., 1965). H. M. Hamill, Jr., ed., *Dictatorship in Spanish America* (New York, 1965). I. Horowitz, et al., eds., *Latin American Radicalism: A Documentary Report on Left and Nationalist Movements* (New York, 1969). J. J. Johnson, *Political Change in Latin America: The Emergence of the Middle Sectors* (Stanford, Calif., 1958). Robert Kern and Robert Dolkart, eds., *The Caciques: Oligarchical Politics and the System of Caciquismo in the Luso-Hispanic World* (Albuquerque, N. Mex., 1973). Ronald McDonald, *Party Systems and Elections in Latin America* (Chicago, 1971). Martin Needler, *Latin American Politics in Perspective* (Princeton, N.J., 1963); *Political Development in Latin America: Instability, Violence, and Evolutionary Change* (New York, 1968). William Pierson and Federico Gil, *Governments of Latin America* (New York, 1957). Frederick B. Pike, ed., *Freedom and Reform in Latin America* (Notre Dame, Ind., 1959). Frederick Pike and Thomas Stritch, eds., *The New Corporatism: Social-Political Structures in the Iberian World* (Notre Dame, Ind., 1974). Claudio Véliz, ed., *The Politics of Conformity in Latin America* (New York, 1967). Edward J. Williams, *Latin American Christian Democratic Parties* (Knoxville, Tenn., 1967).

International Relations. Samuel Bemis, *The Latin American Policy of the United States* (New York, 1943). Harry Bernstein, *Making an Inter-American Mind* (Gainesville, Fla., 1961). Alexander DeConde, *Herbert Hoover's Latin-American Policy* (Stanford, Calif., 1951). Donald Dozer, *Are We Good Neighbors? Three Decades of Inter-American Relations, 1930–60* (Gainesville, Fla., 1959); ed., *The Monroe Doctrine: Its Modern Significance* (New York, 1965). J. C. Drier, ed., *The Alliance for Progress: Prob-*

lems and Perspectives (Baltimore, 1962). Herbert Feis, *The Diplomacy of the Dollar: First Era, 1919–32* (Baltimore, 1950). C. G. Fenwick, *The Organization of American States: The Inter-American Regional System* (Washington, 1963). Federico Gil, *Latin American–United States Relations* (New York, 1971). Lincoln Gordon, *A New Deal for Latin America: The Alliance for Progress* (Cambridge, 1963). E. O. Guerrant, *Roosevelt's Good Neighbor Policy* (Albuquerque, N. Mex., 1950). R. D. Hussey and R. Burr, *Documents on Inter-American Cooperation*, 2 vols. (Philadelphia, 1955). S. G. Inman, *Inter-American Conferences, 1826–1954* (Washington, 1965). J. A. Logan, *No Transfer: An American Security Principle* (New Haven, Conn., 1961). J. L. Mecham, *A Survey of United States–Latin American Relations* (Boston, 1965); *The United States and Inter-American Security* (Austin, Tex., 1961). Edward S. Milenky, *The Politics of Regional Organization in Latin America: The Latin American Free Trade Association* (New York, 1973). J. W. Nystrom and N. A. Haverstock, *The Alliance for Progress* (Princeton, N.J., 1966). Dexter Perkins, *A History of the Monroe Doctrine* (Boston, 1955). J. F. Rippy, *Latin America in World Politics*, 3d ed. (New York, 1938); *Globe and Hemisphere* (Chicago, 1958). C. N. Ronning, ed., *Intervention in Latin America* (New York, 1970). A. P. Whitaker, *The United States and the Independence of Latin America, 1800–30* (Baltimore, 1941); *The United States and South America: The Northern Republics* (Cambridge, 1948); *The Western Hemisphere Idea: Its Rise and Decline* (Ithaca, N.Y., 1954). Bryce Wood, *The Making of the Good Neighbor Policy* (New York, 1961). George Wythe, *The United States and Inter-American Relations: A Contemporary Appraisal* (Gainesville, Fla., 1964).

Nationalism.   Samuel Bailey, ed., *Nationalism in Latin America* (New York, 1971). Gerhard Masur, *Nationalism in Latin America: Diversity and Unity* (New York, 1966). Carl Solberg, *Immigration and Nationalism: Argentina and Chile,* *1890–1914* (Austin, Tex., 1970). A. P. Whitaker and David Jordan, *Nationalism in Contemporary Latin America* (New York, 1966).

The Church.   John Considine, *The Church in the New Latin America* (Notre Dame, Ind., 1964). J. L. Mecham, *Church and State in Latin America: A History of Politico-Ecclesiastical Relations*, rev. ed. (Chapel Hill, N.C., 1966). Frederick Pike, ed., *Conflict Between Church and State in Latin America* (New York, 1963). Karl Schmitt, ed., *The Roman Catholic Church in Modern Latin America* (New York, 1972).

The Military.   Willard Barber and C. N. Ronning, *Internal Security and Military Power: Counter-Insurgency and Civic Action in Latin America* (Columbus, 1966). Edwin Lieuwen, *Army and Politics in Latin America* (New York, 1960); *Generals vs. Presidents: Neomilitarism in Latin America* (New York, 1964). John Johnson, *The Military and Society in Latin America* (Stanford, Calif., 1964); ed., *The Role of the Military in Underdeveloped Countries* (Princeton, N.J., 1962). Mauricio Solaún and Michael A. Quinn, *Sinners and Heretics: The Politics of Military Intervention in Latin America* (Urbana, Ill., 1973).

Communism.   Luis E. Aguilar, ed., *Marxism in Latin America* (New York, 1968). Robert Alexander, *Communism in Latin America* (New Brunswick, N.J., 1957). R. E. Poppino, *International Communism in Latin America: A History of the Movement, 1917–63* (New York, 1964).

Labor.   Victor Alba, *Politics and the Labor Movement in Latin America* (Stanford, Calif., 1968). Robert Alexander, *Labor Relations in Argentina, Brazil, and Chile* (New York, 1962); *Organized Labor in Latin America* (New York, 1965). Moises Poblete Troncoso and Ben Burnett, *The Rise of the Latin American Labor Movement* (New York, 1960). Sinclair Snow, *The Pan-American Federation of Labor* (Durham, N.C., 1964).

Socioeconomic. R. N. Adams, et al., *Social Change in Latin America Today: Its Implications for United States Policy* (New York, 1960). F. C. Benham and H. A. Holley, *A Short Introduction to the Economy of Latin America* (New York, 1960). Marvin Bernstein, ed., *Foreign Investments in Latin America: Cases and Attitudes* (New York, 1966). James Cockcroft, et al., eds., *Dependence and Underdevelopment: Latin America's Political Economy* (Garden City, N.Y., 1972). Harold Davis, *Latin American Social Thought* (Washington, 1961). Celso Furtado, *Development and Underdevelopment,* tr. by R. de Aguiar and E. Drysdale (Berkeley, Calif., 1964). Wendell Gordon, *The Political Economy of Latin America* (New York, 1965). Simon Hanson, *Five Years of the Alliance for Progress* (Washington, 1967). Albert Hirschman, *Journeys Toward Progress: Studies of Economic Policy Making in Latin America* (New York, 1963). Albert Lauterbach, *Entrepreneurs in Latin America: Business Attitudes in a Developing Economy* (Ithaca, N.Y., 1966). Alberto Martinez Piedra, ed., *Socioeconomic Change in Latin America* (Washington, 1970). John Powelson, *Latin America: Today's Economic and Social Revolution* (New York, 1964). J. F. Rippy, *British Investments in Latin America* (Minneapolis, 1959); *Latin America and the Industrial Age,* 2d ed. (New York, 1947). Victor Urquidi, *The Challenge of Development in Latin America,* tr. by M. Urquidi (New York, 1964). Raymond Vernon, ed., *How Latin America Views the U. S. Investor* (New York, 1966).

Other General Topics. Germán Arciniegas, *Latin America: A Cultural History,* tr. by J. Mac-Lean (New York, 1966); *The State of Latin America* (New York, 1952). Harold Benjamin, *Higher Education in the American Republics* (New York, 1965). Harry Bernstein, *Modern and Contemporary Latin America* (Philadelphia, 1952). James Bryce, *South America: Observations and Impressions,* rev. ed. (New York, 1914). Stephen Clissold, *Latin America: A Cultural Outline* (New York, 1965). Carlos Dávila,

We of the Americas (Englewood Cliffs, N.J., 1949). Carlos Fuentes, et al., *Whither Latin America?* (New York, 1963). F. García Calderón, *Latin America: Its Rise and Progress* (New York, 1913). W. Rex Crawford, *A Century of Latin American Thought,* rev. ed. (Cambridge, 1961). Lewis Hanke, *Do the Americas Have a Common History? A Critique of the Bolton Thesis* (New York, 1964). Marvin Harris, *Patterns of Race in the Americas* (New York, 1964). Pedro Henriquez-Urena, *Literary Currents in Hispanic America* (Cambridge, 1945). I. Horowitz, ed., *Masses in Latin America* (New York, 1970). John Johnson, ed., *Continuity and Change in Latin America* (Stanford, Calif., 1967). Tom B. Jones, *South America Rediscovered* (Minneapolis, 1949). Benjamin Keen, ed., *Readings in Latin-American Civilization* (New York, 1955). Seymour Lipset and Aldo Solari, eds., *Elites in Latin America* (New York, 1967). Magnus Morner, ed., *Race and Class in Latin America* (New York, 1970). Richard M. Morse, et al., eds., *The Urban Development of Latin America, 1750–1920* (Stanford, Calif., 1971). Luis Quintanilla, *A Latin American Speaks* (New York, 1943). Robert E. Scott, ed., *Latin American Modernization Problems: Case Studies in the Crises of Change* (Urbana, Ill., 1973). T. L. Smith, ed., *Agrarian Reform in Latin America* (New York, 1965). Rodolfo Stavenhagen, ed., *Agrarian Problems and Peasant Movements in Latin America* (Garden City, N.Y. 1970). Watt Stewart, *Henry Meiggs: Yankee Pizarro* (Durham, N.C., 1946). Arturo Torres-Rioseco, *The Epic of Latin American Literature,* rev. ed. (New York, 1946). Claudio Véliz, ed., *Obstacles to Change in Latin America* (New York, 1965). Leopold Zea, *The Latin American Mind,* tr. from Spanish (Norman, Okla., 1963).

Individual Countries and Regions

Argentina. Samuel Baily, *Labor, Nationalism, and Politics in Argentina* (New York, 1967). J. R. Barager, *Why Perón Came to Power* (New York, 1968). G. I. Blanksten, *Perón's*

Argentina (Chicago, 1953). Alison W. Bunkley, *The Life of Sarmiento* (Princeton, N.J., 1952). Miron Burgin, *The Economic Aspects of Argentine Federalism, 1820–1852* (Cambridge, Mass., 1946). J. F. Cady, *Foreign Intervention in the Rio de la Plata* (Philadelphia, 1929). Alberto Ciria, et al., *New Perspectives on Modern Argentina* (Bloomington, Ind., 1972). Alberto Conil Paz, *Argentina's Foreign Policy, 1930–1962* (Notre Dame, Ind., 1966). Thomas B. Davis, Jr., *Carlos de Alvear: Man of Revolution* (Durham, N.C., 1955). Henry S. Ferns, *Argentina* (New York, 1969); *Britain and Argentina in the Nineteenth Century* (Oxford, 1960). Aldo Ferrer, *The Argentine Economy*, tr. by M. Urquidi (Berkeley, Calif., 1966). T. R. Fillol, *Social Factors in Economic Development: The Argentine Case* (Cambridge, 1961). Marvin Goldwert, *Democracy, Militarism, and Nationalism in Argentina, 1930–1966* (Austin, Tex., 1972). S. G. Hanson, *Argentine Meat and the British Market* (Stanford, Calif., 1938). Roger Haigh, *Martín Güemes: Tyrant or Tool? A Study of the Sources of Power of an Argentine Caudillo* (Fort Worth, Tex., 1968). José Luís de Imaz, *Los Que Mandan (Those Who Rule)*, tr. by C. A. Astiz and M. F. McCarthy (New York, 1970). Mark Jefferson, *Peopling the Argentine Pampa* (New York, 1926). W. H. Jeffrey, *Mitre and Argentina* (New York, 1952). John J. Kennedy, *Catholicism, Nationalism, and Democracy in Argentina* (Notre Dame, Ind., 1958). Clifton B. Kroeber, *The Growth of the Shipping Industry in the Rio de la Plata Region, 1794–1860* (Madison, Wis., 1957). Ricardo Levene, *A History of Argentina*, tr. and ed. by W. S. Robertson (Chapel Hill, N.C., 1937). Thomas F. McGann, *Argentina, The United States and the Inter-American System, 1880–1914* (Cambridge, 1957). Madaline Nichols, *The Gaucho* (Durham, N.C., 1942). Harold F. Peterson, *Argentina and the United States, 1810–1960* (Albany, N.Y., 1964). Robert Potash, *The Army and Politics in Argentina, 1928–1945* (Stanford, Calif., 1969). Ysabel F. Rennie, *The Argentine Republic* (New York, 1945). José

Luís Romero, *A History of Argentine Political Thought*, tr. by T. F. McGann (Stanford, Calif., 1963). D. F. Sarmiento, *Life in the Argentine Republic in the Days of the Tyrants: or Civilization and Barbarism*, tr. by Mrs. H. Mann (New York, 1868). James R. Scobie, *Argentina: A City and a Nation* (New York, 1971; 1st ed. 1964); *Revolution on the Pampas: a Social History of Argentine Wheat, 1860–1910* (Austin, Tex., 1964). Peter G. Snow, *Argentine Radicalism: The History and Doctrine of the Radical Civic Union* (Iowa City, 1965); *Political Forces in Argentina* (Boston, 1971). C. C. Taylor, *Rural Life in Argentina* (Baton Rouge, La., 1948). Richard J. Walter, *Student Politics in Argentina: The Reform and Its Effects, 1918–1964* (New York, 1968). Felix Weil, *Argentine Riddle* (New York, 1944). A. P. Whitaker, *The United States and Argentina* (Cambridge, 1954); *Argentine Upheaval: Peron's Fall and the New Regime* (New York, 1956); *Argentina* (Englewood Cliffs, N.J., 1964). J. W. White, *Argentina: The Life Story of a Nation* (New York, 1942).

Bolivia. Robert J. Alexander, *The Bolivian National Revolution* (New Brunswick, N.J., 1958). C. W. Arnade, *The Emergence of the Republic of Bolivia* (Gainesville, Fla., 1957). J. Valerie Fifer, *Bolivia: Land, Location, and Politics Since 1825* (New York, 1972). Dwight B. Heath, et al., *Land Reform and Social Revolution in Bolivia* (New York, 1969). Herbert S. Klein, *Parties and Political Change in Bolivia, 1880–1952* (New York, 1969). Olen E. Leonard, *Bolivia: Land, People and Institutions* (Washington, 1952). William L. Lofstrom, *The Promise and Problem of Reform: Attempted Social and Economic Change in the First Years of Bolivian Independence* (Ithaca, N.Y., 1972). James M. Malloy, *Bolivia: The Uncompleted Revolution* (Pittsburgh, 1970); and Richard S. Thorn, eds., *Beyond the Revolution: Bolivia Since 1952* (Pittsburgh, 1971). Harold Osborne, *Bolivia: A Land Divided*, 2d ed. (London, 1955). James W. Wilkie, *The Bolivian Revolution and*

United States Aid Since 1952: Financial Background and Context of Political Decisions (Los Angeles, 1969). C. H. Zondag, The Bolivian Economy, 1952–1965 (New York, 1966).

Brazil. Fernando de Azevedo, Brazilian Culture: An Introduction to the Study of Culture in Brazil, tr. by W. R. Crawford (New York, 1950). Werner Baer, Industrialization and Economic Development in Brazil (Homewood, Ill., 1965). J. M. Bello, A History of Modern Brazil, 1889–1964, tr. by J. L. Taylor (Stanford, Calif., 1966). Leslie Bethell, The Abolition of the Brazilian Slave Trade: Britain, Brazil and the Slave Trade Question, 1807–1869 (Cambridge, 1970). E. Bradford Burns, A Documentary History of Brazil (New York, 1966); A History of Brazil (New York, 1970); Nationalism in Brazil (New York, 1968); Perspectives on Brazilian History (New York, 1967). J. P. Calógeras, A History of Brazil, tr. and ed. by P. A. Martin (Chapel Hill, N.C., 1939). Robert Conrad, The Destruction of Brazilian Slavery, 1850–1888 (Berkeley, Calif., 1973). Sergio Corrêa Da Costa, Every Inch a King: A Biography of Dom Pedro I, First Emperor of Brazil, tr. by Samuel Putnam (New York, 1950). João Cruz Costa, A History of Ideas in Brazil, tr. by Suzette Macedo (Berkeley, Calif., 1964). Euclides Da Cunha, Rebellion in the Backlands (Os Sertões), tr. by Samuel Putnam (Chicago, 1957). John W. F. Dulles, Anarchists and Communists in Brazil: 1900–1935 (Austin, Tex., 1973); Unrest in Brazil: Political-Military Crises 1955–1964 (Austin, Tex., 1970); Vargas of Brazil: A Political Biography (Austin, Tex., 1967). Peter L. Eisenberg, The Sugar Industry of Pernambuco, 1840–1910 (Berkeley, Calif., 1974). Florestan Fernandes, The Negro in Brazilian Society, tr. by Jacqueline D. Skiles, A. Brunel, and Arthur Rothwell, ed. by Phyllis B. Eveleth (New York, 1967). Gilberto Freyre, New World in the Tropics: The Culture of Modern Brazil (New York, 1959); The Mansions and the Shanties: The Making of Modern Brazil, tr. and ed. by Harriet de Onis (New York, 1963); The Masters and the Slaves, tr. and ed. by Samuel Putnam, 2nd English ed. rev. (New York, 1956). Celso Furtado, The Economic Growth of Brazil: A Survey from Colonial Times, tr. by R. W. de Aguiar and E. C. Drysdale (Berkeley, Calif., 1963). Charles A. Gauld, The Last Titan, Percival Farquhar: American Entrepreneur in Latin America (Stanford, Calif., 1964). Richard Graham, Britain and the Onset of Modernization in Brazil 1859–1914 (Cambridge, 1968); A Century of Brazilian History Since 1865 (New York, 1969). C. H. Haring, Empire in Brazil: A New World Experiment with Monarchy (Cambridge, 1958). Marvin Harris, Town and Country in Brazil (New York, 1956). Lawrence Hill, Brazil (Berkeley, Calif., 1947); Diplomatic Relations Between the United States and Brazil (Durham, N.C., 1932). Emanuel de Kadt, Catholic Radicals in Brazil (New York, 1970). Daniel Kidder and J. C. Fletcher, Brazil and the Brazilians (Philadelphia, 1857). Joseph Love, Rio Grande do Sul and Brazilian Regionalism, 1882–1930 (Stanford, Calif., 1971). A. K. Manchester, British Preeminence in Brazil: Its Rise and Decline (Chapel Hill, N.C., 1933). Anyda Marchant, Viscount Mauá and the Empire of Brazil: A Biography of Ireneu Evangelista de Sousa, 1813–1889 (Berkeley, Calif., 1965). R. M. Morse, ed., From Community to Metropolis: A Biography of São Paulo, Brazil (Gainesville, Fla., 1958). Carolina Nabuco, The Life of Joaquim Nabuco, tr. and ed. by Ronald Hilton (Stanford, Calif., 1950). Roy Nash, The Conquest of Brazil (New York, 1926). J. F. Normano, Brazil: A Study of Economic Types (Chapel Hill, N.C., 1935). Donald Pierson, Negroes in Brazil: A Study of Race Contact at Bahia (Chicago, 1942). Rollie E. Poppino, Brazil: The Land and People, 2nd ed. (New York, 1973). Samuel Putnam, Marvelous Journey: Four Centuries of Brazilian Literature (New York, 1948). Arthur Ramos, The Negro in Brazil, tr. by Richard Pattee (Washington, 1939). S. H. Robock, Brazil's Developing Northeast: A Study of Regional Planning and Foreign Aid (Washington, 1963). Riordan Roett, ed., Brazil in the Sixties (Nashville, Tenn., 1972). John

Saunders, ed., *Modern Brazil: New Patterns and Development* (Gainesville, Fla., 1971). Philippe Schmitter, *Interest Conflict and Political Change in Brazil* (Stanford, Calif., 1971). Ronald M. Schneider, *The Political System of Brazil: Emergence of a "Modernizing" Authoritarian Regime, 1964–1970* (New York, 1971). Charles W. Simmons, *Marshal Deodoro and the Fall of Dom Pedro II* (Durham, N.C., 1966). Thomas L. Skidmore, *Politics in Brazil, 1930–1964: An Experiment in Democracy* (New York, 1967). T. Lynn Smith, *Brazil: People and Institutions*, 2nd ed. (Baton Rouge, La., 1954); and Alexander Marchant, *Brazil: Portrait of Half a Continent* (New York, 1951). Stanley J. Stein, *The Brazilian Cotton Manufacture: Textile Enterprise in an Underdeveloped Area, 1850–1950* (Cambridge, 1957); *Vassouras: A Brazilian Coffee Country, 1850–1900* (Cambridge, 1957). Robert B. Toplin, *The Abolition of Slavery in Brazil* (New York, 1972). Charles Wagley, *An Introduction to Brazil* (New York, 1963); *Amazon Town: A Study of Man in the Tropics* (New York, 1953). Mary W. Williams, *Dom Pedro the Magnanimous, Second Emperor of Brazil* (Chapel Hill, N.C., 1937). John D. Wirth, *The Politics of Brazilian Development, 1930–1954* (Stanford, Calif., 1970). Donald Worcester, *Brazil: From Colony to World Power* (New York, 1973). George Wythe, et al., *Brazil: An Expanding Economy* (New York, 1949). Jordan M. Young, *The Brazilian Revolution of 1930 and the Aftermath* (New Brunswick, N.J., 1967).

Chile. Alan Angell, *Politics and Labour Movement in Chile* (London, 1972). Harold Blakemore, *British Nitrates and Chilean Politics 1886–1896: Balmaceda and North* (London, 1974). Robert N. Burr, *By Reason or Force: Chile and the Balancing of Power in South America, 1830–1905* (Berkeley, Calif., 1965); *The Stillborn Panama Congress* (Berkeley, 1962). G. J. Butland, *Chile: An Outline of Its Geography, Economics, and Politics*, 3rd ed. (London, 1956). Alvin Cohen, *Economic*

Change in Chile 1929–1959 (Gainesville, Fla., 1960). Paul Ellsworth, *Chile: An Economy in Transition* (New York, 1945). Luís Galdames, *A History of Chile*, tr. and ed. by I. J. Cox (Chapel Hill, N.C., 1941). F. C. Gil, *The Political System of Chile* (Boston, 1966). Leonard Gross, *The Last Best Hope: Eduardo Frei and Chilean Democracy* (New York, 1967). Ernest Halperin, *Nationalism and Communism in Chile* (Cambridge, 1965). Jay Kinsbruner, *Chile: A Historical Interpretation* (New York, 1973); *Diego Portales* (The Hague, 1967). Markos Mamalakis and Clark W. Reynolds, *Essays on the Chilean Economy* (Homewood, Ill., 1965). George M. Mcbride, *Chile: Land and Society* (New York, 1936). Frederick M. Nunn, *Chilean Politics, 1920–1931: The Honorable Mission of the Armed Forces* (Albuquerque, N. Mex., 1970). James Petras, *Politics and Social Forces in Chilean Development* (Berkeley, Calif., 1969). Frederick B. Pike, *Chile and the United States, 1880–1962* (Notre Dame, Ind., 1963). John R. Stevenson, *The Chilean Popular Front* (Westport, Conn., 1970, 1st ed. 1942). Theodore H. Moran, *Multinational Corporations and the Politics of Dependence: Copper and Chile* (Princeton, N.J., 1975).

Colombia. Harry Bernstein, *Venezuela and Colombia* (Englewood Cliffs, N.J., 1964). David Bushnell, *Eduardo Santos and the Good Neighbor, 1938–1942* (Gainesville, Fla., 1967); *The Santander Regime in Gran Colombia* (Newark, Del., 1954). Robert H. Dix, *Colombia: The Political Dimensions of Change* (New Haven, Conn., 1967). Orlando Fals-Borda, *Peasant Society in the Colombian Andes* (Gainesville, Fla., 1955). Vernon L. Fluharty, *Dance of the Millions* (Pittsburgh, 1957). J. M. Henao and G. Arrubla, *History of Colombia*, tr. and ed. J. F. Rippy (Chapel Hill, N.C., 1938). John D. Martz, *Colombia: A Contemporary Political Survey* (Chapel Hill, N.C., 1962). William P. McGreevey, *An Economic History of Colombia, 1845–1930* (Cambridge, 1971). E. Taylor Parks, *Colombia and the United States, 1765–1934*

(Durham, N.C., 1935). James Payne, *Patterns of Conflict in Colombia* (New Haven, Conn., 1968). T. Lynn Smith, *Colombia: Social Structure and the Process of Development* (Gainesville, Fla., 1967).

Ecuador. George I. Blanksten, *Ecuador, Constitutions and Caudillos* (Berkeley, Calif., 1951). C. R. Enock, *Ecuador* (New York, 1914). Lilo Linke, *Ecuador: Country of Contrasts*, 3rd ed. (New York, 1960). M. C. Needler, *Anatomy of a Coup d'Etat: Ecuador 1963* (Washington, 1964). J. V. D. Saunders, *The People of Ecuador: A Demographic Analysis* (Gainesville, Fla., 1961). Thomas E. Weil et al., *Area Handbook for Ecuador* (Washington, 1973). D. H. Zook, Jr., *Zarumilla-Marañón: The Ecuador-Peru Dispute* (New York, 1964).

Mexico. J. C. Ashby, *Organized Labor and the Mexican Revolution under Lázaro Cárdenas* (Chapel Hill, N.C., 1967). Carleton Beals, *Porfirio Díaz: Dictator of Mexico* (Westport, Conn., 1971; 1st. ed. 1932). William H. Beezley, *Insurgent Governor: Abraham González and the Mexican Revolution in Chihuahua* (Lincoln, Neb., 1973). Marvin D. Bernstein, *The Mexican Mining Industry, 1890–1950* (Albany, Ga., 1965). Alfred Hoyt Bill, *Rehearsal for Conflict: The War with Mexico, 1846–1848* (New York, 1947). F. R. Brandenberg, *The Making of Modern Mexico* (Englewood Cliffs, N.J., 1964). Anita Brenner, *The Wind that Swept Mexico: The History of the Mexican Revolution, 1910–1942* (Austin, Tex., 1971; 1st ed. 1943). Fanny Calderón de la Barca, *Letters*, ed. by H. T. and M. H. Fisher (Garden City, N.Y., 1966). W. H. Callcott, *Santa Anna: The Story of an Enigma Who Was Once Mexico* (Norman, Okla., 1936); *Church and State in Mexico, 1822–1857* (Durham, N.C., 1926); *Liberalism in Mexico, 1857–1929* (Stanford, Calif., 1931). Peter Calvert, *The Mexican Revolution, 1910–1914: The Diplomacy of Anglo-American Conflict* (New York, 1968); *Mexico* (New York, 1973). Howard F. Cline, *The United States and Mexico*, rev. ed. (Cambridge, 1963); *Mexico, Revolution to Evolution, 1940–1960* (London, 1962). James D. Cockroft, *Intellectual Precursors of the Mexican Revolution: 1900–1913* (Austin, Tex., 1968). Michael P. Costeloe, *Church Wealth in Mexico: A Study of the Juzgado de Capellanías in the Archbishopric of Mexico, 1800–1856* (Cambridge, 1967). Charles C. Cumberland, *Mexican Revolution: The Constitutionalist Years* (Austin, Tex., 1972); *Mexican Revolution: Genesis Under Madero* (Austin, Tex., 1952); *Mexico: The Struggle for Modernity* (New York, 1968). Josephus Daniels, *Shirt-Sleeve Diplomat* (Chapel Hill, N.C., 1947). John W. F. Dulles, *Yesterday in Mexico* (Austin, Tex., 1961). Richard Fagen and William Tuohy, *Politics and Privilege in a Mexican City* (Stanford, Calif., 1972). W. P. Glade, Jr., and C. W. Anderson, *The Political Economy of Mexico* (Madison, Wis., 1963). Pablo González Casanova, *Democracy in Mexico*, tr. by D. Salti (New York, 1970). Charles A. Hale, *Mexican Liberalism in the Age of Mora, 1821–53* (New Haven, Conn., 1968). Roger Hansen, *The Politics of Mexican Development* (Baltimore, 1970); *Mexican Economic Development: The Roots of Rapid Growth* (Washington, 1971). Joan Haslip, *Imperial Adventurer: Emperor Maximilian of Mexico* (London, 1971). Robert S. Henry, *The Story of the Mexican War* (Indianapolis, 1950). Frank A. Knapp, Jr., *The Life of Sebastián Lerdo de Tejada, 1823–89* (New York, 1968; 1st ed. 1951). Oscar Lewis, *The Children of Sanchez: Autobiography of a Mexican Family* (New York, 1961). Edwin Lieuwen, *Mexican Militarism: The Political Rise and Fall of the Revolutionary Army, 1910–1940* (Albuquerque, N. Mex., 1968). George McBride, *The Land Systems of Mexico* (New York, 1923). Archie P. McDonald, ed., *The Mexican War: Crisis for American Democracy* (Lexington, Mass., 1969). Michael C. Meyer, *Huerta: A Political Portrait* (Lincoln, Neb., 1972); *Mexican Rebel: Pascual Orozco and the Mexican Revolution, 1910–15* (Lincoln, Neb., 1967). Sanford Mosk, *Industrial Revolution in Mexico* (Berkeley, Calif., 1950). Edith O'Shaughnessy, *A Diplomat's Wife in Mexico* (New York, 1916). Vincent Padgett, *The Mexican Political System* (New York, 1966). Henry B. Parkes, *A History of Mexico*, rev. ed. (Boston, 1969). Octavio Paz, *Labyrinth of Solitude: Life and Thought in Mexico* (New York, 1962). David M. Pletcher, *The Diplomacy of Annexation: Texas, Oregon, and the Mexican War* (Columbia, S.C., 1973); *Rails, Mines and Progress* (Ithaca, N.Y., 1958). Joel R. Poinsett, *Notes on Mexico: Made in the Autumn of 1822* (New York, 1969, 1st published 1824). Robert Quirk, *An Affair of Honor: Woodrow Wilson and the Occupation of Veracruz* (Lexington, Mass., 1962); *The Mexican Revolution, 1914–18: The Convention of Aguascalientes* (Bloomington, Ind., 1960); *The Mexican Revolution and the Catholic Church, 1910–29* (Bloomington, Ind., 1973); *Mexico* (Englewood Cliffs, N.J., 1971). Robert W. Randall, *Real del Monte: A British Mining Venture in Mexico* (Austin, Tex., 1972). Robert Redfield, *Tepoztlán: A Mexican Village* (Chicago, 1930); and Alfonso Villa Rojas, *Chan Kom: A Maya Village* (Washington, 1934). Nelson Reed, *The Caste War of Yucatan* (Stanford, Calif., 1964). Clark W. Reynolds, *The Mexican Economy: Twentieth-Century Structure and Growth* (New Haven, Conn., 1970). J. F. Rippy, *Joel R. Poinsett, Versatile American* (Durham, N.C., 1935). Ralph Roeder, *Juarez and His Mexico*, 2 vols. (New York, 1947). Stanley R. Rose, *Francisco I. Madero, Apostle of Mexican Democracy* (New York, 1955); ed., *Is the Mexican Revolution Dead?* (New York, 1966). Ramon E. Ruiz, *Mexico, the Challenge of Poverty and Illiteracy* (San Marino, Calif., 1963). Walter V. Scholes, *Mexican Politics During the Juarez Regime, 1855–72* (Columbia, S.C., 1969; 1st ed. 1957). Robert E. Scott, *Mexican Government in Transition*, rev. ed. (Urbana, Ill., 1964). Robert Jones Shafer, *Mexican Business Organizations: History and Analysis* (Syracuse, N.Y., 1973); *Mexico: Mutual Adjustment Planning* (Syracuse, N.Y., 1966). E. N. Simpson, *The Ejido: Mexico's Way Out* (Chapel Hill, N.C., 1937). Lesley B. Simpson, *Many Mexicos*, 4th ed. (Berkeley, Calif., 1966). O. A. Singletary, *The Mexican War* (Chicago, 1960). Frank Tannenbaum, *The Mexican Agrarian Revolution* (New York, 1929); *Peace by Revolution: An Interpretation of Mexico* (New York, 1935). Waddy Thompson, *Recollections of Mexico* (New York, 1847). Alfred Tischendorf, *Great Britain and Mexico in the Era of Porfirio Diaz* (Durham, N.C., 1961). Frederick Turner, *The Dynamic of Mexican Nationalism* (Chapel Hill, N.C., 1968). H. G. Ward, *Mexico in 1827*, 2 vols. (London, 1828). D. A. Walker, *The Nacional Financiera of Mexico* (Cambridge, 1961). Nathan Whetten, *Rural Mexico* (Chicago, 1948). James Wilkie, *The Mexican Revolution: Federal Expenditures and Social Change Since 1910* (Berkeley, Calif., 1967); and Albert Michaels, eds., *Revolution in Mexico: Years of Upheaval, 1910–40* (New York, 1969). John Womack, Jr., *Zapata and the Mexican Revolution* (New York, 1969).

Paraguay. Paul H. Lewis, *The Politics of Exile: Paraguay's Febrerista Party* (Chapel Hill, N.C., 1968). Charles J. Kolinski, *Independence or Death! The Story of the Paraguayan War* (Gainesville, Fla., 1965). George Pendle, *Paraguay: A Riverside Nation*, 2nd ed. (London, 1956). Joseph Pincus, *The Economy of Paraguay* (New York, 1968). Philip Raine, *Paraguay* (New Brunswick, N.J., 1956). H. G. Warren, *Paraguay: An Informal History* (Norman, Okla., 1949). C. A. Washburn, *History of Paraguay*, 2 vols. (Boston, 1871). Pablo Max Ynsfran, *The Epic of the Chaco* (Austin, Tex., 1950). David H. Zook, Jr., *The Conduct of the Chaco War* (New York, 1960).

Peru. American University, Foreign Area Studies, *U.S. Army Area Handbook for Peru* (Washington, 1965). Carlos Astiz, *Pressure Groups and Power Elites in Peruvian Politics* (Ithaca, N.Y., 1969). François Bourricaud, *Power and Society in Contemporary Peru*, tr. by Paul Stevenson (New York, 1970). James C. Carey, *Peru and the United States, 1900–1962* (Notre Dame, Ind., 1964). Thomas M. Davies, Jr., *Indian Integration in Peru: A Half Century* *of Experience, 1900–1948* (Lincoln, Neb., 1974). W. J. Dennis, *Tacna and Arica* (New Haven, 1931). Thomas R. Ford, *Man and Land in Peru* (Gainesville, Fla., 1955). Jack W. Hopkins, *The Government Executive of Modern Peru* (Gainesville, Fla., 1967). Harry Kantor, *The Ideology and Program of the Peruvian Aprista Movement* (Washington, 1966; 1st ed. 1953). Peter F. Klarén, *Modernization, Dislocation and Aprismo: Origins of the Peruvian Aprista Party, 1870–1932* (Austin, Tex., 1973). Abraham F. Lowenthal, ed., *The Peruvian Experiment: Continuity and Change Under Military Rule* (Princeton, N.J., 1976). Robert H. K. Marett, *Peru* (New York, 1969). Harold Osborne, *Indians of the Andes: Aymaras and Quechuas* (Cambridge, 1952). R. J. Owens, *Peru* (New York, 1963). James L. Payne, *Labor and Politics in Peru: The System of Political Bargaining* (New Haven, Conn., 1965). Frederick B. Pike, *The Modern History of Peru* (New York, 1967). Watt Stewart, *Chinese Bondage in Peru: A History of the Chinese Coolies in Peru, 1849–1874* (Durham, N.C., 1951).

Uruguay. Marvin Alisky, *Uruguay: A Contemporary Survey* (New York, 1969). Russell H. Fitzgibbon, *Uruguay, Portrait of a Democracy* (New Brunswick, N.J., 1954). S. G. Hanson, *Utopia in Uruguay* (New York, 1938). W. H. Koebel, *Uruguay* (London, 1911). George Pendle, *Uruguay*, 2d ed. (London, 1957). John Street, *Artigas and the Emancipation of Uruguay* (Cambridge, 1959). Philip B. Taylor, Jr., *Government and Politics of Uruguay* (New Orleans, 1960). Milton I. Vanger, *José Batlle y Ordóñez: Creator of His Times, 1902–1907* (Cambridge, 1963). Martin Weinstein, *Uruguay, The Politics of Failure* (Westport, Conn., 1975).

Venezuela. R. J. Alexander, *The Venezuelan Democratic Revolution: A Profile of the Regime of Rómulo Betancourt* (New Brunswick, N.J., 1964). Harry Bernstein, *Venezuela and Colombia* (Englewood Cliffs, N.J., 1964). Winfield Burggraaeff, *The Venezuelan Armed Forces in Politics, 1935–1959* (Columbia, S.C., 1972). R. B. Cunninghame Graham, *José Antonio Páez* (Philadelphia, 1929). Robert Gilmore, *Caudillism and Militarism in Venezuela, 1810–1910* (Athens, Ga., 1964). John Lavin, *A Halo for Gómez* (New York, 1954). Edwin Lieuwen, *Venezuela*, 2d ed. (New York, 1965); *Petroleum in Venezuela: A History* (Berkeley, Calif., 1954). John V. Lombardi, *The Decline and Abolition of Negro Slavery in Venezuela: 1821–1854* (Westport, Conn., 1971). W. D. and A. L. Marsland, *Venezuela Through Its History* (New York, 1936). John Martz, *Acción Democrática: Evolution of a Modern Political Party in Venezuela* (Princeton, N.J., 1966). Thomas Rourke, *Gómez, Tyrant of the Andes* (New York, 1936). Mary Watters, *A History of the Church in Venezuela, 1810–1930* (Chapel Hill, N.C., 1933). A. P. Whitaker, *The United States and South America: The Northern Republics* (Cambridge, 1948). George S. Wise, *Caudillo: A Portrait of Antonio Guzmán Blanco* (New York, 1951).

Central America: (a) *In General*. R. N. Adams, *Cultural Survey of Panama-Nicaragua-Guatemala-El Salvador-Honduras* (Washington, 1957). L. E. Bumgartner, *José del Valle of Central America* (Durham, N.C., 1963). Carlos M. Castillo, *Growth and Integration in Central America* (New York, 1966). Robert S. Chamberlain, *Francisco Morazán: Champion of Central American Federation* (Coral Gables, Fla., 1950). Thomas L. Karnes, *The Failure of Union: Central America, 1824–1960* (Chapel Hill, N.C., 1961). C. D. Kepner, *Social Aspects of the Banana Industry* (New York, 1936). J. D. Martz, *Central America: The Crisis and the Challenge* (Chapel Hill, N.C., 1959); *Justo Rufino Barrios and Central American Union* (Gainesville, Fla., 1963). Stacy May and Galo Plaza Lasso, *The United Fruit Company in Latin America* (Washington, 1958). Dana G. Munro, *The Five Republics of Central America* (New York, 1918). F. D. Parker, *The Central American Republics* (New York, 1964). Mario

Rodríguez, A *Palmerstonian Diplomat in Central America, Frederick Chatfield, Esq.* (Tucson, Ariz., 1964); *Central America* (Englewood Cliffs, N.J., 1965). E. G. Squier, *Travels in Central America*, 2 vols. (New York, 1853). J. L. Stephens, *Incidents of Travel in Central America, Chiapas, and Yucatan*, new ed., ed. by R. L. Predmore (New Brunswick, N.J., 1949). Sol Tax, et al., *Heritage of Conquest: The Ethnology of Middle America* (Glencoe, Ill., 1952).

(b) *Costa Rica.* American University, Foreign Area Studies, *Area Handbook for Costa Rica* (Washington, 1970). John P. Bell, *Crisis in Costa Rica: The 1948 Revolution* (Austin, Tex., 1971). John and Mavis Biesanz, *Costa Rican Life* (New York, 1944). James L. Busey, *Notes on Costa Rican Democracy* (Boulder, Colo., 1962). Chester Lloyd Jones, *Costa Rica and Civilization in the Caribbean* (Madison, Wis., 1935). Donald E. Lundberg, *Adventure in Costa Rica* (Tallahassee, Fla., 1960). Stacey May, et al., *Costa Rica: A Study in Economic Development* (New York, 1952). Watt Stewart, *Keith and Costa Rica* (Albuquerque, N. Mex., 1964).

(c) *Guatemala.* Richard Adams, et al., *Crucifixion by Power: Essays on Guatemalan National Social Structure, 1944–1966* (Austin, Tex., 1970). J. J. Arévalo, *The Shark and the Sardines*, tr. by June Cobb and R. Osegueda (New York, 1961). William J. Griffith, *Empires in the Wilderness, Foreign Colonization and Development in Guatemala, 1834–1944* (Chapel Hill, N.C., 1965). M. P. Holleran, *Church and State in Guatemala* (New York, 1949). Chester Lloyd Jones, *Guatemala, Past and Present* (Minneapolis, 1940). Vera Kelsey, *Four Keys to Guatemala*, rev. ed. (New York, 1961). R. A. LaBarge, *Impact of the United Fruit Company on the Economic Development of Guatemala, 1946–1954* (New Orleans, 1960). Ronald M. Schneider, *Communism in Guatemala, 1944–1954* (New York, 1959). K. H. Silvert, *A Study in Government: Guatemala* (New Orleans, 1954).

Nathan L. Whetten, *Guatemala: The Land and the People* (New Haven, Conn., 1961). Ralph L. Woodward, Jr., *Class Privilege and Economic Development: The Consulado de Comercio of Guatemala, 1793–1871* (Chapel Hill, N.C., 1966).

(d) *Honduras.* W. S. Stokes, *Honduras* (Madison, Wis., 1950).

(e) *Nicaragua.* American University, Foreign Area Studies, *Area Handbook for Nicaragua* (Washington, 1970). A. H. Z. Carr, *The World and William Walker* (New York, 1963). I. J. Cox, *Nicaragua and the United States, 1909–1927* (Boston, 1927). William A. Kamman, *A Search for Stability: United States Diplomacy Toward Nicaragua, 1925–1933* (Notre Dame, Ind., 1968). W. O. Scroggs, *Filibusters and Financiers: The Story of William Walker and His Associates* (New York, 1916).

(f) *Panama.* John and Mavis Biesanz, *The People of Panama* (New York, 1955). M. P. DuVal, Jr., *And the Mountains Will Move: The Story of the Building of the Panama Canal* (Stanford, Calif., 1947); *Cadiz to Cathay: The Story of the Long Struggle for a Waterway Across the American Isthmus* (Stanford, Calif., 1940). L. O. Ealy, *The Republic of Panama in World Affairs, 1903–1950* (Philadelphia, 1951). J. H. Kemble, *The Panama Route, 1848–1869* (Berkeley, Calif., 1943). Sheldon B. Liss, *The Canal: Aspects of United States-Panamanian Relations* (Notre Dame, Ind., 1967).

(g) *El Salvador.* Thomas P. Anderson, *Matanza: El Salvador's Communist Revolt of 1932* (Lincoln, Neb., 1971). Alastair White, *El Salvador* (London, 1973).

The Island Republics: **(a)** *In General.* Germán Arciniegas, *Caribbean: Sea of the New World* (New York, 1946). John E. Fagg, *Cuba, Haiti, and the Dominican Republic* (Englewood Cliffs, N.J., 1965). Chester L. Jones, *The Carib-*

bean Since 1900 (New York, 1936). Dana G. Monro, *Intervention and Dollar Diplomacy in the Caribbean, 1900–1921* (Princeton, N.J., 1964). Dexter Perkins, *The United States and the Caribbean* (Cambridge, 1947). J. F. Rippy, *The Caribbean Danger Zone* (New York, 1949). A. C. Wilgus, ed., *The Caribbean*, 17 vols. (Gainesville, Fla., 1951–67).

(b) Cuba. Luis E. Aguilar, *Cuba 1933: Prologue to Revolution* (New York, 1972). Edward Boorstein, *Economic Transformation of Cuba* (New York, 1968). Fidel Castro, *History Will Absolve Me*, tr. from the Spanish (New York, 1961). Charles E. Chapman, *A History of the Cuban Republic* (New York, 1927). Arthur F. Corwin, *Spain and the Abolition of Slavery in Cuba* (Austin, Tex., 1967). Theodore Draper, *Castro's Revolution: Myths and Realities* (New York, 1962); *Castroism: Theory and Practice* (New York, 1965). Richard R. Fagen, *The Transformation of Political Culture in Cuba* (Stanford, Calif., 1972). R. H. Fitzgibbon, *Cuba and the United States, 1900–1935* (Menasha, Wis., 1935). Philip S. Foner, *A History of Cuba and Its Relations with the United States, 1492–1845* (New York, 1962); *The Spanish-Cuban-American War and the Birth of American Imperialism: 1895–1902*, 2 vols. (New York, 1972). Boris Goldenberg, *The Cuban Revolution and Latin America* (New York, 1965). Eduard Gonzalez, *Cuba Under Castro: The Limits of Charisma* (Boston, 1974). Richard B. Gray, *José Martí, Cuban Patriot* (Gainesville, Fla., 1962). Ramiro Guerra y Sánchez, *Sugar and Society in the Caribbean* (New Haven, Conn., 1964). Maurice Halperin, *The Rise and Decline of Fidel Castro: An Essay in Contemporary History* (Berkeley, Calif., 1972). David F. Healy, *The United States in Cuba, 1898–1902* (Madison, Wis., 1963). Franklin W. Knight, *Slave Society in Cuba During the Nineteenth Century* (Madison, Wis., 1970). D. L. Larson, ed., *The Cuban Crisis of 1962: Selected Documents and Chronology* (Boston, 1963). Jorge Manach, *Martí: Apostle of Freedom*, tr. by C. Taylor (New

York, 1953). Herbert L. Matthews, *The Cuban Story* (New York, 1961). Wyatt McGaffey and Clifford Barnett, *Cuba: Its People, Its Society, Its Culture* (New Haven, 1962). Lowry Nelson, *Rural Cuba* (Minneapolis, 1950). James O'Conner, *The Origins of Socialism in Cuba* (Ithaca, N.Y., 1970). Fernando Ortiz, *Cuban Counterpoint: Tobacco and Sugar*, tr. by Harriet de Onis (New York, 1947). H. M. Patcher, *American-Soviet Confrontation: A Case Study of the Cuban Missile Crisis* (New York, 1963). Rámon E. Ruiz, *Cuba, the Making of a Revolution* (Cambridge, 1968). Dudley Seers, ed., *Cuba, the Economic and Social Revolution* (Chapel Hill, N.C., 1964). Robert F. Smith, *Background to Revolution: The Development of Modern Cuba* (New York, 1966); *The United States and Cuba: Business and Diplomacy, 1917–1960* (New York, 1960); *What Happened in Cuba? A Documentary History* (New York, 1963). Hugh Thomas, *Cuba or the Pursuit of Freedom* (London, 1971). H. C. Wallich, *Monetary Problems of an Export Economy: The Cuban Experience, 1914–1947* (Cambridge, 1950). Loree Wilkerson, *Fidel Castro's Political Programs from Reformism to Marxism-Leninism* (Gainesville, Fla., 1965).

(c) Dominican Republic. American University, Foreign Area Studies, *Area Handbook for Dominican Republic* (Washington, 1966). Juan Bosch, *The Unfinished Experiment: Democracy in the Dominican Republic* (New York, 1965). Robert D. Crassweller, *Trujillo: The Life and Times of a Caribbean Dictator* (New York, 1966). A. R. Espaillat, *Trujillo: The Last Caesar* (Chicago, 1963). J. B. Martin, *Overtaken by Events: The Dominican Crisis from the Fall of Trujillo to the Civil War* (New York, 1966). Jose A. Moreno, *Barrios in Arms* (Pittsburgh, 1970). Selden Rodman, *Quisqueya, A History of the Dominican Republic* (Seattle, 1964). Tad Szulc, *Dominican Diary* (New York, 1965). Charles C. Tansill, *The United States and Santo Domingo, 1798–1873: A Chapter in Caribbean Diplomacy* (Baltimore, 1938). Sumner Welles,

Naboth's Vineyard: The Dominican Republic, 1844–1902, 2 vols. (New York, 1966; 1st ed. 1928). Howard J. Wiarda, *Dictatorship and Development: The Methods of Control in Trujillo's Dominican Republic* (Gainesville, Fla., 1968).

(d) Haiti. Stephen Alexis, *Black Liberator: The Life of Toussaint L'Ouverture*, tr. by W. Stirling (New York, 1949). Harold Courlander, *The Drum and the Hoe: Life and Lore of the Haitian People* (Berkeley, Calif., 1960). H. P. Davis, *Black Democracy*, rev. ed. (New York, 1936). M. J. Herskovits, *Life in a Haitian Valley* (New York, 1937). C. L. R. James, *The Black Jacobins: Toussaint L'Ouverture and the San Domingo Revolution*, 2nd ed. (New York, 1963). J. G. Leyburn, *The Haitian People* (New Haven, Conn., 1941). R. W. Logan, *The Diplomatic Relations of the United States with Haiti, 1776–1891* (Chapel Hill, N.C., 1941). Arthur C. Millspaugh, *Haiti Under American Control, 1915–1930* (Boston, 1931). L. L. Montague, *Haiti and the United States, 1714–1938* (Durham, N.C., 1940). Charles Moran, *Black Triumvirate: A Study of L'Ouverture, Dessalines, Christophe—The Men Who Made Haiti* (New York, 1957). Selden Rodman, *Haiti: The Black Republic* (New York, 1954). Robert I. Rothberg and C. K. Clague, *Haiti: The Politics of Squalor* (Boston, 1971). Hans Schmidt, *The United States Occupation of Haiti, 1915–1934* (New Brunswick, N.J., 1971).

INDEX